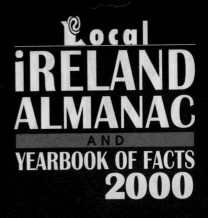

Local iRELAND ALMANAC
AND
YEARBOOK OF FACTS
2000

The Ultimate
Annual Almanac and Yearbook of Facts
MILLENNIUM EDITION

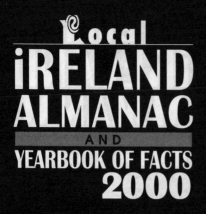

iRELAND ALMANAC AND YEARBOOK OF FACTS 2000

published by **LOCAL IRELAND**
merrion house, merrion road, dublin 4.

© **DnD Research Ltd** 1999

Editorial Staff
Helen Curley *(Editor)*
Damian Dowds and Dónal Campbell *(Research)*
Anita Gallagher *(Assistant Researcher)*

Printed by Techman Ireland Ltd.,
www.techman.ie

ISBN 0 9536537 0 6

The Ultimate
Annual Almanac and Yearbook of Facts
MILLENNIUM EDITION

EDITOR'S INTRODUCTION

WELCOME to the Millennium edition of the *Local Ireland Almanac and Yearbook of Facts*. No other book provides you with the detailed statistical information which accurately reflects the essence of our country today. Ireland on the eve of the 21st century is a forward-looking society, confident and fully engaged with business, arts, culture, sport and education, all of which are covered in detail in this publication.

It is fitting that at the beginning the new millennium, we are launching the Almanac simultaneously with our new website - www.localalmanac.ie - a first for an Irish reference book of this stature. We believe that the textual and electronic formats will complement and enhance each other, and we are excited at the prospect of developing both in the future.

A special feature of this year's edition is the Millennium chapter. Although we are all aware of the landmarks in the world history of the millennium, few publications provide you with a guide to Ireland's history over the last one thousand years. We include a detailed chronology of Ireland over the past millennium, as well as providing you with a synopsis of the main events which defined each of the past ten centuries

Other new features within the Almanac have been developed with the user in mind. To make the book more reader friendly we have introduced an 'at a glance' statistics table at the beginning of each chapter. This table provides a handy summary of the detailed facts and figures from each field of Irish life, from arts to agriculture.

Our yearbook chronicles the year from October 1st, 1998, to September 30th, 1999, and includes what we deem to be the most important news stories from this 12-month period. The year in question has been a frustrating one in terms of the Northern Ireland peace process. The two incidents which defined last year - the Belfast Agreement and the Omagh Bombing - gave a strong impetus to the Peace Process. It has been galling to see the drive for peace, which was so hard won, being so casually cast aside during the farcical abandonment of the Northern Ireland Executive this summer. The Peace Process and the other important stories of 1998-1999 are handily summarised in the Almanac's Chronology of the Year chapter.

One important element within the almanac is the contribution of in-depth articles from experts within Irish life. These contributors are not pundits who trot out fashionable views, but are experts in their chosen field. You may or may not like what they have to say, but it will certainly provide you with food for thought.

The compilation of the book and the website has been an enormous undertaking, which has been enhanced by the contributions of the staff at Local Ireland. I would like to take this opportunity to thank them and all the people around the country, North and South, who gave of their time, expertise and knowledge so freely, both from the public sector and in a voluntary capacity. This book is a testament to their generosity.

Helen Curley

HELEN CURLEY *(Editor)*
October 1999

Merrion House, Merrion Road, Dublin 4.
Tel 01-218 7600 *Fax* 01-283 9805
email almanac@local.ie *website:* www.localalmanac.ie

CONTENTS

Articles

FREQUENTLY USED
ABBREVIATIONS

approx. approximately
assoc. association
avg. Average
assoc. association
b. born
c. circa
Co County / Company
d. died
e.g. *exempli gratia* for example
excl. excluding
Hse house
i.e. *id est* that is
incl. including
Lwr Lower
Ltd Limited
mph miles per hour
mtn mountain
no. Number
Nth north
plc Public Limited Company
rev. revised
Sth south
v versus

£bn billion pounds
£m million pounds
AD *anno Domini*
AIB Allied Irish Banks
AIDS acquired immune deficiency syndrome
BBC British Broadcasting Corporation
BC before Christ
BIK Benefit(s) in Kind
BIM Bord Iascaigh Mhara
BT British Telecom
CAB Criminal Assets Bureau
CEO Chief Executive Officer
CIÉ Coras Iompair Éireann
CSO Central Statistics Office.
DPP Director of Public Prosecutions
EBR Exchequer Borrowing Requirement
EBS Educational Building Society
ESB Electricity Supply Board.
EPA Environmental Protection Agency
ESRI Economic and Social Research Institute
EU European Union
GAA Gaelic Athletic Association
FAI Football Association of Ireland
FÁS Foras Áiseanna Saothair
GATT General Agreement on

Tariffs and Trade
GDP Gross Domestic Product
GNP Gross National Product
H.E. His / Her Excellency
IBEC Irish Business and Employers' Confederation
IDA Industrial Development Agency
IDB Industrial Development Board
IFA Irish Football Association.
IMRO Irish Music Rights Organisation Ltd.
IRMA Irish Recorded Music Association
IRFU Irish Rugby Football Union
IT Institute(s) of Technology
IR£ Irish punt (pound)
MEP Member of the European Parliament
NATO North Atlantic Treaty Organisation
NI Northern Ireland
NIO Northern Ireland Office
OECD Organisation for Economic Cooperation and Development
OBE Order of the British Empire
PfP Partnership for Peace (NATO-led organisation)
PRSI Pay Related Social Insurance
RHA Royal Hibernian Academy of Arts.
RIAI Royal Institute of Architects in Ireland RIAI
RIAM Royal Irish Academy of Music
RIR Royal Irish Regiment
RoI Republic of Ireland
RTÉ Radio Telefís Éireann
RUC Royal Ulster Constabulary
Stg£ Pound sterling
TBA To be announced
UN United Nations
UNESCO United Nations
US / USA United States of America
UTV Ulster Television
VAT Value Added Tax
VEC Vocational Education Committee
VHI Voluntary Health Insurance
WHO World Health Organisation
WWI World War I
WWII World War II

POLITICAL PARTIES:
Republic of Ireland

C na G Cumann na nGaedheal
DL Democratic Left
FF Fianna Fáil
FG Fine Gael
GP Green Party
Ind Independent
Lab Labour Party
PD Progressive Democrats
SF Sinn Féin
SP Socialist Party
TD Teachta Dála
WP Workers Party

Northern Ireland
All Alliance
DUP Democratic Unionist Party
Ind Independent
MP Member of Parliament
N Nationalist
N Nationalist Party
NILP Northern Ireland Labour Party
NIWC Northern Ireland Women's Coalition
Other Lab Other Labour Groupings
Other N Other Nationalist groups
Other U Other Unionist groups
PUP Progressive Unionist Party
SDLP Social and Democratic and Labour Party
SF Sinn Féin
U Unionist/Ulster Unionist Party
UKUP United Kingdom Unionist Party
UUP Ulster Unionist Party

European Union
PES Party of European Socialists
EPP European People's Party
UFE Union for Europe
ELR Liberals

Education Institutions
DCU Dublin City University (incl. St Patrick's College Drumcondra)
DIT Dublin Institute of Technology
HEA Higher Education Athority
NCAD National College of Art and Design
NCEA National Council for Educational Awards
NUI National University of Ireland
QUB Queen's University Belfast
RCSI Royal College of Surgeons

SPM St Patrick's College,
Maynooth
TCD Trinity College Dublin
UCC University College Cork
UCD University College Dublin
UCG University College Galway
UL University of Limerick (incl.
Mary Immaculate College
Limerick)

Measurements:
*Commonly used SI imperial and
metric measurements:*

°C degrees centigrade
cm centimetre
dwt deadweight

lw liveweight
ft foot
g grams
ha hectares
in inch
kg kilogram
km kilometre
kV kilo volts
kW kilo watts
l litre
lbs pounds
lwt liveweight
m metre
Mt million tonnes
MW mega watts
t tonnes

Media Chapter
est Established
Ed Editor
News News Editor
Pol Political Editor
Bus Business Editor
Arts Arts Editor
Features Features Editor
Sport Sports Editor
Ads Advertising Manager
ABC cir
Audit Bureau of Circulation
Price Price £IRL
Fin Finance Editor
NI Northern Ireland Editor

 # Additional Notes

Reading the tables
-        no information
n/a   Not applicable
p   provisional figures
e   estimated figures

Political Structures and Titles *See also Politics chapters*
Refrences are frequently made to following:
the Dáil: the Irish house of elected representatives
the Seanad: the Irish Senate
the Taoiseach: the prime minister
the Tánaiste: the deputy prime minister
TD: Teachta Dála: deputy to the Dáil (member of the house of representatives)
MP: member of parliament (British House of Commons)

Telephone numbers: The telephone numbers provided in the Local Ireland Almanac for both the North and South consist of the local area code and telephone number.

To call from the Republic of Ireland to Northern Ireland, users must dial 08 before the area code and phone number; e.g. to call Belfast, dial 08+01232 (the area code), followed by the phone number. For calls made from Northern Ireland to the Republic, users should place the international dialling code 00+353 before the local area code and phone number e.g. to call Dublin, dial 00+353+1 (the area code is 01 - delete the zero), followed by the phone number.

A new telephone numbering system is being introduced in Northern Ireland in order to create capacity for new numbers. A new area code (028) will be introduced as the code for all of Northern Ireland, while the local five- and six-figure numbers will become eight-figure local numbers. After 22 April 2000 the new eight-figure local number can be used to dial locally, and the new national number for Northern Ireland will come into use after 16th September, 2000.

In addition, local five figure numbers in the Republic of Ireland are being increased by two digits in many regions, but users may continue to dial old numbers.

MILLENNIUM

Local History in Ireland: Past Problems, Present Promise

By **Dr Ciaran Brady**

HE writing of local history in Ireland has itself a long and distinguished history. Appropriately enough, it might be said, because the earliest surviving sources for Irish history as a whole - the great corpus of Gaelic genealogies and the rich compilations of Irish annals - were themselves intensely local in character, detailing the (often specious) descents of powerful local dynasties or retelling the history of the island (and sometimes the whole world) from the perspective of the area in which the annals were compiled. Yet the origins of Ireland's tradition of local history are more complex and more discontinuous than such a simple lineage might suggest. For the problems of comprehension and interpretation presented by such materials prevented their use by all but the most expert eyes; while the most readily available sources for Ireland's localities provided an interpretative frame of both a narrow and subtly deceptive character.

The earliest efforts at writing local history in a recognisably modern form appeared in the mid-eighteenth century in a series of cyclopedic surveys compiled by Charles Smith and others bearing standard titles such as The ancient and present state of the county of Cork ditto Down ditto Kerry etc. Over the next century or so such works, which combined strings of historical records with contemporary statistical material were succeeded by more strictly sequential histories of counties and towns such as James Hardiman's History of the town and county of Galway (1820), E.P. Shirley's History of Monaghan (1878) P.H. Hore's six volume History of the town and county of Wexford (1900-1910) and many more. And at the same time these individual efforts were supplemented by a more collective effort in local research which filled the pages of the such great antiquarian journals as the Ulster Journal of Archaeology and similar publications for Kilkenny, Waterford, Kerry, Limerick and Galway. The amount of material produced in these journals - covering places, families, monuments, castles and events - was massive, and their files are still a fertile resource for anyone embarking on local research. Yet the manner in which such work was produced raised some serious critical difficulties.

It was, in the first place, the work of a leisured class of gentlemen scholars who, though not all were landlords and not all would have considered themselves part of the Protestant establishment, were nevertheless fully accepting of the status quo in which that establishment held sway. The potential for conservative bias inherent in such a group was, moreover, re-inforced by the very materials on which they relied to write their history. Being largely unaware or unable to handle Gaelic materials, the sources they most commonly employed were those generated by the English governing and administrative system - court records, plantation maps and surveys, and the correspondence, memoirs and histories written by English administrators and settlers in justification of their actions. The extent of the prejudice relayed from these sources depended on the disposition and the critical acumen of the historians; and not all were simple apologists. Yet a deeper implicit bias can be discerned in the defining units of locality which almost all of the scholars uncritically adopted: the county, the borough, the plantation estate, the parish of the established church. The validity of such units, of course, can hardly be doubted. But their unquestioned status either diminished the significance or excluded altogether those alternative structures of communal identity which had both preceded and survived under the administrative units imposed by the governing elite.

Even in the nineteenth century such an exclusivist view of the locality did not go unchallenged. Yet the manner of the challenge was itself problematic. A tradition of Gaelic scholarship- from Roderick O'Connor in the seventeenth century to Eugene O'Curry and John O'Donovan in the nineteenth - continued to reveal an alternative history of localities, and the persistence of underground identities was nurtured in the poetry, oral traditions and folkways of 'the hidden Ireland'. But the esoteric character of the former and the diffuse and fluid nature of the latter rendered both incapable of launching a serious attack upon the scholarly authority of the dominant school. The most articulate and effective source of opposition came instead from the educated Catholic clergy, professionals and teachers who began to exert a powerful influence on Irish cultural life from the mid-nineteenth century on. This new local history borrowed the forms of the dominant tradition, expressing itself both in individual volumes of research and in the publications of local journals. The scholarship too was frequently impressive: thorough, accurate and linguistically skilled. And the range of prejudice was equally broad, running from restrained accounts of the sufferings of the faithful in Penal times to outright confessional bigotry. But once more a deeper bias was to be found within the school's preferred units of analysis: not the county, but the diocese, the Catholic parish, the local Catholic family and the ancient monastic foundation. Thus it was that, amidst the great efflorescence of Irish local history in the nineteenth and early twentieth centuries, a curious and debilitating symmetry between the dominant schools of local history. And, as each group burrowed industriously away within its own closed framework, the possibility of critical interaction between both was excluded and the opportunity for questioning the narrow and static assumptions adopted by each was lost.

It was from these circumstances, I believe, that the divergence between the activities of the amateurs in the localities and the work of the academics in the universities began to become marked. Sometimes simply characterised as a gap in historical skills between the amateur and the 'professional', the difference was at once less stark and more interesting. Most of the practitioners of local history displayed, as I have suggested, remarkably high levels of skill in archival research, documentary research and literary presentation, and deep political prejudice was not unknown in the groves of academe. A deeper reason lay in the academic historians' preoccupation with national over local history. Such a difference in perspective did not necessarily entail a breakdown in relations: because for long the academics had been happy to raid the localities for evidence in support of some national event or other, and the locals had been happy to supply the material. The real difficulty arose only when the assumptions underlying the high political history of the national historians were themselves exposed to serious philosophical and ideological attack which questioned the very status of history as a distinct body of knowledge.

The response of the academics to this fundamental challenge was slow but steady. And gradually, by taking on board many of the conceptual tools of their critics - Marxian economics, for example, and Weberian sociology - by learning to accept that their interpretations were no longer authoritative but forever subject to criticism and revision, the university historians reconstructed their subject. It was here, however, that differences arose between the centre and the localities as battle-hardened academics adopted both an interpretative technique and an expressive idiom which seemed both unnecessary and irrelevant to the practice of local historical research. For many decades this gap between the academics and the amateurs was often painfully evident in the pages of local journals. But now there are clear signs that this disjunction has been well-nigh overcome.

In part this has been because the practitioners of local history have themselves become aware of the problems that surround their pursuit and have adopted techniques of the academics in order to meet them. But more importantly it has been because the academics, in adopting the perspectives of economists, geographers, anthropologists have at last perceived the importance of local and regional communities as powerful forces in their own right shaping the political and social fabric of the country as a whole. In accepting too the complexity and hidden meanings of historical narrative they have begun to see also new ways of reading and interpreting ancient histories, poems folklore and popular culture which has made such material more central to the historical recordthan ever before. In these ways even as the locality is becoming more pertinent to the concern of the general historian, so the academics are aiding in a radical reappraisal of the traditional sources and interpretative frames of the local historian. The success of this convergence is already evident in the spate of local studies of the highest calibre which the recent commemorations of the Famine and 1798 have called forth, in the lengthening series of collective county histories which are currently underway, but most importantly of all in the establishment in universities and colleges of centres dedicated to the development of local history. All these testimony to the fact that, despite its troubled origins, local history has now become a fully integrated pursuit and integral too to the practice of history as a whole.

Dr Ciaran Brady
October 1999

The author is a Senior Lecturer in Modern History at Trinity College Dublin and joint editor of the periodical **Irish Historical Studies.**

Significant Events by Century

Eleventh Century - Battle of Clontarf

The Battle of Clontarf took place on Good Friday, April 23 1014 and lasted all day. It has been portrayed as the defining battle which broke Norse power in Ireland. In fact it was a rebellion by the Irish of Leinster who secured Norse allies, against Brian Boru's high kingship. High king since 1002, Brian responded to a call for help from his ally Mael Sechnaill in 1013 by attacking Leinster and blockading the city of Dublin from September until December. The blockade was unsuccessful and the Norse king of Dublin, Sitric, used the winter months to build alliances with the Norse in the Orkneys and the Isle of Man. Brian returned to Leinster in the spring of 1014 and battle commenced on Good Friday. The Leinstermen and their Norse allies were defeated but the price of Brian's victory was high. Brian, too old to fight, was killed in his tent while son Murchad and many of his other leaders were killed in the battle. The loss of these leaders saw the fortunes of the Munster kings on the wane for some years afterwards while the Leinstermen enjoyed a degree of independence.

Twelfth Century - Church Reform

The twelfth century saw various reforms within the church in Ireland with Synods at Cashel in 1101, Ráith Bressail in 1111, at Kells in 1152 and again at Cashel in 1172. The Synod of Cashel of 1101 saw the king of Munster, Muirchertach Ua Briain grant Cashel to the church. The Synod forbade marriage to close members of the family and condemned lay encroachment on the church. The Synod of Ráith Bressail while not introducing territorial dioceses brought a new degree of church organisation establishing two arch-dioceses, Cashel and Armagh, dividing each into twelve dioceses. The Synod of Kells established an additional two arch-dioceses, Dublin and Tuam, and reassigned the 24 dioceses appropriately. Armagh enjoyed the primacy among the four arch-dioceses and the Synod succeeded in ending the control of Armagh by laymen; it was subsequently headed by a bishop. The Synod at Cashel in 1172 was held at Henry II's request and legislated for and improved system of tithes and wills.

Thirteenth Century - Norman Invasion

The arrival of invaders along the south east coast in 1169 and 1170 marks the beginning of the Norman conquest of Ireland. The most famous of the invaders was Richard de Clare (Strongbow), recruited by Diarmait MacMurchada the deposed king of Leinster to retake his kingship. Strongbow acceded to the Leinster kingship following Diarmait's death in 1171. This development was a cause of concern for Henry II, the king of England who feared Strongbow might use his power base in Ireland to retake lands in England which Henry had denied him. Henry II landed at Waterford in October 1171 and Strongbow and a number of Irish kings recognised Henry as their overlord. The Treaty of Windsor of 1175 saw the high king of Ireland, Ruaidrí Ua Conchobair accept Henry as overlord of Leinster and Meath and the cities of Waterford, Wexford and Dublin and saw Henry accept Ua Conchobair as king of the unconquered parts of the country.

Fourteenth Century - The Black Death

The Black Death is the name for the bubonic and pneumonic pandemic transmitted by fleas and rats in Europe in the 1340s. It was first recorded at the coastal town of Drogheda in August 1349 and soon after at Howth and Dalkey. While the inhabitants of Dublin and Drogheda were first to feel its effects it moved quickly inland and had spread to Limerick before the year was out. The plague was at its most deadly in population centres resulting in the more urbanised Anglo-Irish being more severely affected than the Gaelic Irish. The plague recurred at various stages throughout the middle ages with another severe outbreak in 1361. It is estimated that up to half of the population of Ireland may have been wiped out before 1400.

Fifteenth Century - The Wars of the Roses in Ireland

The Wars of the Roses was a civil war between the houses of Lancaster and York in England beginning in the 1450s and continuing intermittently until 1487. Ireland had proved troublesome for the English kings throughout the period by providing a launching pad for invasions and subsequently supporting pretenders. Richard, duke of York (who had close links with the earls of Desmond and Kildare from his time as Chief Governor) led an invasion in 1460. In 1462 the Lancastrian Sir John Butler was defeated in battle by Thomas Fitzgerald (a Yorkist) at Carrick-on-Suir; Fitzgerald was appointed Chief Governor a year later. The succession of the Lancastrian Henry Tudor (Henry VII) to the throne in 1485 was followed two years later by the arrival in Ireland of Lambert Simnel, a Yorkist pretender to the throne. Simnel was crowned king of England in Dublin and led an unsuccessful invasion of England to claim the throne. In 1491 another pretender, Perkin Warbeck, arrived in Ireland and was received as the rightful king. Although the Lancastrian succession was well in place at least some of the Irish lords remained Yorkist in sympathy a situation which did not change until Garret More Fitzgerald was appointed Lord Deputy in 1496.

Sixteenth Century - The Reformation

In 1536 the Irish Parliament passed the Act of Supremacy recognising Henry VII as the head of the Church of Ireland. Doctrinally there was little change although an act providing for the dissolution of the monasteries followed a year later. The reformation adopted a more doctrinally Protestant dimension during the reign of Edward VI, with the Book of Common Prayer (containing all the services and the Thirty-Nine Articles) imposed in the teeth of significant clerical and lay opposition. The reign of Elizabeth I saw the height of the Reformation in Ireland with an Act of Uniformity passed in 1560 making attendance at Protestant services compulsory (those who did not would be fined) and a revised Book of Common Prayer issued. The reformation did not take root as strongly in Ireland as it did in England because the government legislated only in a small part of the country because it lacked sufficient clerics –particularly Irish-speaking clerics– to spread the reformation and because it was opposed by the Anglo-Irish of the Pale who resented the trend of appointing men of English birth to high office in Church and government. Finally the Catholic Church put in place its own counter-reformation before the end of the sixteenth century which reclaimed some of those who had converted to Protestantism.

Seventeenth Century - The Williamite War

The Williamite War, fought between 1689 and 1691, was an Irish civil war which was part of a greater European war. It was fought between the Catholic James II, who was deposed as king of England in 1688, and the Protestant William III who, along with his wife Mary, replaced him. James arrived in Ireland with French troops in March 1689 and laid an unsuccessful siege at Derry while Williamite forces recorded a number of victories in south Ulster and north Connacht. A major Williamite expeditionary force arrived in Ulster in August but did not proceed southwards. William arrived in Ireland in June 1690 to take charge of the army which defeated the Jacobites at the river Boyne west of Drogheda. The victory ensured Williamite control of Dublin and the eastern part of the country. The Jacobites retreated across the Shannon rebutting Williamite attacks at Athlone and Limerick. However a seaborne force captured Cork in September and the Jacobites quickly ceded control of Munster. Athlone was captured by Williamite forces in June 1691 and the Jacobite army was routed at the Battle of Aughrim, the most strategically important victory of the war. The final act of the war was the siege laid at Limerick in September 1691 which was concluded by the Treaty of Limerick. The Treaty guaranteed Jacobite soldiers free passage to the continent, secured the estates of those who remained and promised Catholics the freedom to practice their religion.

Eighteenth Century - The 1798 Rebellion

The 1798 Rebellion was the product of an alliance between two secret societies, the Society of United Irishmen, and the Defenders. Inspired by the ideals and successes of the American and French revolutions, radicals (Presbyterian and Catholic) found common cause in overthrowing British rule in Ireland and establishing an independent republic. Beset by informers many of the United Irishmen leaders were arrested prior to the outbreak of rebellion on May 23, 1798. The rebellion was uncoordinated and the expected French invasion was insignificant and came too late. The rebellion was confined to the south-east (Wexford and Waterford), eastern Ulster (Down and Antrim), Dublin and surrounding counties and later in north Connacht. Government forces crushed the rebels in Leinster executing many of those who surrendered. The rebels in Ulster were also quickly defeated but those in Wexford enjoyed some success. They captured the towns of Enniscorthy and Wexford, massacring militia and Protestant civilians in the process but, were finally defeated at Vinegar Hill. The final significant act of the rebellion was the landing of French troops at Killala in August. The troops defeated government forces at Castlebar but surrendered at Ballinamuck in county Longford. Theobald Wolfe Tone, the last remaining United Irishmen leader at large, was captured at Lough Swilly in November and was convicted of treason and sentenced to death by hanging, but died after inexpertly cutting his own throat.

Nineteenth Century - The Great Famine

Over-dependence on the potato and the decimation of that crop in the period 1845-49 caused the Great Famine. Despite a pronounced economic decline in the period after the Napoleonic Wars the population of Ireland grew exponentially. It has been estimated that the staple diet of up to three million people was the potato, supplemented occasionally by meat or fish. The potato crops of 1845, 1846 and 1848 were drastically reduced when afflicted by the fungal disease *Phytophthora infestans* – potato blight. The crop of 1847 was largely unaffected but a seed potato shortage meant that a smaller acreage than normal had been sown. Government responses to the famine shaped the consequences. The Tory government of Robert Peel distributed maize meal and instituted a programme of public works. The Whig government of Lord John Russell, however, which assumed office in June 1846, extended the programme of public works but ended the practice of distributing food. As is the norm in times of famine disease was more deadly than starvation, with typhus, relapsing fever and dysentery the most prevalent diseases. Reliable figures are not available for how many died or how many emigrated but the census of 1851 recorded a population of 6.5 million, down from 8.2 million in 1841. The western seaboard was the area most severely affected by the famine and the poorest socio-economic class, landless labourers, were virtually wiped out.

Twentieth Century - Independence

The proclamation of the Irish Republic during Easter week in 1916 provided the inspiration for Irish nationalists to pursue a course of national independence. Sinn Féin MPs returned at the 1918 General Election met in January 1919 to form a national assembly (Dáil Éireann) and the first encounter of the War of Independence occurred on the same day. The War of Independence was formally concluded by the Anglo-Irish Treaty, signed in December 1921. The treaty established the Irish Free State as a self governing dominion of the Commonwealth and provided for a Boundary Commission to determine the border between the new state and Northern Ireland. The Treaty was narrowly ratified by the Dáil with many TDs unhappy at the retention of the link to the crown and an Oath of Allegiance to the monarch. When Civil War broke out in June 1922 government forces secured victory and the existence of the new state was ensured. The report of the Boundary Commission was suppressed in 1925 after it emerged that the Free State would be required to cede territory to Northern Ireland. The Constitution of 1937 removed all mention of the crown, putting an elected President as head of state. Ireland formally left the Commonwealth in 1949 with the Declaration of the Republic.

Chronology of the Irish Millennium

Events, laws, acts and persons appearing in small capitals in the chronology are featured elsewhere in the Almanac.
Entries with an arrow indicate the next entry in a chain of events

1001-1299

1005 BRIAN BORU (→ 1014), high-king 1002-1014, visits Armagh and confirms its primacy in the Church.

1014 Battle of Clontarf. Brian Boru defeats the rebellious Leinstermen and their Viking allies decisively but is killed himself.

1028-36 Christchurch Cathedral, Dublin, built.

1095 First Crusade proclaimed by Pope Urban II. Irish join in great numbers.

1124 Round tower at Clonmacnoise completed.

1142 First Cistercian monastery in Ireland founded at Mellifont.

1152 Synod of Kells-Mellifont establishes diocesan organisation of Church, with four dioceses - Armagh, Dublin, Cashel and Tuam. Armagh enjoys the primacy.

1169 Normans arrive in Ireland at invitation of exiled Leinster king, DIARMAIT MAC MURCHADA (→ 1171)

1169-c.1300 Normans conquer much of Leinster, north and east Ulster, Munster and parts of Connacht.

1171 (May) RICHARD DE CLARE (STRONGBOW) succeeds Diarmait Mac Murchada as king of Leinster.

1171 (October) Henry II, king of England, lands at Waterford.

1175 Treaty of Windsor: High-king Ruairdhí Ua Conchobair (Rory O'Connor) recognises Henry II as his overlord, while Henry recognises Ua Conchobair as high-king of unconquered parts of Ireland.

1177 Prince John (son of Henry II) appointed lord of Ireland. Becomes king of England 1199.

1204 Normans start building Dublin Castle.

1216 (October) John, king of England, dies. Succeeded by Henry III as king and lord of Ireland. (→ 1254)

1216 (November) Magna Carta issued for Ireland.

1254 Henry's son Edward is styled 'Lord of Ireland.' (→ 1272)

1272 Henry III dies, succeeded by Edward I. (→ 1307)

The 1300s

1301-5 Irish mercenaries fight with Edward I in Scotland. The Scots, led by William Wallace, were defeated in 1305.

1307 Edward I dies, succeeded by Edward II. (→ 1327)

1315 Edward Bruce (crowned king of Scotland 1306) arrives in Ulster. Crowned king of Ireland in 1316 but never reigned. Killed 1318 at Battle of Faughart.

1327 Edward II abdicates, his queen rules until their son Edward III comes of age in 1330. (→ 1377)

1348 First record of Black Death in Ireland. Occurrences at Howth and Drogheda.

1366 Parliament at Kilkenny. STATUTE OF KILKENNY enacted, designed to prohibit assimilation of Anglo-Irish and Gaelic Irish.

1377 Edward III dies, succeeded by Richard II. (→ 1399)

1395 Richard II defeats Leinster Irish in battle. Most Irish kings and rebel Normans submit to him.

1399 Richard II deposed, Henry IV crowned king of England, also Lord of Ireland. (→ 1413)

The 1400s

1413 Henry IV succeeded by Henry V. (→ 1422)

1422 Henry V succeeded by Henry VI. (→ 1461)

1460 Irish parliament declares that only acts passed by it are binding on the country. (→ 1494)

1461 Edward IV assumes English Crown and with it the lordship of Ireland. (→ 1470)

1470 Henry VI reinstalled to the English Crown. (→ 1471)

1471 Edward IV restored to the throne. (→ 1483)

1479 Gearóid Mór Fitzgerald, the eighth earl of Kildare, appointed Lord Deputy (king's representative in Ireland). (→ 1496)

1483 (April) Edward V, son of Edward IV succeeds to throne on his father's death. (→ June)

1483 (June) Edward V deposed, replaced by Richard III. (→ 1485)

1485 Henry Tudor kills Richard III at Battle of Bosworth and becomes king as Henry VII. (→ 1509)

1487 First recorded use of a firearm in Ireland.

1494 Edward Poynings appointed Lord Deputy. POYNINGS' LAW enacted by parliament at Drogheda. All legislation passed by subsequent Irish parliaments to be approved by the king. Act not amended until 1782.

1495 Parliament makes reference to the English Pale in Ireland in a statute.

1496 Earl of Kildare reappointed Lord Deputy. (→ 1513)

The 1500s

1504 Battle of Knockdoe. Clanricard and O'Brien defeated by forces of the Pale, the Lord Deputy and O'Donnell, king of Tír Conaill. Estimated 2,000 combatants killed.

1509 Death of Henry VII. Accession of his son Henry VIII. (→ 1541)

1513 Gearóid Óg Fitzgerald, ninth earl of Kildare, appointed Lord Deputy following the death of his father.

1534 (June) THOMAS FITZGERALD (SILKEN THOMAS) son of Gearóid Óg rebels against English rule. Surrenders August 1535 and imprisoned. Executed February 1537.

1534 Gearóid Óg dies in Tower of London.

1536 Reformation parliament, held in Dublin, recognises Henry VIII as temporal head of the Church in Ireland.

1537 Act of Irish parliament provides for suppression of monasteries throughout the country.

1541 Act of Irish parliament recognises Henry VIII as king of Ireland (→ 1547). The English king had hitherto been styled 'lord of Ireland'.

1541 First instance of the system of 'surrender and regrant' where Irish lords recognised the king as sovereign, revoked their Gaelic title, assumed an English title and gained a royal grant of their lands.

1547 Accession of Edward VI following death of his father, Henry VIII. (→ 1553)

1549 Act of Uniformity orders the use of the Book of Common Prayer in England and Ireland.

1553 Mary I accedes to the throne on the death of Edward VI. (→ 1558) Pace of Reformation halted.

1557 Plantation of Laois and Offaly begins.

1558 Death of Mary I. Accession of the virgin queen, Elizabeth I (→ 1570; → March 1603). Reformation gains new impetus.

1562 Shane O'Neill, earl of Tyrone in rebellion. Submits to Lord Deputy in 1563 but continues warring with local lords until his death in 1567.

1570 Elizabeth I excommunicated by the Pope.

1568-74 Desmond Rebellion in Munster.

1579-83 Further rebellion in Munster. Earl of Desmond killed in 1583.

1582 Pope Gregory XIII reforms calendar - 4/10/1582 to be followed by 15/10/1582 - and year to commence on January 1. Britain and Ireland adopt Gregorian calendar 1782.

1583 HUGH O'NEILL takes the Gaelic title of The O'Neill. Conferred with English title of Earl of Tyrone in 1587.

1587 First grant of land in the plantation of Munster.

1588 Spanish Armada founders off Irish coast, 25 ships wrecked, survivors aided in Connacht and Ulster but put to death elsewhere.

1592 Trinity College Dublin established.

1595-1603 Nine Years War - Rebellion of Hugh O'Neill, earl of Tyrone, and Red Hugh O'Donnell who enlist Spanish support (troops land at Kinsale in 1601).

The 1600s

1601 Battle of Kinsale - Forces of O'Neill and O'Donnell heavily defeated by Lord Deputy Mountjoy.

1603 (March) Accession of James I (James VI of Scotland), first of Stuart line, following the death of Elizabeth I. (→ 1625)

1603 (March) Treaty of Mellifont. O'Neill submits to Mountjoy and pledges loyalty to the Crown.

1607 'Flight of Earls'. Earls of Tyrone and Tirconnell leave Ireland, sailing from Lough Swilly. Their lands are forfeited to the Crown. (→ 1609)

1608 CAHIR O'DOHERTY–the last Irish chieftain–in rebellion, sacks Derry. Killed in Donegal, his lands are forfeited to the Crown.

1609 Beginning of the plantation of Ulster in counties Donegal, Derry, Tyrone, Armagh, Cavan and Fermanagh.

1625 Death of James I, accession of Charles I. (→ January 1649)

1632 Compilation of the ANNALS OF THE FOUR MASTERS, a significant historical work, begins and is completed 1636.

1641 A rising, ostensibly in support of Charles I, begins in Ulster and spreads southwards. Thousands of Protestants reported massacred.

1649 (January) Execution of Charles I. England a republic until 1660.

1649 (August) Oliver Cromwell lands in Ireland. Massacre of Catholics in Drogheda and Wexford.

1653 Acts providing for the transplanting of Catholic Irish to Connacht and Ulster Presbyterians to Munster. Their lands are subsequently taken by Cromwellian soldiers and English settlers.

1660 Charles II proclaimed king in Dublin following restoration of the monarchy. (1685)

1673 Non-Anglicans excluded from public office by Test Act.

1685 Accession of James II on the death of Charles II. (→ 1689)

1688 James II flees to France from England.

1689 (February) William and Mary crowned as joint monarchs. (→ 1694; → 1702)

1689 (April) Siege of Derry. Jacobites (followers of James II) lay siege to the city until July when seaborne supplies arrive.

1690 William defeats James at river Boyne (July 1); James departs for France (July 4); unsuccessful siege at Limerick by Williamite forces (August 9 - 30).

1691 Jacobites defeated at Battle of Aughrim (July 12).

1691 Siege of Limerick (August 25 - September 24) followed by a truce allowing the signing of the TREATY OF LIMERICK (October 3), which guaranteed Catholic rights of worship and free passage of Jacobite soldiers to France.

1691 (December) First of the PENAL LAWS passed, Catholics excluded from parliament and public office by means of oath of supremacy.

1692-1703 Williamites begin confiscation of land from those who supported James.

1694 Death of Mary II.

The 1700s

1702 William III dies and is succeeded by Queen Anne. (→ 1714)

1714 Queen Anne dies without an heir, succeeded by George I, first of the Hanoverian line. (→ 1727)

1718 Significant numbers of Ulster Scots (largely Presbyterian) begin emigration to North America.

1719 Toleration Act passed for dissenting protestants. Legal toleration of their religion.

1720 Declaratory Act - British parliament affirms its right to legislate for Ireland. (→ 1782)

1727 George I succeeded by George II. (→ October 1760)

1737 First edition of *The Belfast Newsletter*.

1740-1 Severe famine in Ireland; several hundred thousand die.

1745 The Rotunda Maternity Hospital is founded in Dublin.

1745 (May) Battle of Fontenoy (part of the War of Austrian Succession) at which Irish troops, known as the Wild Geese, distinguished themselves.

1752 George II brings Britain and Ireland into line with Europe by adopting Gregorian Calender - 2/9/1752 followed by 14/9/1752.

1756 Work begins on construction of Grand Canal.

1760 (March) CATHOLIC COMMITTEE founded in Dublin to lobby for removal of penal laws.

1760 (October) George III becomes king on death of his grandfather George II. (→ 1820)

1778 VOLUNTEER MOVEMENT founded in Belfast.

1782 Ireland attains legislative independence. Declaratory Act 1720 repealed, and Poynings' Law 1494 amended. (→ 1801)

1783 Bank of Ireland begins trading.

1791 Society of UNITED IRISHMEN founded in Belfast. (→ 1798)

1793 CATHOLIC RELIEF ACT - Catholics given rights to vote, to third level education and to hold all but the highest offices of state.

1795 (September) ORANGE ORDER founded in Armagh.

1795 (October) Roman Catholic seminary opens at Maynooth.

1797 (July) Fourteen are killed in violence at an Orange parade in Stewartstown, Co. Tyrone.

1798 (May) United Irishmen rebellion begins. Fighting confined to Leinster and Ulster. Government forces defeat the rebels.

1798 (August) French troops land in Mayo in support of the rebellion. Surrender on September 8.

1798 (November) THEOBALD WOLFE TONE, leader of United Irishmen, arrested at Buncrana. Convicted of treason by court martial and sentenced to death. Commits suicide before sentence can be carried out.

The 1800s

1800 ACT OF UNION passed to provide for legislative and political union between Great Britain and Ireland.

1801 Union of Great Britain and Ireland commences.

1803 Rebellion in Dublin led by ROBERT EMMET. Emmet hanged for treason September 20.

1813 Four men are killed following violence at an Orange parade in Belfast.

1814 APPRENTICE BOYS OF DERRY formed.

1820 Death of George III, accession of George IV. (→ 1830)

1822 Act of parliament provides for an all-Ireland police force. (→ 1836)

1823 CATHOLIC ASSOCIATION founded in Dublin to lobby for Catholic Emancipation. (→ April 1829)

1825 Unlawful Societies (Ireland) Act passed, Catholic Association dissolves, as does the Grand Lodge of the Orange Order (reconstituted 1828). Law ignored by Orange lodges parades continue.

1828 DANIEL O'CONNELL elected to House of Commons but unable to take his seat because he is Roman Catholic.

1829 (April) CATHOLIC EMANCIPATION granted. Roman Catholics permitted to enter parliament and hold the high offices of state.

1829 Sixteen die in violence accompanying Orange marches during the summer.

1830 Death of George IV, accession of William IV. (→ 1837)

1831 (June) 'Tithe war' begins. Recurring outbreaks of violence caused by the collection of Anglican tithes from members of all religious denominations.

1831 (November) Scheme for nationwide primary schooling initiated - the first in the world.

1832 Party Procession Act passed curtailing marches.

1834 First railway line in Ireland comes into operation.

1836 (April) Grand Lodge of the Orange Order dissolves to avoid suppression.

1836 (May) IRISH CONSTABULARY formed, earned 'Royal' prefix 1867. (→ May 1922;→ August 1923)

1837 Queen Victoria accedes to the throne on death of William IV. (→ January 1901)

1838 TOTAL ABSTINENCE MOVEMENT founded in Cork by Fr. Theobald Matthew and William Martin.

1839 (January 6) 'Night of the Big Wind,' storms cause widespread damage.

1840 Daniel O'Connell forms LOYAL NATIONAL REPEAL ASSOCIATION to lobby for the repeal of the Union between Ireland and Great Britain.

1841 Census. Population of Ireland - 8,175,124. (→ 1851)

1841 First edition of *The Cork Examiner*.

1843 Daniel O'Connell organises 'Monster meetings' in support of Repeal throughout the country; the biggest is at Tara (an estimated 750,000 attend).

1845 (June) Party Processions Act lapses, Orange Order reformed.

1845 (July) Queen's Colleges Act provide for the establishment of new third level colleges. (→ 1849)

1845 (September) First report of potato blight. Beginning of the Famine. Crop decimated in 1846. 1847 (Black '47) is worst year. Blight and famine continue until 1850. In excess of one million die and more than one million emigrate.

1848 YOUNG IRELAND rebellion in Munster easily put down. Leaders transported.

1849 Opening of Queen's Colleges at Belfast, Cork and Galway.

1850 (March) Party Processions Act renewed, police empowered to seize weapons and emblems.

1850 (August) IRISH TENANT LEAGUE formed to lobby for rights of tenant farmers.

1851 Census. Population of Ireland 6,552,385. (→ 1861)

1854 Catholic University of Ireland (now University College Dublin) opens.

1855 First edition of *The Irish News*.

1858 IRISH REPUBLICAN BROTHERHOOD founded in Dublin. A sister movement, the FENIAN BROTHERHOOD founded in New York 1859. (→ February-March 1867)

1859 First edition of *The Irish Times*.

1861 Census. Population of Ireland - 5,798,967. (→ 1871)

1867 (February-March) Fenian rising in Munster easily suppressed.

1867 (July) Orange procession opposing Party Processions Act leads to a reduction in powers of the Act. Marches now permitted in non-contentious areas. Party Processions Act repealed 1872.

1869 IRISH CHURCH ACT provides for disestablishment of Church of Ireland.

1870 (August) Gladstone's first LAND ACT. (→ August 1881)

1871 Census. Population of Ireland - 5,412,377. (→ April 1881).

1872 Ballot Act. Secret voting introduced.

1873 (May) ISAAC BUTT forms the HOME RULE LEAGUE, precursor of IRISH PARLIAMENTARY PARTY.

1877 CHARLES STEWART PARNELL becomes leader of Home Rule Confederation of Great Britain, elected chairman of Irish Parliamentary Party 1880. (→ 1890)

1879 IRISH NATIONAL LAND LEAGUE formed in Dublin to agitate for land reform. Proscribed 1882.

1879-82 'The Land War'. Huge increase in rural crime. Directed almost exclusively at landlords and their agents.

1880 'Boycotting' of land agent CHARLES CUNNINGHAM BOYCOTT in Mayo.

1881 (April) Census. Population of Ireland 5,174,836. (→ April 1891)

1881 (August) Gladstone's second LAND ACT. (→ August 1885)

1882 Murders of the Chief Secretary and his Under Secretary (the principal government officials in Ireland) in the Phoenix Park by the INVINCIBLES.

1884 GAELIC ATHLETIC ASSOCIATION founded in Thurles.

1885 (May) IRISH LOYAL AND PATRIOTIC UNION formed to oppose Home Rule and maintain the union.

1885 (August) ASHBOURNE ACT provides government loans to tenant farmers for land purchase. (→ August 1891)

1886 First HOME RULE BILL defeated in House of Commons. (→ September 1893)

Fifty people lose their lives in sectarian rioting in Belfast.

1888 (November) Borough of Belfast created a city by charter.

1888 Pioneer and Total Abstinence Association founded by James Cullen SJ.

1890 Parnell ousted from leadership of Irish Parliamentary Party. He is cited as co-respondent in the William O'Shea divorce petition. Unacceptable to Liberal Party and Catholic hierarchy, causes split in party. (→ 1900)

1891 (March) Anti-Parnellite Irish National Federation founded.

1891 (April) Census. Population of Ireland - 4,704,750. (→ March 1901)

1891 (August) BALFOUR ACT. Extends tenant purchase scheme and establishes Congested Districts Board. (→ August 1903)

1891 First edition of the *Evening Herald*.

1892 (June) Ulster Convention at Belfast. Delegates vote to oppose workings of a Home Rule parliament.

1892 (June) Primary school education made compulsory.

1893 (July) CONRADH NA GAEILIGE (the Gaelic League) formed.

1893 (September) HOME RULE BILL passed in the House of Commons but defeated in House of Lords. (→ September 1914)

1894 (April) IRISH AGRICULTURAL ORGANISATION SOCIETY founded.

1894 (April) Trade Union Congress held for first time.

1898 Local Government (Ireland) Act. Establishes county and district councils.

1899 (May) IRISH LITERARY THEATRE founded in Dublin.

1899 (October) Beginning of the Boer War.

1900-1909

1900 Irish Parliamentary Party reunites with JOHN REDMOND as leader.

1901 (January) Queen Victoria dies. Accession of Edward VII. (→ 1910)

1901 (March) Census. Population of Ireland - 4,458,775. (→ April 1911)

1903 (March) St. Patrick's Day, March 17, declared a bank holiday.

1903 (June) Independent Orange Order founded in Belfast.

1903 (August) WYNDHAM ACT. Culmination of the series of land acts dating back to 1870.

1905 (March) ULSTER UNIONIST COUNCIL formed to oppose Home Rule.

1905 First edition of the *Irish Independent*.

1907 (April) SINN FÉIN LEAGUE founded (adopts name Sinn Féin 1908).

1907 (July) Irish Crown jewels stolen. They have never been recovered.

1908 (August) IRISH UNIVERSITIES ACT, instituting the National University of Ireland (NUI).

1908 (December) IRISH TRANSPORT AND GENERAL WORKERS' UNION (ITGWU) founded in Dublin.

1910-1919

1913 Irish becomes a compulsory subject for matriculation in NUI.

1910 Death of Edward VII, accession of George V.

1911 (April) *Titanic* launched in Belfast.

1911 (April) Census. Population of Ireland - 4,390,219. (→ April 1926)

1911 (August) Parliament Act abolishes veto powers of House of Lords.

1912 (April) *Titanic* sinks on her maiden voyage.

1912 (June) Labour Party founded at Clonmel, Co. Tipperary.

1912 (September) ULSTER SOLEMN LEAGUE AND COVENANT signed by 218,000 men pledging to use all necessary means to oppose Home Rule.

1913 (January) ULSTER VOLUNTEER FORCE founded in Belfast. (→ July 1916)

1913 (August) Beginning of the Dublin 'Lock-Out', where Dublin Employers' Federation shuts out members of ITGWU from their places of employment. Continues until January 1914.

1913 (November) IRISH CITIZENS ARMY founded in Dublin to protect the locked-out workers.

1913 (November) IRISH VOLUNTEERS founded in Dublin as a response to formation of UVF. (→ September 1914)

1914 (March) Curragh Incident - British officers serving at the Curragh indicate that they will not aid the imposition of Home Rule in Ulster.

1914 (April) Gunrunning by Ulster Volunteers at Larne passes off without incident.

1914 (July) Four civilians killed by troops when Irish Volunteers engage in gunrunning at Howth.

1914 (August 4) Britain declares war on Germany. The 36th Ulster Division is established, drawing on UVF membership. War ends November 1918.

1914 (September) HOME RULE BILL passed but suspended because of World War I.

1914 (September) Split in Irish Volunteers. Majority answer John Redmond's call to join the war. Remainder become National Volunteers under leadership of ÉOIN MAC NEILL.

1915 IRB reorganised and Military Council formed. Plans for an Irish rebellion at advanced stage.

1916 (April) Easter Rising in Dublin. Independent Irish Republic proclaimed. Rebellion suppressed within five days; over 3,000 injured and 450 killed.

1916 (May) Fifteen of the leaders of the Rising executed, including the seven signatories of the proclamation - THOMAS J. CLARKE, SEÁN MACDIARMADA, THOMAS MACDONAGH, PADRAIG PEARSE, EAMONN CEANNT, JAMES CONNOLLY and JOSEPH PLUNKETT.

1916 (July) Battle of the Somme begins (continues until November), the 36th Ulster Division decimated.

1916 (August) SIR ROGER CASEMENT hanged for his part in the Easter Rising.

1918 (November 11) Armistice day. End of World War I.

1918 (November) Universal Suffrage granted. Women win right to vote and right to sit in parliament.

1918 (December) Final all-Ireland general election to Westminster parliament. Seats: SF: 73, UUP: 25, Nat: 6, Ind: 1. (→ May 1921;→ November 1922)

1919 (January 21) Sinn Féin MPs, in keeping with their declared policy of abstention, do not take their seats at Westminster and meet as Dáil Éireann at the Mansion House in Dublin.

1919 (January 21) Two policemen killed in Tipperary in first engagement of War of Independence. War ends July 1921.

1919 (June) First non-stop transatlantic flight completed when Alcock and Brown land in Galway.

1919 (October) Irish Volunteers swear allegiance to the Irish Republic becoming the IRISH REPUBLICAN ARMY.

The 1920s

1920 (January) First British soldiers are recruited by RIC, commonly termed the BLACK AND TANS.

AUXILIARIES recruited from July onwards.

1920 (March) Lord Mayor of Cork, Tomás Mac Curtáin, shot dead by crown forces outside his home in Cork.

1920 (November) 'Bloody Sunday'. Fourteen British secret agents assassinated by IRA in Dublin. Black and Tans retaliate by shooting into a crowd watching a Gaelic football match at Croke Park, killing 12.

1920 (December) Black and Tans and Auxiliaries destroy centre of Cork city.

1920 (December) GOVERNMENT OF IRELAND ACT - Provides for the partition of Ireland and two Home Rule parliaments, one in Dublin, one in Belfast. (→ June 1921)

1921 (May) General election to Northern Ireland (NI) parliament. Seats: UUP: 40, Nat: 6, SF: 6. (→ April 1925)

1921 (May) One hundred and twenty-four Sinn Féin and four independent MPs are returned unopposed to the Parliament of Southern Ireland. (→ June 1922)

1921 (May) Custom House in Dublin is destroyed by IRA.

1921 (June) NI parliament opened by George V, prorogued March 1972.

1921 (June) Parliament of southern Ireland meets in Dublin. Only the four independent MPs turn up; the 124 Sinn Féin MPs refuse to accept its legitimacy and do not take their seats.

1921 (July) Truce agreed between IRA and British army.

1921 (July) Fifteen Catholics killed and 68 seriously injured in one day when members of Orange Order, aided by police officers attack Catholic areas in Belfast.

1921 (August) Sinn Féin MPs elected to the parliament of southern Ireland meet in the Mansion House as the second Dáil.

1921 (December) ANGLO-IRISH TREATY signed in London establishing the Irish Free State (IFS). (→ January 1922; → December 1922; → December 1925)

1922 (January) Anglo-Irish Treaty approved by Dáil Éireann by 64 votes to 57. Split in Sinn Féin; those in opposition to the Treaty walk out. MICHAEL COLLINS becomes the chairman of the Provisional Government.

1922 (May) Royal Ulster Constabulary established.

1922 (May) IRA declared an illegal organisation in NI.

1922 (June) General election in IFS. Seats: Pro-treaty SF: 58, anti-treaty SF: 36, Lab: 17, Farmers' Party 7, others 10. Pro-treaty Sinn Féin form the government. (→ August 1923)

1922 (June) Civil War breaks out in IFS, ends May 1923.

1922 (August) Chairman of Provisional Government and Commander in Chief of the Free State forces, Michael Collins, assassinated in Cork.

1922 (October) Dáil Éireann ratified the CONSTITUTION OF THE IFS (approved by British parliament in December).

1922 (November) Provisional Government orders the first of 77 executions of anti-treaty prisoners.

1922 (November) NI elections to Westminster. Seats: UUP: 11, Nat: 2. (→ December 1923)

1922 (December) Executive Council of the IFS takes office with W.T. COSGRAVE as President.

1922 (December) NI parliament opts out of the IFS.

1923 (March) CUMANN NA NGAEDHEAL founded from pro-treaty Sinn Féin.

1923 (May) Civil war ends.

1923 (August) Garda Síochána established by act of Free State Dáil.

1923 (August) General election in Free State. Seats: Cumann na nGaedheal 63, SF 44, Lab. 14, Farmers' Party 15, others 17. Cumann na nGaedheal form government. (→ June 1927)

1923 (September) IFS becomes member of the League of Nations. (→ December 1955)

1923 (November) W.B. YEATS receives Nobel Prize for literature. (→ November 1926)

1923 (December) NI elections to Westminster. Seats: UUP 11, Nat. 2. (→ October 1924)

1924 (March) Mutiny in IFS army.

1924 (September) BBC starts radio broadcasts from Belfast as 2BE.

1924 (October) NI elections to Westminster. UUP win all 13 seats. (→ May 1929)

1925 (April) General election to NI parliament. Seats: UUP 32, Nat. 10, other U. 4, other Lab. 3, other Nat. 2, Ind. 1. (→ May 1929)

1925 (July) Shannon hydro-electric scheme approved by Dáil.

1925 (December) Governments of Britain, NI and IFS agree to rescind powers of the Boundary Commission.

1926 (January) 2RN, the forerunner of RTE commences radio broadcasts.

1926 (April) Census. Population of NI - 1,256,561. (→ February 1937) Population of IFS - 2,971,992. (→ April 1936)

1926 (May) FIANNA FÁIL founded by ÉAMON DE VALERA.

1926 (November) GEORGE BERNARD SHAW receives Nobel Prize for literature. (→ October 1965)

1927 (June) General election in IFS. Seats: Cumann na nGaedheal 47, FF 44, Lab. 22, Farmers' Party 11, National League 8, SF 5, others 16. Cumann na nGaedheal remain in office. (→ September)

1927 (July) KEVIN O'HIGGINS, Minister for Justice in IFS, assassinated.

1927 (August) Éamon de Valera and Fianna Fáil take Oath of Allegiance and take their seats in Dáil Éireann.

1927 (September) Cumann na nGaedheal 62, FF 57, Lab 13, Farmers' Party 6, others 15. Cumann na nGaedheal retain in office. (→ February 1932)

1929 (April) Proportional Representation abolished in NI parliamentary elections.

1929 (May) General election to NI parliament. Seats: UUP 38, Nat.11, other U. 3. (→ November 1931)

1929 (May) NI elections to Westminster. Seats: UUP 11, Nat. 2. (→ October 1933)

1929 (July) CENSORSHIP OF PUBLICATIONS ACT in IFS establishes a board with wide-ranging powers of censorship.

1929 (October) Shannon hydro-electric scheme comes into operation.

The 1930s

1931 (September) First edition of the *Irish Press*. (→ May 1995)

1931 (October) IRA declared an illegal organisation in IFS.

1931 (October) NI elections to Westminster. Seats: UUP 11, Nat. 2. (→ November 1935)

1931 (December) STATUTE OF WESTMINSTER passed by British parliament. Gives Dominion parliaments equal status with Imperial parliament at Westminster.

1932 (February) Quasi-fascist ARMY COMRADES ASSOCIATION - BLUESHIRTS - founded.

1932 (February) General election in Free State. Seats: FF 72, Cumann na nGaedheal 57, Lab. 7, Farmers' Party 4, others 13. Fianna Fáil form the new government. (→ January 1933)

1932 (June) Payment of land annuities to Britain withheld. Beginning of economic war between Ireland and Britain, ends April 1938.

1933 (January) General election in Free State. Seats: FF 77, Cumann na nGaedheal 48, Lab. 8, National Centre Party 11, others 9. Fianna Fáil remain in office. (→ July 1937)

1933 (May) Oath of Allegiance removed from constitution of IFS.

1933 (September) FINE GAEL formed by amalgamation of Cumann na nGaedheal, Centre Party and National Guard (Blueshirts). ÉOIN O'DUFFY first leader.

1933 (November) General election to NI parliament. Seats: UUP 36, Nat. 9, other U. 3, other Nat. 2, other Lab. 2. (→ February 1938).

1935 (July) Nine are killed and 2,241 Catholics across NI are intimidated out of their homes in riots accompanying 12th of July parades by the Orange Order.

1935 (November) NI elections to Westminster. Seats UUP 11, Nat. 2. (→ July 1945)

1936 (January) Death of George V, accession of Edward VIII. (→ December 1936)

1936 (April) Census in IFS. Population - 2,968,420. (→ May 1946)

1936 (May) Senate of IFS abolished by Dáil.

1936 (August) Aer Lingus established as national airline of the IFS.

1936 (November) Irish brigade, under leadership of Éoin O'Duffy, join General Franco's fascists in Spanish Civil War.

1936 (December) Abdication of Edward VIII, accession of George VI. (→ February 1952).

1936 (December) EXTERNAL RELATIONS ACT passed by Dáil during abdication crisis in Britain. It removes all reference to the Crown from the constitution.

1936 (December) CONNOLLY COLUMN, under leadership of FRANK RYAN, join socialists in Spanish Civil War.

1937 (February) Spanish Civil War (Non-intervention) Act forbids involvement of Free State citizens in the war.

1937 (February) Census in NI Population - 1,279,745. (→ April 1951)

1937 (July 1) CONSTITUTION OF ÉIRE is ratified by referendum, comes into effect December 29.

General election in Free State. Seats: FF 69, FG 48, Lab. 13, others 8. Fianna Fáil remain in government. (→ June 1938)

1938 (February) General election to NI parliament. Seats: UUP 39, Nat. 8, other U. 3, other Lab. 2. (→

June 1945)

1938 (April) Economic War with Britain ends, and Britain transfers the 'treaty ports' to Éire.

1938 (June) General election in Éire. Seats: FF 77, FG 45, Lab. 9, others 7. Fianna Fáil remain in government. (→ 1943)

1938 (June) DOUGLAS HYDE inaugurated as the first President of Ireland. (→ June 1945)

1939 (September 2) De Valera announces Éire will remain neutral during World War II.

Britain declares war on Germany (September 3).

State of national emergency declared (September 3), not rescinded until 1976.

The 1940s

1941 (April/May) German air-raids on Belfast kill almost 1,000.

1941 (May) Germans bomb North Strand in Dublin, killing 34.

1942 American troops arrive in NI.

1943 General election in Éire. Seats: FF 67, FG 32, Lab 17, CLANN NA TALMHAN 14, others 8. Fianna Fáil form the government. (→ May 1944)

1944 (May) General election in Éire. Seats: FF 76, FG 30, Clann na Talmhan 11, Lab. 8, others 13. Fianna Fáil remain in office. (→ February 1948)

1944 (December) Coras Iompair Éireann established as national transport company.

1945 (May 8) War ends in Europe (Ends in Pacific on August 14).

1945 (June) General election to NI parliament. Seats: UUP 33, Nat.10, other Lab. 4, other U. 2, Ind. 2, other Nat. 1. (→ February 1949)

1945 (June) SEÁN T. Ó CEALLAIGH inaugurated as second President. (→ June 1959)

1945 (July) N.I. elections to Westminster. Seats: UUP 9, Nat. 2, others 2. (→ 1950)

1946 (May) Census in Éire. Population - 2,955,107. (→ April 1951)

1946 (June) Bórd na Móna established.

1947 EDUCATION ACT in NI provides free secondary school education for all.

1948 (February) General Election in Éire. Seats: FF 68, FG 31, Lab. 14, CLANN NA POBLACHTA 10, Clann na Talmhan 7, others 17. Inter-party government formed by Fine Gael, Labour, Clann na Poblachta, Clann na Talmhan and independents. (→ May 1951)

1948 (December) REPUBLIC OF IRELAND ACT passed by Dáil. Republic declared on April 18, 1949, accompanied by a formal withdrawal from the British Commonwealth.

1949 (February) General election to N.I. parliament. Seats: UUP 37, Nat. 9, other U. 2, Ind. 2, other Nat.1, other Lab. 1. (→ October 1953)

1949 (February) Government announces it cannot join North Atlantic Treaty Organisation because of Britain's sovereignty in NI.

1949 (May) Council of Europe established. Ireland and Britain amongst founding members.

1949 (June) IRELAND ACT passed at Westminster recognising Ireland's withdrawal from the Commonwealth and reaffirming the constitutional position of NI.

The 1950s

1950 NI elections to Westminster. Seats: UUP 10, Nat. 2. (→ October 1951)

1951 (April) Census. Republic of Ireland (RoI) population - 2,960,593. (→ April 1956) NI population - 1,370,921. (→ April 1961)

1951 (April) Opposition to the Mother-and-Child Scheme from the Roman Catholic hierarchy results in resignation of Minister for Health and collapse of the government.

1951 (May) General election in RoI. Seats: FF 69, FG 40, Lab. 16, Clann na Talmhan 6, Clann na Poblachta 2, others 14. Fianna Fáil form minority government. (→ May 1954)

1951 (October) NI elections to Westminster. Seats: UUP 9, Nat. 2, others 1. (→ May 1955)

1951 (November) E.T.S. WALTON awarded Nobel Prize for Physics.

1952 (February) Death of George VI, accession of Elizabeth II.

1952 (July) Bord Fáilte, Irish tourist board, established by Act of Dáil Éireann.

1953 (January) Car ferry between Stranraer and Larne sinks with loss of 130 lives.

1953 (May) BBC begins television transmissions from Belfast.

1953 (October) General election to NI parliament. Seats: UUP 38, Nat. 7, other Lab. 3, other Nat. 2, other U. 1, Ind. 1. (→ 1958)

1954 (April) Flags and Emblems (Display) Act in NI makes it an offence to interfere with the Union Jack and empowers police to remove flags or emblems likely to incite trouble.

1954 (May) General election in RoI. Seats: FF 65, FG 50, Lab. 19, Clann na Talmhan 5, Clann na Poblachta 3, others 5. Inter-party government formed by Fine Gael, Labour, Clann na Talmhan and Clann na Poblachta. (→ 1957)

1955 (May) NI elections to Westminster. Seats: UUP 10, SF 2. (→ October 1959)

1955 (July) Led by BRIAN FAULKNER, MP, and protected by 300 RUC officers, 12,000 Orangemen march along a contentious route at Annalong, Co. Down.

1955 (December) RoI admitted to United Nations Organisation.

1956 (April) Census in RoI. Population - 2,898,264. (→ April 1961)

1956 (December) Beginning of IRA border campaign, ends February 1962.

1957 General election in RoI. Seats: FF 78, FG 40, Lab. 12, Clann na Poblachta 5, Clann na Talmhan 3, others 9. Fianna Fáil form government. (→ October 1961)

1958 General election to NI parliament. Seats: UUP 37, Nat. 7, other Lab. 6, other Nat. 1, Ind. 1. (→ May 1962)

1959 (June) Éamon de Valera elected President (→ June 1966)

Proposal to abolish proportional representation in Republic defeated by referendum.

1959 (October) NI elections to Westminster. Seats: UUP 12. (→ 1964)

1959 (October) First broadcast by Ulster Television.

The 1960s

1960 (November) Nine Irish soldiers killed while serving as UN peacekeepers in Belgian Congo. (→ April 1980)

1961 (April) Census. RoI population - 2,818,341. (→ April 1966) NI population - 1,425,042. (→ October 1966)

1961 (October) General election in RoI. Seats: FF 70, FG 47, Lab. 16, Clann na Talmhan 2, Clann na Poblachta 1, others 8. Fianna Fáil remain in office. (→ April 1965)

1961 (December 31) Inaugural television broadcast of Radio Telefís Éireann. (→ November 1978)

1962 (May) General election to NI parliament. Seats: UUP 35, Nat. 9, other Lab. 7, others 1. (→ November 1965)

1962 (July) The first motorway in NI, the M1 from Belfast to Lisburn, opens.

1963 (June) President of the United States, John Fitzgerald Kennedy, pays official visit to Ireland.

1964 NI elections to Westminster. Seats: UUP 12. (→ March 1966)

1965 (January) Taoiseach SEÁN LEMASS and Prime Minister TERENCE O'NEILL meet in Belfast followed by a meeting in Dublin in February.

1965 (April) General election in RoI. Seats: FF 72, F.G. 47, Lab. 22, Clann na Poblachta 1, others 2. Fianna Fáil form government. (→ June 1969)

1965 (June) New Towns Act in NI provides for establishment of Craigavon.

1965 (November) General election in NI. Seats: UUP 36, Nat. 9, other Lab. 4, others 3. (→ February 1969)

1966 (March) Nelson's pillar in Dublin is blown up.

1966 (March) NI elections to Westminster. Seats: UUP 11, Republican Lab. 1. (→ June 1970)

1966 (April) Census. RoI population - 2,884,002. (→ April 1971)

1966 (June) Éamon de Valera re-elected President. (→ May 1973)

1966 (October) Census in NI. Population - 1,484,775. (→ April 1971)

1967 (January) NI CIVIL RIGHTS ASSOCIATION (NICRA) formed.

1968 (August) Higher Education Authority established in Republic.

1968 (August) NICRA holds its first demonstration.

1968 (October) Proposal to abolish proportional representation defeated by referendum in RoI.

1969 (January) Civil rights march attacked by loyalists at Burntollet, Co. Derry.

1969 (February) General election in NI. Seats: UUP 39, Nat. 6, other Lab. 4, others 3. (→ March 1972)

1969 (June) General election in RoI. Seats: FF 75, FG 50, Lab. 18, others 1. Fianna Fáil remain in government. (→ February 1973)

1969 (August) British troops move into NI, following sustained clashes between Bogside residents and the 'B' SPECIALS in Derry sparked off by the annual Apprentice Boys march.

1969 (October) SAMUEL BECKETT awarded Nobel Prize for literature. (→ October 1995)

1969 (December) Act of NI parliament establishes Ulster Defence Regiment (UDR), disbanded 1992.

The 1970s

1970 (January) Split in Sinn Féin between abstentionists (PROVISIONAL SINN FÉIN) and non-abstentionists (OFFICIAL SINN FÉIN). IRA splits along same lines.

1970 (April) 'B' Specials disbanded.

1970 (April) ALLIANCE PARTY OF NI founded.

1970 (May) Irish Government ministers CHARLES HAUGHEY and NEIL BLANEY charged with procuring arms for the IRA, Blaney's charges are dropped; Haughey is acquitted.

1970 (June) NI elections to Westminster. Seats: UUP 8, others 4. (→ February 1974)

1970 (August) SOCIAL DEMOCRATIC AND LABOUR PARTY founded.

1971 (February) Decimal currency introduced in both NI and the RoI. Pre-decimal 240 pence pound replaced with 100 pence pound. (→ March 1979)

1971 (April) Census. RoI population - 2,978,248. (→ April 1979) NI population - 1,536,065. (→ April 1981)

1971 (August) Internment without trial reintroduced in NI. Measures aimed at nationalist community in particular. Continues until December 1975. All parades and marches are banned for six months.

1971 (September) DEMOCRATIC UNIONIST PARTY founded by IAN PAISLEY.

1971 (September) Protestant paramilitary organisation, the ULSTER DEFENCE ASSOCIATION (UDA) formed.

1972 (January) 'Bloody Sunday' - 13 civilians on civil rights march in Derry shot dead by British army paratroopers. One man later dies from his injuries.

1972 (February) British embassy in Dublin is attacked and burned following 'Bloody Sunday'.

1972 (March) NI parliament prorogued and direct rule from Westminster introduced.

1972 (May) RoI's proposed entry to European Economic Community (EEC) approved by referendum. (→ December 1972)

1972 (December) Referendum in the RoI lowers the voting age to 18 and removes the special position of the Roman Catholic church from the constitution. (→ July 1979)

1973 (January) RoI joins European Economic Community along with Britain and Denmark.

1973 (February) General election in RoI. Seats: FF 69, FG 54, Lab. 19, others 2. Fine Gael and Labour form coalition government. (→ June 1977)

1973 (March) Referendum in NI on remaining within United Kingdom: 98.9% in favour, 1.1% against (nationalists boycott poll).

1973 (May) ERSKINE CHILDERS elected President; inaugurated June 25. (→ December 1974)

1973 (June) Elections to NI Assembly. Seats: UUP 23, SDLP 19, Alliance 8, DUP 8, VANGUARD UNIONIST PROGRESSIVE PARTY 7, others 13. Assembly prorogued May 1974.

1973 (July) NORTHERN IRELAND CONSTITUTION ACT. NI parliament abolished and provision made for a 12-

member executive.

1973 (December) Tripartite Conference results in SUNNINGDALE AGREEMENT. Power-sharing executive for NI agreed upon.

1974 (January) Power-sharing executive takes office. (→ May)

1974 (February) NI elections to Westminster. Seats: UUP 7, DUP 1, SDLP 1, VUPP 1. (→ October)

1974 (May) ULSTER WORKERS' COUNCIL declares general strike in opposition to power-sharing executive. Executive falls after two weeks.

1974 (October) SEÁN MACBRIDE shares Nobel Peace Prize. (→ November 1976)

1974 (October) NI elections to Westminster. Seats: UUP 6, DUP 1, SDLP 1, VUPP 1, others 1. (→ May 1979)

1974 (December) CEARBHALL Ó DÁLAIGH inaugurated as President following death of Erskine Childers. (→ December 1976)

1975 (May) Election to NI Convention. Seats: UUP 19, SDLP 17, VUPP 14, DUP 12, Alliance 8, others 8. Convention dissolved January 1976.

1976 (March) Special category status for persons convicted of paramilitary offences phased out, followed by Republican protests in Long Kesh. (→ March 1981)

1976 (July) British ambassador to the Republic killed in IRA bomb attack in Dublin.

1976 (August) Peace People founded.

1976 (November) Betty Williams and Mairead Corrigan, founding members of the Peace People awarded Nobel Peace Prize. (→ December 1998)

1976 (December) DR. PATRICK HILLERY inaugurated as President following resignation of Cearbhall Ó Dálaigh. (→ November 1990)

1977 (June) General election in RoI. Seats: FF 84, FG 43, Lab. 17, others 4. Fianna Fáil return to government. (→ June 1981)

1978 (November) Second national television channel established by RTÉ. (→ October 1996)

1979 (January) Oil tanker explodes at Whiddy Island oil terminal Cork, killing 50.

1979 (March) Ireland joins European Monetary System, ending parity between Punt and Sterling.

1979 (April) Census in RoI. Population - 3,368,405. (→ April 1981)

1979 (May) General election in NI. Seats: UUP 5, DUP 3, SDLP 1, others 3. (→ June 1983)

1979 (June) Elections to European parliament. Seats in RoI: FF 5, FG 4, Lab. 4, others 2. Seats in NI: SDLP 1, UUP 1, DUP 1. (→ June 1984)

1979 (July) Referendum on protection of adoption system and altering university representation in the Seanad passed. (→ September 1983)

1979 (August) Earl Mountbatten is killed by IRA bomb explosion on his boat off the Co. Sligo coast. Three others including two teenagers also die. Eighteen British soldiers are killed in an explosion in Co. Down on same day.

1979 (September/October) Pope John Paul II visits Ireland, celebrating public mass at Knock, Drogheda and Dublin and a private mass at Maynooth.

The 1980s

1980 (April) Two Irish soldiers serving as UN peacekeepers shot dead in Lebanon. (→ March 1989)

1981 (February) Forty-eight die as fire sweeps through Stardust Ballroom in Artane, Dublin. Over 160 injured.

1981 (March) Republican hunger strike to regain special category status, led by BOBBY SANDS, begins in Long Kesh.

1981 (April) Imprisoned hunger striker Bobby Sands elected to House of Commons in Fermanagh & South Tyrone by-election. He and nine other prisoners died during the protest before it was called off in October. Sixty-four died in accompanying disturbances throughout NI.

1981 (April) Census. RoI population - 3,443,405. (→ April 1986) NI population - 1,481,959. (→ April 1991)

1981 (June) General Election in RoI. Seats: FF 78, FG 65, Lab. 15, WORKERS' PARTY 1, others 7 (including two hunger strikers). Fine Gael and Labour form coalition government. (→ February 1982)

1981 (August) Death of hunger striker Kieran Doherty TD.

1982 (February) General election in RoI. Seats: FF 81, FG 63, Lab. 15, WP 3, others 3. Fianna Fáil form minority government. (→ November)

1982 (October) Election to NI. Assembly. Seats: UUP 26, DUP 21, SDLP 14, Alliance 10, SF 5. Assembly dissolved July 1986.

1982 (November) General election in RoI. Seats: FF 75, FG 70, Lab. 16, WP 2, others 3. Fine Gael and Labour form coalition government. (→ February 1987)

1982 (December) Seventeen killed in INLA bombing of a disco in Co. Derry.

1983 (May) New Ireland Forum meets for first time. (→ May 1984)

1983 (June) NI elections to Westminster. Seats: UUP 11, DUP 3, SDLP 1, SF 1, others 1. (→ January 1986)

1983 (August) Twenty-two republicans convicted on the word of supergrass Christopher Black (18 have their convictions quashed within three years).

1983 (September) Referendum prohibiting legalisation of abortion in RoI passed. (→ June 1984)

1983 (September) Thirty-nine IRA inmates escape from Long Kesh, 20 are quickly recaptured.

1984 (May) REPORT OF THE NEW IRELAND FORUM published.

1984 (June) Ronald Regan, President of the United States, pays official visit to Ireland.

1984 (June) Elections to European parliament. Seats in Republic: FF 8, FG 6, others 1. Seats in NI: SDLP 1, UUP 1, DUP 1. (→ June 1989)

Referendum on extending voting rights to non-citizens in RoI passed. (→ June 1986)

1984 (October) IRA bomb the Brighton hotel where the Conservative Party conference is being held. Five are killed and many members of the British cabinet narrowly escape serious injury or death.

1985 (June) Air India jet crashes off Co. Kerry coast with loss of 329 lives.

1985 (October) First commercial flight from Knock airport.

1985 (November) ANGLO-IRISH AGREEMENT signed by British and Irish governments. Setting up British/Irish governmental conference.

1985 (December) PROGRESSIVE DEMOCRATS founded.

1986 (January) Fifteen by-elections in NI caused by simultaneous resignation of all unionist MPs in protest at the Anglo-Irish Agreement. Seats: UUP 10, DUP 3, SDLP 1, others 1. (→ June 1987)

1986 (June) Referendum in RoI rejects legalisation of divorce. (→ May 1987)

1986 (April) Census in RoI. Population 3,540,643. (→ April 1991)

1987 (January) Government reveals that one-third of the country's haemophiliacs contracted HIV through the transfusion of contaminated blood.

1987 (February) General election in RoI. Seats: FF 81, FG 51, PD 14, Lab. 12, WP 4, others 4. Fianna Fáil form minority government. (→ June 1989)

1987 (March) National Lottery launched in the RoI.

1987 (May) Eight members of the IRA and one passer-by killed in a British army ambush at Loughgall, Co. Armagh.

1987 (May) Referendum in RoI ratified SINGLE EUROPEAN ACT. (→ June 1992; → January 1993)

1987 (June) NI elections to Westminster. Seats: UUP 9, DUP 3, SDLP 3, SF 1, others 1. (→ April 1992)

1987 (November) IRA bomb kills eleven civilians at Remembrance Day service in Enniskillen.

1988 Dublin celebrates its Millennium Year.

1988 (March) Week of unrest in NI following killing of three IRA members in Gibraltar by SAS. Three mourners killed at their funerals by loyalist gunman. Two soldiers killed at subsequent funerals.

1988 (August) Eight British soldiers killed in an IRA explosion near Ballygawley, Co. Tyrone.

1988 (October) British government introduces a broadcasting ban, based on the Republic's Section 31, on direct statements by paramilitary organisations. (→ August 1994)

1989 (January) Forty-five die in British Midland air crash on London-Belfast route.

1989 (February) Belfast lawyer Pat Finucane shot dead by the UFF amid claims of security force collusion.

1989 (March) Three Irish soldiers serving with the UN in Lebanon killed by a landmine.

1989 (May) Church of Ireland General Synod votes in favour of the ordination of women.

1989 (June) General election in RoI. Seats: FF 77, FG 55, Lab. 15, WP 7, PD 6, others 6. Government formed by Fianna Fáil/Progressive Democrat coalition. (→ November 1992)

1989 (June) Elections to European Parliament. Seats in RoI: FF 6, FG 4, Lab. 1, WP 1, PD 1, others 2. Seats in NI: UUP 1, SDLP 1, DUP 1. (→ June 1994)

1989 (September) Ten British army bandsmen are killed by an IRA bomb explosion at their headquarters in Deal.

1989 (October) 'Guildford Four,' imprisoned in October 1975, have their convictions quashed and are released.

The 1990s

1990 (January) Beginning of the six-month Irish presidency of the European Community.

1990 (April) Minor earthquake (5.2 on the Richter scale) felt along the east coast of Ireland.

1990 (May) Report of the Stevens inquiry finds evidence of collusion between the UDR and loyalist paramilitaries.

1990 (June) First punt pound coins minted.

1990 (August) Brian Keenan, Irish hostage in the Lebanon, released after four-and-a-half years in captivity.

1990 (November) MARY ROBINSON becomes seventh President of Ireland and the first woman to hold the office. (→ October 1997)

1991 Dublin was European City of Culture for the year.

1991 (January) Fourteen are killed during violent storms in the first weekend of the new year.

1991 (March) The 'Birmingham Six', convicted of the 1974 Birmingham pub bombings which killed 18, have their convictions quashed and are released having spent more than 16 years in prison.

1991 (April) Census. RoI population - 3,525,719. (→ April 1996) NI population - 1,577,836.

1991 (April) Talks begin in NI under the chairmanship of Sir Ninian Stephens, they break down in July.

1991 (October) Tribunal of Inquiry into the Irish beef industry begins.

1992 (January) Eight workmen die when their van is blown up by an IRA bomb at Teebane crossroads, Co. Tyrone.

1992 (February) Five men are shot dead in a betting shop on Belfast's Ormeau Road by the UDA. Four IRA members are killed by the British army following an attack on Cookstown RUC station.

1992 (February) The Supreme Court overturns the Attorney General's injunction against a 14 year-old girl, preventing her travelling to Britain to procure an abortion in what became known as the 'X-Case'.

1992 (April) NI elections to Westminster. Seats: UUP 9, SDLP 4, DUP 3, others 1. (→ May 1997)

1992 (May) Bishop Eamon Casey resigns as Bishop of Galway following revelations that he had an 18-year-old son in the United States and had used diocesan funds to pay maintenance.

1992 (June) MAASTRICHT TREATY ON EUROPEAN UNION ratified by referendum in RoI. (→ November 1992)

1992 (July) Three of the 'UDR Four' are released when the NI Court of Appeal finds their convictions unsafe.

1992 (October) President Robinson becomes the first head of state to visit hunger stricken Somalia.

1992 (November) General election in RoI. Seats: FF 68, FG 45, Lab. 33, PD 10, DEMOCRATIC LEFT 4, others 6. Coalition government formed by Fianna Fáil and Labour. (→ November 1994)

1992 (November) Referendum on abortion in RoI. Right to travel and right to information passed. Availability of abortion (the 'substantive issue') rejected. (→ November 1995)

1993 (January) Single European market comes into effect.

1993 (March) IRA bomb in Warrington kills two children and provokes widespread and sustained public outcry.

1993 (July) Tribunal of Inquiry into the beef industry comes to an end having met for 226 days.

1993 (October) IRA bomb explodes prematurely on Belfast's Shankill road killing ten including the bomber; loyalist gunmen retaliate one week later by killing seven at a pub in Greysteel, Co. Derry.

1994 (January) Irish government revokes the Section 31 broadcasting ban.

1994 (June) Elections to European Parliament. Seats in RoI: FF 7, FG 4, GREEN PARTY 2, Lab. 1, Ind. 1. Seats in NI: UUP 1, SDLP 1, DUP 1.

1994 (June) Six Catholics killed by the UVF in a Co. Down pub while watching the Republic of Ireland v. Italy World Cup soccer match.

1994 (August) IRA ceasefire begins. (→ February 1996) Loyalist paramilitary ceasefire begins in October. British government lifts broadcasting ban.

1994 (November) Fianna Fáil/Labour coalition collapses, replaced by Fine Gael/Labour/Democratic Left 'rainbow' coalition. (→ June 1997)

1995 (February) Taoiseach John Bruton and British Prime Minister John Major launch the FRAMEWORK DOCUMENT.

1995 (May) *The Irish Press* newspaper goes out of business with the loss of 600 jobs.

1995 (October) Derry poet SEAMUS HEANEY awarded the Nobel Prize for Literature.

1995 (November) Referendum on legalisation of divorce in the Republic passed. (→ November 1996)

1995 (November) President Clinton visits Ireland receiving a rapturous welcome in Belfast, Derry and Dublin. Addresses a full sitting of both houses of the Oireachtas.

1996 (February) IRA ceasefire ends with bombing of London's Docklands. (→ July 1997)

1996 (April) Census in RoI. Population 3,621,035.

1996 (May) Elections to NI Forum. Seats: UUP 30, DUP 24, SDLP 21, SF 17, Alliance 7, other U. 7, other Lab. 2, others 2, Forum dissolved April 1998.

1996 (June) Multi-party talks under the chairmanship of George Mitchell get under way at Stormont. Sinn Féin refused entry because of the absence of an IRA ceasefire. (→ April 1998)

1996 (July) Ireland assumes a six-month presidency of the European Union.

1996 (July) NI experiences its worst rioting in 15 years following the decision of the RUC to ban an Orange Order march along the nationalist Garvaghy Road and the subsequent reversal of that decision.

1996 (July) Swimmer Michelle Smith becomes Ireland's most successful Olympian winning three gold medals and one bronze medal at the Olympic Games in Atlanta Georgia.

1996 (October) RTÉ launch new Irish language channel, Telifís na Gaeilige.

1996 (November) Referendum in RoI on the denial of bail to likely reoffenders ratified. (→ October 1997)

1997 (May) NI elections to Westminster. Seats: UUP 10, SDLP 3, SF 2, DUP 2, others 1.

1997 (June) The SDLP's Alban Maginness was installed as Belfast's first ever nationalist Lord Mayor

1997 (June) General Election in Republic. Seats: FF 77, FG 54, Lab. 17, PD 4, WP 4, GP 2, SF 1, others 6. Fianna Fáil and Progressive Democrats form coalition government.

1997 (July) NI witnessed a five days of sustained rioting following the RUC's decision to force an Orange Order march along the nationalist Garvaghy Road

1997 (July) The IRA restored their August 1994 ceasefire.

1997 (September) Sinn Féin are admitted to multi-party talks at Stormont, substantive negotiations in the three stranded process began in October.

1997 (October) MARY MCALEESE elected President, the first person from north of the border to hold the office. Inaugurated November 11th.

Referendum on cabinet confidentiality passed. (→ May 1998).

1997 (December) Gerry Adams led the first Sinn Féin delegation to 10 Downing Street since the signing of the Anglo-Irish treaty.

1998 (April) THE 'GOOD FRIDAY' AGREEMENT between the Irish and British governments and several parties in Northern Ireland was signed establishing NI Assembly, North/South bodies and replacing the Anglo-Irish Agreement.

1998 (May) The Good Friday Agreement was ratified by referenda in NI and RoI. AMSTERDAM TREATY ratified by referendum in RoI.

1998 (May) Elections to the NI Assembly. Seats: UUP 28, SDLP 24, DUP 20, SF 18, All. 6, UKUP 5, NIWC 2, PUP 2, others 3.

1998 (August) In the single worst atrocity of the 'Troubles' a group calling itself the 'Real IRA' detonated a bomb in Omagh town centre on a busy Saturday afternoon. Twenty-nine people, many of them women and children lost their lives and scores more were injured.

1998 (September) The President of the United States, Bill Clinton visited Belfast, Omagh, Armagh, Dublin and Limerick on a short Irish visit.

1998 (November) A peace tower commemorating the Irishmen who died during World War One was opened by President McAleese and Queen Elizabeth II at Mesen, Belgium.

1998 (December) JOHN HUME and DAVID TRIMBLE were jointly awarded the Nobel Peace Prize in Oslo.

Movements and Organisations

● **ABBEY THEATRE**
Founded: Dublin 1904.
Founders: William Butler Yeats, Lady Gregory and Edward Martyn.
Profile: The national theatre of Ireland, it was established to produce plays written by Irish playwrights and dealing with Irish themes. Staged works by Yeats, Synge and O'Casey. Has received government funding since 1924. Went into artistic decline from early 1930s until late 1960s.

● **AMNESTY ASSOCIATION**
Founded: 1868.
Founder: John Nolan.
Profile: Campaigned for the release of Fenians imprisoned after the 1867 rebellion, who were being held under harsh conditions in British jails. Prominent figures for whom amnesties were secured were O'Donovan Rossa and John O'Leary. The organisation lapsed in the 1870s and 1880s but was reformed in the early 1890s to campaign for the release of remaining Fenian prisoners. Dynamite expert Thomas J. Clarke was the last of the Fenian prisoners to be released in September 1898, and the association was wound up.

● **ANCIENT ORDER OF HIBERNIANS**
Founded: 1641 (reformed United States 1836).
Profile: Traditionally associated with nationalism and the defence of the Catholic faith. Marches continue to be held annually on the Feast of the Assumption, 15th August.

● **APPRENTICE BOYS**
Founded: Derry, 1814.
Profile: A political Protestant society, it commemorates the Siege of Derry (April-July 1689). Takes its name from the 13 apprentices who shut the city's gates to Catholic troops. The organisation was affiliated to the Ulster Unionist Council from 1911 until the mid 1970s. Continues to hold marches throughout Northern Ireland with its main demonstration on the Saturday closest to August 12.

● **AUXILIARIES (THE)**
Founded: July 1920 (first recruits enlisted).
Profile: A force similar to the Black and Tans, its members were drawn from demobilised officers of the British army. The force was even less under the control of the RIC than the Black and Tans. The Auxiliaries demise accompanied that of the RIC.

● **BLACK AND TANS**
Founded: January 1920 (first recruits enlisted)
Profile: Formed to supplement the RIC, it recruited demobilised British soldiers to maintain operational strength, following widespread resignations and dismissals from the RIC. The name derived from the force's mufti uniform which consisted of both army and police issue.

The Black and Tans were given a free hand in their fight against the IRA and acted with extreme lawlessness. The fierceness of their reputation was based on their attacks on innocent civilians and major atrocities such as the burning of Cork City and Balbriggan, Co. Dublin, and Bloody Sunday at Croke Park in November 1921, when they shot into the crowd and killed eleven spectators and one player. Their demise accompanied that of the RIC.

● **BLUESHIRTS**
Founded: February 1932.
Profile: A political movement, with Edmund Cronin as its first leader, it was formally known as the Army Comrades Association. Consisting mainly of veterans of the Free State army, the association adopted a distinctive uniform of a blue shirt and black beret (hence the name). Former Garda Commissioner Eoin O'Duffy was elected as leader in July 1933 and changed the name of the movement to the National Guard. It was an anti-communist, quasi-fascist organisation and drew inspiration from Mussolini and his Blackshirt movement.

In October 1933, it merged with Cumann na nGaedheal and the National Centre Party to form Fine Gael with O'Duffy as its first president. It declined in the years 1934-36, but in November 1936, O'Duffy, with the blessing of members of the Catholic hierarchy, raised an 'Irish Brigade' to fight with Franco in the Spanish Civil War. They returned in June 1937.

● **BROY HARRIERS**
Formed: 1933.
Founder: Eamon Broy (Garda Commissioner).
Profile: An armed auxiliary police force whose membership was largely drawn from former members of the anti-Treaty IRA. The group was formed in reaction to the alarm caused in government and throughout the state with the formation of the Blueshirts. It was disbanded in 1935 when the Blueshirts had dissipated.

● **CATHOLIC ASSOCIATION**
Founded: May 1823.
Founders: Daniel O'Connell and Richard Lalor Shiel.
Profile: A nationwide movement, it agitated for Catholic Emancipation. It collected a 'Catholic Rent' which mobilised Catholic society as never before. In 1826, it succeeded in having four pro-emancipation MPs elected. O'Connell's victory in the 1828 Clare by-election forced the British government to grant Catholic Emancipation on April 13, 1829, but the Act disenfranchised many Catholic voters. Disbanded February 12, 1829.

● **CATHOLIC COMMITTEE**
Founded: March 1760.
Founders: Dr. John Curry, Charles O'Connor and Thomas Wyse.
Profile: Organised the small urban Catholic middle-class and lobbied government for a relaxation of the Penal Laws. Met with considerable success in early 1790s, culminating in a Catholic Relief Act in 1793, which repealed many of the Penal Laws. Suppressed

1811.

● CLAN NA GAEL
Founded: June 1867 in New York.
Founder: Jerome Collins.
Profile: A secret organisation, it recognised the Supreme Council of the Irish Republican Brotherhood as the legitimate government of Ireland. The Clan supported Parnell and Davitt's 'New Departure' in the 1880s. The movement played an active role in plans for the 1916 Rising, especially in procuring German aid. It survived the aftermath of the Rising but became embroiled in bitter personal disputes between its leading members. Divided over the Civil War, the organisation petered out in the early 1940s.

● CLANN NA TALMHAN
Founded: Galway, 1938.
Founder: Michael Donnellan.
Profile: A political party representing the small western farmer, it contested the general election of 1943 and won 14 seats. At each subsequent election, the number of seats it won decreased; by 1961, its representation was reduced to just two TDs. Part of the Inter-Party coalition governments of 1948-51 and 1954-57, its leader Joseph Blowick was twice Minister for Lands. The party did not contest the 1965 general election.

● CLANN NA POBLACHTA
Founded: July 1946.
Founder: Sean MacBride (former IRA Chief-of-Staff).
Profile: A republican party, it formed part of the Inter-Party coalition of 1948-51 and held two central ministerial portfolios: MacBride at Foreign Affairs and Dr. Noel Browne at the Department of Health. The controversy engendered by Dr. Browne's 'Mother and Child' scheme brought about the fall of the government in May 1951 and split the party. It was never again to be a political force and did not fulfil its promise of providing a viable republican alternative to Fianna Fáil. Winning only one seat in both the 1961 and 1965 general elections, it formally dissolved in 1965.

● COMDHÁIL NÁISIÚNTA NA GAEILGE
(National Congress of the Irish Language)
Founded: October 1943.
Profile: A co-ordinating body for Irish language organisations, including Conradh na Gaeilge.

● CONGESTED DISTRICTS BOARD
Established: August 1891 by the 'Balfour' Land Act
Profile: A government appointed board of commissioners whose function was to give aid to designated congested areas (in the province of Connacht and in the counties of Clare, Cork, Donegal, Limerick and Kerry). Funded by income from the sale of church land accruing from the 1869 Irish Church Act, it made grants available to improve the infrastructure, to modernise methods of farming and to aid indigenous industries, such as fishing and the blossoming cottage industries.

The Board was empowered to purchase estates and distribute the land to small farmers, often involving re-location. Dissolved in 1923 by the Free State government, its functions were transferred to the Land Commission.

● CONGRESS OF IRISH UNIONS
Formed: April 1945.
Founder: William O'Brien.
Profile: A breakaway from the Irish Trades Union Congress and the Labour Party, because of "communist tendencies within the ITUC." In February 1959, it reunited with the ITUC to form the Irish Congress of Trade Unions.

● CONNOLLY COLUMN
Formed: December 1936.
Founder: Frank Ryan.
Profile: The column was a group of republican volunteers who joined the Abraham Lincoln Battalion in the 15th International Brigade and fought with the socialists against Franco in the Spanish Civil War (1936-39).

● CUMANN NA nGAEDHEAL
Founded: September 1900.
Founders: Arthur Griffith and William Rooney.
Profile: An umbrella group for small anti-English organisations. The organisation called on the IPP to abstain from Westminster in 1902 and organised protests against the visit of Edward III in July 1903. It became part of Sinn Féin in 1907. It had no link to the political party of the same name founded by W.T. Cosgrave in 1923.

● CUMANN NA nGAEDHEAL
Founded: March 1923.
Leader: W.T. Cosgrave (its first and only leader).
Profile: Consisting of the pro-Treaty wing of Sinn Féin, Cumann na nGaedheal formed every government from the Provisional Government in 1922 until 1932 due to the republican policy of abstentionism.

The party played an important role in the formation and consolidation of the fledgling Free State, ruthlessly pursuing the anti-treaty IRA, executing 77 republicans during the Civil War and crushing the real threat that the IRA posed. The party also provided for the establishment of the Garda Síochána, the Electricity Supply Board, the Shannon hydro-electric scheme and the Agricultural Credit Corporation.

In the field of foreign affairs, the party set about pursuing the freedoms implicit in the Treaty. Its members were prominent at Commonwealth conferences in exploring these freedoms. Their greatest success came in 1931 with the Statute of Westminster, which put the parliaments of the Dominions (including Ireland) on an equal footing with the Imperial Parliament at Westminster.

The party lost power in 1932, and less than a year later it merged with the Blueshirts and the National Centre Party to form Fine Gael.

● DEFENDERS
Founded: Armagh, July 1784.
Profile: A nationalist secret society found largely in Ulster, absorbed into the United Irishmen in the 1790s.

● DEMOCRATIC UNIONIST PARTY
Founded: 1971 *(See Politics Chapter)*.

● FARMERS' PARTY

Formed: 1922.

Profile: The party contested Dáil elections between 1922 and 1932, winning eleven seats in its first election in 1922, its best return came in 1923 when it secured 15 seats. Support was drawn from more affluent farmers, and the party generally supported the Cumann na nGaedheal government. Following a disastrous election in 1932 when it won only four seats, its members went on to found the National Centre Party.

● FENIAN BROTHERHOOD

Founded: April 1859 in New York.

Founder: John O'Mahony.

Profile: An American auxiliary of the IRB, its name came to be used when describing both groups. Chiefly concerned with the procurement of weapons for the IRB, it staged an abortive attack at New Brunswick in Canada in 1866. Formally merged with the IRB in 1916.

● FIANNA FÁIL

Founded: 1926 (*See Politics Chapter*)

● FINE GAEL

Founded: 1933 (*See Politics Chapter*)

● GAELIC ATHLETIC ASSOCIATION (GAA)

Founded: November 1, 1884 in Thurles, Co. Tipperary.

Founders: Michael Cusack and Maurice Davin, under the patronage of the Archbishop of Cashel, Dr. T.W. Croke.

Profile: Gaelic games had been slipping into decline because of disorganisation and apathy. The GAA hoped to preserve and cultivate Irish pastimes such as gaelic football and hurling. Initially the GAA's main efforts were concentrated in athletics but Gaelic Games quickly became its main focus. Unashamedly nationalist in outlook, it prohibited members from playing foreign games (such as rugby, hockey and soccer) until 1971 and continues to exclude members of the security forces in Northern Ireland from membership.

The association spread gradually until it established itself in every parish in the country providing Gaelic pastimes to vast numbers of people and becoming the largest organisation (sporting or otherwise) in the country, a distinction it retains. A voluntary and completely amateur organisation (save for a handful of administrators) its major games attract crowds in excess of 65,000.

● THE GAELIC LEAGUE – CONRADH NA GAEILGE

Founded: July 1893.

Founders: Dr. Douglas Hyde, Eoin MacNeill and Fr. Eugene O'Growney.

Profile: The League sought to preserve the Irish language as a spoken language and de-Anglicize Ireland. Successes included the recognition of St. Patrick's Day as a national holiday (1903) and the inclusion of Irish as a matriculation subject in the NUI (1908).

The League sent teachers (or timirí) around the country to set up classes and had up to 600 branches countrywide by 1908. Infiltrated by the IRB in 1915, Douglas Hyde resigned as president because of the increasingly political role it was fulfilling. Following the formation of the Free State in 1922, it lobbied successfully for Irish to be made a compulsory subject in both primary and secondary schools. The League remains one of the largest Irish language organisations in the country.

● HOME RULE LEAGUE

Founded: November 1873 in Dublin.

Founder: Isaac Butt.

Profile: With the objective of self-government for Ireland, it was a precursor to the Irish Parliamentary Party. It won 60 seats in the 1874 general election.

● INDEPENDENT IRISH PARTY

Founded: September 1852 in Dublin.

Profile: An amalgamation of the Irish Tenant League, the Irish Brigade and 41 liberal MPs who were sympathetic to the plight of the tenant farmers. It demanded land reform, the repeal of the Ecclesiastical Titles Act and the disestablishment of the Church of Ireland. Beset by splits and defections, it petered out by the mid 1850s.

● INVINCIBLES

Founded: 1881.

Profile: An extremist group which broke away from the IRB. In May 1882, it assassinated the Chief Secretary and the Under Secretary (the top government officials in Ireland) in what became known as the Phoenix Park Murders. Its leaders were tried in May 1883, convicted of the murders and hanged.

● IRISH AGRICULTURAL ORGANISATION SOCIETY

Founded: April 1894.

Founders: Sir Horace Plunkett and Fr. Thomas Finlay

Profile: Established to co-ordinate the activities of the nationwide Co-operative Movement (established in 1890). It allowed dairy producing farmers to collectively sell their produce, it provided credit to farmers and purchased agricultural goods in bulk to sell to its members.

● IRISH CITIZEN ARMY

Founded: November 1913 in Dublin.

Founders: James Connolly and James Larkin.

Profile: Formed to protect workers from police attacks during the 1913 Dublin Lock-Out. Following the Lock-Out, Connolly turned his attention to the creation of a workers' republic. His intention to stage a Citizen Army rebellion caused alarm within the IRB, and their leaders informed him of plans for the Easter 1916 rebellion. Connolly pledged his army's support for the Rising and when it came, the Citizen's Army fought with distinction. It also fought in the War of Independence and on the anti-treaty side in the Civil War. Disbanded in 1923 after the Civil War ended.

● IRISH CONFEDERATION

Founded: January 13, 1847, in Dublin by Young Irelanders who had seceded from the Loyal National Repeal Association.

Profile: A militant nationalist organisation, it promoted an independent, self-sufficient Ireland and linked self-determination to the land question. 1848 saw revolutions throughout Europe, and inspired by this, the Confederation drafted plans for an Irish rebellion. By July, the government had suspended *habeas corpus* and proscribed the Confederation. In July, it staged a poorly planned and ill-timed rebellion which was easily defeated. The movement, having lost its leaders through arrest and transportation, collapsed.

● **IRISH LITERARY THEATRE**
Founded: May 1899 in Dublin.
Founder: William Butler Yeats.
Profile: A literary society dedicated to the promotion of Irish culture and customs through the production of plays written and set in Ireland. The first society to stage a play in the Irish language (Douglas Hyde's *Casadh an tSúgáin*). Dissolved in 1904 and was absorbed into the Abbey Theatre.

● **IRISH LOYAL AND PATRIOTIC UNION**
Founded: May 1885.
Profile: A political association of unionist landlords, businessmen and scholars opposed to Home Rule. Contested the 1885 general election but won little support. Superseded in 1891 by the Irish Unionist Alliance.

● **IRISH NATIONAL LAND LEAGUE**
Founded: October 1879 in Dublin.
Founders: Charles Stewart Parnell and Michael Davitt.
Profile: The League aimed to protect tenant rights through the securing of the 'three Fs' and sought the complete abolition of landlordism. Ostensibly a moral force organisation which developed and utilised the tactic of 'boycotting', it enjoyed the support of the Fenians, Clann na Gael and the IRB. The appeal of the League was wide and all classes of society, encompassing all religions, were members. The Land Act of August 1881 was a major success, but it was accompanied by a Coercion Act which banned the League. The League was reformed by Parnell in October 1882 under the name of the National League where the emphasis was on Home Rule rather than land reform.

● **IRISH NATIONAL LIBERATION ARMY**
Formed: Dublin, 1975.
Profile: A splinter republican paramilitary group responsible for some of the most ruthless attacks in Northern Ireland during the 'troubles'. Initially, it drew members from those disenchanted with the 'Official' IRA. It later attracted members from the fringes of the 'Provisionals'. The INLA has been plagued by feuds since the late 1980s, resulting in the deaths of many of its members. The organisation called a ceasefire in August 1998, in the aftermath of the Omagh bombing.

● **IRISH PARLIAMENTARY PARTY (IPP)**
Formed: 1882, it evolved from the Home Rule League.
Profile: With the securing of Home Rule as its primary objective, it gained widespread support through its action and leadership on the land question, the single biggest issue of the day. Ineffective under the leadership of Isaac Butt, save for its filibustering obstruction of business at Westminster, it met with huge success especially with regard to the land question under the leadership of Charles Stewart Parnell (elected chairman May 1880).

The party became the model for modern political parties in that it developed an extensive grass roots constituency organisation, established a party whip and had its members take a party pledge to vote *en bloc*. These innovations and the skill of its leadership helped achieve significant land reform and brought Home Rule to the top of political agenda at Westminster. Despite its success, the party, under pressure from Gladstone's Liberal Party and the Catholic hierarchy in Ireland, split in 1890 following revelations about Parnell's adulterous affair with Katharine O'Shea.

Reunited under the leadership of John Redmond in 1900, it went on to secure the passage of the third Home Rule Bill in 1914, the implementation of which was suspended until after World War I. The 1916 Rising and executions, along with British government attempts to introduce conscription in 1918, precipitated a huge swell in support for Sinn Féin at the expense of the IPP. Their representation at Westminster fell from 70 MPs in 1910 to 6 in 1918. Sinn Féin replaced the party as the major party within nationalism. The Northern rump of the party reconstituted itself as the Nationalist Party of Northern Ireland in 1921, but southern members joined Cumann na nGaedheal after 1923.

● **IRISH REPUBLICAN ARMY (IRA)**
Founded: January 1919 (The oath to the Republic taken by the Volunteers in can be seen as the starting point of the IRA).
Profile: It successfully adopted and developed guerrilla warfare during the War of Independence and created such a state of disorder that the British authorities sued for a truce. The Anglo-Irish Treaty was not accepted by the IRA, and a split ensued along pro- and anti-Treaty lines. There followed a bloody and bitter civil war where erstwhile comrades fought one another; those who supported the Treaty became the army of the Free State, and the republicans became known as the 'Irregulars'. Defeat for the Irregulars followed, and a truce was called in May 1923. The IRA formally withdrew from Sinn Féin in November 1925. The organisation was proscribed in Northern Ireland in 1922 and in the Free State in 1931

The IRA staged an offensive in England (January 1939-March 1940) which resulted in further anti-republican legislation being passed in both jurisdictions in Ireland. It was relatively inactive from then until the period 1956-62 when it engaged in a 'Border Campaign'. The advent of the Civil Rights movements in the late 1960s saw an increasingly political and non-militaristic IRA emerge particularly in the south. The arrival of British troops in Northern Ireland in August 1969 precipitated a decisive split between the Marxist, southern-based leadership, whose commitment to physical force was on the wane, and northern members, who were less concerned with ideology now that British troops were once again in Ireland. The movement split in December 1968 into 'Provisional' (largely northern-based) and 'Official' (largely southern-based) wings.

(See also Official IRA and Provisional IRA)

● IRISH REPUBLICAN BROTHERHOOD (IRB)
Founded: 17 March, 1858 in Dublin.
Founder: James Stephens.
Profile: A secret, republican, oath-bound society its 1867 rebellion was easily put down. It survived this setback and later in the century infiltrated nationalist movements such as the Gaelic Athletic Association, the Gaelic League and the Land League. Reorganised in 1904, it infiltrated the Irish Volunteers and with the outbreak of World War One, its military council began planning the Easter 1916 rebellion. Following the Rising it was again reorganised (all of its leaders had been executed) and exerted much influence between 1916 and 1919. Its influence declined during the War of Independence, and a split occurred during the Civil War. The movement disbanded in 1924.

● IRISH SOCIALIST REPUBLICAN PARTY
Founded: May 1896 in Dublin.
Founder: James Connolly.
Profile: A small socialist nationalist party, it was reorganised and renamed the Socialist Party of Ireland in 1903. In 1921 the Socialist Party was reorganised as the Communist Party of Ireland.

● IRISH SOCIETY
Profile: The Society of London companies entrusted with the strategic plantation of Derry. It fortified the towns of Derry and Coleraine, established other small towns and villages and brought English settlers. Some of the companies sold their holdings in the early 18th century while the remainder sold theirs in the late 19th century. In 1952 the Foyle Fisheries was sold by the Society.

● IRISH TENANT LEAGUE
Founded: August 1850 in Dublin.
Founders: Charles Gavan Duffy and Frederick Lucas.
Profile: Drawing its membership from larger tenant farmers, it aimed to secure the 'three Fs' - fair rent, fixity of tenure and free sale. Following the 1852 general election, it combined with the Irish Brigade to form the Independent Irish Parliamentary Party which had the allegiance of about 40 MPs. The League collapsed in 1855 when Lucas died and Duffy emigrated.

●IRISH TRANSPORT AND GENERAL WORKERS' UNION
Founded January 1909 in Dublin.
Founder: James Larkin.
Profile: Formed as a breakaway from the British National Union of Dock Labourers, it survived the disastrous Dublin Lock-Out. Increasing in size throughout the revolutionary period, internal bickering, power struggles and splits tore at the union from 1923 until 1959. Formally joined the Irish Congress of Trade Unions in 1959.

● IRISH UNIONIST ALLIANCE
Founded: 1891.
Profile: The successor to the Irish Loyal and Patriotic Union - its membership comprised mainly southern unionists opposed to Home Rule. Despite its rather small membership, the alliance exerted considerable influence at Westminster and in the House of Lords in particular. Rendered obsolete by the passing of the Home Rule Bill in 1914.

● IRISH VOLUNTEERS
Founded: November 1913 in Dublin.
Founders: Éoin MacNeill and Bulmer Hobson.
Profile: Formed as a response to the formation of the UVF, the Volunteers secured arms in a gun-running episode at Howth on July 26, 1914. Membership had reached around 180,000 at the outbreak of World War I when, in September 1914, leader of the Irish Parliamentary Party, John Redmond, called on the Volunteers to join "in defence of right, of freedom and religion in this war." Over 170,000 did, renaming themselves the National Volunteers. Approximately 11,000 remained with the Irish Volunteers.

Many of the senior posts of the Irish Volunteers were occupied by members of the IRB's Supreme Council, and the Volunteers fought in the 1916 Rising. Reorganised in 1917, the Volunteers became a powerful and increasingly belligerent force. When the first Dáil met in 1919, the Volunteers took an oath to the Republic and fought in the War of Independence as the Irish Republican Army.

● IRREGULARS
Profile: The name given to the anti-Treaty IRA which fought the Free State army during the Civil War (June 1922-April 1923). Led by Liam Lynch, his death in April 1923 was swiftly followed by a truce.

● THE LABOUR PARTY
Founded: 1912 *(See Politics Chapter)*

● LADIES LAND LEAGUE
Founded: October 1880 in New York.
Founder: Fanny Parnell (established in Ireland in January 1881 by her sister Anna, both women were sisters of Charles Stewart Parnell).
Profile: The League stepped into the breach when the Land League was banned in 1881 and was vociferous in the campaign against landlordism. The first Irish political movement organised by women, it met with opposition from elements within the Catholic Church and the Irish Parliamentary Party who found their radicalism unacceptable. When Charles Stewart Parnell was released from prison in May 1882, he cut their funding and in August 1882 suppressed the movement entirely.

● LAND LEAGUE OF MAYO
Founded: August 1879 in Westport, Co. Mayo
Founder: Michael Davitt.
Aims: Securing the 'three Fs' of fair rent, fixity of tenure and free sale.
Profile: Precursor of the Irish National Land League.

● LOYAL NATIONAL REPEAL ASSOCIATION
Founded: April 1840.
Founder: Daniel O'Connell.
Profile: The Association aimed to secure repeal of the Act of Union and create an Irish legislature subservient

to Westminster. Organised along the same lines as the Catholic Association, it used mass agitation and organised 'monster meetings'. Its finest year was 1843 with over 750,000 attending a monster meeting at Tara. The onset of famine in 1845, tensions between O'Connell and the 'Young Irelanders', which came to a head in 1846, and O'Connell's death in 1847 led to the movement fading out without realising its objective.

● NATIONAL COUNCIL
Founded: June 1903.
Founder: Arthur Griffith.
Profile: Formed to oppose the 1903 visit of Edward III, its members included senior figures from Cumann na nGaedheal. Became part of Sinn Féin in 1908.

● NATIONAL LEAGUE
Founded: October 17, 1882, in Dublin.
Founder: Charles Stewart Parnell.
Profile: It replaced the proscribed Land League, securing Home Rule was its primary objective with land reform of lesser importance. It also served as the 'grass roots' organisation of the Irish Parliamentary Party. The movement provided finance and delegates for the IPP and had the support of the majority of the Catholic clergy. The League, split along the same lines as the IPP in 1890, faded into oblivion and was replaced by the United Irish League in 1900, when the IPP was reunited.

● NORTHERN IRELAND CIVIL RIGHTS ASSOCIATION
Founded: Belfast, February 1967.
Profile: Aimed to secure the introduction of universal suffrage; an end to gerrymandering; the disbanding of the 'B' SPECIALS; the repeal of the Special Powers Act; and the fair allocation of public housing. The Association was organised along the same lines as the British National Council for Civil Liberties. The main weapon employed by the association was protest marches, the first of which was held in Dungannon in August 1968. Marches were organised throughout the late 1960s and early 1970s and often led to clashes with the RUC. The association's influence declined from the mid 1970s.

● 'OFFICIAL' IRISH REPUBLICAN ARMY
Profile: Formed following the split in the IRA in late 1969. It was allied to 'Official' Sinn Féin and was more Marxist than its 'provisional' counterpart. A feud ensued between the two wings of the IRA with casualties on both sides. The official IRA has ceased to operate since it called a ceasefire on May 29, 1972, but strongly contested allegations have persisted that the group continued to exist and carried out robberies and assassinations well into the 1980s.

● 'OFFICIAL' SINN FÉIN
Formed: January 1970.
Profile: Formed following a split with what became known as 'Provisional' Sinn Féin, the party was led by Tomás MacGiolla and applied a socialist analysis to the conflict in the North. The party was organised throughout the 32 counties and, in 1977, changed its name to Sinn Féin The Workers' Party. Since 1982 the party has been known as The Workers' Party.

● ORANGE ORDER
Founded: Armagh, September 1795 after serious disturbances between Catholics and Protestants at the Diamond in Loughgall.
Profile: The Order came into existence as a Protestant response to the relaxation of the anti-Catholic penal laws at the end of the 18th century. It comprised Protestant males who pledged their allegiance to the Crown (as long as it remained Protestant) and their Protestant faith. The Order commemorates the Battle of the Boyne (1690) and the Battle of the Somme (1916) with marches each summer. The main marches are held at different county centres throughout Northern Ireland on July 12.

The Order has played a significant role in Irish politics; it was prominent in the formation of the Ulster Unionist Council in 1905, it organised the Solemn League and Covenant in 1912 and harnessed Protestant opposition to Home Rule. With its membership concentrated in Northern Ireland, it played a central role in the formation of the Northern Ireland state - each of Northern Ireland's six Prime Ministers were Orangemen. In recent years, restrictions have been placed on where it can march.

● PEEP O' DAY BOYS
Founded: July 1784 in Armagh.
Profile: A Protestant secret society founded after a sectarian clash with the Defenders. Precursor of the Orange Order.

● PEOPLE'S DEMOCRACY
Founded: Belfast, October 1968.
Founders: Michael Farrell and Bernadette Devlin.
Profile: A socialist organisation, it demanded an end to discrimination against Catholics in Northern Ireland, one man-one vote and the revoking of the Special Powers Act. The group was involved in one of the bloodiest encounters of the Civil Rights era when unarmed marchers were attacked by baton-wielding loyalists at Burntollet on January 4th, 1969. Some of its leaders were interned in August 1971, and with the increasing violence of the 'troubles', it became less significant.

● PHOENIX SOCIETY
Founded: 1856, in Skibbereen, Co. Cork.
Founder: Jeremiah O'Donovan (O'Donovan Rossa).
Profile: Outwardly, it had the appearance of a debating society, but it was, in reality, a revolutionary society and precursor to the Irish Republican Brotherhood into which it was subsumed in 1859.

● 'PROVISIONAL' IRISH REPUBLICAN ARMY
Profile: Formed following a split in the IRA in late 1969. The split was led by the IRA's northern command who felt that the ideological swing to the left by the southern-based leadership was detrimental to the movement as a whole. With the traditional enemy, in the form of the British army, on the streets of Northern Ireland, the 'Provisionals' felt that it was time to leave politics behind and respond in a military fashion. From 1969 until 1994 they waged a relentless war against the British Army and RUC and also attacked civilians. The ruling Army

Council declared a ceasefire in August 1994, which ended in February 1996 but was restored in July 1997 and remains in force.

● ROYAL IRISH CONSTABULARY (RIC)

Formed: 1836 as Irish Constabulary, earned prefix 'Royal' after suppressing the 1867 Fenian Rising.
Profile: A quasi-military national police force, it was hugely unpopular due to its role in enforcing evictions and quelling the agrarian violence endemic in the late 19th century. Its members suffered terribly during the War of Independence; many resigned out of fear or disapproval of the tactics of the Black and Tans, and many more were dismissed because of their nationalist sympathies. Disbanded in 1922 following the Anglo-Irish Treaty, its northern members were absorbed into the Royal Ulster Constabulary by an Act of the Northern Ireland Parliament in May 1922.

● SINN FÉIN

Founded: 1905 *(See Politics Chapter).*

● SOCIAL DEMOCRATIC AND LABOUR PARTY:

Founded: 1970 *(See Politics Chapter)*

● TOTAL ABSTINENCE MOVEMENT

Founded: 1838.
Founders: Fr. Theobald Matthew and William Martin.
Profile: With the aim of promoting abstinence from alcohol in Ireland, it reputedly recorded 5 million pledges in Ireland. Revenue from alcohol dropped from £1.4 million in 1839 to £350,000 in 1844.

● ULSTER DEFENCE ASSOCIATION

Founded: September 1971.
Profile: Established to co-ordinate the loyalist vigilante groups endemic in the early 1970s. A working class loyalist paramilitary organisation, it was heavily involved in the Ulster Workers' Council strike which toppled the Power Sharing Executive in 1974. Through its terrorist wing - the Ulster Freedom Fighters - it killed many civilians; the killings continued until 1994. Part of the Combined Loyalist Military Command, it declared a ceasefire in October 1994. The UDA was proscribed in 1992.

● ULSTER DEFENCE REGIMENT (UDR)

Established: December 1969 (by Act of Parliament).
Profile: A largely part-time force under the command of the British Army. Many of its members were drawn from the disbanded 'B' Specials, and its original aim of recruiting from both communities was never realised (only 3% of the force were Catholic). The UDR was used as a back up for RUC patrols. Its members were targeted both on and off duty by the IRA and INLA, and 197 members were killed from its inception until it was disbanded in 1992. The Regiment was amalgamated with the Royal Irish Rangers in 1992 to form the Royal Irish Regiment.

● ULSTER SPECIAL CONSTABULARY

Formed: 1922.
Profile: An auxiliary part-time police force established to supplement the Royal Ulster Constabulary and defend the newly founded Northern Ireland from IRA attack. Membership of the force was exclusively Protestant. There were three grades - A, B and C. The 'A' and 'C' specials were used only in the 1920s, while the 'B' specials went on to gain notoriety, especially in the late 1960s when they attacked civil rights marches. The force was disbanded in April 1970, and many of its members joined the newly established Ulster Defence Regiment.

● ULSTER UNIONIST COUNCIL

Founded: March 3, 1905 in Belfast.
Profile: A political organisation founded at a conference of Ulster unionist MPs, its members were drawn from the Orange Order, the Apprentice Boys of Derry, unionist associations, MPs and peers.

The Solemn League and Covenant in 1912, the formation of the Ulster Volunteer Force in 1913 and the Larne gun-running in 1914 were all organised under its auspices. In 1913 it appointed a Provisional Government for Ulster to take effect should Home Rule become law. The Council initially opposed partition but went on to play a significant role in the formation of Northern Ireland. Its political arm, the Ulster Unionist Party governed Northern Ireland from 1921 until 1972. The council remains in place today as an executive for the Ulster Unionist Party.
(For Ulster Unionist Party see Politics Chapter)

● ULSTER VOLUNTEER FORCE (UVF)

Founded: January 1913.
Profile: Formed to oppose the implementation of Home Rule by military force if necessary, James Craig and Sir Edward Carson were prominent members of its leadership. Guns were procured and landed at Larne in April 1914. The outbreak of World War I and the suspension of Home Rule resulted in the UVF becoming the 36th (Ulster) Division of the British Army. The division was all but wiped out in the Battle of the Somme (July-November 1916). Following partition the force was disbanded and its members recruited by the RUC.

The UVF was re-established in 1966 by Gusty Spence, amongst others. It immediately declared war on the IRA but was banned by Prime Minister Terence O'Neill in June of that year. It called a cease-fire in October 1994 under the auspices of the Combined Loyalist Military Command.

● ULSTER WORKERS' COUNCIL

Formed: 1974.
Profile: Formed to oppose the Sunningdale Agreement and the imposition of Direct Rule. It organised the loyalist strike of May 14-29, 1974 (enforced by loyalist paramilitaries). The cutting off of electricity supplies ensured the success of the strike, and the executive fell on May 28. Prominent members of the UWC co-ordinating committee were the leaders of the main unionist parties, including Harry West (UUP), Rev. Ian Paisley (DUP) and William Craig (VUPP). The UDA, the UVF and other loyalist paramilitary groups also had members on the co-ordinating committee.

The committee organised an abortive loyalist strike in May 1977 which failed to get unanimous unionist support. The council was reorganised in 1981.

● UNITED IRISHMEN

Founded: October 1791 in Belfast.

Founders: Thomas Russell, Theobald Wolfe Tone and James Napper Tandy.

Profile: A revolutionary oath-bound secret society. Inspired by the American and French revolutions, it aimed to secure an Irish republic and attracted radical Presbyterians in the north and an almost equal mix of Catholics and Protestants in the Dublin area. Procured French aid for its rising in 1798, which tragically turned into a sectarian massacre in Wexford and which the government put down with great force. The rising's leaders were executed and the movement crushed.

● **UNITED ULSTER UNIONIST COUNCIL**

Formed: January 1974.

Profile: A coalition of unionist interests formed to oppose the Sunningdale Agreement ranging from the Ulster Unionist Party, the Democratic Unionist Party to the Vanguard Unionist Progressive Party. The Council opposed all aspects of the Sunningdale Agreement, and the Council of Ireland proposals in particular. It called for the removal of the power-sharing executive and co-operated fully with, and gave support to, the Ulster Workers' Council (UWC) strike in May 1974 which paralysed Northern Ireland and brought down the power-sharing executive.

It suffered a split in 1975 when the VUPP suggested some form of coalition that would include the SDLP. The Council collapsed when paramilitary groups were admitted and when prominent MPs, John Dunlop and Rev. Ian Paisley, supported the abortive 1977 loyalist strike which the UUP opposed.

● **VANGUARD UNIONIST PROGRESSIVE PARTY**

Founded: March 1973.

Founder: William Craig.

Profile: A unionist political party whose roots were in the Ulster Vanguard, with the majority of its members drawn from the ranks of the UUP. The party contested the 1973 Northern Ireland Assembly election, winning seven seats, and it won three Westminster seats in two general elections in 1974. Opposed to Direct Rule, the Sunningdale Agreement and the power sharing executive, it became part of the United Ulster Unionist

Council and was prominent in the Ulster Workers' Council strike in 1974. A split occured in 1977 when its leader suggested some form of voluntary coalition with the SDLP. In 1978, it ceased to function as a party. Current Ulster Unionist Party leader, David Trimble, was a prominent member and was deputy leader of the party (1977-78).

● **THE VOLUNTEER MOVEMENT**

Founded: March 1778.

Profile: Armed corps established to help defend Ireland against French or Spanish invasion. Lobbied for free trade, legislative independence and relaxation of the Penal Laws. Suppressed March 1793.

● **WHITEBOYS**

Emerged: Munster October 1761.

Profile: Generic term for different Catholic secret societies. Engaged in violent disturbances related to resentment at taxes and changes from arable to dairy farming as well as to sectarianism.

● **WILD GEESE**

Profile: The name given to the 14,000 Irish Jacobite soldiers (commanded by Patrick Sarsfield), who left Ireland after the Treaty of Limerick (October 1691) and distinguished themselves on European battlefields in the 18th century. The Wild Geese also refers to other Irish soldiers who fought in continental Europe throughout the 18th century. The most celebrated action of the Wild Geese occurred at the Battle of Fontenoy in 1745.

● **YOUNG IRELANDERS**

Profile: The name given to the adherents of the nationalism expounded by Thomas Davis, Charles Gavan Duffy and John Blake Dillon in *The Nation* (first published October 1842). Not content with repeal, they wanted to achieve an independent Ireland and were prepared to use physical force. Their acceptance of physical force led to their break with the Repeal movement in 1846 when O'Connell sought a pledge stipulating that force could never be justified.

Significant Documents

● **STATUTE OF KILKENNY**

Enacted: 1366 by the Irish Parliament at Kilkenny.

A series of apartheid-type laws forbidding English settlers assimilating with native Gaelic Irish and adopting their culture. Gaelic laws, customs and language were banned among the settlers, as was marriage between the 'races'. The laws were ultimately ineffective and were revoked in 1537.

● **POYNINGS' LAW**

Enacted: December 1, 1494 (named after the Lord Deputy, Sir Edward Poynings).

• Forbade the Irish parliament to convene without the King's prior permission.

• All intended legislation had to be approved by him. The law was almost completely repealed in 1782, the only part of it which remained was the Crown's right to

veto a bill.

● **THE ANNALS OF THE FOUR MASTERS**

Compiled: Between 1632 and 1636.

The Annals are a history of Ireland compiled in book form by religious scribes (completed by Michael O'Clery and others on August 10, 1636) in Donegal Town.

● **TREATY OF LIMERICK**

Signed: October 3, 1691,

Signatories: Patrick Sarsfield and the Williamite General Ginkel.

• Irish soldiers allowed to join other Jacobites in France.

• Roman Catholics to be allowed rights of worship, to retain their property and to practice their professions.

The articles dealing with religious freedoms for

Catholics were not honoured by the British parliament which, within two months, put in place an anti-Catholic Oath of Supremacy and, in the years 1695-1709, enacted a comprehensive series of penal laws.

● PENAL LAWS (1695-1709)

The collective name for a series of laws designed to secure the privileged position of members of the Church of Ireland, the established Church. The laws were aimed at eradicating the Roman Catholic religion in the country and showed little tolerance towards Presbyterianism.

Included were restrictions on rights to education, the bearing of arms, the purchase of land, taking a seat in parliament and holding any government office. The Roman Catholic clergy, including virtually all of the hierarchy, was banished in 1697 (although some priests were permitted to stay) and the ordination of new priests was forbidden.

A Toleration Act for Protestant Dissenters was passed in 1719, while Catholics had to wait until late in the century for many of their restrictions to be formally repealed and until 1829 before they were eligible to sit in parliament or hold high public office.

● CATHOLIC RELIEF ACTS (1774-93)

Enacted: April 9, 1793.

A series of acts which repealed the penal laws.
• Catholics permitted to purchase and own land.
• Catholics permitted to practice law.
• Catholics permitted to hold selected public and military positions.
• Parliamentary franchise extended to Catholics.
• Official bar on Catholics receiving university degrees removed.

● ACT OF UNION

Enacted: July 2, 1800 (effective January 1, 1801).
• Legislatures of Great Britain and Ireland joined.
• Irish Parliament abolished.
• One hundred Irish MPs, 28 Lords and 4 bishops to sit in the Houses of Parliament at Westminster.
• Church of Ireland amalgamated with Church of England.

The act was superseded by the Government of Ireland Act, 1920, and the Anglo-Irish Treaty of 1921.

● ROMAN CATHOLIC RELIEF ACT

Enacted: April 13, 1829.
• Oaths of Allegiance, Supremacy and Abjuration replaced, enabling Roman Catholics to sit in the Houses of Parliament; belong to any corporation; and hold the higher offices of State.

● IRISH CHURCH ACT

Enacted: July 26, 1869 (effective January 1, 1871).
• Churches of England and Ireland separated.
• Church of Ireland disestablished (i.e. the dissolution of the legal union of Church and State).
• Property of the Church of Ireland confiscated.
• Grants to Maynooth College and the Presbyterian Church discontinued (although compensation paid).
• Ecclesiastical Courts disbanded.
• Tithes due to Church of Ireland by all denominations abolished
• Provision made for tenants residing on Church of Ireland lands to purchase their holdings.

● LAND ACTS

Landlord and Tenant (Ireland) Act (Gladstone)

Enacted: August 1, 1870.
• Attempted (but failed) to legalise the 'Ulster Custom' of not evicting tenants who had paid their rent in full and allowing tenants to sub-let their holdings.
• Landlords required to pay compensation for any improvements made by a tenant to his holding.
• The 'Bright Clause' provided tenants with a government loan of 66% of the cost of their holdings to enable them to buy their farms.

Land Law (Ireland) Act (Gladstone)

Enacted: August 22, 1881.
• The 'Three Fs' (Fair rents, Fixity of tenure and Free Sale) were incorporated in statute.
• **Fair rents:** To be decided by arbitration at a Land Commission hearing.
• **Fixity of tenure:** Tenants who had their rent fully paid could not be evicted. A Land Court was established to arbitrate in tenant-landlord disputes.
• **Free sale:** Payment for any improvements made would be ensured by the Land Court.
• A land purchase scheme was put in place providing a 75% loan to tenants wishing to purchase their holdings.

Purchase of Land (Ireland) Act (Ashbourne)

Enacted: August 14, 1885.
• £5 million made available to tenants to purchase their holdings. Grants were made available for 100% of the value of the holding.
In 1888, money available was increased to £10 million.

Purchase of Land (Ireland) Act (Balfour)

Enacted: August 5, 1891.
• £33 million made available to tenants to purchase their holdings.
• A Congested Districts Board established to administer aid to designated congested areas.

Irish Land Act (Wyndham)

Enacted: August 14, 1903.
• £83 million made available to tenants to buy out their lands. Landlords got a bonus if they sold their entire estate.

● HOME RULE BILLS

1886

• Two-tier Irish legislature with limited powers.
• Ireland would not be represented at the Imperial Parliament at Westminster.
• Lord Lieutenant to remain as representative of the Crown in Ireland and gave royal assent to Bills.
• Revenue would come from taxes collected in Ireland (excluding customs and excise tariffs) and a portion of Imperial taxes.
• Control of the Royal Irish Constabulary (RIC) to remain with the Imperial Parliament.
Bill defeated June 8, 1886 in House of Commons by 341 votes to 311.

1893

As 1886 except it proposed to send Irish MPs to Westminster.
Bill defeated September 9, 1893, in House of Lords by

419 votes to 41.

1914

Introduced in the House of Commons in 1912 it was defeated in the Lords, whose veto had been reduced to two years by the 1911 Parliament Act. The Bill was signed into law by the King on September 18, 1914, but its implementation was suspended, with the agreement of the Ulster Unionists and Irish Parliamentary Party, for the duration of World War One.
• Two-tier Irish legislature to be established.
• Ireland to send 42 MPs to the House of Commons.
• Revenue to come from taxes collected within Ireland and custom and excise tariffs.
• Control of the RIC to remain with the Imperial Parliament but would revert to the Irish parliament after six years.

● IRISH UNIVERSITIES ACT

Enacted: British parliament August 1, 1908
• Royal University abolished.
• Established two new bodies, the National University of Ireland (consisting of University Colleges Cork, Dublin and Galway and other smaller colleges) and the Queen's University of Belfast.
• The governing body of the National University, although officially non-denominational, had a significant number of Roman Catholic bishops.

● ULSTER'S SOLEMN LEAGUE AND COVENANT

Signed: 28 September, 1912 (218,000 male signatories).
• A pledge to oppose Home Rule by 'using all means which may be found necessary' and, in the event of a Home Rule parliament being foisted on Ireland, to refuse to recognise its authority.

● PROCLAMATION OF THE IRISH REPUBLIC

Issued: April 24, 1916 (beginning of the Easter Rising).
Signatories: (On behalf of the Provisional Government) Thomas Clarke, Seán MacDiarmada, Thomas MacDonagh, Padraig Pearse, Eamonn Ceannt, James Connolly and Joseph Plunkett. All seven were executed within three weeks.
• Asserted the right of the people of Ireland to the ownership of a sovereign and independent republic.
• Proclaimed the Irish Republic as a 'Sovereign Independent State'.
• Guaranteed religious and civil liberty, equal rights and equal opportunities to all its citizens.
• Resolved to pursue the 'happiness and prosperity of the whole nation and of all its parts' and to cherish all of the children of the nation equally.
• Established a Provisional Government until such time as a permanent national government could be elected by universal suffrage.

● GOVERNMENT OF IRELAND ACT

Enacted: December 23, 1920.
• Home Rule Act of 1914 repealed.
• Proposed to establish two Home Rule parliaments - one in Belfast to legislate for the counties of Antrim, Armagh, Derry, Down, Fermanagh and Tyrone - and one in Dublin to legislate for the other 26 counties.
• Control of finance and defence would be retained by

Westminster.
• A Council of Ireland, comprising MPs from both Irish parliaments to deal with matters of mutual interest proposed. The council would have limited powers and would pave the way for an end to partition if both parliaments assented to it.

The act was superseded in the Free State by the Anglo-Irish Treaty of 1921 and in Northern Ireland by the Northern Ireland Constitution Act and the Northern Ireland Assembly Act, both of which were passed by the British parliament in 1973.

● THE ANGLO-IRISH TREATY

Signed: December 6, 1921.
Irish Signatories: Arthur Griffith, Michael Collins, Robert Barton, Edmund Duggan and George Gavan O'Duffy.
British Signatories: David Lloyd George, Austen Chamberlain, Lord Birkenhead, Winston Churchill, L. Worthington-Evans, Hamar Greenwood and Gordon Hewart.
Ratified: British parliament December 5, 1921.
Ratified: Dáil Éireann January 7, 1922 by 64 votes to 57.
• Established the Irish Free State (IFS) as a nation of the British Empire with Dominion status, i.e. same as status of Canada, Australia etc.
• Established a new Irish parliament, Dáil Éireann.
• Crown to be represented by a Governor General.
• All members of the IFS Parliament required to swear an Oath of Allegiance to the IFS Constitution, the Crown and the British Empire.
• IFS to assume a portion of United Kingdom's war debt.
• The British military to retain control of the coastal defence of the IFS and the ports of Berehaven, Queenstown, Belfast Lough and Lough Swilly.
• Size of the Irish army limited.
• Northern Ireland had choice of opting out of the IFS within one month of the Treaty being signed.
• In the event of Northern Ireland opting out of the IFS, a three-person Boundary Commission was to be established. The remit of the Commission was to determine the border, in accordance with the wishes of the inhabitants, as far as those wishes were compatible with economic and geographic conditions.
• Religious discrimination expressly forbidden in both jurisdictions.

● CIVIL AUTHORITIES (SPECIAL POWERS) ACT (NORTHERN IRELAND)

Enacted: Northern Ireland parliament on April 7, 1922.
Delegated a series of wide-ranging powers to the Minister for Home Affairs permitting him to take any steps necessary to preserve the peace. These powers included:
• Arrest without warrant.
• Internment without trial.
• Flogging.
• Execution.
• Banning of organisations or publications.
Initially, it was renewed every year, but in 1928 it was renewed for five years and in 1933 it was made permanent. Rescinded in 1972.

● **CONSTITUTION OF THE IRISH FREE STATE**
Ratified by: Dáil Éireann October 25, 1922 and by the British parliament December 5, 1922.
• Irish Free State declared a co-equal member of the British Commonwealth of Nations.
• The legislature of the new state established (the King, the Senate and the Dáil).
• The Irish language recognised as the national language with official recognition of status of the English language.
• *Habeas corpus* ensured.
• Freedom to practice religion and the free expression of opinion assured
• All citizens entitled to free elementary education.
• The Oath of Allegiance, as agreed in the Treaty, included.
• Articles relating to eligibility to vote and run for public office also included.
Superseded by the 1937 Constitution.

● **CENSORSHIP OF PUBLICATIONS ACT**
Enacted: Dáil Éireann July 1929.
• Established a censorship board of five members empowered to censor or ban publications, the main targets being obscenity and information about birth control. The nature of the act resulted in thousands of books, including many by Ireland's most eminent authors, being banned.
No adequate avenue for appeal was provided until the act was amended in 1967.

● **STATUTE OF WESTMINSTER**
Enacted: British parliament December 11, 1931.
• Conferred equal status on the parliaments of the British Dominions (including Ireland) with the Imperial parliament at Westminster.
• Dominion parliaments empowered to pass any law and amend or repeal any existing or future law enacted by Westminster.
• Dominion parliaments not obliged to implement any British act with which they did not agree.

● **EXTERNAL RELATIONS ACT**
Enacted: Dáil Éireann, December 12, 1936 (during the abdication crisis of Edward VIII).
• Crown recognised only for purposes of external association (i.e. accreditation of diplomats and international agreements).
• The Constitution Amendment (No. 27) Bill, passed on December 11, deleted all reference to the crown from the Irish Free State Constitution.
The Act made the Free State a republic in all but name.

● **CONSTITUTION OF IRELAND**
Ratified: By referendum on July 1, 1937. *See Law and Defence chapter.*

● **EDUCATION ACT**
Enacted: Northern Ireland parliament - 27 November, 1947.
• Grants towards the building and extension of schools provided.
• Financial assistance provided to any student, irrespective of denomination or economic background, to attend university having attained the required educational standards.
• Universal secondary schooling established.

● **REPUBLIC OF IRELAND ACT**
Enacted: Dáil Éireann - December 21, 1948 (effective from April 18, 1949)
• 1936 External Relations Act repealed.
• The 26 counties of Éire declared a Republic.
• Republic of Ireland leaves British Commonwealth of Nations.

● **IRELAND ACT**
Enacted: British parliament June 2, 1949.
• Recognised the Republic of Ireland's withdrawal from the British Commonwealth.
• Affirmed the position of Northern Ireland within the United Kingdom and stated that no change could be effected on its status without the consent of the Northern Ireland parliament.
• Irish citizens would not be considered as aliens in Britain.
• Free travel area between the Britain and Ireland enshrined.

● **NORTHERN IRELAND ASSEMBLY ACT**
Passed by the British parliament May 3, 1973. It proposed:
• A 78-member Assembly elected from the 12 Westminster constituencies by proportional representation. The Assembly would also have law making powers.

● **NORTHERN IRELAND CONSTITUTION ACT**
Passed by the British parliament (July 18, 1973), it superseded the Government of Ireland Act. In it:
• The Northern Ireland Parliament was abolished.
• The Office of Governor was abolished.
• Basic legislation for a system of devolved government, complementary to the Northern Ireland Assembly Act, was laid out including provision for the creation of a 12-member Executive with limited functions.
• The constitutional status of Northern Ireland within the United Kingdom was guaranteed and would not change save for a majority indicating the desire to do so in a border poll.
• In the absence of a devolved administration taking office, provision is made for the functions to be carried out by a Secretary of State and team of junior ministers.

● **SUNNINGDALE AGREEMENT**
Signed December 9, 1973, by Taoiseach Liam Cosgrave, British Prime Minister Edward Heath and leaders of the UUP, SDLP and Alliance parties. Its main points were:
• The Irish government accepted there would be no change in the constitutional status of Northern Ireland without the consent of a majority of people living there.
• The British government affirmed Northern Ireland's position within the United Kingdom but stated that if a majority demonstrated indicated a desire to join a united Ireland they would legislate for that.
• A Council of Ireland, consisting of seven ministers

from both Northern Ireland and the Republic, was to be established to deal with matters of mutual concern.
• On law and order, proposals relating to extradition, the establishing of a common law enforcement area and policing were made.

● **PREVENTION OF TERRORISM (TEMPORARY PROVISIONS) ACT**
Passed by the British Parliament November 29, 1974, it provided for:
• Exclusion orders banning individuals suspected of terrorism from Northern Ireland, Britain or the United Kingdom as a whole.
• Extended detention for terrorist suspects. Police may detain suspects for 48 hours without charge and for a further five days subject to approval from the Home Secretary or the Secretary of State for Northern Ireland.
• The banning of certain organisations.
• In 1988 remission for those convicted of terrorist offences was reduced from 50 to 33 per cent.

● **EUROPEAN MONETARY SYSTEM**
Established: March 13, 1979.
By entering the European Monetary System the Republic of Ireland ended one-for-one parity between the Irish and British currencies which had existed since independence.

● **REPORT OF THE NEW IRELAND FORUM**
Published May 2, 1984, it was the report of the Forum (convened May 1983) which took submissions from Fianna Fáil, Fine Gael, Labour, the SDLP, the Roman Catholic Church and other smaller (and invariably nationalist) organisations on a potential Northern Ireland settlement. Its main findings were:
• All parties favoured a unitary 32-county state.
• Joint authority in Northern Ireland could be exercised by the British and Irish governments or federal arrangements could be put in place.
• All parties pledged to remain open to other views which could contribute to political development.
The Report was rejected by unionists, Sinn Féin and the British government.

Explanatory Notes:
Prior to January 1801, all Acts referred to were Acts of the Irish parliament (with all, excluding the Statute of Kilkenny, subject to Poynings' Law). From 1801 until 1921 all Acts referred to were Acts of the British parliament. Acts referred to from 1922 onwards are distinguished as Acts of Dáil Éireann, the Northern Ireland parliament or the British parliament, as appropriate.

Anniversaries

25 Years (1975)

May 8: Northern Ireland Convention meets (breaks up March 3, 1976).
July 31: Three members of Miami showband ambushed and killed in Co. Down, 2 UVF men die in same attack.
October 3: Dr Tiede Herrema kidnapped in Limerick, release of republican prisoners demanded by abductors. Herrema released unharmed 7 November.
December 5: End of internment in NI.

Died
Vincent Barry, b. 1908, an organic chemist he developed a treatment for leprosy.
Tom Dreaper, b. 1898, horse trainer who trained the magnificent Arkle.
Seamus Murphy b. 1907, sculptor who specialised in stone sculpture.
Eamon de Valera b. 1882, veteran of 1916 Rising, founder and leader of Fianna Fáil, Taoiseach 1932-48, 1951-54 and 1957-59, President 1959-75.

Born
Jason Sherlock, Dublin Gaelic footballer, winner of All-Ireland SFC medal in 1995.
Keith Gillespie, Northern Ireland international soccer player.

50 Years (1950)

Holy Year. Celebrated by Catholics.
June 6: Labour Party and National Party reunite after 6 year split.

Born
Don Baker, blues musician.
Gabriel Byrne, actor, starred in *The Usual Suspects* and *Into the West.*
Peter Cassells, General Secretary of the Irish Congress of Trade Unions
Mary Dorcey, poet and novelist, works include *The Tower of Babel* and *A Noise from the Woodshed.*
Maire Geoghegan-Quinn, politician, TD 1975-97, Minister for Justice 1993-94, retired from public life 1997.
Desmond Hogan, writer his work includes *A Farewell to Prague.*
Donal Hurley, classical composer.
Neil Jordan, film director his films include *The Crying Game, Michael Collins* and *The Butcher Boy.*
Brian Keenan, writer, kidnapped in Beirut 1986 released 1990, wrote *An Evil Cradling* about his experiences.
Medbh McGuckian, poet, collections include *Venus and the Rain* and *The Grateful Muse.*
Martin McGuinness, politician MP since 1997, senior member of Sinn Féin's Ard Comhairle.
Mícheál Ó Súilleabháin, composer and Professor of Music at the University of Limerick.
Philip Orr, Rugby international capped 58 times, won the Triple Crown in 1982 and 1985.
Christy Roche, Horse trainer and former Champion Jockey, winner of both the Irish and English derbies as a jockey.
Dick Spring, politician, TD since 1981, leader of The Labour Party 1982-97, Tánaiste 1982-87 and 1993-97, Minister for Foreign Affairs 1993-97 he was heavily involved in the Northern Ireland Peace Process.

Desmond Smyth, Managing Director of Ulster Television since 1983.

Charles Tyrrell, artist.

Michael Warren, sculptor specialising in wood sculpture.

Ted Walsh, Horse Trainer and former Champion Jockey.

Bill Whelan, composer, a member of the band Planxty, he wrote the music for the hugely successful *Riverdance.*

Died

Sara Allgood, b. 1883, stage actress appeared in Yeats's *Cathleen ní Houlihan.*

Osborn J. Bergin, b. 1873, member of Gaelic League, Professor of Early and Medieval Irish at UCD 1909-40.

Arthur Conway, b. 1875, Professor of Mathematical Physics at UCD 1909-40, President of UCD 1940-47.

Rex Ingram, b. 1893, film director his films include *The Four Horsemen of the Apocalypse* and *Baround.*

Robert McAllister, b. 1870, Professor of Celtic Archaeology at UCD 1909-42 and an expert on ogham translation.

Muiris Ó Súileabháin, b. 1904, author of *Fiche Bliain ag Fás* about life on the Blasket Islands.

George Bernard Shaw, b. 1856, playwright and Nobel Laureate his most famous plays include *John Bull's Other Island, Man and Superman* and *Saint Joan.*

James Stephens, b. 1882, writer his novels include *The Charwoman's Daughter* and *The Crock of Gold.*

75 Years (1925)

July: Shannon hydro-electric scheme commenced.

December: Governments in NI, IFS and Britain agree to rescind powers of the Boundary Commission.

Born

George Colley, TD 1961-83, served as Minister for Finance and Minister for Education. Defeated candidate in Fianna Fáil leadership elections in 1966 and 1979, d. 1983.

Paddy Devlin, founding member of the Social Democratic and Labour Party in 1970.

Con Houlihan, the doyen of Irish sports journalism he worked for *The Kerryman, The Evening Press* and *The Sunday World.*

Val Mulkerns, novelist, work includes *The Summerhouse* and *A Friend of Don Juan.*

Maureen Potter, theatrical actress, cabaret performer and comedienne.

Barbara Warren, painter whose work is known internationally.

Died

Darrell Figgis, with Erskine Childers he landed arms for the Irish Volunteers at Howth in July 1914. Involved in drafting the Constitution of the Irish Free State he was a TD 1922-25, d. 1925.

Centenary (1900)

January 30: Nationalist MPs vote to reunite Irish Parliamentary Party 10 years after the Parnell split.

June 27: Irish Education Act abolishes fees for primary education and makes school attendance compulsory for 6-14 year olds.

September 29: Belfast Labour Party formed, the first Labour Party in Ireland.

Born

James Beddy, civil servant, first chairman of IDA, d. 1976.

Daniel Binchy, IFS Minister to Berlin 1929-32, d. 1989.

Vincent Byrne, veteran of 1916 Rising, member of Michael Collins' 'Squad', d. 1992.

William Collis, doctor and rugby international, won seven caps with Ireland 1924-26, d. 1975.

Eugene Coughlan, hurler, won five All-Ireland SHC medals with Cork including one as captain in 1931.

John Doherty, traditional musician renowned for his fiddle playing, d. 1979.

Sir Tyrone Guthrie, theatre producer and founder of the eponymous theatre in Minneapolis, d. 1971.

Patricia Lynch, author, primarily of children's books most famous of which is *The Turf Cutter's Donkey,* d. 1972.

Maurice MacGonigal, landscape painter and President of Royal Hibernian Academy 1962-78, d. 1979.

Seosamh MacGrianna, Irish language author, d. 1990.

William Norton, Labour Party TD 1926-27 and 1932-63, party leader 1932-60, d. 1963.

Seán Ó Faoláin, author whose works include *King of the Beggars* and *Midsummer Night Madness,* d. 1991

Noel Purcell, actor who appeared in the films *Mutiny on the Bounty* and *Captain Boycott,* d. 1985.

Died

Sir Frederick William Burton, b. 1816, portrait artist, director of National Gallery in London.

Oscar Wilde, b. 1854, playwright and wit his most famous comedies include *The Importance of Being Earnest* and *Lady Windemere's Fan,* he also wrote the autobiographical *Ballad of Reading Gaol.*

Sesquicentenary (1850)

February 24: Paul Cullen ordained Archbishop of Armagh, created Cardinal 22 June 1866.

September 3: Charter providing for the establishing of the Queen's University in Ireland.

Bicentenary (1800)

August 1: Irish Parliament enacts the Act of Union, meets for the last time on August 2nd.

Born

Thomas Grubb, optician and astronomer, helped build telescope at Birr, d. 1878.

Anna Maria Hall author, noted works include *Sketches of Irish Character,* d. 1881.

William Parsons, astronomer, the 3rd Earl of Rosse built the world's biggest telescope (Leviathan) at Birr in 1842, d. 1867.

Died

Richard Hennessy, b. 1720, fought in the War of the Austrian Succession retired and established the famous Cognac distillery which bears his name.

Eibhlín Dhubh Ní Chonaill, b. 1740s, originator of the famous lament *Caoineadh Airt Uí Laoire.*

Quatercentenary (1600)

Nine Years War in progress, fighting in Munster, Connacht, Thomond, Offaly, Kerry, south Leinster, Louth and Donegal.

Born
Piaras Feirtéir, chieftain and poet, d. 1653.
Heber McMahon, Bishop, soldier and member Confederation of Kilkenny, d. 1650.

Quincentenary (1500)

Galway City damaged by fire.

Septcentenary (1300)

Parliament held at Dublin.

Millenary (1000)

January: Brian Boruma captures Dublin, Sitric Silkbeard, king of Dublin, submits.

CHRONOLOGY OF THE YEAR

October 1998

1: According to the annual report by the Comptroller and Auditor General, a total of £14.5m was paid out by the Department of Social, Community and Family Affairs in cases involving fraud or suspected fraud last year. Other government overspending included a Revenue write-off in unpaid tax of £280m and a bill of almost £98m in overtime to state employees in 1997, up a massive 27% on 1996, with the gardai and prison service once again accounting for the bulk of the bill.

1: The National Cancer Registry issued a report which found that Ireland has the highest incidence of bowel cancer in Europe.

1: David Andrews, Minister for Foreign Affairs, was at the centre of a controversy over promotions in his department. Mr Andrews admitted he promoted three civil servants who had been "stuck" in middle management jobs without interviewing them. A series of documents showed that he was once asked to tell the Taoiseach of the "deep unhappiness" over promotions among officials in the department.

1: There was a drop of more than 10,000 in the unemployment figures, bringing the total unemployed down to the lowest level for nine years.

1: Fears about Ireland's soaring economy resurfaced as latest figures showed the country has by far the highest inflation of the 11 EU states launching the single currency on January 1, 1999.

2: A disturbing report has revealed that one-third of the world's natural resources have been wiped out in 25 years, and that the Irish have been among the heaviest users of natural resources in that period.

3: With an impending funding crisis at Tallaght Hospital, Minister Brian Cowen sent in a team of management consultants to prevent further haemorrhaging of finances.

3: The Irish Penal Reform Trust warned that the massive prison building programme proposed by the government, allocating a further 2,000 prison places, is "an extravagant waste of taxpayer's money" as there is no research to suggest that these prison places are necessary.

6: The executive directors of First Active, which was recently floated on the stock exchange, have received large profits based on the former building society's first day of trading. Shares in the former building society rose by 29% and were boosted by a strong recovery on world stock markets.

7: Minister Joe Walsh pledged the Government's total opposition to any reduction in EU aid for Irish farmers.

8: The Government promised that banks and building societies will be forced to pay outstanding DIRT tax on fraudulent non-resident accounts. The statement was made following revelations that AIB only paid a fraction of a £100m DIRT bill it owed the state on bogus non-resident accounts operated during the early 1990s.

9: Elaine Moore, who was held in Britain on terrorist charges, returned to Dublin a free woman, promising she would not return to Britain "for a long time".

9: The IRFU admitted that two Irish rugby players were being investigated after giving positive drugs tests last season, one of them at a Five Nations Championship match.

TOP NEWS STORY

Deadlock in Peace Process

Date *Ongoing*

One word defined the Peace Process in the North this year - impasse.

At the heart of the impasse was Unionist retrenchment over powersharing and the vagueness over decommissioning inherent in the Belfast Agreement. Added to that was a public weariness over "event politics" where prime ministers and presidents had to nurse the process along, without Northern Irish leaders making visible contributions themselves.

The whole process was characterised by a one step forward, two steps back pattern . . . In October: Martin McGuinness and David Trimble met with the British Prime Minister in Downing Street to talk about the deadlock over decommissioning; there was no satisfactory outcome.

In December, on the wave of optimism accompanying the Nobel Peace Prize, significant progress was made with the confirmation of North-South bodies and ministries in Northern Ireland. January was marked by paramilitary beatings and murder and ended with the commemoration of Bloody Sunday - a satisfactory inquiry into which has still to take place. In March the deadline for the formation of the executive loomed and David Trimble told Sinn Féin that the "settlement train" was leaving with or without them.

Deadlines were moved and the Tony-Bertie alliance came on board to formulate the Hillsborough

10: Tanáiste Mary Harney strongly recommended to the Cabinet that the best way to ensure industrial development in the west, midland and border areas was to divide Ireland into rich and poor regions. If these areas were allowed to keep their Objective One EU grant status for 2000-2006, it would allow for a greater increase in state aid and EU investment.

11: Revelations were made that Peter Sutherland, former bank chairman of the AIB, set up a committee of AIB directors in 1991 to look into allegations made by Tony Spollen, a former head of the AIB's internal audit department. Spollen complained about management inaction over the tax owed on the bogus non-resident accounts, which he estimated at £100m. The management committee concluded that Mr. Spollen's complaints were unfounded, and he was informed that he was to move his post. He subsequently resigned.

12: Mark Nash has been found guilty of murdering his former girlfriend's sister, Ms Catherine Doyle, and brother-in-law, Carl Doyle, at their home in Caran, Co. Roscommon, in August 1997, and causing grievous bodily harm to his girlfriend. He also confessed to murdering two elderly women patients from Grangegorman Psychiatric Hospital.

13: Mr. Dermot Quigley, chairman of the Revenue Commissioners, denied in front of the Dáil Public Accounts Committee that the commissioners made any sort of a settlement with AIB over writing off £86m in DIRT tax. However, internal AIB documents showed that it was offered a deal whereby DIRT due on bogus non-resident accounts from prior to April 1990 would not have to be paid. The Revenue was strongly criticised by the committee.

14: Garda Martin Shankey-Smith successfully appealed a six-month prison sentence for knocking down and killing 28-year-old Alan Jones. Mr Jones died in December 1997 after being struck by the garda's sports car as he left a disco in Portarlington, Co. Laois.

15: The AIB's chief executive, Mr Tom Mulcahy, appeared before the Dáil Public Accounts Committee maintaining that the Revenue Commissioners had authorised a settlement on tax arrears.

15: Tom Crosby, a Roscommon Fianna Fáil councillor, told Rooskey District Court that would rather "rot in prison" before he would pay £500 in compensation to Mr Seán Doherty TD for assaulting the TD at a private meeting in Tarmonbarry, Co. Roscommon.

18: The Irish Association of Suicidology found suicide figures for the first quarter of 1998 increased by 81% over the same period in the previous year. In 1997, 433 people in Ireland committed suicide - a 14% increase on 1996.

19: Mr Martin McGuinness, chief negotiator for Sinn Féin, and Mr David Trimble, the First Minister, concluded separate meetings with the British Prime Minister at 10 Downing Street by insisting that the other must make the next move to break the impasse over arms decommissioning.

19: Ann McGuinness has become the first woman in Ireland to be appointed county manager. She was awarded the post in Co. Westmeath.

20: Michael Flatley, star of Lord of the Dance, has reached an out-of-court settlement with his former manager in London who sued him for an estimated £10 million breach of contract.

20: The three men convicted for killing LVF leader Billy Wright in the Maze prison in December 1997 were given a life sentence for the murder.

21: Naas Circuit Court has dismissed the civil case taken by a young Co. Kildare couple against a developer who increased the price of a house by £20,000 after accepting a deposit from the couple. This practice - so-called gazumping - has become more familiar in the current housing market.

22: The ISPCC announced that child begging in Dublin has reached a high level, with 2,872 sightings of begging incidents reported between October 1997 and September 1998.

22: The Cork South-Central by-election was won by Simon Coveney of Fine Gael. He won the seat formerly held by his father who died earlier this year.

25: The Irish Hospital Consultants' Association accused the Department of Health of wasting £88m each year on acute hospital beds occupied by people who should be placed in other facilities.

25: Mr Walter Regan reported that he and others who worked for the Limerick Steamship Co. could have dumped toxic, possibly nuclear, waste from Windscale (now Sellafield) in the Irish Sea in the late 1950s-early 1960s.

26: Joshua Kipkemboi won the 98FM Dublin City Marathon (in a time of 2:20) for the second year in a row.

27: Dr Conor Cruise O'Brien resigned from the UK Unionist Party following statements he made in Sunday newspapers outlining how unionists might have to enter negotiations for a 32-county republic. The statements were dismissed by the UKUP as "absolutely without foundation".

28: Dublin city centre was brought to a standstill for six hours during an angry protest by an estimated 40,000 farmers over demands to boost income. The Irish Farmers' Association has threatened to pull out of Partnership 2000 if these demands were not met.

31: Mr Brian Service, a 35-year-old Catholic with no political or paramilitary connections, was shot dead near his home in the Ardoyne by an obscure loyalist group known as the Red Hand Defenders.

November 1998

1: A Romanian family - the Constinas - who have lived in the state for five years won a last minute reprieve on their deportation order after widespread media coverage of their plight.

2: The report of a review into the railway system, commissioned by Minister Mary O'Rourke, found there was a predictable risk of a fatal train derailment within two years if immediate action was not taken and recommended an investment of £590m in the railway system over the next 15 years.

2: Four of the 12-man crew of a Spanish fishing trawler died and two more went missing during storm-force winds, south-west of Mizen Head. The remaining crew member were rescued by another trawler in the area.

4: The state successfully appealed, for the first time, an award of £20,000 in damages for hearing disability to a former soldier.

5: The Moriarty tribunal heard evidence in private from two witnesses who were questioned about the identity of the Ansbacher depositors. Mr. Pádraig Collery is a former employee of Guinness & Mahon bank and Ms Joan Williams was the long-time secretary of the late Mr Des Traynor, the main Irish figure involved in the operation of the accounts.

7: Mr Seamus Mallon and Mr David Trimble, the North's Deputy First and First Ministers issued a joint statement, promising that the murder of Brian Service would not derail the peace process.

9: Taoiseach Bertie Ahern presented the 1998 Irish Person of the Year Award to Ms Sophia McColgan. She and her siblings were horrendously abused for years by their father and fought a long public court battle against the North Western Health Board for not intervening.

10: The Duke of Edinburgh made his first official visit to the Republic to announce details of a millennium award scheme for young people to be jointly awarded by Gaisce (the President's award scheme) and his own award scheme.

11: President Mary McAleese and Queen Elizabeth joined King Albert of Belgium at a ceremony commemorating World War I in Mesen. They opened a peace tower in memory of the 50,000 Irishmen, who died in the war. The tower was built by young work trainees from both sides of the border.

12: Judge Raymond Groarke commended Philip and Maire Eustace for taking on the Irish Permanent which attempted to evict the couple from their home. The financial institution admitted it had overcharged them for two years and blamed a systems failure for the error.

14-15: At the annual SDLP conference, party leader John Hume noted that unionists and nationalists had at last taken their future into their hands and seized control of their history, rather than letting history hold them.

15: The government expressed concern that leaks to the media from the affidavit of the chief witness in the Flood tribunal, Mr James Gogarty, would undermine the tribunal's investigations into planning abuses and corruption. Extracts in a Sunday newspaper included an allegation that "money would have to be paid" to six serving Dublin county councillors in 1989 to obtain rezonings of land.

16: After vigorous lobbying from the independent TD, Jackie Healy-Rae, Kerry and Clare are to be included among the poorest regions in the plan to divide Ireland in its application for future EU structural funds.

17: After the government agreed on a new regionalisation plan for maximising EU funds, a number of Fianna Fáil TDs criticised Cabinet members for their role in including Clare and Kerry in

TOP NEWS STORY

Declaration - a framework for establishing the executive and a basis for the decommissioning process. Sinn Féin came out strongly against the proposal that voluntary decommissioning would begin a few weeks after the formation of the executive, and the Taoiseach and Prime Minister met to discuss the decommissioning issue.

At Sinn Fein's May Ardfheis, ministers were nominated for the executive. The political manoeuvring continued in June, and the Northern Ireland Human Rights Bureau reported that paramilitaries had killed five people and exiled 600 others since the signing of the Belfast Agreement.

Again the Taoiseach and the Prime Minister met to try and formulate an acceptable agreement before the June 30th deadline. This resulted in the *Way Forward* initiative, whereby ministers would be nominated by July 15th with a devolution order being laid before the British Parliament and a failsafe mechanism suspending the executive if decommissioning failed to take place. By this stage, the process was into the volatile marching season. The British government passed the *Way Forward* in the face of strong opposition from Unionists and Conservatives.

David Trimble returned to Belfast on July 14th to meet with the UUP policy-making executive - a meeting which lasted just some 15 minutes with the inevitable outcome of UUP rejection of the initiative. The next day, the d'Hondt process was triggered at the Northern Ireland Assembly. Neither David Trimble nor any of the UUP attended, while other Unionists refused to nominate ministers. This resulted in a cabinet comprising the poor regions nominated for maximum EU funding.

17: The OECD warned in its draft annual economic review that the Minister for Finance should limit public spending and tax cuts in the forthcoming budget to "what is required to retain the consensus-based approach to wage formation".

18: It was revealed that following representations by the former Taoiseach, Albert Reynolds, the Iraqi government undertook to pay up to £170m owing to the Goodman group of companies. This undertaking would negate a compensation claim of over £80m by one of the Goodman companies against the Irish government.

18: Mr Michael McGimpsey, the Ulster Unionist security spokesman, warned that if moves were made to disband the RUC, the Belfast Agreement could collapse.

19: A report from the UN Committee Against Torture has called for a ban on plastic bullets, the closure of Castlereagh and other RUC detention centres and the reorganisation of the RUC.

19: The Dept. of Justice handed over all the files relating to the passports-for-investment scheme to the Moriarty tribunal. The tribunal received up to 160 files in recent days.

21-22: At the Fianna Fáil Ard Fheis, Taoiseach Bertie Ahern told delegates that a peaceful Ireland would be a prosperous Ireland and that it was only a matter of time before Ireland was united.

24: Rail workers led an unofficial strike which disrupted mainline services throughout the country and brought thousands of extra cars on to the roads.

24: Patrick John Kelly, a Christian Brother, was remanded in custody for sentence after admitting 53 charges of sexual assault and gross indecency on boys between 1977 and 1988.

25: Two men from north Mayo, Mr Paddy Doherty and Mr Declan Sweeney, were drowned after their car went into the sea while they were chasing a fox.

25: A report from Families Against Intimidation and Terror has stated that there were more than 400 incidents linked to paramilitary groups with 55 killings and 61 "punishment" killings in Northern Ireland in the ten months to November.

26: British Prime Minister Tony Blair addressed a joint sitting of the houses of the Oireachtas, stating that Ireland and Britain had both grown up and had come too far to go back now - a new generation was in power in each country.

26: The Moriarty tribunal investigated accounts held by the late Mr P.V. Doyle (of the Doye hotel group) in Gunness and Mahon Bank which may have been used for the benefit of former Taoiseach Charles Haughey. It emerged that full disclosure of the accounts of

the National Gallery's private fundraising committee, chaired by Mr Haughey until June this year, was being sought by at least two members of the gallery's board of governors.

27: Paul Ward was sentenced to life imprisonment for his involvement in the murder of Veronica Guerin.

28/29: Dr Patrick McKeon, consultant psychiatrist at St Patrick's Hospital, noted at the launch of a new antidepressant drug that 200,000 people in the state are affected by depression and predicted that by 2020, the illness will become second only to heart disease a cause of "lost years of healthy life".

30: Train drivers on mainline and DART services embarked on another train strike, despite much negotiation and appeals to call off the strike.

December 1998

1: The Minister of State for Foreign Affairs, Liz O'Donnell, reiterated her case for a large increase in Ireland's aid budget, stating that it was a "measure of our commitment to civilised values" and threatened to resign if the increase wasn't forthcoming.

2: In the budget, the Minister for Finance announced the introduction of a tax reform package, with £581m in reductions for lower earners. This budget saw increases in Vehicle Registration Tax, with heavier levies on high powered cars, increases in education expenditure - particularly adult literacy, a new unemployment assistance scheme for low income farmers and increases in the price of cigarettes. The budget was also kind to gamblers abolishing taxes for on-track betting and reducing taxes for off-course betting.

2: Residents in the Co. Donegal village of Kerrykeel protested against the erection of mobile phone antennae by Esat Digifone and were embroiled in serious clashes with gardaí.

3: A report released by the Human Rights Watch (an important human rights monitoring body) had both praise and criticism for former president Mrs Robinson, stating she was at her best on "Algeria, Rwanda and Colombia".

5: The Minister for Social Community and Family Affairs met officials from his department to clear up confusion over Christmas bonus payments, proposing that the bonus be paid on the same basis as previous years.

7: Gardaí carried out house-to-house inquiries in Connemara after the body of schoolgirl Siobhán Hynes was found dead. A post-mortem revealed she had been murdered.

8: President Clinton asked Northern Irish politicians to move the peace process forward, reminding them to "obey not only the letter of the Good Friday Agreement but its spirit as well".

9: Fruit of the Loom in Co. Donegal confirmed the transfer of its T-shirt sewing operations to

Morocco from next year with the loss of 770 jobs but undertook that there would be no other job losses in 1999. The IDA agreed to waive up to £5m in penalties on the company when it guaranteed 1,300 jobs for at least a year.

9: The Irish Life and Irish Permanent have agreed on the terms of a £2.8bn merger - the largest of its kind in Irish business history.

10: Mr John Hume and Mr David Trimble were awarded the Nobel Peace Prize at a ceremony in the City Hall, Oslo. The two men were presented with gold medals and their Nobel diplomas. Their cheques for £344,000 will be sent to them in the new year.

12: The Labour Party and Democratic Left voted at their respective delegate conferences to merge the two parties.

14: There is to be an inquiry by the Institute of Obstetricians and Gynaecologists in Ireland into the actions of an obstetrician who worked as a consultant at Our Lady of Lourdes Hospital in Drogheda, following reports that he carried out an abnormally high number of hysterectomies on young mothers. He is said to have performed as many as nine unnecessary hysterectomies.

14: The UK Unionist Party assembly bloc divided over accusations by its leader, Mr Bob McCartney, that his colleagues were politically immature and counter accusations that the UKUP leader "impugned' their integrity.

15: It was revealed that a taxation appeal commissioner reduced a tax assessment of £2m on Mr Charles Haughey to zero. The assessment was made against the former Taoiseach after the McCracken tribunal reported last year that he received £1.3m from the businessman Ben Dunne between 1987 and 1991.

15: Another medical inquiry was announced, this time by the Royal College of Surgeons in Ireland, into a consultant, following concerns over his cases, including two in which patients died.

15: A report on the Tallaght Hospital, commissioned by the Minister for Health, has found that the hospital was in a "financial crisis of the most serious kind" after only six months of operation and was "already significantly in arrears in paying its creditors".

16: Taoiseach Bertie Ahern confirmed that his brother-in-law, Ronan Kelly, was the appeal commissioner who dismissed the £2m tax assessment against Charles Haughey.

17: After 18 hours of negotiations, significant strides have been made in the implementation of the Belfast Agreement with the confirmation of North-South bodies and ministries in Northern Ireland. The six North-South bodies will govern inland waterways, aquaculture, trade and business development, food safety, the Irish and Ulster-Scots languages, and EU funding programmes, while the number of departments was increased from six to ten. These comprise Agriculture and Rural Development; Environment; Regional Development; Social Development; Education; Higher and Further Education, Training and Employment; Enterprise, Trade and Investment; Culture, Arts and Leisure; Health, Social Services and Public Safety; Finance and Personnel.

18: The Loyalist Volunteer Force became the first paramilitary organisation in the North to hand over weapons to the international decommissioning body.

19: According to the European Monitoring Centre for Drugs and Drug Addiction, Ireland has the fourth highest rate of cannabis-related arrests, with 63% of drug related arrests relating to cannabis. Three-quarters of these arrests were for use rather than supply.

24: Gay Byrne's long running morning radio show came to an end after 26 years on RTÉ's Radio 1.

24: Two brothers died in a drowning accident close to Sligo town centre, after returning from Christmas Eve celebrations.

26: The worst storms to hit Ireland since Hurricane Debbie in 1961 struck the country with winds of over 109 mph hitting the

TOP NEWS STORY

nationalists and republicans, an imbalance which automatically led to the executive's suspension (the ministerial portfolios were allotted to Mark Durkan: Finance & Personnel; Bairbre de Bruin: Enterprise Trade & Investment; Sean Farren: Regional Development; Martin McGuinness: Agriculture and Rural Services; Denis Haughey: Social Development; Mary Nellis: Culture Arts & Leisure; Alban Maginnis: Environment). As a result of this farcical process Seamus Mallon announced his bitter disappointment with his Unionist colleagues and resigned.

Once again outside negotiators had to be called in. Former senator George Mitchell - the deal maker - arrived in September in the aftermath of Unionist ire over the report from the Patten Commission to reform the RUC and wranglings over whether the IRA had broken the ceasefire. It seemed the process was unravelling fast.

Finally, at the end of this frustrating 12-month period, the process lost Northern Secretary Mo Mowlam who was replaced by Peter Mandelson. Her 'promotion' was possibly the inevitable outcome of the prime minister allowing himself to be directly on call to Unionists and their desire for someone more conformist.

At this stage there is little expectation that George Mitchell will be able to negotiate a resolution between the two sides, and there is an ominous feeling that the North is heading towards a resumption of violence.

western seaboard. An estimated 1,800 ESB poles were knocked down, leaving 160,000 households without electricity. The storm was responsible for three deaths and inflicted severe damage on many houses. In the North, the storm left eight families homeless and one man dead.

28: Cathal Goulding, former chief-of-staff of the IRA and leading member of the Irish Left, died. He spent 16 years in British and Irish jails and was a key figure in the IRA split that led to the formation of the Workers' Party.

28: A publican was found murdered on his premises in Clondra, Co. Longford. In Dublin, one man was killed and two others injured in a stabbing incident.

29: Many households, particularly in the north-west, were hit again by new storms following a night of freezing conditions. Around 12,000 people were still without power. It was estimated that over £100m in storm damage was caused. Northern Ireland Electricity was heavily criticised for not providing customers with information during the power cuts.

30: Ronnie Flanagan, the RUC Chief Constable and Reg Empey of the UUP were included in the British New Year's honours list.

31: Figures released for 1998 include the number of fatalities for car accidents, which decreased slightly from from those of the previous year to 463. A total of 48 people died violently in 1998, compared to 53 in 1997, and more than 30 people were murdered, seven of whom were women. One indicator of the continuing roar of the Celtic Tiger was car sales, which increased from 137,000 to 145,000 in 1998. Met Éireann officially described the year as warm, wet and dull, with Autumn being the wettest recorded in 15 years. There has been a succession of warmer than normal years since 1994. The weather in February was the mildest for that month on record.

January 1999

1: The rate of the currencies participating in the euro was irrevocably fixed by the EU's finance ministers in Brussels. The euro, worth IR£0.787564, was introduced into cashless transactions, such as cheques, direct debits and credit transfers, in the Republic of Ireland.

1: The first baby of 1999 was born at the Rotunda Hospital in Dublin. Lloyd Pilson was brought into the world at five seconds past midnight.

4: An armed robbery was attempted on a Brinks-Allied van carrying £500,000. The robbery took place in Dalkey, Co. Dublin, but the getaway car stalled. The gang fired two shots as they escaped.

5: Exchequer figures released indicated a budget surplus of £747m. The Minister for Finance announced the sum would go towards reducing the national debt.

5: The Rape Crisis Centre found that the number of rapes reported to them increased by one-third in 1998. Child sex abuse was up by 13%.

7: After the bad weather of the past year, thousands of farm animal faced starvation due to fodder shortages.

7: The Comptroller and Auditor General, Mr John Purcells, criticised the Department of Energy for selling state land at Glen Ding woods in Co Wicklow in 1992 to Roadstone Dublin Ltd. At the time of the sale, the company's chairman was Des Traynor, who was personal financier to Charles Haughey, the then taoiseach.

8: Sarah Flannery of Scoil Muire Gan Smál, Co Cork, won the Young Scientist of the Year for her invention of a new mathematical algorithm to encrypt information sent by computer. Computer firms worldwide have been in contact with her, but she has decided to put the code into the public domain.

9: The government has offered to pay for all school sites and buildings - the first time in the history of the state that it has took on such a responsibility.

11: Four men - Pearse McCauley, Jeremiah Sheehy, Michael O'Neill and Kevin Walsh - went on trial for the murder of Detective Garda Jerry McCabe. Detective McCabe was shot dead during an failed robbery in Adare in 1996.

11: Brian Moore, the renowned Belfast-born novelist, died at his home in Malibu, California.

12: Mr James Gogarty (81), the former building company executive and main witness in the Flood Tribunal, began giving his evidence with details of the relationship with his former employer, the millionaire builder, Mr Joseph Murphy.

12: Following a meeting between the British Ambassador, Dame Veronica Sutherland, and the Minister for Public Enterprise, a joint review of evidence will be made into the 1968 Tuskar Rock air disaster in which 61 people lost their lives. There are allegations that the British Defence Forces accidently shot down the Aer Lingus aircraft.

13: In the first case of its kind, a national school principal, Laurence Begley, was fined for assaulting a 12-year-old student.

13: The artist Derek Hill was granted honorary citizenship of Ireland by President Mary McAleese.

14: James Gogarty told the Flood tribunal of his arguments with Joseph Murphy Structural Engineering to agree on a pension that would secure his future.

16: Jeffrey and Jennifer Bramley flew back to Britain with their foster daughters Jade and Hannah Bennett after hiding out in Tralee, Co Kerry, for around 17 weeks. They left Britain after arguments with the authorities over guardianship of the girls.

16: EU commissioner Pádraig Flynn made a

controversial appearance on the *Late Late Show*. He made derogatory comments about property developer, Tom Gilmartin, who allegedly made a payment of £50,000 to Mr Flynn during the late 1980s.

18: Arising out of the appearance of Pádraig Flynn on the *Late Late Show*, Taoiseach Bertie Ahern defended Mr Flynn's performance as EU Commissioner but would not comment on whether he would endorse him for another term as EU Commissioner.

19: At the Flood Tribunal, James Gogarty alleged that Ray Burke was paid £80,000 by two builders in 1989. He made further allegations, focusing on a £50,000 cheque which he received in 1990 to buy his silence. He never cased the cheque but kept it as evidence.

19: Dr David McCutcheon, the head of Tallaght hospital, resigned following arguments between himself and the Minister for Health and department officials over the hospital budget.

20: The FAI announced plans to build a £65m stadium in south-west Dublin.

20: James Gogarty told the planning tribunal he was handed a £50,000 cheque by Michael Bailey, a building developer, at a north Dublin hotel to buy his silence for the payment he gave to Ray Burke, the former minister for foreign affairs. On a separate note, a gun was found at the tribunal in the men's toilets. It transpired that the gun was left there accidentally by a Garda detective.

20: Darren Kavanagh, who thought he was stealing house windows, was jailed for 18 months for stealing £250,000 worth of Microsoft Windows software.

20: On his official visit to the Middle East, Taoiseach Bertie Ahern became the first European head of state permitted to fly into Gaza, where he met with Yasser Arafat for talks about the Wye Agreement. Previously in the day, he visited a number of sites in Jerusalem, including the Holocaust memorial at Yad Vashem for a wreath-laying ceremony.

21: The UN Secretary General, Kofi Annan, arrived for an official visit to Ireland. He met the Minister for Foreign Affairs, Mr David Andrews, and visited the UN Peacekeeping School at the Curragh.

21: The ISPCC was investigated by the Garda National Fraud Investigation as part of a "routine inquiry". The inquiry followed allegations made by the *Sunday Business Post* that the Society underpaid its collectors by underestimating amounts collected (it must pay a percentage commission to its collectors on money raised in street collections).

21: An Oireachtas Committee was told by Teagasc officials of an unprecedented shortage of fodder in the country, reporting that animals were starving and that government aid was urgently needed.

23: Conflict arose over the number and content of meetings and conversations in 1989 between businessman Tom Gilmartin and Taoiseach Bertie Ahern: Mr Ahern recalled one meeting while Mr Gilmartin states that they had four meetings in total.

24: The Irish Amateur Swimming Association was wound up after 100 years in existence and replaced by a new body - Swim Ireland. However, there was heated debate between delegates and the executive of the new body, some of whom were on the executive of the IASA when there was investigations into cases of sexual abuse within the IASA.

25: Taoiseach Bertie Ahern met with the Tánaiste Mary Harney to tell her "all the details as he knew them" about Tom Gilmartin's alleged payment of £50,000 to EU Commissioner Pádraig Flynn.

25: Gerry Adams, president of Sinn Féin, was angry at David

TOP NEWS STORY

Nobel Peace Prize
Date *10th December, 1998*

It was acknowledged that the award was more of an incentive to push the peace process forward. To this end, it has partially failed. While the consensus was that John Hume totally deserved the prize, David Trimble's nomination was viewed as a carrot and stick approach to compel Unionist commitment to the process.

Others, including no lesser a figure than President Bill Clinton, pointed out that there was a third person missing - Gerry Adams who, at considerable risk to himself and his party, participated fully in negotiations with John Hume from the very beginning.

Nonetheless, Ireland celebrated with both leaders in winning such a prestigious award. John Hume became the second person from Derry (the first being Seamus Heaney) to win the Nobel Prize. *The text of his speech is given further on in this publication.*

The Flood Tribunal
Date *Ongoing*

If the impasse dominated the news in the north, the one word on everyone's lips in the Republic of Ireland was Tribunal. We were in turn amused, angered and possibly bored by the tribunals.

Billed as the greatest free show in town, the star of this tribunal was the octogenarian James Gogarty, whose battling with barristers and professed desire for the truth "warts and all" was riveting. The exchanges between Justice Flood and the various senior counsels were amusing sub-plots, as was the incident of the gun

Trimble's suggestion that the Northern peace process may be 'parked' if the IRA did not start decommissioning.

26: Taoiseach Bertie Ahern stated he had three meetings with Tom Gilmartin, and not one, as he previously recalled. He did not confirm whether he had questioned Pádraig Flynn about a £50,000 payment, asserting that it was a matter for the tribunal.

26: A Catholic family in the largely Protestant area of Greenisland, Co. Antrim, were the victims of a bomb attack, when a pipe bomb was planted under their car.

27: Eamon Collins, a former republican who helped murder a number of people while in the IRA and who turned supergrass (later retracting his confessions), was found dead with massive injuries near Newry. He wrote a book, *Killing Rage,* which detailed his involvement in the IRA.

27: Taoiseach Bertie Ahern addressed the Dáil with regard to allegations made by the businessman, Tom Gilmartin, over meetings they had. The Taoiseach stated he never asked Mr Gilmartin for a financial contribution to Fianna Fáil. Mr Gilmartin confirmed that Mr Ahern did not solicit a contribution, but had asked if he had given one.

27: The PDs signalled their continued support for the government following the Taoiseach's statement to the Dáil.

28: The Moriarty tribunal opened with Mr Haughey's counsel asking for the tribunal to be adjourned as adverse publicity might jeopardise Mr Haughey's right to fair criminal trial, which Justice Moriarty refused. The tribunal heard that Mr Haughey had a bank loan with the AIB of £1.43m at a time when he lectured the nation on overspending.

28: Terry Madden, (51) a community activist who was married with three children in Monasteraden, Co. Sligo, was found dead with gunshot wounds to his leg. The murder occurred as Mr Madden left for a meeting.

28: A former army private received an award for £219,000 in the High Court for the army's non-treatment of his post-traumatic stress disorder.

28: A senior official from the ISPCC was arrested in connection with the gardaí fraud investigation into the society.

30: Ulster won a momentous victory over the French club, Colomiers, in the European Rugby Cup final at Lansdowne Road. Over 30,000 Ulster supporters travelled to Dublin to attend the game.

31: Mr Paddy Fox, a former IRA prisoner, was abducted from his car in Co. Monaghan and beaten up. He is alleged to be an outspoken critic of the Sinn Féin leadership and the Belfast Agreement.

31: Ireland's oldest synagogue - the 107-year-old Orthodox synagogue on Adelaide Road in Dublin - closed. The closure was due to the falling numbers of Jews in Ireland.

31: The annual commemoration of the 27th anniversary of Bloody Sunday (marking when 13 people were shot dead by British paratroopers on January 30th, 1972) took place in Derry, with around 10,000 people taking part. In London, 500 people marched to commemorate the anniversary.

February 1999

1: In the light of Apple Computers' global restructuring, the company announced 450 job losses at its factory in Cork with a decision to move production of its new iMac computer to other low-cost locations. Ironically, the job cuts follow the huge success of the company's new iMac computer.

1: Two prisoners were convicted for their roles in the 1997 siege at Mountjoy Prison in which prison officers were held hostage and threatened. Eamonn Seery (34) was sentenced to two years imprisonment and Edward Ferncombe (27) to three years.

1: Commissioner Padraig Flynn said to RTÉ's Tommie Gorman that he would not be clarifying his position before giving evidence to the Flood tribunal.

1: Lord Alderdice has increased his chances of staying on as speaker of the Northern Assembly after a DUP-backed motion of no confidence in him was rejected.

1: Mr James Gogarty informed the Flood tribunal that on June 19th, 1994, sometime after 2 am, he received threatening phone calls from Joseph Murphy jnr of Joseph Murphy Structural Engineering (JMSE). Justice Flood allowed the counsel for Ray Burke, the Murphy group, Bovale Developments and others to cross-examine Mr Gogarty when he has finished giving his evidence. He also ruled that if any material was to be put to Mr Gogarty during the cross-examination, it should first be circulated to all relevant parties.

2: The Moriarty Tribunal heard how Charles Haughey asked Ben Dunne for money shortly after becoming Taoiseach in 1987.

2: Dr John Lockington, a long standing member of the Orange Order who says he will not take part in joint worship with Catholics, has been elected as the new Moderator of the Presbyterian Church.

3: The trial over the murder of Garda Jerry McCabe took a dramatic twist as the four men convicted of his murder pleaded guilty when the charges against them were reduced from capital murder to manslaughter. Widespread outrage was expressed by gardaí, politicians and members of the public. Taoiseach Bertie Ahern gave assurances that the men would not receive early release under the terms of the Good Friday agreement.

3: A number of London-based Irish passengers, who caused a Jamaica-bound flight to be diverted when they became involved in a fight on board the airplane, left for London after being stranded in Norfolk, Virginia.

4: It was revealed that during negotiations on the Good Friday Agreement, Sinn Féin attempted to pressure the government into including the men who were charged with Garda Jerry McCabe's murder on the list of those eligible for early release.

4: New legislation (drafted to replace the Aliens Act which was ruled unconstitutional in January) will allow non-nationals threatened with deportation to make a case as to why they should not be deported. They can use their domestic situation, length of stay and links with the country in their application.

4: The Moriarty tribunal heard from Padraig Collery, a banker with Guinness & Mahon who operated the Ansbacher accounts with Mr Des Traynor. He stated that an £80,000 payment from Dunnes Stores in 1992 was channelled through the accounts to Mr Charles Haughey.

5: The four men convicted of killing Det Garda Jerry McCabe were sentenced in the Special Criminal Court: Kevin Walsh received 14 years, Pearse McCauley - 14 years, Jeremiah Sheehy - 12 years, Michael O'Neill - 11 years. Justice Johnston noted that Walsh had shown no sign of regret. The sentences were criticised by the Garda Representative Association and politicians. Martin McGuinness of Sinn Féin believed that the killers would qualify for early release under the Belfast Agreement, but the Taoiseach ruled this out.

5: Unemployment fell to its lowest figure - 209,500 - in 15 years.

5: Franz Fischler, the EU Agriculture Commissioner, ended his two day visit to Ireland on a disappointing note, telling farmers that the Agenda 2000 reforms will cut EU support for farming. Farmers claimed they would lose £260m in income and indicated they would protest in Brussels on February 22nd when the agriculture ministers meet to finalise the reforms.

5: The gardaí were asked to try to find out the source of a story from the Flood tribunal which appeared in the *Irish Independent,* in which journalist Sam Smyth claimed that the developer, Mr Michael Bailey, drew £50,000 in cash from his bank in November 1989, stating that it was to pay Mr James Gogarty.

8: President Mary McAleese attended the funeral of King Hussein of Jordan, along with many other leaders, monarchs and presidents from around the world.

9: James Gogarty finished giving his evidence and will be given a week's rest, in deference to his age, before his cross-examination begins.

13-14: At the 70th Fine Gael Ard Fheis, delegates focused on the timing of a General Election in the light of the scandals arising from the tribunal which are threatening the current government.

15: The US biotechnology company, Monsanto, was accused by environmental group Genetic Concern of 'deliberately misleading the public' in relation to its running of experiments here in Ireland. An independent opinion poll showed that 88% of Irish consumers wanted GM food clearly labelled.

15: Dr Patrick Wall, the chief executive of the Food Safety Authority of Ireland, was of the opinion that GM foods are of no direct benefit to the consumer. Dr Patrick O'Reilly of Monsanto rejected these claims and stated that on a global level, GM crops were already leading to less pesticide use. He also noted that GM organisms have been used widely in the food and drinks industry for some years without adverse effects.

15: Taoiseach Bertie Ahern rejected criticisms that he compounded the government's difficulties by making himself too available for comment to the media.

16: The Moriarty Tribunal heard details of Charles Haughey's financial dealings with the AIB in the 1970s, during which time he ran up debts of more than £1m. It was revealed Haughey

TOP NEWS STORY

accidently left by a garda detective in the men's toilets at the tribunal and found by a vigilant lawyer.

The Flood Tribunal was set up in October 1997 to inquire into the planning history of 726 acres of land in north County Dublin. These were the subject of a letter written by property developer Michael Bailey to Mr James Gogarty, then of Joseph Murphy Structural Engineering (JMSE), in June 1989. Mr Gogarty alleged during the tribunal that the former Minister for Foreign Affairs, Ray Burke, received payments amounting to £80,000 while Mr Burke stated he received £30,000.

The tribunal was also given powers to inquire into all improper payments made to politicians in connection with the planning process, including allegations that Luton-based property developer Tom Gilmartin made payments to former EU Commissioner Pádraig Flynn.

One of the more dramatic developments in the tribunal was the behaviour of one witness, George Redmond, the former assistant Dublin city and county manager, whose dealings and 'savings' have come to dominate newspaper headlines in recent months.

In February he was arrested at Dublin airport with a bag containing £200,000 in cash which he had collected from a bank in the Isle of Man. His activities were and still are under investigation by the Criminal Assets Bureau (CAB), but the recent revelations of the hundreds of thousands of pounds he had stashed away in various bank accounts, while on a take-home pay of £19,000 in 1988, were beyond even the estimations of the CAB. The story continues . . .

threatened the AIB that he could be "a very troublesome adversary" if the bank took any action against him.

17: In the light of revelations by Dr Garret FitzGerald that AIB and Ansbacher cancelled his debt of £200,000 in 1993, three former taoisigh - Liam Cosgrave, Albert Reynolds and John Bruton - stated they never had bank debts written off.

17: Up to 15,000 farmers protested throughout Ireland against the proposed reform of the CAP in the EU.

18: The government was criticised after revelations that an interest-free loan was given to Fianna Fáil by a passport investor in 1993.

18: The government proposed new legislation be introduced to compel most sex offenders to sign a register.

18: An award of some £2.15m was made to Blaise Gallagher, a six-year-old boy with cerebral palsy who is quadriplegic in settlement of an action against the National Maternity Hospital and a consultant obstetrician.

19: The Director of Consumer Affairs, Ms Carmel Foley, ordered an investigation into business practices at Superquinn after Senator Feargal Quinn admitted he looked for support funds - "hello money" - when his supermarket chain, Superquinn, opened new supermarkets.

19: George Redmond, the former assistant Dublin city and county manager was arrested at Dublin airport with a bag containing £200,000 in cash. He had flown to the Isle of Man that morning where he collected the money and flew back to Dublin. He had earlier contacted a Manx bank to arrange the collection. He was expected to be one of the main witnesses at the Flood Tribunal. After his arrest, he was questioned by the Criminal Assets Bureau.

22: The Minister for Agriculture, Joe Walsh, flew to Brussels to attend the Agenda 2000 negotiations. The IFA president, Tom Parlon, stated that the survival of the family farm in Ireland depended on negotiations over cuts in subsidies for beef and milk.

24: Eurostat, the EU statistical body, has objected to the inclusion of Clare and Kerry in the proposed disadvantaged areas in Ireland that are to qualify for EU structural funds. The government disputed the ruling.

24: Colm Murphy from Armagh was charged in connection with the Omagh bombing.

25: The English have been in Ireland longer than previously thought - evidence of a pre-Viking Anglo Saxon dwelling was found in the Temple Bar area of Dublin city. English archaeologists confirmed the house was similar to hundreds in England.

26: Anne Maria Sacco was found not guilty of participating in her husband Franco's murder. A 15-year-old shot Franco at his house in Templeogue, and it was alleged that Anna

Maria had handed the girl a loaded shotgun and told her to shoot her husband. The girl had seen Anna Maria beaten by her husband on a number of occasions. She was subsequently convicted of murder, but was released by the Court of Criminal Appeal because there was no place suitable for her to be detained.

26: Nuala Ahern MEP complained about the killing of 1,300 badgers by the Department of Agriculture. The department had the animals killed as part of an experiment to eradicate bovine TB.

March 1999

1: David Trimble threatened republicans that he intends to press for the transfer of powers to a new executive, even if Sinn Féin does not take part.

1: Ireland remains below average EU and OECD educational attainment levels: Some 53% of 26 to 54-year-olds have not finished secondary school, and experts have indicated that unless action is directed towards disadvantaged communities, Ireland will still be below average in 2015. An ESRI report found wide gaps in exam performance between schools, primarily as a result of economic and social factors.

1: Gardaí believe that they have enough evidence to bring major charges against suspects in the Omagh bombing, but they also believe that the man responsible for directing the bombing has fled the country. The man is a former senior Provisional IRA figure who defected at the calling of a second ceasefire and set up his own terrorist group.

2: Controversy erupted over a speech made by Archbishop Desmond Connell to the Life Society in St Patrick's College, Maynooth. In the speech the archbishop criticised planned children stating they suffered as a result of their planning.

6: Arson attacks were carried out on the homes of two Catholic women in a Protestant enclave in north Belfast.

6: Belfast sisters, Bronagh and Karen Mullan, won the National Song Contest with *When You Need Me* and will represent Ireland at the Eurovision Song Contest in Israel.

6: David Trimble issued an unprecedented invitation to Sinn Féin to meet for talks in an attempt to break the impasse over decommissioning. Senior UUP figures denied there was a secret deal in progress to allow Sinn Féin into the power-sharing executive.

7: Ireland's Eddie Irvine won his first Formula One Grand Prix for Ferrari in Melbourne, Australia. The Irish Jordan team also had reason to celebrate with Heinz Harald Frentzen taking second place in the race.

8: The minister for Foreign Affairs and the Northern Secretary met in Dublin Castle to sign four treaties establishing the institutions central to the Good Friday Agreement. Dr Mowlam also put back the deadline for the creation of the Northern Ireland executive from March 10th to Easter week, a move which has infuriated First Minister David Trimble.

8: The minister for Education, Micheal Martin, announced a £9m initiative to reduce class sizes in primary schools. The initiative aims to reduce classes to an average of 30 and will involve 150 extra teaching posts.

8: The North Western Health Board is to fly home Robert Drake, the gay American writer, who was hospitalised after being severely beaten in Sligo.

8: Robert Drake, an American writer who was hospitalised after being severely beaten in Sligo was flown home to America by the North West Health Board.

9: The British budget yielded a windfall for the Republic's border counties. With the rise in petrol and cigarettes, many motorists from the North continued to make the journey across the border to fill their tanks.

9: Mr Alan Byrne was shot and wounded as he was walking to work in Dublin's south inner city. He was to be a witness at the trial of nine men charged with the manslaughter of Josie Dwyer, a heroin addict who was beaten to death in 1996. Gardaí are investigating whether the IRA may be linked to the shooting.

9: The government studied the latest report by the economic consultant, Dr Peter Bacon, on the housing market. A series of measures to boost housebuilding and stabilise the market is expected in the wake of the report. In particular, a new scheme may be introduced which would give buyers a 70% stake in their property with the balance acquired for a specified period by a trust or similar organisation, giving the purchaser the option to acquire the remaining equity after a given period of at least ten years.

9: The Dáil has agreed to ask the Flood tribunal if EU Commissioner Pádraig Flynn was free to answer the allegation that he received £50,000 intended for Fianna Fáil.

10: Mr Walsh, the Minister for Agriculture, attended the meeting in Brussels at which agreement was reached for a farm package for Agenda 2000 including new proposals on beef compensation payments.

10: The Flood tribunal was adjourned when a large amount of new information from Bovale Developments was made available.

10: Security guard Pat O'Donnell was killed when two car thieves rammed a heavy gate at an underground car park in Dublin city centre.

11: There were threatened cuts to electricity supply over an industrial dispute at ESB stations.

11: British paratrooper Lee Clegg was found guilty of attempting to wound with intent Martin Peake, the driver of a stolen car. However Clegg was acquitted of passenger Karen O'Reilly's murder. The court also found that Clegg had lied in his evidence.

12: New jobs were announced for employment blackspots in the North West and the West.

13: Fr Seán Fortune, a priest who was to be tried for numerous sex offences in the Wexford parish where he served until he went on administrative leave in 1995, committed suicide. Fr Fortune left a suicide note in which he apologised to his family and blamed the media for his trial.

13: Ireland's St Patrick's Day festival kicked off with a massive fireworks display in Dublin. The 30-minute extravaganza cost £400,000 and was billed as the greatest ever seen in Europe.

14: A gun attack was carried out at a local soccer match in Dublin by a man who was a pillion passenger on a motor bike. Four people were taken to hospital with injuries after the shooting.

15: The Central Criminal Court decided to continue the trial of

TOP NEWS STORY

The Moriarty Tribunal
Date *Ongoing*

The Flood Tribunal may have been the greatest free show in town, but the Moriarty Tribunal showed that emperor's clothes included bespoke shirts from Paris totalling £16,000.

This tribunal was established in September 1997 to investigate payments to former Taoiseach Charles Haughey and Michael Lowry and extended the investigations of the McCracken tribunal. It set out to establish the source of all payments to Mr Haughey and whether any decisions made by him when he was in government were associated with these payments.

The tribunal (along with Mr Haughey's former mistress) revealed the former taoiseach lived a lavish lifestyle well beyond his means at a time when he was urging the rest of the country to tighten their belts and practice economic restraint. In a further twist, the tribunal discovered that a cheque for £20,000, intended to pay for a liver transplant for politician Brian Lenihan, ended up in an account for Celtic Helicopters, a firm run by Mr Haughey's son Ciarán, and further allegations were made that this cheque may have gone towards paying Mr Haughey's expenses.

The tribunal also uncovered that he was not alone in his lifestyle and clandestine banking habits; that the top echelon of society were secreting money away in Ansbacher accounts at a time when high taxes were crippling the rest of the country.

The tribunals may have uncovered a vipers pit of corruption, but they prove to be an

Joseph Delaney with the remaining eleven members of the current jury. One member of the jury was excused from serving when he discovered that he had indirect contact with the defendant which might taint his judgement. The jury confirmed they were happy with security arrangements around the trial.

15: In what was seen as a major setback for the peace process, Rosemary Nelson, one of Northern Ireland's most high-profile solicitors, was murdered in a car bomb explosion. Mrs Nelson represented nationalists in many important cases (the Garvaghy Road Residents' Coalition and the family of Robert Hamill) and she was the subject of loyalist paramilitary and alleged RUC threats in the past. The Red Hand Defenders, a loyalist paramilitary group, admitted responsibility for the killing.

15: All 20 members of the EU commission, including Ireland's Mr Pádraig Flynn, resigned en masse following a report which was highly critical of the executive, singling out Ms Édith Cresson and the president of the Commission, Jacques Santer, for particular criticism.

15: A joint Garda-RUC investigation was underway into the rape and subsequent death of a 91-year-old woman. The Garda and the RUC issued an appeal for men aged 16–70 along the Tyrone-Donegal border to submit to a voluntary DNA test in the area.

15: The Flood tribunal was resumed a only to adjourn for another week in the wake more media leaks, this time by Ursula Halligan in the *Sunday Times*. The tribunal chairman ruled that Mr Gogarty had suffered a very nervous upset over the article and that it was to be brought to the attention of the Gardaí who were already investigating previous media leaks.

16: The National Hunt Festival at Cheltenham, one of the most popular pilgrimages for Ireland's punters, opened with the Irish favourite, Istabraq, owned by JP McManus, winning the Smurfit Champion Hurdle.

16: RUC Chief Constable Ronnie Flanagan announced that David Phillips, the Chief Constable of Kent, had been asked to oversee the investigation into solicitor Rosemary Nelson's murder. The FBI was also invited to help with the investigation.

17: St. Patrick's Day events were staged all over the world, and the Dublin parade brought out thousands on what was an unseasonably warm and sunny day. When President Clinton was presented with shamrock by Taoiseach Bertie Ahern, he urged Northern Irish politicians to set their sights above the current short-term difficulties.

18: Thousands of people attended the funeral of Ms Rosemary Nelson in Lurgan.

18: The 1998 report by the ombudsman, Mr Kevin Murphy, indicated that £15m in arrears are to be paid to more than 4,000 people on social welfare and that at least £500,000 is to be paid out to house-owners who overpaid their local authority loans.

20-21: The growing political crisis in the North, fuelled by the murder of Ms Rosemary Nelson, saw David Trimble assuring those at the UUP conference that there would be IRA decommissioning. Gerry Adams stated that Sinn Féin would try to find some accommodation.

21: A 13-year-old became one of the youngest victims of a punishment beating when a gang of masked loyalists attacked him in Newtownards, Co Down.

22: Kathleen Bell from Galway, who killed her partner, had the murder charge against her rejected by a court which convicted her of manslaughter. The charge was dropped when the details of a long history of abuse against her emerged.

22: In the Flood Tribunal, Liam Lawlor TD (FF) admitted that he was the TD associated with George Redmond. the former assistant city and county manager. However, he denied meeting Jim Kennedy, the arcade owner with whom George Redmond had invested £100,000.

23: There have been calls for an independent inquiry in Rosemary Nelson's murder in the wake of a report into allegations of death threats made by the RUC to Rosemary Nelson. The report, compiled by the Independent Commission on Police Complaints, encountered a number of obstacles, one of which was the behaviour of the chief inspector who "appeared to have difficulties in co-operating productively" with the barrister charged with leading the inquiry.

23: The director of consumer Affairs confirmed that she had received accusations up to six months ago that the Tesco supermarket chain were overcharging.

25: The Chief Constable of the RUC, Sir Ronnie Flanagan, rejected calls to withdraw his force from the investigation into the murder of Rosemary Nelson.

26: After days of protracted negotiations, the German EU presidency produced a compromise agreement on Agenda 2000. Irish negotiators expressed deep disappointment on all three key priority areas to Ireland: transition arrangements, cohesion funding and farm spending.

28: Speculation intensified around the case of a Dublin architect who was freed after serving only one year of a four-year sentence on a charge of dangerous driving causing death. Philip Sheedy was sentenced by Judge Joseph Matthews in October 1997. A review date was set for October 1999. However, last November the then Dublin Circuit Court judge Mr Cyril Kelly - now a High Court judge - suspended the remaining three years for good behaviour.

29: The IRA announced it had identified the location of the bodies of nine people killed by the organisation in the 1970s and 1980s and buried in secret. The British and Irish governments said that any new evidence uncovered would not be used in subsequent criminal proceedings.

29: The Taoiseach and the British Prime Minister met at Hillsborough Castle for the opening round of meetings on decommissioning of paramilitary weapons. Earlier, the taoiseach confirmed the government's intention to press ahead with joining the NATO-sponsored Partnership for Peace programme in the autumn. The declaration came against a backdrop of protests against the NATO bombing of Yugoslavia.

30: The talks between Mr Ahern and Mr Blair continued in Belfast. Efforts were being made to incorporate guarantees from the Deputy First Minister, Mr Séamus Mallon, that the SDLP would cooperate in excluding Sinn Féin from government if decommissioning failed to take place by a specific date.

30: The Central Bank issued a warning on rising wages, living costs and house prices. It said Irish consumers were facing an annual increase in the cost of living of as much as 3.2%, well above what would be indicated by the consumer price index.

30: The Minister for Justice, Mr O'Donoghue, confirmed that he was conducting an investigation into the Sheedy case. Further inquiries were being carried out under the direction of the Chief Justice, Mr Justice Hamilton.

31: The participants in the Belfast talks reported some progress following the issuing of the IRA's Easter statement which said "we wholeheartedly support efforts to secure a lasting resolution to the conflict".

31: Seven environmentalists who admitted their involvement in the sabotaging a genetically modified food crop site were applauded by supporters as they left a Co Wexford district court. Six were given the Probation Act, and one was bound to keep the peace.

31: It was announced that in 2003, Ireland will host the first Special Olympic World Summer Games to be held outside the US.

April 1999

1: The Hillsborough Declaration was agreed by Taoiseach Bertie Ahern and British Prime Minister Tony Blair, setting out a framework for progress towards establishing the Northern Ireland executive.

1: The retail chain Superquinn was found to have breached the Groceries Order Act by asking suppliers for "hello money". The Director of Consumer Affairs threatened the company with High Court proceedings if it did not halt the practice.

1: The Minister for Justice, Mr O'Donoghue, told the Dáil "a certain individual" had asked the county registrar to list the case of Philip Sheedy for review in the Circuit Criminal Court. He said the individual would be given a right to reply before being named.

1: The Health and Safety Authority and the Irish Aviation Authority confirmed that they were investigating safety standards in Ryanair's aircraft maintenance and ground handling operations, following accidents earlier this year.

1: Hundreds of people were evacuated from Belmullet, Co Mayo, following an outbreak of fire in a local factory.

2: Sinn Féin issued a strong negative response to the outcome of the Hillsborough talks. Gerry Adams repeated that Sinn Féin could not deliver IRA decommissioning "no matter how this is presented". This phrase is the strongest indication so far that the provisional republican movement will not tolerate the

expensive way of doing so. Figures issued by the Government in May showed that both tribunals cost almost £6 million up to that period. The Flood tribunal cost an average of £6,222 per day for 82 public and private sittings, while the Moriarty tribunal cost £1,840,592 in legal fees alone, with barristers earning well in advance of £1,000 a day for their services in both tribunals.

Public Accounts Committee on non-resident accounts.
Date *Ongoing*

The Public Accounts Committee (PAC) looked into the massive tax fraud associated with bogus non-resident accounts.

The background to its investigation was that banks and building societies allowed, and sometimes allegedly encouraged, Irish residents to set up non-resident accounts as a way of avoiding DIRT Tax.

The PAC is currently investigating the revelations that Allied Irish Banks (AIB) only paid a fraction of an alleged £100m DIRT bill it owed the state on bogus non-resident accounts, which were being operated during the early 1990s.

Mr Tony Spollen, the former head of the AIB's internal audit department, complained about management inaction over the tax liability on the bogus accounts, which estimated at the time to be around £100m. In 1991 the chairman of the AIB at that time, Peter Sutherland, set up a top-level committee of directors to look into the matter. The only outcome of this investigation was that Mr Spollen's complaints were unfounded and that he was to move his post. He

declaration's proposal for some "voluntary" IRA decommissioning four weeks after ministers are nominated for an executive.

3: The government is to send £2m in aid to Kosovar refugees, and plans are afoot to admit 1,000 of the refugees into the country.

4: A new study indicated "disturbing evidence of underachievement by a relatively large body of students" who sat the junior and leaving cert examinations.

6: The government announced record returns for the first quarter of 1999, with the exchequer taking in £287m more than it spent.

6: The annual teachers' union conferences began, and issues over pay were at the top of the agenda.

6: Supreme Court Judge Hugh O'Flaherty made a full statement of his involvement with the case concerning Philip Sheedy, the architect who was freed from prison after serving just one year for killing a pedestrian through dangerous driving.

7: The latest CSO release shows the seasonally adjusted unemployment figure at 201,600, the lowest since October 1983.

7: Ten members of Youth Defence, the radical anti-abortion group, appeared before Dublin District Court in connection with charges of disorderly conduct after they punched and hit gardaí with placards during a demonstration last year.

8: The Attorney General advised the government there was no need for a referendum to join the NATO-backed Partnership for Peace organisation.

9: Pranksters severed the head from the famed landmark statue of writer Pádraic Ó Conaire at Eyre Square in Galway.

9: A man in his 30s was injured in a bomb attack by a dissident loyalist paramilitary group, the Orange Volunteers, on the Barleycorn pub near Antrim town. The injured man received leg and chest wounds.

10: The Catholic church in Harryville, Co. Armagh, was once again under siege as loyalists picketed the church during Saturday evening mass.

12: Mr Justice Hugh O'Flaherty told the Chief Justice's inquiry that he did not discuss the Philip Sheedy case with Mr Justice Kelly.

12: Broadcaster Gay Byrne is to be given the freedom of Dublin City.

12: Mo Mowlam discussed the UN report on alleged collusion between members of the security forces and paramilitaries with its author, the UN rapporteur, Mr Param Cumaraswamy. The report accused Sir Ronnie Flanagan, chief constable of the RUC, of "indifference", an allegation that is strongly denied by the Northern Ireland Police Authority.

13: The North Western Health Board has admitted mistaken results with the cervical smears relating to 2,000 women, with nearly 70 of these tests being mistakenly reported as normal.

14: The Minister of State for Foreign Affairs, Liz O'Donnell, has confirmed that the Hillsborough Declaration would be used as the basis for resolving the decommissioning crisis.

15: Taoiseach Bertie Ahern and Prime Minister Tony Blair met in London and have arranged a number of bilateral talks to resolve the impasse over decommissioning.

16: The Chief Justice, Mr Justice Liam Hamilton, issued a highly critical report into the handling of the Philip Sheedy case by two senior judges - Mr Justice Hugh O'Flaherty of the Supreme Court and Mr Justice Cyril Kelly of the High Court. The report found that Mr O'Flaherty's intervention caused Sheedy's case to be relisted; that this intervention was inappropriate, unwise and damaging to the administration of justice; that the Sheedy hearing by Mr Kelly lasted only minutes; that Mr Kelly failed to conduct case in a manner befitting a judge; and that Mr Kelly compromised the administration of justice.

18: In light of the report from the Chief Justice's inquiry into the Sheedy case, Supreme Court Judge Hugh O'Flaherty announced his resignation.

19: Bilateral talks were held in London by Taoiseach Bertie Ahern and Prime Minister Tony Blair with the UUP, Sinn Féin and the SDLP to resolve the decommissioning issue.

19: Dublin's county councils and corporation announced plans to provide 66,000 extra house sites in an attempt to relieve the current housing shortage.

20: High Court Judge Cyril Kelly and the Dublin County Registrar, Michael Quinlan, announced their respective resignations with regard to their roles in the Philip Sheedy case.

20: The Doyle Hotel Group has been taken over by Jury's, making it the biggest hotel group in the country.

21: Telecom Éireann began the first phase of its flotation on the stock market by issuing invitations to register for shares to the 2.8 million people recorded on the electoral register.

22: The first £1 million homes development in Ireland went on sale in Carrickmines, South Dublin, with all 15 homes being sold within four hours.

22: Northern Ireland's First Minister, David Trimble, met the Pope in the Vatican as part of a delegation of Nobel laureates.

22: British Scientists reported that more than one-third of the plutonium waste being emitted into the Irish Sea is unaccounted for.

23: Scaffolding contractors met for several hours to discuss the worsening unofficial strike by 800 scaffolders in Dublin. Most city-centre sites closed because of the dispute, and pickets were extended to suburban sites. It was estimated that about 500 building workers were laid off in Dublin because of the strike. Several hundred more workers were issued with protective notice by their employers.

24: Sinead O'Connor, who has been ordained a priest, announced that she wanted to be known as Mother Bernadette Mary O'Connor and that she rejected criticisms of her ordination as an act of simony (she donated £150,000 to fund a hernia operation for Bishop Michael Cox who ordained her).

26: Martin Comerford (36) was found shot dead in Ranelagh, Dublin, just hours before he was due in court. He was on trial for the murder of Anthony Beatty in 1997.

27: Drug Dealer 'Cotton Eye' Joe Delaney was sentenced to life for the murder of Mark Dwyer. In pronouncing the sentence, Justice John Quirke spoke of the "unspeakable savagery" of the crime (Dwyer was badly tortured before being killed). Gardaí saw the trial as the first successful one against organised crime.

28: In the wake of the Philip Sheedy affair, Mr Justice Hamilton, the Chief Justice, announced the setting up of a judicial body to ensure high standards of judicial conduct, as well as a system for handling complaints about judges.

28: The sale of Cablelink, the company owned by Telecom Éireann and RTÉ, was suspended with the emergence of irregularities in the sale, including interested parties rigging the outcome. The High Court issued an order preventing the sale of Cablelink to NTL or any other company until 30th April, 1999.

29: The governor of the Central Bank, Mr Maurice O'Connell, accused banks and building societies of lending too much to mortgage borrowers, fuelling excessive increases in house prices.

May 1999

1: Lyric FM, Ireland's new classical music radio station, was launched in Limerick.

2: The Coalition faced a major crisis with the revelation in the *Sunday Tribune* that Taoiseach Bertie Ahern did not comply with Tánaiste Mary Harney's request to confirm to the Dáil that he made representations to the Department of Justice on behalf of Philip Sheedy.

3: Taoiseach Bertie Ahern announced the Tánaiste never asked him to reveal to the Dáil about his role in the Sheedy affair.

3: Yasser Arafat, the president of the Palestinian Authority, visited Ireland and met the Taoiseach at Government Buildings. He asked for help in garnering international support for the Middle East peace process.

4: The Tánaiste announced she would not talk to the Taoiseach until he issued a statement confirming that she requested him to put his role in the Sheedy affair on the Dáil record.

5: In a letter to the Committee on Justice, Equality and Women's Rights, former Justice Hugh O'Flaherty refused to appear before the Oireachtas on constitutional grounds. He was to appear before a committee to explain his role in the Sheedy affair.

5: The Flood Tribunal discussed the role played by Taoiseach Bertie Ahern, Tánaiste Mary Harney and Minister Dermot Ahern in the inquiry into Ray Burke's dealings in planning irregularities.

5: Dr Mo Mowlam, the Northern Secretary, met with relatives of Pat Finucane, the solicitor who was murdered in 1989. They wish to open a public inquiry into his death.

6: The government will not dispute Mr Hugh O'Flaherty's refusal to appear before an Oireachtas committee investigating the Sheedy case.

6: Cablelink, the sale of which was previously held up due to irregularities with the sale, was sold to NTL, an Anglo American consortium, for over £500m.

TOP NEWS STORY

subsequently resigned.

PAC was also told of other accounts used for tax fraud - a senior tax inspector, Mr Tony Mac Cárthaigh, told the DIRT hearings that special low Tax Savings Accounts (SSAs), held by thousands of depositors since 1993 and totalling £162.9m, were the "greatest haven for tax evasion today". In addition the Revenue does not have the powers to properly investigate the SSAs.

What the above incidents illustrate, along with the Flood and the Moriarty tribunals, is the extraordinary depth of corruption in Irish politics, banking and business and the fact that this corruption was systemic. No-one seemed to be untainted by it, even the Central Bank, the watchdog for our economy.

Although the tribunals serve a cathartic need in the country to reveal our gamekeepers turned poachers, and may form the basis for further criminal investigations, in the future we may be better served by a thorough review of the Irish political system and Irish Finance legislation which seemed to better serve fraud that compliance with the law.

A Year of Political Scandal

Date *Ongoing*

The revelations of the Moriarty and Flood tribunals ensured that it was a busy year for the Government for all the wrong reasons.

The start of the Government's *annus horibilis* was tame enough: The Minister for Foreign Affairs, David Andrews, had an unprecedented public spat with his Secretary General, Padraic

6: The new president of the EU Commission, Mr Romano Prodi, made David O'Sullivan head of his cabinet. This is the most senior permanent EU post ever held by an Irish official.

7: A cross-border investigation was launched after gardaí arrested a man from Armagh and seized cannabis resin worth about £850,000 near Balbriggan, Co Dublin. The man was arrested after he drove the wrong way along part of the Balbriggan bypass.

7: A ten-point plan drawn up by groups representing Ireland's estimated 360,000 people with disabilities was issued to candidates for the European and local elections.

8-9: At Sinn Féin's annual Ard Fheis, the ministerial nominees to the Northern Ireland executive were officially announced: Martin McGuinness and Bairbre de Brún. However, the party made it clear that unless Tony Blair pressurised David Trimble to form a cabinet that includes Sinn Féin loyalist attacks could wreck the peace process.

8: According to a new EU report, at least 10% of those involved traffic accidents in the EU are on drugs.

8: Seán D. Dublin Bay Rockall Loftus, one of Dublin's most colourful local politicians, announced his retirement after 25 years in politics.

9: Thirty-one merchant seamen received valour awards at Dublin Castle for their service on Irish ships during the Emergency. Thirteen Irish-registered ships were lost during World War II, and 156 Irish seamen were killed.

10: Mr Patrick Ward (38) was fatally injured in a shooting at a Traveller funeral in Ballymote, Co Sligo. Six men were arrested in connection with the killing, and a man suffering from gunshot injuries was kept under garda surveillance in Sligo General Hospital.

11: Mr Cathal Dervan, currently the sports editor for *Ireland on Sunday*, settled his libel action for an undisclosed sum for damages arising out of an article written by Eamon Dunphy in the *Sunday Independent*. The article referred to an unnamed journalist as "a scurvy little pup" and "a media non-entity".

12: The US First Lady, Mrs Hillary Clinton, visited Galway city to deliver the inaugural address at Galway University's millennium lecture series which marked 150 years of student enrolment. She was also made the First Freewoman of the city of Galway.

12: Mr Ray Burke, the former minister for foreign affairs, was interviewed by Flood Tribunal lawyers about the evidence he will give concerning the payment of at least £30,000 to him at a meeting in his house in June 1989. The tribunal would not be able to hear his evidence until after the break for elections on June 14th. Burke was to be questioned on his contacts with the Fianna Fail leader, Mr Ahern,

immediately before he was appointed minister for foreign affairs in 1997.

13: The Minister for Finance, Charlie McCreevy, met union leaders, employers and other groups to consider the National Development Plan for the next six years, The plan outlines ways in which to spend £22bn on regional development, the largest investment package in the history of the Republic. The plan's proposals include developing new cities at Athlone and Sligo and expanding the existing cities of Limerick, Waterford and Galway. Smaller regional centres are planned, and the plan prioritises the creation of a world ecommerce centre for the Border, Midlands and Western region where telecommunications infrastructure is at its poorest.

13: Government figures indicated that the Flood and Moriarty tribunals have cost nearly £6m to date.

14 A new report, entitled "Rosemary Nelson - the life and death of a human rights defender", blamed allegations from RUC officers denouncing her as a "Provo solicitor" for her death. The document contains a detailed chronology of events leading up to the killing of Ms Nelson by a loyalist device in March. Eyewitness accounts of the heavy security presence near Ms Nelson's home in the days before the attack are cited in the report, which asks how a group of loyalist paramilitaries felt confident enough to enter the nationalist area of Lurgan on the night in question and attach an under-car booby trap device.

14: The Taoiseach and the Tanaiste insisted that no referendum was needed on Ireland's joining Partnership for Peace. The NATO-led PfP programme involves joint training and military exercises between states. These include almost all of Europe's NATO, former Warsaw Pact, neutral and non-aligned states.

14: Former *Sunday Independent* journalist Terry Keane admitted on RTÉ's *Late Late Show* that she had an affair over many years with former Taoiseach Charles Haughey. She appeared on the show to disclose the affair and publicise a series of articles on her life to be published in the *Sunday Times*.

15: The UN Committee on Economic, Social and Cultural Rights criticised Ireland's lack of legislation in addressing the detention of mentally handicapped people in psychiatric hospitals, the rights of physically disabled people and the discrimination faced by the Traveller community. It also highlighted the increase in tobacco use as the single most important health problem facing the government.

16: British Prime Minister Tony Blair designated 30th June as the final deadline for the devolution of power to the Northern Ireland Assembly. The announcement was given when the Unionists reneged on proposals previously agreed on by David Trimble with the SDLP, Sinn Féin and the Irish government. This failure has occurred even though Gen John de Chastelain's report on decommissioning, due out at the end of June, would have noted actual decommissioning in progress.

17: The UUP has announced that it will not be changing its position before or after the June EU elections.

17: The number of candidates declaring for the EU elections totals 42: 8 FF, 7 FG, 5 Lab, 4 SF, 4 NLP, 3 GP but none from the PDs.

19: Maurice O'Connell, the governor of the Central Bank, stated that interest rates would not be subjected to further cuts for some time and that a slow down in the economy is imminent.

19: The Environmental Protection Agency issued a report on Irish waters which indicated evidence of a decline in water quality, with one-third of Irish rivers being classified as polluted.

19: The government held off on tendering out the contract for the delivery of social welfare payments. These are currently administered by An Post and removing them from the organisation would jeopardise hundreds of rural post offices.

20: The government reiterated its decision to become involved in the NATO-led PfP without resorting to a referendum. The Minister for Foreign Affairs, David Andrews, said the decision against a referendum was "based on crystal-clear legal advice".

21: Gay Byrne's last *Late Late Show* attracted one of the biggest television audiences in RTÉ's history. The show usually attracted between 800,000 and 700,000 viewers, but this one had TAM ratings well in excess of a million. The show ran for a record 37 years on air - the longest running chat show in the history of television.

21: After 21 years of waiting, Cork's Jack Lynch Tunnel under the River Lee tunnel was officially opened by Taoiseach Bertie Ahern. The £105m tunnel is the first of its kind in the Republic and the largest project undertaken by any local authority in the State.

24: The Minister for Education, Michael Martin, announced a £2m initiative to help 1,100 primary and post-primary schools in disadvantaged areas develop plans to improve their teaching and management.

24: The anti-smoking lobby in Ireland was highly critical of the decision to appoint the Formula 1 motor racing team owner, Eddie Jordan, as a tourism and sporting ambassador for Ireland.

24: The FBI announced that it was no longer actively involved in the investigation into the murder of the Lurgan solicitor, Ms Rosemary Nelson. The bureau was available on a "stand-by" basis to help the investigation, but it would be up to the RUC to decide what further help the FBI could give.

25: The Taoiseach was asked in the Dáil why he counter-signed blank cheques drawn on the Fianna Fáil leader's account in 1989 and how £25,000 was used for Charles Haughey's benefit. Mr Ahern was also questioned on whether funds intended to pay for the late Brian Lenihan's liver operation ended up in this account. Mr Ahern insisted he had acted properly and brought the matter to the attention of the Moriarty tribunal so that any significance could be determined by the inquiry. He said that in most recent contacts with the tribunal, they had "again forcefully reiterated the necessity for confidentiality outside of public sittings".

25: Senior Scotland Yard police officer, John Stevens, re-opened inquiry into the 1989 murder of the Belfast solicitor Patrick Finucane. However, the Belfast-based human rights group, the Committee on the Administration of Justice, criticised his role as leader of the inquiry, claiming contradictions between different accounts of the previous involvement by Mr Stevens in investigating the Finucane murder. A Scotland Yard spokesman rejected the claim, stating that Mr Stevens' previous involvement

TOP NEWS STORY

Mac Kernan, over the Minister's direct intervention in promoting three civil servants. Then independent TD Jackie Healy-Rae announced that his vigorous lobbying resulted in Kerry and Clare being included in Ireland's poorest regions, a move which jeopardised the country's application for EU funding.

It was EU Commissioner Pádraig Flynn who plunged the government into hot water when he appeared on RTÉ's Late Late Show in January and impugned the reputation of Luton-based property developer, Mr Tom Gilmartin, who allegedly made a payment of £50,000 to Mr Flynn with regards to a development in Dublin and subsequently met with the current Taoiseach.

First of all the Taoiseach denied meeting him, then he accepted that he may have met him once and finally admitted to admitting him on three occasions. By this time, the Sheedy affair began to hit the headlines, and the Taoiseach was once again in trouble, having allegedly made representation to the Department of Justice on behalf of Philip Sheedy. At this stage (May), he was juggling many balls in the air - his intervention in the crisis in the North, his defence of his role in the signing of blank cheques drawn on the Fianna Fáil leader's account, as well as his role in the Sheedy affair.

Fortunately, the summer break was on its way, but even that held hidden dangers. Tánaiste Mary Harney and Minister for Finance Charlie returned from their break after holidaying in the South of France villa of Ulick McEvaddy, an aviation entrepreneur, who submitted proposals for a new airport terminal in Dublin and who had spoken to the ministers in with the Finucane case was in the context of a wider investigation of alleged collusion between the security forces and terrorists.

25: EU Social Affairs Commissioner Pádraig Flynn denounced the decision by European social affairs ministers to extend the deadline for member-states to reduce junior hospital doctors' maximum working week to 48 hours.

25: After more than two years of lobbying by the Irish Haemophiliacs Society, the government published the terms of reference for a tribunal of inquiry into the infection of haemophiliacs with HIV and hepatitis C through contaminated blood. Of Ireland's approximately 400 haemophiliacs, some 210 have been infected with Hepatitis C and an estimated 103 with HIV. These two diseases have been responsible for all but two of 68 haemophiliac fatalities over the past 15 years.

27: The Minister for Arts, Heritage, Gaeltacht and the Islands, Síle de Valera, introduced a groundbreaking new Broadcasting Bill in the Dáil. The first major bill on broadcasting since 1988, it introduces Ireland to the world of digital television, provides for 35 channels, defines public service broadcasting and provides aid to the Irish film industry. RTÉ will remain a major operator in the industry, but will lose control of its transmission system. The Bill is due to be enacted by Christmas 1999, with RTÉ transmitting its first digital programmes by the second half of 2000.

28: The Government extended without competition An Post's contract to deliver social welfare payments.

28: The first "disappeared" body, that of Eamonn Molloy, was found in a coffin under a bush in a country graveyard just south of the border. His family made arrangements for his funeral, 24 years after he disappeared. The IRA admitted abducting, murdering and burying eight other people.

28: Dr Patrick Wall, the chief executive of the Food Safety Authority of Ireland, warned that the rapid growth of premises in Ireland, from corner shops to petrol stations, selling "ready-to-go" convenience foods is threatening the ability to produce safe food.

29: Six sites in Louth, Monaghan, Meath and Wicklow were identified to the Independent Commission for the Location of Victims Remains as the burial places of IRA victims. The commission was informed that the body of Jean McConville, who was abducted in 1972, was buried under a car park at a beach, in Co Louth. After extensive excavation, nothing was found.

29: At the 1999 Eurovision Song Contest in Jerusalem, Ireland received one of its lowest scores in the history of the contest for *When You Need Me*, sung by Bronagh and Karen Mullan. Sweden won the contest with *Take Me to Your Heaven*, sung by Charlotte Neilsson.

30: The EU task force on money-laundering, the Financial Action Task Force, set up after the G7 summit in Paris in 1989 to counter international money-launderers, praised CAB and Ireland's anti-organised crime legislation and recommended it as a model for anti-organised crime forces in other countries. The task force report is expected to recommend other EU countries to follow Ireland's example on countering organised crime through asset seizure. Already, the British Home Office is considering laws on seizure based Irish legislation.

30: Some 40,000 members of the Pioneer Total Abstinence Association gathered for a rally at Croke Park to celebrate its 100th anniversary.

30: Controversy surrounding the Bloody Sunday inquiry intensified as families of the 14 victims reacted to the support of the British Secretary for Defence, Mr George Robertson, for the soldiers concerned. The 17 members of the Parachute Regiment were claiming anonymity in the inquiry into the 1972 killings, on the grounds that they would be in danger if their names were revealed.

31: Pte William Kedian (21), from Station Road, Ballyhaunis, Co Mayo, was killed, and Pte Ronnie Rushe (23), from Co Offaly, was seriously injured in mortar fire in South Lebanon. Pte Kedian, the 18th Irish fatality in action in Lebanon, was hurrying his comrades from their sleeping quarters into a bunker after a mortar round landed. The Israeli army admitted responsibility, and a formal complaint by the Irish government was issued to Israel, along with a UN protest.

31: EU foreign ministers reacted angrily to UEFA's refusal to postpone or cancel a match between Yugoslavia and the Republic scheduled for today.

June 1999

1: The Minister for Justice, John O'Donoghue, announced the "revolving-door" system in prisons would end in the autumn, with the introduction of restrictions on the temporary release of prisoners and new bail laws.

2: The Department of Agriculture moved quickly to detain all Belgian poultry and egg produce in circulation in the Republic, following concerns that it could contain a cancer-causing dioxin. The EU ordered the removal from sale and destruction of all Belgian chickens, eggs and poultry products throughout Europe.

2: The government's consultation process on genetically modified foods was derailed by the withdrawal of 19 organisations, all opponents of the way GM foods are being introduced to Ireland.

2: The trial began in the Special Criminal Court of Brian Meehan, a Dublin man accused of the murder of journalist Veronica Guerin.

2: According to a report published by the

Northern Ireland Human Rights Bureau, loyalist paramilitaries and the Provisional IRA killed five people and exiled 600 others since the signing of the Belfast Agreement.

2: The government refused visas to the Yugoslav soccer team, due to the situation in Kosovo, causing the Yugoslavia v. Ireland match to be cancelled.

3: Ireland's largest disability organisation warned that less than one- quarter of Ireland's 350,000 people with disabilities would be likely to vote in the European and local elections.

3: The secretary general of the Department of Health told a Dáil committee that the government would have to pay out £377m in compensation to people infected with the hepatitis C virus.

3: Supermarkets removed products with Belgian poultry and egg ingredients from their shelves after strong warnings from the Food Safety Authority and the Department of Health about their safety.

5: Loyalist extremists were blamed for killing Elizabeth O'Neill (59), who died after a pipe-bomb was thrown through a window of her home on the loyalist Corcrain estate in Portadown. Mrs O'Neill was a Protestant, married to a Catholic.

7: Four tourists, three of them Irish - Alan Daly (35), John Thomas Geough (28) and Emma Duke (28) - were drowned while white-water rafting on an Austrian river. Their raft broke its moorings, dropped into a whirlpool and capsized. Austrian police began an investigation into the deaths.

7: Ireland's triple Olympic swimming champion, Michelle de Bruin, failed in her appeal against a four-year ban imposed last summer by FINA, the sport's governing body. The Court of Arbitration for Sport, in Lausanne, Switzerland, upheld the ban for tampering with a drugs test. In a statement from her solicitors, Michelle de Bruin acknowledged her career had come to an end, but continued to proclaim her innocence.

7: The Republic is now the second most expensive place in Europe to buy a house after Finland, according to data published by the brokerage firm Dresdner Kleinwort Benson. A typical urban home now costs more than 18 times the average annual disposable income, compared with just 8.3 times in the US.

8: The Taoiseach and British Prime Minister Tony Blair announced a series of intensive meetings in a final attempt to break the deadlock in the Northern talks before the June 30th deadline.

9: Ms Anne Heraty and Mr Paul Carroll, a husband-and-wife team who set up a recruitment consultancy business 10 years ago will be worth a combined £13m when their CPL Group is floated on the Dublin and London stock exchanges later this month.

10: Nora Wall, a former nun was found guilty of raping a 10-year-old girl at St Michael's Child Care centre, run by the Sisters of Mercy in Co Waterford around 1987–88. Ms Wall (51), formerly Sister Dominic, was the then director of the centre, and was convicted of the crime along with Paul "Pablo" McCabe. After leaving the order Wall worked in a hostel for women and children in Dublin and a Romanian orphanage.

10: The government is to sell its entire 50.1% shareholding in Telecom Éireann when the company is floated on the stock market in July.

10: A record price of £8.3m was paid for a house at Brighton Road in Foxrock, Co Dublin.

11: Less than 50% of the electorate voted in the local and European elections and the referendum on local government in the Republic. Sinn Féin made significant gains in the local elections, increasing its vote from 2.1% in the 1991 local elections to 3.5%, and it trebled the level of its representation to 21 seats. Dana Rosemary Scallon took the last seat in the Connacht-Ulster European Parliament constituency and made it clear she would be calling for another referendum on abortion.

TOP NEWS STORY

question about a £150m rail project. However, the Taoiseach stood beside the members of his cabinet and felt they had no questions to answer; it was business as usual.

And what a lucrative business it is. In September we found out that members of the Oireachtas claimed £5.4 million in expenses over the past year, with the average claim for the year coming in around £25,000. Our most expensive TD was Tom Enright, the FG TD for Laois-Offaly, whose expenses bill amounted to just under £45,000.

Rosemary Nelson's Murder
Date *15th March*

Back to the North and one event that was viewed as a major setback for the peace process - the murder of solicitor Rosemary Nelson in Lurgan. Although it was a relatively quiet year with regards to violence by Northern Ireland's standards, her death when her car was blown apart by loyalist paramilitaries was a particularly gruesome one.

Ms Nelson represented many high-profile nationalist cases, such as that of the Garvaghy Road Residents' Coalition and the family of Robert Hamill, who was kicked to death while RUC officers looked on. Because of these cases, she was an easily targeted person and had received many death threats in the past, to which shad alerted the authorities and the media.

Ironically, some of the death threats were allegedly made by official authorities - RUC officers - within her hearing and to people she represented. Added to this were the allegations by UN rapporteur Param Cumaraswamy

In Northern Ireland, UUP MEP Jim Nicholson retained his seat despite a sharp drop in party support. The DUP leader, Rev Ian Paisley, and John Hume of the SDLP also retained their seats, with Dr Paisley topping the poll in the constituency for the fifth time.

12: Ms Joan FitzGerald, the wife of former Taoiseach Garret FitzGerald, died at her home in Dublin.

13: Dublin Women's Mini Marathon brought 36,868 participants onto the streets.

13: Unionist politicians blamed republicans for the previous night's murder of Newry drugs dealer Paul 'Bull' Downey. Mr Downey was the second major drugs dealer to be murdered in the area in just over a month.

15: The Taoiseach said the Irish and British governments would "set aside" the Belfast Agreement and seek alternative means of political progress if a breakthrough was not made by June 30th. In Belfast, British Prime Minister Tony Blair said the governments would "have to look for another way forward" if the deadline was missed.

15: Despite large mortgage rate cuts, inflation figures for May exceeded analysts' expectations, rising by 0.5% rather than the anticipated 0.3%.

16: The Bank of Ireland's planned £13bn merger with Britain's Alliance and Leicester collapsed. Analysts said the breakdown left both banks discredited, and one suggested they were extremely vulnerable to takeover. In a separate development shares in AIB fell heavily over fears that the bank might be excluded from the Dow Jones Eurostox-50 index when the index is restructured later this month.

16: The Taoiseach described as "inappropriate" the relationship his former special adviser Paddy Duffy had with Dillon Consultants. Dillons advised NTL, which bought Cablelink last month.

16: A survey of Dublin prostitutes suggested that 38% of female sex workers using drugs have attempted suicide, and two-thirds of those who are mothers do not live with their children.

17: The FAI was fined about £20,000 by UEFA because the Ireland v. Yugoslavia match failed to go ahead after the Yugoslavs were refused visas by the government.

17: Gardaí uncovered 60 kg of cannabis resin in a conifer forest at Glenaknouckana in Co Cork.

18: The Independent Commission for the Location of Victims' Remains suspended two of the searches for the IRA victims which started three weeks ago and was reviewing progress at the six other sites.

20: Ten people were being questioned by detectives on both sides of the border in connection with the bombing of Omagh last August.

20: The UUP leader, David Trimble, invited dissident MP Jeffrey Donaldson to rejoin his talks team in preparation for the negotiations with Tony Blair over his June 30th devolution deadline.

21: The Department of Agriculture confirmed that dog carcasses destroyed by local authorities can end up in the food chain in the meat and bonemeal fed to pigs and poultry.

21: The Department of Health has confirmed that the Minister, Brian Cowen, ordered the rewriting of a draft of the Government Green Paper on abortion some months ago without informing the Cabinet sub-committee supervising the preparation of the document.

21: An Oireachtas committee rejected a proposal to set up a tribunal into the Sheedy case.

21: The BBC programme *Panorama* examined collusion in Northern Ireland and alleged that the RUC Chief Constable, Sir Ronnie Flanagan, told a UN rapporteur, Dr Param Cumaraswamy, that some lawyers in Northern Ireland were "working for the paramilitaries". Sir Ronnie has denied the claim.

22: The Taoiseach announced that the Northern Ireland executive must be established before paramilitary weapons are disposed of, adding to the pressure on David Trimble to soften his stance before the June 30th deadline.

22: The Department of Social, Community and Family Affairs found that the number of one-parent families claiming assistance increased by almost 9% in the past 18 months. There were 67,738 one-parent families in the Republic in May 1999 compared to 58,960 at the beginning of 1998. Of the present number, just over 50,000 are unmarried parents.

23: The Moriarty tribunal investigated bank accounts belonging to Charles Haughey, the former Taoiseach, to which more than £1.5 million was lodged between 1979 and 1987. The accounts were in Mr Haughey's name and were held in Guinness & Mahon bank, Dublin, and are understood to be separate from the more secretive Ansbacher deposits, which were also held in the bank.

23: The home of the Guinness family in Ireland was sold to the Government for £23m. The Farmleigh property in the Phoenix Park, Dublin, passed into state ownership after a contract was agreed between the Office of Public Works and Lord Iveagh.

23: The drinks group Cantrell & Cochrane payed £68m for Ireland's biggest snack-food manufacturer, Tayto.

24: William Alfred Stobie (48), who served in the UDR, was arrested in connection with the killing of the Belfast solicitor, Pat Finucane, in 1989. It is the first arrest in the case since the Deputy Commissioner of the Metropolitan Police, John Stevens, began investigating it in April.

25: Taoiseach Bertie Ahern and British Prime Minister Tony Blair flew to Belfast to present a joint proposal in a final, dramatic bid to save the Belfast Agreement. The principles for resolving the arms decommissioning impasse were agreed in the Stormont talks but major differences remained on timing and implementation. The Taoiseach and the Prime Minister will return to Belfast on Monday for negotiations ahead of Wednesday's deadline for agreement.

27: The UUP leader, David Trimble, challenged Sinn Fein to get a promise from the IRA to disarm by May 2000. But Sinn Fein's chief negotiator, Martin McGuinness, said he could not speak on behalf of the IRA. Seamus Mallon, deputy leader of the SDLP, interpreted Mr Trimble's challenge as indicating an acceptance that the demand for prior disarmament would not be met.

27: Duty-free stores at cross-channel ferry companies and airports experienced a brisk trade as consumers stocked up in advance of the abolition of duty-free sales for travel within the EU on June 30th.

28: The Parades Commission banned the Portadown District of the Orange Order from marching down the Garvaghy Road on Sunday, 4th July. The decision followed the breakdown of talks between Garvaghy Road residents and the Order. The Commission also re-routed the Long March in support of Protestant rights and the Portadown Orangemen away from nationalist areas of Lurgan, Co Armagh.

28: An appeal by the *Sunday Times* newspaper arising out of the libel case taken against it by Albert Reynolds concluded in the House of Lords, and a decision is expected in October.

29: After 30 days of searching, gardai uncovered the bodies of two of the "disappeared", believed to be John McClory (17) and Brian McKinney (22), murdered by the IRA in 1978 for allegedly stealing weapons.

29: Unionist and Sinn Fein spokesmen were cautious about the degree of progress made in the Stormont talks despite an upbeat assessment by the British and Irish governments. Official sources suggested substantial progress had been made in the talks with Sinn Fein which was said to have hardened its verbal commitment to the principle of decommissioning and to using its influence to persuade the IRA to dispose of weapons in the context of the full implementation of the Belfast Agreement.

29: It was revealed that since its new board members were appointed last year, the Adoption Board granted all requests from adult adoptees for original birth certificates.

30: Upwards of half-a-million people were estimated to have applied for shares in Telecom Éireann.

July 1999

1: An Air Corps helicopter crashed on Tramore beach with the loss of all four crew members - Capt David O'Flaherty, Capt Michael Baker, Sgt Paddy Mooney and Cpl Niall Byrne. It was the worst accident in Air Corps history.

1: It was revealed that Mr Justice Moriarty (of the Moriarty tribunal) had shares worth £500,000 in Cement Roadstone Holdings. Mr Justice Moriarty said he had asked the attorney general to inform party leaders just before his appointment. At that time, the government rejected an opposition bid to have the sale of Glen Ding wood to CRH by the government included in the remit of the tribunal.

1: A teenager who urinated at an O'Connell Street, Dublin, cash machine was ordered by a judge to stand beside it with a placard saying "I apologise."

2: In a joint statement, entitled *The Way Forward,* Taoiseach Bertie Ahern and Prime Minister Tony Blair proposed the nomination of ministers on July 15th with a devolution order being laid before the British parliament next day. The initiative aims to ensure the

TOP NEWS STORY

on a BBC current affairs programme that Sir Ronnie Flanagan, the Chief Constable of the RUC, had stated some lawyers in Northern Ireland were "working for the paramilitaries" - a statement the Chief Constable denied making. Furthermore, the RUC as an organisation was branded by many as being at the very least negligent in its duty to protect Ms Nelson.

In the midst of the shockwaves over Rosemary Nelson's death, the inquiry into the murder of another Northern Irish solicitor, Pat Finucane, who was murdered ten years previously was re-opened. Like Rosemary Nelson, he was a solicitor who took on nationalist cases, when no-one else would do so and again like Rosemary Nelson, there were rumours of security force complicity associated with his death.

The inquiry has been dogged by controversy from the start. There were questions over the suitability of appointing Scotland-yard officer John Stevens to head the inquiry. These questions over his suitability were amplified when after the arrest of William Stobie for the murder, the respected Northern political editor of the *Sunday Tribune,* Ed Moloney, was ordered to hand over his notes taken in an interview with William Stobie some years previously (Mr Stobie had claimed he was an RUC informer at the time of the killing and that he told his police handler an attack was imminent although he did not know who was to be targeted). There appeared to be more emphasis placed on arraigning Mr Moloney than on the inquiry itself. Amnesty International commented that his prosecution would have an "intimidatory" effect on investigative journalism in the North.

full implementation of the Belfast Agreement with the creation of new institutions, including a devolved government. The legislation includes a "failsafe" mechanism to reassure unionists who are concerned that the IRA would try to hold onto weapons after Sinn Féin had taken its place in government. The proposed legislation provides for the suspension of the Northern Executive if IRA decommissioning fails to take place.

3: A syndicate comprising 40 Dublin Bus employees won the £2.96m Lotto jackpot (£74,000 each). They went on to celebrate their win on an open-top bus which drove through the centre of Dublin.

4: Some 5,000 loyalists gathered outside the hilltop church at Drumcree to protest the ban on their march down the Garvaghy Road. They were watched by hundreds of British soldiers and RUC who were part of a huge security operation to uphold the decision to prevent Orangemen from marching. After the church service, six Orangemen marched to the main barricade where they spoke to a senior RUC officer. There was very little trouble, with just one minor skirmish towards evening.

5: According to the Patterson, Kempster & Shorthall (PKS) update, construction in the Republic will grow at more than 10% this year, and by at least 7% in 2000. However, the review warned that strains were beginning to show due to skills shortages, which could lead to higher wages and ultimately dampen growth. Construction is seen as a key indicator of business confidence in the economy.

6: Prime Minister Tony Blair put UUP leader David Trimble under sustained pressure to accept the British/Irish strategy - *The Way Forward.*

6: The former Fianna Fáil minister, Ray Burke, entered the witness box at the Flood Tribunal. He has not been seen in political circles since he resigned from the Dáil and the Cabinet in October 1997.

7: A man was arrested in connection with the deaths of the three sisters who died in a fire on Inisbofin island.

7: The Attorney General, David Byrne, was announced as the new EU commissioner by Taoiseach Bertie Ahern. Barrister Michael McDowell, the former PD TD, is to replace him as Attorney General.

8: Telecom Éireann was floated on the stock exchange, with shares starting trade at £3.07.

10: According to a UN report, Ireland is second only to the US in having the highest levels of poverty in the industrialised world.

10: Taoiseach Bertie Ahern has rejected UUP calls for a guarantee that the government will support the continuation of an all-party executive if the IRA does not deliver on weapons decommissioning.

11: Train drivers took unofficial industrial action

which led to interruptions in rail services between Dublin and Cork and Kerry. The action resulted in a fall in the number of passengers carried on the affected routes from a norm of 9,000 to 4,500.

12: The marches of July 12th passed off without incident. Ormeau Park in Belfast was fenced off with barbed wire to keep marchers and spectators at the Orange Order parade away from the nationalist end of the park from which the march was banned by the Parades Commission.

12: A highly organised armed gang hired a crane to steal a 40ft container of cigarettes, worth about £1m, off a freight train at Dunleer, Co Louth.

12: Telecom shares are up 20% - £3.67 - on their flotation price of £3.07.

12: The National Adult Literacy Agency reported that Ireland has one of the worst levels of adult literacy the industrialised world (23% of adults have only basic literacy levels) and stated that Industry must help to combat high levels of illiteracy.

13: In the House of Commons, the British government carried its new Northern Ireland Bill by 312 votes to 19 to implement the *Way Forward* proposals and provide Prime Minister Tony Blair's "failsafe" mechanism. There was strong opposition to the Bill from Unionists and Conservatives. The British government promised to reflect on issues raised by former prime minister, Mr John Major.

13: A 51-year-old former army sergeant was charged with the murder of Ms Phyllis Murphy who was raped and killed in Co Kildare shortly before Christmas 1979. The man was arrested by detectives investigating the random killings of women in the Wicklow Mountains and eastern Midlands over the past 20 years.

14: David Trimble returned to Belfast to hold a meeting of his policy-making executive committee, which lasted only 15 minutes. David Trimble and the UUP rejected *The Way Forward* strategy. There was angry reactions by many to the decision: Sinn Féin attacked the way amendment after amendment was added into the strategy to appease the Unionists.

14: More than 600 jobs are at stake with the threatened closure of Tara Mines in Co. Meath. Talks are ongoing between staff and management, and the County Manager, Brian Fitzgerald, is to bring in the leaders of IBEC and SIPTU to help negotiations.

14: The Minister for Tourism and Sport, Jim McDaid, announced the building of Ireland's first 50 metre swimming pool, which is to be sited in Limerick.

15: At the morning meeting of the Northern Ireland Assembly, the d'Hondt process was triggered. Neither David Trimble nor any member of the UUP attended, while all other Unionists refused to nominate any ministers.

This left the cabinet made up of nationalists and republicans (Mark Durkan: Finance & Personnel; Bairbre De Bruin: Enterprise, Trade & Investment; Sean Farren: Regional Development; Martin McGuinness: Agriculture & Rural Development; Bríd Rodgers: Higher & Further Education; Pat Doherty: Education; Joe Hendron: Health & Social Services; Denis Haughey: Social Development; Mary Nellis: Culture, Arts & Leisure; Alban Maginness: Environment). After the nominations, the deputy first minister, Seamus Mallon, resigned. Because the cabinet was not balanced between Unionists and Nationalists, it was suspended, and a review of the Good Friday Agreement will have to be introduced.

15: Senator George Mitchell, former chairman of the Northern talks, was invited to meet Taoiseach Bertie Ahern and Prime Minister Tony Blair in London on Tuesday to talk about the peace process.

16: It emerged that Pat Cox MEP is to become the president of the European Parliament early next year after an agreement between the Liberals' parliamentary group headed by Mr Cox and the European People's Party, the parliament's largest grouping. He will be Ireland's first president of the EU parliament.

19: The father of Brian Meehan, the man on trial for the murder of Veronica Guerin, was shot and wounded at his home in Kimmage, Dublin.

19: The north Belfast house of a Catholic mother and her children was targeted in a petrol bomb attack.

20: At a meeting in Downing Street with the Taoiseach and the British Prime Minister, Senator George Mitchell confirmed that he will act as the "facilitator" in the review of the peace process. He later met with David Trimble, who also met Taoiseach Bertie Ahern at the Irish embassy in London and announced that he would not be resigning as Northern Ireland's First Minister.

20: The Comptroller & Auditor General found evidence of widespread tax evasion through false accounts in the banking system. The Revenue Commissioners are now going to pursue the millions of pounds owed in DIRT payments by the financial institutions.

20: The Bloody Sunday inquiry team, led by Lord Saville, deferred the inquiry for six months, until 27th March, 2000. The delay caused upset but little surprise to the relatives of the victims. The delay is mainly due to court hearings and appeals to ensure that British soldiers involved in the shootings, due to give evidence to the inquiry, can maintain their anonymity.

21: The IRA released a statement, rejecting demands for decommissioning "in the current political context" but did not rule out the prospect of weapons decommissioning, pledging its "definitive commitment" to the success of the peace process. The statement falls short of what the Irish and British governments had hoped for - an IRA statement agreeing with Sinn Féin's position on decommissioning.

21: In an unprecedented attack, Sgt Andrew Callanan was burnt to death at Tallaght Garda station, when a man set the reception area of the station alight. A man in his thirties was charged in connection with the killing,

21: The cabinet gave the go-ahead for drafting a £33.4bn national development plan which would outline spending on the economic and social development of Ireland over the next seven years.

22: Just weeks after Telecom Éireann's flotation, Minister Mary O'Rourke agreed in principal to floating Aer Lingus on the stock market, which could leave the company valued anywhere between £650m and £1bn. The agreement was made with the proviso that Aer Lingus makes a successful alliance with British

TOP NEWS STORY

The Philip Sheedy Affair
Date *Ongoing*

From miscarraiges of justice in the North to subvertion of the judicial system in the Republic.

The Philip Sheedy affair began at a Tallaght roundabout with the death of a young mother Mrs Anne Ryan, who was killed by a drunk driver, Philip Sheedy, an architect. He was sentenced to four years in prison but was freed after serving only one year. A friend of the Ryan family saw him. They were angered that he was freed after serving only a year and informed the Gardaí who in turn alerted the DPP. Rumours began to circulate as to improper practices within the courts over his appeal.

Two inquiries were set up, one led by the Chief Justice, Mr Justice Liam Hamilton, the other by the Minister for Justice, Mr O'Donoghue, as to how the Sheedy appeal case came to be listed in the Circuit Criminal Court without the knowledge of the DPP or the Gardaí. Mr Justice Liam Hamilton's inquiry resulted in a damning report into the handling of the case by the two senior judges involved in the affair: Mr Justice Hugh O'Flaherty and Mr Justice Cyril Kelly of the High Court.

The report found that but for Mr O'Flaherty's intervention, the case may not have been relisted in the way it was; that this intervention was inappropriate, unwise and damaging to the administration of justice; that the Sheedy hearing by Mr Kelly lasted only minutes; that Mr Kelly failed to conduct the case in a manner befitting a judge; and that Mr Kelly compromised the administration of justice. Both judges subsequently resigned, although former Justice O'Flaherty refused to appear before an

Airways and American Airlines.

22: The DPP charged George Redmond, the former assistant Dublin city and county manager, with failing to make tax returns. This badly affects the Flood tribunal's investigations into planning corruption.

23: In a fatal traffic accident between a stolen car and a Vauxhall Corsa in County Antrim, three people were killed and four were seriously injured. Two of the dead were a married couple while their three year-old son was critically injured.

23: Tánaiste Mary Harney announced the creation of some 1,300 new jobs in the Cork and Kerry region by next September.

24: Dr John Cosgrave discovered the largest known composite (non-prime) Fermat number at St Patrick's College, Drumcondra, Dublin. The creator of the computer program used by Dr Cosgrave, French scientist Yves Gallot, is credited as co-discoverer. The discovery is likely to go forward as one of the major discoveries of the end of the millennium. The series of Fermat numbers quickly rises into figures of astronomical size, and the story of their discovery has been a measure of the progress of computation.

25: More than 25,000 people took part in the annual pilgrimage up Croagh Patrick in Co Mayo.

25: The Republic of Ireland U-18s lost their bid to retain their title as European champions, coming third at the European Soccer Youth championship in Sweden.

26: The SDLP leader, John Hume, stressed there are no new proposals needed for the Belfast Agreement and that the three main principles of the agreement must underpin its full implementation.

26: Ennis man Eric Considine (23) was arrested after the killing of a Belgian national, Walter Van Dael (42), at a tourist hostel in Ennis, Co Clare. Gardaí were following "a definite line of inquiry" into the death.

27: A plot to smuggle weapons from the US through the post was foiled in a joint operation by the Gardaí, British police and FBI. Three people were arrested at a house in Inverin, Co Galway, while stateside, four people were arrested - three in Florida and one in Philadelphia.

27: The Court of Criminal Appeal quashed a conviction for the rape of a 10-year-old girl against Nora Wall, after the DPP admitted that certain information had not been given to the defence. Ms Wall, and her co-defendant, Paul McCabe, were released on bail, but remain charged with the offences.

27: A new government ruling allowed more than 2,000 asylum-seekers to work in Ireland while their applications are processed. The ruling only applies to those who are in the state for more than 12 months and are still awaiting a decision on their case.

27: The Flood tribunal could face further significant delays in its investigation into planning corruption after it lost a Supreme Court appeal. The decision means that the tribunal will no longer be able to compel people to attend for interview before its lawyers.

28: Following a reshuffle of the British Cabinet, Dr Mo Mowlam retained her post as secretary of state for Northern Ireland, despite unionist objections. She will be at Stormont for the publication of the Patten Report on the RUC and the review of the Belfast Agreement. However, Northern Ireland Minister of State, Paul Murphy, was moved from his political development post to become secretary of state for Wales.

28: It was announced that cars more than eight years old (an estimated 440,000 vehicles) have to pass a road-worthiness test from 2000.

28: The families of the Bloody Sunday victims were disappointed at the Appeal Court ruling stating that the soldiers who opened fire in Derry in 1972 will not be named in open court.

29: In a juryless trial, the Special Criminal Court convicted Brian Meehan of the murder of journalist Veronica Guerin after it accepted the evidence of the state witness, Russell Warren, that Meehan had driven the stolen motorcycle used in the killing.

29: In the second such statement given in a month, former Taoiseach Charles Haughey denied cheque fraud in relation to a £20,000 cheque given to him for the medical expenses of the late Brian Lenihan. The statement arose out of the Moriarty tribunal's investigations into whether funds donated for Mr Lenihan were used to pay Mr Haughey's expenses.

30: The Provisional IRA was linked to the US-based plot to import arms. One of the people arrested for posting guns from Florida to Ireland was believed to be a senior Provisional IRA figure.

30: A part-time taxi driver, Charles Bennett (22), was found shot in the head on waste ground in west Belfast. It was alleged that he was detained for four days before being shot twice in the head. The IRA are suspected of the shooting.

30: In the last day of the Flood tribunal hearings before its seven-week break, the developer, Michael Bailey, said he was the victim of a "total set-up" by James Gogarty which he could not explain.

30: The Supreme Court ruled that it is impossible to say what the offence of blasphemy is.

31: A man was arrested and arms seized during disturbances between loyalists and nationalists on Saturday in Portadown, during which gunfire was aimed at Catholics.

August 1999

1: Fine Gael leader John Bruton demanded that the Taoiseach and the British Prime Minister identify what types of action by paramilitaries would disqualify their associated parties from participation in the Northern Ireland executive. Sinn Féin continued to insist that the IRA ceasefire remained intact.

2: The Taoiseach rejected John Bruton's call to specify what political penalties might be imposed on Sinn Féin if the Provisional IRA is found to have authorised recent arms smuggling and the murder of Charles Bennett.

2: Seven people were killed in traffic accidents in Ireland over the August bank-holiday week-end, three of them in a head-on crash in Co Cork, bringing the total number of people who have died in road traffic accidents so far this year to 237.

2: Although the National Disability Authority Bill has passed all stages in the Oireachtas, it has no staff and no CEO.

3: Security and republican sources confirmed that the Provisional IRA was responsible for the murder of Charles Bennett. Two men have been arrested in connection with the killing.

4: Tony Blair's chief of staff, Jonathan Powell, had talks with Orange Order leaders to try to resolve the impasse at Drumcree. A separate meeting between Mr Blair's adviser and the Garvaghy Road Residents Coalition was called off.

4: The Minister for Justice, John O'Donoghue, announced that gardaí will have to videotape interviews with persons suspected of serious crimes. Garda representative groups, the Irish Council for Civil Liberties and Opposition politicians welcomed the announcement. Audio/ video recording facilities, costing £10m will be installed in 200 Garda stations.

4: An Exchequer surplus of some £5.82bn was noted at the end of July - the highest ever recorded. Although the surplus included the once-off £3.6bn from the flotation of Telecom Éireann, the figures show that the economy is continuing to grow very strongly.

4: A further £500m was wiped off the value of AIB as disappointment with the bank's interim results added to fears that it may be dropped from a key European index of blue-chip shares.

5: The Report by the Victims' Commission recommended that a private inquiry into the 1974 Dublin and Monaghan bombings, which killed 33 people and injured over 400, be set up in the autumn. However, the victims and relatives of the bombings have criticised the failure to recommend a public tribunal of inquiry and voiced concerns about a cover-up. A similar inquiry was also recommended into the 1976 murder of Séamus Ludlow in Co Louth; there were rumours that the SAS were involved, an allegation which the British army vehemently denied.

5: The Victims' Commission report contained a wide range of measures to meet the need of victims of violence in Northern Ireland. It recommended a review of the criminal injuries compensation scheme and further compensation for past victims of violence.

5: An Army bomb disposal team removed a 60-year-old unexploded live shell from a house in Whitehall, Dublin, and made it safe. The shell was found by Robbie O'Connor in his attic. More than 100 houses were evacuated and the M1 motorway in north Dublin closed.

5: Government spending on adult literacy was increased to nearly £5.7m this year. However, only 2% of those with literacy difficulties were being reached by current programmes.

6: The IRA issued a statement announcing that the killing of Charles Bennett did not constitute a breach of the ceasefire. The

TOP NEWS STORY

Oireachtas inquiry to explain his role. The whole affair threatened to destabilise the criminal justice system and jeopardised the reputation of the judiciary. In its wake, a judicial body was established to ensure high standard of conduct and a system for handling complaints about judges.

The Celtic Tiger
Date *Ongoing*

The Celtic Tiger kept on roaring this year, although fears surfaced about the economy overheating.

At the launch of the euro on 1st January, Ireland emerged as the country with by far the highest inflation among the eleven EU states participating in the single currency. The OECD warned in its draft annual economic review that the Minister for Finance should check public spending and limit any tax cuts.

Furthermore, with the country's increased growth came setbacks in the form of cuts in EU cohesion funding and farm spending.

However, other international organisations pointed out Ireland's economic success (along with Austria, Denmark and the Netherlands) and said the country's prosperity was contrary to the popular economic belief that public sector cuts are the only way towards economic growth. The ILO believed that significant employment growth can be achieved using the European welfare state model, as exemplified by Ireland, which has a well-established social protection system with a strong government role.

statement did not deny responsibility for the murder and noted that the army council had not sanctioned an operation to smuggle arms from Florida.

11: Thousands of Irish people viewed the last solar eclipse of the millennium. Most of Ireland came under a partial eclipse, ranging from 85–98%. Temperatures dropped by up to 2 degrees celsius and the sky darkened around 11:11 a.m., as the eclipse reached its limit. The ESB reported that electricity demand fell by 3.5% around this time. Despite repeated warnings some people looked directly at the sun, and Dublin's Eye and Ear Hospital received up to 40 phone calls from people fearful that they may have damaged their eyes. The next total eclipse to pass over Ireland will be in 2090.

12: Enterprise Oil's second test of the Corrib gas field, which lies 70 km off Achill island, indicated that the area is rich in gas (just slightly smaller than the Kinsale gas field) and could eventually supply up to half of the Irish market's gas requirements. All oil and up to 50% of gas are imported, so this find could result in significant savings to the country's energy import bill.

13: Three lending institutions - First Active, EBS Building Society and Irish Life Homeloans - increased mortgage rates on their fixed-interest products.

13: An international study on heart disease mortality rates in the developed world rated the Republic fourth-highest out of 30 countries, immediately followed by Northern Ireland.

14: The RUC were heavily criticised following the force's removal of protesters from the Lower Ormeau Road to make way for an Apprentice Boys' march. About 300 people who staged a sit-down protest were dragged from the road, and there was fighting between police and protesters. Widespread public disorder erupted in Derry in the aftermath of the Apprentice Boys' parades march along the city's walls. More than 130 petrol-bombs were thrown resulting in millions of pounds worth of damage to the city centre. Most of those involved in the violence were young, and many of the incidents were spontaneous. Martin McGuinness, Sinn Féin's chief negotiator, condemned the violence, saying those involved were wrong.

15: The first anniversary of the Omagh bombing was commemorated by ceremonies in Omagh, Buncrana and Dublin.

16: In what was viewed as one of the worst periods for fatal accidents for a long time, at least eight people died in car crashes on Irish roads since Friday - six in the Republic and two in the North.

16: A Newry businessman, Richard McFerran, was shot dead in Dundalk. He had survived another attempt on his life last year in a

dispute stemming from the man's personal life.

17: The Department of Education offered schools with high numbers of early school leavers large sums of money in order to stem the flow of early school leavers. Many schools will be offered well over £100,000 each and some more than £200,000. In the past three years the proportion of secondary students going on to the Leaving Certificate levelled off at around 83%.

18: This year's Leaving Certificate results were released to more than 64,000 students. The CAO received applications for college places from 64,996 people, a slight increase on last year's 64,741.

18: The Garda Commissioner, Pat Byrne, announced a major investigation into the sex industry. The investigation was in response to the recent public debate surrounding the banning of *In Dublin* magazine by the Censorship of Publications Board on the grounds that the magazine had "usually or frequently been indecent or obscene". The publication's 'health studios' ads were believed to be the cause of the ban.

19: According to a report into the level of drug use and related illnesses in Irish prisons, 20% of prisoners who inject drugs said they began doing so while in custody. The report also found that Irish prisoners had high infection rates of hepatitis C.

19: The government announced it is planning to impose a tax on the 1.2bn plastic bags handed out free each year in shops and supermarkets, in an attempt to reduce pollution.

19: The High Court overturned Censorship of Publications Board's ban on *In Dublin* magazine. Mr Justice O'Donovan described the actions of the board as "incredible" and "reprehensible" and added that the board had been unfair to the magazine's publisher, Michael Hogan, in refusing to meet him and had been "nothing less than reprehensible" in suppressing its predetermination of the magazine's future.

20: Members of the Lower Ormeau Concerned Community group, including the group's spokesman, Gerard Rice, appeared before Belfast Magistrates Court charged with obstruction and disorderly conduct, following their staged sit-down protest on the Lower Ormeau Road to an Apprentice Boys parade. The Department of Foreign Affairs has voiced concern about the arrests to Downing Street.

20: The International Monetary Fund (IMF) sent a strong warning to the government asking it not cut taxes in the next budget, as doing so could fuel inflation. The organisation also warned of the risks which a sharp fall in prices could pose to borrowers and to the banks.

20: The Department of Health and Children found that one in four children is not being vaccinated against measles. According to medical specialists, this low figure means a measles epidemic is imminent.

20: The Department of Enterprise announced the scheduled reduction of places on the Community Employment (CE) scheme over the next five years.

22: The Northern Ireland Office said that with the signing of the Belfast Agreement, breaches of ceasefire might result in a halt to the early prisoner release scheme. Martin McGuinness stated that such a move could endanger Sinn Féin's participation in the September review of the peace process.

23: The annual report from the Department of Social, Community and Family Affairs indicated that anti-fraud measures saved the department £164m last year. The report also showed considerable variation in the time taken to process applications for various payments.

23: The Criminal Assets Bureau agreed that documents belonging to George Redmond could be revealed to the Flood tribunal.

23: The Irish Marine Emergency Service reported that a Y2K-type glitch affected certain GPS navigational systems but that none of the incidents were serious.

23: The Taoiseach indicated the Tánaiste and the Minister for Finance could participate in any cabinet decisions on a new terminal for Dublin Airport, despite holidaying in the south of France at a villa owned by aviation entrepreneur Ulick McEvaddy, who is promoting a terminal project for the site. The Taoiseach said that he did not believe the two Ministers had any questions to answer regarding their stay. Mr McEvaddy told the High Court three weeks ago he had been lobbying politicians to try to block EU rules which he claimed would cost his aircraft business more than £26m if implemented.

23: There was good news for most students in this year's CAO points allocation, unless they wanted one of the elite "high points" courses such as law and medicine. More students will get into college than at any time in the past. with 74,769 offers of places in the first round of the CAO allocation. The courses demanding the highest points are medicine and law with French at TCD at 570 points.

24: A well-known Waterford local politician and his wife were arrested by gardaí investigating financial irregularities of over £100,000 at the Ulster Bank branch in the city.

24: Dr Mo Mowlam met with the Minister for Foreign Affairs, David Andrews, to discuss both the IRA cessation and the September 6th review of the Belfast Agreement. Afterwards she disagreed with Mr Andrews' view that the IRA ceasefire was still intact.

24: Irish banks and building societies faced new competition in the form of the Bank of Scotland, which offered to sell the cheapest mortgage deals to Irish consumers - a 4.1% variable rate.

24: An unofficial demarcation dispute at the ESB station in Ferbane, Co Offaly, threatened to spread to Moneypoint and other electricity supply stations.

24: According to new audience research figures, RTÉ lost its dominance of the national airwaves for the first time. RTÉ Radio 1's market share fell by 2% to 29%, while 2FM held its 20% market share. In contrast, Today FM and the independent local stations increased their market reach. However, RTÉ's newest station, Lyric FM, was performing well above expectations.

25: A new planning bill, published by the Department of the Environment, outlines a radical new provision where building developers will have to sell up to 20% of their land to local authorities for "affordable housing" in exchange for planning permission for private housing.

25: The Economic and Social Research Institute stated that Irish growth will remain strong - a diametrically opposite view to the International Monetary Fund's criticism of Irish economic policy.

TOP NEWS STORY

All throughout the year, the Exchequer reported record returns: it announced a £5.82bn surplus at the end of July - the highest ever recorded. Although the surplus included the once-off monies accrued from the flotation of Telecom Éireann (now Eircom), the figures demonstrated that the economy continued to grow very strongly.

The Telecom Éireann flotation demonstrated how confident Irish people were in the economy. An army of small investors - around half a million people - bought shares in the company's stock market flotation, although the shares slumped in early September, due to selling of shares by foreign investors who believe that the long-term prospects for the Irish economy are negative.

Fears of inflation persisted throughout the year and were confirmed by figures released at the end of August, when inflation rose to 1.4% - the highest in the euro zone - and it is forecast to rise to 2.2% by the end of the year. Other experts believe that real price rises are far higher than those measured by the Consumer Price Index and that most people face price rises of 5%, particularly for services.

The Housing Crisis
Date *Ongoing*

House prices in the Republic of Ireland continued to soar this year. According to one of Europe's leading brokerage firms, Ireland is now the second most expensive place in Europe to buy a house after Finland. An average town house in the Republic of Ireland now costs more than 18 times the

25: The government announced it is to introduce a uniformed warden service, run by local authorities, to assist gardaí with implementing traffic and parking laws and to act as rangers in public parks.

25: The 31-year-old woman from Portlaoise, who was the first person in the country to be diagnosed with CJD, a human form of BSE in cattle, died at her home.

25: The Minister for Foreign Affairs, David Andrews, travelled to the Indonesian-controlled island of East Timor, to lead EU observers in monitoring the island's referendum on independence. Violence had broken out between the pro-independence movement and the loyalist autonomy militia in the island's capital, Dili.

26: Mo Mowlam ruled that the IRA have not broken the ceasefire. Her decision drew widespread criticism from the Unionist parties.

27: A private helicopter crashed near Ballinamuck, Co. Longford. Both the pilot and the passenger aboard the helicopter were killed.

28: The IRA issued a death threat to a number of teenagers in Dungannon, warning them that if they did not leave the country by Saturday night they would be killed. Two of the teenagers left for England and the others went into hiding.

29: Four people died after their boat containing four adults and four children capsized off the Louth coast, near Clogherhead.

29: The High Court ruled that the founder of a pregnancy advice agency had unlawful custody of a baby born to a college student who had sought help from the agency last summer. The 21-year-old gave up her baby for adoption by the founder and his wife. The High Court case was brought by the health board against the man, his wife and the baby's mother.

31: Two former secretaries of the Department of Finance told the Dail Oireachtas Committee on Public Accounts that despite frequent proposals from the civil service, the various politicians who held office in the 1980s showed no appetite for tackling the widescale tax evasion through bogus non resident accounts.

31: British Prime Minister Tony Blair resisted demands from the UUP for a delay in the review of the Belfast Agreement and strongly supported Dr Mo Mowlam's ruling that the IRA ceasefire has not broken down.

31: The Labour Court gave a £100m pay award to nurses. The latest Labour Court ruling will see the wage bill for nurses in the health services rise by 23% since 1997.

September 1999

1: Sinn Féin and the UUP still refused to state whether they will engage in the review designed to break the stalemate over IRA decommissioning and the formation of the Northern Ireland executive.

1: The government approved the publication of a Green Paper on abortion that will lead to another referendum.

1: The soccer match which was delayed by the war in Kosovo - Republic of Ireland v. Yugoslavia - finally kicked off at Lansdowne Road. Ireland beat Yugoslavia 2-1.

2: The Northern editor of the *Sunday Tribune,* Ed Moloney, was given seven days to comply with a court order instructing him to hand over notes of conversations he had with William Stobie, the man now charged with the murder of Belfast solicitor Pat Finucane. Amnesty International has said any prosecution of Mr Moloney would have an "intimidatory" effect on investigative journalism, while Human Rights Watch said the decision set a "dangerous precedent".

2: A senior tax inspector, Tony Mac Cárthaigh, told the DIRT hearings that the Special Savings Accounts (SSAs), held by thousands of depositors since 1993, provided the "greatest haven for tax evasion today" and that the Revenue didn't have the powers to police properly SSAs. Mr Mac Cárthaigh further described his exchanges with AIB, saying it was "extraordinary" that the bank would not admit to its "wrongdoings".

2: At the end of August, the Exchequer reported a £2.2bn surplus of revenue over spending. Market economists predicted that the Minister for Finance, Charlie McCreevy, could afford tax cuts of £1bn.

3: The chief nursing unions rejected the £100m Labour Court award and threatened strike action in order to get pay parity with teachers and other professionals.

3: The Irish Permanent, Ireland's biggest mortgage lender, reduced its home loan rates, in response to Bank of Scotland's recent arrival on to the Irish market.

4: Raonaid Murray (17), was murdered in Dublin as she walked towards her home.

5: Figures released under the Freedom of Information Act indicated that TDs and senators received £5.4m in expenses, with members of the Oireachtas claiming almost £450,000 a month in expenses between April 1998 and April 1999. This money is largely unvouched and is not subject to tax. Tom Enright (FG), TD for Laois-Offaly, received the largest amount at almost £45,000, while Rory Kiely (FF) from Limerick and Brian Mullooly (FF) from Roscommon topped the expenses list for Seanad members, receiving over £41,000 each.

6: Senator George Mitchell began the review of the Belfast Agreement at Stormont. The UUP and Sinn Fein both decided to take part, but the UUP refused to engage directly with Sinn Féin or fringe loyalist parties. The DUP did not participate but met with Senator Mitchell to voice its objections.

6: The Homeless Initiative reported that there are 2,900 homeless adults in Dublin, Kildare and Wicklow, a figure more than double previous estimates.

6: A major report from the European Commission criticised Ireland for providing one of the poorest childcare systems in Europe. The Commission, in its assessment of the Irish National Action Plan (NAP) on employment, stated that the government was not doing enough to assist women's return to work.

6: The Heritage Council warned that Ireland's archaeological monuments are under increasing threat. The Council estimated that around 34% of these monuments were destroyed since 1840 and concluded that present destruction rates could see Ireland's entire archaeology levelled by the year 2101. The main cause of monument destruction was land improvement, with the greatest damage occurring in Meath and Wexford.

7: Telecom Éireann relaunched itself as Eircom, while the Irish-language channel formerly known as Teilifís na Gaeilge was relaunched as TG4.

8: The Minister for Foreign Affairs, in an angry reaction to what he called the failure of the international community to protect the people of East Timor, said the UN's credibility of the was on the line after a massacre by the Indonesian-backed militia when the people of East Timor voted for independence from Indonesia.

8: The government issued a statement warning nurses, gardaí and CIÉ workers that it will not give "unsustainable" pay rises that would damage the economic progress made through social partnership.

8: Ireland may be given £1.74bn in total in EU rural development cash until 2006. The total makes up 50–70% of the funding for four programmes co-financed by the government: the early retirement scheme, the rural environmental protection scheme, the disadvantaged areas scheme and the forestry scheme.

8: ESAT Telecom bought Postgem/Ireland OnLine for £115m.

8: Donal Buckley, an inspector of taxes, told the DIRT Inquiry of how officials in the Tipperary branch of Bank of Ireland helped a taxpayer "and his wife" to open 166 bank accounts throughout the country.

9: The Patten commission report was officially released. With some 180 proposals, it called for the speedy devolution of significant police and criminal justice issues and the renaming of the RUC as the Northern Ireland Police Service. The report contains many key proposals covering areas like accountability, recruitment, ethos, composition, training and structure of the RUC. First Minister David Trimble described it as "the most shoddy piece of work I have seen in my entire life", and there were strong objections from RUC officers themselves.

9: The government appointed James Hamilton as the new Director of Public Prosecutions in succession to Eamonn Barnes.

9: Applications for divorce rose significantly in the first three months of this year, particularly in Dublin where 475 couples moved to end their marriages.

9: The Department of Education announced major changes in the content of the primary school curriculum, including the introduction of science.

9: Ed Moloney, the Northern Editor with the *Sunday Tribune* was allowed to challenge the legal ruling that he must hand over his notes relating to the murder of Belfast solicitor Pat Finucane.

9: The Minister for Tourism, Sport and Recreation, Dr Jim McDaid, announced the number of visitors to Ireland has increased by 129% in 10 years, making the country the fastest growing tourism destination in the EU.

10: Both the AIB and Bank of Ireland cut their variable mortgage rates to below 4%, in response to the Bank of Scotland's entry

TOP NEWS STORY

average annual disposable income, compared with just 8.3 times the annual disposable income in the US.

The latest report by Peter Bacon, the economic consultant to the government on the housing market, introduced a series of measures to boost house building and dampen soaring prices. The most notable recommendation of the report was a new scheme to give buyers a 70% stake in the property with the balance acquired for a given period by a specially set-up trust.

The Department of the Environment also proposed a Bill to stabilise the housing market. The most radical initiative in this bill was the provision where building developers will have to sell up to 20% of their land to local authorities for affordable housing in return for planning permission for private hosing on the remainder.

An interesting development in the property sector is the entry of the Bank of Scotland into the Irish housing market. Its offer of a mortgage rate lower than 4% forced Irish lenders to cut their interest rates in response to competition rather than an across-the-board cut in rates. Some banks are now allowing people to apply for much higher mortgages than permitted. The Bank of Ireland was censured for offering mortgages on up to three times the main salary plus 1.24 times the subsidiary income.

And this year's records: the highest price paid for private accommodation was £8.3m for a house in Foxrock, Co Dublin. Ireland's first exclusive development of £1 million homes in Dublin was sold out in a matter of hours.

The outlook for the housing industry is summarised by the

into the Irish market.

11: Around 300 non-consultant hospital doctors marched through Dublin to protest against long hours and low rates of pay.

11: Of the 17,000 people who expressed an interest in working in Ireland at the London 'EXPO Ireland' exhibition, 60% were British.

12: Cork triumphed with a one-point victory over Kilkenny in the 1999 All-Ireland Senior Hurling Final.

12: Gardaí and the RUC Chief Constable, Sir Ronnie Flanagan, stated over the week-end that the 'Real IRA' was reorganising.

12: The Minister for Finance, Charlie McCreevy, announced that the Exchequer would have a £5.8bn surplus this year. However, he stated that granting the pay increases sought by nurses and other public service workers would "wreck the Celtic Tiger".

13: During the meeting of the UUP ruling committee, David Trimble dismissed suggestions of a threat to his leadership of the UUP and reiterated that his party will continue to be involved in the Mitchell review of the Belfast Agreement at Stormont. The UUP's 120-member executive strongly rejected the Patten report.

13: Taoiseach Bertie Ahern, Tánaiste Mary Harney and the Minister for Finance, Mr Charlie McCreevy, met leaders of the Irish Congress of Trade Unions and the Irish Business and Employers' Confederation separately in an effort to salvage Partnership 2000, with nurses' pay being one of the central issues addressed at the meeting.

13: A huge coral reef was discovered off Ireland's west coast. Dr Anthony Grehan of NUI Galway helped discover the reef, measuring some 64 km long and 350 m high, in the Rockall Trough. The deep-water corals could be tens of thousands of years old.

13: The town of Clonakilty won the top prize in the 1999 Tidy Towns competition.

14: On his official visit to the Russian Federation, Taoiseach Bertie Ahern, conveyed the sympathy of the Irish people to the Russian Deputy Prime Minister, Ilya Klebanov, on the 300 people who were killed in bomb attacks in Moscow over the past two weeks. He promised to help Russia in its fight against terrorism.

14: According to the Victims' Charter, published by the government, victims of crime will have the right to have a review of their case when the DPP decides not to prosecute. All victims will be entitled to clearly defined treatment by government agencies.

14: Pádraig Flynn retired as EU Commissioner and was praised for his pioneering role in moulding EU social policy, particularly on employment. David Byrne, who succeeds him, was installed as EU Commissioner at the European Parliament in Strasbourg.

14: Official figures on AIDS showed an apparent tenfold increase in the number of people developing AIDS this year in Ireland. Of the 682 AIDS cases reported to date, almost 50% have died. However, the number of people testing positive with HIV remained relatively stable.

14: Johnny Adair, nicknamed "Mad Dog" for his notorious involvement in directing loyalist violence in the early 1990s, was freed under the Belfast Agreement's early release scheme.

14: Around 1,000 building workers marched through Dublin city centre to protest at recent deaths in the industry.

15: Although all Garda leave has been cancelled for the millennium, industrial action could still upset plans for policing the celebrations.

15: Irish inflation rose by 0.6% in August following the end of the summer sales, bringing the annual rise in the cost of living to 1.4%, the highest in the EU. Experts believe that real price rises are far higher than measured by the Consumer Price Index with most people facing rises of up to 5%, particularly for services.

16: The Defence Forces' elite Army Ranger Wing (ARW) was to be sent to East Timor as part of the UN mission in the area.

16: The government published its White Paper on Private Health Insurance, which will see the privatisation of the VHI. The paper proposed to invest £50–£60m of public money into the VHI and recommendations to increase competition in the private health insurance market.

16: Eamonn Barnes, who retired as DPP, admitted that "appalling mistakes" were made in prosecutions owing to the lack of co-ordination and cohesion between the offices of the DPP and the Chief State Solicitor.

16: Dr Mary Upton, the sister of the late Labour TD, Dr Pat Upton, will be the party's candidate for the Dublin South Central by-election, expected to take place on October 21st.

16: A Co Clare man received the first jail sentence in Ireland's history under conservation laws for removing lorryloads of limestone from the Burren.

16: The Minister for the Marine set up a new division within the Department to address safety regulation among pleasure craft users after the high number of accidents among pleasure craft users this summer.

17: Eircom shares fell far below their original flotation to a new low of £2.89. The decrease was a blow for the many small investors who participated in the company's public flotation.

17: The Environmental Protection Agency licensed Ireland's first "green" hazardous waste treatment plant in Sheriff Street, Dublin.

18: The 32-County Sovereignty Movement, the dissident republican group, says it plans to expand in North to build "the strongest republican opposition ever to British rule".

18: Sir John Hermon, the former RUC chief

constable, addressed a rally in Belfast to save the RUC.

19: Tánaiste Mary Harney and the Minister for Finance, Charlie McCreevy, were in the line of fire after it emerged that they discussed a £150m rail project with businessman Ulick McEvaddy only weeks before holidaying at his villa in the south of France. The Taoiseach supported the Tánaiste and the Minister for Finance saying they did not act inappropriately in their dealings with Mr McEvaddy.

19: A 14-year-old girl accused the man at the centre of the X case of an alleged sexual assault while she was a passenger in the taxi the man now drives for a living. Questions were raised as to how a convicted sex offender was granted a Public Service Vehicle licence enabling him to drive a taxi. The Garda Traffic Department subsequently revoked the man's licence.

20: The Flood tribunal resumed after the summer break, opening with the much anticipated questioning the former Dublin assistant city and county manager, George Redmond, on payments he received from Joseph Murphy Structural Engineering. He told the tribunal that he had received payments other than his employment income from people who sought advice about land, leases and investing.

20: Noel Dempsey, the Minister for the Environment, met Central Bank officials to discuss a breach of mortgage guidelines by Bank of Ireland. The bank gave people much higher mortgages than permitted - up to three times the main salary plus 1.25 times the second income. Mr Dempsey warned that he would introduce legislation to limit the money lent to house buyers.

20: The two main civil service unions - the Public Service Executive Union and the Civil and Public Service Union - announced they will be seeking a pay review for their 17,000 members.

20: Richie Green (49), vice-chairman of the Irish National Organisation of the Unemployed, and his daughter, Christina (18) were killed when a stolen car crashed into their car in inner-city Dublin.

20: The government published a Green Paper outlining a series of "green tax" proposals to lessen Ireland's increasing energy consumption and carbon dioxide emissions. Ireland was expected to go over the limit on greenhouse gases next year for the first time, despite being only halfway through the 20-year period of the agreement set by the UN Kyoto protocol.

21: Sinn Féin and the Ulster Unionists held direct talks at Stormont in the presence of Senator George Mitchell in an effort to break the deadlocked political process. It was the first meeting between the Sinn Féin president, Gerry Adams, and the UUP leader, David since July. The talks were deemed constructive for further negotiations.

22: At the Flood tribunal, the amount of payments made to George Redmond when he was assistant Dublin city and county manager started to emerge and exceeded all previous estimates, even those made by the Criminal Assets Bureau. In 1988 he had investments totalling £660,000. In that year alone he received £171,000, which he lodged in a variety of bank accounts. The next year he lodged over £94,000, at a time when his salary was just £29,000. Lawyers subsequently discovered that he had 33 accounts in a number of financial institutions, many of which were opened under two Irish variations of his name.

22: The novelist Colm Tóibín was shortlisted for this year's Booker Prize for his fourth novel, *The Blackwater Lightship*.

22: Around 450 passengers were left stranded after Irish Ferries' SIPTU crew members took industrial action over the sacking of a shop steward, who allegedly raped a female crew member.

22: The Central Bank warned that the economy is very close to

TOP NEWS STORY

forecast from the Patterson Kempster & Shorthall review, which predicted that construction will grow at more than 10% in 1999 and at least 7% in 2000, but that there were strains on the sector due to skills shortages, which could eventually dampen growth.

Industrial unrest
Date *Ongoing*

Now that the Government has a £5.8 billion surplus in its coffers, it's finding it very hard to preach pay restraint and it looks as though the country is heading towards a winter of discontent.

The most high profile of the threatened strikes, as we go to press, is that of the nurses.

During the summer, the Labour Court gave a £100m pay award to the country's 27,000 nurses - an offer which was rejected by the major nursing unions. At the moment, public sympathy is very much with the nurses, who are understandably seeking pay parity with similarly qualified professionals.

However, if the nursing unions' demands are granted, other public sector workers will follow suit with pay demands, particularly paramedics, Gardaí, teachers and bus and train drivers, who have already threatened action.

At this stage it seems unlikely that the Government will be able to create a new consensus with regards to the successor to Partnership 2000, which was viewed by economists at home and abroad as one of key factors in kick starting our economy in the early 1990s. The question most people are asking is: will large-scale pay rises for the country's public sector plunge the country back into recession?

overheating, with rising house prices one of the main symptoms. It warned the government not to inject too much money into the economy through tax reductions. Some experts believe that by the end of the year, house prices may have risen by 25% despite the implementation of the Bacon Report recommendations and the removal of tax breaks for investors.

22: New child-abuse guidelines were published which will compel health boards to establish registers of children at risk of abuse.

22: The High Court was told that in 1987 more than half of the directors of Cement Roadstone Holdings (CRH), held money in the Ansbacher accounts, suggesting that a large number of the directors knew an unlicenced bank was being operated from their headquarters by the then chairman, Des Traynor. It was estimated that £50m was stashed through complex systemic fraud in Ansbacher Cayman, Ireland. Revenue Commissioners began a detailed examination of the tax affairs of the 120 people connected with the accounts. An authorised officer's report containing the names of the investors was passed to the Revenue by Tánaiste Mary Harney. It was thought that prominent Irish politicians and business executives are among the people named.

22: Nurses overwhelmingly rejected a £100m Labour Court pay offer and are expected to strike in October. Taoiseach Bertie Ahern warned the 27,500 nurses that the government will stand firm against their latest pay demands in his first direct intervention in the current public sector pay disputes.

23: The IMF forecasted a 7% growth for Ireland next year with an inflation rate at 2%.

23: As part of the Jubilee 2000 delegation which is urging rich countries to write off unpayable Third World debts, Bono and Bob Geldof were introduced to Pope John Paul II during a private audience in order to enlist his support for their cause.

23: The Public Accounts Committee heard that a committee was set up within the Bank of Ireland group in 1986 to examine ways of avoiding DIRT payments on behalf of its customers

23: Senator Mitchell concluded the third week of his review over the deadlock in the North, saying there was no viable alternative to the accord. Mr Trimble said the peace process is "a darn sight more robust than people give it credit".

25: The opposition parties demanded that the government publish the names of the 120 Ansbacher account-holders.

26: Meath beat Cork by three points in the All-Ireland Gaelic football final at Croke Park.

26: Eight people, including two gardaí, were killed in a number of road accidents over the weekend.

27: A tribunal of inquiry into the infection of haemophiliacs through contaminated blood products opened in Dublin.

27: The Bloody Sunday inquiry began a week of public hearings in the Guildhall, Derry, dealing with legal issues.

27: The pound fell to almost 80 pence sterling - its lowest level in more than 15 years against sterling.

27: The Irish Commissioner for Food Safety, David Byrne, urged EU farm ministers to back the testing of beef and fish for dioxins. A Belgian study revealed excessive PCB residue levels in 1% out of a sample of 1,000 cattle tested following the recent food contamination scare.

27: Mr Justice Flood agreed to defer taking evidence from Joseph Murphy snr in Guernsey until Mr Justice Morris decides on a judicial review of his ruling to exclude the press.

28: The National Ploughing Championships opened in Castletownroche, Co Cork, with an estimated 100,000 attending the event despite very muddy conditions.

28: At the Dail Committee on Public Accounts, Tony Spollen, former AIB head of internal audit, alleged that AIB conducted a share price support role for an oil exploration company's shares in the 1980s, using money from staff pension funds.

28: The Minister for Justice, John O'Donoghue, opened a new £13m women's prison at Mountjoy, Dublin.

28: Taoiseach Bertie Ahern, along with business leaders, warned public service workers that pay claims could undermine social partnership at national level.

28: According to the National Rehabilitation Board, nearly 1,000 disabled people a year finish training for employment but cannot get jobs.

28: Presenting the 1999 ESB Community Environment Awards in Dublin, the environmental campaigner, Prof David Bellamy warned that the Celtic Tiger was 'eating up' rural Ireland's landscape.

29: Soldiers who are to appear before the Bloody Sunday applied for their evidence to be heard in London, rather than Derry.

29: The Revenue Commissioners collected £1.6m from 43 settlements totalling £1.6 million with tax defaulters for the period April to June.

29: AIB admitted using staff funds as part of an alleged scheme to support their share prices of an oil exploration company. Five former finance ministers, including Taoiseach Bertie Ahern, Ray McSharry, and John Bruton, also gave evidence at yesterday's sitting of the Public Accounts Committee inquiry into bogus non-resident bank accounts in DIRT tax evasion.

29: Addressing the annual joint meeting of the International Monetary Fund and the World

Bank, the Minister for Finance called for the full implementation of a new international measure to cancel some of the debts of the world's poorest countries.

30: The major Dublin acute hospitals are expected to be hardest hit by the failure of health managers and nursing unions to make headway on ground rules for emergency cover in the event of a national strike.

30: Joseph Murphy senior began to give evidence to the Flood tribunal in private after the chairman ruled that to require the witness to undergo a risk to his life and health in a public hearing would be a deprivation of his rights.

30: Elections to Údarás na Gaeltachta are set to go ahead before Christmas, despite a bid by serving members to have them postponed until next year.

30: The Rev Ian Paisley met the Taoiseach in Dublin to discuss recent attacks on Free Presbyterian churches in the Republic.

30: An average of 15 to 20 new drug-abusers presented themselves to the Merchant's Quay Project in Dublin each week last year for needle-exchange or treatment services.

SPEECH OF THE YEAR

Nobel Lecture

By **John Hume**, *MP, MEP*
Oslo
December 10, 1998

Your Majesties, Members of the Norwegian Nobel Committee, Excellencies, Ladies and Gentlemen.

I would like to begin by expressing my deep appreciation and gratitude to the Nobel committee for bestowing this honour on me today. I am sure that they share with me the knowledge that, most profoundly of all, we owe this peace to the ordinary people of Ireland, particularly those of the North who have lived and suffered the reality of our conflict. I think that David Trimble would agree with me that this Nobel prize for peace which names us both is in the deepest sense a powerful recognition from the wider world of the tremendous qualities of compassion and humanity of all the people we represent between us.

In the past 30 years of our conflict there have been many moments of deep depression and outright horror. Many people wondered whether the words of W.B Yeats might come true

Too long a sacrifice/Can make a stone of the heart.

Endlessly our people gathered their strength to face another day and they never stopped encouraging their leaders to find the courage to resolve this situation so that our children could look to the future with a smile of hope. This is indeed their prize and I am convinced that they understand it in that sense and would take strong encouragement from today's significance and it will powerfully strengthen our peace process.

Today also we commemorate and the world commemorates the adoption 50 years ago of the Universal Declaration of Human Rights and it is right and proper that today is also a day that is associated internationally with the support of peace and work for peace because the basis of peace and stability, in any society, has to be the fullest respect for the human rights of all its people. It is right and proper that the European Convention of Human Rights is to be incorporated into the domestic law of our land as an element of the Good Friday Agreement.

In my own work for peace, I was very strongly inspired by my European experience. I always tell this story, and I do so because it is so simple yet so profound and so applicable to conflict resolution anywhere in the world. On my first visit to Strasbourg in 1979 as a member of the European Parliament, I went for a walk across the bridge from Strasbourg to Kehl. Strasbourg is in France. Kehl is in Germany. They are very close. I stopped in the middle of the bridge and I meditated. There is Germany. There is France. If I had stood on this bridge 30 years ago after the end of the second world war when 25 million people lay dead across our continent for the second time in this century and if I had said: "Don't worry. In 30 years time we will all be together in a new Europe, our conflicts and wars will be ended and we will be working together in our common interests", I would have been sent to a psychiatrist. But it has happened and it is now clear that European Union is the best example in the history of the world of conflict resolution and it is the duty of everyone, particularly those who live in areas of conflict to study how it was done and to apply its principles to their own conflict resolution.

All conflict is about difference, whether the difference is race, religion or nationality. The European visionaries decided that difference is not a threat, difference is natural. Difference is of the essence of humanity. Difference is an accident of birth and it should therefore never be the source of hatred or conflict. The answer to difference is to respect it. Therein lies a most fundamental principle of peace, respect for diversity.

The peoples of Europe then created institutions which respected their diversity – a Council of Ministers, the European Commission and the European Parliament – but allowed them to work together in their common and substantial economic interest. They spilt their sweat and not their blood and by doing so broke down the barriers of distrust of centuries and the new Europe has evolved and is still evolving, based on agreement and respect for difference.

That is precisely what we are now committed to doing in Northern Ireland. Our Agreement, which was overwhelmingly endorsed by the people, creates institutions which respect diversity but ensure that we work together in our common interest. Our Assembly is proportionately elected so that all sections of our people are represented. Any new administration or government will be proportionately elected by the members of the Assembly so that all sections will be working together. There will be also be institutions between both parts of Ireland and between Britain and Ireland that will also respect diversity and work the common ground.

Once these institutions are in place and we begin to work together in our very substantial common interests, the real healing process will begin and we will erode the distrust and prejudices of out past and our new society will evolve, based on agreement and respect for diversity. The identities of both sections of our people will be respected and there will be no victory for either side.

We have also had enormous solidarity and support from right across the world which has strengthened our peace process. We in Ireland appreciate this solidarity and support – from the United States, from the European Union, from friends around the world – more than we can say. The achievement of peace could not have been won without this goodwill and generosity of spirit. We should recall too on this formal occasion that our springtime of peace and hope in Ireland owes an overwhelming debt to several others who devoted their passionate intensity and all of their skills to this enterprise: to the Prime Ministers,Tony Blair and Bertie Ahern, to the President of the United States of America, Bill Clinton and the European President Jacques Delors and Jacques Santer and to the three men who so clearly facilitated the negotiation, Senator George Mitchell, former Leader of the Senate of the United States of America, Harri Holkerri of Finland and General John de Chastelain of Canada. And, of course, to our outstanding Secretary of State, Mo Mowlam.

We in Ireland appreciate this solidarity and support – from the United States; from the European Union, from friends around the world – more than we can say. The achievement of peace could not have been won without this goodwill and generosity of spirit. Two major political traditions share the island of Ireland. We are destined by history to live side by side. Two representatives of these political traditions stand here today. We do so in shared fellowship and a shared determination to make Ireland, after the hardship and pain of many years, a true and enduring symbol of peace.

Too many lives have already been lost in Ireland in the pursuit of political goals. Bloodshed for political change prevents the only change that truly matter: in the human heart. We must now shape a future of change that will be truly radical and that will offer a focus for real unity of purpose: harnessing new forces of idealism and commitment for the benefit of Ireland and all its people.

Throughout my years in political life, I have seen extraordinary courage and fortitude by individual men and women, innocent victims of violence. Amid shattered lives, a quiet heroism has born silent rebuke to the evil that violence represents, to the carnage and waste of violence, to its ultimate futility.

I have seen a determination for peace become a shared bond that has brought together people of all political persuasions in Northern Ireland and throughout the island of Ireland.

I have seen the friendship of Irish and British people transcend, even in times of misunderstanding and tensions, all narrower political differences. We are two neighbouring islands whose destiny is to live in friendship and amity with each other. We are friends and the achievement of peace will further strengthen that friendship and, together, allow us to build on the countless ties that unite us in so many ways.

The Good Friday Agreement now opens a new future for all the people of Ireland. A future built on respect for diversity and for political difference. A future where all can rejoice in cherished aspirations and beliefs and where this can be a badge of honour, not a source of fear or division.

The Agreement represents an accommodation that diminishes the self-respect of no political tradition, no group, no individual. It allows all of us – in Northern Ireland and throughout the island of Ireland– to now come together and, jointly, to work together in shared endeavour for the good of all.

No-one is asked to yield their cherished convictions or beliefs. All of us are asked to respect the views and rights of others as equal of our own and, together, to forge a covenant of shared ideals based on commitment to the rights of all allied to a new generosity of purpose.

That is what a new, agreed Ireland will involve. That is what is demanded of each of us.

The people of Ireland, in both parts of the island, have joined together to passionately support peace. They have endorsed, by overwhelming numbers in the ballot box, the Good Friday Agreement. They have shown an absolute and unyielding determination that the achievement of peace must be set in granite and its possibilities grasped with resolute purpose.

It is now up to political leaders on all sides to move decisively to fulfil the mandate given by the Irish people: to safeguard and cherish peace by establishing agreed structures for peace that will forever remove the underlying causes of violence and division on our island. There is now, in Ireland, a passionate sense of moving to new beginnings.

I salute all those who made this possible: the leaders and members of all the political parties who worked together to shape a new future and to reach agreement; the Republican and Loyalist movements who turned to a different path with foresight and courage; people in all parts of Ireland who have led the way for peace and who have made it possible.

And so, the challenge now is to grasp and shape history: to show that past grievances and injustices can give way to a new generosity of spirit and action.

I want to see Ireland – North and South – the wounds of violence healed, play its rightful role in a Europe that will, for all Irish people, be a shared bond of patriotism and new endeavour.

I want to see Ireland as an example to men and women everywhere of what can be achieved by living for ideals, rather than fighting for them, and by viewing each and every person as worthy of respect and honour.

I want to see an Ireland of partnership where we wage war on want and poverty, where we reach out to the marginalised and dispossessed, where we build together a future that can be as great as our dreams allow.

The Irish poet, Louis MacNiece wrote words of affirmation and hope that seem to me to sum up the challenges now facing all of us – North and South, unionist and nationalist in Ireland.

By a high star our course is set, Our end is life. Put out to sea.

That is the journey on which we in Ireland are now embarked.

Today, as I have said, the world also commemorates the adoption fifty years ago, of the Universal Declaration of Human Rights. To me there is a unique appropriateness, a sort of poetic fulfilment, in the coincidence that my fellow Laureate and I, representing a community long divided by the forces of a terrible history, should jointly be honoured on this day. I humbly accept this honour on behalf of a people who, after many years of strife, have finally made a commitment to a better future in harmony together. Our commitment is grounded in the very language and the very principles of the Universal Declaration itself. No greater honour could have been done me or the people I speak here for on no more fitting day.

I will now end with a quotation of total hope, the words of a former Laureate, one of my great heroes of this century, Martin Luther King Jr.

We shall overcome.

Thank you.

FAMOUS SPEECHES

Proclamation of the Irish Republic

THE PROVISIONAL GOVERNMENT OF THE IRISH REPUBLIC TO THE PEOPLE OF IRELAND

IRISHMEN AND IRISHWOMEN: In the name of God and of the dead generations from which she receives her old tradition of nationhood, Ireland, through us, summons her children to her flag and strikes for her freedom.

Having organised and trained her manhood through her secret revolutionary organisation, the Irish Republican Brotherhood, and through her open military organisations, the Irish Volunteers and the Irish Citizen Army, having patiently perfected her discipline, having resolutely waited for the right moment to reveal itself, she now seizes that moment, and supported by her exiled children in America and by gallant allies in Europe, but relying the first on her own strength, she strikes in full confidence of victory.

We declare the right of the people of Ireland to the ownership of Ireland, and to the unfettered control of Irish destinies, to be sovereign and indefeasible. The long usurpation of that right by a foreign people and government has not extinguished the right, nor can it ever be extinguished except by the destruction of the Irish people. In every generation the Irish people have asserted their right to national freedom and sovereignty: six times during the past three hundred years they have asserted it in arms; standing on that fundamental right and again asserting it in arms in the face of the world, we hereby proclaim the Irish Republic as a Sovereign Independent State, and we pledge our lives and the lives of our comrades-in-arms to the cause of its freedom, of its welfare, and of its exaltation among the nations.

The Irish Republic is entitled to, and hereby claims, the allegiance of every Irishman and Irishwoman. The Republic guarantees religious and civil liberty, equal rights and equal opportunities to all its citizens, and declares its resolve to pursue the happiness and prosperity of the whole nation and of all its parts, cherishing all the children of the nation equally and oblivious of the differences carefully fostered by an alien Government, which have divided a minority from the majority in the past.

Until our arms have brought the opportune moment for the establishment of a permanent National Government, representative of the whole people of Ireland and elected by the suffrages of all her men and women, the Provisional Government, hereby constituted, will administer the civil and military affairs of the Republic in trust for the people.

We place the cause of the Irish Republic under the protection of the Most High God, Whose blessing we invoke upon our arms, and we pray that no one who serves that cause will dishonour it by cowardice, inhumanity, or rapine. In this supreme hour the Irish nation must, by its valour and discipline, and by the readiness of its children to sacrifice themselves for the common good, prove itself worthy of the august destiny to which it is called.

Signed on Behalf of the Provisional Government.

THOMAS J. CLARKE.
SEAN Mac DIARMADA, THOMAS MacDONAGH,
P. H. PEARSE, EAMONN CEANNT,
JAMES CONNOLLY, JOSEPH PLUNKETT.

QUOTES OF THE YEAR

October 1998

"A parent, or someone *in loco parentis*, can, under Irish law hit a child and use the defence of reasonable chastisement. In one court case that amounted to broken limbs."

Cian O Tighearnaigh of the ISPCC, commenting on the decision by the European Court of Human Rights not to recognise corporal punishment as "reasonable chastisement".

"Don't kick the dog in the teeth to see if it is still sleeping."

Gerry Adams asking members of the British Labour Party to cease their demands for the decommissioning of arms by the IRA.

"It was there that terror finally lost its power to divide. Instead, it unified."

British Prime Minister Tony Blair speaking of the effect the Omagh bombing had on the community.

"What we are talking about is the blind robbery of the taxpayer by the rich."

Joe Higgins TD on the AIB's liabilities to the Revenue Commissioners, which were owed to the sum of £86 million.

"The town has been ghettoised to the extent that it has become known as the Soweto of the Six Counties."

Dara O'Hagan, Sinn Féin Assembly member, alleging that Portadown was being strangled by loyalists supporting the Drumcree vigil.

"Unfortunately, when you are standing up for liberties, sometimes the cost of those liberties can be very high."

David Jones, spokesman for the Orange Order in Portadown, speaking on the murder of RUC Constable Frank O'Reilly, killed in a blast bomb thrown by loyalist rioters at Drumcree.

"The British like to think of themselves as honourable peacemakers but they were ignorant, stupid and sometimes brutal too."

Nick Ross, BBC TV presenter and a former student at Queen's University, Belfast, who took part in the Civil Rights protests of the 1960s.

"It's not just as an honour to myself, it's also an expression of total endorsement of the work of very many people."

John Hume on being awarded the 1998 Nobel Peace Prize.

"We hope that it is merited, because there is an element of prematurity about this."

David Trimble on being awarded the 1998 Nobel Peace Prize.

"Like winning the lottery without having purchased a ticket"

Eamon McCann on David Trimble sharing the Nobel Peace Prize with John Hume.

"Both have earned this award but I believe there are others too who deserve credit for their indispensable roles, beginning with Gerry Adams, the Sinn Féin leader, without whom there would have been no peace."

US President Bill Clinton on John Hume and David Trimble being awarded the 1998 Nobel Peace Prize.

"I'll rot in prison before I pay Mr Doherty. I wouldn't trust him with 5p."

Tom Crosby, a Co. Roscommon councillor, who refused to pay a £500 fine to Sean Doherty TD, whom he had previously assaulted.

"She is not bloody Molly Malone, she is Bernie Malone and it is our city too and . . . we have as much right to protest as building labourers or anyone else."

A Tullamore farmer on MEP Bernie Malone's comment that farmers had no right to disrupt her city.

"Irish men are lovely. They're always smiling at me."

Adriana Sklenarikova, the new Wonderbra girl, explains why she likes Irish men.

"This is accountancy not a health service."

Dr David Lillis comments on the decision to reduce beds in University College Hospital Galway.

"Jesus, the lolly flows into your pocket and you don't have to do anything."

A Skibbereen farmer, quoted in German magazine *Der Spiegel* on EU subsidies.

November 1998

"There's no point in being a Fianna Fáil backbencher anymore. Jackie Healy-Rae is running the show."

Liam Aylward TD on Carlow's exclusion from Objective One Status for EU funding.

"I feel profoundly both the history of this event, and I feel profoundly the enormity of the honour that you are bestowing upon me. From the bottom of my heart, *go raibh mile maith agaibh.*"

British Prime Minister Tony Blair in his historic address to the Dáil.

"Daniel O'Connell, a man who married his cousin and was rightly accused of all kinds of sexual deviancy. No surprise that the prime minister, with a cabinet of many self-confessed homosexuals and partnerships without marriage, would find a place for him."

Rev Dr Ian Paisley commenting on British Prime Minister Tony Blair's lauding of Daniel O'Connell in his speech to the Dáil.

"He is a liar, a cheat, a hypocrite, a knave, a thief, a loathsome reptile which needs to be scotched."

Rev Ian Paisley on David Trimble.

"As long as even one member of the RUC is a member of a new police force, that force will not be acceptable."

Fr Des Wilson commenting to the Patten Commission on Policing.

"Those whom we commemorate here were doubly tragic. They fell victim to a war against oppression in Europe. Their memory, too, fell victim to a war for independence at home in Ireland . . . Respect for the memory of one set of heroes was often at the expense of respect for the memory of the other."

President Mary McAleese at Armistice Day commemorations in Belgium.

"I'll give you a good reason. The IRA won't do it. That's the reason."

Martin McGuinness of Sinn Féin when questioned why the IRA would not start the process of decommissioning.

"I think that it would be ridiculous to pretend that there haven't been problems between North and South. And I think any initiative which can somehow overcome these rather artificial divisions can only be good."

The Duke of Edinburgh during a visit to Dublin.

"We are talking about a naked man, wrapped in cling film, tied to a lamp post, in broad daylight."

Laura Magahy, managing director of Temple Bar Properties, pointing out some of the incidents which led to stag and hen parties being banned from the Temple Bar area of Dublin.

December 1998

"Most profoundly of all, we owe this peace to the ordinary people of Ireland, particularly those in the North who have lived and suffered the reality of our conflict."

John Hume in his acceptance speech at the Nobel Peace Prize-giving ceremony.

"Burke is the best model for what might be called politicians of the possible - politicians who seek to make a working peace, not in some perfect world that never was, but in this, the flawed world which

is our only workshop."

David Trimble on Edmund Burke, the 18th-century political philosopher, in his acceptance speech at the Nobel Peace Prize-giving ceremony.

"If I'd known I was half as popular, not only would I have stayed but I would have asked for more money."

Gay Byrne on his retirement from radio.

"He was more or less acting like Senator George Mitchell."

Solicitor Hugh Campbell on behalf of his client, Joseph Joyce, who was found in possession of three wooden bats on his way to 'mediate' in a travellers' row.

"He was hardly going to play rounders or baseball."

Judge James O'Sullivan on Mr Joyce.

"I thought it was a swamp monster first, but then I saw it was my mom."

A young girl giving evidence in the Central Criminal Court where her father, David Murphy, was convicted of the murder of his wife, Patricia, in May 1996.

"The reason they are being prevented is that the minister is fearful that they will become involved in Irish life and, in effect, stop being statistics and start being human beings. It is not easy to deport people when they have been someone's neighbour, friend or work colleague."

Liz McManus TD on the ban on asylum seekers working in the Republic.

"Can one imagine Archbishop John Charles McQuaid would have been so reticent?"

Church of Ireland Gazette editorial on the silence of the Catholic church with regard to the Taoiseach's partner, Celia Larkin, and her public role.

"You are umbilically tied to him and it will strangle you."

John Gormley TD on the Taoiseach's failure to distance himself from the former Taoiseach with regard to the controversial dismissal of Charles Haughey's tax assessment of £2 million.

"You do not seem to appreciate the enormity of what you have done . . . you are not a demon, though some less responsible sections of the media have attempted to demonise you. You are a human being who did a dreadful, evil thing which has left this young girl heavily psychologically scarred for the rest of her life."

Mr Justice John Quirke to the rapist at the centre of the 'C' case.

"I hope somebody forgives them because I never will. But as long as they're caught and justice is done then maybe things will change."

Tracey Devine, a survivor of the Omagh bomb, on the bombers after her four-month stay in hospital.

"Our equipment matches the best in the world but

this year's storms were as bad or worse than last year's, and last year's were unprecedented. Unfortunately, there is very little we can do to help them withstand the worst that nature throws at them."

Michael Kelly, a spokesman for the ESB, giving an explanation on why thousands of homes across the country were without electricity over Christmas.

January 1999

"It was the British who banished poitín. I am in favour of upholding the law, but not Cromwell's law."

Tommie Mac Donnchada of Leitir Móir, Connemara.

"No incidents have been reported that may impair the smooth start of the system."

Statement from the European Central Bank on the introduction of the new Euro into trading.

"A start to decommissioning would do more to create confidence between the communities than any other single step."

British Prime Minister Tony Blair.

"Dear old Mr Gogarty will give his evidence, be treated nicely and then totter off."

Colm Allen, Senior Counsel, at the Flood Tribunal.

"They [the lawyers] are laughing at me and they are getting £1,350 a day for laughing at me. I came here to the tribunal to get the truth, warts and all and if I did wrong I am ready to take my place in the queue to pay for it."

James Gogarty the main witness at the Flood Tribunal.

"I am a very silly old man."

Joseph Freer, a 76 year old pensioner convicted of importing heroin.

"The shooting seemed to go on and on. It seemed like for ages. I jumped on to the footpath and put my hands up. I thought I was going to die."

William Jackson, a witness in the Garda McCabe murder trial.

"I remember saying 'Will we get a receipt for this money?' . . . Mr Bailey said 'Will we fuck!' "

James Gogarty, recounts to the Flood Tribunal the conversation he had with the building developer on the way to deliver a cheque to Ray Burke.

"Despite the fact that I have never expressed the least interest in this sad and sordid little episode, I am resigned to seeing it rehashed and reprinted over and over again."

John Boorman, the film director, denying the persistent rumour that he is going to make a film on Bishop Eamon Casey.

"I have no recollection of any telephone conversation with Mr Gilmartin and equally, therefore, I have no recollection of any conversation with him relating to contributions to the party or Mr Flynn".

Taoiseach Bertie Ahern in response to allegations made by Tom Gilmartin that he had advised him of a £50,000 donation to Fianna Fáil through Mr Padraig Flynn.

"Last Sunday he hardly knew me, by Monday he could remember one meeting and by Tuesday he recalled three."

Tom Gilmartin on the Taoiseach's memory.

"It is a bit unfair that when you correct the record quickly, you are accused of a loss of memory, senility or something else."

Taoiseach Bertie Ahern in reference to his recall of meetings with Tom Gilmartin.

"It meant a great deal for me that the prime minister chose to land with his plane at Gaza International Airport and send out the right message. With this gesture prime minister, you have touched my heart and the hearts of the Palestinian people."

Yasser Arafat, the Palestinian president, to Taoiseach Bertie Ahern, who became the first European leader to fly into Gaza.

"It shows that love can conquer evil and that with the courage and the will to live, you can have a new future."

Sandy Smith, a victim of the Omagh bomb announcing her wedding in June.

"On the instructions of my clients, let's be quite clear, Mr Gogarty is a malicious and artful liar, sir, and that is the case we'll be putting to Mr Gogarty."

Michael Cush Counsel for JMSE at the Flood Tribunal.

"There's nobody I'm as sorry for as the victims of my violence because they are at the greatest loss and I don't know how I can ever say sorry enough."

Eamon Collins, author and IRA informer, who was murdered at the end of January.

"The employee, who staunchly asserts his innocence and who denies any wrongdoing, has informed us he believes it is in the best interests of the society and the services it provides that he should absent himself for the present. The society . . . has agreed to grant the employee paid leave."

Statement from the ISPCC after a senior official was arrested and questioned by gardaí who were investigating allegations of fraud within the charity.

February 1999

"There is absolutely no doubt in my mind that Jerry McCabe was murdered and an attempt was made to murder Ben O'Sullivan and if a piece of car hadn't got in the way, he would be dead as well."

John Healy, president of the Garda Representative Association, commenting on the trial of Detective Garda Jerry McCabe's killers.

"To describe what happened in Adare as anything less than murder is a travesty of the truth."

Des O'Malley TD on the trial of Garda McCabe's killers. Those who killed Garda McCabe pleaded guilty and were convicted of manslaughter.

"The Machiavellian machinations indulged by you make this one of the worst cases I have ever dealt with. These were vile acts, acts so disgusting on boys whom you pounced on. You exploited their frailty, taking control of their bodies both mentally and physically."

Judge Frank O'Donnell, jailing Christian Brother Patrick John Kelly for eight years for sexual assault.

"When I was going to school we were all afraid of him. He was both bad and mad and he used to beat the shit out of me . . . He was sexually molesting me one day and I hit him. He beat the pulp out of me and when I went home with a black eye my father said I probably deserved it."

A former male pupil of paedophile Christian Brother Donal Dunne, who was jailed for two years for sex abuse.

"Mr Haughey told me he was asking a few friends to make a contribution of £5,000 each . . . I presumed that a lot of members of the party had been asked to contribute."

Dr John O'Connell, former minister for health, on Charles Haughey's request for a financial contribution to Celtic Helicopters, a company jointly owned by Ciarán Haughey, his son.

"A Flynn must support a Flynn."

Beverly Cooper-Flynn TD before her expulsion from Fianna Fáil for defying the party Whip and voting against a Dáil motion asking her father, Padraig, to explain a donation made by Tom Gilmartin.

"Even though it was company money, they were like my own pound notes."

Ben Dunne at the Moriarty Tribunal.

"I am not a man who takes too much interest in elections."

Ben Dunne at the Moriarty tribunal.

"We're free, Nelson Mandela, we're free."

Members of the Irish traveller family who caused a Jamaica-bound flight to be diverted when they became involved in a fight on board the airliner. They were taken off the plane and left stranded in Norfolk, Virginia.

"From the Dock? Put me in the dock, that's where they want me in the dock. Oh Jesus, oh Mother of God!"

James Gogarty responding to Garrett Cooney,

Counsel for JMSE, after Cooney complained about Gogarty's habit of making 'long rambling speeches from the dock'.

"We will struggle on without him, but we will never forget him."

Labour Party leader Ruairí Quinn on Pat Upton the Labour TD who died suddenly.

"I don't have a bank account in the Isle of Man."

George Redmond, the former assistant Dublin city and county manager.

"I don't need to say anything. Sure you'll make it all up."

George Redmond on his arrest after returning from the Isle of Man with £300,000.

"The shocking thing, the big surprise, is to find the pre-Viking evidence is not of diagnostically Irish type houses and the closest parallels are found in England."

Linzi Simpson, the excavation director who discovered 'a strange house,' a pre-Viking Anglo-Saxon dwelling similar to hundreds in England, at the archeological dig in Dublin's Temple Bar. This discovery indicate that English settlers may have been in Ireland longer than previously thought.

"I want a just vengeance. God allows me a vengeance. He allows me to feel like this because my wife of 40 years contributed to this country by having three fine children. These people destroyed that."

Laurence Rush, whose wife died in the Omagh bomb, on her killers.

March 1999

"People were actually crying, which I assure you is most unusual."

Haruyoshi Totsukawa, executive director of Riverdance promoters in Japan, describing the show's debut in the country.

"What I did say was a throwaway comment. Regrettably, I said they were lying out in the grass in the sun, sunning themselves. I did not compare them at that stage to pedigree dogs. It was never my intention to be derogatory or abusive or insulting."

John Flannery, a Mayo Fine Gael councillor, who was acquitted in court of inciting hatred against the travelling community through public remarks that he made.

"A farrago of deceit and untruth."

Mr Justice Kerr on the trial of British paratrooper Lee Clegg, convicted of murdering teenager Karen Reilly. Clegg was acquitted on appeal.

"These soldiers were the elite. They were supposed to be well-trained and they slaughtered these two

young people."
Dr Joe Hendron, SDLP Assembly member, on Clegg's acquittal.

"**Will she stop substituting oul' blather for real action in this regard?**"
Emmet Stagg TD to Mary O'Rourke, minister for Public Enterprise, on an ESB dispute at Moneypoint.

"**The only blather I hear is from the deputy. He is great at it . . . This is the arch-blatherer of Dáil Éireann.**"
Mary O'Rourke in reply.

"**You must understand that, political donations to political parties or to individuals, there's nothing illegal about that. There never was.**"
Pádraig Flynn.

"**The worst threat is that I am going to be killed. They [RUC interrogators] told one guy 'you're going to die when you get out and tell Rosemary she's going to die too.'** "
Rosemary Nelson, the Lurgan solicitor who was murdered by loyalists, speaking on RUC intimidation before her death.

"**Allegations of intimidation of solicitors were part and parcel of a political agenda to portray the RUC as part of the unionist tradition.**"
Quote attributed to **RUC Chief Constable Ronnie Flanagan** in a 1997 UN report into police intimidation of lawyers.

"**The impression has been given that complaints of child sex abuse were made to me in respect of which I made no response. It is untrue, however, to say I did nothing about them.**"
Bishop Brendan Comiskey denying he did nothing about the child sex abuse allegations that were made to him against Fr Seán Fortune.

"**The greedy have always said that we have to make money before we can share it. That time has now come.**"
Paul Sweeney, an economist for SIPTU.

"**When someone is kicked to death in full view of police officers, it seems strange a conviction is not possible and that sufficient evidence was not able to be presented.**"
Bríd Rodgers, SDLP Assembly member, after Marc Hobson was found not guilty of Robert Hamill's murder.

April 1999

"**I don't need publicity. If I fart I get it.**"
Sinead O'Connor.

"**There are a lot of people around Portadown who aren't very impressed that David Trimble has gone off to meet the Pope and hasn't got more involved**

in trying to get the situation here [Drumcree] resolved.**"
Portadown Orange Order spokesman **David Jones.**

"**Our view is if you park the peace process there will be no Good Friday agreement to come back to. It will be gone.**"
Sinn Féin chairman **Mitchel McLaughlin.**

"**In the circumstances, I conclude that Judge [Cyril] Kelly's handling of this case compromised the administration of justice . . . I also conclude that Mr Justice [Liam] O'Flaherty's intervention was inappropriate and unwise, that it left his motives open to misinterpretation and that it was therefore damaging to the administration of justice.**"
Chief Justice Liam Hamilton on the handling of the Philip Sheedy affair. Sheedy was freed after serving less than one quarter of his sentence, but later returned to prison voluntarily.

"**We kill over 400 people a year on our roads and there is hardly a word. There are about 40 murders and we solve 87 per cent of them and there is still uproar.**"
Garda Commissioner **Pat Byrne.**

May 1999

"**I don't think I can live with the inauthenticity of movies anymore. I don't like watching them, especially my own stuff.**"
Liam Neeson announcing his intention to stop making movies.

"**People are not collateral damage.**"
Mary Robinson, the United Nations Commissioner for Human Rights on military terminology employed during the air war in Kosovo.

"**They [the Progressive Democrats] should be called The Old Man Liver Party. They're afraid of living and scared of dying.**"
Labour TD **Pat Rabbitte.**

"**If I hadn't become a priest I'd be dead . . . If you can't go to the church for redemption where can you go?**"
Sinead O'Connor.

"**The party might be getting out of control.**"
Maurice O'Connell, governor of the Central Bank, on Ireland's economy.

"**We must start by apologising. On behalf of the State and of all citizens of the State, the Government wishes to make a sincere and long overdue apology to the victims of childhood abuse for our collective failure to intervene, to detect their pain, to come to their rescue.**"
An Taoiseach Bertie Ahern.

"Pat Finucane was associated with the IRA and he used his position as a lawyer to act as a contact between suspects in custody and republicans on the outside."

Former RUC Chief Constable **Sir John Hermon** on Belfast solicitor Pat Finucane who was murdered in 1989 amid widespread claims of RUC collusion.

"On the human level, she's a very intelligent, engaging, attractive lady, and David Trimble and I will always welcome attractive ladies."

Seamus Mallon on Hillary Clinton

"I can't explain what happened. I just cut them. I didn't realise what I was doing."

Heroin addict **Robert Hughes** who was imprisoned for four years for pulling toe and finger nails off a four-year-old girl.

"The real question for members of the Orange Order to address is whether they wish to be regarded as members of a religious or political movement."

Church of Ireland Primate of All-Ireland **Archbishop Robin Eames.**

"It's a sad day for Irish sport. I'm sorry that the joy some people got from Michelle's success has been overshadowed now. But sport must be protected."

Kay Guy, who carried out the test which led to De Bruin's banning from competition.

June 1999

"This is a First World country with a Third World infrastructure."

John Bruton.

"No guns, no government."

David Trimble, Ulster Unionist Party Leader quashing the idea of an Executive being formed without prior IRA decommissioning of weapons.

"It remains the Government's firm position that there is no need for a referendum [on the Partnership for Peace]. No other country, not even Switzerland, has had a referendum – and they have one most weekends."

An Taoiseach, Bertie Ahern.

"You can't maintain a state-of-the art economy on the basis of sticking plaster services."

IMPACT president **Bill Gallagher** on the provision of public services.

"The purpose in having the Queen in Cardiff and Edinburgh is to kill off the suggestion that devolution is a means of ending the Union. The reason for not having the Queen in Belfast is because that's not the message the Labour Party wants to convey in Northern Ireland . . . because the opposite is the purpose."

Peter Robinson, deputy leader of the Democratic Unionist Party.

"Ulster Unionists talk about the need to jump together, but I cannot jump far with Mr Trimble on my back."

Gerry Adams.

"We'd rather she was buried here. It's a beautiful area. It beats being under the foundations of someone's house. We were told she was buried in west Belfast."

Séamus McKendry, during the search for his mother-in-law – who was 'disappeared' by the IRA in the 1970s – at Carlingford in County Louth.

"I think the decision not to allow the game to go ahead is the right one. At no stage did we seek to have the game called off on political grounds, but we consider the government made the correct move."

Bernard O'Byrne, Chief Executive of the FAI after the Government denied visas to the Yugoslav team

"In our Western world the church seems to be in retreat. In this island many people are being lost to secularism and materialism. People in general have no interest in God. His day is abused. His house is neglected. His word is ignored."

Presbyterian Moderator **Dr John Lockington.**

"To see a tough guy like Steve collapsing on the canvas like that was frightening."

Steve Collins' trainer on the incident which led to Collins, a former world middleweight champion, retiring from boxing.

"Believe it or not, I am popular. I am a very nice guy, a really good laugh. I am. I am."

TV presenter **Eamon Holmes** blows his own trumpet.

"A miracle."

Dana Rosemary Scallon on winning a seat in the European Parliament.

"This woman has come in from abroad and she is here now for the first time and she is elected. It is a tremendous feat, but I don't understand the reasons for it. I'm baffled."

Defeated Fianna Fáil candidate **Noel Treacy** on Dana Rosemary Scallon's election to the European Parliament.

"That will make some sense out of the nonsense of the millennium."

Bono urging the cancellation of the Third World debt by industrialised countries.

"Don't fool yourself that it is about the issue of decommissioning. It's about more than that. It's because they [unionists] don't want to see a Fenian in government."

Martin McGuinness.

"While part of our country is still occupied by British troops, no welcome should be given to these warmongers."

Sinn Féin Councillor **Larry O'Toole** on the visit by a British warship to Dublin

"One thing I would say to the unionists is that they can always walk away from this if the [decommissioning] commitments aren't made at a later date... They can bring this down at any time by simply walking out if the commitments aren't kept."

US President, **Bill Clinton** advocating the formation of a power-sharing Executive in Northern Ireland.

"I'm gay and I have had gay romances, but now, for the first time in my life, I am in a relationship with someone I love."

Boyzone's **Stephen Gately.**

"Whether it's one's city by birth or by adoption, let us all make Dublin a city in which its inhabitants can share a common sense of belonging."

Lord Mayor of Dublin, **Mary Freehill.**

July 1999

"It was the nicest chequered flag I've ever seen, nicer than Australia . . . this was really hard work; there was so much going on, so many things to do to win."

Formula One Driver **Eddie Irvine** on his Grand Prix win at Austria, his second of the season.

"This evidence [points to] only one conclusion: that the accused was a fundamental part of the conspiracy or plot to murder Veronica Guerin, that he participated fully in the event,"

The findings of the Special Criminal Court which convicted Brian Meehan of the murder of journalist Veronica Guerin on June 26, 1996.

"It is now necessary I resign as Deputy First Minister. I do so with great reluctance and recognition of the awesome responsibility we all have towards lasting peace and the future of all the people of the north of Ireland."

Seamus Mallon at the NI Assembly.

"He [David Trimble] was in Glengall Street today, tomorrow he will be in Downing Street and the day after he will probably be in Sesame Street"

Mark Durkan of the SDLP on David Trimble's failure to show up for the nomination of the Executive.

"Today has been a good day for Northern Ireland. Democracy has triumphed. There are no IRA men in the government of Northern Ireland."

Rev Dr Ian Paisley on the non-formation of the Northern Ireland Executive.

"The issue of decommissioning was never an issue between unionists and nationalists, it was an issue between unionism. A battle within unionism for the hearts and minds of taking people absolutely nowhere."

David Ervine a Progressive Unionist Party Assembly member.

"I'm just an ordinary guy who got lucky."

Boyzone's **Ronan Keating.**

"If Armagh win the Ulster title it will be the only orange parade down the Garvaghy Road this year."

Derry footballer **Joe Brolly** speaking after Armagh beat Derry in the Ulster SFC semi-final. Armagh went on to win the title.

"I can't be expected to tear up immigration law in this country at the whim of retired revolutionaries in Democratic Left."

Minister for Justice **John O'Donoghue** on the rights of asylum seekers to work in Ireland.

"Why are you not off catching real criminals."

Former Miss Ireland **Andrea Roche** to a garda who caught her speeding.

"I'm not arrogant enough or stupid enough to think Manchester United will break the bank to keep me."

Roy Keane on his contract negotiations with Manchester United which ended inconclusively.

"A world-class Lear in long johns, with an ego about one-twentieth the size of a Hollywood bit player."

US magazine *Newsweek* on actor Donal McCann who died in July.

"There are still too many unanswered questions regarding this murder, which I, and many others believe was state-sponsored, state-sanctioned and state-arranged."

David Wright, father of the murdered Portadown loyalist, Billy Wright who is campaigning for an inquiry into his son's murder. Three INLA members have already been convicted of the murder.

"I would say to any young man or woman, leave the dreaded tobacco out of your life."

Former world snooker champion **Alex Higgins** who has throat cancer.

"It will provide a crucial measure of protection for the soldiers most at risk from terrorist reprisals."

Britain's secretary for defence **George Robertson**, on the English Court of Appeal's decision to grant soldiers involved in Bloody Sunday anonymity at the forthcoming public inquiry.

"There is neither a danger nor a threat to the soldiers. We don't want them harmed. We want them to be part of the inquiry."

John Kelly, whose brother was murdered on Bloody Sunday

"The only exercise I get these days is walking

behind the coffins of my friends who take exercise."
Actor **Peter O'Toole.**

August 1999

"[The relatives] would have no confidence in any private inquiry"
Frank Massey, on the recommendations of the Victims' Commission to hold a private rather than a public inquiry into the 1974 Dublin and Monaghan bombings. Mr Massey's daughter was killed in the Dublin bombing.

"An inquiry held in private is not acceptable . . . [there is] strong evidence in the hands of the Irish Government that there was British military involvement in the bombings"
Sinn Féin TD **Caoimhghín Ó Caoláin** on the Victims' Commission recommendations.

"Any assessment of whether a ceasefire has been breached is one based on security intelligence, obviously, but also on fine political judgment from the ministers involved and the two governments."
Liz O'Donnell, the Junior Minister for Foreign Affairs on the criteria for judging the state of the IRA ceasefire.

"It's not the first time that Mr Andrews has spoken without getting his mind fully in gear. I wouldn't attach any great significance to it."
David Trimble on the disagreement between the Minister for Foreign Affairs, David Andrews, and Mo Mowlam, over the state of the IRA's ceasefire.

"Everybody got it, very few were spared. She beat us with sticks, pots and pans, a chain but mostly with her fists."
Regina Walshe, the victim of former nun Nora Wall who was convicted of rape.

"[It's] in sharp contrast to its complete inactivity in the face of 15 months of violent Orange protests in Portadown."
John Gormley, Lower Ormeau Concerned Community spokesman, on the RUC's heavy-handed move against nationalist protesters on the Ormeau Road which resulted in scores of injuries and several arrests.

"For us, there were no flowers, no cards, nothing."
Paddy O'Brien, contrasts public opinion after the Dublin bombings in 1974, in which he was injured, and the Warrington bombing in 1993.

"Ireland was a good place, and many tears were shed when we left. But Kosovo is my home, and the place for my family."
Murtex Demiri, on his return to Kosovo.

"Our prison overtime is out of line with the rest of the world. We are haemorrhaging money."
Head of the Independent Prison Authority, **Seán Aylward.**

"Clearly this is a matter of great concern for the company and its customers."
A spokesman for **In Dublin** magazine after it had been banned by the Censorship of Publications Board for carrying lewd and obscene advertisements.

"The Celtic Tiger benefits 5-10 per cent of people in the upper strata of society, but most people in Ireland don't even get to hold the Tiger's tail for a day."
Actor **Gabriel Byrne.**

"There has . . . been speculation about the recent killing of Charles Bennett. Let us emphasise that there have been no breaches of the IRA cessation, which remains intact."
IRA statement

"The day of the plastic bag is coming towards an end."
Minister for the Environment **Noel Dempsey** who plans to introduce a tax on plastic bags.

"I'm still around but when I go there won't be too many socialists left. This is a very, very sad occasion for me."
Lord [formerly Gerry] Fitt on the death of Paddy Devlin, with whom he formed the Social Democratic and Labour Party in 1970.

"I do not believe that there is a sufficient basis to conclude that the IRA ceasefire has broken down . . . The peace we have now is imperfect, but better than none."
Mo Mowlam's assessment of the IRA ceasefire.

"This decision is absolutely disgraceful. After a number of murders by the IRA and gun-running from America, to suggest the ceasefire is intact is a sick joke."
Ulster Unionist MP **Jeffrey Donaldson.**

"Dolphins will always require food, shelter or sex, and Belmullet is obviously providing for one or other of these basic needs."
Environmentalist **Shay Fennelly**, on the school of dolphins which arrived in Broadhaven Bay in Co Mayo.

"We like to say it's about beauty with a purpose."
Miss Ireland co-ordinator **Róisín McQueenie.**

September 1999

" 'No guns, no government.' Four words, two no's."
Martin McGuinness on the double negativity of the Ulster Unionists.

". . . the greatest haven for tax evasion today."
Tony Mac Cárthaigh, senior tax inspector with the Revenue Commissioners, on the special low-tax sav-

ings accounts, Special Savings Accounts.

"[Mr Blair is] engaged in a process of appeasing evil."
David Trimble.

"A common slut."
Leitrim priest **Father James Duffy** on unmarried mother Sonia O'Sullivan - a comment which prompted widespread public criticism.

"I am sorry if I hurt her and regret in particular the use of the word slut."
Father Duffy apologises.

"Am I to believe that no politician had any association with anything that happened during that decade? It's news to me."
Maurice Doyle, a former senior civil servant and governor of the Central Bank, to the Public Accounts Committee of the Dáil which is investigating bogus non-resident accounts.

"Nobody is going to agree to live inside a mafia state."
David Trimble on the need for IRA decommissioning before Sinn Féin enters government.

"If he begins the review next week, I will not be there."
John Taylor, deputy leader of the UUP announcing his intention to withdraw from the review of the Good Friday Agreement.

"I think there might be bandages, blood and crutches on the plane going out tomorrow because we've really worked hard out there tonight, but I'm delighted."
Republic of Ireland soccer manager **Mick McCarthy** on his side's 2-1 victory over Yugoslavia in the European Championships.

"They were very well behaved and a credit to themselves."
Chief Superintendent Michael Finnegan on the 80,000 fans who travelled to Slane to see Robbie Williams in concert.

"If this is not the way forward, I simply do not know what is."
Chris Patten, Chairman of the Independent Commission on Policing for Northern Ireland, presenting its report.

"A great insult to the RUC and the community . . . The most shoddy piece of work I have ever seen."
David Trimble gives his reaction to the report.

"It is better to play badly and win than play well and lose. One of the worst feelings in football is to go home knowing that you've been mugged."
Mick McCarthy who saw his Republic of Ireland team lose to a injury time goal by Croatia in Zagreb.

"I wouldn't have wanted to go to my grave without Brian being properly buried. For years I've had nowhere to mourn him. Now I'll be able to go to his grave and talk to him, I'll have somewhere to bring flowers and to cry."
Margaret McKinney on her son who was 'disappeared' by the IRA in 1978.

"A dispirited man showing no indication of the slightest optimism."
Bob McCartney MP on Senator George Mitchell.

"The Senator was in good form all day. But, if there was a moment when he became dispirited, it was probably at the prospect of having to listen to Bob McCartney."
Statement from Senator Mitchell's spokesperson.

"The people I have known either for 10 years, 20 years or 30 years from business, gambling, holidays, men and women of all types of reputation, I intend to be seen with them, go out with them, and the only thing I'd be worried about is that some of my friends would be afraid to invite me on holidays in the future."
Minister for Finance, **Charlie McCreevy**, on holidaying in businessman Ulick McEvaddy's French villa.

"They pose a very significant threat . . . I'm talking about the coalition of the so-called "Real! IRA", Continuity IRA and some members of the INLA."
Sir Ronnie Flanagan, Chief constable of the RUC on realignments among republican dissidents.

"The Minister [for Finance] appears to believe that social partnership is about nothing more than pay restraint."
Peter Cassells, general secretary of the Irish Congress of Trades Unions.

"Anyone who walks down any Irish street in clerical dress today soon knows the difference from 10 to 15 years ago. There has, to put it politely, been a lowering of esteem for all clergy, and it is often expressed very impolitely indeed."
The Very Rev Robert MacCarthy, Dean of St Patrick's Cathedral.

"I want to stay active. I've learned a lot along the road of life. If my expertise can be of use to me and others, then it is available, and so be it. If no one wants it, so be it. I don't mind."
Former EU Commissioner **Padraig Flynn**.

"Those who perpetrated the level of fraud as seen in the Ansbacher accounts should go to jail."
Peter Cassells, general secretary of the Irish Congress of Trades Unions.

"I would have no difficulty with that."
Taoiseach Bertie Ahern.

"[I was] a very heavy saver and over the years I made investments of various sorts."

George Redmond, attempting to explain how, on a take-home salary of £19,000 he managed to lodge £265,000 in 1988 and 1989 and had net investments totalling £660,000.

"I accept it was in the area of inappropriate."

George Redmond on accepting money from property developers.

"I would not be here if I were convinced that it couldn't be done. I'm still hopeful, notwithstanding the difficulties."

George Mitchell on the prospects for the Good Friday Agreement.

"I've a lot of respect for the dogs in the street. They're customers of mine from time to time."

Albert Reynolds, pet food producer and a former Minister for Finance, to the Public Accounts Committee when it was put to him that even 'the dogs in the street' knew of the existence and extent of bogus non-resident accounts.

"The Government wants people prosecuted and to get any revenue lost repaid with interest and penalties. Early publication would damage the process that has already brought us to this stage."

Government spokesman on an opposition call for the names of all Ansbacher account holders to be published following the leaking of some of the names to the media.

"What about the names already out in the public arena? What about their right to due process and to fair procedures?"

Fine Gael's **Nora Owen,** whose sister, MEP Mary Banotti, was among one of the names leaked.

"It is well known that for a huge body of people Christmas and the New Year is an unbearable time. For them, what will the millennium be like?"

Right Rev Paul Colton, The Church of Ireland Bishop of Cork, Cloyne and Ross.

"Ah lookit, this is the Mecca of the game, you know. It's like reaching the promised land. I'm as happy as I was the first time we did this. You know, to see a group of young lads pick up the mantle and grow together and achieve something, it's marvellous to see."

Meath manager **Seán Boylan** on his team's All-Ireland football final victory.

"It's only once in a lifetime that you have a millennium."

John Ussher, president Irish Taxi Drivers' Federation president, defending treble fares during the New Year period.

OBITUARIES

October 1998

BLAIR, Billy (1908–1998) former Deputy Lord Mayor of Belfast (1984) and Unionist Councillor.

BURKE, Jack (1922–1998) Honorary Secretary of the Bowling League of Ireland for the past 16 years. Founding member of Blackrock Athletic Club. Winner of the Bowling League of Ireland Triples Championship (1986). President of the Bowling League of Ireland (1981), the Irish Bowling Association (1985) and the BIBC (1996).

CARROLL, Noel (1942–1998) former middle-distance runner for Ireland and Chief Executive of Dublin Chamber of Commerce. Represented Ireland at the 1964 and 1968 Olympic Games and was a former European 800m champion. Became well-known as public relations officer for Dublin Corporation (1972–96) and was appointed Chief Executive of Dublin Chamber of Commerce in 1996.

CARRON, John (1909–1998) Nationalist Party MP for Fermanagh South (1964–72) in the Stormont Parliament, where he was spokesman on community relations. Helped found the Fermanagh Nationalist Registration Association. Awarded the Pro Ecclesia Et Pontifice by Pope John XXIII for his services to the church and local Catholic population.

LEHANE, Ollie (1943–1998) racehorse breeder. Best known as the owner of the dual Irish St. Leger winner, *Oscar Schindler*.

O'DRISCOLL, Dr T. J. (Tim) (1908–1998) former director general of Bord Fáilte (1956–71). The first chairman of An Córas Tráchtála (1951) and chairman of An Taisce (1971). Served in the Department of Foreign Affairs (1950–51) and was Irish Ambassador to the Netherlands (1955–56). Father of Democratic Left TD Liz McManus. Set up the Tidy Towns Competition and was executive director of the European Travel Commission (1971–86).

QUAID, Tommy (1956–1999) former Limerick Hurler and trainer. Limerick goalkeeper for 20 years and winner of three National League Titles (1985, 1986 &

1992). Also won an All-Star award (1992), and an All-Ireland runners-up medal in 1980, when beaten by Galway and Railway Cup medals. Killed following an accident at work.

REA, Willie (1939–1998) former amateur and professional boxer.

November 1998

AUSTIN, David (1936–1998) former director of the Jefferson Smurfit Group. Joined the Group in 1969 and was divisional managing director, executive vice-president, marketing and human resources in 1983. Retired in 1987.

BRENNOCK, Col. John former director of the Army School of Music. Joined the Army in 1936, and was appointed the director of its school of music in 1971. High point of his career was as musical conductor for the ceremonies in the Phoenix Park during the Pope's visit in 1979.

CLANCY, Paddy (1922–1998) Irish folk musician and member of the Clancy Brothers and Tommy Makem group. The group was one of the ground-breaking folk groups which emerged in Ireland during the 1960s. Adopted and introduced American Folk, coupled with Irish traditional material. Toured extensively in Ireland and abroad.

CRADDOCK, Tom (1931–1998) former Irish International golfer and golf course architect. Won the Irish Amateur Open in 1958. An international golfer (1955-70), won the Lytham Trophy in 1969, played in the European team Championship on 22 occasions and became Texaco Golf Sports Star of the Year in 1965.

DEMPSEY, Martin (1924–1998) actor and singer and one of the founder members of the Irish National Opera Company. Appeared in many RTÉ programmes including the *Dubliners*.

FITZGIBBON, Denis former RTÉ Radio presenter, known as Din Joe, presented the RTÉ radio programme 'Take the Floor'. Was also Managing Director of Toyota Ireland.

December 1998

BAIRD, Brian (1929–1998) former UTV newsreader and English lecturer at Stranmillis College, Belfast. Also worked for the BBC in Belfast.

GOULDING, Cathal (1922–1998) former IRA Chief of

Staff and leading socialist agitator. Joined Fianna Éireann in the 1930s with Brendan Behan, revived the IRA in Dublin in 1945, appointed chief of staff in 1961. Spent 16 years in prison for his political activities and was the last person to be charged in the Republic with incitement to violence after a graveside oration in 1975. A key figure in the splits of the 1970s that led to the formation of what became the Workers' Party and Provisional Sinn Féin, of which he was highly critical. Regarded those who left the Workers' Party to form Democratic Left as having compromised their socialism.

HEARNE, Maurice (1934–1998) columnist and sub-editor and with Independent Newspapers, retiring in early 1998. Former sub-editor in *The Irish Press*. Worked in London for the Press Association, the *Financial Times* and the *Daily Mirror*.

KEYES, Michael (1936–1998) former Munster rugby footballer. Winner of the Munster Senior and Munster Junior Cups in 1957, capped for Munster in the Interprovincial Championship in 1959 and 1961, president of the Cork Constitution Club (1980-81), also serving as a selector and PRO.

LEAHY, Dr. Patrick (1917–1998) Ireland's leading campaigner for euthanasia. Suffering from cancer, Leahy made headlines in 1998 when he told Irish radio from Thailand that he had gone there to commit suicide to end his suffering. First courted controversy in the 1970s when he admitted prescribing contraceptives for patients and was also a supporter of abortion rights. Later became Ireland's most prominent campaigner for euthanasia, saying he had helped about 50 people to die. Went to Thailand to commit suicide, but discovered euthanasia was illegal there as well. Died in his sleep at home in Dublin.

MALLON, Ita (1908–1998) former *Irish Independent* Woman's page editor until the 1970s and Irish political general news correspondent for the London-based agency *Central News*. Joined the staff of the Irish Independent in 1949 where she worked as a drama critic, book reviewer and feature writer.

McADOO, Dr. Henry (1916–1998) former Church of Ireland Archbishop and theologian. Ordained in 1939, appointed Dean of Cork (1952-62); elected Bishop of Ossory, Ferns and Leighlin (1962) and the Archbishop of Dublin (1977-85). Co-chaired the Anglican-Roman Catholic International Commission.

WAYMAN, Patrick A. astronomer and former director of Dunsink Observatory from 1964, general secretary of the International Astronomical Union (1979-82), senior Professor in the astronomy section of the School of Cosmic Physics of the Dublin Institute for Advanced Studies until his retirement. Wrote *Dunsirk Observatory 1975-1985: A Bicentennial History* in 1987.

January 1999

KELLY, Brother Jerome former superior general of the Presentation Brothers Order (1981). Principal of the Presentation Brothers College in Cork (1969-81). Founded the group Students Harness Aid for the Relief of the Elderly (SHARE) in 1970.

LOWRY, Lord Robert (1919–1999) former Lord Chief Justice for Northern Ireland (1971-88). Called to the Bar of Northern Ireland in 1947, became QC in 1956 and a High Court Judge (1964-71). Chaired the Constitution Convention at Stormont (1975-76). Made a Life Peer in 1979. Worked as Law Lord in London and appointed a Lord of Appeal in Ordinary (1988-94).

MOORE, Brian (1921–1999) novelist and screenwriter. Published more than 20 novels. Although moved from Belfast to America as a young man, many of his books dealt with Irish themes or Irish characters. Among his more widely known books are *The Lonely Passion of Judith Hearne* which was made into a film, *The Feast of Lupercal* (1957), *The Luck of Ginger Coffey* (1960), *The Emperor of Ice-Cream* (1965), *Catholics* (1972, made into a film later), *Black Robe* (1985, made into a film later), *The Magician's Wife* (1997). Won numerous awards and nominated and won may literature prizes.

February 1999

BERNELLE, Agnes (1923–1999) cabaret artiste and actress. Born in Berlin the daughter of a renowned Jewish-Hungarian theatre impresario who gave Marlene Dietrich her first job. The family fled to London where she married Desmond Leslie, heir to Castle Leslie in Monaghan. In 1963 she moved to Ireland and gave a memorable one-woman show, featuring the music of Kurt Weil and Bertolt Brecht at the Dublin Theatre Festival. She performed with Marc Almond, Gavin Friday, Marianne Faithful and many more. Appeared in numerous stage and film productions including *Hear My Song, Sweetie Barrett* and *Still Life*.

BYRNE, P. F. (1922–1999) former Independent newspaper journalist, radio columnist and theatre and film reviewer. Compiled a weekly column of ghost stories for the *Evening Herald* which were later published as books of Irish Ghost Stories. Member of Old Dublin Society, he was editor of its journal.

CARR, Tom (1909–1999) one of Northern Ireland's most respected painters. Exhibited in the Royal Academy Gallery, Oireachtas and RHA and was a member of the Royal Society of Watercolour Painters and an honorary member of the RHA. Winner of the Royal Ulster Academy gold medal (1973) and the Oireachtas landscape award (1976).

JONES, Jack (1918–1999) former *Irish Press* and *Irish Times* journalist. Was features editor for the *Irish Times* in the 1960s, but returned to the *Irish Press* in the in late 1960s as chief sub-editor and assistant editor until his retirement in 1985.

MURDOCH, Dame Iris (1919–1999) novelist and philosopher. Although born in Dublin, regarded as a British writer and philosopher. Studied philosophy under Ludwig Wittgenstein and elected a fellow of St. Anne's College, Oxford, in 1948. An author of 27 novels, her first novel was *Under the Net* (1953). Among her most successful novels are *The Bell* (1958) and her finest work is considered to be *The Sea, The Sea* which won the Booker Prize in 1978. Among her other publications are plays and philosophical and critical studies, including *Metaphysics as a Guide to Morals* (1992). Made a dame in 1987.

TULLY, Jimmy (1975–1999) former Inter-county footballer with Longford. Killed in an accident. Played club football with Fr. Manning Gaels.

UPTON, Pat (1944–1999) Labour TD for Dublin South Central and university lecturer. Labour Party Spokesperson on Science and Technology and Consumer Affairs since June 1997. Senator, Agricultural Panel (1989-92). Elected to the Dáil in 1992: member of parliamentary assembly of the Council of Europe (1994-95), member of Dublin City Council (1991-93), south Dublin County Council (1993-94), General Council of County Councils (1991-96) and the Eastern Health Board (1996).

March 1999

MURRAY, Alf (1915–1999) former GAA president (1964-67). Played senior football with Armagh and won two Railway Cup medals (1942, 1943). Secretary of the Armagh County Board. Represented Armagh on the Ulster Council for 26 years.

O'DWYER, Prof. William Francis (1916–1999) former President of An Bord Altranais (1964-78). Was also president of the Irish Medical Association (1963), the Medical Societies in UCD (1956) and RSCI (1963). Appointed Professor of Medicine, RCSI (1975). Member of many boards including the Medical Registration Council, the National Health Council and the Dublin Regional Hospital Board.

O'SULLIVAN, Tadhg (1927–1999) former Irish Ambassador. Joined the Department of External Affairs (1949), serving in Dublin, Brussels and Berne. Appointed Counsellor to the Permanent Irish Mission in the UN (1961). Appointed Ambassador to Nigeria (1970), Austria (1974), the U.S., the Soviet Union (1985) and France (1987).

RYAN, Noel (1942–1999) chief executive of the Irish Horseracing Authority from January 1995. Obtained law degree from UCD (1960), and joined the Civil Service. Appointed Assistant Secretary at the Department of Justice (1984-85), Secretary of the Department of Foreign Affairs (1985-90) and Director General of the Incorporated Law Society (1990).

April 1999

ACTON, Charles music critic with *The Irish Times* and a leading figure in Irish music. In his 31 years as a critic, covered a wide range of music, from world music through classical music to traditional Irish. Campaigned successfully for Arts Council funding, contemporary music, Irish composers, opera, and RTÉ and sat on the board of governors of the RIAM.

NOONE, Gerry former sports editor with The Irish Times. Played soccer for Bohemians, worked on the *Evening Press* and joined *The Irish Times*, promoted to chief sports sub-editor, assistant sports editor, then deputy and finally sports editor.

ROHAN, Patrick Kilian (1916–1999) former director of Met Éireann. Joined the Meteorological Service in 1940 during the flying-boat era at Foynes. Appointed Meteorological Office chief at Shannon Airport (1948–1970). Played an key role in international aviation meteorology: served as vice-president of the Commission for Aeronautical Meteorology of the World Meteorological Organisation (1964-67), helped create the quick exchange of data for aviation, and became the first chairman of the Meteorological Telecommunications Network for Europe. Made Head of Climatology in Dublin in 1970 and was one of the first to see the computer's potential in weather analysis. Wrote *The Climate of Ireland* (1976) - the first complete guide to Ireland's climate. Made assistant director of the Meteorological Service in 1975 and finally director, became president of the European Centre for Medium Range Weather Forecasts in 1980.

May 1999

McCREA, Sir William (1904–1999) astrophysicist in the fields of relativity and cosmology. Born in Dublin, but grew up in England. In 1929, awarded a Ph.D. from Cambridge and wrote a series of papers on the sun, which were the first accurate models of the atmosphere of a star. In 1934, posited that expanding universe models of general relativity could be derived within a Newtonian framework. Moved to Queen's University Belfast, where he stayed until 1944, after which he took over as professor of mathematics and head of department at Royal Holloway College. Appointed research professor of theoretical astronomy at the University of Sussex in 1966. In the late 1960s, distanced himself from the single Big Bang theory and advanced that a series of bangs occurred at different times and places in the cosmos.

Knighted in 1985. Contributed papers to journals and wrote books on astrophysics and science history.

Ó MUIRÍ, Éamonn (1945–1999) pioneer in Irish language television. Worked for Gael Linn and Conradh na Gaeilge, Joined RTÉ in 1969, fronting the current affairs programme *Féach*. Retained an objective perspective in his reporting during the 1980's Hunger Strike, when many came under pressure to skew reportage. During the 1980s, co-produced documentaries, one of which, *The Heart of the Mater*, won a Jacobs Award. Returned to television journalism, first to *Iris*, then to *Prime Time*. Was heavily involved in the National Union of Journalists and the Irish Heart Transplant Association.

June 1999

DENNEHY, Tim (1919–1999) one of the pioneers of the public relations industry in Ireland. One of the first head of public relations in state-sector bodies. When the Northern Troubles broke in 1969, co-ordinated a team of press officers sent to embassies around the world to give the Irish viewpoint. Set up his own PR firm and was an influential members of the Public Relations Institute of Ireland - was elected its president three times and made a Fellow in 1997. During the 1979 Papal visit, director of the national press centre where 3,000 journalists covered the event, dubbed by Reuters as the best-organised media event it had ever covered.

HUME, Cardinal Basil (1923–1999) Archbishop of Westminster and leader of the Catholic Church in England and Wales. Abbot of the Benedictine monastery at Ampleforth, appointed archbishop of Westminster in 1976. Was very influential in getting the convictions of the Guildford Four and Maguire Seven quashed which led to them being officially deemed victims of a miscarriage of justice. His interest in the case began with a visit to Giuseppe Conlon in December 1978 after which he found it difficult to believe that Conlon was guilty of the crime for which he was imprisoned.

FITZGERALD, Joan (1923–1999) credited with having a huge influence on Irish political life through her marriage to former taoiseach Dr Garret FitzGerald. Actively involved in Dr FitzGerald's career in academia and his two terms as Taoiseach. Known for an astute political intuition - was instrumental in various political appointments like that of Peter Sutherland as European Commissioner. Had an interest in theology, a deep awareness of European culture, and a social conscience. Her illness - lymphodoemia, exacerbated by arthritis - confined her to bed but this in no way diminished her activities. Once said. "It's not good for politicians to come home to adoring wives. They need criticism".

FRASER, Sir Ian (1901–1999) former president of the Royal College of Surgeons in Ireland. Led the team which introduced the use of penicillin on military casualties in 1941. Became senior surgeon in Belfast's Hospitals. Received many honours, including a knighthood and presidencies of the Royal College of Surgeons in Ireland and the British Medical Association. Held links with the Northern Ireland Police Authority and UDR, and was twice the target of IRA bombs. Published his memoir, *Blood, Sweat And Tears,* in 1989.

O'CONNOR, Peter (1912–1999) best known for fighting with the International Brigade in the Spanish Civil War. Fought in the battle of Jarama in February 1937, which claimed the lives of 19 Irishmen, but given a mixed reception on returning home due to the 1930s propaganda about "the Reds in Spain". Took an active part in refounding the Communist Party of Ireland and remained a member until his death. Was also active in the Labour Party. Wrote *A Soldier of Liberty* - an autobiography.

O'KEEFFE, Paddy (1921–1999) former Group Chief Executive of AIB. After the 1970 amalgamation of the AIB, credited with creating new regional structures within the newly-formed bank and expanding the bank abroad - played a leading role in the purchase of The First National Bank of Maryland in the US.

O'KELLY de GALWAY *née Cummins,* **Countess Mary** (1905–1999) only Irish person in the Belgian Resistance during WWII and a survivor of the Nazi concentration camps. Travelled to Brussels to teach and worked as a translator at the Canadian Embassy, establishing contacts with the Resistance. Arrested and interned in camps, the horrific details of which were recorded in the RTÉ radio documentary *In the Shadow of Death.* Decorated by King Leopold of Belgium and General Eisenhower after the war. Married Belgian barrister Count Gui O'Kelly de Galway, a descendant of the Galway Wild Geese and returned to Ireland.

SHANAHAN, Neil (1979–1999) Motor racing driver and one of Ireland motor racing's most promising talents.Took up Formula Ford racing 1600 in 1997 after four successful seasons as a karter. Went on to take 10 titles and won the prestigious RIAC Dunlop Driver of the Year award twice in a row. He was chosen for the Van Diemen works team which launched the careers of Ayrton Senna and Eddie Irvine. Died in a motor racing accident at Oulton Park circuit in Cheshire.

SWEETMAN, William (1903–1999) editor of the *Irish Press* (1937–1951) and District Justice. While the Irish Press' first London Editor, was one of the few journalists to whom Ghandi would give an interview when he visited London. Hired notable young writers during his time as editor: Brendan Behan, Edna O'Brien and Cearbhall Ó Dálaigh. Left the Press in 1951, when Major Vivion de Valera assumed control over editorial policies. Returned to law and appointed a District Justice to Mayo and then Offaly.

WHITELAW, Viscount William (1918–1999) First Secretary of State for Northern Ireland. Sent to Belfast in 1972 to implement direct rule from Westminster. With soaring violence (467 deaths in

1972), entered into a truce with the Provisional IRA, conceding political status for prisoners and having secret talks in London with IRA leaders. However, the initiative floundered, and Whitelaw sent thousands of British soldiers into Catholic areas. Many of his ideas - power-sharing and a Council of Ireland with formal cross-Border links - remained central to the political initiatives that followed. Was Margaret Thatcher's loyal deputy which led her to state the infamous phrase "every prime minister needs a Willie". Elevated to the House of Lords in 1983, was leader of the House until he retired from politics in 1988.

WILSON, Gilbert (1918–1999) Church of Ireland Bishop of Kilmore, Elphin and Ardagh. Ordained in 1942 and continued to work until an advanced age. His works included practical handbooks as well as scholarly and theological books and articles.

July 1999

DEASY, Richard (1916–1999) leader of the National Farmers' Association (NFA). Became leader of the NFA when it confronted the government for better conditions for farmers. Led an historic march for farmers' rights in 1966. The government gave way after a national blockade of roads and railways. Retired from the NFA in 1967 but took part in the October 1998 protest by 40,000 farmers in Dublin.

DUNSANY, Lady Sheila Plunkett (1912–1999) art collector and fashion connoisseur and wife of Baron Dunsany. Best-known as patron of the fashion designer, Sybil Connolly, also collected the works of notable Irish artists, including Jack Yeats. She was also involved with the Multiple Sclerosis Society and the ICA.

GALLAGHER, Major General John (1923–1999) soldier. Served initially in the Western Command and was as an instructor at the Military College. Appointed as Officer Commanding the 1st Infantry Group, which was hastily formed and deployed along the border when the Northern Ireland Troubles erupted in 1969. Served with three UN peacekeeping missions. Promoted to Brigadier General in 1980, Quartermaster General in 1981 and Major General - the second highest rank in the Defence Forces. Retired in 1984. A talented Gaelic footballer, won two Ulster final medals and was a member of the Irish basketball team at the Olympics in London in 1948. Had a special interest in military history and languages. In 1998, at the age of 75, was conferred with a B.Sc. (Hons) in mathematics and received a Master's in mathematics shortly before his death.

KENNEDY, John Fitzgerald Jr (1960–1999) publisher and scion of the famous Irish-American Kennedy dynasty. The only son of the late President John F. Kennedy, featured frequently in press photographs during Kennedy's term in the White House; one of the most famous images of the American century is of him saluting his father's casket. Spent four years as an assistant district attorney but left to publish

George, a popular journal on US politics. It was often speculated that he would run for political office. Killed in an aeroplane accident off the coast of Massachusetts along with his wife and her sister.

MARTIN, Fr Malachi Brendan (1921–1999) novelist and former Jesuit priest. Although born in Kerry and a best-selling novelist here, was better known in the US. Requested a release from his vows in 1964. Moved to New York and was soon established as an author. The idea of a church under threat was a constant theme in his writings - as was the concept of exorcism. Books include *The Final Conclave, Hostage to the Devil: The Possession and Exorcism of Five Living Americans, The Pilgrim, The Encounter,* and *The Jesuits*. At his request, Rome restored his faculty to say Mass. Was also interested in Semitic languages, oriental history, and Jesus in Islamic and Jewish sources.

McCANN, Donal (1943–1999) one of Ireland's most renowned theatre actors. Began his acting career working for the Abbey theatre and moved to RTÉ, appearing in *Strumpet City*. Returned to theatre with acclaimed performances in Brian Friel's *Faith Healer,* and *Translations* as well as O'Casey's *Juno and the Paycock*. Most acclaimed success was his recent portrayal of Thomas Dunne in Sebastian Barry's internationally acclaimed *The Steward of Christendom*. His many film appearances include John Huston's adaptation of Joyce's *The Dead, December Bride, Budawanny,* and *Poitín* - the first Irish language film.

McPHAIL, Tom (1952–1999) former news editor at the *Irish Press* and later, Granada Television, and co-founder of Irish International news agency. Co-founded the agency in 1982 to supply court coverage which required minimal editing for the national media.

O'DONNELL, Dr Mary (1919–1999) one of the pioneers in the treatment of cerebral palsy in Ireland and a director of Cerebral Palsy Ireland. Her most famous "old boy" was Christy Brown, who dedicated one of his plays, *The Guiding Light,* to her.

PILKINGTON, Joe (1940–1999) actor and artist. He is best known for his his role in The Riordans, one of the most popular series on RTÉ in the 1960s and 1970s, playing Eamonn, the young Traveller. Began his acting career in Dublin theatre, and appeared in many films, including *Durango and The American, The Boxer, The Butcher Boy, A Man of No Importance* and his most famous film appearance - *The Ballroom of*

Romance. Received enthusiastic reviews for his part in *The Hanging Gale*, the BBC series about the Great Famine. Moved to west and acquired a reputation as an excellent photographer and a painter.

ROCHE, Tom (1916–1999) co-founder of Roadstone and creator the National Toll Roads. Set up he a gravel business, Castle Sand Company in 1944 which went public in 1949 as Roadstone. Moved to take over the gilt-edged Cement group in 1970 which led to the creation of CRH, headed by former taoiseach Sean Lemass, became non-executive chairman after Lemass died. CRH is one of the largest companies on the Irish Stock Exchange. A visionary in relation to civil engineering projects, formed the National Toll Roads, the company that owns the East-Link and the West-Link toll bridges. Ownership of this company will transfer to the state after 30 years.

August 1999

DEVLIN, Paddy (1925–1999) founding member of the SDLP, trade unionist and a staunch critic of paramilitary violence. Interned in prison (1942–1945) for IRA activities, became a trade union activist and in 1950 joined the Irish Labour Party. Won a council seat in Belfast and won the Falls seat in the 1969 elections to the Stormont parliament. Formed a new political grouping in 1970 with Gerry Fitt and others - the Social Democratic and Labour Party (SDLP). Appointed minister for health and social services in the short-lived 1974 Sunningdale power-sharing executive. Turned to writing when Stormont collapsed and stayed politically involved through the Peace Train organisation. Wrote a book on the fall of the power-sharing executive and another on outdoor relief in Belfast in the inter-war years, as well as his autobiography, *Straight Left*.

HANLON, Supt Frank (1935–1999) former head of the Fraud Squad and press officer for the Garda Síochána. Joined the Garda Síochána in 1956, moved to the Fraud Squad in 1963 and rose through the ranks to head the unit as an inspector. Was a member of a working party on the computerisation of outdated Garda administrative procedures. Appointed public relations officer in 1985 and set about improving the tense relations between Gardaí and the media. His compassionate response to the Air India disaster in 1985 was widely acknowledged, and his work during the Jennifer Guinness kidnapping was highly praised. Video recordings of his press conferences were used in police training across the world. Retired in 1987.

JOHNSON, Nevill (1911–1999) leading Modernist painter associated with the Victor Waddington Galleries in Dublin and the Irish Exhibition of Living Art. Although English in origin, settled in Belfast in 1934. Visited Paris in the mid-1930s, where he saw his first Cubist pictures, which deeply influenced him to the end of his career, together with Surrealism. After WWII, met the Dublin-based gallery-owner, Victor Waddington and accepted a gallery contract from him. His one-man exhibition at the Waddington Galleries in 1946 established him. Showed regularly at the gallery and the annual Irish Exhibition of Living Art until the late 1950s. Published a book of photographs, showing Dublin in the 1950s, *The People's City*, which won an award at the Leipzig International Book Art Fair. Had settled in Dublin and was seen as one of Ireland's leading Modernists. Did not, however, exhibit again until 1964 but was reintroduced to Dublin in 1979. Published an autobiography entitled *The Other Side of Six*.

LAWLOR, Michael J. (1905–1999) former News Editor (Radio) at Radio Éireann and RTÉ (1945–1970). Died August, 1999

LYSAGHT, Liam (1913–1999) former chief state solicitor (1970–1978). Credited with being one of those professional civil servants who built the modern Irish state. Was Chief State Solicitor at the height of the conflict in Northern Ireland. It was during his tenure that Ireland successfully referred a test case against Britain to the European Court of Human Rights alleging the torture of prisoners in Northern Ireland.

McLACHLAN, Peter (1936–1999) former director of the Belfast Voluntary Welfare Society and unionist member for South Antrim in the Northern Ireland assembly, elected in 1973. Strongly supported Brian Faulkner's attempt to set up a power-sharing executive with the nationalist Social Democratic and Labour party. Was also involved as a leader with the Peace People, from which he resigned in 1980. One of his last acts was to urge David Trimble to find a way of implementing the power-sharing provisions of the Belfast Agreement on Northern Ireland.

MOYNIHAN, Dr Maurice (1902–1999) long–serving former governor of the Central Bank, credited with significantly contributing towards building the Ireland's civil service. Joined the Civil Service in 1925 and became secretary to the Fianna Fáil government (1937–1960). As such, he was involved in all government policies and programmes and joined Philip O'Donoghue and John Hearne on the committee set up by de Valera to draft the new Constitution. Appointed governor of the Central Bank and played a key role in revamping Irish banking whereby the Central Bank assumed a pre-eminent role status, with the commercial banks exchanging most of their sterling holdings for Irish currency from the Central Bank. Most importantly, perhaps, was the operation that led to the transfer of the Exchequer Account from the Bank of Ireland to the Central Bank. Was editor of Speeches and Statements by Eamon de Valera 1917-1973 and his history of the Central Bank, *Currency and Central Banking in Ireland 1922-60*, is an accepted authority on the subject.

MURPHY, Myles (1943–1999) aviation navigation expert. Appointed chief air traffic control officer at Shannon Airport and played a major role in ensuring that the Republic was equipped with state-of-the-art air traffic control equipment and systems. Was the first Irishman to be appointed chairman of the North Atlantic Systems Planning Group (1995) and played a key role in making Ireland the first European provider of Reduced Vertical Separation Minima in 1997, doubling the number of flight levels available to aircraft and providing massive fuel savings.

MURRAY, Bishop Donal (1918–1999) former bishop of the diocese in Nigeria. Ordained in 1946 and consecrated bishop of the diocese of Makurdi in 1968. Began a large building programme including cottage hospitals and health clinics, as well as secondary schools. Had the unusual distinction of having established an order of nuns - the Sisters of the Nativity. Raised much of the money for these programmes through the World Mercy charity. Remained as bishop until 1989. Although his diocese was not involved directly in the Biafran war, he gave refuge to many priests, at least one of whom credited him with saving his life.

RENARD-GOULET, Yann (1914–1999) sculptor. Born in Brittany and a passionate Breton nationalist which brought him into conflict with the French authorities. Escaped to Ireland with his family after being condemned to death in absentia. The family became Irish citizens. Won a commission in 1950 to design the Dublin Brigade Memorial for the Custom House and his art course became a recognised qualification for teaching art. Favoured idealistic images of freedom fighters in heroic monuments. His works include the famous Ballyseedy Memorial in Tralee and a bust of Parnell for the House of Commons. Became a member of Aosdána in 1982 and was RHA Professor of Sculpture.

STRONG, Eithne (1923–1999) poet. Worked as a civil servant and a teacher. Married the writer and psychoanalyst Rupert Strong in 1943. As a mother of nine children, returned to Trinity College to study modern languages in 1969. Wrote both in Irish and English throughout her life. A prolific writer, her poetry included: An Gor (1942); Songs of Living (1961); Sarah, in Passing (1974); Cairt Oibre (1980); Flesh: The Greatest Sin (1982); Nobel (1988); An Sagart Pinc (1990) and Spatial Nosing (1993) as well as two novels, *Degrees of Kindred* (1979) and *The Love Riddle* (1993). She gave poetry readings all over the world as well as at home.

September 1999

BARRY, Kevin (1930–1999) engineer and director of the large British building company, Wimpey (1979–1983), and chief executive of Wimpey Highlands Fabricators. His association with Wimpey gave him a vital role in the development of the North Sea oil industry. Developed the project to bring oil ashore from the oil rigs in the Forties field and to build a number of platforms for extracting North Sea oil. Awarded an OBE in 1989.

CROWLEY, Conor (1928–1999) chartered accountant and founding partner of Stokes Kennedy Crowley (now KPMG, one of Ireland's best-known firms). A partner in Kennedy Crowley, founded by his father, played a major role in the development of the accountancy firm's practice and of the business of many of its clients. Involved in advising many of the leading multinational companies which set up in the Republic and in the early years of the IFSC.

GREEN, Richard (1951-1999) vice-chairman of the Irish National Organisation of the Unemployed. Qualified as a carpenter, the economic recession of the 1980s forced him into unemployment. Became involved in various community schemes and started his own business RG Training, which helped people back into employment. Joined the Irish National Organisation of the Unemployed in 1992 and was elected its vice-chairman in 1997. Was seen a critical figure in the organisation and a tireless campaigner for the unemployed and a tireless campaigner against Dublin's drug problem. Was killed with his daughter, Christina (18), when a stolen car crashed into their car. Died 20th September, 1999

HOUSTON, Christina (1913–1999) publications editor at the Royal Irish Academy (RIA). Joined the RIA in 1940. Worked in the conservation laboratory, repairing and cleaning manuscripts (the RIA holds the world's largest collection of Irish-language manuscripts). Became editor in 1967. During her tenure, published numerous papers and catalogues. Retired in 1978.

McAULEY, Charles (1910–1999) noted Ulster artist whose work focused on the Glens of Antrim. Spent most of his life there, and based his subject matter on its landscape and people. His work was brought to the wider audience with the publication by the Glens of Antrim Historical Society of *The Day of the Corncrake* in 1984, in which reproductions of his paintings were set alongside poetry about the Glens by John Hewitt.

MOLLOY, John (1929–1999) actor and revue artist. Regarded as one of Dublin theatre's most versatile performers during the 1960s and 1970s when he performed many popular one-man shows and played in several leading productions. His television work included the RTÉ soap, *Tolka Row*, and a BBC television production of *The Playboy of the Western*

World. Also wrote revues, one-man shows, musicals, and television plays and a novel called *Alive Alive-Oh.* Died in San Francisco where he went to live in 1981.

NACHSTERN, Arthur (1911–1999) violinist with the RTÉ Symphony Orchestra for 45 years. Born in Odessa, studied at the Odessa Conservatoire, played in the Leningrad Philharmonic and Warsaw Philharmonic and Opera Theatre orchestra. Moved to Ireland to join the nascent Radio Éireann Symphony Orchestra along with 25 other foreign musicians. Became an Irish citizen in 1952. Was well-regarded for his technical virtuoso and playing style. Was deputy leader of the orchestra for many years and led it in recording Seán Ó Riada's *Mise Éire.*

WARD, Andrew (1925–1999) the longest serving Secretary of the Department of Justice (1971–1986) and one of the foremost of all Irish public servants. Served in the department at a difficult time - the North was out of control, Anglo-Irish relations were bad, and the department itself had serious internal difficulties. During his term, the scope of the department expanded greatly: Anglo-Irish and North-South relations improved . His major contribution was to the drafting of the Anglo-Irish Agreement in 1985 and his skilled negotiations at that time. Brought about marked improvements in one of the most important government departments and left it in a far healthier state than he had inherited it.

POLITICS

An Argument against the Revision of the Electoral System

By Seán Donnelly

I would like at the outset to state my total opposition to the recent proposals by the Minister for the Environment Mr Noel Dempsey, to revise our electoral system. I believe our present system has served us well and is a fair and democratic one.

One of the proposals is to reduce the number of Dáil Deputies. This would assume we have too many at present and by reducing this number we would get a more efficient service and there would be some financial savings. The number of TDs has risen from 128 (excluding the first Dáil) to 166 since 1981 (*see Table 1*). But the population that these deputies serve has risen from 2,971,992 in 1922 to 3,621,035 at present. In 1957 each TD served 19,172 people which has risen to 21,813 at present and this is the highest since 1923. If we look at the electorate figures the discrepancy is more pronounced as the present figure of 16,514 is well above the 11,000 odd figure in the late 20s early 30s. A similar trend is seen when those who actually vote are taken into account with each TD today representing on average 10,777 actual voters, more than double the 1922 figure. Looking at the average figures for the last 26 elections our present population per seat is 5% above the average. But for the electorate the figures are most striking as the present electorate per seat is over 30% above the historical average.

Looking at these representation figures a strong case can be made for actually increasing the number of Dáil Deputies rather than decreasing them.

(Table 1) ● GENERAL ELECTIONS 1922-1997							
Dáil	Seats	Population	Pop/Seat	Electorate	Elec/Seat	Valid	Valid/Seat
3. 1922	128	2,971,992	23,219	1,031,342	8,057	621,587	4,856
4. 1923	153	2,971,992	19,425	1,784,918	11,666	1,053,955	6,889
5. 1927	153	2,968,420	19,401	1,730,177	11,308	1,146,460	7,493
6. 1927	153	2,968,420	19,401	1,728,093	11,295	1,170,869	7,653
7. 1932	153	2,968,420	19,401	1,691,993	11,059	1,274,026	8,327
8. 1933	153	2,968,420	19,401	1,724,420	11,271	1,386,558	9,062
9. 1937	138	2,955,107	21,414	1,775,055	12,863	1,324,449	9,597
10. 1938	138	2,955,107	21,414	1,697,323	12,299	1,286,259	9,321
11. 1943	138	2,955,107	21,414	1,816,142	13,160	1,331,709	9,650
12. 1944	138	2,955,107	21,414	1,776,950	12,876	1,217,349	8,821
13. 1948	147	2,960,593	20,140	1,757,139	11,953	1,323,083	9,001
14. 1951	147	2,960,593	20,140	1,780,806	12,114	1,328,575	9,038
15. 1954	147	2,898,264	19,716	1,763,209	11,995	1,335,203	9,083
16. 1957	147	2,818,341	19,172	1,738,278	11,825	1,227,020	8,347
17. 1961	144	2,818,341	19,572	1,670,860	11,603	1,172,295	8,141
18. 1965	144	2,884,002	20,028	1,682,569	11,685	1,253,123	8,702
19. 1969	144	2,978,248	20,682	1,735,388	12 051	1,318,954	9,159
20. 1973	144	2,978,248	20,682	1,783,604	12,386	1,346,834	9,353

21. 1977	148	3,368,217	22,758	2,118,606	14,315	1,603,028	10,831
22. 1981	166	3,443,405	20,743	2,275,450	13,708	1,718,212	10,351
23. 1982	166	3,540,643	21,329	2,275,450	13,708	1,668,135	10,049
24. 1982	166	3,540,643	21,329	2,335,153	14,067	1,688,631	10,172
25. 1987	166	3,525,719	21,239	2,445,515	14,732	1,777,165	10,706
26. 1989	166	3,525,719	21,239	2,448,810	14,752	1,656,813	9,981
27. 1992	166	3,621,035	21,813	2,557,036	15,404	1,724,853	10,391
28. 1997	166	3,621,035	21,813	2,741,262	16,514	1,788,985	10,777
Average	151	3,120,044	20,704	1,917,906	12,641	1,374,774	9,067

I would next like to examine how fair our present system has been to date. *Table 2* lists the results for all General Elections since Proportional Representation was first used in 1922. I have examined the results for the major parties, the Non party or Independents and finally the smaller parties. The table shows the % of the first preference votes achieved by the various parties in each election. This is compared with the % share of the seats won, and finally the two results are proportioned.

(Table 2) ● GENERAL ELECTIONS 1922-1997

Elec.	Sts	%v	%s	s/v%	%v	%s	s/v%	%v	%s	s/v%	%v	%s	s/v%	%v	%s	s/v%
1922	128	21.3	28.1	132.0	38.5	45.3	117.7	21.3	13.3	62.4	11.1	7.8	70.4	7.8	5.5	70.1
1923	153	27.4	28.8	105.0	39.0	41.2	105.6	10.6	9.2	86.3	10.9	11.1	101.9	12.1	9.8	81.0
1927	153	26.1	28.8	110.2	27.5	30.7	111.7	12.6	14.4	114.1	14.1	10.5	74.2	19.7	15.7	79.6
1927	153	35.2	37.3	105.8	38.7	40.5	104.7	9.1	8.5	93.4	9.1	8.5	93.4	7.9	5.2	66.2
1932	153	44.5	47.1	105.8	35.3	37.3	105.5	7.7	4.6	59.4	10.5	9.2	87.1	2.0	2.0	98.0
1933	153	49.7	50.3	101.3	30.5	31.4	102.9	5.7	5.2	91.7	5.0	5.9	117.6	9.1	7.2	79.0
1937	138	45.2	50.0	110.6	34.8	34.8	100.0	10.3	9.4	91.5	9.7	5.8	59.8	0.0	0.0	0.0
1938	138	51.9	55.8	107.5	33.3	32.6	97.9	10.0	6.5	65.2	4.7	5.1	107.9	0.0	0.0	0.0
1943	138	41.9	48.6	115.9	23.1	23.2	100.4	15.7	12.3	78.5	9.6	8.0	83.0	9.7	8.0	82.2
1944	138	48.9	55.1	112.6	20.5	21.7	106.0	8.8	5.8	65.9	9.1	8.0	87.6	12.7	9.4	74.2
1948	147	41.9	46.3	110.4	19.8	21.1	106.5	8.7	9.5	109.5	8.3	8.2	98.4	21.3	15.0	70.3
1951	147	46.3	46.9	101.4	25.8	27.2	105.5	11.4	10.9	95.5	9.6	9.5	99.2	6.9	5.4	78.9
1954	147	43.4	44.2	101.9	32.0	34.0	106.3	12.1	12.9	106.8	5.5	3.4	61.8	7.0	5.4	77.7
1957	147	48.3	53.1	109.9	26.6	27.2	102.3	9.1	8.2	89.7	6.6	6.1	92.8	9.4	5.4	57.9
1961	144	43.8	48.6	111.0	32.0	32.6	102.0	11.6	11.1	95.8	6.7	5.6	82.9	5.9	2.1	35.3
1965	144	47.7	50.0	104.8	34.1	32.6	95.7	15.4	15.3	99.2	2.1	1.4	66.1	0.7	0.7	99.2
1969	144	45.7	52.1	114.0	34.1	34.7	101.8	17.0	12.5	73.5	3.2	0.7	21.7	0.0	0.0	35.0
1973	144	46.2	47.9	103.7	35.1	37.5	106.8	13.7	13.2	96.3	3.9	1.4	35.6	1.1	0.0	0.0
1977	148	50.6	56.8	112.2	30.5	29.1	95.3	11.6	11.5	99.0	5.6	2.7	48.3	1.7	0.0	0.0
1981	166	45.3	47.0	103.7	36.5	39.2	107.3	9.9	9.0	91.3	4.3	3.0	70.0	4.0	1.8	45.2
1982	166	47.3	48.8	103.2	37.3	38.0	101.7	9.1	9.0	99.3	3.0	2.4	80.3	3.3	1.8	54.8
1982	166	45.2	45.2	100.0	39.2	42.2	107.6	9.4	9.6	102.5	3.0	1.8	60.2	3.2	1.2	37.7
1987	166	44.1	48.8	110.6	27.1	30.7	113.4	6.4	7.2	113.0	4.4	2.4	54.8	18.0	10.8	60.2
1989	166	44.2	46.4	104.9	29.3	33.1	113.1	9.5	9.0	95.1	3.9	3.0	77.2	13.1	8.4	64.4
1992	166	39.1	41.0	104.8	24.5	27.1	110.6	19.3	19.9	103.0	6.0	3.0	50.2	11.1	9.0	81.4
1997	166	39.3	46.4	118.0	28.0	32.5	116.2	10.4	10.2	98.5	7.0	3.6	51.6	15.3	7.2	47.2
Avg	151	42.7	46.1	108.0	31.3	33.0	105.5	11.4	10.3	90.5	6.8	5.3	78.0	7.8	5.3	67.6

Elec. = Election **Sts** = Seats **%v** = % Vote **%s** = % Seat **s/v%** = Seats / Votes %

As can be seen from the figures Fianna Fáil have always got a bigger share of the seats than their vote should have warranted. The lowest figure they got was a break-even position in November 1992, when they won 45.2% share of the seats with the same share of the vote. For all of the other 25 elections FF got more than 100% with the 1997 figure of 118 one of their best ever and the best achieved by any of the major parties. On average FF got 46% of the seats with just 42.7% of the vote, a factor of 108.0.

Fine Gael has also done well despite not matching their main rival's performance. FG has fallen below the 100% level on 3 occasions, 1938, 1965 and their poorest result 95.3% in 1977, (coincidentally FF's best result). One of FG's best results was in November 1982 when Garrett FitzGerald became Taoiseach having won 42.2% of the seats with 39.2% of the vote. Like FF 1997 was also one of FG's best results as they won 32.5% of the seats with

28% of the vote or a factor of 116.2 well above their historical average of 105.5.

Whereas the 2 major parties have benefited considerably from the PR system the smaller parties have not done so well. The Labour Party has got a bigger share of the seats than votes on only 6 occasions for and average factor of 90.5. The position for the Independents is much gloomier as on most occasions they got fewer seats than their share of the vote warranted.

Thus the present system has benefited the two larger parties in particular. The least that can be said is that it was not a disadvantage to them. The smaller parties including the not so small Labour Party have lost out in this system, but considering that in recent times much of the parties including the small parties have achieved the ultimate aim of participating in Government, then the system has not been too unfair.

If Noel Dempsey's aim is to try and bring all parties to the break-even level (100%) then his attempts are to be welcomed. Somehow or other I cannot see a FF Minister wishing to give away their present huge advantage for the sake of improving their opponents chances. I stopped believing in Santa Claus a long time ago!

One of the reasons put forward by Mr Dempsey for his proposed changes is the fact that TDs are dragged in all directions by the present system in the multi seat constituencies, that this competition between TDs would disappear in a single seat constituency set up. I believe that we already have something very close to that anyway. Most constituencies are divided up among the TDs and they have their own separate areas and strongholds. How often at a count when there is alarm at the poor showing of one of the candidates have we heard "But sure his area hasn't come in yet". For all intents and purposes we already have single seat constituencies.

The final point of Mr Dempsey's proposal I would like to deal with is the introduction of the List System where half or so of the TDs would be selected by that system. The many arguments against this have already been well made. The conclusion to be drawn from this proposal is we need a different type of TD than the one elected by the people i.e. one that is more qualified to deal with Dáil business and leave the mundane constituency work to those other less well talented. I believe this to be anti-democratic. If a person is not capable of being elected then he or she does not deserve to enter the Dáil. Wouldn't we all like to play in the Cup Final without the necessary drudgery of many long nights training! Let the people decide!

In conclusion I believe the present electoral system has served us well and the only possible reason for changing it, is to ensure that Fianna Fáil get an even greater benefit than at present.

Seán Donnelly
October 1999

The author is a political analyst and has recently published a new book Elections '99.

REPUBLIC OF IRELAND

Introduction

NAME OF STATE: Article 4 of the 1937 Constitution states 'The name of the State is Éire, or in the English language, *Ireland"*. From independence in 1922 until the enactment of the constitution, the state was known as Saorstat Éireann or the Irish Free State. The Republic of Ireland Act 1948 allowed for the state to be described as the Republic of Ireland, but Article 4 naming the state as Éire has not been altered.

The name Éire is derived from the name Ériu, a goddess in Irish mythology. Julius Caesar gave Ireland its Latin name when he referred to it as *Hibernia* in the first century BC, while the ancient Greek cartographer Ptolemy referred to Ireland as *Iouernia*.

HEAD OF STATE: The Head of State is the President. Presidential elections are held every seven years and the President is elected by the direct vote of the people. The current president is Mary McAleese *(pictured left)*.

OFFICE OF PRESIDENT: The office and function of the President of Ireland is dealt with in Articles 12 and 13 of the Constitution. The supreme command of the defence forces is vested in the President (subject to the 1954 Defence Act), who also receives and accredits ambassadors. While the President does not have any executive powers and acts mainly on the advice and authority of the government, she/he does hold a limited number of functions. All Bills passed by the Oireachtas are promulgated by the President who may, after consultation with the Council of State*, refer any Bill (excluding money bills) to the Supreme Court to attest its constitutionality. In the event of the President becoming incapacitated the Council of State will carry out the functions of the Presidency.

The members of the Council of State are the incumbent Taoiseach, Tánaiste, Ceann Comhairle, Cathaoirleach of the Seanad, Attorney General, President of the High Court and the Chief Justice. Other members are any previous Taoisigh, President, or Chief Justice willing to serve and up to seven nominees of the President.

THE PRESIDENT AND THE DÁIL: The President appoints the Taoiseach on the nomination of Dáil Éireann and appoints government ministers on the advice of the Taoiseach. The Taoiseach also advises the President on accepting the resignations of ministers and on the summoning and dismissing of the Dáil. The President reserves the right, as yet unexercised, to refuse the dissolution of the Dáil. The President can be impeached by a two thirds majority of the Oireachtas.

ELECTIONS: The President is elected by the direct vote of the people. Irish citizens resident in the Republic are entitled to vote in a Presidential election. A Presidential candidate must be an Irish citizen over the age of 35 years. The duration of a term of office is seven years and no more than two terms can be served.

PARLIAMENT: The Republic of Ireland is a parliamentary democracy governed by the Oireachtas which consists of the President and the Legislature. The Legislature has two houses, Dáil Éireann, which is a house of representatives, and Seanad Éireann, which is a senate or upper house. The basis of the political system was set out in the Constitution of Ireland, enacted by referendum in July 1937. The power of the Oireachtas is vested in the people.

Members of government are usually elected by the Dáil during the first meeting after an election. A new government however, can be formed without an election. Nominations for all ministerial positions are proposed by the Taoiseach and voted on by the Dáil, and on approval by the Dáil the President formally appoints the ministers. The government,which acts collectively, is the executive power in the state and must, under the constitution, consist of no less than seven and no more than fifteen members. Ministers of State are also elected by the Dáil and appointed by the President and while not members of the Government assist Ministers. At present there are 15 ministers and 17 Ministers of State.

The sole and exclusive power of making laws is vested in parliament. The government presents its proposals to either the Dáil or Seanad in the form of Bills or Motions. These must pass five stages (or readings) in whichever House they are initiated. Non-government members are permitted to initiate Bills which are referred to as Private Members' Bills. The introduction is the first stage while the general principles of the Bill are debated in the second stage. On completion of the House goes into committee – or a specific Oireachtas committee meets–to consider the Bill in detail and substantial amendments are permitted. The fourth stage is the report of the committee and further amendments are permitted while the final stage is a general debate on the contents of the Bill. When the Bill is passed by a House it is then sent to the other House where it goes through a similar process. Finally, when it completes this process it is sent to the President for promulgation. Bills must be passed within 90 days by the Seanad with the exception of Money Bills which must be passed within 21 days.

The Dáil has exclusive responsibility for initiating Money Bills or Bills to amend the Constitution. The Seanad has only limited powers in amending Money Bills and any Bill passed by the Dáil which is rejected by the Seanad may be enacted by a resolution of the Dáil. Similarly any amendments which the Seanad makes to which the Dáil does not agree or if a Bill is neither rejected or accepted within 90 days the Dáil can enact it by resolution.

ELECTIONS: General Elections must be held at least once every five years. One hundred and sixty-six Teachtaí Dála (members of the Dáil) are elected directly in 41 constituencies by Irish and British citizens resident in the Republic of Ireland by a system of proportional representation and a single transferable vote. Seanad Éireann has 60 Seanadoirí (Senators); 11 are nominated by the Taoiseach, 6 are elected by the graduates of Trinity College Dublin and the National University of Ireland, and the remaining 43 are elected by five panels. The electoral constituency of the Seanad comprises of incoming TDs, the outgoing members of the Seanad, and members of county councils and county borough councils. Candidates for the Dáil or Seanad must be aged 21 or older while persons become eligible to vote at 18 years of age.

THE NATIONAL FLAG: The national flag is the tricolour of green, white and orange and enshrined in the Constitution, it has been the official flag since independence in 1922. The tricolour is rectangular, the width being twice the depth. The colours are of equal size, vertically disposed with the green closest to, and the orange furthest from, the staff. The colours signify the union between older Gaelic and Anglo-Norman Ireland (green) and the newer Protestant Planter Ireland (orange), while the white, in the words of Thomas Francis Meagher 'signifies a lasting truce between the Orange and the Green'. In 1848 Meagher received the tricolour as a gift from the citizens of France, on whose flag the Irish tricolour is based. Initially a flag of the 'Young Ireland' movement, it came to be identified as the national flag in the aftermath of the 1916 Rising when it was flown from the General Post Office.

THE ARMS OF STATE: The Arms of State have no official statute or regulation, but the President's seal of office has an heraldic harp engraved on it. It is also emblazoned on the President's standard as a gold harp with silver strings on a sky blue background. The harp, modelled on the 14th century Brian Boru harp, is depicted on the coinage and banknotes of the state and is used by all government departments.

THE NATIONAL ANTHEM: The national anthem is Amhrán na bhFiann (The Soldier's Song). Peadar Kearney (1883-1942) wrote the lyrics, and Patrick Heeney (1881-1911) helped compose the music. Composed in 1907 and first published in 1912 in the newspaper *Irish Freedom* it was immediately adopted by the Irish Volunteers and formally adopted as the national anthem in 1926 replacing 'God Save Ireland'.

Government System

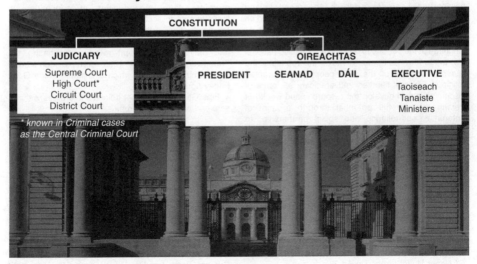

CONSTITUTION

JUDICIARY	OIREACHTAS
Supreme Court High Court* Circuit Court District Court	PRESIDENT SEANAD DÁIL EXECUTIVE Taoiseach Tanaiste Ministers

* known in Criminal cases as the Central Criminal Court

POLITICAL PARTIES

Main Parties

Fianna Fáil
13 Upper Mount Street, Dublin 2.
Tel. (01) 6761551 Fax 6785690
email: info@fiannafail.ie
website: www.fiannafail.ie

Origins: Founded in 1926 by Éamon de Valera. Fianna Fáil (Soldiers of Destiny) was made up of anti-treaty Sinn Féin members, the party did not sit in the Oireachtas until 1927.
First Leader: Éamon de Valera (1926-59).
Current Party Leader: An Taoiseach Bertie Ahern TD since 1994 *(pictured above)*.
Party Chairman: Dr. Rory O'Hanlon TD.
General Secretary: Martin Mackin.
Seats: Dáil Éireann: 76; Seanad Éireann: 30; European Parliament: 6; County Councils/Corporations: 381.
European Alliance: Union for Europe
Former Taoisigh: Six. Éamon de Valera (re-elected six times), Seán Lemass (re-elected twice), Jack Lynch (re-elected twice), Charles Haughey (re-elected three times), Albert Reynolds and Bertie Ahern.
In Government: Fianna Fáil was responsible for the drafting of the Constitution in 1937, maintaining Irish neutrality during World War II, the accession of Ireland into the European Economic Community in 1973, the introduction of major housing developments in the 1960s, and the signing of the Good Friday Agreement in 1998.
Aims: The aims, as set out in 1926, and still broadly holding today, are to establish an agreed Ireland through inclusive political talks with structures based on partnership and equality throughout the island; to restore and promote the Irish language as a living language of the people; to develop a distinctive national life within the European context, incorporating the diverse traditions of the Irish people; to guarantee religious and civil liberties and eradicate all forms of discrimination; to develop the resources and wealth of Ireland to their full potential through a spirit of enterprise, self-reliance and social partnership; to protect the natural environment and heritage of Ireland; to maintain a balance between town and country and between the regions; to promote the family and a wider sense of social responsibility; and to reform the laws and institutions of state, making them more humane and caring.

The party aims to maintain Ireland's status as a sovereign nation within the European Union and pledges to retain neutrality but to take part in genuine peace-keeping missions.

FINE GAEL
51 Upper Mount Street, Dublin 2.
Tel: (01) 6198444 Fax: 6625046

email: finegael@finegael.com
website: www.finegael.com

Origins: Founded in 1933 following the amalgamation of Cumann na nGaedheal, the Centre Party and the Army Comrades Association (the Blueshirts). Fine Gael translates as 'Tribes of the Irish People'
First Leader: General Éoin O'Duffy (1933-34).
Current Party Leader: John Bruton TD since 1990 *(pictured above)*.
Party Chairman: Phil Hogan TD.
General Secretary: Tom Curran.
Seats: Dáil Éireann: 54; Seanad Éireann: 16; European Parliament: 4; County Councils/Corporations: 278.
European Alliance: European People's Party.
Former Taoisigh: Four - John A. Costello (re-elected twice), Liam Cosgrave, Garret FitzGerald (re-elected twice) and John Bruton
In Government: Fine Gael, as major party in coalition governments, was instrumental in the Declaration of the Republic of Ireland in 1949, the signing of the Sunningdale Agreement in 1973, the convening of the New Ireland Forum in 1983 and the signing of the Anglo-Irish Agreement in 1985. The party is committed to constitutional change and has introduced referenda which legalised divorce (1995) and approved the denial of bail to likely re-offenders (1996).
Aims: Fine Gael has a policy of facilitating enterprise through a mixture of state encouragement for private enterprise and direct state involvement. It wants to see decision-making devolved to the appropriate level, particularly involving women and young people, and it promotes fairer opportunities in education, an improvement in social welfare provisions and greater tax equity. On Northern Ireland, the party recognises and respects both the nationalist and unionist traditions and played a significant role in negotiating the Frameworks Document in 1995 which provided a basis for the multi-party talks which culminated in the Good Friday Agreement.

Fine Gael believes that Ireland's future lies within a safe and prosperous Europe.

THE LABOUR PARTY
17 Ely Place, Dublin 2.
Tel. (01) 6612615 Fax: 6612640
email: head_office@labour.ie
website: www.labour.ie

Origins: Founded in 1912 by James Connolly, Jim Larkin and William O'Brien as political wing of Irish Trade Union Congress, the party merged with Democratic Left in January 1999.
First Leader: Tom Johnston (1922-27).
Current Party Leader: Ruairi Quinn TD since 1997 *(pictured above)*.

Party Chairmen: John O'Brien and Pat Brady.
General Secretary: vacant.
Seats: Dáil Éireann: 21; Seanad Éireann: 4; European Parliament: 1; County Councils/Corporations: 83.
European Alliance: Party of European Socialists.
Former Taoisigh: None.

In Government: The party has formed part of seven different coalition governments with its leader holding the position of Tánaiste on each occasion. In government, the party's achievements reflect those of their coalition partners. From 1993 until June 1997, when in government, Labour TDs held the important ministerial portfolios of Finance, Foreign Affairs and Education, among others. Labour Party members were key players in the Northern Ireland Peace Process.

Aims: A socialist party, it hopes to use the four main tenets of socialism, namely, freedom, equality, community and democracy, to build a just society. Twelve trade unions are affiliated to the party, representing 50% of all trade union members in the state.

The party's successful campaign on behalf of its nominated candidate, Mary Robinson, in the 1990 presidential campaign remains one of their finest achievements to date.

Democratic Left merged with the Labour Party in January 1999 with its leader, Proinsias De Rossa, becoming president of the enlarged Labour Party.

PROGRESSIVE DEMOCRATS
25 South Frederick Street, Dublin 2
Tel: (01) 6794399   Fax: 6794757
email: progdems@iol.ie
website: www.iol.ie/pd/

Origins: Formed in 1985 by Des O'Malley, Mary Harney and other former members of Fianna Fáil following a split in that party.
First Leader: Des O'Malley (1985-93).
Current Party Leader: Tánaiste Mary Harney TD since 1993 *(pictured above)*.
Party Chairman: Alderman Declan McDonnell.
General Secretary: John Higgins.
Seats: Dáil Éireann: 4, Seanad Éireann: 4, County Councils/Corporations: 25.
Former Taoisigh: None.
In Government: The party is currently in government and was in government once before, in a coalition with Fianna Fáil (1989-92). As junior coalition partners, they played an important part in Ireland's presidency of the EC (July-December 1990) and in securing the ratification of the Maastricht Treaty in 1992 and negotiating the Good Friday Agreement.

Aims: The party advocates the lowering of tax rates, the abolition of employees' PRSI, the tightening of bail laws, a new constitution and Bill of Rights for Northern Ireland, increased access to adult education and the creation of more prison places. The party favours further integration with Europe and supports the devolution of some decision-making to local level.

THE GREEN PARTY
5A Upper Fownes Street, Dublin 2.
Tel: (01) 6790012   Fax: 6797168
email: greenpar@iol.ie
website: www.greenparty.ie
Origins: Founded in 1981 as the Ecology Party of Ireland, renamed The Green Party in 1986.
Current Co-ordinator: Phil Kearney.
The functions of General Secretary and Party Chairperson are carried out by a 14 member co-ordinating committee.
General Secretary: Functions carried out by a 14 member co-ordinating committee.
Seats: Dáil Éireann: 2; European Parliament: 2; County Councils/Corporations: 8.
European Alliance: Greens.
Former Taoisigh: None.
In Government: The party has never been in government.

Aims: The Green Party supports open government, locally based decision-making, the use of renewable energy sources, recycling, neutral peace keeping in Northern Ireland, workers' co-operatives and small businesses, and the wider use of public transport. The party is opposed to the depopulation of rural areas and consequent over-crowding in cities, pollution, the exploitation of animals, the control of industry by large national and multi-national companies, nuclear power and weapons, land and property speculation, the exploitation of the Third World, and both state and paramilitary violence in Northern Ireland.

SINN FÉIN
See entry in Northern Ireland Political Parties.

Other Parties

Party	Address	Phone
Communist Party of Ireland	James Connolly House, 43 East Essex Street, Temple Bar, D2	01 6711943
Christian Solidarity Party	54a Booterstown Avenue, Blackrock, Co. Dublin	01 2880273
Independent Fianna Fáil	Plunkett O'Boyle Terrace, Letterkenny, Co. Donegal	074 27754
The National Party	16 Revington Park, North Circular Road, Limerick	061 326599
The Natural Law Party	39 Pembroke Lane, Ballsbridge, D4	01 6689773
Muíntír na hÉireann	87 Griffith Avenue, D9	01 2831484
Republican Sinn Féin	Teach Dáithí Ó Conaill, 223 Parnell St, D1	01 8729747
Socialist Party	141 Thomas Street, D8	01 6772592
Socialist Workers' Party	105 O'Hogan Road, Ballyfermot, D10	
The Workers' Party	28 Gardiner Pace, D1	01 8740716

The Government

Taoiseach Bertie Ahern (£111,203)

Tánaiste, and **Minister for Enterprise, Trade and Employment** Mary Harney (£95,624)

Finance
Charlie McCreevy

Foreign Affairs
David Andrews

Justice, Equality and Law Reform
John O'Donoghue

Education and Science
Mícheál Martin

Health and Children
Brian Cowen

Environment & Local Government
Noel Dempsey

Social, Community & Family Affairs
Dermot Ahern

Public Enterprise
Mary O'Rourke

Agriculture and Food
Joe Walsh

Defence
Michael Smith

Marine and Natural Resources
Michael Woods

Arts, Heritage, Gaeltacht and the Islands
Síle de Valera

Tourism, Sport and Recreation
Jim McDaid

Government Chief Whip and Minister of State
Seamus Brennan

Minister of State
Bobby Molloy

Attorney General Michael McDowell SC *(£88,748)*
Ministers (each £88,747)

Ministers of State

Department	Special Responsibilities	Minister
Agriculture and Food	Livestock Breeding and Horticulture	Noel Davern
Agriculture and Food	Food	Ned O'Keefe
Arts, Heritage, Gaeltacht and the Islands	Gaeltacht and the Islands	Eamon Ó Cuiv
Defence		Seamus Brennan
Education and Science		Noel Treacy
Education and Science		Frank Fahey
Education and Science	Adult Education, Youth Affairs and School Transport	Willie O'Dea
Enterprise, Trade and Employment	Science and Technology	Noel Treacy
Enterprise, Trade and Employment	Labour Affairs, Consumer Rights and International Trade	Tom Kitt
Environment and Local Government	Housing and Urban Renewal	Bobby Molloy
Environment and Local Government	Environmental Protection and Awareness and the Environmental Protection Agency	Danny Wallace
Finance	Office of Public Works	Martin Cullen
Foreign Affairs	Overseas Development Assistance and Human Rights	Liz O'Donnell
Health and Children	Children	Frank Fahey
Health and Children	Food Safety and Older People	Tom Moffat
Justice, Equality and Law Reform		Frank Fahey
Justice, Equality and Law Reform	Equality and Disabilities	Mary Wallace
Marine and Natural Resources	Aquaculture and Forestry	Hugh Byrne
Public Enterprise	Energy	Joe Jacob
Tourism, Sport and Recreation	Local Development	Chris Flood
Taoiseach	Government Chief Whip	Seamus Brennan
To the Government		Bobby Molloy

Ministers of State (each £60,813)

Members of the Oireachtas

The Twenty-Eighth Dáil

TDs are listed alphabetically. Constituency is in **bold type** and results are from 1997 General Election except where a by-election taken place held since.
1st pref= 1st preference votes received.

TEACHTAÍ DÁLA (each £38,035)
AHEARN, Theresa (b. 1951) *FG* Ballindoney, Grange, Clonmel, Co. Tipperary. Tel. 052 38142. **Tipperary South** since 1989, 1st pref: 8,494, elected 3rd ct.
AHERN, Bertie (b. 1951) *FF* 'St. Lukes', 161 Lower Drumcondra Road, Dublin 9. Tel. 01 837 4129. Dublin Finglas 1977-81, **Dublin Central** since 1981, 1st pref: 12,175, elected 1st ct.
AHERN, Dermot (b. 1955) *FF* The Crescent, Blackrock, Dundalk, Co. Louth. Tel. 042 21473. **Louth** since 1987, 1st pref: 10,192, elected 1st ct.
AHERN, Michael (b. 1949) *FF* 'Libermann', Barryscourt, Carrigtwohill, Co. Cork. Tel. 021 883592. **Cork East** since 1982 (February) 1st pref: 6,959, elected 6th ct.
AHERN, Noel (b. 1944) *FF* 25 Church Avenue, Drumcondra, Dublin 9. Tel. 01 832 5911. **Dublin North-West** since 1992, 1st pref: 11,075, elected 1st ct.
ALLEN, Bernard (b. 1944) *FG* 7 Mount Prospect, Shanakiel, Cork. Tel. 021 303068. **Cork North-**

Central since 1981, 1st pref: 7,746, elected 1st ct.
ANDREWS, David (b. 1935) *FF* 102 Avoca Park, Blackrock, Co. Dublin. Tel. 01 283 5755. **Dún Laoghaire** since 1965, 1st pref: 8,933, elected 3rd ct.
ARDAGH, Seán (b. 1947) *FF* 168 Walkinstown Road, D12. Tel. 01 456 8736. **Dublin South-Central** since 1997, 1st pref: 4,634, elected 15th ct.
AYLWARD, Liam (b. 1952) *FF* Aghaviller, Hugginstown, Co. Kilkenny. Tel. 056 68703. **Carlow-Kilkenny** since 1977, 1st pref: 11,849, elected 1st ct.
BARNES, Monica (b. 1936) *FG* 5 Arnold Park, Glenageary, Co. Dublin. Tel. 01 285 3751. **Dún Laoghaire** 1982-92 and since 1997, 1st pref: 7,576, elected 7th ct.
BARRETT, Seán (b. 1944) *FG* 'Avondale', 3 Ballinclea Road, Killiney, Co. Dublin. Tel. 01 285 2077. **Dún Laoghaire** since 1981, 1st pref: 9,223, elected 1st ct.
BELL, Michael (b. 1936) *Lab* 122 Newfield Estate, Drogheda, Co. Louth. Tel. 041 38573. **Louth** since November 1982, 1st pref: 4,725, elected 12th ct.
BELTON, Louis J. (b. 1943) *FG* Kenagh, Co. Longford. Tel. 043 22245. Longford-Westmeath 1989-92, **Longford-Roscommon** since 1997, 1st pref: 5,696, elected 8th ct.
BLANEY, Harry (b. 1928) *Ind* Rossnakill, Co. Donegal. Tel. 074 59014. **Donegal North-East** since 1997, 1st pref: 7,484, elected 4th ct.
BOYLAN, Andrew (b. 1939) *FG* Derrygarra, Butlersbridge, Co. Cavan. Tel. 049 31747 **Cavan-Monaghan** since 1987, 1st pref: 4,894, elected 7th ct.

BRADFORD, Paul (b. 1963) *FG* Mourneabbey, Mallow, Co. Cork. Tel. 022 29375. **Cork East** since 1989, 1st pref: 7,859, elected 7th ct.

BRADY, Johnny (b. 1948) *FF* Springville, Kilskyre, Kells, Co. Meath. Tel. 046 40852. **Meath** since 1997, 1st pref: 7,372, elected 10th ct.

BRADY, Martin (b. 1947) *FF* 37 Grangemore Drive, Dublin 13. Tel. 01 848 4509. **Dublin North-East** since 1997, 1st pref: 5,018, elected 10th ct.

BRENNAN, Matt (b. 1936) *FF* Ragoora, Cloonacool, Tubbercurry, Co. Sligo. Tel. 071 85136. **Sligo-Leitrim** since February 1982, 1st pref: 6,461, elected 5th ct.

BRENNAN, Séamus (b. 1948) *FF* 31 Finsbury Park, Churchtown, D14. Tel. 01 295 7171. **Dublin South** since 1981, 1st pref: 8,861, elected 6th ct.

BRISCOE, Ben (b. 1934) *FF* Newtown, Celbridge, Co. Kildare. Tel. 01 628 8426. **Dublin South-West** 1965-69, Dublin South-Central 1969-77, Dublin Rathmines West 1977-81, **Dublin South-Central** since 1981, 1st pref: 4,762, elected 15th ct.

BROUGHAN, Tommy (b. 1947) *Lab* 23 Riverside Road, Coolock, Dublin 17. Tel. 01 847 7634. **Dublin North-East** since 1992, 1st pref: 3,447, elected 8th ct.

BROWNE, John (b. 1936) *FG* Ballinacarrig, Carlow. Tel. 0503 33033. **Carlow-Kilkenny** since 1989, 1st pref: 6,409, elected 8th ct.

BROWNE, John (b. 1948) *FF* Kilcannon, Enniscorthy, Co. Wexford. Tel. 054 35046. **Wexford** since November 1982, 1st pref: 8,646, elected 7th ct.

BRUTON, John (b. 1947) *FG* Cornelstown, Dunboyne, Co. Meath. Tel. 01 825 5573. **Meath** since 1969, 1st pref: 13,037, elected 1st ct.

BRUTON, Richard (b. 1953) *FG* 210 Griffith Avenue, Drumcondra, Dublin 9. Tel. 01 836 8185. **Dublin North-Central** since 1982, 1st pref: 8,196, elected 5th ct.

BURKE, Liam (b. 1928) *FG* 9 Lavets Quay, Cork. Tel. 021 551651. Cork City North-West 1969-77, Cork City 1979*-81, **Cork North-Central** 1981-89 and since 1992, 1st pref: 5,527, elected 9th ct.

BURKE, Ulick (b. 1943) *FG* Eagle Hill, Abbey, Loughrea, Co. Galway. Tel. 0509 45218. **Galway East** since 1997, 1st pref: 6,931, elected 5th ct.

BYRNE, Hugh (b. 1943) *FF* Air Hill, Fethard-on-Sea, Co. Wexford. Tel. 051 397125. **Wexford** 1981-89 and since 1992, 1st pref: 7,003, elected 8th ct.

CALLELY, Ivor (b. 1958) *FF* 7 St. Lawrence Road, Clontarf, Dublin 3. Tel. 01 833 0350. **Dublin North-Central** since 1989, 1st pref: 11,190, elected 1st ct.

CAREY, Donal (b. 1937) *FG* 3 Thomond Villas, Clarecastle, Ennis, Co. Clare. Tel. 065 29191. **Clare** since 1982 (Feb), 1st pref: 7,781, elected 7th ct.

CAREY, Pat (b. 1947) *FF* 69 Bourne View, Ashbourne, Co. Meath. Tel. 01 835 0544. **Dublin North-West** since 1997, 1st pref: 6,188, elected 2nd ct.

CLUNE, Deirdre (b. 1959) *FG* Adare, Rochestown Road, Cork. Tel. 021 364934. **Cork South-Central** since 1997, 1st pref: 4,602, elected 9th ct.

COLLINS, Michael (b. 1940) *FF* Red House Hill, Patrickswell, Co. Limerick. Tel. 061 355081. **Limerick West** since 1997, 1st pref: 6,985, elected 6th ct.

CONNAUGHTON, Paul (b. 1944) *FG* Mountbellew, Ballinasloe, Co. Galway. Tel. 0905 79249. **Galway East** since 1981, 1st pref: 6,445, elected 5th ct.

COOPER–FLYNN, Beverley (b. 1966) *FF* 2 Manor Village, Westport Road, Castlebar, Co. Mayo. Tel. 094 26800. **Mayo** since 1997, 1st pref: 8,353, elected 7th ct.

COSGRAVE, Michael J. (b. 1938) *FG* 22 College Street, Baldoyle, Dublin 13. Tel. 01 832 2554. Dublin Clontarf 1977-81, **Dublin North-East** 1981-92 and since 1997, 1st pref: 4,173, elected 8th ct.

COUGHLAN, Mary (b. 1965) *FF* The Lodge Cranny, Inver, Co. Donegal. Tel. 073 36511. **Donegal South-West** since 1987, 1st pref: 6,597, elected 6th ct.

COVENEY, Simon (b. 1972) *FG* Laharn, Minane Bridge, Co. Cork. Tel. 021 887227. **Cork Central** since 1998,* 1st pref: 16,212, elected 3rd ct.

COWEN, Brian (b. 1960) *FF* Ballard, Tullamore, Co. Offaly. Tel. 0506 52047. **Laois-Offaly** since 1984,* 1st pref: 10,865, elected 1st ct.

CRAWFORD, Seymour (b. 1944) *FG* Drumkeen, Aghabog, Monaghan. Tel. 047 54038. **Cavan-Monaghan** since 1992, 1st pref: 6,552, elected 7th ct.

CREED, Michael (b. 1963) *FG* Codrum, Macroom, Co. Cork. Tel. 026 41177. **Cork North-West** since 1989, 1st pref: 8,041, elected 2nd ct.

CULLEN, Martin (b. 1954) *FF* Abbey House, Abbey Road, Ferrybank, Waterford. Tel. 051 851112. **Waterford** 1987-89 and since 1992, 1st pref: 5,353, elected 9th ct.

CURRIE, Austin (b. 1939) *FG* 'Tullydraw', Ballyowen Lane, Lucan, Co. Dublin. Tel. 01 626 5047. **Dublin West** since 1989, 1st pref: 5,256, elected 9th ct.

D'ARCY, Michael (b. 1934) *FG* 7 Avenue Court, Gorey, Co. Wexford. Tel. 055 28177. **Wexford** 1977-87, 1989-92 and since 1997, 1st pref: 6,561, elected 7th ct.

DALY, Brendan (b. 1940) *FF* Cooraclare, Kilrush, Co. Clare. Tel. 065 59040. **Clare** 1973-92 and since 1997, 1st pref: 7,420, elected 9th ct.

DAVERN, Noel (b. 1945) *FF* Tannersrath, Fethard Road, Clonmel, Co. Tipperary. Tel. 052 22991. **Tipperary South** 1969-81 and since 1987, 1st pref: 8,995, elected 1st ct.

De ROSSA, Proinsias (b. 1940) *Lab* 5 Main Street, Finglas, Dublin 11. Tel. 01 6183003. **Dublin North-West** since 1982, 1st pref: 3,701, elected 10th ct.

De VALERA, Síle (b. 1954) *FF* 9 Chapel Lane, Ennis, Co.Clare. Tel. 065 21100. Dublin mid county 1977-81, **Clare** since 1987, 1st pref: 8,025 elected 7th ct.

DEASY, Austin (b. 1936) *FG* Kilrush, 'Marquis', Dungarvan, Co. Waterford. Tel. 051 293115. **Waterford** since 1977, 1st pref: 7,335, elected 7th ct.

DEENIHAN, Jimmy (b. 1952) *FG* Finuge, Lixnaw, Co. Kerry. Tel. 068 40235. **Kerry North** since 1987, 1st pref: 8,689, elected 2nd ct.

DEMPSEY, Noel (b. 1953) *FF* Newtown, Trim, Co. Meath. Tel. 046 31146. **Meath** since 1987, 1st pref: 8,701, elected 7th ct.

DENNEHY, John (b. 1940) *FF* Avondale, Westside Estate, Togher, Cork. Tel. 021 962908. **Cork South-Central** 1987-92 and since 1997, 1st pref: 6,524, elected 9th ct.

DOHERTY, Seán (b. 1944) *FF* Coothall, Boyle, Co. Roscommon. Tel. 079 67005. **Roscommon–Leitrim** 1977-81, Roscommon 1981-89, Longford-

Roscommon since 1992, 1st pref: 5,768, elected 7th ct.

DUKES, Alan (b. 1945) *FG* Tullywest, Kildare. Tel. 045 521912. Kildare 1981-97, **Kildare South** since 1997, 1st pref: 6,260, elected 3rd ct.

DURKAN, Bernard J. (b. 1945) *FG* Timard, Maynooth, Co. Kildare. Tel. 01 628 6063. Kildare 1981-February 1982 and November 1982-97, **Kildare North** since 1997, 1st pref: 6,653, elected 3rd ct.

ELLIS, John (b. 1952) *FF* Fenagh, Ballinamore, Co. Leitrim. Tel. 078 44252. **Sligo-Leitrim** 1981-November 1982 and since 1987, 1st pref: 7,051, elected 5th ct.

ENRIGHT, Tom (b. 1940) *FG* 3 John's Mall, Birr, Co. Offaly. Tel. 0509 20839. **Laois-Offaly** 1969-92 and since 1997, 1st pref: 8,375, elected 5th ct.

FAHEY, Frank (b. 1951) *FF* 4 Carrig Bán, Menlo, Galway. Tel. 091 771020. **Galway West** Feb. 1982-92 and since 1997, 1st pref: 9,321, elected 1st ct.

FARRELLY, John V. (b. 1954) *FG* Hurdlestown, Kells, Co. Meath. Tel. 046 41290. **Meath** 1981-92 and since 1997, 1st pref: 5,348, elected 10th ct.

FERRIS, Michael (b. 1931) *Lab* Rosanna, Tipperary. Tel. 062 52265. **Tipperary South** since 1989, 1st pref: 5,681, elected 5th ct.

FINUCANE, Michael (b. 1943) *FG* Ardnacrohy, Newcastle West, Co. Limerick. Tel. 069 62742. **Limerick West** since 1989, 1st pref: 5,476, elected 7th ct.

FITZGERALD, Frances (b. 1950) *FG* 116 Georgian Village, Castleknock, Dublin 15. Tel. 01 821 1796. **Dublin South-East** since 1992, 1st pref: 5,501, elected 9th ct.

FLANAGAN, Charles (b. 1956) *FG* Glenlahan, Stradbally Road, Portlaoise, Co. Laois. Tel. 0502 60707. **Laois-Offaly** since 1987, 1st pref: 8,104, elected 5th ct.

FLEMING, Seán (b. 1958) *FF* 'Silveracre', Castletown, Portlaoise, Co. Laois. Tel. 0502 32692. **Laois-Offaly** since 1997, 1st pref: 5,481, elected 5th ct.

FLOOD, Chris (b. 1947) *FF* 22 Birchview Lawn, Kilnamanagh, Tallaght, Dublin 24. Tel. 01 451 8574. **Dublin South-West** since 1987, 1st pref: 5,195, elected 7th ct.

FOLEY, Denis (b. 1934) *FF* 2 Staughton's Row, Tralee, Co. Kerry. Tel. 066 21174. **Kerry North** 1981-89 and since 1992, 1st pref: 5,376, elected 4th ct.

FOX, Mildred (b. 1971) *Ind* Lower Calary, Kilmacanogue, Co. Wicklow. Tel. 01 287 6386. **Wicklow** since 1995,* 1st pref: 5,590, elected 9th ct.

GILDEA, Thomas (b. 1939) *Ind* Stranaglough, Glenties, Co. Donegal. Tel. 075 51757. **Donegal South-West** since 1997, 1st pref: 5,592, elected 6th ct.

GILMORE, Eamon (b. 1955) *Lab* 1 Corbawn Close, Shankill, Co. Dublin. Tel. 01 282 1363. **Dún Laoghaire** since 1989, 1st pref: 7,534, elected 7th ct.

GORMLEY, John (b. 1959) *GP* 71 Stella Gardens, Irishtown, Dublin 4. Tel. 01 660 9148. **Dublin South-East** since 1997, 1st pref: 4,296, elected 11th ct.

GREGORY, Tony (b. 1947) *Ind* 5 Sackville Gardens, Ballybough, Dublin 3. Tel. 01 618 3488. **Dublin Central** since 1982 (February), 1st pref: 5,261, elected 7th ct.

HANAFIN, Mary (b. 1959) *FF* 7 Oaklands Drive, Rathgar, Dublin 6. Tel. 01 283 6533. **Dún Laoghaire** since 1997. 1st pref: 5,079, elected 7th ct.

HARNEY, Mary (b. 1953) *PD* 11 Serpentine Terrace, Ballsbridge, Dublin 4. Tel. 01 676 5033. **Dublin South-West** since 1981, 1st pref: 4,713, elected 7th ct

HAUGHEY, Seán (b. 1961) *FF* Chapelfield Lodge, Baskin Lane, Kinsealy, Dublin 17. Tel. 01 845 0111. **Dublin North-Central** since 1992, 1st pref: 7,760, elected 2nd ct.

HAYES, Brian (b. 1969) *FG* 27 The Dale, Kingswood Heights, Tallaght, Dublin 24. Tel. 01 462 6545. **Dublin South-West** since 1997, 1st pref: 6,487 elected 5th ct.

HEALY–RAE, Jackie (b. 1931) *Ind* Main Street, Kilgarvan, Co. Kerry. Tel. 064 85315. **Kerry South** since 1997, 1st pref: 7,220, elected 5th ct.

HIGGINS, Jim (b. 1945) *FG* Devlis, Ballyhaunis, Co. Mayo. Tel. 0907 31140. Mayo East 1987-97, **Mayo** since 1997, 1st pref: 6,945, elected 7th ct.

HIGGINS, Joe (b. 1949) *SP* 155 Briarwood Close, Mulhuddart, Dublin 15. Tel. 01 820 1753. **Dublin West** since 1997, 1st pref: 6,496, elected 6th ct.

HIGGINS, Michael D. (b. 1941) *Lab* Letteragh, Rahoon, Circular Road, Galway. Tel. 091 524513. **Galway West** 1981-November 1982 and since 1987, 1st pref: 4,856 elected 11th ct.

HOGAN, Philip (b. 1960) *FG* Grovine, Kilkenny. Tel. 056 61572. **Carlow-Kilkenny** since 1989, 1st pref: 9,642, elected 1st ct.

HOWLIN, Brendan (b. 1956) *Lab* Whiterock Hill, Wexford. Tel. 053 24036. **Wexford** since 1987, 1st pref: 9,510, elected 1st ct.

JACOB, Joe (b. 1939) *FF* Main Street, Rathdrum, Co. Wicklow. Tel. 0404 46528. **Wicklow** since 1987, 1st pref: 6,150, elected 8th ct.

KEAVENEY, Cecilia (b. 1968) *FF* 'Loreto', Moville, Co. Donegal. Tel. 077 82177. **Donegal North-East** since 1995,* 1st pref: 8,317, elected 4th ct.

KELLEHER, Billy (b. 1968) *FF* Ballyphilip, White's Cross, Glanmire, Cork. Tel. 021 821045. **Cork North-Central** since 1997, 1st pref: 5,419, elected 11th ct.

KENNEALLY, Brendan (b. 1955) *FF* 38 Viewmount Park, Waterford. Tel. 051 855964. **Waterford** since 1989, 1st pref: 5,971, elected 9th ct.

KENNY, Enda (b. 1951) *FG* Tucker Street, Castlebar, Co. Mayo. Tel. 094 25027.Mayo West 1975*-97, **Mayo** since 1997, 1st pref: 8,568, elected 7th ct.

KILLEEN, Tony (b. 1952) *FF* Kilnaboy, Corofin, Co. Clare. Tel. 065 27895. **Clare** since 1992, 1st pref: 8,169, elected 7th ct.

KIRK, Séamus (b. 1945) *FF* Rathiddy, Knockbridge, Dundalk, Co. Louth. Tel. 042 31032. **Louth** since November 1982, 1st pref: 5,667, elected 9th ct.

KITT, Michael P. (b. 1950) *FF* Castleblakeney, Ballinasloe, Co. Galway. Tel. 0905 78148. **Galway North East** 1975*-77, Galway East since 1981, 1st pref: 5,436, elected 5th ct.

KITT, Tom (b. 1952) *FF* 3 Pine Valley Drive, Rathfarnham, Dublin 16. Tel. 01 493 8200. **Dublin South** since 1987, 1st pref: 9,904, elected 1st ct.

LAWLOR, Liam (b. 1945) *FF* Somerton, Lucan, Co. Dublin. Tel. 01 628 0507. **Dublin West** 1977-81,

February-November 1982 and since 1987, 1st pref: 4,241, elected 9th ct.

LENIHAN, Brian (b. 1959) *FF* 'Longwood', Somerton Road, Strawberry Beds, Dublin 20. Tel. 01 821 4058. **Dublin West** since 1996,* 1st pref: 6,842, elected 6th ct.

LENIHAN, Conor (b. 1963) *FF* 6 Aylmer Road, Newcastle, Co. Dublin. Tel. 01 458 7276. **Dublin South-West** since 1997, 1st pref: 4,436, elected 7th ct.

LOWRY, Michael (b. 1954) *Ind* Glenreigh, Holycross, Thurles, Co. Tipperary. Tel. 0504 43182. **Tipperary North** since 1987, 1st pref: 11,638, elected 1st ct.

MARTIN, Micheál (b. 1960) *FF* 'Lios Laoi', 16 Silver Manor, Ballinlough, Cork. Tel. 021 295218. **Cork South-Central** since 1989, 1st pref: 9,652, elected 1st ct.

McCORMACK, Pádraic (b. 1942) *FG* 3 Renmore Park, Galway. Tel. 091 753992. **Galway West** since 1989, 1st pref: 7,221, elected 7th ct.

McCREEVY, Charlie (b. 1949) *FF* Hillview House, Kilcullen Road, Naas, Co. Kildare. Tel. 01 6288912. **Kildare** 1977-97, Kildare North since 1997, 1st pref: 6,905 elected 4th ct.

McDAID, James (b. 1949) *FF* 2 Sylvan Park, Letterkenny, Co. Donegal. Tel. 074 21652. **Donegal North-East** since 1989 1st pref: 6,538, elected 5th ct.

McDOWELL, Derek (b. 1958) *Lab* 3 Dunluce Road, Clontarf, D3. Tel. 01 833 6138. **Dublin North-Central** since 1992, 1st pref: 2,848, elected 11th ct.

McGAHON, Brendan (b. 1936) *FG* Annaverna, Ravensdale, Dundalk, Co. Louth. Tel. 042 32620. **Louth** since November 1982, 1st pref: 4,346, elected 12th ct.

McGENNIS, Marian (b. 1953) *FF* 44 Bramley Walk, Castleknock, D15. Tel. 01 821 2340. **Dublin Central** since 1997, 1st pref: 3,132, elected 10th ct.

McGINLEY, Dinny (b. 1945) *FG* Bunbeg, Letterkenny, Co. Donegal. Tel. 075 31719. **Donegal South-West** since 1982, 1st pref: 5,679, elected 6th ct.

McGRATH, Paul (b. 1948) *FG* Carna, Irishtown, Mullingar, Co. Westmeath. Tel. 044 40746. Longford-Westmeath 1989-92, **Westmeath** since 1992, 1st pref: 5,218, elected 4th ct.

McGUINNESS, John (b. 1955) *FF* Windsmoor, Brooklawn, Ballyfoyle Road, Kilkenny. Tel. 056 70581. **Carlow-Kilkenny** since 1997, 1st pref: 5,990, elected 8th ct.

McMANUS, Liz (b. 1947) *Lab* 1 Martello Terrace, Bray, Co. Wicklow. Tel. 01 286 8407. **Wicklow** since 1992, 1st pref: 5,226, elected 9th ct.

MITCHELL, Gay (b. 1951) *FG* 192 Upper Rathmines Road, Dublin 6. Tel. 01 490 3744. **Dublin South-Central** since 1981, 1st pref: 8,910, elected 1st ct.

MITCHELL, Jim (b. 1946), *FG* 4 Rathdown Crescent, Terenure, Dublin 6. Tel. 01 490 4574. Dublin Ballyfermot 1977-81, Dublin West 1981-92, **Dublin Central** since 1992, 1st pref: 5,185, elected 10th ct.

MITCHELL, Olivia (b. 1947) *FG* 18 Ballawley Court, Dundrum, Dublin 16. Tel. 01 295 3033. **Dublin South** since 1997, 1st pref: 8,775, elected 8th ct.

MOFFATT, Tom (b. 1940) *FF* Ballina House, Castle Road, Ballina, Co. Mayo. Tel. 096 22868. Mayo East 1992-97, **Mayo** since 1997, 1st pref: 5,735, elected 8th ct.

MOLLOY, Robert (b. 1936) *PD* Rockbarton, Salthill, Galway. Tel. 091 521765. **Galway West** since 1965, 1st pref: 5,914, elected 11th ct.

MOLONEY, John (b. 1953) *FF* 27 Patrick Street, Mountmellick, Co. Laois. Tel. 0502 24391. **Laois-Offaly** since 1997, 1st pref: 8,271, elected 4th ct.

MOYNIHAN, Donal (b. 1968) *FF* Gortnascarty, Ballymakeera, Macroom, Co. Cork. Tel. 026 45019. **Cork North-West** November 1982-89 and since 1992, 1st pref: 7,867, elected 3rd ct.

MOYNIHAN, Michael (b. 1941) *FF* Meens, Kiskeam, Mallow, Co. Cork. Tel. 029 76200. **Cork North-West** since 1997, 1st pref: 8,299, elected 2nd ct.

MOYNIHAN–CRONIN, Breeda (b. 1953) *Lab* 10 Muckross Grove, Killarney, Co. Kerry. Tel. 064 34993. **Kerry South** since 1992, 1st pref: 4,988, elected 7th ct.

NAUGHTEN, Denis (b. 1973) *FG* Ardkennan, Drum, Athlone, Co. Roscommon. Tel. 0902 37100. **Longford-Roscommon** since 1997, 1st pref: 6,652, elected 7th ct.

NEVILLE, Dan (b. 1946) *FG* Kiltannan, Croagh, Co. Limerick. Tel. 061 396351. **Limerick West** since 1997, 1st pref: 7,026, elected 6th ct.

NOONAN, Michael (b. 1943) *FG* 18 Gouldavoher Estate, Fr. Russell Road, Limerick. Tel. 061 229350. **Limerick East** since 1981, 1st pref: 10,092, elected 1st ct.

Ó CAOLÁIN, Caoimhghín (b. 1953) *SF* 21 Dublin Street, Monaghan. Tel. 047 82917. **Cavan-Monaghan** since 1997, 1st pref: 11,531, elected 1st ct.

Ó CUÍV, Eamon (b. 1950) *FF* Corr na Móna, Co. na Gaillimhe. Tel. 092 48021. **Galway West** since 1992, 1st pref: 8,250, elected 1st ct.

O'DEA, Willie (b. 1952) *FF* 2 Glenview Gardens, Farranshore, Co. Limerick. Tel. 061 54488. **Limerick East** since February 1982, 1st pref: 12,581, elected 1st ct.

O'DONNELL, Liz (b. 1956) *PD* 23 Temple Gardens, Rathmines, Dublin 6. Tel. 01 4910363. **Dublin South** since 1992 1st pref: 5,444, elected 8th ct.

O'DONOGHUE, John (b. 1956) *FF* Garranearagh, Caherciveen, Co. Kerry. Tel. 066 72413. **Kerry South** since 1987, 1st pref: 7,204, elected 5th ct.

O'FLYNN, Noel (b. 1951) *FF* 'Melvindale House', Coolowen, Blarney, Co. Cork. Tel. 021 382500. **Cork North-Central** since 1997, 1st pref: 4,943, elected 11th ct.

LEAS CEANN COMHAIRLE
£60,813
O'HANLON, Rory (b. 1934) *FF* Carrickmacross, Co. Monaghan. Tel. 042 61530. **Cavan-Monaghan** since 1977, 1st pref: 7,325, elected 7th ct.

O'KEEFFE, Batt (b. 1945) *FF* 8 Westcliffe, Ballincollig, Co. Cork. Tel. 021 871393. **Cork South-Central** 1987-89 and since 1992, 1st pref: 7,279, elected 7th ct.

O'KEEFFE, Jim (b. 1941) *FG* Old Chapel, Bandon, Co.

Cork. Tel. 023 41399. **Cork South-West** since 1977, 1st pref: 7,454, elected 3rd ct.

O'KEEFFE, Ned (b. 1942) *FF* Ballylough, Michelstown, Co. Cork. Tel. 022 25285. **Cork East** since 1982 (November), 1st pref: 8,737, elected 1st ct.

O'KENNEDY, Michael (b. 1936) *FF* Gortlandroe, Nenagh, Co. Tipperary. Tel. 067 31484. **Tipperary North** 1969-81, February 1982-1992 and since 1997, 1st pref: 9,895, elected 2nd ct.

O'MALLEY, Des (b. 1939) *PD* 11 Cecil Street, Limerick. Tel. 01 4962565. **Limerick East** since 1968, 1st pref: 4,358, elected 9th ct.

O'ROURKE, Mary (b. 1937) *FF* 'Aisling', Arcadia, Athlone, Co. Westmeath. Tel. 0902 75065. **Longford-Westmeath** 1982-92, Westmeath since 1992, 1st pref: 7,262, elected 3rd ct.

O'SHEA, Brian (b. 1944) *Lab* 61 Sweetbriar Lawn, Tramore, Co. Waterford. Tel. 051 381913. **Waterford** since 1989, 1st pref: 5,271, elected 9th ct.

O'SULLIVAN, Jan (b. 1950) *Lab* 7 Lanahone Avenue, Corbally, Limerick. Tel. 061 312316. **Limerick East** since 1998,* 1st pref: 10,619, elected 5th ct.

OWEN, Nora (b. 1945) *FG* 17 Ard na Mara, Malahide, Co. Dublin. Tel. 01 845 1041. **Dublin North** 1981-87 and since 1989, 1st pref: 5,956, elected 7th ct.

CEANN COMHAIRLE (£88,747)

PATTISON, Seamus (b. 1936) *Lab* 6 Upper New Street, Kilkenny. Tel. 056 21295. **Carlow-Kilkenny** since 1961, 1st pref: 9,026, elected 8th ct.

PENROSE, William (b. 1956) *Lab,* Ballintue, Ballynacargy, Mullingar, Co. Westmeath. Tel. 044 73264. **Westmeath** since 1992, 1st pref: 8,037, elected 2nd ct.

PERRY, John (b. 1956) *FG* Main Street, Ballymote, Co. Sligo. Tel. 071 83372. **Sligo-Leitrim** since 1997, 1st pref: 5,786, elected 6th ct.

POWER, Seán (b. 1960) *FF* Castlekealy, Caragh, Naas, Co. Kildare. Tel. 045 432289. **Kildare** 1989-97, Kildare South since 1997, 1st pref: 5,665, elected 4th ct.

QUINN, Ruairí (b. 1946) *Lab* 23 Strand Road, Sandymount, Dublin 4. Tel. 01 260 2852. **Dublin South-East** 1977-81, Dublin South-East since 1982 (February), 1st pref: 6,113, elected 10th ct.

RABBITTE, Pat (b. 1949) *Lab* 56 Monastery Drive, Clondalkin, Dublin 22. Tel. 01 459 3191. **Dublin South-West** since 1989, 1st pref: 5,094, elected 7th ct.

REYNOLDS, Albert (b. 1932) *FF* Mount Carmel House, Dublin Road, Longford. Tel. 043 45070. **Longford-Roscommon** since 1992, Longford-Westmeath since 1977-92, 1st pref: 8,742, elected 3rd ct.

REYNOLDS, Gerry (b. 1961) *FG* Tully, Ballinamore, Co. Leitrim. Tel. 078 44016. **Sligo-Leitrim** 1989-92 and since 1997, 1st pref: 6,743, elected 6th ct.

RING, Michael (b. 1953) *FG* The Paddock, Westport, Co. Mayo. Tel. 098 25734. **Mayo West** 1994*-97, Mayo since 1997, 1st pref: 10,066, elected 3rd ct.

ROCHE, Dick (b. 1947) *FF* 2 Herbert Terrace, Herbert Road, Bray, Co. Wicklow. Tel. 01 286 3211. **Wicklow** 1987-92 and since 1997, 1st pref: 6,101, elected 8th ct.

RYAN, Eoin (b. 1953) *FF* 19 Vavasour Square, Sandymount, Dublin 4. Tel. 01 660 0082. **Dublin South-East** since 1992, 1st pref: 6,494, elected 7th ct.

RYAN, Seán (b. 1943) *Lab* 1 Burrow Road, Portrane, Co. Dublin. Tel. 01 618 3432. **Dublin North** 1989-97 and since 1998,* 1st pref: 11,012, elected 14th ct.

SARGENT, Trevor (b. 1960) *GP* 37 Tara Cove, Baile Brigín, Co. Átha Cliath. Tel. 01 841 2371. **Dublin North** since 1992 1st pref: 5,614, elected 7th ct.

SHATTER, Alan (b. 1951) *FG* 57 Delbrook Manor, Dundrum, D16. Tel. 01 298 3045. **Dublin South** since 1981, 1st pref: 8,094, elected 8th ct.

SHEEHAN, P.J. (b. 1933) *FG* Main Street, Goleen, Co. Cork. Tel. 028 35236. **Cork South-West** since 1981, 1st pref: 8,008, elected 3rd ct.

SHORTHALL, Róisín (b. 1954) *Lab* 12 Iveragh Road, Gaeltacht Park, Whitehall, Dublin 9. Tel. 01 837 0563. **Dublin North-West** since 1992, 1st pref: 4,084, elected 10th ct.

SMITH, Brendan (b. 1956) *FF* 3 Carrickfern, Cavan, Co. Cavan. Tel. 049 62366. **Cavan-Monaghan** since 1992, 1st pref: 8,998, elected 6th ct.

SMITH, Michael (b. 1940) *FF* Lismackin, Roscrea, Co. Tipperary. Tel. 0505 43157. **Tipperary North** 1969-73, 1977-February 1982, and since 1987, 1st pref: 6,999, elected 7th ct.

SPRING, Dick (b. 1950) *Lab* Cloonanorig, Tralee, Co. Kerry. Tel. 066 25337. **Kerry North** since 1981, 1st pref: 10,699 elected, 1st ct.

STAGG, Emmet (b. 1944) *Lab* 736 Lodge Park, Straffan, Co. Kildare. Tel. 01 627 2149. Kildare 1987-97, **Kildare North** since 1997, 1st pref: 5,964, elected 5th ct.

STANTON, David (b. 1957) *FG* Geragh Cross, Coppingerstown, Midleton, Co. Cork. Tel. 021 632867. **Cork East** since 1997, 1st pref: 5,117, elected 8th ct.

TIMMINS, Billy (b. 1959) *FG* Shrughaun, Baltinglass, Co. Wicklow. Tel. 0508 81655. **Wicklow** since 1997, 1st pref: 5,171, elected, 9th ct.

TREACY, Noel (b. 1952) *FF* Gurteen, Ballinasloe, Co. Galway. Tel. 0905 77094. **Galway East** since 1982,* 1st pref: 6,531, elected 5th ct.

WADE, Eddie (b. 1948) *FF* Cahernorry, Drombanna, Co. Limerick. Tel. 061 351467. **Limerick East** since 1997, 1st pref: 4,798, elected 8th ct.

WALL, Jack (b. 1945) *Lab* Castlemitchell, Athy, Co. Kildare. Tel. 0507 32874. **Kildare South** since 1997, 1st pref: 5,834, elected 5th ct.

WALLACE, Dan (b. 1942) *FF* 13 Killeen's Place, Farranree, Cork. Tel. 021 307465. **Cork North-Central** since 1982 (November), 1st pref: 5,273, elected 10th ct.

WALLACE, Mary (b. 1959) *FF* Ennistown, Fairyhouse Road, Ratoath, Co. Meath. Tel. 01 825 6259. **Meath** since 1989, 1st pref: 7,669, elected 8th ct.

WALSH, Joe (b. 1943) *FF* 5 Emmet Square, Clonakilty, Co. Cork. Tel. 023 33575. **Cork South-West** 1977-81 and since 1982 (February), 1st pref: 7,586, elected,

3rd ct.

WOODS, Michael J. (b. 1935) *FF* 13 Kilbarrack Grove, Dublin 5. Tel. 01 832 3357. **Dublin North-East** since 1977, 1st pref: 5,735, elected 7th ct.

WRIGHT, G.V. (b. 1947) *FF* 58 The Moorings, Malahide, Co. Dublin. Tel. 01 845 2642. **Dublin North** 1987-89 and since 1997, 1st pref: 7,007, elected 5th ct.

YATES, Ivan (b. 1959) *FG* Blackstoops, Enniscorthy, Co. Wexford. Tel. 054 33793. **Wexford** since 1981, 1st pref: 10,024, elected 1st ct.

*First Elected at by-election

FORMER MEMBERS OF 28TH DÁIL

Jim Kemmy (Lab) Limerick East, died 25 September 1997.

Ray Burke (FF) Dublin North, resigned 7 October 1997.

Hugh Coveney (FG) Cork South Central, died 14 March 1998.

Pat Upton (Lab) Dublin South Central, died 22 February 1999.

The Twenty-First Seanad

Senators are listed alphabetically and the panel to which they belong is in **bold type**.

SENATORS each £24,068

BOHAN, Eddie (b. 1932) *FF* 18 Orwell Park, Dublin 6. Tel. 01 475 4068. **Industrial & Commercial Panel.**

BONNER, Enda (b. 1949) *FF* Gweedore Road, Dungloe, Co. Donegal. Tel. 074 21722. **Taoiseach's Nominee.**

BURKE, Paddy (b. 1955) *FG* 161 Knockaphunta, Westport Road, Castlebar, Co. Mayo. Tel. 094 22568. **Agricultural Panel.**

CAFFERY, Ernie (b. 1936) *FG* Garden Street, Ballina, Co. Mayo. Tel. 096 22352. **Industrial & Commercial Panel.**

CALLANAN, Peter *FF* Ballymountain, Innishannon, Co. Cork. Tel. 021 775192. **Agricultural Panel.**

CASSIDY, Donie (b. 1945) *FF* Church Street, Castlepollard, Co. Westmeath. Tel. 044 61176. **Labour Panel.**

CHAMBERS, Frank (b. 1949) *FF* Main Street, Newport, Co. Mayo. Tel. 098 41145. **Taoiseach's Nominee.**

COGHLAN, Paul (b. 1944) *FG* 95 New Street, Killarney, Co. Kerry. Tel. 064 31733. **Industrial & Commercial Panel.**

CONNOR, John (b. 1944) *FG* Cloonshanville, Frenchpark, Co. Roscommon. Tel. 0907 70046. **Agricultural Panel.**

COOGAN, Fintan (b. 1944) *FG* Menlo Park, Galway. Tel. 091 764282. **Administrative Panel.**

Leas Cathaoirleach £35,372
COSGRAVE, Liam T. (b. 1956) *FG* Leinster House, Kildare Street, Dublin 1. Tel. 01 288 5575. **Industrial & Commercial Panel.**

COSTELLO, Joe (b. 1945) *Lab* 75 Lr. Sean McDermott Street, Dublin 1. Tel. 01 836 5698. **Administrative Panel.**

COX, Margaret (b. 1963) *FF* 7 Fr. Griffin Road, Galway. Tel. 091 586892. **Industrial & Commercial Panel.**

CREGAN, Denis (b. 1940) *FG* 7 Elm Grove, Ballinlough, Cork. Tel. 021 291863. **Labour Panel.**

CREGAN, John *FF* Church Street, Drumcollogher, Co. Limerick. Tel. 01 6183028. **Labour Panel.**

DARDIS, John (b. 1945) *PD* Belmont House, Newbridge, Co. Kildare. Tel. 045 431665. **Taoiseach's Nominee.**

DOYLE, Joe (b. 1936) *FG* 14 Simmonscourt Terrace, Donnybrook, Dublin 4. Tel. 01 269 2391. **Administrative Panel.**

DOYLE, Avril (b. 1949) *FG* Kitestown House, Crossabeg, Co. Wexford. Tel. 053 42873. **Agricultural Panel.**

FARRELL, Willie (b. 1928) *FF* 5 Mullaghmore Road, Clifoney, Co. Sligo. Tel. 071 63119. **Industrial & Commercial Panel.**

FINNERAN, Michael (b. 1947) *FF* Feevagh Dysart, Ballinasloe, Co. Roscommon. Tel. 0903 22245. **Administrative Panel.**

FITZGERALD, Liam (b. 1949) *FF* 117 Tonlegee Road, Raheny, Dublin 5. Tel. 01 847 0632. **Labour Panel.**

FITZGERALD, Tom (b. 1939) *FF* Dingle Heights, Ballinaboola, Dingle, Co. Kerry. Tel. 066 51543. **Taoiseach's Nominee.**

FITZPATRICK, Dermot (b. 1940) *FF* 18 Navan Road, Dublin 7. Tel. 01 838 7515. **Taoiseach's Nominee.**

GALLAGHER, Pat (b. 1963) *Lab* 8 Hophill Avenue, Tullamore, Co. Offaly. Tel. 0506 52744. **Industrial & Commercial Panel.**

GIBBONS, Jim (b. 1954) *PD* St Anne's, Athy Road, Carlow. Tel. 0503 43657. **Taoiseach's Nominee.**

GLYNN, Camillus (b. 1941) *FF* Newbrook Road, Cloonmore, Mullingar, Co. Westmeath. Tel. 044 40116. **Administrative Panel.**

HANAFIN, Des (b. 1930) *FF* Parnell Street, Thurles, Co. Tipperary. Tel. 0504 21338. **Labour Panel.**

HAUGHEY, Edward *FF* Ballyedmond Castle, Rostrevor, Co. Down. Tel. 08016937 38706. **Taoiseach's Nominee.**

HAYES, Tom (b. 1952) *FG* Cahervillahow, Golden, Cashel, Co. Tipperary. Tel. 062 72194. **Agricultural Panel.**

HAYES, Maurice *Ind* 5 Bullseye Park, Downpatrick, BT30 6RX. Tel. 01 618 3418. **Taoiseach's Nominee.**

HENRY, Mary (b. 1940) *Ind* 12 Burlington Road, Dublin 4. Tel. 01 668 3663. **University of Dublin.**

JACKMAN, Mary (b. 1943) *FG* 5 Newtown, Castletroy, Limerick. Tel. 061 335511. **Labour Panel.**

KEOGH, Helen (b. 1951) *PD* 12 Beech Court, Killiney, Co. Dublin. Tel. 01 285 8433. **Taoiseach's Nominee.**

KETT, Tony (b. 1951) *FF* 54 Whitethorn Road, Artane, Dublin 5. Tel. 01 831 8821. **Administrative Panel.**

KIELY, Rory (b. 1934) *FF* Cloncrippa, Feenagh, Kilmallock, Co. Limerick. Tel. 063 85033. **Agricultural Panel.**

KIELY, Dan (b. 1943) *FF* Doonard, Tarbert, Co. Kerry. Tel. 068 36163. **Labour Panel.**

LANIGAN, Mick (b. 1938) *FF* St Judes, Chapel Avenue, Kilkenny. Tel. 056 22650. **Industrial &**

Commercial Panel.

LEONARD, Ann (b. 1969) ***FF*** Stranagarvagh, Smithboro, Co.Monaghan. Tel. 047 57020. **Taoiseach's Nominee.**

LYDON, Don (b. 1938) ***FF*** 16 Stillorgan Park Avenue, Stillorgan, Co. Dublin. Tel. 01 288 8741. **Labour Panel.**

MANNING, Maurice (b. 1943) ***FG*** 13 Haddington Place, Dublin 4. Tel. 01 660 8058. **Cultural & Educational Panel.**

McDONAGH, Jarlath (b. 1945) ***FG*** Sligo House, Turloughmore, Co. Galway. Tel. 091 797143. **Labour Panel.**

MOONEY, Paschal (b. 1947) ***FF*** Carrick Road, Drumshanbo, Co. Leitrim. Tel. 078 41236. **Cultural & Educational Panel.**

MOYLAN, Pat (b. 1946) ***FF*** Cuba Avenue, Banagher, Co. Offaly. Tel. 0509 51113. **Agricultural Panel.**

CATHAOIRLEACH £44,886
MULLOOLY, Brian (b. 1935) ***FF*** Church Street, Strokestown, Co. Roscommon. Tel. 078 33550. **Labour Panel.**

NORRIS, David (b. 1944) ***Ind*** 18 North Great George's Street, Dublin 1. Tel. 01 872 4614. **University of Dublin.**

Ó MURCHÚ, Labhras (b. 1939) ***FF*** An Boithrin Glas, Caiseal Mumhan, Co. Thiobraid Arann. Tel. 062 61552. **Cultural & Educational Panel.**

O'BRIEN, Francis (b. 1943) ***FF*** Latton, Castleblayney Co Monaghan. Tel. 042 41152. **Agricultural Panel.**

O'DONOVAN, Denis (b. 1955) ***FF*** Montrose House, Slip, Bantry, Co. Cork. 027 51541. **Industrial & Commercial Panel.**

O'DOWD, Fergus (b. 1948) ***FG*** 24 St. Mary's Villas, Drogheda, Co. Louth. Tel. 041 33392. **Administrative Panel.**

O'MEARA, Kathleen (b. 1960) ***Lab*** Lisheen, Portroe, Nenagh. Co Tipperary. Tel. 067 34190. **Agricultural Panel.**

O'TOOLE, Joe (b. 1947) ***Ind*** Kilsallaghan, Co. Dublin. Tel. 01 835 1338. **National University of Ireland.**

ORMONDE, Ann ***FF*** 2 Arburn Road, Dublin 4. Tel. 01 260 1577. **Cultural & Educational Panel.**

QUILL, Mairin (b. 1936) ***PD*** 1 Wellesley Terrace, Wellington Road, Cork. Tel. 021 551677. **Taoiseach's Nominee.**

QUINN, Fergal (b. 1936) ***Ind*** Leinster House, Kildare Street, Dublin. Tel. 01 618 3222. **National University of Ireland.**

RIDGE, Therese (b. 1941) ***FG*** 4 St. Patrick's Avenue, Clondalkin, Dublin 22. Tel. 01 457 3438. **Labour Panel.**

ROSS, Shane (b. 1949) ***Ind*** Leinster House, Kildare Street, Dublin 2. Tel. 01 282 1896. **University of Dublin.**

RYAN, Brendan (b. 1946) ***Ind*** Simon Community, Anderson Quay Cork. Tel. 021 502213. **National University of Ireland.**

TAYLOR–QUINN, Madeline (b. 1951) ***FG*** Frances Street, Kilrush Co. Clare. Tel. 065 51656. **Cultural & Educational Panel.**

WALSH, Jim ***FF*** Montgarrett Castle, New Ross, Co. Wexford. Tel. 051 421771. **Agricultural Panel.**

FORMER MEMBERS OF 21st SEANAD
Sean Ryan (Lab) elected to Dáil Éireann 13.03.98.
Paddy McGowan (FF) died 04.10.99

The European Parliament

AHERN, Nuala (b. 1949) ***GP, Greens*** 5 Oaklands, Greystones, Co. Wicklow. Tel. 01 287 6574. **Leinster** 1st pref: 47,184, elected 3rd ct.

ANDREWS, Niall (b. 1938) ***FF, UFE*** 43 Molesworth St, Dublin 2. Tel. 01 679 4368. **Dublin** 1st pref: 44,176, elected 7th ct.

BANOTTI, Mary (b. 1939) ***FG, EPP*** 43 Molesworth St, Dublin 2. Tel. 01 662 5100. **Dublin** 1st pref: 56,593, elected 1st ct.

COLLINS, Gerry (b. 1938) ***FF, UFE*** The Hill, Abbeyfeale, Co. Limerick. Tel. 01 6184277. **Munster** 1st pref: 83,106, elected 2nd ct.

COX, Pat (b. 1952) ***Ind, ELR*** 21 Cook St, Cork. Tel. 021 278488. **Munster** 1st pref: 63,954, elected 5th ct.

CROWLEY, Brian (b. 1964) ***FF, UFE*** 39 Sundays Well Rd, Cork. Tel. 021 394598. **Munster** 1st pref: 154,195, elected 1st ct.

CUSHNAHAN, John (b. 1948) ***FG, EPP*** 2nd Floor, 31 Cecil St, Limerick. Tel. 061 418289. **Munster** 1st pref: 46,100, elected 6th ct.

De ROSSA, Proinsias (b. 1940) ***Lab, PES*** Leinster House, Kildare St, Dublin 2. Tel. 01 618 3003. **Dublin** 1st pref: 28,748, elected 8th ct.

DOYLE, Avril (b. 1949) ***FG, EPP*** Leinster House, Kildare St, Dublin 2. Tel. 01 618 3034. Leinster 1st pref: 67,881, elected, 2nd ct.

FITZSIMONS, Jim (b. 1936) ***FF, UFE*** 43 Molesworth St, Dublin 2. Tel. 01 662 3065. **Leinster** 1st pref: 58,750, elected 3rd ct.

GALLAGHER, Pat the Cope (b. 1948) ***FF, UFE*** Dungloe, Co. Donegal. Tel. 075 21276. **Connacht-Ulster** 1st pref: 66,055, elected 5th ct.

HYLAND, Liam (b. 1933) ***FF, UFE*** Fearagh Ballacolla, Portlaoise, Co. Laois. Tel. 0502 34051. **Leinster** 1st pref: 58,477, elected 3rd ct.

McCARTIN, John Joseph (b. 1939) ***FG, EPP*** Mullyaster, Newtowngore, Carrick-on-Shannon, Co. Leitrim. Tel. 049 33395. **Connacht-Ulster** 1st pref: 63,632, elected 6th ct.

McKENNA, Patricia (b. 1957) ***GP, Greens*** 43 Molesworth St, Dublin 2. Tel. 01 661 6833. **Dublin** 1st pref: 35,659, elected 7th ct.

SCALLON, Dana Rosemary (b. 1950) ***Ind, EPP*** Fortalleza' Circular Rd, Dangan Upper, Galway. Tel. 091 582258. **Connacht-Ulster** 1st pref: 51,086, elected 6th ct.

Party Strength

Party	Dáil	Seanad	Euro Parliament	Local Government
Fianna Fáil	76	30	6	381
Fine Gael	54	16	4	278
Labour	21	4	1	83
Progressive Democrats	4	4	-	25
Green Party	2	-	2	8
Sinn Féin	1	-	-	21
Socialist Party	1	-	-	2
Independents	6	6	2	85
TOTAL	165*	60	15	883

* The by-election caued by the death of Pat Upton has not been held at time of going to print.
Local Government excludes Urban District Councils and Town Commissions.

Election Results

Local Government

First Preferences

11 June 1999	FF	FG	Lab	PD	GP	SF	Others
Carlow Co. Council	6,397	5,501	2,263	793	658	0	1,963
Cavan Co. Council	12,476	10,166	177	0	138	2,330	2,082
Clare Co. Council	23,505	12,231	1,429	907	792	446	6,566
Cork Co. Council	49,555	48,318	14,997	3,406	1,488	2,566	12,485
Cork Corporation	13,973	8,448	6,826	2,739	2,375	1,327	6,714
Donegal Co. Council	27,089	15,831	3,329	636	103	2,843	15,523
Dublin Corporation	41,921	22,089	21,886	3,039	9,515	9,717	15,656
Dún Laoghaire-Rathdown	18,109	14,285	10,369	3,670	4,208	697	6,010
Fingal Co. Council	12,993	9,912	9,149	1,218	3,958	675	9,844
Galway Co. Council	26,703	16,404	837	3,567	0	384	12,387
Galway Corporation	4,897	3,181	1,865	3,752	292	185	3,268
Kerry Co. Council	25,672	14,951	5,945	0	246	3,810	13,365
Kildare Co. Council	16,509	7,072	8,235	1,891	1,743	506	9,874
Kilkenny Co. Council	13,839	10,297	3,336	267	592	0	3,631
Laois Co. Council	8,643	5,158	962	0	0	416	2,083
Leitrim Co. Council	7,017	6,761	285	0	0	1,286	895
Limerick Co. Council	22,298	15,692	941	4,775	337	361	4,032
Limerick Corporation	4,994	4,737	3,255	1,265	0	143	3,591
Longford Co. Council	4,866	6,851	54	0	0	0	5,459
Louth Co. Council	10,952	9,167	2,573	721	1,279	4,079	6,523
Mayo Co. Council	23,548	18,980	1,021	0	239	860	4,734
Meath Co. Council	18,417	13,285	2,929	0	703	926	7,458
Monaghan Co. Council	10,369	7,018	176	0	493	6,709	2,136
Offaly Co. Council	9,880	6,879	1,887	0	0	439	6,909
Roscommon Co. Council	9,632	11,133	256	771	50	0	6,746
Sligo Co. Council	10,267	25,849	2,859	212	0	1,206	3,886
South Dublin Co. Council	16,171	7,813	7,409	2,776	3,135	4,226	12,817
Tipperary NR Co. Council	14,639	7,894	2,805	0	0	450	5,395
Tipperary SR Co. Council	14,910	10,417	4,575	648	0	0	6,577
Waterford Co. Council	10,352	7,439	3,874	387	371	59	2,373
Waterford Corporation	2,679	2,708	1,267	504	452	0	5,625
Westmeath Co. Council	10,519	5,859	6,024	0	0	0	976
Wexford Co. Council	15,851	14,410	5,568	0	657	1,618	5,003
Wicklow Co. Council	13,603	8,846	8,479	0	1,109	803	8,247
TOTAL	533,245	395,582	147,842	37,944	34,933	49,067	220,833

Seats Won

11 June 1999	FF	FG	Lab	PD	GP	SF	Others
Carlow Co. Council	9	7	3	1	1		
Cavan Co. Council	13	9				2	1
Clare Co. Council	18	9		1			4
Cork Co. Council	19	21	4	1			3
Cork Corporation	12	8	5	2	1	1	2
Donegal Co. Council	14	8	1				6
Dublin Corporation	20	9	14		2	4	3
Dún Laoghaire-Rathdown	10	8	6	3	1		
Fingal Co. Council	6	5	6	1	1		5
Galway Co. Council	16	9		2			3
Galway Corporation	5	4	2	4			
Kerry Co. Council	12	6	3			1	5
Kildare Co. Council	9	5	5	2			4
Kilkenny Co. Council	12	11	1				2
Laois Co. Council	14	10					1
Leitrim Co. Council	10	8				2	2
Limerick Co. Council	14	10		3			1
Limerick Corporation	6	5	3				3
Longford Co. Council	8	10			1		2
Louth Co. Council	14	7	1			1	3
Mayo Co. Council	16	13	1				1
Meath Co. Council	13	12				1	3
Monaghan Co. Council	8	6				6	
Offaly Co. Council	9	7	1				4
Roscommon Co. Council	9	12		1			4
Sligo Co. Council	9	11	2			1	2
South Dublin Co. Council	8	3	7	2	1	2	3
Tipperary NR Co. Council	12	5	1				3
Tipperary SR Co. Council	12	9	1				4
Waterford Co. Council	11	8	3				1
Waterford Corporation	4	3	2	1			5
Westmeath Co. Council	12	6	5				
Wexford Co. Council	9	8	1				3
Wicklow Co. Council	8	6	5			1	4
TOTAL	**381**	**278**	**83**	**25**	**8**	**21**	**87**

Dáil By-Election

Cork South Central (23 October 1998)
Reason for Election: Death of Hugh Coveney (FG).
Candidates: 9; **Electorate:** 86,195; **Turnout:** 49.9%; **Total Valid Poll:** 43,007; **Quota:** 21,504. **First Count:** Simon Coveney (FG) 16,212; Sinead Behan (FF) 12,658; Toddy O'Sullivan (Lab) 8,171; Dan Boyle (GP) 3,461; Henry Cremin (SF) 1,158; Peter Kelly (PD) 971; Benny Cooney (Ind) 197; Brian McEnery (NLP) 150; Jim Tallon (Ind) 29. **Third Count:** Simon Coveney (FG) 23,230; Sinead Behan (FF) 16,379. **Elected:** Simon Coveney (FG).

European Parliament

11 June 1999
CONNACHT-ULSTER
Seats: 3; **Candidates:** 11; **Electorate:** 541,552; **Turnout:** 61.35%; **Total Valid Poll:** 320,151; **Quota:** 80,038. **First Count:** Pat 'The Cope' Gallagher (FF) 66,055; John Joseph McCartin (FG) 63,632; Dana Rosemary Scallon (Ind) 51,086; Noel Treacy (FF) 47,933; Marian Harkin (Ind) 47,372; Sean McManus (SF) 20,457; Gerard Gibbons (Lab) 10,522; Liam Sharkey (Ind) 5,334; Ming Luke Flannagan (Ind) 5,000; Paul Campbell (NLP) 1,920; Paul Raymond (Ind) 840. **Elected:** Pat 'The Cope' Gallagher (FF) 98,258 – 5th Ct; John Joseph McCartin (FG) 75,275 – 6th Ct; Dana Rosemary Scallon (Ind) 72,855 – 6th Ct.

DUBLIN
Seats: 4; **Candidates:** 13; **Electorate:** 793,200; **Turnout:** 36.14%; **Total Valid Poll:** 280,671; **Quota:** 56,135. **First Count:** Mary Banotti (FG) 56,593; Niall Andrews (FF) 44,176; Patricia McKenna (GP) 35,659; Proinsias De Rossa (Lab) 28,748; Jim Mitchell (FG) 27,873; Ben Briscoe (FF) 25,065; Seán Crowe (SF) 18,633; Bernie Malone (Lab) 15,890; Joe Higgins (Socialist) 10,619; Gerard Casey (CSP) 9,425; Ciaran Goulding (Ind) 5,546; Adam Godwin (Ind) 1,438; John Burns (NLP) 1,006. **Elected:** Mary Banotti (FG) 56,593 – 1st Ct; Niall Andrews (FF) 71,423 – 7th Ct; Patricia McKenna (GP) 56,992 – 7th Ct; Proinsias De Rossa (Lab) 47,018 – 8th Ct.

LEINSTER

Seats: 4; Candidates: 8; Electorate: 706,392; Turnout: 50.55%; Total Valid Poll: 342,339; Quota: 68,468. First Count: Avril Doyle (FG) 67,881; Jim Fitzsimons (FF) 58,750; Liam Hyland (FF) 58,477; Alan Gillis (FG) 48,729; Nuala Ahern (GP) 47,184; Sean Butler (Lab) 38,112; Arthur Morgan (SF) 20,015; Desmond Garrett (NLP) 3,191. Elected: Avril Doyle (FG) 69,495 – 2nd Ct; Nuala Ahern (GP) 66,808 – 3rd Ct; Jim Fitzsimons (FF) 66,117 – 3rd Ct; Liam Hyland (FF) 65,496 – 3rd Ct.

MUNSTER

Seats: 4; Candidates: 10; Electorate: 822,907; Turnout: 56.12%; Total Valid Poll: 448,579; Quota: 89,716. First Count: Brian Crowley (FF) 154,195; Gerard Collins (FF) 83,106; Pat Cox (Ind) 63,954; John Cushnahan (FG) 46,100; Jim Corr (FG) 31,363; Martin Ferris (SF) 29,060; Paula Desmond (Lab) 28,270; Ben Nutty (GP) 10,257; Stewart Luck (NLP) 1,267; Denis Riordan (Ind) 1,007. Elected: Brian Crowley (FF) 154,195 – 1st Ct; Gerard Collins (FF) 117,783 – 2nd Ct; Pat Cox (Ind) 95,004 – 5th Ct; John Cushnahan (FG) 78,232 – 6th Ct.

Referendum

REFERENDUM ON LOCAL GOVERNMENT 11 JUNE, 1999

Region	Electorate	Total Poll	Spoiled	Turnout	Yes (%)	No (%)
Connacht–Ulster	525,344	329,083	28,538	62.64%	238,843 (79.47)	61,702 (20.53)
Dublin	779,670	283,403	13,678	36.35%	203,168 (75.32)	66,557 (24.68)
Leinster	687,309	355,027	25,545	51.65%	254,773 (77.33)	74,709 (22.67)
Munster	799,086	458,368	41,305	57.36%	328,066 (78.66)	88,997 (21.34)
Overall	2,791,409	1,425,881	109,066	51.08%	1,024,850 (77.83)	291,965 (22.17)

Leaders of State

Presidents of Ireland

Name	Party	Born	In	Inaugurated	Terms	Retired*	Died
Douglas Hyde	Ind	17.01.1860	Roscommon	25.06.1938	1	24.06.1945	12.07.1949
Seán T. Ó Ceallaigh	FF	25.08.1882	Dublin	25.06.1945	2	24.06.1959	23.11.1966
Éamon de Valera	FF	14.10.1882	New York	25.06.1959	2	24.06.1973	29.08.1975
Erskine H. Childers	FF	11.12.1905	London	30.05.1973	1	17.11.1974	17.11.1974
Cearbhall Ó Dálaigh	Ind	12.02.1911	Wicklow	19.12.1974	1	22.10.1976	21.03.1978
Patrick Hillery	FF	02.05.1923	Clare	03.12.1976	2	02.12.1990	
Mary Robinson	Ind	21.05.1944	Mayo	03.12.1990	1	12.09.1997	
Mary McAleese	FF	27.06.1951	Belfast	11.11.1997	1		

* *Presidents Ó Dálaigh and Robinson resigned from office, President Childers died while in office.*

Douglas Hyde

Seán T. Ó Ceallaigh

Éamon de Valera

Erskine Childers

Cearbhall Ó Dálaigh

Patrick Hillery

Mary Robinson

Mary McAleese

Taoisigh

Name	Party	Born	Place	TD	Taoiseach	Died
William T. Cosgrave	CnaG	06.06.1880	Dublin	1917-44	1922-32	16.11.1965
Éamon de Valera	FF	14.10.1882	New York	1917-59	1932-48, 1951-54, 1957-59	29.08.1975
John A. Costello	FG	20.06.1891	Dublin	1933-69	1948-51, 1954-57	05.01.1976
Seán Lemass	FF	15.07.1899	Dublin	1924-69	1959-66	11.05.1971
Jack Lynch	FF	15.08.1917	Cork	1948-81	1966-73, 1977-79	
Liam Cosgrave	FG	13.04.1920	Dublin	1943-81	1973-77	
Charles J. Haughey	FF	16.09.1925	Mayo	1957-92	1979-81, 1982, 1987-92	
Dr Garret FitzGerald	FG	09.02.1926	Dublin	1969-92	1981-82, 1982-87	
Albert Reynolds	FF	03.11.1932	Roscommon	1977-	1992-94	
John Bruton	FG	18.05.1947	Dublin	1969-	1994-97	
Bertie Ahern	FF	12.09.1951	Dublin	1977-	1997-	

From 1922 to 1937 the head of government was known as President of the Executive Council.

William T Cosgrave

Eamon de Valera

John A. Costello

Seán Lemass

Jack Lynch

Liam Cosgrave

Charles J. Haughey

Dr Garret FitzGerald

Albert Reynolds

John Bruton

Former Ceann Comharile

Ceann Comhairle (Dáil Éireann)	Term
Michael Hayes	1922-32
Frank Fahey	1932-51
Patrick Hogan	1951-67
Cormac Breslin	1967-73
Seán Treacy	1973-77
Joseph Brennan	1977-80
Pádraic Faulkner	1980-81
John O'Connell	1981-82
Tom FitzPatrick	1982-87
Seán Treacy	1987-97
Séamus Pattison	1997-

Former Cathaoirleach

Cathaoirleach (Seanad Éireann)	Term
Lord Glenavy	1922-28
Thomas Westropp Bennett	1928-36
Seán Gibbons	1938-43
Seán Goulding	1943-48
Timothy J. O'Donovan	1948-51
Liam Ó Buachalla	1951-54
Patrick F. Baxter	1954-57
Liam Ó Buachalla	1957-69
Michael Yeates	1969-73
Micheal Cranitch	Jan-Jun 1973
James Dooge	1973-77
Seamus Dolan	1977-81
Charlie McDonald	1981-82
Tras Honan	1982-83
Patrick J. Reynolds	1983-87
Tras Honan	1987-89
Seán Doherty	1989-92
Seán Fallon	1992-95
Liam Naughten	1995-96
Liam T. Cosgrave	1996-97
Brian Mullooly	1997-

Seanad Éireann was abolished in 1936 and restablished under the 1937 Constitution

Former Party Leaders

THE LABOUR PARTY
Tom Johnson ....(1922-27)
T.J. O'Connell ....(1927-32)
William Norton...(1932-60)
Brendan Corish ....(1960-77)
Frank Cluskey ....(1977-81)
Michael O'Leary ....(1981-82)
Dick Spring ....(1982-97)
Ruairí Quinn ....(1997-)

CUMANN NA nGAEDHEAL
William T. Cosgrave ....(1922-33)

FIANNA FÁIL
Éamon de Valera..(1926-59)
Seán Lemass ....(1959-66)
Jack Lynch ....(1966-79)
Charles J. Haughey......................................(1979-92)
Albert Reynolds..(1992-94)
Bertie Ahern ....(1994-)

FINE GAEL
Eoin O'Duffy ....(1933-34)
William T. Cosgrave ....(1935-44)
Richard Mulcahy ....(1944-59)
James Dillon ....(1959-65)
Liam Cosgrave ....(1965-77)
Garret FitzGerald ....(1977-87)
Alan Dukes ....(1987-90)
John Bruton ....(1990-)

CLANN NA POBLACHTA
Seán MacBride ....(1946-65)

PROGRESSIVE DEMOCRATS
Desmond O'Malley ....(1985-93)
Mary Harney...(1993-)

DEMOCRATIC LEFT
Proinsias De Rossa......................................1992-99

Constitutional Referenda, 1937-99

Date	Issue	Turnout (%)	For (%)	Against (%)
01.07.1937	Endorse new constitution	75.8	56.5	43.5
17.06.1959	Introduction of plurality voting system (replacing proportional representation)	58.4	48.2	51.8
16.10.1968	Establishing TD-population ratio	65.8	39.2	60.8
16.10.1968	Introduction of plurality voting system (replacing proportional representation)	65.8	39.2	60.8
10.05.1972	EEC membership	70.9	83.1	16.9
07.12.1972	Lower voting age to 18	50.7	84.6	15.4
07.12.1972	Abolish 'special position' of the Catholic church	50.7	84.4	15.6
05.07.1979	Protect adoption system	28.6	99.0	1.0
05.07.1979	Alteration of university representation in Seanad Éireann	28.6	92.4	7.6
07.09.1983	Prohibit legalisation of abortion	53.7	66.9	33.1
14.06.1984	Extend voting rights to non-citizens	47.5	75.4	24.6
26.06.1986	Legalisation of divorce	60.8	36.5	63.5
24.05.1987	Permit signing of Single European Act	44.1	69.9	30.1
18.06.1992	Ratification of Maastricht Treaty on European Union	57.3	69.1	30.9
25.11.1992	Restrict availability of abortion	68.2	34.6	65.4
	Right to travel	68.2	62.4	37.6
	Right to information	68.2	59.9	40.1
24.11.1995	Right to divorce	62.2	50.3	49.7
28.11.1996	Restriction on right to bail	29.2	74.8	25.2
30.10.1997	Cabinet Confidentiality	47.2	52.6	47.4
22.06.1998	Ratification of Amsterdam Treaty	56.2	61.7	38.3
22.06.1998	Northern Ireland Agreement	56.3	94.4	5.6
11.06.1999	Local Government	51.1	77.8	22.2

The European Commission

Name	Born	Nationality	Portfolio
Romano Prodi	b. 1939	Italian	President
Neil Kinnock	b. 1942	British	Vice President

Continued from previous page

Name	Born	Nationality	Portfolio
			Administrative Reform
Loyola de Palacio	b. 1950	Spanish	Vice President
			Relations with European Parliament, Transport and Energy
Mario Monti	b. 1943	Italian	Competition
Franz Fischler	b. 1946	Austrian	Agriculture and Fisheries
Erkki Liikanen	b. 1950	Finnish	Enterprise and Information Society
Frits Bolkestein	b. 1933	Dutch	Internal Market
Philippe Busquin	b. 1941	Belgian	Research
Pedro Solbes Mira	b. 1942	Spanish	Economic and Monetary Affairs
Poul Nielson	b. 1943	Danish	Development and Humanitarian Aid
Gunter Verheugen	b. 1944	German	Enlargement
Chris Patten	b. 1944	British	External Relations
Pascal Lamy	b. 1947	French	Trade
David Byrne	b. 1947	Irish	Health and Consumer Protection
Michel Barnier	b. 1951	French	Regional Policy and Cohesion
Viviane Reding	b. 1951	Luxembourgeois	Education and Culture
Michaele Schreyer	b. 1951	German	Budget
Margot Wallström	b. 1954	Swedish	Environment
Antonio Vitorino	b. 1957	Portuguese	Justice and Home Affairs
Anna Diamantopoulou	b. 1959	Greek	Employment and Social Affairs

Appointed September 1999

Former Irish Commissioners

Name	Term	Portfolio
Patrick J. Hillery	1973-76	Social Affairs
Richard Burke	1977-80	Transport, Taxation and Consumer Protection, Relations with European Parliament, Education, Science and Research
Michael O'Kennedy	1981-82	Presidents Delegate, Personnel and Administration, Statistical Office, Publications Office
Richard Burke	1982-84	Personnel and Administration, Joint Interpreting and Conference Services, Statistical Office, Publications Office
Peter Sutherland	1985-88	Competition, Social Affairs, Education and Training From 1986: Competition and Relations with European Parliament
Ray McSharry	1989-93	Agriculture and Rural Development
Pádraig Flynn	1993-99	Social Affairs and Employment, Internal and Judicial Affairs, Questions linked to Immigration, Relations with Economic and Social Committee

NORTHERN IRELAND

Introduction

Explanatory notes on Northern Ireland

Northern Ireland contains the counties of Antrim, Armagh, Derry, Down, Fermanagh and Tyrone. Part of the United Kingdom of Great Britain and Northern Ireland, it was established by the Government of Ireland Act 1920. The Northern Ireland parliament opted out of the Irish Free State in December 1922 under the terms of the Anglo-Irish Treaty. From 1921 until 1972 Northern Ireland had its own parliament which dealt with local matters while the Imperial parliament at Westminster dealt with wider matters such as the Crown, taxation and defence.

Following the outbreak of communal violence in 1968, the Stormont Parliament was prorogued in March 1972 to be replaced by direct rule from Westminster, embodied in the powers vested in the Secretary of State. The Northern Ireland Constitution Act 1973 provided for devolved government in the form of a power sharing executive. The executive took office in January with ministers from the UUP, the SDLP and Alliance. It was brought down in May of that year by the Ulster Workers' Council strike. The collapse was followed by the reintroduction of direct rule.

Since May 1974 Northern Ireland has been ruled directly from Westminster under the terms of the Northern Ireland Act 1974 by the Secretary of State for Northern Ireland who is a member of the British government. The Secretary of State is responsible for the departments in the Northern Ireland Office and has a team of junior ministers who head these departments. The departments are Agriculture, Economic Development, Education, Environment, Finance and Personnel and Health and Social Services.

The most recent constitutional initiative, the 'Good Friday' Agreement provides for a 108-member Northern Ireland Assembly. It envisages the creation of an Executive which will assume responsibility for the local government departments within the Northern Ireland Office, although certain powers (such as security, taxation, defence and excise) will remain with the Westminster parliament. Northern Ireland also has 26 district and borough councils which have limited powers of local government.

The United Kingdom is a constitutional monarchy with the monarch as head of state. The parliament consists of the head of state (the monarch), and two houses of Parliament: the House of Commons (a house of representatives) and the House of Lords (consisting of members of the Peerage). All bills passed by the houses of parliament must be promulgated by the monarch.

The House of Commons has 659 members of which Northern Ireland returns 18. All MPs are elected by the 'first past the post' system. A number of Northern Ireland peers sit in the House of Lords.

The House of Lords comprises 1,289 eligible hereditary peers, law lords, life peers and Anglican bishops as of July 1, 1999.

HEAD OF STATE The Head of State is Elizabeth II Alexandra Mary of Windsor. Born London, April 21, 1926, she ascended to the throne on February 6, 1952, and was crowned at Westminster Abbey on June 2, 1953. Married Philip Mountbatten November 20, 1947. They have four children: Charles, Prince of Wales; Anne, the Princess Royal; Andrew, the Duke of York; and Prince Edward. The Queen is represented in Northern Ireland by a Lord Lieutenant in each county or city; they are The Lord O'Neill (Antrim), Colonel E. Wilson (Belfast), The Earl of Caledon (Armagh), W.J. Hall (Down), The Earl of Erne (Fermanagh), Sir Michael McCorkell (Derry), J.T. Eaton (Derry City) and the Duke of Abercorn (Tyrone).

NAME OF STATE: The name of the state is Northern Ireland, and it is part of the United Kingdom of Great Britain and Northern Ireland. Established by the Government of Ireland Act 1920, it consists of six of the nine counties of the historic province of Ulster.

THE NATIONAL FLAG: The national flag is the union flag. It is a combination of the cross of St. George (a red cross on a white background), the cross of St. Andrew (a diagonal white cross on a blue background) and the cross of St. Patrick (a diagonal red cross on a white background). From partition in 1922 until the imposition of direct rule in 1972 the flag was a six-pointed star enclosing a red hand surmounted by a crown at the centre of a red cross on a white background.

THE NATIONAL ANTHEM: The national anthem is 'God Save the Queen'.

NATIONALIST NON-ALLEGIANCE: It is a widely recognised fact that a substantial majority of nationalists do not give their allegiance to the Northern Ireland state. This historical and political reality has been evident in the intermittent civil unrest since the foundation of the Northern state. Since 1969 there has been a serious escalation in this unrest which has resulted in more than 3,000 deaths.

The Northern Ireland 'Good Friday' Agreement has provided for a North/South Ministerial Council which, as well as providing Northern Ireland nationalists with an institutional expression of their Irish identity, will deal with matters which affect the whole of the island of Ireland.

British Government System

● Britain is a Constitutional Monarchy. The Queen is head of state and head of the Anglican Church.
● The House of Commons has 659 members elected on a 'first past the post' basis. Northern Ireland returns 18 members to the House of Commons.
● The Queen appoints the leader of the party who can command a majority in the House of Commons and appoints him/her as Prime Minister. The Prime Minister in turn appoints the members of the cabinet.
● The cabinet acts collectively.
● All acts passed by the Houses of Parliament must be promulgated by the Queen, i.e. given a royal assent.
● As head of the Judiciary, the Lord Chancellor is responsible for the appointment of judges and magistrates. The Lord Chancellor also has a seat in cabinet.
● Britain does not have a written constitution but rather a series of documents and legislation which govern the functions of state. These are: common law, legislation (from the Houses of Parliament), conventions, the law and custom of parliament, European Union law and works of authority.

Northern Ireland Government System

The new arrangements for the governance of Northern Ireland can be divided into three interlocking and interdependent strands. In the first strand, executive authority will be vested in up to 12 Ministers who are part of the 108-member Northern Ireland Assembly, allocated in proportion to party strengths. The Assembly will govern the internal affairs of Northern Ireland in areas such as health, education and agriculture, while other areas such as security, taxation and justice will remain the responsibility of the Secretary of State and the Westminster government. Decisions taken by the executive must be ratified by the Assembly by securing the support of a majority of both nationalists and unionists.

A North/South ministerial council will be established in the second strand. It will draw members from both the Irish government and the Northern Ireland Executive and will participate in consultation, co-operation and action on matters of mutual interest.

The third strand is a British-Irish Council where representatives are drawn from elected parliaments and assemblies in Northern Ireland, the Republic of Ireland, Scotland, Wales, the Isle of Man, the Channel Islands and the House of Commons. It is envisaged the Council will meet twice yearly to discuss matters of mutual interest.

At time of going to print (September 1999) a Northern Ireland Executive had not been appointed, the North/South ministerial council had not been appointed and the British-Irish Council had not convened. Consequently, responsibility for the Northern Ireland Office departments remained with the Secretary of State.

Political Parties

Main Parties

Ulster Unionist Party
3 Glengal Street, Belfast BT12 5AE
Tel: (01232) 324601
Fax: (01232) 246738
email: uup@uup.org
website: www.uup.org

Founded: 1905 as Ulster Unionist Council
First Leader: Edward James Saunderson.
Current Leader: David Trimble MP *(pictured)*.
Party President: Josias Cunningham
General Secretary: David Boyd
Seats: European Parliament: 1; House of Commons: 10; NI Assembly: 28; Local Councils: 176.
Assembly Designation: Unionist
European Alliance: European People's Party.

History: Initially opposed to partition, it formed each government in Northern Ireland from 1921 until 1972. Since the introduction of direct rule from Westminster, the party has consistently been the single largest party in Northern Ireland in terms of MPs and councillors and is currently the largest party in the Assembly.

The UUP was divided over the power-sharing arrangement in 1974. The participation of leader Brian Faulkner brought about his resignation and saw the majority of the party enter into a loose pan-unionist coalition with the DUP and the Ulster Vanguard. When this arrangement collapsed in the late 1970s, the UUP plotted a more independent course, refusing to enter into electoral pacts in marginal constituencies. It opposed the 'rolling devolution', suggested by Secretary of State James Prior in 1982, and the Anglo-Irish Agreement in 1985. The opposition to the Agreement saw the revival of tactical cooperation with the DUP in marginal constituencies and this has remained the case in each Westminster election since. A majority of the party, including its 300 member Party

Executive, support the Good Friday Agreement but a number of its MPs have made their opposition to it clear and have actively opposed its full implementation.

Aims: The party has as its aims the maintenance of Northern Ireland under the Crown as an integral part of the United Kingdom; the safeguarding of British citizenship for the people of Northern Ireland; the promotion of a democratic system of local government; and that any change in the constitutional status must be brought about by the consent of a majority within Northern Ireland. The party opposes the inclusion of Sinn Féin in a Northern Ireland Executive without the prior decommissioning of IRA weapons.

SOCIAL DEMOCRATIC AND LABOUR PARTY
121 Ormeau Road
Belfast BT7 1SH
Tel: (01232) 247700
Fax: (01232) 236699
email: sdlp@indigo.ie
website: www.indigo.ie/sdlp

Founded: 1970 amalgamation of Northern Ireland Labour Party, Republican Labour, the Nationalist Party and leading figures from the civil rights movement.
First Leader: Gerry Fitt.
Current Leader: John Hume MP, MEP *(pictured).*
Party Chairman: Jim Lennon
General Secretary: Mrs Gerri Cosgrove
Seats: European Parliament: 1; House of Commons: 3; NI Assembly 24; Local Councils: 120.
Assembly Designation: Nationalist
European Alliance: Party of European Socialists
History: The party had representatives on the short-lived Power Sharing executive in 1974 and contributed to the New Ireland Forum in 1983. The party opposed 'rolling devolution' in 1982 but strongly supported the Anglo-Irish Agreement in 1985 and subsequent initiatives such as the Downing Street Declaration and Frameworks Document. The SDLP played a major part in the negotiations leading up to the 'Good Friday' Agreement and is the largest nationalist party in the Northern Ireland Assembly.

The party has performed well in all Northern Ireland elections since its inception and has consistently had representatives elected to Westminster and the various Northern Ireland Assemblies and Forums. Since 1979 John Hume, the current party leader, has been a member of the European Parliament.

Aims: A moderate left-of-centre nationalist party, it promotes a united Ireland, freely negotiated and agreed by people both north and south, and contests elections on the following points: the abolition of all forms of discrimination and the promotion of equality among all citizens; the promotion of culture and the arts and the recognition and cherishing of their diversity; the public ownership of all essential services and industries; and the protection of the environment. The party supports full implementation of the Good Friday Agreement including the establishment of an inclusive Northern Ireland Executive and the decommissioning of paramilitary weapons before May 2000.

SINN FÉIN
Conway Mill, Conway Street,
Belfast BT13 2DE
Tel. (01232) 230261
Fax: (01232) 231723
email: sinnfein@iol.ie
website: www.sinnfein.ie

Founded: 1905 (as Sinn Féin League); 1970 as Provisional Sinn Féin.
First Leader: Arthur Griffith; Ruairi Ó Brádaigh (Provisional Sinn Féin).
Current Leader: Gerry Adams MP *(pictured).*
Party Chairman: Mitchell McLaughlin.
General Secretary: Lucilita Bhreatnach.
Assembly Designation: Nationalist
Seats: European Parliament: None; House of Commons: 2; Dáil Éireann: 1; NI Assembly: 18; NI Local Councils: 73; RoI Local Councils: 21.
History: Sinn Féin (translated as 'We Ourselves') was founded in 1905 as an umbrella group for small nationalist organisations. It won an overwhelming majority in the 1918 general election, and its members met to form Dáil Éireann. The party split in 1922 over the signing of the Anglo-Irish treaty and its republican rump withdrew from the Dáil. Small, abstentionist and ineffective, the party suffered a further split in 1970 when two factions emerged, Official Sinn Féin (later to become the Workers' Party) and Provisional Sinn Féin.

Provisional Sinn Féin revived its electoral fortunes in the period after the 1981 Hunger Strike, contesting each election in Northern Ireland from 1982 onwards. The party Ard Fheis of 1986 ended the policy of abstentionism from the Oireachtas and a further split occurred. The party has had members elected to the House of Commons, Dáil Éireann and to most local councils in both Northern Ireland and some in the Republic. The party's Ard Fheis of May 1998 voted to end the policy of abstentionism with regard to the Northern Ireland Assembly and members duly took up their seats.

Aims: Sinn Féin is a republican party committed to ending the union with Britain and as part of the 'republican movement' has consistently been described, despite vehement denials, as the political wing of the IRA. The party is committed to the establishment of an agreed, inclusive Ireland and believes that a non-sectarian and pluralist society is the way forward. The party was instrumental in brokering the IRA ceasefire of August 1994. Sinn Féin was admitted to the multi-party talks following the restoration of the IRA ceasefire in July 1997 and was involved in the negotiations which culminated in the Good Friday Agreement of April 1998. The party supports the establishment of an inclusive Northern Ireland Executive and has pledged to use its influence to bring about the decommissioning of paramilitary weapons under the schedule set out in the Good Friday Agreement.

DEMOCRATIC UNIONIST PARTY
91 Dundela Avenue, Belfast BT4 3BU
Tel. (01232) 471155
Fax: (01232) 471797
email: info@dup.org.uk
website: www.dup.org.uk

Founded: 1971 by Rev Dr Ian Paisley and Desmond Boal.
First and Current Leader: Rev Dr Ian Paisley MP, MEP *(pictured)*.
Party Chairman: James McClure.
General Secretary: Alan Ewart.
Seats: European Parliament: 1; House of Commons: 2; NI Assembly: 20; Local Councils: 90.
Assembly Designation: Unionist
European Alliance: Independent.
History: The DUP was founded in 1971 by the leader of the Protestant Unionist Party, Rev Dr Ian Paisley, and former Ulster Unionist MP, Desmond Boal. Opposed to the 1974 Power Sharing arrangement, it initially secured a vote of around 10%. Its major break-throughs came in 1979 when it won three Westminster seats and its leader, Dr Paisley, topped the poll in the European Parliament election. Staunch in its opposition to the Anglo-Irish Agreement in 1985, it found common ground with the UUP and all subsequent elections have seen electoral co-operation in a number of marginal constituencies. The party opposed initiatives such as the Downing Street Declaration and the Frameworks Document and, after withdrawing from multi-party negotiations in September 1997 when Sinn Féin was admitted, opposed the Good Friday Agreement in coalition with the United Kingdom Unionist Party and anti-Agreement elements within the Ulster Unionist Party.
Aims: The party aims to secure, uphold and maintain Northern Ireland's position as an integral part of the United Kingdom. It supports the imposition and mainte-nance of the rule of law throughout Northern Ireland so that all citizens are equal under the law and equally subject to it. Finally, the party aims to devise and urge a policy of social betterment and equal opportunity for all sections of the community in the economic, educa-tional and social welfare spheres. The party opposes the participation of Sinn Féin in the Northern Ireland Executive in the absence of IRA decommissioning.

ALLIANCE PARTY OF NORTHERN IRELAND
88 University Street, Belfast, BT7 1HE
Tel. (01232) 324274
Fax: (01232) 333147
email: alliance@allianceparty.org
website: www.allianceparty.org

Founded: 1970
First Leader: Phelim O'Neill
Current Leader: Sean Neeson *(pictured)*.
Party Chairman: Peter Osborne
General Secretary: Richard Good
Seats: European Parliament: none; House of Commons: none; NI Assembly 6; Local Councils: 42.
Assembly Designation: Other
History: Founded in 1970 the party attracted support from disaffected unionists following the O'Neill split and from supporters of the Northern Ireland Labour Party. Its members took part in the 1973 Sunningdale confer-ence and went on to take up ministries in the Power

Sharing executive in 1974. Strongly in favour of 'rolling devolution' in the 1982 Convention, it lost support when it gave qualified support to the Anglo-Irish Agreement in 1985. The party helped negotiate and then campaigned for a yes vote in the referendum on 'Good Friday' Agreement.
Aims: The party is neither unionist or nationalist and is committed to the creation of a fair, just, peaceful and prosperous society in Northern Ireland, based on respect for all sections of the community and on the widest possible participation in government. The party utterly opposes the use of violence, and promotes the protection of human rights and believes that no change in the constitutional status of Northern Ireland should occur without the consent of the people.

PROGRESSIVE UNIONIST PARTY
182 Shankill Road, Belfast, BT13 2BH.
Tel. (01232) 326233
Fax: (01232) 249602
email: pupni@shankillh.freeserve.co.uk
website: www.pup.org

Founded: 1977
First and Current Leader: Hugh Smith OBE *(pictured)*.
Party Chairman: William Smyth.
General Secretary: William Mitchell.
Seats: European Parliament: None; House of Commons: None; NI Assembly: 2; Local Councils: 5.
Assembly Designation: Unionist
History: The Progressive Unionist Party was formed in 1977. It has close links with the Ulster Volunteer Force and played a major part in the negotiating of the Combined Loyalist Military Command ceasefire of October 1994. The party participated in all stages of the negotiations which led to the 'Good Friday' Agreement and campaigned for a yes vote in the referendum which ratified it.
Aims: The party is committed to maintaining the Union with Great Britain and believes that the principle of power-sharing with nationalists is the best method for the governance of Northern Ireland. Dedicated to a non-sectarian, pluralist and equitable society, it believes that a written constitution and Bill of Rights should be implemented to safeguard human rights, minorities and institutions.

NORTHERN IRELAND WOMEN'S COALITION
50 University St, Belfast BT7 1HB
Tel: (01232) 233100
Fax: (01232) 240021
email: niwc@iol.ie
website:www.pitt.edu/~novosel/north-ern.html

Founded: 1996
The party does not elect a leader or chairperson.
Co-ordinator: Ann McCann (assembly member Monica McWilliams is pictured).
Seats: European Parliament: None; House of

Commons: None; NI Assembly: 2; Local Councils: 1.
Assembly Designation: Other.
History: Established to raise the profile of women in Northern Irish politics. The party had two delegates at the multi-party talks which culminated in the 'Good Friday' Agreement. Campaigned for a yes vote in the referendum and had two members elected to the Northern Ireland Assembly, Monica McWilliams and Jane Morrice.
Aims: The party advocates policy-building as opposed to political division and supports the Northern Ireland Assembly as a forum where representatives can solve the community's common problems.

NORTHERN IRELAND UNIONIST PARTY
Parliament Buildings, Stormont, Belfast BT4 3XX. Tel. (01232) 521533. Fax: (01232) 521845. email: niup@niassambly.gov.uk website: www.niup.org

Founded: 1999
First & Present Leader: Cedric Wilson *(pictured)*.

Party Secretary: Dr Clifford Smyth
Seats: European Parliament: None; House of Commons: None; NI Assembly: 4; Local Councils: 1.
Assembly Designation: Unionist.

The Northern Ireland Unionist Party was founded when four Assembly members of the United Kingdom Unionist Party ceded from the party in late 1998. It opposes the implementation of the Good Friday Agreement and perceives it as presenting a threat to the Union. The party particularly opposes the inclusion of Sinn Féin in a future Northern Ireland government and advocates a form of devolved government to which all the people of Northern Ireland can give their allegiance.

Other Parties

THE CONSERVATIVE PARTY 2 May Ave, Bangor, Co. Down. Tel. (01247) 469210
THE GREEN PARTY 537 Antrim Road, Belfast 15 Tel. (01232) 776731
LABOUR NORTHERN IRELAND 54 Wynne Hill, Hill Street, Lurgan, Co. Armagh Tel. (01762) 324303
NATURAL LAW PARTY 103 University Street, Belfast 7 Tel. (01232) 311466

ULSTER DEMOCRATIC PARTY 36 Castle Street, Lisburn, Co. Antrim Tel. (01846) 667056
ULSTER INDEPENDENCE MOVEMENT 316 Shankill Road, Belfast BT13 1AB Tel. (01232) 236815
UNITED KINGDOM UNIONIST PARTY 10 Hamilton Road, Bangor, Co. Down BT20 4LE Tel. (01247) 272994
UNITED UNIONIST ASSEMBLY PARTY Parliament Buildings, Belfast BT4 3XX. Tel. (01232) 521464
WORKERS' PARTY 6 Springfield Road, Belfast 12 Tel. (01232) 328663

Party Strength

PARTY	EUROPEAN PARLIAMENT	HOUSE OF COMMONS	NI ASSEMBLY	LOCAL COUNCILS
UUP	1	10	28	176
SDLP	1	3	24	120
DUP	1	2	20	90
SF	-	2	18	73
UKUP	-	1	1	3
All	-	-	6	42
NIUP	-	-	4	1
NIWC	-	-	2	1
PUP	-	-	2	5
Others	-	-	3	68
TOTAL	3	18	108	579

Former Party Leaders

ULSTER UNIONIST PARTY
Edward James Saunderson	(1905-06)
Walter H. Long	(1906-10)
Sir Edward Carson	(1910-21)
Sir James Craig	(1921-40)
John Miller Andrews	(1940-43)
Sir Basil Brooke	(1943-63)
Capt. Terence O'Neill	(1963-69)
Maj. James Chichester-Clark	(1969-71)
Brian Faulkner	(1971-74)
Harry West	(1974-79)
James Molyneaux	(1979-95)
David Trimble	(1995-)

SOCIAL DEMOCRATIC AND LABOUR PARTY
Gerry Fitt	(1970-79)

John Hume...(1979-)

DEMOCRATIC UNIONIST PARTY
Rev. Ian Paisley ....(1971-)

PROVISIONAL SINN FÉIN
Ruairí Ó Brádaigh ....(1970-83)
Gerry Adams ....(1983-)

ALLIANCE PARTY
Phelim O'Neill ....(1972-73)
Oliver Napier ....(1973-84)
John Cushnahan...................................(1984-87)

John Alderdice.....................................(1987-98)
Sean Neeson ....(1998-)

ULSTER DEMOCRATIC PARTY
John McMichael ....(1981-1987)
Raymond Smallwoods ....(1987-1994)
Gary McMichael ....(1994-)

PROGRESSIVE UNIONIST PARTY
Hugh Smyth...(1977-)

Elected Representatives

Members of Parliament

Election results are from 1997.
*First elected at by-election.

ADAMS, Gerry (b. 1948) **SF** 51-55 Falls Rd, Belfast 12. Tel. 01232 230261. **Belfast West** 1983-92 and since 1997, 1st pref: 25,662, maj: 7,909.

BEGGS, Roy (b. 1936) **UUP** 41 Station Road, Larne BT40 3AA. Tel. 01574 273258. **Antrim East** since 1983, 1st pref: 13,318, maj: 6,389.

DONALDSON, Jeffrey (b. 1962) **UUP** 38 Railway Street, Lisburn BT28 1XP. Tel. 01846 668001. **Lagan Valley** since 1997, 1st pref: 24,560, maj: 16,925.

FORSYTHE, Clifford (b. 1929) **UUP** 19 Fountain Street, Antrim BT41 4BG. Tel. 01849 460776. **Antrim South** since 1983, 1st pref: 23,108, maj: 16,611.

HUME, John MEP (b. 1937) **SDLP** 5 Bayview Terrace, Derry BT48 7EE. Tel. 01504 265340. **Foyle** since 1983, 1st pref: 25,109, maj: 13,664.

MAGINNIS, Ken (b. 1938) **UUP** 20 Brooke Street, Dungannon BT71 7AN. Tel. 01868 723265. **Fermanagh & South Tyrone** since 1983, 1st pref: 24,862, maj: 13,688.

MALLON, Seamus (b. 1936) **SDLP** 15 Cornmarket, Newry BT35 8BG. Tel. 01693 67933. **Newry & Armagh** since 1986,* 1st pref: 22,904, maj: 4,889.

McCARTNEY, Robert (b. 1936) **UKUP** 10 Hamilton Rd, Bangor BT20 4LE. Tel. 01247 272994. **North Down** since 1995,* 1st pref: 12,817, maj: 1,449.

McGRADY, Eddie (b. 1935) **SDLP** Saul Street, Downpatrick BT30 6NQ. Tel. 01396 61288. **South Down** since 1987, 1st pref: 26,181, maj: 9,933

McGUINNESS, Martin (b. 1950) **SF** 15 Cable Street, Derry. Tel. 01504 361949. **Mid Ulster** since 1997, 1st pref 20,294, maj: 1,883.

PAISLEY, Ian MEP (b. 1926) **DUP** 17 Cyprus Avenue, Belfast BT5 5NT. Tel. 01232 454255. **Antrim North** since 1971, 1st pref: 21,495, maj: 10,574.

ROBINSON, Peter (b. 1948) **DUP** 51 Gransha Rd, Dundonald, Belfast BT16 0HB. Tel. 01232 473111. **Belfast East** since 1979, 1st pref: 16,640, maj: 6,754.

ROSS, Willie (b. 1936) **UUP** 89 Teevan Rd, Turmeel,

Dungiven BT47 4SL. Tel. 015047 41428. **Londonderry East** since 1974, 1st pref: 13,558, maj: 3,794.

SMYTH, Martin (b. 1931) **UUP** 117 Cregagh Rd, Belfast BT6 0LA. Tel. 01232 457009. **Belfast South** since 1982,* 1st pref: 14,201, maj: 4,600.

TAYLOR, John (b. 1937) **UUP** 6 William Street, Newtownards BT23 4AE. Tel. 01247 814123. **Strangford** since 1983, 1st pref: 18,431, maj: 5,852.

THOMPSON, Willie (b. 1939) **UUP** 156 Donaghanie Rd, Beragh, Omagh BT79 0XE. Tel. 01662 758214. **West Tyrone** since 1997, 1st pref: 16,003, maj: 1,161.

TRIMBLE, David (b. 1944) **UUP** 2 Queen Street, Lurgan BT66 8BQ. Tel. 01762 328088. **Upper Bann** since 1990, 1st pref: 20,836, maj: 9,252.

WALKER, Cecil (b. 1924) **UUP** 20 Oldpark Rd, Belfast BT14 6FR. Tel. 01232 755996. **Belfast North** since 1983, 1st pref: 21,478, maj: 13,024.

Assembly Members

Where a constituency office address is unavailable the address of Parliament Buildings has been included. The full address is:
Parliament Buildings, Stormont, Belfast BT4 3XX.

ADAMS, Gerry MP **SF** 51-55 Falls Rd, Belfast 12. Tel. 01232 230261. **West Belfast** 1st pref: 9,078, elected 1st ct.

ADAMSON, Ian **UUP** Parliament Buildings. Tel. (01232) 521529. **East Belfast** 1st pref: 3,447, elected 15 ct.

AGNEW, William **UUAP** Parliament Buildings. Tel. (01232) 521033. **North Belfast** 1st pref: 2,976, elected 1st ct.

ALDERCICE, Lord **All** Parliament Buildings. Tel. (01232) 521130. **East Belfast** 1st pref: 6,144, elected 1st ct.

ARMITAGE, Pauline **UUP** 12 Dunmore St, Coleraine BT52. Tel. (01232) 520305. **Londonderry East** 1st pref: 3,315, elected 9th ct.

ARMSTRONG, Billy **UUP** Parliament Buildings. Tel. (01232) 520305. **Mid Ulster,** 1st pref: 4,498, elected 6th ct.

ATTWOOD, Alex *SDLP* 60 Andersonstown Rd, Belfast. Tel. (01232) 807808. **West Belfast** 1st pref: 4,280, elected 10th ct.

BEGGS, Roy Jnr *UUP* 32c North St, Carrickfergus BT38 7AQ. Tel. (01960) 362995. **East Antrim** 1st pref: 5,764, elected 1st ct.

BELL, Billy *UUP* 2 Sackville St, Lisburn BT27 4AB. Tel. (01846) 605672. **Lagan Valley** 1st pref: 5,965, elected 5th ct.

BELL, Eileen *All* 27 Maryville Rd, Bangor BT20 3RH. **North Down** 1st pref: 3,669, elected 9th ct.

BENSON, Tom *UUP* Parliament Buildings. Tel. (01232) 520307. **Strangford** 1st pref: 1,623, elected 17th ct.

BERRY, Paul *DUP* 78 Market St, Tandragee BT62 2BW. Tel. (01762) 841668. **Newry & Armagh** 1st pref: 7,214, elected 4th ct.

BIRNIE, Esmond *UUP* Parliament Buildings. Tel. (01232) 520304. **South Belfast** 1st pref: 2,875, elected 8th ct.

BOYD, Norman *NIUP* Parliament Buildings. Tel. (01232) 521733. **South Antrim** 1st pref: 4,360, elected 7th ct.

BRADLEY, Patrick J *SDLP* 10 Corrogs Rd, Newry, Co. Down. Tel. (016937) 62062. **South Down** 1st pref: 5,571, elected 10th ct.

BYRNE, Joe *SDLP* 9B Dromore Rd, Omagh, Co. Tyrone. Tel. (01662) 250065. **West Tyrone** 1st pref: 6,495, elected 4th ct.

CAMPBELL, Gregory *DUP* 31 Long Commons, Coleraine BT52 1LH. Tel. (01265) 327327. **East Derry** 1st pref: 6,099, elected 1st ct.

CARRICK, Mervyn *DUP* 15a Mandeville St, Portadown BT62 3PB. Tel. (01238) 564200. **Upper Bann** 1st pref: 4,177, elected 13th ct.

CARSON, Joan *UUP* Parliament Buildings. Tel. (01232) 521557. **Fermanagh & South Tyrone** 1st pref: 4,400, elected 10th ct.

CLOSE, Seamus *All* 123 Moira Rd, Lisburn BT28 1RJ. **Lagan Valley** 1st pref: 6,788, elected 1st ct.

CLYDE, Wilson *DUP* 69 Church St, Antrim BT41 4BA. Tel. (01849) 462286. **South Antrim** 1st pref: 6,034, elected 6th ct.

COBAIN, Fred *UUP* 23a York Rd, Belfast BT15 3GU. Tel. (01232) 594802. **North Belfast** 1st pref: 2,415, elected 11th ct.

COULTER, Rev Robert *UUP* 30a Ballymoney St, Ballymena BT43 6AL. Tel. (01266) 42264. **North Antrim** 1st pref: 5,407, elected 10th ct.

DALLAT, John *SDLP* 8 Gortnacrane Rd, Kilrea, Co. Derry. Tel. (012665) 40798. **East Derry** 1st pref: 4,760, elected 1st ct.

DAVIS, Ivan *UUP* 2 Sackville St, Lisburn BT27 4AB. Tel. (01846) 668001. **Lagan Valley** 1st pref: 3,927, elected 9th ct.

DeBRUN, Bairbre *SF* Unit 8, Twin Spires, 155 Northumberland St, Belfast BT12. Tel. (01232) 521675. **West Belfast** 1st pref: 4,711, elected 9th ct.

DODDS, Nigel *DUP* 256 Ravenhill Rd, Belfast BT6 8GJ. Tel. (01232) 454255. **North Belfast** 1st pref: 7,476, elected 1st ct.

DOHERTY, Arthur *SDLP* 59 St Catherine's St, Limavady, Co. Derry. Tel. (015047) 50287. **East Derry** 1st pref: 4,606, elected 8th ct.

DOHERTY, Pat *SF* 12 Bridge St, Strabane, Co. Tyrone. Tel. (01504) 886824. **West Tyrone** 1st pref: 7,027, elected 1st ct.

DOUGLAS, Boyd *UUAP* Parliament Buildings. Tel. (01232) 521141. **East Derry** 1st pref: 3,811, elected 9th ct.

DURKAN, Mark *SDLP* 7B Messines Tce, Racecourse Rd, Derry. Tel. (01504) 360700. **Foyle** 1st pref: 4,423, elected 6th ct.

EMPEY, Sir Reg *UUP* Parliament Buildings. Tel. (01232) 521335. **East Belfast** 1st pref: 5,158, 12th ct.

ERVINE, David *PUP* 321 Newtownards Rd, Belfast BT4 1AG. Tel. (01232) 221020. **East Belfast** 1st pref: 5,114, elected 7th ct.

FARREN, Sean *SDLP* 30 Station Rd, Portstewart, co. Derry. Tel. (01265) 833042. **North Antrim** 1st pref: 6,433, elected 6th ct.

FEE, John *SDLP* 2 Bridge St, Newry, Co. Down. Tel. (01693) 67933. **Newry & Armagh** 1st pref: 3,166, elected 8th ct.

FORD, David *All* Feamore, Barnish, Kells BT42 3PR. **South Antrim** 1st pref: 3,778, elected 10th ct.

FOSTER, Sam *UUP* 1 Regal Pass, Enniskillen BT74 7NT. Tel. (01365) 342846. **Fermanagh & South Tyrone** 1st pref: 5,589, 5th ct.

GALLAGHER, Tommy *SDLP* 1st Floor, 39 Darling St, Enniskillen, Co. Fermanagh. Tel. (01365) 342848. **Fermanagh & South Tyrone** 1st pref: 8,135, elected 1st ct.

GIBSON, Oliver *DUP* 12 Main St, Beragh, Omagh BT79 0SY. Tel. (016627) 57000. **West Tyrone** 1st pref: 8,015, elected 1st ct.

GILDERNEW, Michelle *SF* 60 Irish St, Dungannon, Co. Tyrone. Tel. (01868) 722776. **Fermanagh & South Tyrone** 1st pref: 4,703, elected 9th ct.

GORMAN, Sir John *UUP* 77a High St, Bangor BT20 5BD. Tel. (01247) 470300. **North Down** 1st pref: 4,719, elected 6th ct.

HANNA, Carmel *SDLP* 17 Elmwood Mews, 102 Lisburn Rd, Belfast. Tel. (10232) 683535. **South Belfast** 1st pref: 3,882, elected 10th ct.

HAUGHEY, Denis *SDLP* 54A William St, Cookstown, Co. Tyrone. Tel. (016487) 63349. **Mid Ulster** 1st pref: 6,410, elected 6th ct.

HAY, William *DUP* 9 Ebrington Tce, Waterside, Derry BT47 1JS. Tel. (01504) 346271. **Foyle** 1st pref: 6,112, elected 8th ct.

HENDRON, Dr Joe *SDLP* 40 Bristow Park, Belfast. Tel. (01232) 665452. **West Belfast** 1st pref: 6,140, elected 1st ct.

HILDITCH, David *DUP* 22 High St, Carrickfergus BT38 7AA. Tel. (01960) 329980. **East Antrim** 1st pref: 4,876, elected 8th ct.

HUME, John MP, MEP *SDLP* 5 Bayview Tce, Derry. Tel. (01504) 265340. **Foyle** 1st pref: 12,581, elected 1st ct.

HUSSEY, Derek *UUP* 48 Main St, Castlederg BT81 7BP. Tel. (01662) 679299. **West Tyrone** 1st pref: 4,622; elected 8th ct.

HUTCHINSON, Billy *PUP* 135 Shore Rd, Belfast BT15 3PN. Tel. (01232) 772307. **North Belfast** 1st pref: 3,751, elected 11th ct.

HUTCHINSON, Roger *NIUP* Parliament Buildings. Tel. (01232) 521743. **East Antrim** 1st pref: 2,866, elected 13th ct.

KANE, Gardiner *DUP* 142a Main St, Bushmills BT57 8QE. Tel. (01265) 730373. **North Antrim** 1st pref: 3,638, elected 12th ct.

KELLY, Gerry *SF* 19 Hallidays Rd, Belfast BT15. Tel. (01232) 740817. **North Belfast** 1st pref: 5,610, elected 10th ct.

KELLY, John *SF* 70 Tirkane Rd, Maghera, Co. Derry. Tel. (01648) 45122. **Mid Ulster** 1st pref: 5,594, elected 6th ct.

KENNEDY, Danny *UUP* 3 Mallview Tce, Armagh BT61 9AN. Tel. (01861) 511655. **Newry & Armagh** 1st pref: 5,,495, elected 6th ct.

LESLIE, James *UUP* 30a Ballymoney St, Ballymena BT43 6AL. Tel. (01266) 42262. **North Antrim** 1st pref: 3,458, elected 12th ct.

LEWSLEY, Patricia *SDLP* 34 Alina Gardens, Areema, Dunmurry, Belfast. Tel. (01232) 290846. **Lagan Valley** 1st pref: 4,039, elected 9th ct.

MAGINNESS, Alban *SDLP* 228 Antrim rd, Belfast. Tel. (01232) 220520. **North Belfast** 1st pref: 6,196, elected 1st ct.

MALLON, Seamus MP *SDLP* 2 Bridge St, Newry, Co. Down. Tel. (01693) 67933. **Newry & Armagh** 1st pref: 13,582, elected 1st ct.

MASKEY, Alex *SF* Connolly House, 147 Andersonstown Rd, Belfast BT11. Tel. (01232) 808404. **West Belfast** 1st pref: 4,330, elected 10th ct.

McCARTHY, Kieran *All* 3 Main St, Kirkubbin BT22 2SS. **Strangford** 1st pref: 2,947, elected 17th ct.

McCARTNEY, Robert MP *UKUP* 10 Hamilton Rd, Bangor BT20 4LE. Tel. (01247) 272994. **North Down** 1st pref: 8,188, ellected 1st ct.

McCLARTY, David *UUP* 12 Dunmore St, Coleraine BT52. Tel. (01265) 327294. **East Derry** 1st pref: 5,108, elected 5th ct.

McCLELLAND, Donovan *SDLP* 18 Roseville Crescent, Randalstown, Co. Antrim. Tel. (018494) 64615. **South Antrim** 1st pref: 4,309, elected 8th ct.

McCREA, Rev Dr William *DUP* 10 Highfield Rd, Magherafelt BT45 5JD. Tel. (01648) 32664. **Mid-Ulster** 1st pref: 10,339, elected 1st ct.

McDONNELL, Alasdair *SDLP* 150 Ormeau Rd, Belfast. Tel. (01232) 242474. **South Belfast** 1st pref: 4,956, elected 6th ct.

McELDUFF, Barry *SF* Main St, Carrickmore, Co. Tyrone. Tel. (016627) 61744. **West Tyrone** 1st pref: 4,963, elected 9th ct.

McFARLAND, Alan *UUP* 77a High St, Bangor BT20 5BD. Tel. (01247) 470300. **North Down** 1st pref: 4653, elected 6th ct.

McGIMPSEY, Michael *UUP* 127-145 Sandy Row, Belfast BT12 5ET. Tel. (01232) 245801. **South Belfast** 1st pref: 4,938, elected 5th ct.

McGRADY, Eddie MP *SDLP* 32 Saul St, Downpatrick, Co. Down. Tel. (01396) 612882. **South Down** 1st pref: 10,373, elected 1st ct.

McGUINNESS, Martin MP *SF* Burn Road, Cookstown BT80 8DN. Tel. (016487) 65850. **Mid Ulster** 1st pref: 8,703, elected 1st ct.

McHUGH, Gerry *SF* 7 Market St, Enniskillen BT74 7DS. Tel. (01365) 328214. **Fermanagh & South Tyrone** 1st pref: 5,459, elected 7th ct.

McLAUGHLIN, Mitchel *SF* Ráth Mór Shopping Mall, Bligh's Lane, Creggan, Derry. Tel. (01504) 309264.

McMENAMIN, Eugene *SDLP* Laurel Drive, Strabane, Co. Tyrone. Tel. (01504) 883529. **West Tyrone** 1st pref: 3,548, elected 9th.

McNAMEE, Pat *SF* 38 Irish St, Armagh BT61 7EP. Tel. (01861) 511797. **Newry & Armagh** 1st pref: 4,570, elected 8th ct.

McWILLIAMS, Prof Monica *NIWC* 50 University St, Belfast BT7 1HB. Tel. (01232) 233100. **South Belfast** 1st pref: 3,912, elected 10th ct.

MOLLOY, Francie *SF* 7 The Square, Coalisland, Co. Tyrone. Tel. (018687) 48689. **Mid Ulster** 1st pref: 6,008, elected 6th ct.

MORRICE, Jane *NIWC* 108 Dufferin Avenue, Bangor, Co. Down. Tel. (01247) 470739. **North Down** 1st pref: 1,808, elected 12 ct.

MORROW, Maurice *DUP* 62b Scotch St, Dungannon BT70 1BJ. Tel. (01868) 752799. **Fermanagh and South Tyrone** 1st pref: 3,987, elected 10th ct.

MURPHY, Conor *SF* Parliament Buildings. Tel. (01232) 521630. **Newry & Armagh** 1st pref: 4,839, elected 8th ct.

MURPHY, Mick *SF* 17 Circular Rd, Castlewellan BT30. Tel. (01396) 616377. **South Down** 1st pref: 6,251, elected 6th ct.

NEESON, Sean *All* 44 Milebush Pk, Carrickfergus BT38 7QR. **East Antrim** 1st pref: 5,247, elected 1st ct.

NEILIS, Mary *SF* 15 Cable Street, Derry. Tel. (01504) 377551. **Foyle** 1st pref: 3,464, elected 8th ct.

NESBITT, Dermot *UUP* 19 Causeway Rd, Newcastle BT33, 0DL. Tel. (01396) 724400. **South Down** 1st pref: 5,480, elected 8th ct.

O'CONNOR, Danny *SDLP* 55c Main St, Larne, Co. Antrim. Tel. (01574) 270033. **East Antrim** 1st pref: 2,106, elected 13th ct.

O'HAGAN, Dara *SF* 77 North St, Lurgan, Co. Armagh. Tel. (01762) 349675. **Upper Bann** 1st pref: 4,301, elected 10th ct.

O'NEILL, Eamon *SDLP* 60 Main St, Castlewellan, co. Down. Tel. (013967) 78833. **South Down** 1st pref: 3,582, 11th ct.

PAISLEY, Rev Dr Ian MP, MEP *DUP* 17 Cyprus Avenue, Belfast BT5 5NT. Tel. (01232) 454255. **North Antrim** 1st pref: 10,590, elected 1st ct.

PAISLEY, Ian Jnr *DUP* 46 Hill Street, Ballymena BT43 6BH. Tel. (01266) 41421. **North Antrim** 1st pref: 4,459, elected 2nd ct.

POOTS, Edwin *DUP* 46 Bachelors Walk, Lisburn BT28 1XN. Tel. (01846) 603003. **Lagan Valley** 1st pref: 5,239, elected 7th ct.

RAMSEY, Sue *SF* c/o Conway Mill, 5-7 Conway St, Belfast BT13. **West Belfast** 1st pref: 3,946, elected 8th ct.

ROBINSON, Iris *DUP* 96 Belmont Avenue, Belfast BT4 3DE. Tel. (01232) 473111. **Strangford** 1st pref: 9,479, elected 1st ct.

ROBINSON, Ken *UUP* 32c North St, Carrickfergus BT38 7AQ. Tel. (01960) 362995. **East Antrim** 1st pref: 2,384, 13th ct.

ROBINSON, Mark *DUP* 215a Lisburn Rd, Belfast. Tel. (01232) 298569. **South Belfast** 1st pref: 2,872, elected 8th ct.

ROBINSON, Peter MP *DUP* 51 Gransha Rd,

Dundonald, Belfast BT16 0HB. Tel. 01232 473111. **East Belfast** 1st pref: 11,219, elected 1st ct.

ROCHE, Patrick *NIUP* Parliament Buildings. Tel. (01232) 521533. **Lagan Valley** 1st pref: 5,361, elected 9th ct.

RODGERS, Brid *SDLP* 41 North St, Lurgan BT67 9AG. Tel. (01762) 322140. **Upper Bann** 1st pref: 9,260, elected 1st ct.

SAVAGE, George *UUP* 6 Bridge St, Banbridge BT32. Tel. (018206) 24114. **Upper Bann** 1st pref: 669, elected 14th ct.

SHANNON, Jim *DUP* Parliament Buildings. Tel. (01232) 521128 **Strangford** 1st pref: 1,415, elected 18th ct.

SHIPLEY-DALTON, Duncan *UUP* Parliament Buildings. Tel. (01232) 520317. **South Antrim** 1st pref: 4,147, elected 9th ct.

TAYLOR, John MP *UUP* 6 William St, Newtownards, BT23 4AE. Tel. (01247) 814123. **Strangford** 1st pref: 9,203, elected 1st ct.

TIERNEY, John *SDLP* 5 Bayview Tce, Derry. Tel. (01504) 265340. **Foyle** 1st pref: 3,778, elected 7th ct.

TRIMBLE, David MP *UUP* 2 Queen St, Lurgan, BT66 8BQ. Tel. (01762) 328088. **Upper Bann** 1st pref: 12,238, elected 1st ct.

WATSON, Denis *UUAP* Parliament Buildings. Tel. (01232) 521148. **Upper Bann** 1st pref: 4,855, elected 14th ct.

WEIR, Peter *UUP* 77a High St, Bangor BT20 5BD. Tel.

(01247) 470301. **North Down** 1st pref: 2,775, elected 12th ct.

WELLS, Jim *DUP* 18 Lisburn St, Ballynahinch BT24 8BD. Tel. (01238) 564200. **South Down** 1st pref: 4,826, elected 11th ct.

WILSON, Cedric *NIUP* Parliament Buildings. Tel. (01232) 521533. **Strangford** 1st pref: 3,078, elected 18th ct.

WILSON, Jim *UUP* Parliament Buildings. Tel. (01232) 521292. **South Antrim** 1st pref: 6,691, elected 1st ct.

WILSON, Sammy *DUP* 13 Castlereagh Rd, Belfast BT6 9AX. Tel. (01232) 459400. **East Belfast** 1st pref: 3,853, elected 12th ct.

European Parliament

HUME, John MP *SDLP/PES* 5 Bayview Tce, Derry. Tel. (01504) 265340. **Northern Ireland** 1st pref: 190,731, elected 1st ct.

PAISLEY, Rev Dr Ian MP *DUP/Ind* 17 Cyprus Avenue, Belfast BT5 5NT. Tel. (01232) 454255. **Northern Ireland** 1st pref: 192,762, elected 1st ct.

NICHOLSON, Jim *UUP/EPP* 3 Glengall St, Belfast BT12 5AE. Tel. (01232) 439431. **Northern Ireland** 1st pref: 119,507, elected 3rd ct.

Northern Ireland Office Ministers

Sec. of State
Dr. Mo Mowlam

Secretary of State for Northern Ireland..Dr Mo Mowlam MP
Dr Mowlam was replaced as NI Secretary of State by Peter Mandelson on October 11, 1999.
Ministers of State
Department Finance and Personnel..Adam Ingram MP
Department of Health & Social Services...George Howarth MP

Parliamentary Under Secretaries of State
Department of Economic Development ....John McFall MP
Department of Education ....John McFall MP
Department of the Environment ....Lord Dubs
Department of Agriculture..Lord Dubs

Salaries of Elected Representatives

WESTMINSTER	£stg	NORTHERN IRELAND ASSEMBLY	£stg
Member of Parliament	47,008	Assembly Member	29,292
Parliamentary Under Secretary of State	69,339	Presiding Officer	45,069
Minister of State	77,047	Minister	45,069
Minister	106,716	Deputy First Minister	54,876
Prime Minister	147,816	First Minister	60,164

An Assembly Member who is also an MP or MEP is entitled to one-third of the basic salary.

Secretaries of State

Term	Secretary of State	Party
1972-73	William Whitelaw	Conservative
1973-74	Francis Pym	Conservative
1974-76	Merlyn Rees	Labour
1976-79	Roy Mason	Labour
1979-81	Humphrey Atkins	Conservative
1981-84	Jim Prior	Conservative
1984-85	Douglas Hurd	Conservative
1985-89	Tom King	Conservative
1989-92	Peter Brooke	Conservative
1992-97	Patrick Mayhew	Conservative
1997-99	Dr Mo Mowlam	Labour
1999-	Peter Mandelson	Labour

Elections To Westminster, 1922-1997

DATE	NO. OF SEATS	UUP	N	DUP	SDLP	SF	OTHER U	OTHER N	OTHER Lab.	VUPP
15.11.1922	13	11	2	-	-	-	-	-	-	-
06.12.1923	13	11	2	-	-	-	-	-	-	-
29.10.1924	13	13	-	-	-	-	-	-	-	-
30.05.1929	13	11	-	-	-	-	-	2[1]	-	-
27.10.1931	13	11	2	-	-	-	-	-	-	-
14.11.1935	13	11	-	-	-	-	-	2[2]	-	-
05.07.1945	13	9	2	-	-	-	1	-	1	-
23.02.1950	12	10	-	-	-	-	-	2[3]	-	-
25.10.1951	12	9	-	-	-	-	-	2[3]	1	-
26.05.1955	12	10	-	-	-	2	-	-	-	-
08.10.1959	12	12	-	-	-	-	-	-	-	-
15.10.1964	12	12	-	-	-	-	-	-	-	-
31.03.1966	12	11	-	-	-	-	-	-	1	-
18.06.1970	12	8	-	-	-	-	1	2[4]	1	-
28.02.1974	12	7	-	1	1	-	-	-	-	3
10.10.1974	12	6	-	1	1	-	-	1[5]	-	3
03.05.1979	12	5	-	3	1	-	2	1	-	-
09.06.1983	17	11	-	3	1	1	1	-	-	-
11.06.1987	17	9	-	3	3	1	1	-	-	-
09.04.1992	17	9	-	3	4	-	1	-	-	-
01.05.1997	18	10	-	2	3	2	1	-	-	-

1: ....Other N = National League   2: ....Other N = Nationalist Abstentionists
3:.................Other N = Anti-Partition League   4:...............Other N = Unity Candidates
5:.................Other N = Independent

Constitutional Referenda

Date	Issue	Turnout %	For %	Against %
March 8, 1973	Northern Ireland remaining within the United Kingdom	59	98.9	1.1
June 5, 1975	United Kingdom remaining within the EEC	47	52.1	47.9
May 22, 1998	Good Friday Agreement	81.1	71.1	28.9

NI Prime Ministers

Name	Born	MP	Prime Minister	Died	Aged
James Craig	08.01.1871, Belfast	1921-40	7 Jun 1921–24 Nov 1940	24.11.1940	69
John M. Andrews	17.07.1871, Co. Down	1921-53	25 Nov 1940–28 Apr 1943	06.08.1956	85
Basil Brooke	09.06.1888, Co. Fermanagh	1929-67	28 Apr 1943–25 Mar 1963	18.08.1973	85
Captain Terence O'Neill	10.09.1914, London	1946-70	25 Mar 1963–28 Apr 1969	13.06.1990	75
James Chichester Clarke	12.02.1923, Co. Derry	1960-71	1 May 1969–20 Mar 1971	-	-
Brian Faulkner	18.02.1921, Co. Down	1949-72	23 Mar 1971–24 Mar 1972	03.03.1977	56

All NI Prime Ministers were members of the Ulster Unionist Party
→ For profiles see Who Was Who chapter

The Peace Process

When John White, of the Progressive Unionist Party, publicly paid a warm tribute to An Taoiseach, Bertie Ahern, on Good Friday, April 10th, it was, for many, a defining moment in the entire peace process. Symbolically, it was the breaking of the last taboo.

The sight of a hardline former loyalist paramilitary paying tribute to an Irish Taoiseach suggested that the peace process had broken down not only old suspicions and hostilities between the two parts of the island but also eased much of the old enmity between political leaders who hold diametrically opposed views on the future governance of this island.

When the Northern "troubles" broke out in the late 1960s, there were no mechanisms in place to resolve what were very serious communal difficulties.

After Bloody Sunday in Derry (1972), Dublin called home its ambassador to London. The burning of the British Embassy in Dublin around the same time further strained relationships. And the alleged involvement of the British Intelligence Services in the bombings in Dublin and Monaghan (1974) heralded the era of what was later to be known as 'megaphone' diplomacy.

It wasn't until the early 1980s that the two governments began to co-operate more closely in an effort to find a widely acceptable political solution.

Here are some of the key signposts along the way:

ANGLO-IRISH INTERGOVERNMENTAL COUNCIL: Following a meeting in Dublin in 1980 between An Taoiseach, Charles Haughey, and British Prime Minister, Margaret Thatcher, the Council was set up to provide a formal framework within which relationships between the two countries could be explored. The work of the council laid the groundwork for the Anglo-Irish Agreement.

ANGLO-IRISH AGREEMENT: Signed in November 1985, the Anglo-Irish Agreement was received with great hostility by unionists in the North. In the agreement (signed by Mrs. Thatcher and Garret FitzGerald, the then Taoiseach), an Intergovernmental Conference was established, chaired jointly by a representative of each Government and served by a permanent Joint Secretariat based at Maryfield, just outside Belfast.

The unionist hostility was premised on the fact that the Agreement enabled the Irish Government to put forward views and proposals on many aspects of Northern Ireland affairs. The agreement brought co-operation between the two countries to unprecedented levels.

ROUND-TABLE TALKS: In an effort to get movement in the North, the British and Irish Governments convened round table talks during 1991/1992, involving the main constitutional parties in the North. Under the chairmanship of Australian Sir Ninian Stephens the talks were based on the three-strand approach long promulgated by SDLP leader, John Hume. The strands were: 1) Relationships within Northern Ireland; 2) Relationships within the island of Ireland; 3) Relationship between Ireland and Britain. No overall agreement was reached.

JOINT DECLARATION: A Joint Declaration was issued by An Taoiseach, Albert Reynolds, and British Prime Minister, John Major, on December 15, 1993. The Declaration set out the basic principles which, it was felt, would be required to underpin any political settlement. At the core of this document were the principles of self-determination and consent. One of the key phrases contained in the document was that the British Government had "no selfish strategic or economic interest in Northern Ireland". In regard to the principle of consent, the British also affirmed that they would uphold the democratic wish of a greater number of the people in the North on the issue of whether they would prefer to support the Union or a sovereign united Ireland.

The Irish Government stated ". . . the democratic right of self-determination by the people of Ireland, as a whole, must be achieved and exercised with and subject to the agreement and consent of the majority of the people of Northern Ireland."

Of particular importance was the offer in the Declaration to those engaged in paramilitary violence that if they established a commitment to exclusively peaceful means and were willing to abide by the democratic process they would be free to participate fully, in the due course, in the dialogue between the two governments. This, along with SDLP leader John Hume's extensive talks with Sinn Féin President, Gerry Adams, sowed the seeds for the IRA ceasefire.

IRA CEASEFIRE: After 25 years of a sustained campaign, the IRA announced, on August 31, 1994 a "complete cessation of military operations". The Combined Loyalist Military Command announced a similar cessation on October 13, 1994. Both Governments moved swiftly to engage Sinn Féin, and the two loyalist parties, the Progressive Unionist Party (PUP) and the Ulster Democratic Party (UDP), in political dialogue.

FRAMEWORK DOCUMENT: Officially titled "A New Framework for Agreement", the Framework Document sought to apply the principles enunciated in the Joint Declaration. It envisaged balanced constitutional change on both sides and new political structures covering all three relationships. It also committed the Governments to comprehensive negotiations with the Northern Ireland parties and that any agreement resulting from those negotiations be put to the people, North and South, for democratic ratification.

INTERNATIONAL BODY: The entire process stalled during 1995 because unionists refused to engage in talks with Sinn Féin without prior IRA decommissioning. In an attempt to move things forward, the Governments established an International body under the chairmanship of US Senator George Mitchell to provide an independent assessment of how best to handle the decommissioning issue.

In its report in January, 1996, the International Body recommended that all parties participating in negotiations should commit themselves to six principles of democracy and non-violence. It also suggested that the parties might consider a proposal whereby decommissioning might occur during negotiations.

IRA CEASEFIRE ENDS: Amidst a welter of recriminations, much of it directed against An Taoiseach, John Bruton, the IRA ceasefire ended on February 9, 1996, with a huge explosion at Canary Wharf in London. Republicans claimed that they had delivered on their side of the bargain –by delivering a ceasefire– but once that had been achieved, the two Governments had stalled the entire process.

MULTI-PARTY TALKS: After much delay, nine parties assembled in June 1996 for multi-party talks involving the two governments. Sinn Féin was excluded in the absence of an IRA ceasefire. The talks were chaired by Senator Mitchell who was assisted by former Finnish Prime Minister, Harri Holkeri and former Canadian General, John de Chastelain. Progress at the talks was painfully slow, much time being devoted to procedural detail.

IRA RENEW CEASEFIRE: On Friday, July 20, 1997, the IRA announced a renewal of its ceasefire, thus clearing the way for Sinn Féin's entry into the talks on September 9. In protest at the Sinn Féin entry, two unionist parties, the DUP and the UKUP, then left the talks. The largest unionist party, the UUP, under the leadership of David Trimble, decided to stay.

SUBSTANTIVE NEGOTIATIONS BEGIN: More than three years after the IRA first called its ceasefire, substantive negotiations finally got underway on September 24, 1997. The three-strand agenda on relationships within these islands provided the basis for the negotiations.

PROPOSITIONS ON HEADS OF AGREEMENT: On January 12, 1998, the Governments published a series of proposals/suggestions which they hoped would focus the negotiations. Sinn Féin reacted angrily to these "Heads of Agreement" claiming they were more kindly disposed to the unionist position. Against this background, Senator Mitchell imposed a deadline of April 9 for the ending of negotiations.

THE GOOD FRIDAY AGREEMENT: On Friday, April 10 (Good Friday), one day after the agreed deadline, the Northern Ireland parties agreed a comprehensive

political settlement. The two Governments immediately signed a new British-Irish Agreement committing themselves to give effect to the provisions of this multi-party agreement. The main points agreed were the setting up of a new Assembly in the North, a North-South Ministerial Council, the establishment of a British-Irish Council and a British-Irish inter-governmental Conference to promote bilateral co-operation at all levels in matters of mutual interest.

AGREEMENT REFERENDA: On May 22, 1998, referenda were held in both parts of the island to ratify the Agreement. In the North, 71.1% supported it while in the South, 94.4% voted to allow the Government to become party to the Agreement. The combined 'Yes' vote on the island of Ireland was 85%. The referendum in the Republic allows for the change of the Irish Constitution; the Irish nation will be defined in terms of its people, rather than its territory, in the new wording for Article 2 of the Irish Constitution. The new Article 3 will enshrine the principle of consent while "expressing the wish of the majority of the Irish people for a united Ireland". The British government will repeal, through legislation, the 1920 Government of Ireland Act.

ASSEMBLY ELECTIONS: On June 25, 1998, elections took place to elect members to the new Assembly. For the first time in a Northern election, a nationalist party, the SDLP, received the largest share of first preference votes cast. Eventually, under the PR system, the Ulster Unionist Party emerged as the largest party,

ASSEMBLY MEETS: At the inaugural meeting of the new Assembly on July 1st, 1998, UUP leader, David Trimble, was elected Northern Ireland's First Minister while the SDLP's Seamus Mallon was elected Deputy First Minister. On September 7, an unprecedented meeting took place - First Minister, David Trimble met Sinn Féin President, Gerry Adams, during a round table discussion with Northern party leaders.

DEPARTMENTS AGREED: A series of meetings culminating on December 17th led to agreement on six cross border bodies and ten government departments. The cross border bodies will govern trade and business development, EU funding programmes, inland waterways, aquaculture, food safety and the Irish and Ulster-Scots languages.

The government departments are: Finance and Personnel; Enterprise, Trade and Investment; Regional Development; Agriculture and Rural Development; Higher and Further Education; Education; Health and Social Services; Social Development; Culture, Arts and Leisure; Environment.

HILLSBOROUGH DECLARATION: Easter week saw a hectic round of meetings for the second consecutive year. Agreement on the appointment of ministers was not forthcoming from the parties and on April 1 the Taoiseach, Bertie Ahern and the British Prime

Minister Tony Blair set out their ideas on the way forward in the Hillsborough Declaration.

The Declaration proposed that the nomination of ministers should be followed within a month by a collective act of reconciliation incorporating the verifiable beginning of paramilitary decommissioning. Around this time powers would be devolved to the Northern Ireland Assembly and the institutions which were laid out in the Good Friday Agreement would be established. At this time the British authorities would engage on further moves of normalisation and demilitarisation. However, should any of the steps not be completed within the agreed time-frame it would be for the Assembly to confirm the nomination of ministers.

THE WAY FORWARD: For the second time in three months a marathon session of talks aimed at implementing the Good Friday Agreement ended in disagreement among the parties. The British and Irish governments issued a joint statement entitled *The Way Forward* on July 2nd, 1999. The document laid out a schedule for the implementation of the agreement with the D'Hondt procedure to nominate ministers to be run on July 15 and that devolution of powers take place on July 18. The International Commission on Decommissioning was to lay out a timetable for decommissioning and present reports in September and December 1999 with all decommissioning to be completed by May 2000. Furthermore the governments undertook to implement a 'failsafe clause' and suspend the operation of the institutions in the event of commitments to decommissioning or devolution not being fulfilled. The report of the decommissioning commission was published the same day stating that the May 22, 2000 deadline was attainable in the event of the paramilitary organisations appointing an individual to liaise with the commission on the modalities of decommissioning.

NON-APPOINTMENT OF THE EXECUTIVE: The non-attendance of the UUP and the refusal of other unionist parties to appoint ministers reduced the proceedings of the Northern Ireland Assembly to farce on July 15. The Presiding Officer duly triggered the d'Hondt mechanism but no-one other than the SDLP or Sinn Féin appointed ministers thus causing the suspension of the executive as it did not reflect party strength in the Assembly. The ministers appointed were: Mark Durkan (SDLP) Finance and Personnel; Bairbre De Bruin (SF) Enterprise Trade and Employment; Sean Farren (SDLP) Regional Development; Martin McGuinness (SF) Agriculture and Rural Development; Bríd Rodgers (SDLP) Higher and Further Education; Pat Doherty (SF) Education; Joe Hendron (SDLP) Health and Social Services; Denis Haughey (SDLP) Social Development; Mary Neilis (SF) Culture, Arts and Leisure; Alban Maginness (SDLP) Environment. The Deputy First Minister, Seamus Mallon resigned before the the Assembly adjourned. The Secretary for State, Dr Mowlam, announced a review of the Agreement to commence in September. The review, which commenced on September 6th under the chairmanship of George Mitchell, is ongoing at time of going to print.

REFORM OF THE RUC: The Patten Commission published its report complete with 175 recommendations for the reform of the RUC on September 9th. Amongst its main recommendations were the reduction in size of the force, renaming of the force as the Northern Ireland Police Service and the establishment of a new Police Authority drawing members from the Assembly.

Related Documents

● **THE ANGLO-IRISH AGREEMENT**

Signed November 15, 1985, by Taoiseach Garret FitzGerald and British Prime Minister Margaret Thatcher. Its main points were:
• Both governments affirmed that change in the status of Northern Ireland could only come about through the consent of a majority of the people of Northern Ireland. While recognising that such a majority did not exist, the governments declared that they would legislate for a change in Northern Ireland's status should a majority wish to establish a united Ireland.
• An Intergovernmental Conference was established to deal with political, security and legal matters and promote cross-border co-operation.
• The possibility of establishing an Anglo-Irish Parliamentary body was left for decision of the respective parliaments.

● **DOWNING STREET DECLARATION**

Signed December 15, 1993, by Taoiseach Albert Reynolds and British Prime Minister John Major. Its

main provisions were as follows:
• The British government affirmed that it was for the people of Ireland alone, and the two parts respectively, to exercise their right of self-determination, and it stated it had no 'selfish strategic or economic interest in Northern Ireland'.
• The Irish government accepted that Irish self-determination must be achieved and exercised with the consent and agreement of a majority of people in Northern Ireland.
• The Irish government pledged that in the case of a balanced constitutional accommodation it would put forward and support changes to the Irish Constitution which would reflect the principle of consent.
• Both governments confirmed that democratically mandated parties who demonstrated a commitment to exclusively peaceful methods would be free to participate fully in the democratic process.
• The Irish government announced its intention to establish a Forum for Peace and Reconciliation.

● FRAMEWORKS DOCUMENT

Signed by Taoiseach John Bruton and British Prime Minister John Major on February 22, 1995, it set out what both governments saw as the possible format of the talks process. The guiding principles as set out in paragraph ten were:
• The principle of self-determination must be in keeping with the principle of consent.
• Agreement must be pursued and achieved through exclusively democratic and peaceful methods.
• Any new political arrangements must afford parity of esteem to both traditions.
The document also set out three interlocking strands as a basis for areas of negotiation, these were:
• **Structures within Northern Ireland.** Locally elected representatives would exercise "shared administrative and legislative control over agreed matters."
• **North/South Institutions.** These institutions would be consultative, harmonising and executive. A parliamentary forum drawing members from a Northern Assembly and the Dáil would also be established.
• **East/West Structures.** A new agreement between the sovereign governments "reflecting the totality of relationships between the two islands" supported by a permanent secretariat.
The document concludes with the governments agreeing that the matters raised should be examined in negotiations between democratically mandated parties committed to peaceful means and that the outcome to these negotiations should be submitted for ratification through referenda, north and south.

● THE 'MITCHELL' REPORT

Published January 22nd, 1996, it is the report of the International Body on the Decommissioning of Illegal Arms. The body was chaired by US Senator George Mitchell and included former Finnish Prime Minister Harri Holkeri and Canadian General John de Chastelain.
• The six 'Mitchell principles' of democracy to which all parties at the multi-party talks had to 'affirm their total and absolute commitment' were:
(1) to use democratic and exclusively peaceful means to resolve political issues;
(2) to the total disarmament of paramilitary weapons;
(3) to agree that disarmament must be independently verifiable;
(4) to renounce the use of force by themselves or by other organisations;
(5) to accept the outcome of negotiations no matter how repugnant it may be and to use only democratic methods to alter the outcome;
(6) to call an end to "punishment" killings and beatings.
• The report recommended that the decommissioning of illegally held paramilitary weapons should take place during multi-party talks as a tangible confidence building measure.
• The report also recommended the holding of elections as a further confidence-building measure.

● THE 'NORTH' REPORT

Published in 1997, it is the report of the Independent Review of Parades and Marches under the chairmanship of Dr Peter North with members Father Oliver Crilly

and the Reverend John Dunlop. Recommendations include:
• the establishing of a five-person Independent Parades Commission, appointed by the Northern Ireland Secretary of State.
• responsibility for decisions on contentious parades should lie with the Commission rather than with the RUC.

● THE GOOD FRIDAY AGREEMENT

The Settlement was signed on Good Friday, 10 April, 1998 by Taoiseach Bertie Ahern, Prime Minister Tony Blair and the participants at the multi-party talks namely the Alliance Party, the Labour Party, the Northern Ireland's Women Coalition, the Progressive Unionist Party, the Social Democratic and Labour Party, Sinn Féin, the Ulster Democratic Party and the Ulster Unionist Party. *(Both Sinn Féin and the Ulster Unionist Party submitted the Agreement to their parties for ratification.)*

Constitutional Issues
• The British government will repeal, through legislation, the 1920 Government of Ireland Act.
• The Secretary of State for Northern Ireland may order a poll on the status of Northern Ireland on the question of remaining within the United Kingdom or unification with the Republic. Such polls must be held at least seven years apart.
• The Irish government will submit Articles two and three of Bunreacht na hÉireann for amendment by referendum.

Strand One
• Northern Ireland Assembly to be established with 108 seats. Six members will be returned by proportional representation from the 18 Westminster constituencies.
• Assembly to elect a 12-member executive committee of ministers. The ministerial committee will be headed by a First Minister and Deputy First Minister. Ministerial posts will be allocated in proportion to party strength.

Strand Two
• A North/South Ministerial Council to be established within one year, consisting of ministers from the Dáil and the Assembly. Its remit will be to consider matters of mutual interest through consultation, co-operation and action. The Council will be accountable to the Assembly and the Oireachtas.

Strand Three
• A British-Irish Council, supported by a permanent secretariat, is to be established, drawing members from the Assembly, the Dáil, the House of Commons, the Isle of Man, the Channel Islands and the new Assemblies in Scotland and Wales.

British-Irish Intergovernmental Conference
• A new British-Irish Agreement will establish a new Conference to replace that set up by the Anglo-Irish Agreement in 1985.

Rights, Safeguards and Equality of Opportunity
• The European Convention on Human Rights will be incorporated into Northern Ireland law.
• A Human Rights Commission and a statutory Equality Commission will be established in Northern Ireland.
• The Irish government will establish a Human Rights Commission. A joint North-South committee of these Commissions will also be established.

• The British government will take resolute action to promote the Irish language.

Decommissioning

• Participants will use their influence to achieve decommissioning of all illegally held arms in the possession of paramilitary groups within two years of the May referenda in the context of an overall settlement.

Security, Policing, Justice and Prisoners

• The British government will seek to normalise security in Northern Ireland through reducing the numbers and role of security forces, removing security installations and ending emergency powers.
• The Irish government will initiate a review of the Offences Against the State Acts with a view to reforming and dispensing with certain provisions.
• An independent commission will make recommendations on the future of policing in Northern Ireland by May of 1999.
• A review of criminal justice will be undertaken by the British government.
• The British and Irish governments will legislate for the accelerated release of paramilitary prisoners whose organisations are observing a ceasefire.

On May 22nd the Settlement was ratified by referendum in both Northern Ireland and the Republic of Ireland.

● **THE REPORT OF THE INTERNATIONAL COMMISSION ON DECOMMISSIONING**

The Report was due to be published on June 29 but was postponed until July 2 at the request of the British and Irish governments. The members of the Commission were General John de Chastelain, Brigadier Tauno Nieminen and Ambassador Donald C. Johnson.

The Report found that the UDA, IRA, INLA and the Real IRA had not nominated points of contact with the Commission by the end of June. The UVF and the LVF had appointed points of contact and the LVF were the only organisation to carry out an act of decommissioning.

The Commission, cognisant of the guidelines laid down by the British and Irish governments defined the process of decommissioning as being underway when a paramilitary organisation gives an unambiguous commitment to complete the process by May 22, 2000 and when it commences, through an authorised representative, detailed discussions about the location, timing, amounts and types of decommissioning it will engage in. The Commission will draw up a detailed timetable in consultation with the nominated representative of each group to ensure the process is completed by May 2000.

● **THE 'PATTEN' REPORT**

Published on September 9th 1999, it is the report of the Commission set up to investigate policing in Northern Ireland. The Commission was chaired by Chris Patten and its members were: Maurice Hayes, Gerald Lynch, Kathleen O'Toole, Clifford Shearing, Sir John Smith, Peter Smith and Lucy Woods. The Commission received 2,500 written submissions and held 40 public meeting across Northern Ireland which were attended by up to 10,000 people. The main recommendations of the report are:

Accountability

• The Police Authority should be replaced by a new 19 member Policing Board. Ten Assembly members should serve on the Board selected on the d'Hondt system.
• Responsibility for policing should be devolved to the Executive as quickly as possible.
• A District Policing Partnership Board should be established in each District Council Area. The function of the Board is to express public concerns to the police, to purchase additional services from the police or private agencies and provide a forum where the public can address questions directly to the police.
• Legislation on covert policing should be compliant with the European Convention on Human Rights.

Policing in a Peaceful Society

• Police stations should become less forbidding, with existing stations modified, as the security situation permits.
• Police cars should continue to replace armoured Landrovers.
• The role of the army should be diminished and police patrols without military support should commence as security situation permits.
• Anti-terrorism legislation in Northern Ireland should be brought into line with legislation in Britain.
• The holding centres at Castlereagh, Strand Road and Gough Barracks should be closed without delay.

Public Order Policing

• Investment should be made to find a suitable replacement for Plastic Baton Rounds (PBR). The use of PBRs should be limited to a small number of specially trained officers.

Management and Personnel

• Officers should not have inordinately long postings in specialist area of the police.
• A substantial fund to benefit widows, injured officers and their families should be established.
• A rigorous programme of civilianisation of jobs should be implemented.

Structure of the Police service

• Each District Council Area should have a separate district command.
• Special Branch and Crime Branch should be amalgamated with a substantial reduction in the number of officers serving in the new command.
• The Full-Time Reserve should be abolished replaced by an enlarged (up to 2,500) Part-Time Reserve.

Size of the Police Service

• The envisaged size of the new police service should be 7,500 provided the security situation does not deteriorate significantly.
• A generous early retirement scheme for regular officers and full time reservists should be put in place for those over 50.

Composition and Recruitment of the Police Service

• A system of equal recruitment of Protestants and Catholics should be implemented. The implementation of this in conjunction with early retirement this would result in a force with approximately 30% Roman Catholic officers in ten years.
• Community leaders should take steps to remove all discouragements to –and make a priority of encourag-

ing– members of their communities joining the police. The GAA is specifically requested to repeal its Rule 21 which prohibits members of the police from membership of the Association.

• All officers including serving officers and future recruits should be required to register their interests and associations.

Training, Education and Development

• A purpose-built police training college should be built forthwith.

Culture, Ethos and Symbols

• The Royal Ulster Constabulary should not be disbanded but should be renamed the Northern Ireland Police Service.

• The new police force should adopt a new symbol, badge and flag which are free from association with either the British or Irish states.

• The Union flag should no longer be flown over police stations.

Cooperation with other Police Services

• The new police service should have written protocols with the Garda Síochána covering key aspects of cooperation.

• A long-term personnel exchange programme between the Northern Ireland police and the Garda Síochána should be established in key fields.

• Liaison officers from each service might be posted to the central headquarters and border area headquarters of the other.

• A joint database should be established in key areas such as drugs, smuggling and terrorism.

• A commissioner from somewhere other than Britain or Ireland should be appointed to supervise the implementation of these recommendations.

PUBLIC ADMINISTRATION

Central Government

Republic of Ireland Government Departments

AN ROINN TALMHAÍOCHTA AGUS BIA
Department of Agriculture and Food
Agriculture House, Kildare Street, Dublin 2.
Tel. (01) 607 2000 **Fax** (01) 661 6263
email: infodaff@indigo.ie
website: www.irlgov.ie/daff

Minister: Joe Walsh TD.
Ministers of State: Noel Davern TD, Ned O'Keefe TD.
Secretary General: John Malone. (£92,914)
Description: The department's functions are to promote and develop the agri-food sector, maximise its contribution to the national and rural economy, maintain the maximum number of viable farms in Ireland, discharge legal and administrative functions as required under Irish and EU law, ensure food safety and protect general consumer welfare, safeguard the environment and to support rural development and maintain high standards of animal and plant health/welfare.
State Bodies / Agencies: The National Stud, Bord na gCon, Irish Horseracing Authority, TEAGASC, An Bord Bia, An Bord Glas.

AN ROINN EALAÍON, OIDREACHTA, GAELTACHTA AGUS OILEÁN
Department of Arts, Heritage,
Gaeltacht & the Islands
43-49 Mespil Road, Dublin 4.
Tel. (01) 667 0788 **Fax** (01) 667 0827
email: webmaster@ealga.irgov.ie
*website:*www.irlgov.ie/ealga/

Minister: Síle de Valera TD.
Minister of State: Eamon Ó Cúiv TD.
Secretary General: Tadhg Ó hEaláithe. (£87,991)
Description: In order to enrich the quality of life and sense of identity of the Irish people and preserve their inheritance for present and future generations, the department aims to foster and promote Ireland's culture and heritage, specifically the Irish language. In particular, the department is responsible for the cultural, social and economic welfare of the Gaeltacht; encourages the preservation and extension of use of the Irish language; supports and develops cultural institutions responsible for heritage and contemporary arts; and formulates and implements national policy relating to arts and culture,

broadcasting and the audiovisual Industry and heritage.

State Bodies / Agencies: National Archives, National Gallery, National Library, National Museum (Collins Barracks) National Concert Hall, Chester Beatty Library, Hunt Museum, The Irish Architectural Archive, The Irish Manuscripts Commission, The Irish Museum of Modern Art, Marsh's Library, The Arts Council, The Heritage Council, Bord Scannán na hÉireann (The Irish Film Board), Radio Telefís Éireann, Independent Radio and Television Commission, Údarás na Gaeltachta, Bord na Gaeilge.

AN ROINN COSANTA
Department of Defence
Colaiste Caoimhín, Mobhi Road, Glasnevin, Dublin 9.
Tel. (01) 804 2000 **Fax** (01) 837 79933
email: defence@iol.ie
website: www.irlgov.ie/defence

Minister: Michael Smith TD.
Minister of State: Séamus Brennan TD.
Secretary General: David O'Callaghan. (£87,991)
Description: The department is responsible for the administration, training, organisation, maintenance, equipment, management, discipline, regulation and control of the defence forces. The department must ensure that it provides value-for-money military services which meet the needs of the government and the public and encompass an effective civil defence capability.
State Bodies / Agencies: Coiste an Asgard, the Irish Red Cross Society, the Army Pensions Board.

AN ROINN OIDEACHAIS AGUS EOOLAIOCHTA
Department of Education and Science
Marlborough Street, Dublin 1.
Tel. (01) 873 4700 **Fax** (01) 872 9553
*email:*webmaster@educ.irlgov.ie
website: www.irlgov.ie/educ/

Minister: Mícheál Martin TD.
Ministers of State: Willie O'Dea TD, Noel Treacy TD, Frank Fahey TD.
Secretary General: Mr. John Dennehy. (£87,991)
Description: The department manages public, private, post-primary, and special education and subsidises third level institutions in the Republic of Ireland. It is responsible for formulating and implementing national policies in relation to education. It is also responsible for

several national youth agencies.

State Bodies / Agencies: Advisory Council for English Language Schools, Dublin Institute for Advanced Studies - Council; School of Celtic Studies; School of Cosmic Physics; School of Theoretical Physics, Gaisce, the Higher Education Authority (HEA), Institiúd Teangeolaíochta Éireann, LEARGAS, National Centre for Guidance in Education, National Council for Curriculum and Assessment, National Council for Educational Awards, National Council for Vocational Awards, Secondary Teachers' Registration Council, Teastas - the Irish National Certification Authority.

AN ROINN FIONTAR, TRÁDÁLA AGUS FOSTAÍOCHTA

Department of Enterprise, Trade and Employment
Kildare Street, Dublin 2.
Tel. *1890 220 222/(01) 631 2121*
Fax *(01) 676 2654*
email: *webmaster@entemp.irlgov.ie*
website: *www.irlgov.ie/entemp/*

Minister: Mary Harney TD.
Ministers of State: Tom Kitt TD, Noel Treacy TD.
Secretary General: Paul Haran. (£92,914)
Description: The department aims to promote employment by encouraging enterprise, ensuring competitiveness, securing an educated and skilled workforce, tackling exclusion from the labour market, promoting a fair employment environment and implementing an effective business system.
Semi-State Agencies: Shannon Free Airport Development Company, IDA Ireland, Forbairt (Enterprise Ireland), Forfas, Crafts Council of Ireland, Health and Safety Authority, FAS, Nitrigin Éireann Teoranta.

AN ROINN COMHSHAOIL AGUS RIALTAS ÁITIÚIL

Department of Environment and Local Government
Custom House, Dublin 1.
Tel. *(01) 8882000* **Fax** *(01) 8882638*
email: *secretary_general@environ.irlgov.ie*
website: *www.environ.ie/*

Minister: Noel Dempsey TD.
Ministers of State: Danny Wallace TD, Robert Molloy TD.
Secretary General: Jimmy Farrelly. (£87,991)
Description: The department is responsible for environmental programmes and other services associated with the local government system. It aims to ensure, in partnership with local authorities and its own agencies, that Ireland has a high quality environment where infrastructure and amenities meet economic, social and environmental needs and where development is properly planned and sustainable.
State Bodies / Agencies: An Bord Pleanála, Rent Tribunal, Environmental Protection Agency, Medical Bureau of Road Safety, National Safety Council, Building Regulations Advisory Body, An Chomhairle Leabharlanna, Dublin Docklands Development

Authority, Dublin Transportation Office, Temple Bar Properties, Temple Bar Renewal, National Building Agency, National Roads Authority, Local Government Computer Services Board, Local Government Management Services Board, Fire Services Council, Housing Finance Agency.

AN ROINN AIRGEADAIS

Department of Finance
Government Buildings, Upper Merrion Street, Dublin 2.
Tel. *(01) 676 7571* **Fax** *(01) 678 9936*
email: *webmaster@finance.irlgov.ie*
website: *www.irlgov.ie/finance/*

Minister: Charlie McCreevy TD.
Minister of State: Martin Cullen TD.
Secretary General: Patrick Mullarkey. (£98,309)
Description: The department is responsible for the administration and business of the public finance of Ireland, including the collection and expenditure of the revenues of Ireland from whatever source arising. Additional functions are to promote and co-ordinate economic and social planning (including sectoral and regional planning), identify development policies, review the methods adopted by departments of state to implement such policies and generally advise the government on economic and social planning matters. The work of the Department of Finance is distributed between six divisions. The department is responsible for public expenditure, taxation, the budget, economic policy and managing the public service.
Divisions: Budget and Economic, Public Expenditure, Personnel and Remuneration, Finance Division, Corporate Services and Organisation, Management and Training Divisions.
State Bodies / Agencies: ACC Bank, the Central Bank of Ireland, the Civil Service Commission, the Economic and Social Research Institute, ICC Bank, the Institute of Public Administration, the National Lottery, the National Treasury Management Agency, the Office of Public Works, the Office of the Ombudsman, the Office of the Revenue Commissioners, the Ordnance Survey, the State Laboratory, the Trustee Savings Bank, the Valuation Office.

AN ROINN GNÓTHAÍ EACHTRACHA

Department of Foreign Affairs
Iveagh House, 80 St Stephen's Green, Dublin 2.
Tel. *(01) 4780822* **Fax** *(01) 6621007*
email: *library1@iveagh.irlgov.ie*
website: *www.irlgov.ie/iveagh/*

Minister: David Andrews TD.
Minister of State: Liz O'Donnell TD.
Secretary General: Pádraic MacKernan. (£92,914)
Description: The department aims to promote and protect the interests of Ireland and its citizens abroad and to pursue peace, partnership and reconciliation on the island of Ireland. Its responsibilities include monitoring developments and advising the Government in relation to Northern Ireland, co-ordinating Irish policies in the context of membership of the European Union and

developing European integration, managing Irish Aid (the Government's development co-operation programme), assisting the promotion of Ireland's external trade and economic interests, negotiating and ratifying international treaties and conventions, granting passports and visas.

Divisions: Administration and Consular, Anglo-Irish, Protocol and Cultural, Political, Economic, Development Cooperation, Legal, Inspectorate.

AN ROINN SLÁINTE AGUS LEANAÍ
Department of Health and Children
Hawkins House, Hawkins Street, Dublin 2.
Tel. *(01) 635 4000* ***Fax*** *(01) 635 4001*
email: *webmaster@health.irlgov.ie*
website: *www.doh.ie*

Minister: Brian Cowen TD.
Ministers of State: Frank Fahey TD, Dr. Tom Moffatt TD.
Secretary General: Jerry O'Dwyer. (£92,914)
Description: The department has overall responsibility for the administration and controlling of health services throughout the country. It also formulates and implements policy on the provision of these services.
State Bodies / Agencies: Beaumont Hospital Board, Blood Transfusion Service Board, Board for the Employment of the Blind, Board of the Adelaide and Meath Hospital Dublin incorporating the National Children's Hospital, an Bord Altranais (Nursing Board), an Bord Radharcmhastóirí (Opticians Board), an Bord Uchtala (Adoption Board), Comhairle na Nimheanna, Comhairle na n-Ospideal, Dental Council (An Comhairle Fiacloireachta), Drug Treatment Centre Board, Dublin Dental Hospital Board, Food Safety Authority of Ireland, General Medical Services (Payments) Board, Health Research Board (An Bord Taighde Slainte), Health Service Employers Agency, Hospital Bodies Administrative Bureau, Hospitals Trust Board, Irish Medicines Board (Bord Leigheasra na h-Eireann), Leopardstown Park Hospital Board, Medical Council, National Ambulance Advisory Council, National Cancer Registry Board, National Council on Ageing and Older People (National Council for the Elderly), National Rehabilitation Board, Office for Health Management, Postgraduate Medical and Dental Board, St. James's Hospital Board, St. Luke's and St. Anne's Hospital Board, Tallaght Hospital Board, Voluntary Health Insurance Board, Women's Health Council.

AN ROINN DLÍ AGUS CIRT, COMHIONANNAIS AGUS ATHCHIRITHE DLÍ
Department of Justice, Equality and Law Reform
72-76 St. Stephen's Green, Dublin 2.
Tel. *(01) 678 9711* ***Fax*** *(01) 661 5461*
email: *pagemaster@justice.irlgov.ie*
website: *www.irlgov.ie/justice/*

Minister: John O'Donoghue TD.
Ministers of State: Mary Wallace TD, Frank Fahey TD.
Secretary General: Tim Dalton. (£92,914)
Description: The department manages the courts,

prisons and police force in keeping with law and order. It is also responsible for terminating inequality for all social groups that face discrimination in any form. It oversees citizenship matters, EU matters, the courts, the Garda Síochána, immigration, prisons and the probation and welfare service.

State Bodies / Agencies: Land Registry and Registry of Deeds, Probation and Welfare Service, Legal Aid Board, Employment Equality Agency, Film Censor's Office, Censorship of Publications Board, Probation and Welfare Service, Office of the Commissioners for Charitable Donations and Bequests, Criminal Injuries Compensation Tribunal, Office of the Data Protection Commissioner, Forensic Science Laboratory, State Pathology Service.

AN ROINN NA MARA AGUS ACMHHAINNÍ NÁDÚRTHA
Department of the Marine and Natural Resources
Leeson Lane, Dublin 2.
Tel. *(01) 619 9200* ***Fax*** *(01) 661 8214*
email: *contact@marine.irlgov.ie*
website: *www.irlgov.ie/marine/*

Minister: Michael Woods TD.
Minister of State: Hugh Byrne TD.
Secretary General: Tom Carroll. (£87,991)
Description: The department supports the availability of efficient, competitive sea transport and port services; the long-term contribution of the fisheries sectors to the national economy; the sustainable management and development of the marine coastal zone for economic, tourism and leisure purposes; the exploration of minerals and hydrocarbons and their development for the optimum benefit to the Irish economy within the highest safety and environmental protection standards; and the development of the marine and natural resources sectors through effective research and technology development. It is also responsible for the prevention, as far as possible, of loss of life at sea through high safety standards and effective emergency response services and for the preservation and protection of the quality of the marine environment.

State Bodies/Agencies: Bord Iascaigh Mhara, Central Fisheries Board, Coillte Teoranta, the Regional Fisheries Boards (Eastern, Northern, North Western, Shannon, Southern, South Western, Western), Marine Institute, Arramara Teoranta, Salmon Research Agency, Foyle Fisheries Commission, Port Companies (Dublin, Dun Laoghaire, Port of Cork, Shannon Estuary, Drogheda, Galway, Foynes, New Ross), Harbour Authorities under the Harbours Acts 1946-76: Annagassan, Arklow, Ballyshannon, Baltimore/ Skibbereen, Bantry, Buncrana, Dingle, Dundalk. Kilrush, Kinsale, River Moy/Ballina, Sligo, Tralee and Fenit, Waterford, Westport, Wexford, Wicklow, Youghal.

AN ROINN FIONTAR POIBLÍ
Department of Public Enterprise
44 Kildare Street, Dublin 2.
Tel. *(01) 670 7444* ***Fax*** *(01) 677 3169*
email: *webmaster@tec.irlgov.ie*
website: *www.irlgov.ie/tec/*

Minister: Mary O'Rourke TD.
Minister of State: Joe Jacob TD.
Secretary General: John Loughrey. (£92,914)
Description: The department develops and implements national policies in relation to aviation and airports; rail and road transport; telecommunications; postal, radio and meteorological services; the supply and use of energy; and the exploration and extraction of minerals and petroleum. It is also responsible for investigating hazards to health from ionising radiation and radioactive contamination of the environment.
State Bodies / Agencies: Aer Lingus, Aer Rianta, An Post, Bord Gais Éireann, Bord na Mona, Córas Iompair Éireann, Electricity Supply Board, Irish National Petroleum Corporation, the Irish Aviation Authority, Radiological Protection Institute of Ireland, Telecom Éireann. *(now privatized - Eircom)*

AN ROINN GNÓTHAÍ SÓISIALACHA, POBAIL AGUS TEAGHLAIGH
Department of Social, Community and Family Affairs
Aras Mhic Dhiarmada, Store Street, Dublin 1.
Tel. *(01) 874 8444* **Fax** *(01) 704 3868*
email: webweaver@welfare.eirmail400.ie
website: www.dscfa.ie

Minister: Dermot Ahern TD.
Secretary General: Eddie Sullivan. (£87,991)
Description: The department formulates policies relating to the social security system within the country and is responsible for the administration of this system. It deals with the provision of social welfare services, pensions, child benefits, social welfare appeals, disability and injury benefits, unemployment schemes and employment support services.
State Bodies/Agencies: The Social Welfare Appeals Office, Combat Poverty Agency, Pensions Board, National Social Services Board.

ROINN AN TAOISIGH
Department of the Taoiseach
Government Buildings, Upper Merrion St, Dublin 2.
Tel. *(01) 662 4888* **Fax** *(01) 660 3281*
email: webmaster@taoiseach.irlgov.ie
website: www.irlgov.ie/taoiseach/

Taoiseach: Bertie Ahern TD.
Minister of State: Seamus Brennan TD.
Secretary General: Patrick Teahon. (£92,914)
Description: The department is responsible for communication between government departments and the President, for the National Economic and Social Council and for Government Information Services. The Taoiseach carries out functions under the Constitution and under statute, including the administration of public services, the co-ordination of local policies and the administration of the collection, compilation, abstraction and publication of statistics. The department also takes responsibility for a number of programmes, including the co-ordination of local development policy, support at

central government level for development of the West and the Strategic Management Initiative in the public service.
State Bodies / Agencies: The National Economic and Social Council, Government Information Services, Central Statistics Office, Law Reform Commission, Information Society Commission.

AN ROINN TURASÓIREACHTA, SPÓIRT AGUS ÁINEASA
Department of Tourism, Sport and Recreation
Kildare Street, Dublin 2.
Tel. *(01) 662 1444* **Fax** *(01) 676 6154*
email: dtsr@iol.ie
website: www.irlgov.ie/dtt

Minister: Dr. Jim McDaid TD.
Minister of State: Chris Flood TD.
Secretary General: Margaret Hayes. (£87,991)
Description: The department aims to contribute to Ireland's economic and social progress by developing a sustainable tourism sector that promotes high standards in marketing, service quality and product development; an active culture in sport and recreation; and a better partnership approach to local development with an emphasis on enhancing the quality of life in communities with high levels of social deprivation. The day-to-day implementation of these policies has been devolved to the four bodies listed below.
State Bodies / Agencies: Bord Fáilte Éireann (the Irish Tourist Board), Shannon Development, CERT (the State Tourism Training Agency), the Irish Sports Council.

For salaries of Ministers and Ministers of State see Politics chapter.

Northern Ireland Government Departments

NORTHERN IRELAND OFFICE
Level 3, Block B, Castle Buildings, Stormont, Belfast BT4 3SG
Tel. *(01232) 520700* **Fax** *(01232) 528473*
email: press.nio@nics.gov.uk
website: www.nio.gov.uk
Secretary of State: Dr Marjorie Mowlam MP*
Minister of State: Adam Ingram MP.
Permanent Secretary: Joe Pilling
Description: The Northern Ireland Office deals in particular with political and constitutional matters as they relate to Northern Ireland as well as law and order, policing and criminal justice policy and community relations.
Executive Agencies: The Northern Ireland Prison

Service, the Compensation Agency and the Forensic Science Agency of Northern Ireland.

DEPARTMENT OF AGRICULTURE FOR NORTHERN IRELAND
Dundonald House, Upper Newtownards Road, Belfast BT4 3SB.
Tel. (01232) 520100 **Fax** (01232) 525015
email: library@dani.gov.uk
website: www.dani.gov.uk
Parliamentary Under Secretary of State: Lord Dubs of Battersea
Permanent Secretary: Peter Small.
Description: The department is responsible for encouraging sustainable economic growth and the development of the countryside in Northern Ireland by promoting the competitive development of the agri-food, fishing and forestry sectors of the economy; by being both proactive and responsive to the needs of consumers with regard to food; and by being responsible for the welfare of animals and the conservation of the environment. In addition, it aims to strengthen the economy and social infrastructure of disadvantaged rural areas.

Executive Agencies: The Rivers Agency, The Forest Service.
State Bodies: The Agricultural Research Institute of Northern Ireland; The Fisheries Conservancy Board for Northern Ireland, The Foyle Fisheries Commission, The Livestock and Meat Commission for Northern Ireland, The Northern Ireland Fishery Harbour Authority, The Pig Production Development Committee, The Drainage Council for Northern Ireland, The Agricultural Wages Board for Northern Ireland, The Lower Bann Advisory Committee.

**DEPARTMENT OF ECONOMIC DEVELOPMENT**
Netherleigh, Massey Avenue, Belfast BT4 2JP.
Tel. (01232) 529900 **Fax** (01232)
email: webmaster@nics.gov.uk
website: www.dedni.gov.uk
Parliamentary Under Secretary of State: John McFall MP.
Permanent Secretary: Gerry Loughran.
Description: The department is responsible for providing an optimum framework for strengthening economic development in Northern Ireland. Its aims are the promotion of economic growth, leading to increased employment in Northern Ireland; the achievement of a fair and flexible labour market; the targeting of programmes at regions of social and economic deprivation and at the needs of the long-term unemployed; and the administration of the DED's financial and human resources. The DED is organised on a model that is similar to a holding company with specific operation subsidiary businesses or bodies.
State Bodies / Agencies: The Industrial Development Board (IDB), the Training and Employment Agency (T&EA), the Industrial Research and Technology Unit (IRTU). *DED-sponsored non-departmental bodies:* the Local Enterprise Development Unit, the Commission for Racial Equality, the Northern Ireland Tourist Board, the

Labour Relations Agency, the Fair Employment Commission, the Equal Opportunities Commission, the General Consumer Council, the Health & Safety Agency.

DEPARTMENT OF EDUCATION FOR NORTHERN IRELAND
Rathgael House, 43 Balloo Road, Bangor, Co. Down, BT19 7PR.
Tel. (01247) 279279 **Fax** (01247) 279100
email: deni@nics.gov.uk
website: www.deni.gov.uk
Parliamentary Under Secretary of State: John McFall MP
Permanent Secretary: Nigel Hamilton.
Description: The department plays a strategic role in developing and implementing education policies and it is concerned with the whole range of education, from nursery education through to further and higher education, as well as sport and recreation, youth services, the arts and culture (including libraries) and the development of community relations within and between schools. The department administers the Teachers' Superannuation Scheme and pays teachers' salaries on behalf of the Education and Library boards (Belfast, South Eastern, North Eastern, Southern and Western), the Council for Catholic Maintained Schools, some Voluntary Grammar and Grant-Maintained Schools.
State Bodies/Agencies: Arts Council of Northern Ireland, Council for Catholic Maintained Schools, National Museums and Galleries of Northern Ireland, Northern Ireland Council for the Curriculum, Examinations and Assessment, Northern Ireland Higher Education Council, Northern Ireland Museums Council, Sports Council for Northern Ireland, Five Education and Library Boards, Staff Commission for Education and Library Boards, Youth Council for Northern Ireland.

DEPARTMENT OF THE ENVIRONMENT FOR NORTHERN IRELAND
Clarence Court, 10-18 Adelaide Street, Belfast BT2 8GB.
Tel. (01232) 540540. **Fax** (01232) 540021
email: press.office@doeni.gov.uk
website: www.nics.gov.uk/doehome.htm
Parliamentary Under Secretary of State: Lord Dubs of Battersea
Permanent Secretary: Ronnie Spence.
Description: The department is responsible for a wide range of services including planning, roads, water and works services, housing and transport policies and fire services. It also administers specific controls over local government and manages certain lands and properties, urban regeneration, country parks, nature reserves, areas of outstanding natural beauty, environmental protection, the registration of titles of land and deeds and the listing and preservation of historic buildings, ancient monuments and archaeological surveys.
Executive Agencies: Environment and Heritage Service, Construction Service, Roads Service, Land Registers of NI, Public Record Office (NI), Driver and Vehicle Testing Agency (NI), Driver and Vehicle Licensing (NI), Water Service, Rate Collection Agency, Ordnance Survey of NI, Planning Service.

DEPARTMENT OF FINANCE AND PERSONNEL

Balloo Annex, Rathgael House, Balloo Road, Bangor, Co. Down BT19 7NA
Tel. (01232) 520400 Fax (01247) 858109
email: pso.mail@dfpni.gov.uk
website: www.dfpni.gov.uk
Minister of State: Adam Ingram MP
Permanent Secretary: Pat Carvill.
Description: The department supervises and controls the expenditure of the Northern Ireland departments and liaises with the Treasury and the Northern Ireland Office on a number of financial and socio-economic areas. It also develops and administers the equal opportunities policy for the civil service in Northern Ireland and is responsible for personnel, pay, pensions, conditions of service and the coordination of pay policies in the civil service.
State Bodies / Agencies: the Law Reform Advisory Committee for Northern Ireland, the Northern Ireland Economic Council, the Statute Law Committee for Northern Ireland, the Valuation and Lands Agency, the Government Purchasing Agency, the Northern Ireland Statistics and Research Agency, the Business Development Service.

DEPARTMENT OF HEALTH AND SOCIAL SERVICES

Castle Buildings, Stormont, Belfast BT4 3SJ.

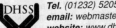

Tel. (01232) 520500 Fax (01232) 520572
email: webmaster@dhssni.gov.uk
website: www.dhss.gov.uk
Parliamentary Under Secretary of State: George Howarth MP
Secretary: Clive Gowdy.
Description: The department aims to maintain and improve the health and social well-being of the people of Northern Ireland by formulating policies and strategies, providing health and personal social services and securing the planning and delivery of these services through the Health and Social Services Boards, the Health Trusts and general practitioners. The department is also responsible for child support, social security and a wide range of social legislation, in addition to providing financial support for those who are retired, sick, disabled, unemployed or in need through the Social Security Agency.
State Bodies / Agencies: the Child Support Agency; Central Services Agency; Northern Ireland Blood Transfusion Service Agency; the Health Estates; Health Promotion Agency; NI Regional Medical Physics Agency; NI Guardian Ad litem Service Agency; the Mental Health Commission for Northern Ireland; the National Board for Nursing, Midwifery and Health Visiting for Northern Ireland; the Northern Ireland Council for Post-Graduate Medical and Dental Education; the Social Security Agency.

Local Government

RoI Corporations and County Councils

General Council of County Councils,
3 Greenmount House,
Harold's Cross Road, Dublin 6W.
Tel: (01) 4548700
The General Council of County Councils champions the cause of Ireland's 34 county and city councils embracing almost 900 elected members. The Council lobbies central government on issues concerning elected members, supports councillors in their role of service to their communities, and works to promote an appreciation of the value of local democracy among interest groups and the public at large.

● **CARLOW COUNTY COUNCIL**
County Offices, Carlow.
Tel: (0503) 31126. Fax: (0503) 41503.
County Manager: Tom Dowling (£54,926)
County Secretary: Jim Kearney (£30,443-40,066)
County Engineer: Dermot O'Riordan (£38,393-47,085)
Council meeting: 1st Monday of each month
Councillors: Rody Kelly FF; Fred Hunter FG; Michael Deering FG – Cathaoirleach; Jim Townsend Lab; Enda Nolan FF; Mary McDonald FG; Arthur McDonald FF; Denis Foley FG; Walter Lacey PD; John Browne, TD FG; Michael Abbey FG; Jimmy Murnane FF; Joe McDonald FF; Declan Alcock FG; Mary White GP; Michael Meaney Lab; Dolores Barron FF; PJ Kavanagh FF; William Paton Lab; John Pender FF; MJ Nolan FF.

● **CAVAN COUNTY COUNCIL**
Courthouse, Cavan.
Tel: (049) 31799. Fax: (049) 61565.
County Manager: Brian Jonnston (£54,926)
County Secretary: Breege Kelly (£30,443-40,066)
County Engineer: John Tiernan (£38,393-47,085)
Council meeting: 2nd Monday of each month
Councillors: Michael Giles FF; Joe O'Reilly FG; Aiden Boyle FG; Anthony P. Vesey FF; T.P. Smith FF – Cathaoirleach; Charlie Boylan SF; Gerry Murray FF; Patrick Conaty FF; Madeline Argue FG; Andrew Boylan, TD FG; Diarmuid Wilson FF; Clifford Kelly FF; Peter McVitty FG; Winston Turner Ind; Eddie Feeley FF; Sean Smith FF; Pauline Tully SF; Danny Brady FF; Robert Fausset FG; Francie Fitzsimons FF; Francis McDermott FF; Turlough Smith FF; Paddy O'Reilly FG; Maura Maguire-Lynch FG; Dessie Boylan FG.

● **CLARE COUNTY COUNCIL**
New Road, Ennis, Co. Clare.
Tel: (065) 21616 Fax: (065) 28233.
email: clarecoco.ie
County Manager: William Moloney (£59,046)
County Secretary: Michael McNamara (£30,443-40,066)
County Engineer: Tom Carey (£38,393-47,085)
Council meeting: 2nd Monday of each month

Councillors: Richard Nagle FF; Bill Chambers FF; John Crowe FG; Patricia McCarthy Ind; Tom Burke FF; Pat McMahon FF; Joe Arkins FG; Tony Mulcahy FG; Michael Hillery FF; Martin Lafferty Ind; Pat Keane FF; Tom Prendeville FF; P.J. Kelly FF; Madeline Taylor-Quinn, MCC FG; Flan Garvey FF; Mary Mannion PD; Michael BegleyFF; Christy Curtin Ind; Bernard Hanrahan FF; Peter Considine FF; Joe Carey FG; Sonny Scanlon FG; Tommy Brennan Ind; James Breen FF; Pat Daly FF; Tony McMahon FG; Patrick O'Gorman FF; Pat Hayes FF; Colm Wiley FF; Sean Hillery FF – Cathaoirleach; Paul Bugler FG; Pat Breen FG.

● CORK COUNTY COUNCIL
County Hall, Cork.
Tel: (021) 276891. Fax: (021) 276321.
email: cccajc@iol.ie **website:** *corkcoco.com*
County Manager: Maurice Moloney (£67,283)
County Secretary: John O'Neill (£30,443-40,066)
County Engineer: Brendan Devlin (£38,393-47,085)
Council meeting: 2nd and 4th Mondays of each month
Councillors: Dan Fleming FF; Deirdre Forde FF; Barry Cogan FF; John Collins FG; Simon C. Coveney, TD FG; Michael Donegan FF; Frank Metcalfe FG; Gerard Murphy FG; Marie Murphy FF; Derry Canty FG; Donal Moynihan, TD FF; Batt O'Keeffe, TD FF; Gerry Kelly FG; Tomas Ryan FG – Cathaoirleach; Vivian Callaghan FF; John Patrick O'Shea FG; Noel Harrington FG; Patrick J. Sheehan, TD FG; Denis O'Donovan, MCC FF; Alan Coleman FF; Kevin Murphy FG; Peter Callanan, MCC FF; Paul Bradford, TD FG; Michael Creed, TD FG; PJ Walsh FG; Michael McCarthy Lab; Tom O'Neill FF; Paula Desmond Lab; Peter Kelly PD; Kevin O'Keeffe FF; Annette McNamara FF; Aileen D. Pyne FG; Dan Joe Fitzgerald FF; Patrick Buckley FG; Frank Crowley FG; Tadg O'Donovan FG; Donal F. O'Rourke FF; Tom Sheahan FG; Maura Cal McCarthy FG; Christy O'Sullivan Ind; Ted Murphy Ind; Art Supple FF; Maurice Ahern FF; Noel Collins Ind; Michael Hegarty FG; John Mulvihill Lab; Frank O'Flynn FF; Joe Sherlock Lab.

● CORK CORPORATION
City Hall, Cork.
Tel: (021) 966222. Fax: (021) 314238.
City Manager: Jack Higgins (£63,165)
Assistant City Managers: Dan Buggy, Denis McCarthy (Acting) (£39,820-46,686)
City Engineer: Kevin Terry (£38,393-47,085)
Council meeting: 2nd and 4th Mondays of each month
Councillors: Brian Bermingham FG; Noel O'Flynn, TD FF; Dan Boyle GP; Denis 'Dino' Cregan, MCC FG; Tom O'Driscoll FF; Sean Martin FF; Tim Falvey FF; P.J. Hourican FG; Colm Burke FG; Michael Ahern, TD Lab; Mary Shields FF; John Dennehy, TD FF; Damian Wallace FF – Lord Mayor; Kathleen Lynch Lab; Con O'Connell Ind; Bernard Allen, TD FG; Michael O'Connell Lab; Don O'Leary SF; Mairin Quill, MCC PD; Tim Brosnan FF; Liam Burke, TD FG; Billy Kelleher, TD FF; John Kelleher Lab; Terry Shannon FF; Deirdre Clune, TD FG; Jim Corr FG; Joe O'Flynn Lab; Donal Counihan FF; John Minihan PD; David McCarthy FF; Con O'Leary Ind.

● DONEGAL COUNTY COUNCIL
County House, Lifford, Co. Donegal.
Tel: (074) 72222 Fax: (074) 41205.
email: donegalcoco.ie
County Manager: Michael McLoone (£59,046)
County Secretary: Eunan Sweeney (£30,443-40,066)
County Engineer: Jack McInerney (£38,393-47,085)
Council meeting: Last Monday of each month
Councillors: Charles Bennett FG; David Alcorn FF; Thomas Pringle Ind; Declan McHugh FF; Sean McEniff FF; Peter Kennedy FF – Cathaoirleach; John Boyle FG; Gerry Crawford FF; Enda Bonner, MCC FF; Mary Coughlan, TD FF; Alice Bonnar FF; Pádraig Doherty FG; Bernard McGuinness FG; JJ Reid FG; Patrick McGowan FF; Joe McHugh FG; Noel McGinley FF; Niall Blaney IFF; Bernard McGlinchey FF; Seán Maloney Lab; Jimmy Harte FG; Jim Sheridan FG; Cecilia Keaveney, TD FF; Rena Donaghey FF; Albert Doherty IFF; Francis Conaghan FF; Dessie Larkin IFF; Thomas Gildea, TD Ind; Paddy Kelly IFF.

● DUBLIN CORPORATION
Civic Offices, Wood Quay, Dublin 8.
Tel: (01) 6796111. Fax: (01) 6792226.
email: dublinc@iol.ie
City Manager: John Fitzgerald (£82,388)
Assistant City Managers: Sean Carey, Philip Maguire, Owen Keegan, Matt Twomey (Acting) (each £54,926)
City Engineer: Michael Phillips (£38,393-47,085)
Council meeting: 1st Monday of each month
Councillors: Deirdre Heney FF; Nicky Kehoe SF; Chris Giblin FG; Dermot Fitzpatrick, MCC FF; Brendan Carr Lab; Marian McGennis, TD FF; Eamonn O'Brien Lab; Noel Ahern, TD FF; Ivor Callely, TD FF; Michael Mulcahy FF; Maurice Ahern FF; Gerry Breen FG; Derek McDowell, TD Lab; Finian McGrath Ind; John Stafford FF; Gay Mitchell, TD FG; Sean Ardagh, TD FF; Vincent Jackson Ind; Ruairi McGinley FG; Tony Gregory, TD Ind; Martin Brady, TD FF; Tommy Broughan, TD Lab; Niamh Cosgrave FF; Liam Fitzgerald, MCC FF; Sean Kenny Lab; Eric Byrne Lab; Christopher Andrews FF; Ciarán Cuffe GP; Dessie Ellis SF; Kevin Humphreys Lab; Mary Mooney FF; Catherine Byrne FG; John Gallagher Lab; Eoin Ryan, TD FF; Eamonn Ryan GP; Mary Freehill Lab – Lord Mayor; Pat Carey, TD FF; Michael Donnelly FF; Michael Conaghan Lab; Dermot Lacey Lab; Joe Doyle, MCC FG; Tony Kett, MCC FF; Joe Costello, MCC Lab; Royston Brady FF; Christy Burke SF; Roisin Shorthall, TD Lab; Tony Taaffe FF; Sean Haughey, TD FF; Richard Bruton, TD FG; Anthony Creevey Lab; Larry O'Toole SF; Frances Fitzgerald, TD FG.

● DÚN LAOGHAIRE-RATHDOWN
County Hall, Dún Laoghaire, Co. Dublin.
Tel: (01) 2054700. Fax: (01) 2806969.
email: dlrcoco.ie **website:** *www.dlrococo.ie*
County Manager: Derek Brady (£63,165)
County Engineer: Barry Casey (Acting) (£38,393-47,085)
Council meeting: 2nd Monday of each month
Councillors: Fiona O'Malley PD; Barry Andrews FF; Frank Smyth Lab; Niamh Bhreathnach Lab; Denis

O'Callaghan Lab; James Murphy FF; Olivia Mitchell, TD FG; Trevor Matthews FF; Vincent MacDowell GP; Donal Marren FG; Don Lydon, MCC FF; Bernie Lowe FF; Tony Kelly FF; Helen Keogh, MCC PD; Pat Hand FG; Maria Corrigan FF; Eamon Gilmore, TD Lab; Betty Coffey FF; Victor Boyhan PD; Liam T. Cosgrave, MCC FG; Louise Cosgrave FG; Aidan Culhane Lab; Eoin Costello FG; Jane Dillion-Byrne Lab; William Dockrell FG; Mary Elliott FG; Tony Fox FF; Larry Butler FF – Cathaoirleach.

● FINGAL COUNTY COUNCIL
PO Box 174, 46-49 Upper O'Connell Street, Dublin 1.
Tel: *(01) 8727777.* **Fax:** *(01) 8725782.*
County Manager: William Soffe (£63,165)
County Engineer: Danny O'Connor (£38,393-47,085)
Council meeting: 2nd Monday of each month
Councillors: Gerry Lynam Ind; Michael J. Cosgrave, TD FG; Liam Creaven FF; Joe Higgins, TD SP; Michael O'Donovan Lab; Margaret Richardson FF; Sheila Terry IND – Cathaoirleach; Tom Morrissey PD; Joan Maher FG; Ned Ryan FF; Clare Daly SP; Joan Burton Lab; Heidi Jane Bedell GP; Sean Dolphin FG; G.V. Wright, TD FF; Peter Coyle Lab; David O'Connor Ind; Tom Kelleher Lab; Michael J. Kennedy FF; Sean Ryan, TD Lab; Dermot Murray FF; Sean Sweeney Lab; Cathal Boland FG; Anne Devitt FG.

● GALWAY COUNTY COUNCIL
PO Box 27, Liosbán Retail Centre,
Tuam Road, Galway.
Tel: *(091) 509000* **Fax** *(091) 509010*
email: galwaycoco.ie
County Manager: Donal O'Donoghue (£59,046)
County Secretary: Tom Kavanagh (£30,443-40,066)
County Engineer: John Colleran (£38,393-47,085)
Council meeting: 2nd Friday and last Monday of each month
Councillors: Pól O Foighil FG; Michael Cunningham FF; Ulick Burke, TD FG; Seamus Walsh Ind; Connie Ní Fhatharta FF; Michael Mullins FG; Josie Conneely FF; James Joyce FF; Pat O'Sullivan FF; Michael Fahy FF; Jarlath McDonagh, MCC FG; Tomás Mannion FF; Seamus Gavin Ind; Joe Burke PD; Tiarnan Walsh FG; Kathleen Quinn FF; Tom McHugh FG; Paddy McHugh FF – Cathaoirleach; Noel Grealish PD; Paul Connaughton, TD FG; Pat Hynes Ind; Tim Rabbitt FF; J.J. Mannion FG; Mary Hoade FF; Joe Callanan FG; Michael Regan FF; Jimmy McClearn FG; Matt Loughnane FF; Michael Connolly FF; Sean O'Neachtain FF.

● GALWAY CORPORATION
City Hall, College Road, Galway.
Tel: *(091) 568151.* **Fax:** *(091) 567493*
email: tclerk@galwaycorp.ie
City Manager: Joe Gavin (£54,926)
Assistant Town Clerk: Martina Moloney
City Engineer: Tom Kilgarriff (£38,393-47,085)
Council meeting: 1st and 3rd Mondays of each month
Councillors: Angela Lupton FG; John Mulholland FG; Catherine Connolly Lab; Padraic McCormack, TD FG; Paul Colleran PD; Donal Lyons PD; Margaret Cox,

MCC FF; Martin Quinn FF; Micheal Ó hUiginn FF; Fintan Coogan, MCC FG; Val Hanley FF; Terry O'Flaherty PD; Declan McDonnell PD – Mayor; Michael Leahy FF; Tom Costello Lab.

● KERRY COUNTY COUNCIL
County Buildings, Tralee, Co. Kerry.
Tel: *(066) 7121111.* **Fax:** *(066) 7121169*
County Manager: Martin Nolan (£59,046)
County Secretary: Joe McGrath (Acting) (£30,443-40,066)
County Engineer: Tom Curran (£38,393-47,085)
Council meeting: 3rd Monday of each month
Councillors: Jackie Healy-Rae, TD Ind; Breandan MacGearailt FF; Michael D. O'Shea FF; Seamus Cosai Fitzgerald FG; Breda Moynihan-Cronin, TD Lab; Brian O'Leary FF; Tom Fleming FF; Michael Gleeson SKIA (Other); Michael Healy-Rae Ind; Michael Cahill FF; Paul O'Donoghue FF; Michael Connor-Scarteen FG; P.J. Donovan FG; Billy Leen Ind; Brendan Cronin Ind; Maeve Spring Lab; Ned O'Sullivan FF; Martin Joseph Ferris SF; Bobby O'Connell FG; Thomas McEllistrim FF; Ted Fitzgerald FF – Cathaoirleach; Denis Foley, TD FF; Pat Leahy Lab; Jimmy Deenihan, TD FG; Tim Buckley FG; Daniel Kiely, MCC FF; John Brassil FF.

● KILDARE COUNTY COUNCIL
St. Mary's, Naas, Co. Kildare.
Tel: *(045) 873800* **Fax:** *(045) 876875.*
email: secretar@kildarecoco.ie
County Manager: Niall Bradley (£59,046)
County Secretary: Tommy Skehan (£30,443-40,066)
County Engineer: Jimmy Lynch (£38,393-47,085)
Council meeting: Last Monday of each month
Councillors: Paul Kelly FF; John O'Neill FF; John Dardis, MCC PD; Jim Keane Lab; Anthony Lawlor Ind; Mary Glennon Ind; Sean Power, TD FF; John McGinley Lab; Timmy Conway PD; Fionnuala Mary Dukes FG; Catherine Murphy Lab; Martin Miley FF; Billy Hillis FG; Jack Wall, TD Lab; Sean O Fearghail FF; P.J. Sheridan FF – Cathaoirleach; Michael Fitzpatrick FF; Jim Reilly FG; Tony McEvoy Ind; Geraldine Conway FF; Emmet Stagg, TD Lab; Rainsford Hendy FG; Fiona O'Loughlin FF; Kathleen Walsh Ind; Senan Griffin FG.

● KILKENNY COUNTY COUNCIL
County Hall, John Street, Kilkenny
Tel: *(056) 52699.* **Fax:** *(056) 63384*
email: secretar@kilkennycoco.ie
County Manager: PJ Donnelly (£59,046)
County Secretary: Philip O'Neill (£30,443-40,066)
County Engineer: Don O'Sullivan (£38,393-47,085)
Council meeting: 3rd Monday of each month
Councillors: Pat Dunphy FG; Dixie Doyle Ind; Joan Murphy FF; Tom Brennan FF; Andy Cotterell FG; Paul Cuddihy FG; Ann Blackmore FF; Billy Ireland FG; Joe Cody Lab; Mary Hilda Cavanagh FG; Pat Millea FF; Martin Carroll FF; John Brennan FG; Catherine Connery FG; Liam Aylward, TD FF; John Coonan FF; John Paul Phelan FG; Phil Hogan, TD FG; Michael Lanigan FF; Bobby Aylward FF; John McGuinness, TD FF; Dick Dowling FG; Tom Maher FG; James J. Brett FF – Cathaoirleach; Teresa Mullen Ind; Cora Long FF.

● **LAOIS COUNTY COUNCIL**
County Hall, Portlaoise, Co. Laois.
Tel: *(0502) 22044.* **Fax:** *(0502) 22313.*
email: *secretar@laoiscoco.ie*
County Manager: Michael Malone (£54,926)
County Secretary: Louis Brennan (£30,443-40,066)
County Engineer: Gerry McGlinchey (£38,393-47,085)
Council meeting: Last Monday of each month
Councillors: Catherine Fitzgerald FF; Joseph Digan FF; David Goodwin FG; Seamus McDonald FF; John A. Moloney, TD FF; Mary Wheatley FF; James Daly FG; John Robert Moran FG; Michael Rice FF; Michael Costello FF; Michael Turley Ind; James Deegan FG; Michael Lalor FG; Martin Phelan FG; John Bonham FG; Joseph Dunne FF – Cathaoirleach; Kieran Phelan FF; Sean Fleming, TD FF; John Joe Fennelly FF; Jerry Lodge FF; Mary Sweeney FG; Charles Flanagan, TD FG; William Aird FG; Martin Rohan FF; Ray Cribbin FF.

● **LEITRIM COUNTY COUNCIL**
Governor House, Carrick-on-Shannon, Co. Leitrim.
Tel: *(078) 20005.* **Fax:** *(078) 21023.*
County Manager: Paddy Fahy (£54,926)
County Secretary: Sean Kielty (£30,443-40,066)
County Engineer: Michael McGoey (£38,393-47,085)
Council meeting: 1st Monday of each month
Councillors: John McTernan FG; Liam McElgunn FF; Liam McGirl SF; Seán McGowan FF; Thomas Mulligan FG; Gerry McGee FF; James J. Shortt FF; Sinéad Guckian FF; Frank Dolan FG; Mary Bohan FF; Gerry Dolan Ind; Jim McPadden FG; Siobhan McGloin FG; Michael Colreavy SF; Tony Ferguson FF – Cathaoirleach; Francis Gilmartin FF; Enda Stenson Ind; Gerard Reynolds, TD FG; Tommy McCartin FG; Caillian Ellis FF; Damian Brennan FG; Aodh Flynn FF.

● **LIMERICK COUNTY COUNCIL**
County Buildings, 79-84 O'Connell Steet, Limerick.
Tel: *(061) 318477.* **Fax:** *(061) 318478.*
email: *secretar@limerickcoco.ie*
County Manager: Roibeard Ó Ceallaigh (£59,046)
County Secretary: Paddy O'Connor (£30,443-40,066)
County Engineer: Tom Barry (£38,393-47,085)
Council meeting: Last Monday of each month
Councillors: Paddy Hourigan FG; Leonard Enright FF; Cormac Hurley FG; Sandra Marsh FF; Pat McAuliffe FF; Dan Neville, TD FG; David Naughton FG; John Griffin FF; John Cregan FF; Eddie Creighton PD; John Gallahue Ind; Tim O'Malley PD; James Houlihan FG; Mary Harty FG; Seamus Ahern FF; Michael Finucane, TD FG; Sean Broderick FG; John Cregan, MCC FF; Eddie Wade, TD FF; Brigid Teefy PD; Noreen Ryan FF; Joe Meagher FF; Mary Jackman, MCC FG; Michael O'Kelly FF – Cathaoirleach; Kevin Sheehan FF; Michael Brennan FF; Richard Butler FG; John Clifford FF.

● **LIMERICK CORPORATION**
City Hall, Limerick.
Tel: *(061) 415799.* **Fax:** *(061) 418342.*
email: *manager@limerickcorp.ie*
City Manager: Brendan Keating (£59,046)
Assistant Town Clerk: Con Murray

City Engineer: Seamus O'Sullivan (£38,393-47,085)
Council meeting: 2nd Monday of each month
Councillors: Catherine Leddin Ind; Dick Sadlier FF; Joe Leddin Lab; Maria Byrne FG; Pat Kennedy FG; Diarmuid Scully FG; Peter Power FF; John Ryan Lab; Ger Fahy FG; John Cronin FF; Michael Hourigan FG; Jan O'Sullivan, TD Lab; John Gilligan Ind; Larry Cross FF; Kieran O'Hanlon FF; Michael Kelly Ind; Jack Bourke FF – Mayor.

● **LONGFORD COUNTY COUNCIL**
Great Water Street, Longford.
Tel: *(043) 46231.* **Fax:** *(043) 41233.*
County Manager: Michael Killeen (£54,926)
County Secretary: Michael Clancy (Acting) (£30,443-40,066)
County Engineer: Alex O'Sullivan (Acting) (£38,393-47,085)
Council meeting: 3rd Monday of each month
Councillors: Gerry Brady FG; James Bannon FG; Paddy Belton FG; Adrian Farrell FG; Sean Farrell FG; Michael Nevin FF; Barney Steele FF; Sean Lynch Ind; Denis Glennon FF; Mae Sexton PD; Peter Murphy IND; – Cathaoirleach; Alan Mitchell FG; John Nolan FF; Peter Kelly FF; Luie McEntire FF; Brian Lynch FF; Maura Kilbride-Harkin FG; Frank Kilbride FG; Martin Farrell FG; James Coyle FF; Victor Kiernan FG.

● **LOUTH COUNTY COUNCIL**
County Offices, Dundalk, Co. Louth.
Tel: *(042) 35457.* **Fax:** *(042) 35449.*
County Manager: John Quinlivan (£59,046)
County Secretary: Joe Boland (£30,443-40,066)
County Engineer: Tony Kearon (£38,393-47,085)
Council meeting: 3rd Monday of each month
Councillors: Maria O'Brien Campbell FF; Oliver Tully FG; Fergus O'Dowd, MCC FG; Peter Savage FF – Cathaoirleach; Donal Lynch FF; Mary Grehan Ind; Noel Lennon FF; Jim D'Arcy FG; Martin Bellew Ind; Declan Breathnach FF; Seamus Keelan FF; Miceál O'Donnell FF; Patsy Kirwan Lab; Arthur Morgan SF; Thomas Clare FF; Nicholas McCabe FF; Tommy Reilly FF; Finnan McCoy FG; Jim Lennon FG; Frank Godfrey Ind; Jacqui McConville FF; Jimmy Mulroy FF; Michael O'Dowd FG; Seamus Byrne FF; Sean Collins FF; Terry Brennan FG.

● **MAYO COUNTY COUNCIL**
Áras an Chontae, Castlebar, Co. Mayo.
Tel: *(094) 24444.* **Fax:** *(094) 23937.*
email: *secretar@mayocc.ie*
County Manager: Des Mahon (£59,046)
County Secretary: Padraig Hughes (£30,443-40,066)
County Engineer: Joe Beirne (£38,393-47,085)
Council meeting: 2nd Monday of each month
Councillors: Beverley Cooper-Flynn, TD FF; Henry Kenny FG; Frank Chambers, MCC FF; Michael Ring, TD FG; Peter Sweeney FF; John M. Flannery FG; Jimmy Maloney FF; Joseph Mellett FG; Gerry Murray FF; John Carty FF; John Cribbin FG; Richard Finn Ind; Margaret Adams FF; Paddy Burke, MCC FG; Brian Golden FF; Johnny Mee Lab; Gerry Coyle FG; Pat Kilbane FG; Frank Leneghan FF; Tim Quinn FF;

Michael Burke FG; Jim Mannion FG; Damien Ryan FF; Ernie Caffrey, MCC FG; Stephen Molloy FF – Cathaoirleach; Sean Bourke FF; Eddie Staunton FG; Seamus Weir FG; Patrick McHugh FF; Annie May Reape FF; Al McDonnell FF.

● **MEATH COUNTY COUNCIL**
County Hall, Railway Street, Navan, Co. Meath.
Tel: (046) 21581. **Fax:** (046) 21463.
County Manager: Joe Horan (£59,046)
County Secretary: Danny McLoughlin (£30,443-40,066)
County Engineer: Oliver Perkins (£38,393-47,085)
Council meeting: 1st Monday of each month
Councillors: Damien English FG; John Brady, TD FF; John V. Farrelly, TD FG; Gerry Gibney FG; Michael Lynch FG; Jimmy Weldon FF; Patrick Fitzsimons FF; Jim Holloway FG; James Mangan FF; Patsy O'Neill FG; Joe Reilly SF; Tommy Reilly FF; Jimmy Cudden Ind; Hugh Gough FF; Brian Fitzgerald Indv– Cathaoirleach; John Fanning FG; Oliver Brooks FF; Mary Bergin FG; Liz McCormack FF; Seamus Murray FF; Peter Higgins FG; Jimmy Fegan FF; Gabriel Cribbin FF; William Carey FG; Shaun Lynch FG; Anne Dillon-Gallagher FG; Tom Kelly Ind; Nick Killian FF; Conor Tormey FF.

● **MONAGHAN COUNTY COUNCIL**
County Offices, Monaghan.
Tel: (047) 30500. **Fax:** (047) 82739.
County Manager: Joe Gavin (£54,926)
County Secretary: Michael Fitzpatrick (£30,443-40,066)
County Engineer: Billy Moore (£38,393-47,085)
Council meeting: 1st Monday of each month
Councillors: Noel Keelan SF; Brenda McAnespie SF; Seymour Crawford, TD FG; Ann Leonard, MCC FF; Hugh McElvaney FG; Aidan Murray FG; Rosaleen O'Hanlon FF; Caoimhghin O'Caolain, TD SF; Brian McKenna SF; Jackie Crowe SF; Padraig McNally FF; Brian MacUaid SF; Francis O'Brien, MCC FF; Gary Carville FG; Willie McKenna FF; Brendan Hughes FF – Cathaoirleach; Owen Bannigan FG; Shane O'Hanlon FF; Patsy Treanor FF; Patrick McKenna FG.

● **OFFALY COUNTY COUNCIL**
Courthouse, Tullamore, Co. Offaly.
Tel: (0506) 46800. **Fax:** (0506) 46868.
email: secretar@offalycoco.ie
County Manager: Niall Sweeney (£54,926)
County Secretary: Bernadette Kinsella (£30,443-40,066)
County Engineer: William Wall (£38,393-47,085)
Council meeting: 3rd Monday of each month
Councillors: Percy Clendennen FG; Noel Bourke FF; Gerard Killally FF; Tom Nolan FF; John Foran FG; Francis Weir Ind; Peter Ormond Ind; Pat Moylan, MCC FF; Joe Dooley FF; Marcella Corcoran-Kennedy FG; Eamon Dooley FF – Cathaoirleach; Connie Hanniffy FG; Pat Gallagher, MCC Lab; Barry Cowen FF; John Flanagan FF; Tommy McKeigue FG; Thomas C. Dolan Ind; Molly Buckley Ind; Michael Fox FG; Tom Feighery FF; Olwyn Enright FG.

● **ROSCOMMON COUNTY COUNCIL**
Courthouse, Roscommon.
Tel: (0903) 37100 **Fax:** (0903) 37108.
email: secretar@roscommoncoco.ie
County Manager: Eddie Sheehy (£54,926)
County Secretary: Derry O'Donnell (£30,443-40,066)
County Engineer: Vincent Brennan (£38,393-47,085)
Council meeting: 4th Monday of each month
Councillors: Gerry Donnelly FG; Tom Crosby Ind; Sean Beirne FG; Eugene M. Murphy FF; Gene Byrne Ind; Danny Burke Ind; Michael McGreal FG – Cathaoirleach; Hugh Lynn PD; John Murray FG; Anthony Geraghty FF; Paddy McGarry FF; Kitty Duignan FG; Oliver Moore FG; John Curran FF; Tom Foxe Ind; Terry Leyden FF; Desmond Bruen FF; Martin Connaughton FF; Frank Feighan FG; Michael Finneran, MCC FF; Charlie Hopkins FG; John Cummins FF; Gerry Garvey FG; Michael Scally FG; Denis Naughten, TD FG; John Connor, MCC FG.

● **SLIGO COUNTY COUNCIL**
Riverside, Sligo.
Tel: (071) 56666. **Fax:** (071) 41119.
email: sligococo.ie
County Manager: Hubert Kearns (£54,926)
County Secretary: Tim Caffrey (£30,443-40,066)
County Engineer: Frank Gleeson (£38,393-47,085)
Council meeting: 3rd Monday of each month
Councillors: Sean McManus SF; Ita Fox FG; Patsy Barry FF; Joe Leonard FG; Albert Higgins FF; Tony McLoughlin FG; Jimmy McGarry FG; Declan Bree Lab; Padraig Branley FF; Jimmy Devins FF; John Perry, TD FG; Gerry Murray FG; Roddy McGuinn FF; Brian Scanlon Lab; Leo Conlon FG; Michael 'Boxer' Conlon FF; Eamon Scanlon FF; Michael Fleming FG; Aidan Colleary FF; Patrick Joseph Cawley FG; Margaret Gormley IND; Joseph Queenan FF; Paul Conmy FG; Mary Barrett FG – Cathaoirleach; Alfie Parke Ind.

● **SOUTH DUBLIN COUNTY COUNCIL**
PO Box 4122, Town Centre, Tallaght, Dublin 24.
Tel: (01) 4149000. **Fax:** (01) 4149111.
email: secretariatdept@sdublincoco.ie
County Manager: Frank Kavanagh (£63,165)
County Engineer: Frank Coffey (£38,393-47,085)
Council meeting: 2nd Monday of each month
Councillors: Don Tipping Lab; Charlie O'Connor FF – Cathaoirleach; Therese Ridge, MCC FG; Brian Hayes, TD FG; Joanna Tuffy Lab; Derek Keating Ind; Deirdre Doherty-Ryan FF; Mick Billane Lab; Colm Tyndall PD; Mark Daly SF; Paul Nicholas Gogarty GP; Sean Crowe SF; Jim Daly FF; John Hannon FF; Pat Rabbitte, TD Lab; Sheila Donnelly Ind; Cait Keane PD; John Lahart FF; Stanley Laing FG; Ann Ormonde, MCC FF; Eamonn Walsh Lab; Maire Ardagh FF; Robert Dowds Lab; John Curran FF; Colm McGrath Ind; Eamon Maloney Lab.

● **TIPPERARY (NORTH RIDING) COUNTY COUNCIL**
Courthouse, Nenagh, Co. Tipperary.
Tel: (067) 31771. **Fax:** (067) 33134.
email: secretary@northtippcoco.ie

County Manager: Risteard Ó Domhnaill (Deputy)
County Secretary: Peter Hogan (Acting) (£30,443-40,066)
County Engineer: Tom Haugh (Acting) (£38,393-47,085)
Council meeting: 3rd Monday of each month
Councillors: Mae Quinn FG; John Carroll FF; Tom Harrington FF; Maire Hoctor FF; Sean Mulrooney FF; John Hogan FF; Joe Hennessy FF; Martin Kennedy Ind; Noel Coonan FG; Kathleen O'Meara, MCC Lab; John Egan FF – Cathaoirleach; John Hanafin FF; Harry Ryan FF; Willie Kennedy Ind; Michael Lowry, TD Ind; Denis Ryan FG; Jim Casey FF; Tony McKenna FF; Tom Berkery FG; Mattie Ryan FF; Gerard Darcy FG.

● **TIPPERARY (SOUTH RIDING) COUNTY COUNCIL**
Áras an Chontae, Emmet Street,
Clonmel, Co. Tipperary
Tel: (052) 25399. Fax: (052) 24355.
email: secretare@southtippcoco.ie
County Manager: Edmond Gleeson (£59,046)
County Secretary: Michael Fitzgerald (£30,443-40,066)
County Engineer: Edmond Flynn (£38,393-47,085)
Council meeting: 1st Monday of each month
Councillors: Thomas Wood FG; Michael Anglim FF; Niall Dennehy FF; Phil Prendergast Ind; Pat Norris FF – Cathaoirleach; Christy Kinahan Ind; Brendan Griffin FG; Mattie McGrath FF; Tom Hayes, MCC FG; Derry Foley FG; Sean McCarthy FF; Denis Landy Lab; Susan Meagher FF; Denis Bourke FF; Eddie O'Meara Ind; John Fahey FG; Pat O'Meara FF; Tom Ambrose FF; Seamus Healy Ind; Jack Crowe FG; Dan Costigan FG; Michael Fitzgerald FG; Michael Maguire FF; Joe Donovan FF; Sean Nyhan FG; Barry O'Brien FF.

● **WATERFORD COUNTY COUNCIL**
Árus Brúgha, Dungarvan, Co. Waterford.
Tel: (058) 42822. Fax: (058) 42911.
County Manager: Donal Connolly (£54,926)
County Secretary: Peter Carey (£30,443-40,066)
County Engineer: John O'Flynn (£38,393-47,085)
Council meeting: 2nd Monday of each month
Councillors: Patrick Kenneally FF – Cathaoirleach; Pat Leahy FF; Ollie Wilkinson FF; Tom Cunningham FF; Gerard Barron Lab; Thomas Cronin FF; Billy Kyne Lab; Tom Higgins FG; John Deasy FG; Fiachra O'Ceilleachair Lab; Lola O'Sullivan FG; Nora Flynn FG; Geoff Power FF; Pat Daly FF; Nuala Ryan FF; John Carey FG; Dan Cowman FF; Paudie Coffey FG; Mary Greene FG; Kieran O'Ryan FF; Willie McDonnell FG; James Tobin FF; Betty Twomey Ind.

● **WATERFORD CORPORATION**
City Hall, Waterford.
Tel: (051) 873501. Fax: (051) 879124.
City Manager: Eddie Breen (£54,926)
Assistant Town Clerk: Mary Ryan
City Engineer: Tom Mackey (£38,393-47,085)
Council meeting: 2nd Monday of each month
Councillors: Oliver R. Clery PD; Pat Hayes Lab – Mayor; Hilary Quinlan FG; Sean J. Dower FF; Davy Walsh WP; Tom Cunningham FG; Michael Ivory FF;

Martin O'Regan WP; Maurice Cummins FG; Tom Murphy FF; Seamus Ryan Lab; John Halligan WP; Laurence O'Neill Ind; Mary Roche FF; David Daniels Ind.

● **WESTMEATH COUNTY COUNCIL**
Mullingar, Co. Westmeath.
Tel: (044) 40861. Fax: (044) 42330.
County Manager: Ann McGuinness (£59,046)
County Secretary: Ciaran McGrath (£30,443-40,066)
County Engineer: Noel Fay (Acting) (£38,393-47,085)
Council meeting: 4th Monday of each month
Councillors: Paul McGrath, TD FG; Donie Cassidy, MCC FF; Tom Bourke FF; Camillus Glynn, MCC FF; Betty Doran Lab; Willie Penrose, TD Lab; Patrick McLoughlin FG; PJ O'Shaughnessy FF; Dan McCarthy Lab; Jim Bourke FF; Frank McDermott FG; Kieran Molloy FF; Brendan McFadden FG; Mark Cooney FG; Mick Dollard Lab; Tom Allen FF; Kevin 'Boxer' Moran FF; Michael Ryan FF; Egbert Moran FF; Tom Cowley FF; Joseph Flanagan FG; Mark Nugent Lab; PJ Coghill FF – Cathaoirleach.

● **WEXFORD COUNTY COUNCIL**
County Hall, Spawell Road, Wexford.
Tel: (053) 42211. Fax: (053) 43406.
email: postmaster@wexfordcoco.ie
County Manager: Seamus Dooley (£59,046)
County Secretary: John Pierce (£30,443-40,066)
County Engineer: Philip Callery (£38,393-47,085)
Council meeting: 2nd Monday of each month
Councillors: Jimmy Curtis FF; Pat Codd FG; Josephine Doyle FF; Ivan Yates, TD FG; John A. Browne, TD FF; Jack Bolger FG; Michele Sinnott FF; Joe Murphy FF; Jim Walsh, MCC FF; Larry O'Brien FG; Seamus Whelan FF; Denis Kennedy FF; Brendan Howlin, TD Lab; Leo Carty Ind; Padge Reck Ind; Gus Byrne FF; Anna Fenlon FG; Lorcan Allen FF; Deirdre Bolger FG; Michael J. D'Arcy, TD FG; Seán Doyle Ind – Cathaoirleach.

● **WICKLOW COUNTY COUNCIL**
Aras an Chontae, Wicklow.
Tel: (0404) 20100 Fax: (0404) 67792.
email: wicklowcoco.ie
County Manager: Blaise Treacy (£59,046)
County Secretary: Bryan Doyle (£30,443-40,066)
County Engineer: Michael Looby (£38,393-47,085)
Council meeting: 1st and 2nd Mondays of each month
Councillors: Bill O'Connell FF; Tommy Cullen Lab; Billy G. Timmins, TD FG; Sylvester Bourke FG; Dick Roche, TD FF; Andrew Doyle FG; James O'Shaughnessy Lab; Pat Doyle FF; Noel Jacob FF; Liam Kavanagh Lab; Veronica O'Reilly Ind; Pat Doran FF; George Jones FG – Cathaoirleach; Vincent Blake FG; Deirdre DeBurca GP; John Byrne Lab; Michael D. Lawlor FF; Pat Vance FF; Joe Behan FF; Liz McManus, TD Lab; Mildred Fox, TD Ind; James Ruttle Ind; Nicky Kelly Ind; Derek Mitchell FG.

NI Borough, City and District Councils

● ANTRIM BOROUGH COUNCIL
The Steeple, Antrim BT41 1BJ.
Tel: (01849) 463113. Fax: (01849) 464469.
email: contact@antrim.gov.uk
Chief Executive: Mr. S.J. Magee.
Mayor: F.R.H. Marks.
Councillors:T.A. Burns (SDLP); M. Rea (UUP); T.E. Wallace (UUP); S. Dunlop (DUP); K.R. Swann (UUP); D.R.J. Ford (All); R. Thompson (UUP); S.W. Clyde (DUP); R.J. Loughran (SDLP); H.J. Cushinan (SF); D. McClelland (SDLP); J. Graham (UUP); O.C.J. Keenan (SDLP); J.B. McConnell (All); A.D. Watson (UUP); F.R.H. Marks (UUP); A.S. Ritchie (UUP); R.J. McClay (DUP).
Council Meeting Dates: 2nd Tuesday of each month.

● ARDS BOROUGH COUNCIL
2 Church Street, Newtownards, Co. Down BT23 4AP.
Tel: (01247) 824000. Fax: (01247) 819628.
Chief Executive: David Fallows
Mayor: Alan McDowell
Councillors: Thomas Benson (UUP); Paul Carson (UUP); Linda Cleland (All); Kathleen Coulter (All); Margaret Craig (UUP); Robin Drysdale (DUP); George Ennis (DUP); Ronald Ferguson (UUP); Robert Gibson (UUP); David Gilmore (DUP); Hamilton Gregory (DUP); Tom Hamilton (UUP); Jeffrey Magill (UUP); Wilbert Magill (Ind); Jim McBriar (All); Bobby McBride (Ind); Daniel McCarthy (SDLP); Kieran McCarthy (All); Alan McDowell (All); David McNarry (UUP); Richard Shannon (DUP); John Shields (UUP); David Smyth (UUP).
Council Meeting Dates: Last Wednesday each month.

● ARMAGH CITY AND DISTRICT COUNCIL
Council Offices, The Palace Demesne, Armagh BT60 4EL.
Tel: (01861) 529600. Fax: (01861) 529601.
email: info@armagh.gov.uk
Chief Executive: Desmond Mitchell
Mayor: Thomas Canavan
Councillors: Margaret Black (DUP); Pat Brannigan (SDLP); Anna Maria Brolly (SDLP); John Campbell (SDLP); Thomas Canavan (SDLP); James Clayton (UUP); Evelyn Corry (UUP); Brian Cunningham (SF); Gordon Frazer (UUP); Brian Hutchinson (DUP); Thomas Kavanagh (SDLP); Sharon McClelland (UUP); Sean McGirr (SF); James McGleenan (SDLP); James Kernan (SDLP); Sylvia Roberts (UUP); Charles Rollston (UUP); Noel Sheridan (SF); Eric Speers (UUP); James Speers (UUP); Robert Turner (UUP); Olive Whitten (UUP).
Council Meeting Dates: Last Monday each month.

● BALLYMENA BOROUGH COUNCIL
Ardeevin, 80 Galgorm Road, Ballymena, Co. Antrim BT42 1AA.
Tel: (01266) 660300. Fax: 01266 660400
email: townclerk@ballymena.gov.uk
Chief Executive: Mervyn Rankin
Mayor: James Currie
Councillors: J. Alexander (Ind); Miss J.A. Dunlop (All); S.C. Henry (Ind); P.J. McAvoy (SDLP); J.E. McKernan (UUP); M.T. Mills (DUP); W. Wright (Ind); D. Armstrong (UUP); D. Clyde (UUP); Miss M. Gribben (SDLP); S.J. Hanna (DUP); T.G.A. Scott (UUP); R. Coulter (UUP); R. Gillespie (DUP); I. Johnston (UUP); T. Nicholl (DUP); S. Gaston (DUP); M. Clarke (DUP); P.T.C. Brown (UUP); J. Currie (UUP); H. Nicholl (DUP); D. O'Loan (SDLP); D.A. Tweed (DUP); W. Moore (UUP).
Council Meeting Dates: 1st Monday of each month.

● BALLYMONEY BOROUGH COUNCIL
Riada House, 14 Charles Street, Ballymoney, Co. Antrim BT53 6DZ.
Tel: (012656) 62280. Fax: (012656) 65150.
email: ballmoneybc@psilink.co.uk
Chief Executive: John Dempsey.
Mayor: William Logan
Councillors: William Logan (UUP); William T. Kennedy (DUP); Harry Connolly (SDLP); Joseph Gaston (UUP); Robert McComb (Ind); Samuel McConaghie (DUP); Frank Campbell (DUP); Cecil Cousley (DUP); John Finlay (DUP); Robert Halliday (DUP); Malachy McCamphill (SDLP); Francis McCloskey (SDLP); Thomas McKeown (UUP); John Watt (UUP); Bill Williamson (Ind); Robert Williamson (DUP).
Council Meeting Dates: 1st and 3rd Monday of each month.

● BANBRIDGE DISTRICT COUNCIL
Civic Building, Downshire Road, Banbridge BT32 3JY.
Tel: (018206) 62991. Fax: (018206) 62595.
email: info@banbridgedc.gov.uk
Chief Executive: Robert Gilmore.
Chairperson: Wilfred McFadden.
Councillors: Joan Baird (UUP); Derick Bell (UUP); William Bell (UUP); Mel Byrne (SDLP); Cyril Vage (DUP); Paul Walsh (Ind); Tom Gribben (UUP); David Herron (DUP); William Martin (UUP); William McCracken (UUP); Catherine McDermott (SDLP); Violet Cromie (UUP); Seamus Doyle (SDLP); John Hanna (UUP); John Ingram (UUP); Malachy McCartan (Ind); Wilfred McFadden (DUP).
Council Meeting Dates: 1st Monday of each month.

● BELFAST CITY COUNCIL
City Hall, Belfast, Co. Antrim BT1 5GS.
Tel: (01232) 320202. Fax: (01232) 438075
email: info@belfastcity.gov.uk
Chief Executive: Brian Hanna.
Lord Mayor: Bob Stoker.
Councillors: Margaret Crooks (UUP); Thomas Ekin (All); Carmel Hanna (SDLP); Catherine Molloy (SDLP); Harry Smith (DUP); Bob Stoker (UUP); David Browne (UUP); Tom Campbell (All); Nigel Dodds (DUP); Danny Lavery (SF); Nelson McCausland (UUP); Alban Maginness (SDLP); Fred Cobain (UUP); Frank McCoubrey (UDP); Chris McGimpsey (UUP); Eric

Smyth (DUP); Hugh Smyth (PUP); Jim Clarke (UUP); Sean Hayes (SF); Steve McBride (All); Alasdair McDonnell (SDLP); Michael McGimpsey (UUP); Tom Hartley (SF); Francis McCann (SF); Seán McKnight (SF); Marie Moore (SF); Margaret Walsh (SDLP); Mick Conlon (SF); Billy Hutchinson (PUP); Bobby Lavery (SF); Gerard Brophy (SF); Martin Morgan (SDLP); Fred Proctor (UUP); Margaret Clarke (UUP); Robert Cleland (DUP); Reg Empey (UUP); David Ervine (PUP); Mervyn Jones (All); Sammy Wilson (DUP); Alex Attwood (SDLP); Michael Browne (SF); Gerard O'Neill (SF); Chrissie McAuley (SF); Alex Maskey (SF); Ian Adamson (UUP); David Alderdice (All); Wallace Browne (DUP); Alan Crowe (Ind); Danny Dow (All); Robin Newton (DUP); Jim Rodgers (UUP).
Council Meeting Dates: 1st weekday of the month (except Fridays and bank holidays).

● CARRICKFERGUS BOROUGH COUNCIL
Town Hall, Carrickfergus, Co. Antrim BT38 7DL.
Tel: (01960) 351604. Fax: (01960) 366676.
email: info@carrickfergus.org
Chief Executive: Adrian Donaldson.
Mayor: T. Greighton.
Councillors: W. Ashe (DUP); Mrs M. Beattie (DUP); J. Brown (Ind); R. Cavan (All); Mrs J. Crampsey (All); T. Creighton (UUP); S. Crowe (Ind); S. Dickson (All); E. Ferguson (UUP); W. Hamilton (Ind); D. Hilditch (DUP); C. Johnston (Ind); S. McCamley (UUP); Mrs N. McIlwrath (All); S. Neeson (All); J. Reid (UUP); N. Wady (Ind).
Council Meeting Dates: 1st Monday of each month.

● CASTLEREAGH BOROUGH COUNCIL
368 Cregagh Road, Belfast, Co. Antrim BT6 9EZ.
Tel: (01232) 799021. Fax: (01232) 704158.
email: chief@castlereagh.gov.uk
Chief Executive: Adrian Donaldson.
Mayor: Mrs M.B. Chambers
Councillors: Mrs M.B. Chambers (DUP); J. Beattie (Ind); R.P. Mitchell (All); Mrs I. Robinson (DUP); P.D. Robinson (DUP); Ms S.E. Cummings (UUP); W.H. Abraham (Ind); C. Hall (UUP); A. Carson (UUP); W. Clulow (DUP); G.T.A. Dillon (UKUP); Mrs S. Duncan (All); J. Dunn (DUP); S. Geddis (DUP); A.D.J. Hegney (SDLP); M. Henderson (UUP); Miss R. Hughes (SDLP); T. Jeffers (DUP); Mrs K. Morton (DUP); J. Norris (DUP); P. Osborne (All); Mrs G. Rice (All); S.M. Robinson (DUP).
Council Meeting Dates: 4th Thursday of each month.

● COLERAINE BOROUGH COUNCIL
Cloonavain, 41 Portstewart Road, Coleraine, Co. Derry BT52 1EY.
Tel: (01265) 52181. Fax: (01265) 53489.
email: townclerk@colerainebc.gov.uk
Chief Executive: H.W.T. Moore
Mayor: Norman Frederick Hillis
Councillors: Norman Hillis (UUP); Olive Church (UUP); Christine Alexander (Ind); Pauline Armitage (UUP); William King (UUP); William McClure (DUP); William Watt (UUP); David Barbour (UUP); Elizabeth Toye-Black (UUP); Robert Bolton (Ind); John Bradley

(DUP); William Creelman (DUP); John Dallat (SDLP); Barbara Dempsey (All); Elizabeth Johnston (UUP); David McClarty (UUP); Gerard McLaughlin (SDLP); Robert McPherson (UUP); William Matthews (All); Eamon Mullan (SDLP); Eamon O'Hara (All); Robert Stewart (DUP).
Council Meeting Dates: 4th Tuesday of each month.

● COOKSTOWN DISTRICT COUNCIL
Council Offices, Burn Road, Cookstown, Co. Tyrone BT80 8DT.
Tel: (016487) 62205. Fax: (016487) 64360.
email: mjm@cookstown.gov.uk
Chief Executive: Mr. M.J. McGuckian
Chairman: Walter Greer.
Councillors: Finbar Conway (SF); Samuel Glasgow (UUP); James McGarvey (SDLP); John Fitzgerald-McNamee (SF); Samuel Parke (Ind); Mary Baker (SDLP); Sean Campbell (SF); Thomas Greer (UUP); Patrick McAleer (SF); Anne McCrea (DUP); Patsy McGlone (SDLP); Sean Begley (SF); Denis Haughey (SDLP); William John Larmour (Ind); William Joseph Larmour (UUP); Trevor Wilson (UUP).
Council Meeting Dates: 2nd Tuesday of each month.

● CRAIGAVON BOROUGH COUNCIL
Civic Centre, Lakeview Road, Craigavon, Co. Armagh BT64 1AL.
Tel: (01762) 341199. Fax: (01762) 312444.
email: info@craigavon.gov.uk
Chief Executive: Trevor Reaney.
Chairperson: Dolores Kelly.
Councillors: Dolores Kelly (SDLP); Frederick Crowe (UUP); Mervyn Carrick (DUP); Samuel Gardiner (UUP); James McCammick (UUP); Joseph Trueman (UUP); Ruth Allen (DUP); William Allen (DUP); Johnathan Bell (UUP); Sydney Cairns (UUP); Meta Crozier (UUP); Joseph Duffy (Ind); Ignatius Fox (SDLP); John Hagan (All); Arnold Hatch (UUP); Breandan MacCionnaith (Ind); Mary McAlinden (SDLP); Kieran McGeown (SDLP); Sean McKavangh (SDLP); Mary McNulty (SDLP); Patricia Mallon (SDLP); Francie Murray (SF); Mark Neale (UUP); John O'Dowd (SF); George Savage (UUP); Kenneth Twyble (UUP).
Council Meeting Dates: 1st and 3rd Monday of each month.

● DERRY CITY COUNCIL
98 Strand Road, Derry BT48 7NN.
Tel: (01504) 365151. Fax: (01504) 264858.
email: derrycc@derrycity.gov.uk
Chief Executive: John Keanie.
Mayor: Patrick Ramsey.
Councillors: A. Davidson (UUP); Annie Courtney (SDLP); Cathal Crumley (SF); E. Hamilton (UUP); Gerard O'hEara (SF); Gerard Peoples (SDLP); Gregory Campbell (DUP); J. Clifford (SDLP); J.Kerr (SDLP); J.M. Mc Laughlin (SF); J.M.Durkan (SDLP); Jim Guy (Ind); John Tierney (SDLP); Joseph Miller M. Garfield (DUP); K.Mc Closkey (SDLP); Lynn Feming (SF); M. Hutcheon (SF); M. Nelis (SF); Martin Bradley (SDLP); Mary Bradley (SDLP); P. Ramsey (SDLP); P.Kelly (SDLP); Patrick Anderson (SF); Richard Dallas (UUP);

S.Gallagher (SDLP); S.Mc Nichol (SDLP); Tony Hassan (SF); William Hay (DUP); William O'Connell (SDLP).
Council Meeting Dates: 4th Tuesday of each month.

● DOWN DISTRICT COUNCIL
24 Strangford Road, Downpatrick,Co. Down BT30 6SR.
Tel: (01396) 610800. Tel: (01396) 610801.
Chief Executive Designate: John McGrillen
Chairperson: Peter Fitzpatrick
Councillors: William Alexander (Ind); Reginald Bicker (UUP); William Biggerstaff (UUP); Catherine Carr (NIWC); Francis Casement (SDLP); Albert Colmer (UUP); Peter Craig (SDLP); Dermot Curran (SDLP); William Dick (DUP); John Doris (SDLP); Gerald Douglas (UUP); Peter Fitzpatrick (SDLP); Gerard Mahon (SDLP); Anne Marie McAleenan (SDLP); Francis McDowell (SF); Patrick McGreevy (SF); John McIlheron (UUP); Carmel O'Boyle (SDLP); Eamonn O'Neill (SDLP); Samuel Osborne (UUP); Margaret Ritchie (SDLP); Patrick Toman (SDLP); Anne Trainor (SDLP).
Council Meeting Dates: 3rd Monday of each month.

● DUNGANNON DISTRICT COUNCIL
Council Offices, Circular Road, Dungannon, Co. Tyrone BT71 6DT.
Tel: (01868) 720300. Fax: (01868) 720333.
email: gladys.smith@dungannon.gov.uk
Chief Executive: Mr. W. Beattie
Chairperson: Jim Kavanagh
Councillors: A. McGonnell (SDLP); W.J. McIlwrath (DUP); S.F. Flanagan (SF); N.R.D. Mulligan (UUP); R.L. Mulligan (UUP); N. Badger (UUP); J. Canning (Ind); J.I. Cavanagh (SDLP); B. Doris (SF); F. Molloy (SF); M. Gillespie (SF); D.J. Brady (UUP); P. Daly (SDLP); J. Ewing (DUP); J. Hamilton (UUP); D.C.G. Irwin (UUP); M.J. Carson (UUP); G.C. Cullen (DL); V. Currie (SDLP); J. Reilly (UUP); V. Kelly (SF); M. Morrow (DUP).
Council Meeting Dates: 2nd Monday of each month.

● FERMANAGH DISTRICT COUNCIL
Town Hall, Enniskillen, Co. Fermanagh BT74 7BA.
Tel: (01365) 325050. Fax: (01365) 322024.
email: liz.connor@fermanagh.gov.uk
Chief Executive: Aideen McGinley.
Chairman: D. Nixon.
Councillors: D. Nixon (UUP); G. Gallagher (SDLP); H. Andrews (UUP); G. Cassidy (SF); J. Dodds (DUP); W. Elliott (UUP); R. Ferguson (UUP); E. Flanagan (SDLP); S. Foster (UUP); T. Gallagher (SDLP); Basil Johnston (UUP); Bert Johnston (DUP); B. Kerr (UUP); D. Kettyles (Ind); R. Lynch (SF); B. McCaffrey (SF); P. McCaffrey (Ind); C. McClaughry (UUP); G. McHugh (SF); A. McPhillips (Ind); F. McQuillan (UUP); R. Martin (SF); C. Noble (UUP).
Council Meeting Dates: 1st Monday of each month.

● LARNE BOROUGH COUNCIL
Smiley Buildings, Victoria Road, Larne, Co. Antrim BT40 1RU.
Tel: (01574) 272313. Fax: (01574) 260660.

Chief Executive: Colm McGarry.
Mayor: Joan Drummond.
Councillors: Jack McKee (DUP); John Matthews (All); Thomas Robinson (UUP); John Beggs (UUP); Roy Craig (Ind); William Cunning (Ind); Mrs Joan Drummond (UUP); David Fleck (UUP); John Hall (UUP); Bobby McKee (DUP); Robert Mason (Ind); Desmond Nixon (Ind); Daniel O'Connor (SDLP); Rachel Rea (DUP).
Council Meeting Dates: 1st Monday of each month.

● LIMAVADY BOROUGH COUNCIL
7 Connell Street, Limavady, Co. Derry BT49 0HA.
Tel: (015047) 22226. Fax: (015047) 22010.
Chief Executive: John Stevenson
Mayor: John McKinney
Councillors: Gerard Lynch (SDLP); Stanley Gault (UUP); Michael Coyle (SDLP); Ian Grant (UUP); John McKinney (SDLP); Michael Carten (SDLP); Ronald Cartwright (UUP); Barry Doherty (SDLP); Arthur Doherty (SDLP); John Dolan (UUP); Douglas Boyd (Ind); Max Gault (UUP); Desmond Lowry (SDLP); Malachy O'Kane (SF); George Robinson (DUP).
Council Meeting Dates: 4th Wednesday of each month.

● LISBURN BOROUGH COUNCIL
The Square, Hillsborough, Co. Down BT26 6AH.
Tel: (01846) 682477. Fax: (01846) 689016.
email: derek.mccallan@lisburn.gov.uk
Chief Executive: Norman Davidson.
Mayor: Peter O'Hagan.
Councillors: W.E. Falloon (UUP); M. Ferguson (SF); W. Gardiner-Watson (UUP); I.M. Gray (SF); J. Tinsley (DUP); K.C. Hull (UUP); W.H. Lewis (UUP); H. Lewsley (SDLP); J.H. Lockhart (UUP); F.C. McCammond (All); W. McDonnell (SDLP); P. O'Hagan (SDLP); D. Adams (UDP); T.D. Archer (UUP); Rev W.J. Beattie (DUP); W.B. Bell (UUP); W.G. Bleakes (Con); P.A. Butler (SF); C. Calvert (DUP); E.J. Campbell (All); S.A. Close (All); R. Crawford (Ind); I. Davis (UUP); W.J. Dillon (UUP); J.G. McMichael (UDP); L. Martin (UUP); G. Morrison (UUP); E.C. Poots (DUP); S. Ramsey (SF); K.S. Watson (UUP).
Council Meeting Dates: 4th Tuesday of each month.

● MAGHERAFELT DISTRICT COUNCIL
50 Ballyronan Road, Magherafelt, Co. Derry BT45 6EN.
Tel: (01648) 32151. Fax: (01648) 31240.
email: mdc@magherafelt.demon.co.uk
Chief Executive: John McLaughlin
Chairman: Frank McKendry
Councillors: George Shiels (UUP); Seamus O'Brien (SF); Patrick Kilpatrick (SDLP); Joseph McBride (SDLP); Rev Dr William McCrea (DUP); Paul McLean (DUP); T.J. Catherwood (DUP); John Junkin (UUP); Patrick McErlean (SDLP); Margaret McKenna (SF); Paul Henry (SF); Patrick Groogan (SF); Kathleen Lagan (SDLP); R.A. Montgomery (Ind); Frank McKendry (SDLP); John Kelly (SF).
Council Meeting Dates: 2nd Tuesday each month.

● MOYLE DISTRICT COUNCIL

Sheskburn House, 7 Mary Street, Ballycastle, Co. Antrim BT54 6QH.
Tel: (012657) 62225. **Fax:** (012657) 62515.
email: info@moyle-council.org
Chief Executive: Richard G. Lewis
Chairman: Archie McIntosh
Councillors: Seamus Blaney (Ind); William Graham (UUP); Helen Harding (UUP); George Hartin (DUP); Gardiner Kane (DUP); Richard Kerr (SDLP); David McAllister (DUP); James McCarry (SF); Christopher McCaughan (All); Andrew McConaghy (Ind); Randal McDonnell (Ind); Archie McIntosh (SDLP); Robert McIlroy (UUP); Oliver McMullan (Ind); Malachy McSparran (SDLP).
Council Meeting Dates: 2nd and 4th Monday of each month.

● **NEWRY AND MOURNE DISTRICT COUNCIL**
Council Offices, O'Hagan House, Monaghan Row, Newry, Co. Down BT35 8DJ.
Tel: (01693) 65411. **Fax:** (01693) 65313.
email: finance@newryandmourne.gov.uk
Chief Executive: Kevin O'Neill
Chairperson: Josephine O'Hare
Councillors: W. Burns (DUP); M. Cunningham (SDLP); I.B. Hanna (UUP); D.E. Haughian (SDLP); B. Reilly (UUP); P.J. Bradley (SDLP); H. Carr (SDLP); J. McCart (SDLP); M. Murphy (SF); C. Mussen (Ind); J. O'Hare (SDLP); A.V. Williamson (Ind); B. Curran (SF); F. Feely (SDLP); D. Hyland (SF); E. Markey (Ind); W. McCaigue (UUP); H. McElroy (SDLP); J. Patterson (Ind); D. Kennedy (UUP); A. Lewis (SF); J.P. McCreesh (SF); S. McGinn (SDLP); W.A. Moffett (UUP); C. Smyth (SDLP); P. Brennan (SF); J. Fee (SDLP); PJ McDonald (SF); P.D. McNamee (SF); P. Toner (SDLP).
Council Meeting Dates: 1st Monday of each month.

● **NEWTOWNABBEY BOROUGH COUNCIL**
1 The Square, Ballyclare, Co. Antrim BT39 9BA.
Tel: (01960) 352681. **Fax:** (01960) 340417.
Chief Executive: Norman Dunn
Mayor: Jay Bingham
Councillors: J.K. Blair (Ind); E.J. Crilly (UUP); I. Hunter (UUP); J.A. Kell (UUP); T.P. McTeague (SDLP); J.J. Rooney (All); Mrs E. Snoddy (DUP); T.J. Bingham (UUP); W.P. Girvan (DUP); P.B. McCudden (All); Mrs V. McWilliam (UUP); E. Turkington (UUP); A. Beattie (Ind); D. Hollis (UUP); R.J. Kidd (NLP); T.G. Kirkham (UDP); M.F. Langhammer (Ind); W.J. Webb (Ind); W.A.F. Agnew (Ind); Mrs L. Frazer (All); Mrs B.J. Gilliland (UUP); W.T. Greer (PUP); G.L. Herron (Ind); W.R. Johnston (UUP); K.W. Robinson (UUP).

Council Meeting Dates: 4th Monday of each month.
● **NORTH DOWN BOROUGH COUNCIL**
Town Hall, The Castle, Bangor, Co. Down BT20 4BT.
Tel: (01247) 270371. **Fax:** (01247) 271370.
Chief Executive: Trevor Polley
Mayor: Marian Smith
Councillors: A. Chambers (Ind); R.L. Cree (UUP); T.M. Fitzsimons (All); I. Henry (UUP); A.J. Lennon (Ind); B.R. Mulligan (Ind); Mrs E. Roche (NIUP); Mrs I.R. Cooling (DUP); S. Currie (PUP); Mrs R.M. Dunlop (UUP); S.A. Farry (All); Mrs V. Kingham (UKUP); Mrs A. Thompson (Ind); Mrs E. Bell (All); R. Davies (UUP); W.D. Keery (UKUP); Mrs M. Smith (UUP); E.J.F. Steele (Ind); Mrs A. Wilson (All); B.A.S. Wilson (Ind); G.M. Dunne (DUP); R.J. Good (All); Mrs E. McKay (UUP); Mrs S.K. O'Brien (All); D.W. Ogborn (Ind).
Council Meeting Dates: 4th Tuesday of each month.

● **OMAGH DISTRICT COUNCIL**
The Grange, Mountjoy Road, Omagh, Co. Tyrone BT79 7BL.
Tel: (01662) 245321. **Fax:** (01662) 252380.
email: info@omagh.gov.uk
Chief Executive: John McKinney
Chairman: Allan Rainey.
Councillors: Vincent Campbell (SDLP); Oliver Gibson (DUP); Ann Gormley (All); Francis Mackey (Ind); Patrick McGowan (Ind); Reuben McKelvey (UUP); John McLaughlin (Ind); Drew Baxter (DUP); Terence Brogan (SF); Joe Byrne (SDLP); Sean Clarke (SF); Michael McAnespie (SF); Patsy McMahon (SF); Seamus Shields (SDLP); Thomas Buchanan (DUP); Patrick McDonnell (SDLP); Crawford McFarland (UUP); Kevin McGrade (SF); Liam McQuaid (SDLP); Cathal Quinn (SF); Allan Rainey (UUP).
Council Meeting Dates: 1st Tuesday of each month.

● **STRABANE DISTRICT COUNCIL**
47 Derry Road, Strabane, Co. Tyrone BT82 8DY.
Tel: (01504) 382204. **Fax:** (01504) 382264.
email: strabanedc@nics.gov.uk
Chief Executive: Daniel McSorley
Chairman: Ignatius Murtagh
Councillors: Ivan Barr (SF); Ann Bell (SDLP); Allan Bresland (DUP); Martin Conway (SF); John Donnell (DUP); James Emery (UUP); Derek Hussey (UUP); T. Kerrigan (DUP); Thomas McBride (SDLP); Charles McHugh (SF); Eugene McMenamin (SDLP); Jarlath McNulty (SF); Eugene Mullen (SDLP); Ignatius Murtagh (SDLP); James O'Kane (Ind); Edward Turner (UUP).
Council Meeting Dates: 2nd and 4th Tuesday of each month.

Diplomatic Missions

Missions Accredited to Ireland

● **DUBLIN**

APOSTOLIC NUNCIATURE H.E. The Most Rev. Luciano Storero, Dean of the Diplomatic Corps, 183 Navan Road, Dublin 7. Tel. (01) 8380577

ARGENTINA (1964) H.E. Mr Victor E. Beaugé, 15 Ailesbury Drive, Ballsbridge, Dublin 4. Tel. (01) 2691546

AUSTRALIA (1946) H.E. Mr Robert George Halverson,

2nd Floor, Fitzwilton House, Wilton Terrace, Dublin 2. Tel. (01) 6761517.

AUSTRIA (1966) H.E. Dr Michael Breisky, 15 Ailesbury Court, 93 Ailesbury Road, Dublin 4. Tel. (01) 2694577.

BELGIUM (1958) H.E. Alain Guillaume, 2 Shrewsbury Road, Dublin 4. Tel. (01) 2692082.

BRAZIL, FEDERATIVE REPUBLIC OF (1974) Mr Armando Sérgio Frazão, Europa House, Block 9, Harcourt Centre, 41-45 Harcourt House, Dublin 2. Tel. (01) 4756000.

BRITAIN (1939) H.E. Mr Ivor Roberts, 29 Merrion Road, Dublin 4. Tel. (01) 2053700.

BULGARIA, REPUBLIC OF (1991) H. E. Mr Peter Poptchev (Chargé d'Affaires), 22 Burlington Road, Dublin 4. Tel. (01) 6603293.

CANADA (1940) H.E. Mr Ron Irwin, 4th Floor, 65-68 St. Stephen's Green, Dublin 2. Tel. (01) 4781988.

CHINA, PEOPLE'S REPUBLIC OF (1980) H.E. Mr Zheng Jinjiong, 40 Ailesbury Road, Ballsbridge, Dublin 4. Tel. (01) 2691707.

CYPRUS, REPUBLIC OF (1997) H.E. Mr Nicholas Emiliou, 71 Lower Leeson Street, Dublin 2. Tel. (01) 6763060.

CZECH REPUBLIC (1993). H.E. Mr Lubos Novy, Ambassador Extraordinary & Plenipotentiary, 57 Northumberland Road, Dublin 4. Tel. (01) 6681135.

DENMARK (1973) H.E. Ulrick A. Federspiel, 121-122 St. Stephen's Green, Dublin 2. Tel. (01) 4756404.

EGYPT, ARAB REPUBLIC OF (1975) H.E. Hassan Wafik Salem, 12 Clyde Road, Ballsbridge, Dublin 4. Tel. (01) 6606566.

ESTONIA, REPUBLIC OF Ms Triin Parts, Chargé d'Affaires a.i., 24 Merlyn Park, Ballsbridge, Dublin 4. Tel. (01) 2691552.

FINLAND (1962) H.E. Mr Timo Jussi Jalkanen, Russel House, Stokes Place, St. Stephen's Green, Dublin 2. Tel. (01) 4781344.

FRANCE (1930) H.E. Mr Henri Benoit de Coignac, 36 Ailesbury Road, Dublin 4. Tel. (01) 2691666.

GERMANY, FEDERAL REPUBLIC OF (1951) H.E. Dr Hartmut Holger Hillgenberg, 31 Trimleston Avenue, Booterstown, Blackrock, Co. Dublin. Tel. (01) 2693011.

GREECE (1977) H.E. Ms. Maria Zografou, 1 Upper Pembroke Street, Dublin 2. Tel. (01) 676 7254.

HUNGARY, REPUBLIC OF (1977) H.E. Dr Géza Pálmai, 2 Fitzwilliam Place, Dublin 2. Tel. (01) 6612902.

INDIA (1951) H.E. Mrs Chokila Iyer, 6 Leeson Park, Dublin 6. Tel. (01) 497 0843.

IRAN, ISLAMIC REPUBLIC OF (1976) H.E. Mr Hassan Taherian, 72 Mount Merrion Avenue, Blackrock, Co. Dublin. Tel. (01) 288 0252.

ISRAEL (1994) H.E. Mr Zvi Gabay, Carrisbrook House, 122 Pembroke Road, Dublin 4. Tel. (01) 668 0303.

ITALY (1937) H.E. Dr Ferdinando Zezza, 63-65 Northumberland Road, Ballsbridge, Dublin 4. Tel. (01) 660 1744.

JAPAN (1964) H.E. Mrs Kazuko Yokoo, Nutley Building, Merrion Centre, Nutley Lane, Dublin 4. Tel. (01) 269 4244.

KOREA, REPUBLIC OF (1983) H.E. Mr Ki-Ho Chang, 15 Clyde Road, Ballsbridge, Dublin 4. Tel. (01) 6608800.

MEXICO (1980) H.E. Mr Daniel Dultzin Dubin, 43 Ailesbury Road, Ballsbridge, Dublin 4. Tel. (01) 2600699.

MOROCCO, KINGDOM OF (1959) Vacant, Chargé d'Affaires: Mrs. Najat Zhor Dine, 53 Raglan Road, Dublin 4. Tel. (01) 660 9449.

NETHERLANDS (1956) H.E. Mr Peter van Vliet, 160 Merrion Road, Ballsbridge, Dublin 4. Tel. (01) 2693444.

NIGERIA, FEDERAL REPUBLIC OF (1963) H.E. Chief Elias Nathan, 56 Leeson Park, Dublin 6. Tel. (01) 6604366.

NORWAY (1950) H.E. Mr Helge Vindenes, 34 Molesworth Street, Dublin 2. Tel. (01) 662 1800.

POLAND, REPUBLIC OF (1990) H.E. Mr Janusz Skolimowski, 5 Ailesbury Road, Ballsbridge, Dublin 4. Tel. (01) 283 0855.

PORTUGAL (1965) H.E. Mr João de Vallera, Knocksinna House, Knocksinna Road, Foxrock, Dublin 18. Tel. (01) 289 4416.

ROMANIA (1995) Vacant, Chargé d'Affaires: Mr George Maior, 47 Ailesbury Road, Ballsbridge, Dublin 4. Tel. (01) 269 2852.

RUSSIAN FEDERATION (1974) H.E. Mr Evgueni N. Mikhailov, 184-186 Orwell Road, Rathgar, Dublin 14. Tel. (01) 492 2048.

SLOVAK REPUBLIC (1993) Chargè d'Affaires Mr Marcel Pesko, 20 Clyde Road, Ballsbridge, Dublin 4. Tel. (01) 660 0012.

SOUTH AFRICA, REPUBLIC OF (1995) Vacant, 2nd

Floor, Alexandra House, Earlsfort Centre, Earlsfort Terrace, Dublin 2. Tel. (01) 661 5553.

SPAIN (1950) H.E. Mr José Maria Sanz-Pastor Mellado, 17a Merlyn Park, Ballsbridge, Dublin 4. Tel. (01) 283 8827.

SWEDEN (1959) H.E. Mr Peter Osvald, 13-17 Dawson Street, Dublin 2. Tel. (01) 671 5822.

SWITZERLAND (1939) H.E. Mr Willy Hold, 6 Ailesbury Road, Ballsbridge, Dublin 4. Tel. (01) 269 2515.

TURKEY, REPUBLIC OF (1972) H.E. Mr Sabir Gunaltay Sibay, 11 Clyde Road, Ballsbridge, Dublin 4. Tel. (01) 668 5240.

UNITED STATES OF AMERICA (1950) H.E. Mr Michael J. Sullivan, 42 Elgin Road, Ballsbridge, Dublin 4. Tel. (01) 668 8777.

● **LONDON**

ALBANIA (1996) Mr Agim Fagu, 4th Floor, 38 Grosvenor Gardens, London SW1 WOEB. Tel. (0044171) 730 5709.

ALGERIA (1983) H.E. Mr Ahmed Benyamina, 54 Holland Park, London W11 3RS. Tel. (0044171) 2217800.

AZERBAIJAN REPUBLIC H.E. Mr Mahmud Mamed-Kuliyev, 4 Kensington Court, London W8 5DL. Tel. (0044171) 937 6463.

BAHRAIN, STATE OF (1981) H.E. Sheikh Abdul Aziz bin Mubarak Al Khalifa, 98 Gloucester Road, London SW7 4AU. Tel. (0044171) 370 5132.

BANGLADESH, PEOPLE'S REPUBLIC OF H.E. Mr A. H. Mahmood Ali, 28 Queen's Gate, London SW7 5JA. Tel. (0044171) 584 0081.

BELARUS, REPUBLIC OF (1996) H.E. Mr Vladzimir R. Shchasny, 6 Kensington Court, London W8 5DL. Tel. (0044171) 9373288.

BRUNEI (1987) H.E. Pehin Dato Dato Jaya Abdul Latif, 19 Belgrave Square, London SW1X 8PG. Tel. (0044171) 581 0521.

BULGARIA, REPUBLIC OF (1991) H.E. Mr Valentin Dobrev, 186-188 Queens Gate, London SW7 5HL. Tel. (0044171) 584 9400.

CHILE (1992) H.E. Mr Mario Artaza, 12 Devonshire Street, London W1N 2FS. Tel. (0044171) 580 6392.

CROATIA, REPUBLIC OF (1996) H.E. Mr Andrija Kohakovic, 19-21 Conway Street, London W1P 5HL. Tel. (0044171) 378 2022.

ESTONIA, REPUBLIC OF (1994) H.E. Raul Mälk, 16 Hyde Park Gate, Kensington, London SW7 5DG. Tel.

(0044171) 589 3428.

ETHIOPIA (1994) Dr Beyene Negewo (Agrée), 17 Prince's Gate, London SW7 1PZ. Tel. (0044171) 5897212.

GEORGIA H. E. Mr Teimuraz Mamatsashvili, 3 Hornton Place, London W8 4LZ. Tel. (0044171) 937 8233.

GHANA, REPUBLIC OF H.E. Mr James E. K. Aggrey-Orleans, 13 Belgrave Square, London SW1X 8PN. Tel. (0044171) 235 4142.

ICELAND (1951) vacant, 1 Eaton Terrace, London SW1 W 8EY. Tel. (0044171) 590 1100.

INDONESIA (1984) H.E. Mr Nana Sutresna Sastradidjaja, 38 Grosvenor Square, London W1X 9AD. Tel. (0044171) 499 7661.

IRAQ, REPUBLIC OF vacant

JORDAN, HASHEMITE KINGDOM OF (1984) vacant, 6 Upper Phillimore Gardens, Kensington, London W8 7HB. Tel. (0044171) 9373685.

KAZAKHHSTAN, REPUBLIC OF H.E. Mr Kanat Saudabaev, 35 Thurlowe Square, London SW7 2DS. Tel. (0044171) 581 4646.

KENYA, REPUBLIC OF (1984) H.E. Mr Mwanyengela Ngali, 45 Portland Place, London W1N 4AS. Tel. (0044171) 636 2371.

KUWAIT, STATE OF (1996) H.E. Mr Khaled Abdul Aziz Al-Duwaissan, 2 Albert Gate, Hyde Park House, Knightsbridge, London SW1X 7JU. Tel. (0044171) 590 3400.

LATVIA, REPUBLIC OF (1994) Mr Normans Penke, 45 Nottingham Palace, London W1M 3FE. Tel. (0044171) 312 0040.

LEBANON (1974) H.E. Dr Mahmoud Hammoud, 21 Palace Garden Mews, London W8 4QM. Tel. (0044171) 229 7265.

LIBYA Vacant.

LITHUANIA (1996) H.E. Mr Justas V. Paleckis, 184 Gloucester Place, London W1H 3HN. Tel. (0044171) 486 6401.

LUXEMBOURG (1973) H.E. Mr Joseph Weyland, 27 Wilton Crescent, London SW1X 8SD. Tel. (0044171) 235 6961.

MACEDONIA, FORMER YUGOSLAV REPUBLIC OF (1996) H.E. Mr Stevo Crvenkovski, 10 Harcourt House, 19-19a Cavendish Square, London W1M 9AD. Tel. (0044171) 499 5152.

MALAYSIA (1969) H.E. Dato Mohamed Amir Jaafar, 45/46 Belgrave Square, London SW1X 8QT. Tel.

(0044171) 235 8033.

MALTA (1990) H.E. Mr Richard Muscat, 36/38 Piccadilly, London W1V 0PQ8. Tel. (0044171) 2924800.

NAMIBIA (1996) vacant, 6 Chandos Street, London W1M 0LQ. Tel. (0044171) 636 6244.

NEW ZEALAND (1966) H.E. Mr Paul Clayton East, New Zealand House, Haymarket, London SW1 4TQ. Tel. (0044171) 930 8422.

OMAN, SULTANATE OF (1988) H.E. Mr Hussain Ali Abdullatif, 167 Queens Gate, London SW3 1HY. Tel. (0044171) 225 0001.

PHILIPPINES (1984) H.E. Mr Cesar B. Bautista, 9a Palace Green, London W8 4QE. Tel. (0044171) 9371600.

QATAR, STATE OF (1976) H.E. Mr Ali Jaidah, 1 South Audley Street, London W1Y 5DQ. Tel. (0044171) 4932200.

RWANDA, REPUBLIC OF H.E. Dr Zac Nsenga, Uganda House, 58-59 Trafalgar Square, London WC2N 5DX. Tel. (0044171) 930 2570.

SAUDI ARABIA (1981) H.E. Dr Ghazi Abdulrahman Algosaibi, 30 Charles Street, London W1X 7DM. Tel. (0171) 917 3000.

SINGAPORE, REPUBLIC OF (1975) H.E. Mr Joseph Y. Pillay, 9 Wilton Crescent, London SW1X 8SA. Tel. (0044171) 235 8315.

SLOVENIA, REPUBLIC OF (1996) H.E. Mr Marjan Setinc, Suite 1, Cavendish Court, 11-15 Wigmore Street, London W1H 9LA. Tel. (0044171) 495 7775.

SRI LANKA, DEMOCRATIC REPUBLIC OF vacant, 13 Hyde Park Gardens, London W2 2LU. Tel. (0171) 2621841.

SUDAN, REPUBLIC OF vacant, 3 Cleveland Row, St. James's, London SW1A 1DD. Tel. (0171) 8398080.

TANZANIA, UNITED REPUBLIC OF (1979) H.E. Dr Abdulkader A. Shareef, 43 Hertford Street, London W1Y 8DB. Tel. (0044171) 499 8951.

THAILAND (1976) H.E. Mr Vidhya Rayananonda, 29/30 Queen's Gate, London SW7 5JB. Tel. (0044171) 259 5005.

TUNISIA, REPUBLIC OF (1978) vacant, 29 Prince's Gate, London SW7 1QG. Tel. (0044171) 584 8117.

UGANDA (1996) H. E. Prof George Barnabas Kirya, 58-59 Trafalgar Square, London WC2N 5DX. Tel. (0044171) 839 5783.

UKRAINE (1996) Prof Volodymyr Vassylenko, 78 Kensington Park Road, London W11 2PL. Tel.

(0044171) 727 6312.

UNITED ARAB EMIRATES (1990) H.E. Easa Saleh Al-Gurg, 30 Princes Gate, London SW7 1PT. Tel. (0044171) 581 1281.

URUGUAY, ORIENTAL REPUBLIC OF (1996) H.E. Mr Augustín Espinosa Lloveras, 2nd Floor, 140 Brompton Road, London SW3 1HY. Tel. (0044171) 584 8192.

VENEZUELA (1981) H.E. Mr Roy Chaderton-Matos, 1 Cromwell Road, London SW7. Tel. (0044171) 5844206.

YUGOSLAVIA, FEDERAL REPUBLIC OF H.E. Dr Milos Radulovic, 5 Lexham Gardens, London W8 5JJ. Tel. (0044171) 370 6105.

ZAMBIA (1983) H.E. Prof Moses Musonda, 2 Palace Gate, Kensington, London W8 5NG. Tel. (0044171) 589 6655.

ZIMBABWE, REPUBLIC OF (1984) vacant, 429 The Strand, London WC2R 0SA. Tel. (0044171) 8367755.

● PARIS

PAKISTAN (1962) Vacant, 18 Rue Lord Byron, 75008 Paris. Tel. (00331) 45622332.

● BRUSSELS

JAMAICA H.E. Mr Douglas Anthony Clive Saunders, Avenue Palmerston 2, 1000 Brussels. Tel. (00322) 230 1170.

Irish Diplomatic and Consular Missions Abroad

ARGENTINA (CHILE, URUGUAY & VENEZUELA) H.E. Art Agnew, Suipacha 1380, 2nd Floor, 1011 Buenos Aires. Tel. (00541) 3258588.

AUSTRALIA (INDONESIA & NEW ZEALAND) H.E. Richard O'Brien, 20 Arkana Street, Yarralumla, A.C.T. 2600. Tel. (00616) 2733022.

AUSTRIA (SLOVAK REPUBLIC & SLOVENIA) H.E. Thelma Doran, Hilton Centre, Landstrasse Haupstrasse 2A,1030 Vienna. Tel. (00431) 7154246.

BELGIUM H.E. Eamon Ryan, 89-93 Rue Froissart, B-1040 Brussels. Tel. (00322) 2305337.

BRITAIN H.E. Ted Barrington, 17 Grosvenor Place, London SWIX 7HR. Tel. (0171) 2352171.

CARDIFF (Consulate General) Consul General Conor O'Riordan, Temple Court, Cathedral Road, Cardiff,

CF1 9HA. Tel. (00441222) 786596.

EDINBURGH (Consulate General) Consul General Dan Mulhall, 16 Randolph Crescent, Edinburgh, EH3 7TT. Tel. (0044131) 2267711.

CANADA (*JAMAICA*) H.E. Paul Dempsey, Suite 1105, 130 Albert Street, Ottawa, Ontario K1P 5G4. Tel. (001613) 2336281.

CHINA, PEOPLES REPUBLIC OF (*PHILIPPINES*) H.E. Joe Hayes, No. 3 Ri Tan Dong Iu, Beijing 100600. Tel. (008610) 65322914.

CZECH REPUBLIC (*UKRAINE*) H.E. Marie Cross, Velvyslanectví Irska, Trziste 13, 11800 Praha 1, Czech Republic. Tel. (004202) 57530061.

DENMARK (*ICELAND & NORWAY*) H.E. James Sharkey, Østbanegade 21, 2100 Copenhagen. Tel. (0045) 31423233.

EGYPT (*JORDAN / WEST BANK / GAZA, LEBANON, SYRIA & SUDAN*) H.E. Peter Gunning, 3 ABU EL FIDA Street (7th Floor), Zamalek, Cairo. Tel. (00202) 3408264. (Postal Address: *P.O. Box 2681, Zamalek, Cairo*).

ETHIOPIA Chargé d'Affaires Pauline Conway, House No. 413, Higher 24, Kebele 13. Tel. (002511) 710835. (Postal Address: *P.O. Box 9585, Addis Ababa*).

PERMANENT REPRESENTATION OF IRELAND TO THE EU H.E. Denis O'Leary, 89/93 Rue Froissart, 1040 Brussels. Tel. (00322) 2308580.

FINLAND (*ESTONIA*) H.E. Gearóid Ó Broin, Erottajankatu 7 A, 00130 Helsinki. Tel. (003589) 646006. (Postal Address: *P.L. 33, 00131 Helsinki*).

FRANCE H.E. Patrick O'Connor, 12 Avenue Foch, 75116 Paris. Tel. (00331) 44176700.

GERMANY H.E. Noel Fahey, Godesberger Allee 119, 53175 Bonn. Tel. (0049228) 959290. (Postal Address: *53131 Bonn*).

GREECE (*ALBANIA, CYPRUS, ROMANIA & FEDER-AL REPUBLIC OF YUGOSLAVIA*) H.E. Pádraic Cradock, 7 Leoforos Vasileos, Konstantinou, GR 106 74 Athens. Tel. (00301) 7232771.

HOLY SEE H.E. Eamon O'Tuathail, Villa Spada, Via Giacomo Medici 1, 00153 - Rome. Tel. (003906) 5810777.

HUNGARY (*BULGARIA*) H.E. Declan Connolly, H-1054 Budapest, Szabadság tér 7. Tel. (00361) 3029600. (Postal Address: *Bank Centre, Granite Tower, Szabadság tér 7, 1944 Budapest*).

INDIA (*BANGLADESH, SINGAPORE & SRI LANKA*) H.E. James Flavin, 230 Jor Bagh, New Delhi 110003. Tel. (009111) 4626733.

IRAN (*PAKISTAN*) H.E. Thomas Lyons, Avenue Mirdamad, Khiaban Razane Shomali No. 10, Tehran 19116. Tel. (009821) 2227672.

ISRAEL H.E. Brendan Scannell, The Tower, 17th Floor, 3 Daniel Frish Street, Tel Aviv 64731. Tel. (009723) 6964166.

ITALY (*LIBYA, MALTA, SAN MARINO & TURKEY*) H.E. Joseph Small, Piazza di Campitelli 3, (Scalla A, int. 2), 00186 Rome. Tel. (003906) 6979121.

JAPAN H.E. Declan O'Donovan, Ireland House 5F, 2-10-7 Kojimachi, Chiyoda-Ku, Tokyo 102. Tel. (00813) 32630695.

KOREA H.E. Brendan Moran, Daehan Fire and Marine Insurance Building, 15th Floor, 51-1 Namchang-Dong, Chung-Ku, 100-060 Seoul. Tel. (00822) 7746455.

LESOTHO (Consulate General) Consul General Tom Wright, Christie House, Plot No. 856, Maseru. Tel. (00266) 314068. (Postal Address: *Private Bag A67, 2nd Floor Christie House, Orpen Road, Lesotho, Southern Africa*).

LUXEMBOURG H.E. Geraldine Skinner, 28 Route D'Arlon, L-1140 Luxembourg. Tel. (00352) 450610.

MALAYSIA (*BRUNEI, VIETNAM & THAILAND*) H.E. Brendan Lyons, No. 4 Jalan Penggawa, Off Jalan U Thant, 55000 Kuala Lumpur, Malaysia. Tel. (00603) 4563763.

MOZAMBIQUE Chargé d'Affaires Justin Carroll, Rua Don Juau 213, Maputo. Tel. (00258) 1491440.

NETHERLANDS H.E. John Swift, Dr Kuyperstraat 9, 2514 BA The Hague. Tel. (003170) 3630993.

NIGERIA (*GHANA*) H.E. Joe Lynch, P.O. Box 2421, 34 Kofo Abayomi Street, Victoria Island, Lagos. Tel. (002341) 2617567. (*Postal Address: Embassy of Ireland, P.O. Box 2421, Lagos*).

DELEGATION OF IRELAND TO THE O.S.C.E. H.E. Brendan McMahon, 1030 Vienna, Austria. Tel. (00431) 7157698;
12 Avenue Foch, 75116 Paris. Tel. (00331) 44176700.

POLAND (*LATVIA & LITHUANIA*) H.E. Patrick McCabe, ul. Humanska 10, 00-789 Warsaw. Tel. (004822) 496633.

PORTUGAL (*BRAZIL & MOROCCO*) H.E. John Campbell, Rua da Imprensa a Estrela 1-4, 1200 Lisbon. Tel. (003511) 3929440.

RUSSIA (*ARMENIA, AZERBAIJAN, BEL- ARUS, GEORGIA, KAZAKHSTAN & UZBERKISTAN*) H.E. Ronan Murphy, Grokholski Pereulok 5, Moscow 129010. Tel. (007095) 7420907.

SAUDI ARABIA (*BAHRAIN, KUWAIT, OMAN, QATAR & UNIED ARAB EMIRATES*) H.E. Michael Collins, Diplomatic Quarter, Riyadh. Tel. (009661) 4882300. (Postal Address: *P.O. Box 94349, Riyadh 11693*).

SOUTH AFRICA (*BOTSWANA, NAMIBIA & ZIMBABWE*) H.E. Hugh Swift, Delheim Suite, Tulbach Park, 1234 Church Street, 0083 Colbyn, Pretoria. Tel. (002712) 3425062. (*Postal Address: P.O. Box 4174, Pretoria 0001*).

SPAIN (*ALGERIA, ANDORRA & TUNISIA*) H.E. Pádraig Murphy, Ireland House, Paseo de la Castellana 46-4, 28046 Madrid. Tel. (003491) 5763500.

SUDAN Irish Aid Office, P.O. Box 299, Wad Medani. Tel. (00249) 512279.

SWEDEN H.E. Martin Bure, Ostermalmsg-atan 97, P.O. Box 10326, 100 55 Stockholm. Tel. (00468) 6618005.

SWITZERLAND (*BOSNIA-HERZEGOVINA, CROATIA, LIECHTENSTEIN, FORMER YUGOSLAV REPUBLIC OF MACEDONIA*) H.E. Bernard Davenport, Kirchenfeld- strasse 68, CH-3005 Berne. Tel. (004131) 3521442.

TANZANIA Chargé d'Affaires Isolda Moylan McNally, 1131 Msasani Road, Oysterbay, Dar-es-Salaam. Tel. (0025551) 667816.

TURKEY H.E. Antoin MacUnfraidh, Sheraton Hotel, Noktali Sokak, Ankara 06700. Tel. (0090312) 4672356.

UGANDA (*BURUNDI & RWANDA*) Chargé d'Affaires Brendan Rogers, P.O. Box 7791, Kampala. Tel. (0025641) 344344.

UNESCO Embassy of Ireland, 12 Avenue Foch, 75116 Paris. Tel. (00331) 44176700.

UNITED NATIONS, NEW YORK H.E. Richard Ryan, 1 Dag Hammarskjold Plaza, 885 Second Avenue, 19th Floor, New York, N.Y. 10017. Tel. (001212) 4216934.

UNITED NATIONS, GENEVA H.E. Anne Anderson, 45-47 Rue de Lausanne, 1202 Geneva 2. Tel. (004122) 7328550.

UNITED STATES OF AMERICA (*MEXICO*) H.E. Sean O'huiginn, 2234 Massachusetts Avenue N.W., Washington D.C. 20008. Tel. (001202) 4623939.

NEW YORK (Consulate General) Consul General Barrie Robinson, Ireland House, 345 Park Avenue, 17th Floor, New York, N.Y. 10154-0037. Tel. (001212) 3192555.

BOSTON (Consulate General) Consul General Orla O'Hanrahan, Chase Building, 535 Boylston Street, Boston Mass. 02116. Tel. (001617) 2679330.

CHICAGO (Consulate General) Consul General Eamonn Hickey, 400 North Michigan Avenue, Suite 911, Chicago, Illinois 60611. Tel. (001312) 3371868.

SAN FRANCISCO (Consulate General) Consul General Kevin Conmy, 44 Montgomery Street, Suite 3830, San Francisco, C.A. 94104. Tel. (001415) 3924214.

ZAMBIA Chargé d'Affaires John Neville, 6663 Katima Mulilo Road, P.O. Box 34923, 10101 Lusaka. Tel. (002601) 290650.

POPULATION

The Irish at the dawn of a New Millennium

To say that Ireland has undergone remarkable change - socially, politically and economically - in the space of the 36,433 days of the 20th century to date would be a colossal understatement of fact. Ireland today is barely recognisable from the struggling island which ushered in the year 1900. Now, some 99 years later as a new century and a new millennium dawns, a glance at the main census figures reveal an island changed utterly.

Republic of Ireland

● **VITAL STATISTICS** The last Census in the Republic of Ireland was conducted on the night of April 28, 1996. It revealed a population of 3,626,087 persons. This constituted an increase of 2.8% or 100,368 persons from the previous Census in 1991 and an increase of 404,264 from the figure at the turn of the century (1901) of 3,221,823.

● **DISTRIBUTION** Some parts of the Republic are growing faster than others. The fastest-growing province was Leinster with an increase of 3.4% (63,753) between 1991 and 1996 with counties Kildare (+10.1%), Dublin (+3.2%) and Wicklow (+5.6%) achieving most growth. Naas in county Kildare, meanwhile, was the fastest growing major urban area with an increase of 26.3% in the five years between censuses. The province of Leinster, bolstered by the urban density of the capital city, Dublin, has the largest population of Ireland's provinces with some 1,924,702 persons or 53.07% of the population now living there. Munster has 1,033,903 (28.5%) persons and Connacht 433,231 (11.95%). The province of Ulster, consisting of the three counties in the Republic (Donegal, Monaghan and Cavan), had a population of 234,251 (6.46%).

County Kildare achieved the biggest growth of all counties since 1991 with 10.1% (+12,336 persons) with Wicklow next with an increase of 5.6% (+5,418 persons). Leitrim had the largest fall in population with a decrease of 1% (-244 persons).

● **AGE** The Republic has a relatively young population. In April 1996, the average age of an Irish person was 33.6 years. Furthermore, 23.9% (859,424) of the population were under 15 years of age, one of the highest percentages in Europe (the EU average is 18.6%). It is estimated that by the year 2001, four out of every ten people will be under the age of 25 - a much higher percentage than in any other European country.

South Dublin has Ireland's youngest population with an average age of 29.4 years, while Leitrim has the oldest population with an average age of 37.3 years.

At the other end of the scale only 413,882 (11.4%) were aged 65 years or more - with the EU average higher at 14.1%.

● **DEPENDENCY** Because of its young population Ireland has a high dependency ratio. This ratio is arrived at by accounting for the number of persons aged 0-14 years and 65+. This number is calculated as a ratio of the rest of the population as it is generally accepted that members of the above age groups are not economically active and therefore dependent on the rest of the population. The ratio for the Republic at the last Census was 0.539, down from 0.616 in 1991.

● **GENDER** Females outnumber males in the Republic by 25,623 (1,825,855 females to 1,800,232 males). 50.35% of the population is female, 49.65% is male. This has been the national trend since the 1986 census when females outnumbered males in the Republic for the first time since the census of 1901.

● **RELIGIOUS COMPOSITION** The Republic of Ireland is predominantly a Catholic country - in 1991 (the last census to request one's religious denomination) 3,228,327 (91.7%) of the population professed to be Catholic while the main Protestant churches (Church of Ireland, Presbyterian and Methodist) numbered 101,076 (2.8%). Minority religions account for 1.3% and 4.2 % either proclaim themselves to be of 'no religion" or refuse to claim any denomination.

● **ETHNIC COMPOSITION** In 1996, 251,624 persons or just 1 in 14 residents were born outside of the Republic. The most common country of birth amongst those born in other countries is England and Wales, accounting for 139,330 persons. Some 39,567 people born in Northern Ireland now reside in the Republic, as do 15,619 American citizens.

● **DENSITY AND URBANISATION** Population density in Ireland is low with just 53 persons per sq km compared with the British average of 142. The Irish figure compares with a UK figure of 244, an United States average of 29 and a Japanese figure of 334 persons per square kilometre.

Well over half (58%) of the State's population now live in towns. Compare this to the figure at the turn of the century (from the 1901 Census) of 28.3% and it is evident that one of the greatest sociological changes to occur in Ireland in the 20th century is urbanisation. The Republic now has 132 urban areas or towns with a population in excess of 1,500 and 23 in excess of 10,000. The major cities of Cork, Limerick, Galway and Waterford have a collective population of 360,609 - 9.9% of the total population of the island. The capital, Dublin, meanwhile continues to push towards the 1,000,000 mark. The 1996 population was recorded at 952,692 persons (26.2% of the entire population). On current estimated growth rates, Dublin's population is expected to exceed 2 million by 2011.

● **BIRTHS** In 1996, 50,390 children were born in the Republic - the annual birth rate per 1,000 persons being 13.9%. The rate has declined annually - in 1980 the number of births was 74,388. In 1996, 12,484 births were recorded outside marriage (24.8%).

● **MARRIAGE** In 1996, 44.9% of the population were recorded as having been married at some stage of their lives - this included persons now separated and persons widowed. The same year, 16,255 marriages were registered, that is 4.5% per 1,000 persons. The number of marriages has declined annually since 1980 when there were 21,792. In 1990 the average age for a first marriage for a female was 26.6 years.

Marriage breakdown has increased in the Republic of Ireland: in 1996 there were 87,800 separated persons compared with 55,100 at the previous census in 1991.

● **MORTALITY** In 1996, 31,723 deaths were recorded in Ireland (8.7 per 1,000 persons).

Males at birth have a life expectancy in the Republic of 71.01 years while females fare better at 76.70 years. This constitutes a huge increase from the early days of the State when 1925-27 figures indicated male life expectancy at 57.4 and females 57.9. Females at birth in the Republic can expect to outlive their male counterparts by an average 5.69 years.

Heart disease continues to be the biggest killer in the Republic, the principal cause of some 13,897 deaths in 1996 - a decrease of 370 from the previous year.

● **EDUCATION** Education has played a major role in Ireland's recent international emergence, both culturally and economically. The state had some 959,651 persons (26.4% of the population) receiving full time education between 4,229 First Level, Second Level and Third Level institutions during 1996/97.

● **ECONOMY/EMPLOYMENT** Ireland's economy has undergone a quite remarkable transformation in recent years - and is now one of the best performing economies in the industrial world. Indeed Ireland has had the fastest growth rate in the OECD (Organisation for Economic Cooperation and Development) since 1995. GDP grew by 9.5% between 1995-96 and 1996-97, and the economy is now expected to expand by about 7% this year.

In employment terms, a simple comparison of the 1993 and 1999 figures indicates the huge progress made. The unemployment rate in 1993 was 15.5% while provisional 1999 figures indicated this had fallen to just 6.8%. Some 203,231 persons were on the Live Register in July 1999. Between April 1997 and Summer 1998 the number of persons in employment is estimated (by the IDA) to have grown by 95,000 persons - the highest annual increase on record. This steep rise in labour opportunities combined with the drastic fall in unemployment has resulted in the substantial fall in the unemployment rate.

The Labour force numbered 1,533,964 persons in 1996 (42.3% of the population) with some 386,656 more males in employment than females.

Vital Statistics

Island of Ireland: Population Statistics "at a glance"

Republic of Ireland

	1996	1998[1]	% Change
Total Population	3,626,087	3,704,900	+2.17%
Aged 0-14	859,424	835,200	-2.8%
Aged 15-24	632.890	652,600	+3.1%
Aged 25-44	1,016,091	1,053,400	+3.67%
Aged 45-64	703,800	743,400	+5.62%
Aged 65+	413,882	420,300	+1.5%
Male	1,800,232	1,839,100	+2.1%
Female	1,825,855	1,865,800	+2.18%
Fastest Growing County	Kildare (1991-96) +10.1	n/a	n/a
Slowest Growing County	Leitrim (1991-96) -1.0	n/a	n/a
Births	50,390[3]	53,551	+6.27%
Within Marriage	37,906	38,418	+1.3%
Outside Marriage	12,484	15,133	+21.2%
Infant Mortality Rate[2]	6	6.2	+3.3%
Deaths	31,723[3]	31,352	-1.16%
Males	16,672	16,482	-1.13%
Females	15,051	14,870	-1.2%
Marital Status			
Marriages	16,255[3]	16,783	+3.24
Ever married (excl. widowed)	1,444,405		
Widowed	184,400		
Single	1,997,282		

1 *Estimates (April 1998).*
2 *Deaths rates of infants under one year of age, per 1,000 births.*
3 *Provisional.* **Source** *CSO*

Northern Ireland

	1991	1996[1]	% Change
Population	1,577,836	1,663,300	+5.41%
Aged 0-14	385,100	n/a	n/a
Aged 15-24	253,700	n/a	n/a
Aged 25-44	433,000	n/a	n/a
Aged 45-64	306,800	n/a	n/a
Aged 65+	199,100	n/a	n/a
Male	769,071	n/a	n/a
Females	808,765	n/a	n/a
Population Growth	(1981-1991) +40,663	(1991-1996) +85,464	n/a
Births	26,265	24,582	-6.4%
Within Marriage	20,959	18,215	-13.09%
Outside Marriage	5,306	6,367	+19.99%
Infant Mortality Rate[2]	7.4	5.8	n/a
Deaths	15,096	15,218	+0.8%
Males	7,533	7,418	-1.5%
Females	7,563	7,800	+3.13%
Marital Status			
Marriages	9,221	8,297	-10%
Total Married	661,000	-	n/a
Widowed	96,700	-	n/a
Single	773,700	-	n/a

1 *Estimates (mid-year population).* 2 *Deaths rates of infants under one year of age, per 1,000 births.* **Source** *CSO*

Population of the Island of Ireland

Year	Total
1821	6,800,000
1831	7,800,000
1841	8,177,744
1851	6,554,074
1861	5,798,564
1871	5,412,377
1881	5,174,836
1891	4,704,750
1901	4,458,775
1911	4,390,219

Year	Total
1926	4,228,553
1951	4,331,514
1961	4,243,383
1971	4,514,313
1981	4,975,601
1991	5,103,555

The collective figures above for the island of Ireland are arrived at by adding the Census data for the RoI and NI on years that the Censuses coincide.

Up to and including the Census of 1911, the island of Ireland population figures are from the UK Census. The 1911 Census was the last to measure the population of the Island of Ireland as a whole (following partition in 1920 the censuses were conducted separately North and South.)

RoI: Main Census Information (1926-1996)

Year	Total Persons	Births Registered	Deaths Registered	Marriages Registered	Natural Increase	Change in Population	Est. net Migration	Intercensal Period
1926	2,971,992	968,742	731,409	230,525	237,333	-167,696	-405,029	1911-26
1936	2,968,420	583,502	420,323	136,699	163,179	-3,572	-166,751	1926-36
1946	2,955,107	602,095	428,297	159,426	173,798	-13,313	-187,111	1936-46
1951	2,960,593	329,270	201,295	80,868	127,975	+5,486	-122,489	1946-51
1956	2,898,264	312,517	178,083	79,541	134,434	-62,329	-196,763	1951-56
1961	2,818,341	302,816	170,736	76,669	132,080	-79,923	-212,003	1956-61
1966	2,884,002	312,709	166,443	80,754	146,266	+65,661	-80,605	1961-66
1971	2,978,248	312,796	164,644	95,662	148,152	+94,246	-53,906	1966-71
1979	3,368,217	548,413	267,378	171,705	281,035	+389,969	+108,934	1971-79
1981	3,443,405	146,224	65,991	42,728	80,233	+75,188	-5,045	1979-81
1986	3,540,643	333,457	164,336	95,648	169,121	+97,238	-71,883	1981-86
1991	3,525,719	277,546	158,300	91,141	119,246	-14,924	-134,170	1986-91
1996	3,626,087	249,455	157,389	82,804	92,066	+100,368	+8,302	1991-96

1 *The 1926 Census was the first to record the 26 counties that made up the Irish Free State (Republic of Ireland) following the partition of the island of Ireland in 1920.* **Source** *CSO*

NI: Main Census Information (1926-1991)

Year	Total Persons	Births Registered	Deaths Registered	Natural Increase	Change in Population	Est. net Migration	Intercensal Period
				(In period mentioned in last column)			
1926[1]	1,256,561	431,148	317,545	113,603	+6,030	107,573	1911-26
1937	1,279,745	280,641	199,806	80,835	+23,184	57,651	1926-37
1951	1,370,921	402,187	243,744	158,443	+91,176	67,267	1937-51
1961	1,425,042	298,808	152,459	146,349	+54,121	92,228	1951-61
1966	1,484,775	182,489	85,055	97,434	+59,733	37,701	1961-66
1971	1,536,065	148,706	72,578	76,128	+51,290	24,838	1966-71
1981*	1,532,196	274,786	167,232	107,554	-3,869	111,423	1971-81
1991	1,577,836	273,227	158,167	115,060	+45,640	69,420	1981-91

1 *The 1926 Census was the first to record the Northern Ireland state following the partition of the island of Ireland in 1920.*

* *1981 Census figures are partially estimated because of a non-response from a section of the population. Due to a protest over the Hunger Strikes, many households were not included in the 1981 Census; the population effect was estimated at 44,500. This effect must be taken into account with regard to all Northern Ireland population tables.*

Population Distribution

RoI: Population/Area by Province and Persons (1996)

Province	Total population	Total area (hectares)	Persons per square kilometre
Leinster	1,924,702	1,980,066	97
Munster	1,033,903	2,467,410	42
Connacht	433,231	1,771,056	24
Ulster *(part of)*	234,251	808,776	29
TOTAL: Republic of Ireland	3,626,087	7,027,308	52

RoI Population: Rural and Town (1996)

Province	Total population	Aggregate Town area	Aggregate Rural area
Leinster	1,924,702	1,415,149 (73.52%)	509,553 (26.47%)
Munster	1,033,903	514,228 (49.73%)	519,675 (50.26%)
Connacht	433,231	126,908 (29.29%)	306,323 (70.70%)
Ulster (part of)	234,251	51,706 (22.07%)	182,545 (77.92%)
Total: Republic of Ireland	3,626,087	2,107,991 (58.13%)	1,518,096 (41.86%)

Population Density: International Comparisons

Country	Persons per km²	Country	Persons per km²	Country	Persons per km²
Netherlands	380	Luxembourg	163	IRELAND	53
Belgium	334	Denmark	123	United States	29
Japan	334	France	108	Sweden	22
United Kingdom	244	Portugal	108	Finland	15
Germany	230	Austria	96	Norway	14
Italy	191	Greece	80	Canada	3
Switzerland	172	Spain	78	Iceland	3

RoI: Population by Province (1841-1996)

Census Year	Leinster	Munster	Connacht	Ulster (part of)*	Total (State)	Actual change	% change
1841	1,973,731	2,396,161	1,418,859	740,048	6,528,799		
1851	1,672,738	1,857,736	1,010,031	571,052	5,111,557	-1,417,242	-21.70
1861	1,457,635	1,513,558	913,135	517,783	4,402,111	-709,446	-13.87
1871	1,339,451	1,393,485	846,213	474,038	4,053,187	-348,924	-7.92
1881	1,278,989	1,331,115	821,657	438,259	3,870,020	-183,167	-4.51
1891	1,187,760	1,172,402	724,774	383,758	3,468,694	-401,326	-10.3
1901	1,152,829	1,076,188	646,932	345,874	3,221,823	-246,871	-7.11
1911	1,162,044	1,035,495	610,984	331,165	3,139,688	-82,135	-2.54
1926	1,149,092	969,902	552,907	300,091	2,971,992	-167,696	-5.34
1936	1,220,411	942,272	525,468	280,269	2,968,420	-3,572	-0.12
1946	1,281,117	917 306	492,797	263,887	2,955,107	-13,313	-0.45
1951	1,336,576	898,870	471,895	253,252	2,960,593	+5,486	+0.18
1956	1,338,942	877,238	446,221	235,863	2,898,264	-62,329	-2.10
1961	1,332,149	849,203	419,465	217,524	2,818,341	-79,923	-2.75
1966	1,414,415	859,334	401,950	208,303	2,884,002	+65,661	+2.32
1971	1,498,140	882,002	390,902	207,204	2,978,248	+94,246	+3.26
1979	1,743,861	979,819	418,500	226,037	3,368,217	+389,969	+13.09
1981	1,790,521	998,315	424,410	230,159	3,443,405	+75,188	+2.23
1986	1,852,649	1,020,577	431,409	236,008	3,540,643	+97,238	+2.82
1991	1,860,949	1,009,533	423,031	232,206	3,525,719	-14,924	-0.42
1996	1,924,702	1,033,903	433,231	234,251	3,626,087	+100,368	+2.84

* Ulster (part of) consists of Donegal, Monaghan and Cavan. **Source** *for all RoI figures above: CSO*

RoI: Population by County, Actual/Percentage Change (1901/1996)

County	1901	1996	Actual change	% change
Republic of Ireland	3,221,823	3,626,087	+404,264	+12.54
LEINSTER	1,152,829	1,924,702	+771,873	+66.95
Carlow	37,748	41,616	+3,868	+10.24
Dublin	448,206	1,058,264	+610,058	+136.11
Kildare	63,566	134,992	+71,426	+112.36
Kilkenny	79,159	75,336	-3,823	-4.82
Laois	57,417	52,945	-4,472	-7.78
Longford	46,672	30,166	-16,506	-35.36
Louth	65,820	92,166	+26,346	+40.02
Meath	67,497	109,732	+42,235	+62.57
Offaly	60,187	59,117	-1,070	-1.77
Westmeath	61,629	63,314	+1,685	+2.73
Wexford	104,104	104,371	+267	+0.25
Wicklow	60,824	102,683	+41,859	+68.81
MUNSTER	1,076,188	1,033,903	-42,285	-3.92
Clare	112,334	94,006	-18,328	-16.31
Cork	404,611	420,510	+15,899	+3.92
Kerry	165,726	126,130	-39,596	-23.89
Limerick	146,098	165,042	+18,944	+12.96
Tipperary	160,232	133,535	-26,697	-16.66
Waterford	87,187	94,680	+7,493	+8.59
CONNACHT	646,932	433,231	-213,701	-33.03
Galway	192,549	188,854	-3,695	-1.91
Leitrim	69,343	25,057	-44,286	-63.86
Mayo	199,166	111,524	-87,642	-44.00
Roscommon	101,791	51,975	-49,816	-48.93
Sligo	84,083	55,821	-28,262	-33.61
ULSTER (part of)	345,874	234,251	-111,623	-32.27
Cavan	97,541	52,944	-44,597	-45.72
Donegal	173,722	129,994	-43,728	-25.17
Monaghan	74,611	51,313	-23,298	-31.22

Source CSO

NI: Population by Council Area, Actual/Percentage Change (1981/1991)

District Council	1981	1991	Actual change	Percentage change
NORTHERN IRELAND	1,532,619	1,573,282	+40,663	2.65%
Antrim	45,029	44,322	-707	-1.57%
Ards	57,808	64,026	+6,218	+10.75%
Armagh	49,237	51,331	+2,094	+4.25%
Ballymena	54,829	56,032	+1,203	+2.19%
Ballymoney	22,952	23,984	+1,032	+4.49%
Banbridge	30,118	33,102	+2,984	+9.90%
Belfast	314,360	283,746	-30,614	-9.73%
Carrickfergus	28,633	32,439	+3,806	+13.29%
Castlereagh	60,802	60,649	-153	-0.25%
Coleraine	46,752	51,062	+4,310	+9.21%
Cookstown	28,265	30,808	+2,543	+8.99%
Craigavon	73,281	74,494	+1,213	+1.65%
Derry	89,126	94,918	+5,792	+6.49%
Down	53,208	57,511	+4,303	+8.08%
Dungannon	43,895	45,322	+1,427	+3.25%
Fermanagh	51,609	54,062	+2,453	+4.75%
Larne	29,084	29,181	+97	+0.33%

Continued from previous page

District Council	1981	1991	Actual change	Percentage change
Limavady	26,972	29,201	+2,229	+8.26%
Lisburn	84,022	99,162	+15,140	+18.01%
Magherafelt	32,503	35,874	+3,371	+10.37%
Moyle	14,400	14,617	+217	+1.50%
Newry and Mourne	76,596	82,288	+5,692	+7.43%
Newtownabbey	72,266	73,832	+1,566	+2.16%
North Down	66,283	70,308	+4,025	+6.07%
Omagh	44,300	45,343	+1,043	+2.35%
Strabane	36,289	35,668	-621	-1.71%

Population of Main Irish Towns

● Republic of Ireland

Town	1991	1996	% change
1. Dublin (Dublin)	929,090	952,692	+2.5
2. Cork (Cork)	174,400	179,954	+3.2
3. Limerick (Limerick)	75,436	79,137	+4.9
4. Galway (Galway)	50,853	57,363	+12.8
5. Waterford (Waterford)	41,853	44,155	+5.5
6. Dundalk (Louth)	30,061	30,195	+0.4
7. Bray (Wicklow)	26,953	27,923	+3.59
8. Drogheda (Louth)	24,656	25,282	+2.5
9. Swords (Dublin)	17,705	22,314	+26.0
10. Tralee (Kerry)	17,862	19,950	+11.6
11. Kilkenny (Kilkenny)	17,669	18,696	+5.8
12. Sligo (Sligo)	17,964	18,509	+3.0
13. Ennis (Clare)	16,058	17,726	+10.3
14. Clonmel (Tipperary)	15,562	16,182	+3.98
15. Wexford (Wexford)	15,393	15,862	+3.0
16. Athlone (Westmeath)	15,358	15,544	+1.2
17. Carlow (Carlow)	14,027	14,979	+6.8
18. Naas (Kildare)	11,141	14,074	+26.3
19. Malahide (Dublin)	12,088	13,539	+12.0
20. Leixlip (Kildare)	13,194	13,451	+1.9

● Northern Ireland

Town	1981	1991	% change
1. Belfast (Antrim)	314,270	279,237	-11.14
2. Derry (Derry)	62,697	72,334	+15.37
3. Newtownabbey (Antrim)	56,149	57,103	+1.69
4. Bangor (Down)	46,585	52,437	+12.5
5. Lisburn (Antrim)	40,391	42,110	+4.2
6. Ballymena (Antrim)	28,166	28,717	+1.95
7. Newtownards (Down)	20,531	24,301	+18.3
8. Newry (Down)	19,026	22,975	+20.7
9. Carrickfergus (Antrim)	17,633	22,885	+29.7
10. Lurgan (Armagh)	20,991	21,905	+4.35
11. Portadown (Armagh)	21,333	21,299	-0.15
12. Antrim (Antrim)	22,342	20,878	-6.5
13. Coleraine (Derry)	15,967	20,721	+29.7
14. Larne (Antrim)	18,224	17,575	-3.56
15. Omagh (Tyrone)	14,627	17,280	+18.1
16. Armagh (Armagh)	12,700	14,640	+15.2
17. Banbridge (Down)	9,650	12,529	+29.8
18. Strabane (Tyrone)	10,340	11,981	+15.8
19. Enniskillen (Fermanagh)	10,429	11,436	+9.6
20. Limavady (Derry)	8,015	10,764	+34.2

Population Structure

RoI & NI: Population by Gender

	● Republic of Ireland			● Northern Ireland		
Year	Total	Males	Females	Total	Males	Females
1901	3,221,823	1,610,085	1,611,738	1,236,952	589,955	646,997
1911	3,139,688	1,589,509	1,550,179	1,250,531	602,539	647,992
1926	2,971,992	1,506,889	1,465,103	1,256,561	608,088	648,473
1936	2,968,420	1,520,454	1,447,966	n/a	n/a	n/a
1937	n/a	n/a	n/a	1,279,745	623,154	656,591
1946	2,955,107	1,494,877	1,460,230	n/a	n/a	n/a
1951	2,960,593	1,506,597	1,453,996	1,370,921	667,819	703,102
1961	2,818,341	1,416,549	1,401,792	1,425,042	694,224	730,818
1966	2,884,002	1,449,032	1,434,970	1,484,775	723,884	760,891
1971	2,978,248	1,495,760	1,482,488	1,536,065	754,676	781,389
1981[1]	3,443,405	1,729,354	1,714,051	1,532,196	749,480	782,716
1986	3,540,643	1,769,690	1,770,953	n/a	n/a	n/a
1991	3,525,719	1,753,418	1,772,301	1,577,836	769,071	808,765
1996	3,626,087	1,800,232	1,825,855	n/a	n/a	n/a

Source *for all RoI figures above* = CSO

RoI & NI: Population by Age

Age Group	Republic of Ireland (000s)				Northern Ireland (000s)		
	1971	1981	1991	1996	1971	1981	1991
0-4 yrs	315,655	353,004	273,743	250,394	156.2	130.8	128.3
5-9 yrs	316,940	349,487	318,503	282,943	157.1	134.2	129.2
10-14 yrs	298,557	341,238	348,328	326,087	143.6	148.9	127.9
15-19 yrs	267,727	326,429	335,026	339,536	126.3	144.5	127.6
20-24 yrs	215,251	276,127	266,572	293,354	114.9	122.3	126.1
25-29 yrs	172,993	246,053	246,321	259,045	101.9	100.0	122.2
30-34 yrs	151,351	231,958	249,071	260,929	86.7	98.7	113.5
35-39 yrs	149,107	193,829	237,889	255,676	82.4	92.5	99.3
40-44 yrs	152,729	165,924	225,683	240,441	84.3	81.2	97.9
45-49 yrs	160,124	151,850	187,762	225,400	86.1	76.1	89.9
50-54 yrs	159,082	149,680	156,806	186,647	80.1	76.0	76.6
55-59 yrs	154,847	149,606	142,549	153,807	78.5	75.1	71.1
60-64 yrs	134,066	139,266	134,566	137,946	72.0	68.0	69.3
65-69 yrs	111,751	133,919	130,752	126,809	60.2	63.4	65.0
70+ yrs	218,068	235,035	272,148	287,073	105.8	120.5	134.1
TOTAL:	2,978,248	3,443,405	3,525,719	3,626,087	1,536.1	1,532.2	1,578.0

Sociological Data

RoI & NI: Overview of Births (1998)

Category	Leinster	Munster	Connacht	Ulster*	Total RoI	Northern Ireland**
Births: Total[1]	29,954	14,741	5,740	3,116	53,551	24,582
Female	14,510	7,181	2,748	1,532	25,971	
Male	15,444	7,560	2,992	1,584	27,580	

*Part of ** 1996 figures 1 Births classified to county of residence of mother. **Source** for all RoI figures above = CSO

RoI: Births Registered

	Number of Births				Rate per 1,000 pop.	
Year	Jan-Mar	Apr-June	July-Sept	Oct-Dec		Total
1985	15,913	16,012	15,683	14,642	17.6	62,250
1990	13,321	13,989	13,285	12,359	15.1	52,954
1995	12,516	12,579	12,488	10,947	13.5	48,530
1997	12,980	13,679	14,211	11,441	14.3	52,311
1998	13,405	13,729	14,027	12,390	14.5	53,551

	Number of Births Outside Marriage				Rate per 1,000 pop.	
Year	Jan-Mar	Apr-June	July-Sept	Oct-Dec		Total
1985	1,316	1,341	1,295	1,316	8.5	5,268
1990	1,863	1,883	2,027	1,887	14.5	7,660
1995	2,851	2,644	2,804	2,489	22.2	10,788
1997	3,656	3,445	3,723	3,068	26.6	13,892
1998	3,872	3,671	3,896	-	-	-

NI: Overview of Births

Description	1991	1992	1993	1994	1995	1996
Births: live	26,265	25,572	24,909	24,289	23,860	24,582
Rate per 1,000 of population	16.5	15.9	15.3	14.8	14.5	14.8

RoI: Marriages Registered

Year	Jan-Mar	Apr-June	July-Sept	Oct-Dec	Rate per 1,000 pop.	Total
1985	2,470	4,368	7,998	3,955	5.3%	18,791

Continued from previous page

Year	Jan-Mar	Apr-June	July-Sept	Oct-Dec	Rate per 1,000 pop.	Total
1990	2,172	4,278	7,758	3,630	5.1%	17,838
1995	1,751	3,711	6,451	3,691	4.3%	15,604
1998	1,642	3,689	7,530	3,922	4.5%	16,783

NI: Marriages Registered

Description	1991	1992	1993	1994	1995	1996
Marriages	9,221	9,392	9,045	8,683	8,576	8,297
Rate per 1,000 of population	5.8	5.8	5.5	5.3	5.2	5.0

Population by Religious Denomination (1991)

	Total pop.	Catholic	Church of Ire.	Presbyterian	Methodist	Other
RoI	3,525,719	3,228,327 (91.56%)	82,840 (2.34%)	13,199 (0.37%)	5,037 (0.14%)	196,316
NI	1,577,836	605,639 (38.38%)	279,280 (17.7%)	336,891 (21.35%)	59,517 (3.77%)	296,509

→ *For detailed breakdown see Religion Chapter.* **Source** *for all RoI figures above: CSO*

RoI: Divorce Statistics

	● Year Ending July 31, 1998			● August 1, 1998 to March 31, 1999			
	Applications			Applications			
Circuit Court Office	Received	Granted	Refused	Received	Granted	Refused	Withdrawn Struck out
Carlow	34	9	0	42	24	0	0
Carrick-on-Shannon	9	6	3	7	3	0	0
Castlebar	62	27	0	39	31	0	0
Cavan	26	12	2	10	13	0	0
Clonmel	64	31	1	31	21	0	0
Cork	268	131	0	175	122	0	0
Dublin	1,277	715	0	1,150	626	0	58
Dundalk	76	35	0	56	32	1	0
Ennis	48	25	0	46	22	0	0
Galway	59	61	0	66	41	0	0
Kilkenny	45	18	0	34	22	0	0
Letterkenny	57	19	0	16	7	0	0
Limerick	105	34	0	77	62	0	2
Longford	17	16	0	16	9	0	0
Monaghan	26	11	0	9	10	0	0
Mullingar	42	20	0	39	24	0	0
Naas	67	28	1	49	29	0	8
Portlaoise	16	8	0	14	6	0	2
Roscommon	11	10	0	13	10	0	0
Sligo	18	15	0	18	17	0	1
Tralee	89	31	0	35	37	0	1
Trim	54	26	0	56	35	0	0
Tullamore	20	14	0	22	9	0	0
Waterford	72[1]	21[1]	0[1]	65[2]	32[2]	0[2]	0[2]
Wexford	88	53	0	42	28	0	0
Wicklow	75	32	0	57	22	0	0
Total Circuit:	2,725	1,408	7	2,184	1,294	1	72
High Court	36	13	0				
Supreme Court	0	0	0				
TOTAL:	2,761	1,421	7				

1 *From January 1, 1998 to December 31, 1998.*
2 *Waterford figures are to end of April 1999.*

NI: Divorce Statistics

Grounds	High Court 1996	High Court 1997	High Court 1998	County Court 1996	County Court 1997	County Court 1998	Total 1996	Total 1997	Total 1998
Adultery	113	118	159	63	67	72	176	185	231
Behaviour	301	311	375	175	218	201	476	529	576
Desertion	7	7	11	6	8	6	13	15	17
Separation (2 years & consent)	484	502	569	586	632	669	1,070	1,134	1,238
Separation (5 years)	326	283	363	332	348	418	658	631	781
Other Grounds	18	27	40	8	11	21	26	38	61
TOTAL:	1,249	1,248	1,517	1,170	1,284	1,387	2,419	2,532	2,904

Occupational Statistics

RoI: Occupations by Industrial Group

Industrial Group[1]	Persons	Male	Female
Agriculture, forestry, fishing	133,969	121,000	12,969
Building & construction	87,452	82,287	5,165
Commerce	191,932	111,519	80,413
Insurance, finance & business services	80,065	39,774	40,291
Electricity, gas & water supply	11,709	9,791	1,918
Manufacturing Industries	249,131	171,728	77,403
Mining, quarrying & turf production	5,774	5,352	422
Personal services	98,810	35,852	62,958
Professional services	241,476	83,296	158,180
Public administration and defence	78,210	51,246	26,964
Transport, communication & storage	78,224	60,501	17,723
Recreational services	23,435	14,019	9,416
Other industries	27,049	16,282	10,767
TOTAL:	1,307,236	802,647	504,589

1 *Census of Population 1996. Source CSO*

NI: Occupations by Industrial Group

Industrial Group[1]	Persons	Male	Female
Agriculture, forestry, fishing	23,962	22,274	1,688
Construction	41,079	38,489	2,590
Banking, Insurance, finance, business services & leasing	40,075	21,200	18,875
Other services	210,204	83,708	126,496
Energy and water supply industries	7,180	6,120	1,060
Extraction of minerals & ores (not fuels); manufacture of metals, mineral products and chemicals	9,147	7,566	1,581
Metal goods, engineering and vehicle industries	32,929	26,451	6,478
Other manufacturing industries	60,174	33,992	26,182
Transport and communication	24,484	19,604	4,880
Distribution, hotels & catering; repairs	103,228	55,273	47,955
On Government employment/training	13,245	8,649	4,596
Other industries	6,971	4,462	2,509
Place of work outside NI and Britain	2,272	1,612	660
TOTAL:	574,950	329,400	245,550

1 *Census of Population 1991.*

Migration

Estimated Migration classified by gender and Country of Destination/Origin

Year ending April	Emigrants					Immigrants					Net migration
	UK	Rest of EU	USA	Rest of world	Total	UK	Rest of EU	USA	Rest of world	Total	
	000										
Persons											
1993	16.4	7.3	5.6	5.8	35.1	17.5	6.6	5.0	5.7	34.7	-0.4
1994	14.8	5.5	9.6	4.9	34.8	15.2	5.8	4.3	4.8	30.1	-4.7
1995	13.3	5.1	8.2	6.6	33.1	15.6	6.3	3.8	5.5	31.2	-1.9
1996	14.1	5.1	5.2	6.8	31.2	17.6	7.2	6.4	8.0	39.2	-8.0
1997[1]	12 9	4.1	4.1	7.9	29.0	20.0	8.1	6.6	9.3	44.0	15.0
1998[1]	8 5	4.3	4.3	4.1	21.2	21.1	8.7	4.9	9.3	44.0	22.8
Males											
1993	8.2	3.4	3.1	3.0	17.6	9.0	2.9	2.5	3.1	17.4	-0.2
1994	7 7	2.6	5.0	2.2	17.6	7.8	2.7	2.1	2.2	14.8	-2.7
1995	7 8	2.5	4.6	3.2	18.2	7.3	2.6	1.8	3.1	14.7	-3.4
1996	6.7	2.2	2.7	3.6	15.3	8.4	3.2	2.8	4.3	18.8	3.5
1997[1]	6.4	1.9	2.5	3.8	14.7	10.2	3.9	2.7	4.8	21.6	6.9
1998[1]	4.5	1.8	2.7	1.9	10.8	11.0	3.4	2.6	4.8	21.8	11.0
Females											
1993	8.2	3.9	2.5	2.9	17.5	8.4	3.8	2.5	2.6	17.3	-0.2
1994	7.1	2.9	4.6	2.7	17.3	7.4	3.1	2.2	2.6	15.3	-2.0
1995	5.4	2.6	3.6	3.4	14.9	8.2	3.7	2.1	2.5	16.5	1.6
1996	7.4	2.8	2.5	3.2	15.9	9.2	3.9	3.6	3.7	20.4	4.4
1997[1]	6.4	2.2	1.6	4.1	14.3	9.8	4.2	3.9	4.5	22.4	8.0
1998[1]	4.0	2.6	1.6	2.2	10.4	10.1	5.3	2.3	4.5	22.2	11.8

1 *Preliminary*
Source CSO

Estimated Immigration by Nationality

(000s) Nationality	1993	1994	1995	1996	1997	1998
Irish	20.0	16.8	17.6	17.7	20.5	23.2
UK	6.2	6.3	5.8	8.3	8.2	8.3
Rest of EU	3.3	3.3	3.2	5.0	5.5	5.8
USA	2.5	2.0	1.5	4.0	4.2	2.2
Rest of world	2.6	1.7	3.1	4.2	5.5	4.5
Total	34.7	30.1	31.2	39.2	44.0	44.0

Source CSO

IRELAND: COUNTIES & TOWNS

County Antrim

"From the Irish Aontroim - solitary farm"

● **GEOGRAPHY**
Province: Ulster
Location: maritime county set in the north-east corner of Ireland
County Size: 9th in Ireland
Land area: 1,093 sq. miles
Highest point: Trostan Mountain (551 m)
Main Geographical Features: The county could be described as a basaltic tableland. Its most remarkable feature is the Giant's Causeway, found in the north-western corner of the county and designated a World Heritage Site. About 35 million years ago, fissures split north-east Ireland and south-west Scotland and were accompanied by much volcanic activity. Great amounts of molten material welled up, with the resulting cooling lava solidifying into the basaltic columns of the Giant's Causeway. The causeway is made up of approximately 40,000, mostly hexagonal, basaltic columns that are packed tightly together. Further east along the coast can be found the Glens of Antrim; nine river valleys which are bisected by rivers and waterfalls and full of wild flowers and birds. The occasional tectonic foundering, characteristic of 250 million years ago, resulted in many small basins opening up around the north-east region e.g. Belfast Lough, Lough Neagh, and the Rathlin Trough. Rock salt and gypsum deposits are sometimes found in these areas.
Main Rivers: Bann; Bush; Main; Glenshesk; Six Mile Water.
Main Lakes: L Neagh; L Beg.
Main Bays: Red; Church; Belfast Lough; Larne Lough.
Main Islands: Rathlin.
Areas of Geographical interest: Giant's Causeway, Carnfunnock Country Park (parklands which slope down to the sea, contains a maze, a time garden with sundials and an old walled garden), Glenariff Forest Park (glen walk with three waterfalls), Portrush Countryside Centre, Benvarden Garden (a walled garden dating back to the 1780s, with a Victorian woodland pond).

● **HISTORY**
Prehistory: The Antrim coast is where Ireland's first inhabitants - nomadic boatmen from Scotland - landed circa 7000 BC.
Medieval: Normans conquered the county and began building castles; John de Courcy built a huge castle in 1180 at Carrickfergus, and Richard de Burgh, the Earl of Ulster, first built Dunluce Castle, a fortification that clings on to the sea cliffs on the north. Edward Bruce, King of Scotland, landed in Larne in 1315 and besieged Carrickfergus Castle for more than a year. This established a pattern for the castle and town of Carrickfergus for the following centuries (primarily due to the site's strategic importance at the entrance of Belfast Lough). The MacDonnells had possession of Dunluce Castle and its surrounding lands in the late 15th century, while the rest of the Antrim region was ruled over by the MacQuillans, the O'Neills and the Hebridean Scots of the Glens (the Glens were one of the last places in Northern Ireland where Scots Gaelic was spoken).
English: the establishment of Hebridean Scots in the Glens indicates that Antrim was unofficially planted long before the formal plantation of other counties in Ulster in 1610. The whiskey distillery at Bushmills, which is still in operation, was established in 1608, making it the world's oldest legal distillery. Antrim was one of the few counties in Ireland to be directly affected by the Industrial Revolution. It, along with Armagh and Monaghan, was a county of domestic linen production and consequently, was heavily populated (particularly in southern Antrim). This led to tension over occupation of land, dislocation and ultimately, the growth of Belfast as a major industrial centre with a large Protestant working class.
Areas of Historical Interest: Old Bushmills Distillery, the Dunluce Centre (which narrates the legends of the North Antrim coast), Carrickfergus Castle, Antrim Castle Gardens (restored 17th-century garden, laid out in a similar style to the gardens at Versailles but on a smaller scale, which was favoured for Anglo-Dutch gardens), Irish Linen Centre (recreates Ulster's Linen industry heritage with weaving workshop and looms), Leslie Hill in Ballymoney (Georgian mansion with large 18th-century walled garden).

● **THE COUNTY**
Total Population: 562,216 *(e)*
County Capital & Largest City: Belfast *see profile*
Main Towns: Antrim, Ballymena, Ballycastle, Belfast, Carrickfergus, Larne, Lisburn, Newtownabbey.
Main Business Contact: Ledu The Small Business Agency: Ledu House, Upper Galwally, Belfast. Tel 01232-491 031
No of Golf Clubs: 23 (14 x 18; 6 x 9; 1 x 45), 12 in Belfast (7 x 18; 4 x 9; 1 x 27).
Blue Flag Beaches: 1 - Ballycastle
Other Attractions: Fantasy Island in Portrush, Waterworld in Portrush, Carrick-a-rede Rope Bridge (the famous landmark bridge linking the mainland to a rocky outcrop).

Belfast City

"From the Irish Beal Feiriste - the mouth of the Farset, a river flowing through Belfast"

● **HISTORY**

Origins: The area was first settled circa 1177 around an ancient fort. Its growth as a city stems from the 17th century with the arrival of English settlers and Huguenot refugees who developed linen weaving in the area. **Growth:** One of the few areas in Ireland to be directly affected by the Industrial Revolution, consequently, it grew as a major industrial centre with a large Protestant working class. In the 1790s, it was plunged into the throes of rebellion when the Society of United Irishmen was founded by a native son - Henry Joy McCracken. However, by the end of the 19th century, the city was strongly unionist due to its growing Protestant proletariat and the city became the centre of opposition to Home Rule in Ireland. In 1888, the borough was established as a city by charter. After the partition of Ireland, Belfast was established as the capital of the self-governing British province of Northern Ireland, a form of governance that continued until the imposition of direct rule from London in 1972. It was bombed during World War II and over 1,000 of its citizens lost their lives. The Troubles from the 1960s onwards also served to badly scar the city, both structurally and economically.

● **TODAY**

Location south-east corner of Antrim, on the River Lagan and surrounded by high hills, a small portion of the city edges into Co. Down

Population: 279,237 (-11.14% from 1981 Census).

Tourist Attractions Botanic Gardens (1828; noted for its rose gardens, herbaceous borders and a Tropical Palm House dating back to 1839 - a cast iron conservatory similar those at Kew and Dublin Botanic Gardens), Cave Hill Country Park (as well as being the site of Neolithic caves and geological features, the United Irishmen planned 1798 Rebellion here), Belvoir Forest Park, Sir Thomas & Lady Dixon Park (its 130 acres contain over 25,000 rose bushes; the international rose trials are held here), Belfast Zoo (contains a wide variety of species and includes an underwater viewing area), Streamvale Open Dairy Farm, Colin Glen Forest Park (a 200-acre park at the foot of the Black Mountain), Lagan Lookout Centre (explains the River Lagan's weir, as well as the river's industrial and folk heritage), Grovelands (contains a variety of small ornamental gardens), Ulster Museum (its antiquities collection includes gold from the Spanish Armada, an art gallery and natural science collection), Ormeau Baths Gallery, Grand Opera House (1894; highly decorated Late Victorian building), The Waterfront Hall, Malone House & Barnett Demesne (an restored regency house in parkland, with extensive daffodil gardens and a sundial lawn), Linenhall Library (1788; for promoting knowledge, it contains rare books and a vast store of political documents), the political murals around Belfast, Belfast City Hall (completed in 1906 from Portland Stone, its statues include a memorial to those who lost their lives on board the Titanic), St Anne's Cathedral (neo-Romanesque Protestant cathedral, dating back to 1904), Crown Liquor Saloon (the only pub owned by the National Trust, this Victorian drinking palace boasts a beautiful marble, glass and wood interior), Stormont (at various stages it held the parliament of Northern Ireland, and is the site of government offices)

● **TRANSPORT**

Main Routes: Belfast is served by major routes A1-N1 (to Dublin); M2-A6 (to Derry).
Miles from Derry (73); Dublin (104); Galway (190); Cork (264).
Nearest Travel Centre (Bus): Ulsterbus, Europa Bus Centre & Laganside Bus Centre 01232-320 011.
Nearest Rail Station: Central Station, Belfast 01232-899 400.
Nearest Airport: Belfast City Airport 01232-734 828; Belfast International Airport 01849-484 848.
Nearest Ferry Port: Belfast; Larne (+21 miles).

County Armagh

"From the Irish Ard Macha - Macha's Height - it refers to Queen Macha who reputedly built a fortress on top of a hill around the mid-first millennium BC"

● **GEOGRAPHY**
Province: Ulster
Location: inland county in the north-east of Ireland
County Size: 29th in Ireland
Land area: 484 sq. miles
Highest point: Slieve Gullion (575 m)
Main Geographical Features: Armagh's rolling hilly terrain is due to its being part of Ireland's drumlin belt. South Armagh is home to the Ring of Gullion, with its varied mountain topography of volcanic-shaped hills. The gentle landscape of the north-east of the county is ideal for fruit growing, which has led Armagh to be called the Orchard County. Records reveal that apples have been grown in Armagh for more than 3,000 years (the Bramley apple has proven to be the easiest species to grow in the northern climate, and an orchard trust has been established by local growers to keep alive traditional orchards and old apple varieties that are currently under threat from the cheaper, more standard varieties).
Main Rivers: Blackwater; Bann.
Main Lakes: L Neagh; Loughgall.

Http://www.localalmanac.ie/counties/

Areas of Geographical interest: Oxford Island National Nature Reserve (situated on L Neagh), Gosford Forest Park (surrounding a huge castle, it contains an arboretum, a walled garden and has associations with Dean Swift, being mentioned in one of his poems), Peatlands Country Park (peatlands with small loughs and outdoor exhibits on peat ecology and a narrow gauge railway through the bogs), Lough Neagh Discovery Centre (wildlife, management and history of Lough Neagh), Slieve Guillion Mountain and Forest Park.

● HISTORY
Prehistory: Navan Fort, *Emain Macha,* two miles west of the city of Armagh, was home to the kings of Ulster. Although traces of man at the site date back to 5500 BC, it is thought that Navan Fort was at its height from 700 BC. A major building complex begun to develop by the Late Bronze Age, including roundhouses and compounds at Navan Fort, a ritual pool at the King's Stables and a hill-fort known as Haughey's Fort. The discovery of a barbary ape skull at Navan Fort plus other important objects suggests that it had become a place of great importance around this time. The Late Bronze Age King's Stables are lose to the fort and contain the only prehistoric artificial pool known in the British Isles. Beside Navan Fort is Loughnashade. At the end of the 18th century, four great bronze horns were found decorated in the Celtic style. The Celts often sacrificed precious goods in water as offerings, indicating that Loughnashade was a sacred lake. The theatre director Tyrone Guthrie envisaged Navan as the one site in Ireland where all peoples in Ireland could be brought together for a great cultural celebration.
Early Christian: Lore has it that Armagh became the centre of Irish Christianity during the fifth century with the arrival of St. Patrick, but in reality, a collection of hagiographic writings on St. Patrick, compiled between AD 670 and 690, attempted to bring the primacy of the Irish church to Armagh. This attempt proved successful, and Armagh's primacy within the Irish Church was officially confirmed in 1005 by Brian Boru, the high king of Ireland at that time. Armagh retains its position as ecclesiastical capital of Ireland.
Medieval During medieval times, Armagh was ruled over by the O'Neills.

English: Armagh was planted in 1610 along with other counties in Ulster. In 1646, Owen Roe O'Neill rose up against the settlers at the Battle of Benburb. In the centuries that followed, bloody conflicts continued between the native Irish and the Protestant settlers. The Orange Order was founded in Armagh in 1795 and united disparate Protestant groups. During the 18th century, Richard Robinson, the Church of Ireland Primate, used a large portion of his personal wealth to convert Armagh into a city of Georgian splendour rivalling Dublin, and many of the city of Armagh's public buildings date to this time, including Armagh Observatory.
Areas of Historical Interest: Tannaghmore Gardens and Museum (also contains a rare breeds farm), St Patrick's Trian (tells the Armagh story and an adaptation of *Gulliver's Travels*), Armagh Planetarium (contains the Robinson Dome with a 10-inch telescope, other astronomical instruments and allows visitors to explore the universe with computers), Navan Centre (interpretive centre near the famous Navan hill fort), Armagh's Palace Stables Heritage Centre (restored Georgian stable block featuring a day in the life of the Palace), The Argory (1824; house overlooking the River Blackwater, has an acetylene gas lighting system, formal Victorian gardens and a lime walk), St Patrick's Cathedral (a church has stood on this site for 1,500 years, although it has been destroyed and rebuilt over 17 times), Armagh County Museum (contains an exhibition on local history), Derrymore House (18th century thatched cottage-orné manor house, designed by John Sutherland, a follower of 'Capability' Brown), Ardress (18th century house with its own apple orchard, recently planted with old apple varieties).

● THE COUNTY
Total Population: 141,585 *(e)*
County Capital: Armagh
Largest Town: Craigavon *see profile*
Main Towns: Craigavon, Portadown, Lurgan and Keady
Main Business Contact: Ledu The Small Business Agency: Contact Ledu House, Upper Galwally, Belfast. Tel 01232-491 031.
No of Golf Clubs: 7 (7 x 18).

Craigavon New Town

From the name of the first prime minister of Northern Ireland, James Craig - Lord Craigavon

● HISTORY
Origins: Craigavon New Town was initially proposed by Professor Sir Robert Matthew in the Belfast Regional and Survey Plan in 1963. The area brought together the two existing Boroughs of Lurgan and Portadown and a number of small villages in the area. These towns and villages share a common industrial heritage in Ulster's historic linen industry when Irish linen was exported throughout the world
Growth: The new town was proposed to help relieve the urban pressure on Belfast (30 miles away) as well as rejuvenate the area. The Craigavon Development Commission was formed in 1965. The Commission proceeded with the development of Craigavon. Craigavon District Council came into being in June 1973 following the reorganisation of local government in 1973, and it achieved Borough status from 1st October 1973 under the charter of the former Borough of Lurgan. Craigavon has a mixed economy with over one-third of employment in the manufacturing sector. Business parks have been constructed to meet specialist requirements of industries in the area, and Craigavon also benefits from Northern Ireland's highly developed STAR telecommunications network.

● **TODAY**
Location set in the north-east corner of Armagh beside the shores of Lough Neagh, the largest fresh water lake in the British Isles, Craigavon occupies 100 sq miles (260 sq km). To the east, west and south lie the hills of Armagh. Also to the south is the City of Armagh, Ireland's ecclesiastical capital.
Population Urban: 65,000 & Borough: 78,200.
Tourist Attractions Oxford Island National Nature Reserve (Ecolab, Birdwatching Hides, Exhibition, Guided Walks), Newry Canal (1742; first summit-level canal in the country, which greatly enhanced Portadown's position as a trading town), Moneypenny's Lock & Lockhouse, The Peacock Gallery (situated at Pinebank House in the central Brownlow area), Craigavon Watersport Centre, Craigavon Golf & Ski Centre (outdoor artificial ski slope and golf facility), Cascades Leisure Centre, Waves Leisure Centre in Lurgan, Craigavon Leisure Centre, Maghery Country Park, Coney Island (the only remaining inhabited island on L Neagh), Ulster Way (goes along the River Bann and Newry Canal), Lurgan Public Park (200 acres of wooded areas), Brownlow House, Portadown Public Park, the Central Park in Brownlow (centres on a listed 18th-century Georgian farmhouse), Kinnego marina (accommodates L Neagh Sailing Club established in 1877, one of the oldest yacht clubs in Northern Ireland).

● **TRANSPORT**
Main Routes: Armagh is served by major routes A27-N1 (to Dublin); M1 (to Belfast); A3-N12-N54-N3-N55-N6 (to Galway); A28-A5 (to Derry).
Miles from Dublin (89); Belfast (23); Galway (166); Cork (249).
Nearest Travel Centre (Bus): Armagh Bus Station 01861-522 266; Craigavon Bus Station 01762-342 511.
Nearest Rail Station: Lurgan Station 01762-322 052.
Nearest Airport: Belfast City Airport 01232-734 828; Belfast International Airport 01849-484 848.
Nearest Ferry Port: Belfast (+23 miles); Larne (+44 miles).

County Carlow

"From the Irish Ceatharlach - quadruple lake, possibly referring to the flooding of the rivers Barrow and Burrin"

● **GEOGRAPHY**
Province: Leinster
Location: inland county (one of the few inland counties that does not constitute part of the central plain) in the south-east of the country
County Size: 31st in Ireland
Land area: 346 sq. miles
Highest point: Mt Leinster (793 m)
Main Geographical Features: The Castlecomer Plateau, which Carlow shares with County Kilkenny, contains coal shale - a geological feature that has given Carlow an industrial tradition, unusual in Ireland. The county is bounded in the east by the granite walls of the Blackstairs Mountains and is split in three by rivers flowing southwards. The R. Barrow is navigable for a distance of 68km and was used right up to the 1960s for commercial transport
Main Rivers: Burren, Barrow.
Areas of Geographical interest: Barrow Way (a 70-mile walking route which follows the towpath along the River Barrow), Eagle Hill (views take in most of the county), Altamount Gardens in Tullow (one of Ireland's finest formal gardens - holds wildlife and rare shrubs), Sth Leinster Way (part of this signposted walk, 34 km, goes through Carlow), boat cruising on the Barrow.

● **HISTORY**
Pre-Christian The most impressive prehistoric monument in the county is the Browne's Hill Dolmen, believed to be the largest type of this kind of megalith in Europe with a capstone weighing around 100 tonnes. Dolmens are the ruined chamber at the centre of megalithic tombs, which are found all around Ireland. These tombs are divided into four types: Court tombs, Portal tombs, Passage tombs and Wedge tombs.
Early Christian During early Christian times, Carlow's rich river valleys were the sites for many monastic settlements, including the settlement at St. Mullins, most of which were destroyed by the Vikings. Other important monastic sites include St Lazerian's (initially founded in 632, it was one of the foremost monasteries in Leinster and had at one time 1,500 monks. Killeshin monastery is noted for its beautifully carved Romansque doorway.
Medieval Carlow's strategic position between Kilkenny and the east coast and its river links led to widespread Viking attacks - most of the monastic settlements were destroyed by the Vikings. The invading Normans conquered Ireland by establishing themselves on a territory they took from the native Irish and by setting up fortifications and eventually castles. This system was plainly carried out in the Carlow area: by the middle of the 14th century over 150 castles had been built. While none survive intact, some imposing ruins remain. These castles were built to a similar plan with a four-towered keep and were probably the first of their kind in Europe. In the 14th century, Art MacMurrough Kavanagh of Borris became king of Leinster and a thorn in the side of the Anglo-Norman armies. His attacks on the Pale were so frequent that Richard II was himself compelled to confront the chieftain with an estimated 10,000 strong expeditionary force. However, Art Oge, as he was known, inflicted defeat upon defeat on the king, giving Richard's enemies the chance to usurp the English throne.
English: Carlow was planted by the English during the Cromwellian plantation of the 1650s. County Carlow and County Wexford were the sites of most of the fiercest fighting in the 1798 rebellion, and more than 640 rebels were slaughtered in the county.

Areas of Historical interest: Browne's Hill Dolmen, Haroldstown Dolmen, 'Old Derry' House and site of the first monastery founded by St. Diarmuid, Royal Oak village and Stone Fort of Rathgall (where ancient kings are allegedly buried) St Moling's Mill (a blessed well and bath house), St Mullin's Abbey (7th century), St Lazerian's Cathedral (foremost monastic houses), Borris Castle (residence of the McMurrough Kavanaghs - rulers of Leinster), Black Castle (1181; built by Hugh de Lacy - one of the Ireland's earliest Norman castles), Ballymoon Castle (14th century), Clonmore Castle, Carlow Museum, Duckett's Grove (extensive Gothic ruin, former home of the Duckett family from the 17th century to 1915), Clonmore abbey (holds many ancient Celtic crosses), Huntington Castle, Dunleckney Manor (18th century; built by Walter Bagenal, founder of Bagenalstown).

● **THE COUNTY**
Total Population: 41,616 *(1996)*
Growth rate: a 1.6% increase since 1991
County Capital and Largest Town: Carlow *see profile*
Main Towns: Borris, Muinebeag, Tullow.
Main Business Contact: Carlow County Enterprise Board, 98, Tullow Street, Carlow. Tel 0503-30880.
No of Schools: National 43; Secondary 11.
No of Golf Clubs: 3 (2 x 18; 1 x 9)

Carlow Town

See county name

● **HISTORY**
Origins: There may have been a monastic settlement in the area in early Christian times founded by St Comgall. The town's origins date back to the building of Carlow Castle (1207–1213)
Growth: The castle is attributed to William Marshal, Earl of Pembroke and Lord of Leinster to guard a vital river crossing. Carlow was an important military fortress strategically situated at the confluence of the River Barrow and the River Burren and on the south eastern corner of the Pale. A charter was granted to William Marshal in 1210, allowing the town's citizens to form guilds, be exempt from tools and to do sell their properties. Carlow town would have organically grown around the outer ramparts of the mediaeval castle. In 1361, Edward III's son, Lionel, moved the King's Exchequer in Ireland temporarily to Carlow and constructed a wall around the town. The castle was attacked many times: James FitzGerald seized it in 1494, but soon surrendered it to Sir Edward Poynings. During the 1641 rebellion, the castle was attacked and the town burnt by rebels, but the Earl of Ormonde's forces rescued the town's Protestant inhabitants, who were sheltering in the castle. King James I granted the town another charter, allowing to return members to parliament. The rebels of 1798 besieged the castle and the garrison, but were soon overcome and slaughtered. It remained in relatively good repair. In 1814, a Dr Middleton planned to convert the castle into an asylum and to demolish the interior he used explosive charges which undermined its foundations resulting in the collapse of all but two towers.

● **TODAY**
Location north-east corner of Carlow on the Barrow and the Burren River
Population: 14,979 (+6.8% on 1991 Census)
Tourist Attractions Carlow Castle (the oldest building in the town), Carlow Cathedral (1833; designed after the Beftroi tower in Bruges, Belgium), St Mary's Church of Ireland (1727, its interior contains monuments attributed to the architect, Richard Morrison), the Croppies Grave (a memorial to the 1798 massacre in Carlow Town), Carlow Courthouse (1830; designed by William Vitruvius Morrison, its magnificent exterior points to the fact that the building was allegedly intended for Cork city), St Patrick's College Catholic seminary (1793; supposedly the seminary in longest continuous use in the world), Graiguecullen bridge (1569), the Town Hall (1884; contains Carlow Museum), the Liberty Tree (sculpture by John Behan in memory of the 1798 rebellion), Carlow Brewing Company (local microbrewery, specialising in Celtic beers).

● **TRANSPORT**
Main Routes: Carlow is served by major routes N9-N7 (to Dublin); N9-N7-N1-A1-M1 (to Belfast); N9-N10-N76-N24-N8 (to Cork); N80-N7-N62-N52-N65-N6-N18 (to Galway).
Miles from Dublin (53); Belfast (157); Galway (116); Cork (116).
Nearest Travel Centre (Bus): Contact Plunkett Station, Waterford Tel 051-879 000.
Nearest Rail Station: Carlow Tel 0503-31633.
Nearest Airport: Dublin Airport Tel 01-8141111.
Nearest Ferry Port: Dublin (+53 miles); Rosslare (+55 miles).

County Cavan

"From the Irish Cabhán - *a hollow"*

● **GEOGRAPHY**
Province: Ulster
Location: inland county and the most southerly of the nine Ulster Counties, it is bounded by six other counties.
County Size: 19th in Ireland
Land area: 730 sq. miles
Highest point: Cuilcagh Mtn (667 m)
Main Geographical Features: Cavan is divided into the eastern highlands, the Erne valley and the mountainous region of west Cavan.
Main Rivers: Shannon; Erne; Blackwater; Annalee.
Main Lakes: L Gowna; L Oughter; L Sheelin; L Ramor.
Rivers: Blackwater, Annalee and the two great river systems of the Shannon, the longest river in Ireland which rises from the Shannon Pot on the southern slopes of the Cuilcagh Mountain, and the Erne which rises east of Lough Gowna. The Shannon-Erne waterway is a a 6.5 km cross-border canal which links the Shannon and Erne river systems
Areas of Geographical interest: Dún a Rí Forest Park, Killykeen Forest Park (home to stoats, hare, mink, squirrels and otters), the Shannon Pot (the source of the River Shannon), the Spa Wells at Swanlinbar.

● **HISTORY**
Legends: A favourite legend is that the ancient town of Cavan lies beneath the waters of the Green Lake.
Prehistory: There are 59 megalithic tombs in Cavan, the best known example of which is Cohaw (a double court tomb, erected 3000–2500 BC) and Duffcastle Dolmen. Cavan with its many lakes has well over 100 confirmed and suspected crannog sites. Crannógs were built on small natural or man-made islands in lakes, rivers or swamps and were made of mud, stones and wood surrounded by a wooden palisade. Another significant field monument in the county is the Black Pig's Dyke, an ancient frontier fortification, which was built near Dowra. The fortification dates back to around 500 BC (the Iron Age) and was thought to have been an interrupted defensive system built to stop cattle raiding from the south.
Early Christian: An early Christian saint, St Killian, established a monastery and links with Würzburg, (then in Franconia, now Germany).The saint is still celebrated in Germany at Kilianfest. He was one of a number of Irish monks who travelled to the continent to act as teachers and missionaries. Irish monks were viewed as being a unique strand of Christianity, in that they they were neither part of the old Roman empire nor part of an invasion force, and they made major contributions to continental monasteries during this period.
Medieval In the ninth century, the county formed the eastern part of the ancient kingdom of Breifne ruled over by the Clan Uí Raghallaigh - the O'Reillys, while Leitrim formed the western part of the Kingdom and was ruled by the O'Rourkes. The O'Reilly family seat was at Clogh Oughter, a castle in the true sense of the word in that it was a military fortification, designed to withstand prolonged attack. Clogh Oughtair is the best surviving example of a medieval stone castle in County

Cavan. Most other surviving castles in Cavan are tower houses - a much smaller structure than a castle - designed to provide secure accommodation and refuge during raids but not to withstand siege. The O'Reilly clan held onto to the area up until the 16th century.
English: In 1584, the lord-deputy of Ireland designated East Breifne as the present county of Cavan and although it was formerly part of Connacht, Cavan was incorporated with the counties that formed Ulster. In order to lessen the influence of the O'Reillys, the land was parceled into seven baronies, each of which was settled on separate branches of the family. After the death of the last, no successor was elected under the distinguishing title of O'Reilly and early in the reign of James I, the lord deputy came to Cavan and had a commission into the ownership of all the lands. British planters were granted land; two boroughs were created - Cavan and Belturbet - and received grants. In 1610, the town of Virginia was also established - it derives its name from Elizabeth I of England, the Virgin Queen. Besides the O'Reillys, the land was populated by the Mac Gaurans, who elected their own king and queen. Cavan was one of the three Ulster counties to be incorporated into the Irish Free State in 1921.
Areas of Historical Interest: The Black Pig's Dyke at Dowra, 'Finn McCool's Fingers' (bronze age stones at Shantemon), The Cohan Megalithic Tomb, Moneygashel Ring Fort, St Killian's Heritage Centre at Mullagh (built in association with the Diocese of Würzburg), County Cavan Heritage and Genealogical Research Centre, Cavan County Museum in Ballyjamesduff (as well as containing exhibits from prehistoric times, the museum also houses the 'Pighouse' collection of more than 3,000 artifacts of rural from 18th century to present day), Cavan Crystal Factory (Ireland's second oldest glass-making factory), Lough Oughter Castle (ancient seat of the O'Reillys), Kildallon (the ancestral home of Edgar Allen Poe), Drumlane medieval church and round tower (dating back to the 13th century, has fine carvings on the exterior), Kilmore Cathedral, Trinity Island, Kill Graveyard, Cavan Abbey, Omard Cross, Drumlane Abbey, Crover Castle, The Bridge of Finea, Killeshandra old Church, Phil Sheridan's birthplace, Bawnboy Workhouse, Turbot Island Motte and Bailey, Cohaw Court Tomb, Killycluggin Stone, Ballyhaise House, Farnham House, Killycluggin Stone ('La Tene' style stone).

● **THE COUNTY**
Total Population: 52,944 *(1996)*
Growth rate: 0.3% increase since 1991.
County Capital and Largest Town: Cavan *see profile*
Main Towns: Cootehill, Bailieboro, Kingscourt, Belturbet
Business Contact: Cavan County Enterprise Board, 17 Farnham Street, Cavan. Tel 049-32427.
No of Schools: National 81; Secondary 10.
No of Golf Clubs: 6 (2 x 18; 4 x 9).
Other Tourist Attractions: the GAA Gallery, Corlegga Goat Cheese Farm, the Railway Project, Belturbet.

Cavan Town

See county name

● HISTORY

Origins: early in the reign of James I, the lord deputy came to Cavan and held a commission into the ownership of all the lands; British planters were to be granted land, and two of the boroughs were created and received grants - those of Cavan and Belturbet. The town grew as a prosperous trading and administrative centre for the county.

● TODAY

Location centre of the county
Population: 5,623 (+7% on 1991 Census).
Tourist Attractions Lifeforce Mill (a restored working mill, founded in 1846 but on the site of a much earlier mill, in the centre of Cavan Town), Cana House (genealogy records).

● TRANSPORT

Main Routes: Cavan is served by major routes N3 (to Dublin); N3-N54-N2-A3-M1 (to Belfast); N55-N6-N62-N8-N25 (to Cork); N3-N5-N6-N18 (to Galway).
Miles from Dublin (67); Belfast (88); Cork (187); Galway (103).
Nearest Travel Centre (Bus): Bus Éireann 049-31353; Bus Office 049-32533.
Nearest Rail Station: Carrick-on-Shannon, Co Leitrim 078-20036.
Nearest Airport: Dublin Airport 01-814 1111; Knock 094-67222.
Nearest Ferry Port: Dublin (+67 miles).

County Clare

"From the Irish An Clár - the plain."

● GEOGRAPHY

Province: Munster
Location: maritime county on the west coast of the country which could be referred to as a peninsula; bounded by Lough Derg in the east, by the Shannon estuary in the south, by the Atlantic Ocean in the west and by Galway Bay in the north-west.
County Size: 7th in Ireland
Land area: 1,262 sq. miles
Highest point: Slieve Glennagallaigh (533 m)
Main Geographical Features: The county has some of the most interesting and diverse topography in Ireland, including the bare limestone karst landscape of the Burren caused by glaciation and erosion. Around 250 million years ago, Ireland occupied the latitude where Egypt now lies and had a desert climate. The desert climate left it open to strong erosion, baring the limestone over the central region of the country. The exposure of this limestone left it open to weathering by acidic rain, resulting in a karstic landscape of the burren, with its Turloughs (shallow lakes which are dry in the summer but flood in the winter), underground cave systems and diverse flora and fauna. Other interesting features in the county include the Cliffs of Moher and the beaches of the Atlantic Coast.
Main Rivers: Doonbeg; Fergus.
Main Lakes: L Graney.
Main Rivers: Liscannor; Kilbaha.
Main Islands: Mutton; Scattery; Inishmore (pop. 1).
Areas of Geographical interest: Ailwee Caves, the Burren National Park (with its 28 species of butterfly, unique Alpine plants, the Cliffs of Moher (with their contrasting layers of black shale and sandstone they provide a dramatic sight as they rise to a height of 200m and extend for 8 km), Dolphin Watch at Carrigaholt (gives observers the chance to see Ireland's only resident group of bottlenose dolphins), Kilkee Bay (rated as one of the best diving locations in Europe), Lahinch Seaworld.

● HISTORY

Prehistory: Evidence of human habitation in Clare dates back to the Stone Age. There are around 120 dolmens and wedge tombs in the Burren National Park, the most famous being Poulnabrone Dolmen. Archaeological excavations in 1999 at Roughan Hill on the south-east perimeter of the Burren, Co Clare, have revealed one of the most extensive and well-preserved prehistoric landscapes in Europe. American archaeologists have uncovered a megalithic tomb over 5,500 years old in a preserved prehistoric landscape set among contemporary neolithic / early Bronze Age farmsteads, settlements and 4,400-year-old field walls. The unique environmental conditions of the Burren have preserved these archaeological features. The system of settlements could be vitally important in uncovering the lifestyle of Ireland's prehistoric farmers. The area extending from the south-eastern edge of the Burren to Doolin, because of its light, well drained soil and the gentle typography, was home to a thriving farming community in prehistoric times.

There is evidence that the Burren was, at one stage, densley covered by field walls and Final Neolithic/Early Bronze Age settlements, indicating the area was intensively farmed: mound walls occur widely across the Burren and there is a dense distribution of the late Neolithic/Early Bronze Age wedge tombs and early Bronze Age burials in earlier monuments. It is suggested that they were built sometime between the loss of the tree cover in the earlier Neolithic and the subsequent soil loss in the Bronze Age. This suggests that humans were responsible for the loss of trees and subsequent loss of soil, through continual tree felling, field wall construction, and finally, soil erosion.

Medieval Brian Boru, the high king of Ireland, who defeated the Vikings, had overlordship of Clare. The Normans failed to secure a permanent hold in the county, and the English did not appear in Clare until Murrough O'Brien was made Earl of Thomond in 1541. **English:** A subsequent 17th-century earl of Thomond supported King Charles but reluctantly allowed Cromwell's forces to garrison at Bunratty Castle. The wars of this period ravaged the county, leaving it ruined by famine and depopulation. Although the native people were oppressed by the Penal Laws of the 18th century, they led the way towards civil and religious liberty. It was they who returned Daniel O'Connell as a Member of Parliament, which led to Catholic Emancipation in 1829, earning Clare the title of the Banner County. However, the county fared badly during the Great Famine, and its population fell from 286,000 in 1841 to half this number in 1871.

Areas of Historical Interest: Bunratty Castle and Folk Park, Dromoland Castle, Dunguaire Castle, Dysert O'Dea Castle and its archaeology centre, Knappogue Castle (erected in 1467 by the MacNamaras), Leamaneagh Castle, Newtown Castle, Cahermore Stone Fort, Gleninsheen Wedge Tomb, Poulnabrone Dolmen (possibly the most famous dolmen in Ireland, dating back to 2500–2000 BC), Craggaunowen Bronze Age lake dwellings (recreated historic site which shows how people lived during the bronze), Holy Island (the site of a 7th century monastic ruins on Lough Derg), Kilrush (an 18th century market town that has been designated a Heritage Town), Scattery Island centre in Kilrush (which details the island's medieval monastic history and flora and fauna), St Flannan's Cathedral in Killaloe (dating back to 1182 with an ancient stone, covered in Ogham and Nordic runes) .

● **THE COUNTY**
Total Population: 94,006 *(1996)*
Growth rate: 3.4% increase since 1991
County Capital and Largest Town: Ennis *see profile*
Main Towns: Ennis, Kilkee, Killaloe, Kilrush, Shannon Town
Main Business Contact: Clare County Enterprise Board, Enterprise House, Mill Road, Ennis, Co Clare. Tel 065-41922.
No. of Schools: National 123; Secondary 19.
No. of Golf Clubs: 10 (7 x 18; 1 x 9; 1 x 12; 1 x 36).
Blue Flag Beaches / Marinas: 10 - Kilrush Creek Marina, Mountshannon Marina, Cappagh Pier (Kilrush), White Strand (Miltown Malbay), Lahinch, Fanore, Ballycuggeran, Mountshannon, Kilkee, White Strand (Doonbeg)
Other Tourist Attractions: Boating centre of Killaloe on Lough Derg, Lisdoonvarna (once a Victorian spa resort but now better known for its matchmaking festival).

Ennis Town

"From the Irish Inis *- an island, alluding to the town's origins between two streams of the River Fergus"*

● **HISTORY**
Origins: The Franciscan Ennis Friary, from which the medieval town grew, dates back to the 1204 and was founded by the medieval O'Briens (Kings of Thomond, who were the feudal overlords in the area).
Growth: Ennis's beginnings as an administrative and market town for the area date back 400 years to when it was chosen as the capital for the newly designated county of Clare. It was granted the right to hold fairs and markets in 1610. There are a number of buildings in the town which date back to the 17th century. Daniel O'Connell, who was elected MP for the county gave his name to the town's main street and square. Ennis is renowned for its music and its developments in IT - it was designated by Eircom (formerly Telecom Éireann) to be Ireland's first Information Age Town and as such it is the largest community technology project in the country.

● **TODAY**
Location south central Clare on the River Fergus
Population: 17,726 (+10.3 % on 1991 Census).
Tourist Attractions the O'Connell Street Monument, Manchester Martyrs' Memorial, Steeles Rock, the De Valera Library, Ennis Friary (in use until the early 17th century, it contains many carvings of which the McMahon tomb is the most renowned example), Ennis Sculpture Initiative, Cois na hAbhana, St Peter and Paul's Cathedral, River Fergus, St Columba's Church, Dromore Wood (an area of 1,000 acres just outside Ennis with a wide range of habitats).

● **TRANSPORT**
Main Routes: Ennis is served by major routes N18-N7-M7-N7 (to Dublin); N18-N66-N6-N55-N54-N12-A3-M1 (to Belfast); N18-N21-N20 (to Cork); N18 (to Galway).
Miles from Dublin (147); Belfast (205); Cork (83); Galway (42).
Nearest Travel Centre (Bus): Bus Éireann, Ennis Bus Station 065-624177.
Nearest Rail Station: Ennis 065-40444.
Nearest Airport: Shannon Airport 061-471 444.
Nearest Ferry Port: Cork (+83 miles).

County Cork

"From the Irish Corcaigh - marsh, referring to the swampy estuary of the Lee upon which Cork city was founded"

● **GEOGRAPHY**
Province: Munster
Location: maritime county on the south-west coast
County Size: 1st in Ireland
Land area: 2,878 sq. miles
Highest point: Knockboy (710 m)
Main Geographical Features: The prevailing tropical weathering of 35 million years ago had huge effects on the Irish landscape. Most of the chalk deposited in Ireland was eroded around this time, and this erosion left 'clay with fints', examples of which can be seen just south of Cork city. Long ridges of sandstone traverse the county, and the county's main rivers flow west to east along the valleys between these limestone ridges, each turning sharply southwards to empty into the sea. About 25 million years ago, the river pattern we see today could have begun. River valleys, particularly those in the south, cut deeply into the terrain, although the particular routes taken by the Blackwater, Lee and Bandon rivers may not have dated to the same time; their north-south sections are perhaps older than the eastward-flowing reaches and could have started on the earlier chalk surface. The Gulf Stream touches Ireland first at Cork, providing warm, mild weather that ensures lush growth in the county's fertile farmlands. Little bays and harbours are indented all along the county
Main Rivers: Lee; Blackwater; Bandon; Sullane; Awbeg; Illen; Bride.
Main Bays: Youghal; Clonakilty; Roaringwater; Dunmanus; Bantry; Garnish.
Main Islands: Spike (pop. 103); Inishbeg (pop. 19); Sherkin (pop. 98); Hare (pop. 16); Clear (pop. 145); Long (pop. 9); Whiddy (pop. 34); Bear (pop. 212); Dursey (pop. 9); Haulbowline (pop.110); Inchydoney (pop. 102); Ringarogy (pop. 76); Ballycottin (pop. 27).
Coastline: 680 miles (one-fifth of national coastline).
Areas of Geographical interest: Ireland's only cable car service is in Cork (linking Dursey Island with the mainland at Beara peninsula), Healy Pass in the Caha Mtns), Gougane Barra National Park, Mizen Head (Ireland's most southerly point), Garinish Island (turned into an exotic garden in 1910 - with subtropical flora and neo-Classical follies), Fota Wildlife Park and Arboretum (contains over 70 different animal species).

● **HISTORY**
Prehistory: The heaviest concentration of stone circles in Ireland and Britain is to be found in the south-west region, with around 80 such monuments located in the Cork-Kerry area. The purpose of these ancient rings remains a mystery. It is certain they have some sort of ritualistic associations and could possibly have an astrological purpose.
Early Christian: Cork's early Christian history centres around St. Finbarr who founded a church in the area of Cork city
Medieval Viking raiders attacked the region around AD 820 but later integrated with the local population. When the Anglo-Norman force attacked in 1172, the Danes and the McCarthy clan had to submit.

English: The Battle of Kinsale, the event that heralded the end of Gaelic Ireland, took place off the coast of Cork in 1601, when the Irish along with their Spanish allies, were defeated. Cork was also prominent in two other Irish historic failures - when the French entered Bantry Bay in 1689 and again in 1798 to aid the Irish. Cork played a prominent role in all struggles for Independence, and Michael Collins, Ireland's best known revolutionary, came from Cork.
Areas of Historical Interest: Labbacallee (a huge pre-historic monument), Dromberg Stone Circle (dating back to about 150 BC, it is aligned with the sun at the winter solstice), Bantry House (built in 1720 and home of the Earls of Bantry, renowned for its views and 18th century collections), Blarney Castle and the Blarney stone, Castle Curious (a folly tower), Desmond Castle, Dunmanus Castle, Roche Castle, Timoleague Abbey (founded in the the 13th century by the Franciscans), Dunkathel House (near Glanmire, a neo-Classical country house rebuilt in 1785 for a wealthy Cork merchant and containing a fine collection of furniture and art), the Royal Gunpowder Mills in Ballincollig (built in 1794 and used during the Napoleonic wars by the British for gunpowder production - one of Cork's foremost industries by the mid-19th century), the West Cork Museum (contains many mementos of Michael Collins), the Queenstown Story (an exhibition that tells how Cobh was the embarkation point for many thousands of Irish emigrants and convicts), West Cork Regional Museum in Clonakilty, Charles Fort (est. in 1670s by Kinsale by the British against invading forces, it is one of the finest examples of a star-shaped fort in Ireland), Youghal Clock Tower.

● **THE COUNTY**
Total Population: 293,323 - excluding Cork City *(1996)*
Growth rate: 3.6% increase since 1991
County Capital and Largest Town: Cork *see profile*
Main Towns: Bantry, Clonakilty, Cobh, Cork, Fermoy, Kinsale, Mallow, Mitchelstown, Skibbereen, Youghal.
Main Business Contact: Cork City Enterprise Board, Albert Quay House, Albert Quay, Cork. Tel 021-961 828.
North Cork County Enterprise Board, 26 Bank Place, Mallow, Co Cork. Tel 022-43235.
South Cork County Enterprise Board, Exham House, Fingerpost, Douglas, Cork. Tel 021-895 977.
West Cork County Enterprise Board, 8 Kent Street, Clonakilty, Co Cork Tel 023-34700.
No of Schools: National 371; Secondary 91.
No of Golf Clubs: 29 (19 x 18; 8 x 9; 2 x 27).
Blue Flag Beaches / Marinas: 10 - Kinsale Yacht Club Marina, Barleycove, Garrylucas, Garryvoe, Inchydoney, Owenahincha, The Warren, Tragumna, Clay-castle (Youghal), Front Strand (Youghal)
Other Tourist Attractions: The many bays and harbours indented all along the county's coastline make Cork an ideal location for sailing (the oldest yacht club in the world is based in Cork at Crosshaven and dates back to 1720) Kinsale Town (Ireland gourmet food centre), Midleton (the home of Jameson Whiskey and the James Heritage Centre which tells the story of Irish whiskey), Schull Planetarium, Skibbereen (crafts centre).

Cork City

See county name

● **HISTORY**

Origins: As indicated by its name, the city was originally a monastic site founded by St Finbarr in AD 650. The town was successively raided by the Vikings and the Normans.

Growth: Because of its location on one of Ireland's largest natural harbours, Cork City thrived from the medieval ages onwards. It was Ireland's main point of contact with continental Europe (there is a continental atmosphere in the city's narrow alleys, waterways and Georgian architecture). It also allowed the city a greater autonomy, enabling it to maintain a reputation for resistance, leading to it being named 'Rebel Cork' (the city was the base for the 19th-century Fenian movement and played a pivotal role in the Irish struggle for independence).

● **TODAY**

Location south-east coast of the county, on the banks of the River Lee, it is a city built on water (it is still flooded during heavy rainfall) with picturesque quays and bridges

Population: 179,954 (+3.18 from 1991 Census).

Tourist Attractions Bishop Lucey Park (with its section of city walls and a gateway from the old cornmarket), the Coal Quay, (an open air market steeped in Cork's folk culture); the Cork Heritage Park, Blackrock; the riverside quadrangle at University College Cork; the Old English Market in Grand Parade (a covered fruit and vegetable market, est. 1610) Patrick's Hill, the Quays (where much of Cork's commercial activity was centred) Cork Opera House, the Crawford Municipal Art Gallery (formerly an art college and originally the city's Custom House dating back to 1724, it now houses studios, picture galleries and a fine sculpture collection which includes some Rodins), Triskel Arts Centre in Tobin Street, the Butter Exchange (dates to 1770, butter was sorted here before being exported abroad and supplied to the British navy), Blackrock Castle, the Fr. Theobald Matthew Monument (a 19th-century temperance advocate), the National Monument on Grand Parade (commemorating those who died in 1798 and 1867), the old gaol in Sunday's Well (includes an exhibition on inmates lives during the 19th and 20th centuries), St Ann's (the church in Shandon with its famous bells, clocks and weathervane), Elizabeth Fort (est. during the 16th century and later converted into a gaol), Red Abbey (13th century Augustinian abbey ruins and the oldest building in the city), St Mary's Dominican church, St. Finbarr's Cathedral (neo-Gothic church finished in 1878), St. Mary's Cathedral, (with its notable carvings).

● **TRANSPORT**

Main Routes: Cork is served by major routes N8-N7-M7-N7 (to Dublin); N8-N80-N52-N1-A1-M1 (to Belfast); N20-N21-N18 (to Galway).

Miles from Dublin (159); Belfast (262); Galway (187).

Nearest Travel Centre (Bus): Bus Éireann, Parnell Place, Cork. Tel 021-508 188.

Nearest Rail Station: Cork. Tel 021-506 766.

Nearest Airport: Cork Airport. Tel 021-313 131.

Nearest Ferry Port: Cork.

County Derry

"From the Irish Doire - Oak Grove"

● **GEOGRAPHY**

Province: Ulster

Location: maritime county in the north-west of Northern Ireland

County Size: 15th in Ireland

Land area: 798 sq. miles

Highest point: Sawel Mtn (680 m)

Main Geographical Features: a hilly terrain particularly in the south-west where the Sperrin Mountains are found. It is bordered on the west by the River Foyle, which flows into Lough Foyle, on the north by the Atlantic Ocean, on the east by County Antrim and on the south by County Tyrone and Lough Neagh.

Main Rivers: Foyle; Bann; Roe.

Main Lakes: L Neagh; L Foyle.

Areas of Geographical interest: Roe Valley Country Park (contains riverside walks, Ulster's first domestic hydro-electric station and ruined linen water mills), Ness Wood Country Park (woodland walks), the Guy L. Wilson Daffodil Garden (at University of Ulster, Coleraine, contains the world's largest collection of daffodils - more than 1,800 types - incl. Irish-bred daffodils and other narcissi in memory of daffodil breeder Guy Wilson, 1885–1962), White Rocks (caves and arches scoured from the limestone cliffs around Portrush), Springhill (early 18th century house, surrounded by gardens, incl. a herb garden and scented camomile lawn).

● **HISTORY**

Prehistory: One of the best known Gold collars of the La Tène style was found at Broighter along with a hoard of plaited chains and torques.

Early Christian: The county's early Christian history is dominated by St. Columba, who died in 597 and who successfully advanced Christianity in both his native land and Scotland. He established a monastery in Derry

546, out of which Derry city grew, and went on to establish a large family of churches around Scotland's Atlantic seaboard including the monastery at Iona.

Medieval The O'Neills held sway over much of the county around the middle ages, although Richard de Burgh the 'Red Earl' of Ulster took control of the little port of Derry with a view to developing it as a stronghold at the beginning of the 14th century. However, he was defeated in battle by Edward Bruce in 1315 and lost control of Ulster for a time. The O'Neills assumed power during the 14th century and shared this power in Derry county with the O'Donnells and the O'Cahans in the 15th century

English: Derry, along with the rest of Ulster, was planted in 1610. Following the plantation, the area was formally assigned county status in 1613 and, along with the city, was renamed Londonderry after the intervention of the London-based society, which rebuilt the city after it was sacked. In 1641, the old Catholic landowners rose against the new Protestant planters in Ulster, but the rising was crushed by Cromwell when he arrived in 1649. During the Jacobite/Williamite war, many of the county's planter population sought refuge in Derry.

Areas of Historical Interest: Bellaghy Bawn (a restored fortified house dating back to 1618 and used in the writings of Bellaghy-born poet, Seamus Heaney), Plantation of Ulster Visitor Centre (tells the story of the plantation of Ulster, including the Flight of the Earls), Garvagh Museum & Heritage Centre (Stone Age artifacts and eel fishery), Mussenden Temple (on the cliffs at Downhill, built as a library by Augustus Hervey, the eccentric earl-bishop of Derry in 1783, and based on the Temple of Vesta outside Rome), Magilligan Point (with its Martello tower, built during the Napoleonic wars to guard the entrance to L. Foyle), Mountsandel Fort, Downhill Castle (the palace ruins of the Earl-Bishop of Derry, with a modern ornamental garden and two artificial lakes), Dungiven Priory and O'Cahan's Tomb (the tomb of an O'Cahan who died in 1385), the Victorian sea front promenade in Portstewart.

● **THE COUNTY**

Total Population: 213,035 *(e)*

County Capitals: Derry, Coleraine, Limavady, Magherafelt.

Largest Town: Derry *see profile*

Main Towns: Coleraine, Derry, Dungiven, Limavady, Maghera, Magherafelt, Portstewart.

Main Business Contact: Ledu The Small Business Agency: 13 Shipquay Street, Derry. Tel 01232-267257.

No of Golf Clubs: 10 (3 x 18; 3 x 9; 3 x 27; 1 x 45).

Blue Flag Beaches: 2 - West Strand (Portrush), Benone Strand.

Other Tourist Attractions: Portstewart Strand (popular beach with over 2 miles of strand), Earhart Centre (exhibition on Amelia Earhart, the first woman to fly the Atlantic solo and who finished her journey here), Coleraine (home to the North West 200, one of the fastest and most dangerous motor cycle races in the world).

Derry City

See county name

● **HISTORY**

Origins: The city's existence can be traced back to pagan times when Calgach, a warrior, made his camp on the 'island' of Derry. St. Columb founded his first monastery in 546 in the vicinity. In 1164, the first bishop of Derry built a cathedral in the city near the monastic site, and Derry came to be known as Doire Columcille, in honour of St. Columb. During Norman times, the city was ruled over by the de Burgos, the earls of Ulster.

Growth: The first defensive fortifications around the city were built by the English in 1566. These were breached in 1608 when Derry was sacked by Cahir O'Doherty. He was subsequently killed in Donegal and the rebellion he incited died. In 1613 the city was chosen as a major plantation project, organised by the London livery companies. The city of London sent master builders and money between 1614 and 1619 to rebuild the ruined medieval city and construct its famous walls. Hence the acquisition of the prefix London, used now by British authorities when referring to the city and county. During the 17th century, Derry endured a number of sieges - those of 1641, 1649 and the Great Siege of 1689, when the apprentice boys locked out the invading Jacobite forces. It was 105 days later that relief came when the Williamites broke the boom across the river. In the 18th century, Derry's reputation as a major port grew from the numbers embarking from its docks to emigrate from the county. Its industrial base in the 19th century as a centre for shipbuilding and shirt manufacturing confirmed its status as an important trading port. During World War II, the city was one of the major naval bases for the Allied troops during the Battle of the Atlantic. Derry became a focal point for conflict during the troubles which started in 1969; it was the site of 'Bloody Sunday' in January 1972, when 13 civilians were shot dead by British army paratroopers during a civil rights march - one man died later from his injuries. Derry has been rejuvenated in recent years with major new building developments and community initiatives,.

● **TODAY**

Location north-west corner of the county on the banks of the River Foyle, which divides the city in two - the Waterside and the Cityside - the latter containing the walls of Derry.

Population: 72,334 (+15.37% from 1981 Census).

Tourist Attractions St. Columb's Cathedral (est. 1633, the first Protestant cathedral to be built after the Reformation; its stained glass windows depict scenes from the 1688/9 siege), Tower Museum, Derry (a multi-award winning museum, the building of which is based on the O'Doherty tower, its tunnels date from the 17th century),

Guildhall (built in 1890, it is the seat of local government in Derry), the Diamond (the main square in the city centre, originally made for Sheffield), Foyle Valley Railway Museum (tells of the narrow gauge railway that carried the Donegal, Londonderry and Lough Swilly railways), Harbour Museum (narrates Derry's maritime history; contains a replica of St Columba's curragh in which he sailed to Iona in 563 AD), Derry's city walls and gates (the only intact city walls on the island of Ireland and one of the finest in Europe, these were built between 1613 and 1618, rising to a height of 8 m and extending in places to 9 m in width), the Calgach Centre (on Butcher Street, contains a heritage library and genealogy centre), The Fifth Province (a interpretive centre that brings to life the history of the Celts), St. Eugene's Cathedral (dates from 1873), the craft village (a centre for crafts and design), Derry's political murals and monuments (including the Bloody Sunday memorial in the Bogside).

● **TRANSPORT**
Main Routes: Derry is served by major routes A6-A5-N2 (to Dublin); A6-M2 (to Belfast); A6-A5-A32-A509-N3-N55-N6-N62-N8 (to Cork) N13-N56-N15-N17 (to Galway).
Miles from Dublin (147); Belfast (74); Cork (271); Galway (173).
Nearest Travel Centre (Bus): Foyle Street, Derry Tel 01504-262 261.
Nearest Rail Station: Waterside, Derry. Tel 01504-342 228.
Nearest Airport: City of Derry Airport. Tel 01504-810 784.
Nearest Ferry Port: Belfast (+74 miles); Larne (+71 miles).

County Donegal

"From the Irish Dún na nGall - the fort of the foreigners"

● **GEOGRAPHY**
Province: Ulster
Location: maritime county on the north-west seaboard of the country
County Size: 4th in Ireland
Land area: 1,876 sq. miles
Highest point: Mt Errigal (752 m)
Main Geographical Features: The oldest rock in Ireland (1,700 million years) is found in Donegal on the island of Inishtrahull - it is believed that ice from the south pole would have covered Donegal (Ireland would have been positioned where South Africa is today). The Ice Age (1,700,000 - 13,000 years ago) comprised many periods of warming up and cooling down. The first stage of this accumulation occurred on higher ground. North facing mountain hollows received the least amount of sun and permanent snow patches formed (corries). Features relating to this period include the shapes of Mts Errigal and Muckish. About 35,000 - 13,000 years ago, large masses of ice developed over the Northern half of the country. The scree surrounding the base of Errigal dates back to this time when ice froze in cracks in the rock and loosened stones. Donegal's dramatic coastline includes the highest sea cliffs in Europe at Slieve League (Bunglas cliff is more than 606 m high). Ireland's most northerly point - Malin Head - is located on the Inishowen peninsula. Donegal holds more than a quarter of the entire sandy coast of all of the Irish counties. This coastal system is home to many unique natural habitats and ecological systems. However, some of these beach and dune systems are under threat from natural shoreline erosion and from growing tourism and development pressures. Plans are now afoot with the University of Ulster to monitor some of the more heavily used beaches in the north-west
Main Rivers: Swilly; Finn.
Main Lakes: L Eske; L Derg; L Foyle; L Swilly.
Main Bays: White Strand; Trawbreaga; Mulroy; Gweedore; Inishfree; Rosses; Gweebarra; Loughros More; McSwyne's; Inver; Donegal.
Main Islands: Rathlin O'Birne; Inishfree Upper (pop. 15); Aran (pop. 602); Owey; Gola; Inishbofin (pop. 24); Inishdooey; Inishbeg; Tory (pop. 169); Aughnish (pop. 3); Cruit (pop. 70); Island Roy (pop.15).
Areas of Geographical interest: Glenveagh National Park (contains the Poison Glen and Glenveagh Castle on the shores of Lough Veagh), Ards Forest Park in Creeslough, Slieve League (the location of Europe's highest sea cliffs), Tory Island, Bloody Foreland, Mt Errigal, Horn Head (rich in birdlife and views), Crohy Head (with its unusual cliff formations), Glengesh Pass, Rosguill, Fanad and Inishowen Peninsulas.

● **HISTORY**
Prehistory: Donegal has numerous historical sites, including dolmens, souterrains, and 40 Bronze Age cairns. The most famous of these sites is the Grianan of Aileach, an ancient fortress and sun temple.
Early Christian: Donegal's rich early Christian history centres around St. Column Cille (Columba of Iona) who gave his name to Glencolumcille and founded Derry.
Medieval Donegal played an active role in Ulster's history until 1921. The O'Donnells and the O'Dohertys ruled the area during medieval times with the inaccessibility of Donegal's highlands helping to preserve its Gaelic culture and language. It was the last county to be taken over by the English - Cahir O'Doherty was the last chieftain in Ireland to be defeated in 1608 (but most of Donegal's chieftains fled to Europe in 1607).
Areas of Historical Interest: The High Cross at Carndonagh (believed to be the oldest in Ireland), Doe Castle (16th century castle erected by Scottish mercenaries, overlooking Sheephaven Bay), O'Doherty Castle in Buncrana (built in 1718), Donegal Castle (Donegal town, originally inhabited by the O'Donnells, but taken over by Sir Basil Brooke after 1607), the Obelisk in Donegal town (commemorates the monks who wrote the Annals of the Four Masters - a history of Ireland up to the end of the 16th century), Donegal Railway Heritage Centre (tells the story of the Co.

Donegal Railway, now defunct), Flight of the Earls Centre in Rathmullan, Grianan of Aileach (ancient fortress and sun temple dating back to the 5th century BC and possibly further back, overlooking Lough Swilly and Lough Foyle, it was used up until the 12th century), Assaroe Abbey (est. 1184 by Cistercians), Colmcille Heritage Centre (tells the story of St Colmcille), Dunree Military Fort (built to counter the threat of French invasion in the 1790s), Donegal Historical Society Museum in Rossnowlagh (contains exhibits of local antiquities).

● THE COUNTY

Total Population: 129,944 *(1996)*
Growth rate: 1.5% increase since 1991
County Capital: Lifford
Largest Town: Letterkenny *see profile*
Main Towns: Ballybofey, Ballyshannon, Buncrana, Bundoran, Carndonagh, Dungloe, Letterkenny, Lifford, Moville

Main Business Contact: Donegal County Enterprise Board, County House, The Diamond, Lifford, Co Donegal. Tel 074-72351.
No of Schools: National 176; Secondary 24.
No of Golf Clubs: 17 (9 x 18; 6 x 9; 1 x 26; 1 x 36).
Blue Flag Beaches: 11 - Bundoran, Carrickfinn, Culdaff, Downings Fintra, (Killybegs), Kilahoey (Dunfanaghy), Lisfannon (Fahan), Marble Hill (Rosapenna), Murvagh (Laghy), Portnoo (Naran), Portsalon (Fanad), Rossnowlagh
Other Tourist Attractions: The Folk Village in Glencolumcille, Lakeside Centre at Dunlewy, Lough Derg (known as St. Patrick's Purgatory where pilgrims voyage to purge their souls, est. circa 1150), Glebe House and Gallery (once the home of Derek Hill, house contains Islamic ceramics, works by famous artists such as Jack Yeats, Picasso and Renoir), Donegal Gaeltacht.

Letterkenny Town

"From the Irish Leitir Ceanain - the fair headed hillside"

● HISTORY
Origins: The area was associated with the O'Cannons, although no evidence remains of forts or castles built by the clan. However, Conwall, which is two miles west of Letterkenny, had an early Christian settlement and was a harbour for the area. Rory O'Cannon, was the last chieftain of the O'Cannon clan and he was killed in 1248. Godfrey O'Donnell succeeded him and King of Tir Chonaill, but his reign was short - he was killed in battle in 1257 against Maurice Fitzgerald the Norman lord who had conquered Sligo. The land in the area was granted to Captain Patrick Crawford in 1611, but he was killed during a siege in 1614. His wife remarried Sir George/John Mulbery and it was he who founded the town around 1620, building a Plantation Castle at the shores of Lough Swilly and erecting a market town with 50 thatched houses and a water mill.
Growth: In 1767 in a special County Infirmaries (Amendment) Act, passed to facilitate the establishing of the County Infirmary at Lifford rather than Letterkenny. By 1821, Letterkenny was a thriving market town. The town had constables, conservators of the streets and two enclosures for impounding trespassing animals. However, Letterkenny's growth as one of the region's main administrative centres occurred after partition in 1921 when Derry was incorporated into Northern Ireland. Recent urban renewal has regenerated the town centre. Its Institute of Technology is one of the most technically advanced in the country with a new library.

● TODAY
Location north-east of the county at the mouth of Lough Swilly
Population: 11,996 (+11.8% from 1991 Census).
Tourist Attractions St Eunan's Cathedral (dates back to the late 19th century, its tower dominates the town skyline), the County Museum

● TRANSPORT
Main Routes: Letterkenny is served by major routes N13-N14-A5-N2 (to Dublin); N13-A6-M2 (to Belfast); N13-N56-N15-N17-N4-N61-N6-N62-N8 (to Cork); N13-N56-N15-N17 (to Galway).
Miles from Dublin (148); Belfast (95); Cork (279); Galway (160).
Nearest Travel Centre (Bus): Bus Éireann, Bus Depot, Letterkenny, Co. Donegal. Tel 074-21309.
Nearest Rail Station: Waterside, Derry Tel 01504-342 228.
Nearest Airport: Donegal Airport. Tel 075-48284; City of Derry Airport. Tel 01504-810 784.
Nearest Ferry Port: Larne (+97 miles).

County Down ▬▬▬▬

"From the Irish an Dún - Fort"

● GEOGRAPHY
Province: Ulster
Location: maritime county on the north-east coast of Ireland and is bounded on three sides by water

County Size: 12th in Ireland
Land area: 318 sq. miles
Highest point: Slieve Foy (590 m)
Main Geographical Features: About 35 million years ago, fissures split north-east Ireland and were accompanied by much volcanic activity. There were many lava

flows across the northern part of Ireland, as well as molten-rock intrusions, which created the Mourne Mountains and Carlingford Mountain. The Mourne Mountains now cover the southern part of the county, with 15 peaks rising to 2,000 ft, while in the east, the Ards Peninsula curves around to protect the waters of Strangford Lough, designated Northern Ireland's premier marine nature reserve. Very little trace of dinosaurs are to be found in Ireland; one of the few exceptions to this are the footprints, dating back 225 million years ago, found on Scrabo Hill, just south of Newtownards

Main Rivers: Lagan; Bann.

Main Bays: Strangford Lough; Helen's Bay; Dundrum Bay; Carlingford Lough.

Main Islands: Copeland; Mew; Chapel; Islandmore; Island Taggart; Light House Island.

Areas of Geographical interest: Strangford Lough (Northern Ireland's premier marine nature reserve due to its marine wildlife, which is among the richest in Europe), Tollymore Forest Park (contains several stone follies - a barn decorated as a church, stone cones, gothic arches bridges - giant sequoia trees and wildlife exhibits), Scrabo Country Park, Castlewellan Forest Park (its arboretum at the foot of the Mourne Mtns, is one of the largest tree and shrub collections in Europe), Murlough National Nature Reserve (sand dune system with heath and woodland), Delamont Country Park (a restored walled garden,   with hide and walks), Kilbroney Park in Rostrevor, Silent Valley in Kilkeel (beautiful parkland and huge water reservoirs), Redburn Country Park, Rowallane Gardens (est. 1903 by Hugh Armitage Moore, contains one of Ireland's best plant collections in its Spring, Rock and Walled Gardens and in the National Collection of penstemons).

● HISTORY

Prehistory: Humans have lived around the county's coast for around 9,000 years

Early Christian: St. Comgall founded a monastery in Bangor in A.D. 558, and monks from the monastery set sail to spread Christianity throughout Europe. The importance of this site in the Dark Ages was such that Bangor features on the famous Mappa Mundi, while London does not. The county also has strong associations with St Patrick (as evidenced in the name of Downpatrick town)

Medieval John de Courcy, the Norman who gained control of east Ulster in the 12th century, pledged to bring the remains of Saints Patrick, Brigid and Columbanus to Bangor. Some believe that this pledge was based on the debt the Normans owed the Irish for keeping the Christian faith alive during the Dark Ages. The monastery was revived by St. Malachy in the 12th century but by 1469 was once more in ruins due to the

dissolution of the Irish monasteries in the 1540s. The monastic lands were taken over by the O'Neills of Clandeboye and remained in their domain until they were divided by King James I between Hugh Montgomery and James Hamilton.

English: Parts of Down were already in Scottish or English hands before the plantation of the rest of Ulster in 1610. During the 18th century, the coast from Newcastle to Greencastle became notorious for smuggling, and merchandise disappeared via mountainous trails, such as the Brandy Pad.

Areas of Historical Interest: Ulster Folk & Transport Museum (contains exhibits made in Ulster from early trams to the 1980s De Lorean car), Ballycopeland Windmill (est. 1784, Northern Ireland's only working windmill), Scrabo Tower (built in 1857 to commemorate the third Marquess of Londonderry), Grey Abbey (est. 1193, contains a physick garden with medicinal plants modelled on those which might have been used by medieval monks), Hillsborough Castle and Fort (the fort, est. 1650, was converted in the 18th century), Down Cathedral (contains a 10th century cross), Down County Museum (in Downpatrick's old jailhouse), Inch Abbey (est 1180 by John de Courcy), Mount Stewart House (built by the Londonderry family, the most famous of whom was Lord Castlereagh, its gardens contain plants from every continent; it has Italian, Spanish, Sunken and Shamrock gardens, as well as the Temple of the Winds, which is being restored), Castle Ward (the home of the Bangor's, built in the 1760s, a mixture of Palladian and Gothic styles with parkland, 40 acres of garden and an 18th century formal canal), Kilclief Castle (dating from the 15th century, one of the oldest tower houses in ireland), Legananny Dolmen, Seaforde (an 18th century walled garden with a hornbeam maze and a butterfly house).

● THE COUNTY

Total Population: 454,411 *(e)*

County Capitals: Banbridge, Downpatrick, Hillsborough, Newry, Bangor

Largest Town: Bangor *see profile*

Main Towns: Ballynahinch, Bangor, Banbridge, Castlewellan, Donaghadee, Downpatrick, Dromore, Hillsborough, Holywood, Kilkeel, Newcastle, Newry, Newtownards, Portaferry

Main Business Contact: Ledu The Small Business Agency: 6-7 The Mall, Newry, Co Down. Tel 01693-62955.

No of Golf Clubs: 25 (17 x 18; 6 x 9; 2 x 36).

Blue Flag Beaches / Marinas: 3 - Bangor Marina, Millisle Lagoon, Tyrella Strand

Other Tourist Attractions: Pickie Family Fun Park, Exploris (an aquarium in Portaferry with thousands of marine animal species), Newry Arts Centre.

Bangor Town

"From the Irish Beanna chor - the curved peaks or horns, referring to the headlands at the opening of the bay"

● HISTORY

Origins: Settlements in the area date back to 3000 BC and Bronze age swords (c. 500 BC) have been found nearby. Iron Age Fortifications are also dotted around the land

Growth: Bangor's fame extends back to the 6th century to a monastery founded by St Comgall on the southern shore of Belfast Lough. The monastery was home for a time to the missionaries Columbanus of Bobbio and St Gall (the town of Gallen in Switzerland takes its name from this saint). One rare manuscript survives from this time, The Bangor Antiphonary (now in Milan), which details the early hymns of the time and indicates that Bangor may have been an important school of Latin. The manuscript was probably transferred to Bobbio to ensure its safety during the Viking raids. By the time of St. Malachy (d. 1148), the monastery had become secularised. He restored monastic life and built the first stone building at the site. Such was the fame of the monastery that Bangor was one of the four Irish sites included in a 1300 *mappa mundi* now kept in Hereford Cathedral. By 1469, the monastery had declined, while the 16th century saw the Tudor dissolution of the monasteries. The area was ruled by the O'Neills of Clannaboy, but in the early 17th century, Con O'Neill was arrested and his lands forfeited to the king. Bangor was taken over by a Scots man, James Hamilton, who set about founding the modern town. He built a 'fayre stone house' and added a settlement of 80 stone houses, and planted the area with English and Scots families. Bangor was granted a borough charter in 1613. The town was disrupted in 1641 by a rebellion of the native Irish in Ulster. In 1710, the town passed from the Hamiltons to the Wards of Castle Ward, who dominated it for the next 250 years. In the 1780s, Colonel Robert Ward extended the town's harbour facilities and introduced the cotton industry which lasted until the 1850s. The town developed into a Victorian seaside resort town when cheap transport in the way of a new railway, built in 1865, enabled the working masses from Belfast to travel. Bangor capitalised on this by constructing piers, promenades, and yacht clubs. The railway also allowed the more wealthier middle classes to live in Bangor and commute to Belfast. This brought about better buildings and water, sanitation and lighting services. In 1864, the town elected its first town commissioners who administered the town until 1899, when the authority became an urban district council. The town reclaimed its status as a borough in 1927. The town underwent a period of rejuvenation in the 1930s, and the population swelled to 14,000, but by the end of World War II, it had become more of a dormitory town for Belfast. In 1973, it lost its borough status when the local government was re-organised all over Northern Ireland. Bangor is still a seaside resort town with a renowned marina and is developing its natural facilities through the Seafront Development Scheme.

● **TODAY**
Location north county Down on the top part of the Ards Peninsula, at the mouth of Helen's Bay in Belfast Lough
Population: 52,437 (+12.5% from 1981 Census).
Tourist Attractions Abbey St (the old stone wall of which is known as Malachy's wall, referring to St Malachy's church which stood in the area), the Town Hall (initially the site of James Jamilton's house, then rebuilt in 1852 as Bangor Castle), the Tower and Tower house (built in 1637 by James Hamilton as a Custom house and watchtower), Bangor Grammar School (initially built in 1856 as Bangor Endowed School with a bequest from Colonel Robert Ward), Bangor Parish Church (built in 1882).

● **TRANSPORT**
Main Routes: Bangor is served by major routes A2-M1-A1-N1-M1-N1 (to Dublin); A2 (to Belfast); A2 -M1-A1-N1-N52-N80-N8 (to Cork); A2-M1-A3-N12-N54-N3-N55-N6-N18 (to Galway).
Miles from Dublin (118); Belfast (13); Cork (278); Galway (204).
Nearest Travel Centre (Bus): Bangor. Tel 01247-271143.
Rail Station: Bangor. Tel 01247-270141.
Nearest Airport: Belfast City Airport. Tel 01232-734828; Belfast International Airport. Tel 01849-484848.
Nearest Ferry Port: Belfast (+13 miles); Larne (+34 miles).

County Dublin

"From the Irish Dubh Linn - black pool"
● **GEOGRAPHY**
Province: Leinster
Location: maritime county on the east coast beside the Irish Sea
County Size: 27th in Ireland
Land area: 49 sq. miles (*Dun Laoghaire/Rathdown*), 173 sq. miles *(Fingal)*, 86 sq. miles *(South Dublin)*
Highest point: Kippure Mtn (752 m)
Main Geographical Features: It could be described, in geological terms, as the seaward extension of the central limestone plain lying to the west. The county is bounded by granite mountains in the south and rich pastureland, bordered by river estuaries and a long sandy coast in the north.
Main Rivers: Liffey; Tolka; Dodder; (Royal Canal,

Grand Canal).
Main Bays: Dublin; Carrigeen; Killiney.
Main Islands: St Patrick's; Lambay (pop. 8); Ireland's Eye; Dalkey; North Bull (pop. 22).
Areas of Geographical interest: Phoenix Park (largest city park in Europe), *Dun Laoghaire/Rathdown:* Booterstown Salt Marsh, Fernhill private gardens in Sandyford, the Dublin Mountains, Killiney Hill, *Fingal:* Botanical Gardens in Glasnevin, Howth Head and Peninsula (provides a panoramic view of Dublin Bay), Howth Castle Gardens (boasts over 2,000 rhododendron varieties), Lambay Island (a noted bird sanctuary), Rush and Skerries seaside resorts. *South Dublin:* Corkagh Regional Park (Clondalkin), Dodder Valley Linear Park (Firhouse), Griffeen Valley Park (Lucan), Sean Walsh Memorial Park, Tymon Regional Park

(Greenhills), the Dublin Mountains.

● HISTORY

Early Christian: Dublin county had a strong early Christian presence; there are well-preserved round towers in Clondalkin and Swords, and monastic ruins can be found at Lusk, Tallaght, Newcastle and Saggart. Recent discoveries this year at an archaeological dig in Dublin's Temple Bar have yielded the pre-Viking remains of 'a strange house' - the closest parallels to which are Anglo-Saxon habitations in England, indicating the English may have been in Ireland much earlier than previously thought.

Medieval The Vikings established a major settlement in Dublin, as reflected in town names such as Howth and the findings at Wood Quay in Dublin, but were finally defeated by Brian Boru at the Battle of Clontarf in Dublin on Good Friday, 1014. The county was part of the Norman Pale from the 12th to the 16th century.

English: Its English past is reflected in the many stately homes and gardens and the model villages found throughout the county. However, Dublin has always been a hotbed of Irish political activity - the Easter 1916 Rising occurred here and paved the way for Irish Independence - and it was in Dublin that most Irish literary and artistic movements began and flourished.

Areas of Historical Interest: *Dun Laoghaire/ Rathdown:* Dalkey Castle and Heritage Centre, Cabinteely House & Park, The Old Oratory of the Sacred Heart Convent in Dun Laoghaire, Dun Laoghaire (the site of Ireland's first railway in 1831 and the National Maritime Museum of Ireland), the James Joyce Museum at Sandycove Martello Tower. *Fingal:* Lusk Heritage Centre, Malahide Castle and the Fry Model Railway Museum, Marino Casino (a small folly house built in the 18th century), Marino Crescent (birthplace of Bram Stoker, the author of *Dracula*), Newbridge House (an important Georgian mansion in Donabate, built in 1737 by renowned architect Richard Castle), Portrane House (once the home of Esther Johnson - Jonathan Swift's lover), Royal Hospital

Kilmainham *South Dublin:* Montpelier Hill (the location of the Hell Fire Club, where the first Earl of Rosse conducted Satanic rites with his friends in the 18th century), Rathfarnham Castle, Grange Castle (Kilcarbery).

● THE COUNTY

Total Population: excl. the city - 189,999 *(Dun Laoghaire/Rathdown);* 167,683 *(Fingal);* 218,728 - a 4.8% increase since 1991 *(South Dublin).* Roughly one-third of the Republic of Ireland's population now live in the Dublin region *(1996)*

Growth rate: 2.5% increase since 1991*(Dun Laoghaire/Rathdown);* 9.8% increase *(Fingal),* 4.8% increase *(South Dublin).*

County Capital: Dublin *see profile*

Main Towns: *Dun Laoghaire/Rathdown* - Blackrock, Dalkey, Dundrum, Dun Laoghaire, Shankhill and Stillorgan; *Fingal* - Balbriggan, Blanchardstown, Malahide, Skerries and Swords; *South Dublin* - Brittas, Clondalkin, Greenhills, Killakee, Lucan, Rathcoole, Rathfarnham, Saggart, Tallaght, Terenure

Main Business Contact: Dublin City Enterprise Board: 17 Eustace Street, D2. Tel 01-677 6068.

Fingal County Enterprise Board: Upper Floor Office Suite, Mainscourt, 23 Main Street, Swords, Co. Dublin. Tel 01-890 0800.

South Dublin County Enterprise Board: No 3 Village Square, Old Bawn Road, Tallaght, Dublin 4. Tel 01-405 7073.

Dun Laoghaire/Rathdown County Enterprise Board: Dundrum Office Park, Main Street, Dundrum, Dublin 16. Tel 01-205 1100.

No of Schools: National 462; Secondary 188.

No of Golf Clubs: 32 in county (24 x 18; 3 x 9; 1 x 23; 4 x 27), 23 in City (10 x 18; 8 x 9; 1 x 20; 1 x 24; 3 x 36).

Blue Flag Beaches: 2 - Seapoint, Killiney.

Other Tourist Attractions: *Dun Laoghaire/Rathdown:* Leopardstown Racecourse, Marlay Park & Craft Centre, Lambert Puppet Theatre & Museum in Monkstown. *Fingal:* Dunsink Observatory,

Dublin City

"From the Irish Baile Átha Cliath - *the town of the hurdle ford, which refers to barriers erected to prevent flooding.*

● HISTORY

Origins: Evidence of human habitation in the area dates back millennia.

Growth: The city's growth as an urban centre began when the Vikings sailed in circa 841, attacking monastic sites and establishing settlements: the earliest evidence of Viking habitation was that of a large burial ground in Islandbridge in the 19th century. Europe's largest city excavation took place in the old medieval quarter of the city during the 1960s, 1970s and 1980s, revealing a great wealth of detail about the Vikings. They contributed greatly to the urbanisation of Ireland, introducing trade, a monetary system, shipbuilding and metalworking into the area. There was an extensive trade with the rest of the Viking world which extended from the Baltic Sea through central Europe to Iceland and beyond. The Vikings were defeated by Brian Boru at Clontarf in 1014 and subsequently integrated with the native Irish. The Normans conquered Dublin, with King Henry II during 1171–72, beginning an era of 700 years of foreign control. The specialisation of crafts and the formation of guilds in the city dates to this time. The Normans built a castle around the area where Dublin Castle now stands and established the Pale around the eastern part of Leinster with Dublin as the seat of Norman Power. In the 18th century, the town was moulded into a Georgian City and became one of the most elegant and cosmopolitan cities of its day. Handel first performed the Messiah in Dublin in 1742. Dublin's reign as a cosmopolitan centre ended in 1800 with the Act of Union, when Dublin ceased to be a political force. The 19th century saw increasing pressure to bring about Home Rule. This culminated in the 1916 Rising in Dublin, during which British gun boats sailed up the Liffey and bombed the city. The War of Independence, along with the internecine turmoil that followed it, left Dublin badly damaged. The city changed very little until the 1960s, when moves were made to address the conditions of the people who lived in Dublin's inner city tenements.

● **TODAY**
Location In the Eastern part of the county it is set in Dublin Bay at the confluence of the Liffey, Dodder, Poddle and Tolka Rivers. The Liffey divides the city into two sides: the north side and the south side.
Population: 952,692 (+2.5% from 1991 Census).
Tourist Attractions St Stephen's Green, Merrion Square, Dublin Zoo (est. 1830 - the 3rd oldest zoo in the world), the Phoenix Park (the biggest urban park in Europe, est. 1662), Waterways Visitor Centre on Grand Canal Quay, Fitzwilliam Square, Iveagh Gardens, the Brazen Head (Ireland's oldest pub), Christ Church Cathedral (built in 1038 by the Danish King Sitric of Dublin, most of the church dates back to Norman times), St. Audoen's Church (one of Ireland's oldest surviving medieval parish churches), St. Michan's Church (built in 1686 and containing naturally mumified bodies and the organ on which Handel is reputed to have played), St. Patrick's Cathedral, Leinster House (how the home of the Oireachtas, initially built for the Duke of Leinster in 1745), Dublin Castle (containing magnificent state apartments), Dublinia (a permanent multi-media exhibition on Dublin's past), Dublin Writers Museum in Parnell Square, the General Post Office (where bullet holes from the 1916 Rising can still be seen), the Mansion House (built in 1710 on Dawson Street), the Guinness Brewery, Kilmainham Gaol (where Ireland's revolutionaries were held and executed in 1916), the National Library (built in 1890 to house the collection of the Royal Dublin Society), the National Museum of Ireland (containing a treasury of Irish gold and silver dating from thousands of years ago, and Viking, Egyptian and Prehistoric exhibitions) at Collins Barracks and Kildare Street, Dublin's Viking Adventure, the Natural History Museum, Trinity College (Ireland's oldest university, built in 1592, and home to the Book of Kells, written in AD 806), Smithfield Market, the Shaw Birthplace (Synge Street, home of the playwright George Bernard Shaw), The Irish Jewish Museum (off Sth Circular Road), City Hall (the meeting place of Dublin Corporation), Dublin Civic Museum, Powerscourt Townhouse (originally the home of Viscount Powerscourt, now a shopping centre), Temple Bar, Custom House, Four Courts, Chester Beatty Library.

● **TRANSPORT**
Main Routes: Dublin is served by major routes M1-N1-M1-N1-A1-M1 (to Belfast); N7-N8 (to Cork); N4-N6-N18 (to Galway).
Miles from Belfast (103); Cork (159); Galway (135).
Nearest Travel Centre (Bus): Busaras, Store Street, Dublin 1. Tel 01-836 6111.
Main Railway Station: Connolly Station, Amien Street, Dublin 1. Tel 01-836 3333.
Nearest Airport: Dublin Airport. Tel 01-814 1111.
Nearest Ferry Port: Dublin; Rosslare (+96 miles).

County Fermanagh

"From the Irish Fear Manach *- the men of Manach"*

● **GEOGRAPHY**
Province: Ulster
Location: an inland county in the north-west of the island
County Size: 25th in Ireland
Land area: 647 sq. miles
Highest point: Cuilcagh Mtn (667 m)
Main Geographical Features: The length of the county is spanned by the Erne River and Lake system, which stretches southwards for 50 miles. The system has recently been joined to the River Shannon via the Shannon-Erne Waterway. Both systems were previously linked by a canal, constructed in 1860. However, it closed to commercial traffic after nine years with the arrival of steam and railways. The county is also home to the extensive Marble Arch cave system, which can be navigated by boat during the drier seasons
Main Rivers: Erne.
Main Lakes: Lower Lough Erne; Upper Lough Erne; L Melvin; L Macnean Upper; L Macnean Lower.
Areas of Geographical interest: Castle Archdale Country Park in Irvinestown, Marble Arch Caves (one of the finest underground cave systems in the country with spectacular stalactites and stalagmites), Drum Manor

Forest Park in Cookstown, Florencecourt Forest Park, Lough Navar Forest Park and scenic drive (offers incomparable views of Lower Lough Erne), Explore Erne Exhibition (14,000 - tells how Lough Erne was formed), Crom Estate (contains 1,900 acres of woods, lakes and farmland supporting a wide diversity of wildlife, designed initially in 1838 by William Sawrey Gilpin, a famous English landscape designer).

● **HISTORY**
Prehistory: Fermanagh's ancient heritage is revealed on the islands of its lakes and the Burren area near Belcoo, an area rich in archaeological monuments, such as portal tombs, wedge tombs and a court tomb. On Boa Island, there are two Celtic Janus (two-faced) statues, possibly dating from the first century
Early Christian: This area also reveals evidence of the county's early Christian Heritage: White Island is home to seven enigmatic statues, housed in an early Christian church; while Devenish Island contains a large monastic ruin, dating back to the sixth century. The monastery holds a 12th-century round tower, which monks used for spotting possible attackers.
Medieval During medieval times, the Maguires held sway over the Fermanagh region and were said to

police the Erne with a private navy of 1,500 boats. **English:** The Maguire's lands were confiscated after the 17th century wars and settled by English and Scottish planters. The many stately homes in the county date from this time onwards.

Areas of Historical Interest: Belleek Pottery (established in 1857 by John Caldwell Bloomfield, the factory is Ireland's oldest parian china factory), Enniskillen Castle, Castle Coole (home to the Earls of Belmore, the finest of the National Trust houses in Northern Ireland, completed in 1798 with a Palladian facade, a colony of greylag geese, woods designed by Ireland's most important landscape gardeners - W King and James Frazer), White Island and Devenish Island's ancient ruins.

● **THE COUNTY**

Total Population: 54,033 *(e)*
County Capital and Largest Town: Enniskillen *see profile*
Main Towns: Irvinestown, Lisnaskea and Roslea.
Main Business Contact: Ledu The Small Business Agency: Ledu House, Upper Galwally, Belfast. Tel 01232-491 031.
No of Golf Clubs: 2 (2 x 18).
Other Tourist Attractions: Fermanagh Crystal, The Sheelin Antique Irish Lace Museum (contains exhibits, dating from 1850–1900, of the five types of lace made in Ireland: Youghal Needlelace, Inishmacsaint Needlelace, Crochet, Limerick lace and Carrickmacross Lace).

Enniskillen Town

"From the Irish Inis Ceithleann - Ceithle's island"

● **HISTORY**

Origins The town emerged with the growth of Enniskillen Castle, which dates back to the 15th century. Once the medieval stronghold of the Maguire chieftains, it houses a heritage centre and the Inniskilling Regimental Museum. With the arrival and the British planters, the town became a garrison town. It developed into a market town for the area and a centre for fishing and boating Although Enniskillen was marred by the IRA bomb which killed 11 people in 1987, it continues to be a thriving market and tourism centre in the area.

● **TODAY**

Location at the centre of Co Fermanagh, on an island between Upper and Lower Lough Erne.
Population: 11,436 (+9.6% since 1981 Census).
Tourist Attractions Enniskillen Castle, Portora Royal School (est. 1618, the school has a place in Irish literary history as the playwrights Oscar Wilde and Samuel Beckett both attended), Cole monument (provides views of the surrounding lakes), the Watergate and Arcaded Barracks (twin turreted towers overlooking the river), the Museum of the Royal Inniskilling Fusiliers, Florence Court House & Gardens (one of the most important 18th-century houses in the country, built by the earls of Enniskillen, its graceful Rococo plasterwork, dating to the mid-18th century, it is known as the home of the Irish Yew, discovered *c.* 1760), Enniskillen Craft and Design Centre.

● **TRANSPORT**

Main Routes: Enniskillen is served by major routes A509-N3 (to Dublin); A4-M1-A3-M1 (to Belfast); A4-A509-N3-N55-N6-N62-N8 (to Cork); A4-N16-N-15-N17 (to Galway).
Miles from Dublin (109); Belfast (86); Cork (224); Galway (114).
Nearest Travel Centre (Bus): Enniskillen. Tel 01365-322 633.
Nearest Rail Station: Sligo. Tel 071-69888.
Nearest Airport: City of Derry Airport. Tel 01504-810 784; Belfast City Airport. Tel 01232-734828; Belfast International Airport. Tel 01849-484848.
Nearest Ferry Port: Belfast (+86 miles); Larne (+107 miles).

County Galway

"From the Irish Abhainn na Gaillimhe - the Galway river, named after Galvia, a mythological princess who drowned in the river.

● **GEOGRAPHY**

Province: Connacht
Location: maritime county on the west coast
County Size: 2nd in Ireland
Land area: 2,349.79 sq. miles
Highest point: Benbaun (727 m)
Main Geographical Features: Large mountain ranges such as the Twelve Bens and the Maamturks fortify the

west coast of the county. Its heavily indented Atlantic coastline provides a myriad of wide bays, sheltered harbours, deep fjords and island clusters. Lough Corrib divides the county in two - the fertile farmlands in the east, and mountainous Connemara, heartland of the Irish language, in the west. The prevailing tropical weathering of 35 million years ago resulted in the mineral ores in the limestone forming complex hydrated compounds - the valuable Lead and Zinc mine at Tynagh, Co. Galway, dates to this period. The Ice Age (1,700,000 - 13,000 years ago) was not a period of continuous ice; a wide variety of surface land features in

Ireland date to this time. At times, general ice sheets covered most of the land, and glaciers deposited unsorted material. Discontinuities in the ice allowed material to gather. This material was subsequently moulded into ovoid masses - *drumlins* - in the direction of the ice flow. Between Roundstone and Slyne Head in Connemara great areas of ice-scoured rock is found with occasional drumlins. Finds in Gort, Co. Galway from 425,000 - 300,000 years ago, show that pine, spruce, hazel, birch and certain herbs were common in this area.

Main Rivers: Suck; Owenglin; Corrib; Cregg; Clare.

Main Lakes: L Mask; L Corrib.

Main Bays: Galway; Mannin; Betraghboy; Kilkieran.

Main Islands: Aran Islands - Inishmore (pop. 838), Inishmaan (pop. 191), Inisheer (pop. 274); Inishbofin (pop. 200); Inishshark; Inishgort; Omey (pop. 4); Lettermullan (pop. 204); Mweenish (pop. 150); Rossroe (pop. 23); Rusheennacholla (pop. 3); Annaghuaan (pop. 104); Furnace (pop. 59); Gorumna (pop. 1,057); Illaunmore (pop. 1); Inchaughaun (pop. 3); Inishbarra (pop. 1); Inisheltsa; Inishnee (pop. 33); Inishtravin (pop. 3); Lettermore (pop. 503).

Areas of Geographical interest: Connemara National Park (takes in the bogs, mountains and coastline of the Connemara region and holds a diverse range of flora and fauna, incl. otters, falcons, reed deer and grey seals), the Aran Islands (known for their strong Irish culture, dry-stone walls and prehistoric stone forts), Killary Harbour (Ireland's best-known fjord), Lough Corrib (known as an angler's paradise, the lake is the second biggest on the island of Ireland and is dotted with islands).

● **HISTORY**

Prehistory: Humans first inhabited the Galway Region over 5,000 years ago. Stone monuments on the Aran Islands date back as far as 2000 BC and include the famous Dun Aengus, a stone fort situated at the edge of a sea cliff and dating back to around the time of Christ. Another monumental find from the area is the Turoe Stone, one metre high and one of the finest examples of the curvilinear Celtic designs of the 3rd century BC La Tène style, which would have been brought over from the continent.

Early Christian: With the arrival of Christianity, monasteries were built at Roscam, Inchagoill Island on L. Corrib and Annaghdown.

Medieval These monasteries attracted the attentions of the Vikings and Roscam was raided in 830. Around 1232, Richard de Burgo, a Norman Baron, attacked Connacht. Galway city expanded with the arrival of English, Welsh and Flemish settlers, but the native Irish regained their power as the Normans adopted the Irish language and tradition. Around this time, 14 prominent merchant families came to power and held this position until Cromwell's attack on the county. Elsewhere, continental orders established monasteries around the county, incl. one at Portumna, (est. *c.*1414 by the Dominicans).

English: The Irish in Galway were finally routed at the Battle of Aughrim in 1691. Following this defeat, the native population lost most of their lands and suffered under the penal laws. They endured further suffering during the Great Famine and the population was decimated. Towards the close of the 19th century, Galway became the centre of the the Irish Literary Renaissance. Lady Gregory's home at Coole Park attracted many writers, and Lady Gregory herself, along with Yeats and Synge founded the Abbey Theatre in Dublin 1904.

Areas of Historical Interest: Dún Aenghus on Inishmore (the Bronze Age fort, protected by chevaux de frize - razor sharp stones put in at an angle), Aughrim Interpretative Centre, Athenry Castle, Aughnanure Castle (built by the O'Flaherty's who controlled west Connacht from the 13th to the 16th centuries), Bunowen Castle (once the home of the pirate queen, Grace O'Malley), Dunguaire Castle (now used for medieval banquets), Portumna Castle and Forest Park (built in the early 17th century for the de Burgo family), Claregalway Abbey), Kylemore Abbey (Gothic castle built for the wife of Mitchell Henry, it became the home of the Benedictine nuns fleeing the continent during WWI and is now a girls' boarding school), Coole Park (the home of Lady Gregory and birthplace of the Irish Literary Renaissance), Derrigimlagh Bog (the location of Marconi's 1907 telegraph station and landing site for Alcock and Brown in 1919 after their transatlantic flight), Rosmuck (with its memorial cottage in honour of 1916 Rebellion leader Padraig Pearse), Thoor Ballylee (the home of W.B. Yeats and inspiration for his poems in 'The Tower'), Clonfert Cathedral (built on a site founded by St Brendan in AD 563, the medieval Cathedral is famed for its heavily decorated Romanesque arches), the ruined Martello Tower at Cleggan Hill.

● **THE COUNTY**

Total Population: 131,613 (excl. Galway city) *(1996)*

Growth rate: 1.6% increase since 1991

County Capital and Largest Town: Galway *see profile*

Main Towns: Ballinasloe, Loughrea, Tuam

Main Business Contact: Galway City/County Enterprise Board: Wood Quay Court, Wood Quay, Galway. Tel 091-565 269.

No of Schools: National 238; Secondary 48.

No of Golf Clubs: 17 (11 x 18; 5 x 9; 1 x 27).

Blue Flag Beaches: 5 - Traught (Kinvara), Tra na mBan (An Spideal), Tra an Doilin (An Cheathru Rua), Cill Mhuirbhigh (Inishmore, Aran Islands), Loughrea Bathing Place

Other Tourist Attractions: Dan O'Hara's Homestead in the Connemara Heritage & History Centre, the Tropical Butterfly Centre in Costelloe.

Galway City

See county name

● HISTORY

Origins: Settlements had been established around the area for millenia, As far back as 1191, the Annals of Loch Cé record the finding of an axe and spearhead in the River. In medieval times, the city was an Anglo-Norman stronghold surrounded by warring Gaelic chieftains.

Growth: Galway as a city was already 500 years old when it was granted its charter in 1484 by Richard III. It had already assumed a commercial importance - Christopher Columbus visited the city while trading from Lisbon in 1477. Around this time 14 wealthy merchant families ruled the city, earning Galway the name of the 'City of the Tribes'. These families were proud of their status and created their own special coat of arms, often without heraldic authority, which they had carved on to the facades of their premises. The tribes held their position for the next 170 years, until 1651 when a Cromwellian force, under Sir Charles Coote, besieged the city. Galway surrendered, and the tribes lost all their power. Although Irish Catholics temporarily regained the city, they soon lost this control following the Battle of Aughrim. During the 18th century, Galway declined in status and in 1841, lost its classification as a city. Nonetheless, it still maintained strong trading links and many industries flourished. Queen's College, Galway, was established in 1845. This was the time of the Great Famine, when many thousands died in the city and its environs. By 1899, the population of Galway had been halved. In 1916, a rising against the British was instigated by Liam Mellowes in the city but failed. The fortunes of the city began to look up in the 1960s, with the expansion of industry and tourism in the country. Galway City is now one of the fastest growing cities in Europe and has a young population by virtue of its third-level institutes and thriving industries. At the centre of its renowned arts scene is the Druid Theatre (which recently celebrated its 25th anniversary), one of Ireland's best known theatrical exports - it won international acclaim in 1998 for its production of *The Beauty Queen of Leenane.*

● TODAY

Location set at the entrance to Galway Bay at the western edge of the county, on the R. Corrib
Population: 57,363 (+12.8% from 1991 Census)
Tourist Attractions Kennedy Park-Eyre Square is the focus point of the city centre, it contains the Quincentennial fountain and the celebrated sculpture of the Galway hooker boat along with statues of Padraig Ó Conaire - beheaded this year - and Liam Mellowes; the Browne Doorway (a 17th century entrance to a mansion in Abbeygate Street) the Claddagh district, the leaping salmon statue at the Salmon Weir Bridge, Leisureland, the Lynch Memorial Window, Nora Barnacle House Museum, the restored Shoemaker and Penrice Towers, Salthill (one of Ireland's busiest seaside resorts), Shop Street (a medieval street that contains the 15th-century Lynch's Castle), Siamsa na Gaillimhe - the Spanish Arch, St. Nicholas Collegiate Church (Galway's most intact medieval building, dating to 1320, which Christopher Columbus supposedly visited), Tí Neachtain (now a pub, but once the home of Humanity Dick, an 18th century MP who advocated for the protection of animals).

● TRANSPORT

Main Routes: Galway is served by major routes N18-N6-N4 (to Dublin); N18-N6-N55-N54-N2-A3-M1 (to Belfast); N18-N20 (to Cork); N17 (to Sligo).
Miles from Dublin (136); Belfast (190); Cork (120); Sligo (86).
Nearest Travel Centre (Bus): Bus Éireann, Ceannt Station, Eyre Square, Galway. Tel 091-562 000.
Nearest Rail Station: Ceannt Station, Eyre Square. Tel 091-561 444.
Nearest Airport: Galway Airport (Carnmore). Tel 091-755 569; Knock International Airport. Tel 094-67222; Shannon Airport. Tel 061-471 444.
Nearest Ferry Port: Cork (+120 miles); Dublin (+136 miles).

County Kerry

"From the Irish Ciarraí *- Ciar's People, referring to an early Celtic tribe who settled in the area."*

● GEOGRAPHY
Province: Munster
Location: maritime county on the south-west of Ireland on the Atlantic seaboard.
County Size: 5th in Ireland
Land area: 1,815.16 sq. miles
Highest point: Carrauntohill (1041 m) - around 250 million years ago, Carrauntoohill would probably have

been 3000m in height, as compared to its current height, due to the erosion which occurred in the country around this time
Main Geographical Features: A great ridge of mountains dominates the county, dividing it into the open countryside of the north and east, which extends into Ireland's Golden Vale, and the mountainous western region that consists of three jutting peninsulas. Kerry is home to Ireland's highest mountains and most westerly point. A very rare fossil (only five others recorded in the world), of a four-footed amphibian in pressure cleaved

slate formed 350 million years ago was found in Valentia, Co. Kerry. The prevailing tropical weathering of 35 million years ago had huge effects on the Irish landscape. Most of the chalk deposited in Ireland was eroded, the one of the few exceptions being scattered deposits lying in karstic sinkholes, the only evidence of which can be found near Farranfore in Kerry. The Ice Age (1,700,000 - 13,000 years ago) consisted of periods of warming up and cooling down. A wide variety of surface land features in Ireland date to this time. The first stage of this accumulation occurred on higher ground. North-facing mountain hollows received the least amount of sun and permanent snow patches formed (corries). The glaciers extending from these corries followed existing valleys and with their surface layer of rocks wore the V-shaped valleys into U-shaped ones. Features relating to this period include the shape Mt Brandon, as well as the Gap of Dunloe and Upper lake at Killarney, which are all ice-scoured. Periglacial deposits (dating back 122,000 - 100,000 years ago) were found on top of peaty muds which was resting on a raised beach and a wave-cut shoreline near Fenit in Co. Kerry. It is likely that this was the deposits of an independent icecap in the Kerry Mountains. Similar exposures are found in Dingle and Ballybunion. Again, 35,000 - 13,000 years ago, when large masses of ice developed over the Northern half of the country, there were independent ice caps once more in Kerry. These ice masses left drumlins in their wake again over the south-west. The Gulf Stream washes the Kerry coast and brings with it several species of sub-tropical, marine animals

Main Rivers: Kenmare; Feale; Galey; Inny; Maine; Laune; Flesk.

Main Lakes: Currane; Caragh; Leane.

Main Bays: Tralee; Brandon; Dingle; St Finan's; Ballinskelligs.

Main Islands: Carrig (pop. 13); Great Blasket Island; Inishvickillane; Beginish (pop. 2); Valencia (pop. 676); Puffin; Great Skellig (pop. 4); Rossmore (pop. 8); Ormond's; Dinish; Deenish; Scariff; Tarbert (pop. 13).

Areas of Geographical interest: Ring of Kerry, Killarney National Park, Crag Cave (located in Castleisland), Carrauntuohill (Ireland's highest mountain), Dingle (home of Fungi the Dolphin and Dingle Sea Life Centre.

● **HISTORY**

Prehistory: Kerry's prehistoric peoples travelled across the county's peninsulas, seeking mineral treasures. Copper was extracted here and sent to Spain some 4,000 years ago. The great forts and castles of the Celtic races and later groups are still highly visible in the county

Early Christian: The county is home to many fine early Christian sites, including the early Christian monastery on the Skellig Islands and the Gallarus Oratory, which at more than 1,000 years old is the oldest church in Ireland and which is structurally intact.

Medieval Although the Normans arrived in the county in the 13th century, it was not until the wars of the 16th and 17th centuries that the county's native Irish came under direct threat.

English: The county was formally demarcated in 1606. Nonetheless, it continued to maintain its unique and rich Irish culture. The Irish language is still spoken here, no doubt helped by the relative isolation imposed by the county's rugged mountains.

Areas of Historical Interest: Derrynane National Park (the home of Daniel O'Connell), National Transport Museum in Killarney.

● **THE COUNTY**

Total Population: 126,130 *(1996)*

Growth rate: 3.5% increase since 1991

County Capital and Largest Town: Tralee *see profile*

Main Towns: Ballybunion, Castleisland, Cahirciveen, Dingle, Kenmare, Killarney, Killorglin, Listowel.

Main Business Contact: Kerry County Enterprise Board: County Buildings, Ratass, Tralee, Co. Kerry. Tel 066-21111.

No of Schools: National 147; Secondary 32.

No of Golf Clubs: 17 (7 x 18; 8 x 9; 1 x 36; 1 x 54).

Blue Flag Beaches: 13 - Ballinskelligs, Ballybunion Nth, Ballybunion Sth, Ballyheigue, Banna (Ardfert), Derrynane (Caherdaniel), Fenit, Inch, Kells, Maherabeg (Castlegregory), Rossbeigh (Glenbeigh), Ventry, White Strand (Caherciveen)

Other Tourist Attractions: Tralee's Aqua Dome, Muckross House and Gardens, Blennerville Windmill.

Tralee Town

"From the Irish Trá Lí - the strand on the (river) Lee"

● **HISTORY**

Origins: Tralee originally formed part of the ancient kingdom of 'Ciar' which dates from the first century. **Growth:** By the 12th century Tralee had grown as a fortified town and was the seat of the Earls of Desmond. The Dominican monastery was founded in 1213. Tralee is now an important gateway for local tourism and enjoys a highly developed business and transport infrastructure with a good telecommunications network, making it the commercial and administrative centre of County Kerry. It has the third highest participation rate in higher education in the country and its Institute of Technology, established in 1977, is developing a new campus, adjoining the site of the new Kerry Technology Park. Tralee is home to Siamsa Tire (the National Folk Theatre of Ireland) and the Rose of Tralee Festival.

● **TODAY**

Location set on the corner of the Dingle Peninsula on the north west coast of Kerry, at the mouth of Tralee Bay, at the foot of the Slieve Mish Mountains

Population: 19,950 (+11.6% from 1991 Census).
Tourist Attractions The multi-million pound Aqua Dome for indoor water activities, the Geraldine experience (recounting Tralee's medieval past) and county museum (located in the Ashe memorial hall), Horse racing and greyhound tracks, the Gaelic football stadium, the Blennerville Windmill (just outside the town).

● **TRANSPORT**
Main Routes: Tralee is served by major routes N21-N7-M7-N7 (to Dublin); N21-N7-N52-A1-M1 (to Belfast); N22 (to Cork); N21-N18 (to Galway).
Miles from Dublin (190); Belfast (275); Cork (73); Galway (126).
Main Nearest Travel Centre (Bus): Bus Éireann, Casement Station, Tralee, Co. Kerry. Tel 066-23566.
Nearest Rail Station: Tralee. Tel 066-7123 522.
Nearest Airport: Kerry Airport, Farranfore, Co Kerry. Tel 066-976 4644; Shannon Airport. Tel 061-471 444.
Nearest Ferry Port: Cork (+73 miles).

County Kildare

"From the Irish Cill Dara - Church of the Oak Tree, alluding to St. Brigid's monastery beneath an oak tree"

● **GEOGRAPHY**
Province: Leinster
Location: inland county in the east of the country
County Size: 24th in Ireland
Land area: 654 sq. miles
Highest point: Dunmurry (234 m)
Main Geographical Features: Part of the Great Central Plain, a limestone base with tracts of low lying peat land, the vast Bog of Allen touches the west of the county, and farmland, Kildare is bounded by the Wicklow mountain range to the east, the foothills of which extend westwards to meet the unique plain known as the Curragh, an area renowned for horse racing, training and breeding. Kildare's river valleys, bogs, woodlands and canals are the preserve of wild fowl, birds and animals, with nature reserves at Pollardstown and Ballinafagh.
Main Waterways: Grand Canal; Blackwater; Royal Canal; Liffey; Barrow.
Areas of Geographical interest: The Curragh, Japanese Gardens in Tully, Peatland World Visitor Centre in Lullymore,

● **HISTORY**
Prehistory: evidence of raths, earthworks and standing stones is found around the Curragh.
Early Christian: This era is marked by Kildare's ties to St. Brigid, the sixth century saint who is one of the three patrons of Ireland.
Medieval The county was the stronghold of the FitzGeralds. They increased their wealth and influence with a combination of political savvy and expedient marriages, with their power reaching its height during the time of Garret Mór, the 8th Earl, known as the 'Great Earl'. The base of power he created lasted until 1534 and the rebellion of his grandson, Silken Thomas. He fought both the Irish and English, and travelled as far as Connacht and Ulster to do battle. He was the first person to use guns in Ireland (1489). His learning was reflected in the comprehensive library of English, French, Latin and Irish books housed at Maynooth Castle. The Great Earl was a Yorkist supporter, and, following the victory of the Lancastrians in the War of the Roses, he supported the claims of the Pretenders to the English throne. Although arrested for treason he was restored to power by Henry VII in 1496 and remained one of Ireland's most powerful men until his death in 1513. Garret Óg succeeded him as Earl of Kildare and Chief Governor and continued to rule in his father's style, until 1519, when Henry VIII adopted a more active policy towards Ireland. Garret Óg was summoned to London in 1534. His son Silken Thomas, to whom had been entrusted the government of Ireland, believed that his father had been executed, and organised a rebellion. Maynooth Castle was breached with the first cannon used in Ireland, the garrison was slaughtered and Silken Thomas arrested. He and his five uncles were executed in London at Tyburn in 1537, bringing an end to the power of the House of Kildare.
English: During the 16th century reign of the Tudors, many English settled in the county. Oliver Cromwell seized many of the Anglo-Norman estates and parceled them out amongst the Cromwellian soldiery and supporters. The restoration of Charles II as English king led to the reinstatement of many Anglo-Normans, including the Earls of Kildare but the disastrous Jacobite rebellion and the ensuing penal laws resulted in the demise of many important Anglo-Norman families. The year 1798 saw the outbreak of rebellion in Ireland. There were strong loyalties to the crown in Kildare but the leaders of the 1798 rebellion had strong connections with Co. Kildare; these included Theobald Wolfe Tone and Lord Edward Fitzgerald, a descendant of the Great Earl. This clash resulted in violent skirmishes in the county: almost 300 United Irishmen were slaughtered by the Crown forces on the Gibbet Rath in 1798. The 18th century saw the erection of many of Kildare's great houses, most notably Castletown House and Carton House. The building of the Grand Canal, begun in 1756 and the Royal Canal in 1789, allowed for the transportation of goods from Dublin and throughout the county. Kildare was spared the worst effects of the Great Famine due to its low population density - the lowest in the country. Military garrisons have been situated in the county over the centuries, and the Curragh has been the main training base for the Irish army since Ireland gained its Independence.
Areas of Historical Interest: Cross of Moone at Timolin, Celbridge (Ireland's largest and finest Palladian House), Maynooth Castle, the Quaker Village of

Ballitore (designed and built by Quakers and the location of the Quaker Museum), Straffan Steam Museum, Wonderful Barn Leixlip (an 18th century conical granary).

● THE COUNTY
Total Population: 134,992 *(1996)*
Growth rate: 10.1% increase since 1991
County Capital and Largest Town: Naas
Main Towns: Athy, Celbridge, Kildare, Leixlip, Maynooth, Naas, Newbridge (Droichead Nua).

Main Business Contact: Kildare County Enterprise Board: The Woods, Clane, Co Kildare. Tel 045-861 707.
No of Schools: National 95; Secondary 27.
No of Golf Clubs: 18 (12 x 18; 5 x 9; 1 x 36).
Blue Flag Beaches: none
Other Tourist Attractions: the Butterfly farm in Straffan, Mondello Park car racing circuit, National Irish Stud and Horse Museum in Tully, Punchestown horse racing course.

Naas Town

"From the Irish Nás na Riogh - the assembly place of kings"

● HISTORY
Origins: As suggested by its Irish name, Naas was the seat of the Kings of Leinster for nearly seven centuries. A dun (or fort) was built in the area, but was burned by Cormac Mac Art (the King of Ireland, AD 254–277) in reparation for the crimes committed by King Dunlang of Leinster. Contemporaneous writings mention the town during the course of St. Patrick's apostolic wanderings. There are strong indications that a church dedicated to St. Patrick or St. Corban was erected in the area afterwards. The last king to dwell at Naas was Cearbhall, who was buried at Cill Corban in AD 904.

Growth: The Barony of Naas was originally granted to Maurice FitzGerald and then to his son, William FitzMaurice, by Henry II in 1176. There followed a settlement by a colony from Wales, which in turn constructed an early Norman church, dedicating it to Saint David of Pembrokeshire (up to the end of the 18th century it was customary in Naas to wear a green leek in honour of the saint). In 1206 and again in 1210, the town was visited by King John and sittings of the parliament were held there. During the medieval ages, the Magdalens Hospitallers of St John of Jerusalem, reputedly had a hospital in the town, giving rise to the present-day town symbol, which is a serpent. In 1409, the town received its first charter, giving it the right to have a corporation. The town was one of the border towns of the Pale and accordingly, from Edward the Bruce in 1316 to Rory Óg O' More in 1577 (he totally destroyed the town by burning it), and throughout the 17th and 18th centuries, the town was subject to repeated attacks. Naas saw the first act of rebellion in 1798, when the Cork mail coach and subsequently, the town barracks, were attacked. Naas also adjoined the Curragh, the position of which as a military training ground extends back to the Fianna, and the Anglo-Normans also used it for military gatherings. From the 16th century onwards armies encamped there and a temporary camp was established in 1805 during the Napoleonic wars. However it was not until 1855 that a permanent camp was established - many famous British regiments trained there and the future King Edward VII attended an infantry course in 1861, causing much concern over his association with an actress, Nellie Clifden. Many British soldiers brought their families with them and settled in the area permanently, while others married local women, resulting in a preponderance of English names in the locality. With its population having grown by over 25% in the 1990s, Naas conforms to, and exceeds, the demographic trends in Co Kildare - more people live in the county now than at any other time in its history. Part of this growth is due to a close proximity to Dublin - many of Kildare's towns serving as dormitory towns. With this growth in population, the town has developed into a shopping and commercial centre for the area. Naas also serves The Curragh - Ireland's premier horseracing course - many of the classic races are run here, and there are vast acres of training grounds and stud land near the town.

● TODAY
Location set in the central eastern part of the county
Population: 14,074 (+26.3% from 1991 Census).
Tourist Attractions: The Curragh, St. David's Church (dating to 12th century, possibly the most important historical building in Naas) The castle and lodge house, Motor Racing at Mondello Park, Naas and PUnchestown racing course, canal bank walks.

● TRANSPORT
Main Routes: Naas is served by major routes N7 (to Dublin); N7-M1-N1-M1-N1-A1-M1 (to Belfast); M7-N7-N8 (to Cork); N7-M7-N7-N62-N52-N65-N6-N18 (to Galway).
Miles from Dublin (20); Belfast (124); Cork (139); Galway (125).
Main Nearest Travel Centre (Bus): Contact Busaras, Store Street, Dublin 1 (01) 836 6111.
Nearest Rail Station: Contact Connolly Station, Amien Street, Dublin 1. Tel 01-836 3333.
Nearest Airport: Dublin Airport. Tel 01-814 1111.
Nearest Ferry Port: Dublin (+20 miles); Rosslare (+86 miles).

County Kilkenny

"From the Irish Cill Chainnigh - *Cainneach's church, founded in Kilkenny City by St. Canice."*

● **GEOGRAPHY**
Province: Leinster
Location: inland county in the south-east of the country **County Size:** 16th in Ireland
Land area: 796 sq. miles
Highest point: Brandon Hill (516 m)
Main Geographical Features: In the north-east of the county lies the Castlecomer Plateau, layered on shale, sandstones and seams of anthracite coal. The county is also noted for its marble, a dark black stone, prized in Georgian and Victorian times, that led to Kilkenny being named the Marble City
Main Lakes
Main Rivers
Areas of Geographical interest: Dunmore Cave (containing some of the best calcite formations found in any Irish cave), Kilfane Glen and Waterfall,

● **HISTORY**
Prehistory Kilkenny was part of the ancient kingdom of Ossory which won for itself a semi-independent position as a state within the kingdom of Leinster, probably in the 1st century AD.
Early Christian In the 6th century, St Canice founded a monastery at Aghavoe, which later became the seat of the diocese of Ossory around the year 1052. By 1178, the "See of Ossory" was removed to the city of Kilkenny, where the foundation of the cathedral church of St. Canice was laid.
Medieval Kilkenny became one of the counties of Leinster in 1210. The city of Thomastown was founded in the 13th century by Thomas FitzAnthony, a Welsh mercenary of the 1169 Norman landings and Governor of Leinster in the 13th century. He built the fortifications at Thomastown, Co. Kilkenny, fragments of which can still be seen today. Similar to Galway, Kilkenny had its own merchant Tribes, including the Shees, the Rothes and the Archers, as well as the tribes of Archdekin, Cowley, Knaresborough, Langton, Lawless, Ley and Ragget. The Statutes of Kilkenny (1366/7) were enacted at a parliament held in the city and were an unsuccessful attempt to stop Anglo-Normans intermarrying with the Gaelic population and adopting the Gaelic language and customs.
English Kilkenny became the capital of Ireland, with the founding of a parliament in 1641 known as the Confederation of Kilkenny. This attempt to unite the resistance to English persecution of Catholicism, though powerful for a while, had greatly diminished by the time Cromwell arrived in 1650. The 'Tithe War' was fought between 1830 and 1838, where the local citizenry rebelled against paying tithes to the established church.the war started in Graiguenamanagh on the Carlow-Kilkenny border when the tithe collector took the cattle of a Catholic priest, Fr Martin Doyle, who organised resistance with the approval of his bishop, James Doyle. The rebellion soon spread to the midlands. According to records of the time, the rebellion resulted in 242 homicides, 1,179 robberies, 401 burglaries, 568 burnings, 280 cases of cattle-maiming, 161 assaults, 203 riots and 723 attacks on houses.
Areas of Historical Interest: The five ancient round towers in the county, Thomastown (founded in the 13th century, has many historic remains), Jerpoint Abbey (est. 1158 - some of the finest Cistercian ruins in Ireland), Inistioge Augustinian priory, Callan Augustinian priory, and Kells Augustinian priory (est. 1193 by Geoffrey FitzRobert), Duiske Abbey (est. 1204, still includes the 9th century Celtic crosses of Akylthawn and Ballyogan), ruins of Grenan Castle, Tullaherin Round Tower dates from the end of the 9th century, St Lachtain's (622, an ancient church, near Freshford, was destroyed by the Vikings but a new church was built around 1100 and the extant Hiberno-Romanesque doorway is all that remains from this period). Ballylarkin Abbey (14th century), Kilcooley (a Cisternian monastery near Urlingford), high crosses (at Kilree, Killamery and Kilkieran).

● **THE COUNTY**
Total Population: 75,336 *(1996)*
Growth rate: 2.3% increase since 1991
County Capital and Largest Town: Kilkenny*see profile*
Main Towns: Callan, Castlecomer, Graiguenamanagh, Thomastown.
Main Business Contact: Kilkenny County Enterprise Board: 42 Parliament Street, Kilkenny. Tel 056-52662.
No of Schools: National 79; Secondary 16.
No of Golf Clubs: 6 (5 x 18; 1 x 9).
Other Tourist Attractions: Bród Tullaroan and the Lory Meagher Heritage Centre, Kilkenny Design Centre, Rice House (the birthplace of Brother Edmund Rice in Callan).

Kilkenny City

See county name

● **HISTORY**
Origins Kilkenny was the ecclesiastical and political capital of the kingdom of Ossory, but it was not until the Normans that it achieved national prominence. **Growth:** Kilkenny city was the medieval capital of Ireland and still retains much of its Norman origins and medieval structure. At the time of the Norman Invasion, in 1172, a wooden fortress was built by Strongbow (Richard de Clare). In 1195, William Marshal, Earl of Pembroke, who succeeded Strongbow, rebuilt the castle on a larger scale, and restored the town. The city of Kilkenny had two townships:

Irishtown, which had its charter from the bishops of Ossory; and Englishtown, established by William Marshal and raised to the status of a city in 1609. The two townships were eventually united in 1843. From the 14th century Kilkenny Castle was the main seat of the Butlers, the Earls and Dukes of Ormonde, who played a large part in Irish history. The city flourished during these centuries and had a number of wealthy merchants and patrons. As the country's medieval capital, Anglo-Norman parliaments were held in Kilkenny from 1293 to 1408, and from 1642 to 1648, including the infamous one in 1366 that led to the unsuccessful Statute of Kilkenny and the Confederation of Kilkenny in 1642, where Irish Catholics sided with Charles I. However, the confederation was dissolved and the Roman Catholic confederacy and surrendered to Oliver Cromwell in 1651. After this, the city's trade passed into Protestant hands, but the town continued to flourish as a centre for brewing, milling, woolen blanket manufacturing and marble stone-cutting. The city went into decline around the 1830s. However, it still retained its distinctive cultural identity and by the mid 20th century it re-emerged as a leader in the arts and crafts in Ireland.

● **TODAY**
Location set in the north central part of the county on the banks of the River Nore
Population: 18,696 (+5.8% from 1991 Census).
Tourist Attractions Castle (purchased by James Butler 3rd Earl of Ormond in 1391, from then on the Castle was the principal seat of the Earls of Ormond). In 1609 James I conferred on the then town of Kilkenny, City status. What were the Castle stables are now occupied by the Kilkenny Design Workshops. St. Canice's Cathedral (c. 1251 and Round Tower). the Exchange and Town Hall (erected 1761), the County Court House (a classical building of 1794), Rothe House (a double court house built in 1594), the Black Abbey (est. 1225, constructed by the Dominicans)

● **TRANSPORT**
Main Routes: Kilkenny is served by major routes N77-N78-N9-N7 (to Dublin); N77-N78-N9-N7-M1-N1-M1-N1-A1-M1 (to Belfast); N76-N24-N8 (to Cork); N77-N7-N62-N52-N65-N6-N18 (to Galway).
Miles from Dublin (71); Belfast (174); Cork (91); Galway (107).
Nearest Travel Centre (Bus): Contact Busaras, Store Street, Dublin 1. Tel 01-836 6111.
Nearest Rail Station: MacDonagh Station, Kilkenny. Tel 056-22024.
Nearest Airport: Dublin Airport. Tel 01-814 1111.
Nearest Ferry Port: Dublin (+71 miles).

County Laois

From Loigis/Loigsi - late Iron Age Pict mercenaries who helped conquer Leinster.

● **GEOGRAPHY**
Province: Leinster
Location: inland county in the east of Ireland and the only county that does not border on another county touching the sea
County Size: 23rd in Ireland
Land area: 664 sq. miles
Highest point: Arderin Mtn (528 m)
Main Geographical Features: It is largely bounded by raised bog, highlands and rivers and the Slieve Bloom mountains. To the south-east of the county is the Castlecomer Plateau and its adjoining uplands, which are layered on Upper Carboniferous shales and sandstones, with some coal seams. The centre is dominated by large tracts of tillage and pasture land, bounded on the east by the Killeshin plateau.
Main Rivers: Barrow; Nore.
Main Lakes: Annaghmore.
Areas of Geographical interest: Slieve Bloom Environmental Park, Heywood Gardens in Ballinakill, Rock of Dunamase.

● **HISTORY**
Prehistory: County Laois is dotted with the remains of Celtic ring-forts, ruined strongholds and monastic buildings. The Office of Public Works has identified more than 1,000 historical sites and monuments in the coun-

ty. The Heath is one of the most important archaeological sites in the country. You can still see the outline of ancient, pre-Christian raths and ring barrows today. Near the area of Timogue there are two ring-forts.These would have been built as protected enclosures around farms around the early Christian period
Early Christian: St Comdhan founded a monastery in Killeshin at the end of the 5th century, the last historical reference to which is in 1082. An oratory here was destroyed in 1041 and the monastery was burned in 1077. The county had a strong Christian establishment by the sixth century, but many of its monasteries fell prey to the Viking hordes, as evidenced by a re-discovered Viking longphort at Dunrally.
Medieval The Normans gained control of the best land in the county by around 1325, but a Gaelic revival occurred during the 14th century. This revival was summarily ended when the O'Mores had their lands confiscated by the English in the 16th century
English: Laois was established out of a number of unrelated Gaelic territories and earlier chiefdoms and referred to as the Queen's County by a parliamentary act in 1556, during the reign of Queen Mary. It, along with Offaly, became the first area to be planted in Ireland. Emo Court is one of the finest examples of the Georgian mansions built by the English The house was designed originally in about 1790 by James Gandon for the first Earl of Portarlington. Gandon also designed the nearby church at Coolbanagher. Laois did not escape the ravages of the Great Famine; its population prior to

it in 1841 was 153, 930, compared to 73,124 in 1881. As a direct result of the famine, Laois like all Irish counties, had its workhouses. Donaghmore workhouse was built in 1850 under the Poor law Act. About 10 per cent of the population of the area were categorised as paupers. They were forced into this institution and subjected to its inhumane system. Family members were segregated according to age and sex, assigned to separate apartments and not allowed to communicate with each other. The breaking up of families was a consciously worked-out policy in order to make the workhouse as unattractive as possible to the poor. They were then forced into a system of hard physical labour and poor diet.

Areas of Historical Interest: Abbeyleix House and Gardens, Ballaghmore Castle, Kinnity Castle, Lea Castle, Dysart Castle, Srahan Castle and Moat, St Canice's Monastery, Emo Court and Gardens (designed originally in about 1790 by James Gandon for the first Earl of Portarlington, one of the finest Georgian houses in the country), the Great Heath of Maryborough (one of the most important archeological sites in Ireland), Killeshin Church (est. around the 12th century, has one of the finest Romanesque doorways in the country), Mountmellick Quaker Museum, Stradbally Steam Museum, Timahoe Church and Round Tower, Ballaghmore Tower House, The Swallows Quarter in Donaghmore, Donaghmore Workhouse and Museum (originally the workhouse at Donaghmore, the building today houses an agricultural museum, which focuses on the day-to-day activities of people in rural Ireland during the past 100 years),

● **THE COUNTY**
Total Population: 52,945 *(1996)*
Growth rate: 1.2% increase since 1991
County Capital and Largest Town: Portlaoise *see profile*
Main Towns: Abbeyleix, Mountrath, Mountmellick, Portarlington
Main Business Contact: Laois County Enterprise Board: IBS House, Dublin Road, Portlaoise, Co Laois. Tel 0502- 61800.
No of Schools: National 68; Secondary 13.
No of Golf Clubs: 5 (4 x 18; 1 x 9).

Portlaoise Town

"From the Irish Port Laoise - the fortress of Laoiseach Ceannmore, a descendant of the Red Branch Knights of Ulster"

● **HISTORY**
Origins: The town is situated near the prominent Rock of Dunamase, the 12th-century fortress of the King of Leinster, Dermot MacMurrough. It was the scene of many battles in the centuries after the Anglo-Norman invasion.
Growth: In 1547, during the reign of Philip and Mary, Port Laoise was established as a fortified area - The Fort Protector (named after the earl of Somerset, ruling at that time in the monority of King Edward VI) - in 1547 as a garrison which served to oust the local O'Moore clan. The fort had an oblong layout, the walls of which contained a round tower and a square tower, protecting a castle (demolished in 1835). In 1556, the Fort was renamed Maryborough. In 1558, the Fort was garrisoned but was continually attacked by the O'Moores. The town received its charter in 1570, which raised it to the status of a borough, which gave the right to have a corporation and return two members to the Irish Parliament. The O'Moore were eventually transplanted to Co Kerry and replaced by English planters. In 1616, a public school was set up and in 1635, the town received the right to hold two fairs. The Earl of Ormond took over the fort in 1642 to ensure it did not fall into the hands of the Confederate Catholics. The O'Neills conquered the town in 1646, but had to surrender it to the king in 1648. The nearby Rock of Dunamase was demolished in 1650 by Cromwellians. Little remains of the original fortification except part of the outer wall of the tower. The fort was taken and demolished in 1650 by the Cromwellians. Afterwards, it was rebuilt as a garrison and market town, becoming the administrative centre of the county. Trade flourished: with wool, flour and other products being traded. Several duels were fought in the town, the most famous being between Colonel Jonah Barrington and a Mr Gilbert. Along with other Irish towns, Maryborough lost the right to elect MPs after the Act of Union. Its common was also taken and divided up between local aristocracy. Its corporation was annulled in the 1830s after an official commission into the workings of corporations in Ireland. The county council was formed in 1899 and in 1920, Maryborough was renamed Portlaoise.
Today: The town is a conduit for many of the important routes in the country. The employment structure reflects a dependence on services as the main source of employment. The town has expanded rapidly over the past 20 years. It is estimated that a high proportion of the total work force (48%) are engaged in services, 15% in industry, and 22% in agricultural employment. Main manufacturing industries include Bord Na Móna. Portlaoise is also known for its large prison (originally built in 1830).

● **GENERAL**
Location Upper central part of the county.
Population: 9,474 (+13.3% from 1991 Census).
Tourist Attractions The Old Library (built in 1782, originally a jail and the location of public executions; then in 1830 the Police barracks), the Courthouse (built in 1762), old Church Tower (dates back to the 16th century, John Wesley reputedly preached in it), the War Memorial (built in 1918 to commemorate those who died in WWI), the Methodist Church (completed 1883, early Gothic design), the Railway Station (built 1845), St Peter's Church of Ireland (1803; its obelisk may have been designed by Gandon), St Peter and Paul Church (1822), Garda Station

(1808; originally used as a military barracks), Convent Tower (built c. 1547, it was connected by underground passages to the fort).

● **TRANSPORT**
Main Routes: Port Laoise is served by major routes N7 (to Dublin); N80-N52-N1-A1-M1 (to Belfast); N8 (to Cork); N7-N62-N65-N6-N18 (to Galway).
Miles from Dublin (52); Belfast (152); Cork (104); Galway (89).
Nearest Travel Centre (Bus): Contact Bus Éireann, Plunket Station, Waterford. Tel 051-879 000.
Nearest Rail Station: Portlaoise Station. Tel 0502-21303.
Nearest Airport: Dublin Airport. Tel 01-814 1111.
Nearest Ferry Port: Dublin (+52 miles).

County Leitrim

"From the Irish Liathdroim - the grey hillridge"

● **GEOGRAPHY**
Province: Connacht
Location: almost an inland county (a tiny stretch of Leitrim touches on the Atlantic coastline near Bundoran) in the north-west of the country
County Size: 26th in Ireland
Land area: 614 sq. miles
Highest point: Benbo Mtn (633 m)
Main Geographical Features: The county is hilly and its soil is exceptionally retentive of water, as evidenced by its many lakes: The county is practically surrounded and bisected by water: its northern borders are defined by Loughs MacNean and Melvin and the River Erne, and the county is divided by the great river Shannon. Some of its hills are rich in mineral deposits and in the past, there were coal and iron ore mines
Main Rivers: Shannon.
Main Lakes: Melvin; Allen.
Coastline: 2 miles
Areas of Geographical interest: the Barr Scenic Route, Glencar Waterfall, the Leitrim Way/Slí Liatroma (a scenic walking route).

● **HISTORY**
Early Christian: the county formed the western part of the ancient kingdom of Breifne and was ruled by the O'Rourkes (while the eastern part was ruled over by the O'Reillys) The Clan held onto to the area until the 16th century. Dromahaire had, by that time, become their principal seat. After the confiscation of the O'Rourke chieftain's territory, the county definition of Leitrim came into being in 1565. The county, in the medieval period, was thickly forested, and five great forests lasted until the l7th century, but they have disappeared leaving bleak tracts of country. By 1879 not one O'Rourke held

land in the county according to a list of landowners of upwards of one acre.
English: the English imposed a policy of land confiscation and plantation on Leitrim at the beginning of the 17th century. Towns such as Carrick-on-Shannon, Manorhamilton and Jamestown were established and fortified during this time. Emigration from famine times onwards caused the population to dramatically drop from a high of 155,000 in the early 19th century to around 25,000 today.
Areas of Historical Interest: Miners Way (historical trail, long-distance walking route), Creevylea Abbey ruin (set on the banks of the Bonet river, Dromahair), Leitrim Heritage Centre, Parke's Castle in Dromahair, the Shannon-Erne Waterway, Lough Rynn House and Gardens in Mohill (100 acres of woodland, open pasture, ornamental gardens and nature trails, baronial hall and arboretum),

● **THE COUNTY**
Total Population: 25,057 *(1996)*
Growth rate: 1.0% decrease since 1991
County Capital and Largest Town: Carrick-on-Shannon see *profile*
Main Towns: Ballinamore, Drumshanbo, Manorhamilton
Main Business Contact: Leitrim County Enterprise Board: Park Lane House, Carrick-on-Shannon, Co Leitrim. Tel 078-20450.
No of Schools: National 43; Secondary 9.
No of Golf Clubs: 2 (2 x 9).
Other Tourist Attractions: Cruising on the River Shannon, Drumcoura City Western Riding Farm in Ballinamore, Sliabh an Iarain Visitor Centre in Drumshanbo, Lough Rynn House and Gardens, Park's Castle in Dromahair, Gerties Famous Canal Stop and Museum in Keshcarrigan.

Carrick-on-Shannon Town

"From the Irish Cara Droma Ruisc - the weir of the marshy ridge"

● **HISTORY**
Origins: The town started as a river crossing, just south of the confluence of the Boyle and Shannon rivers, and is mentioned as such in the Annals of Lough Cé in 1530
Growth: During medieval times, the town occupied a strategic location on the border of the lands ruled by the McDermotts in North Roscommon (Ma Lurg) and those of the O'Rourkes in South Leitrim (Ma Rein). After the defeat of Brian Oge O'Rourke in 1603, his lands were confiscated and granted to Sir Maurice Grifith and later to

the St. George family. Carrick-on-Shannon was transformed into a plantation town when it was turned into a royal borough, with a corporation, by a charter granted by King James I in 1613. This gave the town the right to elect two members of the Irish Parliament. However, this franchise was abolished in 1800 with the Act of Union, and the corporation ceased its operations in 1826. Although the town was almost exclusively Protestant, Catholics did live on the Roscommon side of the river. With the establishment of Leitrim County Council in 1898, the town became the county's administrative capital. The town's fortunes were also increased by the extra trade that flourished due to improvements made to Shannon waterway, that is the building of bridges and quays in the area in 1846, and with the building of the Midland Great Western Railway in 1862. Carrick-on-Shannon is still the administrative capital of the county. Tourism activities centre around cruising on the River Shannon - Carrick is usually the starting point for many cruises. A number of industries have recently started up in the region, bolstering local employment.

● **TODAY**

Location set on the south-western border of the county on the River Shannon
Population: 1,868 (+0.5% from 1991 Census).
Tourist Attractions The Costello Memorial Chapel (reputed to be one of the smallest chapels in the world), Lough Key Forest Park and Botanical Gardens (350 hectares of rolling parklands, forest walks, nature trails, playground, picnic area, restaurant and boat trips), Strokestown Park House and Famine Museum (an early 18th century gentleman's country estate preserved in its entirety and its award winning museum commemorating the Great Irish Famine of the 1840s), Slieve an Iarann Visitor Centre (in Drumshanbo tells the story of the county).

● **TRANSPORT**

Main Routes: Carrick-on-Shannon is served by major routes N4 (to Dublin); N4-N55-N3-N54-N2-A3-M1 (to Belfast); N4-N55-N6-N62-N8 (to Cork); N7-N55-N6-N18 (to Galway).
Miles from Dublin (97); Belfast (123); Cork (182); Galway (75).
Nearest Travel Centre (Bus): Contact Bus Éireann, McDiarmada Station, Sligo. Tel 071-60066
Nearest Rail Station: Carrick-on-Shannon. Tel 078-20036.
Nearest Airport: Knock International Airport. Tel 094-67222; Sligo Airport, Strandhill. Tel 071-68280.
Nearest Ferry Port: Dublin (+97 miles).

County Limerick

"From the Irish Luamanach - a place covered in cloaks, possibly referring to cloaks observed floating on the Shannon after some ancient battle."

● **GEOGRAPHY**
Province: Munster
Location: maritime county on Ireland's south-west coast between Clare and Kerry.
County Size: 10th in Ireland
Land area: 1,030 sq. miles
Highest point: Galtymore Mtn (920 m)
Main Geographical Features: Most of the county is covered in a fertile limestone plain - commonly referred to as the Golden Vale. The county is bounded by the wide mouth of the Shannon estuary to the north-west, the high peaks of the Galtee mountains to the south-east and Co. Kerry to the west
Main Rivers: Shannon; Feale; Deel; Maigue; Camoge.
Main Lakes: L Gur.
Areas of Geographical interest: Curraghchase Forest Park, Mitchelstown Caves.

● **HISTORY**
Prehistory: Human habitation of the region can be traced back to around 3500 BC, with the megalithic remains at Duntryleague dating to this time.
Early Christian: Most of Limerick does not appear to have been settled until the fifth century, with the arrival of Christianity and the establishment of monasteries at Ardpatrick, Mungret and Killeedy. The Ardagh Chalice, which dates from this era, was found in a west Limerick

ring fort.
Medieval The Vikings launched attacks on the county, sailing up the Shannon Estuary in 922 and establishing a settlement on an island in the estuary, which was to form the origins of Limerick City. The Normans attacked in 1194, after Dónal Mór O'Brien, the King of Munster, died, and the county of Limerick was formally recognised in 1210. The Normans built hundreds of castles in the region - Limerick has more castles than any other county in Ireland.
English: The Earls of Desmond, or the Geraldines as they were known, were at the centre of Norman power in Munster and led a revolt against the English in 1571. This rebellion was put down and the Geraldines' lands confiscated. The revolt was to be the start of centuries of wars and sieges centred around Limerick City. The native Irish suffered badly in the Great Famine, and Limerick endured waves of emigration.
Areas of Historical Interest: Abbeys (at Ardpatrick, Glenstal, Lislaughtin, Manister, Mungret and Killeedy), Adare Village and Heritage Centre, castles (numbering more than 400 in total and including Askeaton Island Castle, Castle Matrix - where Edmund Spenser met Sir Walter Raleigh and where the potato was first grown in Ireland - Glenquin Castle, Glin Castle, Portrinard Castle), the de Valera Museum at Bruree, Foynes Flying Boat Museum (tells the story of the early days of transatlantic flights), Reerasta Fort (where the Ardagh Chalice was found).

● **THE COUNTY**
Total Population: (excl. Limerick city) 113,003 *(1996)*
Growth rate: 2.8% increase since 1991
County Capital: Newcastle West
Largest Town: Limerick *see profile*
Main Towns: Abbeyfeale, Kilmallock, Limerick, Newcastle West, Rathkeale
Main Business Contact: Limerick City Enterprise Board: The Granary, Michael Street, Limerick. Tel 061-

312 611.
Limerick County Enterprise Board: County Buildings, 79-84 O'Connell Street, Limerick. Tel 061-319 319.
No of Schools: National 151; Secondary 36.
No of Golf Clubs: 8 (7 x 18; 1 x 9).
Other Tourist Attractions: Croom Mills, the Celtic Park and Gardens in Kilcornan, the Palatine Exhibition at Rathkeale, Lough Gur Interpretative Centre.

Limerick City

See county name

● **HISTORY**
Origins The city's origins date back to when the Vikings sailed up the Shannon Estuary in 922 and founded a settlement on an island.
Growth: With the arrival of the Normans in 1194, St. Mary's Cathedral and the great castle of King John were built. Limerick's charter is 800 years old, making it older than London. The Geraldines' rebellion against the English in 1571 was the first of many such wars and sieges centred around Limerick City, including the year-long siege against Oliver Cromwell in 1651 and the 1690 and 1691 sieges. The 1690 siege resulted in General Patrick Sarsfield leading the Jacobite cause, which was supported by the Catholic Irish. The end of this siege led to the signing of the Treaty of Limerick in 1691, the terms of which were dishonoured by the English parliament. The city's walls were taken down in the 18th century and the city developed westwards into an area known as Newtown Pery, famed for its elegant houses and wide streets. Limerick City began to prosper in the 1950s and 1960s with the industrial development arising from Shannon Airport, the geographical location of which made it the first suitable landing site for long-distance air travel from and to America. Shannon Free Airport Development Company was established in 1959 to ensure that the region maintained its viability in air transport activity. The effects of this agency were quickly felt throughout the Shannon region, particularly in Limerick City. The cultural life of the city has been reinvigorated in recent years through the Irish World Music Centre which was set up by Mícheál Ó Súilleabháin at the University of Limerick in 1994. The centre has become a home of excellence to Irish traditional and contemporary music and dance and RTÉ's new national classical music station, Lyric FM, is based there.

● **TODAY**
Location Set in the north-east of County Limerick on the mouth of the Shannon estuary.
Population: 79,137 (+4.9% from 1991 Census).
Tourist Attractions the Dominican Church, Kilrush Church - dates back to 1201, St. John's Cathedral, St. Mary's Cathedral, the Exchange at Nicholas Street, the Granary in Michael Street, Hunt Museum (includes a fine medieval collection and more than 2,000 works of art donated by John and Gertrude Hunt), John's Square, King John's Castle, Limerick City Walls, Limerick Lace Making at the Good Shepherd Convent in Clare Street, Limerick Museum, the O'Connell Monument, the Rugby Heritage Centre at Thomond Park, Sarsfield Bridge, the Sarsfield Memorial, the Treaty Stone off Thomond Bridge.

● **TRANSPORT**
Main Routes: Limerick is served by major routes N7 (to Dublin); N7-N52-N1-A1-M1 (to Belfast); N21-N20 (to Cork); N18 (to Galway).
Miles from Dublin (123); Belfast (201); Cork (63); Galway (65).
Nearest Travel Centre (Bus): Bus Éireann, Colbert Station, Limerick. Tel 061-313 333.
Nearest Rail Station: Colbert Station, Limerick. Tel 061-418 666.
Nearest Airport: Shannon Airport. Tel 061-471 444.
Nearest Ferry Port: Cork (+63 miles).

County Longford

"From the Irish Longphort Ui Fearraill - the fort or strong-hold of the O'Farrell family; the ford could refer to a ford by the River Camlin."

● **GEOGRAPHY**
Province: Leinster
Location: inland county roughly in the centre of the country

County Size: 30th in Ireland
Land area: 403 sq. miles
Highest point: Corn Hill (276 m)
Main Geographical Features: inland county set in the River Shannon basin (which forms the whole western boundary of the county) and the upper catchment of the River Erne, Longford contains lakeland, bogland, pastureland and wetland. During the Midlandian Main Cold

Stage (80,000 - 65,000 years ago) of the Ice Age in Ireland, huge ice domes were forced to turn to the north and south by advancing Scottish ice. The inland ice was forced through the midlands, and with its retreat, it left till, moraines, sheets of sand and eskers behind.
Main Rivers: Shannon; Royal Canal.
Main Lakes: L Ree; L Gowna; L Kinale.

● **HISTORY**
Legends: Longford figures in many Irish myths; the Black Pig's Dyke can be found near Granard, and the route of the Táin crosses through the county
Prehistory: A trackway of large oak planks was recently discovered in a bog at Corlea. This trackway is very important in archaeological terms, as it is the only find from Ireland that can be dated back to the early Iron Age. An exhibition centre, focusing on the Corlea Trackway, has now been built in the area
Early Christian: St Patrick's associations with the county are evident in some of the placenames, such as Tubberpatrick.
Medieval The region was known as Analé or Annaly (the tribe name of the O'Farrels) and was the principality of the O'Farrels from the 11th century onwards. The clan was descended from Fearghall ('the valiant one'), a hero of the Battle of Clontarf (AD 1014), who had marched westwards and forcibly taken control of the area. At this time Annaly was included in the ancient province of Meath. Henry II made a grant of the land to Hugh de Lacy, but appears to have been a grant in name only as the O'Farrels continued to hold sway. In 1543, when Meath was divided into two counties, Annaly was considered to be part of the Western county.
English: It wasn't until Sir Henry Sidney arrived (1576) that the county was defined, included in the province of Connacht and named Longford after its chief town. Faghan O'Farrel surrendered his lands to Elizabeth I and was granted them under the terms of English law. The O'Farrels lost their property under James I's plantation of the Leinster counties. The O'Farrels did reclaim their castle in 1641, but lost it again with the arrival of Cromwell's forces. Some of the fiercest fighting of the 1798 rebellion occurred in the county, mainly around Ballinamuck. In 1798, after General Humbert landed in Mayo, he took Killala and Ballina, then led his men onto the British garrison of Castlebar, which he took. He marched to Sligo and veered south-eastward through Leitrim into Longford where he faced a force

over five times as strong as his own under Lord Cornwallis and General Lake. The Battle at Ballinmuck ended with Humbert's surrender after barely half an hour. The Irish battalions on the top of the hill watched as the French were treated with all the civilities of a formal surrender, but were themselves then set upon. Many rebels fled into the bog where the cavalry could not follow, but they were surrounded and killed. It is alleged that 500 were buried in mass graves. In October, the main French force of over 3,000 finally arrived off the coast of Donegal, with the leader of the United Irishmen, Theobald Wolfe Tone on board. The French fleet was intercepted and Wolfe Tone captured. The rebellion had already been defeated by then, although occasional skirmishes continued for several years. The Great Famine in 1847 took a heavy toll on the county's population, and during this time, a Longford-Argentine connection was established, resulting from the many families in the county who emigrated to Argentina. During the early 1920s War of Independence General Sean MacEoin, 'the Blacksmith of Ballinalee', led the North Longford Flying Column. He went on to become Minister for Justice and for Defence.
Areas of Historical Interest: Corlea Trackway Exhibition Centre, the Black Pig's Dyke (one of the most visible ancient boundary formations in the country), Ardagh Heritage Village (built in the 1860s along a Swiss design), Carrigglas Manor, Cashel Museum in Newtowncashel, Castleforbes Demesne, the Cistercian Abbeys at Abbeylara and Abbeyshrule, Longford County Museum, the ruins of Rathcline Castle are about two miles from Lanesborough, Ballinamuck Battlefield Centre.

● **THE COUNTY**
Total Population: 30,166 *(1996)*
Growth rate: 0.4% decrease since 1991
County Capital and Largest Town: Longford *see profile*
Main Towns: Ballymahon, Edgeworthstown, Granard
Main Business Contact: Longford County Enterprise Board: Great Water Street, Longford. Tel 043-46572.
No of Schools: National 43; Secondary 10.
No of Golf Clubs: 1 (1 x 18).
Other Tourist Attractions: Clondra's Teach Cheoil, Goldsmith Country (maps out the countryside celebrated by the poet Oliver Goldsmith), Lilac Activity Centre in Lanesboro, Michael Casey's Bog Oak sculptures at Barley Harbour.

Longford Town

See county name

● **HISTORY**
Origins: There is mention of an ancient monastic site in the area which was founded by a disciple of St Patrick. The town was the stronghold of the O'Farrels of Annaly and gave its name to the county.
Growth: In 1400, under the auspices of the O'Farrels, a Dominican abbey was founded in the town. The abbey was dissolved during the Tudor dissolution of monastic houses. James I granted the town the privilege of holding a market and fair. By this time a castle was founded in the town, the possession of which appeared to have been taken from the O'Farrels and granted to Lord Francis Aungier. In 1641, the O'Farrels retook the castle and killed the garrison barracked there. The castle was retaken with the arrival of Cromwell's forces. In 1657, Lord Aungier was granted a charter for the town which allowed him to build a manor with the power of holding court and a jail,

as well as the right to appoint bailiffs and burgesses for the town. After the Act of Union, the town was disenfranchised from returning members to parliament. During the 1830s, Longford was the principal market town for the region and had thriving trades: merchants and curers shipped quantities of pork and bacon to Dublin, London and Liverpool and large quantities of butter were exported for the English markets. The town also had a brewery and whiskey distillery. By this time a branch of the Royal Canal had been brought to the town and this enabled the cheap and quick transport of such products to Dublin and beyond, and the town was a stop on the mail-coach road to Carrick-on-Shannon.

● **TODAY**
Location centre of the western half of the county, on the River Camlin
Population: 6,984 (+2.3% from 1991 Census).

● **TRANSPORT**
Main Routes: Longford is served by major routes N4 (to Dublin); N4-N55-N54-N2-A3-M1 (to Belfast); N4-N55-N62-N8 (to Cork); N6 (to Galway).
Miles from Dublin (76); Belfast (123); Cork (162); Galway (67).
Main Nearest Travel Centre (Bus): Contact Busaras, Store Street, Dublin 1. Tel 01-836 6111.
Nearest Rail Station: Longford. Tel 043-45208.
Nearest Airport: Dublin Airport. Tel 01-814 1111.
Nearest Ferry Port: Dublin (+76 miles).

County Louth

"From the Irish Lú - the river Lud or a hollow"

● **GEOGRAPHY**
Province: Leinster
Location: maritime county on the east coast situated half-way between Dublin and Belfast on the border.
County Size: 32nd in Ireland
Land area: 318 sq. miles
Highest point: Slieve Foy (590 m)
Main Geographical Features: underlying rock is limestone, but the pressure of the Ice Age caused the surface to crumble and form rich soil, eventually giving rise to well-wooded areas and sandy beaches.
Main Rivers: Fane; Glyde; Dee;
Main Lakes: Carlingford.
Main Bays: Dundalk.
Areas of Geographical interest: Carlingford Forest Park, Dundalk Bird Sanctuary

● **HISTORY**
Prehistory: Flint shaped in palaeolithic times was found near the town of Drogheda and is believed to be one of the oldest in Ireland. The area including Co Louth was part of the ancient province of Ulster, which covered the area north of a line drawn between Bundoran and Drogheda.
Early Christian: Monasterboice in south Louth was an important centre in early Christian times
Medieval The Vikings established settlements in nearby Carlingford in 931. In the late 12th century, the De Verdons were the first Norman family to take a grant of the North part of the county, and they founded a fortified town in 1189 at Dundalk. Louth was on the border of the Pale at the gateway to Ulster, and as such it was targeted for attack by the Ulster clans and others. The O'Neills launched many incursions into the area from 1392 onwards. Around 1492, there was terrible famine in the area.
English: Oliver Cromwell's most infamous attack in Ireland was made against Drogheda in 1649, when his forces murdered about 2,600 of the towns inhabitants. Charles II granted lands in the area to Lord Dungannon and Sir Robert Reynolds in 1667. Louth had barely recovered from the Crowellian invasion, when it was plunged into the wars between the Jacobites and the Williamites. General Schomberg garrisoned in the area. Although his army did not capitulate to the Jacobites, he lost one-third of his men through sickness. Later on William camped at Dundalk and proceeded on to Ardee and fought the Battle of the Boyne.
Areas of Historical Interest: Dromiskin Cross, Dundalk Motte and Bailey, Dun Dealgan, Dundalk Museum, King John's Castle at Carlingford, 'The Mint' (15th century tower in Carlingford), Old Mellifont Abbey at Collon, Monasterboice's inscribed crosses and round tower, Prolleek dolmen, Seatown Windmill (one of Ireland's largest surviving windmills).

● **THE COUNTY**
Total Population: 92,166 *(1996)*
Growth rate: 1.6 % increase since 1991.
County Capital and Largest Town: Dundalk *see profile*
Main Towns: Ardee, Drogheda, Dundalk.
Main Business Contact: Louth County Enterprise Board: Partnership Court, The Ramparts, Dundalk, Co Louth. Tel 042-932 7099.
No of Schools: National 73; Secondary 17.
No of Golf Clubs: 7 (6 x 18; 1 x 9).

Dundalk Town

"From the Irish Dun Dealgan - the fort of Dalga, who was the father of the famous warrior from Irish legend - CuChulainn"

● **HISTORY**

Origins: Evidence has been found of prehistoric and early Christian settlements in the area. An Iron age fort near the town was supposedly Cuchulainn's home, although a Norman motte now covers it. In the late 12th century, the De Verdons founded a fortified town in the area.

Growth: Two large medieval settlements were found in Dundalk. The centre of the town still retains its medieval layout, which is based on a linear north-south axis. King John granted the town a charter in 1220, and the continental orders, such as the Franciscans, set up abbeys in the town. Edward Bruce, during the Scots-English war, captured Dundalk and burned it around 1316. The town was granted a royal charter in 1356, allowing it a seneschal, provost, burgesses and merchants' guilds. The O'Neills attacked the town on many occasions, and a trench was established around the town in 1458 to prevent further attacks, but Shane O'Neill continued to lay siege to the town in 1562, 1563, 1566 and 1567, effectively destroying it. He was invited to talk to Elizabeth I; however, he was murdered soon after and was succeeded by Hugh O'Neill. Dundalk became the focus of the English attack on Hugh. He guarded the area, to prevent attacks northwards. After much fighting, the English sought a truce, but the Irish earls rejected their settlement terms and engaged in the Nine Years War against the English. The town had a brief peace before the 1641 Catholic rising. During the Cromwellian era, General Monk was put in charge of the garrison at Dundalk. In 1699 Lord Dungannon introduced the linen trade to the town, in the wake of the law forbidding the export of Irish wool. Buildings were constructed to house the looms for linen spinning and weaving. Lord Dungannon's interest in the town passed to the earls of Roden (who still hold the ground landlordship in parts of the town). At the beginning of the 19th century, a scheme of public building was undertaken, but tragedy struck in the form of famine (1817) and a cholera epidemic (1832). In 1833, as with other towns in Ireland, there was an inquiry into the town corporation. The old corporation was abolished and a new body, the town commissioners, was elected. By the end of the 19th century, Dundalk was flourishing and evidence of the town's prosperity is reflected in the Italianate facades of some of the town houses, with their flamboyant 'Dundalk' style. Dundalk acts as an administrative business and shopping capital both for Co Louth and many of the adjoining counties. It is strategically located between the country's two capitals being 50 miles equidistant from Dublin and Belfast and its border location has led to business and community links with the Northern Irish border town of Newry. The town has also a state-of-the-art telecommunications infrastructure and there are plans afoot to link it to the fibre optic system in Northern Ireland via Newry.

● **TODAY**

Location North-east of the county, at the mouth of Dundalk Harbour.
Population: 30,195 (+0.4% from 1991 Census).
Tourist Attractions Dundalk Museum / Interpretive Centre (converted from the old Carroll's bonded warehouses), the Town Hall, St Patrick's Cathedral, the Court House, the former Jail, the Louth County Council Offices, Proleek Dolmen, Dun Dealgan, Bellurgan Forest, Dundalk Racecourse, Dundalk Greyhound Track, Dundalk Bay (a designated wetland of ecological, botanical, zoological and ornithological importance.

● **TRANSPORT**

Main Routes: Dundalk is served by major routes N1 (to Dublin); N1-A1-M1 (to Belfast); N52-N80-N8 (to Cork); N52-N6 (to Galway).
Miles from Dublin (53); Belfast (52); Cork (202); Galway (148).
Nearest Travel Centre (Bus): Bus Office, Dundalk. Tel 042-933 4075.
Nearest Rail Station: Dundalk. Tel 042-9335529.
Nearest Airport: Dublin Airport. Tel 01-814 1111.
Nearest Ferry Port: Dublin (+53 miles); Belfast (+52).

County Mayo

"From the Irish Maigh Eo - plain of yew-trees"

● **GEOGRAPHY**
Province: Connacht
Location: maritime county on the west coast
County Size: 3rd in Ireland
Land area: 2,159 sq. miles
Highest point: Mweelrea Mtn (819 m)
Main Geographical Features: Its topography varies from the relatively flat land in east Mayo through island-

dotted lakes to the bare quartzite mountains along Mayo's indented Atlantic coastline. During the Irish Ice Age (1,700,000 - 13,000 years ago), there were many periods of warming up and cooling down, which had a significant result on the Irish landscape. Around 300,000 - 130,000 years ago, ice flows from Scotland, Mayo, Donegal carried rocks from their original source in these regions and deposited them elsewhere in the country: rocks of Pre-Cambrian gneiss from north Mayo can be found on beaches in Kerry. The last ice in Mayo

melted around 13,000 years ago.
Main Rivers: Oweniny; Deel; Moy.
Main Lakes: Carrowmore Lake; L Conn; L Allen; Beltra L; L Mask; L Carra; L Cullin.
Main Bays: Killala; Broad Haven; Blacksod; Clew; Newport; Westport.
Main Islands: Inishkea North; Inishkea South; Inishbiggle (pop. 48); Clare (pop. 136); Inishturk (pop. 83); Caher; Achill (pop. 2,718); Clynish (pop. 5); Collan More; Inishcottle (pop. 7); Inishgort (pop. 2); Inishtyre (pop. 7); Inishnakilliew (pop. 6).
Areas of Geographical interest: the Inishkea bird sanctuaries, Downpatrick Head, the new Mayo National Park in the Owenduff-Nephinbeg area (Ireland's sixth suck park, with a visitors' centre at Ballycroy and encompassing some of the best Atlantic blanket bog in Europe), Moy river (renowned for its angling, exceptional salmon fishery and a choice of over 100 game and coarse fish), Lough Conn (spans 15 square miles, holds an estimated 1 million Trout), Killala Bay (holds a large range of species of seafish and marine mammals), the Nephin mountain range, the Moy Valley.

● **HISTORY**
Prehistory: The first colonisation of Mayo probably took place around the time the first people arrived in Ireland (sometime *c.* 7000 BC) during the Mesolithic period. Around 4000 BC, the first farmers arrived in Ireland. They started burying their dead collectively in large stone-built chambered tombs known as megalithic tombs - the earliest surviving architectural structures in the country. Examples of all sorts of Megalithic tombs survive in Mayo. The Northern part of the county holds extensive tracts of blanket bog, which developed from the late 3rd millennium BC onwards and in places covered the field systems, the communities and tombs of the early farmers. Corralled field systems with stone walls have been discovered embedded in the bog, west of Ballycastle in County Mayo. The Behy/Glenlura region - the 'Céide Fields' - contains a 1,500 hectare archaeological site, the most extensive Stone Age monument in the world. Mayo has many other neolithic monuments: 34 wedge-tombs, 24 stone circles, close to 300 ancient cooking-sites - 'fulachta fiadh'. The county has also several monuments from the Early Iron Age (c. 400BC-AD 400): over 250 crannógs (lake-dwellings); over 100 promontory forts, and many ringforts and souterrains.
Early Christian: The county's early Christian history shows significant associations with St. Patrick. The Cross at Cong is the most famous relic of this period, coming from the site of a 6th century monastery founded by St Fechin. According to legend, St. Patrick spent considerable time in County Mayo, and spent 40 days and nights on the summit of Croagh Patrick fasting and praying. From the middle of the sixth century onwards, hundreds of small monastic settlements were established around the country, many of which became very important. Some examples of well-known early monastic sites include Mayo, founded in 7th century by Saint Colmán of Lindisfarne, who had to leave Whitby in England and eventually moved to the *Maigh Eo* near Balla. Their monastery came to be called 'Mayo of the

Saxons' and was famed as a centre of learning for both English and Irish monks. The eventually became an abbey of Augustinian Canons in the late 14th century and survived until the dissolution of the monasteries after the Reformation.
Medieval The Normans arrived in Mayo in 1235; their invasion meant the suppression of the Gaelic clan of the O'Connors of Connacht, but they soon adopted Gaelic customs and began to marry with the native Irish. Common Mayo surnames today with Norman origins include Barrett, Burke, and Walsh, to name but a few. The Normans started towns and introduced the building of abbeys or friaries for new continental orders - Augustinians, Carmelites, Dominicans and Franciscans. Almost all of these abbeys were dissolved during the Reformation in the 16th century. From mid-15th century onwards, the O'Donnells, one of the warring clans from Donegal, frequently attacked North Connacht.
English: By the late 1560s the lord deputy, Sir Henry Sidney, had the submission of the de Burgos the Gaelicised Norman lords of Mayo. County Mayo was established around 1570 and was named after the famous monastery and diocese. Mayo was home at this time to one of the most remarkable women in Irish history, Grainuaile - Gráinne Ní Mháille (anglicised to Grace O'Malley), a pirate queen who lived along the county's coast. The Cromwellian settlement of Mayo, Galway, Roscommon and Clare left many Mayo landowners displaced to make way for the new arrivals. In the 18th century because of the 'the penal laws', many Mayo people emigrated including William Brown (1777-1857), 'the father of the Argentine Navy'. In 1798, after the United Irishmen had been defeated in counties Down and Wexford, General Humbert landed at Kilcummin strand, on Killala bay, with an army of the French Republic. A short engagement, 'the races of Castlebar', ended in defeat for the British government forces. However, Humbert was later defeated at Ballinmuck, and anyone suspected of having been involved in the rising was executed. The Great Famine had a catastrophic effect on the county: It is estimated that over 100,000 died in Mayo during this time. There are still many visible reminders of the Famine, including workhouse sites (there were nine in the county), famine graves and deserted villages. There was wide-scale emigration from Mayo from this time onwards. In 1879, Michael Davitt set up the Mayo Land League, which eventually became a national organisation and led to tenant farmers becoming landowners. During the Land Wars of the 1880s, Mayo gave a new word to the English language by creating a new form of non-violent protest - boycotting - which originated from the ostracisation of a landlord's agent, Captain Charles Cunningham Boycott.
Areas of Historical Interest: Céide Fields near Ballycastle (dating back 5,000 years, one of the oldest enclosed farms in the World, its interpretive centre is built to an award winning design), Cong (famous for its cross and as the location of the film *The Quiet Man*), Michael Davitt Museum, Moore Hall, Rosserk Abbey, Rathfran Abbey, Moyne Abbey, Ballintubber medieval abbey (founded in 1216), the round Tower and ancient Cathedral at Killala, the great Famine walks at

Bonniconlon, the North Mayo Heritage Centre at Enniscoe near Crossmolina, the Foxford Woollen Mills (its history centre gives 100 years of sights, sounds and smells of the Woollen Industry), the Dolmen of the four Maols, The portal-tombs (at Ballyknock, Claggan, Gortbrack North, Knocknalower, Achill and Killasser). Aughagower, Inishmaine, Ballintubber, Errew, Kilmore Erris, Balla, Cong, Killala, Turlough, Moyne near Cross, and island settlements off the Mullet peninsula like Inishkea North, Inishkea South and Duvillaun More.

● THE COUNTY

Total Population: 111,524 *(1996)*
Growth rate: 0.7% increase since 1991
County Capital: Castlebar
Largest Town: Ballina *see profile*
Main Towns: Ballina, Ballinrobe, Ballyhaunis, Charlestown, Claremorris, Crossmolina, Swinford,

Westport.
Main Business Contact: Mayo County Enterprise Board: Spencer Street, Castlebar, Co Mayo. Tel 094-24444.
No of Schools: National 191; Secondary 29.
No of Golf Clubs: 10 (6 x 18; 4 x 9).
Blue Flag Beaches: 8 - Bertraw (Westport), Carrowmore, Clare Island, Dooega (Achill), Dugort (Achill), Keem (Achill), Keel (Achill), Golden Strand (Achill), Elly Bay (Belmullet), Mullaghroe, Mulranny, Old Head (Louisburgh), Ross (Killala)
Other Tourist Attractions: Croagh Patrick (one of the main pilgrimage points in Ireland), Foxford Woollen Mills Visitor Centre, Knock Marian Shrine and Folk Museum, Westport House and Children's Zoo, the Sculpture Trail along the North Mayo coast.

Ballina Town

"From the Irish Béal an Átha - the mouth of the Ford."

● HISTORY
Origin The area around the River Moy, one of the most famous salmon rivers in Ireland, has been the site of human habitation for eons.
Growth The ecclesiastical centres of Moyne Abbey and Rosserk Friary, dating back to the 15th century, indicate that there was a settlement in the area in medieval times. However, prior to the 18th century Ballina was a small hamlet. It wasn't until around 1700 that it was developed into a town by a Scots Presbyterian, John Knox. In 1798, General Humbert and the United Irishmen took Ballina, and went on to capture the British garrison of Castlebar. The town is an important administrative and market centre for the north Mayo area.
● TODAY
Location In the north-east of the county, on the River Moy at the mouth of Killala Bay the Ox mountains to the East and the Nephin mountain range to the West
Population: 8,762 (+7.2% from 1991 Census).
Tourist Attractions St Muredach's Cathedral (on the banks of the Moy), Presbyterian Church Walshe Street (founded in 1846, the building to the left of the church was formerly an orphanage attached to the congregation), Moy river (renowned for its angling, exceptional salmon fishery and a choice of over 100 game and coarse fish), nearby Lough Conn (spans 15 square miles, holds an estimate 1 million Trout), Killala Bay (over 30 species of seafish), the nearby Ox and Nephin mountain ranges, walking in the Moy Valley.

● TRANSPORT
Main Routes: is served by major routes N57-N5-N4 (to Dublin); N59-N17-N15-N16-A4-M1-A3-M1 (to Belfast); N57-N58-N5-N60-N84-N18-N21-N20 (to Cork); N57-N58-N5-N60-N84 (to Galway).
Miles from Dublin (154); Belfast (167); Cork (184); Galway (74).
Nearest Travel Centre (Bus): Bus Office, Ballina. Tel 098-71800.
Nearest Rail Station: Ballina. Tel 096-71818.
Nearest Airport: Knock International Airport. Tel 094-67222.
Nearest Ferry Port: Dublin (+154 miles).

County Meath

"From the the Irish An Mhí - the middle."
● GEOGRAPHY
Province: Leinster
Location: set in the east of the country, a small part of Meath touches the coast
County Size: 14th in Ireland
Land area: 905 sq. miles
Highest point: Sliabh na Galligh (279 m)
Main Geographical Features: a rich limestone plain provides the basis of the county's fertile farmlands. Meath is bordered by the Irish sea in the east and by

County Dublin in the south.
Main Waterways: Boyne; Stonyford; Royal Canal; Skane; Blackwater.
Main Lakes: L Sheelin; L Bracken.
Areas of Geographical interest: Grove Gardens, Butterstream Gardens (at Fordstown, Kells), Sonairte - the National Ecology Centre in Laytown.

● HISTORY
Prehistory: Once part of the ancient fifth province of Ireland, Meath has been inhabited for more than 8,000

years. The county was the centre of prehistoric Ireland and the place from which the ancient roads of Ireland radiated. In the Boyne Valley lie the celebrated megalithic burial grounds at Newgrange, Knowth and Dowth, some of the oldest Neolithic structures in Europe, predating the Egyptians pyramids and Stonehenge. Newgrange (c. 3200) could lay claim to being possibly the oldest astronomically aligned Stone Age structure in the world. It was discovered during the 17th century, along with heavily decorated curb stones. An active solstice site, there is a waiting list of several years to get in to Newgrange to see the sun's rays penetrate the tomb at dawn on the day of winter solstice. New evidence has been found indicating that Knowth - A Neolithic cemetery of up to 20 passage tombs, once the Royal Residence of the Kings of Breaga - like Newgrange, could also have an astronomical function. Other important archaeological finds in the county include the Tara Brooch, found in Bettystown.

Early Christian: The county is referred to as Royal Meath, as it was once home to the kings of pagan and early Christian Ireland at Tara. Arguably the most important early Christian artifact - The Book of Kells - came from Kells in Meath

English: The Boyne Valley has been significant in most eras in Irish history from prehistory to the Battle of the Boyne in 1690, when King James II was vanquished by King William III for the crown of England. The British army defeated Irish rebels during the 1798 rebellion at Tara, and Daniel O'Connell held a 'monster' rally here in 1843, leading an estimated one million people to protest against the Act of Union

Areas of Historical Interest: Brú na Bóinne Visitor Centre (starting point for the visits to the megalithic tombs at Newgrange & Knowth), Hill of Tara (seat of the ancient high kings of Ireland), St. John's/Trim Castle (contains the largest castle fortifications in Ireland and was the location of the film *Braveheart*), Loughcrew (a series of hills with passage graves), St. Mary's Abbey (where the Duke of Wellington was educated), Kells High Crosses, St. Colmcille's Hut in Kells.

● **THE COUNTY**

Total Population: 109,732 *(1996)*
Growth rate: 4.1% increase since 1991
County Capital and Largest Town: Navan *see profile*
Main Towns: Ashbourne, Athboy, Dunshaughlin, Kells, Navan, Slane, Trim.
Main Business Contact: Meath County Enterprise Board: Navan Enterprise Centre, Trim Road, Navan, Co Meath. Tel 046-27444.
No of Schools: National 103; Secondary 20.
No of Golf Clubs: 12 (7 x 18; 3 x 9; 2 x 27).
Other Tourist Attractions: Hill of Slane (where St Patrick lit the Pascal fire), The Power & Glory Visitor's Centre at Trim.

Navan Town

"From the Irish An Uaimh - the Cave"

● **HISTORY**

Origins: In early Christian times the town was known as *Nuachongbhail* - the new dwelling - a name associated with monastic sites and their surrounds, and there are early Christian sites in the area - the ruins of Donaghmore Round Tower and Church are still visible.

Growth: The town itself dates back to Norman times (a Norman Motte, early Abbey and Norman Castle remain at nearby Athlumney), when Hugh De Lacy granted Joscelyn De Aguelo (later Gaelicised to Nangle) the lands of the town. The town was subsequently walled and was defended as an outer boundary of the Pale. As such, the town was subjected to frequent attacks, particularly during the 15th and 16th century, from the O'Neills and other Ulster clans. With the intermittent peace of the 18th century, the town began to prosper. A canal was opened to Drogheda which allowed the cheap and quick transport of commercial goods. Trades such as milling, distilling and paper making flourished. The town is the administrative centre for the county, and many people are employed in services industries. Europe's largest zinc mine is located nearby and is a major employer.

● **TODAY**

Location at the centre of the county on the confluence of the Boyne and Blackwater Rivers.
Population: 12,810 (+9.4% from 1991 Census).
Tourist Attractions Tower at Donaghmore, Athlumney Motte (an early Norman structure), Newgrange (within 20 minutes drive - this prehistoric burial site is in fact older than the pyramids of Egypt and one of the world's first great pieces of architecture), Slane Castle (venue for major music concerts), Dalgan Park (home to missionaries and priests and open as a visitor centre), Sonáirte (Ireland's national ecology centre), Hill of Tara (site of the residence of the High Kings of Ireland), Hill of Slane (allegedly the site of St. Patrick's Pascal Fire, which introduced Christianity), Newgrange Farm (a genuine working farm with traditional farm animals and a display of vintage machinery), Navan Racecourse, Fairyhouse (home of the Irish Grand National is only a short drive away).

● **TRANSPORT**

Main Routes: is served by major routes N3 (to Dublin); N51-N2-N52-N1-A1-M1 (to Belfast); N51-N52-N80-N8-N8-N25 (to Cork); N52-N6-N18 (to Galway).
Miles from Dublin (28); Belfast (85); Cork (183); Galway (124).
Nearest Travel Centre (Bus): Contact Bus Office, Drogheda. Tel 041-35023.
Nearest Rail Station: Contact Drogheda Station. Tel 041-9838749.
Nearest Airport: Dublin Airport. Tel 01-814 1111.
Nearest Ferry Port: Dublin (+28 miles); Dún Laoghaire (+36 miles).

County Monaghan

"From the Irish Muineachán - the place of the shrubs"

● **GEOGRAPHY**
Province: Ulster
Location: An inland county, in the central north-east of the country
County Size: 28th in Ireland
Land area: 500 sq. miles
Highest point: Mullyash Mtn (320 m)
Main Geographical Features: Its rolling hilly landscape and myriad of lakes indicate that it is part of the drumlin belt in Ireland, a swath of small steep-sided hills that were formed during the Ice Age (1,700,000 - 13,000 years ago). The Irish Ice Age was not a period of continuous ice; there were numerous periods of warming up and cooling down. At times, general ice sheets covered most of the land, and these depressed the land underneath with their weight. Glaciers deposited unsorted debris - *boulder clay*. Breaks in the ice allowed this material to gather, and it was subsequently moulded into ovoid masses - *drumlins* - in the direction of the ice flow. These drumlins give rise today to the "basket of eggs" terrain so evident in Monaghan today. Bones of woolly mammoth, giant Irish deer, spotted hyena, Norwegian lemming, red deer, reindeer, brown bear, arctic fox, mountain hare dating back to the the Drumlin Phase of the Ice Age (34,000 - 26,000 years ago) have been found, suggesting that the country experienced a continental climate at the time.
Main Rivers: Finn; Blackwater
Main Lakes: L. Muckno.
Areas of Geographical interest: Fane River Park and River Walk, Lough Muckno Leisure Park, Rossmore Forest Park.

● **HISTORY**
Prehistory: Monaghan was occupied before the bronze age, and its many low hills were natural sites for the tombs, forts and cairns of the county's early settlers.
Early Christian: The county was part of the ancient Kingdom of Uladh or 'Ulster'. As the power of this kingdom declined, the Monaghan area was subsumed into the Oriel Kingdom and was ruled by the O'Carrolls.
Medieval After the Normans invaded in 1169, the MacMahons rose to power. In the 1580s, they participated in the Elizabethan policy of surrender and regrant, whereby the Gaelic clans were integrated into the English system but maintained their lands.
English: During the reign of the Tudors, local Irish chieftains incurred land confiscation for treasonable action (such as adhering to traditional administrative practices) and this is what happened to the McMahons. In 1590, Hugh Roe MacMahon was executed for breaking his surrender and regrant agreement. The land was divided between lords and freeholders and church lands were granted to government officials. Hugh O'Neill contested this action, and it was one of the major factors that led to the Nine Years War. The county was one of the three Ulster counties to be included in the Irish Free State in 1922.
Areas of Historical Interest: Castle Leslie in Glaslough, Clones Fort and Clones Medieval Abbey, the early Christian ruins at Donagh Graveyard, Hope Castle, Monaghan County Museum (a centre that features archaeology, folk life, crafts, transport, coinage, industry and the arts).

● **THE COUNTY**
Total Population: 51,266 *(1996)*
Growth rate: 0.1% decrease since 1991
County Capital and Largest Town: Monaghan *see profile*
Main Towns: Castleblaney, Carrickmacross, Clones.
Main Business Contact: Monaghan County Enterprise Board: Courthouse, Monaghan. Tel 047-71818
No of Schools: National 66; Secondary 11.
No of Golf Clubs: 5 (2 x 18; 3 x 9).
Other Tourist Attractions: the antique lace exhibition at Clones, Heritage Centre at St. Louis Convent in Monaghan, Patrick Kavanagh Rural and Literary Resource Centre at Iniskeen, Tyrone Guthrie Centre (Annamakerrig House - a retreat for writers and artists).

Monaghan Town

See county name

● **HISTORY**
Origins: The town was built near a crannóg, which would have been built in early Christian times. A garrison was established in the town at the time of the partition of Monaghan, which arose from the execution of Hugh Roe McMahon in 1590.
Growth: The present town has its beginnings in 1613 during the plantation of James I. Monaghan became a thriving centre for the linen industry. It was also a centre for lace making. The town was populated mainly by Scottish Calvinists. Around this time it was built around three squares: the Market Square - the older buildings of which date back to the 18th century; Church Square; and the Diamond, which was the original market place.

● **GENERAL**
Location North central part of the county
Population: 5,842 (-1.7% from 1991 Census).
Tourist Attractions Market House (18th century building, now the tourist office), Rossmore Memorial (an ornate

Victorian drinking fountain, the County Museum (which contains exhibits from Monaghan's linen and lace-making past), St Macartan's Cathedral (a Gothic Revival Building).

● **TRANSPORT**
Main Routes: is served by major routes N2 (to Dublin); N54-N2-A3-A27-A3-M1 (to Belfast); N54-N3-N55-N62-N8-N25 (to Cork); N54-N55-N6-N18 (to Galway).
Miles from Dublin (79); Belfast (58); Cork (216); Galway (132).
Main Nearest Travel Centre (Bus): Bus Éireann, Bus Office, Monaghan. Tel 047-82377.
Nearest Rail Station: Contact Newry Station. Tel 01693-62971.
Nearest Airport: Belfast City Airport. Tel 01232-734 828; Belfast International Airport. Tel 01849-484848.
Nearest Ferry Port: Belfast (+58 miles); Dublin (+79 miles).

County Offaly

"From the Irish Uíbh Fhailí - *Failghe's People."*

● **GEOGRAPHY**
Province: Leinster
Location: an inland county, located at the heart of Ireland
Size: 18th in rank among counties
County Size: 18th in Ireland
Land area: 771 sq. miles
Highest point: Arderin Mtn (528 m)
Main Geographical Features: Offaly is bordered by Slieve Bloom mountains in the south-east and the River Shannon in the west. The county's Clara bog is one of the largest remaining relatively intact raised bogs in Western Europe and is now recognised as being of international importance. Offaly's bogs and wetlands are home to several species of native and migrant birds; a total of 87 species have been recorded to date. In January this year, a rare species of snail - *Vertigo geyeri* - was discovered on Killaun Bog, near Birr, Co. Offaly. The snail species is believed to have originated in the glacial age and is one of the three listed for protection in Ireland.
Main Rivers: Shannon; Gowlan; Blackwater; Brosna; Grand Canal; Tullamore.
Main Lakes: L Boora; Annaghmore.
Areas of Geographical interest: Slieve Bloom Environment Park, the Blackwater Bog (a raised bog of major significance near Clonmacnoise).

● **HISTORY**
Early Christian: Offaly is home to Clonmacnoise, one of the largest and most important monastic sites in Ireland. The ruins of Clonmacnoise include a cathedral, three high crosses, two round towers and eight churches. In addition, Ireland's earliest Irish language manuscript was produced here and Ireland's last high king - Rory O'Connor - is buried here.
Medieval In the past, the Shannon acted as the main route for the county. The Danes sailed up the Shannon to Clonmacnoise and raided it.
English: After the English conquered the area in 1556 Offaly was known as King's County and was, along with Laois, the first region in Ireland to be planted by the English. The English also built the Martello Tower in Banagher and the Napoleonic fortifications at Lusmagh and Shannonbridge. Birr was settled by the Parsons family, later earls of Rosse, in the 1620s and by 1641 was seeking county town status from Daingean or

Philipstown. Offaly was known as King's County until 1920. Thomas Moore, an Elizabethan soldier, received lands at Croghan Hill in east Offaly in the 1570s as part of the first Offaly plantation. The county town at that time was Daingean which was owned by the Ponsonby family, and although Tullamore had a much larger population by the 18th century, the political influence of the Ponsonby's was such that Daingean was the county seat until 1833. The Grand Canal was linked to Tullamore in 1798 and to the Shannon in 1804, increasing passenger and goods traffic through Offaly. The canal boats provided a direct link with Dublin at low cost facilitating the transport of turf, bricks, grain for malting and Tullamore limestone from the local quarries. As with most other Irish counties outside the Pale in the post famine period, the population of Offaly dropped considerably from almost 147,000 in 1841,to 53,000 in 1926.
Areas of Historical Interest: Birr Castle Demesne (within its confines can be found a fabulous array of rare and exotic plants, as well as a giant telescope dating from 1845, once the largest in the world. A new telescope and observatory have recently been installed, and the demesne is the home of Ireland's new science museum), Clonmacnoise monastic ruins, Clonmacnoise and West Offaly Railway, Durrow Abbey and High Cross, Kinnitty Castle, Leap Castle at Clareen, Cloghan Castle, artillery fortifications at Shannonbridge and Lusmagh (from Napoleonic times), the Martello Tower at Banagher, monastic ruins at Lynally, Clareen and Birr.

● **THE COUNTY**
Total Population: 59,080 *(1996)*
Growth rate: 1% increase since 1991
County Capital and Largest Town: Tullamore *see profile*
Main Towns: Banagher, Birr, Edenderry, Ferbane
Main Business Contact: Offaly County Enterprise Board: Cormac Street, Tullamore, Co Offaly. Tel 0506-52971.
No of Schools: National 67; Secondary 13.
No of Golf Clubs: 5 (5 x 18).
Other Tourist Attractions: Tullamore Dew Heritage Centre.

Tullamore Town

"From the Irish Tulach Mhor - the big mound or hill, probably referring to the hilly ground in the town"

● **HISTORY**

Origins: Although Tullamore lies in the ancient district of Fear Ceall, and in an area was famous for its monastic centres, the town did not begin to flourish until the 18th century. The oldest house in Tullamore is a tower house, known as Sragh Castle, dating back to 1588.

Growth: Thomas Moore received lands in the area in the 1570s as part of the Elizabethan plantation. The Moores neglected their lands throughout the 17th century, and during this time, Tullamore had a castle, a water mill and a few cottages in the 1620s and a population of not much more than 100. In the early 1700s the political influence of the Moore family brought a barracks for 100 foot soldiers in 1716. The building of the barrack provided an impetus to business - Huguenots from Portarlington and Quakers from Mountmellick and Edenderry soon established trades in the town. Indications of the town's growth date back to 1767 when it was decided to locate the County Infirmary at Tullamore instead of Daingean. Although the town's growth in this era was very much a function of landlord influence, structural forces such as the need to create a market centre east of the isolated lands of west Offaly and the county's bog lands were also growth factors. Other important industries were distilling and linen industry; by the 1780s Offaly was second only to the Ulster counties in the manufacture of linen. In 1785 the famous balloon fire in Tullamore occurred (an air balloon caught fire in the third attempt to make such an ascent in Ireland, and some 100 houses were burnt in the area). The Grand Canal was linked to Tullamore in 1798 and to the Shannon in 1804, increasing passenger and goods traffic through the town enormously and leading to the building of goods stores. Tullamore petitioned in 1784 and 1786 to become the county town but this did not happen until 1833. After the 1840s, merchants and farmers came to influence the town's progress through public boards. The main sources of employment up to the 1930s were in malting, distilling, stone quarrying and distribution. Tullamore has 50% of Offaly's business and draws from a hinterland of at least 30,000 people. Shops and services are a significant source of employment for the town, although IDA-backed foreign industries are significant employers as well. The town is still famous for its "Tullamore Dew" whiskey and "Irish Mist Liqueur". The whiskey is now made in Midleton, Co. Cork and the liqueur blended in Tullamore.

● **TODAY**

Location set in the centre of the county, the town is located on the Tullamore river which divides it. To the north is the the Eiscir Riada, known locally as the Arden Hills. To the south lie the Slieve Bloom mountains while to the east and west are flat boglands. Tullamore has managed to preserve much of its original townscape, laid out on a grid-iron pattern.

Population: 10,039 (+6.4% from 1991 Census).

Tourist Attractions The Catholic Church (initially built 1802, demolished and rebuilt in 1902, destroyed by fire in 1983 and rebuilt with an impressive timber interior and some Harry Clarke Studio windows), St. Catherine's Church of Ireland (designed by Francis Johnston, completed 1815), the former county jail (built 1826 in a gothic-style), the courthouse (built 1835, to a neo-classical design), Charleville Castle (erected between 1800–1812, designed by Francis Johnston, considered one of the finest Gothic style country houses in Ireland and the home of the former owners of the town, the earls of Charleville), the Town Hall (erected 1789) the county infirmary (erected in 1788), the Grand Canal (a linear park and a line to the Shannon for pleasure craft).

● **TRANSPORT**

Main Routes: is served by major routes N52-N6-N4 (to Dublin); N52-N1-A1-M1 (to Belfast); N80-N8-N25 (to Cork); N80-N6-N18 (to Galway).

Miles from Dublin (66); Belfast (133); Cork (128); Galway (82).

Nearest Travel Centre (Bus): Contact Busaras, Store Street, Dublin 1. Tel 01-836 6111.

Nearest Rail Station: Tullamore. Tel 0506-21431.

Nearest Airport: Dublin Airport. Tel 01-814 1111.

Nearest Ferry Port: Dublin (+66 miles); Dún Laoghaire (+70 miles).

County Roscommon

"From the Irish Ros - a wooded or pleasant gentle height and Coman - the name of the county's famous saint and the first bishop of the see."

● **GEOGRAPHY**

Province: Connacht

Location: an inland county towards the western quarter of the country

County Size: 11th in Ireland

Land area: 984 sq. miles

Highest point: Slieve Bawn (264 m)

Main Geographical Features: Two-thirds of it is bounded by water and one-third of the county is under bog, mostly in the west. Tectonic 'sagging' from around around 35 million years ago possibly resulted in the Shannon basin around the east Roscommon area. In

the north of the county, at Arigna, on the border with Leitrim, there are deposits of anthracite coal, which were mined commercially until recently.
Main Rivers: Suck; Lung; Breedoge; Shannon.
Main Lakes: L Skean; L Cloonacolly; L Cloonagh; L Errit; L Glinn; L Key; L Drumharlow; Clogher L; Cavetown L; L Annaghmore; L Forbes; L Ree; L Funshinagh.
Areas of Geographical interest: Arigna Scenic Drive, Lough Key Forest Park and Botanical Gardens (350 hectares of parklands, forest walks, nature trails, playground, picnic area, restaurant and boat trips), Rock of Doon near Boyle.

● HISTORY
Prehistory: Many traces of early colonisation are evident in Roscommon; the county has numerous burial mounds, megalithic tombs and ring forts.
Early Christian: Rathcroghan, at the centre of the county, was home to the kings of Connacht from the earliest times and later became home to the high kings of Ireland.
Medieval The O'Conors and the MacDermotts, two of Roscommon's great families, were among the leading Gaelic clans in medieval Ireland. During medieval times, the McDermotts and the O'Beirnes ruled the lands in North Roscommon (Ma Lurg). One of the most important histories of the time, the Annals of Loch Cé were compiled in the Boyle area, probably by the Cistercians in Boyle Abbey from 1191 up to 1228, and by the Ó Maolchonaire family in the mid-15th century

and the Ó Duibhgeannáin family in the 16th century.
English: Nearly all of the county's lands were confiscated during the various English plantations. These were subsequently reclaimed by the Irish Land Commission in the 1920s and 1930s.
Areas of Historical Interest: Rathcroghan and Carnfree Ancient Celtic Sites, Boyle Cistercian Abbey, Clonalis House in Castlerea, Dr. Douglas Hyde Interpretive Centre in Frenchpark, Roscommon Abbey and County Museum, the Old Schoolhouse Museum in Ballintubber, Strokestown Park House and Famine Museum (an early 18th century gentleman's country estate preserved in its entirety and its award winning museum commemorating the Great Irish Famine of the 1840s),

● THE COUNTY
Total Population: 51,975 *(1996)*
Growth rate: 1.1% increase since 1991
County Capital: Roscommon
Largest Town: Boyle *see profile*
Main Towns: Boyle, Castlerea, Elphin, Roscommon, Strokestown.
Main Business Contact: Roscommon County Enterprise Board: Abbey Street, Roscommon. Tel 0903-26263.
No of Schools: National 95; Secondary 11.
No of Golf Clubs: 6 (2 x 18; 4 x 9).
Other Tourist Attractions: Keadue Village, King House in Boyle.

Roscommon Town

See county name

● HISTORY
Origins The town had its beginnings in the early Christian abbey of St Coman, which had close ties with ecclesiastical settlement of St Ciaran at Clonmacnois **Growth** The town grew up as a settlement around the Norman castle, north of the town, which was built in 1269, and the Dominican abbey priory founded in 1253 by Felim O'Conor, King of Connacht. The Gaelic clans captured the castle and burnt it, but it was rebuilt in 1280 by the Normans, who eventually integrated with the native Irish in the area. A large part of Roscommon belonged to the O'Kelly family before the Cromwellian plantation of the 17th century, which removed many Irish Catholics from the good lands of the county to the poorer parts. According to legend, Roscommon town had the unique distinction of having a female executioner, Lady Betty, who had her sentence for murder suspended on the proviso that she became the hangman without fee or reward. Roscommon is now a vibrant town with a growing indigenous industry base.

● TODAY
Location situated in the south central section of the county, in the rich farmland of Roscommon.
Tourist Attractions Roscommon Castle (1280), ruins of the Dominican Priory, Bank of Ireland (once the town's courthouse and Catholic church), the Sacred Heart Church (built in 1903).

● TRANSPORT
Main Routes: is served by major routes N61-N6-N4 (to Dublin); N61-N5-N4-N55-N3-N54-N12-A3-M1 (to Belfast); N61-N6-N62-N8-N25 (to Cork); N61-N6-N18 (to Galway).
Miles from Dublin (91); Belfast (139); Cork (156); Galway (51).
Nearest Travel Centre (Bus): Ceannt Station, Eyre Square, Galway. Tel 091-562 000.
Nearest Rail Station: Roscommon. Tel 0903-26201.
Nearest Airport: Knock International Airport. Tel 094-67222.
Nearest Ferry Port: Dublin (+91 miles).

County Sligo

"From the Irish Sligeach - *abounding in shells."*

● **GEOGRAPHY**
Province: Connacht
Location: maritime county on the north-west coast of Ireland
County Size: 21st in Ireland
Land area: 709 sq. miles
Highest point: Truskmore (647 m)
Main Geographical Features: The county's topography is characterised by unusually shaped hills rising from steep valleys, including Benbulben at the prow of Kings Mountain; Knocknarea, and the ancient Ox Mountains, the oldest mountain range in Sligo at 600 million years old.
Main Rivers: Moy; Owengarve.
Main Lakes: Easky L; Templehouse Lake; L Gill; L Arrow; L Skean; Colgagh L; L Gara.
Main Bays: Sligo; Drumcliff; Ballysadare.
Main Islands: Inishmurray; Coney (pop: 6); Ardboline.
Areas of Geographical interest: the Glen (an area of botanical importance near Strandhill), Gleniff Horseshoe, Rosses Point (with a world-renowned golf course and a metal man - an early 19th century navigational aid), Benbulben and the Ox Mountains.

● **HISTORY**
Prehistory: Sligo has a preponderance of ancient burial sites, from court cairns, passage graves on the Bricklieve Mountains, and dolmens. The reasons why this is so are not clear, and many theories abound as to why the Stone Age peoples constructed them - from the confluence of ley lines to ancient battles fought in the area. Evidence of human habitation in Sligo dates back almost 6,000 years; one of the largest Stone Age cemeteries in Europe and the oldest in Ireland is situated to the west of Sligo town at Carrowmore. This summer, evidence emerged of a neolithic settlement nearby on the side of Knocknarea.
Early Christian: The remains of early Christian monasteries can be found on Inishmurray Island and at Drumcliffe. Near Drumcliffe, Saints Columcille and Finian fought a battle in the sixth century for the copy of a psalter that Columcille had secretly made. Columcille's self-imposed exile to Iona was a direct result of this battle, one of the earliest battles over copyright.

Medieval The town of Sligo was established in Viking times, and an abbey and castle were founded by the Norman Maurice Fitzgerald during the 13th century. Many other castles were built in the county, including ones at Ballinafad and Ballymote.
English: Most historical events in Sligo reflect the fact that the area was of strategic importance as one of the main conduits to the north. As a result, the region, particularly Sligo town, suffered attacks from both the northern chieftains and the English. In 1588 some ships of the Spanish Armada were wrecked by a storm at Streedagh beach, and the timbers of the ships can still be seen at low tide. Some of the crew aboard the ships managed to escape the English and were sheltered by local people, eventually returning back to Spain. The county played a role in the 1798 Rebellion, when the French-Irish force marched over the Curlews on the Sligo-Roscommon border and engaged the British in battle. A statue is erected in memory of Bartholemew Teeling in the town of Collooney for the role he played in the rebellion.
Areas of Historical Interest: Misgan Maeve (a Stone Age cairn on Knocknarea and the alleged burial site of Queen Maeve; Sligo's Neolithic monuments (at Carrowmore, Carrowkeel, Creevykeel and Heapstown), Carrowmably martello tower near Dromore West, Innismurray Island (with its early Christian remains), Lissadell House (home to the Gore-Booth family), Sligo Abbey, Tobernalt (a holy well outside Sligo town).

● **THE COUNTY**
Total Population: 55,821 *(1996)*
Growth rate: 1.3% increase since 1991
County Capital and Largest Town: Sligo
Main Towns: Ballymote, Grange, Tubbercurry
Main Business Contact: Sligo County Enterprise Board: Sligo Development Centre, Cleveragh Road, Sligo. Tel 071-46792.
No of Schools: National 75; Secondary 16.
No of Golf Clubs: 5 (2 x 18; 2 x 9; 1 x 27).
Blue Flag Beaches: 3 - Enniscrone, Rosses Point, Mullaghmore
Other Tourist Attractions: the Caves of Keshcorran (where legend notes Diarmuid and Gráinne took refuge), the Lake Isle of Innisfree on Lough Gill, Yeats's grave at Drumcliffe, seaside resorts (Enniscrone, Easkey, Mullaghmore, Rosses Point, Strandhill).

Sligo Town

See county name

● **HISTORY**
Origins There has been a settlement in the area for millenia, as the nearby Stone Age tombs at Carrowmore suggest.
Growth Sligo town proper has its origins Norman times when Maurice Fitzgerald built a castle in 1245 and an abbey in 1253 on the southern shores of the Garavogue river. This section of the town retains some of its medieval street structure and recent building developments uncovered a medieval lime kiln near to the original castle site. The tower of the Church of Ireland Cathedral is the oldest building in the town, with its base dating back to the 13th century. The abbey was burned down in 1414 and the current extensive stone structure was erected soon after.

Many prominent families were interred in the abbey, a practice which continued well after the dissolution of the monasteries at the time of the Reformation until the 19th century. In 1641, Sir Frederick Hamilton attacked the castle and the town and razed them to the ground, killing many town's inhabitants. Although the abbey still stands, nothing remains of the castle. The garrison stationed at the town during the 17th century played an active role in the Cromwellian and Jacobite wars of that period. During the 18th century, the town began to prosper as a trading port. The channel out to Sligo Bay contains one of four surviving metal men in the world. Dating back to 1822, these point the safest channel for ships to sail. The Pollexfens and the Middletons were the main trading merchants in Sligo, with their ships plying a steady trade with Liverpool and other English and American ports. The town suffered from a cholera epidemic in 1832, when it was estimated that 600 of the towns people died. As well as goods, many people from the surrounding counties emigrated from the port of Sligo. It is estimated that in the wake of the Great Famine, at least 50,000 left from the town. The town's status as a port declined towards the end of the 19th and beginning of the 20th century.

● **TODAY**
Location in the north-west of the county on the Garavogue River
Population: 18,509 (+3% from 1991 Census).
Tourist Attractions Sligo Abbey (est. 1253), St John's Church of Ireland Cathedral (elements of which date back to the 13th century; William Pollexfen, W.B. Yeats' grandfather is buried here as are other members of his family. Parts of the church were designed by the famous architect Richard Cassels), the Cathedral of the Immaculate Conception, Sligo Peace Park, Lough Gill, Sligo Model Arts Centre, Sligo County Museum, Hazelwood Sculpture Trail.

● **TRANSPORT**
Main Routes: is served by major routes N17-N4 (to Dublin); N15-N16-A4-M1-A3-M1 (to Belfast); N17-N4-N61-N6-N62-N8-N25 (to Cork); N17 (to Galway).
Miles from Dublin (135); Belfast (130); Cork (205); Galway (86).
Main Nearest Travel Centre (Bus): Bus Éireann, McDiarmada Station, Sligo. Tel 071-60066.
Nearest Rail Station: Sligo. Tel 071-69888.
Nearest Airport: Sligo Airport, Strandhill, Co Sligo. Tel 071-68280. Knock International Airport. Tel 094-67222.
Nearest Ferry Port: Dublin (+135 miles); Belfast (+130 miles).

County Tipperary

"From the Irish Tiobraid Arann - *the well of Ára"*

● **GEOGRAPHY**
Province: Munster
Location: the country's largest inland county, located in the south of Ireland
County Size: 6th in Ireland
Land area: 1,647 sq. miles
Highest point: Galtymore Mtn (920 m)
Main Geographical Features: Tipperary's diverse geology has yielded coal mines and slate quarries. The county's great central-southern limestone plain, which extends into County Limerick, is better known as the Golden Vale and is famed for its fertile farmlands. Tipperary is bordered by several mountain ranges - the Galtees and the Knockmealdowns in the south, the Silvermines and Arra Mountains in the west, Devilsbit mountain in the north and the Slieveardagh Hills and Slievenamon in the south-east.
Main Rivers: Shannon; Little Brosna; Nenagh R; Ballintotty; Nore; Drish; Multeen; Suir; Moyle.
Main Lakes: L Derg.
Areas of Geographical interest: Glen of Aherlow, Mitchelstown Caves (containing some of Europe's finest calcite formations).

● **HISTORY**
Early Christian: the most prominent of Tipperary's historical sites is the Rock of Cashel, which was the centre of ecclesiastical and secular life in Munster from the end of the fourth century until medieval times. One of the most impressive buildings in the Cashel complex is Cormac's chapel which features idiosyncratic carvings and ornate arches. The kings of Munster ruled from Cashel until Brian Boru came to power. In 1101 Muircheartach O'Brien gave the Rock of Cashel to the church.
Medieval Tipperary was spared most of the ravages of the Viking attacks, and when the Normans arrived, the county was placed in the hands of the Butlers, whose royal patronage protected the county from all plantations except that of Cromwell.
English: The Cromwellian Plantation had disastrous consequences for most of the native Irish; some remained on their lands as tenant farmers, while others moved to the bogland areas. Those who stayed had to pay exorbitant rents, pushing them into joining the Whiteboy movement in the 18th century and carrying out violent reprisals against the English overlords. This ran concurrently with faction fighting that led the county to be christened 'Turbulent Tipperary'. By the middle of the 19th century, the county had a strong Fenian following. It defiantly elected John Mitchel, a Young Ireland transportee on two occasions and played a full political role in the formation of Ireland's fledgling state. It is the only county in Ireland that is divided into ridings, which date back to 1838 when the English authorities decided that the county's large population (it was the third highest populated county at the time) and its

alleged lawlessness necessitated that the county be split. It is still administered as the North Riding and the South Riding. The county councils for the South and North Riding were created under the Local Government Act of 1898.

Areas of Historical Interest: the Bianconi Coach Road (on Slieve na Muck), Cashel of Kings Heritage Centre, Fethard Augustinian Friary and Folk Farm and Transport Museum, GAA Museum (Lár na Pairce in Thurles), Holycross Abbey (one of the most picturesque monasteries in Ireland), Ormonde Castle in Carrick-on-Suir, the Rock of Cashel, the county museums at Tipperary and Clonmel.

● **THE COUNTY**
Total Population: 133,535 *(1996)*

Growth rate: 0.8% increase since 1991
County Capitals: Nenagh *(North Riding)*, Clonmel *(South Riding)*
Largest Town: Clonmel *see profile*
Main Towns: Cahir, Carrick-on-Suir, Cashel, Roscrea, Templemore, Tipperary, Thurles
Main Business Contact: Tipperary ( ) County Enterprise Board: Summerhill, Nenagh, Co Tipperary. Tel 067-33086. Tipperary (SR) County Enterprise Board: 1 Gladstone Street, Clonmel. Tel 052-29466.
No of Schools: National 170; Secondary 34.
No of Golf Clubs: 11 (9 x 18; 2 x 9).
Other Tourist Attractions: Bru Boru Heritage Centre, GPA Bolton Library (some of the collection of which dates from the beginning of the age of printing).

Clonmel Town

"From the Irish Cluain Meala - pasture of honey."

● **HISTORY**
Origins There is mention of the Vikings sailing up the River Suir and establishing a settlement in the area.
Growth: As with most other Irish towns, Clonmel's beginning as a proper town an be traced back to the Normans. The town was walled in the 14th century and came under the protection of Maurice Fitzgerald, the first earl of Desmond. He introduced the Dominican and Franciscan orders to the town, and it became a centre for trading in the area. In 1516, the town came under siege from the earl of KIldare. Oliver Cromwell attacked it in 1650, and the town's inhabitants surrendered. In 1675, during the reign of King Charles II, the "Main Guard" was built to house the king's representatives. By the 18th century, the town became the centre for agricultural trade: flour and other cereals were milled, butter and bacon were traded and brewing and distilling was conducted. In the 19th century, the town continued to flourish as a market town, and had its own army barracks and a cotton factory (established in 1837). One unique development in Clonmel during the 19th century was Charles Bianconi's national mail coach system which began running from Hearn's hotel in Clonmel in 1815.

● **TODAY**
Location set on the southern border of Tipperary on the River Suir.
Population: 16,182 (+3.98% from 1991 Census).
Tourist Attractions the town walls (dating from the 15th century), Old St Mary's Church (which has been the site of a church since the 1220s), the Abbey of St Francis (dating back to 1269), the West Gate (built in 1831 on the site of the town walls' original west gate), Tipperary South Riding County Museum (large collection of items of local interest, including artifacts from Charles Bianconi's mail coach business as well as items associated with Charles Kickham. The museum is also home to a permanent art exhibition which features paintings by many of Ireland's best known artists).

● **TRANSPORT**
Main Routes: is served by major routes N24-N76-N77-N78-N9-N7 (to Dublin); N24-N76-N77-N78-N9-N7-N1-M1-N1-A1-M1 (to Belfast); N24-N8-N25 (to Cork); T49-N8-N62-T21-N52-N65-N6-N18 (to Galway).
Miles from Dublin (102); Belfast (205); Cork (60); Galway (115).
Nearest Travel Centre (Bus): Contact Plunket Station, Waterford. Tel 051-879 000.
Nearest Rail Station: Clonmel. Tel 052-21982; Thurles. Tel 0504-21733.
Nearest Airport: Cork Airport. Tel: 021-313131; Shannon Airport. Tel 061-471 444.
Nearest Ferry Port: Cork (+60 miles).

County Tyrone

"From the Irish Tír Eoghain - the territory of Eoghan, one of the sons of Niall of the Nine Hostages - St Patrick's abductor"
● **GEOGRAPHY**
Province: Ulster
Location: inland county in the centre of Ulster and the largest county in Northern Ireland.

County Size: 8th in Ireland
Land area: 1,211 sq. miles
Highest point: Mullaghclogha (634 m)
Main Geographical Features: The Sperrin mountains dominate the Tyrone skyline, and the county is bounded by Armagh, Derry, Donegal, Fermanagh, Monaghan and Lough Neagh.

Main Rivers: Foyle; Derg; Owenreagh; Strule; Glenelly; Owenkillew; Blackwater; Ballinderry.

Main Lakes: L Neagh.

Areas of Geographical interest: Benburb Valley Park (contains ruins of Benburb Castle and walks along the River Blackwater), Parkanaur Forest Park (home to a herd of white fallow deer and daffodil and rhododendron plantations), Drum Manor Forest Park (originally an 18th century demesne, now a forest park with shrub gardens, artificial lakes, walled butterfly garden and arboretum), Gortin Glen Forest Park (five-mile forest drive), Sperrin Heritage Centre (containing natural history and gold-mining exhibits).

● **HISTORY**

Prehistory: Evidence of human settlement dates back 6,000 years. The Beaghmore Stone Circles, near Cookstown, attest to this ancient inhabitation, as do other burial chambers, monuments and cairns found throughout the county. The hilltop enclosure of Tullyhogue Fort served for a time as the inauguration site for the Celtic kings of Ulster.

Early Christian: Examples of Tyrone's early Christian remains include the Ardboe High Cross, which depicts biblical scenes, and Donaghmore High Cross.

Medieval Tyrone is renowned for its connection with the O'Neills, the clan from which it takes its name. Their domain at one stage incorporated parts of Tyrone, Armagh, Derry and Donegal. They ruled over Ulster for more than four centuries and hindered the English in their attempts to colonise the region.

English: After the defeat of the chieftains at the Battle of Kinsale in 1601, however, the O'Neill's power waned and they eventually left Ireland, an event that has been termed the 'Flight of Earls'. Their lands fell to the crown, and in 1610, Tyrone, along with most of the counties in

Ulster was planted by Scottish and English settlers. Many inhabitants of the area, particularly those of Presbyterian Scottish Stock, suffered religious persecution during the 18th century along with the native Irish and emigrated from Tyrone to America in the early 1700s. There is a strong connection culturally between Tyrone and the Appalachian mountain region in Virginia. In particular, the musical culture of the emigrants has had a formative influence on American folk music.

Areas of Historical Interest: Ulster American Folk Park (tells the story of 200 years of emigration to America), Ulster History Park (narrates the history of human settlement in Ulster), An Creagan Visitor Centre (tells archaeological history and stories of the Omagh area), Grant Ancestral Home (the ancestral home of 18th US president in Ballygawley), Ardboe High Cross (richly decorated high cross dating back to the 10th century).

● **THE COUNTY**

Total Population: 152,827 (e)

County Capitals: Cookstown, Omagh, Dungannon, Strabane

Largest Town: Omagh see profile

Main Towns: Augher, Castlederg, Clogher, Cookstown, Coalisland, Dungannon, Strabane.

Main Business Contact: Ledu The Small Business Agency: 47 Kevlin Avenue, Omagh, Co Tyrone. Tel 01662-245 763.

No of Golf Clubs: 8 (5 x 18; 3 x 9).

Other Tourist Attractions: Tyrone Crystal, Corn Mill Heritage Centre (tells the story of Coalisland's industrial history).

Omagh Town

"From the Irish An Oigh Maigh - *the virgin or sacred plain."*

● **HISTORY**

Origins: There have been ancient settlements around the meeting point of the rivers, but the town is said to owe its beginnings to the establishment of an early monastery in 792.

Growth: The warring O'Neills maintained a fortress in the present town, which was particularly active during the reign of Art O'Neill in the 15th century. In 1471, Henry O'Neill captured Omagh fort or castle from Art and granted it to his eldest son Con. The earl of Kildare, who later became lord deputy in Ireland, attacked the O'Neill fortress in 1498 and again in 1507. When the abbey was dissolved by the Tudors in 1600, its lands were granted to Sir Henry Piers. With the Plantation of Ulster, Omagh was granted to Lord Castlehaven in 1609 and then to Captain Edmund Leigh, who went on to build a fort in the town. In 1641, Sir Phelim O'Neill marched against the Castle of Omagh, the garrison of which immediately surrendered to him. King James I visited the town on his way to Derry in 1689 and found the town in ruins. Omagh was rebuilt in the 18th century. Lord Mountjoy owned a vast swathe of land in the area and trade and industry began to develop once again. Around 1768, it became the county town, having taken the title from Dungannon, a courthouse and jail were built reflecting this progression. These buildings along with the town's churches are to be found on the hill above the meeting of the rivers, well out of the danger of flooding. By 1847, the town had a brewery and by 1846, it was one of the stops on the Dublin-Derry mail road. In 1852, it also had two railway stations which served the Omagh–Dungannon line and the Derry–Enniskillen line (closed in the 1960s). The 'new' military barracks were built in 1881. Today the town is still recovering from the 1998 bombing of the town centre which was the worst single atrocity of the current troubles, affecting hundreds of people from Omagh and its hinterland.

● **TODAY**

Location centre of the county on the Strule River, which meets the Rivers Camowen and Drumragh. It is sur-

rounded by hills, the steepest of which is Mullaghcarn.
Population: 17,280 (+18% from 1981 Census).
Tourist Attractions the county court house which was built in 1814, the Jail (built in 1804), Presbyterian Church (dates back to 1721, although there was a congregation in the town from 1664, this building is now known as Montgomery's Printing Works), Trinity Presbyterian Church (built in 1850), Church of Ireland (dates back to 1777), the Sacred Heart Church (consecrated in 1899, designed in neo-Gothic style), Drumragh Parish Church (1764; one of the first Catholic churches to be built in Ireland after the relaxation of the Penal Laws. Gortin Forest

● **TRANSPORT**
Main Routes: Omagh is served by major routes A5-N2 (to Dublin); A5-A4-M1 (to Belfast); A32-A509-N3-N55-N6-N62-N8-N25 (to Cork); A32-N16-N17 (to Galway).
Miles from Dublin (112); Belfast (70); Cork (241); Galway (140)
Nearest Travel Centre (Bus): Omagh. Tel 01662-242711.
Nearest Rail Station: Waterside, Derry. Tel 01504-342228.
Nearest Airport: City of Derry Airport. Tel 01504-810784.
Nearest Ferry Port: Belfast (+70 miles); Larne (+73 miles).

County Waterford

"From the Norse Vethrafjorthr - *weather haven"*
● **GEOGRAPHY**
Province: Munster
Location: maritime county on the south-eastern seaboard.
County Size: 20th in Ireland
Land area: 713.08 sq. miles
Highest point: Knocknaree Mtn (679 m)
Main Geographical Features: The diversity of the landscape found in Waterford is based on the three main rock types - the old red sandstone of the mountain ranges, the shale found in the north and the limestone belt found in the south-west. The Comeragh, Knockmealdown, and Monavullagh mountain ranges dominate the landscape and border the county to the north and north-west. Around 25 million years ago, the river valleys, particularly those in the south such as the Barrow, cut deeply into the terrain, while their lower reaches were drowned by the sea. Today the tide runs up many of these rivers for several kilometres. Other current features which date back to this time are Etch plains where chemical weathering produced flat plains. Examples of this type of land feature around found in Cappoquin.
Main Rivers: Nier; Clodiagh; Suir; Blackwater; Bride; Glenaboy; Finisk.
Main Lakes: Belle Lake.
Main Bays: Muggort's Bay; Clonea Bay.
Areas of Geographical interest: Mount Congreve Gardens in Kilmeadan, the Nire Valley (a scenic area, with glens and waterfalls), Tourin House and Gardens, the Vee (a spectacular scenic route through the Knockmealdown mountains).

● **HISTORY**
Viking: Waterford Harbour's wide sea route into the heart of the country led to the county being the focus of Viking, Norman and English activity. The county was subject to four centuries of an active Viking presence, as reflected in many of the town names, such as Helvick, meaning rock shelf in Norse.

Norman: There followed subsequent waves of Norman invasion and settlement. The city of Waterford was designated a royal city c. 1171 and became one of Ireland's major ports and merchant centres.
English: Waterford was involved in many of the turbulent events of the 18th and 19th centuries. Waterford's population showed a talent for surviving and prospering; Thomas Francis Meagher, a fervent nationalist, was sentenced to death in 1848, but he escaped to the U.S. and went on to become Governor of Montana. The county has a unique feature for the east coast in that it has a surviving Gaeltacht area - Ring - located near Dungarvan.
Areas of Historical Interest: Mount Mellerey Abbey, Portlaw (a model village founded by a Quaker family), Waterford's Castles (King John's Castle at Dungarvan, Dunhill Castle, Knockmaun Castle).

● **THE COUNTY**
Total Population: 52,140 (excluding Waterford Borough) *(1996)*
Growth rate: 1.6% increase since 1991
County Capital: Dungarvan
Largest Town: Waterford *see profile*
Main Towns: Dungarvan, Tramore, Waterford
Main Business Contact: Waterford City Enterprise Board: Enterprise House, New Street Court, Waterford. Tel 051-852 883. Waterford County Enterprise Board: Cross Bridge Street, Dungarvan, Co Waterford. Tel 058-44811.
No of Schools: National 79; Secondary 21.
No of Golf Clubs: 8 (7 x 18; 1 x 9).
Blue Flag Beaches: 3 - Counsellors Strand (Dunmore East), Bonmahon, Clonea Strand.
Other Tourist Attractions: Dromana (a Hindu-Gothic gate lodge), Laserworld, the Master McGrath Monument (possibly the only public monument to a greyhound in Ireland), Waterford Crystal Factory, West Waterford Vineyards at Cappoquin.

Waterford City

See county name

● **HISTORY**
Origins: The city was founded about 850AD by the Vikings who used the city as a naval base.
Growth The town rapidly developed under their rule as they introduced trade, currency and shipbuilding. Reginald the Dane was said to have built a tower, reputed to be the oldest mortar and stone tower in Europe, in 1003 and still in perfect condition. All around the city are remnants of the old walls the vikings built to fortify the city. The seven watch towers placed at intervals along the wall can still be seen. From Norman times one Waterford became the principal city of south-east Ireland. Dermot MacMurrough, king of Leinster, hired mercenaries - Normans, Flemish, and Welsh - to help him overcome the Norse forces. One of these mercenaries, Strongbow (Richard de Clare), married MacMurrough's daughter and stayed in Ireland. This alarmed Henry II who declared Waterford a royal city, which meant that it had remain loyal to him and his heirs. History suggests that it did. Waterford withstood a six-week siege in 1487 when Lambert Simnel, "the Pretender" was crowned in Dublin and in 1497 when Perkin Warbeck challenged the kingship. In return for the city's loyalty, Henry bestowed the motto upon the city *Urbs intacta manet Waterfordia*. The city remained strongly Catholic. In 1649, Cromwell challenged the city's walls twice, with the second siege lasting three months. He finally withdrew in return for the port. Waterford was finally surrendered to William III in 1690. One of Waterford's most famous exports is Waterford Crystal, which was manufactured in the city since the 18th century. The city remains a thriving port.

● **TODAY**
Location set in the east of the county on the River Suir at the mouth of Waterford Harbour.
Population: 44,155 (+5.5% from 1991 Census).
Tourist Attractions: Reginald's Tower, (built 1003 AD and now the Civic Museum), Waterford's town walls (including a fortified gateway at Spring Garden Alley and the Norman walls), Waterford's Catholic cathedral (finished in 1796), Christchurch Church of Ireland cathedral (designed by John Roberts) St. Olaf's, (named after a Viking saint), Greyfriars (the French Church, which was used as a monastery, hospital, and finally a place of Huguenot worship), the Municipal Library, the City Hall (1788) and the Court House (designed by Sir Richard Morrison in 1849).

● **TRANSPORT**
Main Routes: is served by major routes N24-N9-N7 (to Dublin); N24-N9-N7-M1-N1-M1-N1-A1-M1 (to Belfast); N25 (to Cork); N24-N9-N10-N77-N7-N62-N52-N65-N6-N18 (to Galway).
Miles from Dublin (101); Belfast (204); Cork (77); Galway (137).
Main Nearest Travel Centre (Bus): Bus Éireann, Plunket Station, Waterford. Tel 051-879 000.
Nearest Rail Station: Plunket Station, Waterford. Tel 051-873 401.
Nearest Airport: Waterford Airport. Tel 051-875 589.
Nearest Ferry Port: Rosslare (+51 miles); Cork (+77 miles).

County Westmeath

"From the Irish an Iar Mhí - Iar meaning west and Mí, the central place."

● **GEOGRAPHY**
Province: Leinster
Location: An inland county at the heart of Ireland
County Size: 22nd in Ireland
Land area: 710 sq. miles
Highest point: Mullaghmeen (260 m)
Main Geographical Features: Westmeath's northern regions are dotted with drumlins - small steep-sided hills that were formed by the melting glaciers of the Ice Age during the Drumlin Phase of the Ice Age (34,000 - 26,000 years ago), when glaciers deposited unsorted debris which was subsequently moulded into ovoid masses - drumlins - in the direction of the ice flow. The central and southern regions of Westmeath are flatter, with bogs and lakes. The southern part contains a long line of low hills, or eskers, yet another feature dating from the Ice Age, formed during a cold stage (80,000 - 65,000 years ago). Huge ice domes were forced to turn to the north and south by advancing Scottish ice. The inland ice was forced through the midlands, and with its retreat, it left till, moraines, sheets of sand and eskers behind.
Main Rivers: Tang; Royal Canal; Deel; Black; Inny; Riffey; Yellow, Gaine;
Main Lakes: L Ree; L Iron; L Owel; L Ennell; Brittas L; L Bane; L Derravaragh; L Lene.
Areas of Geographical interest: The Royal Canal Bank Walk, the many bogs which are subject to increasing scientific interest

● **HISTORY**
Prehistory: Lough Derravaragh was reputedly one of the lakes were the children of Lír lived for hundreds of years while transformed by an evil spell into swans. Two centuries prior to St. Patrick's arrival, the county was home to the seat of the High King of Ireland at Uisneach, near Mullingar, which was also the meeting point of the five ancient provinces of Ireland.
Early Christian: St. Patrick brought Christianity to

Westmeath in the fifth century, and there are a number of notable, early monastic sites in the county, particularly that of Fore, established by St. Fechin.

Medieval The Normans arrived in the region c. 1170, and their numerous mottes-and-baileys can still be seen around the county.

English: The county was originally part of the ancient province of Meath, but in 1542, an act of law by Henry VIII designated it as a separate county. Westmeath has played a prominent role in Ireland's history, as one of its principal towns, Athlone, is a major crossing point on the River Shannon and was the site of many major battles.

Areas of Historical Interest: Athlone Castle Interpretative Centre, the Catstone on Uisneach Hill, the Dower House of the Pollard Family at Castlepollard, Fore Abbey, St. Fechin's Church, Gigginstown House and Mearescourt House in Mullingar, the Military Museum at Columb Barracks, Tullynally Castle and Gardens in Castlepollard, Tyrrellspass Castle and Museum.

● **THE COUNTY**
Total Population: 92,166 *(1996)*
Growth rate: 1.6 % increase since 1991
County Capital: Mullingar **Largest Town:** Athlone see *profile*
Main Towns: Athlone, Kilbeggan, Kinnegad, Moate.
Main Business Contact: Westmeath County Enterprise Board: Enterprise Centre, Bishopsgate Street, Mullingar, Co Westmeath. Tel 044-49222.
No of Schools: National 77; Secondary 15.
No of Golf Clubs: 5 (5 x 18).
Blue Flag Beaches: 2 - Lilliput (Lough Ennell, Mullingar), The Cut (Lough Lene, Collinstown).
Other Tourist Attractions: An Dun Transport and Heritage Museum in Athlone, Mullingar Bronze and Pewter Visitor Centre, Locke's Distillery (one of the world's oldest licensed whiskey distilleries).

Athlone Town

"From the Irish Áth Luain - the ford of Luan, initially Áth Mór, the Great Ford; Luan reputedly kept a hostelry near the river banks and acted as a guide across the river."

● **HISTORY**

Origins: The earliest evidence of human habitation in the area is a megalithic tomb on the western part of the town. Bronze age implements have been recovered from the river bed, and the area may have been the site of an early Christian monastery.

Growth: The town owes its existence to its strategic location as one of the main river crossings on the Shannon. Toirrdelbach Ua Conchobair, the king of Connacht (1122-56), recognised this fact and built a number of bridges in the area to aid the expansion of his kingdom into Meath. The Normans arrived in 1210 and spanned a bridge over the river and started building the extant stone castle on the western side of the town. Monasteries were also established: by the Benedictines on the western shore and the Franciscans on the eastern shore. The arrival of the Normans brought about the commencement of trading and urban life. However, by 1300, the Norman town went into decline. After 1400, Gaelic clans in the area had regained their power, and the Norman castle passed alternately into the hands of the O'Kellys and the Gaelicised Norman family, the Dillons. In 1537, English government forces took retook the castle and completed a new stone bridge across the Shannon (which remained until 1840s) under the auspices of Sir Henry Sidney. The bridge facilitated the English incursion into Connacht, and the town became the seat of English government in the area in 1569. By 1599, Athlone had received its first charter, which gave it its own corporation and the right to return two members to parliament. Between 1618 and 1622, the president of Connacht, Viscount Wilmot, arranged for the townsmen to be granted the titles of their property on the proviso that they built houses in the English manner, erect a town wall (and pay Wilmot a bribe of £4,000). When Cromwell's forces occupied the town, they completed the fortification of the Leinster town and transplanted most of the Catholic townsmen to Connacht. During the Jacobite war in 1690, the Williamites captured the Leinster town and after much fighting, the Connacht town. General Ginkel was made Earl of Athlone. In 1672, the town passed into the possession of the Earl of Ranelagh. During the 18th century, the town began to prosper: its population grew, a wide variety of trades were plied, schools were established (both Catholic and Protestant) and a the local yacht club was founded in 1770 (the second oldest in Ireland). The town's barracks were extended during the 18th and 19th centuries. By the 19th century, the town's layout began to take on much of its present structure, with improvements to Shannon navigation added in the form of a by-pass canal, as well as railway lines and roads. The 19th century also saw the rise and fall of William Keogh, an MP for the town, who incurred the wrath of the townspeople by abandoning the Catholic Association 1852 to hold government office. He went on to become a judge and later committed suicide. The town was also the birthplace of the famous Irish tenor, John McCormack. Today, the town is home to many high technology industries.

● **TODAY**

Location At the centre of Ireland, on the Westmeath–Roscommon border, the town straddles the River Shannon, with the Leinster part of the town in Westmeath and the Connacht part in Roscommon
Population: 15,544 (+1.2% from 1991 Census).
Tourist Attractions The castle (dates from 1210, the oldest building in the town), the Megalith tomb at Drum (dating back 2500 BC), Sailing on Lough Ree, Lissoy (just outside Athlone, frequently visited by the poet Oliver Goldsmith), Athlone Library's local history collection.

● **TRANSPORT**
Main Routes: is served by major routes N6-N4 (to Dublin); N55-N3-N54-N12-A3-M1 (to Belfast); N6-N62-N8-N25 (to Cork); N6-N18 (to Galway).
Miles from Dublin (78); Belfast (136); Cork (136); Galway (58).
Main Nearest Travel Centre (Bus): Bus Éireann, Bus Depot, Athlone, Co. Westmeath. Tel 0902- 73322.
Nearest Rail Station: Athlone. Tel 0902-73300.
Nearest Airport: Dublin Airport. Tel 01-814 1111; Shannon Airport. Tel 061-471 444.
Nearest Ferry Port: Dublin (+78 miles).

County Wexford

"From the Norse Weissfiord - the fjord of the flats"

● **GEOGRAPHY**
Province: Leinster
Location: a maritime county set in the south-east corner of Ireland
County Size: 13th in Ireland
Land area: 909 sq. miles
Highest point: Mount Leinster (793 m)
Main Geographical Features: Known as the 'Model County', Wexford enjoys the best of Irish weather. It is bounded by the sea on the east - St. George's Channel - and by hills and rivers on the west. A wide variety of surface land features in Ireland date from the Ice Age. One strange feature, common in the south east, the irregular freezing gave rise to were pingos - dome-like masses which when melted left residual domes with a central hollow.
Main Rivers: Slaney; Barrow; Corock; Bann.
Main Lakes: Lady's Island Lake; Tacumshin Lake.
Main Bays: Wexford Bay; Rosslare Bay; Ballyteige Bay; Bannow Bay; Sandeel Bay; Lumsdin's Bay; Tacumshin Bay.
Major Offshore Islands: Saltee Islands, Tuskar Rock, Bannow (pop: 5).
Areas of Geographical interest: Wexford Wildfowl Reserve.

● **HISTORY**
Prehistory: Around 350 BC, Gaelic invaders attacked conquered the south-east naming the area Uí Cheannselaig. However, they did not inhabit the sea flats near Wexford town - leaving it to the realms of mystery and the sea people (it was known as Forth and had its own dialect up until the last century).
Medieval The Vikings attacked and settled the main town of Wexford, from the 9th to the 12th centuries
Norman: The Normans captured the town of Wexford after they landed in the country in 1169. The coast of Wexford was particularly cruel to maritime travellers, the treacherous tides, currents and moving sandbanks resulting from the meeting of the Irish Sea and the Atlantic Ocean. The area was also subject to heavy ocean-going traffic from the English and continental

ports. There have been sea wrecks in the area for centuries (well over 200 ships), from Viking Long boats to World War II submarines. One of the earliest lighthouses in north-west Europe - Hooke Lighthouse - was erected off the county's coast. The native Irish benefited from the misfortunes of others at sea - it is reported that in south Wexford, where trees were not plentiful, locals used the timbers of shipwrecks in all types of construction.
English: The county suffered Cromwell's attacks in 1649, when he attacked the town and murdered 200 people. The men of Wexford were among the main instigators in the 1798 Rebellion. Their opposition to the English came to a head at the famous Battle of Vinegar Hill in Enniscorthy
Areas of Historical Interest: Dunbrody Abbey and Visitor Centre, Hook Lighthouse (one of the oldest lighthouses in Europe, dating from the 12th century), Tintern Abbey, Wexford's Castles (Ballyhack Castle, Enniscorthy Castle, Ferns Castle, Johnstown Castle and Gardens, Rathmacknee Castle, Slade Castle), Wexford County Museum in Enniscorthy, Wexford's high crosses (at Arthurstown, Ballinaray, Carrick and Killesk), Wexford town (a designated heritage town).

● **THE COUNTY**
Total Population: 104,371 *(1996)*
Growth rate: 2.3% increase since 1991
County Capital and Largest Town: Wexford *see profile*
Main Towns: Bunclody, Enniscorthy, Gorey, New Ross, Tramore
Main Business Contact: Wexford County Enterprise Board: 16/17 Mallin Street, Cornmarket, Wexford. Tel 053-22965.
No of Schools: National 104; Secondary 20.
No of Golf Clubs: 7 (5 x 18; 1 x 9; 1 x 27).
Blue Flag Beaches / Marinas: 5 - Kilmore Quay Marina, Courtown, Curracloe, Duncannon, Rosslare.
Other Tourist Attractions: Craanford Mills, John F. Kennedy Park, (marks the birthplace of the late president's grandfather), Irish National Heritage Park at Ferrycarrig, Woodville Victorian Walled Garden in New Ross.

Wexford Town

See county name

● **HISTORY**
Origins: settlements were made in the area from prehistoric times, the earliest mention being that of Loc Garman, which was named after a Gaelic queen. However, the region because of its situation on the margins of the sea was more a home to outsiders - it was even known as for Tuatha Mara - the place of the sea people. In his seminal work 'Geography', Ptolemy named the town *Menapia* in AD 140, after a continental group from Belgium.

Growth: The Wexford coat of arms motto 'By fire and water' sums up the town's history. By the 9th century, the Vikings had established a territory in the area of the town. It was from this settlement that the modern town of Wexford developed. Trade grew up between the Vikings and neighbouring Irish clans. In 1169, Dermot MacMurrough offered the town to mercenaries in exchange for their help in regaining the Leinster kingship. The Normans entered Ireland by way of Wexford, capturing the town by siege. Churches were built in the town, its walls were reinforced and extended to hold the old Gaelic township of Loc Garman. In 1317, the town was granted its first charter, which was further ratified by subsequent English monarchs: Queen Elizabeth in 1559, James I in 1609 and James II in 1687. Cromwell besieged the town and massacred its inhabitants in 1649. The 19th century saw significant urban renewal in the town, with schools, church and quays extended as the town prospered as a maritime trading centre. The town has expanded across the new bridge, with new industries being set up in the area. Culturally, the expansion has taken the shape of the internationally renowned Wexford Opera Festival which first took place in 1951.

● **TODAY**
Location in the north east corner of the county at the mouth of Wexford Harbour
Population: 15,862 (+3% from 1991 Census)

● **TRANSPORT**
Main Routes: served by major routes N11 (to Dublin); N11-M1-N1-M1-N1-A1-M1 (to Belfast); N25 (to Cork); N25-R732-R700-N77-N7-N62-N52-N65-N6-N18 (to Galway).
Miles from Dublin (88); Belfast (187); Cork (115); Galway (157).
Nearest Travel Centre (Bus): Contact Bus Éireann, Plunket Station, Waterford. Tel 051-879 000.
Nearest Rail Station: O'Hanrahan Station, Wexford. Tel 053-22522; Rosslare Harbour Port & Station. Tel 053-33114.
Nearest Airport: Dublin Airport. Tel 01-814 1111.
Nearest Ferry Port: Rosslare (+12 miles).
Other Tourist Attractions: Theatre Royal (home to Wexford Festival Opera), Redmond Square, Bride Street church, Selskar Abbey, Commodore John Barry statue, Rowe Street church, Westgate Heritage Centre, County Hall and St Liberius church.

County Wicklow

"From the Norse Vykinglo - *Viking meadow."*

● **GEOGRAPHY**
Province: Leinster
Location: small maritime county on the east coast
County Size: 17th in Ireland
Land area: 782 sq. miles
Highest point: Lugnaquilla (927 m)
Main Geographical Features: Intrusions of granite provided the basis of the Wicklow mountains 440 million years ago. A raised granite ridge runs through the county, containing two of the highest passes in the country - the Sally Gap and the Wicklow Gap - which are major routes to the east and west for the county. To the north of this ridge is Dublin city, and to the east is the tranquil valley of Glendalough. The county is crisscrossed by rivers and is known as the 'Garden of Ireland.' A wide variety of Wicklow's topography was shaped during Ireland's Ice Age between 1,700,000 - 13,000 years ago. Gradually, over many cold periods, permafrost - a layer of permanent frozen subsoil - formed to a depth of around 20m. The first stage of this accumulation occurred on higher ground. North facing mountain hollows received the least amount of sun and permanent snow patches formed corries. The glaciers extending from these corries followed existing valleys and with their surface layer of rocks wore the V-shaped valleys into U-shaped ones, as can be seen in the shapes of the Wicklow Mountains. During the last cold stage of the Ice Age (35,000 - 13,000 years ago) large masses of ice developed over the northern half of the country and there were independent ice caps in Wicklow. These ice masses melted about 13,000 years ago.

Main Rivers: Liffey; Dargle; Slaney; Kings; Derry; Avonbeg; Avonmore; Ow; Aughrim; Vartry; Avoca; Lackan.
Main Lakes: L Bray Upper; L Bray Lower; L Tay; Broad L.
Main Bays: Brittas Bay.
Areas of Geographical interest: Blessington lakes, Lugnaquilla (Ireland's second highest mountain), National Garden Exhibition Centre at Kilquade, Powerscourt Gardens (containing the ruins of Powerscourt House and Powerscourt waterfall - Ireland's highest waterfall), Wicklow's seaside resorts (Brittas Bay, Arklow, Clogga, Sliver Strand, Bray and Greystones).

● **HISTORY**
Early Christian: The county's history is directly related to its physical setting. Glendalough was established as a monastic city from a sixth century hermitage set up by St. Kevin in the peaceful setting of 'the Glen of Two Lakes'.
Medieval Although the county's highlands assisted in protecting the county's Gaelic heritage, the lowlands of the west and the east coast were more susceptible to the successive raids launched by the Vikings, the Normans and the English. Dermot McMurrough, a

Wicklow chieftain and king of Leinster, invited the Normans to help him repossess his lands, and it was this act that led to English taking power and that ultimately directed the course of Irish history.

English: The English sojourn in the county is marked by the many stately homes and gardens scattered around the county, the most notable of these being Powerscourt and Russborough House. Many of Wicklow's villages still reflect their English origins as estate villages. The Irish kept their hold on the highlands, providing refuge to rebels, and the people of Wicklow played a prominent role in the 1798 rebellion. However, after the rebellion, the British built the Military Road through the county to provide them with easier access to the rebel strongholds.

Areas of Historical Interest: Avondale House (the home of Charles Stewart Parnell), Glendalough (with its many monastic ruins, has an interpretive centre to detail the ancient history of the area), the Maritime Museum in Arklow, Russborough House (an 18th century Palladian mansion that houses the internationally renowned Sir Alfred Beit art collection), Wicklow Historic Gaol, Wicklow Mountains National Park, Avoca (home to Ballykissangel), Powerscourt Estate and Gardens, the Wicklow Way (a walking route of 132 km through the county), the National Garden Exhibition Centre in Kilquade), Avoca Handweavers and Gardens, the Wicklow and Sally Gaps.

● **THE COUNTY**
Total Population: 102,683 *(1996)*
Growth rate: 5.6% increase since 1991
County Capital: Wicklow
Largest Town: Bray *see profile*
Main Towns: Arklow, Bray, Greystones, Wicklow
Main Business Contact: Wicklow County Enterprise Board: 1 Main Street, Wicklow. Tel 0404- 67100.
No of Schools: National 85; Secondary 21.
No of Golf Clubs: 21 (16 x 18; 5 x 9).
Blue Flag Beaches: 3 - Greystones South, Brittas Bay Nth, Brittas Bay Sth.
Other Tourist Attractions: Arklow Pottery, the National Aquarium at Bray.

Bray Town

"From the Norse Brae *- the brow of the hill, the hill being Bray Head."*

● **HISTORY**
Origins: there have been settlements in the area, dating back to prehistoric and early Christian times. Before the Normans, the area was known as Uí Briuin Cuallan and was shared between the Dublin Vikings and the son-in-law of Diarmuid Mac Murchada.
Growth: the town's beginnings date back to 1171, when the manor of Bré at the ford of the Dargle river was granted to Walter de Ridlesford, who built a castle overlooking the river in 1173. A Norman town, with its own mill grew up around the ford. The lands in the area passed into the possession of the Monastery of St Thomas. However, in 1316, the castle was destroyed by the Gaelic clans of the O'Byrnes and O'Tooles, who frequently attacked the area. In the 14th century, the area the town now occupies was already known as Much Bre and Lytle Bre. In 1402, the citizens of Dublin launched a battle against the Wicklow clans on a hill in the present town. With the dissolution of the abbies by the Tudor dynasty, the lands around Bré passed into the hands of Sir William Brabazon. By 1657, the now established village had taken on the anglicised name of Bray. A bridge was built over the Dargle in 1666, a barracks was constructed in 1692 and occupied by the military (until 1818) and by 1700, the village, with a population of about 560 souls, extended from Sunnybank to Quinsboro' Road. A regular coach service through the village was established by 1770, with a mail service dating back to 1790. With the frequent traffic, trade grew and Quin's Hotel (now the Royal) was set up as a coaching in 1776. In 1854, this regular traffic was further supplement by the extension of the Dublin–Kingstown Railway to the village. Immediately following this, exotic Turkish baths were constructed, a long grass walkway was laid out beside the seafront, men's and women's bathing areas were set out, hotels and fine terraced houses were built - the Victorian seaside resort of Bray was born. Posters of time herald the town as "Bright and breezy Bray, the Brighton of Ireland". But Bray was more than a resort. It had its own gas works and its own brewery and was Ireland's earliest commuter town. Many other industrial and commercial buildings were added to the town during this time, including the town hall and market (1881), and in 1898, Bray received its own urban district council. The population of the town grew considerably in this period and continued to grow after 1900. Always a tourist centre, the town became more so during the war years when many English and Scottish travelled here to escape rationing at home.
Today: Bray continues to grow rapidly (its population has grown by 3.9% between 1991 and 1996) - in line with all of the towns in the Dublin area. Much of its population commute to work in the city, but a growing number of industries have relocated to Bray.

● **GENERAL**
Location Just south of Dublin city, set on the east coast on the River Dargle at the foot of Bray Head and the Sugar Loaf Mountain
Population: 27,923 (+3.59% from 1991 Census).
Tourist Attractions: The Town Hall and Market (1881), The Old Court House (est. 1841, now a Heritage Centre), the promenade and sea-wall (est. 1886), Esplanade Tce (built by Oscar Wilde's father, Sir William Wilde, during the Victorian era), Raheen a Cluig (dates from AD 1200, an old church at the foot of Bray Head), the Obelisk (at the

front of the Heritage Centre, erected to Dr Christopher Thompson for his tireless work during the 1876 typhoid epidemic), No. 1 Martello Tce (where James Joyce lived as a young boy), Bray Bridge (first constructed in 1660, the present bridge dates back to 1856) the Harbour and Lighthouse (dates back to 1891), Sculpture of William Dargan (created by Ruth Romney in the Old Court House), St. Paul's Church (est. 1609, it is one of the earliest post-Reformation churches in the country), Holy Redeemer Church (dates back to 1792, the present building was constructed in 1824), the People's Park (the last area of the town's common land), St. Andrew's church (the Presbyterian church, est. 1859), Prince of Wales Terrace (a fine example of early Victorian town residences), the Railway Station (another example of Victorian architecture), Kilruddery House and Gardens (home to the Brabazon family - the earls of Meath - since 1618), the Cliff Walk (takes in Bray Head, Greystones and the Sugar Loaf Mountain), the National Sea Life Aquarium, the Martello Tower (built in 1805 to protect the coast from attack during the Napoleonic Wars).

● **TRANSPORT**

Main Routes: is served by major routes N11 (to Dublin); N11-M1-N1-M1-N1-A1-M1 (to Belfast); N11-N7-N8 (to Cork); N11-N4-N6-N18 (to Galway).
Miles from Dublin (13); Belfast (118); Cork (172); Galway (151)
Main Nearest Travel Centre (Bus): Busaras, Store Street, Dublin 1. Tel 01-836 6111
Nearest Rail Station: Bray. Tel 01-286 2236
Nearest Airport: Dublin Airport. Tel 01-814 1111.
Nearest Ferry Port: Dublin (+13 miles).

THE ECONOMY

An Irish Ecommerce Renaissance?

By Gerry McGovern

ALMOST four years ago I wrote in a report for Forbairt (now Enterprise Ireland) that there was the opportunity for a new Irish renaissance if we took the Digital Age seriously and fully embraced the Internet. Today, I see a lot of progress but there is still a lot more to do.

Ireland has the skills and resources to become a powerhouse in the Digital Age. The new age is all about fostering an Information Society. Naturally, such a society is driven by information and much of that information, certainly that which is found on the Internet, is in written form. The Irish are excellent writers and communicators and these skills are central to the new economy. The Irish are excellent programmers, have an outstanding musical heritage and are developing a strong visual arts tradition. These are the fundamental skills in a new society and economy where the dominant resources are not so much those you dig out of the ground, but those you mine from the imagination.

Culture is a huge raw material today, and when combined with the above skills, it can create product of high value. Rural Ireland should not be as isolated anymore, if we can embrace teleworking technologies which allow your work to travel and not you. Anyone who experiences the traffic mayhem in Dublin and its very demeaning of the basic quality of life, must surely wish for something better. Teleworking can bring people and jobs back to rural Ireland while at the same time rescuing our cities from the traffic slums they have become.

When I graduated from college in 1984, the lucky ones got low-paying, low-hope jobs in Ireland, while the rest headed to London or America. The idea that you might set up a business was laughable. It is hard to believe how different a world we live in today. Confidence, once thought extinct on these shores, has blossomed. Young people think they can take on the world and win, and it's great. The older generations are infused too and banks will actually give you money today without demanding a lean on your soul. No longer are you valued by the amount of bricks and mortar you have. Today, more and more financiers recognise the value of intellectual assets, of software.

The Government has led the way in making Ireland ecommerce friendly. Our ministers 'get it' and their civil servants get it even more. We are seeing bold, visionary initiatives that seek not to imitate but to lead.

So, it is all rosy in the cyber-garden? While our Government does indeed get it, there is still a fundamental shift in thinking that it and its agencies must make if Ireland is to truly prosper. Over the last 30 years the IDA has done a magnificent job in attracting foreign multinationals to locate here. That strategy is no longer so valid in the age before us. We are no longer the cheap labour-force we once were. Turning Ireland into a hub where other ecommerce entities can supply Europe is the wrong approach. Ireland must become a centre. Irish companies need to build brands and sell products into the new economy. It is time we moved from a labour force to a driving force.

While Irish business claims to recognise the importance of the Internet and ecommerce, there is precious little evidence that they are taking serious action to back up their beliefs. We simply don't understand that America exists in another universe when it comes to the Internet. Many of the brands that will dominate the 21st Century are already built and they are nearly all American. Irish business needs to spend and spend big if they are to really exploit the opportunities the Internet offers.

It may be easier to get a loan today but venture capital in Ireland is still quite lame. America, again, recognises that venture capital is about ventures and taking big risks to win big. This is an era of big risks and big failures but also huge success. But let's be realistic. The Internet is the most ferociously competitive marketplace in the world. Yes, co-operation and free information may be abundant, but the Internet takes no prisoners. Behind the shine of the new it is a hard, cruel world where those who don't cut it disappear into the million-deep website graveyard.

If anyone asks you what exactly ecommerce is, tell them that 90% of ecommerce is information. Providing quality information on a consistent basis is not cheap. It requires a well-planned information infrastructure and quality people who know what they're talking about and write well. If you get an order from Chile, how are you going to deliver it? How do you deal with taxes? How do you deal with returns? One of the biggest problems ecommerce websites face today is either a lack of a comprehensive stock offering or else a poor integration with their traditional stock control systems. Too many people are being told some days after ordering something that it's out of stock. That's not good enough.

But the biggest challenge to a successful ecommerce brand today is marketing. First-mover advantage usually brings with it both word-of-mouth and media promotion. What happens when you don't have first-mover advantage? You better have a big marketing budget. Over 50% of Internet users go to less than fifty websites. When you launch you're out there with the 10 million other websites desperately trying to attract people. An average ecommerce website in America that will spend $2-3 million on development and $10 million on marketing and advertising. The Americans understand that success on the Internet is all about marketing.

While the nineties has brought huge prosperity to Ireland we have still some catching up to do. Computer and Internet usage could be stronger. Without these foundations, it is hard to grow an ecommerce economy. Of course any successful ecommerce entity must export, particularly to the United States. However, having a vibrant home market where you can learn and solidify a bit is always welcome.

The Internet does not make the world a fairer place. It increases the divide between rich and poor. If people think that basic literacy is a major problem to overcome today, then they should also realise that technological literacy (the ability to use a computer, search the Internet, etc.) is a basic requirement for entry into the Information Society. Left alone, the divide between information rich and information poor will widen. Major initiatives are required here if we are not to create an even more unequal society.

In 1995, my company, Nua, started with three people and a £5,000 personal bank overdraft. Today, we have over 100 people and are profitable. Having returned home in the early nineties I had made a decision that I would make it here or nowhere. I believe that we can and will create something great. Let us not forget, however, that a civilised society is a just society. We should measure our progress in relation to how it improves the lives of all our citizens, not just the lucky few.

Gerry McGovern
gerry@nua.ie
October 1999

The author is founder and CEO of Local Ireland Ltd and Nua Ltd, both of which are on the cutting edge of Internet business and information development. He is also author of *The Caring Economy: Internet Business Principles*.

Statistics at a Glance

Republic of Ireland

● **MAIN FIGURES "AT A GLANCE"**

Euro......................................0.787564 (Irish Pounds)
Number 1 Company ....Intel Ireland
Taxes Collected....................................IR£14,280m[1]
Trade (Imports)..............................IR£31,096.7m
Trade (Exports) ....IR£44,777.3m
Coins Produced................................174.7m
Notes Produced................................136.3
GDP..IR£54,722m[2]
GDP Growth..10.4%
Inflation 2.6%
Employment in Financial Services...............44,200[3]
Letter Post Items Delivered........................669.8m
Planning Permissions Granted.....................37,223
Average New House Prices ....IR£93,724

1 provisional; 2 estimate;
3 includes banking, building societies and insurance only.

Northern Ireland

● **MAIN FIGURES "AT A GLANCE"**

Number 1 Company...............Viridian (NI Electricity)
Trade (Imports)..Stg£14,175[1]
Trade (Exports)...Stg£5,142[1]
GDP ....Stg£15,468m
GDP Growth...2.1%[2]
Inflation ....2.1%[2]
Employment in Financial Services...............68,000

1 1997 figures;
2 UK figures;
5 includes banking, building societies and insurance only.

The Euro

Fixed Conversion Rates between the Euro and Currencies of the participating Member States

EU Member State	Euro	Conversion Rate*
Austria	1 euro =	13.7603 Austrian schilling
Belgium	1 euro =	40.3399 Belgian franc
Finland	1 euro =	5.94573 Finnish markka
France	1 euro =	6.55957 French franc
Germany	1 euro =	1.95583 German mark
IRELAND	**1 EURO =**	**0.787564 IRISH POUND**
Italy	1 euro =	1936.27 Italian lira
Luxembourg	1 euro =	40.3399 Luxembourg franc
Netherlands	1 euro =	2.20371 Dutch guilder
Portugal	1 euro =	200.482 Portuguese escudo
Spain	1 euro =	166.386 Spanish Peseta

* (as of Jan. 1st 1999)

The Euro is the single currency that has been introduced by the Economic and Monetary Union (EMU) to replace all national currencies of the following participating EU Member States (Austria, Belgium, Finland, France, Germany, Ireland, Italy, Luxembourg, Netherlands, Portugal and Spain). The Euro came into existence in January 1999, but the notes and coins will not be in circulation until January 2002.

Companies

RoI: Profile of Top 30 Companies

1
Intel Ireland Computer chip manufacturer £m Turnover 3300.00(e) Employees 4,100 Chief Executive John McGowan Address Collinstown Industrial Park, Leixlip, Co Kildare Telephone 01-6067000.

2
CRH Building materials manufacturer and supplier £m Turnover 3213.00 £m Profit 253.20 Employees 22,708 Chief Executive Don Godson Address Belgard Castle, Clondalkin, Dublin 22 Telephone 4591111.

3
Dell Products Europe (BV) PC manufacturer and sales £m Turnover 3000.00 Employees 3,800 Chief Executive Padraic Allen Address Raheen Industrial Estate, Co Limerick Telephone 061-304091.

4
Jefferson Smurfit Group Print and packaging £m Turnover 2570.86 £m Profit 150.17 Employees 2,535 Chief Executive Dr Michael Smurfit Address Beech Hill, Clonskeagh, Dublin 4 Telephone 01-2696622.

5
Glanbia Dairy/meat producer £m Turnover 2369.60 £m Profit 60.02 Employees 12,000 Chief Executive Ned Sullivan Address AW House, Kilkenny Telephone 056-72200.

6
Microsoft European Operations Centre Software manufacturer and distributor £m Turnover 2256.00 Employees 800 Chief Executive Kevin Dillon Address Blackthorn Road, Sandyford Industrial Estate, Dublin 18 Telephone 01-2953826.

7
Fyffes Fruit and vegetable importer and distributor £m Turnover 1501.00 £m Profit 62.10 Employees 3,179 Chief Executive David McCann Address 1 Beresford Street, Dublin 7 Telephone 01-8095555.

8
The Irish Dairy Board Exporters of dairy produce £m Turnover 1400.00 £m Profit 24.00 Employees 3,117 Chief Executive Noel Cawley Address Grattan House, Lower Mount Street, Dublin 2 Telephone 01-6619599.

9
Telecom Eireann (now Eircom) Telecommunications £m Turnover 1350.00 £m Profit 222.69 Employees 11,560 Chief Executive Alfie Kane Address St Stephen's Green West, Dublin 2 Telephone 01-6714444.

10
Kerry Group Food processing £m Turnover 1344.10 £m Profit 78.60 Employees 12,500 Chief Executive Denis Brosnan Address Princes Street, Tralee, Co Kerry Telephone 066-7182000.

11
Dunnes Stores Retail chain £m Turnover 1250.00(e) Employees 9,500 Chief Executive Margaret Heffernan Address 67 Upper Stephen Street, Dublin 8 Telephone 01-4751111.

12
Electricity Supply Board Electricity supply £m Turnover 1191.15 £m Profit 131.60 Employees 7,500 Chief Executive Ken O'Hara Address Lower Fitzwilliam Street, Dublin 2 Telephone 01-6765831.

13
Musgrave Wholesale distribution £m Turnover 983.40 Employees 2,100 £m Profit 28.50 Chief Executive Seamus Scally Address Airport Road, Cork Telephone 021-963700.

14
Oracle Europe Software manufacturer and sales £m Turnover 900.00 Employees 720 Chief Executive John Appleby Address Oracle House, Herbert Street, Dublin 2 Telephone 01-8031000.

15
Guinness Ireland Brewing £m Turnover 831.00 £m Profit 161.00 Employees 2,300 Chief Executive Brian Duffy Address St James's Gate, Dublin 8 Telephone 01-4533645.

16
Tesco Ireland Supermarket retail £m Turnover 810.00(e) Employees 10,000 Chief Executive Maurice Pratt Address PO Box 3, Gresham House, Marine Road, Co Dublin Telephone 01-2808441.

17
Aer Lingus Air transportation £m Turnover 802.30 £m Profit (48.0) Employees 5,090 Chief Executive Garry Cullen Address Head Office, Dublin Airport, Co Dublin Telephone 01-7052222.

18
Irish Distillers Group Distillers £m Turnover 760.00 £m Profit 58.90 Employees 2,010 Chief Executive Richard Burrows Address Bow Street Distillery, Smithfield, Dublin 7 Telephone 01-8725566.

19
DCC Industrial holding company £m Turnover 702.80 £m Profit 36.50 Employees 2,170 Chief Executive Jim Flavin Address DCC House, Brewery Road, Stillorgan, Co Dublin Telephone 01-2831011.

20
Irish Food Processors Meat process and export £m Turnover 700.00 Employees 2,950 Chief Executive Laurence Goodman Address 14 Castle Street, Ardee, Co Louth Telephone 041-6853754.

21
Swords Laboratories Pharmaceutical manufacturer £m Turnover 690.00 Employees 358 Chief Executive Tibor Racz Address Watery Lane, Swords, Co Dublin Telephone 01-8406611.

22
IAWS Group Agri business £m Turnover 675.30 £m Profit 26.20 Employees 950 Chief Executive Philip Lynch Address 151-156 Thomas Street, Dublin 8 Telephone 01-6121200.

23
Janssen Pharmaceutical (Irl) Pharmaceutical intermediaries £m Turnover 650.00 Employees 450 Chief

Executive Bryan Mohally *Address* Little Island, Co Cork *Telephone* 021-353321.

24

Dairygold Co-op Society Dairy products £m *Turnover* 617.00 £m *Profit* 16.70 *Employees* 2,898 *Chief Executive* Denis Lucey *Address* Fermoy Road, Mitchelstown, Co Cork *Telephone* 025-24411.

25

Apple Computers Computer manufacturing £m *Turnover* 600.00(e) *Employees* 950 *Chief Executive* Joe Gantly *Address* Hollyhill Industrial Estate, Cork *Telephone* 021-392088.

26

Glen Dimplex Small domestic appliance manufacturer £m *Turnover* 600.00 *Employees* 6,000 *Chief Executive* Martin Naughton *Address* Ardee Road, Dunleer, Co Louth *Telephone* 01-2838277.

27

Independent Newspapers Print and publishing £m *Turnover* 598.80 £m *Profit* 100.10 *Employees* 8,782 *Chief Executive* Liam Healy *Address* 1/2 Upper Hatch Street, Dublin 2 *Telephone* 01-4758432.

28

Golden Vale Dairy products £m *Turnover* 564.50 £m *Profit* 16.20 *Employees* 2,010 *Chief Executive* Jim Murphy *Address* Charleville, Co Cork *Telephone* 063-81501.

29

Gateway 2000 PC manufacturer and sales £m *Turnover* 545.00(e) *Employees* 1,900 *Chief Executive* Mike Swallwell *Address* Clonshaugh Industrial Estate, Coolock, Dublin 17 *Telephone* 01-7972000.

30

EMC (Benelux) BV Computer data storage £m *Turnover* 525.00 (e) *Employees* 650 *Chief Executive* Veronica Perdisatt *Address* Ovens, Co Cork *Telephone* 021-281500.

Source: Business & Finance Magazine February 1999 edition.

(e) = estimate

NI: Profile of Top 10 Companies

1

NIE/Viridian Electricity service *Established* 1973 £m *Turnover* 512.2 £m *Pre-Tax Profit* 86.6 *Employees* 2,160 *Chief Executive* Patrick Haren *Town* Belfast.

2

Short Brothers Plc Aircraft manufacturers *Established* 1936 £m *Turnover* 432.5 £m *Pre-Tax Profit* 43.8 *Employees* 8,158 *Chief Executive* George Quigley *Town* Belfast.

3

Glen Electric Ltd Heating appliance manufacturers *Established* 1973 £m *Turnover* 409.4 £m *Pre-Tax Profit* 22.4 *Employees* 3,473 *Chief Executive* Martin Naughton *Town* Newry.

4

Powerscreen International Plc Screening equipment manufacturers *Established* 1970 £m *Turnover* 310.6 £m *Pre-Tax Profit* (-47.5) *Employees* 1,951 *Group Managing Director* Don Campbell *Town* Dungannon.

5

FG Wilson (Engineering) Ltd Manufacturers and assembly of diesel generators *Established* 1966 £m *Turnover* 247.7 £m *Pre-Tax Profit* 27.8 *Employees* 1,953 *President* Dick Nitto *Town* Larne.

6

United Dairy Farmers Milk marketing *Established* 1995 £m *Turnover* 233.9 £m *Pre-Tax Profit* 1.8 *Employees* 705 *Managing Director* David Stewart *Town* Belfast.

7

Harland & Wolff Group Shipbuilders *Established* 1861 £m *Turnover* 222.9 £m *Pre-Tax Profit* 5.1 *Employees* 1,920 *Chief Executive* Per Nielson *Town* Belfast.

8

Dunnes Stores (Bangor) Ltd Supermarket proprietors *Established* 1969 £m *Turnover* 218.5 £m *Pre-Tax Profit* 23.3 *Employees* 1,615 *General Manager* Eddie Kane *Town* Newry.

9

John Henderson Ltd Grocery wholesalers and retailers *Established* 1923 £m *Turnover* 196.2 £m *Pre-Tax Profit* 3.0 *Employees* 1,094 *Chief Executive* John Agnew *Town* Newtownabbey.

=10

J & J Haslett Ltd Grocery wholesalers and retailers *Established* 1854 £m *Turnover* 178.1 £m *Pre-Tax Profit* 6.2 *Employees* 692 *Chief Executive* Harry Morrison *Town* Belfast.

=10

Charles Hurst Group Commercial vehicles and car dealers *Established* 1938 £m *Turnover* 178.1 £m *Pre-Tax Profit* 3.8 *Employees* 549 *Chief Executive* Ken Surgenor *Town* Belfast.

Source: Ulster Business/Dun & Bradstreet August 1999 edition.

RoI: Location of Acquisitions

Location	1994 (%)	1995 (%)	1996 (%)	1997 (%)	1998 (%)
Republic of Ireland	41	51	40	36	41
UK	30	31	29	29	27
Other European Countries	11	8	12	10	13
United States	13	7	15	17	14
Rest of World	5	3	4	8	5
Total:	100	100	100	100	100

Rol: Top Ten Domestic Acquisitions by Irish Companies, 1998

Rank	Acquirer	Target Company	Nature	Value IR£000s
1	Irish Life	Irish Permanent	Financial Services	2,800,000
2	Tedcastle Oil Products	ADM Londis	Food, Drink & Agri	45,000
3	CBT Group	Knowledge Well	IT / Communication	34,000
4	Heiton Holdings	Cooper Clarke Group	Construction & Property	22,900
5	Golden Vale	Rye Valley Foods	Food, Drink & Agri	19,400
6	DCC	B M Browne	Medical	14,900
7	MBO	Betatherm Corporation	Engineering	12,700
8	Protaras	Peterhead Group	Construction & Property	12,600
9	DCC	Burmah Ireland	Natural Resource	11,500
10	MBO	NZI Life	Financial Services	10,000

Rol: Top Ten Foreign Acquisitions by Irish Companies, 1998

Rank	Acquirer	Target Company	Nature	Value IR£000s
1	Elan Corporation	Neurex (USA)	Medical	498,000
2	Kerry Group Plc.	Dalgety (Europe)	Food, Drink & Agri	394,000
3	CRH Plc.	Ibstock (UK)	Construction & Property	130,000
4	Green Property	Trafford Park Estates (UK)	Construction & Property	130,000
5	CBT Group	Forefront (USA)	IT / Communication	108,000
6	Elan Corporation	GWC Health (USA)	Medical	107,000
7	Elan Corporation	Nano Systems (USA)	Medical	101,000
8	Jefferson Smurfit Group	MacMillan Bathurst (Canada)[1]	Print & Packaging	83,000
9	Greencore Plc.	Pauls Malt (UK)	Food, Drink & Agri	74,000
10	Dunloe Ewart	Sydney & London Prop Ltd. & Gross Hill Prop Ltd. (UK)	Construction & Property	72,600

[1] 50%

Taxation and Budgets

Rol: Tax Tables 1999-2000

Applies to April 1999 - April 2000 unless otherwise stated.

INCOME TAX

Rates:

	Single	Married
24% on First	IR£14,000	IR£28,000
46% on Balance		

Main Allowances: IR£

Single Person	4,200
Married Couple	8,400
Widowed Person*	4,200
P.A.Y.E. Allowance	1,000
Child Allowance (Incapacitated)	1,000
Dependent Relative Allowance	110
Age 65 or over (single)	400
Age 65 or over (married)	800

* Widow in year of bereavement - IR£8,400

RELIEFS

● **VHI & BUPA Premiums**

Relief for 1999-2000 is available at 24% only for the premium paid in.

● **Rents**

Relief is allowed at the standard rate of tax of 24% for persons under 55 and at 46% for persons 55 or over.

	Single £	Widowed £	Married £
under 55	500	750	1,000
55 or over	1,000	1,500	2,000

● **Pension Contributions**

Relief is available for contributions to revenue approved schemes at the marginal rate. Contributions are limited to 15% of net relevant earnings.

● **Mortgage Interest**

Relief is at the standard rate of tax only of 24%. The maximum relief is:

	Single	Married	Widow
Existing Mortgages	1,900	3,800	2,870

Special rates apply to first time buyers

● **Medical Expenses**

Relief is available at the taxpayer's marginal rate for

Continued from previous page

expenses paid in excess of £200 (£100 single person).

P.R.S.I. & LEVIES

The P.R.S.I. rates are:

	IR £ 0-25,400	IR £ 25,400-35,000	IR £ over 35,000
Employees	4.5%	2%	2%
Employer*	12%	12%	Nil
Self-Employed	5%	2%	2%

* 8.5% if earning less than IR£14,560.

The Health levy is 2% on all income (less benefits in kind), and applies only where annual income is over £11,250

CORPORATION TAX

Rates:
Standard Rate* 28%
Manufacturing Rate 10%
* *A rate of 25% applies to the first IR£100,000 of taxable income.*

NI: Tax Tables 1999-2000

Applies to April 1999 - April 2000 unless otherwise stated.

INCOME TAX

Rates: *Stg£*
10% on first 1,500
23% on next...26,500
40% on balance...

Main Allowances:
Personal Allowance 4,335
Married Couple's Allowance[1] 1,970
Additional Widow's Bereavement Allowance[1] .1,970
Additional One-Parent Families' Allowance* ...1,970
Blind Person's Allowance 1,380
Age Allowance 65-74 (single)[2] 5,720
Age Allowance 65-74 (married)[2] 5,125
Age Allowance 75 and over (single)[2] 5,980
Age Allowance 75 and over (married)[2]..............5,195

1 *Relief restricted to 10%*
2 *Excess over basic allowances withdrawn by £1 for every £2 of income over £16,800.*

RELIEFS

● **Individual Savings Accounts (ISAs)**

	Maxi ISA (£)	Mini ISA (£)
Stocks and Shares	up to 7,000	3,000
Cash	up to 3,000	3,000
Life Insurance	up to 1,000	1,000

Only one Maxi ISA or up to three Mini ISAs can be invested in per each tax year.

CAPITAL GAINS TAX

Rates:
Personal Exemption £1,000
Standard Rate 20%
Development Land Gain 40%

CAPITAL ACQUISITIONS TAX

CLASS THRESHOLDS:

Relationship to Disponer:	IR£
Child, minor child of deceased child	192,900
Other blood relatives	25,720
None of the above	12,860

Rates of Tax	Inheritance	Gift
Threshold Amount	nil	nil
next IR£10,000	20%	15%
next IR£30,000	30%	22.5%
Balance	40%	30%

PROBATE TAX: Charged at a rate of 2% on estates valued over IR£11,250.

● **Pension Contributions**

Relief for private pension contributions is limited as follows:

	% of Net Relevant Earnings	
Age	P.P.P.	R.A.P.
35 or under	17.5	17.5
36-45	20.0	17.5
46-50	25.0	17.5
51-55	30.0	20.0
56-60	35.0	22.5
61 or over	40.0	27.5

The general earnings cap is £STG 90,600.
PPP - Personal Pension Policy
RAP - Retirement Annuity Policy

● **National Insurance:**
Earnings limits are as follows:

	Lower Earnings Limit - Annual Stg£	Upper Earnings Limit - Annual Stg£
Class 1 employee	3,432	26,000
Class 2 employee	3,770	26,000
Class 4 employee	7,530	26,000
Employer	3,432	-

Class 1 Employees not contracted out rates:

Weekly Earnings £STG	Employees %	Employers %
Below 66	nil	nil
66 -83	10	nil
83 -500	10	12.2
Over 500	0	12.2

Continued from previous page

Class 1 Employees contracted out rates:

Weekly Earnings £STG	Employees	Employers SRS	MPS
Below 66	nil	nil	nil
66-83	8.4%	nil	nil
83-500	8.4%	9.2%	11.6%
over 500	0	12.2%	12.2%

SRS - Salary Related Scheme
MPS - Money Purchase Scheme

CORPORATION TAX

Rates:
Standard Rate 30%
Small Companies Rate................................20%

Small Companies Rate Limit £300,000
Marginal Relief Limit...................................£1,500,000
Marginal Rate 32.5%

CAPITAL GAINS TAX

Rates:
Individual Annual Exemption £7,100
Trusts £3,550

INHERITANCE TAX

Rates:
Chargeable Value up to £231,000.........................0%
Chargeable Value over £231,000.......................40%

RoI: Budget Highlights (December 1998)

Changes in Rates	Old Rate %	New Rate %
Corporation Tax	32	28
Health Levy	1.25	2
DIRT on Special Savings Accounts	10	20
Off-course Betting Tax	10	5
Self-employed Pension Contributions	15	30

Other Changes	Amount
Decrease in Auto LPG	1.8p per litre
Increase on packet of 20 Cigarettes	5p
Increase on Cigars (25g approx.)	7p
Increase on Fine Cut Tobacco (25g approx.)	6p
New Employers' P.R.S.I. ceiling	£35,000
New Employees' P.R.S.I. ceiling	£25,400
Increase in Social Welfare Payments	£3 per week
Increase in Old Age Pensions	£6 per week
Increase in Child Benefit - first and second child	£3 per month
Increase in Child Benefit - third and subsequent children	£34 per month
Increase in Family Income Supplement Income Level	£8 per week
Increase in PRSI Allowance	£200
Increase in Single Personal Allowance	£1,050
Increase in Married Personal Allowance	£2,100
Increase in Personal Tax Allowance for blind person	£500
Increase in Personal Tax Allowance for blind couple	£1,000
New Lower Tax Band for single person	£14,000
New Lower Tax Band for married couple	£28,000

NI: Budget Highlights (March 1999)

Changes in Rates	Old Rate %	New Rate %
Stamp Duty for Houses worth more than £250,000	2	2.5
Corporation Tax	31	30
Starting Rate of Income Tax	20	10
Basic Rate of Income Tax (from April 2000)	23	22

Other Changes	Amount
Increase on packet of 20 cigarettes	17.5p per packet
Increase in Unleaded Petrol	3.79p per litre
Increase in Leaded Petrol	4.25p per litre
Increase in Diesel	6.14p per litre
Increase in Ultra-low Sulphur Diesel	4.69p per litre
Increase in Insurance Premium Tax (from July 1999)	1p
Increase in Capital Gains Tax Exemption	£300

→ Continued from previous page

Other Changes	Amount
Decrease in Tax cut on Pools	17.5%
New Winter Allowance for the Elderly	£100 a year
New Child Benefit for first child	£15 per week
New Child Benefit for second and subsequent children	£10 per week
Increase in Landfill Tax	£1 per tonne
Decrease in Vehicle Excise Duty for small cars (from July 1999)	£55

RoI: Taxation Yields

Sector	1996 (IR£m)	1997 (IR£m)	1998 (IR£m)
P.A.Y.E.	3,894	4,357	4,755
Self-Employed	527	644	736
Income Tax from Non-PAYE Sources	158	208	251
V.A.T.	3,109	3,707	4,267
Excise:	2,304	2,523	2,825
Excise Duty on Tobacco	533	573	616
Excise Duty on Alcohol	552	579	608
Tax on Motor Vehicles	353	396	484
Excise Duty on Hydrocarbons	795	895	1,028
Other Indirect Taxes	71	79	87
Corporation Tax	1,428	1,697	2,059
Stamp Duty	332	424	541
Residential Property Tax	14	3	1
Other Capital Taxes	166	221	305
Revenue Investigations and Audits	133	132	133
Other	31	47	27
Total Net Tax Receipts	12,096	13,963	15,900

RoI: Taxes Collected

Year	Total Arrears (£m)	Taxes Collected (£m)	Year	Total Arrears (£m)	Taxes Collected (£m)
1988	3,501	6,100	1994	2,057	9,427
1989	2,985	6,242	1995	1,978	9,870
1990	2,718	6,763	1996	1,690	11,468
1991	2,538	7,247	1997	1,329	12,794
1992	2,437	8,037	1998	1,167	14,280[1]
1993	2,215	8,524	1 Provisional		

Trade

RoI: Trade by Area

Area (£m)	1997			1998[1]		
	Imports	Exports	Balance	Imports	Exports	Balance
European Union:						
Britain and Northern Ireland	8,945.4	8,706.4	-239.0	10,438.4	9,946.4	-492.0
Other Member States	5,604.4	15,198.0	9,593.6	6,290.5	20,327.6	14,037.1
Total: European Union	14,549.8	23,904.4	9,354.6	16,728.9	30,274.0	13,545.1
Other Countries	10,633.0	10,581.6	-51.4	13,385.4	13,708.0	322.6
Unclassified	699.4	850.4	151.0	982.4	795.3	-187.1
Total:	25,882.2	35,336.4	9,454.2	31,096.8	44,777.3	13,680.5

NI: Trade

Year	Imports	Exports	Year	Imports	Exports
1992	12,937	4,392	1995	14,952	5,083
1993	13,859	4,688	1996	14,918	4,981
1994	14,830	4,958	1997	14,175	5,142

RoI: Composition of Imports & Exports

Sector (£m)	Imports			Exports		
	1996	1997	1998[1]	1996	1997	1998[1]
Food & Live Animals	1,545.8	1,656.3	1,808.0	4,143.2	3,624.5	3,955.2
Beverages & Tobacco	233.4	275.8	322.4	517.8	549.6	568.7
Crude Materials, Inedible, except Fuels	407.3	448.2	511.2	556.7	607.6	582.4
Mineral Fuels, Lubricants & Materials	823.7	897.6	789.1	116.6	147.3	119.1
Animal & Vegetable Oils etc.	82.3	83.0	94.2	28.0	28.7	39.0
Chemicals & Related Products	2,762.1	3,210.6	3,402.9	6,724.3	8,933.0	14,206.2
Manufactured Goods	2,422.8	2,682.1	2,929.1	1,358.4	1,378.2	1,412.9
Machinery & Transport Equipment	9,468.2	11,750.5	15,705.5	10,627.7	13,359.9	16,414.0
Miscellaneous	2,862.2	3,122.8	3,423.5	4,601.9	4,760.4	5,268.5
Other	1,821.5	1,755.1	2,110.9	1,732.4	1,947..2	2,211.4
Total:	22,429.3	25,882.0	31,096.8	30,407.0	35,336.4	44,777.4

1 *Provisional*

RoI: Volume / Price of Exports and Imports

Year	Volume Index Imports	Volume Index Exports	Price Index Imports	Price Index Exports
1990	100.0	100.0	100.0	100.0
1991	100.8	105.6	102.3	99.3
1992	105.6	121.1	100.2	96.6
1993	113.0	133.4	105.4	103.9
1994	127.9	153.2	108.1	103.8
1995	146.3	184.0	112.7	105.7
1996	160.9	202.2	111.4	105.1
1997	184.8	232.4	112.0	106.3
1998[1]	216.3	288.5	114.6	109.1

1 *Provisional*

NI: Top 5 Export Markets

Country (£m)	Textiles, Clothing & Leather	Food, Drink & Tobacco	Engineering	Other	Total
Republic of Ireland	81.2	165.1	66.7	297.6	610.6
Germany	13.1	19.4	160.2	105.9	298.6
USA	13.5	10.3	294.7	39.8	358.3
Asia	20.7	17.7	192.9	40.9	272.2
France	16.2	41.1	51.2	53.2	161.7

NI: Manufacturing Companies Export Sales

	1992-93 (Stg£m)	1993-94 (Stg£m)	1994-95 (Stg£m)	1995-96 (Stg£m)	1996-97 (Stg£m)	1997-98[1] (Stg£m)
Total Sales:	6,827	7,267	7,848	8,618	8,749	9,150
Northern Ireland	2,425	2,578	2,631	2,794	2,782	2,808
External Sales:	4,402	4,689	5,217	5,824	5,697	6,342
Britain	2,422	2,514	2,614	2,811	2,978	3,176
Export Sales:	1,980	2,175	2,603	3,013	2,989	3,166
Republic of Ireland	498	544	631	678	734	792
Rest of European Union	879	916	1,047	1,218	1,140	1,092
Rest of World	603	715	925	1,117	1,115	1,282

1 *Provisional*

NI: Destination of Sales

Destination	1996/97		1997/98	
	(Stg£m)	%	(Stg£m)	%
Northern Ireland	2,782	32	2,808	31

Continued from previous page

Destination	1996/97		1997/98	
	£m	%	£m	%
Republic of Ireland	734	8	792	9
Britain	2,978	34	3,176	34
Rest of EU	1,140	13	1,092	12
Rest of World	1,115	13	1,092	14
Total:	8,749	100	9,150	100

NI: Sales by Sector

Sector (£m)	1996-97	Export		1997-98	Export	
	Sales	Sales	Exports	Sales	Sales	Exports
Food, Drink & Tobacco	2,726	1,526	574	2,802	1,579	499
Textiles, Clothing & Leather	1,167	1,036	281	1,112	1,007	260
Electrical & Optical Equipment	829	773	502	909	837	534
Transport Equipment	742	687	342	982	919	572
Other Machinery & Equipment	671	558	368	605	514	309
Chemicals & Man-Made Fibres	600	494	407	570	477	393
Rubber & Plastics	502	390	211	497	382	226
Paper & Printing	440	183	105	441	183	107
Other Non-Metallic Mineral Products	364	103	65	352	109	60
Basic Metals / Products	330	112	70	388	161	114
Wood & Wood Products	286	87	40	295	81	42
Other Manufacturing	167	85	46	197	93	50
Total:	8,824	6,034	3,011	9,150	6,342	3,166

Finance

Selected Exchange Rates of IR£[1]

Currency (Country)	1992	1993	1994	1995	1996	1997	1998
Dollar (Canada)	2.0629	1.8913	2.0471	2.2011	2.1826	2.1003	2.1177
Franc (France)	9.0037	8.2970	8.2949	8.0010	8.1869	8.8483	8.3976
Mark (Germany)	2.6562	2.4228	2.4254	2.2974	2.4081	2.6285	2.5049
Drachma (Greece)	324.68	335.63	362.98	371.39	385.13	413.94	420.65
Lira (Italy)	2,095.87	2,301.58	2,412.07	2,612.81	2,468.65	2,581.37	2,472.49
Peseta (Spain)	174.20	186.24	200.25	199.87	202.69	221.96	212.67
Pound (UK)	0.9692	0.9764	0.9778	1.0165	1.0257	0.9268	0.8602
Dollar (US)	1.7073	1.4668	1.4989	1.6039	1.6007	1.5179	1.4259

1 *based on Dublin Market Averages*

RoI: Coin and Note Circulation

Coins / Notes	1997				1998			
	Number		Value		Number		Value	
	Million	% of Total	£ Million	% of Total	Million	% of Total	£ Million	% of Total
Coins:								
1p	752.0	38.5	7.5	3.7	816.3	38.2	8.2	3.7
2p	445.5	22.8	8.9	4.4	472.0	22.1	9.4	4.2
5p	284.6	14.6	14.2	7.0	331.1	15.5	16.6	7.4
10p	172.4	8.8	17.2	8.5	188.7	8.8	18.9	8.5
20p	137.9	7.1	27.6	13.7	151.4	7.1	30.3	13.6
50p	64.2	3.3	32.1	15.9	70.8	3.3	35.4	15.9
£1	94.6	4.9	94.6	46.8	104.2	4.9	104.2	46.7
Total: Coins	1,951.2	100.0	202.1	100.0	2,134.4	100.0	229.9	100.0
Notes:								
10/-	1.2	0.8	0.6	0	1.2	0.7	0.6	-
£1	13.8	9.1	13.8	0.6	13.6	8.2	13.6	0.5

→ Continued from previous page

Coins / Notes	1997				1998			
	Number		Value		Number		Value	
	Million	% of Total	£ Million	% of Total	Million	% of Total	£ Million	% of Total
£5	20.4	13.6	102.2	4.2	21.6	12.9	107.9	3.8
£10	23	15.3	230.2	9.5	25.1	15.0	250.7	8.9
£20	85.6	56.8	1711.3	70.8	95.5	57.2	1,910.2	67.8
£50	6.1	4	303.7	12.6	9.1	5.4	453.8	16.1
£100	0.5	0.4	54.6	2.3	0.8	0.5	79.1	2.8
Total: Notes	150.6	100	2,416.4	100	166.9	100.0	2,816.0	100.0

RoI: Number of Notes and Coins Produced

Coin (millions)	1996	1997	1998
1p	41.5	62.7	67.0
2p	32.5	18.1	26.5
5p	40	45.9	51.6
10p	12	17.2	10.0
20p	10.6	17.4	15.0
50p	0	8.3	0
£1	0	0	4.6
Total:	136.6	169.6	174.7

Note (millions)	1996	1997	1998
£5	24.2	36.3	33.9
£10	30.3	36.6	52.2
£20	57.5	51.3	50.2
£50	10.8	0	0
£100	0.8	4.6	0
Total:	123.6	128.8	136.3

RoI: Balance of Payments - Capital and Financial Account

Year	Capital Transfers	Private Capital	Official Capital	Transactions of Credit Insts.	Official External Reserves	Total	Net Residual
1990	229	-1,862	59	727	-443	-1,290	1,514
1991	378	-1,141	254	-381	-280	-1,169	960
1992	463	-743	-167	-1,344	1,201	-589	269
1993	513	-471	542	-844	-1,756	-2,016	768
1994	251	-1,375	-1,335	140	102	-2,217	1,219
1995	511	-1,824	24	1,798	-1,443	-934	-136
1996	489	-535	38	-1,229	55	-1,182	6
1997	578	-2,661	-2,180	-303	754	-3,812	2,450
1998	661	-2,991	-1,255	4,350	-1,645	-879	-168

RoI: Balance of Payments - Current Account

Year (IR£m)	Merchandise	Services	Invisibles Factor Incomes	Transfers	Total	Current Balance
1990	1,797	-513	-2,921	1,412	-2,022	-225
1991	2,066	-668	-2,796	1,608	-1,856	210
1992	3,501	-1,217	-3,209	1,245	-3,181	320
1993	4,826	-1,366	-3,521	1,309	-3,578	1,248
1994	5,396	-1,978	-3,575	1,156	-4,397	999
1995	7,459	-2,991	-4,508	1,110	-6,390	1,070
1996	8,756	-3,782	-5,151	1,354	-7,579	1,176
1997	11,084	-4,690	-6,321	1,290	-9,721	1,362
1998	15,396	-7,711	-7,676	1,039	-14,348	1,047

RoI: Expenditure on Gross National Product

IR£m	1997	1998[1]	1999[2]
Personal Consumption Expenditure	25,191	27,964	30,992
Public Net Current Expenditure	6,669	7,387	7,931
Gross Domestic Fixed Capital Formation: building and construction	6,254	7,544	9,106

Continued from previous page

IR£m	1997	1998[1]	1999[2]
machinery and equipment	3,194	3,685	3,993
Total: Gross Domestic Fixed Capital Formation	9,448	11,229	13,099
Value of physical changes in stocks	539	457	421
Gross Domestic Expenditure	41,847	47,037	52,443
Exports of Goods and Services	40,614	50,905	58,557
Final Demand	82,461	97,942	111,000
Imports of Goods and Services	34,220	43,220	49,828
Gross Domestic Product	48,241	54,722	61,172
Net Factor Income from Rest of World	6,322	7,676	9,037
Gross National Product	41,919	47,046	52,135

1 Estimate   2 Forecast

RoI: Capital and Financial Accounts

IR£m	1997	1998
Capital Transfers	578	661
Private Capital:		
Semi-State Companies	47	314
Other	-2,708	-3,306
Total: Private Capital	-2,661	-2,992
Official Capital:		
Exchequer Foreign Borrowing	-1,055	-697
Irish Government Securities	-1,122	-656
Other	-4	98
Total: Official Capital	-2,181	-1,255
Credit Institutions Transactions	-303	4,350
Official External Reserves:		
Reserve Position in the IMF	-45	-151
Gold	6	-17
SDR Holdings	-18	-18
Other External Assets	381	-1,627
Counterpart to Valuation Charges	430	168
Total: Official External Reserves	754	-1,645
Total:	-3,813	-881

RoI: External Reserves

IR£m	1995	1996	1997	1998
Reserves (at beginning of year)	4,041	5,473	4,960	4,636
Changes in Reserves:				
Interventions involving Irish Pounds	935	-20	-1,098	-
Foreign Exchange Swaps	-	-	-	1,120
Government Direct External Borrowings	-672	-1,009	-1,041	-748
Government Interest Payments Abroad	-885	-613	-537	-534
EU Receipts	1,599	1,578	1,984	1,772
Other	455	-449	368	202
Total: Changes in Reserves	1,432	-513	-324	1,812
Reserves (at end of year)	5,473	4,960	4,636	6,448

RoI: Current Account

Sector (IR£m)		1996	1997	1998	1999[1]
Current Expenditure:	Central Fund Services	3,161	3,505	3,434	3,407
	Supply Services	9,501	10,367	10,979	11,994
Total: Current Expenditure		12,662	13,872	14,413	15,401
Current Revenue:	Taxation	12,520	14,158	16,129	17,335
	Non Tax	434	333	375	401
Total: Current Revenue		12,954	14,491	16,504	17,736
Current Budget Surplus		292	619	2,091	2,335
% of GNP		0.8%	1.5%	4.4%	4.5%

1 Post-Budget Estimate / forecast

RoI: Government Revenue - Expenditure & Borrowing

IR£m	1998	1999[1]
Current Government Revenue:		
Customs and Excise	2,982	3,249
VAT	4,270	4,837
Income Tax	5,736	5,944
Corporation Tax	2,065	2,289
Motor Vehicle Duties	0	0
Stamp Duties	540	599
Other Tax Revenue	536	417
Total: Tax Revenue	16,129	17,335
Non-tax Revenue	374	401
Total: Current Government Revenue	16,503	17,736
Current Government Expenditure:		
Central Fund Services	3,434	3,407
Non-capital Supply Services	10,979	11,994
Total: Current Government Expenditure	14,413	15,401
Current Budget Deficit	-2,090	-2,335
Exchequer Borrowing for Capital Purposes	1,344	1,410
Total Exchequer Borrowing	-746	-925

1 *Post budget estimates*

RoI: Current Expenditure 1999*

Sector	£m	% of Expenditure
Health	3,371	17.8
Security	1,454	7.7
Infrastructure	56	0.3
Service of Public Debt	2,542	13.4
Education	2,603	13.8
Social Welfare	5,103	27.0
Other Social Services	142	0.8
Economic Services (industry, agriculture, tourism)	1,404	7.4
Other	2,225	11.8
TOTAL	18,900	100.0

* Post Budget Estimate

RoI: National Debt

IR£M	1977	1987	1990	1996	1997	1998
Domestic Debt	3,190	14,001	16,235	21,194	22,401	23,631
Foreign Debt	1,039	9,693	8,848	8,718	8,288	7,376
Total National Debt	4,229	23,694	25,083	29,912	30,689	31,007
General Government Debt	-	24,636	26,600	32,100	32,300	31,300

RoI: Currency Composition of the National Debt

Currency (IR£m)	1997	1998
Irish Pounds	22,582	22,353
Sterling	2,185	1,763
US Dollar	1,712	-
Deutschemark	1,621	5,251
Swiss Franc	1,132	-
French Franc	904	188
Euro	178	-104
Dutch Guilder	165	137
Japanese Yen	139	-
Belgian Franc	71	-47
Total:	30,689	29,541

Rol: Currency Composition of Foreign Debt

Currency	1996 IR£m	1997 IR£m	1998[1] IR£m
Sterling	2,430	2,185	1,974
US Dollars	1,741	1,712	1,502
Deutschemark	1,326	1,621	1,793
Swiss Francs	988	1,132	1,139
Dutch Guilder	122	165	165
Belgium Francs	42	71	72
ECU	244	178	237
Japanese Yen	411	139	443
French Franc	1,208	904	922
Others	206	182	194
Total:	8,718	8,288	8,441

1 As at March 31

NI: Local Authority Expenditure

Sector (Stg£m)	Current 94/95	Current 95/96	Current 96/97	Capital 94/95	Capital 95/96	Capital 96/97
Agriculture, Fisheries and Forestry	0	0	0	1	2	1
Energy	6	6	7	7	7	7
Roads & Transport	1	1	1	6	6	6
Environmental Services	102	106	115	17	18	20
Education, Arts and Libraries	56	57	63	18	18	19
Total:	165	170	186	49	51	53

NI: Public Expenditure

Sector (Stg£m)	94-95	95-96	96-97	97-98*	98-99*	99-00*
Law, Order and Protective Services	959	934	901	929	912	923
National Agriculture and Fisheries Support	141	152	186	176	164	165
N.I. Agriculture, Forestry and Fisheries Support	160	132	151	152	137	137
Industry, Energy, Trade and Employment	432	430	474	488	459	444
Transport	177	174	172	165	161	161
Housing	226	246	248	243	243	240
Environmental and Miscellaneous Services	208	217	243	205	171	160
Fire Service	40	42	43	44	44	44
Education, Arts and Libraries	1,295	1,355	1,401	1,376	1,383	1,401
Health and Personal Social Services	1,418	1,518	1,600	1,645	1,672	1,690
Social Security	2,232	2,380	2,586	2,652	2,750	2,854
Other Public Services	75	62	85	56	56	55
Euro-Regional Funded Expenditure	62	63	95	94	103	89
Total	7,425	7,705	8,185	8,225	8,255	8,363

* Forecast

NI: Gross Domestic Product

Year	GDP in Northern Ireland (£m)	% of UK GDP	GDP per head in Northern Ireland (£)	% of UK GDP
1990	10,145	2.1	6,383	76.9
1991	11,062	2.2	6,908	80.1
1992	11,647	2.2	7,197	80.2
1993	12,437	2.3	7,622	81.0
1994	13,123	2.3	7,993	80.7
1995	13,907	2.3	8,434	81.4
1996	14,545	2.3	8,745	80.2
1997	15,468	2.3	9,235	80.4

International Economic Statistics

Area (%)	Real GDP Growth 1998	Real GDP Growth 1999[1]	Inflation 1998	Inflation 1999[1]	Current Balance of Payments as % of GDP 1998	Current Balance of Payments as % of GDP 1999[1]
Euro Area:						
Belgium	2.9	1.9	1.0	1.3	4.2	4.3
Germany	2.8	1.7	0.9	0.7	-0.2	0.0
Spain	3.8	3.3	2.0	2.2	-0.3	-1.4
France	3.2	2.3	0.3	0.7	2.8	2.6
Ireland	10.4	7.5	2.6	2.9	1.9	0.5
Italy	1.4	1.4	2.4	1.7	2.0	1.9
Netherlands	3.8	2.2	1.8	1.9	5.6	5.3
Austria	3.3	2.2	0.9	0.7	-2.1	-2.0
Portugal	3.9	3.1	2.8	2.5	-4.3	-4.5
Finland	4.7	3.3	0.7	1.1	5.8	5.8
Total: Euro Area	2.9	2.1	1.3	1.2	1.4	1.2
Denmark	2.9	1.6	1.7	2.3	-1.4	-1.5
Greece	3.5	3.0	4.7	2.7	-3.0	-2.9
Sweden	2.9	2.4	0.5	0.7	2.1	1.5
UK	2.1	0.7	2.1	2.4	0.1	0.1
Total: EU	2.8	1.9	1.5	1.4	1.1	1.0
US	3.9	3.6	0.8	1.3	-2.7	-3.4
Canada	3.0	2.9	1.2	1.7	-2.1	-1.9
Japan	-2.8	-0.9	0.4	-0.3	3.2	3.0

1 *Estimate*

Banking and Post Offices

Rol: Banking, Building Societies & Insurance Employment

Year (as at December)	Banks	Building Societies	Insurance	Total
1993	22,500	2,600	10,500	35,600
1994	23,000	2,800	10,500	36,300
1995	23,300	2,900	11,000	37,200
1996	24,600	3,000	10,600	38,200
1997	25,900	3,200	11,300	40,400
1998[1]	28,600	3,300	12,300	44,200

1 *September 1998 figures*

NI: Financial Employment

	1995	1996	1997	1998[1]
Males	32,000	36,000	30,000	26,000
Females	25,000	48,000	43,000	42,000
Total	57,000	84,000	73,000	68,000

1 *Approximate*

Rol: Post Office Statistics

Operational Statistics	1993	1994	1995	1996	1997	1998
Mail:						
Letter Post - Items Delivered (m)	518.1	551.7	559.8	578.0	646.6	669.8
Pieces of mail per capita	146.9	156.5	158.8	159.6	176.6	180.8
System Size:						
Number of Delivery Points (m)	1.178	1.208	1.232	1.261	1.296	1.313
Post Office Network:						
No. of Company Post Offices	95	95	96	96	96	97
No. of Sub-Post Offices	1,876	1,854	1,838	1,825	1,818	1,814

Continued from previous page

Operational Statistics	1993	1994	1995	1996	1997	1998
Other Company Premises	38	38	40	41	45	48
No. of Motor Vehicles	2,147	2,208	2,214	2,239	2,275	2,389
Personnel:						
Headquarters	469	461	459	463	475	560
Savings Services	211	204	190	184	193	218
Remittance Services	75	71	68	67	71	82
Inspection	35	38	45	40	50	65
Postmen/Women	4,323	4,058	4,066	3,876	4,045	4,160
Postal Sorters	530	648	766	759	888	926
Post Office Clerks	1,165	1,125	1,154	1,244	1,246	1,201
Other Grades	827	765	737	718	729	728
Temporary	879	711	515	681	609	635
Subsidiary Companies	-	20	25	78	139	192
Total Group Employees	8,532	8,101	8,025	8,110	8,445	8,767
Postmasters engaged as Agents	1,976	1854	1,838	1,825	1,818	1,814
Financial:						
Operating Costs (IR£ m)	273.0	287.1	297.8	319.1	354.8	381.0
Profit for the Financial Year (IR£ m)	4.8	5.8	7.2	6.1	6.3	5.0
Letter Post Turnover (IR£ m)	179.8	192.0	194.4	207.3	231.3	241.4
SDS Turnover (IR£ m)	27.1	29.7	32.7	36.7	42.3	46.9

Housing

RoI: Planning Permissions Granted

	1995	1996	1997	1998
New Constructions:				
Dwelling	10,298	12,016	13,729	16,719
Other	5,861	5,301	5,068	5,180
Total: New Constructions	16,159	17,317	18,797	21,899
Extensions	9,417	10,422	11,150	12,576
Alterations and Conversions	2,983	2,799	2,686	2,748
Total:	28,559	30,538	32,633	37,223

RoI: Planning Permissions Granted by Region, 1998[1]

Region	New Construction Dwellings	Other	Extension	Alteration & Conversion	Total
Border	774	191	396	94	1,455
Dublin	249	259	787	179	1,474
Mid-East	261	90	245	68	664
Midlands	349	94	166	41	650
Mid-West	484	154	289	80	1,007
South-East	692	199	343	85	1,319
South-West	619	139	338	103	1,199
West	897	170	374	62	1,503
Total:	4,325	1,296	2,938	712	9,271

1 *October - December 1998*

RoI: New Houses Completed

Year	Social Housing	Private Housing	Total
1992	1,482	20,982	22,464
1993	2,090	19,301	21,391
1994	3,275	23,588	26,863
1995	3,971	26,604	30,575
1996	3,593	30,132	33,725
1997	3,388	35,454	38,842
1998	3,256	39,093	42,349

RoI: House Prices

Location	New IR £				Second-Hand IR £			
	1995	1996	1997	1998	1995	1996	1997	1998
Dublin	68,259	76,439	94,326	124,243	70,045	82,246	102,436	138,234
Cork	60,334	67,219	75,242	87,735	55,756	60,762	69,364	86,580
Galway	69,135	73,283	86,160	92,798	61,721	69,321	78,882	99,310
Limerick	57,766	65,589	71,188	81,859	48,119	55,969	61,180	76,088
Waterford	55,090	62,835	71,473	84,257	46,788	49,582	57,121	73,633
Other Areas	56,570	64,652	74,042	91,449	50,538	58,480	67,572	87,731
National Average	61,192	68,336	78,739	93,724	55,495	62,727	72,759	93,596

RoI: House Sales & House Completions

Local Authority House Sales, 1996-98 County Council Area	1996	1997	1998	House Completions, 1996-98 County Council Area	1996	1997	1998
Carlow	18	24	17	Carlow	403	656	603
Cavan	20	9	12	Cavan	325	440	495
Clare	34	49	42	Clare	966	1,435	1,221
Cork	74	94	121	Cork	2,461	3,222	3,903
Cork County Borough	59	73	65	Cork County Borough	859	1,132	1,266
Donegal	77	87	91	Donegal	1,548	1,507	1,883
Dublin County Borough	516	331	190	Dublin County Borough	4,125	3,427	3,777
Dun-Laoghaire/Rathdown	50	54	23	Dun-Laoghaire/Rathdown	1,053	712	549
Fingal	33	59	98	Fingal	2,024	2,707	2,618
Galway	93	37	33	Galway	1,093	1,295	1,849
Galway County Borough	38	30	27	Galway County Borough	1,047	1,223	1,026
Kerry	177	165	100	Kerry	1,024	1,242	1,638
Kildare	18	33	18	Kildare	1,900	2,095	2,509
Kilkenny	17	35	45	Kilkenny	562	628	701
Laois	20	25	46	Laois	404	399	452
Leitrim	17	13	14	Leitrim	221	265	295
Limerick	23	50	20	Limerick	800	903	1,197
Limerick County Borough	103	89	47	Limerick County Borough	539	946	906
Longford	6	18	10	Longford	316	292	310
Louth	179	101	118	Louth	969	1,191	1,171
Mayo	35	49	81	Mayo	1,097	1,431	1,527
Meath	27	29	25	Meath	1,154	1,318	1,421
Monaghan	41	36	28	Monaghan	334	295	423
Offaly	31	55	60	Offaly	347	382	624
Roscommon	8	11	9	Roscommon	332	292	305
Sligo	31	27	15	Sligo	563	666	903
South Dublin	103	97	286	South Dublin	2,244	2,479	2,013
Tipperary N.R.	22	58	44	Tipperary N.R.	520	749	823
Tipperary S.R.	137	96	70	Tipperary S.R.	407	478	557
Waterford	32	38	37	Waterford	393	539	520
Waterford County Borough	56	63	59	Waterford County Borough	433	574	539
Westmeath	17	32	10	Westmeath	702	929	1,105
Wexford	63	79	72	Wexford	992	1,446	1,484
Wicklow	109	93	73	Wicklow	1,168	1,147	1,335
Total:	2,284	2,139	2,006	Total:	33,325	38,442	41,948

NI: Average House Prices

District Council Area	1998	1999[i]
Antrim / Ballymena	57,844	62,737
Belfast	63,237	71,240
Coleraine / Limavady	62,485	63,379
Craigavon / Armagh	59,380	63,537
Derry / Strabane	58,205	60,805
East Antrim	59,783	62,315
Enniskillen / Fermanagh / S. Tyrone	64,291	67,341

→ *Continued from previous page*

District Council Area	1998	1999¹
Lisburn	69,715	72,568
Mid Ulster	58,492	57,672
Mid & South Down	70,118	74,999
North Down	72,191	77,964
Northern Ireland Average House Prices	57,978	61,213

1 *First two quarters of 1999*

RoI: Percentage Share of Mortgage Market

Year	Banks & Other Agencies	Building Societies	Local Authorities
1993	36.0	62.9*	1.1
1994	45.0	54.4*	0.6
1995	67.2*	32.4	0.4
1996	65.4*	34.3	0.3
1997	63.7*	36.1	0.2
1998	64.2*	35.7	0.1

* *Includes Irish Permanent*

RoI: Tenure of Borrowers for Housing

Year	Owner Occupied		Private Tenant		Local Authority Tenant		Parents' Residence		Other	
	New (%)	Second Hand (%)	New (%)	Second Hand (%)	New (%)	Second Hand (%)	New (%)	Second Hand (%)	New (%)	Second Hand (%)
1993	32.0	44.3	23.1	24.1	1.4	2.8	41.1	26.3	2.4	2.6
1994	35.5	45.3	26.4	21.1	2.4	4.9	33.9	25.8	1.9	2.8
1995	40.8	54.8	24.6	18.5	1.3	2.9	30.5	21.0	2.8	2.8
1996	46.4	60.3	22.8	16.5	1.1	3.3	27.3	17.2	2.4	2.7
1997	52.6	65.0	22.9	16.8	1.1	1.7	21.4	14.2	2.0	2.3
1998	50.1	65.8	23.4	16.0	0.7	1.2	23.8	15.4	1.9	1.6

RoI: Public Capital Expenditure on Housing

Constituents (£m)	1993	1994	1995	1996	1997	1998
Local Authority Housing	92.6	157.1	180.3	191.9	218.2	242.2
Voluntary Housing	20.5	27.5	33.8	33.0	27.3	27.0
Shared Ownership	35.0	44.4	50.0	50.0	43.1	50.2
House Purchase and Improvement Loans etc.	24.2	19.2	18.0	20.6	18.8	19.9
Private Housing Grants	15.3	26.5	33.9	26.7	36.6	36.9
Other Housing	2.0	4.0	3.0	4.0	4.1	5.0
Total:	189.6	278.7	319.0	336.2	348.1	381.2

RoI: Consumer Price Index

Item	1994	1995	1996	1997	1998
Alcohol	120.1	123.3	126.4	129.6	134.4
Clothing and Footwear	105.1	104.0	102.9	95.5	90.0
Durable Household Goods	109.1	110.3	111.3	111.4	112.1
Food	107.4	110.7	112.9	114.9	119.7
Fuel and Light	105.8	105.9	107.6	107.5	107.6
Housing	111.5	118.0	117.8	121.6	123.1
Services and Related Expenses	119.5	123.0	124.4	126.4	130.8
Tobacco	128.6	135.4	142.4	147.7	154.2
Transport	111.1	112.7	115.4	118.6	120.4
Other Goods	112.4	115.8	118.6	120.0	123.5
Total	112.4	115.2	117.1	118.8	121.7
Energy Products	101.2	101.8	105.6	108.8	108.1

Base Year (1985) =100

INDUSTRY, ENERGY & TRANSPORT

The Construction Industry in Ireland

By **Michael J.T. Webb**

THE tower cranes on the skyline of Dublin, Limerick, Cork and Galway are a visible indication of the current strength of the Irish construction industry. Construction has generally been the barometer of the Irish economy. Today that barometer reflecting the Irish economy as a whole, is high and tending to overheat.

Construction has replaced agriculture as Ireland's largest employer and Ireland's largest economic sector.

In 1999 investment in construction and machinery (GFCF) will account for 27% of GNP - an exceptionally high rate of investment which arguably cannot be sustained.

The total output of the Irish construction industry is expected to reach IR£10 - 400 million in 1999 - a high figure by Irish terms but a figure exceeded by each of Europe's top 10 contractors in 1999.

The output of the Irish construction industry has doubled over the past 5 years and the strains are beginning to show. Initially the increase in volume took up some of the slack within the industry. Increased activity led to a return to Ireland of many skilled tradesmen from Britain and further afield. Productivity within the industry increased significantly. After an inexplicable delay the number of apprentices entering the industry has substantially increased. As an open economy Ireland is open to the import of most building materials and equipment from Northern Ireland, Britain and continental Europe so the supply and price levels of materials remain competitive.

However, five years on, the benign effect of these factors has been absorbed and labour and skills shortages are becoming obvious. Different trade groups have flexed their muscles to obtain higher rewards in an increasingly profitable industry.

The construction industry has shown tremendous skill and flexibility in coping with ever increasing demand. However increases in wage levels and in contractors margins have led to price increases significantly in excess of the general level of inflation.

In 1999 with general inflation running at 2% to 3% prices for new construction (as measured by the PKS Tender Index) rose by 8% following a similar trend in 1997 and 1998.

The outlook despite the skills shortages remains rosy. The rate of increase will probably decline but significant increases are expected in the years to come.

For the year 2000 the PKS projection is for growth in volume of 5% while the ESRI are even more optimistic with a + 7% projection. Projections for 2001, 2002 and 2003 suggest increases in volume of 2% to 4% each year.

In recent years the growth has been across all sectors. Housing has been the most buoyant with significant year on year increases. However the supply of serviced land in the Dublin area has been an inhibitor to the supply of new housing meeting the demand. The demand has been fuelled by returning emigrants as well as a steadily increasing workforce and changes in demographic trends.

Commercial and retail construction has also shown real growth in recent years.

Industrial building fuelled by incoming giants like Hewlett Packard and IBM has showed steady increases.

Public building - universities, schools and hospitals - has increased year by year supported by EU Structural and Cohesion Funds.

EU Funds have also had a major impact on the civil engineering sector of the industry. Despite considerable EU funding being available delays in land acquisition and in the planning process have meant that many programmes are late and the sector has shown minimal growth until 1999. Hopefully the release of a number of road contracts and the advent of 6 Public Private Partnership - PPP projects will help to revive the one sector which probably can cope with much greater demand.

Although many of the major construction projects have been in the greater Dublin region most other urban centres have also benefited. Limerick and Galway have been particularly busy while Cork, the Republic's second city, has only recently began to catch up. Major building projects are also to be seen in most towns throughout Ireland.

From 2000 much of Ireland's EU investment will be channelled to the western seaboard where wealth is still below the EU average. Cities and town such as Galway, Sligo and Athlone will benefit.

The past five years have been exciting ones for the Irish construction industry and one can confidently predict that the cranes will remain on the skyline for a number of years to come.

Michael J.T. Webb
October 1999

The author is Managing Partner of Patterson Kempster & Shorthall *PKS*, Ireland's leading quantity surveying / construction cost management firm. He is also the president of the European Committee for Construction Economics and is editor of the *PKS Review of the Construction Industry*.

INDUSTRY

Overview

Republic of Ireland

● MAIN FIGURES "AT A GLANCE"

Total in Employment	1,520.5m
Unemployed	203,231*
Unemployment Rate (%)	7.5%
Average Weekly Earnings	IR£298.11
Number of industrial disputes	34
Union Membership	521,036
Total IDA-assisted employment	115,981
Average cost per IDA job created/sustained	IR£10,891

Live Register figures

Northern Ireland

● MAIN FIGURES "AT A GLANCE"

Total in Employment	681,000
Unemployed	56,000
Unemployment Rate (%)	7.6%
Average Weekly Earnings	Stg£333
Number of industrial disputes	7 (1997)
Union Membership	204,910
Total IDB-assisted employment	86,137
Average cost per IDB job created/sustained	Stg£8,638

Employment/Unemployment

Employment by Sector

● REPUBLIC OF IRELAND (000s)	1994			1998		
Sector	Males	Females	Total	Males	Females	Total
Agriculture, Forestry & Fishing	132.09	14.78	146.87	120.0	16.0	136.0
Other Production Industries	178.02	73.94	251.96	210.6	93.3	303.8
Construction	85.92	5.55	91.47	133.0	7.7	140.7
Wholesale & Retail	99.54	69.54	169.08	115.9	96.3	212.2
Hotels & Restaurants	31.08	37.26	68.34	40.0	55.3	95.2
Transport, Storage, Communication	44.74	11.17	55.91	62.0	20.9	83.1
Financial and Other Services	61.74	52.59	114.33	84.1	85.8	169.8
Public Administration; Defence; Social Security	42.72	23.64	66.36	45.7	27.2	73.0
Education & Health	53.63	127.80	181.43	59.8	153.6	213.3
Other	36.77	38.04	74.81	43.0	49.9	92.9
TOTAL:	766.25	454.31	1220.56	914.4	606.0	1,520.5

● NORTHERN IRELAND	1996			March 1999[1]		
Sector	Males	Females	Total	Males	Females	Total
Agriculture, Hunting, Forestry & Fishing	16,470	2,340	18,810	14,000	1,960	15,960
Mining & Quarrying	1,700	160	1,860	1,670	170	1,840
Manufacturing	69,840	33,210	103,050	74,060	31,600	105,660
Electric, Gas & Water Supply	4,110	480	4,590	3,560	430	3,980
Construction	20,190	2,370	22,560	25,920	2,810	28,730
Wholesale & Retail Trade: Repairs	41,660	46,480	88,140	45,900	51,610	97,510
Hotels & Restaurants	10,700	17,390	28,090	13,160	19,720	32,880
Transport, Storage & Communications	16,910	5,140	22,050	18,210	6,470	24,690
Financial Intermediation	5,260	8,360	13,620	5,200	9,240	14,450
Real Estate Renting & Business Activities	14,750	17,670	32,420	19,210	21,890	41,400
Public Administration & Defence	35,630	23,860	59,490	34,620	24,410	59,030
Education	17,380	44,920	62,300	17,590	48,280	65,870
Health & Social Work	16,260	75,020	91,280	15,710	77,530	93,240
Other Service Activities	13,470	12,300	25,770	14,330	13,510	27,840
TOTAL:	284,330	289,700	574,030	303,130	309,640	612,770

1 Provisional figures

RoI: Labour Force Statistics

Economic Status	April 1994	April 1995	April 1996	April 1997	1998
In Labour Force	1,431.6	1,459.2	1,507.5	1,539.0	1,645.5
Males	898.1	909.2	925.1	937.3	991.3
Females	533.5	550.0	582.4	601.7	654.1
In Employment	1,220.6	1,281.7	1,328.5	1,379.9	1,520.5
Full Time	1,083.2	1,127.8	1,176.4	1,210.0	1,269.8
Part Time	137.4	153.9	152.1	169.9	250.6
Unemployed	211.0	177.4	179.0	159.0	125.0
seeking full time work	186.4	153.5	151.3	136.6	104.3
seeking part time work	24.6	24.0	27.7	22.4	20.65
Not in Labour Force	1,255.7	1,264.2	1,259.2	1,276.1	1,231.3
Total persons aged 15 or over	2,687.3	2,723.4	2,766.7	2,815.1	2,876.8
Unemployment rate %	14.7	12.2	11.9	10.3	7.5
Participation rate %	53.3	53.6	54.5	54.7	57.2

Public Sector Employment Figures

● REPUBLIC OF IRELAND Sector	1994 (000s)	1996 (000s)	1998 (000s)
Civil Service	31.1	32.1	31.9
Prison Officers	2.4	2.5	2.6
Administrative Civil Servants	26.0	26.9	26.6
Industrial Civil Servants	2.0	2.1	2.0
Others in the Civil Service	0.7	0.6	0.7
Defence	14.2	13.6	12.7
Garda Síochána	10.9	10.7	11.0
Education	61.7	64.5	65.8
Primary	21.4	21.6	21.7
Education: Secondary	16.9	17.8	17.9
Education: Third Level	7.5	8.4	8.9
VECs (Including RTCs)	15.9	16.7	17.3
Regional Bodies	30.8	30.7	31.6
Local Authorities	29.2	29.0	30.0
Others	1.6	1.7	1.6
Semi-State Companies	65.0	63.0	63.4
Commercial	57.1	54.9	55.0
Non-Commercial	7.9	8.1	8.4
Total Public Sector (excluding Health)	213.7	214.6	216.4

● NORTHERN IRELAND Sector (March 1999)	Male	Female	Total
NI Central Government	30,970	16,351	47,321
Bodies under the aegis of NI Central Government	17,440	48,853	66,293
UK Central Government	3,299	2,930	6,229
Local Government (District Councils)	5,586	3,680	9,266
Public Corporations	19,336	49,163	68,499
Total Public Sector Employment Jobs	76,631	120,977	197,608
% of Employee Jobs	25.3%	39.1%	32.2%

RoI: Employment in Manufacturing, Transportable Goods and All Industries

(Average) (000s) Year	Manufacturing	Transportable Goods	All Industries
1990	191.9	197.1	211.2
1991	195.1	200.1	213.9
1992	198.0	202.8	216.5
1993	199.1	203.8	217.8
1994	202.4	207.2	220.8

Continued from previous page

(Average) (000s) Year	Manufacturing	Transportable Goods	All Industries
1995	214.0	218.6	231.6
1996	222.8	227.6	240.1
1997	236.2	241.0	252.9
1998*	239.2	244.0	255.7

* Figures from March 1998

NI: Employment in Manufacturing, Construction and Services.

(March 1999)	Male Full time	Male Part time	Female Full time	Female Part time	Total Persons	% change since last yr
Manufacturing	71,730	2,330	26,710	4,890	105,660	-1.1%
Construction	25,190	730	1,870	940	28,730	+1.4%
Services	147,530	36,400	132,940	139,730	456,600	+2.1%
Other[1]	8,360	10,860	880	1,680	21,780	-2.8%
Total	252,820	50,320	162,400	147,240	612,770	+1.3%

1 *Covers Agriculture, Hunting, Forestry and Fishing; Mining and Quarrying; Electricity, Gas and Water Supply.*

RoI: Persons on Live Register[1] by County

Province County	July 1998 Total persons	July 1999 Total persons	July 1999 Total Male	July 1999 Total Female
CONNACHT	**28,781**	**25,879**	**14,769**	**11,110**
Galway	12,670	11,165	6,523	4,642
Leitrim	1,863	1,576	832	744
Mayo	8,804	7,957	4,526	3,431
Roscommon	2,010	2,015	1,172	843
Sligo	3,434	3,166	1,716	1,450
LEINSTER	**122,645**	**102,868**	**58,320**	**44,548**
Carlow	3,346	2,977	1,561	1,416
Dublin	69,129	55,737	32,698	23,039
Kildare	6,625	5,638	2,907	2,731
Kilkenny	3,556	3,130	1,734	1,396
Laois	2,635	2,478	1,304	1,174
Longford	2,414	2,123	1,179	944
Louth	9,315	8,041	4,565	3,476
Meath	3,561	3,193	1,750	1,443
Offaly	3,492	3,032	1,720	1,312
Westmeath	3,712	3,662	1,912	1,750
Wexford	8,153	7,378	4,007	3,371
Wicklow	6,707	5,479	2,983	2,496
MUNSTER	**62,838**	**56,627**	**30,959**	**25,668**
Clare	4,323	3,780	1,983	1,797
Cork	24,445	21,446	11,699	9,747
Kerry	8,401	7,522	4,363	3,159
Limerick	9,841	9,290	4,985	4,305
Tipperary	8,438	7,566	4,169	3,397
Waterford	7,390	7,023	3,760	3,263
ULSTER	**18,549**	**17,857**	**10,851**	**7,006**
Cavan	2,559	2,288	1,342	946
Donegal	12,634	12,420	7,762	4,658
Monaghan	3,356	3,149	1,747	1,402
STATE	**232,813**	**203,231**	**114,899**	**88,332**

1 *The Live Register is not designed to measure unemployment as it includes part-time workers (up to three days a week), seasonal and casual workers who are entitled to Unemployment Assistance or Benefit.*

NI: Persons on Unemployment Benefit by Area

District Council Area	July 1999 Total persons	July 1999 Total Male	July 1999 Total Female
NORTHERN IRELAND TOTAL	52,968	39,727	13,241
Antrim	1,064	729	335
Ards	1,652	1,183	469
Armagh	1,601	1,113	488
Ballymena	1,460	1,028	432
Ballymoney	792	610	182
Banbridge	686	468	218
Belfast	12,384	9,789	2,595
Carrickfergus	956	660	296
Castlereagh	1,136	797	339
Coleraine	1,965	1,430	535
Cookstown	883	628	255
Craigavon	1,950	1,459	491
Derry	5,160	4,068	1,092
Down	1,895	1,343	552
Dungannon	1,274	906	368
Fermanagh	2,147	1,599	548
Larne	694	496	198
Limavady	1,099	822	277
Lisburn	2,348	1,803	545
Magherafelt	1,036	703	333
Moyle	635	476	159
Newry & Mourne	3,339	2,619	720
Newtownabbey	1,684	1,211	473
North Down	1,712	1,204	508
Omagh	1,774	1,298	476
Strabane	1,642	1,285	357

International Unemployment Rates

Country	1996	1997	1998	1999[1]
United States	5.4	4.9	4.5	4.2
Japan	3.4	3.4	4.1	4.7
Belgium	9.7	9.4	9.5	9.0
France	12.4	12.3	11.7	11.3
Germany	8.9	9.9	9.4	9.0
IRELAND	11.6	9.9	7.8	6.8
NORTHERN IRELAND			8.0	7.6[2]
Luxembourg	3.0	2.8	2.8	2.8
Norway	4.9	4.1	3.3	2.9
Spain	22.2	20.8	18.8	16.4
United Kingdom	8.2	7.0	6.3	6.3

1 Figures are based on January -May 1999 (5 months) and are provisional. 2 April-June 1999

Wages & Earnings

RoI: Industrial Workers
Gross Earnings and Hours Worked

Year	Avg. Weekly Earnings (IR£)	Average Hours Worked	Avg. Earnings Per Hour (IR£)
1990	225.16	41.4	5.43
1991	235.23	41.0	5.73
1992	244.27	40.6	6.01
1993	258.00	40.5	6.36
1994	265.13	41.0	6.47
1995	270.70	40.9	6.62
1996	278.68	40.9	6.82

➤ *Continued from previous page*

Year	Avg. Weekly Earnings (IR£)	Average Hours Worked	Avg. Earnings Per Hour (IR£)
1997	286.14	40.9	7.00
1998	298.11	40.5	7.35

* Provisional figures for January - September 1998

NI: Industrial Workers
Gross Earnings and Hours Worked

Year	Average Weekly Earnings Male (Stg£)	Increase on Previous Year (%)	Average Weekly Earnings Female (Stg£)	Increase on Previous Year (%)
1992	298.2	9.5%	224.2	11.2%
1993	313.6	5.2%	232.5	3.7%
1994	319.2	1.8%	236.7	1.8%
1995	330.9	3.7%	251.4	6.2%
1996	337.4	2%	256.9	2.2%
1997	355.9	5.5%	265.2	3.2%
1998	368.0	3.4%	278.0	4.8%

| April 1998 | Male | | | Female | | | Male & Female | | |
	Manual	Non Manual	All	Manual	Non Manual	All	Manual	Non Manual	All
Average Gross Weekly earnings (Stg£)	284	444	368	182	297	278	265	370	333
Average Gross Hourly earnings (Stg£)	6.49	11.35	9.03	4.65	8.14	7.54	6.15	9.74	8.45
Average Total Weekly hours	43.7	39.5	41.5	39.3	37.0	37.4	42.9	38.3	39.9
Average Weekly Overtime hours	4.5	1.8	3.1	1.1	0.6	0.7	3.8	1.2	2.1

Production

RoI: Industrial Production Index

Industrial Sector (1997)*	No. of Local Units (No.)	Gross output (£m)	Industrial inputs (£m)	Net output (£m)	Wages & salaries (£m)	Persons engaged (No.)
Mining & quarrying	127	511.7	165.6	346.1	113.8	5,286
Manufacture of:						
Food products, beverages & tobacco	842	10,074.8	5,870.9	4,203.9	757.3	46,327
Textiles and textile products	372	737.9	404.1	333.8	186.5	16,835
Leather and leather products	30	57.6	37.6	20.0	10.8	1,036
Wood, wood products	229	424.3	262.0	162.4	65.5	5,175
Pulp, paper and paper products, publishing and printing	572	4,139.3	959.3	3,180.0	434.1	22,688
Chemicals, chemical products and man-made fibres	250	8,074.8	2,008.2	6,066.6	451.4	21,002
Rubber and plastic products	262	775.8	399.6	376.2	152.4	10,064
Other non-metallic mineral products	290	861.2	381.0	480.2	177.7	10,120
Basic metals and fabricated metal products	533	1,176.2	692.5	483.7	214.9	14,184
Machinery, equipment	373	1,146.3	599.5	546.9	227.6	15,046
Optical and electrical equipment	443	12,054.4	7,452.4	4,602.0	920.6	56,948
Transport equipment	130	661.3	374.6	286.7	168.3	9,423
N.e.c., recycling, manufacture of coke, refined petroleum products, nuclear fuel	413	1,210.5	742.5	468.0	159.4	11,606
Electricity, gas & water supply	90	1,833.3	752.5	1,080.7	302.7	12,193

⟶ Continued from previous page

Industrial Sector (1997)*	No. of Local Units (No.)	Gross output (£m)	Industrial inputs (£m)	Net output (£m)	Wages & salaries (£m)	Persons engaged (No.)
Summary						
Transportable Goods Industries	4,866	41,906.2	20,349.7	21,556.5	4,040.1	245,740
Manufacturing Industries	4,739	41,394.5	20,184.1	21,210.4	3,926.4	240,454
All Industries	4,956	43,739.5	21,102.2	22,637.2	4,342.9	257,933

Source: CSO

NI: Industrial Production Index

● Output: Production Industries	Weights	1994	1995¹	1996	1997	1998
Production Industries	1000.0	96.3	100.0	102.3	107.6	110.3
Manufacturing	859.9	95.9	100.0	101.7	107.8	110.9
Electricity, Gas & Water	124.2	98.3	100.0	104.9	104.1	105.9
Mining & Quarrying	15.9	103.2	100.0	111.1	121.7	112.5

● Output: Manufacturing Industries	Weights	1994	1995¹	1996	1997	1998
Food, Drink & Tobacco	190.6	101.0	100.0	101.6	103.5	105.4
Leather, Textiles & Textile Products	120.4	98.8	100.0	98.8	98.7	91.0
Chemical & Chemical Products	74.7	105.6	100.0	99.7	124.9	124.8
Basic & Fabricated Metals	36.5	93.3	100.0	108.3	121.2	129.5
Engineering & Allied Industries	236.5	87.4	100.0	102.2	111.0	120.2
Total Other Manufacturing	201.1	96.2	100.0	102.5	104.8	108.5

Industrial Disputes/Unions

RoI: Industrial Disputes in progress during 1998

Description	Public Sector¹	Private Sector²	Totals
Number of Disputes	15	19	**34**
Official Disputes	7	12	**19**
Unofficial Disputes	8	7	**15**
Days Lost	8,267	29,107	**37,374**
Number of Firms involved	39	24	**63**
Number of Workers	3,987	4,073	**8,060**

Companies/bodies involved and Number of Days lost:

1 Limerick Corporation (8.5); Cork Corporation (1); St Ita's Hospital (1); Local Authorities/Health Boards (5); A&E and PTS Ambulance Services (42); Regional Orthodontic Dept (1); Aer Lingus Catering (3.5); National Gallery of Ireland (2); Iarnrod Éireann (1); Midland Health Board (1.5); Bus Éireann (3); Boyneview House, St Mary's Hospital and Cottage Hospital (6); Duchas (40); Courtenay NS, CBS Scoil na mBraithe; Plas Mhuire Boy's NS, Kilbrian NS, Redhills NS, Castletara NS, Baile Mhic Airt NS, Cul na Smear NS, Carrabane NS, Scoil Gharghain, Dooagh NS, Central Model NS and Ferrybank NS (1); Bord Gais (1).

2 Weatherglaze Systems Ltd (10); Ryanair (25); IJM Timber Engineering Ltd (9); Showerings/Grants (Ireland) Ltd (2); Arcon Mines Ltd (69); Roche (Ireland) Ltd (26); Esmonde Motors Ltd (9); Zoe Developments (1, 24); Iceland Frozen Foods (4); EVE Holdings (1); Otis Lifts, Schindler (50 to 64, 1), Irish Lift Services, Ennis Lifts, Mid-West Lift Services, CJ Boyle & Co, Industrial Logistics, Pickerings (50 to 64); Smurfit Corrugated Cases (3); Leixlip and District Credit Union (9); ABB Transformers Plc (4); James McMahon (14); Castlemahon Food Products Ltd (1.5); XBL (8).

NI: Industrial Disputes

Year	Stoppages	Workers Affected	Working Days Lost
1990	24	12,479	18,322
1991	12	16,805	16,926
1992	5	3,905	7,734
1993	7	15,870	15,723
1994	14	3,849	4,949
1995	7	4,391	4,919
1996	3	4,660	20,201
1997	7	6,000	13,800

Rol & NI: Union Membership

ICTU: Total members 725,946 (Rol: 521,036 in 48 unions; NI 204,910 in 33 unions) in 63 unions. Overlap occurs for unions organised in Rol and NI.

Union Group	Rol Union Members	NI Union Members
General Unions	208,704	53,991
Public Service Unions	110,395	87,610
Postal & Telecommunications	19,600	6,688
Electrical, Engineering Unions	39,820	23,946
Construction Unions	23,612	2,840
Other Industry Unions	8,198	3,287
Distribution / Transport Unions	42,224	7,229
Professional / White Collar Unions	67,722	19,319
Others	761	0
TOTAL	521,036	204,910

State Assisted Employment

Rol: IDA Ireland Analysis

Description	1993	1994	1995	1996	1997	1998
New Jobs Filled	8,225	9,890	11,689	13,273	14,836	15,996
Number of Companies	877	912	965	1,047	1,111	1,140
Employment	78,571	83,524	90,037	97,279	107,171	115,981
Net Change in Full Time Employment	+2,682	+4,953	+6,513	+7,242	+9,892	+8,810
% Net Change Full Time Employment	+3.5%	+6.3%	+7.8%	+8.0%	+10.2%	+8.2%
Job Losses	-5,543	-4,937	-5,176	-6,031	-4,944	-7,186
Job Losses as % of Total Jobs	7.1%	5.9%	5.8%	6.2%	4.6%	6.2%
Temporary Employment	5,268	9,033	11,533	9,598	13,338	14,995

NI: IDB Northern Ireland Analysis

Description	94/95	95/96	96/97	97/98
Number of Projects	76	63	91	83
Jobs Promoted	4,994	5,678	6,005	7,137
Jobs Safeguarded	3,802	2,484	5,577	4,254
Total Investment (Stg£m)	394	507	638	713
IDB Assistance (Stg£m)	102	151	158	155
IDB Contribution	26%	30%	25%	22%

Rol: IDA Employment & New Jobs by Region

	Total Employment					New Jobs				
Region	1994	1995	1996	1997	1998	1994	1995	1996	1997	1998
North West / Donegal	6,705	6,911	6,747	6,736	6,568	441	405	297	279	312
West	7,671	8,429	8,891	9,778	10,758	1,038	1,005	954	1,444	1,157
Mid West	10,114	10,663	11,071	11,261	12,180	1,345	1,142	1,239	925	1,812
South West	11,760	12,323	12,924	13,650	15,102	1,027	1,477	1,163	1,510	2,496
South East	8,340	8,636	9,410	9,878	9,802	646	784	1,459	935	1,173
East	28,354	32,468	37,808	45,132	50,552	4,147	6,146	7,547	8,667	8,220
North East	4,781	4,960	4,378	4,484	4,790	726	432	85	440	419
Midlands	5,799	5,647	6,050	6,252	6,229	520	298	529	636	407
TOTAL:	83,524	90,037	97,279	107,171	115,981	9,890	11,689	13,273	14,836	15,996

NI: IDB Employment & Employment by Area

	No. of IDB supported companies		Employment in IDB supported companies	
Region	93/94	97/98	93/94	97/98
Antrim	34	35	2,805	3,268
Ards	24	23	3,034	2,477

➤ *Continued from previous page*

Region	No. of IDB supported companies		Employment in IDB supported companies	
	93/94	97/98	93/94	97/98
Armagh	16	16	1,271	1,161
Ballymena	23	23	4,469	4,861
Ballymoney	9	9	1,759	1,673
Banbridge	9	12	873	890
Belfast	109	131	16,598	15,259
Carrickfergus	11	13	716	1,163
Castlereagh	21	18	2,653	2,962
Coleraine	15	18	2,156	2,660
Cookstown	8	11	1,050	1,068
Craigavon	77	75	9,826	9,983
Derry	36	39	7,257	7,741
Down	13	13	1,218	985
Dungannon	35	36	3,300	3,821
Fermanagh	30	29	2,880	3,403
Larne	9	11	1,607	2,107
Limavady	5	6	1,192	1,785
Lisburn	42	35	3,138	3,626
Magherafelt	24	25	1,908	2,486
Moyle	3	3	254	253
Newry & Mourne	29	31	2,498	3,017
Newtownabbey	40	38	4,238	4,395
North Down	12	13	1,603	1,652
Omagh	7	9	1,071	1,211
Strabane	10	12	2,113	2,230
TOTAL	651	684	81,487	86,137

RoI: Average Cost Per Job Created and Sustained*

Period	Irish	Overseas	Overall Average
1984/1990	£11,419	£23,475	£16,768
1985/1991	£11,476	£21,477	£16,028
1986/1992	£10,948	£19,707	£14,998
1987/1993	£10,777	£17,395	£13,961
1988/1994	£10,092	£14,229	£12,204
1989/1995	£9,746	£12,869	£11,399
1990/1996	£9,694	£12,558	£11,273
1991/1997	£9,505	£11,853	£10,875
1992/1998	£9,693	£11,806	£10,891

* For IDA Ireland and Enterprise Ireland-backed companies.

NI: Average Cost Per Job Created*

1992	1993	1994	1995	1996	1997	1998
Stg£3,357	Stg£2,490	Stg£2,842	Stg£6,573	Stg£9,301	Stg£10,517	Stg£8,638

* For IDB Northern Ireland-backed companies.

RoI: State Expenditure in support of Job Creation

1990	1991	1992	1993	1994	1995	1996	1997	1998
£387.5m	£411.5m	£381.5m	£414.8m	£408.0m	£461.0m	£527.8m	£551.8m	£605.4m

RoI: New Jobs by Sector*

Sector	1994	1995	1996	1997	1998
Pharmaceuticals/Heathcare	1,044	804	1,342	1,461	1,714
Electronics/Engineering	5,394	7,234	7,345	7,617	6,652
Textile/Clothing/Footwear	504	344	222	149	109
Miscellaneous Industry	793	636	339	844	450

Continued from previous page

Sector	1994	1995	1996	1997	1998
International Services	2,155	2,671	4,025	4,765	7,071
TOTAL	9,890	11,689	13,273	14,836	15,996

* IDA Ireland supported companies

RoI: IDA Employment by Sector*

Sector	1994	1995	1996	1997	1998	% change
Pharmaceuticals/Heathcare	13,615	14,206	15,276	16,119	17,422	8.1%
Electronics/Engineering	42,837	47,609	51,726	57,195	59,401	3.9%
Textile/Clothing/Footwear	8,010	7,664	6,961	6,047	5,509	-8.9%
Miscellaneous Industry	8,456	8,399	7,821	8,349	8,139	-2.5%
International Services	10,606	12,159	15,495	19,461	25,510	31.1%
TOTAL	83,524	90,037	97,279	107,171	115,981	8.2%

* IDA Ireland supported companies

NI: IDB Employment by Sector[1]

Sector	No. of Companies 93/94	No. of Companies 97/98	Employment 93/94	Employment 97/98	External Sales (£m) 93/94	External Sales (£m) 97/98	Turnover (£m) 93/94	Turnover (£m) 97/98
Food, Drink & Tobacco	114	98	17,492	15,736	1,353	1,277	2,257	2,126
Textiles, Clothing & Leather	107	97	22,838	20,431	799	905	905	989
Wood & Wood Products	12	17	1,222	1,496	44	73	125	185
Paper, Printing & Publishing	27	31	2,627	2,957	113	123	175	201
Chemical Industry & Fibres	13	16	2,747	3,140	350	415	382	456
Rubber & Plastic	28	37	3,849	4,565	222	328	262	378
Non-Metallic Mineral Products	21	26	1,780	2,425	50	70	122	153
Basic Metals & Fabricated Metal	18	24	1,358	1,744	30	72	89	135
Machinery & Equipment	26	35	4,295	5,685	304	471	314	483
Electrical & Optical Equipment	33	42	6,378	10,396	431	723	440	746
Transport Equipment	21	18	11,835	10,632	545	617	556	633
Other Manufacturing	34	32	2,078	1,944	92	104	192	219
All Manufacturing	454	473	78,399	81,151	4,333	5,178	5,819	6,704
Tradable Services	41	50	3,088	4,986	129	213	313	427
All Client Companies	495	523	81,487	86,137	4,462	5,391	6,132	7,131

1 IDB supported companies

RoI: Origin of Overseas Companies[1]

Country/Area of Origin	Number of Companies	Employment 1998
United States	465	73,836
United Kingdom	178	12,074
Germany	156	10,526
Rest of Europe	231	11,479
Asia / Pacific	55	4,892
Rest of World	55	3,174
TOTAL:	1,140	115,981

1 IDA Supported Companies

NI: Top Export Markets for IDB Companies[1]

Rank	Country/Area	£m
1	Republic of Ireland	£611
2	United States	£358
3	Germany	£299
4	Asia	£272
5	France	£162
6	Canada	£157
7	Italy	£137
8	Netherlands	£121
9	Spain	£112
10	Middle East	£85

1 IDB Supported Companies (1997/98)

Mining

RoI: Mining & Quarry Production

Description	Volume	Value £000
Quarrying of limestone, gypsum and chalk	2,509,015,743*	21,286
Operation of gravel and sandpits *including the following:*		154,166
Silica Sands *(quartz sands or industrial sands)*	178,617,201	892
Construction sands *(excl. metal-bearing sands of HS 26)*	2,458,060,814	7,211
Gravel, pebbles, shingle and flint	6,940,691,414	26,236
Crushed stone used for concrete aggregates, for roadstone and for other construction use	15,263,956,357	64,136
Coated roadstone *(tarred macadam)*	1,948,244,372	53,490
Total Value of Sales excluding confidential groups[1]		175,452

1 *Volume and value on the following products is confidential: Non-ferrous metal ores, excluding uranium and thorium ores; Common clays and shale for construction use; Kaolinic clays; Aluminium ores and concentrates; Lead ores and concentrates; Zinc ores and concentrates; Granite; Sandstone; Marble granules, chippings and powder; Granules, chippings and powder of stone; Gypsum and anhydrite; Industrial diamonds; Natural graphite and Magnesia*

* *Volume for Limestone (excl. crushed limestone aggregate and calcareous dimension) only.* Source: CSO

Mining Activity (000 tonnes of metal concentrates)

● Zinc	1996	1997	1998
Output in Ireland	164.5	193.0	180.6
Proportion of global output	2.3%	2.6%	2.4%

● Lead	1996	1997	1998
Output in Ireland	45.3	45.0	36.5
Proportion of global output	1.5%	1.5%	1.2%

Exploration Activity

	1996	1997	1998
Exploration in Ireland (IR£m)	7.14	8.05	-
Proportion of global exploration	0.213%	0.218%	(est) 0.3%+
Proportion of European expenditure	4.01%	5.59%	(est) 10%+
Number of current prospecting licenses (at year end)	428	401	397

Source: *Department of the Marine and Natural Resources*

NI: Mining & Quarry Production

Category of Rock	Quantity 000 Tonnes			Selling Value £000		
	1996	1997	1998	1996	1997	1998
Basalt and Igneous Rock	6,974	6,286	6,107	17,007	16,570	16,324
Sandstone	4,941	6,042	6,584	12,023	14,493	17,306
Limestone	4,122	3,500	3,892	10,793	10,534	10,930
Sand and Gravel	7,684	5,138	5,300	16,880	10,542	11,973
Others	1,392	625	473	6,622	3,394	2,456
TOTAL:	25,133	21,591	22,356	63,325	55,533	58,989

NI: Persons Employed in Mines & Quarries

Mineral	Inside Pit or Excavation		Outside Pit or Excavation		Management/ Administration		Total Employed	
	1997	1998	1997	1998	1997	1998	1997	1998
Basalt and Igneous Rock	137	116	259	256	104	140	500	512
Sandstone	143	150	124	159	96	99	363	408
Limestone	59	59	78	72	103	104	240	235
Sand and Gravel	101	111	100	110	106	76	307	297
Others	39	33	18	26	11	12	68	71
TOTAL:	479	469	579	623	420	431	1,478	1,523

ENERGY

Overview

Republic of Ireland

● MAIN FIGURES "AT A GLANCE"

Number of Power Stations	23
Total Output (Kilowatt hours)	18,845m
Number of Electricity customers	1,528,359
Imported Bituminous coal not agglomerated	2,664,249

Northern Ireland

● MAIN FIGURES "AT A GLANCE"

Number of Power Stations	4
Total capacity	2,243
Number of Electricity customers	673,100
Coal Shipments into NI (000 tonnes)	2,422

Demand & Supply

RoI: Primary Energy Demand

Energy Source	1995	1996	1997	1998
Oil	49%	50%	50%	51%
Natural Gas	19%	20%	20%	20%
Coal	18%	17%	17%	17%
Peat	12%	11%	10%	10%
Hydro/Renewables	2%	2%	3%	2%

NI: Primary Energy Supply

Energy Source	(million therms) 1997
Oil	937
Coal	627
TOTAL	1,565

NI: Energy Consumption by Source

Source	(million therms) 1997
Coal	320
Gas	-
Electricity	237
Petroleum	200
TOTAL	758

Electricity

RoI: Electricity Supply Board (ESB) Statistics

Description	1996	1997	1998	Change on 1997
New Houses Connected	33,097	38,452	44,619	+16%
Turnover (£m)	1,104	1,191	1,261	+5.9%
Surplus (£m)	132	108	197	+9.3%
Sales (million units)	15,707	16,726	17,440	+5.5%
Customers	1,442,416	1,483,740	1,528,359	+3%

NI: Northern Ireland Electricity (NIE) Statistics

Description	1993-94	1994-95	1995-96	1996-97	1997-98
Sales (million kWh)	6,412.0	6,529.0	6,715.0	6,876.0	6,930
Consumers	633,647.0	643,776.0	654,625.0	665,000.0	673,100

Continued from previous page

Description	1993-94	1994-95	1995-96	1996-97	1997-98
Turnover *(£ million)*	481.9	497.7	524.7	560.9	502.0
Operating Costs *(£ million)*	117.8	113.9	114.2	129.6	109.5
Capital Expenditure *(£ million)*	41.9	58.5	66.5	64.5	66.4

RoI: Electricity Supply Board (ESB) Growth

Year	Units sold to customers (Millions)	Rev from elec sales (£000)	Average price - units sold (pence)	Customers (Total)
1929/30	43.2	478	1,108	48,606
1939/40	318.6	1,946	0.612	172,545
1949/50	626.1	4,774	0.763	310,639
1959/60	1,692.2	14,724	0.871	610,946
1969/70	4,411.6	39,400	0.892	788,500
1979/80	8,508.3	300,024	3.505	1,043,428
1990	11,768.0	756,074	6.425	1,278,870
1995	14,699.1	913,143	6.212	1,407,772
1996	15,706.6	979,524	6.236	1,442,416
1997	16,725.9	1,056,400	6.318	1,483,740
1998	17,440.0	1,103,300	6.326	1,528,359

Power Stations

RoI: Power Stations by Type and Capacity*

Generating Station	Kilowatt hours (millions)			
	1993	1994	1995	1996
Hydro-Electric: Total	733	884	683	689
Ardnacrusha	331	395	268	288
Erne	259	320	275	258
Lee	82	104	87	92
Liffey	46	50	37	47
Clady	15	15	16	4
Pumped Storage: Total	247	278	255	260
Turlough Hill	247	278	255	260
Peat: Total	1,835	1,867	1,976	2,144
Allenwood	-	-	-	-
Ferbane	223	201	171	162
Lanesboro'	485	556	581	603
Cahirciveen	14	7	11	14
Gweedore	7	7	3	0
Rhode	286	282	393	366
Bellacorrick	181	159	239	220
Shannonbridge	639	655	578	779
Coal / Oil: Total	8,908	9,461	9,634	9,610
Moneypoint	6,567	6,662	6,995	6,963
Arigna	29	-	-	-
Great Island	86	200	221	244
Tarbert	1,631	1,846	1,688	2,147
Poolbeg	595	753	730	256
Gas: Total	4,405	4,318	5,008	6,142
Marina	302	695	634	791
Aghada	1,760	1,041	1,823	1,858
North Wall	710	835	669	921
Poolbeg	1,633	1,747	1,882	2,572
TOTAL	16,128	16,808	17,556	18,845

* Information on capacity/output from Power Stations post-1996 are no longer made public by the ESB.

NI: Power Stations by Type and Capacity

Name	Type	Capacity (Mega Watts)
Ballylumford	Gas / Gas Oil	1,067
Belfast West	Coal	240
Kilroot	Fuel Oil / Coal or Gas Oil	578
Coolkeeragh	Fuel Oil / Gas Oil	358

Fuel Production/Price

RoI: Bord na Móna Production and Sales Statistics

Description	1994/95	1995/96	1996/97	1997/98	1998/99
Production:					
Machine Turf (000 tonnes)	94	77	62	52	41
Milled Peat (000 tonnes)	3,646	6,658	5,049	2,744	3,104
Briquettes (000 tonnes)	365	344	291	244	276
Horticulture (000 cu metres)	1,142	1,702	1,452	1,616	1,615
Sales:					
Machine Turf (000 tonnes)	97	86	88	67	48
Milled Peat:					
To ESB (000 tonnes)	2,994	3,145	3,284	3,005	2,873
To Bord na Móna Factories (000 tonnes)	995	868	728	612	1,013
Total	3,989	4,013	4,012	3,617	3,886
Briquettes (000 tonnes)	363	294	283	263	276
Horticulture (000 cu metres)	1,562	1,710	1,393	1,536	1,664
Value of Sales:					
Machine Turf (£000s)	3,224	2,581	2,363	2,088	1,520
Milled Peat to ESB (£000s)	54,926	57,613	56,477	52,071	42,126
Briquettes (£000s)	27,151	23,326	22,089	21,438	26,586
Coal (£000s)	0	9,073	11,069	9,906	27,507
Horticulture (£000s)	41,587	45,409	45,959	42,132	35,503
Environmental Products (£000s)	2,732	3,050	4,930	6,000	7,735
Exports included above (£000s)	20,050	21,674	18,737	22,062	23,381

RoI: Coal Imports into Republic of Ireland

Type	January-December 1998		January-December 1997	
Country	(Quantity)	(Value)	(Quantity)	(Value)
● Anthracite, whether or not pulverised, not agglomerated				
Total	120,081	8,287	109,321	7,378
EU Countries	15,460	791	15,836	1,017
Non-EU Countries	104,621	7,496	93,485	6,361
● Bituminous coal, not agglomerated				
Total	2,664,249	84,565	3,109,497	102,201
EU Countries	125,486	6,545	138,841	6,583
Non-EU Countries	2,538,763	78,020	2,970,656	95,618
● Coal, not agglomerated (excluding anthracite and bituminous				
Total	64,164	4,609	90,839	5,784

NI: Coal Shipments into Northern Ireland

Use	1993	1994	1995	1996	1997
Domestic (000 tonnes)	1,082	1,211	932	919	997
Industrial (000 tonnes)	147	190	206	246	132
Electricity (000 tonnes)	1,256	1,225	1,660	1,525	1,293
TOTAL: (000 tonnes)	2,485	2,626	2,798	2,690	2,422

RoI & NI: Average Price of Petrol/Diesel

	● REPUBLIC OF IRELAND				● NORTHERN IRELAND			
Year	Premium Leaded	Regular Leaded	Unleaded Petrol	Diesel	4 Star	Super Unleaded	Unleaded	Derv
1987	58.87	57.93	-	-	37.9	-	-	34.58
1988	58.19	57.06	-	-	37.38	-	-	34
1989	61.49	60.57	61.71	-	40.39	-	38.29	36.18
1990	63.02	59.92	60.90	-	44.87	-	42.03	40.48
1991	62.26	-	59.89	-	48.47	47.31	45.06	43.81
1992	59.04	-	58.27	-	50.28	48.38	46.11	45.01
1993	59.43	-	56.57	-	54.12	52.91	49.44	49.2
1994	59.77	-	56.03	-	56.87	55.98	51.56	51.53
1995	60.57	-	56.34	-	59.7	58.55	53.77	54.24
1996	63.69	-	59.14	-	61.63	63.67	56.52	57.71
1997	66.68	-	59.86†	57.42	67.22	71.31	61.82	62.47
1998	68.76	58.51	70.24	54.96	71.1	77.79	64.79	65.50

TRANSPORT

Air

Republic of Ireland

● MAIN FIGURES "AT A GLANCE"

Passengers: Dublin (1998) 11,641,100
Passengers: Shannon (1998) 1,840,008
Passengers: Cork (1998) 1,315,224
Freight at above airports (1998) ....191,505 tonnes

Airport Statistics

● DUBLIN AIRPORT
Location Lat. 532517N, Long. 061612W
Elevation 242 ft. AMSL
Runway 1 10/28 Length 2637 metres
Width 45 metres plus 15 m shoulders
Surface concrete, Category III
Runway 2 16/34 Length 2072 metres
Width 61 metres Surface asphalt, Category I
Runway 3 11/29 Length 1356 metres
Width 61 metres Surface asphalt-concrete
Refuelling Full refuelling facilities available
Operational Hrs 24 hrs
Postal Address Dublin Airport, Co. Dublin, Ireland
Tel 01-814 1111 Fax 814 4614.
Passengers 11,641,100
Aircraft Movements 162,086
Terminal Freight incl. mail (metric tonnes) 134,650

● CORK AIRPORT
Location Lat. 515029N, Long. 082928W
Elevation 502 ft. AMSL
Runway 1 17/35 Length 2133 metres
Width 45 metres plus 15 m shoulders

Northern Ireland

● MAIN FIGURES "AT A GLANCE"

Passengers: Belfast International (1998)..2,627,000
Passengers: Belfast City (1998) 1,310,000
Passengers: City of Derry (1998)...................54,615
Freight at above airports (1998) ....46,806 tonnes

Surface asphalt, Category II
Runway 2 07/25 Length 1310 metres
Width 45 metres
Surface concrete
Refuelling Full refuelling facilities available
Operational Hrs 24 hrs
Postal Address Cork Airport, Co. Cork, Ireland
Tel 021-313 131 Fax 965 166.
Passengers 1,315,224
Aircraft Movements 37,742
Terminal Freight incl. mail (metric tonnes) 12,818

● SHANNON AIRPORT
Location Lat. 524207N, Long. 085529W
Elevation 46 ft. AMSL
Runway 1 06/24 Length 3199 metres
Width 45 metres plus 16 m shoulders
Surface asphalt, Category II
Runway 2 13/31 Length 1720 metres
Width 45 metres
Surface asphalt-concrete
Refuelling Full refuelling facilities available
Operational Hrs 24 hrs

Postal Address Shannon Airport, Co. Clare, Ireland.
Tel 061-471444 **Fax** 47 1719.
Passengers 1,840,008
Aircraft Movements 45,776
Terminal Freight incl. mail (metric tonnes) 44,037

● **KNOCK AIRPORT**
Location Lat. 53°54' 36.49N, Long. 08°49' 04.27W
Elevation 665 ft. AMSL
Runway 09/27 Length 2,300 metres
Width 45 metres
Surface Asphalt, Category 4D
Refuelling Full refuelling facilities available
Operational Hrs 8 hrs
Postal Address Knock International Airport
Charlestown, Co Mayo, Ireland.
Tel 094-67222 **Fax** 67232
Passengers 195,032
Aircraft Movements 5,736

● **DONEGAL AIRPORT**
Location Lat. 550230N, Long. 082025W
Elevation 30 ft. AMSL
Runway 03/21 Length 1,500 metres
Width 30 metres Surface Bitumen Macadam
Refuelling Full refuelling facilities available
Operational Hrs 0900 - 1800 hrs
Postal Address Donegal Airport, Carrickfinn,
Kincasslagh, Co Donegal, Ireland.
Tel 075-48284 **Fax** 48483
Passengers 15,120 (1998)
Aircraft Movements 2,334 (1998)
Terminal Freight incl. mail (metric tonnes) 4.1 (1998)

● **KERRY AIRPORT**
Location Lat. 521052N, Long. 093153W
Elevation 113 ft. AMSL
Runway 1 08 Length 2,000 metres
Width 45 metres Surface tarmac
Runway 2 26 Length 2,000 metres
Width 45 metres Surface tarmac Category I
Refuelling Full refuelling facilities available
Postal Address Kerry Airport, Farranfore, Co Kerry.
Tel 066-976 4644 **Fax** 976 4134
Passengers 157,173

● **SLIGO AIRPORT FACTFILE**
Location Lat. 541648N, Long. 083555W
Elevation 20 ft. AMSL
Runway 1 11/29 Length 1,200 metres
Width 30 metres plus 5 m shoulders
Surface bitumen Category III
Refuelling Jet A1/Avgas
Operational Hrs 0830-1730 hrs
Postal Address Sligo Airport, Strandhill, Co Sligo.
Tel 071-68280 **Fax** 68396
Passengers 26,100 (1998)
Aircraft Movements 4,200 (1998)
Terminal Freight incl. mail (metric tonnes)
136 (1998)

● **WATERFORD REGIONAL AIRPORT**
Location Lat. 52116.8N, Long. 070512.5W
Elevation 119ft AMSL

Runway Length 1,433 metres
Surface asphalt
Refuelling Jet A1, AVGAS
Operational Hrs 0900-1700 daily;
1000-1800 weekends
Postal Address Killowen, Co Waterford
Tel 051-875589 **Fax** 872288
Passengers 18,978 (1998)
Aircraft Movements 10,173 (1998)
Terminal Freight incl. mail (metric tonnes) 1.6 (1998)

● **GALWAY AIRPORT**
Location Lat. 531800.63N, Long. 0085629.73W
Elevation 81 ft. AMSL
Runway 26/08 Length 1,350 metres
Width 30 metres
Surface tarmac, Category II
Refuelling Jet A1/Avgas
Postal Address Galway Airport, Carnmore, Co Galway.
Tel 091-755569 **Fax** 752876
Passengers 150,000 (1998)
Aircraft Movements 12,000 (1998)
Terminal Freight incl. mail (metric tonnes) 5.7 (1998)

● **BELFAST INTERNATIONAL AIRPORT**
Location Lat 543925N Long 0061350W
Elevation 267 ft. AMSL
Runway 1 25 Length 2,777 metres
Width 45 metres plus 7.5m shoulders
Surface asphalt, Category 3B
Runway 2 07 Length 2,777 metres
Width 45 metres plus 7.5m shoulders
Surface asphalt
Runway 3 17 Length 1,798 metres
Width 45 metres plus 7.5m shoulders
Surface asphalt Catagory I
Refuelling On request
Operational Hrs 24 hrs
Postal Address Belfast International Airport, Belfast
BT29 4AB
Tel 028-484848 **Fax** 482096
Passengers 2,627,000 (1998)
Aircraft Movements 96,448 (1998)
Terminal Freight incl. mail (metric tonnes) 38,825

● **BELFAST CITY AIRPORT**
Location Lat. 543725N, Long. 055152W
Elevation 15 ft. AMSL
Runway 1 04/22 Length 1,820 metres
Width 61 metres
Surface concrete/asphalt
Refuelling Full refuelling facilities available
Operational Hrs 16 hrs
Postal Address Belfast City Airport, Belfast BT3 8JN
Tel 01232-734828 **Fax** 739102
Passengers 1,310,000 (1998)
Aircraft Movements 34,560 (1998)
Terminal Freight incl. mail (metric tonnes)
120 (1998)

● **CITY OF DERRY AIRPORT**
Location Lat. 550234N, Long. 0070939W
Elevation 23 ft. AMSL
Runway 1 08/26 Length 1,852 metres

Width 45 metres
Surface asphalt, Category I
Runway 2 03/21 Length 1,204 metres
Width 45 metres
Surface asphalt
Refuelling Full refuelling facilities available
Operational Hrs 0830hrs - 1800 hrs
Postal Address City of Derry Airport, Airport Road,
Co Derry.

Tel 01504-810784 Fax 811426
Passengers 54,615 (1998)
Aircraft Movements 15,051 (1998)
Terminal Freight incl. mail (metric tonnes)
7,861 (1998)

RoI: International Airport Traffic & Aircraft Statistics

Passengers		1998	1996	1994
● Dublin Airport	Transatlantic	674,328	477,881	397,656
	Great Britain	6,919,221	5,624,094	4,185,817
	Europe	3,384,545	2,454,181	1,973,801
	Domestic	539,444	464,510	369,158
	Transit	123,562	70,630	54,551
	Total	11,641,100	9,091,296	6,980,983
● Shannon Airport	Transatlantic	548,559	512,271	432,149
	Great Britain	557,117	467,151	331,165
	Europe	170,475	214,756	187,817
	Domestic	158,425	145,256	117,674
	Transit	405,432	401,216	465,627
	Total	1,840,008	1,740,650	1,534,432
● Cork Airport	Transatlantic	141	1,148	113
	Great Britain	800,326	698,393	483,269
	Europe	266,246	215,883	143,306
	Domestic	233,378	195,107	168,107
	Transit	15,133	13,789	5,393
	Total	1,315,224	1,124,320	800,188
● Overall	Transatlantic	1,223,028	991,300	829,918
	Great Britain	8,276,664	6,789,638	5,000,251
	Europe	3,821,266	2,884,820	2,304,924
	Domestic	931,247	804,873	654,939
	Transit	544,127	485,635	525,571
	Total	14,796,332	11,956,266	9,315,603
● Terminal Freight incl. Mail (Metric Tonnes)				
	Dublin	134,650	107,004	72,655
	Shannon	44,037	35,463	29,314
	Cork	12,818	4,214	2,294
	Total	191,505	146,681	104,263

Aircraft Movements		1998	1996	1994
● Dublin Airport	Commercial - Scheduled	132,558	110,551	94,145
	Commercial - Non-Scheduled	12,259	11,122	10,268
	Commercial - Training	1,092	563	491
	Others	16,177	17,807	25,127
	Total	162,086	140,043	130,031
● Shannon Airport	Commercial - Scheduled	14,218	11,578	8,598
	Commercial - Non-Scheduled	7,528	9,912	10,053
	Commercial - Training	16,663	19,147	15,174
	Others	7,367	6,594	6,116
	Total	45,776	47,231	39,941
● Cork Airport	Commercial - Scheduled	15,490	14,538	10,268
	Commercial - Non-Scheduled	2,786	4,413	3,604
	Commercial - Training	14,908	17,844	12,530
	Others	4,558	4,098	3,279
	Total	37,742	40,843	29,681
● Overall	Commercial - Scheduled	162,266	136,667	113,011
	- Non-Scheduled	22,573	25,447	23,925
	- Training	32,663	37,554	28,195

➤ *Continued from previous page*

Aircraft Movements	1998	1996	1994
● Overall .... Others	28,102	28,499	34,522
Total	245,604	228,167	199,653

NI: Airport Passengers

Year	Belfast International	Belfast City	City of Derry	Totals
1986	1,854,000	210,000	12,000	2,076,000
1988	2,176,000	400,000	13,000	2,589,000
1990	2,294,000	548,000	41,000	2,883,000
1992	2,241,000	612,000	28,000	2,881,000
1994	2,039,000	1,228,000	34,000	3,301,000
1995	2,346,000	1,280,000	64,000	3,691,000
1996	2,351,000	1,361,000	64,000	3,776,000
1998	2,627,000	1,310,000	54,615	3,991,615

Aer Lingus Fleet Statistics*

● AIRBUS A330-300
Number 5 **Powered by** Two General Electric CF6-80E1 engines **Seats** 315-327 **Chief Routes** New York, Newark, Boston and Chicago.

Reg.	Serial	Delivered	Name
EI-SHN	54	02 May 94	St. Flannan
EI-DUB	55	11 May 94	St. Patrick
EI-CRK	70	18 Nov 94	St. Brigid
EI-JFK	86	11 July 95	St. Colmcille
EI-ORD	59	01 July 97	St. Maeve

● AIRBUS A330-200
Number 1 **Powered by** Two General Electric CF6-80E1 engines **Seats** 267-275 **Chief Routes** Los Angeles, New York, Newark, Boston and Chicago.

Reg.	Serial	Delivered	Name
EI-LAX	269	29 April 99	St. Mella

● BOEING 737-400
Number 6 **Powered by** Two CFM-56-3B2 engines **Seats** 156 **Chief Routes** London and European.

Reg.	Serial	Delivered	Name
EI-BXA	24474	12 July 89	St. Conleth
EI-BXB	24521	27 Oct 89	St. Gall
EI-BXC	24773	26 April 90	St. Brendan
EI-BXD	24866	01 June 90	St. Colman
EI-BXI	25052	29 April 91	St. Finnian
EI-BXK	25736	23 April 92	St. Caimin

● BOEING 737-500
Number 8 **Powered by** Two CFM-56-3B1 engines **Seats** 117 **Chief Routes** Short-haul network.

Reg.	Serial	Delivered	Name
EI-CDA	24878	30 Oct 90	St. Columba
EI-CDB	24919	19 Dec 90	St. Albert
EI-CDC	24968	10 Jan 91	St. Munchin
EI-CDD	24989	04 Feb 91	St. Macartan
EI-CDE	25115	28 May 91	St. Jarlath
EI-CDF	25737	27 March 92	St. Cronan
EI-CDG	25738	14 April 92	St. Moling
EI-CDH	25739	27 April 92	St. Ronan

AER LINGUS is the Republic of Ireland state airline.

● FOKKER 50
Number 5 **Powered by** Two Pratt & Whitney PW125B engines **Seats** 50 **Chief Routes** Domestic and UK regional.

Reg.	Serial	Delivered	Name
EI-FKA	20118	30 Sep 88	St. Fintan
EI-FKC	20177	23 Mar 90	St. Fidelma
EI-FKD	20181	12 April 90	St. Mel
EI-FKE	20208	28 Jan 91	St. Pappin
EI-FKF	20209	07 Feb 91	St. Ultan

● BRITISH AEROSPACE BAE146-300
Number 6 **Powered by** four Textron Lycoming ALF502R-5 engines **Seats** 110 **Chief Routes** Between Dublin and UK

Reg.	Serial	Delivered	Name
EI-CLG	E3.131	08 June 95	St. Finbarr
EI-CLH	E3.146	02 June 95	St. Aoife
EI-CLI	E3.159	19 April 95	St. Eithne
EI-CLJ	E3.155	01 Mar 96	St. Senan
EI-CLY	E3.149	17 April 97	St. Eugene
EI-CTM	E3.129	23 Mar 99	St. Fiacra

● BRITISH AEROSPACE BAE146-200
Number 2 **Powered by** Four Textron Lycoming ALF502R-5 engines **Seats** 93 **Chief Routes** Between Dublin and UK.

Reg.	Serial	Delivered	Name
EI-CSK	E2.062	03 April 98	St. Ciara
EI-CSL	E2.074	08 May 98	St. Cormac

● AIRBUS A321
Number 5 **Powered by** Two General Electric CFM56 engines **Seats** 168 **Chief Route** London.

Reg.	Serial	Delivered	Name
EI-CPC	815	08 May 98	St. Fergus
EI-CPD	841	19 June 98	St. Davnet
EI-CPE⁻	926	11 Dec 98	St. Enda
EI-CPF	991	09 April 99	St. Ita
EI-CPG	1023	01 May 99	St. Aidan

Aer Lingus Factfile

● MAIN FIGURES "AT A GLANCE"

Founded	April 1936
Turnover (December 1998)	£901.4 million
Net Profit for year 1998	£53.7 million
Total passengers carried	5.8 million
Transatlantic Passengers	776,000
Ireland-London Passengers	2.0 million

● MAIN FIGURES "AT A GLANCE"

Ireland-UK Provincial Passengers	1.1 million
Continental Europe Passengers	1.1 million
Strength of current fleet	38 planes
Cargo Tonnes carried	45,000 tonnes
Number of Employees	7,327

Ryanair Factfile, Route Network & Fleet Statistics

● MAIN FIGURES "AT A GLANCE"

Founded	June 1985
Total passengers carried	5.1 million (1998)
Strength of current fleet	26 planes
Number of routes	34
Number of employees	1,112

● RYANAIR ROUTE NETWORK 1999 - Dublin to: Birmingham London (Stansted/Luton/Gatwick) Bristol Cardiff Bournemouth Glasgow (Prestwick) Leeds (Bradford) Liverpool Manchester Teesside. London (Stansted) to: Cork Kerry Brussels (South) Knock Stockholm (South) Glasgow (Prestwick) Oslo (South) Rimini Venice (Treviso) Pisa Carcassonne (Toulouse) Saint Etienne (Lyon) Kristianstad (Malmo) Paris (Beauvais) Frankfurt Genoa Turin Ancona Biarritz Dinard. Glasgow Prestwick to: Paris (Beauvais)

● RYANAIR 737-800 PROFILE

Number of parts: Approximately 300,000 **Seating** 737-800 (162 to 189 passengers) **Configurations** Four to six abreast with one aisle **Length** 737-800 (129 feet 6 inches, 39.5 metres) **Wingspan** 737-800 (112 feet 7 inches, 34.3 metres) **Tail height** 737-800 (41 feet 2 inches, 12.5 metres) **Exterior fuselage diameter** 12 feet 3 inches (3.73 metres) **Interior cross-section**

width 11 feet 7 inches (3.63 metres) **Engines** CFM56-7B24 (produced by CFMI, a 50/50 joint company of General Electric and Snecma of France) 24,000 Lbs thrust each **Maximum take off weight** 174,200 pounds, 79 tonnes **Fuel capacity** 6,878 U.S. gallons (all three models) **Maximum range** 2,925 nautical miles **Cruise speed** Mach 0.785 **Cargo capacity** 737-800 1,591 feet 3 45m3 **Average price** 737-800 US$48-$54 million **Total orders** 934 (as of 6/9/98) **Total customers** 42 (as of 6/9/98) **Programme launch** 5th September 1994 **Rollout** 30th June 1997 **First flight** 31st July 1997 **Flight testing** 10 airplanes (4 -700's, 3 -800's, 3 -600's) **Certification** FAA 13/3/98, JAA 9/4/98 (737-800) **First delivery** 22nd April 1998 (737-800) September 1998 **In service** 24th April 1998 (737-600) (737-800)

● 737-800 vs 737-200A (Generic Comparison)

Higher 41,00ft vs 37,000ft **Faster** +37mph (59kph) @ cruise **Further** +1,000 nautical miles **Less Fuel Burn/Seat** -30% **Lower Emissions** 40% less by mass; 12.3kg less/ flight - 22 tonnes less/year **Quiet** 2 8 d b (only 1/5 of 737-200) **Seats** 59 more seats

Ryanair is a wholly independent Irish airline.

Rail

Iarnród Éireann (Irish Rail) Factfile

● MAIN FIGURES (1998) "AT A GLANCE"

Total Customer Revenue	£136.6m
Mainline Customer Revenue	£86.5m
Bray/Howth Suburban Customer Revenue	£16.1m
Company Profit	£4.4m
Accumulated deficit (as of 31.12.98)	£41.5m
Total Number of Passengers	32.1m
Suburban Passenger journeys	+22m
Mainland Rail Passenger journeys	10m
Freight Revenue	£16.8m
Road Freight Profit	£1.2m
Total track kilometres (1997)	2,682

● GEOGRAPHICAL ANALYSIS OF PASSENGER REVENUE

Region	1997 (£m)	1998 (£m)	% Change
South West	27.2	30.6	+11.8
West	13.1	14.0	+6.6

Region	1997 (£m)	1998 (£m)	% Change
South East	4.3	5.3	+20.8
Belfast	4.4	6.1	+32.4
Branch Lines	0.8	0.7	-13.3
DART	14.6	16.1	+9.8
Other Suburban	7.9	6.9	-13.5
TOTAL:	**72.3**	**79.7**	**+9.7**

● COMMUNICATIONS

Iarnród Éireann - Irish Rail
Connolly Station, Amiens St, Dublin 1
Tel: 01-8363333 Email: INFO@irishrail.ie

Northern Ireland Railways Factfile

● **MAIN FIGURES (1998) "AT A GLANCE"**

Total Customer Revenue £9,959,000
Company Profit ....£850,652 (after tax)
Total Number of Passengers 27,207
Local Passenger journeys 4,964,709
Cross-Border Passenger journeys 846,997
Number of Employees...671
Network Kilometres 211
Number of Rail Stations...57
Number of Locomotives ....6 + 30 power cars

● **MAIN FIGURES (1998) "AT A GLANCE"**

Number of Passenger Coaches ..64 + 30 power cars
Number of Drivers 65
Number of available Seats................................6,635
Busiest Route ....Belfast-Dublin

Sea

RoI: Traffic & Passenger Movement at Principal Ports

	1996	1997	1998
Total: Freight Vehicles / Trailers	**431,929**	**423,886**	**533,125**
Dublin	340,983	323,209	399,000
Dun Laoghaire	14,695	25,954	42,000
Rosslare	70,147	70,072	92,125
Cork	6,104	4,651	
Total: Passengers	**3,955,250**	**4,039,260**	**4,479,000**
Dublin	784,940	961,000	1,290,000
Dun Laoghaire	1,856,650	1,624,065	1,719,000
Rosslare	1,313,660	1,454,195	1,470,000
Total: Number of Arrivals	**12,721,000**	**12,413,000**	**10,358,000**
Dublin	6,256,000	6,209,000	6,596,000
Dun Laoghaire	1,726,000	1,396,000	1,362,000
Rosslare	2,355,000	2,405,000	2,400,000
Cork	2,384,000	2,403,000	
Total: Accompanied Private Cars and Buses	**796,917**	**867,609**	**594,775**
Dublin	138,722	186,203	244,160
Dun Laoghaire	287,644	271,156	310,022
Rosslare	283,085	342,765	40,593
Cork	87,466	67,485	

NI: Sea Transport Movement by Traffic Tourist Vehicles

Year	Belfast		Larne		Totals		Total
	Inward	Outward	Inward	Outward	Inward	Outward	
1991	1,804	1,935	196,263	190,910	198,067	192,845	390,912
1992	43,536	43,868	180,087	174,241	224,250	218,250	442,500
1993	60,153	60,205	201,903	196,118	262,056	256,323	518,379
1994	57,723	57,927	215,578	208,959	273,301	266,886	540,187
1995	75,972	73,139	226,119	220,252	302,091	293,391	595,482
1996	201,899	193,489	98,186	95,779	300,085	289,268	589,353
1997	208,784	208,927	86,661	85,113	295,445	294,040	589,485
1998	201,885	201,913	94,647	95,216	296,532	297,129	593,661

● **TONNAGE OF GOODS THROUGH THE PRINCIPAL PORTS (inward traffic - 000 tonnes)**

Year	Belfast	Larne	Derry	Warrenpoint	Other Ports	Totals
1993	7,349	2,328	768	1,270	2,144	13,859
1995	8,271	2,496	1,013	1,111	2,061	14,952
1998	9,168	1,900	1,094	1,072	1,257	14,491

● **TONNAGE OF GOODS THROUGH THE PRINCIPAL PORTS (outward traffic - 000 tonnes)**

Year	Belfast	Larne	Derry	Warrenpoint	Other Ports	Totals
1993	1,603	2,006	21	679	379	4,688
1995	1,873	2,177	31	572	430	5,083
1998	3,066	1,488	33	491	232	5,310

RoI: Ship Register (December 1998)

Vessel Description	Number	Combined Gross Tonnage
Merchant > or equal to 100 gross tons	40	145,320
Barges and Dredgers > 100 gross tons	17	4,610
Lightships, Tugs, Training and Estuarial Car Ferries	43	11,770
Yachts, Pleasure Craft and Sail Training	473	6,400
TOTAL	573	168,100

Road

RoI & NI: Public Transport (Bus)

● BUS ÉIREANN (IRISH BUS)[1] 1998

Total Revenue	£105.5m
Total Operating Costs	£107.1m
Company Profit	£3.6m
Passenger Journeys	84,392,000
Number of Employees	2,500
Vehicle Kilometres	64,595,000
Size of Fleet	1,300+
Number of School Buses	2,300
Average Age of Fleet	6.7 years
Number of Drivers	approx. 900

1 Provides the national bus service outside Dublin.

● BUS ÁTHA CLIATH (DUBLIN BUS)[2] 1998

Total Customer Revenue	£105.1m
Total Operating Costs	£111.8m
Company Profit	£1.3m
Total Number of Passengers	187.9m
Number of Employees	2,924
Size of Fleet	950
Number of Drivers	2,100

2 Operates the Dublin City bus services.

● ULSTERBUS (NI BUS)[3] 1998

Kilometres Operated	48,613,000
Passenger Journeys	49,358,000
Bus Miles	30,208,000
Passenger Receipts	£52,867,000
Bus Fleet	1,171
Average Age of Buses	11.31 years
Number of Staff	2,111

3 Operates inter-urban express services and rural services.

● CITYBUS (NI BUS)[4] 1998

Kilometres Operated	11,150,000
Passenger Journeys	21,863,000
Bus Miles	6,928,000
Passenger Receipts	£16,638,000
Bus Fleet	265
Average Age of Buses	9.51 years
Number of Staff	652

4 Citybus operates mostly within the boundaries of the Belfast City Council area.

Source: DOE

RoI: Cross-Border Passenger Movement

	Rail		Road bus scheduled services		Total rail and road bus scheduled services	
Year	Outward	Inward	Outward	Inward	Outward	Inward
1990	180,000	189,000	309,000	305,000	489,000	494,000
1991	226,000	238,000	386,000	387,000	612,000	625,000
1992	227,000	243,000	418,000	412,000	645,000	655,000
1993	255,000	280,000	417,000	412,000	671,000	692,000
1994	306,000	337,000	411,000	407,000	717,000	744,000
1995	377,000	415,000	430,000	427,000	807,000	842,000
1996	374,000	388,000	430,000	429,000	804,000	817,000
1997	344,000	374,000	517,000	516,000	861,000	890,000
1998	354,000	371,000	579,000	579,000	933,000	951,000

RoI: Vehicle & Driver Statistics

● No. of Mechanically Propelled Vehicles by Taxation Class

Taxation Class	1998	1997	Actual change	% Change
Private Cars	1,196,901	1,134,429	+62,472	+5.51
Goods Vehicles	170,866	158,158	+12,708	+8.04
Agricultural Tractors	72,703	73,523	-820	-1.12
Motorcycles	24,398	24,424	-26	-0.11
General Haulage Tractors	576	583	-7	-1.20
Exempt Vehicles	11,748	10,336	+1,412	+13.66
Small Public Service Vehicles	11,249	10,340	+909	+8.79

Continued from previous page

● No. of Mechanically Propelled Vehicles by Taxation Class

Taxation Class	1998	1997	Actual change	% Change
Large Public Service Vehicles	6,104	5,845	+259	+4.43
Schoolbuses	1,090	1,162	-72	-6.20
Excavators, Trench Diggers etc	3,898	3,590	+308	+8.58
Mobile Machines & Forklift Trucks	5,560	4,757	+803	+16.88
Hearses	699	698	+1	+0.14
Small Dumpers	599	455	+144	+31.65
Off-Road Dumpers	271	254	+17	+6.69
Vintage Vehicles	4,082	3,776	+306	+8.10
Motor Caravans	109	0	+109	-
TOTAL	1,510,853	1,432,330	+78,523	+5.48

● No. of Vehicles by Type of Fuel (at 31.12.97)

Fuel	Number	%
Petrol	1,019,930	71.21%
Diesel	411,075	28.70%
Liquid Petroleum Gas (LPG) and others	1,325	0.09%
Total	1,432,330	100%

● Age of Vehicles (at 31.12.97)

Vehicle	Private Cars	Goods Vehicles
4 Years old and over	732,731 (65%)	96,302 (61%)
6 Years old and over	581,884 (51%)	74,849 (47%)

● New Vehicles - Licensed for First Time

Vehicle	1998	1997	1996
Private Cars	138,538	125,818	109,333
Goods Vehicles	23,811	18,895	16,445
Agricultural Tractors etc.	2,318	1,848	2,233
Motor Cycles	3,117	2,717	2,412
Others	4,740	3,808	3,541
Total	172,524	153,086	133,964

● Second Hand Vehicles

Vehicle	1998	1997	1996
Private Cars	39,565	41,554	44,500
Goods Vehicles	5,388	4,888	4,927
Agricultural Tractors	3,040	3,065	3,627
Others	4,643	4,263	4,138

● Driving Licensing: Classification of Licences (at 31.12.97)

License	1997	1992
Full	1,395,920 (76%)	1,092,078 (77%)
Provisional	452,970 (24%)	330,907 (23%)
Total	1,848,890 (100%)	1,422,985 (100%)

NI: Vehicle & Driver Statistics

● No. of All Vehicles registered by Body Type and Taxation Group (at December 1998)

Vehicle	Number
Cars	592,831
Taxis	391
Motorcycles	14,384
Tricycles	68
Light Goods Vehicles	45,198
Heavy Goods Vehicles	24,771
Buses/Coaches	5,105
Agricultural Vehicles	8,842
Others	3,770
TOTAL	**695,360**

● No. of mechanically-propelled road vehicles registered for the first time during 1998

Vehicle	Number
● Private Cars	
New Cars PLG	61,864
New Cars exempt (Government owned)	18
New Cars exempt (non-Government owned)	8,438
Used Cars PLG	28,848
Used Cars exempt (Government owned)	1
Used Cars exempt (non-Government owned)	1,321
Total Cars	**100,490**
● Hackneys	
Total Hackneys	482

Continued from previous page

● No. of mechanically-propelled road vehicles registered for the first time during 1998

Vehicle	Number
● Light Goods Vehicles	
Light Goods	10,060
Light Goods exempt (Government owned)	162
Light Goods exempt (non-Government owned)	294
Total Light Goods vehicles	10,516
● Heavy Goods Vehicles	
Heavy Goods	421
Heavy Goods exempt (Government owned)	61
Heavy Goods exempt (non-Government owned)	37
Total Heavy Goods vehicles	519
● Tractors	
Tractors	962

Vehicle	Number
Tractors exempt (Government owned)	19
Tractors exempt (non-Government owned)	92
Total Tractors	1,073
● Motor Cycles	
Motor Cycles	4,283
Motor Cycles exempt (Government owned)	5
Motor Cycles exempt (non-Government owned)	135
Total Motor Cycles	4,423
Total of other exempt vehicles	103
Total of other non-exempt vehicles	0
TOTAL ALL VEHICLES	117,606

● Age of Vehicles by Taxation Class (at December 1998)

Vehicle	Average Age (yrs)
Private and Light Goods	4.32
Motor Cycles, Scooters and Mopeds	4.74
Hackney and Bus	7.54

RoI: Vehicle Registration Marks by County

Index & County	Council Office
CW: Carlow	Athy Road, Carlow
CN: Cavan	Courthouse, Cavan
CE: Clare	Courthouse, Ennis
C: Cork	Carrigrohane Road, Cork
DL: Donegal	County Building, Lifford
G: Galway	County Building, Galway
KY: Kerry	Moyderwell, Tralee
KE: Kildare	Friary Road, Naas
KK: Kilkenny	John's Green, Kilkenny
LS: Laois	County Hall, Portlaoise
LM: Leitrim	Priest's Lane, Carrick-on-Shannon
LK: Limerick	O'Connell Street, Limerick
LD: Longford	Great Water Street, Longford
LH: Louth	The Crescent, Dundalk
MO: Mayo	Courthouse, Castlebar

Index & County	Council Office
MH: Meath	County Hall, Navan
MN: Monaghan	North Road, Monaghan
OY: Offaly	O'Connor Square, Tullamore
RN: Roscommon	Abbey Street, Roscommon
SO: Sligo	Cleveragh Road, Sligo
TN: Tipperary, N.Riding	Kickham Street, Nenagh
TS: Tipperary, S.Riding	Emmet Street, Clonmel
WD: Waterford	Courthouse, Dungarvan
WH: Westmeath	County Buildings, Mullingar
WX: Wexford	County Hall, Wexford
WW: Wicklow	County Buildings, Wicklow
L: Limerick City	City Hall, Merchants Quay, Limerick
W: Waterford City	6-8 Lombard Street, Waterford
D: Dublin	River House, Chancery Street, Dublin 7.

NI: Vehicle Registration Marks by County

Index Mark	County
IA; DZ; KZ; RZ;	Antrim
IB; LZ;	Armagh
IJ; BZ; JZ; SZ;	Down
IL;	Fermanagh
IW; NZ; YZ;	Derry

Index Mark	County
JI; HZ; VZ;	Tyrone
OI; XI; AZ; CZ; EZ; FZ; GZ; MZ; OZ; PZ; TZ; UZ; WZ;	Belfast City
UI;	Derry City

Issued by: Dept. of the Environment for N. Ireland,
The Vehicle Licensing Central Office, County Hall, Castlerock Rd, Coleraine, Co. Derry BT51 3HS.

RoI: Twenty Most Popular Newly Licensed Cars

Car	Number (1997)	Car	Number (1997)
Ford	16,235	Mitsubishi	3,639
Volkswagen / Audi	15,771	Honda	3,304
Opel	14,656	Seat	2,839
Toyota	12,409	Hyundai	2,339
Nissan	11,917	Citroen	2,189
Fiat / Lancia	9,292	Mercedes	1,730
Renault	7,768	BMW	1,694
Peugeot / Talbot	5,426	Volvo	1,575
Mazda	4,414	Suzuki	1,348
Austin / Rover	3,937	Subaru	473

NI: Twenty Most Popular Newly Licensed Cars

Make	Number	Make	Number
Ford	8,798	Mazda	1,521
Renault	8,629	BMW	1,468
Vauxhall	6,549	Honda	1,267
Peugeot	4,966	Mitsubishi	1,235
Volkswagen	3,491	Fiat	1,232
Citroen	3,243	Mercedes	1,087
Nissan	3,234	Seat	1,075
Rover	3,065	Audi	1,042
Toyota	3,041	Suzuki	718
Hyundai	1,655	Daewoo	568

RoI: Cost of Selected New Cars

Make	Model	Type	Republic of Ireland (IR£)*
Alfa Romeo	Spider	2.0 16v TS Lusso	£33,000
Audi	A3	1.6 100 BHP	£18,355
BMW	3 Series	Compact 316i	£19,950
BMW	5 Series	Saloon 520i	£34,600
Citroen	Xsara	1.4 VL Coupé 3dr	£12,495
Fiat	Punto	60 Team 3dr	£8,995
Ford	Ka	1.3i KA 3dr	£8,910
Ford	Fiesta	Encore 1.3i 3dr	£10,210
Ford	Puma	1.4i 3dr	£16,035
Ford	Escort	1.4i 5dr	£12,870
Ford	Mondeo	LX 1.6i	£17,245
Honda	Civic	1.4i 3dr	£12,815
Honda	Accord	1.8i S Vtec 4dr	£20,710
Hyundai	Atoz	1.0 5dr GLSi	£8,595
Hyundai	Lantra	1.6 4dr GLSi Executive	£14,495
Jaguar	Classic	XJ8 3.2 V8	£55,600
Jeep	Wrangler	2.5 Petrol Sport Soft top	£20,525
Jeep	Cherokee	2.5 TD Sport 4dr	£29,980
Lexus	GS 300	Suede Velvet	£50,950
Mazda	121	LX S 1.3i 3dr	£9,250
Mazda	323	LX 1.3i BHB S	£11,580
Mercedes-Benz	A-Class	A140	£15,500
Mitsubishi	Colt	1.3 GL A/B 3dr	£11,640
Mitsubishi	Lancer	1.3 GLX A/B Saloon	£12,630
Mitsubishi	Galant	2.0 GLS A/C Saloon	£22,435
Nissan	Micra	1.0 GX 3dr	£10,195
Nissan	Primera	1.6 Sri 4dr	£16,985
Nissan	Patrol	2.8 SE Diesel LWR Estate 3dr	£36,000
Opel	Corsa	Champion X1.0XE 3dr	£10,100
Opel	Astra	GL 1.2XE 3dr	£13,250
Peugeot	106	Zest 1.0 5sp 3dr	£9,345

Continued from previous page

Make (August 1999 Prices)	Model	Type	Republic of Ireland (IR£)*
Porche	911	Carrera	£104,000
Renault	Clio	1.2 3dr	£10,150
Renault	Megane	(Hatchback) RN 1.4 ABS 5dr	£13,500
Renault	Laguna	RT 1.6 ABS	£17,100
Rover	Mini	1.3i	£10,650
Saab	9-3	2.0 3dr	£23,150
Skoda	Felicia	LX	£8,620
Subaru	Vivio	GLi 5dr	£7,920
Toyota	Starlet	1.3 3dr	£10,870
Toyota	Corolla	H/B Linca Terra	£12,995
Volkswagen	Polo	1.0 3dr 50HP	£10,200
Volkswagen	Golf	1.4 16v 75 BHP 3dr	£13,610
Volkswagen	Passat	1.6 100HP B5	£17,900
Volvo	S40	1.6	£18,900

Source: SIMI (Society of the Irish Motor Industry) *Price list for August 1999

NI: Cars Imported by Country of Origin, 1998

Country	Number	Country	Number
New Cars (NI)	55,081	Used Cars (re-registered)	20,146
Republic of Ireland	6,733	Republic of Ireland	3,604
Continent	50	Continent	5,098
TOTAL:	61,864*	TOTAL:	28,848*

* Does not include vehicles which are exempt from excise.

RoI: Used Car Imports by Country of Origin

Country of Origin	Net Registration	% of Total 1998
Northern Ireland and Britain	10,557	28.1%
Japan	23,043	61.3%
Germany	1,665	4.4%
France	1,715	4.6%
Italy	250	0.7%
Sweden	153	0.4%
Spain	75	0.2%
Others	150	0.4%

RoI: Cost of keeping a car on the Road

Standing Charges per annum (£)	up to 1000	1001-1250	1251-1500	1501-1750	1751-2000	2001-2500	2501-3000	3001-4000
Car Licence[1]	98	160	186	262	323	477	607	849
Insurance[2]	730	830	970	1,060	1,230	1,400	1,550	1,650
Driving Licence[3]	4	4	4	4	4	4	4	4
Depreciation[4]	938	1,188	1,313	1,500	1,688	1,813	2,250	2,750
Interest on capital[5]	188	238	263	300	338	363	450	550
Garage/Parking[6]	1,820	1,820	1,820	1,820	1,820	1,820	1,820	1,820
AA Subscription[7]	55	55	55	55	55	55	55	55
Total	£3,833	£4,295	£4,611	£5,001	£5,458	£5,932	£6,736	£7,678
Costs Per Mile (in pence)								
10,000	38.330	43.950	46.110	50.001	54.580	59.320	67.360	76.780
5,000	76.560	85.900	92.220	100.002	109.160	118.640	134.720	153.560
15,000	25.553	28.633	30.740	33.334	36.386	39.546	44.906	51.186
20,000	19.165	21.475	23.055	25.000	27.290	29.660	33.680	38.390
Operating Costs Per Mile (in pence)								
Petrol[8]*	6.069	6.868	7.457	8.700	9.666	10.440	11.863	14.500

Continued from previous page

Operating Costs Per Mile (in pence)								
Oil[9]	0.152	0.185	0.202	0.223	0.272	0.300	0.323	0.385
Tyres[10]	1.195	1.302	1.528	2.003	2.102	2.245	3.495	5.126
Servicing[11]	1.102	1.595	1.755	1.795	2.029	2.000	2.093	2.402
Repairs[12]	4.906	5.850	6.105	6.732	7.309	8.905	10.105	12.575
Total (pence)	**13.424**	**15,800**	**17.047**	**19.453**	**21.378**	**23.890**	**27.879**	**34.988**

Total Costs Per Mile (based on 10,000 miles)								
Standing Charges	38.330	42.950	46.110	50.001	54.580	59.320	67.360	76.780
Operating Costs	13.424	15.800	17.047	19.453	21.378	23.890	27.879	34.988
Total (pence)	**51.754**	**58.750**	**63.157**	**69.454**	**75.958**	**83.210**	**95.239**	**111.768**

*57.45 per litre (Unleaded) for each penny more, or less, add or subtract							
	0.105	0.119	0.129	0.151	1.167	0.181	0.206	0.251

Figures are average. Vehicles have been valued at £7,500 - £9,500 - £10,500 - £12,000 - £13,500 - £14,500 - £18,000 - £22,000 respectively. 1 £98 - £160 - £186 - £262 - £323 - £477 - £607 - £849 respectively. 2 Average rates for Third Party, Fire & Theft Policies. 3 £4.00 per annum. 4 Based on mileage of 10,000 miles per annum, and assuming economical life of 80,000 miles or 8 years. 5 Car value if invested at 2.5% per yr. 6 £35 per wk. 7 £55 per yr. 8 Petrol at £2.61 per gallon (57.4 p per litre) - Unleaded; £3.15 per gallon (69.3p per litre) - Leaded. 9 Allowance for variable consumption and cost of replacement after oil changes. 10 Estimated tyre life 30,000 miles. 11 General servicing as recommended by manufacturers. 12 Estimated on the basis of total cost of repairs, replacements and renovations over 8 yrs or 80,000 miles.

Source: Automobile Association (AA)

RoI: Speed Laws

Vehicle Type	MPH Built-up Areas	MPH Elsewhere	MPH Motorways
Cars (*includes light goods vehicles & motorcycles*)	30	60	70
Single Deck Buses - *not carrying standing passengers*	30	50	-
Single Deck Buses - *carrying standing passengers*	30	40	-
Double Deck Buses	30	40	-
Goods Vehicles (*including Articulated vehicles*) - *gross vehicle weight in excess of 3,500 Kgs*	30	50	-
Any vehicle drawing another	30	50	-

NI: Speed Laws

Vehicle Type	MPH Built-up Areas	MPH Elsewhere		MPH Motorways
		Single Carriage	Dual Carriage	
Cars (*including car-derived vans & motorcycles*)	30	60	70	70
Cars towing caravans or trailers (*including car-derived vans & motorcycles*)	30	50	60	60
Buses and Coaches (*not exceeding 12 metres in overall length*)	30	50	60	70
Goods vehicles (*not exceeding 7.5 tonnes maximum laden weight*)	30	50	60	70[1]
Goods vehicles (*exceeding 7.5 tonnes maximum laden weight*)	30	40	50	60

1 60 MPH if articulated or towing a trailer.

RoI & NI: Length of Public Roads

● REPUBLIC OF IRELAND	
Road	Length (kms)
National Primary	2,749.00
National Secondary	2,694.70
Regional	11,690.29
Local	78,610.41
TOTAL	**95,744.40**

● NORTHERN IRELAND	
Road	Length (kms)
Motorway	110
Class I	2,240
Class II	2,880
Class III	4,720
Unclassified	14,390
TOTAL	**24,340**

RoI: Length of Public Roads

Road Authority (km)	National Primary	National Secondary	Regional	Local	Total
County Council					
Carlow	23.40	53.60	157.70	948.20	**1,182.90**
Cavan	65.20	60.70	399.00	2,470.20	**2,995.10**
Clare	54.50	179.80	597.50	3,307.60	**4,139.40**
Cork	220.60	257.70	1,321,100	10,260.70	**12,060.00**
Donegal	150.40	153.70	688.30	5,307.80	**6,300.20**
Dun Laoghaire-Rathdown	20.30	0.00	103.40	492.90	**616.60**
Fingal	61.80	0.00	196.70	757.20	**1,015.70**
Galway	153.50	276.80	765.70	5,293.00	**6,489.00**
Kerry	94.80	333.80	460.30	3,807.20	**4,696.10**
Kildare	112.40	25.60	387.80	1,692.80	**2,218.60**
Kilkenny	146.40	67.90	313.30	2,536.50	**3,064.10**
Laois	83.50	79.40	280.80	1,664.90	**2,108.60**
Leitrim	56.50	0.00	334.20	1,774.60	**2,165.30**
Limerick	136.40	53.40	462.60	2,929.00	**3,581.40**
Longford	43.20	55.00	153.39	1,317.00	**1,568.59**
Louth	74.00	51.90	196.00	951.00	**1,272.90**
Mayo	134.30	267.40	586.24	5,244.98	**6,232.92**
Meath	121.80	76.90	474.70	2,438.68	**3,112.08**
Monaghan	74.30	31.00	289.30	2,077.20	**2,471.80**
Offaly	18.00	120.30	338.70	1,499.40	**1,976.40**
Roscommon	100.90	145.00	346.10	3,358.00	**3,950.00**
Sligo	108.20	47.80	221.80	2,337.00	**2,714.80**
South Dublin	31.10	21.70	99.42	608.48	**760.70**
Tipperary N.R.	65.90	100.60	341.70	2,198.00	**2,706.20**
Tipperary S.R.	119.50	39.10	426.44	2,300.00	**2,885.04**
Waterford	68.10	35.70	377.90	2,100.60	**2,582.30**
Westmeath	96.60	84.20	228.80	1,767.00	**2,176.60**
Wexford	150.10	15.10	438.70	2,758.40	**3,362.30**
Wicklow	53.70	42.00	423.70	1,540.20	**2,059.60**
County Council Total	**2,639.40**	**2,676.10**	**11,411.19**	**75,738.54**	**92,465.23**
County Borough Corporations					
Cork	38.50	2.80	38.30	324.40	**404.00**
Dublin	35.70	5.90	168.90	965.50	**1,176.00**
Galway	12.20	7.70	30.90	162.90	**213.70**
Limerick	15.00	2.20	17.50	144.80	**179.50**
Waterford	8.20	0.00	23.50	122.70	**154.40**
County Borough Corps Total	**109.60**	**18.60**	**279.10**	**1,720.30**	**2,127.60**
Borough Corporations					
Clonmel				45.10	**45.10**
Drogheda				62.95	**62.95**
Kilkenny				24.10	**24.10**
Sligo				43.60	**43.60**
Wexford				20.00	**20.00**
Borough Corporations Total				**195.75**	**195.75**
Urban District Councils Total				**955.82**	**955.82**
Overall Totals	**2,749.00**	**2,694.70**	**11,690.29**	**78,610.41**	**95,744.40**

NI: Length of Public Roads

Divisions/Council Areas	Motorway km	Class I Dual Carriage km	Single Carriage km	Class II km	Class III km	Unclass-ified km	Total km
Ballymena Division:	28.97	22.37	349.83	410.01	655.93	1,853.28	3,320.39
Belfast Division:	27.72	24.90	138.31	118.21	130.91	1,194.24	1,634.28
Coleraine Division:	0.00	12.21	357.23	524.98	580.74	1,828.37	3,303.54
Craigavon Division:	23.86	36.39	397.04	565.78	1,038.59	3,108.03	5,169.69
Downpatrick Division:	19.32	41.59	362.74	331.65	608.26	1,899.87	3,263.44

➤ *Continued from previous page*

Divisions/Council Areas	Motorway km	Class I Dual Carriage km	Single Carriage km	Class II km	Class III km	Unclass- ified km	Total km
Omagh Division:	12.70	5.63	493.86	925.01	1,707.94	4,509.12	7,654.26
GRAND TOTAL:	112.57	143.09	2,099.02	2,875.64	4,722.37	14,392.92	24,345.59

RoI & NI: Minimum Age for Driving by Category

● **REPUBLIC OF IRELAND**

Vehicle Type	Categories	Minimum Ages for Driving
Motorcycles	A, A1	18, 16
Cars	B, EB	17
Trucks	C, EC, C1, EC1	18
Buses	D, ED	21
Minibuses	D1, ED1	21
Work Vehicles/Tractors	W	16

● **NORTHERN IRELAND**

Vehicle Type	Categories	Minimum Ages for Driving
Motorcycles	A, A1	17
Moped	P	16
Cars	B	17
Trucks	C, C1, C+E	18/21
Buses	D, D1	21
Tractors	F	16/17

AGRICULTURE, FISHERIES & FORESTRY

Republic of Ireland

- **MAIN AGRICULTURE FIGURES "AT A GLANCE"**
- Minister for Agriculture & Food ....Joe Walsh TD
- Persons farming 281,900
- Land area farmed ....4,341,000 ha
- Number of Farms 147,800
- Average Farm Size ....29.4 hectares
- Number of Cattle 7,794,600
- Number of Sheep 8,373,400
- Gross Output £3,260.2m

Northern Ireland

- **MAIN AGRICULTURE FIGURES "AT A GLANCE"**
- Parliamentary Under-Secretary of State ..Lord Dubs
- Persons farming 61,096
- Land area farmed ....1,068,370 ha
- Number of Farms 31,817
- Average Farm Size ....33.6 hectares
- Number of Cattle 1,767,300
- Number of Sheep 2,986,600
- Gross Output..................................Stg£1,104.2m

Farms

Rol: Size and Number of Farms

Hectares	1992 (000's)	1993 (000's)	1994 (000's)	1995 (000's)	1997 (000's)
Less than 5	16.6	16.6	15.2	14.8	11.1
5 and less than 10	22.2	22.2	20.9	20.5	18.4
10 and less than 20	46.1	44.9	42.4	40.6	40.1
20 and less than 30	29.9	29.4	28.7	29.1	29.1
30 and less than 50	27.6	27.4	26.8	28.1	28.3
50 and less than 100	15.4	5.2	15.5	16.1	16.6
100 or more	3.9	3.7	3.9	4.1	4.2
TOTAL:	**161.7**	**159.4**	**153.4**	**153.3**	**147.8**

NI: Size and Number of Farms

	1994 (000's)	1995 (000's)	1996 (000's)	1997 (000's)	1998 (000's)
Number of Farms	28,404	27,937	27,547	32,118	31,817

- **1998 Figures**

Hectares	Number of Farms	Hectares
0.1 - 9.9	7,837	41,898
10.0 - 19.9	7,090	103,401
20.0 - 29.9	4,871	120,130
30.0 - 49.9	5,676	219,589
50.0 - 99.9	4,719	321,779
100.0+	1,624	261,573
TOTAL	**31,817**	**1,068,370**

Selected EU Countries Cattle farms and Rol ranking

Country	Farms	Animals	Average Herd Size	Country	Farms	Animals	Average Herd Size
France	300,312	20,153,560	67.1	IRELAND	132,677	6,991,728	52.7
Germany	286,794	15,740,000	54.9	Britain	129,499	11,272,490	87.0
Italy	227,220	7,166,377	31.5	Netherlands	52,085	4,410,640	84.7
Spain	197,600	5,883,680	29.8	Denmark	27,605	2,004,210	72.6
Austria	107,824	2,197,940	20.4	Luxembourg	1,944	205,193	105.6

People

RoI: Number of Persons farming

Category	1994 (000)	1995 (000)	1996 (000)	1997 (000)
Holder	153.0	153.0	149.3	147.6
Spouse	68.2	59.0	71.5	54.4
Other family worker	73.5	66.0	66.4	66.0
Regular non-family workers	15.6	15.5	13.8	13.9

NI: Number of Persons farming

Category	1994	1995	1996	1997	1998
Farmers and Partners	41,107	39,805	39,914	39,237	38,832
Spouses of farmers	6,208	6,807	6,810	7,001	7,042
Other workers	15,820	16,341	15,770	15,639	15,222
Total Agricultural labour force	63,135	62,953	62,494	61,877	61,096

RoI & NI: Agriculture (Forestry & Fisheries) in relation to population and labour force

● Republic of Ireland (1998)	(000)	● Northern Ireland (1997)	(000)
All Persons in Labour Force	1,645.5	All Persons in Labour Force	726.7
In Employment	1,520.5	Unemployed	60.8
Unemployed	125.0	Total at work	665.9
Not in Labour Force	1,231.3	Total in employment in Agriculture	38.8
Total Persons aged 15 or over	2,876.8		
Unemployment Rate %	7.5	Agriculture as % of Total at work	5.8%
All persons in employment in Agriculture, Forestry, fishing	136.0		

RoI: Age structure of Farm holders

Age	Number	%	Age	Number	%
-34 yrs	17,700	12%	55-64 yrs	33,400	22.6%
35-44 yrs	28,700	19.4%	65+ yrs	32,300	21.9%
45-54 yrs	35,500	24.1%	Total Farm holders	147,600	

Land Use and Crop Production

RoI: Land use

Product (000 hectares)	1993	1994	1995	1996	1997	1998*
Cereals:						
Wheat	79.2	74.1	70.7	85.7	93.9	83.8
Oats	20.2	20.9	19.9	20.9	20.6	19.4
Barley	180.8	169.7	178.6	181.4	189.8	190.7
Other	4.7	5.3	4.7	5.5	5.6	6.6
Total	284.9	270	273.9	293.5	309.9	300.6
Crops:						
Beans & Peas	6.1	5.6	4.8	4.8	4.8	6.5
Oilseed Rape	3.4	6.4	4.1	3.5	4.4	5.6
Potatoes	21.6	21.4	22.4	24.3	18.2	18.5
Sugar Beet	32.2	35.4	35.1	32.3	32.3	32.9
Turnips	5.2	5.6	5.3	5.4	5.2	4.6
Fodder Beet	10.9	9.8	8.9	9.9	9.1	7.3
Kale & Field Cabbage	1.8	1.8	1.5	1.6	1.7	1.1
Vegetables for Sale	4.6	4.8	4.7	4.6	4.7	5.1
Fruit	1.6	1.7	1.6	1.5	1.7	1.6

Continued from previous page

Product (000 hectares)	1993	1994	1995	1996	1997	1998*
Nursery Stock, Bulbs & Flowers	1	1.3	1.2	1.1	1.2	1.2
Other	30.5	36.6	36	24	21.0	23.0
Total	118.9	130.4	125.6	113	104.3	107.4
Pasture:						
Silage	872.3	917.4	933.6	956.1	931.5	950.4
Hay	425.9	410.1	357.2	371.5	338.8	282.7
Pasture	2,202.5	2,201.3	2,238.9	2,178.4	2,273.0	2,327.3
Total	3,500.7	3,528.8	3,529.7	3506	3,543.3	3,560.4
Total: Cereals, Crops & Pasture	3,904.5	3,929.2	3,929.2	3,912.5	3,957.6	3,968.4
Rough Grazing in Use	499.7	461.5	459.5	429	473.9	446.4
TOTAL LAND IN USE:	4,404.2	4,390.7	4,388.7	4,341.5	4,431.6	4,414.8

* Figures are based on the month of June.
The area under cereal in June 1998 showed a decrease of 3% from the previous June.

NI: Land use

Product (000 hectares)	1994	1995	1996	1997	1998
Agricultural Crops:	56.1	54.9	55.0	56.6	55.9
Oats	2.2	2.3	2.2	2.4	2.6
Wheat	7.2	6.6	6.9	6.9	7.1
Winter Barley	6.0	6.8	7.3	7.7	7.7
Spring Barley	28.3	26.7	26.9	28.7	27.1
Mixed Corn	0.1	0.1	0.1	0.1	0.1
Potatoes	8.7	9.0	8.8	7.8	7.5
Arable Crop Silage	1.8	2.0	1.6	1.7	2.0
Other field crops	1.8	1.4	1.1	1.2	1.7
Horticulture Crops:	3.3	3.2	3.2	3.1	3.2
Fruit	1.8	1.7	1.7	1.6	1.7
Vegetables	1.4	1.3	1.4	1.4	1.4
Other horticultural crops	0.1	0.1	0.1	0.1	0.2
Grass	813.0	817.4	819.3	825.1	830.6
Total crops and grass	872.4	875.5	877.5	884.8	889.8
Rough Grazing	176.3	170.9	169.0	164.1	159.1
Woods and Plantations	8.2	8.1	8.2	8.2	8.2
Other Land	14.7	13.2	12.9	11.8	11.3
Total agricultural holdings area	1,071.6	1,067.8	1,067.6	1,068.9	1,068.4

RoI: Crop Production by selected crop

Crops (000 tonnes)	1995	1996	1997	1998
Cereals: Total	1,796	2,142	1,944	1,876
Wheat	583	771	725	667
Oats	129	146	132	125
Barley	1,084	1,225	1,087	1,084
Root Crops: Total	2,165	2,228	1,947	2,091
Potatoes	618	733	472	539
Sugar Beet	1,547	1,495	1,475	1,552
Total Crops	3,961	4,370	3,891	3,967

NI: Crop Production by selected crop

Crops (000 tonnes)	1995	1996	1997	1998
Cereals: Total	235.2	243.1	238.8	214.8
Wheat	51.2	51.7	48.5	49.6
Oats	11.0	10.8	12.3	11.8
Barley	173.0	180.6	178.0	153.4

Continued from previous page

Crops (000 tonnes)	1995	1996	1997	1998
Non-Cereal Crops: Total	**288.1**	**285**	**273.8**	**246.2**
Potatoes	287.1	284.2	272.2	243.7
Oilseed Rape	1.0	0.8	1.6	2.5
Hay	280.0	267.6	233.2	94.4
Grass Silage	7,921.7	8,528.9	8,186.1	7,837.4
TOTAL CROPS:	**8,725**	**9,324.6**	**8,931.9**	**8,392.8**

RoI: Organic Farming Practices in Ireland

	Land Area			Number of Farms		
Year	Organic	Conversion	Total	Organic	Conversion	Total
1993	2,073	3,387	5,459	77	80	238
1994	1,601	3,789	5,390	103	92	195
1995	2,829	9,805	12,634	91	285	498
1996	3,545	16,951	20,496	245	519	764
1997	6,926	16,665	23,591	294	514	808
1998	15,009	13,695	28,704	498	436	887*

** Under the column 'Number of Farms', the organic and conversion number do not correspond with the figure in the total column due to the number of farmers who have land in conversion as well as being of full organic status. In 1998 47 farms were in conversion as well as of full organic status. **Source:** Irish Organic Farmers and Growers Association (IOFGA)*

Livestock

RoI: Livestock by number

Livestock (000s)	1995	1996	1997	1998
Cattle: Total	**7,122.1**	**7,422.9**	**7,659.8**	**7,794.6**
Cows	2,322.9	2,413.1	2,492.5	2,525.5
Heifers in Calf	326.8	340.9	362.2	329.9
Bulls	37.9	40.7	43.4	44.2
Other Cattle	4,434.5	4,628.2	4,761.7	4,895
Sheep: Total	**8,369.4**	**7,934**	**8,185.1**	**8,373.4**
Breeding Ewes	4,537.3	3,587.5	3,584.7	3,622.1
Rams	117.3	109.7	111.4	113.4
Other Sheep	3,714.8	4,236.8	4,489.0	4,637.9
Pigs: Total	**1,547.3**	**1,620.9**	**1,699.6**	**1,818.6**
Breeding Pigs	174.3	183.5	191.7	199.9
Other Pigs	1,373.0	1,437.4	1,507.9	1,618.7
Poultry	66,004	69,094	71,758	71,082

NI: Livestock by number

Livestock (000s)	1995	1996	1997	1998
Cattle: Total	**1,699.1**	**1,759.3**	**1,731**	**1,767.3**
Dairy Cows	271.5	281.1	279.2	287.7
Beef Cows	308.6	315.4	323.9	344.7
Heifers in Calf	88.8	97.5	109.1	101.8
Bulls for service	14.8	15.6	16.5	17.1
Other Cattle	1,015.4	1,049.7	1,002.3	1016
Sheep: Total	**2,753.6**	**2,753.2**	**2,880.1**	**2,986.6**
Breeding Ewes	1,345.3	1,341.6	1,384.1	1,449.8
Other Sheep	1,408.3	1,411.6	1,496.0	1,536.8
Pigs: Total	**564.2**	**565.2**	**616.7**	**653.4**
Sows and Gilts	60.4	60.8	63.8	66.9
Other Pigs	503.8	504.4	552.9	586.5
Poultry	16,003.3	15,899.5	15,607.8	15,170.6
Goats	3.8	3.6	3.5	3.6
Horses & Ponies	9.6	9.8	9.9	9.8

RoI: Production of Dairy Products

Products (000 tonnes)	1996	1997	1998
Butter	141.7	138.6	131.2
Cheese	97.2	95.7	92.4
Whole Milk Powder	28.3	33.8	32.1
Chocolate Crumb	69.1	69.4	39.8
Butteroil	11.1	9.8	9.2
Skimmed Milk Powder	118.8	101.6	90.9
Casein & Caseinates	41.9	42.4	42.6

Agro-Economics

RoI & NI: Land Sales and Average Price

● Republic of Ireland	1994	1995	1996	1997	1998
Transaction Size (hectares)	18.4	12.9	14.5	12.75	17.95
Number of Transactions	1,015	1,600	1,272	882	479
Average Price per hectare (£)	4,212	4,402	5,282	5,392	6,800

● Northern Ireland	1994	1995	1996	1997
Transaction Size (hectares)	4,605	4,050	3,425	2,912
Number of Transactions	420	355	223	257
Value (£ '000)	23,285	24,097	18,561	22,879

RoI & NI: Agricultural Wages

Minimum Weekly Wage Rate	1994	1995	1996	1997
Republic of Ireland IR£	137.24	139.98	147.07	152.25
Northern Ireland Stg£	168.53	167.96	193.82	-

RoI: Gross Agricultural Output

Agricultural Products	1996 (£m)	1997 (£m)	1998 (£m)
GROSS AGRICULTURAL OUTPUT:	3,538.4	3,315.4	3,260.2
Livestock: Total	1,844.5	1,760.6	1,685.4
(of which) Cattle	1,147.7	1,093.0	1,088.4
(of which) Pigs	293.4	254.3	221.6
(of which) Sheep & Lambs	203.0	196.2	162.9
Livestock Products: Total	1,240.0	1,145.3	1,156.4
(of which) Milk	1,209.4	1,116.3	1,131.8
Crops: Total	454.0	409.5	418.4
(of which) Cereals	158.7	125.9	109.0
(of which) Potatoes	38.5	40.2	61.3
(of which) Sugar Beet	58.7	55.7	58.0

RoI: Horticultural Output Value

OUTPUT VALUE (£m)	1994	1995	1996	1997	1998*
Mushrooms	60.1	61.4	72.7	80.3	85.1
Other Fresh Vegetables	48.3	45.2	53.6	46.6	46.0
Fresh Fruit	11.2	14.6	16.1	7.5	10.7
Total	119.6	121.2	142.4	134.4	141.8

* Provisional figure

● 1998 Market % Value Share	Fresh Vegetables	Nursery Products	Selected Fruit & Berries
TOTAL VALUE = £272.5 million	70.3%	12.5%	16.1%

NI: Gross Agricultural Output

Agricultural Products	1996 (£m)	1997 (£m)	1998 (£m)
GROSS AGRICULTURAL OUTPUT:	1,367.2	1,272.5	1,104.2
Livestock & Livestock Products: Total	1,148.1	1,037.5	907.5
Finished Cattle & Calves	416.3	379.7	317.7
Finished Sheep & Lambs	107.7	99.3	93.6
Finished Pigs	123.6	99.1	66.8
Poultry	97.1	96.0	91.3
Eggs	45.6	39.0	37.2
Milk	342.8	308.5	286.0
Other	15.1	15.9	14.9
Field Crops: Total	66.1	50.3	56.0
Potatoes	22.0	14.6	21.9
Cereals	36.9	30.7	26.6
Other Crops	7.2	5.0	7.5
Horticultural Products: Total	56.8	60.5	55.8
Fruit	6.1	9.8	5.0
Vegetables	10.1	10.2	10.8
Mushrooms	32.0	30.4	29.9
Flowers	8.6	10.1	10.2
Capital Formation (breeding livestock)	49.5	79.8	44.1
Agricultural contract work	30.1	30.5	31.5
Milk quota leasing	12.9	10.2	5.5
Inseparable non-agricultural activities (using farm resources)	3.6	3.7	3.7

RoI: Gross Output in selected Foods, Drinks sector

(£m)	1985	1990	1995	1998
Meat	1,497	2,004	2,554	2,559
Dairy	1,586	2,068	2,258	2,277
Grain etc	501	556	759	675
Bread	225	215	321	329
Sugar	126	124	422	438

RoI & NI: Agricultural Output Price Index

● Republic of Ireland:	1994	1996	1997
Milk (litre)	0.218	0.233	0.214
Bullocks (100kg lw)	131	110.4	108.2
Heifers (100 kg lw)	122.3	103	99.8
Pigs (kg head)	27.1	35.8	31.0
Sheep (kg head)	46.3	53.6	56.7
Wheat (tonne)	94.1	95.6	80.0
Feed Barley (tonne)	88.7	90.7	78.0
Malting Barley (tonne)	95.8	110.9	86.6
Potatoes (tonne)	184	93	163.0
Sugar Beet (tonne)	44.4	40.9	40.9

● Northern Ireland: Price / unit	1994	1996	1998
Milk (litre)	0.212	0.241	0.193
Finished Steers, heifers & young bulls (kg dwt)	2.23	1.84	1.37
Finished Sheep & Lambs (kg dwt)	2.16	2.54	1.96
Finished Clean Pigs (kg dwt)	0.95	1.31	0.71
Potatoes - ware main crop (tonne)	118	76	110
Barley (tonne)	112	116	84
Wheat (tonne)	114	125	88
Mushrooms (tonne)	1,190	1,225	1,150
Apples (tonne)	119	158	275

RoI: Value of Imports and Exports

Products (£m) of which	Imports			Exports		
	1995	1996	1997	1995	1996	1997
Live Animals	58.4	64.6	108.4	175.4	149.4	116.1
Meat and Meat Products	142.3	142.2	153.7	1,252.0	1082.2	1,054.7
Dairy Products	133.7	144.2	163.4	994.1	757.2	828.4
Corn Crops and Processed Cereal Products	142.8	135.6	138.7	28.1	35.5	49.4
Vegetables and Fruit	192.8	209.3	193.9	87.0	91.6	106.0
Sugar Products	52.3	53.4	65.0	40.9	42.3	52.8
Animal Foodstuffs	168.2	152.6	125.5	50.4	47.5	38.0
Hides and Skins	3.2	4.3	5.7	71.2	66.2	72.1
Flax and Wool	26.4	22.7	23.1	24.2	22.6	15.3
Animal and Vegetable Materials	55.4	63.1	59.7	65.4	71.8	64.6
Lard, Oils and Fats	5.4	6.9	4.2	21.3	22.7	21.8
Casein and Caseinates	9.9	8.2	6.9	137.6	110.1	101.5
TOTAL:	990.8	1,007.0	1,048.2	2947.6	2,499.1	2,520.7

RoI: Export of Live Cattle by number and destination

Destination	1996	1997	1998
France	3,000	1,000	1,000
Italy	9,000	4,000	31,000
Netherlands	11,000	1,000	15,000
Spain	17,000	15,000	84,000
Belgium	2,000	1,000	3,000
United Kingdom	10,000	27,000	5,000
Total EU Countries	52,000	49,000	139,000
Egypt	106,000	5,000	-
Libya	33,000	-	-
Lebanon	-	2,000	27,000
Total non-European Union Countries	139,000	7,000	27,000
OVERALL TOTAL	191,000	56,000	166,000

NI: Imports and Exports of Livestock

Imported & Exported Stock (000s)	1993/94	1994/95	1995/96	1996/97	1997/98	1998/99
Cattle Imports from RoI: Total	43.7	17.5	19.5	13.3	23.6	4.8
Steers, Heifers, Young Bulls	28.7	8.4	9.2	1.4	7.7	1.3
Store Cattle	13.4	7.3	9.1	10.4	13.6	2.4
Other Cattle	1.5	1.8	1.2	1.5	2.3	1.0
Cattle Imports from Britain: Total	n/a	n/a	23.0	3.6	3.9	1.8
Slaughter	n/a	n/a	7.6	0.1	0.3	-
Further Keep	n/a	n/a	15.4	3.5	3.7	1.8
Cattle Exports to Britain & other countries[1]	n/a	n/a	4.8	7.4	6.7	7.3
Sheep Imports from the Republic of Ireland:						
Slaughter	n/a	n/a	117.1	106.6	100.2	96.6
Sheep Imports from Britain: Total	n/a	n/a	9.5	19.3	41.1	45.4
Slaughter	n/a	n/a	4.6	12.3	32.8	39.1
Further Keep	n/a	n/a	4.8	7.0	8.3	6.4
Sheep Exports to Britain & Other Countries[1]	n/a	n/a	121.6	71.0	91.6	145.9

1998/99 figures are provisional. 1: Excluding Republic of Ireland

RoI: Subsidies and Levies

Payments	1994 (£m)	1995 (£m)	1996 (£m)	1997 (£m)	1998 (£m)
Headage: Total	136.6	118.0	116.2	126.4	123.3
Cattle Headage	93.8	80.2	81.4	88.8	87.6
Beef Cow Headage	19.0	17.0	11.3	13.4	12.5
Sheep Headage	20.8	20.4	22.5	23.9	22.6

Continued from previous page

Payments	1994 (£m)	1995 (£m)	1996 (£m)	1997 (£m)	1998 (£m)
Livestock Premiums, Compensation Packages and Arable Aid: Total	458.8	547.4	672.9	620.6	711.2
Suckler Cow Premium	89.9	112.2	157.7	121.3	176.7
Special Beef Premium	122.5	169.8	167.1	157.8	198.0
Deseasonalisation Premium	15.6	15	16.8	23.8	26.4
Ewe Premium	117.3	108	113.2	73.6	94.2
Extensification Premium	47.5	59.8	60.5	66.9	80.1
Special BSE Compensation Package	0	0	69.0	31.2	7.6
Agri-Monetary Compensation	0	0	0	50.4	16.3
Arable Aid	66	82.5	88.6	95.7	94.5
Fodder Scheme 1998					12.1
Cull Ewe Scheme					5.3
Disease Eradication Schemes	17.2	20.9	28.9	34.4	36.6
Milk Payments	36.6	18.4	17.3	38.9	14.3
Forestry Premium Scheme	1	4.2	12.6	10.9	16.4
Installation Aid for Young Farmers	2.3	4.2	6.5	7.0	3.4
Rural Environment Protection Scheme	1.2	30.9	56.4	101.4	132.8
Others	15.8	4.0	0.7	0.8	0.0
TOTAL PAYMENTS	669.5	747.5	911.4	940.4	1,038.0
TOTAL LEVIES	31.8	36.3	30.5	23.1	24.9
PAYMENTS less LEVIES	637.7	711.2	878.9	917.3	1,013.1

NI: Subsidies and Levies

Payments (£m)	1994	1995	1996	1997	1998
Cereals	4.9	7.5	8.2	8.8	8.3
Other Crops	0.3	0.2	0.1	0.2	0.4
Cattle Premiums: Total	88.9	101.9	222.3	188.9	153.9
(including) Beef Special Premium	28.9	36.4	40.3	39.1	37.6
(including) Suckler Cow Premium	29.9	38.7	43.5	42.7	40.4
(including) Extensification Supplement	15.0	16.4	18.3	21.3	20.2
(including) Deseasonalisation Premium	4.7	-	-	6.0	5.6
(including) Hill Livestock Compensatory Allowance	10.5	10.4	10.5	24.2	11.8
(including) Over 30 Months Scheme	-	-	83.0	29.5	25.3
Sheep Premiums	31.8	39.6	27.7	25.5	33.7
Pigs	-	-	-	-	0.5
Total other direct payments	1.0	1.3	2.9	3.9	5.2
TOTAL PAYMENTS	126.8	150.4	261.1	227.3	202.0
TOTAL LEVIES	2.5	9.9	4.4	1.2	5.3

Communications

RoI & NI: Agricultural Bodies

Department of Agriculture and Food Kildare Street, Dublin 2. Tel. (01) 607 2000.

Irish Farmers' Association Irish Farm Centre, Bluebell, Dublin 12. Tel. (01) 450 0266.

Irish Organic Farmers & Growers Association Harbour Building, Harbour Road, Kilbeggan Co Westmeath. Tel. (0506) 32563

Teagasc 19 Sandymount Avenue, Ballsbridge, Dublin 4. Tel. (01) 6376000

The Irish National Stud Company Tully, Co. Kildare. Tel: (045) 521251

An Bord Bia Elm House, Clanwilliam Court, Lower Mount Street, Dublin 2. Tel: (01) 668 5155

An Bord Glas (The Horticultural Development Board) 8-11 Lower Baggot Street, Dublin 2. Tel: (01) 676 3567

Irish Dairy Board Grattan House, Mount Street Lower, Dublin 2. Tel: (01) 661 9599

Department of Agriculture for Northern Ireland Dundonald House, Upper Newtownards Road, Belfast BT4 3SB. Tel: (01232) 520100

Livestock and Meat Commission for Northern Ireland Lissue House, 31 Ballinderry Road, Lisburn BT28 2SL. Tel: (01846) 633000

United Dairy Farmers 456 Antrim Road, Belfast BT15 5GD. Tel. (01232) 372237.

Northern Ireland Agricultural Producers Association 15 Molesworth Street, Cookstown, Co. Tyrone BT80 8NX. Tel. (016487) 65700.

Royal Ulster Agricultural Society Showgrounds, Balmoral, Belfast BT9 6GW. Tel. (01232) 665225.

Ulster Farmers' Union 475 Antrim Road, Belfast BT15 3DA. Tel. (01232) 370222.

FISHERIES

Republic of Ireland

● MAIN FIGURES "AT A GLANCE"
Total Fish Landings (tonnes)......................336,935*
No 1 Fishing Port[1] ....Killybegs
Fish Exports by Production (£m)[1] 228.3
Export Markets; European Union (£m)[1] 169,869
Export Markets;
Non-Europeann Union (£m)[1] 58,493

*Provisional figures. **1** 1997 figures.*

Northern Ireland

● MAIN FIGURES "AT A GLANCE"
Total Fish Landings (tonnes) 24,956.52
Total Fish Landings (£)............................20,243,214
No 1 Fishing Port...Kilkeel
Total Fish landed by NI Vessels (tonnes) 37,688
Total Fish landed in NI Ports (tonnes) 24,956.51

*Provisional figures. **1** 1997 figures.*

Landings

RoI: All Fish Landings

● 1997	Live Weight (Tonnes)	Landed Weight (Tonnes)	Value (IR£)	● 1998*	Live Weight (Tonnes)	Value (IR£)
Demersal..............	45,081.8	40,7717.1	51,551,618.41	Demersal..............	43,383	52,751,061
Pelagic	216,342.5	216,342.5	46,671,454.85	Pelagic	248,016	62,684,466
Total Wetfish.......	261,424.3	257,119.6	98,223,073.26	Total Wetfish.......	291,399	115,435,527
Shellfish...............	46,562.6	42,859.2	46,551,022.70	Shellfish...............	45,536	46,356,694
Total: All Fish	307,986.9	299,978.8	144,774,095.96	Total: All Fish	336,935	161,792,221

Provisional figures

NI: All Fish Landings into Northern Ireland

Species	1997 tonnes	(Stg£)	1998 tonnes	(Stg£)
Pelagic & Demersal				
(including) Herring...................	7,241,138	726,263	4,713,244	532,150
(including) Mackerel.................	1,082,672	227,241	3,711,472	822,308
(including) Horse Mackerel	1,816,798	226,466	757.8	88,320
Total Wet Fish...................	**20,156,870**	**10,075,029**	**17,695,322**	**9,681,183**
Total Shellfish...................	**7,838,507**	**11,916,758**	**7,261.20**	**10,562,031**
TOTAL ALL FISH	**27,995,377**	**21,991,787**	**24,956.52**	**20,243,214**

RoI: Landings & Value of Seafish at Top Irish Ports

Rank (1997)	Port	County	Live Weight (Tonnes)	Landed Weight (Tonnes)	Value (IR£)
1	Killybegs	Donegal	114,627.7	114,290.0	28,459,524.38
2	Castletownbere	Cork	12,763.3	11,909.0	10,967,408.60
3	Dingle	Kerry	7,946.9	7,200.9	8,120,480.38
4	Howth	Dublin	5,963.9	4,580.6	7,937,852.25
5	Dunmore East	Waterford	10,598.0	10,020.7	5,974,550.22
6	Rossaveal	Galway	9,141.6	8,629.6	4,709,430.72
7	Greencastle	Donegal	4,092.6	3,804.0	4,638,285.81
8	Union Hall	Cork	2,911.8	2,654.4	3,214,247.50
9	Baltimore	Cork	3,509.7	3,406.8	2,737,355.00
10	Kilmore Quay	Wexford	1,625.8	1,481.0	2,629,259.00

NI: Liveweight & Estimated Value of all Fish Landed in Northern Ireland Ports

Port	1994 Tonnes	(£)	1996 Tonnes	(£)	1998 Tonnes	(£)
Ardglass	5,845.52	2,960,194	8,129.24	3,195,349	6,227.69	3,346,142
Kilkeel	7,587.96	7,368,142	9,340.92	8,751,366	9,014.09	8,680,274
Portavogie	6,118.92	6,312,225	5,450.88	5,883,804	5,259.83	6,396,220
Other NI Ports	1,327.42	1,368,899	4,929.02	1,578,870	4,454.90	1,820,578
TOTAL	20,879.82	18,009,460	27,850.06	19,409,389	24,956.51	20,243,214

RoI: Sea Fish Landed by Irish Vessels into Irish Ports

Species	1993 Quantity (tonnes)	Value (£000)	1994 Quantity (tonnes)	Value (£000)	1995 Quantity (tonnes)	Value (£000)	1996 Quantity (tonnes)	Value (£000)
Wetfish:								
Demersal	33,427	37,719	35,826	38,370	43,428	45,448	44,162	48,246
Pelagic	219,301	31,180	225,851	32,861	305,472	40,306	256,901	50,409
Shellfish	33,962	28,368	33,257	35,096	44,166	40,667	43,666	43,100
GRAND TOTAL:	286,690	97,267	294,934	106,327	393,066	126,421	344,729	141,755

Liveweight & Estimated Value of all Fish Landed by Northern Ireland Vessels

Area of Landing	1994 Tonnes	(Stg£)	1996 Tonnes	(Stg£)	1998 Tonnes	(Stg£)
Northern Ireland	20,225	17,588,560	22,189	18,260,114	23,805	19,551,117
Scotland	1,683	972,997	3,340	2,021,629	4,713	2,084,276
England & Wales	3,387	1,117,189	3,405	1,226,744	544	576,956
Isle of Man	716	125,110	693	184,007	2	2,200
Republic of Ireland	693	571,501	1,337	420,867	1,785	291,608
Other EC Countries	1,673	1,838,233	1,961	2,562,150	5,839	3,271,283
TOTAL	28,377	22,213,590	32,925	24,675,511	37,688	25,777,440

RoI: Foreign Landings by Irish Vessels

	1996 Live Weight (Tonnes)	Landed Weight (Tonnes)	Value (IR£)	1997 Live Weight (Tonnes)	Landed Weight (Tonnes)	Value (IR£)
Wetfish: Demersal	3,299.5	3,213.3	4,750,155.00	3,287.3	3,216.8	5,408,466.40
Wetfish: Pelagic	41,020.1	41,020.1	14,889,794.00	63,938.5	63,938.5	12,689,358.80
Shellfish	65.3	64.5	168,300.00	94.9	94.3	269,617.20
TOTAL:	44,384.9	44,297.9	19,808,249.00	67,320.7	67,249.7	18,367,442.40

RoI: Persons Engaged in Sea Fishing

Personnel	1992	1993	1994	1995	1996
Full-Time	3,280	3,300	3,300	3,200	3,200
Part-Time	4,420	4,400	4,400	4,300	4,300
TOTAL:	7,700	7,700	7,700	7,500	7,500

RoI: Irish Fisheries Quotas for 1998

Species	ICES Area	1998 Quota	Species	ICES Area	1998 Quota
Cod	IIa	405	Cod	VI	1,820

Continued from previous page

Species	ICES Area	1998 Quota
Cod	VIIb-k	2,040
Cod	VIIa	4,675
Haddock	VI	2,020
Haddock	VII	4,440
Saithe	VI	440
Saithe	VII	2,480
Pollock	VI	150
Pollock	VII	1,300
Whiting	VI	2,620
Whiting	VII (exVIIa)	7,510
Whiting	VIIa	2,880
Plaice	VI	880
Plaice	VIIa	1,365
Plaice	VIIbc	240
Plaice	VIIfg	80
Plaice	VIIhjk	540
Sole	VI	95

Species	ICES Area	1998 Quota
Sole	VIIa	115
Sole	VIIbc	85
Sole	VIIfg	25
Sole	VIihjk	325
Hake	VI,VII	1,830
Monk	VI	860
Monk	VII	2,020
Megrim	VI	630
Megrim	VII	3,710
Nephrop	VI	170
Nephrop	VII	8,485
Mackerel	VI,VII	65,300
Herring	VIaN	11,590
Herring	VIaS	25,450
Herring	VIIA MANX	2,340
Herring	Celtic Sea	19,180
TOTAL		178,095

RoI: Fish Exports by Production

Product	1996 Value £m	%	1997 Value £m	%
Fish Live / Fresh / Chilled *(excl. fillets)*	56.0	22.2	58.5	25.6
Frozen Fish *(excl. fillets)*	67.1	26.5	55.4	24.3
Shellfish Live / Fresh / Chilled / Frozen	50.6	20.0	52.7	23.1
Fish Fillets Fresh / Chilled / Frozen	39.8	15.8	26.3	11.5
Fish & Shellfish Prepared / Preserved	17.6	7.0	18.9	8.3
Fish Dried Salted / Smoked etc.	10.1	4.0	9.2	4.0
Fish Meal / Oil etc.	11.3	4.5	7.3	3.2
TOTAL:	252.5	100.0	228.3	100.0

RoI: Geographical Spread of Export Markets

Country (£000)	1987	1990	1995	1996	1997
European Union: Total	84,175	120,444	151,953	179,629	169,869
Non-European Union: Total	39,765	34,723	61,138	72,834	58,493
TOTAL EXPORTS:	123,940	155,167	213,091	252,463	228,362

RoI: Value of Fish Exports

Country	£m	%
European Union: Total	179.8	71.2
Non-European Union: Total	72.7	28.8
TOTAL:	252.5	100.0

RoI: Inland Fisheries: Licenses Issued

	1996	1997	1998
Drift	778	852	871
Draft	497	492	494
Other	172	174	170
Rod	28,261	29,881	29,848

RoI: Aquaculture Production Trends

Year	Tonnes	Value (£m)	Average £/tonne
1988	4,075	19.5	4,785
1992	9,696	30.4	3,135
1996	14,025	37.3	2,659
1997	15,440	39.9	2,584

FORESTRY

Republic of Ireland

● MAIN FIGURES "AT A GLANCE"
Total Forest Cover..............................613,806 ha
Total Planted Forest (public & private) .....500,371 ha
% of Ireland's total land area 8.9%
Other EU Member State land area average 33%

Area planted*..............................9,897 ha.
Timber sold (million m³)*...................................2.36
Plants produced*...........................51 million
Forest Roads built*.............................307 km
Employment average*...............................1,068
Timber Revenues*........................£59.44 million
Total Revenues*....................£82.48 million
1998 Profits*...........................£15.06 million

*Information refers to afforestation managed by Coillte - The Irish Forestry Board which is responsible for the management of public forests in the Republic of Ireland.

Northern Ireland

● MAIN FIGURES "AT A GLANCE"
Forested area................................61,042 ha
Timber production (roadside) ...93,200 cubic metres
Timber production (standing) .169,200 cubic metres
New Planting...112 ha
Replanting....................................622
Employment 366
Timber Revenues..................Stg£5.2 million
Turnover ....Stg£5.9 million

*Information refers to afforestation managed by The Forest Service - an Executive Agency within the Department of Agriculture for Northern Ireland which is responsible for the implementation of forestry policy in Northern Ireland

Afforestation

RoI: Land Areas Afforested

Year	Total	Coillte	Farmer	Other	Total non Coillte	Farmer as % of non Coillte
1984	5,476	5,192	n/a	n/a	284	-
1986	6,969	4,689	n/a	n/a	2,280	-
1988	11,708	7,112	n/a	n/a	4,596	-
1990	15,817	6,670	4,025	5,122	9,147	44
1992	16,699	7,565	5,115	4,019	9,134	56
1994	19,355	6,518	9,114	3,723	12,837	71
1996	20,981	4,426	15,026	1,528	16,555	91
1998	12,928	2,926	8,923	1,079	10,002	89

RoI: Land Areas Afforested by County

1998 County	Total (ha.)	Private (ha.)	State (ha.)	Area	% Planted
Carlow	6,295.25	1,904.35	4,390.9	89,635	7.023
Cavan	8,902.54	3,498.8	5,403.74	189,060	4.708
Clare	39,302.63	16,031.76	23,270.87	318,784	12.328
Cork	69,140.64	19,455.79	49,684.85	745,988	9.268
Donegal	50,602.17	15,835.53	34,766.64	483,058	10.475
Dublin	5,524.83	3,341.83	2,183	92,156	5.995
Galway	54,491.5	14,342.1	40,149.4	593,966	9.174
Kerry	39,276.31	20,017.5	19,258.81	470,142	8.354
Kildare	9,069.661	3,922.661	5,147	169,425	5.353
Kilkenny	16,990.17	6,950.27	10,039.9	206,167	8.240
Laois	23,245.76	6,549.76	16,696	171,954	13.518
Leitrim	20,263.53	7,542.29	12,721.24	152,476	13.289
Limerick	18,232.84	6,404.77	11,828.07	268,580	6.788
Longford	5,243.25	2,351.48	2,891.77	104,387	5.022
Louth	3,226.4	1,819.4	1,407	82,334	3.918

Continued from previous page

County	Total (ha.)	Private (ha.)	State (ha.)	Area	% Planted
Mayo	47,293.36	14,465.85	32,827.51	539,846	8.760
Meath	4,562.36	3,876.36	.686	233,587	1.953
Monaghan	5,374.93	1,580.38	3,794.55	129,093	4.163
Offaly	13,679.43	7,599.43	.6,080	199,774	6.847
Roscommon	17,042.99	7,818.01	9,224.98	246,276	6.920
Sligo	17,632.94	7,919.94	9,713	179,608	9.817
Tipperary	43,438.32	11,627.8	31,810.52	425,458	10.209
Waterford	28,354.39	8,055.21	20,299.18	183,786	15.427
Westmeath	12,638.5	7,162.05	5,476.45	176,290	7.169
Wexford	14,890.26	5,666.86	9,223.4	235,143	6.332
Wicklow	3,9091.09	8,469.04	30,622.05	202,483	19.305
TOTAL	613,806.1	214,209.2	399,596.8	6,889,456	8.909

Source: Department of the Marine and Natural Resources

NI: Land Areas Afforested by County

Category	Antrim	Derry	Down/Armagh	Fermanagh	Tyrone	Total
Forested Area (ha):						
High Forest	10,635	9,461	6,106	18,448	12,484	57,134
Recreation	94	18	104	26	85	327
Amenity	104	124	363	19	243	853
Conservation	271	310	255	1,112	224	2,172
Research	92	22	15	186	41	356
Christmas Trees	20	21	23	9	44	117
Total (ha)	11,216	9,956	6,866	19,800	13,121	60,959
Plantable Reserve (ha)	16	0	2	235	32	285
Awaiting Replant (ha)	74	237	46	193	120	670
Other Unplanted Area (ha)	2,404	1,666	1,529	5,886	2,312	13,797
TOTAL AREA* (ha):	13,710	11,859	8,443	26,114	15,585	75,711

* Information refers to afforestation managed by The Forest Service - an Executive Agency within the Department of Agriculture for Northern Ireland which is responsible for the implementation of forestry policy in Northern Ireland

RoI: Coillte Afforestation by Species

Species Area (ha)	1997 Total Area (ha)	1998 Total Area (ha)	%
Conifers:			
Sitka Spruce	216,702	221,557	+2.2
Lodgepole Pine	67,373	63,275	-6.1
Norway Spruce	17,618	17,912	+1.6
Larch	8,637	9,010	+4.2
Scots Pine	8,624	7,444	-14.7
Douglas Fir	7,933	8,016	+1.0
Other Conifers	5,432	5,434	-
Total*	332,319	332,648	-

Species	1997 Total Area (ha)	1998 Total Area (ha)	%
Broadleaves			
Beech	3,445	3,616	+4.8
Oak	2,876	2,912	+1.2
Ash	1,967	2,129	+7.9
Birch	1,517	1,738	+13.5
Other Broadleaves	1,131	1,161	+2.6
Sycamore	533	693	+26.1
Total*	11,469	12,249	+6.6

* Information refers to afforestation managed by Coillte Teoranta - The Irish Forestry Board.

Forest Cover by European Country

Country	Forest Area 000s ha	%	Ownership (%) Public	Private
Belgium	620	20	41.9	58.1
France	13,110	24	25.7	74.3
Germany	10,490	29	56.2	43.8
IRELAND	529	8	74.6	25.4
Italy	6,750	22	39.7	60.3
Luxembourg	85	33	46.3	53.7
Netherlands	334	9	48.0	52.0
Portugal	2,755	31	24.0	76.0
Spain	8,388	17	33.5	66.5
Britain	2,207	9	43.4	56.6

Plantation & Output

RoI: Coillte Plantation by Area

Year	Area Planted (ha)	Year	Area Planted (ha)
1989	10,062	1994	10,614
1990	10,352	1995	11,734
1991	12,006	1996	10,548
1992	11,513	1997	9,984
1993	11,248	1998	9,897

RoI: Coillte Statistics by Region - Plantation, Timber Sales, Road Construction & Employment

Region		1994	1995	1996	1997	1998
Eastern Region:	Land planted (ha.)	1,087	1,126	1,079	1,111	1,122
	Timber sold (m³)	400,000	354,000	340,000	264,127	292,884
	Roads built (km)	9	72	48	39	28
	Direct employment	273	255	221	205	210
Southern Region:	Land Planted (ha)	1,575	1,590	1,614	2,576	2,018
	Timber Sold (m³)	292,000	367,400	411,000	547,560	591,395
	Roads built (km)	48	61	84	76	69
	Direct employment	250	205	176	163	152
Mid-Southern Region:	Land Planted (ha)	1,858	2,202	1,772	2,012	2,356
	Timber Sold (m³)	292,000	367,400	274,000	476,383	555,504
	Roads built (km)	53	81	73	64	55
	Direct employment	266	240	193	176	168
Western Region:	Land Planted (ha)	1,717	1,732	1,804	1,458	1,489
	Timber Sold (m³)	201,000	261,000	245,000	228,216	266,223
	Roads built (km)	17	30	28	26	44
	Direct employment	214	148	115	110	106
North-Western Region:	Land Planted (ha)	1,764	2,478	1,883	1,645	1,597
	Timber Sold (m³)	293,000	265,000	297,000	290,006	351,514
	Roads built (km)	38	57	46	54	50
	Direct employment	233	197	196	182	173
Midlands Region:	Land Planted (ha)	1,365	1,158	885	1,182	1,315
	Timber Sold (m³)	256,000	232,000	263,000	255,318	300,895
	Roads built (km)	21	31	35	47	57
	Direct employment	154	140	121	118	115

NI: Plantation by Area

Description	1993-94	1994-95	1995-96	1996-97	1997-98	1998-99
Annual Planting Area (ha):						
State	816	826	774	643	725	663
New Planting	365	296	158	140	94	109
Replanting	451	530	616	503	631	554

* Plantation by The Forest Service. Table does not include private plantation.

NI: Plantation by Species

Species (by % planted)	1992-93	1993-94	1994-95	1995-96	1996-97	1997-98	1998-99
Sitka Spruce	68	70	74	75	76	77	77
Lodgepole Pine	6	4	2	2	1	3	1
Larch	13	10	9	7	8	8	6
Norway Spruce	2	1	1	1	1	-	1
Other Conifers	3	4	3	4	4	4	6
Broadleaved Species	8	11	11	11	10	8	9
TOTAL*:	100	100	100	100	100	100	100

* Plantation by The Forest Service. Table does not include private plantation.

NI: Forestry Statistics by Timber Production, Turnover & Employment

Production (000m³)	1992-93	1993-94	1994-95	1995-96	1996-97	1997-98	1998-99
Thinning	20.8	18.0	21.8	23.1	25.2	23.0	15.7
Clear Felling	174.5	191.6	191.4	200.9	200.0	202.1	234.0
Firewood	2.5	3.1	1.5	1.9	1.2	1.5	1.7
Scattered Windthrow	0.6	0.3	0.4	0.2	0.2	0.4	0.0
Clear Windthrow	1.3	9.9	6.8	5.7	4.3	2.2	10.9
TOTAL:	199.7	222.9	221.9	231.8	230.9	229.2	262.3

Turnover (Stg£000)	1998	1999
	6,101	5,961*

* For the year ended 31 March 1999

● PERSONS EMPLOYED IN FORESTRY (1999)

Sector	Numbers
Industrial:	243
Professional and Technical	70
Administrative (Headquarters)	53
OVERALL TOTAL	366

Source: The Forest Service

HEALTH & SAFETY

The Current Plight of Postgraduate Doctors-in-training in Ireland

By Dr Steve Harris

SINCE the beginning of June 1999, postgraduate doctors-in-training (also known as non-consultant hospital doctors) have been appealing in earnest for a drastic improvement in their professional working conditions and further training. At present, there are approximately 2,800 postgraduate doctors-in-training working in over 40 hospitals across the Republic of Ireland. These are the doctors who, around the clock, provide care for patients in the Accident & Emergency Department and on the hospital wards as well as patients in the outpatient clinics. For the vast majority of the general public who need urgent medical care, these are the first doctors they will meet on admission to hospital. The patient has to rely on these doctors' ability to provide the best care at a time which is often the most frightening of their lives.

Common sense dictates that long continuous hours of clinical duties adversely affect the ability of doctors in providing this high standard of patient care. However, many doctors work in excess of 80, if not over 100, hours each week. Surprisingly, few people outside clinical medicine realise this fact. Probably even less people realise the full extent of the inhumane treatment of doctors, who are one of the most dedicated and hardest working professions.

Treating people with serious, painful diseases is a vocation in the true sense of the word, as the professional carer hopes to put the needs of the patient first. "To treat others as I and my family would want to be treated in a time of illness" is a belief held strongly by many doctors. Caring for the patient's relatives is also an essential part in caring well for the patient. They are the crucial link in the patient's care and often provide further invaluable information. If the family members are reassured and cared for, the patient will naturally feel more reassured. Are doctors able to do all this under the current circumstances?

On starting medical school, many students, most of whom are very academically talented, hold the ideal of helping others by being a good doctor. For them, the next six years of college consist of hours of study and examinations. They have to face tough challenges whilst learning to communicate and care for patients both in hospital and in the community. The newly qualified doctor then starts working in a clinical team led by a consultant. The hierarchy of the clinical hospital team usually consists of the following: the Intern, the newly qualified doctor and most junior of the team, who is provisionally registered by the Medical Council; the Senior House Officer (SHO), a doctor who is fully registered and qualified usually two to four years; the Registrar, a doctor who has usually been qualified several years, and may have also qualified as a member of one of the

Postgraduate colleges; the Specialist Registrar, a doctor who is on one of the recently created Higher Training Schemes and is a member of one of the Postgraduate colleges; the Consultant, the fully trained doctor and the permanent staff member, who ultimately is the main clinical decision maker of the team.

Often the less experienced Interns and SHOs are the main providers of patient care in hospitals after the normal working day. Generations of doctors-in-training have been forced to work long continuous hours of clinical duty in poor working facilities with little provision for further training, and poor or non-existent overtime rates of pay. Postgraduate Doctors-in-training have felt trapped for years without an effective and active means of protesting about their problems. Beliefs such as "We went through it, so you should go through it" and the need for a reference from each consultant, has meant that it is very difficult to call for changes without possibly injuring one's own career chances.

Times are changing. Students now come from a variety of backgrounds, and the number of women in medicine is also increasing. These and many other factors are bound to usher in many changes in clinical medicine in the future. However, many doctors have become disillusioned by the slow and inadequate rate of real change. The 1987 strike action by doctors of the Irish Medical Organisation (IMO) did little in the long term to solve their problems. In fact, it caused more division amongst doctors, both senior and junior, and resulted in many consultants forming a separate Union, namely the Irish Hospital Consultants Association. More recently, GPs have formed another Union, the Alliance of GPs. Many doctors hope to renew their faith in the negotiating skills of the Irish Medical Organisation based on the evidence of concrete changes. Doctors and other Healthcare staff believe that, without real positive changes, the standard of patient care will inevitably suffer as a consequence.

The European Council of Health Ministers issued a directive in May 1999 advocating to the European Parliament a 13-year postponement regarding the review of the working hours and conditions of postgraduate doctors-in-training in Europe. They believe that these doctors only really work 48 hours a week, and that any on-call work was either deemed as training, or was much less onerous work than daytime clinical duties.

Nothing could be further from the truth. Many junior doctors are involved in the care of very sick patients. On-call work over night can mean literally no sleep. A skeleton staff care for all the patients in the hospital, as well as caring for all the new patients who are admitted as emergencies. Understandably, severe stress and exhaustion are the major complaints. Many of the on-call doctors then start a new day's work with no rest or sleep. Add these facts to the reality that:

1. Doctors contracts are frequently broken in many ways by Health Boards.
2. Permanent consultancy posts in Ireland are rare.
3. Pay for overtime is usually at 50% of the normal rate, with no pay at all for most doctors who work over 65 hours.
4. There is little provision made for postgraduate/specialist training.

Many people expressed their amazement at the ignorance of the Health Ministers in perpetuating this inhuman system of healthcare for patients and staff alike. In response to the announcement of the EU directive in May 1999, doctors staged a national working-lunchtime protest on Wednesday, June 9th, 1999, to demand that this ridiculous decision be overturned. It was the first public demonstration by doctors in many years. Many reports came of "a sea of white coats" outside the foyer doors of virtually every hospital, showing the strength of feeling. The IMO happened to be meeting with the Department of Health that afternoon. It was obvious that there was serious discontent about the directive, and so a government statement was issued promising to review the problems of doctors hours urgently. Reassurance given that the advice of the EU directive would not be followed. However, the unrest amongst many doctors continued. With news from the Government that there was approximately £5 billion surplus in the Nation's budget, doctors and other healthcare staff waited eagerly to hear whether there were serious plans to upgrade the healthcare service.

The news, in July 1999, of a £38 billion National Development Plan for 2000–2006 offered the opportunity for government to plan for the health of the nation. In the spirit of partnership 2000, a working lunchtime appeal by doctors, nurses and other healthcare staff took place on Wednesday, August 11th, 1999, in several large hospitals. The Appeal was for Patient Care Reform to become the major part of the proposed National Development Plan. In terms of the Professional Carers at the coalface - that is doctors, nurses and ambulance crews - this would mean an urgent review of staffing levels and resources; working conditions, including fair pay for every hour worked; and further higher training. To emphasize their commitment to this appeal, a National March for Patient Care Reform, with about 400 healthcare staff, took place through the centre of Dublin on Saturday, 11th September, 1999. At the end of the march, speeches were made by a founder of the Irish Patients Association, a postgraduate doctor-in-training and an MEP, who representing the three main strands of the healthcare service; namely, patients, staff and resources. The march was the first successful public demonstration of its kind for many years, and good media attention served to further heighten public awareness.

However, the campaign for improvements in patient care by doctors is just beginning. Many healthcare staff believe that one of the keys to success is the direct involvement of the general public. People in Ireland must realise that a long awaited review of patient care should be demanded urgently by themselves. People are the essential wealth of any country. The responsibility of every nation with an active conscience is to care for its people who are afflicted by disease and hardship. This means providing an effective and compassionate national healthcare service for the next millennium.

We live in the hope that our pleas will be heard.

Dr Steve Harris
October 1999

The author is a Specialist Registrar in General Medicine/Endocrinology & Diabetes at Cork University Hospital. He became a member of the Royal College of Physicians in Ireland in 1996. He is also a member of the Irish Medical Organisation since July 1999 and is one of a group of people who are campaigning for improving the working lives of doctors-in-training, and patient care.

Health at a glance

Republic of Ireland

No. of births *1998* 53,551
Births outside marriage 15,133 (28.3%)
Total Period Fertility Rate ....1.93 children per female
.............*(below population replacement level of 2.1)*
Birth rate - teenage mothers..16.4 per 1,000 females
Infant Deaths *1998* 330
Infant Mortality rate.....................6.2 per 1,000 births
No. of deaths *1998*.......................................31,352
Malignant Cancers 7,493
Circulatory System Diseases 13,191
Respiratory System Diseases......................4,134
Rate ....8.5 per 1,000 people
Suicides *1998* 504
No. accidents 1,925
In-Patient Admissions *1997* 236,817
In-Patients Discharged / Deaths *1997* 536,236
Occupancy Rate *1997* 83.3%
Average Length of Stay in Days *1997* 6.5
Casualty Attendances *1997* 1,213,321
Day Cases *1997* 249,472
No. psychiatric In-patients 5,575
Dialysis Treatments *1997* 60,759
In-patient waiting lists ....33,924.
Personnel in health services *1997*...............135,700
No. medical card holders..1,218,728 (33.6% of pop.)
Capital Spending on Health *1997* ....IR£122.685m
Non-capital Spending *1996* ....IR£2,354.216m

Source Dept of Health and Children

Northern Ireland

No. of births *1997/8* 24,105
Changes in birth rate ....2% less than 1996/7
Infant Deaths *1997/8*...137
Infant Mortality rate.....................5.6 per 1,000 births
No. of deaths *1997*..9,971
Cancer (Benign & Malignant) 1,791
Circulatory System Diseases 3,339
Respiratory System Diseases..........................1,543
Suicides *1997/8*..126
No. of Road accident Deaths..............................150
Inpatients *1997/8* 410,493
In-Patients Discharged / Deaths *1997/8*.......306,161
Occupancy rate *1997/8* 81%
Avg length of stay *1997/8* ....8.7 Days
Casualty attendances *1997/8* 664,549
Day cases *1997/8*.......................................104,332
Compulsory admissions to mental hospitals..1,072
No. of Children in care 150
Ordinary admissions waiting list *1997/8*.......25,421
Highest In-patient Activity Royal Group Hospital HSS
Highest allocation of beds ....Geriatric; Mental Illness
Highest throughput ....Altnagelvin Group HSS trust
Personnel *(hospital- and community-based)* 43,618
Most Infectious Disease ....Chicken pox (59%)
Occurrence of Meningitis ....1% of all notifications
Number of Children in Care *1998*....................2,354
Expenditure on health *(31/3/98)* ....Stg£5,222m

Source Dept of Health and Social Services

Health Boards

RoI Health Boards

● **EASTERN HEALTH BOARD** *(covers Dublin city and county, Co Kildare, Co Wicklow)*
Dr Steevens Hospital, Dublin 8. 01-679 0700 freephone: 1800-520520. email: ehbmis@iol.ie **CEO:** Mr P McLoughlin. **No. employed by Board:** 9,398. **Population in health board:** 1,293,964 *(dependency ratio on working-age population: 0–14 yrs 33.5%; 65+ yrs 14.3%; Total 47.8%)* **No. people covered by medical cards** (1996): 352,944 *(27% of area pop.)* **Dialysis treatments:** 27,397 **Births** *(1998)* 22,185 **Marriages** *(1998)* 5,285 **Deaths** *(1998)* 10,230 **Major causes of death** (1996): 1 Cancer 2 Heart Disease **Suicide rate** 9.62 per 100,000 pop. **No. employed by Board:** 9,398.

● **MIDLAND HEALTH BOARD** *(covers Co Laois, Co Longford, Co Offaly, Co Westmeath)*
Arden Rd, Tullamore, Co. Offaly. Tel: (0506) 21868 email: info@mhb.ie. **CEO:** Mr Denis Doherty. **No. employed by Board:** 3,325. **Population in health board:** 206,000 *(dependency ratio on working-age population: 0–14 yrs 40.3%; 65+ yrs 19.5%; Total 59.8%)* **No. people covered by medical cards** (1996): 80,446 *(39% of area pop.)* **Dialysis treatments:** 0. **Births** *(1998)* 2,157 **Marriages** *(1998)* 976 **Deaths** *(1998)* 1,731 **Major causes of death:** 1 Heart Disease 2 Cancer **Suicide rate** 9.16 per 100,000 pop. **Waiting List** (1998): 850 Nos in the Intellectual Disability database: 1,904 (4.35 people per 1,000 population).

● **MID-WESTERN HEALTH BOARD** *(covers Co Clare, Limerick city and county, Co Tipperary NR)*
31-33 Catherine St, Limerick. 061-316 655. email: eolas@mwhb.ie **CEO:** Mr Stiofan de Burca **No. employed by Board:** 4,139. **Population in health board:** 316,875 *(dependency ratio on working-age population: 0–14 yrs 37.2%; 65+ yrs 18.4%; Total 55.6%)* **No. people covered by medical cards** (1996): 106,961 *(34% of area pop.)* **Dialysis treatments:** 4,550 **Births** *(1998)* 3,971 **Marriages** *(1998)* 1,569 **Deaths** *(1998)* 2,910 **Major causes of death:** 1 Heart Disease 2 Cancer **Suicide rate** 9.69 per 100,000 pop.

● **NORTH-EASTERN HEALTH BOARD** *(covers Co Cavan, Co Louth, Co Meath, Co Monaghan)* Navan Rd., Kells, Co. Meath. 046-40341. email: nehbms@indigo.ie **CEO:** Mr Donal O'Shea **No. employed by Board:** 4,440. **Population in health board:** 305,703 *(dependency ratio on working-age population: 0–14 yrs 40.1%; 65+ yrs 18%; Total 58.1%)* **No. people covered by medical cards** (1996): 122,993 *(40% of area pop.)* **Dialysis treatments:** 2,498 **Births** *(1998)* 3,537 **Marriages** *(1998)* 1,474 **Deaths** *(1998)* 2,318 **Major causes of death:** 1 Heart Disease 2 Cancer **Suicide rate** 12.3 per 100,000 pop.

● **NORTH-WESTERN HEALTH BOARD** *(covers Co Donegal, Co Leitrim, Co Sligo)* Manorhamilton, Co. Leitrim. 072-55123. Web: www.nwhb.ie **CEO:** Mr Pat Harvey. **No. employed by Board:** 4,198. **Population in health board:** 210,122 *(dependency ratio on working-age population: 0–14 yrs 40.1%; 65+ yrs 22.7%; Total 62.8%)* **No. people covered by medical cards** (1996): 102,569 *(49% of area pop.)* **Dialysis treatments:** 4,583 **Births** *(1998)* 2,810 **Marriages** *(1998)* 1,086 **Deaths** *(1998)* 2,126 **Major causes of death:** 1 Heart Disease 2 Cancer **Suicide rate** 8.93 per 100,000 pop.

● **SOUTH-EASTERN HEALTH BOARD** *(covers Co Carlow, Co Kilkenny, Co Tipperary SR, Co Waterford, Co Wexford)* Lacken, Dublin Rd., Kilkenny. 056-51702. email: aylwardb@sehb.ie **CEO:** Mr John Cooney. **No. employed by Board:** 5,645. **Population in health board:** 391,046 *(dependency ratio on working-age population: 0–14 yrs 38.3%; 65+ yrs 18.7%; Total 57%)* **No. people covered by medical cards:** 141, 734 *(36% of area pop.)* **Dialysis treatments:** 4,839 **Births** *(1998)* 5,250 **Marriages** *(1998)* 2,018 **Deaths** *(1998)* 3,340 **Major causes of death:** 1 Heart Disease 2 Cancer (U-15: accidents and poisoning; U-65: Cancer; O-65: Cardiovascular disease) **Suicide rate** 15.44 per 100,000 pop.

● **SOUTHERN HEALTH BOARD** *(covers Cork city and county, Co. Kerry)* Wilton Rd, Cork. 021-545 011. email: communications@shb.ie **CEO:** Mr Sean Hurley **No. employed by Board:** 7,227. **Population in health board:** 546,209 *(dependency ratio on working-age population: 0–14 yrs 36.3%; 65+ yrs 18.8%; Total 55.1%)* **No. people covered by medical cards** (1996): 186,363 *(34% of area pop.)* **Dialysis treatments:** 9,756. **Births** *(1998)* 7,935 **Marriages** *(1998)* 2,502 **Deaths** *(1998)* 5,039 **Major causes of death:** 1 Heart Disease 2 Cancer **Suicide rate** 15.77 per 100,000 pop.

● **WESTERN HEALTH BOARD** *(covers Co Galway, Co Mayo, Co Roscommon)* Merlin Park Regional Hospital, Galway. 091-751 131 email: ceowhb.iol.ie **CEO:** Dr Sheelah Ryan **No. employed by Board:** 5,974. **Population in health board:** 351,874 *(dependency ratio on working-age population: 0–14 yrs 38.6%; 65+ yrs 22.5%; Total 61%)* **No. people covered by medical cards** (1996): 153,272 *(44% of area pop.)* **Dialysis treatments:** 7,136 **Births** *(1998)* 5,706 **Marriages** *(1998)* 1,873 **Deaths** *(1998)* 3,658 **Major causes of death:** 1 Heart Disease 2 Cancer **Suicide rate** 14.62 per 100,000 pop

NI Health & Social Services Boards

The Health and Social Services Boards - Eastern, Northern, Southern and Western - in Northern Ireland plan and commission Northern Ireland's health and social services. The HSS (Health and Social Services) Trusts provide these services, which can be hospital- and/or community-based. These services are then bought by the health boards from HSS Trusts and General Practitioners on behalf the people who live in the health board area.

● **EASTERN HEALTH AND SOCIAL SERVICES BOARD** Champion House, 12–22 Linenhall Street, Belfast BT2 8BS. Tel: 01232-321313. **Area population** 667,500 **Total Births** 10,914 **Ambulance response times:** 96% of Ambulances arrived within 18 minutes. **Patient journeys** 159,220. **HSS Trust Staff** 22,091 **HSS Trusts covered:** Ulster Community & Hospitals *(est. 1/4/1998)* Health & Care Centre, 39 Regent St, Newtownards, Co Down BT23 4AD. Tel: 01247-816666 *(Acute/Community category).* **North & West Belfast** *(est. 1/9/93)* Glendinning Hse, 6 Murray St, Belfast BT1 6DP. Tel: 01232-327156 *(Community category).* **South & East Belfast** *(est. 1/9/93)* Trust Headquarters, Knockbracken Healthcare Park, Saintfield Road, Belfast BT8 8BH Tel: 01232-790673 *(Community category).* **Belfast City Hospital** *(est. 23/11/92)* 51 Lisburn Rd, Belfast BT9 7AB. Tel: 01232 329241. *(Acute category).* **Royal Group of Hospitals and Dental Hospital** *(est. 1/4/92)* 274 Grosvenor Rd, Belfast BT12 6BP. Tel: 01232 240503. *(Acute category).* **Green Park** *(est. 23/11/92)* 20 Stockman's Lane, Belfast BT9 7JB. Tel: 01232 669501 *(Acute category).* **Mater Infirmorum Hospital** *(est. 1/3/94)* 45-51 Crumlin Rd, Belfast BT14 6AB. Tel: 01232-741211 *(Acute category).* **Down Lisburn** *(est. 1/9/93)* Lisburn Health Centre, 25 Linenhall St, Lisburn BT28 1BH. Tel: 01846 501309 *(Acute/Community category).*

● **NORTHERN HEALTH AND SOCIAL SERVICES BOARD** County Hall, 182 Galgorm Road, Ballymena, County Antrim BT42 1QB. Tel: 01266 653333. **Area population** 411,200 **Total Births** 4,217 **Ambulance response times** 95% of Ambulances arrived within 21 minutes. **Patient journeys** 92,866. **HSS Trust Staff** 8,427 **HSS Trusts covered:** Causeway *(est. 11/1/95)* 8E Coleraine Rd, Ballymoney BT53 6BP, Co Antrim. Tel: 012656-66600 *(Acute/Community category).* **Homefirst Community** *(est. 1/2/96)* The Cottage, 5 Greenmount Ave, Ballymena,

Co Antrim BT43 6DA. Tel: 01266-633700 *(Community category).* **United Hospitals** *(est. 9/11/95)* Antrim Area Hospital, Bush Hse, 45 Bush Rd, Antrim BT41 2RL. Tel: 01849-424673 *(Acute category).*

● **SOUTHERN HEALTH AND SOCIAL SERVICES BOARD** Tower Hill, Armagh BT61 9DR. Tel: 01861-410041. **Area population** 298,800 **Total Births** 4,833 **Ambulance response times** 95% of Ambulances arrived within 21 minutes. **Patient journeys** 85,919. **HSS Trust Staff** 6,917 **HSS Trusts covered:** **Craigavon Area Hospital Group** *(est. 23/11/92)* 68 Lurgan Rd, Portadown, Craigavon BT63 5QQ, Co. Armagh. Tel: 01762 334444 *(Acute category).* **Craigavon & Banbridge** *(est. 23/11/93)* Bannvale Hse, Moyallen Rd, Gilford BT63 5JX, Co Down. Tel: 01762-831983 *(Community category).* **Newry & Mourne** *(est. 23/11/93)* 5 Downshire Place, Newry BT34 1DZ, Co Down. Tel: 01693-60505 *(Acute/Community category).* **Armagh & Dungannon** *(est. 5/9/95)* St Luke's Hospital, Loughgall Rd, Armagh BT61 7NQ. Tel: 01861-522381 *(Acute/Community category).*

● **WESTERN HEALTH AND SOCIAL SERVICES BOARD** 15 Gransha Park, Clooney Road, Derry BT47 1TG. **Area population** 271,400 **Total Births** 4,141 **Ambulance response times** 95% of Ambulances arrived within 21 minutes. **Patient journeys** 45,900. **HSS Trust Staff** 7,183 **HSS Trusts covered:** **Altnagelvin Hospitals** *(est. 9/11/95)* Altnagelvin Area Hospital, Glenshane Rd, Derry BT47 1SB. Tel: 01504-345171 *(Acute category).* **Foyle** *(est. 9/11/95)* Riverview Hse, Abercorn Rd, Derry BT48 6SA. Tel: 01504-266111 *(Community category).* **Sperrin Lakeland** *(est. 25/3/96)* Trust Headquarters, Strathdene Hse, Tyrone & Fermanagh Hospital, Omagh, Co Tyrone BT79 0NS. Tel: 01662-244127 *(Acute/Community category).*

Other HSS Trusts

NORTHERN IRELAND AMBULANCE SERVICE *(est. 30/3/95)* Ambulance Service Headquarters, 12-22 Linenhall St, Belfast BT2 8BS. Tel: 01232-246113 **Category** Ambulance **Chairman** Mr Ivor Oswald **CEO** Mr Paul McCormick.

Source: Dept. of Health and Social Services

Spending

RoI: Capital Expenditure on Health Services

Health Programme, 1997	Health Board (£m)	Voluntary (£m)	Total (£m)
General Hospitals	39.482	38.523	78.005
Community Health & Welfare	20.686	6.493	27.179
(incl. community protection, welfare homes & child welfare)			
Psychiatric	2.470	0.014	2.487
Handicapped	9.610	3.230	12.840
(incl. mental handicap, rehabilitation, deaf, blind and Cheshire Homes)			
Miscellaneous	0.009	1.244	2.174
TOTAL	73.181	49.504	122.685

Source Dept of Health & Children

RoI: Non-capital Expenditure on Health Services

Health Programme, 1997	1994 (£m)	1995 (£m)	1996 (£m)
Community Protection[1]	40.232	48.218	54.738
Community Health[2]	371.626	405.948	433.948
Community Welfare[3]	200.729	180.217	133.377
Psychiatric Services[4]	215.850	227.852	233.199
Programme for the Handicapped[5]	222.756	257.742	267.519
General Hospitals[6]	1,146.609	1,226.510	1,276.548
General Support[7]	92.856	1.244	107.597
GROSS TOTAL	2,290.658	1.244	2,506.926
Income[8]	144.900	1.244	152.710
NET TOTAL	2,145.758	49.504	2,354.216

Source: Dept of Health & Children

1 *Prevention of infectious disease, child health exams, food hygiene & standards, drugs advisory service, health promotion and preventative services.*
2 *GP services, subsidies for drug purchases, refunds of drug purchases for long-term illnesses, home nursing services, domiciliary maternity services, family planning, and dental, ophthalmic and aural services.*
3 *Home helps, meals-on-wheels, milk supplies, pre-school supports, child residential services, Welfare homes for the aged, other child-care and adoption services and cash payments, grants and allowances for disabled, handicapped, voluntary welfare bodies and others.*

4. *Diagnostic, care and preventative services for psychiatric ailments.*
5 *Care programmes for mentally handicapped, rehabilitation services and assessment and care of the blind, deaf, and those otherwise handicapped.*
6 *Services to regional, public voluntary, general, district and long stay hospitals and nursing homes.*
7 *Administration, research, pensions and finance charges. 8 charges for private and semi-private stays, deductions and payments.*

RoI Funding Sources

Sources*	1995 (£000s)	1996 (£000s)	1997 (£000s)
Exchequer	2,031.49	2,079.96	2,412.69
Health contributions	215.88	215.58	229.50
EU Regulations Receipts	51.61	58.66	69.72
Income from services *(minor sources eg canteen etc.)*	146.74	152.71	161.39
TOTAL	**2,445.72**	**2,506.91**	**2,873.30**

Source CSO
* *for non-capital health services*

NI expenditure on health services

Expenditure by the Two main Social Programmes, 31/3/98	Stg£ m
Northern Ireland Consolidated Fund:	
Health & Social Services	1,826
Social Security *(non-contributory)*	1,993
Department Administration*	201
Northern Ireland Insurance Fund:	
Social Security *(contributory)*	1,202
TOTAL	5,222

Source Dept. of Health and Social Services
*incl. the cost of the Social Security and Child Support Agencies

Personnel

RoI Numbers Employed in Public-health Services

Employment Health Sector, 31.12.97	East	Midland	Mid-Western	North-East	North-West	South-East	Southern	Western	Other Hospitals*	Other Homes*	Total
Management/Admin	1,340	348	504	415	585	609	864	759	2,250	476	**8,151**
Medical/Dental	552	206	281	205	246	378	543	423	1,803	47	**4,684**
Nursing	3,334	1,305	1,660	1,374	1,545	2,462	3,096	2,458	7,886	2,144	**27,264**
Para-Medical	936	254	308	225	301	352	497	447	1,883	373	**5,576**
Support Services	2,690	1,000	1,011	1,005	1,294	1,513	1,903	1,618	3,537	2,890	**18,461**
Maintnce/Tech	246	86	163	58	90	117	220	179	366	94	**1,618**
Total (health board)	9,099	3,200	3,926	3,281	4,061	5,432	7,123	5,883	17,725	6,024	**65,755**

Source: Dept of Health and Children Personnel Census.
*Other Hospitals refers to Voluntary/Joint Board Hospitals. Other Homes refers to Mental Handicap Homes.

NI Hospital-based staff by HSS Trust

Hospital-based Staff by HSS Trust, 31/3/98	Medical & Dental	Professional & Technical	Nursing & Midwives	Social Services	Admin.	Other	Total
Altnagelvin Hospitals	180	154	792	1	217	86	1,430
Armagh & Dungannon	72	107	831	9	133	143	1,295
Belfast City Hospital	322	288	1,554	0	395	453	3,012
Causeway	92	110	578	0	130	161	1,071
Craigavon Area Hospital Group	142	101	719	8	151	71	1,192
Craigavon / Banbridge	11	6	88	0	15	0	120
Down Lisburn	134	117	764	1	120	40	1,176
Foyle	10	19	420	12	20	13	494
Green Park	69	218	850	0	204	40	1,381
Homefirst Community	42	38	316	2	51	77	526
Mater Infirmorum Hospital	75	82	364	0	147	150	818
Newry & Mourne	62	51	352	1	105	172	743
North & West Belfast	14	22	518	3	48	191	796
Royal Group of Hospitals & Dental Hospital	559	433	2,114	3	800	828	4,737

Continued from previous page

Hospital-based Staff by HSS Trust, 31.03.98	Medical & Dental	Professional & Technical	Nursing & Midwives	Social Services	Admin.	Other	Total
South & East Belfast	33	44	362	9	48	163	659
Sperrin Lakeland	88	123	991	0	166	149	1,517
Ulster Community & Hospitals	223	236	1,154	2	338	382	2,335
United Hospitals	209	272	1,449	0	444	537	2,911
TOTAL	2,337	2,421	14,216	51	3,532	3,656	26,213

Source Dept of Health & Social Services

NI Community-based staff by HSS trust

● Northern Ireland - Community-based Staff by HSS Trust, 31.03.98	Medical & Dental	Professional & Technical	Nursing & Midwives	Social Services	Admin.	Other	Total
Armagh & Dungannon	24	65	216	134	109	80	628
Causeway	11	66	133	162	230	808	1410
Craigavon / Banbridge	13	61	227	722	160	132	1315
Down Lisburn	19	93	319	347	209	279	1266
Foyle	43	75	304	298	257	1009	1986
Homefirst Community	40	193	499	630	581	566	2509
Newry & Mourne	12	40	143	191	119	119	624
North Down & Ards	12	98	286	395	180	789	1760
North & West Belfast	42	121	306	460	220	392	1541
South & East Belfast	16	138	521	536	290	1109	2610
Sperrin Lakeland	31	64	262	255	134	1010	1756
TOTAL	263	1014	3216	4130	2489	6293	17405

Source Dept of Health & Social Services

EU Comparison: Number of Doctors per 100,000, 1996

Country	No. of Doctors / 100,000 people	Country	No. of Doctors / 100,000 people
Austria	339.0*	Italy	570.0
Belgium	378.0	Luxembourg	228.0*
Denmark	291.0*	Netherlands	n/a
Finland	285.0	Norway	295.0
France	82.0*	Portugal	301.0
Germany	341.0	Spain	422.0
Greece	393.0**	Sweden	300.0***
Iceland	301.0*	Switzerland	322.0
IRELAND	211.0	Britain	175.0

Source Eurostat
*1994; **1995; ***1993

Hospital Statistics

Acute Hospital Statistics

● Republic of Ireland by Health Board, 1997	avg avail. in-patient beds	In-patient admissions	Discharges & Deaths	Day Cases	% bed occupancy	avg length of stay	avg no. day beds available	Casualty attend.s
Eastern	4,947	190,999	191,028	133,699	85.6	7.6*	326	540,342
Midland	473	28,135	28,076	6,896	90.7	5.6	29	54,472
Mid-Western	752	41,693	41,718	15,426	90.8	6.0	51	110,840
North-Eastern	911	41,358	41,426	11,715	75.9	6.1	27	98,969
North-Western	662	34,129	34,135	16,302	77.4	5.1*	22	47,923
South-Eastern	1,114	58,994	59,166	15,637	79.1	5.4	53	110,134
Southern	1,771	83,423	82,550	32,714	80.8	6.3	68	142,771
Western	1,231	58,086	58,137	17,083	82.7	6.4	36	107,870
Total Health Boards	6,828	332,551	331,627	108,538	82.2	6.1*	282	680,188
Voluntary Hospitals	5,033	204,266	204,609	140,934	84.8	7.2*	330	533,133
Overall Total	11,861	536,817	536,236	249,472	83.3	6.5*	612	1,213,321

➤ *Continued from previous page*

● Northern Ireland by HSS Trust, 1997/8	avg Available Beds[1]	Occupied Beds	Deaths & Discharges	Day Cases	Through put[2]	avg Length of Stay[3]	Waiting List	Operated Cases	A&E[4] Attendances
Altnagelvin Hospitals	495.4	377.5	27627	8810	55.8	5	2,140	13,540	50,956
Armagh & Dungannon	632.1	512.3	10475	3636	16.6	17.9	506	4,923	35,407
Belfast City Hospital	781.5	645	39737	13532	50.8	5.9	3,518	10,768	53,210
Causeway	339.2	238.8	12740	4161	37.6	6.8	431	6,907	31,691
Craigavon / Banbridge	80	70.1	1117	0	14	22.9			
Craigavon Area Hospital Grp	464.5	345.2	22560	7979	48.6	5.6	2,442	9,992	44,414
Down Lisburn	647.4	543.2	16588	4734	25.6	12	450	8,241	56,063
Foyle	318.3	274.4	1568	0	4.9	63.9			
Green Park	476.3	344.5	12070	3137	25.3	10.4	3,470	5,450	
Homefirst Community	384	360.6	1773	0	4.6	74.2			
Mater Infirmorum Hospital	210.6	182.8	11635	3086	55.3	5.7	164	5,615	44,950
Newry & Mourne	272.6	195.6	13836	3450	50.8	5.2	416	6,228	30,511
North & West Belfast	482	419.4	470	0	1	325.7			
Royal Group of Hospitals and Dental Hospital	913.2	718.7	45392	24819	49.7	5.8	6,311	22,767	104,805
South & East Belfast	384	343	1359	0	3.5	92.1			
Sperrin Lakeland	623.3	482.1	19587	4368	31.4	9	1,102	6,514	37,613
Ulster Community & Hospitals	652.7	565.5	31743	10839	48.6	6.5	2,224	21,827	80,417
United Hospitals	848.7	661.3	35884	11781	42.3	6.7	2,247	11,428	94,512
TOTAL	9,005.8	7,280.0	306,161	104,332	34	8.7	25,421	134,200	664,549

RoI Source *Dept of Health and Children.*
* The 'avg. length of stay' in days calculations totals excl. Inc Orthopaedic, NRH, Peamount, Baldoyle (Eastern Health Board) and Manorhamilton (North-Western Health Board) because of their specialties which involve much longer stays than acute hospitals.

NI Source *Dept of Health & Social Services*
1 Avg no. of Available / Occupied beds during the year in wards open overnight.
2 refers to the avg no. of ordinary admissions treated in the available beds open overnight (excl. day cases)
3 Figure is calculated by multiplying avg daily no. of occupied beds by days in the year and dividing the sum by no. of Deaths & Discharges
4 refers Accident and Emergency attendances.

NI: Programme of Care Statistics

Programmes of Care 1997/8	available beds	discharges & deaths	avg length of stay	through -put	outpatient referrals	outpatient attendances*	outpatient DNAs**
Acute Services	4324	227756	5	53	348863	850456	180529
Maternity & Child Health	826	53394	3	65	25302	86379	4868
Elderly Care	1775	12613	44	7	4518	13748	1611
Mental Health	1317	9651	46	7	13741	72767	21475
Learning Disability	764	2747	88	4	197	3100	448

Source Dept of Health & Social Services
*initiated by consultant
** DNA: did not attend

Psychiatric Patient Statistics

● Republic of Ireland	In-patient Numbers			Out-patient numbers	
	1994	1995	1996	Day Centres	Day Hospitals
Total	6,197	5,807	5,575	14,779	17,418

Source Dept of Health and Children.

● Northern Ireland In-patient No.s, 1997/8	Avg available beds	Avg occupied beds	Deaths & Discharges	Day Cases	% Day Cases	Avg length of stay
Total	1,317.0	1,204.8	9,651	93	1.0	45.6

Source Dept of Health and Social Services

NI: HSS Trusts Providing Community Services

Northern Ireland - HSS Trusts by type of service	Mentally Ill	Learning Disability	Visually Impaired	Hearing Impaired	Physically Disabled	Materially Handicapped	Not Known	Total
Armagh & Dungannon:								
Home Help Service	85	45	196	230	590	1,378	0	2,524
Meals on Wheels	0	0	0	0	0	0	0	0
Contact with healthcare providers	1,104	644	647	926	2,438			5,759
Causeway :								
Home Help Service	25	5	52	7	234	946	0	1,269
Meals on Wheels	0	1	1	0	10	10	100	122
Contact with healthcare providers	469	447	253	244	700			2,113
Craigavon / Banbridge:								
Home Help Service	35	32	9	2	301	1,304	0	1,683
Meals on Wheels	4	0	0	0	49	289	0	342
Contact with healthcare providers	809	490	454	320	653			2,726
Down Lisburn:								
Home Help Service	6	31	118	46	190	2,005	0	2,396
Meals on Wheels	2	6	34	5	23	386	0	456
Contact with healthcare providers	1,156	921	618	345	827			3,867
Foyle:								
Home Help Service	7	22	29	42	275	1,461	0	1,836
Meals on Wheels	0	3	0	0	10	0	469	482
Contact with healthcare providers	690	964	477	837	919			3,887
Homefirst Community:								
Home Help Service	283	110	124	40	1,027	2,783	0	4,367
Meals on Wheels	6	4	10	2	43	144	0	209
Contact with healthcare providers	3,465	1,299	804	575	2,621			8,764
Newry & Mourne:								
Home Help Service	165	35	126	99	216	1,009	0	1,650
Meals on Wheels	13	3	0	0	8	261	0	285
Contact with healthcare providers	606	523	466	614	671			2,880
North Down & Ards:								
Home Help Service	20	16	36	29	65	1,661	0	1,827
Meals on Wheels	24	4	17	7	10	595	0	657
Contact with healthcare providers	984	666	372	305	242			2,569
North & West Belfast:								
Home Help Service	33	13	110	44	217	3,230	0	3,647
Meals on Wheels	13	3	18	6	43	266	0	349
Contact with healthcare providers	743	859	581	496	1,426			4,105
South & East Belfast:								
Home Help Service	63	26	150	147	279	3,649	0	4,314
Meals on Wheels	18	3	0	0	0	0	887	908
Contact with healthcare providers	1,557	853	827	932	972			5,141
Sperrin Lakeland:								
Home Help Service	68	17	59	61	751	1,125	780	2,861
Meals on Wheels	9	3	20	15	129	289	0	465
Contact with healthcare providers	1,228	627	368	388	2,757			5,368

Source Dept of Health & Social Services

Ambulance Statistics

Northern Ireland - Journey Priority, 1997/8	Eastern	Northern	Southern	Western	Total
Emergency	32,367	14,485	8,046	8,241	63,139
of which Cardiac calls	*497*	*873*	*853*	*655*	*2,878*
Urgent	15,161	10,002	6,017	5,936	37,116
Special or Planned	111,692	68,379	71,856	31,723	283,650
TOTAL	**159,220**	**92,866**	**85,919**	**45,900**	**383,905**

Source Dept of Health & Social Services

Mortality Rates

Deaths classified by cause

● Republic of Ireland - *Cause of Death (1998)*	Male	Female	Total
Infectious & Parasitic Diseases	111	83	194
Cancer (Benign & Malignant)	4,022	3,471	7,493
Diabetes mellitus, Nutritional diseases, Anaemias	249	230	479
Meningitis	4	8	12
Ulcers, Appendicitis	79	88	167
Liver, Nephritic Disease	266	255	521
Circulatory System Diseases	6,835	6,356	13,191
Pneumonia, influenza, Bronchitis, Emphysema and Asthma	1,183	1,419	2,602
Genito-urinary System Diseases	11	-	11
Pregnancy, Childbirth etc. Complications	-	3	3
Congenital Anomalies	102	96	198
Perinatal Complications	78	56	134
Ill-defined Conditions	82	125	207
Poisoning & Injury	1,101	439	1,540
Other Diseases	2,360	2,240	4,600
TOTAL	**16,483**	**14,869**	**31,352**
External Causes	1,732	779	2,511
Total + External Causes	*18,215*	*15,648*	*33,863*

Source *Dept. of Health and Children*

● Republic of Ireland - *Cause of Death*	1966	1973	1980	1988	1993	1998
All Circulatory System Diseases	17,678	17,452	16,977	14,952	14,529	13,191
All Cancers	5,173	5,803	6,288	7,154	7,589	7,493
All Accidents, Poisoning & Violence	1,169	1,583	1,713	1,427	1,377	1,747
of which: Motor Traffic Accidents	350	604	569	460	411	429
of which: Suicide	69	105	216	266	327	504

Source: Dept of Health & Social Services

● Northern Ireland - *Cause of Death*	1988 Male	1988 Female	1993 Male	1993 Female	1997 Male	1997 Female
Infectious & Parasitic Diseases	30	16	23	32	24	37
Cancer (Benign & Malignant)	1742	1667	1917	1786	1878	1791
Endocrine, Nutritional, Metabolic & Immunity Diseases	35	38	28	47	56	50
Diseases of the Blood and Blood-forming Organs	10	8	9	20	7	13
Mental Disorders	16	19	27	29	79	59
Nervous System and Sense Organ Diseases	82	70	92	97	118	117
Circulatory System Diseases	3877	3867	3497	3640	3166	3339
Respiratory System Diseases	1216	1352	1244	1512	1121	1543
Digestive System Diseases	160	198	195	250	187	263
Genito-urinary System Diseases	125	125	121	140	91	152
Pregnancy, Childbirth etc. Complications	-	2	-	-	-	-
Skin, Musculoskeletal and Connective Tissue Diseases	23	67	19	49	13	56
Congenital Anomalies	53	38	71	45	27	32
Perinatal Complications	53	47	35	27	38	29
Ill-defined Conditions	21	23	14	28	35	57
Poisoning & Injury	550	284	439	200	404	189
TOTAL	**7993**	**7821**	**7731**	**7902**	**7244**	**7727**

Source: Dept of Health & Social Services

EU Comparison: Mortality rates/100,000 population by principal causes

Country, 1995	all causes	diseases of circ. system	heart disease	stroke	malignant cancers	respiratory tract cancer	female breast cancer	accidents, poison & violence	traffic accidents	suicide
Austria*	732.3	367	147.9	84.1	184.6	33.9	30.1	51.9	11	19.9

Continued from previous page

Country, 1995	all causes	diseases of circ. system	heart disease	stroke	malignant cancers	respiratory tract cancer	female breast cancer	accidents, poison & violence	traffic accidents	suicide
Belgium****	770.2	267.7	81	66.8	214.5	53.4	35.5	56.3	15.4	17.2
Britain	770.7	317.2	181	74.4	206.5	48.6	36	28.6	5.8	7.1
Denmark	868.5	316.5	163.9	68.2	234.2	55.1	42.6	55.9	10.2	16
Finland	772.4	354	207.4	90.9	163	31.3	25.1	79.1	7.5	26.1
France**	639.7	182.8	54.3	46	194.3	34.8	28.2	64.5	13.5	19.4
Germany	764.1	343.8	151.2	78.3	196.7	36.3	31.7	41.2	10.7	13.9
Greece	700.5	340.9	90.4	122.9	163	39.2	22.9	39.6	21.6	3.2
IRELAND*	847.4	369.5	204.9	75	206	42	35.6	37.2	11	10.6
Italy***	695.5	284.8	90	85.5	199.9	42.2	29.5	40.8	13.3	7.2
Luxembourg	724.4	284.8	90.8	86.9	208.7	45.2	36.2	53.9	15.5	14.2
Netherlands	724.5	269.3	110.5	62	206.8	50.6	36.6	29.8	7.4	9.2
Portugal	877.5	352.5	74.5	187.4	170.8	22.3	25	55.5	23.3	7.5
Spain**	674.5	245.9	70.3	75.4	179.7	34.8	24.6	37.6	13.3	7.4
Sweden	647.7	295.9	158.1	61	161.3	24.6	24.8	40.3	5.3	14.2
EU Average	725.1	289.8	117.3	76.4	195.1	39.5	30.6	43.6	11.6	11.7

Source World Health Organisation
*1996; **1994; ***1993; ****1992.

Infant Mortality rates

● Republic of Ireland - *Infant mortality*	1966	1971	1976	1981	1986	1991	1998
Rates Per 1,000 live births *under 1 year*	25.0	18.0	15.5	10.3	8.9	7.6	6.2
Numbers *under 1 year*	1552	1214	1052	746	547	401	330
Perinatal rate / 1,000 live & still births *U-28 days*	28.6	22.8	19.7	13.4	11.8	9.5	n/a

Source Dept. of Health and Children

● Northern Ireland - *Stillbirths and infant deaths*	1951/5	1961/5	1971/5	1981/5	1991/5	1997
Rates Per 1,000 live births *(under 1 year old)*	36.6	26.5	21.1	11.8	6.7	5.6
Numbers *(under 1 year old)*	1,054	879	610	323	168	137

Source Dept of Health & Social Services

● EU Comparison - *by Country, 1994*	Infant Mortality Rate	Neo-Natal Mortality Rate	Perinatal Mortality Rate
Austria	6.3	3.9	6.2
Belgium	7.6	4.3*	8.3*
Denmark	5.6	3.5**	7.4**
Finland	4.7	3.5	5.4
France	5.8p	3.3(d)	7.7***
Germany	5.6	3.2	6.4
Greece	7.9	5.6	9.7
IRELAND *	**5.5**	**3.9**	**9.3**
Italy	6.6p	5.9***	9.4***
Luxembourg	5.3	3.3	6.2
Netherlands	5.6	4.0	8.6
Portugal	8.1	4.8	9.3
Spain	6.0p	4.1**	6.6**
Sweden	4.4	3.0	5.4
Britain	6.2	4.1	8.9
EU Average	6.1p	4.4*	8.1*

Source CSO, Eurostat.
*1991; **1993; ***1992.

Suicide rates

● Suicide Deaths by Age-group	Rep. of Ireland 1997			N. Ireland 1998		
	Male	Female	Total	Male	Female	Total
0-14 years	8	0	8	0	0	0
15-19 years	26	7	33	11	5	16
20-24 years	61	9	70	12	0	12

Continued from previous page

● Suicide Deaths by Age-group	Rep. of Ireland 1997			N. Ireland 1998		
	Male	Female	Total	Male	Female	Total
25-29 years	45	6	51	15	4	19
30-34 years	38	10	48	18	4	22
35-39 years	39	7	46	5	7	12
40-44 years	30	8	38	10	3	13
45-49 years	27	7	34	7	2	9
50-54 years	17	4	21	4	2	6
55-59 years	20	2	22	2	1	3
60-64 years	15	4	19	4	1	5
65-69 years	10	6	16	4	2	6
70-74 years	4	5	9	2	0	2
75-79 years	11	2	13	0	0	0
80-84 years	4	1	5	0	0	0
85+ years	0	0	0	1	0	1
TOTAL	355	78	433	95	31	126

Source Dept. of Health and Children, Source: Dept of Health & Social Services

Suicides by Year	Republic of Ireland			Northern Ireland		
	Male*	Female	Total	Male	Female	Total
1991	283	63	346	93	36	129
1992	304	59	363	90	17	107
1993	260	67	327	103	36	129
1994	280	73	353	107	31	138
1995	321	83	404	91	31	122
1996	323	69	392	99	25	124
1997	355	78	433	95	25	120
1998	n/a	n/a	504	95	31	126

Source Department of Health and Social Services, CSO.
Suicide is the main cause of death in RoI males aged 15-24.

● Republic of Ireland - *Suicide Deaths by County, 1998*

Carlow	5	Limerick County	13
Cavan	10	Longford	1
Clare	14	Louth	14
Cork City	32	Mayo	9
Cork County	48	Meath	11
Donegal	17	Monaghan	8
Dublin City	55	Offaly	9
Dublin County	66	Roscommon	7
Galway City	9	Sligo	9
Galway County	20	Tipperary *(NR)*	8
Kerry	29	Tipperary *(SR)*	16
Kildare	12	Waterford County	7
Kilkenny	10	Waterford City	2
Laois	12	Westmeath	11
Leitrim	5	Wexford	14
Limerick City	9	Wicklow	12

Source CSO

International Comparison: Life Expectancy at Birth

Country	Females	Males	Country	Females	Males
Austria	80.5e	74.2e	Italy	81.3e	74.9e
Belgium	80.5*p	73.8p	Japan	83.2	76.7
Britain	79.4	74.3	Luxembourg	79.6	73.5
Canada	81.3	76.8	Netherlands	80.3	74.7
Denmark	78.2p	73.0p	Norway	81.0	75.4
Finland	80.3e	73.3e	Portugal	78.7	71.4
France	82.1p	74.2p	Spain	81.6e	74.4e
Germany	80.0e	73.7e	Sweden	81.8p	76.7p
Greece	81.4e	75.1e	Switzerland	82.2p	76.1p

Continued from previous page

Country	Females	Males
Iceland	81.3	76.4
IRELAND	78.7p	73.3p

Source Eurostat

Country	Females	Males
US	79.5	72.8

Accident Statistics

RoI External Causes of Death

External Cause, 1998	Male	Female	Total
Accidents and adverse effects	770	391	1161
Car accidents	327	102	429
Accidental falls	156	179	335
Suicide	421	83	504
Homicide	28	11	39
Other external causes	30	13	43

Source Dept. of Health and Children

RoI Accidents in the workplace

Industrial Sector 1997	Injured	Fatalities
Agricultural Sector	43	15
Fishing / Diving	5	5
Mining / Quarrying	101	1
Manufacturing	2,541	2
Electricity, Gas, Water Supply	298	-
Construction	504	15
Wholesale and Retail Trade	203	2
Catering Sector	110	
Transport, Storage, Communications	222	6
Financial Intermediation	47	
Real Estate	138	-
Public Administration and Defence	514	-
Education	99	
Health and Social Welfare	357	-
Other	85	2
TOTAL	5,670	48

Source CSO

RoI Accident Fatalities by Accident Type

● Republic of Ireland Accident Type	1994	1995	1996	1997	1998
Road Deaths	404	437	453	472	461
Water Deaths	203	212	151	167	n/a
Fire Deaths	42	50	58	51	45
Railway accident Deaths	11	7	8	14	n/a

Source CSO

Road Accidents

● Republic of Ireland - Fatalities by road user type	1989	1992	1995	1998
Pedestrians	141	115	113	n/a
Pedal Cyclists	39	35	28	n/a
Motor Cyclists	46	59	57	n/a
Car Users	211	169	193	n/a
Other Road User	23	37	46	n/a
TOTAL	460	415	437	461

Source CSO

● Northern Ireland - Road Accidents and Casualties	1989/90	1992/93	1995/96	1998/99
Number of Accidents	7,237	6,699	2,290	7,460

Continued from previous page

● Northern Ireland - *Road Accidents and Casualties*	1989/90	1992/3	1995/6	1998/9
Fatalities	187	140	139	150
Serious Injuries	2,036	1,868	1,543	1,462
Minor Injuries	9,481	9,361	9,910	11,682
Total Casualties	11,704	11,369	11,592	13,294

Source RUC

RoI: Marine Emergency Incidents

Incidents	1994	1995	1996	1997	1998
Incidents	1,047	1,155	1,396	1,644	1,559
Persons Saved/Assisted	1,459	3.924	4,588	6,531	6,468
Pleasure Craft	189	274	334	348	343
Merchant Craft	25	43	57	59	54
Fishing Craft	168	228	377	417	391
Pollution Reports	36	24	42	46	33
IMES Coastal Units	255	431	423	283	421
S6IN	136	151	125	118	185
IAC Helicopter	70	113	141	122	154
RNLI	240	407	434	511	472
CIRS	15	19	10	20	24
Gardai	129	168	166	146	149
False Alarms	134	153	150	198	149
Hoax	50	36	51	53	40

Source Dept. of Marine

Morbidity Rates

NI Notifications of Infectious Diseases

Type of Disease, 1997	Meningitis*	Chicken-pox	Food poisoning	Gastro-enteritis**	Measles	Rubella	Scarlet Fever	Whooping Cough	Others	Total
Northern Ireland	91	5,253	1,534	896	120	127	425	135	306	8,887

Source Dept of Health and Social Services
* *bacterial & viral Meningitis*
** *refers to cases in children under 2*

NI Immunisations and Vaccinations

Immunisations against TB, 1997/8	Under 1	1-9 yrs	10-13 yrs	14-15 yrs	16+ yrs	Total
N o. Vaccinated	48	2956	19816	1114	278	24212

Children Under 2, 1998	Diphtheria	Polio	Tetanus	Pertussis	MMR*	HIB**
% Immunised	97.2	97.2	97.2	95.6	92.4	97.1

Source Dept of Health and Social Services
*MMR - Measles, Mumps, Rubella
**HIB - Haemophilus Influenzae B

RoI Psychiatric Hospital Admissions

Diagnosis, 1996	Sex		Age					Admissions per 100,000 people*
	Male	Female	U-25	25-44	45-64	65+	unknown	
Organic Psychosis	409	447	18	86	135	600	17	23.6
Schizophrenia	3,286	2,340	552	2,649	1,735	582	108	155.2
Other Psychoses	118	104	53	89	46	25	9	6.1
Depressive	2,802	4,140	527	2,429	2,349	1,480	157	191.4
Mania	1,258	1,592	222	1,278	902	383	65	78.6
Neuroses	695	1,028	329	683	482	200	29	47.5
Personality Disorders	651	820	401	779	189	65	37	40.6
Alcoholic Disorders	4,071	1,364	306	2,364	2,236	476	53	149.9
Drug Dependence	416	149	228	252	58	21	6	15.6

Continued from previous page

| Diagnosis, 1996 | Sex | | Age | | | | | Admissions per |
	Male	Female	U-25	25-44	45-64	65+	unknown	100,000 people*
Mental Handicap	278	202	94	228	113	31	14	13.2
Unspecified	211	275	58	151	123	101	53	13.4
Total	14,195	12,461	2,788	10,988	8,368	3,964	548	735.1

Source Health Research Board.
* These rates are based on the 1996 Census of Population.

Children in Care

● Republic of Ireland - *Health Board 1998*	Cases of confirmed Abuse	Total Children in Care
Eastern	701	1,519
Midland	178	194
Mid-Western	n/a	404*
North-Eastern	636	303*
North-Western	515	183
South-Eastern	n/a	329*
Southern	n/a	522*
Western	211	239

Source Dept. of Health; Eastern, Midland, North-Eastern, North-Western and Western Health Boards.
incl. physical, sexual, emotional abuse and neglect. *As of the 31st Dec. 1996

● Northern Ireland - *HSS Trust 31/3/98*	No.s on Child Protection Register	Total Children in Care
Armagh & Dungannon	24	85
Causeway	32	145
Craigavon / Banbridge	28	130
Down Lisburn	203	245
Foyle	148	278
Homefirst Community	168	447
Newry & Mourne	36	86
North Down & Ards	186	173
North & West Belfast	346	381
South & East Belfast	154	251
Sperrin Lakeland	61	133
TOTAL	**1,386***	**2,354**

Source Dept of Health & Social Services
*incl. physical, sexual, emotional abuse and neglect.

Disability Statistics

● Northern Ireland - *Prevalence of disability by age group*	Male (000s)	Female (000s)	Total (000s)
0-4 years	1.7	1.3	3.0
5-9 years	3.1	2.1	5.2
10-15 years	3.9	2.6	6.5
16-59 years	36.0	39.0	75.0
60-74 years	29.0	36.0	65.0
75+ years	18.0	42.0	60.0
Total	**91.7**	**123.0**	**214.0**

Source Dept of Health & Social Services

RoI Incidence of diseases and disabilities

The statistics below were given by the relevant representative agencies. Because these agencies are voluntary, many do not have the funding to carry out adequate research and therefore base their estimates on European or WHO figures.

● **AIDS Cases reported** 682 to date **recorded deaths** 344 (almost 50%). **No. HIV+** 2,062 (end of May 1999) **Population groups with AIDS** intravenous drug-users - almost 50%, homosexuals and bisexuals 8%, heterosexuals 7%. **No. testing HIV+ in the past year:** 74 in the last six months of 1998, 76 in the first five months of 1999. **Location:** The majority (59 cases) were in the Eastern Health Board region.
Contact CAIRDE, 25 St Mary's Abbey, Dublin 7. Tel: 873 0800. Gay HIV Strategies, Fumbally Court, Fumbally Lane, Dublin 8. Tel: 473 0599

● **ALCOHOLISM** The National Health and Lifestyle Surveys found that 27% of males and 21% of females in Ireland drink more than the recommended amount of alcohol in a week and 29% of children were reported as having a drink in the last month. Higher percentages of men than women drink, but younger age groups are drinking significant amounts on a more regular basis. Alcoholics Anonymous is unable to give any figures into its membership but it has 706 groups, holding a total f 78,000 meetings each year in Ireland. Dept of Health figures show that there are 149 psychiatric admissions per 100,000 persons for alcohol-related disorders (4,071 men and 1,364 women). AL-ANON has 230 groups in Ireland and it estimated that for every alcoholic, six others are affected.

Contact Alcoholics Anonymous, 109 Sth Circular Rd, Leonard's Corner, Dublin 8. Tel: 01-453 8998. AL-ANON (for those in contact with alcoholics), Al-Anon Information Centre, 5 Capel St, Dublin 1. Tel: 01-873 2699. Pioneer Total Abstinence Association, 27 Upper Sherrard St, Dublin 1. Tel: 01-874 9464.

● **ALZHEIMER'S** 33,000 people in Ireland estimated suffering from dementia (incl Alzheimer's which is very difficult to diagnose).

Contact Alzheimer Soc. of Ireland, 43 Northumberland Ave, Dun Laoghaire, Co. Dublin. Tel: 01-284 6616.

● **ARTHRITIS** 13% of population have some form of arthritis; 1 in 7 people, 1 in 3 families, with 2 out of 3 sufferers being women. *Osteoarthritis:* a joint disease, with damage to the joint surface and an abnormal reaction of the underlying bone, affects those over 55, with women 2–3 times more likely to suffer from it. Rheumatoid Arthritis: autoimmune disease involving chronic inflammation of joints. 1% of adults suffer from it, with women 3 times more likely to get it.

Contact Arthritis Foundation of Ireland, 1 Clanwilliam Sq, Grand Canal Qy, Dublin 2. Tel: 01-661 8188 web: www.arthritis-foundation.com email: info@arthritis-foundation.com

● **ASTHMA** It is estimated that 274,000 people suffer from asthma in Ireland

Contact Asthma Society of Ireland, 15–17 Eden Quay, Dublin 1. Tel: 01-878 8511

● **AUTISM** Approx. 5 in 10,000 children suffer from Autism but it is very difficult to diagnose.

Contact Irish Soc for Autism, 16 O'Connell St Lwr, Dublin 1. Tel: 01-874 4684.

● **CANCER** 1 in 3 people develop cancer by 75 years of age, 1 in 13 Irish women will develop breast cancer, and 1 in 6 men and 1 in 7 women will develop skin cancer. **Commonest Cancer** skin, followed by colorectal cancers, the breast, lung, cervical, and prostate cancer. These types of cancer account for more than two-thirds of all cancers. There are almost twice as many women cancer cases as men in the 20–54 age group. The largest number of cancers occur in the 65+ age group.

Contact Irish Cancer Society, 5 Northumberland Rd, Dublin 4. Tel: 668 1855 Cancer Helpline: 1800 200 700 Bonemarrow for Leukaemia Trust, PO Box 6830, St James Hospital, Dublin 8

● **COELIAC DISEASE** Coeliac disease sufferers are hypersensitive to gluten - proteins that are present in wheat. It is estimated that in Europe, 1 in 200 people are coeliacs, while a survey carried out in Derry found 1 in 175 were sufferers.

Contact Coeliac Society of Ireland, Carmichael Hse, Nth Brunswick st, Dublin 7, Tel: 01-872 1471. open 10am -1pm Mon, Wed, Fri.

● **CYSTIC FIBROSIS** (CF) Ireland's most common genetic disease, it affects the glands, and damages many organs, through the sticky mucus produced which blocks up the body's channels. Ireland has the highest incidence of CF sufferers in the world, with 900+ diagnosed; 1 in 20 people carrying the CF gene; 1 baby with CF born every week; and approximately 1 in 500 marriages are between CF carriers.

Contact The Cystic Fibrosis Association of Ireland, 24 Lwr Rathmines Rd, Dublin 6; 496 2433; email: cfhouse@internet-ireland.ie

● **DEAFNESS** People with deafness have difficulty hearing sounds and speaking clearly, and it is seen as a communication impairment which can affect all situations where information is communicated through speech or sound. Around 17% of the population have hearing loss - **mild:** 11.33% of total adult population. **moderate:** 4.99%. **severe:** 0.54%. **profound:** 0.14% of total adult population. At least three-quarters of people with hearing loss are 60+ years and it is more prevalent among men.

Contact National Association for Deaf People *(incl. The Irish Tinnitus Association, the Hard of Hearing Association, Irish Ménière's Support Group)*, 35 Nth Frederick St, Dublin 1. Tel: 01-872 3800. email: nad@iol.ie.

● **DEPRESSION** the Republic's first major survey of depression (carried out in 1999) found that depression is 50% more common than was previously thought, with 7.5% of workers clinically depressed (1 in 14) and 6.7% of GP patients depressed. Previously, the figure was estimated at 5% of the population - 1 in 20 people - but the new figure correlates with the 400% increase in the suicide rate in men under 35 since 1990. Significantly more women than men were found to be depressed. Another significant finding was that one-third of workers said they had experienced depression in the past. By 2020, it is estimated the illness will become second only to heart disease a cause of 'lost years of healthy life'.

Contact AWARE, 72 Lwr Leeson St , Dublin 2. Tel: 01-661 7217

● **DIABETES** is the inability to produce insulin which metabolises sugars in the body. From WHO estimates, it is believed that 70,000 suffer from the condition in Ireland. These figures could double in the next few years as diabetes is growing among younger and older people. Early in the next century, it is estimated 240 million people worldwide will suffer from the disease - officially making diabetes an epidemic.

Contact Diabetes Foundation of Ireland, 76 Gardiner St Lower, Dublin 1. Tel: 01-836 3022.

● **DOWN'S SYNDROME** Health boards have not

compiled statistics but it is estimated that 1 in 600 births are to Down's Syndrome babies.

Contact Down's Syndrome Association of Ire, 41 Lwr Dominick St, Dublin 1. Tel: 01-873 0999

● **DYSLEXIA** Based on international surveys (no major survey has been carried out in Ireland), 8% of population suffer from dyslexia, with 4% needing intervention.

Contact Dyslexia Association of Ireland, 1 Suffolk St, Dublin 1. Tel: 01-679 0276

● **EATING DISORDERS** These include Anorexia Nervosa, where people starves themselves; Bulimia Nervosa, where people binge eat and then purge themselves immediately afterwards; and Binge Eating Disorder, where people consume large amounts of food usually in response to stress. It is roughly estimated that in all, 9,920 Irish people suffer from eating disorders - 0.14% of the population - and that 10% of these will die **Anorexia Nervosa** affects 1.5% of women (3,382 females and 338 males) **Bulimia Nervosa** affects 2.5% of women (5,637 females and 563 males.

Contact BODYWHYS, Central Office, PO Box 105, Blackrock, Co. Dublin. 01-283 4963

● **EPILEPSY** There are estimated to be 20,000+ people with epilepsy in Ireland; 1 in 200 adults, 1 in 100 children (10,000 alone in the Eastern Health Board).

Contact Brainwave - Irish Epilepsy Association, 249 Crumlin Rd, Dublin 12. Tel: 01-455 7500

● **ECZEMA Contact** National Eczema Society, Carmichael Hse, Nth Brunswick St, Dublin 7. Tel: 01-455 7807

● **HAEMOPHILIA** There are estimated to be 350 people suffering from Haemophilia in Ireland, and related disorders bring this number up to 500. The majority of Haemophiliacs in Ireland were infected by contaminated blood products, and a tribunal is now in progress to inquire into how 210 haemophiliacs were infected with hepatitis C between the mid 1970s and 1990 and 103 infected with HIV during the 1980s.

Contact Irish Haemophilia Society, Block C, Iceland Hse, Arran Crt, Arran Qy, Dublin 7. Tel: 01-872 4466.

● **HEAD INJURY** The total numbers diagnosed with head injury in Ireland were 11,223 in 1995, 11,309 in 1996 and 10,980 in 1997. Most of these are discharged into communities with no specialist support services. The majority of people with head injuries are young males (more than twice the number of women) and 57% of those sustaining head injury are under 25 years. The major sources of injury were road traffic accidents (25%), Hospital transfer (5.5%), and accidents in the home (8%).

Contact Headway Ireland, Unit 2, Stewart Hall, Parnell St, Dublin 1. Tel: 01-872 9222

● **HEART DISEASE** It is the most commonest cause of death in Ireland, North and South, with circulatory system related diseases accounting for 13,191 deaths in 1998. Ireland has one of the highest heart disease mortality rates in the EU, with 3.6 per 1,000 people attributable to heart disease.

Contact Irish Heart Foundation, 4 Clyde Rd, Ballsbridge, Dublin 4. Tel: 01-668 5001.

● **HUNTINGTON'S DISEASE** A genetic disease of the central nervous system. There are estimated to be 400 sufferers in Ireland, with a further 2,000 at risk of developing the condition.

Contact Huntington's Disease Association of Ire, Carmichael Hse, Nth Brunswick St, Dublin 7. Tel: 01-872 9931.

● **KIDNEY DISEASE** There are 120 people waiting for transplants and approximately 700 receiving dialysis treatment in Ireland, with the health boards conducting 60,750 dialysis treatments last year.

Contact Irish Kidney Association, Donor Hse, 156 Pembroke Rd, Dublin 4. lo call 1890 455 565

● **LUPUS** A rheumatic disease involving abnormalities in the immune system, affecting joints, muscles, skin, kidneys, nervous system, lungs, heart and blood forming organs. Nine women to every one man is affected, particularly during child-bearing years.

Contact Irish Lupus Support Group, 40 Killester Park, Dublin 5. Tel: 01-831 8524

● **M.E.** There are estimated to be 10,000 sufferers, which include those suffering from ME, chronic fatigue syndrome, fibromyalgia and post-viral syndrome. It is believed that future research into the disease must focus on the role played by the immune system, as well as environmental and genetic factors.

Contact Irish ME/CFS Support Group, PO Box 3075 Dublin 2. Tel: 01-235 0965. Irish ME Trust, 18 Fitzwilliam St Uppr Dublin 2. Tel: 01-676 1413

● **MULTIPLE SCLEROSIS** Approximately 6,000 people in Ireland are diagnosed with MS. contact Michael Hutchinson, neurologist-Vincent's 269 5033,

Contact Multiple Sclerosis Society of Ireland, Royal Hospital in Donnybrook, Bloomfield Ave, Morehampton Rd, Dublin 4. Tel: 01-269 4599

● **SCHIZOPHRENIA** Schizophrenia affects 1% of the population in Ireland, with 155.2 hospital admissions per 100,000 people, the breakdown of which 3,286 males admitted 2,340 females admitted. The percentage is stable worldwide.

Contact Schizophrenia Ireland, 38 Blessington Street, Dublin 7. Tel: 01-860 1620

● **SMOKING** Smoking rates far exceed the targets set by the government, with 31% of respondents to the National Health and Lifestyle Surveys being regular smokers. Although smoking is slightly higher among men (32%) than women (31%), the numbers of women smoking are growing with rates among younger women (40% smoking) actually higher than men (38%).

Contact ASH, 5 Northumberland Road, Dublin 4. Tel: 01-660 7044.

LAW AND DEFENCE

The Irish Prison System: In Need of a Radical Overhaul

By Micheál Mac Gréil, S.J.

THE Irish State's degree of 'unenlightment' in the provision of a constructive and humane method of dealing with offenders has been a source of great disappointment. The current prison system as part of the penal apparatus has changed very little in its essentials since the foundation of the State. The system seems to suffer from institutional self-perpetuation. Granted, some concrete improvements have been carried out in standards of accommodation in some of our prisons and places of detention. Only for the humane quality of prison staff the lives of the prisoners would be unbearable.

From an analysis of the statistics received and a reading of reports, this prison system would appear to be as much a cause of crime as it is its cure. It seems to reinforce the young offender and often result in his (and occasionally her) debasement. This is largely due to official and public attitudes towards imprisonment. Prison is seen as a place of insulation with the primary and almost exclusive emphasis on the custodial function.

Historically viewed, offenders convicted and sentenced to prison are 'deported within the country'. Prior to the 1850s, convicted felons who were not physically punished or executed were deported to Australia, Tasmania, or to the American colonies of Britain. Once these outlets were closed down, new prisons like Mountjoy were built to become 'Van Diemen's Land' at home in Ireland.

Another feature of Irish prisons has been the incarceration of people convicted of 'political crimes'. These included persons involved in land agitation and republican and loyalist causes. It could be argued that this political link was in part responsible for the over-emphasis on curtailment and security.

Ireland (Republic) has one of the highest male proportion of prison inmates, i.e., 98% as compared with 95% in the E.U. This predominance of male prisoners has never been addressed properly to find out what is wrong with our society that leads to the criminalisation of men, especially young men from poorer backgrounds. Perhaps, those engaged in trying to reduce crime might address this issue and discover the cause of this possible anti-male gender discrimination for certain categories of men? The bio-anthropological approach which linked crime to genetically related causes has been thoroughly ruled out by serious criminologists. Therefore, the male crisis must be due to socio-cultural causes rather than male gene-related ones. Ironically, this criminalisation of males from certain socio-cultural backgrounds is at the hands of a predominantly male controlled penal and social system. It is a case of intra-sex rather than inter-sex discrimination.

One of the most discouraging trends in recent times has been the increase of 50% of those committed to prison for serious crimes between 1990 and 1996. Even since 1997 the average daily occupancy of prisons in the Republic has since risen from approximately 2,227 to 2,800 i.e., an increase of 25% in average daily occupancy. The current figures would represent 70 in 100,000 which, incidentally, is still one of the lowest levels of imprisonment in Europe.

This trend is quite disturbing, especially when coupled with the rise in suicide in the Republic over recent years. Sociologists sometimes take imprisonment (representing serious crime largely due to relative deprivation) and suicide (due often to a relatively high level of anomie or normlessness and a lack of social cohesion) to be indicators of the failure of social and cultural conditions capable of satisfying the basic human needs of all the people. These indicators give a different insight into the so-called success or failure of contemporary Irish society despite all the hype about the economic and commercial improvements.

Emphasis on success and competitiveness can be quite dysfunctional and dissociative and may in part be responsible for our socio-cultural pathology. A society based on equality and co-operation would be more conducive to low crime rates and fewer suicides. **Prison numbers and suicides** are probably better indicators of the human quality of a society than are high incomes for some, even the majority of a society! Does it mean, therefore, that there is a negative correlation between the material and economic success of Ireland and the personal, social and cultural quality of life of its citizens? It would appear the 'Celtic Tiger' phenomenon is a mixed blessing!

Prior to the *MacBride Report* of 1980 there was no serious enquiry in the Irish penal system for ninety-nine years, i.e., since the *Royal Commission of Enquiry into Irish Prisons 1881*. Our prison system was inherited from the British colonial administration in 1922 and the Irish Free State more or less followed the previous routine. The most significant structural change was the transfer of control of the prisons from a Prison Board to the Department of Justice in 1928, where it has remained until very recently when a move "towards an independent Prison Agency" was recommended and approved by the Government in the 12th November 1996. The MacBride Report 1980 and the Whitaker Report in 1986 both advocated a change from the Department of Justice back to an independent Board.

This new development is to be welcomed but I feel that the proposed Board's functions are too limited and do not give enough priority to such issues as prevention and recidivism. They are focused more on the proper **prison routine** than on **treatment of offenders.** The proposal in the MacBride Report (which I quote in full below) was far more comprehensive and likely to be more effective that the one now being instituted. MacBride proposed that

> "*The entire responsibility for the treatment of offenders should be invested in a **Treatment of Offenders' Board** consisting of not less than nine members and not more than eleven. Membership of the Board should not include more than two members of the existing prison system or Civil Service.*
>
> *The other members of the Board should be independent persons, appointed because of their expertise and experience in the fields of Education, Religion, Medicine, Social Services, Trade Unions, Business and other relevant disciplines. The organisation under the control of the **Treatment of Offenders' Board** should be divided under the following divisions:*
>
> *(i) **The Security Division:** which would be assigned jointly to the Department of Justice and the Gardaí Síochána. This Division would have sole responsibility for the custodial containment of offenders and security related to places of detention.*

(ii) Rehabilitation Division: This Division should occupy the central role in advising the Board as to the particular type of treatment to be provided for each individual offender. Its motivation should be the rehabilitation of the offender. This will involve education, training, remedial treatment and reintegration of offenders into society. Wherever reasonably possible, custodial detention should be avoided or reduced to a minimum. This Division should be under overall control of a Director chosen by reason of his/her training and experience in social work.

(iii) Preventive Division: This division should analyse and keep under constant review the incidence and causes of juvenile delinquency. Where appropriate, it should consult with the educational and Gardaí authorities as to the incidence of different types of offences. The function of this Division should be to identify the underlying causes of offences and to initiate measures that could be taken to reduce the incidence of certain types of offences. Such measures might involve the provision of educational training facilities. The provision of social and sports activities to reduce the incidence of petty juvenile delinquency in built-up areas should be envisaged.

(iv) Building, Maintenance, Catering and Administrative Division: This Division should be responsible to the Board for the building, maintenance, catering and administration (including financial control) of all institutions under the control of the Board. This Division should be under the control of specialists in the different aspects of the administration.

Each of these four Divisions would report directly to the **Treatment of Offenders' Board.** *The Department of Justice would provide the administrative services for the Board and would exercise supervisory functions on behalf of the Board. The Board would report directly to the Minister and consult with the Minister at regular intervals."*
(MacBride Report, *1980. pp.58 - 60).*

The above rather lengthy extract from the *MacBride Report* is in my opinion a most important recommendation for the restructuring of the Irish Prison System and, if tried, could result in great improvements for the benefit of Irish society and of offenders. In my opinion, the present structures are not conducive to crime reduction or rehabilitation.

In 1997, the average number in custody each day was 2,227 offenders and alleged offenders in custody in the prisons of the Republic. It is planned to provide 3,800 prison places according to current State policy. With extra places it is expected that we will have people to fill them! The curtailment of bail which will be legislated for in the near future is expected to result in an increase of prisoners on remand. It is a rather pessimistic outlook and an admission of failure on behalf of the Government to be providing extra prison places rather than working for a reduction in numbers of prisoners. What a peace dividend? When one examines the following figures one can see the rise and fall of Irish society over the past 120 years. Rise of Irish society is reflected in low numbers in prison.

Year	Number Of Prisoners (Average Daily)
1878	3,910 (All Ireland)
1928	728 Free State/Republic
1960	400 Republic of Ireland
1980	1,200 Republic of Ireland
1997	27,227 Republic of Ireland
1999	2,800 Republic of Ireland

Space does not permit much commentary on the types of offenders one finds in Irish prisons today. Dr Paul O'Mahony's book, *Mountjoy Prisoner: A Sociological and Criminological Profile (Dublin, Oifig an t'Solathair, 1997)* is worth reading in this regard.

Many prisoners have serious drug-related problems. Counselling and psychiatric services are quite inadequate to deal with all the problems. Up to three hundred prisoners are classified as sex offenders and all of these need counselling but only a fraction of places are available.

People are often sent to prison for the wrong reasons. The criminal code needs a serious overhaul. The Courts and the Gardaí are at the receiving end of those committing offences who are sent to criminal prison in accordance with current law.

The purpose of this brief article is to help the reader to reflect on the Irish Penal System. Is it not time that the Irish people become more enlightened about our penal system and what it is telling us about our attitudes, values and structures?

Micheál Mac Gréil, S.J.
October 1999

The author is a Sociologist and Editor of the **MacBride Report on the Irish Penal System** *(1980). He is also author of the seminal works,* **Prejudice and Tolerance in Ireland** *(1977) and* **Prejudice in Ireland Revisited** *(1996). He is currently the chairperson of the Board of Management of the Pioneer Total Abstinence Association.*

Court System, RoI

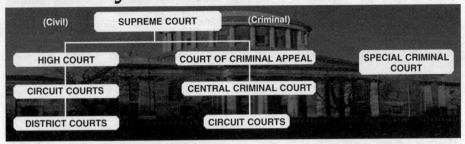

(Civil)   **SUPREME COURT**   (Criminal)

HIGH COURT   **COURT OF CRIMINAL APPEAL**   **SPECIAL CRIMINAL COURT**

CIRCUIT COURTS   **CENTRAL CRIMINAL COURT**

DISTRICT COURTS   **CIRCUIT COURTS**

Judiciary

JUDGES OF THE SUPREME COURT
Chief Justice The Honourable Mr. Justice Liam Hamilton, *b. 1928, app 1994* (£111,204)

style: The Honourable Mr/Ms Justice [name] (£96,377)
Ms. Justice Susan Denham, *b. 1945, app 1993*
Mr. Justice Donal Barrington *b. 1928, app 1996*
Mr. Justice Ronan Keane, *b. 1932, app 1996*
Mr. Justice Francis Murphy, *b. 1932, app 1996*
Mr. Justice Kevin Lynch, *b. 1928, app 1996*
Mr. Justice Henry Barron, *b. 1929, app 1997*

JUDGES OF THE HIGH COURT
President The Honourable Mr. Justice Frederick R. Morris, *b. 1929, app 1990 (President 1998)* (£100,137)

style: The Honourable Mr/Ms Justice [name] (£88,749)
Ms. Justice Mella Carroll, *b. 1934, app 1980*
Mr. Justice Robert Barr, *b. 1930, app 1980*
Mr. Justice Richard Johnson, *b. 1937, app 1987*
Mr. Justice Vivian Lavan, *b. 1944, app 1989*
Mr. Justice Declan Budd, *b. 1943, app 1991*
Mr. Justice Feargus Flood, *b. 1928, app 1991*
Mr. Justice Paul Carney, *b. 1943, app 1991*
Mr. Justice Hugh Geoghegan, *app 1992*
Mr. Justice Dermot Kinlen, *app 1993*
Mr. Justice Brian McCracken, *app 1995*
Ms. Justice Mary Laffoy, *app 1995*
Mr. Justice Michael Moriarty, *app 1996*
Mr. Justice Peter Kelly, *b. 1950, app 1996*
Mr. Justice Thomas Smyth, *app 1996*
Mrs. Justice Catherine McGuinness, *b. 1934, app 1996*
Mr. Justice Diarmuid O'Donovan, *app 1996*
Mr. Justice Philip O'Sullivan, *app 1997*
Mr. Justice Kevin C. O'Higgins, *app 1997*
Mr. Justice John Quirke, *app 1997*
Mr. Justice Nicholas Kearns, *app 1998*
Mr. Justice Matthew P. Smith, *app 1998*
Ms. Justice Fidelma Macken, *app 1998*
The President of the Circuit Court (ex officio)

JUDGES OF THE CIRCUIT COURT
President The Honourable Mr. Justice Esmond Smyth (£88,749)

style: His/Her Honour Judge [name] (£69,840)
Judge Dominic Lynch, Dublin Circuit
Judge Michael Murphy, Cork Circuit
Judge Matthew R. Deery, Northern Circuit
Judge Patrick Joseph Moran, Cork Circuit
Judge Kieran O'Connor, Dublin Circuit
Judge Liam Devally, Dublin Circuit
Judge Harvey Kenny, Western Circuit
Judge Sean A. O'Leary, South Western Circuit
Judge Kevin Haugh, Dublin Circuit
Judge John Buckley, Dublin Circuit
Judge Alison Lindsay, Dublin Circuit
Judge Raymond Groarke, Eastern Circuit
Judge Elizabeth Dunne, Dublin Circuit
Judge Patrick Frank O'Donnell, Dublin Circuit
Judge Michael White, unassigned
Judge Olive Buttimer, South Eastern Circuit
Judge Joseph Matthews, unassigned
Judge Patrick John McCartan, unassigned
Judge Carroll Moran, unassigned
Judge Jacqueline Linnane, unassigned
Judge John O'Hagan, unassigned
Judge Yvonne Murphy, Dublin Circuit
Judge John Clifford, Cork Ciircuit
Judge Brian McMahon, unassigned

JUDGES OF THE DISTRICT COURT
President: Judge Peter Smithwick (£69,840)

Dublin Metropolitan Court (each £58,020)
Judge Peter Smithwick, Judge James P. McDonnell, Judge Desmond Windle, Judge Timothy H. Crowley, Judge James Scally, Judge David Anderson, Judge Thomas E. O'Donnell, Judge Mary Devins, Judge Sean Delap, Judge Brian Kirby, Judge Gillian M. Hussey, Judge Clare Leonard, Judge Michael O'Leary, Judge Mary Collins, Judge Catherine A. Murphy, Judge Miriam Malone.

District 1: Judge John O'Donnell
District 2: Judge Oliver McGuinness
District 3: Judge Daniel G. Shields
District 4: Judge Mernard M. Brennan
District 5: Judge Donal McArdle
District 6: Judge Flann Brennan
District 7: Judge John F. Garavan
District 8: Judge James J. O'Sullivan
District 9: Judge John F. Neilan

District 10: Judge John P. Brophy
District 12: Judge Albert Louis O'Dea
District 13: Judge Mary O'Halloran
District 14: Judge Michael C. Reilly
District 15: Judge Mary Martin
District 16: Judge Thomas Ballagh
District 17: Judge Humphrey P. Kelleher
District 18: Judge Brendan J. Wallace
District 19: Judge Uinsin MacGruairc, Judge Constantine O'Leary
District 20: Judge Michael Pattwell
District 21: Judge David Riordan
District 22: Judge William Harnett
District 23: Judge Donnchadh O Buachalla

Moveable Judges
Judge Joseph Mangan, Judge William G.J. Hamill, Judge Thomas Fitzpatrick, Judge Desmond Hogan, Judge Gerard J. Haughton, Judge Terence Finn, Judge Murrough B. Connellan, Judge Mary Fahy, Judge William Early, Judge Michael Connellan, Judge John J. O'Neill, Judge James O'Connor.

Court Venues

CIRCUIT COURT
Cork Circuit
Towns: Bandon, Bantry, Clonakilty, Cork, Fermoy, Kanturk, Macroom, Mallow, Midleton, Skibbereen, Youghal.

Eastern Circuit
Towns: Dundalk, Athy, Naas, Trim, Wicklow.

Midland Circuit
Towns: Athlone, Mullingar, Birr, Tullamore, Boyle, Roscommon, Longford, Portlaoise, Sligo.

Northern Circuit
Towns: Buncrana, Donegal, Letterkenny, Carrick-on-Shannon, Manorhamilton, Castleblayney, Monaghan, Cavan.

South Eastern Circuit
Towns: Carlow, Clonmel, Nenagh, Thurles, Tipperary, Dungarvan, Waterford, Kilkenny, Wexford.

South Western Circuit
Towns: Ennis, Kirush, Killarney, Listowel, Tralee, Limerick, Rathkeale.

Western Circuit
Towns: Ballina, Castlebar, Swinford, Westport, Galway, Loughrea.

Dublin Circuit
Town: Dublin.

DISTRICT COURT
District 1: Buncrana, Carndonagh, Donegal, Glenties, Letterkenny.
District 2: Ballyfarnon, Ballymote, Boyle, Collooney, Dowra, Drumkeerin, Easkey, Grange, Inniscrone,
Manorhamilton, Riverstown, Skreen, Sligo, Tubbercurry.
District 3: Achill, Balla, Ballina, Ballinrobe, Ballycastle, Callycroy, Belmullet, Castlebar, Crossmolina, Foxford, Killala, Kiltimagh, Newport, Swinford, Westport.
District 4: Ballaghaderreen, Ballyhaunis, Carrick-on-Shannon, Castlerea, Charlestown, Claremorris, Dunmore, Elphin, Glenamaddy, Kilkelly, Roscommon, Rooskey, Strokestown, Williamstown.
District 5: Arva, Bailieborough, Ballinamore, Ballyconnell, Ballyjamesduff, Belturbet, Cavan, Cootehill, Kingscourt, Mohill, Monaghan, Oldcastle, Virginia.
District 6: Ardee, Ballybay, Carlingford, Carrickmacross, Castleblayney, Drogheda, Dundalk, Dunleer.
District 7: Carna, Clifden, Derreen, Derrynea, Galway, Headford, Kilronan, Letterfrack, Maam, Oughterard, Spiddal, Tuam.
District 8: Athlone, Ballinasloe, Ballyforan, Birr, Borrisokane, Eyrecourt, Loughrea, Moate, Mount Bellew, Kilcormac, Woodford.
District 9: Ballymahon, Ballynacargy, Castlepollard, Delvin, Edenderry, Edgeworthstown, Granard, Kilbeggan, Killucan, Longford, Mullingar, Tullamore.
District 10: Athboy, Ceanannua Mor, Dunshaughlin, Kilcock, Navan, Trim.
District 12: Athenry, Corofin, Ennis, Ennistymon, Gort, Kildysart, Kilkee, Killaloe, Kilrush, Kinvara, Lisdoonvarna, Miltown Malbay, Shannon, Sixmilebridge, Scarriff, Tulla.
District 13: Abbeyfeale, Adare, Askeaton, Bruff, Drumcologher, Kilfinane, Kilmallock, Listowel, Newcastle West, Rathkeale, Rath Luirc, Shanagolden, Tarbert.
District 14: Cappamore, Cappawhite, Limerick City, Nenagh, Newport, Thurles.
District 15: Abbeyleix, Athy, Ballyragget, Carlow, Castlecomer, Mountmellick, Mountrath, Portarlington, Portlaoise, Rathdowney, Roscrea, Templemore, Urlingford.
District 16: Baltinglass, Blessington, Bray, Droichead Nua, Hacketstown, Kildare, Naas.
District 17: Annascaul, Cahirciveen, Castlegregory, Castleisland, Dingle, Kenmare, Killarney, Killorglin, Sneem, Tralee, Waterville.
District 18: Bandon, Bantry, Castletownbere, Clonakilty, Coachford, Dunmanway, Glengarriff, Kinsale, Macroom, Millstreet, Schull, Skibbereen.
District 19: Cork City.
District 20: Ballincollig, Blarney, Buttevant, Carrigaline, Castlemartyr, Castletownroche, Cobh, Fermoy, Kanturk, Mallow, Midleton, Mitchelstown, Riverstown.
District 21: Cahir, Cappoquin, Carrick-on-Suir, Cashel, Clogheen, Clonmel, Dungarvan, Killenaule, Lismore, Tallow, Tipperary, Youghal.
District 22: Callan, Kilkenny, Kilmacthomas, Thomastown, Waterford.
District 23: Arklow, Bunclody, Enniscorthy, Gorey, Muine Bheag, New Ross, Rathdrum, Shillelagh, Tullow, Wexford, Wicklow.

Court System, NI

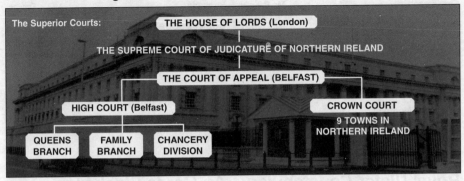

The Superior Courts:

THE HOUSE OF LORDS (London)

THE SUPREME COURT OF JUDICATURE OF NORTHERN IRELAND

THE COURT OF APPEAL (BELFAST)

HIGH COURT (Belfast)

CROWN COURT
9 TOWNS IN
NORTHERN IRELAND

QUEENS BRANCH | **FAMILY BRANCH** | **CHANCERY DIVISION**

Judiciary

THE SUPREME COURT OF JUDICATURE

The Lord Chief Justice of Northern Ireland The Rt Hon Sir Robert Douglas Carswell *(pictured)*
The Rt Hon Lord Justice Nicholson
The Rt Hon Lord Justice McCollum
The Rt Hon Lord Justice Campbell
The Hon Mr Justice Shiel
The Hon Mr Justice Kerr
The Hon Mr Justice Pringle
The Hon Mr Justice Higgins
The Hon Mr Justice Girvan
The Hon Mr Justice Coghlin
The Hon Mr Justice Gillen
Principal Secretary to the Lord Chief Justice: G.W. Johnston

SUPREME COURT OFFICERS

Queen's Bench, Appeals and Clerk of the Crown in Northern Ireland Master: J.W. Wilson; High Court Master: Mrs D.M. Kennedy
Office of Care and Protection Master: F.B. Hall
Bankruptcy and Companies Office Master: C.W.G. Redpath
Chancery Office Master: R.A. Ellison
Probate and Matrimonial Office Master: Miss M.J. McReynolds
Taxing Office Master: J.C. Napier
Court Funds Office Accountant General: H.G. Thompson
Official Solicitor, Royal Courts of Justice vacant

RECORDERS

Belfast: His Honour Judge Hart QC
Derry: His Honour Judge Burgess

COUNTY COURT JUDGES

His Honour Judge Curran QC
His Honour Judge Gibson QC
His Honour Judge Petrie QC
His Honour Judge Smyth QC
His Honour Judge Markey QC
His Honour Judge McKay QC
His Honour Judge Brady QC
His Honour Judge Rodgers
His Honour Judge Foote QC
Her Honour Judge Philpott QC
His Honour Judge Lockie
His Honour Judge McFarland

CHIEF SOCIAL SECURITY COMMISSIONER

His Honour Judge Martin QC

DISTRICT JUDGES (by Division)

Belfast: District Judge Wells
Derry and Antrim: District Judge Keegan
Armagh & South Down and Fermanagh & Tyrone: District Judge Brownlie
Craigavon & Ards: District Judge Wheeler

Court Venues

THE SUPREME COURT OF JUDICATURE

Royal Courts of Justice, Chichester Street, Belfast BT1 3JF

CROWN COURTS

Court	Manager
Armagh	Mr. E. Strain
Ballymena	Mr. T. Long
Belfast	vacant
Craigavon	Mr. J. Halliday
Downpatrick	Mr. P. Kelly
Enniskillen	Mrs. M. Kilpatrick
Londonderry	Mr. G. Richardson
Newtownards	Mr. P. Kelly
Omagh	Mrs. M. Kilpatrick

MAGISTRATES' COURTS

Court	Clerk/Officer
Antrim	Mr. T. Long
Newtownards	Mr. P. Kelly
Armagh	Mr. E. Strain

Ballymena	Mr. T. Long	North Antrim	Mr T. Long
Banbridge	Mr. E. Strain	North Down	vacant
Belfast	Mr. B.W. Sinnamon	Omagh	Mrs. M. Kilpatrick
Castlereagh	Mr. P. Kelly	Strabane	Ms. J. Devine
Craigavon	Mr. J. Halliday		
Down	Mr. P. Kelly		
East Tyrone	Mrs. M. Kilpatrick		
Fermanagh	Mrs. A. Harland		
Larne			
Limavady			
Lisburn	Mr. J. Halliday		
Londonderry	Mr. G. Richardson		
Magherafelt			
Newry and Mourne	Mr. E. Strain		
Newtownabbey	Mr. B.W. Sinnamon		

COUNTY COURTS

Court	Manager
Antrim	Mr. T. Long
Ards	Mr. P. Kelly
Armagh and South Down	Mr. E. Strain
Belfast	vacant
Craigavon County Court	Mr. J. Halliday
Fermanagh and Tyrone	Mrs. M. Kilpatrick
Londonderry	Mr. G. Richardson

Policing

Royal Ulster Constabulary

Rank	Strength 1999
Chief Constable	1
Deputy Chief Constables	1
Assistant Chief Constables	8
Chief Superintendents	39
Superintendents	121
Chief Inspectors	168
Inspectors	489
Sergeants	1,398
Constables	6,271
Total	8,496

Sir Ronnie Flanagan, Chief Constable *(pictured)*.

RUC Full Time Reserve	2,862
RUC Part Time Reserve	1,217

An Garda Síochána

Rank	Strength 1998
Commissioner	1
Deputy Commissioners	2
Assistant Commissioners	10
Chief Superintendents	46
Superintendents	168
Inspectors	262
Sergeants	1,866
Gardaí	8,880
Total	11,235

Pat Byrne, Commissioner *(pictured)*.

Strength of An Garda Síochána

	1991	1992	1993	1994	1995	1996	1997	1998
Males	10,629	10,724	10,560	10,388	10,251	10,114	10,167	10,292
Females	334	298	372	446	546	607	690	832
TOTAL	10,963	11,022	10,932	10,834	10,797	10,721	10,857	11,124

Source An Garda Síochána

Strength of Royal Ulster Constabulary

	1991	1992	1993	1994	1995	1996	1997	1998
Males	7,510	7,688	7,646	7,640	7,528	7,526	7,562	7,523
Females	707	790	818	853	887	897	923	933
TOTAL	8,217	8,478	8,464	8,493	8,415	8,423	8,485	8,456

Source Royal Ulster Constabulary

● **Composition of the RUC by Religious Background**

	Regular		Full-time Reserve		Total	
	Actual	Percentage	Actual	Percentage	Actual	Percentage
Protestant	7,470	88.3%	2,568	87.5%	10,038	88.1%
Catholic	704	8.3%	202	6.9%	906	8.0%
Other	283	3.4%	154	5.6%	448	3.9%
TOTAL	**8,457**		**2,935**		**11,392**	

Souce Report of the Independent Commission on Policing for Northern Ireland.
Note: These figures are correct as of December 31, 1998.

Garda Síochána Regional Statistics, 1998

Description	Northern Region	Western Region	Eastern Region	Southern Region	South Eastern Region	Dublin Region
Population	314,551	443,352	614,854	718,842	452,109	1,082,469
Area (km²)	11,306	17,739	12,864	14,936	12,977	869
Primary/Secondary Roads (km)	745.2	1,328.2	1,117.6	1,152.7	906.5	153.5
Regional Crime	3,419	5,122	11,379	13,133	6,982	45,592
Crime per 1,000 Population	10.87	11.55	18.51	18.27	15.44	42.10
Road Traffic Offences	11,819	18,041	33,444	41,213	20,176	113,478
Garda Strength	1,078	1,061	1,321	1,699	921	3,842
Garda Vehicles	133	126	189	225	128	583
Garda Stations	108	144	126	162	117	44
Garda Districts	14	20	19	22	16	18

Regions - Western: Clare, Galway, Roscommon, Mayo; **Northern:** Sligo, Leitrim, Donegal, Cavan, Monaghan; **Southern:** Kerry, Limerick, Cork; **Eastern:** Louth, Meath, Longford, Westmeath, Laois, Offaly, Carlow, Kildare; **Dublin:** Dublin Area. **South Eastern:** Wexford, Tipperary, Waterford, Kilkenny.
Source An Garda Síochána

Crime

Crime Rate per Garda Division *(per 1,000 population)*

Garda Division	1992	1993	1994	1995	1996	1997
Dublin Metropolitan Area	49.9	53.6	-	56.3	56.4	48.5
Carlow / Kildare	15.4	16.5	16.9	17.2	19.1	20.7
Cavan / Monaghan	10.4	9.6	8.6	9.5	8.2	9.1
Cork City*	-	-	-	-	-	30.9
Cork East*	36.4	36.0	34.4	32.4	29.5	-
Cork North*	-	-	-	-	-	13.5
Cork West	11.2	9.5	9.7	9.7	9.1	9.7
Clare	7.9	7.9	8.8	11.8	11.5	12.1
Donegal	10.9	10.3	12.0	11.1	10.9	12.4
Galway West	19.8	21.8	19.8	19.3	17.6	15.7
Kerry	15.6	12.9	15.8	14.1	12.8	11.5
Laois / Offaly	10.7	11.4	14.3	13.3	11.9	13.0
Limerick	23.5	22.0	22.8	23.8	21.2	19.0
Longford / Westmeath	25.6	18.9	19.3	19.9	19.5	17.1
Louth / Meath	21.3	21.2	22.4	25.5	24.6	23.8
Mayo	7.5	7.4	7.6	8.0	8.1	8.5
Roscommon / Galway East	8.8	9.4	10.0	9.5	8.6	7.9
Sligo / Leitrim	10.2	11.2	11.9	10.0	11.5	12.7
Tipperary	16.4	14.5	13.7	12.8	11.2	11.8
Waterford / Kilkenny	14.0	15.8	17.6	17.3	17.8	20.1
Wexford	18.9	21.3	19.9	15.5	17.1	15.8

* In 1996, the division of Cork East was replaced with two new divisions Cork City and Cork North.

RoI Indictable Offences 1996-98

	1996 known	detected	1997 known	detected	1998 known	detected
Offences against the person (non sexual)	7,339	2,332	5,777	2,039	4,691	1,858
Murder	42	33	38	34	38	34
Manslaughter*	7	5	16	16	16	15
Attempted murder	7	5	1	1	5	5
Dangerous driving causing death	12	12	16	15	29	29
Assault wounding or similar offences*	554	436	591	472	691	571
Endangering railway passengers*	0	0	5	5	0	0
Cruelty to or neglect of children	2	2	0	0	0	0
Child stealing	0	0	1	1	1	1
False imprisonment	16	11	27	22	22	13
Abduction	0	0	4	0	9	3
Use of firearms to resist or escape	0	0	0	0	2	2

Continued from previous page

	1996 known	detected	1997 known	detected	1998 known	detected
Robbery including muggings*	6,547	1,788	4,990	1,442	3,817	1,158
Armed robbery	152	40	88	31	61	27
Sexual offences	**836**	**709**	**1015**	**871**	**992**	**861**
Sexual Assault lincluding aggravated assault	559	469	613	527	609	528
Rape of Females	180	147	256	214	292	244
Buggery	34	33	80	72	29	28
Unlawful carnal knowledge of girls under 17	34	33	42	36	30	29
Incest	11	11	10	10	18	18
Other sexual offences *	18	16	14	12	14	14
Larcenies	**47,943**	**18,473**	**42,533**	**16,969**	**41,022**	**17,313**
Larceny from person (pickpocketing)	3,648	633	3,652	775	3,202	742
Larceny by employee	28	23	16	11	25	20
Offences under Post Office Act	23	19	25	20	15	12
Larceny from vehicles, shops or stalls	25,199	11,750	20,639	10,328	20,065	10,679
Unauthorised takings of vehicles	16	15	17	16	20	19
Larceny of vehicles	1,780	103	2,450	103	1,500	97
Handling of stolen goods	1,665	1,665	1,443	1,442	1,311	1,311
*Other larcenies *	*15,584*	*4,265*	*13,909*	*4,006*	*14,542*	*4,214*
Frauds	**3,758**	**3,240**	**3,349**	**2,903**	**3,134**	**2,734**
Burglaries	**31,741**	**11,025**	**28,963**	**10,438**	**26,765**	**9,422**
Burglary including aggravated burglary	31,065	10,574	28,484	10,083	26,387	9,160
Aggravated Burglary with Firearm*	345	121	179	57	178	63
Possession of Articles with intent	331	330	300	298	200	199
Criminal damage	**8,747**	**4,877**	**8,724**	**5,222**	**8,533**	**5,315**
Arson	249	104	288	142	281	137
Possession of Explosives/making explosives	4	4	5	5	3	3
Causing or attempting to cause explosion	1	0	1	0	1	0
Hijackings	23	7	39	18	24	12
Other Criminal Damage	8,470	4,762	8,391	5,057	8,224	5,163
Other offences	**421**	**400**	**514**	**501**	**490**	**471**
Misuse of Controlled drugs	137	137	276	276	193	193
Extortion/Blackmail	11	10	7	5	6	6
Escape from Custody	10	9	9	9	8	8
Offences under Electoral Act	2	2	2	2	0	0
Threat or Conspiracy to Murder	0	0	0	0	5	5
Possession/Carrying firearms to endanger life	73	64	78	71	71	64
Concealment of Birth	0	0	2	2	1	1
Offences Against the State Act	1	1	1	1	1	1
Offences under Fishery Acts	25	25	37	37	19	19
Firearms, Offensive Weapons Act	47	47	47	46	31	31
Other Indictable Offences*	115	105	55	52	155	143
TOTAL	**100,785**	**41,056**	**90,875**	**38,943**	**85,627**	**37,974**

Source An Garda Síochána

Rol Non Indictable Offences

	1996		1997		1998	
	P	C	P	C	P	C
Assaults	7,811	4,607	8,191	4,381	8,802	5,109
Cruelty to Animals	268	160	143	97	248	173
Offences against Traffic Acts	268,572	122,404	263,207	107,426	238,171	118,766
Other Traffic Act Offences	122,910	53,051	112,613	48,317	98,467	47,856
Offences against Intoxicating Liquor Laws	12,642	8,516	16,110	10,213	15,690	9,890
Criminal Damage	2,393	1,594	3,276	2,172	2,757	1,820
Offences against Police Regulations	652	269	622	185	765	313
Criminal Law Sexual Offences Act, 1993	63	45	502	380	793	539
Criminal Justice (Public Order) Act, 1994	16,384	11,286	25,755	16,375	27,945	17,980
Offences against Revenue Laws	72	32	129	49	87	36

Continued from previous page

	1996		1997		1998	
	P	C	P	C	P	C
Offences against Street Trading Acts	640	192	710	247	741	319
Offences against Vagrancy Acts	242	123	526	394	579	326
Offences against Wireless Telegraphy Act, 1926	87	42	49	20	37	31
Offences against Firearms Acts	845	643	405	250	388	269
Firearms and Offensive Weapons Act, 1990	0	0	1,908	1,295	1,600	1,118
Offences in Relation to Explosives	5	0	5	1	13	6
Offences against Juries Act, 1976	169	122	284	148	390	208
Gaming and Lotteries Act, 1956	0	0	67	36	136	96
Prohibition of Incitement to Hatred Act, 1989	0	0	0	0	1	0
Other non-indictable offences	17,512	10,533	17,240	10,758	15,730	9,979
TOTAL:	**451,267**	**213,619**	**451,742**	**202,744**	**413,340**	**214,834**

P=Proceedings taken, C=Convictions *Source An Garda Síochána*

RoI Indictable Offences Recorded

Year	Crimes Recorded	Detected	Percentage
1988	89,544	29,685	33.15%
1989	86,792	28,781	33.16%
1990	87,658	28,985	33.07%
1991	94,406	31,653	33.53%
1992	95,391	32,400	33.97%
1993	98,979	35,430	35.80%
1994	101,036	39,108	38.71%
1995	102,484	39,754	38.79%
1996	100,785	41,056	40.74%
1997	90,875	38,943	42.85%
1998	85,627	37,972	44.35%

Source An Garda Síochána

NI Notifiable offences

Offence	Recorded 1997/98	Cleared 1997/98	Recorded 1998/99	Cleared 1998/99
Offences Against the Person	4,967	3,072	6,616	3,032
Sexual Offences	1,297	1,194	1,485	1,175
Burglary	13,724	2,414	15,480	2,650
Robbery	1,573	256	1,395	269
Theft	28,318	7,358	34,604	8,226
Fraud and Forgery	3,620	2,074	5,280	2,317
Criminal Damage	4,773	1,318	9,794	1,351
Offences Against the State	457	365	459	359
Other Notifiable Offences	1,193	1,123	1,531	1,332
Total	59,922	19,174	76,644	20,711

NI Notifiable Offences by Region

	Urban		Northern		Southern		Total	
	Recorded	Cleared	Recorded	Cleared	Recorded	Cleared	Recorded	Cleared
Offences Against Person	2,888	1,314	2,191	840	1,537	878	6,616	3,032
Sexual Offences	677	545	441	319	367	311	1,485	1,175
Burglary	7,741	1,402	4,202	640	3,537	608	15,480	2,650
Robbery	823	157	307	79	265	33	1,395	269
Theft	20,188	4,253	7,530	2,260	6,886	1,713	34,604	8,226
Fraud and Forgery	2,999	1,135	1,155	594	1,126	588	5,280	2,317
Criminal Damage	5,129	509	2,289	420	2,376	422	9,794	1,351
Offences Against the State	241	182	105	89	113	88	459	359
Other Notifiable Offences	809	700	472	398	250	234	1,531	1,332
Total	41,495	10,197	18,692	5,639	16,457	4,875	76,644	20,711

Urban Region: Belfast and environs; **Northern Region:** Counties Antrim, Derry, Fermanagh and West Tyrone; **Southern Region:** Counties Armagh, Down and East Tyrone. *Source RUC*

NI Security Situation Statistics

Description	1995/96	1996/97	1997/98	1998/99
Deaths				
RUC	-	-	3	1
Army	-	2	1	1
Civilian	12	12	29	42
Total	12	14	33	44
Injuries				
Punishment Shootings	6	41	73	73
Assaults	246	291	125	172
Total	252	332	198	245
Incidents				
Shootings	65	140	245	187
Bombings	-	50	73	123
Incendiaries	7	7	6	20
Firearms Found	116	103	97	104
Explosives Found (kg)	6.4	2,462.5	661.7	778.4
Persons Charged	476	591	423	441

Source RUC

RoI Firearms, Explosives and Ammuniton Seized

	1996	1997	1998
Firearms			
Rifles/Machine Guns	72	60	153
Hand Guns	91	113	96
Shotguns	153	165	265
Others	380	300	479
Ammunition			
Shotgun Cartridges	2,057	2,340	5,242
Other Ammunition (rounds)	12,199	7,070	15,928
Explosives			
Semtex (kg)	46.7	30.1	0.6
Home made explosives (kg)	139.0	-	3,340
Other explosives (kg)	28.5	6.6	3.6
Other			
Detonators	366	59	117
Timers/Power Units	22	760	16
Mortars and related units	704	24	21
Incendiary Devices	2	15	63
Grenades	23	10	9
Bunkers/Hides	18	10	20
Training Camps/Firing Ranges	1	1	2

Source An Garda Síochána

Parades NI

Parade Statistics, 1998

	Legal	Illegal	Re-routed	Other Conditions	Disorder	Total
Loyalist	2,584	75	59	9	18	2,745
Republican	216	13	-	1	4	234
Other	542	-	-	-	-	542
TOTAL:	3,342	88	59	10	22	3,521

Banned, Restricted and Illegal Parades, 1985-98

Year	Total	Banned	Illegal	Re-routed	Conditions Imposed	Disorder
1985	2,120	3	-	22	-	-

Continued from previous page

Year	Total	Banned	Illegal	Re-routed	Conditions Imposed	Disorder
1986	1,950	1	-	9	-	-
1987	2,109	-	96	11	-	18
1988	2,055	-	8	11	-	21
1989	2,317	-	2	14	-	5
1990	2,713	-	1	10	-	1
1991	2,379	-	4	14	1	1
1992	2,744	-	-	16	16	-
1993	2,662	-	-	12	12	1
1994	2,792	-	-	29	29	-
1995	3,500	-	24	20	20	9
1996	3,162	-	19	25	7	15
1997	3,363	-	8	11	20	6
1998	3,521	-	88	59	10	22

Source RUC

Prisons

Rol Prison Statistics

	1992	1993	1994	1995	1996	1997	1998
Average Daily Population:							
Male Adult	1,955	1,943	1,939	-	-	-	-
Male Juvenile	191	184	164	-	-	-	-
Female	39	44	38	-	-	-	-
TOTAL:	2,185	2,171	2,123	2,109	2,197	2,424	2,567e
Committal Trends:							
Remand	5,078	5,255	4,664	-	-	-	-
Trial	324	845	328	-	-	-	-
Sentenced	4,297	4,357	5,161	-	-	-	-
TOTAL:	9,699	10,457	10,153	9,844e	10,598e	11,620e	11,648e
Number of Prison Officers Employed	-	2,255	2,413	2,440	2,446	2,524	2,775
Average annual Cost per prison place (£)	-	39,475	43,735	44,600	46,140	45,813	53,400

As of June 30 1999 there were 3,313 persons serving a prison sentence of which 138 were female.

e = estimated. *Source Department of Justice*

Rol Deaths in Prisons

Year	Natural Causes	Suicide	Overdose	Total
1990	0	3	1	4
1991	0	4	1	5
1992	1	3	1	5
1993	0	1	2	3
1994	0	3	2	5
1995	0	1	2	3
1996	3	5	1	9
1997	3	3	1	7
TOTAL	7	23	11	41

	● Age Profile				
Year	<21	21-30	31-50	51>	Total
1990	2	1	1	0	4
1991	0	2	3	0	5
1992	2	1	2	0	5
1993	1	1	1	0	3
1994	1	1	3	0	5
1995	0	2	1	0	3
1996	3	3	2	1	9
1997	1	3	1	2	7
TOTAL	10	14	14	3	41

Source *Report of National Steering Group on Deaths in Prisons*

Prisons in the Rol

Institution	Governor	Capacity
Mountjoy	John Lonergan	607
Wheatfield	John O'Sullivan	320
Portlaoise	William Donohoe	205
Castlerea	Daniel Scannell	183
St Patrick's	John Brophy	165
Cork	Frank McCarthy	150

Continued from previous page

Institution	Governor	Capacity
Limerick	Patrick Laffan	145
Arbour Hill	Patrick Dunne	138
Fort Mitchel	Finbarr O'Leary	102
Training Unit	John O'Hara	96
Loughan House	John O'Brien	85
Curragh	Patrick Powell	68
Shanganagh Castle	John Quigley	60
Shelton Abbey	Martin Corrigan	58
Total Prison Places		**2,382**

NI Prison Population

Description of Prisoners	1993	1994	1995	1996	1997	1998
On Remand						
Male	418	427	312	318	333	340
Female	8	12	5	8	9	9
Subtotal	426	439	317	326	342	394
Fine Defaulters						
Male	30	27	28	24	24	29
Female	2	3	1	0	1	2
Subtotal	32	30	29	24	25	31
Immediate Custody						
Male	1,445	1,403	1,382	1,257	1,234	999
Female	30	26	29	21	20	13
Total	1,475	1,429	1,411	1,278	1,254	1012
Non-Criminal						
Male	1	1	5	11	12	9
Female	0	0	0	0	0	1
Subtotal	1	1	5	11	12	10
TOTAL	1,934	1,899	1,762	1,639	1,633	1,402

Source Northern Ireland Prison Service

Military

RoI Defence Staff

Rank	Name	Located
President (Commander in Chief)	Mary McAleese	Phoenix Park
Minister for Defence	Michael Smith, TD	Defence HQ, Dublin
Minister of State for Defence	Seamus Brennan, TD	Government Buildings

Rank	Name	Stationed
Chief of Staff	Lt. Gen. Dave Stapleton *(on left)*	Defence HQ, Dublin
Deputy Chief of Staff (Operations)	Maj. Gen. Bill Dwyer	Defence HQ, Dublin
Deputy Chief of Staff (Support)	Maj. Gen. Colm Mangan	Defence HQ, Dublin
GOC 2nd Eastern Brigade	Brig. Gen. E. Heskin	Cathal Brugha Barracks, Dublin
GOC 4th Western Brigade	Brig. Gen. John Martin	Custume Barracks, Athlone
GOC 1st Southern Brigade	Brig. Gen. Dave Taylor	Collins Barracks., Cork
Commandant Military College	Col. D. Travers	Curragh Camp, Kildare
Flag Officer Commanding Naval Service	Commodore John Kavanagh	Naval Base, Cork
GOC Air Corps/Director Military Aviation	Brig. Gen. Pat Cranfield	Baldonnel, Co. Dublin

RoI Defence Headquarters

Address	Telephone
Defence Forces Headquarters - Parkgate, Dublin 8	(01) 804 2000
2nd Eastern Brigade - Cathal Brugha Barracks, Rathmines, Dublin 6.	(01) 804 6000
1st Southern Brigade - Collins Barracks, Cork.	(021) 514000
4th Western Brigade - Custume Barracks, Athlone, Co. Westmeath	(0902) 21000
Air Corps - Casement Aerodrome, Baldonnel, Dublin 22	(01) 8046689
Naval Service - Haulbowline, Cobh, Co. Cork.	(021) 864700

NI Defence Staff

Position	Name
General Officer Commanding Northern Ireland	Lieutenant General Sir Hew Pike
Chief of Staff, Headquarters Northern Ireland	Brigadier J.M.J. Balfour
Commander, 3rd Infantry Brigade	Brigadier Roger Brunt
Commander, 8th Infantry Brigade	Brigadier P.E.O'R.-B Davidson-houston
Commander 39th Infantry Brigade	Brigadier J.N.R. Houghton (from December 1999 Brigadier W.E.B. Loudon)

NI Defence Headquarters

The Army
Army Headquarters - Thiepval Barracks, Lisburn, Co. Antrim BT28 3SE ....(028) 926 665111
3rd Infantry Brigade - Mahon Barracks, Portadown, Co. Armagh ....(028) 383 351551
8th Infantry Brigade - Ebrington Barracks, Derry BT47 1JU ....(028) 714 3211
39th Infantry Brigade - Thiepval Barracks, Lisburn, Co. Antrim BT28 3SE ....(028) 926 665111
Other Army Locations
Palace Barracks, Holywood, Co. Down ....(028) 904 25121
Abercorn Barracks, Ballykinler, Co. Down ....(028) 446 13111
Lisanelly Barracks, Omagh, Co. Tyrone ....(028) 822 43194
Shackleton Barracks, Ballykelly, Co. Derry ....(028) 717 63221
Territorial Army
St. Patrick's Barracks, Ballymena, Co. Antrim BT43 7BH ....(028) 256 61298
Royal Navy
Palace Barracks, Holywood, Co. Down BT18 9RQ ....(028) 904 27040
Royal Air Force
Aldergrove, Co. Antrim ....(028) 944 22051

RoI Defence Personnel

Year	Permanent Defence Force	Reserve Defence Force	Total
1960	8,965	24,569	33,534
1965	8,199	21,946	30,145
1970	8,574	20,253	28,827
1975	12,059	17,221	29,280
1980	13,383	19,249	32,632
1985	13,778	16,358	30,136
1990	13,233	15,982	29,215
1995	12,742	16,188	28,930
1996	12,107	15,795	27,902
1997	12,006	15,515	27,521
1998	11,463	15,710	27,173
1999	11,255	15,297	26,552

RoI Defence Force Officers By Rank and Gender 1999

Rank	Army		Air Corps		Naval Service		Total
	M	F	M	F	M	F	
Lieutenant-General	1						1
Major-General	2						2
Brigadier-General	5		1		1		7
Colonel	33		2		2		37
Lieutenant-Colonel	113		8		10		131
Commandant	360	5	32		40		437
Captain	372	13	43	2	32		462
Lieutenant	81	10	14	1	27		133
2nd Lieutenant	62		15	1	4	3	85
Sergeants-Major (or equivalent)	29		5		7		41
Battalion Quartermaster Sergeant (or equivalent)	38		4		5		47
Company Sergeant (or equivalent)	134	1	37		58		230
Company Quartermaster Sergeant (or equivalent)	265	1	12		13		291
TOTAL	1,495	30	173	4	199	3	1,904

Rol Defence Forces Overseas Strengths (as of August 6, 1999)

Mission	Location	Brig Gen	Col	Lt Col	Comdt	Capt	Lt	CF	NCO	Pte	Total
● United Nations Troop Missions											
UNIFIL 85th Bn	Lebanon	-	-	1	11	18	11	2	171	315	529
UNIFIL HQ	Lebanon	1	1	4	9	7	-	-	47	8	77
UNFICYP HQ	Cyprus	-	-	1	-	2	-	-	13	-	16
Total		1	1	6	20	27	11	2	231	323	622
● United Nations Observer Missions											
UNNY	United States	-	-	1	-	-	-	-	-	-	1
UNSCOM	Iraq	-	-	-	1	-	-	-	-	-	1
UNSMA		-	1	-	-	-	-	-	-	-	1
UNTSO	Middle East	-	-	1	4	6	-	-	-	-	11
UNIKOM	Iraq & Kuwait	-	-	1	2	2	-	-	-	-	5
UNMOP	Croatia	-	-	-	1	-	-	-	-	-	1
MINURSO	Western Sahara	-	-	1	4	2	-	-	-	-	7
UNAMET	East Timor	-	-	1	2	-	-	-	-	-	3
UNMIK	Kosovo	1	-	1	2	-	-	-	2	-	5
Total		1	1	6	16	10	0	0	2	0	36
● European and International Missions											
SFOR	Bosnia	-	-	1	2	1	-	-	40	3	47
DFA		-	4	-	-	-	-	-	-	-	4
OSCE	Various	-	1	5	7	7	-	-	-	-	20
ECCM	Yugoslavia	-	1	3	6	2	-	-	1	-	13
GOAL	Africa	-	-	-	-	-	-	-	4	-	4
Total			6	9	15	10	0	0	45	3	88
● OVERALL TOTAL		2	8	21	51	47	11	2	278	326	7460

Northern Ireland: Defence Personnel, 1999

Force	Number
Royal Air Force	1,200
Royal Navy	250
Royal Irish Regiment (RIR)	4,350
RIR (Full-time)	2,500
RIR (Part-time)	1,850
Others	11,150
TOTAL	**16,950**

Rol Air Corps

Fixed Wing Aircraft	Role	Number	Speed (knots)	End. (Hours)	Capacity (Persons)
Marchetti SF260[1]	Pilot Training, Ground Attack	8	170	2.45	3
Fouga Magister CM 170[2]	Advanced Pilot Training, Ground Attack	6	365	1.5	2
Beechcraft SKA 200[3]	Transport, Air Ambulance, Pilot Training	1	270	5.5	12
*Cessna 172[4]	Parachuting, Drogue Towing, VIP Flights	7	120	4.5	6
Casa CN235[5]	Maritime Patrols, Parachuting, General Transport	2	210	8	45
Gulfstream IV[6]	Ministerial Air Transport Service	1	475	8	14

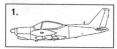
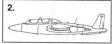
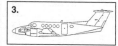
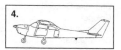
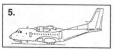

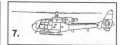

Rotorary Aircraft	Role	Number	Speed (knots)	End. (Hours)	Capacity (Persons)
Gazelle[7]	Pilot Training, VIP Flights, Instrument Training	2	135	2.66	5
*Alouette III[8]	Search & Rescue, Air Ambulance	8	95	2.5	7
Dauphin[9]	Search & Resuce, Air Ambulance, Naval Co-op	5	135	3	10

Continued from previous page

End. = Endurance
* Role includes use in co-operation with Army and Gardai.

Rol Naval Service

Ship	Type	Acquired	Range (N. Miles)	Speed (Knots)	Displacement (Tonnes)	Complement
LE Eithne	Helicopter Patrol Vessel	1984	7,000	19	1,970	9 Officers, 77 Other ranks
LE Deirdre	Offshore Patrol Vessel	1972	7,500	18	972	6 Officers, 41 Other ranks
LE Emer	Offshore Patrol Vessel	1978	7,500	18	972	6 Officers, 41 Other ranks
LE Aoife	Offshore Patrol Vessel	1979	7,500	18	1,020	6 Officers, 41 Other ranks
LE Aisling	Offshore Patrol Vessel	1980	7,500	18	1,020	6 Officers, 41 Other ranks
LE Orla	Coastal Patrol Vessel	1988	2,500	26	712	5 Officers, 34 Other ranks
LE Ciara	Coastal Patrol Vessel	1988	2,500	26	712	5 Officers, 34 Other ranks

Headquarters Defence HQ, Dublin 8. *Main Base* Haubowline, Co. Cork.

● NAVAL SERVICE MARINE ACTIVITY 1997-98

	1997	1998
Sightings	2,136	2,247
Boardings	1,052	1,409
Warnings	98	123
Detentions	49	27

● AIR CORPS MARINE ACTIVITY 1997-98

	1997	1998
Patrol Hours	1,778	1,336
Sightings	6,787	5,620

Source Department of the Marine

Constitution of Ireland
Bunreacht na hÉireann

The Constitution of Ireland was approved by referendum on July 1, 1937, the Dáil having already approved it on June 14, 1937. It came into effect on December 29, 1937, replacing the Constitution of the Irish Free State (1922). The then Taoiseach, Éamon de Valera, played a large part in the drafting of the document which made the Free State a Republic in all but name.

Under the Constitution, the name of the state became Éire (Article 4), and it defined the national territory as "the whole island of Ireland, its islands and the territorial seas" (Article 2). It also stated that laws passed by the Dáil would have effect in the 26 counties only "pending re-integration of the national territory".

Under the heading of the State, the Constitution provided for the name and description of the State, stating Ireland to be a "sovereign, independent democratic state" (Article 5). The powers of government, the national flag, the position of Irish as the national language and the recognition of English as the second official language, citizenship and natural resources are also dealt with under the heading of the State.

The office and function of the President are enshrined in Articles 12 and 13, while the composition, regulation and functions of the Oireachtas (the National Parliament) and both houses therein, the Dáil and the Seanad (the houses of representatives and senate, respectively), are dealt with in Articles 15 to 19.

Articles 20 to 27 deal with the introduction, debate of and passing of legislation. Government, which according to Article 6 derives all legislative, executive and judicial powers from the people, is considered by Article 28, with reference to the exercising of that power, its responsibility to the Dáil, its powers during war or national emergency and the nomination and composition of the cabinet. Foreign Affairs and International Relations, as conducted by the Government, are provided for under Article 29 such as membership of the European Union.

Articles 34 to 39 deal with the Structure Organisation and Powers of the Courts; Articles 30 to 33 being concerned with the establishment of the Offices of the Attorney General, Comptroller and Auditor General and the creation of a Council of State to advise the President.

Articles 40 to 44 are concerned with the fundamental rights of the Citizen under the broad headings of Personal Rights (Article 40); The Family and Education (Articles 41 to 42); Private Property (Article 43); Religion (Article 44). Other unenumerated Rights have been granted by the Courts. Under these Articles, all Citizens are equal before the law and the law undertakes to protect the personal rights of all Citizens. Freedom of expression, assembly and association are guaranteed, subject to Public Order and Morality. The family is recognised as the fundamental unit of society and provision is made for mothers "not obliged by economic necessity to engage in labour to the neglect of their duties in the home" (Article 40.2.2). The institution of marriage was protected by the prohibiting of its dissolution, but with the introduction of the Family

Law (Divorce) Act in 1997, this no longer the case.

The State will endeavour to educate its citizens but recognises and respects that the family is the "primary and natural educator of the Child" (Article 42.1). The right to own private property is guaranteed, as is the Freedom of Religious Conscience and Practice, and the State will not discriminate on grounds of Religious Belief (Article 44.2.3).

Article 45 contains the principles of social policy under which the state operates. Articles 46 and 47 deal with amendments to the Constitution which can only be done by referendum. Articles 48 to 63 deal with the Repeal of the 1922 Irish Free State Constitution and the transitory powers necessary until the new Constitution comes into effect.

Articles Two and Three will be changed when the Good Friday Agreement is implemented.

RELIGION

The Faith That Dare Not Speak its Name

By Michael Paul Gallagher, S.J.

J ust before Easter 1997, I met a young writer who had been a student of mine in UCD's English department some 10 years ago. Perhaps because it was Holy Thursday we found ourselves talking about faith.

Mark (let's call him) has not lost his roots in Catholicism and indeed has deepened his sense of faith over the years. Since I had been living outside Ireland for six years, I asked him how his contemporaries now view religious faith. After all, this has been a period of explosive change for the church here, for its image and its reality.

But I did not realise how much the new culture seems to put religion "off limits" for his generation - in their late 20s or early 30s. "I mentioned to someone," said Mark, "that I was off drink for Lent and her first reaction was shock that I would use such a religious word in polite society. But then it emerged that she too was secretly a believer!"

"Believing is a lonely language in my generation," he added. "It's a bit like Irish. Unless you go to a special club, you don't expect to find others who speak it fluently. Or perhaps being religious is like being gay: it's not something you admit to everyone straight off. Faith has certainly gone shy and yet it's there more often than you think. Scepticism may be the required mask, but it's not the whole picture."

In its way Mark's story echoes some of the lively US debates of recent years on cultural issues. In 1993 Stanley Carter published his bestseller *The Culture of Disbelief*, with the subtitle, *How American Law and Politics Trivialize Religious Devotion*. This expert on constitutional law diagnosed that religion is being made impotent in the public sphere and that faith is reduced to the level of a hobby by the dominant culture.

The message is that "it's perfectly all right to believe that stuff" provided you keep it to yourself. Religion, in short, is not "a fit activity for intelligent, public-spirited adults". So-called "culture wars" can break out when people resist this "liberal" reduction of religion, and these wars reveal major differences over philosophies of life.

For Mr Carter and others "culture" has become not only a fashionable buzz-word, but a key concept for understanding the environment that shapes our attitudes and practices. Culture with a capital "C", meaning the worlds of creativity or mind, has widened to culture with a small "c" - in the sense of invisible assumptions and the more everyday.

In Ireland religion has been a powerful strand in both dimensions of culture. Judged more negatively, the church had a domineering role in the culture of pre-modern Ireland (up to the 1960s) and is now accused of trying to preserve its power in the modern or perhaps postmodern present. But something more subtle may also be happening.

Mark would suggest that current forms of domineering come from another direction and that a certain silencing of religious expressions is caused by the dominant culture around him. The question becomes whether the new cultural mood induces an unhealthy shyness towards faith - even among those who "have" faith.

When distrust of churches hardens into prejudice, it is difficult for theology to be accepted as a real partner in debates about our emerging self-images. The whole religious horizon can be regarded with suspicion, rather like the speech of a tough school principal at a past pupils' reunion. The pupils are long out of school but their memories leave them sceptical of any wisdom he or she might offer.

Thus old agendas make listening impossible. Immature levels of communication reinforce mutual distance between religious and secular positions. Cultural skirmishing rules the day and can remain unrecognised. As Mary Douglas remarks in her book, *Thought Styles,* cultural bias colours thought. Where prejudice holds sway, we remain unfree for dialogue. To reach a decent level of exchange is never easy but it is one of the urgent needs of Ireland just now - for both South and North - to heal different wounds and to overcome different forms of non-listening.

An example from Italy may help. It is not infrequent for a church leader, like Cardinal Martini or Cardinal Ruini, to engage in written face-to-face dialogue with some distinguished representative of "secular culture" such as the writer Umberto Eco or Massimo Cacciari, the philosopher-mayor of Venice. The level of the exchanges is impressively high - intellectually, in terms of mutual courtesy and in wanting to do justice to the vision of the other person.

The goal is to explore various key issues affecting our humanity today, and the themes chosen have ranged from spirituality and art to suffering and social solidarity. Of course divergences emerge but the very attempt to have such conversations in public is evidence of a willingness to search for new understanding together.

Beyond sniping or silencing, beyond point-scoring or skirmishing, we too need honest and discerning dialogue about where our culture has come from and where it is going. And one does not need cardinals to get something under way.

Michael Paul Gallagher
October 1999

The author is a Jesuit priest and apostolate writer who lectures in theology in Rome's Gregorian University for part of the academic year. He is also author of **Clashing Symbols: an introduction to faith and culture.** *This article first appeared in* **The Irish Times.**

Overview

According to the most recent census figures dealing with religious affiliation on the island of Ireland (1991 was the last Census conducted in NI, and the 1991 Census in the Republic was the last to pose questions on religious adherence) approximately 90% of the population of the island (5.1 million people) identified themselves as Christian. Of this figure 75% (3,833,966) belong to the Roman Catholic church, 7.2% (368,467) belong to the Church of Ireland, 6.8% (350,090) belong to the Presbyterian Church, 1.2% (64,554) belong to the Methodist Church and 3.1% (161,191) belong to other denominations.

Members of the Jewish faith in Ireland now account for less than 0.03% of the population (1,400), while 161,191 persons are classified as 'Other' according to the census - denoting minor religions. 6.3% (323,706) inhabitants of the island chose either not to state their religion or to declare themselves non-religious.

RoI & NI: Membership of Religious Denominations

● REPUBLIC OF IRELAND[1]

Year	RC	COI	Presb.	Meth.	Jewish	Other	No Religion	Not Stated
1881	3,465,332	317,576	56,498	17,660	394	-	12,560	-
1891	3,099,003	286,804	51,469	18,513	1,506	-	11,399	-
1901	2,878,271	264,264	46,714	17,872	3,006	-	11,696	-
1911	2,812,509	249,535	45,486	16,440	3,805	-	11,913	-
1926	2,751,269	164,215	32,429	10,663	3,686	-	9,730	-
1936	2,773,920	145,030	28,067	9,649	3,749	-	8,005	-
1946	2,786,033	124,829	23,870	8,355	3,907	-	8,113	-
1961	2,673,473	104,016	18,953	6,676	3,255	5,236	1,107	5,625
1971	2,795,666	97,739	16,052	5,646	2,633	6,248	7,616	46,648
1981	3,204,476	95,366	14,255	5,790	2,127	10,843	39,572	70,976
1991	3,228,327	82,840	13,199	5,037	1,581	45,090	66,270	83,375

● NORTHERN IRELAND

Year	RC	Presb.	COI	Meth.	Breth.	Baptist	Cong.	Unitn.	Other	None	Not Stated
1961	497,547	413,113	344,800	71,865	16,847	13,765	9,838	5,613	23,236	-	28,418
1971	477,919	405,719	334,318	71,235	16,480	16,563	10,072	3,975	40,848	-	142,511
1981	414,532	339,818	281,472	58,731	12,158	16,375	8,265	3,373	72,651	-	274,584
1991	605,639	336,891	279,280	59,517	12,446	19,484	8,176	3,213	79,129	59,234	114,827

1 In 1996, for the first time, the RoI Census did not pose any questions on religious adherence.

RoI: Religious Denomination by Province and County

Province & County	Total Persons	RC	COI	Prot.	Presb.	Meth.	Jewish	Other	No Religion	Not Stated
TOTAL:	3,525,719	3,228,327	82,840	6,347	13,199	5,037	1,581	38,743	66,270	83,375
Connacht:	423,031	397,848	5,321	516	333	286	21	3,208	5,392	10,106
Galway	180,364	168,640	1,358	228	81	76	16	1,772	3,191	5,002
Leitrim	25,301	23,682	721	41	17	61	-	80	217	482
Mayo	110,713	105,839	817	116	101	27	2	601	929	2,281
Roscommon	51,897	50,204	358	28	13	21	2	221	333	717
Sligo	54,756	49,483	2,067	103	121	101	1	534	722	1,624
Leinster:	1,860,949	1,685,334	50,912	3,391	3,799	2,815	1,439	24,829	43,843	44,587
Carlow	40,942	37,767	1,747	42	15	25	5	262	343	736
Dublin	1,025,304	911,454	26,169	2,157	2,716	1,895	1,383	17,571	33,269	28,690
Kildare	122,656	113,828	2,923	147	153	102	9	1,212	1,859	2,423
Kilkenny	73,635	68,699	1,586	74	143	56	2	559	822	1,694
Laois	52,314	48,461	2,417	41	38	94	1	312	256	694
Longford	30,296	28,645	705	24	46	37	-	161	163	515
Louth	90,724	85,770	939	49	137	20	5	907	974	1,923
Meath	105,370	98,766	1,926	133	142	42	2	797	1,236	2,326
Offaly	58,494	55,172	1,604	52	39	142	1	279	323	882

Continued from previous page

Province & County	Total Persons	RC	COI	Prot.	Presb.	Meth.	Jewish	Other	No Religion	Not Stated
Westmeath	61,880	58,508	1,059	80	32	38	-	401	528	1,234
Wexford	102,069	94,832	3,287	169	81	77	8	554	1,052	2,009
Wicklow	97,265	83,432	6,550	423	257	287	23	1,814	3,018	1,461
Munster:	1,009,533	941,675	15,758	1,385	548	1,185	111	9,192	15,402	24,277
Clare	90,918	84,847	699	72	55	43	12	861	1,778	2,551
Cork	410,369	379,011	8,864	792	240	690	57	4,291	7,567	8,857
Kerry	121,894	114,253	1,415	173	46	34	17	920	1,696	3,340
Limerick	161,956	152,364	1,409	158	86	210	15	1,365	2,084	4,265
Tipperary	132,772	125,607	2,132	101	52	147	1	885	1,074	2,773
Waterford	91,624	85,593	1,239	89	69	61	9	870	1,203	2,491
Ulster: (part of)	232,206	203,470	10,849	1,055	8,519	751	10	1,514	1,633	4,405
Cavan	52,796	46,703	3,622	160	710	94	1	240	291	975
Donegal	128,117	111,427	5,602	555	5,412	603	8	866	1,029	2,615
Monaghan	51,293	45,340	1,625	340	2,397	54	1	408	313	815

NI: Religious Denomination by District Council Area

Council Area	Total Persons	RC	Presb.	COI	Meth.	Other	None	Not Stated
TOTAL:	1,577,836	605,639	336,891	279,280	59,517	122,448	59,234	114,827
Antrim	44,516	14,117	13,614	6,384	786	3,600	2,025	3,990
Ards	64,764	7,341	25,219	12,137	3,386	7,069	3,904	5,708
Armagh	51,817	23,518	8,627	10,604	1,236	3,964	825	3,043
Ballymena	56,641	10,392	26,067	6,869	1,442	6,115	1,845	3,911
Ballymoney	24,198	7,311	9,411	3,151	123	2,184	524	1,494
Banbridge	33,482	9,256	9,608	6,362	624	3,977	929	2,726
Belfast	279,237	108,954	47,743	50,242	14,667	20,113	14,756	22,762
Carrickfergus	32,750	2,269	10,166	7,698	3,162	4,390	2,476	2,589
Castlereagh	60,799	5,743	17,445	14,638	5,323	8,481	3,797	5,372
Coleraine	50,438	11,323	15,946	12,550	784	4,214	2,104	3,517
Cookstown	31,082	16,522	4,779	5,288	331	2,131	382	1,649
Craigavon	74,986	30,060	7,718	18,666	3,904	7,190	1,955	5,493
Derry	95,371	66,260	10,539	8,503	853	2,629	1,353	5,234
Down	58,008	32,507	9,025	6,183	559	3,454	1,658	4,622
Dungannon	45,428	25,299	5,822	8,245	912	2,416	384	2,350
Fermanagh	54,033	29,657	1,549	14,283	2,724	2,534	745	2,541
Larne	29,419	6,510	11,136	4,083	1,107	2,771	1,291	2,521
Limavady	29,567	15,281	5,683	4,699	203	1,035	512	2,154
Lisburn	99,458	26,786	20,980	26,286	4,095	9,154	4,780	7,377
Magherafelt	36,293	21,377	5,466	4,372	165	2,632	313	1,968
Moyle	14,789	7,723	2,766	2,587	29	452	254	978
Newry & Mourne	82,943	59,555	8,890	3,861	314	3,376	947	6,000
Newtownabbey	74,035	9,635	23,610	14,976	6,437	8,125	4,476	6,776
North Down	71,832	6,435	23,658	16,591	5,077	7,500	6,140	6,431
Omagh	45,809	29,469	5,141	5,766	785	1,910	570	2,168
Strabane	36,141	22,339	6,283	4,256	489	1,032	289	1,453

Main Christian Churches

The Catholic Church

● **COMMUNICATIONS**
Catholic Press and Information Office
169 Booterstown Avenue, Blackrock, Co. Dublin.
Tel 01-288 5043 *email* cathinfo@cpio.ie

● **ORGANISATION**
The Roman Catholic Church is the largest religious denomination on the island of Ireland, accounting for 75% of the total population. The island is divided into four arch-dioceses: Armagh, Cashel, Dublin and Tuam. The arch-dioceses do not share the civil borders of the corresponding Irish provinces – several of the dioceses have parishes in both the Republic of Ireland and Northern Ireland. The church's ecclesiastical capital is Armagh, in which the Catholic church leader of the island of Ireland - the Primate of All-Ireland - resides. The Catholic church has a huge involvement in education, North and South, providing some 4,412 primary and secondary schools which educate around 650,857 pupils.

● **MAIN FACTFILE**
Primate of All-Ireland ....Most Rev Sean Brady
Members of Catholic Church ....3,989,560[1]
Number of Dioceses...26
Number of Parishes 1,329
Number of Churches...2,646
Number of Archbishops...4
Number of Bishops...31
Number of Priests (active in Diocese) 3,051
Number of members of Religious Orders 12,603
Number of newly ordained priests (1997)................53
Number of Irish Missionaries (1994)....................5,571
Number of Catholic Primary Schools...................3,573
Number of Catholic Secondary Schools 839

1 Current figure released by the Catholic Press Office

Diocese of Armagh
Archbishop:
HE Most Rev. Sean Brady
(Primate of All-Ireland); *(on left)*
Ordained Priest 1964;
installed Archbishop 1996.

Auxiliary: Most Rev. Gerard Clifford (titular Bishop of Geron); *ordained Priest* 1967;
ordained Bishop 1991.
Priests 158; Parishes 62; RC Population 204,500; Churches 146.
Bishops:
Meath: Most Rev. Michael Smith
ordained Priest 1963; *ordained Bishop* 1984.
Priests 127; Parishes 69; RC Population 194,000; Churches 149.
Ardagh and Clonmacnois: Most Rev Colm O'Reilly

ordained Priest 1960; *ordained Bishop* 1983.
Priests 74; Parishes 41; RC Population 71,806; Churches 80.
Clogher: Most Rev. Joseph Duffy
ordained Priest 1958; *ordained Bishop* 1979.
Priests 89; Parishes 37; RC Population 85,022; Churches 86.
Derry: Most Rev. Seamus Hegarty
ordained Priest 1966; *ordained Bishop* (Raphoe) 1982; *installed Bishop* (of Derry) 1994.
Auxiliary, Most Rev. Francis Lagan (titular Bishop of Sidnacestre); *ordained Priest* 1960; *ordained Bishop* 1988.
Priests 135; Parishes 53; RC Population 213,525; Churches 104.
Down and Connor: Most Rev. Patrick Walsh
ordained Priest 1956; *ordained Bishop* 1983.
Auxiliaries, Most Rev. Michael Dallat
(titular Bishop of Thala); *ordained Priest* 1951; *ordained Bishop* 1994.
Most Rev. Anthony Farquhar
(titular Bishop of Ermiana), *ordained Priest* 1965; *ordained Bishop* 1983.
Priests 219; Parishes 88; RC Population 304,436; Churches 152.
Dromore *(Down):* Most Rev. Francis Gerard Brooks
ordained Priest 1949; *ordained Bishop* 1976.
Priests 56; Parishes 23; RC Population 63,200; Churches 48.
Kilmore *(Cavan):* Most Rev. Leo O'Reilly
ordained Priest 1969; *ordained Bishop* 1997; *installed Bishop* 1998
Priests 91; Parishes 36; RC Population 55,465; Churches 97.
Raphoe *(Donegal):* Most Rev. Philip Boyce
ordained Priest 1966; *ordained Bishop* 1995.
Priests 74; Parishes 31; RC Population 82,260; Churches 71.

Diocese of Cashel
Archbishop:
Most Rev. Dermot Clifford
ordained Priest 1964; *ordained Bishop* 1986; *installed Archbishop* 1988.
Priests 116; Parishes 46; RC Population 78,244; Churches 84.
Bishops:
Cloyne *(Cork):* Most Rev. John Magee
ordained Priest 1962; *ordained Bishop* 1987.
Priests 129; Parishes 46, RC Population 121,000; Churches 108.
Cork and Ross: Most Rev John Buckley
(titular Bishop of Leptis Magna)
ordained Priest 1965; *ordained Bishop* 1984; *installed* 1998.
Priests 134; Parishes 68; RC Population 215,500; Churches 124.
Kerry: Most Rev. William Murphy
ordained Priest 1961; *ordained Bishop* 1995.
Priests 109; Parishes 54; RC Population 125,000; Churches 105.
Killaloe *(Clare):* Most Rev. William Walsh

ordained Priest 1959; ordained Bishop 1994.
Priests 112; Parishes 58; RC Population 107,834;
Churches 133.
Waterford and Lismore: Most Rev. William Lee
ordained Priest 1966; ordained Bishop 1993.
Priests 111; Parishes 45; RC Population 132,798;
Churches 85.
Limerick: Most Rev. Donal Murray
ordained Priest 1966; ordained Bishop 1982.
Priests 116; Parishes 60; RC Population 168,527;
Churches 94.

Diocese of Dublin:

Archbishop:
Most Rev. Desmond Connell
(Primate of Ireland), ordained Priest 1951,
ordained Archbishop 1988.
Priests 473, Parishes 200, RC Population 1,041,100,
Churches 238.
Auxiliaries: Most Rev. Martin Drennan (titular Bishop of
Acque Regie); ordained Priest 1968; ordained Bishop
1997.
Most Rev. Raymond Field (titular Bishop of Ard Mor);
ordained Priest 1970, ordained Bishop 1997.
Most Rev. James Moriarty (titular Bishop of Bononia);
ordained Priest 1961; ordained Bishop 1991.
Most Rev. Fiachra Ó Ceallaigh (titular Bishop of Tre
Taverne); ordained Priest 1961, ordained Bishop
1994.
Most Rev. Eamonn Walsh (titular Bishop of Elmham),
ordained Priest 1969, ordained Bishop 1990.
Bishops:
Ferns (Wexford): Most Rev. Brendan Comiskey
ordained Priest 1961; ordained Bishop 1980 (Tibili,
Auxiliary Bishop of Dublin), transferred. 1984.
Priests 111; Parishes 49; RC Population 99,000;
Churches 101.
Kildare and Leighlin (Carlow): Most Rev. Laurence
Ryan; ordained Priest 1956, ordained Bishop 1984.
Priests 102; Parishes 56; RC Population 173,206;
Churches 117.
Ossory (Kilkenny): Most Rev. Laurence Forristal
ordained Priest 1955; ordained Bishop 1980 (titular
Bishop of Rotdon, Auxiliary Bishop of Dublin);
installed Bishop (of Ossory) 1981.
Priests 77; Parishes 42; RC Population 74,227;
Churches 89.

Diocese of Tuam:

Archbishop:
Most Rev. Michael Neary
ordained Priest 1971; ordained Bishop 1992;
installed Archbishop 1995.
Clergy 152; Parishes 56; RC Population 119,223;
Churches 131.
Bishops:
Achonry (Roscommon): Most Rev. Thomas Flynn

ordained Priest 1956; ordained Bishop 1977.
Priests 50; Parishes 23; RC Population 34,000;
Churches 47.
Clonfert (Galway): Most Rev. John Kirby
ordained Priest 1963; ordained Bishop 1988.
Priests 52; Parishes 24; RC Population 32,600;
Churches 47.
Elphin (Sligo): Most Rev. Christopher Jones
ordained Priest 1962; ordained Bishop 1994.
Priests 70; Parishes 38; RC Population 68,000;
Churches 90.
Galway: Most Rev. James McLoughlin
ordained Priest 1954; ordained Bishop 1993.
Priests 70; Parishes 40; RC Population 88,534;
Churches 72.
Killala (Mayo): Most Rev. Thomas A. Finnegan
ordained Priest 1951; ordained Bishop 1987.
Priests 44; Parishes 22; RC Population 36,553;
Churches 48.

Papal Nuncio to Ireland:
HE Most Rev Dr Luciano Storero
(titular Archbishop of Tigimma); ordained Priest 1949;
ordained Archbishop 1970; appointed Apostolic
Nuncio to Ireland 1995.

● **FORMER CARDINALS**
Paul Cullen b. 1803; ordained Archbishop of Armagh
1850; transferred. Dublin 1852; created Cardinal 1866
by Pope Pius IX; d. 1878.
Edward McCabe b. 1816; ordained Bishop 1877;
appointed Archbishop of Dublin 1879; created
Cardinal 1882 by Pope Leo XIII; d. 1885.
Michael Logue b. 1840; ordained Bishop 1879;
appointed Archbishop of Armagh 1887; created
Cardinal 1893 by Pope Leo XIII; d. 1924.
Patrick O'Donnell b. 1856; ordained Bishop 1888;
appointed Archbishop of Armagh 1924; created
Cardinal 1925 by Pope Pius XI; d. 1927.
Joseph McRory b. 1861; ordained Bishop 1915;
appointed Archbishop of Armagh 1928; created
Cardinal 1929 by Pope Pius XI; d. 1945.
John D'Alton b. 1882; ordained Bishop 1942;
appointed Archbishop of Armagh 1946; created
Cardinal 1953 by Pope Pius XII; d. 1963.
William Conway b. 1913; ordained Bishop 1958;
appointed Archbishop of Armagh 1963; created
Cardinal 1965 by Pope Paul VI; d. 1977.
Tomás Ó Fiaich b. 1923; appointed Archbishop of
Armagh 1977; created Cardinal 1979 by Pope John
Paul II; d. 1990.
Cahal Daly b. 1917; ordained Bishop 1967; appointed
Archbishop of Armagh 1990; created Cardinal 1991 by
John Paul II; retired 1996.

Catholic Church statistics by Diocese

Diocese	No. of Parishes	Catholic Population	No. of Churches	No. of Priests active in Diocese	Religious Orders: Clerical	Brothers	Sisters
Armagh	62	204,500	146	158	52	43	349
Dublin	200	1,041,100	238	473	975	505	2,736
Cashel	46	78,244	84	116	65	32	213
Tuam	56	119,223	131	152	28	48	393

Continued from previous page

Diocese	No. of Parishes	Catholic Population	No. of Churches	No. of Priests active in Diocese	Religious Orders: Clerical	Brothers	Sisters
Achorny	23	34,000	47	50	3	1	95
Ardagh	41	71,806	80	74	5	9	278
Clogher	37	85,022	86	89	8	6	170
Clonfert	24	32,600	47	52	39	0	176
Cloyne	46	121,000	108	129	6	25	269
Cork & Ross	68	215,500	124	134	148	88	772
Derry	53	213,525	104	135	5	4	158
Down & Connor	88	304,436	152	219	68	56	369
Dromore	23	63,200	48	56	24	8	141
Elphin	38	68,000	90	70	6	5	150
Ferns	49	99,000	101	111	3	10	275
Galway	40	88,534	72	70	44	23	222
Kerry	54	125,000	105	109	12	23	357
Kildare & Leighlin	56	173,206	117	102	93	54	380
Killala	22	36,553	48	44	3	3	76
Killaloe	58	107,834	133	112	26	25	320
Kilmore	36	55,465	97	91	14	0	85
Limerick	60	168,527	94	116	73	38	363
Meath	69	194,000	149	127	131	42	309
Ossory	42	74,227	89	77	18	51	256
Raphoe	31	82,260	71	74	21	5	67
Waterford & Lismore	45	132,798	85	111	147	65	438
TOTAL:	**1,329**	**3,989,560**	**2,646**	**3,051**	**2,017**	**1,169**	**9,417**

Nullity of Marriage

Year	Applications	Decrees	Year	Applications	Decrees
1987	882	209	1993	347	282
1988	926	188	1994	470	300
1989	915	212	1995	502	355
1990	1,043	216	1996	627	347
1991	402	215	1997	515	582
1992	444	289			

Figures above relate to 32 counties.

Applicants and Entrants to Clergy & Religious Orders

Religious Orders	1994 Applicants	1994 Entrants	1996 Applicants	1996 Entrants	1997 Entrants
Diocesan	193	98	131	52	53
Clerical Religious Orders	130	66	88	39	32
Sisters' Orders	63	33	48	19	20
Brothers' Orders	18	4	11	1	0
TOTAL:	404	201	278	111	105

Mass Attendance among Catholic Population

	RoI	NI
Average Attendance at Weekly Mass	65%	57%
Average Rural Rate of Mass attendance	83%	
Average Urban Rate of Mass Attendance	54%	
Average Mass Attendance among young people (15-24 yrs)	50%	60%
Average Mass Attendance among people (25-34)	51%	39%
Average Mass Attendance among people (35-49)	69%	51%
Average Mass Attendance among older people (50-64 yrs)	81%	72%
Average Mass Attendance among older people (65+ yrs)	88%	79%
Average number receiving weekly Communion	42%	36%
Average number making monthly Confessions	11%	19%

Source: 1997 Survey by the Council for Research & Development, St Patrick's College, Maynooth.

The Church of Ireland

● **COMMUNICATIONS**
Central Office, Church of Ireland House,
Church Avenue, Rathmines, Dublin 6.
Tel 01-4978422
email rcbdub@iol.ie

● **ORGANISATION**
The Church of Ireland is a self-governing church within the worldwide Anglican Communion of Churches. The island of Ireland is divided into the provinces of Armagh and Dublin, led by the Archbishop of Armagh, who is Primate of All Ireland, and the Archbishop of Dublin, who is Primate of Ireland. The provinces are further divided into 12 dioceses. The General Synod is the legislative body which governs the Church. It consists of 660 members who are divided between the House of Bishops and the House of Representatives. The Church of Ireland is heavily involved in education and has its own schools in the Republic of Ireland.

● **MAIN FACTFILE**
Primate ....Most Rev. Robin Eames
Members of Church of Ireland 368,467
Number of Dioceses..12
Number of Parishes 475
Number of Churches..1,106
Number of Archbishops..2
Number of Bishops...10
Number of clergy (active in Diocese).....................489
Number of newly ordained clergy (1998)................17

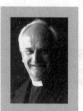

Province of Armagh
Archbishop:
Most Rev. Robin Eames
(Primate of All-Ireland), *(on left)*
ordained 1963;
consecrated 1975;
appointed 1986.
Clergy 47; Parishes 46;
Churches 89.

Bishops:
Clogher: Right Rev. Brian Hannon
ordained 1961; *consecrated* 1986; *appointed* 1986.
Clergy 29; Parishes 35; Churches 70.
Derry and Raphoe: Right Rev. James Mehaffey
ordained 1954; *consecrated* 1980; *appointed* 1980.
Clergy 50; Parishes 50; Churches 121.
Down and Dromore: Right Rev. Harold Miller
ordained 1976; *consecrated* 1997; *appointed* 1997.
Clergy 88; Parishes 80; Churches 117.
Connor: The Right Rev. James Moore
ordained 1956; *consecrated* 1995; *appointed* 1995.
Clergy 85; Parishes 77; Churches 120.
Kilmore, Elphin and Ardagh (Cavan):
Right Rev. Michael Mayes
ordained 1964; *consecrated* 1993; *appointed* 1993.
Clergy 18; Parishes 26; Churches 99.
Tuam, Killala and Achonry:
Right Rev. Richard Henderson

ordained 1986; *consecrated* 1998; *appointed* 1998.
Clergy 8; Parishes 9; Churches 31.
Province of Dublin
Archbishop:
Most Rev. Walton Empey
(Primate of Ireland, Bishop of Glendalough),
ordained 1958; *consecrated* 1981; *appointed* 1996.
Clergy 58; Parishes 55; Churches 107.
Bishops:
Meath and Kildare: Most Rev. Richard Clarke
ordained 1975; *consecrated* 1996; *appointed* 1996.
Clergy 16; Parishes 20; Churches 58.
Cashel and Ossory: Right Rev. John Neill
(Bishop of Cashel, Waterford, Lismore, Ossory, Ferns and Leighlin), *ordained* 1969; *consecrated* 1986; *appointed* 1997.
Clergy 32; Parishes 34; Churches 150.
Cork, Cloyne and Ross: Right Rev. Paul Colton
ordained 1984; *consecrated* 1999; *appointed* 1999.
Clergy 20; Parishes 23; Churches 75.
Limerick and Killaloe: Right Rev. Edward Darling
(Bishop of Limerick, Ardfert, Aghadoe, Killaloe, Kilfenora, Clonfert, Kilmacduagh and Emly),
ordained 1956, *consecrated* 1985, *appointed* 1985.
Clergy 16, Parishes 20, Churches 69.

● **FORMER PRIMATES OF ALL-IRELAND**
William Alexander:
transferred from Derry; *elected* 25 February 1896.
John Baptist Crozier:
transferred from Down; *elected* 2 February 1911.
Charles Frederick D'Arcy:
transferred from Dublin; *elected* 17 June 1920.
John Godfrey Fitzmaurice Day:
transferred from Ossory; *elected* 27 April 1938.
John Allen Fitzgerald Gregg:
transferred from Dublin; *elected* 15 December l938.
James McCann; *transferred from* Meath;
elected 19 February 1959.
George Otto Simms:
transferred from Dublin; *elected* 17 July 1969.
John Ward Armstrong:
transferred from Cashel; *elected* 25 February 1980.

The Presbyterian Church

● **COMMUNICATIONS**
Church House, Fisherwick Place, Belfast BT1 6DW
Tel 01232-322284   Fax 01232-236609
email info@presbyterianireland.org
Website www.presbyterianireland.org

● **ORGANISATION**
The Presbyterian Church in Ireland dates back to 1642, established primarily in the north following the Plantation of Ulster by Scottish settlers. The church has as its chief representative a Moderator (who serves for one year only), elected by the General Assembly of the Church. This Assembly, formed for the first time in 1840, is made up of 21 Presbyteries and five regional Synods drawn from 560 congregations in Ireland. It

meets annually and is responsible for deciding Church laws and policy. Each congregation is entitled to representation at the Assembly. The Synods and Presbyteries also elect Moderators who serve for one year. The Ministry was opened to women in 1972. The Presbyterian Church is the largest Protestant Church in Northern Ireland.

● MAIN FACTFILE

Moderator............................Rt Rev Dr John Lockington
Members of Presbyterian Church in Ireland 350,090
Number of Regional Synods..5
Number of Regions..21
Number of Congregations 560
Number of Ministers..427
Number of women Ministers 18
Largest Parish ....Larne, Co Antrim (2715)

Moderator of the General Assembly
Rt Rev Dr John Lockington
(on left)
ordained 1969, *appointed* 1999.

Synod of Armagh & Down
Moderator of Synod
Rev Campbell Wilson
ordained 1969, *appointed* 1999.
Presbytery of Ards
Rev George F. McKeown
ordained 1980, *appointed* 1999.
Ministers 32; *Congregations* 36; *Presbyterian population* 31,920.
Presbytery of Armagh Rev Anthony D. Davidson
ordained 1982, *appointed* 1999.
Ministers 17; *Congregations* 30; *Presbyterian population* 12,589.
Presbytery of Down Rev Robert E. Boggs
ordained 1966, *appointed* 1999.
Ministers 16; *Congregations* 23; *Presbyterian population* 15,391.
Presbytery of Dromore Rev Alexander S. Thompson
ordained 1987, *appointed* 1999.
Ministers 17; *Congregations* 22; *Presbyterian population* 17,526
Presbytery of Iveagh Rev Colin D. McClure
ordained 1990, *appointed* 1999.
Ministers 17; *Congregations* 28; *Presbyterian population* 11,243
Presbytery of Newry Rev Brian McMillen
ordained 1990, *appointed* 1999.
Ministers 13; *Congregations* 26; *Presbyterian population* 8,813.
Synod of Ballymena and Coleraine:
Moderator of Synod Rev John H. MacConnell
ordained 1966, *appointed* 1999
Presbytery of Ballymena Rev David W. Brice
ordained 1982, *appointed* 1999.
Ministers 30; *Congregations* 31; *Presbyterian population* 24,598
Presbytery of Carrickfergus Rev Frederick A. Bradley
ordained 1980, *appointed* 1999.
Ministers 19; *Congregations* 20; *Presbyterian population* 19,509

Presbytery of Coleraine Rev Dr Brian Kingsmore
ordained 1959, *appointed* 1999.
Ministers 19; *Congregations* 25; *Presbyterian population* 14,370
Presbytery of Route
Rev Robert F.S. Poots OBE
Deputy Clerk of the General Assembly,
ordained 1962, *appointed* 1999,
Ministers 17; *Congregations* 22; *Presbyterian population* 11,722
Presbytery of Templepatrick Rev John Brackenbridge
ordained 1983, *appointed* 1999.
Ministers 17; *Congregations* 20; *Presbyterian population* 15,086
Synod of Belfast
Moderator of Synod Rev Prof James P. Taylor
ordained 1975, *appointed* 1999
Presbytery of North Belfast Rev JN Seawright
ordained 1978, *appointed* 1999.
Ministers 24; *Congregations* 25; *Presbyterian population* 20,405
Presbytery of South Belfast Rev Thomas W. Gordon
ordained 1978, *appointed* 1999.
Ministers 21; *Congregations* 19; *Presbyterian population* 10,955
Presbytery of East Belfast Rev George Moffett
ordained 1980, *appointed* 1999.
Ministers 26; *Congregations* 27; *Presbyterian population* 26,061
Synod of Derry and Omagh
Moderator of Synod Rev Brian A. Hunt
ordained 1980, *appointed* 1999
Presbytery of Derry and Strabane Rev Robert Stirling
ordained 1989, *appointed* 1999.
Ministers 17; *Congregations* 35; *Presbyterian population* 12,390
Presbytery of Foyle Rev Dr Clive Glass
ordained 1990, *appointed* 1999.
Ministers 10; *Congregations* 20; *Presbyterian population* 11,133
Presbytery of Omagh Rev Norman S. Harrison
ordained 1992, *appointed* 1999.
Ministers 12; *Congregations* 29; *Presbyterian population* 7,625
Presbytery of Tyrone Rev Thomas J. Conway
ordained 1988, *appointed* 1999.
Ministers 18; *Congregations* 33; *Presbyterian population* 12,401
Synod of Dublin
Moderator of Synod Rev Georgina J. Mackerel
ordained 1983, *appointed* 1999
Presbytery of Donegal Rev Alan W. Carson
ordained 1998, *appointed* 1999.
Ministers 9; *Congregations* 22; *Presbyterian population* 4,379
Presbytery of Dublin and Munster
Rev James Carson
ordained 1960, *appointed* 1999.
Ministers 23; *Congregations* 39; *Presbyterian population* 4,128
Presbytery of Monaghan Rev David T. Moore

ordained 1993, *appointed* 1999.
Ministers 13; *Congregations* 28; *Presbyterian population* 3,053

● FORMER MODERATORS
OF THE GENERAL ASSEMBLY

Rev. John McC. Hamilton (1900); Rev. James Heron (1901); Rev. John Edgar Henry (1902); Rev. John MacDermott (1903); Rev. Samuel Prenter (1904); Rev. William McMordie (1905); Rev. William McKean (1906); Rev. William Davidson (1907); Rev. John McIlveen (1908); Rev. John Courtenay Clarke (1909); Rev. John Howard Murphy (1910); Rev. John Macmillan (1911); Rev. Henry Montgomery (1912); Rev. William J. Macaulay (1913); Rev. James Bingham (1914); Rev. Thomas M. Hamill (1915); Rev. Thomas West (1916); Rev. John Irwin (1917); Rev. James McGranahan (1918); Rev. J.M. Simms (1919); Rev. H. Patterson Glenn (1920); Rev. W.J. Lowe (1921); Rev. W.G. Strahan (1922); Rev. George Thompson (1923); Rev. R.W. Hamilton (1924); Rev. Thomas Haslett (1925); Rev. R.K. Hanna (1926); Rev. James Thompson (1927); Rev. T.A. Smyth (1928); Rev. J.L. Morrow (1929); Rev. Edward Clarke (1930); Rev. James G. Paton (1931); Rev. James J. Macauley (1932); Rev. William Corkey (1933); Rev. T.M. Johnstone (1934); Rev. A.F. Moody (1935); Rev. F.W.S. O'Neill (1936); Rev. John Waddell (1937); Rev. W.J. Currie (1938); Rev. Prof James Haire (1939); Rev. J.Bishop Woodbum (1940); Rev. W.A. Watson (1941); Rev. W.M. Kennedy (1942); Rev. Phineas McKee (1943); Rev. Andrew Gibson (1944); Rev. Prof Robert Corkey (1945); Rev. Thomas Byers (1946); Rev. Robert Boyd (1947); Rev. Alfred W. Neill (1948); Rev. Gordon D. Erskine (1949); Rev. J.H.R. Gibson (1950); Rev. Hugh McIlroy (1951); Rev. John K.L. McKean (1952); Rev. Principal J.E. Davey (1953); Rev. John Knowles (1954); Rev. James C. Breakey (1955); Rev. T.M. Barker (1956); Rev. Principal R.J. Wilson (1957); Rev. Wm. McAdam (1958); Rev. T.A.B. Smyth (1959); Rev. Austin A. Fulton (1960); Rev. W.A.A. Park (1961); Rev. John H. Davey (1962); Rev. W.A. Montgomery (1963); Rev. James Dunlop (1964); Rev. S. James Park (1965); Rev. Alfred Martin (1966); Rev. William Boyd (1967); Rev John H. Withers (1968); Rev John T Carson (1969); Rev Principal JLM Haire (1970); Rev F. Rupert Gibson (1971); Rev. R.V.A. Lynas (1972); Rev J.W. Orr (1973); Rev G. Temple Lundie (1974); Rev G.H.F. Wynne (1975); Rev. A.J. Weir (1976); Rev T.A. Patterson (1977); Rev. David Burke (1978); Rev. William Craig (1979); Rev. R.G. Craig (1980); Rev. John Girvan (1981); Rev. E.P Gardner (1982); Rev T.J. Simpson (1983); Rev. Howard Cromie (1984); Rev. Robert Dickinson (1985); Rev. Prof. John Thompson (1986); Rev. William Fleming (1987); Rev. A.W.G. Brown (1988); Rev. James Matthews (1989); Rev. Prof. R.F.G. Holmes (1990); Rev. Rodney Sterritt (1991); Rev. John Dunlop (1992); Rev. Andrew R. Rodgers (1993); Rev. David J. McGaughey (1994); Rev. John Ross (1995); Rev. Harry Allen Coleraine (1996); Rev. Samuel Hutchinson (1997); Rev. Samuel John Dixon (1998);

The Methodist Church

● COMMUNICATIONS
1 Glenagherty Drive, Old Galgorm Road, Ballymena, Co.Antrim BT42 1AG.
Tel & Fax 01266-656693

● ORGANISATION
The Methodist Church in Ireland dates from the 18th century and is closely linked with its British counterpart. The church has as its leader a President (who serves for one year only). Administratively, the church consists of 76 Circuits - each circuit usually consisting of several churches. These circuits are further grouped geographically to form a District Synod, of which there are eight in total. Each Synod is presided over by a District Chairman who can serve up to six years. The highest Court of the Methodist Church is The Conference which meets annually.

● MAIN FACTFILE
President ....Rev Dr. Kenneth A. Wilson
Members of Methodist Church in Ireland...........64,554
Number of Regional Synods 8
Number of Circuits 76
Number of Churches 228
Number of Ministers 200
Number of lay preachers..290

President
Rev. Dr. Kenneth A. Wilson
(on left)
ordained 1967; *appointed* 1999.

Secretary
Rev. Edmund T.I. Mawhinney
ordained 1964; *appointed* 1990.
District Chairmen
Belfast: Rev Dr. W.B Fletcher
ordained 1974; *appointed* 1999.
Clergy 51; *Circuits* 14; *Community* 17,113; *Churches* 29.
Down: Rev R.P Roddie
ordained 1964; *appointed* 1997
Clergy 37; *Circuits* 10; *Community* 10,247; *Churches* 22.
Dublin: Rev T.M. Kingston
ordained 1968; *appointed* 1997.
Clergy 18; *Circuits* 8; *Community* 2,284; *Churches* 20.
Enniskillen and Sligo: Rev A.W. Ferguson
ordained 1980; *appointed* 1999.
Clergy 12; *Circuits* 9; *Community* 3,330; *Churches* 32.
North West: Rev P.A. Good
ordained 1972; *appointed*1995.
Clergy 13; *Circuits* 6; *Community* 3,695; *Churches* 27.
Midlands and Southern: Rev S.K. Todd
ordained 1969; *appointed* 1997.
Clergy 12; *Circuits* 10; *Community* 2,084;

Churches 27.
North East: Rev K.H. Thompson
ordained 1973; *appointed* 1997.
Clergy 25; *Circuits* 28; *Community* 12,280;
Churches 24.
Portadown: Rev S.W. Blair
ordained 1985; *appointed* 1999.
Clergy 24; *Circuits* 11; *Community* 7,336;
Churches 44.

● **FORMER PRESIDENTS**
1965 Rev. Robert A. Nelson; **1966** Rev. Samuel J. Johnston; **1967** Rev. R.D. Eric Gallagher; **1968** Rev. Gerald G. Myles; **1969** Rev. George E. Good; **1970** Rev. James Davison; **1971** Rev. Charles H. Bain; **1972** Rev. Edward R. Lindsay; **1973** Rev. Harold Sloan; **1974** Rev. R. Desmond Morris; **1975** Rev. Hedley W. Plunkett; **1976** Rev. Richard Greenwood; **1977** Rev. Robert G. Livingstone; **1978** Rev. John Turner; **1979** Rev. Vincent Parkin; **1980** Rev. W. Sydney Callaghan; **1981** Rev. Ernest W. Gallagher; **1982** Rev. Charles G. Eyre. **1983** Rev. Cecil A. Newall; **1984** Rev. Paul Kingston; **1985** Rev. Hamilton Skillen; **1986** Rev. Sydney Frame; **1987** Rev. William I. Hamilton; **1988** Rev. T. Stanley Whittington; **1989** Rev. George R. Morrison; **1990** Rev. William T. Buchanan; **1991** Rev. J. Winston Good; **1992** Rev. J. Derek H. Ritchie; **1993** Rev. Richard H. Taylor; **1994** Rev. Edmund T.I. Mawhinney; **1995** Rev. Christopher G. Walpole; **1996** Rev. Kenneth Best; **1997** Rev. Norman W. Taggart; **1998** Rev. David J. Kerr.

Other Religions

Baptist Churches In Ireland

● **COMMUNICATIONS**
117 Lisburn Road, Belfast BT9 7AF
Tel 01232-663108 *email* buofi@aol.com

● **ORGANISATION**
The Baptist Union of Ireland was first organised in Ireland in 1640. The association is made up of 108 autonomous local churches of the Baptist faith in Ireland (93 in Northern Ireland and 16 in the Republic of Ireland). Membership in the Union does not interfere with the autonomy of the local church. The operations of the Union are controlled by the Churches' Council, which is made up of at least two representatives from each church in the Union and meets at least twice a year. The Council acts through its Officers and Executive Committee. The Executive Committee is elected by the Churches' Council from among its members, and its role is to supervise the work of the Union.

● **MAIN FACTFILE**
President .... Rev Clifford Morrison
Members of Baptist Church in Ireland 8,376
Number of Pastors 84

Number of Missionaries 16
Number of College Tutors 4
Number of women Pastors .... None (1 lady lay-worker)
Number of Churches 108

The Brethren

● **COMMUNICATIONS**
Crescent Church, 6 University Rd, Belfast BT7 1NH

● **ORGANISATION**
The origins of the Brethren in Ireland can be traced back to Dublin in 1830. The church grew out of meetings for worship among young aristocrats, and their growing assembly became known as 'The Brethren' or Plymouth Brethren'. The Brethren are born-again believers who adhere to the fundamental doctrines of Christianity. The church at local level is autonomous and is governed by elders.

Free Presbyterian Church

● **COMMUNICATIONS**
356 - 376 Ravenhill Rd,
Belfast BT6 8GL
Tel 01232-457106
Web www.freepres.org

● **ORGANISATION**
The Free Presbyterian Church in Ireland was founded in 1953 by Rev Dr Ian Kyle Paisley, following a split in the Presbyterian Church in East Down. The denomination's moderator since that time has been Dr Paisley - who is also a Member of Parliament and, since 1979, an MEP. The church - which is largely based in Northern Ireland - claims to be fundamental in doctrine, evangelical in outreach and Protestant in conviction.

● **MAIN FACTFILE**
Head of Church .... Rev Dr Ian Paisley
Members of Church in Ireland 13,000
Number of Clergy 59
Number of Churches 64

Non-subscribing Presbyterian

● **COMMUNICATIONS**
102 Carrickfergus Road, Larne, Co Antrim BT40 3JX
Tel 028-28 272600

● **ORGANISATION**
The Non-Subscribing Presbyterian Church of Ireland, organised in its present structure in 1910, has its roots in the main body of Irish Presbyterianism. The church is Presbyterian in government - the supreme court of the

church is the General Synod and the Moderator of that Synod usually holds office for two years.

● **MAIN FACTFILE**

Head of Church ....Rev Brian Stuart Cockroft
Members of Baptist Church in Ireland 3,580
Number of Clergy 20
Congregations 34
Number of Presbyteries 3

Islam

● **COMMUNICATIONS**

19 Roebuck Road, Clonskeagh, Dublin 14.
Tel 01-208 0000 *email* iccislam@tinet.ie

● **ORGANISATION**

Islam originated in the Middle East in the 7th Century. The first Muslim organisation in Ireland (The Dublin Islamic Society) was formed in 1959 by Muslim students from South Africa and Malaysia.

The Muslim community in Ireland is multi-racial and multi-cultural, comprising Asian, Middle Eastern, European and Irish adherents. Numbering 11,000 (6,000 of whom reside in Dublin), Muslims now make up the third largest denomination in the Republic after Roman Catholics and the Church of Ireland. There are smaller communities in Belfast, Cork, Mayo, Armagh, Cavan, Donegal, Galway and Limerick. There is no national leader in Ireland although each mosque has a religious leader (imam).

● **MAIN FACTFILE**

Members of Islam faith in Ireland 11,000
Number of Communities 9

Judaism

● **COMMUNICATIONS**

Herzog House, Zion Road, Rathgar, Dublin 6.
Tel 01-4923751

● **ORGANISATION**

The Jewish Community in Ireland, while small in number, dates back over 500 years. The earliest record of a Synagogue in Ireland dates from 1660. The Spiritual head of the Jewish Community in the Republic of Ireland is the Chief Rabbi, under whose supervision all congregations operate. The Jewish population peaked at approximately 5,500 in the late 1940s although numbers have now declined to approximately 1,200 in the Republic and 400 in Northern Ireland. 60-75% of Irish Jews are now aged 50+ years of age.

● **MAIN FACTFILE**

Chief Rabbi ....Gavan Broder
Number of members of Jewish faith in Ireland 1,400
Number of Congregations 2

Number of Synagogues 3
Number of Rabbis / Ministers 2

Lutheran Church

● **COMMUNICATIONS**

24 Adelaide Road, Dublin 2.
Tel 01-676 6548

● **ORGANISATION**

The Lutheran Church is German in origin, dating from to the Protestant Reformation of the 16th century. Established in Dublin in 1697, it is the oldest German institution in Ireland. Its first church building was consecrated in 1725 in Dubin and the city remains the church's main Irish base, with services also conducted at intervals across the country and in Belfast.

● **MAIN FACTFILE**

Head of Church ....Pastor Fritz-Gert Mayer
Members of Church in Ireland 1,100
Number of Pastors 1
Number of Churches 1

Greek Orthodox Church

● **COMMUNICATIONS**

46 Arbour Hill, Dublin 7.
Tel 01-847 4956

● **ORGANISATION**

The Greek Orthodox Church was founded in Ireland in 1981. There is one multi-national Greek Orthodox Community in Ireland, North and South, made up of all Orthodox Christians living here, irrespective of their national identity. Consisting of around 1,000 members, the Orthodox community's headquarters in Ireland are located at Arbour Hill in Dublin.

● **MAIN FACTFILE**

Senior Clergyman in Ireland ....Fr Ireneu Craciun
Members of Church in Ireland 1,000
Number of Churches 4
Number of clergy 1

The Church of Jesus Christ of Latter-Day Saints

● **COMMUNICATIONS**

The Willows, Glasnevin, Dublin 11.
Tel 01-8306899

● **ORGANISATION**

Sometimes referred to as 'the Mormons', the Church was founded in the United States in 1830, and came to

Ireland in the late 1840s. The church in Ireland is divided ecclesiastically into two Stakes (Belfast and Dublin) and one District (Cork). The Belfast Stake, organised in 1974, has approximately 3,500 members across Northern Ireland. The Dublin Stake was created out of the Dublin District in 1995 and has around 1,800 members, while the Cork District has over 400 members.

● **MAIN FACTFILE**

Stake Presidents....................Liam Gallagher (Dublin)
Peter K. Ferguson (Belfast)
District President..........................Michael Kelly (Cork)
Members of Church in Ireland 5,000-6,000
Number of Stakes 2
Number of Districts 1
Number of Churches...15

Religious Society of Friends

● **COMMUNICATIONS**

Swanbrook House, Bloomfield Ave,
Morehampton Rd, Dublin 4
Tel & Fax 01-668 3684

● **ORGANISATION**

The Religious Society of Friends (Quakers) was founded in England in the early 1650s and the first Meeting for Worship in Ireland was established by William Edmundson in Lurgan, Co Armagh, in 1654. The Society is a Christian movement which abstains from formal doctrine, outward sacraments and ordained ministers. Monthly, Quarterly and Yearly Meetings take place, while Meetings for Worship are unprogrammed.

● **MAIN FACTFILE**

Yearly Meeting Clerk ....Rachel M. Bewley-Bateman
Members of members in Ireland 1,605
Number Meetings for Worship 30

The Salvation Army

● **COMMUNICATIONS**

P.O. Box 2098, c/o Dublin Central Mission
Lower Abbey Street, Dublin 1
Tel 01-874 0987

● **ORGANISATION**

The Salvation Army originated in London in 1865 and commenced work in Ireland in May 1888. Headquarters for the Army is Abbey Street Hall in Dublin. As the name suggests, the Salvation Army is militaristic in administration with personnel consisting of adherents, local officers, soldiers and higher officers.

● **MAIN FACTFILE**

Head of Church..........................General John Gowans
Number of members in Ireland ....(R.O.I.) 30

(N.I.) 1,500
Number of churches (N.I.)...21

The Seventh-Day Adventist Church in Ireland

● **COMMUNICATIONS**

20 Bushfield Lawns, Clondalkin, Dublin 22
Tel 01-4641037

● **ORGANISATION**

Originating in the United States in 1863, the first Seventh-Day Adventist Church in Ireland was organised in Dublin around the beginning of the present century. The small Irish Mission, consisting of 335 members North and South, is part of the British Union Conference. The majority of members are Northern based.

● **MAIN FACTFILE**

Head of Church ....Elder Alan D Hodges
Members of Church in Ireland................................335
Number of Churches ....11 (5 in ROI)
Number of Clergy...9

Irish District of Moravian Church

● **COMMUNICATIONS**

The Moravian Mance, Church Rd, Gracehill,
Ballymena, Co Antrim BT42 2NL
Tel 01266-653141

● **ORGANISATION**

The Moravian Church (rooted in Episcopal Protestantism) originated in the early 16th century in Czechoslovakia. The Church in Ireland was founded in Dublin by John Cennick in 1749, but was largely Northern-based. There are five Congregations today which make up the Irish district and all are located north of the border.

● **MAIN FACTFILE**

Head of Church ....Rev Victor D Launder
Members of Church in Ireland................................520
Number of Congregations...5
Number of Churches...5
Number of Clergy...2

Church of Scientology

● **COMMUNICATIONS**

Mission of Dublin,
62-63 Middle Abbey St,
Dublin 1.
Tel 01-8720007

● ORGANISATION

The Church of Scientology was founded in the United States in 1954. The main congregation of Scientologists in Ireland are located in the Mission of Dublin, which was officially incorporated in 1994 but in operation since the late 1980s. There are smaller informal groups in Cork, Belfast and elsewhere.

● MAIN FACTFILE

Head of Church ....John Keane
Members of Church in Ireland ....200+
Number of Churches / Houses of Worship 1
Number of Ministers.....................................1

Jehovah's Witnesses

● COMMUNICATIONS

Watch Tower House,
Newcastle, Greystones, Co. Wicklow.
Tel 01-2810692

● ORGANISATION

Jehovah's Witnesses were founded in Pennsylvania in 1872. They have been in Ireland since the 1890s following the establishment of congregations in Dublin and Belfast. There are now 114 congregations arranged into five circuits. A branch committee of three elders supervises activity throughout Ireland.

● MAIN FACTFILE

Branch Co-Ordinator ....Arthur E Matthews
Number of Witnesses in Ireland..........................4,500
Number of congregations 114
Number of elders...596
Number of Kingdom Halls 92

Bahá'í Faith

● COMMUNICATIONS

24 Burlington Road, Dublin 4.
Tel 01-6683150 email nsairl@iol.ie

● ORGANISATION

The Bahá'í Faith is an independent world religion founded over 150 years ago and was first set up in Ireland on an organised scale in 1948. It is governed by elected councils at local, national and international levels. The jurisdictions of these councils (spiritual assemblies) are contiguous with civil boundaries. There are 174 elected National Spiritual Assemblies, including one for the Republic of Ireland In the Republic of Ireland, there are 20 elected local spiritual assemblies and 9 in Northern Ireland. National and local Assemblies have nine members and are elected annually.

● MAIN FACTFILE

Number of members in Ireland...............approx. 1,000

Number of Spiritual Assemblies: 29

Buddhism

● COMMUNICATIONS

The Friends of the Western Buddhist Order
Dublin Meditation Centre, 2 East Essex Street,
Temple Bar, Dublin 2
Tel 01 671 3187 email fwboirl@iol.ie

● ORGANISATION

Buddhism is an ancient religion which originated in India in the sixth century BC. A number of Buddhist traditions are represented in Ireland (i.e. Tibetan, Theravadin, Zen and Western Buddhism). These groups have regular meetings and organise a range of activities.

One of these Buddhist organisations, The Friends of the Western Buddhist Order, has two semi-monastic residential communities in Ireland which accommodate teaching programmes, meditation meetings and retreats.

The Unitarian Church

● COMMUNICATIONS

112 St Stephen's Green, Dublin 2
Tel 01-4780638

● ORGANISATION

The Unitarian Church originated in Poland and Transylvania in the 16th century, and has had a small presence in Ireland dating back over 300 years. Unitarianism is Judaeo-Christian in its roots but accommodates insights from other world faiths and philosophies. The Church has approximately 120 members in Ireland and is affiliated to the General Assembly of Unitarian and Free Christian Churches in Britain and also to the Non-Subscribing Presbyterian Church in Northern Ireland.

● MAIN FACTFILE

Number of Congregations ....2 (Dublin & Cork)
Number of members of Church in Ireland..............120
Number of Churches..2
Number of Clergy...1

EDUCATION

Adult Literacy in Ireland

By **Inez Bailey, National Adult Literacy Agency (NALA)**

ADULT Literacy in Ireland and internationally, has received unprecedented attention in recent years due to a number of factors. The biggest factor however has been the economy and the demands it places on our society. In order for the economy to boom, people must be flexible and embrace change as required. This is the era of the knowledge society and at its core are the essential skills of literacy and numeracy.

NALA Definition of Literacy

Literacy involves the integration of listening, speaking, reading, writing and numeracy. It also encompasses aspects of personal development - social, economic, emotional - and is concerned with improving self-esteem and building confidence. It goes far beyond mere technical skills of communication. (NALA) Literacy skills play a key role in combating long-term unemployment, access to education, learning and training, breaking the cycle of poverty and dependency as well as building and strengthening the community.

Causes and Effects

The manifestation of literacy difficulties fall into four broad categories:

Educational large classes, poor teaching, limited remedial facilities.
Physical/Psychological poor hearing/vision, specific learning difficulties.
Social & Economic poverty, poor housing, no money for materials.
Family large size, no habit of reading, other difficulties.

Most people who have low literacy skills will also have experienced a combination of the above. The effects of this can be divided as follows:

Positive good memory, observation skills and coping strategies.
Negative generalised sense of failure, negative attitudes to school, poor self esteem, lower social standing, non-participation, isolation and limited employment prospects.

Brief Historical Policy Context

Up to the 1970's there was no recognition of the literacy problem in Ireland. There was no commitment during these years to equality of educational opportunity nor to a critical evaluation of how effective the National School system operated. Sean Moylon, Minister for Education (1951-54) said "It is my opinion that this system of ours, of which there is no comparable system on earth, is very appropriate to this country". By 1960, Charles McCarthy, then General Secretary of the Vocational Teachers' Association of Ireland, said that the population in Ireland ".... is almost universally literate; or more accurately ...

only the unteachable are illiterate. I have nothing more to say on illiteracy . . .". NALA was established in 1980 and from that time campaigned for understanding, recognition and response to the adult literacy problem in Ireland.

International Adult Literacy Survey

By 1995, the Organisation for Economic Co-operation and Development (OECD) International Adult Literacy Survey (IALS) results sparked off the debate and led to the recognition of the adult literacy issue and the policy imbalance being redressed.

Literacy ability was measured against five levels from 1 (lowest) to 5 (highest). Level 1 indicates very low literacy skills, where the individual may, for example, have difficulty identifying the correct amount of medicine to give a child from the information found on the package. At Level 2, respondents can deal only with material that is simple, clearly laid out and in which the tasks involved are not too complex. Level 3 is considered the minimum desirable threshold in developed countries but some occupations require higher skills.

Ireland compared unfavourably to most other countries surveyed with a rating of 25% or 500,000 adults aged between 16-65 at Level 1. The corresponding figure for Sweden was 7% and Britain 21%. A previous survey by the OECD revealed that the proportion of adults in Ireland who have left school at or before the junior cycle of second level is 58% which is among the highest in the EU. In real terms this figure amounts to just over 930,000 people. (OECD, 1996, Lifelong Learning for All, Paris.)

Age was found to be very strongly associated with literacy performance in the Irish sample. In general, the greatest differences are between the younger age groups and those aged 46 years and over. For example 17% of those aged 16-25 are at Level 1 compared with over 44% in the oldest age group (55-65). In respect of gender, there was great similarity between men and women in all countries surveyed.

The OECD survey highlighted that an Irish person at Level 1 would experience the highest incidence of unemployment than people who scored at Level 1 in any other country surveyed (OECD, 1997). The ratio of unemployed to employed people scoring at the lowest literacy level in the Irish survey is 2:1. It is also evident from the survey that literacy level is associated to income. Higher literacy levels result in higher incomes. Literacy activities are most engaged in at work, in particular in higher status occupations. This has major implications for those who are not currently employed as they may not be exercising their literacy skills on a regular basis. Over one-fifth of those interviewed indicated that they never read a book.

Overall the Irish survey concluded that a significant minority of adults do not engage in challenging literacy activities in everyday life. If reading and writing skills are not utilised regularly, they can be lost. Therefore people who may have learnt basic skills can become de-skilled over a period of time - think learning a language and then not practising as opposed to riding a bike!

The Adult Literacy Service and other Providers

Adult Literacy Schemes provide learner centred tuition on an individual and/or group basis to adults with reading and writing difficulties, who in the majority of cases are experiencing varying levels of disadvantage. This service is provided free of charge and is available in most cases during the day and in the evening.

However, in order to meet current demand, tuition is provided by volunteers to the tune of 85%, with Adult Literacy Organisers employed on a full-time basis since last September. Prior to this most worked minimal paid hours (approximately 7 hours per week). There are currently around 2,500 volunteers contributing to the service. As a result of the dependence on volunteers and insufficient budget (£5.6 million shared between 107 schemes), adults can only access two to four hours tuition per week in most schemes, equivalent to two to four weeks full-time study per annum. There are approximately 10,000 adults participating in literacy schemes nationwide, 2% of those estimated to have low literacy skills.

The Green Paper on Adult Education proposes the expansion of the literacy services in order to cater for more adults with literacy difficulties, building on the extra resources made available to local VECs last year. This had led to initiatives in family literacy, intensive basic education and distance learning. In addition, most of the VEC areas have increased the number of Group Tutors available to schemes.

Research Findings - Access and Participation in Irish Adult Literacy Schemes

From 1996 to 1998, NALA carried out a piece of research into access and participation in adult literacy schemes in Ireland. 159 learners participated in interviews outlining their experience of having a literacy difficulty and deciding to do something about it.

In almost all cases the dominant barriers to participation in literacy programmes were negative attitudes to education. Some quotes from the people interviewed illustrate this.

"Well to tell you the truth, I don't even try to tell my friends. I wouldn't even tell my next door neighbour that I'm coming here. There was a chap from our road here and when I seen him first I wanted to hide, like I felt ashamed. I had a chat with him and he said he wouldn't breathe a word . . . You just feel that people might look down on you".
(Man in his thirties)

"And you were constantly told you were stupid....when they asked us was there anybody to would clean the toilets, we'd put up our hands, just to get out of the class. About four of us, who were pals. It was pointless trying to teach us, the teachers said. And it wasn't pointless".
(Woman in her forties)

Many of the interviewees highlighted how their experience of poverty had contributed to their literacy difficulty. As children they knew that 'better off' children were given the attention in school. The attitude of the interviewees' parents was also highlighted as many regretted that their parents did not play a more significant role in their education.

Almost half of the research participants were in paid employment (mainly men) while a significant number of those not in paid employment were working full time in the home (mainly women). Many spoke about their frustration with their jobs or lack of them and felt that their education levels had severely limited their lifestyle options. These people returned to the local literacy service in order to help their children, improve their job prospects or change jobs and simply to meet their own developmental needs.

All detailed a variety of benefits which ensued, including the pleasure of reading the newspaper, increased participation in social and community activities, improved mental health and empowerment. The learners who participated in the survey provided ample evidence that non-formal adult basic education is having a profoundly positive outcome on people who are regarded as 'hard to reach'.

Conclusion

The extent of the adult literacy problem and the current capacity of the adult literacy service and other providers to meet the potential demand in Ireland, presents an enormous challenge to all involved. The combination of employment growth, skills shortages and the demographic dividend, has focused attention on those in the labour force with low educational attainment. The economy has spoken and we are all listening and responding. It is important however to take the widest interpretation of economic needs and bring in those who may be excluded by the focus on the labour force and related needs. The human rights perspective that all adults are entitled to a quality adult basic education service, whatever their goal, must be the underlying principle guiding these developments.

Inez Bailey
October 1999

The author is the director of the National Adult Literacy Agency (NALA) - the co-ordinating, training and campaigning body for all those involved in adult literacy work in Ireland.

Statistics at a Glance

Republic of Ireland

Category (by education level)	Numbers
Students *(1st, 2nd, 3rd)*	933,444
Schools & Colleges *(1st, 2nd, 3rd)*	4097
Teachers *(1st, 2nd level)*	44410
Students doing exams *(2nd)*	129,813
Total spent on Education *(1st, 2nd, 3rd)*	£2,583.3m

Northern Ireland

Category (by education level)	Numbers
Students *(1st, 2nd)*	350,565
Schools & Colleges *(1st, 2nd, 3rd)*	1,337
Teachers *(1st, 2nd level)*	105,41
Students entitled to free meals *(1st, 2nd)*	85,618
Integrated schools *(1st, 2nd)*	24

General

Total Student Enrolment

● Republic of Ireland - *School / College*	1987/88	1992/93	1997/98
Primary Schools:	**565,487**	**521,531**	**460,845**
National Schools (ordinary classes only)	554,008	510,012	446,359
National schools with pupils with special needs	2,904	3,435	7,077
Special National schools	8,575	8,084	7,409
Secondary Schools:	**339,556**	**358,347**	**368,160**
Secondary*	214,798	221,167	217,303
Vocational	84,868	92,003	97,309
Community & Comprehensive	39,890	45,177	53,548
Tertiary Institutions:	**57,221**	**81,050**	**104,439**
HEA Institutions	34,365	48,124	61,308
Institutes of Technology**	20,827	32,198	41,909
National College of Industrial Relations	-	-	628
Non-HEA Primary Teacher Training	1,769	523	391
Home Economics Teacher Training	260	205	203

Source Dept. of Education and Science
* incl. secondary top schools up to 1990/91 inclusive
**incl. Killybegs HTC College, Dublin College of Music, Dun Laoghaire College of Art & Design from 1988/9. incl. Cork School of Music and the Crawford College of Art & Design (both as part of Cork IT) from 1992/3. Incl. the NCI from 1993/4.

● Northern Ireland - *School* by management type	Nursery schools/classes	Primary yr 1–yr 8	Secondary yr8–yr14	Special	Hospital	Independent	Total
Controlled	6,438	87,567	54,734	4,318	143	-	153,200
Catholic Maintained	2,387	85,756	45,936	251	-	-	134,330
Other Maintained	25	1,275	268	106	-	-	1,674
Integrated *(controlled & grant-aided)*	-	4,222	5,269	-	-	-	9,491
Voluntary *(Catholic and other)*	28	2,753	47,743	-	-	-	50,524
Non Grant-aided	-	-	-	-	-	1,346	1,346
TOTAL:	**8,878**	**181,573**	**153,950**	**4,675**	**143**	**1,346**	**350,565**

Source Dept. of Education Northern Ireland

RoI Expenditure on Education

Expenditure by Student & Level	1987/88	1992/93	1997/98 (e)
Expenditure Per Student (1998 Prices)*:			
Primary level	£1,005	£1,350	£1,786
Secondary level	£1,774	£2,136	£2,645
Third level	£4,060	£3,932	£4,016
Expenditure per Level of Education (£m)*:			
Primary level	462.0	654.9	873.6
Secondary level	499.7	732.8	1,024.8
Third level	242.0	398.7	684.9

Continued from previous page

● Republic of Ireland	1987/88	1992/93	1997/98 (e)
Total	1,203.7	1,786.4	2,583.3

Source Dept. of Education and Science
*refers to financial years.

Pupil-teacher Ratios

● Republic of Ireland - Type of School	1987/88	1992/93	1997/98
Primary Schools*	26.7	25.1	21.8
Secondary Schools**	17.6	18.1	17.5

Source Dept. of Education and Science
* Ratios are based on the total enrolment in all national schools.
** Ratios shown are for full-time teachers only and do not incl. full-time equivalent of part-time teachers.

● Northern Ireland - Type of School	1987/8	1996/7	1998/9
Nursery	24.1	23.4	23.7
Primary*	23.5	19.8	19.9
All Secondary	14.8	14.5	14.6
Special	7.2	6.4	6.4
All Grant-aided Schools	18.4	16.7	16.8

Source: Dept. of Education Northern Ireland
* These ratios incl. full-time teachers, part-time teachers and full-time equivalent of part-time teachers. The ratios excl. substitute and peripatetic teachers. All students are included and part-time students are inserted as 0.5 of a full-time student.

Number of Schools and Colleges

● Republic of Ireland - Type of School/College	1987/88	1992/93	1997/98
Primary Schools:	3387	3326	3305
National Schools	3269	3209	3186
National schools with pupils with special needs	175	204	369
Special National schools	118	117	119
Secondary Schools:	817	785	762
Secondary*	502	467	435
Vocational	254	248	246
Community & Comprehensive	61	70	81
Tertiary Institutions:	33	32	30
HEA Institutions**	7	7	10
Institutes of Technology***	18	19	15
Primary Teacher Training	6	4	3
Home Economics Teacher Training	2	2	2

Source Dept. of Education and Science
*incl. secondary top schools up to 1990/91 inclusive.
**incl. Mary Immaculate College of Ed. and St Patrick's College Drumcondra from 1992/3 and 1993/4, respectively.
***incl. Killybegs HTC College, Dublin College of Music, Dun Laoghaire College of Art & Design from 1988/9. incl. Cork School of Music and the Crawford College of Art & Design (both as part of Cork IT) from 1992/3. Incl. the NCI from 1993/4.

● Northern Ireland - Type of School/College	1987/88	1991/92	1998/99
Nursery Schools	-	91	91
Primary Schools	1,071*	938	916
Secondary Schools			
Non-Grammar	249**	161	165
Grammar	-	71	72
Tertiary Institutions			
Further Institutions	-	-	4***
Higher Education Institutions	-	-	17
Special Schools	46	47	47
Hospital Schools	-	3	3
Independent Schools	16	20	22
TOTAL	1,382	1,331	1,337

Source Dept. of Education Northern Ireland
* Figure incl. Nursery schools. **Figure incl. Grammar schools. ***Figure does not incl. the Open University

Multi-denominational Schools

● Republic of Ireland - *Level of School*	1997/98	1998/99
Primary Schools*	n/a	24
(of which are Educate Together schools)	-	18
Primary Students	n/a	3,533
Secondary Schools	319	322
Secondary Students	148,479	148,714

Source Dept. of Education and Science
* Incl. Special Schools run by Health Boards

● Northern Ireland - *Integrated schools*	1991/92	1996/97	1998/99
Number of Schools	11	21	24
Number of Pupils	1,226	3,512	9,491

Source Dept. of Education Northern Ireland

Gaelscoileanna *(Outside the Gaeltacht)*

School Level	Leinster	Munster	Connacht	Ulster *(9 Co.s)*	Total
Primary Schools 1998/9:					
No. of Schools	52	41	12	29	134
Pupil Enrolment (e)	9,526	6,670	2,050	2,157	20,618 (e)
Secondary Schools 1997/8:					
No. of Schools	11	14	2	2	31
Pupil Enrolment (e)	2877	1860	199	340	5276(e)

Source Gaelscoileanna

NI Students at Single-sex / Co-ed Schools

● Northern Ireland - *Type of School*	Boys	Girls	Total
Nursery *(co-educational)*	2,854	2,647	5,501
Primary*			
Single sex	5,614	6,919	12,533
Co-educational	86,898	82,302	169,200
Prep. Departments			
Single sex	532	573	1,105
Co-educational	1,120	992	2,112
Secondary Schools *(non-Grammar)*			
Single sex	10,357	13,369	23,726
Co-educational	36,265	31,767	68,032
Grammar			
Single sex	14,099	15,714	29,813
Co-educational	15,843	16,536	32,379
All Schools			
Single sex	30,602	36,575	67,177
Co-educational	142,980	134,244	277,224

Source Dept. of Education Northern Ireland

European Comparisons

% population 25–59 years completed at least upper Secondary education (1997)

AUS	75.1	ITA	41.4
BEL	60.6	LUX	47.7
DEN	80.0	NL	65.9
FIN	72.6	NOR	44.0*
FRA	62.7	POR	23.8
GER	82.1	SPA	35.1
GRE	49.3	SWE	76.7
ICE	75.0*	SWI	81.0*
IRL	**51.3**	UK	55.3

% 16–18 year olds in education 1996

AUS	82.0	ITA	:
BEL	95.0	LUX	77.0
DEN	83.0	NL	91.0
FIN	90.0	NOR	93.0
FRA	91.0	POR	69.0
GER	92.0	SPA	74.0
GRE	69.0	SWE	94.0
ICE	77.0	SWI	86.0
IRL	**84.0**	UK	70.0

*1996.

Continued from previous page

% of Women in 3rd-level education as a proportion of all students (1996)			
AUS	48.0	ITA	53.0
BEL	50.0	LUX	50.0
DEN	55.0	NL	47.0
FIN	53.0	NOR	58.0
FRA	55.0	POR	56.0
GER	45.0	SPA	53.0
GRE	48.0	SWE	55.0*
ICE	59.0	SWI	39.0
IRL	51.0	UK	50.0

*1995.

% 19–21 year olds in education 1996			
AUS	31.0	ITA	n/a
BEL	62.0	LUX	41.0
DEN	45.0	NL	59.0
FIN	44.0	NOR	48.0
FRA	57.0	POR	39.0
GER	48.0	SPA	50.0
GRE	42.0	SWE	32.0*
ICE	48.0	SWI	42.0
IRL	38.0	UK	41.0

*1995.

Students

Status of School Leavers

● Republic of Ireland - *Status*	1995	1996	1997
Estimated Number in Category	67,500	68,500	68,900
Employed	40.4%	44.0%	41.3%
Unemployed after loss of job	4.5%	4.1%	4.3%
(of which on schemes)	(0.7%)	(0.4%)	(0.4%)
Unemployed and seeking first job	9.9%	8.6%	7.2%
(of which on schemes)	(20.3%)	(18.4%)	(22.7%)
Studying	41.9%	37.5%	41.2%
Unavailable for work	1.9%	3.0%	2.9%
Emigrated	1.4%	2.8%	3.1%
TOTAL	100.0%	16.8%	20.1%

Source Dept. of Education and Science

● Northern Ireland (1996/7)	Male	Female	Total
Students (Higher Education Institutes)	3,203	4,044	7,247
Students (Further Education Institutes)	3,785	4,608	8,393
Employed/in training/seeking employment	5,905	3,770	9,675
Unknown	224	178	402
TOTAL	13,117	12,600	25,717

Source Dept. of Education Northern Ireland

Percentage of Population in Full-time Education

● Republic of Ireland - *Age Group**	1987/88	1992/93	1997/98
Persons aged 5–12 years	100.0%	100.0%	99.9%
Persons aged 13–15 years	98.0%	98.0%	98.7%
Persons aged 16 years	88.7%	92.6%	91.3%
Persons aged 17 years	69.1%	80.8%	81.6%
Persons aged 18 years	42.2%	61.8%	61.4%
Persons aged 19 years	24.7%	40.3%	48.4%
Persons aged 20 years and over**	11.2%	16.8%	20.1%

Source Dept. of Education and Science
Estimates incl. non-aided schools/institutions) and are based on provisional population estimates for each year.
**Figures from 1993/4 onwards excl. student aged 25 and over for percentage calculations.*

● Republic of Ireland - *Age Group*	1992-93	1994-95	1996-97
16 years	45.6%	47.0%	46.7%
17 years	33.2%	36.9%	31.4%
16 and 17 years	39.4%	42.0%	42.2%

Source Dept. of Education Northern Ireland

School Leavers without Formal Qualifications

● Republic of Ireland - *Status*	1995	1996	1997
Estimated Number in Category	2,200	2,700	2,200
Employed	33.8%	27.1%	33.1%
Unemployed after loss of job	7.9%	8.2%	10.6%
(of which on schemes)	(3.1%)	(1.1%)	(2.1%)
Unemployed and seeking first job	45.1%	52.8%	48.6%
(of which on schemes)	(20.3%)	(18.4%)	(22.7%)
Studying	1.4%	1.3%	0.8%
Unavailable for work	11.6%	9.9%	6.5%
Emigrated	0.2%	0.7%	0.4%
TOTAL	100.0%	16.8%	20.1%

Source Dept. of Education and Science

● Northern Ireland - *Status of School Leavers 1997/8*	Males	Females	Total
No. of Students with no qualifications of any kind	505	292	797
% of Students with no qualifications of any kind	3.9%	2.3%	3.1

Source Dept. of Education Northern Ireland

RoI Most Popular Subjects in Secondary Senior Cycle

Subject	Males	Females	Total
Mathematics	59,903	63,503	123,406
English	59,679	63,361	123,040
Irish	58,908	62,594	121,502
Religious Education	52,296	58,056	110,352
French	32,425	45,555	77,980
Physical Education	34,384	42,424	76,808
Biology	20,805	39,726	60,531
Geography	31,716	27,591	59,307
Business Organisation	21,821	26,134	47,955
Home Economics (S & S)	6,202	38,147	44,349
Computer Studies	14,200	19,099	33,299
History	17,504	13,554	31,058
German	10,282	12,719	23,001
Art	8,970	12,363	21,333
Accounting	9,237	10,517	19,754
Physics	14,681	4,990	19,671
Construction Studies	17,951	1,185	19,136
Technical Drawing	15,631	1,112	16,743
Chemistry	6,942	7,349	14,291

Source Dept. of Education and Science

Average number of Foreign Languages taught per Pupil in 2nd-level Education (1996)

Country	No. Languages	Country	No. Languages
AUS	n/a	ITA	1.1
BEL	1.4*	LUX	2.9
DEN	1.9	NL	2.4
FIN	2.4	NOR	n/a
FRA	1.6	POR	1.3
GER	1.2	SPA	1.0
GRE	1.2	SWE	1.7**
ICE	n/a	SWI	n/a
IRL	1.0	UK	n/a

* Incl. data from French-speaking and Flemish speaking communities. **1994.

Teachers
Number of Full-time Teachers

● Republic of Ireland - *Personnel by School Level*	1987/88	1992/93	1997/98
Primary Schools	21,217	20,761	21,100
Secondary Schools (full-time teachers)	19,314	19,807	21,066
Secondary Schools (full-time equivalent of part-time teachers)	n/a	1,386	2,244

Source Dept. of Education and Science

● Northern Ireland - *Personnel by School Level*	1987-88	1991-92	1996-97
Nursery	156	162	180
Primary	7,678	8,044	9,099
Special	525	609	726
Secondary Schools	6,378	5,965	6,553
Grammar Schools			
Preparatory	155	116	173
Secondary	3,268	3,354	3,815
TOTAL:	9,801	9,435	10,541

Source Dept. of Education Northern Ireland
These figures do not include full-time teachers in hospital schools.

Numbers Employed in 3rd-level Education

● Republic of Ireland - *Full-time Staff, Dec. 1997*	Full-time	Part-time	Total
Academic Staff	2,861	1,050	3,911
Professor and Associate Professor	323	27	350
Associate Professor	185	5	152
Statutory / Senior Lecturer	607	27	634
College Lecturer	1,359	371	1,730
Assistant Lecturer	194	494	688
Other teaching staff	139	93	231
Other staff	54	33	87
Non-academic Staff	3,853	987	4,840
Management / Senior Administrators	312	5	317
Administration	1,731	340	2,071
Technical	1,053	292	1,102
Maintenance	704	329	944
Student Services	53	21	74

Source Higher Education Authority
* Figures refer to UCD, UCC, UCG, TCD, SPM, DCU, UL, NCAD.

● Northern Ireland - *Full-time University Staff by Grade*	1996/97	1997/98
Professors	259	281
Readers & Senior Lecturers	473	550
Lecturers, Assistant Lecturers	1,635	1,733
Demonstrators and Others	-	2,564
Total	2,367	5,128

Source Dept. of Education Northern Ireland

RoI Expenditure on salaries

Expenditure by Sector	1987/98 £m*	1992/93 £m*	1997/98 £m*(e)
Primary level (Salaries & Pensions)	399.5	578.0	735.1
Secondary level (Salaries & Pensions)	397.0	591.1	783.0
Third level (Salaries)	150.2	241.8	330.8

Source Dept. of Education and Science
*refers to financial years.

Exams

Rol Number of Pupils taking Public Exams

● Republic of Ireland - *Examination*	1987/98	1992/93	1997/98
Candidates sitting Junior Certificate*..	75,863	66,063	64,612
Candidates sitting Leaving Certificate**.....................................	51,159	61,563	65,201
Total	127,022	127,626	129,813

Source Dept. of Education and Science
*Figures for 1987/88 are for the Group Cert and Intermediate Cert which was replaced by the Junior Cert in 1991/92.
Figures for 1992/93 and 1997/98 excl. participants in the Vocational Training Opportunities Scheme.
**Excl. participants in the Vocational Training Opportunities Scheme. Incl. participants who repeated the Leaving
Certificate, those who were external candidates and those who undertook the Applied Leaving Cert.*

Subjects taken in Leaving Certificate Exams

Subject 1997/98	Total taking exam	No. of Higher papers	Subject	% A1s awarded overall
English	61,304	33,787	Chemistry	6.55
Irish	57,556	17,732	Accounting	4.12
Mathematics	55,913	10,723	Physics	3.44
French	37,085	17,628	Biology	3.36
Biology	30,613	19,024	Technical Drawing	3.06
Geography	29,689	21,484	History	2.54
Home Economics (S & S)	24,181	17,626	Economics	2.50
Business Organisation	24,055	14,561	German	2.19
History	14,842	9,025	Mathematics	1.89
German	11,372	7,234	Business Organisation	1.54
Art	10,323	7,137	Home Economics (S & S)	1.47
Accounting	9,888	6,520	French	1.44
Physics	9,659	6,704	Geography	1.39
Construction Studies	8,608	6,124	Art	1.31
Technical Drawing	7,480	3,428	Construction Studies	1.10
Chemistry	7,325	6,051	English	1.07
Economics	5,394	4,072	Irish	0.77

Source Dept. of Education and Science

Qualifications of School Leavers

● Republic of Ireland - *Exam Grades*	1995	1996	1998
Males			
Candidates with ≥ 3 Grade A2s on higher level papers	691	717	848
Candidates with ≥ 3 Grade B3s on higher level papers	2,811	2,685	3,028
Candidates with ≥ 6 Grade C3s on higher level papers	3,388	3,259	3,570
Candidates with ≥ 4 Grade C3s on higher level papers	7,646	7,229	7,792
Candidates with ≥ 2 Grade C3s on higher level papers	13,727	12,554	13,881
Candidates with ≥ 5 Grade D3s at any level	25,369	23,460	25,330
Females			
Candidates with ≥ 3 Grade A2s on higher level papers	930	878	1,267
Candidates with ≥ 3 Grade B3s on higher level papers	4,106	3,936	5,012
Candidates with ≥ 6 Grade C3s on higher level papers	5,050	4,772	5,902
Candidates with ≥ 4 Grade C3s on higher level papers	10,778	9,854	11,353
Candidates with ≥ 2 Grade C3s on higher level papers	16,760	14,968	16,926
Candidates with ≥ 5 Grade D3s at any level	28,402	25,727	28,697
Total			
Candidates with ≥ 3 Grade A2s on higher level papers	1,621	49,187	2,115
Candidates with ≥ 3 Grade B3s on higher level papers	6,917	1,595	8,040
Candidates with ≥ 6 Grade C3s on higher level papers	8,438	6,621	9,472
Candidates with ≥ 4 Grade C3s on higher level papers	18,424	8,031	19,145
Candidates with ≥ 2 Grade C3s on higher level papers	30,487	17,083	30,807
Candidates with ≥ 5 Grade D3s at any level	53,771	27,522	54,027

Source Dept. of Education and Science
Incl. figures for School, VTOS and Repeat Candidates only

Http://www.localalmanac.ie/education_and_science/

● Northern Ireland - *Exam Grades*	1987/88	1994/95	1997/98
Males	12,658	12,543	12,840
Candidates with ≥ 3 'A' levels	-	-	2,898
Candidates with ≥ 2 'A' levels	2,566	3,288	744
Candidates with 1 'A' level	390	314	249
Candidates with ≥ 5 higher grade GCSEs*	1,150	2,133	2,419
Candidates with 1–4 higher grade GCSEs*	2,573	3,095	3,254
Candidates with lower grade GCSEs*	2,613	2,767	2,368
Candidates with Other Qualifications**	-	-	908
Females	11,730	11,900	12,789
Candidates with ≥ 3 'A' levels	-	-	4,066
Candidates with ≥ 2 'A' levels	2,897	4,262	1,158
Candidates with 1 'A' level	481	344	240
Candidates with ≥ 5 higher grade GCSEs*	1,430	2,629	2,722
Candidates with 1–4 higher grade GCSEs*	3,026	2,676	2,606
Candidates with lower grade GCSEs*	2,027	1,670	1,540
Candidates with Other Qualifications**	-	-	457
Total	24,388	22,326	25,629
Candidates with ≥ 3 'A' levels	-	-	6,964
Candidates with ≥ 2 'A' levels	5,463	7,550	1,902
Candidates with 1 'A' level	871	658	489
Candidates with ≥ 5 higher grade GCSEs*	2,580	4,762	5,141
Candidates with 1–4 higher grade GCSEs*	5,599	5,771	5,860
Candidates with lower grade GCSEs*	4,640	4,437	3,908
Candidates with Other Qualifications**	5,235	1,355	1,365

Source Dept. of Education Northern Ireland
* *Incl. participants who sat GNVQs.*
***Incl. participants who did not sit GCSEs or who received no grades but who obtained other qualifications such as Pitman, City & Guilds, RSA, etc.*

Conversion Table - grades to points for 3rd-Level

NORTHERN IRELAND (A-level results)**	REPUBLIC OF IRELAND LEAVING CERTIFICATE* (Higher-level results)	(Ordinary-level results)
A=10 points	A1=100 points	A1=60 points
B=8 points	A2=90 points	A2=50 points
C=6 points	B1=85 points	B1=45 points
D=4 points	B2=80 points	B2=40 points
E=2 points	B3=75 points	B3=35 points
	C1=70 points	C1=30 points
	C2=65 points	C2=25 points
	C3=60 points	C3=20 points
	D1=55 points	D1=15 points
	D2=50 points	D2=10 points
	D3=45 points	D3= 5 points

Source Dept of Education Northern Ireland; Dept. of Education and Science
* *Six Leaving Certificate subjects are taken into consideration; Bonus points are awarded for maths by UL and DIT.*
** *Two or more A-levels are taken into consideration.*

Third level

Third-level Colleges - Republic of Ireland

● UNIVERSITIES

University of Dublin Trinity College, Dublin 2. ....*(Founded 1592)* ....(01) 677 2941
Dublin City University Glasnevin, Dublin 9. ....*(Founded 1980)* ....(01) 704 5000
University of Limerick Plassey Technological Park, Limerick. ....*(Founded 1972)* ....(061) 330 316
National University of Ireland, 49 Merrion Square, Dublin 2. ....01 - 676 7246
  University College Cork - National University of Ireland, Cork ....*(Founded 1854)* 021-276 871
  National University of Ireland, Dublin (UCD) Belfield, Dublin 4. ....*(Founded 1845)* 01-706 7777
  National University of Ireland, Galway (NUI Galway) Galway. ....*(Founded 1845)* 091-524411

Continued from previous page

National University of Ireland, Maynooth Co. Kildare. ....(Founded 1795) 01-628 5222

● **INSTITUTES OF TECHNOLOGY (ITs)**

DUBLIN IT Admissions office, 30 Upper Pembroke Street, Dublin 2 ....01-402 3445
DIT Aungier Street, Dublin 2...01-402 3000
DIT Bolton Street,Dublin 1 ....01-402 3000
DIT Cathal Brugha Street, Dublin 1 ....01-402 3000
DIT College of Music, Adelaide Road, Dublin 2 ....01-478 4564
DIT Kevin Street, Dublin 8 ....01-402 3000
DIT Mountjoy Square, Dublin 1..01-402 3000
Athlone IT Dublin Road, Athlone, Co. Westmeath..0902-24400
IT Carlow Kilkenny Road, Carlow. 0503-70400
Cork IT Rossa Avenue, Bishopstown, Co. Cork. 021-326 100
Crawford College of Art & Design Cork 021-966 777
Cork School of Music Union Quay, Cork 021-270 076
Dundalk IT Co. Louth. 042-70200
Dun Laoghaire Institute of Art, Design & Technology
Carriglea Park, Kill Ave., Dun Laoghaire, Co. Dublin. 01-280 1138
Galway-Mayo IT Dublin Road, Galway. 091-753 161
Letterkenny IT Port Road, Letterkenny, Co. Donegal. 074-24888
Limerick IT Moylish Park, Limerick. 061-327 688
IT Sligo Ballinode, Sligo. 071-43261
IT Tallaght Dublin 24. ....01-459 8888
IT Tralee Clash, Tralee, Co. Kerry 066-24666
IT Waterford Cork Road, Waterford 051-302 000
Colleges of Art & Design / Music
National College of Art & Design 100 Thomas St, Dublin 8 ....01-671 1377

● **COLLEGES OF EDUCATION AND COLLEGES OF HOME ECONOMICS**

Church of Ireland College of Education 96 Upper Rathmines Road, Dublin 6. ....01-497 0033
Colaiste Mhuire Marino, Griffith Ave, Dublin 9 ....01-833 5111
Froebel College of Education Sion Hill, Blackrock, Co. Dublin. 01-288 8520
Mary Immaculate College of Education South Circular Road, Limerick. 061-314 588
St. Angela's College Lough Gill, Co. Sligo. 071-43580
St. Catherine's College Sion Hill, Blackrock, Co. Dublin...01-288 4989
St. Patrick's College of Education Drumcondra, Dublin 9. ....01-837 6191

● **THEOLOGY & DIVINITY COLLEGES**

All Hallows College Grace Park Road, Dublin 9. ....01-837 3745
Holy Ghost College (Theology & Philosophy) Kimmage Manor, Whitehall Road, Dublin 12...........01-456 0057
Mater Dei Institute of Education Clonliffe Road, Dublin 3. ....01-837 6027
Milltown Institute of Theology & Philosophy Milltown Park, Dublin 6. ....01-269 8802
Pontifical University of Maynooth, Maynooth, Co. Kildare. 01-708 3600
St. John's College (Theology & Philosophy) St John's Hill, Waterford. 051-874199
St. Patrick's College Carlow. 0503-31114
St. Patrick's College (Theology & Philosophy) Thurles, Co. Tipperary 0504-21201
St. Peter's College (Theology) Summerhill, Wexford...053-42071

● **OTHER COLLEGES**

Advisory Council for English Language Schools 36 Lwr Baggot St, Dublin 2 ....01-676 3321
American College in Dublin 2 Merrion Square, Dublin 2 ....01-676 8939
CERT, the State Tourism Training Agency Cert Hse, Amiens St, Dublin 1 ....01-855 6555
Dublin Business School (DBS) 13-14 Aungier Street, Dublin 2.....................................01-475 1024
Dublin Dental Hospital Lincoln Place, Dublin 2..01-612 7200
Dublin Institute for Advanced Studies 10 Burlington Road, Dublin 4 ....01-668 0748
Garda College Training Centre, Templemore, Co. Tipperary. 0504-31522
Griffith College South Circular Road, Dublin 8 ....01-454 5640
Institiúid Teangeolaíochta Éireann 31 Plás Mhic Liam, Baile Átha Cliath 2 ....01-661 0004
Institute of Public Administration 57 - 61 Lansdowne Road, Dublin 4. ....01-668 6233
International Education Board Ireland, IPC House, 35–39 Shelbourne Rd, Dublin 4 .....01-614 4839
Honorable Society of Kings Inns Henrietta St, Dublin 1 ....01-874 4840
Montessori College Mount St. Mary's Road, Dundrum, Dublin 6. ....01-269 2499
Law Society of Ireland Blackhall Place, Dublin 7. 01-6710200
Military College Curragh Camp, Co. Kildare. ....(045) 41301

➤ *Continued from previous page*

● **OTHER COLLEGES**

National College of Industrial Relations Sandford Road, Dublin 6. ....(01) 406 0500
NTDI - Roslyn College, Roslyn Park, Sandymount, Dublin 4 ....01-205 7200
Portobello College South Richmond Street, Dublin 2. ....(01) 6715811
Royal College of Surgeons in Ireland St Stephen's Green, Dublin 2. ....01-402 2228
Royal Irish Academy of Music 36–38 Westland Row, Dublin 2. ....01-676 4412
Shannon College of Hotel Management Shannon, Co. Clare. ....(061) 471444
Hotel Training and Catering College Killybegs, Co. Donegal. 073-31120
Source *Higher Education Authority, Dept. of Education and Science*

Third-level Colleges - Northern Ireland

● **UNIVERSITIES & HIGHER EDUCATION INSTITUTES**

Queen's University of Belfast Belfast, BT7 1NN...............................*(Founded 1845)*.........01232-245 133
University of Ulster University House, Cromore Rd., Coleraine, Derry ......*(Founded 1968)*.............01265-44141
University of Ulster (Jordanstown) Shore Rd., Newtownabbey, Antrim....*(Founded 1968)*.........01232-365 131
University of Ulster (Magee College) Northland Rd., Derry BT48 7JL. 01232-365 621
University of Ulster (at Belfast) York St., Belfast BT15 1ED..................*(Founded 1968)*.........01232-328 515
St. Mary's Teacher Training College 191 Falls Road, Belfast....................................01232-327 678
Stranmillis Teacher Training College Stranmillis Road, Belfast 01232-381 271

● **FURTHER EDUCATION INSTITUTES**

Armagh College of Further Education Lonsdale Street, Armagh....................................01861-522 205
Belfast Institute of Further and Higher Education Park Hse, 87-91 Great Victoria St., Belfast...01232-265 000
Castlereagh College of Further and Higher Education Montgomery Road, Cregagh, Belfast...01232-797 144
Causeway Institute of Further and Higher Education Union St., Coleraine, Co. Derry.................01265-54717
East Antrim Institute of Further and Higher Education 32-34 Pound St., Larne, Co. Antrim 01574-272 268
East Down Institute of Further and Higher Education Market Street, Downpatrick, Co. Down ...01396-615 815
East Tyrone College of Further Education Circular Road, Dungannon, Co. Tyrone 01868-722 323
Fermanagh College Fairview, 1 Dublin Road, Enniskillen, Co. Fermanagh.............................01365-322 431
Limavady College of Further Education Main St., Limavady, Co. Derry 015047-62334
Lisburn College of Further and Higher Education 39 Castle Street, Lisburn, Co. Antrim...........01846-677 225
Newry & Kilkeel College of Further Education Patrick Street, Newry. Co. Down 01693-61071
North Down and Ards Institute of Further and Higher Education
Castle Park Rd, Bangor, Co. Down 01247-271 254
Northern Ireland Hotel & Catering College Ballywillan Road, Portrush, Co. Antrim 01265-823 768
North East Institute of Further and Higher Education Trostan Ave., Ballymena, Co. Antrim.......01266-652 871
North West Institute of Further and Higher Education Strand Road, Derry.............................01504-266 711
Omagh College of Further Education Mountjoy Rd., Omagh, Co. Tyrone.............................01662- 245 433
Upper Bann Institute of Further and Higher Education
26 Lurgan Road, Portadown, Craigavon, Co. Armagh 01762-337 111
Source *Dept. of Education Northern Ireland*

Entry Points for Third Level Education

Subject	Northern Ireland 1998/99 Mean	Republic of Ireland 1999 Upper Range for Degrees*
Agriculture	16.2	370
Architecture	19.2	495-566
Biological Sciences/Biotechnology	19.3	380-490
Business Studies	22.4	405-475
Combined Subjects	19.5	-
Commerce	-	395-440
Communications	-	470-475
Computer Science/Applications/Engineering	-	330-455
Creative Arts	17.9	-
Dentistry	-	525-535
Education	-	465-470
Engineering	21.0	250-490
Hotel/Catering Management	-	320-355
Humanities	20.0	-
Languages	-	420-475

Continued from previous page

Subject	Northern Ireland 1998/99 Mean	Republic of Ireland 1999 Upper Range for Degrees*
Law	22.6	445-540
Mathematical Sciences	19.0	410
Medicine	-	535-560
Medicine & Dentistry	29.5	-
Pharmacy	-	550
Physics	17.7	330-430
Quantity Surveying	-	370-385
Science	-	310-445
Social Science	22.4	415-420
Sport Science	-	460-480
Veterinary Medicine	-	545

Source Dept of Education and Science, CAO
*Not all on this points score were offered places. Certain colleges assess students on points plus performance and / or interview for some degrees, eg music, fine art, education.

Degrees and Diplomas Awarded

● Republic of Ireland - Qualification	1994	1996	1997
Higher Degree	2,510	2,845	2,706
Higher Diploma in Education	1,006	811	827
Postgraduate Diploma in Education	-	129	-
Primary Degree	11,051	13,045	13,537
Primary Degree in Education	422	652	672
Cert & Diploma (NCEA/DIT)	9,928	10,851	11,547
TOTAL	24,917	28,333	29,289

Source Higher Education Authority

● Northern Ireland - Qualifications from NI Institutions*	1995/96	1996/97	1997/98
Doctorates	256	283	162
Other higher degrees	1,349	1,561	1,626
PGCE	415	391	343
Other post-graduate qualifications	972	2,013	2,104
Primary Degree	6,051	6,283	6,500
HND/Dip HE	532	512	702
Other undergraduate qualifications	568	939	1,396
TOTAL	10,143	11,982	12,833

Source Dept of Education Northern Ireland
* incl. full-time & part time students and students from NI, RoI, Great Britain, EU and other overseas countries

Third-level Awards by Field of Study

● Republic of Ireland Students by Subject - 1998	Full-time Male	Full-time Female	Full-time Total	Part-time Male	Part-time Female	Part-time Total	Overall Total
Agricultural Science & Forestry	646	371	1,017	50	20	70	1,087
Architecture	167	133	300	10	3	13	313
Art & Design	232	430	662	7	1	8	670
Arts	5,827	13,124	18,951	999	2,026	3,025	21,976
Business Econ. & Social Studies	573	693	1,266	89	61	150	1,416
Combined Studies	441	501	942	187	189	376	1,318
Commerce	3,717	3,691	7,408	650	497	1,147	8,555
Communications & Information	287	838	1,125	9	8	17	1,142
Dentistry	0	0	0	0	0	0	0
Education	550	1,236	1,786	118	332	450	2,236
Engineering	5,079	1,193	6,272	1,142	398	1,540	7,812
Equestrian Studies	58	130	188	0	1	1	189
European Studies	154	411	565	0	2	2	567
Food Science & Technology	269	502	771	0	0	0	771
Law	514	697	1,211	159	113	272	1,483
Medicine	2,157	4,046	6,203	242	1,331	1,573	7,776
Multi-Faculty	630	1,406	2,036	0	0	0	2,036

Continued from previous page

● Republic of Ireland Students by Subject - 1998	Full-time Male	Full-time Female	Full-time Total	Part-time Male	Part-time Female	Part-time Total	Overall Total
Science	5,797	5,942	11,739	378	320	698	**12,437**
Social Science	12	15	27	2	4	6	**33**
Veterinary Medicine	210	174	384	3	4	7	**391**
TOTAL	**27,320**	**35,533**	**62,853**	**4,045**	**5,306**	**9,348**	**72,201**

Source Higher Education Authority
* *Institutions incl. in figures: UCD, UCC, UCG, TCD, SPM, DCU, UL, NCAD, RCSI.*

● Northern Ireland Students* by Subject - 1998/9	Full-time 1998/99	Part-time 1998/99	Total 1998/99
Business & Administrative Studies	4,660	4,805	9,465
Social, Economic & Political Studies	1,863	2,081	3,944
Education	1,383	298	1,681
Medicine-allied Subjects	3,476	1,865	5,341
Combined Subjects	2,296	1,622	3,918
Engineering & Technology	2,023	817	2,840
Computer Science	1,771	1,250	3,021
Biological Sciences	1,895	173	2,068
Physical Sciences	1,102	69	1,171
Creative Arts & Design	1,323	300	1,623
Languages	1,135	1,153	2,288
Architecture, Building & Planning	1,201	335	1,536
Humanities	831	478	1,309
Law	551	48	599
Librarianship & Information Science	610	28	638
Medicine & Dentistry	1,007	26	1,033
Agriculture & Related Subjects	265	154	419
Mathematical Sciences	468	33	501
TOTAL	**27,860**	**15,535**	**43,395**

Source Dept of Education Northern Ireland
**undergraduates only*

First Destination of 3rd-level Graduates

● Republic of Ireland - Primary & Higher Degree: 1997	Male	Female	Total
Research / Further Study - Ireland	1,035	1,072	2,107
Research / Further Study - Overseas	161	150	311
Teacher Training - Ireland	101	258	359
Teacher Training - Overseas	3	22	25
Other Vocational/Professional Training - Ireland	474	644	1,118
Other Vocational/Professional Training - Overseas	16	27	43
Work Experience - Ireland	21	64	85
Seeking Employment - Ireland	147	115	262
Not available - Ireland	152	202	354
Obtained Full-Time Employment - Ireland	2,631	2,831	5,462
Obtained Full-Time Employment - Overseas	742	764	1,506
Obtained Part-Time Employment - Ireland	59	117	176
Obtained Part-Time Employment - Overseas	41	55	96
TOTAL	**5,583**	**6,321**	**11,904**

● Republic of Ireland Sub-degree Respondents: 1997*	One-year cert %	Certificate %	Diplomas %	Total Number
Research / Further Study - Ireland	38.2	64.5	42.6	2,580
Research / Further Study - Overseas	2.9	2.1	6.6	189
Work Experience - Ireland	n/a	1.6	0.9	62
Seeking Employment - Ireland	n/a	1.5	2.9	96
Not available - Ireland	2.9	0.8	1.8	58
Obtained Full-Time Employment - Ireland	55.9	27.3	40.8	1,553
Obtained Full-Time Employment - Overseas	n/a	1.2	2.9	91
Obtained Part-Time Employment - Ireland	n/a	0.9	1.3	48
Obtained Part-Time Employment - Overseas	n/a	0.1	0.2	5
TOTAL	**100.0**	**100.0**	**100.0**	**4,682**

● Northern Ireland - *1996/97*	Undergraduate	Postgraduate	Total
Further Study/Training	1753	80	1833
Employed in the UK	2559	566	3125
Employed outside the UK	513	150	663
Not available for Study/Employment/Training	169	15	184
Assumed unemployed	376	26	402
Other	268	79	347
TOTAL:	5638	916	6554

NI Source Dept. of Education Northern Ireland

RoI Source Dept of Education and Science
* Includes One-Year Certs, National & DIT Certs, National & DIT Diplomas.

First Destination Occupations of Graduates

● Republic of Ireland *Primary & Higher Degree Holders by Sector, 1997*	Male	Female	Total
Agriculture, Forestry & Fishery Sectors	38	34	72
Manufacturing & Other Non-service Sectors	1,028	637	1,665
Public Services	596	1,085	1,681
Civil Service (Central) & Defence	56	42	98
Local Government	47	50	97
Health Board & Hospital Services	235	475	710
Education (Primary & Secondary)	82	267	349
Education (3rd-level)	120	170	290
Non-commercial state sponsored	56	81	137
Private Services	1,687	1,888	3,575
Wholesale distribution	23	17	40
Retailing	56	114	170
Transport, Communications, Storage	86	135	221
Business and Financial Sectors and Computer Services	796	741	1537
Social & Personal Services	51	142	193
Professional Services, Private Practice	550	508	1058
Other Areas	125	231	356
Other	124	123	247
TOTAL	3,473	3,767	7,240

Source Higher Education Authority

Graduate Employment by Region

● Republic of Ireland - *Region1997**	Primary Degree	Higher Degree	sub-Degree Cert
Ireland	4,444	1,194	1,601
North West & Donegal	78	21	62
West	314	58	161
Mid-west	306	45	120
South-west	458	149	245
South-east	209	50	109
East	2,832	827	767
North-east	61	14	59
Midlands	149	21	74
Northern Ireland	37	9	4
Overseas	1,249	353	96
Britain	397	107	56
Other EU states	457	123	20
Non-EU states	13	8	1
North America	94	31	12
South America	9	3	n/a
Africa	6	18	n/a
Australia	76	19	1
Middle East	30	4	1
Asia	93	6	2
Other	74	34	3
TOTAL	5,693	1,547	1,697

Source Higher Education Authority

Graduate Salaries

● **Republic of Ireland** - *Salary Level, 1997*

	Primary Degree	Higher Degree	Cert & Diplomas*
Under £5,000	2.5%	2.1%	5.4%
£5,000–£6,999	4.4%	2.9%	6.9%
£7,000–£8,999	5.8%	5.2%	11.5%
£9,000–£10,999	10.1%	4.8%	25.4%
£11,000–£12,999	10.6%	7.0%	18.6%
£13,000–£14,999	11.3%	6.8%	11.2%
£15,000–£16,999	17.1%	10.1%	8.2%
£17,000–£18,999	9.2%	7.8%	4.1%
£19,000+	5.9%	20.2%	5.3%
Unknown	23.0%	33.1%	3.4%
TOTAL	100.0%	100.0%	100.0%

Source Higher Education Authority
incl. One-Year Certs, National & DIT Certs, National & DIT Diplomas.

Useful addresses

Aontas - The National Association of Adult Education 22 Earlsfort Tce, Dublin 2 ....01-475 4121
Association of Community & Comprehensive Schools 2 Ascal Herbert, Dublin 4......................01-269 5375
Belfast Education & Library Board 40 Academy Street, Belfast BT1 2NQ....................................01232-564 000
Central Applications Office Tower Hse, Eglinton St, Galway...091-563 318
(The body responsible for processing third-level entry applications for most undergraduate courses.)
Catholic Primary Schools Managers, Veritas Hse, 7/8 Lwr Abbey St, Dublin 1 ....01-874 2171
Church of Ireland Board of Education, Church Ave, Rathmines, Dublin 6.................................01-497 8422
Council for Catholic Maintained Schools 160 High Street, Holywood, Co. Down 01232-426 972
Department of Education and Science, Communications Unit, Marlborough St, Dublin 1 ....01-809 5005
Dept of Education Northern Ireland Rathgael Hse, Balloo Rd, Bangor, Co. Down BT19 7PR 01247-279 279
Educate Together, 9B John Player Hse, 276-288 Sth Circular Rd, Dublin 8................................. 01-473 0309
FÁS - The Training Authority 27–33 Upper Baggot Street, Dublin 4 ....01-607 0500
Forfás Wilton Park Hse, Wilton Place, Dublin 2...01-607 3000
Gaelscoileanna, 7 Cearnóg Mhuirfean, Dublin 2...01-676 3222
Higher Education Authority 3rd Floor, Marine House, Clanwilliam Court, Dublin 2 ....01-661 2748
National Adult Literacy Agency, 76 Lwr Gardiner St, Dublin 1 ....01-855 4332
National Centre for Guidance in Education, Avoca Hse, 189/193 Parnell St, Dublin 1 ....01-873 1411
National Centre for Technology in Education, Dublin City University, Dublin 9 ....1850 70 40 40
National Council for Curriculum and Assessment, 24 Merrion Sq, Dublin 2 ....01-661 7177
National Council for Education Awards, 26 Mountjoy Sq, Dublin 1 ....01-855 6526
National Council for Vocational Awards, Marino Institute of Education, Griffith Ave, Dublin 9.........01-837 2211
North Eastern Education & Library Board
County Hall, 182 Galgorm Road, Ballymena, Co Antrim BT42 1HN 01266-653 333
Open University Holbrook Hse, Holles St, Dublin 2 ....01-678 5399
Open University 40 University Rd, Belfast 01232-245 025
South Eastern Education & Library Board 18 Windsor Ave, Belfast BT9 6EF 01232-564 000
Southern Education & Library Board 3 Charlemont Place, The Mall, Armagh...........................01861-512 200
TEASTAS, the National Certification Authority Marino Inst. of Education, Griffith Ave, Dublin 9 ....01-837 6969
UCAS, the Universities and Colleges' Admissions Centre for the UK ....www.ucas.ac.uk
Western Education & Library Board 1 Hospital Road, Omagh, Co. Tyrone 01662-411 411

MEDIA

Changing the Face of Irish Broadcasting

By **Sile deValera TD,**
Minister for Arts, Heritage, Gaeltacht & The Islands

W E in Ireland have been well served in terms of broadcasting media for many years. Initially RTÉ and its predecessor Radio Éireann provided a national broadcasting service, which became and remains an integral part of our lives. Broadcasting was enhanced and invigorated through the establishment of independent local radio services in the late 1980s and early 1990s. The 1990s also saw the establishment of Teilifís na Gaeilge - a national Irish language television service - and the establishment of Today FM and TV3, our national independent radio and television services, as well as a number of community and special interest radio stations.

In addition to these indigenous services, Irish viewers and listeners have enjoyed access to British television and radio services and have, of course, access to a broad range of English language and other services, which are delivered via satellite

We are now in the midst of revolutionary technological change through the application of digital techniques to broadcast transmission and the convergence of broadcasting, information and telecommunications technologies. Apart from technological change itself, the pace of change is astounding.

It is clear that if we are to ensure that the benefits of these new and changing technologies can be shared by all, a proper statutory structure for broadcasting needs to be established. It was with this objective in mind that I published the Broadcasting Bill, 1999 last May. This is the first major piece of legislation relating to broadcasting matters since 1988. I hope that when enacted, the Broadcasting Bill 1999 will provide the secure statutory basis for the development of indigenous broadcasting services of high quality that are of relevance to Irish society and serve the interests of our citizens well into the new millennium.

Of course broadcasting is no longer what might be called a stand alone medium. As we all know digital technology is bringing about an unstoppable convergence between telecommunications, computers and broadcasting, and creating the global infrastructure for the Information Society. The digital broadcasting infrastructure that will be created will become an essential element in the provision of all kinds of content and services over the same network. The balancing act for me in promoting this new legislation is to try and get the relationship between the cultural and the technological dimension right.

The application of digital technologies to broadcasting provides the opportunity for the provision of a vast additional range of Information Society services and to provide those services on a platform that can compete with telecommunications and other delivery platforms. It is not for me to say which is the better platform. However it is my concern to recognise in my legislative proposals that in addition to technical and economic aspects, social, cultural and democratic aspects are of paramount importance for the development of the Information Society.

Digital services are already available in some countries and the cable and Multichannel Multipoint Distribution System (MMDS) industry have announced plans to upgrade to digital.

Digital terrestrial television services have also been introduced in a number of countries including our nearest neighbour - Britain. The Government has decided that arrangements should be made for the introduction of digital terrestrial television (DTT) in Ireland at the earliest possible date. A new entity is to be created, in which RTÉ will be a minority partner with a significant minority shareholding. That entity will be mandated to build and operate the DTT infrastructure and to promote the development of multimedia services and the Information Society. RTÉ's existing transmission function will be separated from RTÉ as a going concern and RTÉ's equity contribution to the new entity will be met to the extent required by the value of these assets.

It is envisaged that RTÉ will have guaranteed access to the capacity of one of the DTT multiplexes and that TV3 and TnaG will have guaranteed access to another multiplex. The remaining four multiplexes may carry UK terrestrial channels as subscription services as well as premium services such as movie and sports channels. Internet and other interactive services may also be carried. These services would be managed by the Transmission Entity.

A key policy objective is the concept of universal service. Digital terrestrial television services must be made available to all. Universal access to the Internet and other interactive services are also important public policy objectives as DTT has the potential to be an important delivery medium for Information Society services, especially in rural areas. I hope that the DTT transmission network project will be rolled out during the course of the year 2000.

The introduction of DTT and the development of other digital platforms such as digital cable and MMDS will provide the opportunity for the provision of new indigenous teLevision services. The Broadcasting Bill, 1999 recognises this potential and provides a statutory structure under which these services can be provided. My legislative proposals will confer additional functions on the Independent Radio and Television Commission, which after the enactment of the Bill will be known as the Broadcasting Commission of Ireland. It is envisaged that content of all indigenous digital programme services, apart from those governed by existing legislation will be regulated by the Broadcasting Commission of Ireland. It will be the responsibility of the Commission to draw up codes and rules to be complied with in relation to such content. I will expect the Commission to regulate the sector with a light touch.

The Bill proposes that the Commission must prepare codes specifying standards to be complied with in respect of the taste and decency of programme material. It also proposes that the Commission must draw up a code of standards to be complied with in relation to advertising, teleshopping material, sponsorship and other forms of commercial promotion employed in any broadcasting service.

Those wishing to become broadcasters or broadcasting service providers on any platform - DTT, cable or MMDS - will be able to apply to the Broadcasting Commission of Ireland for a broadcasting content contract. I hope that new services at a local and regional level, as well as niche services can be encouraged and developed.

In keeping with the theme that the benefits of digital broadcasting should be shared by all, the legislation specifically proposes that the Commission shall make rules requiring broadcasters to take specific steps to promote the understanding by people with aural or visual impediments of broadcasting services. While it will be a matter for the Commission to draw up the code the legislation clearly envisages a quota regime that will see an ever-increasing amount of programming accessible to those with hearing and visual impairments.

The Bill also clarifies the public service remit of RTÉ in these changing times so that public service broadcasting continues to play its vital role in the digital era. Powers to establish Teilifís na Gaeilge as a separate entity will be provided as well as specific measures to support the local radio sector.

The next few years will see enormous change to the broadcasting map in Ireland and indeed the rest of the world. My objective is that Irish broadcasters and programme makers as well as the providers of new multimedia services have the opportunity to access these new technologies so that the maximum benefit can be derived by all.

Síle de Valera
October 1999

The author is the Minister for Arts, Heritage, Gaeltacht and the Islands and is a TD for the Clare constituency since 1987. She recently published the Broadcasting Bill, 1999, the first major piece of legislation relating to broadcasting matters since 1988.

Television

Radio Telefís Éireann

MAIN FACTFILE
Director General......**Bob Collins**
Chairman of RTÉ Authority
..........................Farrel Corcoran
Director of Television..................
..........................Joe Mulholland
Director of News.........Ed Mulhall
Number of channels..................3
% Home produced 63%
Number of Regional Studios 8
International Offices 3
Number of Staff......................................2,100

COMMUNICATIONS
Donnybrook, Dublin 4.
Tel 01-208 3111   *Fax* 01-208 6080
email press@rte.ie   *Website* www@rte.ie

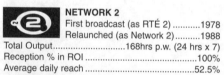

RTÉ 1
First broadcast ....December, 1961
Total Output ...168 hrs p.w. (24 hrs x 7)
Reception % in ROI 100%
Average daily reach 61.8%

NETWORK 2
First broadcast (as RTÉ 2) 1978
Relaunched (as Network 2)..........1988
Total Output.............................168hrs p.w. (24 hrs x 7)
Reception % in ROI 100%
Average daily reach 52.5%

TG4
Ceannasaí ....**Cathal Goan**
Editor, Nuacht ....Michael Lally
First broadcast (TnaG).........1996
Total output..............66.5 hrs p.w.
Irish language output31.5 hrs p.w.
Reception % in ROI 74%
Daily viewers ..... (7-9%) 335,000
Number of Staff 40

Communications:
Baile na hAbhainn, Co na Gaillimhe.
Tel 091-505050 *Fax* 091-505 021.
email: eolas@tg4.ie *Web* www.tg4.ie

TV3 Television Network

MAIN FACTFILE
Managing Director:
......................**Rick Hetherington**
Director of Engineering
.....................................Peter Ennis
Director of Sales: ....Pat Kiely
Director of News: Andrew Hanlon
Director of Programming: Michael

Murphy
First broadcast ....September 1998
Number of channels 1 (TV3)
Total Output ....138 hours p.w.
% Home produced 24.8%
Reception % in ROI 92%
Number of Staff......................................153

COMMUNICATIONS
Westgate Business Park, Ballymount, Dublin 24
Tel 01-419 3333   *Fax* 01-419 3300

British Broadcasting Corporation Northern Ireland

MAIN FACTFILE
Controller: ......**Patrick Loughrey**
Head of Broadcasting:
..........................Anna Carragher
Head of Production:...Paul Evans
Head of News & Current Affairs:
..........................Andrew Colman
Head of Drama:....Robert Cooper
Number of channels 2
(BBC 1 & BBC 2)
Total Output ....685 hours p.w.
Home produced Output...........10hrs (BBC 1 & BBC 2)
Number of Regional Studios 1
Number of Staff: Regional Broadcasting.................336
Number of Staff: Resources....................................248

Communications
Broadcasting House, Ormeau Avenue,
Belfast BT2 8HQ.
Tel 01232-338000 *Fax* 01232-338800.
Website www.bbc.co.uk/ni

Ulster Television PLC.

MAIN FACTFILE
Managing Director:
........................**Desmond Smyth**
Controller of Programming:
...............................Alan Bremner
Head of News and Current Affairs:
...............................Rob Morrison
First broadcast ...... October 1959
Number of channels
..........................2 (UTV, TV-You)
Total Output..144 hours p.w.
Home produced..12 hours p.w.
Reception % in ROI..................................75% (approx)
Number of Regional Studios.......................................1
Number of Staff...150

COMMUNICATIONS
Havelock House, Ormeau Road, Belfast BT7 1EB.
Tel 01232-328122 *Fax* 01232-246695
Website www.utvlive.com

RoI: Channel Penetration

	RTÉ 1 %	N2 %	TV3 %	BBC 1 %	BBC 2 %	UTV %	C4 %	SKY 1 %
Percentage Reception	100	100	85	71	70	64	62	50

RoI: National & Multi Channel Share

Adults Peak time 18.00 - 23.29 Jan-Jun 1999	RTÉ 1 %	NET 2 %	TV3 %	Others %
National Channel Share	41.5	13.7	5.1	44.8
Multi Channel Share	32.7	10.6	3.4	56.7

RoI & NI: Television Licences by number

(1998)	Monochrome	Colour	Total
REPUBLIC OF IRELAND	14,005	901,147	915,152
Leinster	5,443	486,749	492,192
Munster	5,143	262,600	267,743
Connacht	2,654	101,940	104,594
Ulster (part of)	765	49,858	50,623
NORTHERN IRELAND	17,431	406,185	423,616
TOTAL (all-island)	31,436	1,307,332	1,338,768

RTÉ 1: Most Popular Programmes 1998

Rank	Programme	Genre	Day & Date	No. of viewers
1	Father Ted - Tribute	Comedy	Sunday, 1 March	1,163,000
2	The Late Late Show	Talk Show	Friday, 4 December	1,143,000
3	The Eurovision Song Contest	Music	Saturday, 9 May	1,027,000
4	Coronation Street	Soap Opera	Wednesday, 1 April	1,019,000
5	Glenroe	Soap Opera	Sunday, 1 March	998,000
6	Only Fools And Horses	Comedy	Thursday, 1 January	970,000
7	Winning Streak	Game Show	Saturday, 3 January	926,000
8	Babe	Film	Friday, 25 December	921,000
9	The Rose Of Tralee	Entertainment	Wednesday, 26 August	886,000
10	Kenny Live	Talk Show	Saturday, 14 March	881,000
11	Fair City	Soap Opera	Tuesday, 20 January	853,000
12	Falling For A Dancer	Drama	Sunday, 27 September	815,000
13	The Santa Claus	Film	Saturday, 19 December	797,000
14	The Shawshank Redemption	Film	Tuesday, 6 January	791,000
15	Crimeline	Crime	Monday, 7 September	773,000
16	Lethal Weapon 2	Film	Wednesday, 30 December	765,000
17	Dennis The Menace	Film	Saturday, 3 January	761,000
18	Braveheart	Film	Friday, 25 December	758,000
19	Nell	Film	Sunday, 4 January	747,000
20	Die Hard With A Vengeance	Film	Monday, 1 June	733,000
21	Mr Bean	Comedy	Thursday, 1 January	730,000
22	Snapper	Film	Tuesday, 17 March	729,000
23	Upwardly Mobile	Comedy	Friday, 25 December	723,000
24	Eurosong	Music	Sunday, 8 March	712,000
25	One Foot In The Grave	Comedy	Sunday, 8 March	712,000
26	1998 Academy Awards	Awards Show	Tuesday, 24 March	710,000
27	Keeping Up Appearances	Comedy	Monday, 28 December	710,000
28	Home Alone	Film	Saturday, 12 December	684,000
29	Fame And Fortune	Game Show	Friday, 28 August	678,000
30	Other Woman		Sunday, 29 March	671,000

NETWORK 2: Most Popular Programmes 1998

Rank	Programme	Genre	Day & Date	No. of viewers
1	Friends	Comedy	Monday, 7 December	759,000
2	Father Ted	Comedy	Monday, 7 September	685,000
3	Argentina v England	Sport	Tuesday, 30 June	625,000
4	Sunday Game Live (All Ireland Football Finals)	Sport	Sunday, 27 September	603,000

➤ *Continued from previous page*

Rank	Programme	Genre	Day & Date	No. of viewers
5	Holland v Brazil	Sport	Tuesday, 7 July	597,000
6	Ireland v Malta	Sport	Wednesday, 14 October	577,000
7	Home And Away	Soap Opera	Monday, 2 March	550,000
8	France v Brazil	Sport	Sunday, 12 July	540,000
9	Ireland v Argentina	Sport	Wednesday, 22 April	532,000
10	France v Croatia	Sport	Wednesday, 8 July	512,000
11	Dr. No	Film	Wednesday, 14 January	504,000
12	Forever Young	Film	Wednesday, 11 March	487,000
13	Romania v England	Sport	Monday, 22 June	486,000
14	Sunday Game Live (All Ireland Hurling Finals)	Sport	Sunday, 13 September	483,000
15	Sister Act 2	Film	Saturday, 21 November	477,000
16	Sister Act	Film	Saturday, 23 May	474,000
17	Ireland v Germany (UEFA Under-18 Final)	Sport	Sunday, 26 July	462,000
18	Diamonds Are Forever	Film	Wednesday, 11 February	449,000
19	Sleeping With The Enemy	Film	Friday, 2 January	446,000
20	From Russia With Love	Film	Wednesday, 21 January	444,000
21	Ireland v Italy (UEFA Under 16 Final)	Sport	Friday, 8 May	444,000
22	Scotland v Morocco	Sport	Tuesday, 23 June	441,000
23	Barcelona v Manchester United	Sport	Wednesday, 25 November	434,000
24	You Only Live Twice	Film	Wednesday, 28 January	432,000
25	Manchester United v Monaco	Sport	Wednesday, 18 March	429,000
26	Licence To Kill	Film	Wednesday, 7 January	424,000
27	Titanic-Confession	-	Saturday, 21 March	424,000
28	Childline 10th Birthday Celebration	Concert	Saturday, 21 February	403,000
29	Elton John - Tantrums & Tiaras	Concert	Thursday, 1 January	396,000
30	Manchester Utd v Bayern Munich	Sport	Wednesday, 9 December	396,000

TG4 (formerly TnaG): Most Popular Programmes 1999

Rank	Programme	Genre	Day & Date	No. of viewers
1	Carraig An Cheoil	Music	Wednesday, 17 March	55,000
2	Gleann Ceo	Comedy	Sunday, 31 January	43,000
3	Craobh Club AIB	Sport	Sunday, 31 January	43,000
4	Ros Na Rún	Soap Opera	Tuesday, 13 April	42,000
5	Gearóid na Gaisce 27	Animation	Friday, 9 April	41,000
6	Spórt TnaG	Sport	Sunday, 18 April	39,000
7	Ole Ole	Sport	Monday, 7 June	37,000
8	Ard San Aer	Sport	Tuesday, 13 April	36,000
9	Art Ó Ruairc	Animation	Sunday, 24 January	36,000
10	Gradam TnaG i Gceoil	Music	Friday, 1 January	35,000

BBC One Northern Ireland: Most Popular Programmes 1998

Rank	Programme	Genre	Audience Share %	No. of viewers
1	Showbands	Documentary	43	276,000
2	Give My Head Peace	Comedy	39	231,000
3	Making A Difference	-	39	209,000
4	Children In Need	Charity Broadcast	41	208,000
5	Twelfth Live	Current Affairs	62	196,000
6	We Shall Overcome	-	37	186,000
7	Titanic, Made in Belfast	Documentary	27	163,000
8	Back To The Future	Film	43	154,000
9	Newsline (6:30)	Current Affairs	26	151,000
10	Let's Talk	Current Affairs	26	141,000
11	Lives of Our Time	-	23	127,000
12	Spotlight	Current Affairs	23	125,000
13	Opening of NI Assembly	Current Affairs	33	124,000

Continued from previous page

Rank	Programme	Genre	Audience Share %	No. of viewers
14	Election '98	Current Affairs	36	106,000
15	Home Truths	-	22	101,000
16	Let Me Entertain You	Music/Entertainment	19	90,000
17	Match of the Day (NI)	Sport	30	81,000
18	NI Sports Results	Sport	20	77,000
19	Irish Rock & Pop Awards	Music	15	59,000
20	NI Sports Awards	Sport	18	18,000

BBC Two Northern Ireland: Most Popular Programmes 1998

Rank	Programme	Genre	Audience Share %	No. of viewers
1	Pipe Bands	Music	26	101,000
2	Rankin Challenge	Cookery	15	94,000
3	Hand of History	-	9	45,000
4	Country Times	-	10	44,000
5	Awash With Colour	Arts	6	39,000

RoI: Selected Advertising Rates

Station (Rate in bracket)	10 secs £	20 secs £	30 secs £	40 secs £	50 secs £	60 secs £
RTÉ1 and Network 2 (prime rate)	3,500	5,600	7,000	9,310	11,690	14,000
RTÉ 1 and Network 2 (bottom rate)	25	40	50	67	84	100
TnaG (single spot)	60	80	100	-	-	-

Radio

Radio Telefís Éireann

MAIN FACTFILE
Director General ....Bob Collins
Chairman of RTÉ Authority ....Farrel Corcoran
Director of Radio ....Helen Shaw
Director of News ....Ed Mulhall
Number of channels ....5 (see profiles below)
Total Output (per week) ....200 hours
% Home produced 50%
Number of Regional Studios 8
International Offices 3
Number of Staff 2,100

Communications
Donnybrook, Dublin 4.
Tel 01-208 3111 *Fax* 01 208 6080
email press@rte.ie *Website* www@rte.ie

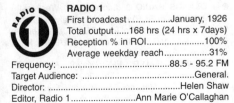

RADIO 1
First broadcast ....January, 1926
Total output ......168 hrs (24 hrs x 7days)
Reception % in ROI 100%
Average weekday reach 31%
Frequency: ....88.5 - 95.2 FM
Target Audience: ....General.
Director: ....Helen Shaw
Editor, Radio 1 ....Ann Marie O'Callaghan

2FM
First broadcast ....May, 1979
Total output: ....168 hrs (24 hrs x 7days)
Reception % in ROI 100%
Average weekday reach 28%
Frequency: ....90 - 92 FM
Target Audience: ....15-34 yrs
Head of 2FM ....John Clarke
Programme Manager ....Liam Thompson
Station email ....2fm@rte.ie

RAIDIÓ NA GAELTACHTA
First broadcast 1972
Total output: .....115.5 hours
(16.5 hrs x 7days)
Reception % in ROI ...100%

Raidió na Gaeltachta
ar fud na tíre

Average daily reach 1%
Frequency: ....90.9- 102.7 FM
Target Audience: ....Gaeltacht / Gaelic speakers
Ceannaire: ....Pól Ó Gallchóir
Leas Ceannaire
agus Eagarthóir Stiúrtha: ....Tomas Mac Con Iomaire
Staff 60

Communications
Casla, Contae na Gaillimhe
Tel 091-506677 *Fax* 091-506666
email rnag@rte.ie *Website* www.rnag.ie

LYRIC FM
First broadcast ....May, 1999
Total output: 168 hours (24 hrs x 7 days)

Frequency: ....96 - 99 FM
Target Audience: ....Classical music audience
Head of Lyric FM.............................Séamus Crimmins

Communications
Cornmarket Square, Limerick.
Tel 061-207300   *Fax* 061-207390
email lyric@rte.ie   *Website* www.lyricfm.ie

RTÉ RADIO CORK
First broadcast.........................June, 1974
Total output: ....38.5 hrs (5.5 hrs x 7)
Frequency: ....89 FM & 729 MW
Target Audience: ....Cork
Head, Broadcasting ....Gerry Reynolds
Producer in charge ....Pat O'Donovan

Communications
Fr. Matthew Street, Cork.
Tel 021-272922   *Fax* 021-273829
email info@rtecork.iol.ie

Today FM

MAIN FACTFILE
First broadcast........January, 1998
Chairperson: ....John McColgan
Chief Executive..Willie O'Reilly
News Editor...Noel Shannon
Reception % in ROI 100%
Average weekday reach 13%
Total output ....168 hrs (24 hrs x 7days)
Frequency: ....100-102 FM
Target Audience: ....25-44 yr. Olds
Number of Staff..50

Communications
124 Upper Abbey Street, Dublin 1.
Tel 01-804 9000 *Fax:* 01-804 9099
email admin@todayfm.com   *Web* www.todayfm.com

BBC Northern Ireland

MAIN FACTFILE
Controller........................Pat Loughrey
Head of Broadcast..............................Anna Carragher
Total Output ....5,500 hrs. per year
Number of Regional Studios 8

Communications
Broadcasting House, Ormeau Avenue,
Belfast, BT2 8HQ
Tel 01232-338000 *Fax* 01232-338800.
Website www.bbc.co.uk/ni

BBC RADIO ULSTER
First broadcast...1924
Total output..18 hrs daily
Average Weekly Reach 15+ 409,000
Frequency: ....92.4 - 95.4 FM
Target Audience: ....General.

BBC RADIO FOYLE
First broadcast..1979
Total output................................15 hrs daily (average)
Average Weekly Reach 15+ 27,000
Frequency: ....93.1 FM
Target Audience: ....General.
Station Manager ....Ana Leddy

Communications
8 Northland Road, Derry BT48 7JD.
Tel 01504-262244 *Fax* 378666

Local Radio (Main Stations)

● **CKR FM** (Carlow, Kildare) Lismard Hse, Tullow St, Carlow; *Tel* 0503-41044; *email* info@ckrfm.com; *Gen Manager* Debra O'Neill; *Frequencies:* 97.3 MHz/97.6 MHz/104.4 MHz; *Listenership Figures* 39%.

● **CLARE FM** (Co Clare) The Abbeyfield Centre, Francis St, Ennis, Co Clare; *Tel* 065-682 8888; *email* info@clarefm.ie; *Gen Manager* Liam O'Shea; *Frequencies* 96.4 MHz/95.5 MHz/95.9 MHz; *Listenership Figures* 46%.

● **CORK 96FM/103FM COUNTY SOUND** (Cork City, Co) Broadcasting Hse, Patrick's Place, Cork; *Tel* 021-551596; *email* 96FM@indigo.ie; *MD* Colm O'Conaill; *frequencies* 96.4 MHz/ 103.7 MHz/103.3 Mhz; *Listenership Figures* 63%.

● **EAST COAST RADIO** (Co Wicklow) 9 Prince of Wales Tce, Bray, Co Wicklow; *Tel* 01-286 6414; *email* online@eastcoastradio.net; *CEO* Seán Ashmore; *Frequencies* 94.9 MHz/96.2 MHz/102.9 MHz/104.4 MHz (Arklow); *Listenership Figures* 33%.

● **FM104** (Dublin City, Co) 3rd Floor, Hume Hse, Pembroke Rd, Ballsbridge, D4; *Tel* 01-6689689; *MD* Dermot Hanrahan; *Frequency* 104.4 MHz; *Listenership Figures* 29%.

● **GALWAY BAY FM** (Galway City, Co) Sandy Rd, Galway; *Tel* 091-770 000; *email* gbfm@galway.net; *CEO* Keith Finnegan. *Frequencies* 95.8 MHz/96.8 MHz; *Listenership Figures* 48%.

● **HIGHLAND RADIO** (Nth Donegal) Pine Hill, Letterkenny, Co Donegal; *Tel* 074-25000; *email* highland@infowing.ie; *Gen Manager* Charlie Collins; *Frequencies:* 103.3 MHz/87.9 MHz/95.2 MHz; *Listenership Figures* 75%.

● **LM FM** (Louth, Meath) Boyne Shopping Centre, Drogheda, Co Louth; *Tel* 041-32000; *email* info@lmfm.tinet.ie; *CEO* Michael Crawley; *Frequencies* 95.5 MHz/104.9 MHz; *Listenership Figures* 39%.

● **MIDLANDS RADIO 3** (Laois, Offaly, Westmeath) The Mall, William St, Tullamore, Co Offaly; *Tel* 0506-51333; *email* mr3@iol.ie; *CEO* Joe Yerkes; *Frequencies* 103.5 MHz/102.1 MHz/96.5 MHz; *Listenership Figures* 35%.

● **MID WEST RADIO FM** (Mayo) Abbey St, Ballyhaunis, Co Mayo; *Tel* 0907-30553; *email* mwr@iol.ie; *Stat Manager* Chris Carroll; *Frequencies* 96.1MHz - 97.1MHz; *Listenership Figures* 57%.

● **NORTH WEST RADIO** (Sligo, Nth Leitrim, Sth Donegal) Market Yard, Sligo; *Tel* 071-60108; *email*

nwr@iol.ie; *Stat Manager* Tommy Marren; *Frequencies* 102.5 MHz & 105.0 MHz; *Listenership Figures* 57%.
● **NORTHERN SOUND** (Cavan, Monaghan) 33 Glaslough St, Monaghan; *Tel* 047-72666; *Stat Manager* Fintan Duffy; *Frequencies* 94.8 MHz/96.3 MHz/97.5MHz; *Listenership Figures* 49%.
● **RADIO KERRY** (Kerry) Maine St, Tralee, Co Kerry; *Tel* 066-712 3666; *Gen Manager* Paul Sheehan; *Frequencies* 97.0 MHz/97.6 MHz/96.2 MHz; *Listenership Figures* 51%.
● **RADIO KILKENNY** (Kilkenny City, Co) 32 Hebron Rd, Kilkenny; *Tel* 056-61577; *email* onair@radiokilkenny.tinet.ie; *CEO* Diarmuid Healy; *Frequencies* 96.6 MHz/96.0 MHz/106.3 MHz; *Listenership Figures* 54%.
● **SHANNONSIDE 104FM** (Roscommon, Longford, Sth Leitrim) Minard Hse, Sligo Rd, Co Longford; *Tel* 043-47777; *email* shannonside@tinet.ie; *CEO* Richard A. Devlin; *Frequencies* 104.1 MHz/95.7 MHz; *Listenership Figures* 49%.
● **SOUTH EAST RADIO** (Wexford) Customs Hse Quay, Wexford; *Tel* 053-45200; *email* wexford@iol.ie; *Stat Manager* Liam Dwyer; *Frequencies* 95.6 MHz/96.2 MHz/96.4 MHz; *Listenership Figures* 58%.
● **TIPPERARY MID WEST RADIO** (Tipperary Sth West) St. Michael's St, Tipperary; *Tel* 062-52555; *Chairperson* Seán Kelly; *Frequencies* 104.8 MHz; *Listenership Figures* 48%.
● **TIPP FM** (Tipperary, excluding Sth west) Davis Rd, Clonmel, Co Tipperary; *Tel* 052-25299; *MD* John O'Connell; *Frequencies* 97.1 MHz/103.9 MHz/95.3 MHz; *Listenership Figures* 43%.
● **W.L.R. FM** (Waterford City, Co) George's St, Waterford; *Tel* 051-877592; *MD* Des Whelan; *Frequencies* 97.5 MHz/95.1 MHz; *Listenership Figures* 57%.
● **95FM** (Limerick City, Co) P.O. Box 295, 88 O'Connell St, Limerick; *Tel* 061-400195; *email* reception@95fm.ie; *MD* Scott Williams; *Frequencies* 95.0MHz/95.3MHz; *Listenership Figures* 60%.
● **98 FM** (Dublin City, Co) The Malt Hse, Grand Canal Quay, D2; *tel* 01-670 8970; *Gen Manager* Ken Hutton; *Frequency* 98.1 MHz; *Listenership Figures* 24%.

Source: The Independent Radio & Television Commission (IRTC).

Other Special Interest and Community Radio Stations

● **ANNA LIVIA FM** (Dublin City, Co) Griffith College, Sth Circular Rd, D8; *Tel* 01-473 4444; *Stat Manager* Mary Long; *Frequencies* 103.8 MHz/103.2 MHz.
● **CORK CAMPUS RADIO** (Cork City) Level 3, Áras na Mac Léinn, University College Cork; *Tel* 021-902008; *Stat Manager* Sinéad O'Donnell; *Frequency* 97.4 MHz.

● **FLIRT FM** (Galway City) c/o The Porters Desk, Concourse, University College Galway; *Tel* 091-750445; *Stat Manager* Yvonne Igoe; *Frequency* 105.6 MHz.
● **NEAR FM** (Dublin Nth East) CDC, Bunratty Drive, D17; *Tel* 01-848 5211; *Chairperson* Jack Byrne; *Frequency* 101.6 MHz.
● **RAIDIÓ NA LIFE** (Greater Dublin) 7 Cearnóg Mhuirfean, Baile Átha Cliath 2; *Tel* 01-661 6333; *Stat Manager* Finnouala Mac Aodha; *Frequencies* 102.2 MHz/106.4 MHz.
● **WIRED FM** (Limerick City) Mary Immaculate College, Sth Circular Rd, Limerick; *Tel* 061-215103; *email* isr@iol.ie; *Stat Manager* Darren Connolly; *Frequency* 96.8 MHz.
● **CONNEMARA COMMUNITY RADIO** (Nth Connemara) Letterfrack, Co Galway; *Tel* 095-41616; *Stat Manager* Mary Ruddy; *Frequencies* 87.8 MHz/106.1 FM.
● **COMMUNITY RADIO CASTLEBAR** (Castlebar Town, Environs) Market Sq, Castlebar, Co Mayo; *Tel* 094-25555; *Stat Manager* Peter Killeen; *Frequency* 102.9 MHz.
● **COMMUNITY RADIO YOUGHAL** (Youghal Town, Environs) Catherine St, Youghal, Co Cork; *Tel* 024-91199; *Chairperson* Rev Peter Rhys-Thomas; *Frequency* 105.1 MHz.
● **DUBLIN SOUTH COMMUNITY RADIO** (Dublin Sth, West Dún Laoghaire/Rathdown) The Old School, Loreto Ave, Rathfarnham, D14; *Tel* 01-4930377; *Chairperson* John O'Brennan; *Frequencies* 104.9 FM.
● **TALLAGHT COMMUNITY RADIO** (Sth West Dublin) Level 3, The Square, Tallaght, D24; *Tel* 01-462 3333; *Stat Manager* Declan McLoughlin; *Frequency* 107.2 MHz.
● **WEST DUBLIN COMMUNITY RADIO** (Dublin West) Ballyfermot Rd, D10; *Tel* 01-626 6011; *Stat Manager* Eugene Bullard; *Frequency* 96 MHz.

Other NI Radio Stations

● **BELFAST CITY BEAT** (Greater Belfast, East Ulster) PO Box 967, Belfast BT9 5DF; *Tel* 01232-205967; *email* citybeat967@dnet.co.uk; *Frequencies* 96.7 FM.
● **COOL FM** (Belfast City, East NI) PO Box 974, Belfast, BT1 1RT; *tel* 01247-817181; *email* music@coolfm.co.uk; *MD* David Sloan.
● **DOWNTOWN RADIO** (Ulster) Newtownards, Co Down BT23 4ES; *Tel* 01247-815555; *email* programmes@downtown.co.uk; *MD* David Sloan; *Frequency* 102.4 FM.
● **Q102 FM** (Nth West, Nth Coast) Old Waterside Railway Station, Duke St, Waterside, Derry BT47 6DH; *Tel* 01504-344449; *email* Q102@iol.ie; *Stat Manager* David Austin; *Frequency* 102.9 FM.

RoI: Weekday Listenership Figures

Period: July 1998 - July 1999		
● NATIONAL LISTENERSHIP FIGURES		
Independents	53%	+1
RTÉ Radio 1	31%	-2

Period: July 1998 - July 1999		
● NATIONAL LISTENERSHIP FIGURES		
2FM	28%	no change
Today FM	13%	+2

Continued from previous page

● DUBLIN LISTENERSHIP FIGURES

RTÉ Radio 1	36%	-1
FM104	29%	+1
98FM	24%	+2
2FM	20%	-1
Today FM	10%	+2

● CORK LISTENERSHIP FIGURES

Cork 96FM/County Sound	63%	+3
RTE Radio 1	31%	-1
2FM	26%	no change
Today FM	14%	+1
RTÉ Cork 89FM	5%	no change

● LOCAL LISTENERSHIP FIGURES (see profiles)

Highland Radio (Donegal)	75%	+7
New 95FM (Limerick)	60%	no change
South East Radio (Wexford)	58%	+3
Mid West Radio (Mayo)	57%	+1
North West Radio (Sligo)	57%	+3

Source: JNLR Weekday listenership figures July 1998 to June 1999 from The Independent Radio & Television Commission (IRTC).

RoI & NI Advertising Rates

Station (Advert period in brackets)	15 secs £	20 secs £	30 secs £	40 secs £	50 secs £	60 secs £
RTÉ Radio 1[1]	1968	2350	2937	3906	4905	5874
2FM[2]	2614	3121	3901	5188	6515	7802
Raidió na Gaeltachta				No commercial advertising carried		
Lyric FM[3]	737	880	1,100	1,463	1,837	2,200
Today FM (7:00a.m. - 7:00p.m.)[4]	103	124	155	206	258	310
Today FM (7:00p.m. - 11:00p.m.)[4]	40	48	60	80	100	120

1 (9 spots - Adults/Men/ABC1) Rate effective October - December 1999
2 (28 spots - Total Audience Package) Rate effective October - December 1999
3 (21 spots - Total Audience Package) 4 Based on Prime Time Package (21 spots); Based on Night Time Package (21 spots)
(All rates above are based on various package deals - not all information is comparable)

Print

National Daily Newspapers

● **BELFAST TELEGRAPH** 124-144 Royal Avenue, Belfast BT1 1EB; *Tel* 01232-264000; *Fax* 554506; *Web* www.belfasttelegraph.co.uk; *Est* 1870; *Ed* Edmund Curran; *News* Paul Connolly; *Pol* Chris Thornton; *Bus* Francess McDonnell; *Arts* Neil Johnston; *Features* John Caruth; *Sport* John Laverty; *Ads* John Leslie; *ABC cir* Price Stg 28p.

● **EXAMINER, The** PO Box 21, Academy Street, Cork; *Tel* 021-272722; *Fax* 275112; *Web* www.examiner.ie; *ISDN* 021 806091; *Est* 1841; *Ed* Brian Looney; *News* Brian Carroll; *Pol* Liam O'Neill; *Bus* Kevin Mills; *Arts* Declan Hassett; *Features* Dan Buckley; *Sport* Tony Leen; *Ads* Padraig Mallon; *ABC cir* 60,579; *Price* 85p.

● **EVENING ECHO** Academy Street, Cork; *Tel* 021-272722; *Fax* 275112; *email* echo_ed@examiner.ie; *ISDN* 021 806091; *Est* 1892; *Ed* Brian Feeney; *News* Ailín Quinlan; *Bus* Brian Winders; *Arts* Declan Hassett; *Features* Vincent Power; *Sport* Mark Woods; *Ads* Padraig Mallon; *ABC cir* 27,914; *Price* 50p.

● **EVENING HERALD, The** Middle Abbey Street, Dublin 1; *Tel* 01-7055333; *Fax* 8731787; *email* herald.letters@independent.ie; *Est* 1891; *Ed* Paul Drury; *News* Martin Brennan; *For* Michael Clare; *Pol* Katir Hannon; *Bus & Fin* Ken Curran; *Arts* Maurice Haugh; *Features* David Robbins; *Sport* David Courtney; *Ads* Yvonne Doyle; *ABC cir* 110,507; *Price* 65p.

● **IRISH INDEPENDENT, The** Middle Abbey Street, Dublin 1; *Tel* 01-7055333; *Fax* 8720304; *Web* www.independent.ie; *email* independent.letters@independent.ie; *Est* 1905; *Ed* Vincent Doyle; *News* P. Molloy; *Bus* F. Mulrennan; *Fin* B. Keenan; *Features* John Spain; *Sport* PJ Cunningham; *Ads* B. McCabe; *ABC cir* 165,657; *Price* 85p.

● **IRISH NEWS, The** 113-117 Donegall Street, Belfast BT1 2GE; *Tel* 01232-322226; *Fax* 337505; *Web* www.irishnews.com; *email* newsdesk@irishnews.com; *ISDN* 01232 311081; *est* 1891; *Ed* Noel Doran; *News* Niall Blaney; *Pol* Billy Graham; *Bus & Fin* James Stinson; *Arts & Features* Anna Marie McFaul; *Sport* John Haughey; *Ads* Paddy Meehan; *ABC cir* Price 50p.

● **IRISH TIMES, The** 10-16 D'Olier Street, Dublin 2; *Tel* 01-6792022; *Fax* 6793910; *Web* www.irish-times.com; *email* postmaster@irish-times.ie; *Est* 1859; *Ed* Conor Brady; *News* Niall Kiely; *NI* Deaglán de Bréadún; *For* Paul Gillespie; *Pol* Geraldine Kennedy; *Bus & Fin* Cliff Taylor; *Arts* Victoria White; *Features* Sheila Wayman; *Sport* Malachy Logan; *Ads* Liam Holland; *ABC cir* 112,623; *Price* 85p.

● **NEWS LETTER, The** 46-56 Boucher Crescent, Belfast, BT12 6QY; *Tel* 01232-680000; *Fax* 664412; *ISDN* 01232 381238; *Est* 1737; *Ed* Geoff Martin; *News* Steven Moore/Ric Clarke; *Pol* Mervyn Pauley; *Bus & Fin* Adrienne Magill; *Features* Geoff Hill; *Sport* Brian Millar; *Ads* Nuala Meenahan; *ABC cir* Price IR 45p.

● **STAR, The** 62A Terenure Road North, Dublin 6W; *Tel* 01-4901228; *Fax* 4902193; *email* news@the-star.ie;

ISDN 01-4055017; *Est* 1988; *Ed* Gerard O'Regan; *News* David O'Connell; *Pol* John Donlon; *Fin* & *Bus* Dave O'Connell; *Arts* Terry McGeehan; *Features* Danny Smyth; *Sport* Connie Clinton; *Ads* Ken Grace; *ABC cir* 89,304; *Price* 60p.

National Weekly Newspapers

● **AN PHOBLACHT/REPUBLICAN NEWS** 58 Parnell Square, Dublin 1; *Tel* 01-8733611; *Fax* 8733074; *Web* http://irlnet.com/aprn; *email* aprn@irlnet.com; *Est* 1979; *Ed* Martin Spain; *NI* Peadar Whelan; *Price* 50p (Thursday).

● **PUBLIC SECTOR TIMES** 1 Eglinton Road, Bray, Co Wicklow; *Tel* 01-2869111; *Fax* 2869074; *email* publicsectortimes@tinet.ie; *Est* 1975; *Ed* Shay Fitzmaurice; *Price* Free (Wednesday).

● **SUNDAY BUSINESS POST, The** 80 Harcourt Street, Dublin 2; *Tel* 01-6026000; *Fax* 679 6283; *Web* www.sbpost.ie; *email* sbpost@iol.ie; *ISDN* 4176938 (PC), 4176932 (Mac); *Est* 1989; *Ed* Damien Kiberd; *News* Aileen O'Toole; *Pol* Mark O'Connell; *Bus* Tod Harding; *Fin* Ruth Marchand; *Arts* & *Features* Daire O'Brien; *Sport* Eoghan Corry; *Ads* Siobhan Lennon, Deirdre Hughes; *ABC cir* 49,621; *Price* £1.10.

● **SUNDAY INDEPENDENT, The** 90 Middle Abbey Street, Dublin 1; *Tel* 01-7055333; *Fax* 7055779; *Web* www.independent.ie; *email* sunday.letters@independent.ie; *ISDN* 01 7055058; *Est* 1906; *Ed* Aengus Fanning; *News* Willie Kealy; *Pol* Jodie Corcoran; *Bus* & *Fin* Shane Ross; *Arts* Ronan Farren; *Features* Anne Harris; *Sport* Adhamhnan O'Sullivan; *Ads* Karen Preston; *ABC cir* 315,599; *Price* £1.00.

● **SUNDAY LIFE** 124 Royal Avenue, Belfast BT1 1EB; *Tel* 01232-264300; *Fax* 554507; *email* b.arnold@belfasttelegraph.co.uk; *Est* 1988; *Ed* Martin Lindsay; *News* Martin Hill; *Features* Sue Corbett; *Sport* Jim Gracey; *Ads* John Leslie; *ABC cir* *Price* 65p.

● **SUNDAY TRIBUNE** 15 Lower Baggot Street, Dublin 2; *Tel* 01-661 5555; *Fax* 661 5302; *email* editorial@tribune.ie; *Est* 1983; *Ed* Matt Cooper; *News, For* Martin Walls; *Pol* Stephen Collins; *Bus* & *Fin* Brian Carey; *Arts* Ciaran Carty; *Features* Roslyn Dee; *Sport* Paul Howard; *Ads* John Holland; *ABC cir* 84,566; *Price* £1.

● **SUNDAY WORLD, The** Rathfarnham Road, Dublin 6; *Tel* 01-4901980; *Fax* 4901838; *email* sunworld@iol.ie; *Est* 1973; *Ed* Colm MacGinty; *News, For* & *Pol* Sean Boyne; *Bus* & *Fin* Aileen Hickie; *Arts* Val Sheehan; *Features* John Sheils; *Sport* Pat Quigley; *Ads* Gerry Lennon; *ABC cir* 308,037; *Price* £1.00.

● **IRELAND ON SUNDAY** 50 City Quay, D2; *Tel* 01-671 8255; *Fax* 671 8882; *email:* info@irelandonsunday.iol.ie; *Est* 1997 (as Ireland On Sunday; June 1996 as The Title); *Ed* Liam Hayes; *News* Ken Whelan; *Sport* Cathal Dervan; *Bus* & *Fin* Dara Doyle; *Arts* Kathy Dillon; *Features* Fionnula McCarthy; *Ads* Karl Louwrens; *ABC cir* 63,476; *Price* £1.00.

● **IRISH FARMERS' JOURNAL** Irish Farm Centre, Bluebell, Dublin 12; *Tel* 01-450 1166; *Fax* 452 0876; *email* editdept@farmersjournal.ie; *Web* www.farmer-

sjournal.ie; *ISDN* 4092822; *Est* 1948; *Ed* Matt Dempsey; *News, Pol* Des Maguire; *For* Matt Dempsey; *Bus* Paul Mooney; *Fin* Paul Meade; *Arts* Steve Treacy; *Features* Alison Healy; *Sport* Micheal O'Muircheartaigh; *Ads* Oliver Hayes; *ABC cir* 76,098; *Price* £1.10.

● **IRISH FAMILY, The** PO Box 7, GPO Mullingar, Co Westmeath; *Tel* 044-42987; *Fax* 45150; *email* irishfamily@tinet.ie; *Web* www.irishfamily.com; *Est* 1994; *Ed* Richard Hogan; *Price* 60p.

Provincial Newspapers

● **ANDERSTOWN NEWS** (Belfast, Co Antrim) 301 Glen Road, Belfast BT11 8BU; *Tel* 01232-619000; *fax* 620602; *email* info@belfast-news.ie; *ISDN* 309018; *Ed* Robin Livingstone; *Sports* Anthony Neeson; *group* none; *Price* Stg 40p; (Thursday).

● **ANGLO-CELT, The** (Cavan/Monaghan) Station House, Cavan; *Tel* 049-4331100; *Fax* 4332280; *email* anglocel@iol.ie; *Est* 1846; *Ed* Johnny O'Hanlon; *Sport* Eamon Gaffney; *Group* none; *ABC cir* 15,643; *Price* 95p; (Wednesday).

● **ANTRIM GUARDIAN** (Antrim) 5 Railway Street, Antrim; *Tel* 01849-462624; *Fax* 465551; *Est* 1972; *Ed* Liam Heffron; *Sport* Alvin McCaig; *Group* Northern Newspaper Group; *Price stg* 60p; (Wednesday).

● **ANTRIM TIMES** (Co Antrim) 45A High Street, Antrim BT41 4AY; *Tel* 01849-428034; *Fax* 428875; *Ed* Des Blackadder; *Group* Morton Newspapers; *Price stg* 50p; (Wednesday).

● **ARGUS, THE** (Dundalk, N Louth) Park Street, Dundalk, Co Louth; *Tel* 042-34632; *Fax* 31643; *Est* 1865; *Ed* Kevin Mulligan; *Group* Independent Newspapers; *Price* £1.00(Wednesday, Friday*) *Price** 50p.

● **ARMAGH DOWN OBSERVER** (Armagh, Down) Ann Street, Dungannon, Co Tyrone BT80 1ET; *Tel* 01868-722557; *Fax* 727334; *Ed* Desmond Mallon; *Group* Observer Group; *Price stg* 40p; (Thursday).

● **ARMAGH OBSERVER** (Armagh) Ann Street, Dungannon, Co Tyrone BT80 1ET; *Tel* 01868-722557; *Fax* 727334; *Est* 1929; *Ed* Desmond Mallon; *Group* Observer Group; *Price Stg* 50p; (Wednesday).

● **AVONDHU, THE** (Nth East Cork, Sth Tipperary, Sth Limerick, West Waterford) 18 Lower Cork Street, Mitchelstown, Co Cork; *Tel* 025-24451; *Fax* 84463; *email* info@avondhupress.ie; *ISDN* 41015; *Est* 1978; *Ed* Liam Howard; *Sports* Robert Peters; *Group* none; *Price* 75p; (Thursday).

● **BALLYMENA CHRONICLE & ANTRIM OBSERVER** (Antrim) Ann Street, Dungannon, Co Tyrone BT80 1ET; *Tel* 01868-722557; *Fax* 727334; *Ed* Desmond Mallon; *group* Observer Group; *Price Stg* 30p; (Wednesday).

● **BALLYMENA GUARDIAN** (mid, east & south Antrim) 83/87 Wellington Street, Ballymena, Co. Antrim BT43 6AD; *Tel* 01266-41221; *Fax* 653920; *Est* 1972; *Ed* Maurice O'Neill; *Sport* Shaun O'Neill; *Group* Northern Newspapers; *Price Stg* 60p; (Wednesday).

● **BALLYMENA TIMES** (Co Antrim, Co Derry) 22 Ballymoney Street, Ballymena, Co. Antrim BT43 6AL; *Tel* 01266-653300; *Fax* 41517; *Est* 1855; *Ed* Des Blackadder; *Sports* Billy Spence; *Group* Morton

● **BALLYMONEY TIMES** (Co Antrim) 19 Church Street, Ballymoney, Co. Antrim BT53 6HS; *Tel* 012656-66216; *Fax* 67066; *Est* 1989; *Ed* Lyle McMullen; *Sports* Billy Weir; *Group* Morton Newspapers; *Price Stg* 60p; (Wednesday).

● **BANBRIDGE CHRONICLE** (Co Down) 14 Bridge Street, Banbridge, Co. Down; *Tel* 018206-62322; *Fax* 24397; *Est* 1870; *Ed* Bryan Hooks; *Sport* Paul Kelly; *group* none; *Price Stg* 60p; (Wednesday).

● **BANBRIDGE LEADER** (Co Antrim, Co Down) 25 Bridge Street, Banbridge, Co Down BT32 3UL; *Tel* 018206-62745; *Fax* 26378; *Ed* Damian Wilson; *Group* Morton Newspapers; *Price Stg* 55p; (Wednesday).

● **BELFAST NEWS** (Belfast E, S, N) c/o Century Newspapers, 45-56 Boucher Crescent, Belfast BT12 6QY; *Tel* 01232-680000; *Fax* 664436; *ISDN* 381238; *Est* 1999; *Ed* Chris Harbinson; *Group* Century Newspapers; *Price* free; (Thursday).

● **BRAY PEOPLE** (Co Wicklow, Co Dublin) 25 Main Street, Bray, Co Wicklow; *Tel* 01-2867393; *Fax* 286 0879; *email* pbyrnes@peoplenews.ie; *Web* www.peoplenews.ie; *ISDN* 205 0732; *Ed* Owen Quinn; *Sports* Sean Nolan; *Group* People Newspapers; *Price* £1.00; (Thursday).

● **CARLOW PEOPLE** (Co Carlow) Lismard House, Tullow Street, Co Carlow; *Tel* 0503-41877; *Fax* 34185; *email* pbyrnes@peoplenews.ie; *Web* www.peoplenews.ie; *Ed* Michael Ryan; *Sports* Sean Nolan; *Group* People Newspapers; *Price* 90p (Tuesday).

● **CHRONICLE, The** (north Antrim & Co Derry) 20 Railway Road, Coleraine, Co Derry BT52 1PD; *Tel* 01265-43344; *Fax* 329672; *Est* 1844; *Ed* Grant Cameron; *Sport* Roger Anderson; *Group* Northern Newspapers; *Price Stg* 60p; (Wednesday).

● **CLARE CHAMPION** (Clare) Barrack Street, Ennis, Co Clare; *Tel* 065-6828105; *Fax* 6820374; *email* editor@clarechampion.ie; *Web* clarechampion.ie *Est* 1903; *Ed* Gerry Collison; *Group* none; *ABC cir* 20,772; *Price* 90p; (Friday).

● **CLONMEL NATIONALIST** (South Tipperary, Co Limerick, Co Waterford, Co Kilkenny) Queen Street, Clonmel, Co Tipperary; *Tel* 052-22211; *Fax* 25248; *Web* www.nationalist.ie; *Est* 1890; *Ed* Tom Corr; *Sports* Michael Heveran; *Group* Kilkenny People Group; *Price* £1.00; (Thursday).

● **COLERAINE TIMES** (Coleraine Borough Council area) 71 New Row, Market Court, Coleraine, Co. Derry BT52 1AF; *Tel* 01265-55260; *Fax* 56186; *Web* www.mortonnewspaper.com; *email* edcr@mortonnewspaper.com; *Est* 1990; *Ed* David Rankin; *Sport* Damian Mullan; *group* Morton Newspapers; *Price Stg* 55p; (Wednesday).

● **COMMUNITY TELEGRAPH** (Greater Belfast & North Down) 124 Royal Avenue, Belfast BT1 1EB; *Tel* 01232-239049; *Fax* 239050; *Est* 1998; *Ed* Nigel Tilson; *Sport* Graham Luney; *Group* Belfast Telegraph Newspapers; (7 titles); *Price* Free; (Wednesday & Thursday).

● **CONNACHT SENTINEL, THE** (Galway City) 15 Market Street, Galway; *Tel* 091-567251; *Fax* 567970; *email* ctribune@iol.ie; *Web* www.ctribune.iol.ie; *ISDN* 567148/9; *Est* 1909; *Ed* John Cunningham; *Sport* John McIntyre; *Group* The Connacht Tribune Ltd.; *ABC cir* 7,089; *Price* 30p; (Tuesday)

● **CONNACHT TRIBUNE, THE** (Galway city, county) 15 Market Street, Galway; *Tel* 091-567251; *Fax* 567970; *Web* www.iol.ie/ctribune; *email* ctribune@iol.ie; *Est* 1909; *Ed* John Cunningham; *Sport* John McIntyre; *Group* none; *ABC cir* 29,006; *Price* 95p; (Thursday).

● **CONNAUGHT TELEGRAPH** (Mayo, parts of Galway, Roscommon, Sligo) Cavandish Lane, Castlebar, Co. Mayo; *Tel* 094-21711; *Fax* 24007; *email* conntel@tinet.ie; *Web* www.con-telegraph.ie; *Est* 1828; *Ed* Tom Gillespie; *Sport* John Melvin; *Cir* 15,265; *Price* 85p; (Wednesday).

● **CORKMAN, THE** (Co. Cork) Clash Industrial Estate, Tralee, Co. Kerry; *Tel* 066-7145500; *Fax* 7145570; *email* kerryman@indigo.ie; *ISDN* 7145068; *Est* 1904; *Ed* Gerard Colleran; *Sport* John Barry; *Group* Independent Newspapers; *Price* £1; (Wednesday).

● **COUNTY DOWN SPECTATOR** (North Down) 109 Main Street, Bangor, Co. Down BT20 4AF; *Tel* 01247-270270; *Fax* 271544; *email* spectator@dial.pipex.com; *ISDN* 465953; *Est* 1904; *Ed* Paul Flowers; *Group* County Down Spectator Group; *Price* 50p; (Thursday).

● **CRAIGAVON ECHO** (Co Armagh, Co Down) 14 Church Street, Portadown, Craigavon, Co. Armagh BT62 3HY; *Tel* 01762-327777; *Fax* 325271; *Ed* Richard Elliott; *Group* Morton Newspapers; *Price* free; (Wednesday).

● **DEMOCRAT, THE** (Tyrone) Ann Street, Dungannon, Co Tyrone BT80 1ET; *Tel* 01868-722557; *Fax* 727334; *Ed* Desmond Mallon; *Group* Observer Group; *Price Stg* 35p; (Thursday).

● **DERRY JOURNAL, The** (Derry city, Donegal) Buncrana Road, Derry BT48 8AA; *Tel* 01504-272200; *Fax* 272260; *email* derryj@sol.co.uk; *Est* 1772; *Ed* Pat McArt; *Sport* Arthur Duffy *Group* Mirror Group; *ABC cir* 26,531; *Price* 70p (Friday); [also Tuesday; *Price* 65p].

● **DERRY PEOPLE/DONEGAL NEWS** (Derry, Donegal) Crossview House, Letterkenny, Co Donegal; *Tel* 074-21014; *Fax* 22881; *Web* www.donegalnews.com; *email* editor@donegalnews.com; *Est* 1901; *Ed* Columba Gill; *Sport* Harry Walsh; *group* North West of Ireland Printing & Publishing Company; *Cir* 11,985; *Price* 70p; (Friday).

● **DONEGAL DEMOCRAT** (Co Donegal, N Sligo, Co Leitrim, W Fermanagh) Donegal Road, Ballyshannon, Co Donegal; *Tel* 072-51201; *Fax* 51945; *email* donegaldemocrat@tinet.ie; *ISDN* 22012; *Est* 1919; *Ed* John Bromley; *Sport* Michael Daly; *Group* Trinity - Mirror; *ABC cir* 17,075; *Price* 75p (Thursday).

● **DONEGAL PEOPLES PRESS** (Co Donegal) 30 Port Road, Letterkenny, Co. Donegal; *Tel* 074-28000; *Fax* 24787; *email* derryj@sol.co.uk; *ISDN* 01504 360079; *Est* 1932; *Ed* Paddy Walsh; *Sport* Tom Comack; *Group* Trinity - Mirror; *ABC cir* 3,922; *Price* 60p; (Wednesday).

● **DOWN RECORDER** (Co Down) 2-4 Church Street, Downpatrick, Co Down; *Tel* 01396-613711; *Fax* 614624; *email* downr@sol.co.uk; *Web* www.down-recorder.co.uk; *ISDN* 01396 617633; *Est* 1836; *Ed* Paul Symington; *Sport* Marcus Crichton; *Group* none; *Price Stg* 50p (Wednesday).

● **DROGHEDA INDEPENDENT** (Co. Louth, Co. Dublin) 9 Shop Street, Drogheda, Co. Louth; *Tel* 041-

9838658; *Fax* 9834271; *email* droindo@tinet.ie; *ISDN* 9871196; *Est* (1884); *Ed* Paul Murphy; *Sport* Hubert Murphy; *Group* Independent Newspapers; *ABC cir* 15,055; *Price* £1.00; (Wednesday).

● **DUNDALK DEMOCRAT** (Louth, Sth & Mid Monaghan, Sth Armagh) 3 Earl Street, Dundalk, Co Louth; *Tel* 042- 9334058; *Fax* 9331399; *email* dundalkdemo@tinet.ie; *Est* 1849; *Ed* Peter Edward Kavanagh; *Sport* Joseph Carroll; *Group* none; *Cir* 16,500; *Price* £1.00 (Friday).

● **DUNGANNON NEWS AND TYRONE COURIER** (Mid-Ulster) 58 Scotch Street, Dungannon, Co Tyrone; *Tel* 01868-722271; *Fax* 726171; *Est* 1880; *Ed* Richard Montgomery; *Sport* Peter Bayne; *Group* Alpha Group; *Price* Stg 60p; (Wednesday).

● **DUNGANNON OBSERVER** (Tyrone) Ann Street, Dungannon, Co Tyrone BT80 1ET; *Tel* 01868-722557; *Fax* 727334; *Ed* Desmond Mallon; *Group* Observer Group; *Price* Stg 40p; (Friday).

● **DUNGARVAN LEADER, The** (mid, west Waterford) 78 O'Connell Street, Dungarvan, Co Waterford; *Tel* 058-41203; *Fax* 45301; *email* dungarvanleader@cablesurf.com; *Est* 1938; *Ed* Colm J. Nagle; *Sport* Michael Power; *Group* none; *Price* 70p; (Wednesday).

● **DUNGARVAN OBSERVER** (Waterford, east Cork, south Tipperary) Shandon, Dungarvan, Co Waterford; *Tel* 058-41205; *Fax* 41559; *email* observer@indigo.ie; *Est* 1912; *Ed* James A. Lynch; *Sport* James O'Keeffe; *Group* none; *Price* 70p; (Wednesday).

● **EAST-ANTRIM ADVERTISER** (Co Antrim) 8 Dunluce Street, Larne, Co Antrim BT40 1JG; *Tel* 01574-272303; *Fax* 260255; *Ed* Hugh Vance; *Group* Morton Newspaper Group; *Price* free; (Monthly).

● **EAST-ANTRIM TIMES** (Belfast, Co Antrim) 8 Dunluce Street, Larne, Co Antrim BT40 1JG; *Tel* 01574-272303; *Fax* 260255; *Ed* Hugh Vance; *Group* Morton Newspapers; *Price* Stg 55p; (Thursday). *Three papers incorporating Larne Times, Carrick Times and Newtownabbey Times..*

● **ENNISCORTHY ECHO** (Co Wexford) Mill Park Road, Enniscorthy, Co Wexford; *Tel* 054-33231; *Fax* 33506/34492; *email* wexfordecho@tinet.ie; ISDN 42134/42135; *Est* 1902; *Ed* Tom Mooney; *Group* Echo Newspapers; *Price* £1.00; (Wednesday).

● **ENNISCORTHY GUARDIAN** (Enniscorthy, Gorey) Castle Hill, Enniscorthy, Co Wexford; *Tel* 054-33833; *Fax* 69937; *email* pbyrnes@peoplenews.ie; *Web* www.peoplenews.ie; *Ed* Michael Ryan; *Sports* Sean Nolan; *Group* People Newspapers; *Price* £1.00; (Wednesday).

● **FARM WEEK** (N. Ireland, Co Donegal, Co Monaghan) 14 Church Street, Portadown, Craigavon, Co. Armagh BT62 3HY; *Tel* 01762-339421; *Fax* 350203; *Est* 1961; *Ed* Hal Crowe; *Group* Morton Newspapers; *Price* Stg 60p; (Friday).

● **FERMANAGH HERALD** (Fermanagh) 30 Belmore Street, Enniskillen, Co. Fermanagh; *Tel* 01365-322066; *Fax* 325521; *Web* www.fermanaghherald.com; *email* editor@fermanaghherald.com; *Est* 1901; *Ed* Dominic McClements; *Sport* Barry O'Donnell; *group* North-West of Ireland Printing & Publishing Company; *Price* Stg 45p; (Wednesday).

● **FERMANAGH NEWS** (Fermanagh) Ann Street, Dungannon, Co Tyrone BT80 1ET; *Tel* 01868-722557; *Fax* 727334; *Ed* Desmond Mallon; *Group* Observer Group; *Price* Stg 30p; (Friday).

● **GALWAY ADVERTISER** (Galway city & county) 2/3 Church Lane, Galway; *Tel* 091-567077; *Fax* 567079; *web* www.galwayadvertiser.ie; *email* news@galwayadvertiser.ie; *est* 1970; *Ed* Ronnie O'Gorman; *Sport* Linley McKensie; *Group* none; *Price* Free; (Thursday).

● **GOREY ECHO** (Co Wexford) Mill Park Road, Enniscorthy, Co. Wexford; *Tel* 054-33231; *Fax* 33506/34492; *email* wexfordecho@tinet.ie; ISDN 42134/42135; *Est* 1902; *Ed* Tom Mooney; *Group* Echo Newspapers; *Price* £1.00; (Wednesday).

● **IMOKILLY PEOPLE** (east Cork, west Waterford) 57 Main Street, Midleton, Co Cork; *Tel* 021-613333; *Fax* 632500; *Web* www.imokillypeople.ie; *email* news@imokillypeople.ie; *Est* 1989; *Ed* Patrick O'Connor; *Group* none; *Price* 95p; (Thursday).

● **IMPARTIAL REPORTER** (Co Fermanagh, Co Tyrone, parts of N. Ireland) 8-10 East Bridge Street, Enniskillen, Co Fermanagh BT74 7BT; *Tel* 01365-324422; *Fax* 325047; *email* info@impartialreporter.com; *Web* www.impartialreporter.com; *ISDN* 323650; *Ed* Denzil McDaniel; *Group* none; *Price* Stg 52p (Thursday).

● **INISH TIMES, THE** (Inishowen Peninsula, Donegal) 42 Upper Main Street, Buncrana, Co Donegal; *Tel* 077-41055; *Fax* 41059; *email* inishted@tinet.ie; *Est* 1999; *Ed* Liam Porter; *Sports* Kevin Callaghan; *Group* none; *Price* 50p (Thursday).

● **KERRYMAN, THE** (Kerry, North Cork) Clash Industrial Estate, Tralee, Co. Kerry; *Tel* 066-7145500; *Fax* 7121608; *email* kerryman@indigo.ie; *ISDN* 7145068; *Est* 1904; *Ed* Gerard Colleran; *Sport* John Barry; *group* Independent Newspaper Group; *ABC cir* 34,749 (2 titles); *Price* £1; (Wednesday).

● **KERRY'S EYE** (Kerry, W Limerick) 22 Ashe Street, Tralee, Co Kerry; *Tel* 066-7149200; *Fax* 7123163; *email* news@kerryseye; *Web* www.kerryseye.com; *ISDN* 7149264; *Est* 1974; *Ed* Padraig Kennelly; *Sport* Padraig Corkery; *Group* none; *Price* £1.00 (Thursday).

● **KILDARE NATIONALIST** (Co. Kildare) Liffey House, Edward Street, Newbridge, Co. Kildare; *Tel* 045-432147; *Fax* 433720; *Web* www.rmbi.ie; *email* news@leinster-times.ie; *Est* 1883; *Ed* Eddie Coffey; *Sports* Paul Donaghy; *Group* Nationalist Group; *Price* £1.00 (Wednesday).

● **KILDARE TIMES** (Kildare) Unit 1, SuperValu S.C., Fairgreen, Naas, Co Kildare; *Tel* 045-895111; *Fax* 895099; *email* kildaretimes@tinet.ie; *Est* 1997; *Ed* Shay Fitzmaurice; *Group* Brandán Media; *Price* Free (Tuesday).

● **KILKENNY PEOPLE** (Kilkenny) 34 High Street, Kilkenny; *Tel* 056-21015; *Fax* 21441; *email* kilkennypeople.ie; *ISDN* 056 72187; *Est* 1892; *Ed* John Kerry Keane; *Sport* John Kuox; *Group* Kilkenny People Group; *ABC cir* 17,138; *Price* £1.00 (Wednesday).

● **KINGDOM NEWSPAPER** (Co Kerry) 65 New Street, Killarney, Co Kerry; *Tel* 064-31392; *Fax* 34609; *email* kingdom@iol.ie; *Web* www.inkerry.com-kingdom.htm; *ISDN* 70016/7; *Ed* Sean Courtney; *Sport* Murt Murphy; *Price* £1.00; (Tuesday).

● **LAOIS NATIONALIST** (County Laois) Coliseum Lane, Portlaoise, Co. Laois; *Tel* 0502-60265; *Fax* 61399; *Web* www.rmbi.ie; *Est* 1883; *Ed* Eddie Coffey; *Sports* Paul Donaghey; *Group* Nationalist Group; *Price* £1.00 (Wednesday).

● **LEADER, THE** (Coleraine, Portrush, Portstewart) 20 Railway Road, Coleraine, Co Derry BT52 1PD; *Tel* 01265-43344; *Fax* 329672; *Est* 1984; *Ed* Jarvis Grant; *Group* Northern Newspaper Group; *Price* Free (Tuesday).

● **LEADER, THE** (Co Antrim, Co Down) 12 Market Square, Dromore, Co Down BT25 1AW; *Tel* 01846-692217; *Fax* 699260; *Ed* Damian Wilson; *Group* Morton Newspapers; *Price* Stg 55p; (Wednesday).

● **LEINSTER EXPRESS** (Laois, Offaly, Carlow, Kildare, N Tipperary) Dublin Road, Port Laoise, Co Laois; *Tel* 0502-21666; *Fax* 0502 20491; *email* L.express@indigo.ie; *Web* www.rmbi.ie; *ISDN* 0502 70077; *Est* 1831; *Ed* John Whelan; *Sport* Brian Keyes; *Group* Leinster Express; *Cir* 13,684; *Price* £1; (Wednesday).

● **LEINSTER LEADER** (Kildare) 19 South Main Street, Naas, Co Kildare; *Tel* 045-897302; *Fax* 045 871168; *email* Michaels@Leinster-Leader.ie; *ISDN* 045 872017; *Est* 1882; *Ed* Michael Sheeran; *Sport* Tommy Callaghan; *group* PNAI; *Cir* 15,480; *Price* £1; (Thursday).

● **LEITRIM OBSERVER** (Co Leitrim, Co Longford, Co Sligo, Co Cavan, Co Donegal) St George's Terrace, Carrick-on-Shannon, Co Leitrim; *Tel* 078-20025/20299; *Fax* 20112; *email* leitrimobserver@tinet.ie; *ISDN* 50006; *Est* 1890; *Ed* Claire Casserley; *Sport* John Connolly; *Group* Morton Newspaper Group; *Cir* 9,750; *Price* £1.00; (Wednesday).

● **LIFFEY CHAMPION** (N Kildare) 3 Captain's Hill, Leixlip, Co Kildare; *Tel* 01-6245533; *Fax* 6243013; *email* champnews@tinet.ie; *Est* 1991; *Ed* Vincent Sutton; *Group* none; *Price* 90p (Thursday).

● **LIMAVADY (ROE VALLEY) SENTINEL** (Co Derry, parts of Co Tyrone and Antrim) 32A Market Street, Limavady, Derry BT40 0AA; *Tel* 015047-64090; *Fax* 22234; *Est* 1829; *Ed* Chris McNabb; *Sports* William McClelland; *Group* Morton Newspaper Group; *Price* Stg 58p (Wednesday).

● **LIMERICK CHRONICLE** (Limerick City and County, Co Dublin, Co Clare, Co Cork) 54 O'Connell Street, Limerick; *Tel* 061-204500; *Fax* 314804; *email* admin@limerickleader.ie; *Web* www..limerick-leader.ie; *ISDN* 204240/204092; *Est* 1889; *Ed* Brendan Halligan; *Sport* Cormac Liddy; *Group* Limerick Leader Ltd.; *Price* 90p; (Tuesday).

● **LIMERICK LEADER** (Limerick City and County, Co Dublin, Co Clare, Co Cork) 54 O'Connell Street, Limerick; *Tel* 061-204500; *Fax* 314804; *email* admin@limerickleader.ie; *Web* www..limerick-leader.ie; *ISDN* 204240/204092; *Est* 1889; *Ed* Brendan Halligan; *Sport* Cormac Liddy; *Group* Limerick Leader Ltd.; *ABC cir* 26,659; (weekend edition) *Price* 30p; (Monday, Wednesday, Thursday, Friday).

● **LISBURN ECHO** (Co Antrim, Co Down) 12A Bow Street, Lisburn, Co. Antrim BT28 1BN; *Tel* 01846-601114; *Fax* 602904; *Ed* David Fletcher; *Group* Morton Newspapers; *VFD cir* 21,844; *Price* free; (Wednesday).

● **LONDONDERRY SENTINEL** (Derry, Co Derry, parts of Co Antrim and Tyrone) Suite 3, Spencer House, Spencer Road, Waterside, Derry BT49 1AA; *Tel* 01504-348889; *Fax* 341175; *Est* 1829; *Ed* Chris McNabb; *Sports* William McClelland; *Group* Morton Newspapers; *ABC cir* 5,315; *Price* Stg 58p (Wednesday).

● **LONGFORD LEADER, The** (Longford, Leitrim, parts of Westmeath, Cavan, Roscommon) Market Square, Longford; *Tel* 043-45241; *Fax* 41489; *email* ads@longford-leader.iol.ie; *Web* www.rmbi.ie; *Est* 1897; *Ed* Eugene McGee; *Sport* Padraic O'Brien; *Group* RNAN; *Cir* 13,500; *Price* £1.00; (Wednesday).

● **LONGFORD NEWS** (Co Longford & surrounding Leitrim, Cavan, Roscommon & Westmeath) Earl Street, Longford; *Tel* 043-46342; *Fax* 41549; *email* info@longford-news.iol.ie; *Est* 1936; *Ed* Derek G. Cobbe; *Sport* Neil Halligan; *Group* Tribune Group; *Cir* 8,800; *Price* 95p; (Wednesday).

● **LURGAN AND PORTADOWN EXAMINER** (Lurgan, Portadown) Ann Street, Dungannon, Co Tyrone BT80 1EB; *Tel* 01868-722557; *Fax* 727334; *Ed* Desmond Mallon; *Group* Observer Group; *Price* Stg 30p; (Wednesday).

● **LURGAN MAIL** (Co Armagh, Co Down) 4 High Street, Lurgan, Craigavon, Co Armagh BT67 9BG; *Tel* 01762-327777; *Fax* 325271; *Ed* Richard Elliott; *Sports* John Bingham; *Group* Morton Newspapers; *Price* Stg 62p (Thursday).

● **MAYO NEWS** (Mayo/Galway) The Fairgreen, Westport, Co. Mayo; *Tel* 098-25311; *Fax* 26108; *Web* www.MayoNews.ie; *email* editor@MayoNews.ie; *Est* 1892; *Ed* Sean Staunton; *Sport* Stephen O'Grady; *Group* none; *Cir* 10,000; *Price* 90p; (Wednesday).

● **MEATH CHRONICLE** (Co Meath, parts of Cavan, Westmeath, Louth, Kildare, Dublin) Market Square, Navan, Co Meath; *Tel* 046-79600; *Fax* 23565; *email* info@meath-chronicle.ie; *Web* www.meath-chronicle.ie; *ISDN* 046 79699; *Est* 1897; *Ed* Ken Davis; *Sport* Conall Collier; *Group* none; *ABC cir* 19,528; *Price* £1.00 (Wednesday).

● **MEATH TOPIC** (Co Meath) 6 Dominick Street, Mullingar, Co Westmeath; *Tel* 044-48868; *Fax* 43777; *email* topic@indigo.ie; *ISDN* 39056/7; *Ed* Dick Hogan; *Group* Topic Newspapers; *Price* 90p; (Thursday).

● **MIDLAND TRIBUNE, THE** (Co Offaly, Co Laois, Co Westmeath, Co Tipperary) Syngefield, Birr, Co Offaly; *Tel* 0509-20003; *Fax* 20588; *email* midtrib@iol.ie; *ISDN* 69100; *Est* 1881; *Ed* John O'Callaghan; *Sport* John Horan; *Group* Tullamore Tribune Group; *ABC cir* 12,000; *Price* £1.00; (Wednesday).

● **MID-ULSTER ECHO** (Cookstown & Magherafelt Council areas) 52 Oldtown Street, Cookstown, Co Tyrone BT80 8BB; *Tel* 016487-61364; *Fax* 642951; *Ed* John Fillis; *Group* Morton Newspapers; *Price* free; (Wednesday).

● **MID-ULSTER MAIL** (Cookstown & Magherafelt Council areas) 52 Oldtown Street, Cookstown, Co Tyrone BT80 8BB; *Tel* 016487-62288; *Fax* 64295; *Web* www.mortonnewspapers.com; *Est* 1890; *Ed* John Fillis; *Sport* Mark Bain; *Group* Morton Newspapers; *Price stg* 60p; (Thursday).

● **MID-ULSTER OBSERVER** (Co Derry, Tyrone) Ann Street, Dungannon, Co Tyrone BT80 1ET; *Tel* 01868-722557; *Fax* 727334; *Ed* Desmond Mallon; *Group*

Observer Group; *Price* Stg 50p; (Wednesday).

● **MOURNE OBSERVER & CO DOWN NEWS** (Sth, East & West Co Down) Castlewellan Road, Newcastle, Co Down BT33 OJX; *Tel* 013967-22666; *Fax* 24566; *Web* www.mourneobserver.com; *Est* 1949; *Ed* Terence Bowman; *Sport* Raymond Stewart; *Group* none; *Price* Stg 50p; (Wednesday).

● **MUNSTER EXPRESS, The** (Waterford city & county, South Tipperary, Kilkenny) 37 The Quay, Waterford; *Tel* 051-872141; *Fax* 873452; *Web* www.munster-express.ie; *Est* 1859; *Ed* Kieran Walsh; *Sports* John O'Connor; *Group* none; *Cir* 17,909; *Price* 90p (Friday).

● **MUSKERRY LEADER, THE** (Mid Cork, Cork city and parts of west and north Cork and Kerry border) Time Square, Ballincollig, Co Cork; *Tel* 021-874490; *Fax* 874493; *email* leadergr@indigo.ie; *Web* http://kol.ie/leadernewspaper; *ISDN* 850043/4; *Est* 1992; *Ed* Eoin English; *Sports* Michael Downing; *Group* Leader Newspapers; *Price* 60p; (Thursday).

● **NATIONALIST AND LEINSTER TIMES** (Carlow & west Wicklow) 42 Tullow Street, Carlow; *Tel* 0503-70100; *Fax* 30301; *Web* www.rmbi.ie; *email* news@leinster-times.ie; *Est* 1883; *Ed* Eddie Coffey; *Sports* Paul Donaghy; *Group* Nationalist Group; *Cir* 15,620 (group); *Price* £1.00 (Wednesday).

● **NATIONALIST AND MUNSTER ADVERTISER** (South Tipperary, Co Limerick, Co Waterford, Co Kilkenny) Queen Street, Clonmel, Co Tipperary; *Tel* 052- 22211; *Fax* 25248; *Web* www.nationalist.ie; *Est* 1890; *Ed* Tom Corr; *Sports* Michael Heveran; *Group* Kilkenny People Group; *ABC cir* 15,785; *Price* £1.00; (Thursday).

● **NENAGH GUARDIAN** (North Tipperary, Co Clare, Co Galway, Co Offaly) 13 Summerhill, Nenagh, Co Tipperary; *Tel* 067-31214; *Fax* 33401; *email* nenaghg@tinet.ie; *Web* www.nenagh-guardian.ie; *ISDN* 50050; *Est* 1838; *Ed* Gerry Slevin; *Group* none; *ABC cir* 7,706; *Price* 90p; (Wednesday).

● **NEW ROSS ECHO** (Co Wexford) Mill Park Road, Enniscorthy, Co. Wexford; *Tel* 054-33231; *Fax* 33506/34492; *email* wexfordecho@tinet.ie; ISDN 42134/42135; *Est* 1902; *Ed* Tom Mooney; *Group* Echo Newspapers; *Price* £1.00; (Wednesday).

● **NEW ROSS STANDARD** (New Ross) 1 North Main Street, Wexford; *Tel* 053-22155; *Fax* 23228; *email* pbyrnes@peoplenews.ie; *Web* www.peoplenews.ie; *ISDN* 60026; *Ed* Michael Ryan; *Sports* Sean Nolan; *Group* People Newspapers; *Price* £1.00; (Wednesday).

● **NEWRY REPORTER, THE** (South Down, Co Armagh, Co Louth) 4 Margaret Street, Newry, Co Down BT34 1DF; *Tel* 01693 67633/6; *Fax* 63157; *ISDN* 257852; *Est* 1863; *Ed* Donal O'Donnell; *Sports* Jimmy Davis; *Group* none; *Price* Stg 50p; (Thursday).

● **NEWTOWNARDS SPECTATOR** (North Down) 109 Main Street, Bangor, Co. Down; *Tel* 01247-270270; *Fax* 271544; *email* spectator@dial.pipex.com; *ISDN* 465953; *Est* 1904; *Ed* Paul Flowers; *Group* County Down Spectator Group; *Price* 50p; (Thursday).

● **NEWTOWNARDS CHRONICLE** (Ards Peninsula) 25 Frances Street, Newtownards, Co Down BT23 3OT; *Tel* 01247-813333; *Fax* 820087; *ISDN* 01247 465953; *Est* 1873; *Ed* John Savage; *Sports* James Waide; *Group* D E Alexander; *Price* Stg 50p; (Thursday).

● **NORTHERN CONSTITUTION** (Coleraine, Magherafelt, S Derry) 20 Railway Road, Coleraine, Co Derry BT52 1PD; *Tel* 01265-43344; *Fax* 329672; *Est* 1875; *Ed* Maurice McAleese; *Sports* Michael Anderson; *Group* Northern Newspaper Group; *Price* Stg 60p (Wednesday).

● **NORTHERN STANDARD** (Co Monaghan, Co Cavan, Co Louth, Co Fermanagh) The Diamond, Monaghan; *Tel* 047-81867/82188; *Fax* 84070; *email* garysmyth@tinet.ie; *Web* www.northern-standard.ie; *Est* 1839; *Ed* Martin Smyth; *Sports* Patrick Smyth; *Group* none; *ABC cir* 14,000 *Price* 70p; (Thursday).

● **NORTHSIDE PEOPLE, THE** (North West & West Dublin) 85-86 Omni Park Shopping Centre, Santry, Dublin 9; *Tel* 01-8621611; *Fax* 8621625; *email* news@northsidepeople.ie; *Web* www.northsidepeople.ie; *ISDN* 806 0066/7; *Est* 1987 (east) 1995 (west); *Ed* Aidan Kelly (west) Tony McCullagh (east); *Group* Dublin People; *ABC cir* 39,442; (west) 52,000 (east); *Price* free; [2 titles] (Wednesday).

● **NORTHWEST ECHO** (Co Derry, Tyrone, Antrim) Suite 3, Spencer House, Spencer Road, Waterside, Derry BT47 1AA; *Tel* 01504-342226; *Fax* 341175; *Ed* Chris McNabb; *Group* Morton Newspapers; *Price* free; (Wednesday).

● **OFFALY EXPRESS** (Offaly, Westmeath, N Tipperary, Kildare, Carlow) Bridge Street, Tullamore, Co Offaly; *Tel* 0506-21744; *Fax* 51930; *email* L.express@indigo.ie; *Web* www.rmbi.ie; *ISDN* 0502 70077; *Est* 1831; *Ed* John Whelan; *Sport* Brian Keyes; *Group* Leinster Express; *Price* £1; (Wednesday).

● **OFFALY INDEPENDENT** (Midlands) 11 Sean Costello House, Athlone, Co Westmeath; *Tel* 0902-72003; *Fax* 74474; *email* westof@iol.ie; *ISDN* 20020; *Ed* Margaret Grennan; *Group* Westmeath Independent Ltd.; *Price* £1.00; (Thursday).

● **OFFALY TOPIC** (Co Offaly) 6 Dominick Street, Mullingar, Co Westmeath; *Tel* 044-48868; *Fax* 43777; *email* topic@indigo.ie; *ISDN* 39056/7; *Ed* Dick Hogan; *Group* Topic Newspapers; *Price* 90p; (Thursday).

● **OUTLOOK, THE** (Mourne Area) Castle Street, Rathfriland, Co Down; *Tel* 018206-30202; *Fax* 31022; *Est* 1939; *Ed* Steven Patton; *Group* Alpha Group; *Price* Stg 40p; (Wednesday).

● **PORTADOWN TIMES** (Co Armagh, Co Down) 14 Church Street, Portadown, Craigavon, Co Armagh BT62 3HY; *Tel* 01762-336111; *Fax* 350203; *Est* 1924; *Ed* David Armstrong; *Group* Morton Newspapers; *Price* Stg 62p; (Friday).

● **ROSCOMMON CHAMPION** (Roscommon, Westmeath, Longford, East Galway) Abbey Street, Roscommon; *Tel* 0903-25051; *Fax* 25053; *email* roscommonchampion@tinet.ie; *Est* 1927; *Ed* Paul Healy; *Sport* Noel Fallon; *Group* Midland Tribune Group; *Cir* 9,100; *Price* 90p; (Wednesday).

● **ROSCOMMON HERALD** (Roscommon & adjoining counties) St. Patrick Street, Boyle, Co Roscommon; *Tel* 079-62004; *Fax* 62926; *email* roherald@indigo.ie; *Web* www.roscommonherald.ie; *ISDN* 079 64044; *Est* 1859; *Ed* Christina McHugh; *Sport* Liam Heagney; *Group* none; *Cir* 16,000; *Price* 90p; (Wednesday).

● **SLIGO CHAMPION, The** (Sligo city & county, east

Mayo, north Roscommon, west Leitrim) Wine Street, Sligo; *Tel* 071-69222; *Fax* 69040; *email* sales@sligochampion.ie; *Est* 1836; *Ed* Seamus Finn; *Sport* Leo Gray; *Group* none; *ABC cir* 15,298; *Price* 85p; (Wednesday).

● **SLIGO WEEKENDER** (Sligo, n Leitrim, s Donegal) Castle Street, Sligo; *Tel* 071-42140; *Fax* 42255; *email* weekend@iol.ie; *Est* 1983; *Ed* Brian McHugh; *Sport* Liam Maloney; *Group* Thomas Crosbie Holdings; *Price* Free; (Friday).

● **SOUTHERN STAR** (Co Cork, except N & NE) Ilen Street, Skibbereen, Co Cork; *Tel* 028 21200; *Fax* 21071; *email* Liam@southernstar.ie; *Est* 1889; *Ed, Sport* Liam O'Regan; *Group* none; *Cir* 15,500; *Price* 90p; (Thursday).

● **SOUTHSIDE PEOPLE, THE** (Dublin South East, Dun Laoghaire-Rathdown Council Area, west of south County Dublin) 85-86 Omni Park Shopping Centre, Santry, Dublin 9; *Tel* 01-862 1611; *Fax* 862 1625/6; *email* kfinlay@indigo.ie; *Web* www.sorthsidepeople.ie; *ISDN* 806 0066/7; *Est* 1980 (east) 1997 (west); *Ed* Ken Finlay; *Group* Dublin People; *Price* free; [2 titles] (Wednesday).

● **STRABANE CHRONICLE** (Strabane district) 10 John Street, Omagh, Co Tyrone BT78 1DT; *Tel* 01662-243444; *Fax* 242206; *email* editor@ulsterherald.com; *Est* 1907; *Ed* Dominic McClements; *Group* none; *Price* stg 38p; (Thursday).

● **STRABANE WEEKLY NEWS** (north Tyrone & east Donegal) 25-27 High Street, Omagh, Co Tyrone BT78 1BD; *Tel* 01662-242721; *Fax* 243549; *Est* 1908; *Ed* Wesley Atchison; *Group* Alpha Newspaper Group; *Price* 45p; (Friday).

● **TIPPERARY STAR** (Tipperary - parts of Kilkenny, Limerick, Laois, Offaly) Friar Street, Thurles, Co. Tipperary; *Tel* 0504-21122; *Fax* 21110; *Web* www.Tipperarystar.ie; *Est* 1909; *Ed* Michael Dundon; *Group* Kilkenny People Group; *ABC cir* 10,021; *Price* £1.00 (Thursday).

● **TUAM HERALD & WESTERN ADVERTISER** (Co Galway) Dublin Road, Tuam, Co Galway; *Tel* 093-24183; *fax* 24478; *email* tuamhrld@iol.ie; *Web* www.tuamherald.ie; *ISDN* 093 70046; *Est* 1837; *Ed* David Burke; *Sport* Jim Carney; *Group* none; *Cir* 10,850; *Price* 80p (Wednesday).

● **TULLAMORE TRIBUNE, The** (Tullamore & Offaly) Church Street, Tullamore, Co. Offaly; *Tel* 0506-21152; *Fax* 21927; *email* tulltrib@iol.ie; *Est* 1978; *Ed* Gerard Scully; *Group* RNAI; *Price* £1.00; (Wednesday).

● **TYRONE CONSTITUTION, The** (mid, west and north Tyrone, north Fermanagh) 25-27 High Street, Omagh, Co Tyrone BT78 1BD; *Tel* 01662-242721; *Fax* 243549; *email* editor@tyroneconstitution.com; *Est* 1844; *Ed* Wesley Atchison; *Sport* Richard Mulligan; *Group* Alpha Newspaper Group; *Price* 65p; (Thursday).

● **TYRONE TIMES** (Dungannon, parts of Co Tyrone) 48 Market Square, Dungannon, Co Tyrone BT70 1JH; *Tel* 01868-752801; *Fax* 752819; *Ed* Paul McCreary; *Sports* Kevin Hughes; *Group* Morton Newspapers; *Price* Stg 55p; (Thursday).

● **ULSTER GAZETTE** (Armagh city & district) 56 Scotch Street, Armagh BT61 7DQ; *Tel* 01861-522639; *Fax* 527029; *Est* 1844; *Ed* Richard Stewart; *Sport*

Stephen Richardson; *Group* Alpha Newspaper Group; *Price* Stg 60p; (Wednesday).

● **ULSTER HERALD** (Omagh district) 10 John Street, Omagh, Co Tyrone BT78 1DT; *Tel* 01662-243444; *Fax* 242206; *email* editor@ulsterherald.com; *Est* 1901; *Ed* Dominic McClements; *Group* none; *Price* Stg 50p; (Thursday).

● **ULSTER STAR** (Co Antrim, Co Down) 12A Bow Street, Lisburn, Co Antrim BT28 1BN; *Tel* 01846-679111; *Fax* 602904; *Ed* David Fletcher; *Sport* Gary Allif; *Group* Morton Newspapers; *Price* Stg 60p; (Friday).

● **WATERFORD NEWS & STAR** (Waterford city, County) 25 Michael Street, Waterford; *Tel* 051-874951; *Fax* 051 856317; *email* editor@waterford-news.ie; *Web* www.waterford-news.ie; *ISDN* 051 301204; *Est* 1848; *Ed* Peter Doyle; *Sport* Peter Doyle; *Group* none; *Price* 90p; (Wednesday).

● **WEEKENDER, THE** (Co Meath) 6 Charter Buildings, Kennedy Road, Navan, Co Meath; *Tel* 046-22333; *Fax* 29864; *email* tebitdo@indigo.ie; *ISDN* 79276/7; *Est* 1984; *Ed* Fergus Barry; *Sports* Noel Coogan; *Group* none; *Price* 70p; (Tuesday).

● **WESTERN PEOPLE, The** (W, NW Mayo) Francis Street, Ballina, Co. Mayo; *Tel* 096-21188; *Fax* 70208; *email* wpeople@iol.ie; *Web* www.westernpeople.ie; *ISDN* 096 60064; *est* 1883; *Ed* Terry Reilly; *Sport* Ivan Neill; *Group* Thos. Crosbie Holdings; *ABC cir* 24,200; *Price* 90p; (Tuesday).

● **WESTMEATH EXAMINER, THE** (Midlands) Hayden House, 19 Dominick Street, Mullingar, Co Westmeath; *Tel* 044-48426 (5 lines); *Fax* 40640; *ISDN* 30092; *Est* 1882; *Ed* Nicholas Nally; *Sports* John Fitzsimons; *Group* none; *Cir* 13,668; *Price* £1.00; (Wednesday).

● **WESTMEATH INDEPENDENT** (Midlands)11 Sean Costello House, Athlone, Co Westmeath; *Tel* 0902-72003; *Fax* 74474; *email* westof@iol.ie; *ISDN* 20020; *Ed* Margaret Grennan; *Group* Westmeath Independent Ltd.; *Price* £1.00; (Thursday).

● **WESTMEATH TOPIC** (Co Westmeath) 6 Dominick Street, Mullingar, Co Westmeath; *Tel* 044-48868; *Fax* 43777; *email* topic@indigo.ie; *ISDN* 39056/7; *Ed* Dick Hogan; *Group* Topic Newspapers; *Cir* 13,786; *Price* 90p; (Thursday).

● **WEXFORD ECHO** (Co Wexford) Mill Park Road, Enniscorthy, Co. Wexford; *Tel* 054-33231; *Fax* 33506/34492; *email* wexfordecho@tinet.ie; *ISDN* 42134/42135; *Est* 1902; *Ed* Tom Mooney; *Group* Echo Newspapers; *Price* £1.00; (Wednesday).

● **WEXFORD PEOPLE** (Co Wexford) 1 North Main Street, Wexford; *Tel* 053-22155; *Fax* 23228; *email* pbyrnes@peoplenews.ie; *Web* www.peoplenews.ie; *ISDN* 60026; *Ed* Michael Ryan; *Sports* Sean Nolan; *Group* People Newspapers; *Price* £1.00; (Wednesday).

● **WICKLOW PEOPLE** (Co Wicklow except N E) Main Street, Wicklow; *Tel* 0404-67198; *Fax* 69937; *email* pbyrnes@peoplenews.ie; *Web* www.peoplenews.ie; *ISDN* 01 205 0732; *Ed* Owen Quinn; *Sports* Sean Nolan; *Group* People Newspapers; *Price* £1.00; (Thursday).

● **WICKLOW TIMES** (Wicklow) 1 Eglinton Road, Bray, Co Wicklow; *Tel* 01-2869111; *Fax* 2869074; *email* wicklowtimes@tinet.ie; *Est* 1988; *Ed* Shay Fitzmaurice;

Group Brandán Media; *Price* free (Wednesday).

Irish papers published abroad

● **IRISH POST, The** (Britain) Cambridge House, Cambridge Grove, Hammersmith, London W6 OLE, England; *Tel* 00-44-181 741 0649; *Fax* 741 3382; *Web* www.irishpost@irishpost.co.uk; *email* irishpost@irish-post.co.uk; *ISDN* 0181 563 0462; *Est* 1970; *Ed* Norah Casey; *ABC cir* 52,000; *Price* Stg 60p (Wednesday).

● **IRISH ECHO** (New York, USA) 309 Fifth Avenue, New York, NY 10016; *Tel* 212-686 1266; *Fax* 686 1756; *Ed* Tom Connelly; (Weekly).

● **NATIONAL HIBERNIAN DIGEST** (USA) 3114 Lynx Lane - Timber Pines, Springhill, FL 34604; *Tel* 352-683 1567; *Fax* 683 1567; *Ed* James J Brennan; (Bi-monthly).

● **IRISH VOICE** (New York, USA) 432 Park Ave Sth, New York, NY 10016; *Tel* 212-684 3366; *Fax* 779 1198; *Ed* Debbie McGoldrick (weekly).

● **IRISH EDITION** (USA) 803 B.Willow Grove Ave, Wyndmoor, PA 19038; *Tel* 215-836 4900; *Fax* 848 2018; *Ed* Jane M Duffin (Monthly).

● **AN SCATHAN** (USA) PO Box 24, Ashland, PA 17921-0024; *Tel* 717-875 2999; *Fax* 875 2234; *Ed* Hugh Doherty (Monthly).

● **FLORIDA IRISH AMERICAN** (USA) 650 E Sample Road, Pompano Beach, FL 33064; *Tel* 954-946 1093; *Fax* 946 6173; *Ed* Sheila Hynes (Monthly).

● **IRISH AMERICAN CELEBRATION** (USA) 3482 Maggie Blvd, Orlando, FL 32811; *Tel* 407-872 7695; *Fax* 872 7784; *Ed* Dan Davis (Quarterly).

● **BUFFALO IRISH CENTRE NEWSLETTER** (New York, USA) 245 Abbott Road, Buffalo, NY 14220; *Tel* 716-825 6700; *Ed* Mary Heneghan (Bi-monthly).

● **IRISH INSIDER NEWSLETTER** (New York, US) PO Box 90387, Rochester, NY 14609; *Tel* 716-482 2843; *Fax* 482 9405; *Ed* Jack & Melissa Rosenberry (Bi-monthly).

● **IRISH AMERICAN NEWS** (USA) 503 5 Oak Park Ave, Ste 204, Oak Park, IL 60304-1224; *Tel* 708-445 0700; *Ed* Clifford Carlson (Monthly).

● **TEXAS IRISH NEWS** (USA) PO Box 13731, Houston, TX 77019; *Ed* Mike Coogan (Monthly).

● **HARP & SHAMROCK SOCIETY OF TEXAS NEWSLETTER** (USA) 19840 Encino Brook, San Antonio, TX 78259; *Tel* 512-497-8435; *Ed* Patrick J. Dowd (Monthly).

● **IRISH AMERICAN POST** (USA) 301 N. Water Street, Milwaukee, WI 53202-5713; *Tel* 414-273 8132; *Fax* 273 8196; *ed* Martin Hintz (Bi-monthly).

● **IRISH GAZETTE** (USA) PO Box 65782, St Paul, MN 55165; *Tel* 612-698-3083; *Ed* James Brookes (Bi-monthly).

● **IRISH CONNECTION, The** (USA) PO Box 36775, Grosse Pointe, MI 48236-9998; *Tel* 313-822-7555; *Fax* 693-8260; *Ed* John Pollard (Bi-monthly).

● **IRISH HERALD, The** (USA) 3516 Geary Blvd, San Francisco, CA 94118; *Tel* 415-752-7977; *Ed* Paul Downey (Monthly).

● **IRISH FOCUS** (USA) 2123 Market Street, San Francisco, CA 94114-1321; *Tel* 415-621-2200; *Ed* John Collins (Monthly).

● **GAEL, The** (USA) 286 Beverly Street, San Francisco, CA 94132; *Tel* 415-586-0142; *Ed* Raymond Hughes (Monthly).

● **DESERT SHAMROCK** (USA) 5025 North Central Ave, Phoenix, AZ 85012; *Tel* 602-242-3203; *Ed* Maureen O'Mahar (Monthly).

● **IRISH NEWS AND ENTERTAINMENT** (USA) 2330 West Third, Los Angeles, CA 90057; *Tel* 818-563-1845; *Ed* Jim McDonough (Monthly).

● **IRISH EYES** (USA) 15414 N7th St, 8-173 Phoenix, AZ 85022; *Tel* 602-866-3226; *Ed* Art O'Hagan (Monthly).

● **BOSTON IRISH REPORTER** (USA) 304 Neponset Ave, Dorchester, MA 02122; *Tel* 617-436-1222; *Ed* Bill Forry (Monthly).

● **IRISH EMIGRANT** (USA) 11 Hamilton Road, Wakefield, MA 01880; *Tel* 617-246-3945; *Eds* Connell & Siobhan Gallagher (Weekly).

Explanation of Newspaper Profile

● **NAME OF NEWSPAPER** (Area served) *Address; Telephone; Fax; email Address; Year established; Editor; Newspaper Group; Price;* (Day published).

National Newspaper Advertising Rates

(£) Newspaper	Mono SCI	Mono 1/2 Pg	Mono Full Pg	Col. SCI	Col. 1/2 Pg	Col. Full Pg
Irish Independent	99	7,750	15,500	135	10,000	20,000
Belfast Telegraph* (Stg)	15.45	4,326	8,652		6,056	11,680
Examiner, The	47	4,400	8,700	56.40	5,280	10,440
Evening Echo	28	1,275	2,550	33.60	1,530	3,060
Evening Herald	68	3,000	6,000	88	3,500	7,000

Continued from previous page

(Rates: effective 1999) Newspaper	Mono SCI (£)	Mono 1/2 Pg (£)	Mono Full Pg (£)	Col. SCI (£)	Col. 1/2 Pg (£)	Col. Full Pg (£)
Irish News (Stg)	7.55	1,834	3,669	9.43	2,293	4,586
Irish Times*	39.50	7,850	15,357		9,135	16,957
News Letter, The* (Stg)	10.75	1,280	2,560	15.05	1,665	3,330
Star, The	64	3,100	6,200	88	4,100	8,200
Sunday Business Post	46	3,700	7,000	61	4,850	9,300
Sunday Independent	110	9,000	18,000	165	11,500	23,000
Sunday Tribune	63	5,445	10,466	93	7,824	15,188
Sunday World *	41	4,750	9,500	62.50	7,100	14,200
Ireland on Sunday*	69.20	3,390	5,981	54.50	2,670	4,710
Irish Farmers' Journal	53.50	2,164	4,327	93.55	3,788	7,576

* Single column cm. Package rates and discount offers are available from most newspapers for block booking.

Selected Provincial Newspaper Rates (1999)

Newspaper	Mono SCI (£)	Mono 1/2 Pg (£)	Mono Full Pg (£)	Col. SCI (£)	Col. 1/2 Pg (£)	Col. Full Pg (£)
Anglo Celt	15.00	1,000.00	1,850.00	20.00	1,300.00	2,600.00
Clare Champion	16.00	1,400.00	2,700.00	19.00	1,650.00	3,200
Connacht Telegraph	12.00	1,080.00	2,268.00	18.00	1,620.00	3,402.00
Connacht Tribune	17.00	1,640.00	3,280.00	24.00	1,920.00	3,676.00
Derry Journal*	10.50	1,260.00	2,525.00	10.50	1,610.00	2,875.00
Derry People/Donegal News	7.90	775.00	1,550.00	N/A	N/A	N/A
Donegal Democrat*	10.20	1,000.00	2,000.00	10.20	1,300.00	2,300.00
Donegal Peoples Press*	7.90	415.00	825.00	7.90	715.00	1,125.00
Drogheda Independent	22.00	2,178.00	4,356.00	27.50	2,722.00	5,445.00
Dundalk Argus	16.00	830.00	1,600.00	24.00	1,220.00	2,370.00
Dundalk Democrat	10.00	795.00	1,590.00	19.00	1,500.00	3,000.00
Kerryman/Corkman	29.50	2,920.00	5,840.00	35.00	3,465.00	6,930.00
Kilkenny People	15.50	1,506.00	3,012.00	19.40	1,882.00	3,765.00
Leinster & Offaly Express*	16.50	865.00	1,730.00	16.50	1,215.00	2,080.00
Leinster Leader*	16.50	1,260.00	2,520.00	16.50	1,760.00	3,020.00
Leitrim Observer	15.00	1,200.00	2,400.00	21.00	1,600.00	3,000.00
Limerick Chronicle	8.00	300.00	600.00	8.50	650.00	950.00
Limerick Leader	21.00	1,900.00	3,600.00	21.00	2,250.00	3,950.00
Longford Leader	15.00	1,350.00	2,500.00	21.00	1,650.00	2,800.00
Longford News	13.50	1,000.00	1,900.00	19.00	1,400.00	2,600.00
Midland/Tullamore Tribune	16.00	800.00	1,500.00	32.00	1,100.00	1,800.00
Mayo News	11.50	552.00	1,104.00	18.00	902.00	1,454.00
Meath Chronicle	16.00	1,360.00	2,720.00	18.00	1,530.00	3,060.00
Munster Express	14.50	1,354.50	2,709.00	21.50	1,754.00	3,924.00
Nationalist & Leinster Times*	16.75	1,500.00	2,500.00	16.75	1,800.00	2,800.00
Nationalist (Clonmel)*	14.50	1,370.00	2,740.00	14.50	1,770.00	3,140.00
Nenagh Guardian	10.00	875.00	1,550.00	15.00	1,166.00	2,066.00
Northern Standard	15.00	1,320.00	2,580.00	N/A	N/A	N/A
People Newspapers*	30.95	1,390.00	2,690.00	30.95	2,390.00	3,690.00
Roscommon Herald*	12.00	850.00	1,500.00	12.00	1,150.00	1,800.00
Roscommon Champion	14.50	800.00	1,300.00	28.00	1,100.00	1,500.00
Sligo Champion*	10.00	750.00	1,450.00	10.00	1,000.00	1,700.00
Southern Star	12.00	1,000.00	2,000.00	20.00	2,000.00	3,500.00
Tipperary Star	13.00	1,230.00	2,450.00	16.25	1,500.00	3,000.00
Tuam Herald*	7.00	588.00	1,175.00	7.00	888.00	1,475.00
Waterford News & Star	13.00	1,290.00	2,574.00	17.55	1,740.00	3,475.00
Western People	19.00	1,800.00	3,500.00	23.00	1,950.00	3,800.00
Westmeath Examiner*	13.00	900.00	1,650.00	13.00	1,150.00	1,900.00
Westmeath/Offaly Independent*	13.00	900.00	1,650.00	13.00	1,150.00	1,900.00

* Single column cm. Rates effective from April 1999

Periodicals, Magazines and Journals

Title	Year Established	Issues per year	Telephone number	Editor	Price
● **ARCHAEOLOGY**					
Archaeology Ireland	1987	4	01-2862649	Tom Condit	£3.95
● **ADVERTISING - MARKETING**					
Irish Marketing Journal	1974	11	01-2950088	Norman Barry	£90.75*
Deadline	1995	10	01-4784322	Seamus Bagnall	*
MAPS		1	01-2960000	Rosemary Delaney	£30
Marketing	1990	10	01-2807735	Michael Cullen	£50*
Marketing Institute Ireland News		6	01-4972711	John Casey	FtM
Marketing News	1989	6	01-4972711	Julie Colby	FtM
● **AGRICULTURE**					
Genuine Irish Old Moore's Almanac		1	01-2960000	Rosemary Delaney	£1.75
Irish Farmers Monthly Journal	1982	12	01-2893305	Paul O'Grady	£1.00
Tillage Farmer, The	1946	6	0503-31487	Michael Grimes	£15.00*
Today's Farm	1990	6	01-6688188	John Keating	C.C.
United News	1996	12	01232-783200	Euel Agnew	£27.50*
● **ARTS / LITERATURE**					
Books Ireland	1976	9	01-2692185	Jeremy Addis (Publisher)	£2.40
Circa Art Magazine	1981	4	01-6765035	Peter FitzGerald	£3.95
Flaming Arrows	1989	1	No Calls	Leo Regan	£2.65
Hibernia	1995	4	01-2808415	Thomas P. Farley	
Poetry Ireland Review		4	01-6714632	Mark Roper	£5.99
● **ASTRONOMY**					
Astronomy & Space	1997	12	01-4598883	David Moore	£3.25
● **BUSINESS - MANAGEMENT - MANUFACTURING - INSURANCE**					
Accountancy Ireland	1969	6	01-6680400	Daisy Downes	£25.00*
Administration	1953	4	01-2697011	Tony McNamara	£11.00
Administration Yearbook & Diary	1965	1	01-2697011	Tony McNamara	£45.00
AMT Magazine	1979	11	01-2847777	Eamon McGrane	£37.00*
Banking Ireland	1898	4	01-6793311	Sean McQuaid	£25.00*
Banking Review, The	1957	4	01-6715311	Felix O'Regan	Free
Business and Finance	1964	50	01-6764587	Vincent Wall	£2.00
Business Contact	1988	12	01-8550477	David O'Riordan	£1.85
Business Plus	1998	12	01-4960666	Niochlas Mulcahy	£1.95
Business Solutions	1999	10	01-6796700	Paul O'Byrne	£71.00*
CMS (Call Management Solutions)	1998	4	01-2847777	John Costello	£2.75
CPA Journal of Accountancy	1943	4	01-6767353	Colleen Quinn	*
Economic & Social Review, The	1969	4	01-6671525	Dr. Frank Barry	£20.00*
European Industry	1983	11	01-6603174	Tony Keegan	£50.00*
Finance Magazine	1987	12	01-6606222	Ken O'Brien	£120.00*
Industrial Relations News	1984	52	01-4972711	Brian Sheehan	£370.00*
Inside Business	1990	10	01-8550477	Claire Reilly	£1.95
Introducing Dublin	1998	4	01-8550477	Karen Hesse	
Irish Broker	1984	12	01-8360366	Joe Flood & Jim Hegarty	£45.00*
Irish Tax Review	1976	6	01-6688222	Frank Carr	£145.20*
IPD News (Institute Personnel Development)	1983	5	01-4972711	Mike McDonnell	FtM
One to One	1993	3	01-6623158	Martina Hughes	Free
Public Sector Times (Civil Service)	1975	52	01-2869111	Shay Fitzmaurice	Free
Public Service Review		6	01-6767271	Tom McKevitt	20p to members
Packaging Business	1997	6	01-6796700	Mike Rohan	£65.00*
Running Your Business	1995	6	01-4902244	Donal McAuliffe	£2.50
Stubbs Gazette	1828	50	01-6764239	Carmel Conroy	£142.00*
Technology Ireland	31yrs	10	01-8082287	Tom Kennedy & Mary Mulvihill	£2.95
Ulster Business	1988	12	01232-783200	Carlton Baxter	£1.95
Visa Card News	1993	3	01-6623158	Martina Hughes	N/C

Title	Year Established	Issues per year	Telephone number	Editor	Price
● **COMMERCIAL**					
Buy & Sell (Ireland's Free Ads Paper)	1990	104	01-6080700	no editor	£1.25
● **COMMUNICATIONS**					
Communications Today	1994	10	01-2847777	John Costello	£37.00*
● **COMPUTERS / TELECOMMUNICATIONS**					
ComputerScope	1985	10	01-8303455	David Darcy	C.C.
Computer Reseller	1997	10	01-4600450	Jeremy Kingston	Direct Mail
Eircell News	1996	4	01-6623158	Martina Hughes	N/C
dot.ie	1996	10	01-4784322	Brian Lavery	£2.95
Irish Computer	1971	12	01-2847777	Declan McColgan	£2.70
IT Times	1997	6	01-4600450	Tony Manson	£2.50
PC Live!	1995	12	01-8303455	John Collins	£2.95
● **CONSTRUCTION**					
Construction		10	01-8550477	Jim Doherty	£39.00*
Construction & Property News	1973	12	01-2800000	Maev Martin	£36.00*
Irish Planning and Environmental Law Journal, The	1994	4	01-8730101	Eamon Galligan	£134.00*
● **DEFENCE**					
Connect	1992	12	01-8042692	Corporal Willie Braine	Free
Constabulary Gazette	1897	12	01232-661091	Bob Catterson	C.C.
Cosantóir, An	1940	10	01-8042690	Sgt. Terry McLaughlin	£1.50
Defence Forces Review	1995	1	01-8062690	Military Editorial Board	£5.00
Garda News	1980	12	01-8309188	Austin Kenny	*
Garda Review	1925	12	01-8550477	Andy Needham	-
● **EDUCATION/COLLEGE**					
An Leabharlann		4	01-6761167	Noreen O'Neill & Kevin Quinn	FtM
Astir	1973	12	01-6719144	Iseult O'Doherty	FtM
CompuSchool	1995	4	01-4537556	Roddy Peavoy	£12.00 C.C.
Dublin's Evening Classes Guidebook	1985	1	01-8305236	Liam Ó hOisín	£2.99
Guide to Post Graduate Study in Ireland, The	1998	1	01-8305236	Miriam Arundle	£5.99
Guideline		5	01-6761975	Michael Roberts	FtM
Irish Journal of Education	1967	1	01-8373789	Thomas Kellaghan	£3.00
InTouch	1997	10	01-8722533	Sinead Shannon	FtM
Parent & Teacher	1995	10	01-4537556	Roddy Peavoy	£12.00 C.C.
Trinity News	1950s	9	01-6082335	Eoghan Williams	Free
UCD Connections		2	01-2960000	Rosemary Delaney	
● **EMPLOYMENT**					
Job News	1992	52	01-2840266	Brendan Barrett	£1.10
Irish Social Worker	1980	4	01-6774838	Kieran McGrath	£6 per issue*
Recruitment	1997	52	01232-319008	Steve Preston	35p
● **ENGINEERING**					
Engineers Journal	1981	10	01-4908256	Leslie Faughnan	£47.25*
Industrial & Manufacturing Engineer	1989	4	01762-334272	Paul Beattie	Stg£2.00
Manufacturing Ireland	1989	10	01-8744180	Willo Litzoun	£35.00*
Plantman Magazine	1970	10	01-4520898	Patrick J. Murphy	£25.00*
Readout	1989	6	01-2822554	Eoin O Riain	C.C.
● **FASHION/STYLE**					
Futura	1969	10	01-2836782	Pat Codyre (Publisher)	£28.00*
d'Side	1993	11	01-6684966	Melanie Morris	£1.95
Himself	1998	10	01-2808415	Francis Cottam	£2.40

Title	Year Established	Issues per year	Telephone number	Editor	Price
● **FISHING**					
Irish Skipper, The	1964	12	075-48935	Mick Browne	95p
● **FIRE/SAFETY**					
Fire & Safety Journal	-	12	01-6713193	Suzanne Hennessey	
● **FOOD - DRINK - RETAIL**					
A Magazine (Arnotts)	1998	2	01-6623158	Lisa Gaughran	£1.50
Bakery World	1972	4	01-2800000	Jeremy Hennessy	£18.00*
Carie Blanche (Blanchardstown)	1997	2	01-6623158	Lisa Gaughran	N/C
Catering and Licensing Review	1979	12	01232-783200	Kathy Jensen	£27.50*
Checkout Ireland	1966	11	01-2300322	Mary Brophy	£50.00*
Consumer Choice	1986	12	01-6686836	Kieran Doherty	£55.00*
Cookbook, The	1997	2	01-6623158	Celine Naughton	£2.50
Dairy & Food Industries Magazine	1992	10	01-2805686	Michael Kenna	£30.00*
Food & Drink Business	1995	10	01-6796700	Mike Rohan	£71.00*
Food & Wine	1997	10	01-2300322	-	£2.40
Food Service Ireland	1998	6	01-6796700	Mike Rohan	£65.00*
Food Technology & Packaging	1997	4	01232-783200	Carlton Baxter	-
Hotel and Catering Review	1974	12	01-2800000	Frank Corr	£30.00*
Irish Food	1989	12	01-2893305	David Markey	Free*
Irish Food & Restaurateur	1997	12	01-2808880	Alice Sheridan	Free
Licensed and Catering News	1944	10	01232-230425	Teresa Dowling	£30.00*
Licensing World	1942	12	01-2800000	Pat Nolan	£30.00*
Mace Lifestyles	1998	6	01232-783200	Kathy Jensen	Stg£1.00
Off Licence	1998	6	01-2800000	Maev Martin	
Retail Forecourt & Convenience Store	1993	6	01232-230425	Larry Nixon	£18.00*
Retail Grocer	1989	10	01232-230425	Larry Nixon	£25.00*
Shelflife	1981	12	01-2847777	John Doyle	£53.00*
SQ Food	1998	2	01-6623158	Petra Carter	£1.95
Ulster Grocer	1972	12	01232-783200	Brian McCalden	£27.50*
Ulster Tatler Wine & Dine	1997	1	01232-663311	Walter Love	£1.50
● **GENERAL**					
Big Issues, The	1994	26	01-8553969	Rosemary Meleady	£2.00
Fortnight	1971	11	01232-232353	John O'Farrell	Stg£2.20
In Dublin	1976	25	01-4784322	Allanna Gallagher	£1.95
Ireland's Eye	1979	12	044-48868	Tom Kiernan	90p
Ireland's Own	1902	52	053-22155	Gerry Breen	55p / 90p
County Down Portrait	1985	1	01232-663311	Richard Sherry	£2.00
Mid Ulster Portrait	1985	1	01232-663311	Richard Sherry	£2.00
North Ulster Portrait	1985	1	01232-663311	Richard Sherry	Stg£2.00
Ulster Tatler	1967	12	01232-663311	Richard Sherry	£2.20
VIP	1999	12	01-6769832	Maura O'Kiely	£1.95
West Belfast Annual	1985	1	01232-663311	Sean McGettigan	£2.00
Irish Roots	1992	4	021-500067	Tony McCarthy	£8.00
● **HARDWARE**					
Irish Hardware	1938	12	01-2800000	Jeremy Hennessy	£30.00*
● **HISTORY**					
Historical Association of Ireland:					
Lives & Times Series	1992	2	01- 7021578	Dr. Ciaran Brady	*
History Ireland	1993	4	01-4535730	Hiram Morgan, Tommy Graham	£3.95
Irish Historical Studies	1938	2	01-7021578	Ciaran Brady, David Hayton	*
● **HEALTH - MEDICAL**					
Bord Altranais News	1984	4	01-6760226	Maria Neary	Free to Nurses
Business Health	-	12	01-6713500	Simon Rowe	
Forum	1991	12	01-2803967	Geraldine Meagan	£72.00*
Health and Safety	-	12	01-6713500	Simon Rowe	

Title	Year Established	Issues per year	Telephone number	Editor	Price
Health & Safety Review	1996	10	01-4972711	Herbert Mulligan	£115.00*
Hospital Doctor of Ireland	1995	6	01-4753300	Maura Henderson	£36.00*
Irish Journal of Psychological Medicine	1981	4	01-2803967	Brian Lawlor	Stg£43.00*
Irish Medical Journal	mid 19th cen	10	01-6767273	Dr. John Murphy	Free/£90.00*
Irish Medical News	1984	50	01-2960000	Niall Hunter	Free/ £2.00
Irish Medical Times	1967	52	01-4757461	Dr. John O'Connell	Free/ £3.00
Irish Optician		6	01-2960000	Valerie Ryan	£20.00*
Irish Pharmacy Journal, The	1923	11	01-6600699	Val Harte	£45.00*
IPU Review	1971	11	01-4931801	Majella Lane	
Journal of the Irish Dental Association	1979	4	01-2830499	Dr. Seamus O'Hickey	Free
MIMs Ireland	1969	12	01-4757461	Andre Letoha	Free to Doctors / £14
Sláinte	1997	4	01-6629452	Sive Hughes	£1.95
World of Irish Nursing	1995	10	01-2803967	Liam Doran	FtM/ £1.10

● HUMAN RIGHTS

Title	Year Established	Issues per year	Telephone number	Editor	Price
Amnesty International	1974	4	01-6776361	Séamas Shiels	£1 / FtM
ICCL News	1990	4	01-8783136	Donncha O'Connell	Free

● INTERIORS - GARDEN

Title	Year Established	Issues per year	Telephone number	Editor	Price
Beyond The Hall Door	1995	1	01-2600899	Hillary Fennell	£3.95
House & Home Magazine	1996	6	01-8550477	Karen Hesse	£1.95
Image Interiors	1995	3	01-2808415	Jane McDonnell	£2.50
Irish Garden, The	1992	10	01-2862649	Gerry Daly and Mary Davies	£2.25
Irish Homes Magazine	1992	6	01-8780444	Berenice Brindley	£1.95
Irish Interiors	10	1	01-6769829	Muriel Bolger	£3.95
Living Space	1997	2	01-6623158	Aine O'Connor	£1.95
Ulster Home	1997	4	01232-663311	Billy McAlister	£2.00
Town Country Homes	1994	10	01762-334272	Andrew Crozier	Stg£2.00

● IRISH LANGUAGE

Title	Year Established	Issues per year	Telephone number	Editor	Price
Feasta	1948	12	066-24169	Pádraig Mac Fhearghusa	£2.50

● LAW/LEGAL

Title	Year Established	Issues per year	Telephone number	Editor	Price
Bulletin of Northern Ireland Law	1970	10	01232-335224	Deborah McBride	Stg£150.00*
Commercial Law Practitioner	1994	11	01-8730101	Thomas B. Courtney	£224.00*
Gazette of the Law Society	1907	10	01-8375018	Conal O'Boyle	£45.00*
Irish Law Times	1983	20	01-8730101	Raymond Byrne	£265.00*
Irish Criminal Law Journal	1991	2	01-8730101	Ivana Bacik	£80.00*
Irish Current Law Statutes Annotated	1998	1	01-8730101	Professor Robert Clark	£490.00*
Irish Journal of European Law	1991	2	01-8730101	J O'Reilly & A Collins	£69.00*
Irish Journal of Family Law	1998	6	01-8730101	Geoffrey Shannon	£115.00*
Irish Law Reports Monthly	1981	14	01-8730101	Hilary Delany	£312.00*
Law Society Gazette	1907	10	01-6724827	Conal O'Boyle	£2.95
Northern Ireland Legal Quarterly	1964	4	01232- 335224	Prof Brigid Hadfield	Stg£50.00*

● MOTORING

Title	Year Established	Issues per year	Telephone number	Editor	Price
Auto Trader		52	01-2950787	None	£1.25
Car Driver	1985	6	01-2600899	Karl Tsigdinos	£1.95
Carsport	1982	12	01232-783253	Patrick Burns	£1.95
Garage Trader	1985	4	01762-334272	Karen McAvoy	Stg£2.00
Irish 4x4 & Off Road	1997	4	096-70941	John Reilly	£1.95
Irish Car	1989	12	096-70941	John Reilly	£1.95
Irish Tyre Trade Journal	1997	4	096-70941	John Reilly	£3.95
Irish Van & Light Truck	1995	4	096-70941	John Reilly	£2.50
Motoring Life	1947	4	01-8780444	Kevin Phenix	£1.75
Motorshow	1997	1	096-70941	John Reilly	£2.95

● MUSIC/ENTERTAINMENT

Title	Year Established	Issues per year	Telephone number	Editor	Price
Big Ticket, The	1998	12	01-4784322	Gareth Murphy	Free
Classical, The	1998	4	01-6624887	Ellen O'Hea	£2.95
Hot Press	1977	24	01-6795077	Niall Stokes	£1.95

Title	Year Established	Issues per year	Telephone number	Editor	Price
Irish Music	1995	12	01-6624887	Sean Laffey	£1.95
New Music News	1990	3	01-6612105	Eve O'Kelly	Free
RTÉ Guide	1961	52	01-2083146	Heather Parsons	£1.00

● POLITICAL/CURRENT AFFAIRS

Title	Year Established	Issues per year	Telephone number	Editor	Price
Comhar	1942	12	01-6785443	Antain Mac Lochlainn	£30.00*
Gay Community News	1988	12	01-6710939	Michael Cronin	Free
Irish Political Studies, Yearbook	1986	1	-	Richard Jay	£15.00/£22.50
Irish Political Studies	1986	1	061-333644	Richard Jay	£15.00
Magill	1977	12	01-4784322	(not confirmed)	£2.40
Phoenix	1983	24	01-6611062	Paddy Prendiville	£1.45
Socialist Voice	1989	26	01-6711943	Eugene McCartan	40p
Unity		52	01-6711943	James Stewart	40p

● PRINTING

Title	Year Established	Issues per year	Telephone number	Editor	Price
Irish Printer	1968	12	01-2800000	Frank Corr	£30.00*

● PROPERTY

Title	Year Established	Issues per year	Telephone number	Editor	Price
Blueprint Home Plans	1981	1	01-8305236	Liam Ó hOisín	£7.95
Commercial Interiors of Ireland	1996	1	01-6769829	Muriel Bolger	
Construction	-	10	01-8550477	Jim Doherty	-
Irish Architect	1839	10	01-2958115	Alan Phelan	£4.50
Irish Building Services News	1964	12	01- 2885001	Pat Lehane	£27.00*
Irish Construction Industry Mag.	1989	11	01-2806888	Tony Cantwell	£49.60*
Irish Forecourt Business	1999	4	01-2863963	Padraic Deane	£4.95
Irish Materials Handling Journal	1999	4	01-2863963	Padraic Deane	
Keystone	1995	6	01232-319008	Steven Preston	Free
Local Authority Times	1986	3	01-6686233	Ellen MacCafferty	
Plan - The Business of Building	1969	10	01-2788162	Che Breen	£45.00*
Property Ireland	1997	6	01-2840266	Brendan Barrett	£1.20
Specify	1980	6	01232-783251	Eddie O'Gorman	£3.00

● RELIGIOUS

Title	Year Established	Issues per year	Telephone number	Editor	Price
Africa		9	0508-73600	Rev. Gary Howley	
Bulletin	1856	4	01-8384164	Tom McSweeney	
Christian Irishman	1710	10	01232-322284	Rev David Temple	Stg65p
Church of Ireland Gazette, The	1853	52	01846-675743	Rev Canon C.W.M Cooper	30p
Doctrine and Life	1951	10	01-8721611	Bernard Treacy	£1.85
Far East, The	1918	8	046-21525	Rev. Alo Connaughton	35p
Fold, The	1953	9	021-312330	Fr. Tom Hayes	£1.00
Furrow, The	1950	11	01-6286215	Fr. Ronan Drury	£1.60
Healing & Development	1940	1	01-2887180	Sr Isabelle Smyth	£2.00
Intercom	1970	10	021-364514	Fr. Bernard Cotter	£25.00*
Irish Catholic, The	1888	52	01-8555619	David Quinn	50p
Irish Theological Quarterly, The	1906	4	01-7083496	Fr. Vincent Twomey	£5.00
Milltown Studies	1978	2	01-2698838	Fr Pat Mullins	£5.00
Outlook	1940s	6	01-2881789	Fr. Brian Gogan	50p
Pioneer	1948	11	01-8749464	Maureen Manning	80p
Presbyterian Herald, The	1943	10	01232-322284	Rev. Arthur Clarke	80p
Religious Life Review	1964	6	01-8721611	Austin Flannery	£1.85
Sacred Heart Messenger, The	1988	6	01-6767491	Brendan Murray	55p
Salesian Bulletin, The	1939	4	01-6275060	Fr. Pat Egan	
Scripture in Church	1970	4	01-8721611	Bernard Treacy	£6.12
Search		2	01-4972821	Rev. S. R. White	£6.00*
Spirituality	1995	6	01-8721611	Tom Jordan	£2.25
Reality	1935	11	01-4922488	Fr. Gerard Moloney	80p
Wider World	1988	4	01232-322284	Alison McCaughan	Stg£2.00
Word, The	1953	12	0903-62608	Rev. Thomas Cahill	75p
SMA - The African Missionary	1914	5	021-292871	Fr. Peter McCawille	£3.00

● SCIENTIFIC

Title	Year Established	Issues per year	Telephone number	Editor	Price
Irish Scientist, The	1994	1	01-2896186	Dr. Charles Mollan	£6.00/£12.00

● SPORT - LEISURE

Title	Year Established	Issues per year	Telephone number	Editor	Price
Angling Holidays in Ireland	1986	1	01-4542727	Cathal Tyrell	
Gaelic Sport	1958	12	01-8550477	Mick Finn	£1.95
Gaelic World	1979	12	01-6798655	Owen McCann	£1.50
Golfer's Companion	1973	7	01-2804077	Gerry Ruddy	£2.00
Highball	1998	11	01-4784322	Eoghan Corry	£1.95
Irish Basketball Magazine	1985	3	01-2841067	Frank Quinn	£1.50
Irish Bridge Journal	1979	6	091-526502	Una Walsh	£9.00
Irish Cycling Review	1983	3	01-2841067	John Brennan	£1.50
Ireland's Equestrian	1994	6	01232-753177	Pat McCrory	Stg£2.50
Irish Golf Review	1997	4	01-6624887	Robert Heuston	£2.95
Irish Golf World	1995	8	01-6624887	Robert Heuston	Free
Irish Greyhound Review	1977	1	01-2841067	Michael Fortune	£7.00
Irish Racing Calendar	1790	52	045445600	Martin Murphy	£190.00*
Irish Racquets Review	1985	3	012841067	Frank Quinn	£1.50
Irish Rugby Review	1983	9	012841067	Karl Johnston	£1.50
Irish Runner	1981	6	014563599	Frank Greally	£1.95
Irish Soccer Magazine	1984	9	012841067	Alan Dalton	£1.50
Northern Ireland Soccer Yearbook	1972	1	01232663311	Malcom Brodie	Stg£2.50
Sportsworld	1960	6	01-8780449	Mark Herbert	£1.75
Sporting Press	1923	52	052-21422	Jerry Desmond	£1.20
Ulster Games Annual	1987	1	01232-663311	Sean McGettigan	£2.00
Ulster Gaelic	1999	12	01868-722477	Paul Quinn	£2.50
Walking World Ireland	1993	6	01-4923030	Martin Joyce	£2.35
Wings	1974	4	01-2804322	Colin MacLochlainn	FtM

● STUDENT/YOUTH

Title	Year Established	Issues per year	Telephone number	Editor	Price
Clár na nÓg	1995	12	01-4784122	Eamonn Waters	Free
Irish YouthWork Scene	1992	4	01-8729933	Fran Bissett	FtM
Student Voice, The	1995	9	01-6710088		Free to USI members

● TOURISM

Title	Year Established	Issues per year	Telephone number	Editor	Price
Be Our Guest		1	01-4976459	Irish Hotels Federation	£3.00
Cara Magazine	1968	4	01-6623158	Vincent de Veau	N/C
Dining in Dublin	1999	2	01-8305236	Sonia O'Donoghue	£3.99
Discover Ireland (series)		1	01-2960000	Rosemary Delaney	Free
Elan Magazine	1997	1	01-2833000	Jason Cooke	Free
Fáilte Welcome		1	01-2960000	Rosemary Delaney	Free
Inside Ireland	1978	4	01-4931906	Brenda Weir	£22.00 D.M.
Ireland of the Welcomes	1952	6	01-6024000	Letitia Pollard	£2.50
Hotels Magazine	1997	11	01-2806888	Tony Cantwell	£49.65*
Visitor		1	01-2960000	Rosemary Delaney	Free

● TRAINING

Title	Year Established	Issues per year	Telephone number	Editor	Price
Arena		6	01-6615588	Mary Rose O'Sullivan	£32.00*
IPD News	1987	6	01-6766655	Mike McDonnell	FtM

● TRAVEL

Title	Year Established	Issues per year	Telephone number	Editor	Price
Business Travel	1994	4	01-4502422	Michael Flood	£3.00
Export & Freight	1974	10	01762-334272	Helen Beggs	Stg£1.60
Fleet Management Magazine	1987	12	01-4976050	Phil O'Kelly	£1.50
Irish Travel Trade News	1972	11	01-4502422	Michael Flood	£3.00
Runway Airports	1970	6	01-7044170	Brian McCabe	Free to Staff

● VETERINARY / ANIMALS

Title	Year Established	Issues per year	Telephone number	Editor	Price
Irish Veterinary Journal	1949	12	01-2893305	Donal Nugent	Free*
Northern Ireland Pets (NIPs)	1994	6	01232-753177	Pat McCrory	Stg£2.00
Irish Field, The	1894	52	01-6792022	Valentine Lamb	£1.70

Title	Year Established	Issues per year	Telephone number	Editor	Price
● **WOMENS**					
Image	1976	12	01-2808415	Sarah McDonnell	£2.40
Irish Brides & Homes Magazine	1983	4	01-4905504	Mary McCarthy	£2.95
Irish Wedding & New Home	1995	4	01-4753300	Vanessa Harriss	£3.95
IT Magazine (Irish Tatler)	1898	12	01-6623158	Morag Prunty	£2.10
Modern Woman	1983	12	046-21442	Margot Davis	£0.50
Northern Ireland Baby Magazine	1993	3	01762-334272	Janice Uprichard	Stg£1.80
Northern Woman	1984	12	01232-783200	Carol-Anne Dornan	£1.95
Parenting Years	1997	4	01232-783200	Carol-Anne Dornan	£1.95
Social & Personal	1934	10	055-29403	Nell Stewart-Liberty	£2.50
U Magazine	1978	12	01-6623158	Lisa Gaughran	£2.00
Ulster Bride	1979	1	01232-663311	Christopher Sherry	£3.00
Ulster Countrywoman	1930s	10	01232-301506	Mildred Brown	75p
VIP	1999	12	01-6769832	Maura O'Kiely	£1.95
Woman's Way	1963	51	01-6623158	Celine Naughton	80p
Woman's Way Annual	1979	1	01-6623158	Celine Naughton	£2.50
Your New Baby	1996	2	01-6623158	Marianne Hartigan	£2.95

* Subscription   **C.C.** Controlled Circulation   **FtM** Free to Members   **N/C** No Charge   **D/M** Direct Mail

 ARTS

Arts at a Glance

Funding through the 1995–1998 Arts Plan ....increased from IR£13m to IR£26m
Public Spending on Arts Rep. of Ireland *(1997)* ....IR£21.98m
   As a % of GDP 0.09
Funding through the 1999–2001 Arts Plan ....IR£100m over 3 yrs (23% increase)
   Total Expenditure (1999) ....IR£28,000,000
   Total Expenditure (2000) ....IR£34,500,000
   Total Expenditure (2001) ....IR£37,500,000
Business Sponsorship of the Arts *(1997)* ....IR£10,217,000 (ten-fold increase over 10 years)
Proportion of applicants for funding to funds 2:1
Economic Significance of the Cultural Industries in the Republic of Ireland
No employed in the cultural industries in Ireland *(1997)*...33,800
   Value of the cultural industries *(1997)* ....IR£441m per year.
   Income earned by direct trading and by grants *(1997)* ....88% and 12%, respectively
   Employment by gender *(1997)* ....women - 54%; men - 46%
   Full-time jobs in the cultural sector..7 out of 10 jobs (mostly on a contract basis)
Public Spending on Arts, Northern Ireland *(1997)*...Stg £17.32m
   As a % of GDP 0.19
Spending on Arts, Northern Ireland *(1998/9)* ....Stg£26,753,216.50
   Spending per capita *(1998/9)* ....Stg££6.25
   Total Spending by local government authorities (1998/9) ....Stg£10,399,443.79
NI National Lottery Awards ....416 awards; total value Stg£26,753,216.50
Source The Arts Council - An Chomhairle Ealaíon; Arts Council of Northern Ireland

General

The Arts Council - An Chomhairle Ealaíon

Board the 11th Arts Council is made up of 17 unpaid members, appointed in 1998 for five years by the government.
Chairman Professor Brian Farrell.
Staff The board is supported by a staff of 32, headed by a director.

Aims To promote excellence and innovation in the arts, to develop participation in, and audiences for the arts, to enhance the arts sectors capacity (the council is the principal channel of government funding for the arts in Ireland). The functions and membership of the Arts Council are governed by the Arts Acts of 1951 and 1973.

Funding comes from the Exchequer and the National Lottery. Smaller amounts come from other bodies for specific schemes or projects and a number of trust funds. It grants funding through revenue grants, capital grants, project grants, awards and bursaries.

Distribution of funds Funds are allocated according to the following headings: Literature, Visual Arts, Architecture, Film & Video, Music, Local Authorities, Opera, Drama, Dance, Development & Partnerships, Multi-Disciplinary Arts, Arts Centres, Community Arts, Arts & Disability, Festivals. Overall, 15% of all schemes and awards are allocated to work centred on children & young people. The Arts Council distributes funds through recurring or revenue grants to organisations, capital grants, funding for schemes, and funding to individuals.
Agencies in receipt of funding The council currently provides funds to some 400 organisations. These agencies are involved in producing and promoting the arts, including theatres, arts centres, art galleries, festivals, opera and dance companies and arts-development and groups involved in arts-promotion.
Individuals in receipt of funding The council currently provides funds to some 450 individuals. These individual artists are entitled to awards, bursaries and travel grants. The Council also supports Aosdána (the affiliation of artists), and administers ARTFLIGHT, a travel scheme run in conjunction with Aer Lingus and the Arts Council of Northern Ireland, and Go See, a travel scheme jointly funded by the British Council in Ireland with support from Bord na Gaeilge. The council, In conjunction with local government authorities and Údarás na Gaeltachta, partly funds 31 arts officer posts throughout the country.

The 1999–2001 Arts Plan:

The Arts council's three aims will be implemented through 12 specific strategies, which are to be funded as follows:

Funding for Key Aims and Strategies	1999 (IR£)	2000 (IR£)	2001 (IR£)
To promote excellence and innovation in the arts	**8,879,716**	**10,846,000**	**11,415,000**
Aid professional formation, practice & career development of artists	3,544,325	4,300,000	4,521,000
Direct funding towards excellence and innovation in promoting the arts	3,507,755	4,356,000	4,544,000
Support artists working through Irish and indigenous arts to achieve their full potential and increase audiences	700,751	835,000	850,000
Foster recognition, acknowledgement, critical assessment & documentation of the arts	1,126,885	1,355,000	1,500,000
To develop participation in, and audiences for, the arts	**10,020,264**	**13,137,000**	**14,695,000**
Support more public participation in the arts	1,177,450	1,425,000	1,650,000
Increase children's and young people's engagement with the arts	2,483,449	2,750,000	3,220,000
Encourage arts organisations and promoters to develop audiences	5,196,790	7,457,000	7,750,000
Develop international audiences for Irish arts and bring international arts to Irish audiences	1,162,575	1,505,000	2,075,000
To enhance the arts sector's capacity	**6,220,230**	**7,342,000**	**7,900,000**
Improve dialogue with the government	167,500	80,000	65,000
Improve local structures for the arts	5,540,310	6,600,000	7,250,000
Help arts organisation to plan and manage better	443,420	570,000	500,000
Rationalise financial supports and improve the application process	69,000	92,000	85,000
Indirect Arts Expenditure through Implementation & Development	*679,790*	*725,000*	*810,000*
Administration	*2,200,000*	*2,450,000*	*2,680,000*
TOTAL EXPENDITURE	**28,000,000**	**34,500,000**	**37,500,000**

Income Sources	1999 (IR£)	2000 (IR£)	2001 (IR£)
Revenue	24,500,000	30,200,000	33,000,000
Capital	3,500,000	4,000,000	4,500,000
TOTAL INCOME	**28,000,000**	**34,500,000**	**37,500,000**

Source *The Arts Council - An Chomhairle Ealaíon*

Arts Council Revenue Funding

Artform/ application 1998	Total Expenditure IR£	Artform/ application 1998	Total Expenditure IR£
Literature	852,500	Arts Centres	1,597,000
Visual Arts	1,606,700	Community Arts	416,500
Architecture	18,500	Festivals	431,250
Film	757,000	Arts & Disability	103,000
Drama	7,690,800	Education Children & Youth	453,000
Opera	1,316,000	Local Authorities	703,000
Music	1,844,300	**TOTAL**	**18,483,050**
Dance	693,500	*Total Revenue Funds*	*23,500,000*

Source: *The Arts Council - An Chomhairle Ealaíon*

International Comparison of Spending on the Arts

Country / Region - Public Spending on Arts (1997)	per capita spending (IR£)	as % of GDP
Australia	25.89	0.19
England	24.23	0.19
Finland	38.51	0.30
Ireland, Northern	17.32	0.19
IRELAND, Rep. of	**21.98***	0.09
Quebec	36.13	0.27
Scotland	27.84	0.21
Sweden	62.14	0.35
US	3.73	0.02

Source *The Arts Council - An Chomhairle Ealaíon*
*incl. Lottery funding. Minus this funding, the total comes to IR£12.36

The Arts Council of Northern Ireland

Status the Arts Council of Northern Ireland is a government agency, which comes under the aegis of the Department of Education for Northern Ireland.
Aims To develop and improve the knowledge, appreciation and practice of the arts; to increase public access to the arts; to encourage and help in the provision of arts facilities, events, services and training; and to distribute funds made available through the National Lottery.
Funding comes from the Department of Education for Northern Ireland and the National Lottery for the Arts.
Distribution of funds The Council distributes funds through revenue grants, project grants, awards and bursaries.

NI Local Government Expenditure on the Arts

Government area	Arts Stg£	Museums Stg£	Cultural Stg£	Total Stg£	per capita
Antrim	288,813.00	-	59,266.00	348,079.00	7.33
Ards	167,825.00	-	-	167,825.00	2.48
Armagh	417,362.00	-	-	417,362.00	7.85
Ballymena	144,823.00	56,914.00	-	201,737.00	3.47
Ballymoney	64,348.00	22,527.00	-	86,875.00	3.49
Banbridge	24,702.00	4,165.00	4,000.00	32,867.00	0.87
Belfast	3,065,500.00		50,800.00	3,116,300.00	10.49
Carrickfergus	61,743.11	36,901.41	-	98,644.52	2.76
Castlereagh	38,766.50	-	-	38,766.50	0.60
Coleraine	206,111.00	41,342.00	-	247,453.00	4.2
Cookstown	31,572.00	-	-	31,572.00	0.99
Craigavon	310,609.00	79,210.00	350.00	390,169.00	4.93
Derry	876,400.00	622,100.00	20,000.00	1,518,500.00	14.50
Down	240,269.00	353,697.00	-	593,966.00	9.71
Dungannon	62,385.00	2,650.00	775.00	65,810.00	1.40
Fermanagh	181,870.94	166,216.68		348,087.62	6.27
Larne	5,000.00	10,134.00		15,134.00	0.50
Limavady	59,277.95	11,461.58		70,739.53	2.30
Lisburn	259,635.00	755,253.00		1,014,888.00	9.52
Magherafelt	42,000.00		10,000.00	52,000.00	1.37
Moyle	19,037.00	13,425.00		32,462.00	2.16
Newry & Mourne	588,582.00	47,989.00		636,571.00	7.50
Newtownabbey	204,355.00	36,870.00	19,644.00	260,869.00	3.28
North Down	135,455.63	232,136.16	15,050.00	382,641.79	5.21
Omagh	102,160.00	3,604.00	13,224.00	118,988.00	2.53
Strabane	46,965.00	56,671.83	7,500.00	111,136.83	3.02
TOTAL	**7,645,567.13**	**2,553,267.66**	**200,609.00**	**10,399,443.79**	**6.25**

Source Arts Council of Northern Ireland

NI National Lottery Awards by Artform

Artform	Value Stg£	No Awards	% of Total
Drama	9,046,491.50	56	33.8
Combined Arts	7,181,917.00	48	26.9
Music	3,218,956.00	155	12.0
Film	2,445,554.00	45	9.1
Community Arts	1,522,793.00	29	5.7
Visual Arts	1,394,716.00	52	5.2
Literature	1,307,561.00	9	4.9
Dance	401,521.00	12	1.5
Opera	216,915.00	7	0.8
Craft	16,792.00	3	0.1
TOTAL	**26,753,216.50**	**416**	**100.0**

Source Arts Council of Northern Ireland
Expenditure does not include spending on the National Museums and Galleries of Northern Ireland, which are funded through the Dept. of Education Northern Ireland

● **RELEVANT BODIES**
The Arts Council - An Chomhairle Ealaíon 70 Merrion Sq, Dublin 2. *Tel* 01-618 0200 *email* info@artscouncil.ie
The Arts Council of Northern Ireland MacNeice Hse, 77 Malone Rd, Belfast BT9 6AQ. *Tel* 01232-385 200.

Architecture

Architecture physically defines the public and private space. The form is promoted both from within the field itself, primarily through the Royal Institute of the Architects of Ireland, and by the Arts Council through publications, exhibitions, award schemes.

● **ARTS COUNCIL AWARDS** Awards available to architects include travel awards, the Apprentice/Assistant Scheme for Visual Artists and Architects, Visual Arts awards and Architecture postgraduate scholarships.
● **SCHOOLS OF ARCHITECTURE** There are three schools of architecture in Ireland, two in the Republic - University College Dublin, Dublin Institute of Technology - and one at Queen's University in Belfast.
● **SOME RELEVANT BODIES**
Royal Institute of the Architects of Ireland (RIAI), 8 Merrion Sq, Dublin 2. *Tel* 01-661 1703. *Web* www.riai.ie
Established 1839 *Membership* 1,700 *Profile* the RIAI is the representative body for professionally qualified architects in Ireland and its qualifications for membership are accepted by the government, the courts and the EU as the required standard. It is affiliated to the Architects Council of Europe and the International Union of Architects. The RIAI aims to advance Architecture and the associated Arts and Sciences, promote high standards of professional conduct and practice and protect the interests of architectural training and education.
The Irish Architectural Archive 73 Merrion Sq, Dublin 2 *Tel* 01-676 3430. *Web* www.archeire.com/iaa *Established* 1976 *Profile* The archive collects the records of Ireland's architectural heritage and makes them available for viewing. The collections housed by archive are the largest body of historic architectural records in Ireland. They include more than 80,000 drawings from the late 17th - 20th centuries. The archive also contains over 300,000 photographs and an extensive reference library, with more than 11,000 items. The holdings contain material - primary and/or secondary - on every famous Irish architect (including, James Gandon, Francis Johnston, Richard Castle, Richard and William Vitruvius Morrison), on every important building period or style, and on most significant buildings in Ireland, north and south.

Arts Council Expenditure

● Rol Arts Council Expenditure	1997 (IR£)
Grants - RIAI	20,000
Grants - Architectural Assoc. of Ireland	5,000
Other Activities	10205
TOTAL	**35,205**

● Rol Arts Council Revenue Decisions1998 (IR£)	
Architectural Association of Ireland	9,500
Gandon Editions	9,000
TOTAL	**18,500**

Source The Arts Council - An Chomhairle Ealaíon

RIAI Regional Awards 1999

The RIAI presents awards to what it deems to be the best of Irish Architecture throughout Ireland in 1999. The exhibition travels to over 20 venues around Ireland and to London.

Project	Winning Architects	Client
Dublin Under £100,000		
Refurbishment of Gresham Hotel Entrance	Arthur Gibney & Partners	Ryan Hotels Ltd.
Extension to Clyde Lane Building	Grafton Architects	Michael Kane
Dublin Over IR£100,000		
25 Eustace St	Arthur Gibney & Partners	Temple Bar Prop. & Irish Landmark Trust
Sacred Heart Oratory, Dun Laoghaire	OPW Architectural Services	Dept Arts, Heritage, Gaeltacht & Islands
Mews Development, Little Strand St	Grafton Architects	Private
Screening Room for Clarence Pictures	Grafton Architects	Clarence Pictures
Restoration/conversion of Kodak Building	Paul Keogh Architects	Quirke Lynch / Cawley Nea
Dublin Over IR£1,000,000		
Housing at Ballybrack	National Building Agency Ltd - Peter Cully	Dun Lao./Rathdown Co. Council
Dublin Dental Hospital	Paul Koralek-Ahrends Burton & Koralek	Dental H.Board & Trinity College
Civic Theatre, Tallaght	Brian Brennan, South Dublin Co. Council	South Dublin Co. Council
Ranelagh Multi-denominational School	O'Donnell & Tuomey	Ranelagh Multi-denominational School
Refurbishment of Heuston Station	Brian O'Halloran & Associates & CIE Architects Dept	Iarnrod Eireann
East Point,Fairview	Scott Tallon Walker Architects	Earlsfort East Point Ltd.
Northern Region Over IR£1,000,000		
Restoration of Stormont Buildings, Belfast	Consarc Design Group Ltd.	Office Accomm.Branch & Construction Service of theEnvironment NI

Southern Region Over IR£100,000
House at Ballycommane, Co.Cork.............Tom Hegarty, O'Riordan Staehli Architects ......John & Sally McKenna
BIM Regional Fisheries Centre, Co. Cork ..Michael Shanahan & Associates........................Bord Iascaigh Mhara
Southern Region Over IR£1, 000,000
Gate Multiplex Cork ....Derek Tynan Architects................Gate Multiplex & CPP International
Eastern Region Over IR£100,000
Hudson House Navan ....O'Donnell & Tuomey ....Richard and Tricia Hudson
Western Region Under IR£100,000
Private House, Killeenaran,Co. Galway......Richard Murphy Architects ....Mr & Mrs Rod Stoneman
Farmhouse Extension, Co. Limerick ....Gerry Lombard Architects ....Private
Western Region Over IR£1, 000,000
Tellabs Ltd. : New Facility ....Michael Healy & Associates ....Tellabs Ltd.
Source RIAI

Dance

● **STATUS OF DANCE IN IRELAND** Although Irish traditional dance is thriving, other forms of dance do not fare as well. There are no dancers professionally employed full-time as creative or performing artists in Ireland; most supplement their income through teaching or through other areas in the creative arts. In addition, there are a very limited number of dance venues around the country. Furthermore, most dance students must travel abroad to further their studies due to the lack of facilities here and many do not return. The artform is, with a few exceptions, Dublin-centred. However, youth interest in dance of all types is very high, and dance in Ireland is a growing artform.
● **THE 1995–1998 ARTS PLAN** initiated a dance touring scheme and provided support for the existing theatre dance companies. It created three new bursaries and instituted a new centre dedicated to dance in Cork.
● **1999–2001 ARTS PLAN** will continue to build on this work. It aims to promote the recognition of choreographers as creative artists, to fund projects in dance development, to fund dance production companies, to introduce a scheme to fund experimental dance, to fund dancers-in-residence schemes, to introduce support for youth dance and dance-in-education initiatives, to fund dance production companies and dance resources, to fund international travel, to promote the special needs of dance training and education, to bring about the creation of an International Dance Festival to be held annually and funded separately from the current funding to dance.
● **ARTS COUNCIL EXPENDITURE ON DANCE** The sector's reliance on Arts Council funding remains higher (accounting for over 70% of turnover) than most other artforms. It also receives a very small proportion of business sponsorship - in the last survey carried out into business sponsorship of the arts, dance received £78,000 - 0.78% - out of the £10m awarded in arts sponsorship.

Arts Council Expenditure

● *RoI Arts Council Revenue Decisions* 1998 (IR£)	
General Grants	455,000
Capital	5,000
Touring	67,000
Education	151,500
Dance Projects	15,000
TOTAL	693,500*

Source The Arts Council - An Chomhairle Ealaíon
Total does not include bursaries to individuals
and other grants awarded

● *NI Awards 1998*	No. of Awards	Stg£
Building	1	20,680
Equipment	4	26,625
Work New to Northern Ireland	2	288,777
New Work	2	43,625
Access	3	21,814
TOTAL	12	401,521

Source Arts Council of Northern Ireland

● **SOME RELEVANT BODIES**
Association for Professional Dancers in Ireland De Valois Centre for Dance and the Performing Arts, 5 Meetinghouse Lane, Dublin 7. *Tel* 01-873 0288 *email* prodance@iol.ie. *Established* 1990 *Profile* It aims to promote support of dancers and choreographers in Ireland by setting up classes, workshops and other activities. It provides information and services for the professional development of dancers and choreographers and for the development of dance and dance theatre in Ireland. It also acts as a lobbying group for professional dancers and publishes the newsletter *Prodance News.*
Ballet Ireland est 1997 0405-57585 086-826 1196
Coiscéim Dance Theatre, Dublin *Tel* 01-670 4134 www.iol.ie/~coisceim
Coimisiun le Rinci Gaelacha, An *See Culture*
Daghda Dance Company, University of Limerick, Plassey, Limerick. *Tel* 061-202700
Dance Collective 34 Station Rd, Syndenham, Belfast BT4 1RF. *Tel* 01232-653 541 *Profile* Promotes and assists all forms of dance in Northern Ireland
Dance Studio 72 Beatrice Rd, Bangor. Tel 01247-457 163 *Profile* The Dance Studio runs the only three-year

vocational training programme for professional dancers in Northern Ireland. The emphasis of the programme is on classical ballet and the age intake is 16. The studio also helps in work towards the ISTD and RAD exams and is the only approved school in Northern Ireland to run the RAD teaching Certificate

Dance Theatre of Ireland, 13 Clarinda Park North Dun Laoghaire, Co Dublin *Tel* 01-280 3455

Firkin Crane, Shandon, Cork. *Tel* 021-507487 *email* firkin@iol.ie *Profile* Ireland's only dedicated dance venue. It houses a 240-seat theatre, rehearsal studios, workshop facilities, with technical resources and qualified, personnel. It is a producing venue for new works, a presenting venue for national and international dance companies and a choreographic research centre. It provides studio facilities for Irish-based dance artistes and an informaton and advice service on dance touring programmes and funding sources.

Inchicore Dance Studies Course Inchicore College of Further Education, Emmet Road, Dublin 8. *Tel* 01-453 5358. *Profile* The course is funded by the VEC and students sit Royal Academy of Dancing exams and can sit a Student Teaching Cert.

Irish Modern Dance Theatre, 37 North Great George's Street, Dublin 1. *Tel* 874 9616. email: imdt@iol.ie *Established* 1991 *Profile* Irish modern dance theatre is an experimental dance theatre company which was founded by choreographer John Scott. The company is noted for incorporating dance in theatre, music, literature and the visual arts. The company infuses strong dramatic works with a mix of dance and seeks to bring experimental dance to Irish audiences as well as maintaining the presence of dance-in-education by giving year-round workshops to schools throughout the country. The company has also pioneered a policy of employing Irish dancers in its work as a priority.

Irish National Youth Ballet *Tel* 01-475 5451

Northern Ireland School of Dance Teachers 40 Glenside Park, Belfast BT14 8BG. *Tel* 01232-719 421

Sallynoggin Senior College Pearse Rd, Dun Laoghaire, Co Dublin. 01-285 2997 EU-funded. Awards: Dept of Education Foundation course for full-time training.

Shawbrook Ballet Theatre Legan, Co Longford. *Tel* 044-57570. Shawbrook School of Ballet is a classical ballet school that runs through the year doing Royal Academy of Dancing exams and regular theatre shows. It runs an intensive summer school.

Drama

● **STATUS OF DRAMA IN IRELAND** Drama is a very well established and popular artform in Ireland. With regard to policy, it has possibly the most developed sectoral consolidation of all the artforms. However, the review of *Theatre in Ireland 1995–1996: Going On* highlighted the need for three-year funding arrangements, with arrangements for rolling over funding so as to ensure that theatres and theatre companies do not encounter periods where they have virtually no funding and cannot continue working. There is a need for funding for touring internationally, as it had been proven than Irish theatre has proved a most marketable product on the international scene. This is exemplified in the spectacular success of the Druid Theatre with the *Beauty Queen of Leenane* in New York, which is one of many Irish cultural success stories internationally. There are also concerns with regard to the taxation of cultural workers which the theatre sector feels need to be addressed. The sector would also like to see the development of theatre for young people and would welcome the co-creation of projects with relevant government bodies. The Drama League of Ireland has already strong relationships with youth theatre. The report also drew attention to the need for a 300-450 seat space in Dublin.

● **PRACTITIONERS** The council currently funds some 23 professional groups who produce around 120 works each year around the country. There are also many youth and amateur movements in the country who contribute the vibrant drama sector.

● **THE 1995–1998 ARTS PLAN** conducted an extensive review of theatre in 1995 and implemented a new policy at the start of its term. This brought about the de-regulation of the theatre touring scheme, which helped with co-production; contract funding extending for more than a year was introduced for certain companies. The effects of this policy were an increase in production and touring, with the result that Irish theatre began to be recognised critically abroad.

● **1999–2001 ARTS PLAN** will continue to build on this work and encourage more experimentation in theatre and the expansion of audiences, particularly young audiences in Ireland.

Arts Council Expenditure

● Rol Arts Council Revenue Decisions	1998 (IR£)
General	5,175,000
Regional Theatres	400,000
Project Grants	215,000
Festivals	335,000
Touring/Venues	412,500
Touring/Companies	310,300
Education	675,000

Continued from previous page

● RoI Arts Council Revenue Decisions	1998 (IR£)
Capital	150,000
Miscellaneous	18,000
TOTAL	7,690,800

Source The Arts Council - An Chomhairle Ealaíon
Total does not include bursaries to individuals and other grants awarded

● NI Awards 1998	No. of Awards	Stg£
Building	7	7,494,421.00
Equipment	13	276,324.00
Feasibility Study	3	40,275.00
New Work	21	355,423.00
Work New to Northern Ireland	3	64,937.00
Access	5	190,324.00
Discretionary Grants	2	5,702.50
Advancement	2	619,085.00
TOTAL	56	9,046,491.50

Source Arts Council of Northern Ireland

● For an up-to-date list of the main theatres and theatre companies in Ireland, see Directory of Arts Venues.

Film

● **STATUS OF FILM IN IRELAND** The value of the Irish film industry reached £123m in 1997, a massive 25% increase on the previous year. The sector employed 1,450 directly and a similar number indirectly. The productions made during this year included Hollywood films like *Saving Private Ryan,* and it was also a very healthy year for the indigenous film industry with the filming of *Dancing at Lughnasa* and *The General,* as well as independent productions for TV, the value of production of which amounted to £18m, again a major increase on previous years. However, animation films have virtually disappeared from the Irish film landscape (its output in 1997 was worth £100,000 in comparison to 1994 when it was worth almost £12m), and the sector is in urgent need of intervention measures. The Arts Council report, *Film in Ireland - The Role of the Arts Council,* pointed out the blurring of the distinction between film as art and film as part of the broad entertainment spectrum and the need for a proper definition to better inform funding and agencies that support the film sector in Ireland. While there was general agreement in the report that the level of film funding was low and did not account for the high costs of filming, there was widely differing views as to what kind of films should be supported by the Arts Council; should it only, for example, fund films that are experimental or fund all Irish-made films regardless of their nature? The Arts Council did take on board that there was an urgent need to ensure proper arrangements for the study of film within the state school curriculum and the need to introduce mechanisms for introducing Irish film to wider audiences in Ireland.

RoI Funding by Type of Production

	Feature Films & Major TV Dramas IR£m	Independent TV Productions IR£m	Animation IR£m	Total IR£m
Irish Funding	59.9	16.2	0.07	76.2
of which				
Section 481	52.4	1.5	0	53.9
Irish Film Board	2.3	0.3	0.02	2.6
RTE	0.7	4.8	0	5.6
TnaG	0	7.4	0	7.4
Other	4.5	2.6	0.05	6.6
Non-Irish Funding	45.3	1.8	0.07	47.2
TOTAL	105.3	18.0	0.1	123.4

Source IBEC - Audiovisual Federation - The Economic Impact of Film Production in Ireland 1997

RoI Expenditure by Type of Production

Type of Production	Total Expenditure IR£m	Of which: Irish Expenditure
Feature Films and Major TV Dramas	105.3	73.3 (70%)
Independent TV Productions[1]	18.0	15.1 (84%)
of which		
RTE	7.2	5.9 (82%)
TnaG	7.7	7.3 (95%)
Other TV Productions	3.1	1.9 (59%)
Animation	0.1	0.1 (97%)
Total	123.4	88.5 (72%)

1 *These independent TV productions are classified by the organisation which was primarily involved with the various productions.*

Source IBEC - Audiovisual Federation - The Economic Impact of Film Production in Ireland 1997

RoI Employment by Type of Production

Type of Production	Total Employment	Of which: Irish Employment	Non-Irish Employment
Feature Films and Major TV Dramas	16,667	15,429 (93%)	1,238 (7%)
Independent TV Productions:	2,593	2,452 (95%)	141 (5%)
of which			
RTE	1,092	1,066 (98%)	26 (2%)
Teilifís na Gaeilge	1,043	1,029 (99%)	14 (1%)
Other TV Productions	458	357 (78%)	101 (22%)
Animation	19	18 (95%)	1 (5%)
Total	19,279	17,899 (93%)	1,380 (7%)

Source IBEC - Audiovisual Federation - The Economic Impact of Film Production in Ireland 1997

RoI Direct Returns to the Exchequer

	Feature Films & Major TV Drama IR£m	Independent TV Productions IR£m	All Productions IR£m
RoI: Direct Returns to the Exchequer - Net Vat	0.7	0.08	0.8
Direct Returns to the Exchequer - PAYE	2.6	0.9	3.6
Direct Returns to the Exchequer - PRSI	1.8	0.4	2.2
Direct Returns to the Exchequer - Corp Tax	0.006	0.04	0.05
Direct Returns to the Exchequer - Schedule D	5.8	0.9	6.6
Direct Returns to the Exchequer - Total Tax	10.9	2.3	13.25

Source IBEC - Audiovisual Federation - The Economic Impact of Film Production in Ireland 1997

RoI Film Production Details Summary

Production Details	1993	1994	1995	1996	1997
Total Funding IR£m	50 5	133.1	100.1	97.3	123.4
Irish Funding IR£m	13.7 (27%)	50.8 (38%)	55.0 (55%)	62.4 (64%)	76.2 (62%)
Non-Irish Funding IR£m	36.7 (73%)	82.3 (62%)	45.1 (45%)	34.9 (36%)	47.2 (38%)
Total Expenditure IR£m	50 5	133.1	100.1	97.3	123.4
Irish Expenditure IR£m	30.5 (61%)	57.0 (43%)	64.1 (64%)	61.8 (64%)	88.5 (72%)
Non-Irish Expenditure IR£m	19.9 (39%)	76.1 (57%)	36.0 (36%)	35.5 (36%)	34.9 (28%)
Total Numbers Employed	4,191	13,858	17,890	11,938	19,279
Total Irish Employment	3,772 (90%)	10,845 (78%)	16,031 (90%)	11,251 (94%)	17,899 (93%)
Total Non-Irish Employment	419 (10%)	3,013 (22%)	1,859 (10%)	687 (6%)	1,380 (7%)
Total Irish Work Hours	845,498	2,276,146	2,232,255	2,093,522	2,556,708
Equivalent Full-time jobs	480	1,291	1,266	1,187	1,450
Total Irish Labour Costs IR£m	13.5	23.3	28.5	26.7	44.2
Irish Labour Costs[1] IR£m	6.0 (45%)	10.2 (44%)	10.6 (37%)	10.0 (38%)	14.7 (33%)
Irish Labour Costs[2] IR£m	7.4 (55%)	13.1 (56%)	17.9 (63%)	16.6 (62%)	29.5 (67%)
Tax Foregone to the Exchequer through Section 35 IR£m	5.4	19.6	18.8	15.1	20.7

Continued from previous page

Production Details	1993	1994	1995	1996	1997
Return to the Exchequer IR£m	7.7	21.0	22.8	21.5	31.2

1 Subject to PAYE   2 Other (Schedule D) IR£m

Source IBEC - Audiovisual Federation - The Economic Impact of Film Production in Ireland 1997

RoI Film Funding Details by type of Production

Source of Funding	Feature Films & Major TV Drama	Independent TV Productions	All Productions
Irish			
Bord Scannán na hÉireann/Irish Film Board	2.3 (2%)	0.3 (1%)	2.6 (2%)
- Radio Telefís Éireann	0.7 (1%)	4.8 (27%)	5.6 (5%)
- Teilifís na Gaeilge	0.0 (-)	7.4 (41%)	7.4 (6%)
- Section 481 (previously 35) Total raised	52.4 (50%)	1.5 (9%)	53.9 (44%)
- An Chomhairle Ealaíon / The Arts Council	0.1 (-)	0.01 (-)	0.1 (-)
- Deferments	0.1 (-)	0.4 (2%)	0.6 (1%)
- Other (including Private Equity, Sponsorship etc.)	4.3 (4%)	1.8 (10%)	6.2 (5%)
Sub Total Irish	**59.9 (57%)**	**16.2 (90%)**	**76.2 (62%)**
Non Irish			
- Broadcasters	3.5 (3%)	0.6 (3%)	4.1 (3%)
- Eurimages	0.0 (-)	0.1 (-)	0.1 (-)
- MEDIA Programme	0.4 (-)	0.0 (-)	0.4 (-)
- Other UK Sources	7.4 (7%)	0.2 (1%)	7.5 (6%)
- Other EU Sources	0.5 (1%)	0.3 (2%)	0.9 (1%)
- US	19.9 (19%)	0.6 (3%)	20.5 (17%)
- Other	13.6 (13%)	0.1 (-)	13.7 (11%)
Sub Total Non-Irish	**45.3 (43%)**	**1.8 (10%)**	**47.2 (38%)**
Total	**105.3 (100%)**	**18.0 (100%)**	**123.4 (100%)**

Source IBEC - Audiovisual Federation - The Economic Impact of Film Production in Ireland 1997

Arts Council Expenditure

● RoI Arts Council Revenue Decisions	1998 (IR£)
Resource & Support Orgs	414,000
Festivals and Exhibitions	180,000
Education	163,000
TOTAL	**757,000**

● NI Awards 1998	No. of Awards	Stg£
Equipment	4	199,890
Production	28	1,991,146
Building	1	35,050
Development	10	128,425
Access	1	75,000
Feasibility Study	1	16,043
TOTAL	**45**	**2,445,554**

Source The Arts Council - An Chomhairle Ealaíon; Arts Council of Northern Ireland
Total does not include bursaries to individuals and other grants awarded

● **SOME RELEVANT BODIES**

Audiovisual Federation of the Irish Business and Employers Confederation (IBEC) Confederation Hse, 84-86 Lower Baggot St, Dublin 2. *Tel* 01-660 1011 *email* audiovisual.fed@ibec.ie *Established* 1992 *Profile* The federation promotes the development of Ireland audiovisual production and distribution industry. Its membership consists of broadcasters (such as RTÉ, TG4, TV3 and UTV), independent film-makers, animators among many others. The federation lobbies the government on the industry view of the development of the sector. Along with Bord Scannán na hÉireann, it seeks to highlight the benefits of the audiovisual sector to the economy.

Bord Scannán na hÉireann - Irish Film Board Rockfort Hse, St Augustine St, Galway. *Tel* 091-561 398*email* film@iol.ie *Web* www.iol.ie/filmboard *Profile* This is a government agency set up to support film production and the dissemination of Irish films at home and abroad. It does this through the provision of loans and equity investment to independent Irish film-makers. The Board also acts in co-operation with other semi-state agencies to improve the marketing, sales and distribution of Irish films and to promote training and development in all areas of film-making. Employment of Irish film workers and the use of Irish services is a vital factor in the Board's consideration of applications. It also publicises the benefits of film making activity in Ireland. It had an annual budget of £1m in 1993, its first year, and currently has a budget of £4m.

Film Base 6 Eustace St, Dublin 2. *Tel* 01-679 6716 *email* filmbase@iol.ie *Profile* The centre is a resource centre for indigenous film and video making in Ireland. It also publishes *Film Ireland*.

Film Institute of Ireland Irish Film Centre, 6 Eustace St, Temple Bar, Dublin 2. *Tel* 01-679 5744 *email* fii@ifc.ie *Web* www.iftn.ie/ifc *Profile* The film institute is charged with promoting film culture in Ireland. It does this through the Irish Film Centre which it owns and manages. The institute administers the Irish Film Archive, the education department and the IFC cinema.

Northern Ireland Film Commission 21 Ormeau Ave, Belfast BT2 8HD. *Tel* 01232-232 444 *email* info@nifc.co.uk *Profile* The commission is the government agency responsible for the development of the film industry and film culture in Northern Ireland. Funded primarily through the Department of Education and the Department of Economic Development, it provides development funds for film projects and television series. It also publishes *Cini* - a quarterly newsletter.

Literature

RoI Book Publishing Turnover and Sales

Category of Publication	1997 IR£m	%	1994 IR£m	%
Educational:				
Primary	7.5	29.4	7.0	30.6
Secondary	16.7	65.5	14.6	63.8
Third Level	1.3	5.1	1.3	5.6
Total: Education	25.5	100.0	22.9	100.0
Non-Education:				
Non-fiction	11.0	79.7	8.2	79.6
Fiction	1.8	13.0	1.2	11.7
Children's	1.0	7.3	0.9	8.7
Total: Non-Educational	13.8	100.0	10.3	100.0
TOTAL	39.3	-	33.2	-
Sales:				
Domestic Sales	34.8	88.5	30.4	91.6
Export Sales (within the EU)	3.3	8.4	1.9	5.7
Export Sales (outside the EU)	1.2	3.1	0.9	2.7
Total: Sales	39.3	100.0	33.2	100.0

Source Clé

RoI Book Publishing Statistics

Category	1997	1994
Employment in Publishing (Full-time)	396	424
Number of Titles Published (New Titles)	841	790
Number of Titles in Print	7,375	6,540

Source Clé

RoI Estimated Retail Value of Published Books

Category of Books	1991 Educ.	Gen.	Total	1994 Educ.	Gen.	Total	1997 Educ.	Gen.	Total
Irish Published Books									
At Invoice Value *(IR£m)*	19.1	6.1	25.2	22.5	7.9	30.4	24.3	10.5	34.8
Margin Used (%)	18.1	37 5	23.9	19.0	42.0	26.6	19.0	43.0	28.1
At Retail Value *(IR£m)*	23.3	9.8	33.1	27.8	13.6	41.4	30.0	18.4	48.4
Imported Books									
Share of Total Market (%)	12.0	82.0	59.0	10.0	81.0	60.0	10.0	79.0	60.0
At Retail Value *(IR£m)*	3.2	44.6	47.8	3.1	58.0	61.1	3.3	69.3	72.6
TOTAL RETAIL MARKET *(IR£m)*	26.5	54.4	80.9	30.9	71.6	102.5	33.3	87.7	121.0

Source Clé

RoI Comparison of Book Publishing Sales

Total Sales by Market	1985 (IR£m)	1991 (IR£m)	1993 (IR£m)	1994 (IR£m)	1997 (IR£m)
General		4.5	8.1	8.9	10.3	13.8
Educational					
Primary		5.4	7.6	6.8	7.0	7.5
Secondary and Third Level		6.4	12.0	12.9	15.9	18.0

Continued from previous page

Total Sales by Market	1985 (IR£m)	1991 (IR£m)	1993 (IR£m)	1994 (IR£m)	1997 (IR£m)
Total Educational	11.8	19.6	19.7	22.9	25.5
Domestic and Export Markets					
Domestic	-	25.2	25.8	30.4	34.8
EU	-	1.5	1.9	1.9	3.3
Outside EU	-	1.0	0.9	0.9	1.2
TOTAL MARKET	16.3	27.7	28.6	33.2	39.3

Source Clé

Arts Council Revenue Decisions

RoI Arts Council Funding Decisions	1998 (IR£)
The Writer	32,200
Writers-in-Residence	35,000
Organisations	243,000
Literary Festivals	43,500
Publishers	388,600
Journals	57,700
Education	52,500
TOTAL	**852,500**

NI Awards Funding	No Awards	Stg£
Building	1,174,171	2
Equipment	10,227	2
New Work	15,900	1
Access	107,263	4
TOTAL	**1,307,561**	**9**

Source The Arts Council - An Chomhairle Ealaíon; Arts Council of Northern Ireland
Total does not include bursaries to individuals and other grants awarded

RoI Eason's Best Selling Books

● September 1998 to September 1999

Rank	Title	Author	Description
1	Angela's Ashes	Frank McCourt	Irish/Fiction
2	Collins Gem Irish Dictionary	(Collins Gem)	Reference/Dictionaries
3	Little Book of Calm	Paul Wilson	Reference/Health
4	Dublin City & District Street Guide	(Ordnance Survey)	Travel/Irish Maps
5	Rachel's Holiday	Marian Keyes	Irish/Fiction
6	To Kill A Mocking Bird	Harper Lee	School/School Text
7	Real Irish Cookery	Mary Caherty	Leisure/Cookery
8	Anam Cara	John O'Donohue	Reference/Philosophy
9	Lucy Sullivan Is Getting Married	Marian Keyes	Irish/Fiction
10	Philadelphia, Here I Come	Brian Friel	School/School Text
11	Mirror Mirror	Patricia Scanlon	Irish/Fiction
12	Bungalow Bliss	(Kells Publishing)	Leisure/DIY
13	Collins Gem French Dictionary	(Collins Gem)	Reference/Dictionaries
14	Are You Somebody	Nuala Ó Faolain	Irish/Non-Fiction
15	Woman To Woman	Cathy Kelly	Irish/Fiction
16	Water Melon	Marian Keyes	Irish/Fiction
17	Roll Of Thunder - Hear My Cry	Mildred D. Taylor	Schools/School Text
18	Isobel's Wedding	Sheila O'Flanagan	Irish/Fiction
19	Gangland	Paul Williams	Irish/Non-Fiction
20	General - Godfather of Crime	Paul Williams	Irish/Non-Fiction
21	Collins Gem English Dictionary	(Collins)	Reference/Dictionaries
22	Caroline's Sister	Sheila O'Flanagan	Irish/Fiction
23	Dublin Street Map	(Ordnance Survey)	Travel/Irish Maps
24	Road Atlas of Ireland	(Ordnance Survey)	Travel/Irish Maps
25	Promises Promises	Patricia Scanlan	Irish/Fiction
26	Sophia's Story	Susan McKay	Irish/Fiction
27	Book Of Kells (Miniature)	(Roberts Books)	Irish/Irish Art
28	Woman Of The House	Alice Taylor	Irish/Fiction
29	Focloir Poca	(An Gum)	Reference/Dictionaries
30	Tara Road	Maeve Binchy	Irish/Fiction
31	Shooting From The Hip - The Pat Spillane Story	Pat Spillane	Sport/Gaelic Football
32	She's The One	Cathy Kelly	Irish/Fiction

Continued from previous page

Rank	Title	Author	Description
33	Plan A Home - Concepts For Irish Homes	(Plan A Home)	Leisure/DIY
34	Goodnight Mister Tom	Michelle Magorian	School/School Text
35	Irish Cooking	Koenmann	Leisure/Cookery
36	Tara Road	Maeve Binchy	Irish/Fiction
37	Animal Farm	George Orwell	School/School Text
38	Pearl	John Steinbeck	School/School Text
39	Emma - Popular Classics	Jane Austen	School/School Text
40	Evening Class	Maeve Binchy	Irish/Fiction
41	Angela's Ashes (Gift Edition)	Frank McCourt	Irish/Fiction
42	The Day Michael Collins Was Shot	(Ryan Media)	Irish/Non-Fiction
43	Dublin City Centre Atlas	(Ordnance Survey)	Travel/Irish Maps
44	Anything But Balls	Willo Ward	Sport/Football
45	Snakes & Ladders	Fergus Finlay	Irish/Political
46	Lord Of The Flies	William Golding	School/School Text
47	Thanks A Million Big Fella	Sam Smyth	Irish/Non-Fiction
48	Glass Lake	Maeve Binchy	Irish/Fiction
49	Feel The Fear And Do It Anyway	Susan Jeffers	Reference/Psychology
50	Love Like Hate Adore	Deirdre Purcell	Irish/Fiction
51	Catcher In The Rye	J.D. Salinger	School/School Text
52	Dreaming Of A Stranger	Sheila O'Flanagan	Irish/Fiction
53	Partner	John Grisham	Fiction/Crime
54	Under The Hawthorn Tree	Marita McKenna	Childrens/Irish Interest
55	Pinch Of This	Frank Moynihan	Leisure/Cookery
56	Little Book Of Calm	Paul Wilson	Reference/Health
57	Student Yearbook & Career - Part 2	Joe Duddy	School/School Text
58	Mammy - Mrs Brown's Boy: The Beginning	Brendan O'Carroll	Irish/Fiction
59	DNU Student Yearbook & Career - Part 2	Joe Duddy	School/School Text
60	Hard Cases	Gene Kerrigan	Irish/Non-Fiction
61	Cay	Theodore Taylor	School/School Text
62	Horse Whisperer	Nicholas Evans	Fiction/Popular Fiction
63	Granny	Brendan O'Carroll	Irish/Fiction
64	Eternal Echoes: Exploring Our Hunger	John O'Donohue	Irish/Celtic
65	Dubliners	James Joyce	School/School Text
66	Street Lawyer	John Grisham	Fiction/Crime
67	Sold Into Marriage	Sean Boyne	Irish/Non-Fiction
68	Sophie's World	Jostein Gaarder	Childrens/Fiction
69	Ireland	(Michelin)	Travel/Irish Maps
70	Chisellers	Brendan O'Carroll	Irish/Fiction
71	God Of Small Things	Arundhati Roy	Fiction/Popular Fiction
72	Crescendo	Mary McCarthy	Irish/Fiction
73	DNU Ireland	(Michelin)	Travel/Irish Maps
74	Road Map Ireland	(Ordnance Survey)	Travel/Irish Maps
75	Street Lawyer	John Grisham	Fiction/Crime
76	Of Mice & Men	John Steinbeck	School/School Text
77	King Scum	Paul Reynolds	Irish/Non-Fiction
78	Taste of Freedom	Liz Ryan	Irish/Fiction
79	Irish Legends For Children	(Carroll)	Childrens/Irish Interest
80	Hannibal	Thomas Harris	Fiction/Popular Fiction
81	Reading In The Dark	Seamus Deane	School/School Text
82	Point Of Origin	Patricia Cornwell	Fiction/Crime
83	Remember Me	Mary McCarthy	Irish/Fiction
84	And No Bird Sang	Mary McCarthy	Irish/Fiction
85	Scalpel	Paul Carson	Irish/Fiction
86	Men Are From Mars Women Are From Venus	John Gray	Reference/Psychology
87	Family Finance 1999/2000	Colm Raffle	Irish/Finance
88	Manchester United Ultimate Yearbook	(Paragon)	Sport/Football

Continued from previous page

Rank	Title	Author	Description
89	Collins Gem German Dictionary	(Collins)	Reference/Dictionaries
90	Finbar's Hotel	Dermot Bolger	Irish/Fiction
91	Last Chance Saloon	Marian Keyes	Irish/Fiction
92	Sky	Deirdre Purcell	Irish/Fiction
93	Dublin - A Grand Tour	Jacqueline O'Brien	Irish/Miscellaneous
94	Falling For A Dancer	Deirdre Purcell	Irish/Fiction
95	W.B. Yeats Images Of Ireland	A &MCCA Le Garsmeur	Irish/Miscellaneous
96	Hard Times (Popular Classic)	Charles Dickens	Fiction/Classics
97	Long Road Home	Danielle Steel	Fiction/Romance
98	Unnatural Exposure	Patricia Cornwell	Fiction/Crime
99	Runaway Jury	John Grisham	Fiction/Crime

Source Eason & Son Ltd

Music & Opera

● **STATUS OF MUSIC IN IRELAND** Despite the fact that support for music and music education in Ireland is not well-structured, the music sector is one of the most dynamic artforms in Ireland with a wide variety of practitioners, from local and community festival practitioners, to specialised ensembles and individual performers and composers. Outside RTÉ, there is little full-time or long-term employment for classically trained musicians. In the consultative review for the Arts Plan 1999 - 2001, relevant bodies pointed out the inadequacies of the music curricula at primary and secondary schools as well as the inadequate support for independent music schools, which are the only institutions open to students outside the capital cities to further their music studies and are obviously inaccessible to those who have no means of funding. In addition to these factors, most Irish musicians, like dancers, travel abroad to finish their training, a factor which limits the development of music in Ireland. There were calls for the arts council to be more adventurous in its policy making and for devolution to regional music bodies. There were also calls for dedicated spaces for the performance of traditional, jazz and improvised music.
● **STATUS OF OPERA IN IRELAND** Opera in Ireland is practised primarily by three companies in Dublin and Wexford, and one in Cork. The artform is very limited in this country due to its need for highly trained singers and practitioners, dedicated venues, high production costs and the lack of an indigenous opera tradition in Ireland. However, it is a growing field, as exemplified by the increasing support for the Wexford Opera Festival.
● **THE 1995–1998 ARTS PLAN** attempted to re-define and broaden its involvement in music of all kinds and this it achieved by providing extra resources to all genres of music. It also attempted to expand audiences for opera and improve cross-border co-operation in the artform
● **1999–2001 ARTS PLAN** will focus on enhancing the provision for professional artists to pursue virtuosoship in the international sphere and promoting the rich culture of participation in music in Ireland. It will seek to achieve these aims through a number of measures, including the funding of masterclasses, festivals and summer schools as well as travel and study by Irish artists abroad. As with the first Arts plan, it will also attempt to expand audiences.

Arts Council Expenditure - Music

Rol Arts Council Funding Decisions	1998 (IR£)	NI Awards Funding	No Awards	Stg£
Support Organisations	877,000	Instruments-Bands	106	1,456,520.50
Concert Promotion	159,750	Instruments-Other	15	193,919.00
Performing Groups	606,000	Equipment	9	145,828.50
Events	69,550	Building	2	66,685.00
Recording / Publications	33,000	New Work	15	61,147.00
Education	99,000	Work New to Northern Ireland	3	299,050.00
TOTAL	1,844,300	Access	4	248,506.00
		Advancement	1	747,300.00
		TOTAL	155	3,218,956.00

Source The Arts Council - An Chomhairle Ealaíon;
Arts Council of Northern Ireland. Total does not include bursaries to individuals and other grants awarded

Arts Council Expenditure - Opera

Rol Arts Council Funding Decisions	1998 (IR£)
Opera Ireland, Dublin	486,000
Opera Theatre Co, Dublin	300,000
Wexford Festival Opera	450,000
TOTAL	1,236,000

NI Awards Funding	No Awards	Stg£
Building	1	45,000
Equipment	1	51,140
Work New to Northern Ireland	2	80,475
New Work	1	40,300
Advancement	2	-
TOTAL	7	216,915

Source The Arts Council - An Chomhairle Ealaíon; Arts Council of Northern Ireland
Total does not include bursaries to individuals and other grants awarded

● **SOME RELEVANT BODIES**
Association of Irish Composers Copyright Hse, Pembroke Row, Dublin 2. *Tel* 01-494 2880 *Profile* The representative body of composers in Ireland, it aims to improve standards of composition and gain support and recognition for composers and their work. It also publishes a newsletter - *AIC News.*
Contemporary Music Centre (CMC) 95 Lower Baggot St, Dublin 2. *Tel* 01-661 2105 *email* info@cmc.ie *Established* 1986 *Profile* In essence, the CMC documents and promotes music in Ireland. It has an archive and large collection of information materials - its library contains the only major specialist collection of music by modern Irish composers. Its facilities are open to performers, composers, teachers, students and the general public, and it will assist people with any questions they have on Irish music. It publishes *New Music News* and is a member of the International Association of Music Information Centres, placing it in contact with similar agencies worldwide.
Music Association of Ireland 69 Sth Great Georges St, Dublin 2. *Tel* 01-478 5368 *email* music.association@indigo.ie *Established* 1984 *Profile* It acts as a lobby group for, and promotes, music in education and the support of the arts. To this end it activities include staging concerts in schools, composer workshops, concerts around the country, EU Youth Orchestra auditions. It also produces a monthly music diary.
Music Network *See Culture*
Wexford Festival Opera Theatre Royal, High St, Wexford. *email* info@wexfordopera.com *Tel* 053-22400 *Established* 1951 *Profile* The festival has established an unique tradition - it is a remarkable success in a town, let alone a country, where opera is not a widely practised artform. Over the years, the festival grew with the addition of more than one opera, recitals, concerts, talks and other events. From its early days, it included works which would not have been widely known and began to attract international attention. It is now one of the highlights of the national arts calendar.
Selection of Main Orchestras in Ireland:
   The Clare Orchestra College Road, Ennis, Co.Clare. *Tel* 065-41774 *email* akr@tinet.ie
   Dublin Youth Orchestras 62 Ailesbury Grove, Dublin 16. *Tel* 01-298 0680
   The Dublin Viols 35 Marlborough Road, Dublin 4. *Tel* 01-668 5349 email: akr@tinet.ie
   Irish Association of Youth Orchestras 6 Alexandra Place,Wellington Rd, Cork. *Tel* 021-507 412
   Irish Chamber Orchestra Foundation Building, University of Limerick. email: ico@iol.ie
   Irish Film Orchestra 10 Beechpark Avenue,Castleknock, Dublin 15. *Tel* 01-8202581
   National Symphony Orchestra Music Department, RTÉ, Donnybrook, Dublin 4. *Tel* 01-208 2779
   National Youth Orchestra of Ireland 37 Molesworth Street, Dublin 2.
   Opera Theatre Co Temple Bar Music Centre, Curved St, Temple Bar, Dublin 2. *Tel* 01-6794962 email: otc@imn.ie
   RTÉ Concert Orchestra Music Department - RTÉ *see National Symphony Orchestra.*
   RTÉ Philharmonic Choir Portobello Studios, Rathmines, Dublin 6. *Tel* 01-208 2979 Web www.rte.ie
   Vanbrugh String Quartet 4 Tirol Avenue, Douglas, Cork.*Tel* 021-893027 email vanbrugh@iol.ie
   St Sepulchres 35 Marlborough Road, Dublin 4. *Tel* 01-668 5349 email: akr@tinet.ie
   Ulster Orchestra Elmwood Hall, 89 University Road, Belfast BT7 1NF.
   Ulster Youth Orchestra Chamber of Commerce Hse, 22 Great Victoria St., Belfast BT2 7LX. *Tel* 01232-278 2877

Visual Arts

● **STATUS OF VISUAL ARTS IN IRELAND** There are an estimated 1,500 visual artists practising in Ireland across a wide range of media: painting, sculpture, installation and new media, such as multimedia. Irish Visual Arts have a higher profile in Ireland and internationally than ever before, and artists are obtaining more commissions for work from at home and abroad. However, the consultative review for the 1999 - 2001 Arts Plan uncovered the problem of a lack of awareness of how artists work and existing Arts Council policy in addressing this. Primarily, this boiled down to the annual funding cycle and its lack of fit with regards to artists' ability to purchase adequate time, space and materials. There has been widespread endorsement of the importance of public art projects and the support of local authority arts officers, and the arts plan will continue to support initiatives in these areas
● **THE 1995–1998 ARTS PLAN** was instrumental in raising the profile of artists in Ireland. It reinforced and expanded the current infrastructure of facilities, studios and galleries, as is evident in the Irish Museum of Modern Art and the municipal galleries in Dublin, Cork, Limerick, Waterford and Sligo. One of the most successful ways in which artists' profile was raised is the "percent for art" scheme whereby a selected artist received a percentage of

the funds from a local authority-EU funded project, such as road or tunnel construction, to create a piece of art alongside the project. The first plan increased awards to individual artists, as well as to organisations and the provision of art space.

● **1999–2001 ARTS PLAN** will continue to provide cnuas to members of Aosdána, to ensure that artists will have the opportunities to exhibit and sell their art - both at home and abroad, to research and formulate policy on artists' re-sale rights, to review existing current funding policies in conjunction with the Arts Council of Northern Ireland, to continue funding galleries and arts events, to support local authorities and others in the realm of public art and to support criticism and education in the visual arts.

Arts Council Expenditure

● Rol Arts Council Funding Decisions	1998 (IR£)
Artists' Organisations	751,000
Studios	74,700
Galleries	525,000
Publications	90,000
Education	45,000
Major Exhibitions	115,000
Major Exhibitions	6,000
TOTAL	1,606,700

Source: The Arts Council - An Chomhairle Ealaíon;
Arts Council of Northern Ireland
Total does not include bursaries to individuals
and other grants awarded

● NI Awards Funding	No Awards	Stg£
Visual Arts		
Public Art	28	961,042
Equipment	10	109,378
Feasibility Study	1	2,000
Building	1	11,880
New Work	4	60,241
Access	8	250,175
TOTAL	52	1,394,716
Craft		
Public Art	2	14,067
Equipment	1	2,725
TOTAL	3	16,792

● **SOME RELEVANT BODIES**

Arthouse Multimedia Centre Curved St, Temple Bar, Dublin 2. *Tel* 01-605 6800 *email* info@arthouse.ie *Web* www.arthouse.ie Creates and promotes new media work and gives training and services to artists wishing to use the latest in communication technology and state of the art software. It has creative studios and exhibition spaces. and has produced one of the most comprehensive resources on Irish Art - Artifact - a CD-ROM on Contemporary Irish Art and information on contemporary artists in Ireland.

Artists Association of Ireland 43Temple Bar, Dublin 2. *Tel* 01-874 0529 *Profile* This is a professional association of visual artists working to improve the conditions of visual artists and visual arts in Ireland. It publishes the Art Bulletin, the Irish Visual Artists Handbook and information on a variety of pertinent issues.

Directory of Arts Venues in Ireland

This directory contains up to date informaton on professional theatre companies, permanent theatres and dedicated gallery spaces in all of the counties, North and South.

Antrim

● **ARTS CENTRES**

Ballyearl Arts Centre Town Hall, Conway Sq, Newtownabbey. 01232-848 287

Clotworthy Arts Centre Antrim Castle Grounds, Randalstown Rd, Antrim. 01849-428 000

Crescent Arts Centre 2-4 University Rd, Belfast. 01232-242 338

Culturlann MacAdhamh Ó Fiaich 216 Falls Rd, Belfast. 01232-239 303

Flax International Arts Centre 7 College Square North, Belfast. 01232-745 241

Harmony Hill Arts Centre 54 Harmony Hill, Lambeg, Lisburn BT27 4ES. 01232-678 219

Old Museum Arts Centre 7 College Sq Nth, Belfast BT1 6AR. 01232-235 053

● **THEATRES & THEATRE COMPANIES**

Aisling Ghéar 12 College Sq Nth, Belfast BT1 6AS.
01232-331 131

Belfast Theatre Co 207 Russell Crt, Belfast BT9 6JX. 01232-596 814

Belfast Youth & Community Theatre Crescent Arts Centre 2-4 University Rd, Belfast BT7 1NH. 01232-310 900

Centre Stage Theatre Co 99 Fitzroy Ave, Belfast BT7 1JU. 01232-249 119

Dubbeljoint Productions 245 Lisburn Rd, Belfast BT9 7EN. 01232-202 222

Kabosh Productions Old Museum Arts Centre, 7 College Sq. Nth, Belfast BT1 6AR. 01232-243 343.

Prime Cut Productions 404 McAvoy House, 17a Ormeau Ave, Belfast BT2 6HD. 01232-313 156

Replay Productions Old Museum Ctre, 7 College Sq North, Belfast BT1 6AR. 01232-322 773.

Ridiculusmus Unit 10F, Owen O'Cork Mill, 288 Beersbridge Rd, Belfast BT5 5DX. 01232-460 630.

Room B Theatre Productions Ltd 118 Benburb St, Belfast BT12 6JJ. 01232-580569.

Shanakee Productions 7 Chesham Parade, Belfast BT6 8GR. 01232-806 263

SHIBBOLE THeatre Co 89-91 Academy St, Belfast BT1 2LS. 01247-853 258

Tinderbox Theatre Co 104 McAvoy House, 17a Ormeau Ave, Belfast BT2 6HD. 01232-329 420

Who the Hell Theatre Co 63 Ardenvohr St, Belfast BT6 8NB. 01232-597 483

Youth Lyric Lyric Theatre 55 Ridgeway St, Belfast BT9 5FB. 01396-831 670

● THEATRE VENUES

Belfast Civic Arts Theatre 41 Botanic Ave, BT7 1JG. 01232-316 901.

Courtyard Theatre Ballyearl Leisure Complex, 585 Doagh Rd, Newtownabbey BT36 8RS. 01232-848 287

Grand Opera House 2-4 Great Victoria St., Belfast BT2 7HR. 01232-240 411

Lyric Players Theatre 55 Ridgeway St, Belfast BT9 5FB. 01232-669 660

Waterfront Hall- BT Studio 2 Lanyon Place, Belfast BT1 3LP. 01232-334 400

● MAJOR EXHIBITION VENUES

Arches Art Gallery 2 Holywood Rd, Belfast. 01232-459 031

Array Studio Group Belfast. 01232-319 248

Bell, The 13 Adelaide Park, Malone Rd, Belfast BT9 6FX 01232-662 998.

Caldwell Galleries Belfast. 01232-323 226

Catalyst Arts 5 Exchange Place, Belfast BT1 2NA. 01232-313 303

Cavehill Gallery 18 Old Cavehill Rd, Belfast BT15 5GT. 01232-776 784

Dalriada Gallery Ballymena. 01266-632 366

Eakin Gallery 237 Lisburn Rd, Belfast. 01232-668 522

Fenderesky Gallery @ Queen's 5-6 Upper Crescent, Belfast BT7 1NT. 01232-235 245

Gallery, The 56-60 Dublin Rd, Belfast. 01232-321 402.

Gilmore Charles 31 Church Rd, Holywood, Belfast.

Linen Hall Library 17 Donegall Sq Nth, Belfast BT1 5GD. 01232 321 707

John Magee Ltd 455 Ormeau Rd, Belfast. 01232-693 830

One Oxford St 1 Oxford St, Belfast BT1 3LA. 01232-310 400

Ormeau Baths Gallery 18a Ormeau Ave, Belfast BT2 8HS. 01232-321 402

Ormonde Gallery Belfast. 01232-321 402

Portrush Gallery Portrush. 01265-823739

Seymour Galleries 20 Seymour St, Lisburn. 01846-662 685

Stables Gallery 27 Ballywindland Rd, Ballymoney BT53 6QT. 012656-65919

Straid Gallery & Art Centre Ballyclare. 01960-354 696

Trooperslane Art Gallery 2 Knockmore Park, Carrickfergus. 01960-364 754

Ulster Arts Club 56 Elmwood Ave, Belfast BT9 6AG. 01232- 660 644

Ulster Museum Botanic Gardens, Belfast. 01232-383 000

Village Gallery 4 Bendooragh Rd, Ballymoney BT53 7ND. 012656-65528

For further information contact the arts officers at: 01849-

428000 (Antrim Borough Council), 01232-325 536 (Belfast City Council), 01266-44111 (Ballymena Borough Council), 01960-351 604 (Carrickfergus Borough Council), 01232 798 572 (Castlereagh Borough Council), 012656-62280 (Ballymoney Borough Council), 01574-272 313 (Larne Borough Council), 01846 678 219 (Lisburn Borough Council), 012657-62225 (Moyle District Council), 01960-352681 (Newtownabbey Borough Council).

Armagh

● THEATRES & THEATRE COMPANIES

Portadown Town Hall 15-17 Edward St, Portadown BT62 3LX. 01762-335 264

Ulster Assoc of Youth Drama *c/o Young Performers Theatre Company (temporary address)*

Young Performers Theatre Co Lurgan Town Hall, 2-6 Union St, Lurgan BT66 8DY. 01762-349 974

Pineback House Arts Centre Tullygally Rd, Craigavon. 01762-41033

● MAJOR EXHIBITION VENUES

Adam Gallery 28 Linenhall St., Armagh. 012657-526 908

Armagh County Museum The Mall East, Armagh. 01861-523 070

Roy Edwards Fine Arts Ltd Maon Rd, Portadown BT62 3EH. 01762-339 116

Brownlow Art Gallery Lurgan. 01762-327 772

Browser Gallery Armagh. 01861-528 660

Craigavon Arts & PeacockGallery Craigavon. 01762-341 618

Hayloft Gallery Palace Stables Heritage Centre, The Palace Demesne, Armagh BT60 4EL. 01861 522 722

The Peacock Pineback House Arts Centre, Tullygally Rd, Craigavon. 01762-341 618

For further information contact the arts officers at: 01861-521 805 (Armagh City & District Council), 0176-341 618 (Craigavon Borough Council).

Carlow

● THEATRES & THEATRE COMPANIES

Bridewell Lane Theatre Bridewell Lane, 7 Tullow St, Carlow. 0503-43307

Uppercrust Theatre Co c/o Bridewell Lane Theatre, 7 Tullow St, Carlow. 0503-30510

● MAJOR EXHIBITION VENUES

Pembroke Studio Carlow Town. 0503-41562

Cavan

● THEATRES & THEATRE COMPANIES

Ramor Theatre Virginia, Co Cavan. 049-854 7074

● MAJOR EXHIBITION VENUES

County Museum Ballyjamesduff. 049-8544 070

For further information contact the arts officer at: 049-4331799 (Cavan Co Council).

Clare

● THEATRES & THEATRE COMPANIES

Danlann an Chlair Ennis. 065-682 0769 (Ticket Master)
Dandelion Puppet Theatre East Clare Community Co-op, Scarriff. 065-6835566
Theatre Omnibus Clare Business Centre, Francis St, Ennis. 065-29952

● MAJOR EXHIBITION VENUES

Burren Painting Centre Lisdoonvarna. 065-74208
De Valera Library Harmony Row, Ennis. 065-21616
Ennistymon Branch Library The Square, Ennistymon. 065-71245
The M'rua Art Centre Bellharbour, Co Clare. 065-707 8005
Seán Lemass Library Town Centre, Shannon. 061-364266
For further information contact the arts officer at: 065-21616 (Clare Co Council).

Cork

● ARTS CENTRES

Ballincollig Gun Powder Mills The Heritage Centre, Ballincollig. 021-874430
Bantry Community Arts Resource Centre Glengarriff Rd, Bantry. 027-51315
Glen Theatre The Heritage & Drama Trust, Banteer, Co Cork
Munster Literature Centre Tig Litriochta, Sullivan's Quay, Cork.
Sirius Commemoration Trust The Old Yacht Club, Cobh. 021-813 612
Triskel Arts Centre Tobin St., Cork. 021-272 022
Village Art Centre The Square, Kilworth, Co Cork. 025-24451
West Cork Arts Centre North St, Skibbereen. 028-22090

● THEATRES & THEATRE COMPANIES

Allihies Centre Allihies, Beara, Co Cork.
Boomerang Theatre Co Teach Barra, Dean St, Cork. 021-316 826
Cork Arts & Theatre Project 6 Knapp's Quay, Cork. 021-508699
Corcadorca Theatre Co 11 Marlboro St, Cork. 021-278 326
Cork Opera House Emmet Place, Cork. 021-274 308
Everyman Palace Theatre 15 MacCurtain St, Cork. 021-503 077
Firkin Crane Centre Shandon, Cork. 021-507 487
Graffiti Theatre Co The Weighmasters House, Shandon, Cork. 021-397 111
Half Moon Theatre c/o Cork Opera House. 021-274 308
Meridian Productions 11-12 Malboro St, Cork. 021-276 837
New Granary Theatre University College, Mardyke, Cork. 021-276 871
Steeple Theatre Co 2 St John's Park, Parkowen, Quaker Rd, Cork. 021-291 536

● MAJOR EXHIBITION VENUES

Art Hive, The Thompson Hse, MacCurtain St, Cork. 021-505 228
Bandon Gallery 83 Nth Main St, Bandon. 023-41360
Bantry Library Bridge St, Bantry. 027-50460
Beara Community Arts The Square, Castletownbere. 027-70765.
Blackcoombe Art Gallery 44a MacCurtain St, Cork. 021-500 040
Boole Library University College Cork, College Rd, Cork. 021-276 871
Charleville Library Main St, Charleville. 063-89769
Crawford Municipal Art Gallery Emmet Place, Cork. 021-273 377
Lavitt's Quay Gallery, Cork-Cork Arts Society 16 Lavitt's Quay, Cork. 021-277 749
O'Kane's Green Gallery Glengarriff Rd, Bantry. 027-50003
Vangard Gallery New St, Macroom. 026-41198
For further information contact the arts officers at: 021-966 222 (Cork Corporation), 021-346 210 (Cork Co Council).

Derry

● ARTS CENTRES

Eden Place Arts Centre Derry. 01504-269 418
Flowerfield Arts Centre 185 Coleraine Rd., Portstewart. 01265-833 959
Foyle Arts Centre Lawrence Hill, Derry. 01504-266 657
The Nerve Centre Magazine St, Derry. 01504-260562
The Playhouse 5-7 Artillery St, Derry BT48 6RG. 01504-264 481

● THEATRES & THEATRE COMPANIES

Big Telly Theatre Co Portstewart Town Hall, The Crescent, Portstewart BT55 7AB. 01265-832 588
The Playhouse 5-7 Artillery St, Derry BT48 6RG. 01504-264 481
Rialto Entertainment Centre 5 Market St, Derry BT48 6EF. 01504-260 516
Riverside Theatre The University of Ulster, Coleraine BT52 1SA. 01265-324 683
Sole Purpose Productions The Playhouse, 5-7 Artillery St, Derry BT48 6RG. 01504-271 126
St. Columb's Theatre & Arts Centre Orchard St, Derry. Tel: (01504) 262800

● MAJOR EXHIBITION VENUES

Apprentice Boys Memorial Hall Society Street, Derry. 01504-263571
Context Gallery The Playhouse, Derry. 01504-264 481
McGilloway Gallery 6 Shipquay St, Derry. BT48 6DN. 01504-366 011
Orchard Gallery Orchard St, Derry BT48 6EG. 01504-269 675
Portstewart Gallery Portstewart 01265-836 177
Riverside Gallery Riverside Theatre, The University of Ulster, Coleraine BT52 1SA. 01265-324 449
The Calgach Centre Butcher St, Derry. 01504-373 177
Verbal Arts Centre Cathedral School Building, London St, Derry BT48 6RQ. 01504-266946
For further information contact the arts officers at: 01265-

52181 *(Coleraine Borough Council)*, 01504-365 151 *(Derry City Council)*, 015047-22226 *(Limavady Borough Council)*, 01648-32151 *(Magherafelt District Council)*.

Donegal

● **ARTS CENTRES**
Central Library & Arts Centre Oliver Plunkett Rd, Letterkenny. 074-29186

● **THEATRES & THEATRE COMPANIES**
Abbey Centre Tirconnel St, Ballyshannon. 072-51375
Butt Drama Circle Balor Theatre Main St, Ballybofey. 074-31840
An Grianán Rectory Field, Port Rd, Letterkenny. 074-20777

● **MAJOR EXHIBITION VENUES**
Cavanacor Corr Gallery Ballindrait, Lifford. 074-41143
Cristeph Gallery Port Road, Letterkenny. 074-26411
Donegal County Museum High Rd, Letterkenny. 074-24613
Ionad Cois Locha - Lakeside Centre Dunlewey. 075-31699
Ionad Teampall Chroin Dungloe. 075-22198
The Gallery Dunfanaghy. 074-36224
The Workhouse Dunfanaghy. 074-36540
Foras Cultúir Uladh - Ulster Cultural Institute Glencolumcille. 073-30248
Glebe House and Gallery Churchill. 074-37071
Tullyarvan Mill Culture and Exhibition Centre Buncrana. 077-61613
For further information contact the arts officer at: 074-21968 (Donegal Co Council).

Down

● **ARTS CENTRES**
Ards Arts Centre Town Hall, Conway Sq, Newtownards BT23 4DD. 01247-810 803
Down Civic Arts Centre 2-6 Irish St., Downpatrick BT30 6BN. 01396-615283
Newry & Mourne Arts Centre 1a Bank Parade, Newry. 01693-66232

● **THEATRES & THEATRE COMPANIES**
Ulster Theatre Co 54 Drumconagher Rd, Crossgar BT30 9JH. 01396-830 166
Assoc. of Ulster Drama Festivals 8 Ward Ave, Bangor BT20 5JW. 01247-270 157
National Operatic & Dramatic Assoc. 10 Ashford Ave, Bangor BT19 6DB. 01247-473 630
Northern Amateur Theatre Assoc. 49 Beverley Gardens, Bangor BT20 4NQ. 01247-473 630

● **MAJOR EXHIBITION VENUES**
Art Gallery, The Hillsborough. 01846 689 896
Castle Espie 78 Ballydrain Rd, Comber. 01247-874 146
Cleft Art Gallery 3 Market Hse, New St, Donaghadee. 01247-888 502
Dromore Community Centre Old Town Hall, Banbridge.
Gallery of Local Art Bangor 01247-453 178

Kristyne Gallery Gilford Castle, Banbridge. 01762-831 108
Lenaderg Lodge Gallery Tourist Information Centre, Banbridge.
Newcastle Art Gallery 18-22 Main St, Newcastle. 013967-23555
North Down Visitors & Heritage Centre Town Hall, Castle Park Ave, Bangor BT20 4BT. 01247-270 371
Priory Art Gallery 10 Shore Rd, Holywood BT18 9HX. 01232-428173
Salem Gallery 29 Mill St, Comber. 01247-874 455
Shambles Art Gallery Dromore Rd, Hillsborough. 01846-682 946
For further information contact the arts officers at: 01247-810 803 (Ards Borough Council), 018206-62991 (Banbridge District Council), 01396-615218 (Down District Council), 01693-66232 (Mourne & Newry District Council), 01247-270 371 (North Down Borough Council).

Dublin

● **ARTS CENTRES**
Ark, The - Children's Cultural Centre Eustace Street, Temple Bar, D2. 01-670 7788
Arts Council, The - An Chomhairle Ealaíon 70 Merrion Square, D2. 01-618 0200
City Arts Centre 23-25 Moss St, D2. 01-677 0643
Northside Arts & Cultural Centre c/o Coolock Development Centre, Bunratty Drive, Coolock, D17. 01-8325419
Project Arts Centre 39 East Essex St, D2. 01-679 6622
Tallaght Community Arts Centre Virginia Hse, Blessington Rd, D24. 01-462 1501

● **THEATRES & THEATRE COMPANIES**
Abbey Theatre Lower Abbey St, D1. 01-874 8741
Ambassador Theatre Parnell St, D1. 01-872 7000
Amharclann de híde An Clós Uachtarach, Caisleán Bhaile Átha Cliath, D2. 01-671 0534
Andrew's Lane Theatre 9-17 Andrew's Lane, Exchequer St, D2. 01-679 7760
Artslab Space 28, 28 North Lotts, D1. 01-872 1882
Barabbas...The Company 7 South Great Georges St, D2. 01-671 2013
Bedrock Theatre Co Halpenny Court, 36-37 Lwr Ormond Quay, D1. 01-872 9300
Beg Borrow & Steal Theatre Co 35 Leinster Ave, North Strand, D3. 01-874 3154
Blackbox Theatre Co 17 Orchard Tce, Phibsboro, D7. Contact: Mr Pat Nolan. 01-679 9599
Brechfest Ormond Centre, 14 Ormond Quay, D1. Contact: Mr Ken McCue. 01-872 3500
Calypso Productions Ltd 7 Sth Great Georges St, D2. 01-450 7104
Corn Exchange 16 Heytesbury Lane, D4. 01-668 2561
Crypt Arts Centre Chapel Royal, Dublin Castle, D2. 01-671 3387
Down-to-Earth 61 Middle Abbey St, D1. 01-873 2566
Draíocht Blanchardstown D15. *(opening 2000)*
Drama League of Ireland PO Box 3094, D8. 01-660 0311
Dry Bread Theatre Co Ltd 21 Effra Rd, Rathmines, D6. 01-496 3983

Dublin Fringe Festival Halpenny Court, 36-37 Ormond Quay, D1. 01-872 9016

Dublin Theatre Festival 47 Nassau St, D2. 01-677 8439

Dublin Theatre Co The High Road, Kilmainham, D8. 01-679 4336

Dublin Youth Theatre 23 Upper Gardiner St, D1. 01-874 3687

Fishamble Theatre Co Shamrock Chambers, 1-2 Eustace St, D2. 01-670 4018

Fly by Night 177 Tonlegee Road, D5. 01-847 9571

Focus Theatre Co 6 Pembroke Place, off Upper Pembroke St, D2. 01-676 3071

Gaiety Theatre South King St, D2. 01-679 5622

Galloping Cat c/o City Arts Centre, 23-25 Moss St, D2. 01-677 0643

Gate Theatre 8 Parnell Sq, D1. 01-874 4045

Gemini Productions Flat 405, Irish Life Centre, D1. 01-874 4304

Groundwork Productions 119 St Stephen's Green, D2. 01-475 6062

Íomha Ildánach Crypt Arts Centre, Chapel Royal, Dublin Castle, D2. 01-671 3387

Jobstown Community Centre Tallaght, D24. 01-280 3455

Lambert Puppet Theatre & Museum Clifton Lane, Monkstown. 01-280 1863

Level 3 23 Beverly Lawns Scholarstown Road, D16. 01-493 3148

Loose Cannon Theatre Co 43 Morehampton Rd, Donnybrook, D4. 01-660 6012

Magpie Theatre Co 137 Viking Harbour, Ushers Island, D8.

Muted Cuped 1 Chester Rd, Ranelagh, D6. 01-496 7645

National Association for Youth Drama 34 Upper Gardiner St, D1. 01-878 1301

National Concert Hall Earlsfort Tce, D2. 01-475 1572

National Theatre Society Ltd *(Abbey & Peacock Theatres),* Abbey Theatre, Lwr Abbey St, D1. 01-874 8741

New Theatre East Essex St, Temple Bar, D2. 01-6703361

Olympia Theatre 72 Dame St, D2. 01-677 7744

Operating Theatre 38 Moyne Rd, Ranelagh, D6. 01-476 2516

Pan Pan Theatre The Old School Hse, Eblana Ave, Dun Laoghaire. 01 280 0544

Passion Machine, 30 Gardiner St, D1. 01-878 8857

Peacock Theatre 01-878 7222

Pink Panda Theatre Co 5 Tymon Grove, Old Bawn, Tallaght, D24.

Players Theatre Trinity Players Drama Group, *c/o Samuel Beckett Theatre.*

Playwrights & Actors Co 9 Nth Frederick St, D1. 01-8747583

Point Theatre East Link Bridge, North Wall Quay, D1. 01-836 6777

Point Depot North Wall Quay, D1. 01-836 6777

Project @ the Mint. 01-679 6622

RDS Ballsbridge, D4. 01-668 0866

Read Co 48 Aughavannagh Rd, D12. 01-473 2285

Rough Magic Ltd 5-6 Sth Great Georges St, D2. 01-671 9278

Samuel Beckett Theatre Trinity College, D2. 01-608 1334

Second Age Ltd 74 Dame St, D2. 01-679 8542

SFX City Theatre 23 Sherrard St Upr, D1. 01-855 4090

Sionnach Theatre Co 43 East Essex St, Temple Bar, D2. 01-670 3361

Smashing Times 5 Meeting Hse Lane, D7. 01-872 7847

St. Anthony's Little Theatre Merchants Quay, D8. 01-670 6991

State of Mime Theatre 43 Windsor Rd, Rathmines, D6. 01-496 1882

Sticks & Stones Co 'Inver', Marlborough Rd, Glenageary, Co. Dublin. 01-2807065

Storytellers' Theatre Co 3rd Floor, 5 Aston Quay, D2. 01-671 1161

Strumpet City Prods. 25 Neville Rd, Rathgar, D6. 01-497 4164

Tallaght Civic Theatre Tallaght, D24. 01-462 7477

Taney Hall Dundrum, D24. 01-280 3455

TEAM Theatre Co 4 Marlborough Place, D1. 01-676 8108.

Theatre Shop 5-6 Sth Great Georges St, D2. 01-671 9278

Theatre Works 1 Richmond Cottages, D1.

Tivoli Theatre 135-138 Francis St, D2. 01-454 4472

Very Special Arts c/o City Arts Centre, 23-25 Moss St, D2. 01-671 6518

Vesuvius Arts Ltd 2nd Floor, 40 Dame St, D2. 01-670 7733

Vicar St 58-59 Thomas St, D8. 01-454 5533

Wildcard Theatre Co 41 Harrington St, off Grantham Place, D8. 01-475 0392

● **MAJOR EXHIBITION VENUES**

Andrew's Lane Theatre 9 St Andrews Lane, D2. 01-6797760

Architecture Centre the Royal Institute of the Architects of Ireland, 8 Merrion Sq, Dublin 2. 01-676 1703

Arthouse Multimedia Centre Curved Street, Temple Bar, D2. 01-605 6800

Black Church Print Studio 4 Temple Bar, D2.

Bridge Gallery 8 Upr Ormond Qy, D7. 01-872 9702

Chester Beatty Library 20 Shrewsbury Rd, D4. 01-269 2386

Cill Rialaig 13 St Stephen's Green, D2. 01-670 7972

Combridge Fine Arts 17 Sth William St, D2. 01-677 4652

Crafts Council Gallery Powerscourt Town Hse, Sth William St, D2. 01-679 7368

Davis Gallery 11 Capel St, D1. 01-872 6969

Designyard 12 East Essex St, D2. 01-677 2694

Douglas Hyde Gallery Trinity College *(Nassau St entrance),* Dublin 2. 01-608 1116

Dublin Photographic Centre 10 Lwr Camden St, D2. 01-660 8513

Dublin Public Libraries Cumberland Hse, Fenian St, D2. 01-661 9000

Dublin Writers Museum 18 Parnell Sq, D1. 01-872 2077

Dun Laoghaire/Rathdown Arts Service Town Hall, Dun Laoghaire, Co Dublin. 01-280 6961

Fire Station Studios 9-11 Lower Buckingham St, D1. 01-855 6735

Frederick Gallery 24 Frederick St Sth, D2. 01-670 7055
Gallery of Photography Meeting Hse Sq, Temple Bar, D2. 01-671 4654
Gorry Gallery 20 Molesworth St., D2. 01-679 5319
Graphic Studio Gallery 8a Cope St *(through the Arch)*, Temple Bar, D2. 01-679 8021
Green on Red 58 Fitzwilliam Sq, D2. 01-671 3414
Gosvenor Room Gallery Ormond Qy, D7. 01-872 1811
Guinness Hop Store Crane Street *(off Thomas St)*, Dublin 8. 01 283 3669
Hallward Gallery 65 Merrion Sq, D2. 01-662 1482
Hugh Lane Municipal Gallery Of Art Charlemont Hse, Parnell Sq Nrth, D1. 01-874 1903
Irish Life Exhibition Ctre Lwr Abbey St, D1. 01-704 2000
Irish Museum of Modern Art Royal Hospital, Military Rd, Kilmainham, D8. 01-612 9900
James Gallery 7 Railway Rd., Dalkey. 01-285 8703
Jo Rain Gallery 23 Anglesea St, D2. 01-677 9966
Kennedy 12 Harcourt St, D2. 01-475 1740
Kerlin Gallery Anne's Lane, Sth Anne St, D2. 01-670 9093
Kevin Kavanagh Gallery 66 Great Strand St, D1. 01-874 0064
Milmo-Penny Fine Art 55 Ailesbury Rd, Ballsbridge, D4. 01-269 3486
National Gallery of Ireland Merrion Sq *(west)*, D2. 01-661 5133
New Art Studio Ltd 2 Mary's Abbey, D7. 01-873 0617
Oisín Gallery 44 Westland Row, D2. 01-661 1315
Oisín Gallery 10 Marino Mart, Fairview, D3. 01-833 3456.
Old Bawn Community School Old Bawn, Tallaght, D24. 01-452 0566
Oriel Gallery 17 Clare St, D2. 01-676 3410
Original Print Gallery 4 Temple Bar, D2. 01-677 3657
Ormond Multi-Media 16-18 Lower Ormond Qy. 01-872 3500
Paul Kane Gallery 53 Sth William St, D2. 01-670 3141
RHA Gallagher Gallery 15 Ely Place, D2. 01-661 2558 *(Ashford Gallery @ the RHA. 01-661 2558)*
Rubicon Gallery 1st Floor, 10 St Stephen's Green, D2. 01-670 8055
Sculptors' Society of Ireland 119 Capel Street, D2. 01-872 2296
Solomon Gallery Powerscourt Townhouse, D2. 01-679 4237
Swords Art & Craft Ctre 10 North St, Swords. 01-840 8258
Taylor Galleries 16 Kildare St, D2. 01-676 6055
Temple Bar Gallery & Studios 5-9 Temple Bar, D2. 01-671 0073
Von Gosseln, Anye 11-13 Suffolk St, D2. 01-671 4079
Waldock Gallery Blackrock Shopping Centre, Blackrock. 01-278 1861
For further information contact the arts officers at: 01-872 2816 (Dublin Corporation), 01-205 4749 (Dun Laoghaire/Rathdown Co Council), 01-872 7777 (Fingal Co Council), 01 462 0000 (Sth Dublin Co Council).

Fermanagh
● **THEATRES & THEATRE COMPANIES**

Ardhowen Theatre & Arts Centre Dublin Rd, Enniskillen. 01365-323 233

● **MAJOR EXHIBITION VENUES**
Ardhowen Theatre & Arts Centre Dublin Rd, Enniskillen. 01365-323 233
Clanart Gallery Enniskillen. 01365-323285
Enniskillen Castle Heritage Ctre Castle Barracks, Enniskillen. 01365-325000
For further information contact the arts officer at: 01365-325 050 (Fermanagh District Council).

Galway
● **THEATRES & THEATRE COMPANIES**
Blackbox Courthouse Sq, Galway. 091-569 755
Druid Theatre Co Chapel Lane, Galway. 091-568 617
Galway Arts Festival 6 Upper Dominick St, Galway. 091-583 800
Macnas Fisheries Field, Salmon Weir Bridge, Galway. 091-561462
Taibhdhearc na Gaillimhe Middle St, Galway. 091-562 024
Town Hall Theatre Courthouse Sq, Galway. 091-569 755

● **MAJOR EXHIBITION VENUES**
An Damhlann - *A Kenny Gallery,* Spiddal Craft Centre, Spiddal. 091-553 733
Artspace Blackbox Theatre, Dyke Rd, Galway. 091-564 522
Ballinasloe Library Ballinasloe. 0905-43464
Clifden Art Gallery Main St, Clifden. 095-21788
Creative Force 12 Cross St, Galway. 091-561 086
Galway Arts Centre 23 Nuns Island, Galway. 091-565 886
Kenny Gallery Middle St, Galway. 091-562 739
Logan Gallery 4a St Anthony's Pl, Woodquay. 091-563 635
Maam Art Gallery Maam. 091-571 109.
University College Galway, University Rd, Galway. 091-524 411
For further information contact the arts officer at: 091-567 722 (Galway Co Council).

Kerry
● **THEATRES & THEATRE COMPANIES**
Siamsa Tíre Theatre / Arts Centre Town Park, Tralee. 066-712 3055.
Arus Padraig Killarney. 064-31524
St. John's Arts and Heritage Centre The Square, Listowel. 068-22566.

● **MAJOR EXHIBITION VENUES**
Bín Bán Gallery, 12 Lower Rock St, Tralee. 066-7122 520
Brushwood Studio Gallery Derryquin, Sneem. 064-45108.
Kerry Branch Library Killarney. 064-32972
Tralee Branch Library, Tralee. 066-712 1200
Wellspring Gallery 16 Denny St, Tralee. 066-712 1218
For further information contact the arts officer at: 066-7121200 (Kerry Co Council).

Kildare

● THEATRES & THEATRE COMPANIES
Crooked House Theatre Co George's St, Newbridge, Co. Kildare. Tel: (0507) 38375
Kilcullen Community Theatre Kilcullen. 045-482004
Moate Theatre Nass. 045-897081

● MAJOR EXHIBITION VENUES
Athy Community Library Athy. 0507-31144
Crookstown Mill Heritage Centre, Ballitore. 0507-23222
Kilcock Art Gallery School St, Kilcock. Tel: (01) 628 7619
Kildare Branch Library Celbridge. 01-627 2207
Kildare Branch Library Basin St, Naas. 045-879111
Maynooth Exhibition Ctre St Patrick's College, Maynooth. 01-628 5222
For further information contact the arts officer at: 045-431 215 (Kildare Co Council).

Kilkenny

● THEATRES & THEATRE COMPANIES
Barnstorm Theatre Co Good Shepherd Centre, Church Lane, Kilkenny. 056-51266
Bickerstaffe Theatre Co 50-51 Upper John St, Kilkenny. 056-51254
Cleere's Theatre Co 28 Parliament St, Kilkenny. 056-62573
County Hall John St, Kilkenny. 056-52699
Watergate Theatre Parliament St, Kilkenny. 056-61674

● MAJOR EXHIBITION VENUES
Berkeley Gallery Grennan Watermill, Thomastown. 056-62453
Butler Gallery Kilkenny Castle, Kilkenny. 056-61106
Kilkenny Co Library Convent Rd, Graiguenamanagh. 0503-24244
For further information contact the arts officer at: 056-52699 (Kilkenny Co Council).

Laois

● MAJOR EXHIBITION VENUES
Dunamaise Theatre & Centre for the Arts Church St, Portlaoise. 0502-63356
Laois County Hall Portlaoise. 0502-22044
For further information contact the arts officer at: 0502-22044 (Laois Co Council).

Leitrim

● THEATRES & THEATRE COMPANIES
The Cornmill Theatre & Arts Centre Carrigallen, Co Leitrim. 049-433 9612
Turbo Prop Theatre Co (Puppet) Manorhamilton, Co Leitrim.

● MAJOR EXHIBITION VENUES
The Glens Centre Manorhamilton, Co Leitrim. 072-55833
Leitrim Sculpture Centre Manorhamilton, Co Leitrim.

For further information contact the arts officer at: 078-20005 (Leitrim Co Council).

Limerick

● THEATRES & THEATRE COMPANIES
Belltable Arts Centre 69 O'Connell St, Limerick. 061-319 866
Island Theatre Co Church St, Kings Island, Limerick. 061-410 433
University Concert Hall University of Limerick, Plassey, Limerick. 061-331 549
Limerick Youth Theatre c/o Belltable Arts Centre.
Friar's Gate Theatre Kilmallock. 063-98727

● MAJOR EXHIBITION VENUES
Anne Fitzgerald Gallery Mungret, Limerick. 061-339 995
Angela Woulfe Gallery 16 Perry Sq, Limerick. 061-310 164
Belltable Arts Centre as above
Bourne-Vincent Gallery (main gallery space) University of Limerick, Plassey, Limerick. 061-213 052
AV Gallery University of Limerick.
Chris Doswell's Gallery Nicholas St, Kings island, Limerick. 061-318 292
Hunt Museum The Custom Hse, Limerick. 061-312 833
Gallery 75 75 O'Connell, Limerick. 061-315 650
Foynes Branch Library Foynes. 069-65365
Limerick City Gallery of Art Pery Square, Limerick. 061-310 633
Newcastle West Library Gortboy, Newcastle West. 069-62273
For further information contact the arts officers at: 061-415 799 (Limerick Corporation), 061-318 477 (Limerick Co Council).

Longford

● THEATRES & THEATRE COMPANIES
Backstage Theatre & Centre For The Arts Farneyhoogan. 043-47888
Shawbrook Ballet Theatre Legan. 044-57570
Bog Lane Theatre Co Bog Lane, Ballymahon. 0902-32273

● MAJOR EXHIBITION VENUES
Atrium Gallery Backstage Theatre, Longford. 043-47888
Carroll Art Gallery Main St, Longford.
Longford Co Library, Town Centre, Longford 043-41124
For further information contact the arts officer at: 043-48376 (Longford Co Council).

Louth

● THEATRES & THEATRE COMPANIES
Droichead Youth Theatre c/o Droichead Arts Centre, Stockwell St, Drogheda. 041-33946
Dundalk Town Hall Crowe St, Dundalk. 042-9332276
Dundalk Youth Theatre Co c/o Town Hall. 042-9332276
Upstate Theatre Co 1 Fair St, Drogheda, Co Louth.

041-44227

● **MAJOR EXHIBITION VENUES**
Ardee Branch Library Market st, Ardee. 041-56080
Artistic License Gallery Dundalk St, Carlingford. 042-73745
The Basement Gallery Town Hall, Dundalk. 042-9332276
County Museum Jocelyn St, Dundalk. 042-9327056
Droichead Arts Centre Stockwell St, Drogheda. 041-33946
Tristanns Gallery 22 Park St, Dundalk. 042-9327466
For further information contact the arts officer at: 042-9332276 (Dundalk UDC).

Mayo
● **THEATRES & THEATRE COMPANIES**
Yew Theatre Co Markievicz Hse, Pearse St, Ballina. 096-71238

● **MAJOR EXHIBITION VENUES**
Andrew Stone Gallery Bridge St, Westport. 098-28870
Art Studio Bridge St, Westport. 098-26732
Ballinglen Arts Foundation Ltd Main St, Ballycastle. 096-43184
Claremorris Library Claremorris.
County Library The Mall, Castlebar. Tel: 094-24444
Custom's Hse Studio Westport. (opening in 2000)
Foxford Exhibition Centre St Joseph's Place, Foxford. 094-56488
Heinrick Böll Academy Achill.
Hillside Gallery 098-27301
Linenhall Arts Centre Linenhall St, Castlebar. 094-23733
McLoughlins Art Gallery Westport.
Western Light Art Gallery Keel, Achill Island. 098-43325
Waterfront Gallery Harbour, Westport. 098-28406
Wright, Sue Lwr Quay, Westport. 098-27343
Yawl Art Gallery Dooega, Achill Island. 098-36137
For further information contact the arts officer at: 094-24444 (Mayo Co Council).

Meath
● **THEATRES & THEATRE COMPANIES**
The Machine Co Hilltown, Dunboyne, Co Meath. 01-8255395
No permanent theatre venue in Meath.
Culturlann na Cille c/o Gaelscoil na Cille, Ashbourne 01-835 1600 Eileen Playmon

● **MAJOR EXHIBITION VENUES**
Navan Library Navan. 046-21134
Trim Library Trim. 046-36014
Torradh Gallery Meath Co Council Civic Offices, Duleek. 01-824 0000

For further information contact the arts officer at: 01-824 0000 (Meath Co Council).

Monaghan
● **THEATRES & THEATRE COMPANIES**
Garage Theatre St Davnet's Complex, Armagh Rd, Monaghan. 047-81597
Patrick Kavanagh Rural & Literary Resource Centre Inniskeen. 042-78560

● **MAJOR EXHIBITION VENUES**
Market House Monaghan. 047-81122
Monaghan County Museum Monaghan. 047-82928
Tyrone Guthrie Centre Newbliss, Co. Monaghan. 047-54003
For further information contact the arts officer at: 047-82928 (Monaghan Co Council).

Offaly
● **THEATRES & THEATRE COMPANIES**
No theatre as yet, one is being planned for Birr at Oxmantown Hall in 2001

● **MAJOR EXHIBITION VENUES**
Tullamore Dew Heritage Centre, Tullamore *(opening in 2000)* 0506-25015
The Heritage Centre, Tullamore.
Offaly County Library Service Tullamore. 0506-21419
Libraries hold exhibitions but as yet there is no dedicated Gallery space.
For further information contact the arts officer at: 0506-46800 (Offaly Co Council).

Roscommon
● **THEATRES & THEATRE COMPANIES**
No Permanent Theatre in Roscommon - plays sometimes staged in the Abbey Hotel, Roscommon.

● **MAJOR EXHIBITION VENUES**
No Dedicated Gallery in Roscommon - exhibitions sometimes hosted in King House, Boyle and the Bank of Ireland.
For further information contact the arts officer at: 0903-37100 (Roscommon Co Council).

Sligo
● **THEATRES & THEATRE COMPANIES**
Blue Raincoat Theatre Co Lwr Quay St., Sligo. 071-70431
Factory Performance Space Lwr Quay St, Sligo. 071-70431
Hawk's Well Theatre Temple St, Sligo. 071-61526

● **MAJOR EXHIBITION VENUES**
K Studios Lwr Quay St, Sligo. 071-42552
Hawk's Well Theatre Temple St, Sligo. 071-61526
Sligo Art Gallery Yeats Memorial Building, Sligo. 071-45847
Sligo County Library *(works of J.B. Yeats)* Stephen St, Sligo.
Model Arts Centre The Mall, Sligo. 071-41405

Taylor's Art Gallery Castlebaldwin. Tel: 071-65138
Castle Studios Castle St, Sligo.
Apple Loft Studios Easkey, Co. Sligo.
For further information contact the arts officer at: 071-56629 (Sligo Co Council).

Tipperary

● **THEATRES & THEATRE COMPANIES**

Galloglass Theatre Co 30 Parnell St, Clonmel. 052-26797
Abymill Theatre Abbey St, Fethard. 052-31254
Regal Theatre Davis Rd, Clonmel 052-21689
Premier Hall Thurles.
South Tipperary Arts Centre Nelson St, Clonmel. 052-27877

● **MAJOR EXHIBITION VENUES**

Carrick-on-Suir Heritage Centre Main St, Carrick-on-Suir. 051-640 200.
Tipperary County Library Service Castle Ave, Thurles. 0504-21555
John Gleeson Auctioneers Slievnamon Rd, Thurles.
Tipperary (SR) Co. Museum Clonmel. 052-25399
For further information contact the arts officer at: 067-31771 (Tipperary Co Council, NR).

Tyrone

● **THEATRES & THEATRE COMPANIES**

Bardic Theatre Donaghmore, Co Tyrone. 01868-723 883
Cookstown Arts Centre *(opening late 1999)*

● **MAJOR EXHIBITION VENUES**

An Creagán Visitor Ctre Creggan, Omagh.
Gateway Museum Grange Court Complex, 21 Moyle Rd, Newtownstewart.
For further information contact the arts officers at: 016487-62205 (Cookstown District Council), 01868-753 626 (Dungannon District Council), 01662-245 321 (Omagh District Council), 01504--382204 (Strabane District Council).

Waterford

● **THEATRES & THEATRE COMPANIES**

Amateur Drama League of Ireland Glenagalt, Rockshire Rd, Waterford. Contact: Ms Jane Leslie 051-32680.
Blossoms Theatre-in-Education Co 11 Ashbrook Rd, Riverview, Waterford. 051-32680.
Forum Theatre The Glen, Waterford. 051-78079
Garter Lane Arts Centre 22a O'Connell St, Waterford. 051-855 038
Red Kettle Theatre Co 33 O'Connell St, Waterford. 051-79688
Theatre Royal The Mall, Waterford. 051-874 402
Waterford Youth Drama 15 Broad St, Waterford. 051-879 377

● **MAJOR EXHIBITION VENUES**

Garter Lane 22a O'Connell St, Waterford. 051-855 038

Lismore Library Lismore. 058-54128
Municipal Arts Gallery Old Greyfriars Building, Waterford.
Waterford Municipal Collection c/o Arts Office, City Mall, The Mall, Waterford. 051-873 501
For further information contact the arts officers at: 051-873 501 (Waterford Corporation), 058-41416 (Waterford Co Council).

Westmeath

● **THEATRES & THEATRE COMPANIES**

Mullingar Youth Theatre Mullingar Arts Centre.
Mullingar Arts Centre Mount St, Mullingar. 044-47777

● **MAJOR EXHIBITION VENUES**

Mullingar Arts Centre Mount St, Mullingar. 044-47777
Rothwell Gallery at Reeves Studio 33 Church St, Athlone. 0902-78507

Wexford

● **THEATRES & THEATRE COMPANIES**

Gorey Little Theatre Pearse St, Gorey. 055-21805
Red Moon Theatre Co Yoletown Studios, Killinick. 053-35014
St Michael's Theatre New Ross. 051-421 255
Theatre Royal High St, Wexford. 053-22400
Tin Drum Theatre 44 Pineridge, Wexford. 053-47453
Wexford Festival Opera c/o Theatre Royal.
Wexford Youth Theatre c/o Youth Info, Francis St, Wexford. 053-23262
Weasel Theatre Co 1 Priory Hall, Spawell Rd, Wexford. 053-23262
Buí Bolg Theatre Group 61 Sth Main St, Wexford. 053-23183
Oyster Lane Theatre Group 32 McClure Meadows, Wexford
Yellow Umbrella Theatre 124 Corish Park Wexford
Spare Cheek Theatre Co Elliot Farm Old Boley, Barntown.
Thunderhead Theatre 3 Roserock Tce, Wexford
Denis Collins Bridge Drama Co The Arts Centre Cornmarket,

● **MAJOR EXHIBITION VENUES**

Kyle Gallery Killurin.
Wexford Arts Centre Cornmarket. 053-23764
Woodland Arts & Crafts Gorey.
The Watchhouse Gallery Market Sq, Enniscorthy. 054-33543
For further information contact the arts officer at: 053-42211 (Wexford Co Council).

Wicklow

● **THEATRES & THEATRE COMPANIES**

Dry Rain Youth Theatre Dargle Rd, Bray. 01-286 6830
Wicklow Youth Theatre Wicklow Working Together Ltd, Enterprise Park, The Murrough, Wicklow Town.
Giltspur Theatre Co 71 Woodbrook Lawn, Boghall Rd, Bray.
No Permanent Theatre space in Wicklow as yet; one

planned for Bray end of 2000

● **MAJOR EXHIBITION VENUES**

Aisling Gallery Newtownmountkennedy. 01-281 9112.

The Hangman Gallery 2 Quinsboro Rd, Bray. 01-286 6208

Renaissance III County Buildings, Wicklow. *Contact Arts Officer*

Signal Art Centre & Gallery 1a Albert Ave, Bray. 01-276 2039

Arklow Community Arts Visual Arts Centre 29 Main St, Arklow. 0402-33575

Bray Heritage Centre Old Courthouse, Main St, Bray. 01-286 7128

Glendalough Visitors Centre Glendalough, Bray. 0404-45325

Tinahely Courthouse Centre Main St, Tinahely. 0402-38529

For further information contact the arts officer at: 0404-20155 (Wicklow Co Council).

CULTURE

The Irish Language

Factfile
on the Irish language

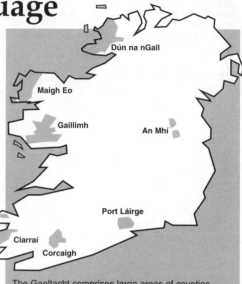

● **THE STATUS OF IRISH:** Irish is constitutionally recognised as the nation's first official language. Government policy states that every citizen has the right to conduct business with the public service through Irish.

● **ORIGIN & DEVELOPMENT OF IRISH:** Introduced by the Celts into Ireland c. 600 BC, Irish originated from the Indo-European family of languages. Around AD 400, Irish was the predominant language in the land and had expanded into areas of Britain conquered by the Irish, particularly Scotland and Wales. With the arrival of the Normans and the development of towns, English became the language of administration and law but Irish continued to be used by the predominantly rural population. However, the renewed drive to impose English in the 16th century ensured that it became the vernacular for the aristocracy, the professional and trading classes. The decline of the Irish language occurred around the time of the Famine when the population was decimated. In post-Famine times, Irish speakers comprised only 25% of the population. Other factors responsible for the decline of Irish included emigration and the fact that Irish was perceived as a language of the poor. With the emergence of various language organisations in the late 19th century and the Irish Free State in 1922, the demise of the language was halted. Modern Irish is a minority language in Ireland today, but is designated as the first language of the Republic. In the North, while the situation is improving, it has a lowlier status than, for example, Welsh in Wales, but with the establishment of North-South bodies in December 1998, one of which is to focus on Irish and Ulster Scots, this situation is set to improve. Modern Irish is grouped into three varieties: Connacht Irish, spoken by communities in Galway, Mayo and the west; Munster Irish, spoken in the south and south west; Ulster Irish, spoken in Donegal and in the north west.

● **RELATED LANGUAGES** Other Celtic languages - Scots Gaelic, Manx, Welsh, Cornish and Breton. The word for Irish - *Gaelic* - is from modern Irish or Scots Gaelic and is a form of the Old Irish *Goídelc*, which refers to an Irish-speaking Celt and is possibly Welsh in origin. However, the word *Gaelic* as a noun for Irish is generally not used in Ireland; Irish is referred to as Gaeilge.

● **EDUCATION** Around 60 Gael Linn-recognised summer colleges offer 3-week courses in Irish; the

The Gaeltacht comprises large areas of counties Donegal, Mayo, Galway and Kerry, all on the west coast, as well as smaller areas of counties Cork, Waterford and Meath.

These are the only areas in Ireland where the Irish language is the preferred spoken language. The total Irish-speaking Gaeltacht population is in excess of 61,035.

● **Irish speakers in Gaeltacht areas**

County	1996	% Irish speakers
Corcaigh *Cork*	2,756	79.9%
Dún na nGall *Donegal*	17,788	76.5%
Gaillimh *Galway*	24,994	72.7%
Ciarraí *Kerry*	6,132	78.1%
Maigh Eo *Mayo*	7,481	67.3%
An Mhí *Meath*	773	57.4%
Port Láirge *Waterford*	1,111	85.9%
TOTAL	61,035	73.8%

Department of Arts, Heritage, Gaeltacht and the Islands supports these courses, and in 1998, 20,000 people attended the summer courses. The number of Gaelscoileanna (Irish medium schools) has risen from 17 in 1977 to 117 in 1998. There are 276 naíonraí (pre-schools) in operation at present. Over 24,000 young people participate in Gaeltacht summer courses each year. Over 2,000 students are currently studying Irish at third level. *See Education Chapter.* There is an estimated figure of over 10,000 adult learners.

● **USE OF IRISH:** According to the latest census figures (1996), 43.5% of the population or 1,430,205 people recorded themselves as having an ability to speak Irish. There is an even distribution of Irish speakers throughout the country, not just in Gaeltacht areas. However, many users were of school-going age, while most of the adult population (20–44 years) rarely or never used Irish. This leads to the conclusion that Irish is perceived as part of the education sector (Irish is a core curriculum subject; most students are required to study Irish from 4 to 18 years). Outside of this sector, the language is more evident in its symbolic rather than day-to-day usage. Outside Ireland, in Europe, Irish is the only official language of a member state that does not share equal status with other official languages. However, the ratification of the Maastricht Treaty gave EU citizens the right to communicate with EU institutions in Irish. In addition, the European Bureau for Lesser Used Languages provides support for Irish.

● **USE OF IRISH LANGUAGE IN THE MEDIA:** TG4 (formerly Teilifís na Gaeilge) attracts around 335,000 viewers daily. Raidió na Gaeltachta, the Irish language radio station broadcasts to Irish speakers nationwide. RTÉ (Raidió Teilifís Éireann) allots a certain amount of time to Irish language broadcasting on both radio and television. Raidió na Life, the Irish Language community station in Dublin, enjoys a listenership of over 20,000. With regard to newspapers, Foinse, the Irish language weekly newspaper, sells over 7,000 copies of each edition. Lá, an Irish newspaper, is published in Belfast. The Irish Times, (circulation 112,600), prints weekly columns in Irish, and Irish Networks and exchanges can now be found on the Internet.

Source: Bord na Gaeilge

Written Irish

● **OGHAM ALPHABET:** Irish is one of the oldest written languages in Europe - its earliest surviving form being ogham. Most ogham inscriptions date back to the fifth and sixth centuries. In ogham, the letters of the alphabet are represented by differing numbers of

● **TEXT:** In early Irish manuscripts, Irish writing took the form of the minuscule Latin script which was used throughout Europe. Even when others changed, Irish scribes continued with this style, and in time it came to be known as Irish script. This form was used right into the 20th century, but was phased out of primary schools by 1964 and secondary schools by 1970. The earliest manuscript text is seen in part of the *Codex Wirziburgensis,* dating back before AD 700. A substantial body of literature followed during the period AD 700–850, with religious and secular verse, prose, homilies, history, law, and commentaries on the Bible. Most surviving manuscripts date to the 11th century and the centuries that followed, but many refer back to earlier texts. This period saw the use of Middle Irish, which was distinguished by the assimilation of Norse. After 1150, Classical Modern Irish emerged with the introduction of a new class of hereditary lay scholars (previously, writing was exclusively the province of monks). Verse compositions by this professional bardic class form most of the writings of this time and include poems dedicated to patrons, and love poetry, as well as stories referring to Fionn Mac Cumhaill and his Oisín. Following the dissolution of many Irish institutions during the 17th century, Irish writing became more fragmented and adopted local idioms. With its revitalisation in Ireland in the 20th century, written Irish was officially standardised. The standardised spelling and morphological forms, compiled by the mid-20th century, is referred to as the *Caighdeán.* Today, written Irish, particularly poetry, is thriving. The two Irish-language publishing houses and the official department of education publishers, An Gúm, print many works. There are over 3,000 Irish books currently in print and over 100 new titles are published each year. Irish language plays are produced on a regular basis by Amharclann de híde, the professional Irish language Theatre Company. The Arts Council and the Northern Ireland Arts Council both support Irish literary efforts through grants to writers, writer-in-residence schemes, publications and publishers, festivals and prizes.

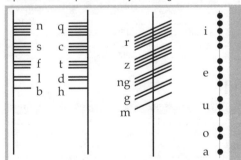

Explanation to Ogham Alphabet

Right-hand side of tree: 'n' 5 strokes, 's' 4 strokes 'f' 3 strokes 'l' 2 strokes 'b' 1 stroke

Left-hand side of tree: 'q' 5 strokes, 'c' 4 strokes 't' 3 strokes 'd' 2 strokes 'h' 1 stroke

Diagonals through the tree: 'r' 5 strokes, 'z' 4 strokes 'ng' 3 strokes 'g' 2 strokes 'm' 1 stroke

Stops on the tree: 'i' 5 dots, 'e' 4 dots, 'u' 3 dots, 'o' 2 dots, 'a' 1 dot.

Source: Bord na Gaeilge

strokes and dots. It is thought to have been a codified form of the Latin alphabet (its relationship with Latin is similar to that between Morse Code and the modern alphabet) and it may have later influenced Irish orthography in the Latin alphabet. It would have been used primarily on stone monuments, but it could have also been used for short texts on wood and bone.

Irish and non-Irish speakers by province

Region by Speakers	1861	1901	1926	1946	1961	1971	1981	1996	% speakers
Connacht									
Irish	409,482	245,580	175,209	154,187	148,708	137,372	155,134	201,195	
Population	913,135	646,932	552,907	492,797	419,465	390,902	424,410	433,231	46.4
Leinster									
Irish	35,704	26,436	101,474	180,755	274,644	341,702	473,225	689,703	
Population	147,635	1,152,829	1,149,092	281,117	1,332,149	1,498,140	1,790,521	1,924,702	35.8
Munster									
Irish	545,531	276,268	198,221	189,395	228,726	252,805	323,704	451,129	
Population	1,513,558	1,076,188	969,902	917,306	849,203	882,002	998,315	1,033,903	43.6
Ulster*									
Irish	86,370	71,426	68,607	64,388	64,342	57,550	66,350	88,178	
Population	517,783	345,874	300,091	263,887	217,524	207,204	230,159	234,251	37.6
TOTAL									
Irish	1,077,087	619,710	543,511	588,725	716,420	789,429	1,018,413	1,430,205	
Population	4,402,111	3,221,823	2,971,992	2,955,107	2,818,341	2,978,248	3,443,405	3,626,087	39.4

Source CSO and Bord na Gaeilge

* From 1926 this refers to counties Cavan, Donegal and Monaghan only. According to the 1991 Northern Ireland Census, 142,003 people over the age of three - approximately 10% of Northern Ireland's population - claim to have some knowledge of Irish. This brings the total number of people with some knowledge of Irish in Ulster to approx. 230,181.

Irish speakers by Age Group

Age Group	3-4	5-9	10-14	15-19	20-24	25-34	35-44	45-54	55-64	65+
Irish Speakers	10%	48%	68%	68%	52%	37%	39%	37%	32%	27%
Numbers	5,471	126,286	209,954	221,561	145,000	186,660	190,202	146,045	90,870	105,156

Source CSO and Bord na Gaeilge

Ability to Speak Irish

Level of ability	1995	1996	1998
Very good	4%	5%	6%
Fairly good	18%	17%	19%
Little ability	41%	42%	43%
No ability	37%	36%	33%

Source Bord na Gaeilge IMS Survey

Ability to Speak Irish by Age Group

Age Group	Fairly good ability	Little / no ability
U-25 years	43%	15%
25–34 years	15%	20%
35–49 years	22%	29%
50+ years	20%	35%

Source Bord na Gaeilge IMS Survey

Frequency of Speaking Irish

Frequency	1993	1995	1998
Daily - several times a week	11%	13%	11%
Once a week	4%	4%	5%
Once a month	4%	5%	4%
Less often	17%	20%	21%
Never	64%	58%	59%

Source Bord na Gaeilge IMS Survey

Roots of Irish Place Names

Ireland contains around 60,000 townlands, each with their own name, and each townland has on average, 20–30 place names, which means that there are literally millions of placenames in Ireland. Most of them describe natural features, land ownership or man-made structures. The following are examples of the more common prefixes and suffixes to Irish placenames.

a

Abha/Abhainn: river. e.g. Awbeg *Abha Bheag* - Little river.
Achadh: field. *Achadh Mór* - Big field. sometimes spelt agha.
Ard: height. *Ardachadh* - the high field
Áth/Átha: ford. Dublin *Baile Átha Cliath* - the town of the hurdle ford.

b

Bádhún: cow fortress (bó dhún), anglicised as bawn. Bawnboy *Bádhún Buí* - the yellow bawn.
Baile: town / townland, anglicised as Bally. Ballinakill *Baile na Coille* - townland of the wood.
Beag: little. Magherabeg *Machaire Beag* - little plain.
Béal: mouth / opening. Bealaha *Béal Átha* - mouth of the ford.
Bealach: road / passage. Baltinglass *Bealach Conglais* - Conglas' Pass.
Beann: mountain peak. Benbulbin *Beann Ghulbain* - Gulban's peak.
Bearna: gap. Barnesmore *Bearnas Mór* - the large gap
Bearna: gap. Barnesmore *Bearnas Mór* - the large gap
Bóthar: road. Boherboy *Bóthar Buí* - the yellow road.
Bruach: bank (of a river). Broughshane *Bruach Sheáin* - Seán's bank.
Buaile: summer pastures / milking place. Boolananave *Buaile na nDamh* - the oxen's milking place.
Buí: yellow. Owenboy *Abhann Bhuí* - the yellow river.

c

Cabhán: valley/hollow, e.g. Cavan.
Caiseal: stone fort, e.g. Cashel.
Caisleán: castle. Castleconnell *Caisleán Uí Chonaill* - Castle of the O' Connells.
Caol: narrow. Kerrykeel *Ceathrú Chaol* - the narrow quarter.
Carn: mound of stones, usually refers to neolithic passage tombs. Carnlough *Carnlach* - place of the cairns.

Cathair:

Cathair: stone fort. Caherdaniel *Cathair Dónaill* - Donal's stone fort.
Ceann: head. Kinsale *Cionn tSáile Beag* - head of the salt water.
Ceathrú: quarter. Carrowkeel *Ceathrú Chaol* - the narrow quarter.
Ceis: wickerwork, usually refers to a wooden road, e.g. Kesh.
Cill: Church. Kildare *Cill Dara* - church of the oak tree.
Cladach: shore, e.g. the Claddagh in Galway city.
Clár: level area or plain. Ballyclare *Bealach Cláir* - the pass of the plain.
Cloch: stone. Clochan *Clochán* - stony place.
Cluain: meadow. Clontarf *Cluain Tarbh* - meadow of the bulls.
Cnoc: hill. Knockboy *Cnoc Buí* - the yellow hill.
Coill/Coillte: wood. Kiltyclogher *Coillte Clochar* - woods of the stony place.
Crann: tree. Cranmore *Crann Mór* - the big tree.
Creag/Creagán: crag, e.g. Cregg and Creggan.
Cuan: bay or harbour, e.g. Coon.
Cúl: back, usually refers to a hill. Coolmore *Cúl Mór* - the big hill.

d

Daragh: oak. Adare *Áth Dara* - ford of the oak.
Doire: oak grove, anglicised to derry, as in Derry city.
Droichead: bridge. Drogheda *Droichead Átha* - bridge of the ford.
Droim: ridge. Drumcondra *Droim Conrach* - ridge of the path.
Dún: fort. Dunlavin *Dún Luáin* - Luán's fort.

e

Éadan: brow. Edenderry *Éadan Doire* - brow of the oak grove.
Éanach: marsh. Raheny *Ráth Eanaigh* - fort of the marsh.
Eiscir: ridge, now used in geology to describe such features from the Ice Age, e.g. Esker.
Eiscir: ridge, now used in geology to describe such features from the Ice Age, e.g. Esker.

Eo:

Eo: yew tree. Mayo *Maigh Eo* - plain of the yew tree.

f

Fada: long. Drumfad *Droim Fhada* - the long ridge.
Fearn: alder. Glenfarne *Gleann Fearna* - glen of the alders.
Fiodh: wood. Finnea *Fiodh an Átha* - the high wood,
Fionn: white. Finglas *Fionn Ghlas* - white stream.

g

Gallán: standing stone. Aghagallon *Achadh an Ghalláin* - field of the standing stone.
Gaoth: inlet. Gweesalia *Gaoth Sáile* - inlet of the sea.
Garbh: rough. Glengarriff *Gleann Garbh* - the rough valley.
Glas: small stream or grey-green. Glasnevin *Glas Naíon* - the child's stream. Glaslough *Glasloch* - grey-green lake.
Gleann: glen. Glendalough *Glean dá Locha* - glen of the two lakes.
Gort: field. Gorteen *Gortín* - little field.
Gráig: small settlement. Graiguenamanagh *Gráig na Manach* - small settlement of the monks.

i

Inbhear: estuary. Inveran *Inbhearán* - the little estuary.
Inis: island. Inishmore *Inis Mór* - the big island.

l

Lag: hollow. Lagan *Lagán* - the little hollow.
Leaba: bed or grave. Labbacallee *Leaba Callighe* - hag's bed.
Leath: half or portion. Lahinch *Leath Inse* - half island or penninsula.
Léim: leap. Limavady *Léim an Mhadaigh* - leap of the dog.
Leitir: hillside. Letterkenny *Leitir Ceanain* - the hillside of Cannanan.

Liag: flagstone. Duleek *Damhliag -* stone church.

Lios: houses enclosed by a rampart or fort. Lismore *Lios Mór -* Big fort.

Loch: lake. Loughrea *Lochch Ria -* grey lake.

(I)

Machaire/Magh: plain. Moycullen *Magh Cuilinn -* plain of holly.

Mainistir: monastery. Monasterevin *Mainistir Eimhín -* Eimhín's monstery.

Mín: smooth area. Meenmore *Mín Mór -* large smooth area.

Móna: bog. Ballymoney *Baile Mónaidh -* townland of bog.

Muileann: mill. Mullingar *Muileann Cearr -* crooked mill.

Mullach: high point. Mullaghmore *Mullach Mór -* the big summit.

P

Páirc: field. Parkreagh *Páirc Riabhach -* striped field.

Poll: hole/pool. Poulaphuca *Poll an Phúca -* pool of the goblin.

Port: port or bank. Portumna *Port Omna -* port of the tree-trunk

---

R

Ráth: earthen fort. Ratoath *Ráth Tó*

- Tó's fort.

Ria: striped or grey. Castlereagh *Caisleán Riabhach -* grey castle.

Rinn: height, point. Rinvyle *Rinn Mhaoile -* height of the bald man.

Rón: seal. Shinrone *Suí an Róin -* the seal's seat.

Ros: promontory or grove. Roscommon *Ros Comáin -* Comán's grove.

Rua: red. Carraroe *Ceathrú Rua -* the red quarter.

S

Sceach: hawthorn. Ballinaskeagh *Baile na Sceach -* townland of the hawthorn.

Sceir: reef, e.g. Skerries.

Sean: old. Shangarry *Seangharraí -* old garden.

Seisceann: marsh. Seskinryan *Seisceann Ríain -* Rían's marsh.

Sliabh: mountain. Slievenamon *Sliabh na mBan -* the women's mountain.

Spidéal: hospital. Ballinspittal *Béal Átha an Spidéil -* the hospital at the mouth of the ford.

Sruth: stream. Ballyshrule *Baile Sruthail -* the townland of the stream.

T

Tamhlact: a burial site. Tallaght

Tamlacht *Maolruáin -* Maolruain's burial site, refers to an ancient Bronze Age burial ground.

Teach: house. Timolin *Tigh Moling -* the house of St Moloing.

Teampall: church. Templemore *Teampall Mór -* the big church.

Tearmann: sanctuary. Termonfechin *Tearmann Feichín -* St Feichín's sanctuary.

Tír: territory. Tyrone *Tír Eoghain -* Eoghan's territory.

Tobar: well. Tubbercurry *Tobar an Choire -* well of the cauldron.

Tóchar: causeway. Ballintogher *Baile an Tóchair -* townland of the causeway.

Trá: beach or strand. Tramore *Trá Mhór -* the big strand.

Tulach: hill. Tullamore *Tulach Mhór -* the big hill.

U

Uaimh: cave. Ballywee *Baile Uaimh -* the townland of caves or cave system.

Uisce: water. Lissaniska *Lios an Uisce -* fort of the water.

Irish Dance

Factfile on Irish Dancing

to Queen Elizabeth's court. One of these was an adaptation of an old Irish peasant dance - the Trenchmore. Another style of dance dating from this time was the Hey - a forerunner of the present day reel.

● **PRE-CHRISTIAN** The earliest reference to dance in Ireland alluded to the Druids, who performed dances honouring the oak tree and the sun. Traces of their circular dances survive in the ring dances of today. When the Celts arrived in Ireland more than 2,000 years ago, they introduced their own folk dances.

● **MEDIEVAL** The 12th century saw the introduction of Norman customs and dances. One of the first written references to Irish dance is in a letter from Sir Henry Sydney to Queen Elizabeth I in 1569. Sydney referred to girl dancers as "very beautiful, magnificently dressed and first class dancers". The dancers formed two straight lines, suggesting they performed an early version of the Rínce Fada.

● **ENGLISH** By the mid-16th century, some of the dances were adapted by English invaders and brought

● **18TH & 19TH CENTURY** The dancing master - a nomadic teacher who travelled around a district - appeared during this period. Each dancing master had his own district and never encroached on that of others; this led to several versions of the same dance emerging from different parts of Ireland, adding to the repertory of Irish dances. The masters introduced group dances to hold the interest of less gifted pupils and giving them the chance to dance. Group set dancing grew from Quadrilles and Lancers, popular forms of dance in Europe, brought to Ireland in the 19th century by Irish soldiers who fought with European armies. Solo dancers were held in high esteem and often doors were taken off hinges and placed on the ground for them to dance on. Céilis - informal evenings of dancing - can be traced back to pre-famine times, when dancing at the cross-roads was a popular rural pastime on summer evenings.

● **20th CENTURY** In 1893 the Gaelic League was founded and encouraged the revival of Irish culture, including dance. The League set up the Irish Dancing Commission, *An Coimisiúin le Rincí Gaelacha*, in 1929 to address local dance variations and establish governing rules. During the 20th century, Irish dance evolved in terms of location, costumes, dance technique and larger stages. As stages became larger, the movement and dance steps of dancers increased. The location of competitions moved from outdoors to predominately indoor locations such as hotels and school halls. Solo dancing changed from being male-dominated to female-dominated (girls dancing solos in competition were rare before the 1920s). Dance styles also evolved; arms and hands were not always held rigid. It seems that conservative mores brought about rigidly-held arms. Hand movements still occur in group dances and modern choreography, as in Riverdance. Today, jigs, reels, hornpipes, sets, half sets, polkas and step dances are all performed.

● **ACCESSORIES** Dance costume has changed greatly: In the 1800s, dance masters wore hats, swallowtail coats, knee breeches, white stockings, and black shoes with silver buckles probably similar to today's hard shoes. With the 1893 revival in Irish culture, the search for a traditional Irish costume began. Pipers adopted the kilt which older male dancers later adopted in the 1910s and 1920s. Today, male dancers wear either kilts or pants. In the 1800s, female dancers wore ordinary dresses and ribbons. After 1893, the typical dance costume consisted of a hooded cloak over a white dress with a sash. By the 1930s the cloak was dropped in place of a shawl which is worn on the back of costumes and attached by brooches or pins. Colors were predominately green, white and saffron on early costumes. In recent times, all colors have come into use. Embroidery, which was minimal in the early 1900s, has steadily increased in use and complexity. Designs were originally based on the ornate strap-work from the Book of Kells, Irish stone crosses, and chalices. Designers are now introducing modern interpretations and patterns and using silver and gold thread in the embroidery. Early descriptions of dancers sometimes noted they were barefoot. Soft shoes were introduced around 1924 for girls dancing reels, jigs, and slip jigs. Boys also adopted their use, but dropped them by the 1970s. Hard shoes have also evolved. Previously, nail heads were used and dancers inserted coins between sole and toe tip to increase loudness. Dancers have now adopted fibreglass toe tips and hollow heels which give much louder taps, changing the emphasis and content of many dances.

● **TODAY** The world-wide success of Riverdance and Lord of the Dance has placed Irish dance on the international stage. Dancing schools in Ireland today are filled with young pupils keen to imitate and learn the dancing styles which brought Jean Butler and Michael Flatley international acclaim. There is also huge interest in Ireland in group set dancing.

● **OTHER COUNTRIES IN WHICH IRISH DANCING IS PRACTICED** Wherever Irish people have emigrated to and settled; this includes the England, Scotland, the US, Australia, Canada, New Zealand.

● **MAIN COMPETITIONS** The Feis is an important part of Irish dance, with group and solo competitions where dancers are graded by age. All four provinces hold dancing championships, and winners of these competitions qualify for the All Ireland Championships. There are also Regional Qualifying Championships held worldwide. The All-Ireland Dancing Championships - Oireachtas Rince na hÉireann - and World Dancing Championships - Oireachtas Rince na Cruinne, established in 1969, are held around Easter, allowing dancers from Ireland, England, USA, Canada, Australia and New Zealand to compete.

● **AN COIMISIÚIN LE RINCÍ GAELACHA** founded by the Gaelic League, it organises and develops the practice of Irish dancing, creates and sets standards for Feiseanna and preserves and promotes its activity as an international organisation. It published the first handbooks detailing the movement of Ceilí dancing in 1939.

● **NUMBERS OF PARTICIPANTS** There are estimated at 200,000 competitors in Irish dance with the ratio of female to male dancers being around 5 to 1.

● **NUMBERS OF TEACHERS** 500 registered in Ireland, 1,300 registered worldwide, including Canada, US, Australia, New Zealand and Britain (this compares to 100 teachers in 1950, which shows how popular Irish dancing has become, helped in no small way with the massive success of *Riverdance - The Show* and Michael Flatley's *Lord of the Dance*

● **NEXT WORLD DANCING CHAMPIONSHIPS** 21–27th April, 2000, in Belfast.

Source: An Coimisiúin le Rincí Gaelacha.

Results - World Dancing Championships

Held in Ennis Co Clare, 27th March - 4th April, 1999, this competition is the biggest in Irish Dancing. There were around 4,000 spectators alone at these Dancing Championships, with competitors arriving from all over the world

Competition	Winner	Dancing School
Men over 21	Raymond Walls	McCaul Academy, Derry
Men 19–21	Conor Holmes	Costello/O'Brien, Limerick
Men 17–19	Nicholas Fallon	King, Merseyside
Boys 15–17	Michael Belvitch	O'Hare, Chicago
Boys 13–15	Alan Kennefick	Cowhie Ryan, Cork

➤ *Continued from previous page*

Competition	Winner	Dancing School
Boys 11–13	James Keegan	Lally, Manchester
Boys 10–11	David Lydon	Costello/O'Brien, Limerick
Women over 21	Noelle Curran	Smith, New Jersey
Women 19–21	Amy Siegel	Smith, New Jersey
Girls 17–19	Deborah O'Keeffe	Cowhie Ryan, Cork
Girls 16–17	Erin Davidson	Oirialla, Dundalk
Girls 15–16	Eimear Murphy	Cadwell Cawte, BÁC
Girls 14–15	Stephanie Power	Costello/O'Brien, Limerick
Girls 13–14	Joanne Kavanagh	McConomy, Derry
Girls 12–13	Ellie Maguire	Maguire O'Shea, London
Girls 11–12	Elaine McConomy-Bradley	McConomy, Derry
Girls 10–11	Tanya Crooks	Donnelly, Belfast
Mixed Céilí under 13	Foireann A	Doherty, Coventry
Girls Céilí under 13	Foireann B	NCOB, Drogheda
Mixed Céilí 13–16	Foireann A	Kiely Walsh, Cork
Girls Céilí 13–16	Foireann B	McLaughlin, Glasgow
Mixed Céilí over 16	Foireann A	McLaughlin, Glasgow
Girls Céilí over 16	Foireann A	McLaughlin, Glasgow
Rince Foirne mixed under 13	Foireann A	Doherty, Coventry
Foirne mixed 13–16	Foireann A	Griffin-O'Loughlin, London
Foirne Girls 13–16	Foireann A	Doherty, Coventry
Foirne mixed over 16	Foireann A	McLaughlin, Glasgow
Foirne mixed over 16	Foireann A	Setanta, Scotland
Damhasdráma	Foireann B	Scoil Rince Dalriada, Belfast

Source: An Coimisiúin le Rincí Gaelacha.

Irish Music

Factfile on Irish Music

● **INTRODUCTION** Irish traditional music includes many types of singing and instrumental music, music of many periods, and performers from Ireland and abroad. However, it all belongs to a common 'oral' tradition, whereby the music is created and performed and carried and preserved in the memory. This means the nature of human memory governs the music's form.

● **REPERTORY** Being oral music, Irish traditional music changes much more than notation-based music. Although most pieces originate from individuals, pieces, after as they pass from performer to performer, becoming the sum of many performances. Change, however, occurs at a slow pace, in accordance with generally accepted principles, and older musical pieces are accorded higher status, with most material coming from the past. Repertories and styles evolved in different regions, and in most regions in Ireland there is a degree of specialisation in certain music - fiddle playing or flute playing, or singing in Irish, and so on, will predominate.

● **INFLUENCES** Irish traditional music is a music of rural origins, but many items and forms of the repertory have come from towns and cities or through them from abroad. It closely resembles other Western European traditional music in its structure, rhythmic pattern, pitch, arrangement, themes of songs, etc. Most of the repertory dates back as far as the 18th and 19th centuries, while some is even earlier in origin, and it is

possible that a number of very old tunes and lyrics have been adapted to modern forms. Printed and manuscript song and music has had an influence on the tradition since at least the 18th century, and throughout the 20th century sound recordings, radio and television have played a part in transmitting the music.

● **TRANSMISSION** The music is passed on from one performer to another, through imitation of more experienced performers. But today, learning also takes place in groups organised for teaching, and occasionally within the school system. Written words or music are only used as an aid to memory, if at all, and never in performance. Most singers don't read music, but many players make some use of notation.

● **PERFORMANCE** Much traditional music is performed almost entirely for recreation, by people who are normally unpaid. There are relatively few full-time professional performers. Solo performance is central to the tradition, but group performance is common. It is played in the home, in the public house and at other social gatherings - parties, weddings, dances, festivals, at concerts, and on radio, television and record.

● **INSTRUMENTAL MUSIC** consists mostly of dance music: reels, jigs, hornpipes, polkas, set dances, mazurkas. Dance music is used for both solo and group dancing. The tunes are played at a fast tempo and are "belted out" for the set, but even in this case the musician will usually try to give tunes that little bit extra in rhythm (called "lift" or "swing") which will add to the dancing. Only a small proportion of the music is made up of slow airs, usually song tunes and planxties (harpers' pieces which date back to the 17th or 18th centuries). Melodies are generally played in one or two sharps, and belong to one of a number of melodic modes, which have mostly seven notes to the scale, but sometimes six or five. Their range does not frequently exceed two octaves, and they end on a variety of final notes. The instruments used for dance music are usually the fiddle, accordion, the Tin Whistle, flute, uilleann pipes, and concertina; percussion instruments rarely feature. Other instruments played in the performance of Irish music include the Banjo, Mandolin, Bodhran, Bones, Spoons, Bouzouki, Guitar, the Harp, the Hammer Dulcimer and Bagpipes. All are forms of instruments found in Western Europe.

● **SINGING** is normally unaccompanied, particularly sean-nós singing. Unison singing, in duet particularly, is common. Instruments are played in unison in combinations of any number. Harmonic accompaniment when possible on an instrument, is generally of a simple kind. Songs are performed in Irish and English, but the more recent songs in English are more widespread. Songs can be quick or slow, strict or relaxed in rhythm.

● **SEAN-NÓS** is a specific style of unaccompanied singing in the Irish language. The three main styles of sean-nós originate from the three Gaeltacht areas: Munster (parts of Cork, Kerry, and Waterford), Connacht (Galway and Mayo) and Ulster (Donegal). The most obvious difference between the styles, is between the Ulster style and the other two. Donegal sean-nós is heavily influenced by Scots Gaelic song, which is less ornamental than sean-nós, while the Munster and Connacht styles are highly ornamented, both with the forms familiar to a traditional instrumentalist and with other more complex forms.

● **GETTING TO HEAR IRISH TRADITIONAL MUSIC** Irish traditional music can be heard in clubs and public houses, and occasionally at local concerts, competitions and festivals. In many parts of the country informal 'sessions', or mixed gatherings of musicians, perform regularly for their own enjoyment. All branches of Comhaltas Ceoltóirí Éireann run regular sessions. Sessions are also held in most Tithe Cheoil and Cultúrlann na hÉireann in Dublin every week throughout the year. Admission is usually free. Concerts of traditional music, or including traditional music, are commonly held throughout the country. Occasionally public recitals by one or two performers are held by non-commercial sponsors such as the Irish World Music Centre at the University of Limerick.

● **ORGANISATION** Comhaltas Ceoltóirí Éireann (CCÉ) is the main body responsible for Irish traditional music and culture. It organises most fleadhs around the country, the first of which (in recent history) was held in 1951. Soon after, the county and the provincial fleadhanna were established. Since then, regional fleadhanna and national fleadhanna in Britain and the US have become annual events. Another import service offered by CCÉ is concert tours abroad. These tours showcase the best in Irish music. CCÉ also holds a national music archive, housed at Cultúrlann na hÉireann, which contains over 4,000 hours of edited material. The CCÉ is in the process of setting up regional archives both in Ireland and overseas. The Co Clare Archive is located in Ennis and others are being located in Westmeath, Tyrone, Sligo, Kerry, Wexford and Tipperary. The following statistics refer to CCÉ activities:

● **NO. OF BRANCHES** 400 (in every county in Ireland, Britain, US, Canada, Australia, Japan, Hungary, Sardinia, Italy).

● **NO. OF CLASSES** More than 600 music classes organised by Comhaltas each week.

● **NO. OF IRISH MUSIC TEACHERS** More than 400 teachers have now qualified (with the TTCT qualification).

● **QUALIFICATIONS AVAILABLE FOR TEACHING IRISH MUSIC** The TTCT - Diploma for traditional music teachers; Performance Certs Through Fás and City & Guilds for musicians, singers and dancers; MA in Irish Traditional Music Performance through the Irish World Music Centre.

● **FLEADHANNA CHEOIL** 44 Fleadhanna Cheoil each year, with over 25,000 competitors taking part

● **FLEADH CHEOIL NA hÉIREANN** The Fleadh, founded in 1951, developed as a competitive event. It grew through the 1960s and 1970s, and eventually qualifying stages had to be arranged, at county and provincial level to cope with large number of potential competitors. Today, almost 50 years later, around 20,000 performers compete in Fleadhanna each year. The Fleadh Cheoil remains biggest, with competitors and onlookers coming from all over the world to participate in competitions in music, dance, singing and the Irish language.

● **CEOL AN GHEIMHRIDH** (March) All-Ireland Finals for the inter-branch competitions held at county and provincial levels.

● **FLEADH NUA** (to be held in Ennis, Co Clare - 25th to 29th May 2000) celebrates 27 years in Ennis and is the first fleadh of the new millennium. The five-day festival includes sessions, céilís and concerts, dancing championships, scoraíocht and pléarácha competitions, lectures and films, a street parade, and workshops in traditional music, singing, set dance and storytelling.

● **CEOLTRAI** A new Comhaltas Winter Competition, which will have competitions at county level for singing, storytelling (in Irish and English) and dancing.

● **FLEADH AMHRÁN & RINCE** (held in Ballycastle, Co Antrim in June) The emphasis of this fleadh is on traditional singing and dancing and includes the inter-provincial set-dance competition.

● **CONCERT TOURS** date back to 1972 when the first official North American Tour took place. It was followed by the Tour of Britain (1973) and the Tour of Ireland (1980). These three tours are now well-established in the music calendar. Other successful tours include the 1997 Tour of Australia and the 1998 Tour of China by

the Brú Ború Group from Cashel.

● **VENUES** Cultúrlann, Dublin; Bru Boru, Tipperary;

● **SCOIL ÉIGSE** a five-day summer school held the week leading up to Fleadh Cheoil na hÉireann in the host town, which offers tuition in all aspects of Irish traditional music, song, and dance.)

Irish Folklore

Factfile on Irish Folklore

● **ORIGINS:** The cultural data transmitted in Irish folklore was accrued both from the indigenous Irish and the successive waves of invaders - Vikings, Normans, Scots and English - and was passed on through a special learned caste - the poets or filí - who where held in high esteem in Irish society. Their enjoyed patronage under the Gaelic chiefs and later, the Norman-Gaelic lords. Although their songs focused on stories and people, they were also thought to contain mystical knowledge that had magical effects.

● **LITERARY ROOTS:** Irish folklore's literary roots date back to the 6th century AD and flourished until the 17th century, when the suppression of all native forms of learning was rigorously enforced by the British overlords.

● **TRANSMISSION:** The early forms of transmission had an elaborate and highly rhetorical style while the oral tradition followed a distinctive highly stylised form, the rhythm and metre of which made it easy to remember for speaking. Indeed, many of the early poems were sung or chanted to the accompaniment of the harps on special occasions. Evidence also suggests that songs were created for everyday life (focusing on various events, work and laments), which were composed with a less complicated rhythm and metre.

During the medieval era, poets borrowed motifs freely from continental troubadour poetry, particularly on the themes of chivalry and love, and incorporated them into the native poems. From the 17th century onwards, the poet's place in society declined. The filí composed more popular stressed rhymes known as *amhrán* (meaning 'song') in Irish as they began to live among the Gaelic peasants. It was around this time, that poems of praise or satire (usually targeting those who were authoritarian, mean or pompous) became popular. A prime example of this type of satire (in this case, a social satire) is Brian Merriman's epic, *Cúirt an Mhean Oíche* - the Midnight Court (1780).

● **THEMES WITHIN IRISH FOLKLORE:**

Genealogical data and litanies on the origins of various names and place names.

Mythologic and historic stories including the adventures of the famous seer-warrior, Finn Mac Cumhaill, his son Oisín, who was spellbound by a beautiful woman and lived with her for 300 hundred

years in Tír na nÓg, the god Lugh, the hero warrior Cú Chulainn, in addition to a pantheon of other warriors and princesses.

Local patron saints whose feats could have been adapted from earlier Celtic deities, and whose feast days are still celebrated at holy wells and other places of pilgrimage around the country (for example, the climbing of Croagh Patrick on the last Sunday in July).

Fairies or the Sí who were created by the early Celts, possibly as explanations of the afterlife. Medieval literature refers to the fairies as the *Tuatha Dé Dannan* (the people of the Goddess Danu). Various phenomena in the country's topography were (and are still) attributed to the fairies - a prime example of this being raths, the ancient round forts that are found all over the country.

International tales including stories of men who marry mermaids, and fairy women, changelings, trickster type tales and stories focusing on local animals and wildlife.

Tales of the supernatural these are concerned with various spirits and ghosts (such as priests who have not celebrated a mass during their lifetime but are condemned to haunt a church or area until they celebrate it), but particularly the banshee, a female spirit which follows families who have an Ó or Mac in their surname. Her terrible keening crying portends the arrival of a death in these families.

As well as this strong emphasis on story and song, the Irish also celebrate festivals of saints; again these were probably adapted from earlier Celtic rituals. These include St Brigid's Day (the 1st of February), May Eve, St. John's Night (or Midsummer's Eve), Lughnasa (in August), Samhain (or Hallowe'en) and many more.

For further information on folklore, See Irish cultural agencies - Department of Irish Folklore, UCD. pastimes.

Profile of Cultural Agencies

BORD NA GAEILGE *7 Cearnóg Mhuirfean, Baile Átha Cliath 2.* **email** eolas@bnag.ie **Tel** 01-639 8400. **Profile** A state board appointed to draft and advise the government on Irish language policies and to promote the language and all its aspects at all levels. Other work includes book distribution and community development projects.

BRÚ BORÚ THEATRE Cashel, Co Tipperary. **email** bruboru@comhaltas.com **Tel** 062-61122 **Established** 1990 **Profile** Located at the foot of the historic Rock of Cashel, Additional Services: Facilities at Brú Ború include a folk theatre, craft centre, information centre, and genealogy suite. From June to September, Brú Ború presents performances of traditional music, song and dance.

AN COIMISIÚIN LE RINCÍ GAELACHA *6 Harcourt Street, Dublin 2.* **email** clrg@tinet.ie **Tel** 01-475 2220. **Established** 1929 **Profile** An Coimisiúin is the governing body in Irish dancing. It organises both the All-Ireland and World Irish Dancing Championships annually.

COMHALTAS CEOLTÓIRÍ ÉIREANN *32 Belgrave Square, Monkstown, Co. Dublin.* Web www.comhaltas.com **email** enquiries@comhaltas.com **Tel** 01-280 0295 **Established** 1951 **Profile** An Irish cultural movement, it promotes Irish traditional music, song, dance and language, through education and performance, both nationally and internationally.

COMHALTAS ULADH *47 Glendale Belfast BT10 0NX* **Tel** 01232-612 707 **Established** 1926 **Profile** covers the ancient province of Ulster, Leathcuinn, which includes the nine counties of Ulster plus Louth. An apolitical body, it focuses on language activities and has 66 local branches, throughout the 10 counties. It runs competitions in spoken Irish at schools; organises summer schools in the Donegal Gaeltacht as well as in schools in Ulster; and publishes books, music, and monthly magazine *An tUltach* (The Ulsterman), established 1924. An index of articles in An Ultach by article and author has been created and a complete unbroken listing of the magazine has been established at Queen's University.

COMHCHOISTE NÁISIÚNTA NA GCOLÁISTÍ SAMHRAIDH Tel 066-915 6100. **Established** 1951. **Profile** The overall body representative of more than 60 summer colleges which organises three-week Irish courses over the summer months, mainly in the Gaeltacht areas.

COMHDHÁIL NÁISIÚNTA NA GAEILGE *46 Kildare Street, Dublin 2.* **email** gachduine@comhdhail.ie **Tel** 01-679 4780. **Established** 1943 **Profile** The steering council of the Irish language, it promotes different voluntary bodies, providing a forum for the exchange of ideas and information, politically and publicly. It

aims to strengthen and consolidate support for the Irish language, so that it remains a living language used in all areas of Irish life. Its activities cover the fields of education, economic affairs, status and rights, social services, the arts, the media and church affairs to name but a few.

COMHLACHAS NÁISIÚNTA DRÁMAÍOCHTA *Tulach na hEigse, Camus, Connemara, Co. Galway.* **email** dramai@tinet.ie **Tel** (091) 574146. **Profile** The National Council of Drama promotes drama in the Irish language through an advice centre, festivals, libraries of play texts and Irish drama courses.

CULTÚRLANN NA HÉIREANN *See Comhaltas Ceoltóirí Éireann* **Established** 1976. **Profile** The Institute offers a wide range of services and facilities, including a Cultural Information Agency, a Training and Education Centre, Library of books and archive of traditional recordings, a recording Studio, classrooms, Administrative Headquarters, the Geantraí Folk Theatre (holds concerts, stage shows and céilís).

AN CUMANN SCOILDRÁMAÍOCHTA *46 Kildare Street, Dublin 2.* **Tel** 01-679 4780. **Profile** Involved in the promotion and development of the Irish language through drama and stage-craft in national schools. It organises an annual national schools' drama festival, *An Fhéile Scoildrámaíochta.*

CONRADH NA GAEILGE *Áras an Chonartha, 6 Harcourt Street, Dublin 2.* **email** cnag@tinet.ie **Tel** 01-475 7401/2. **Established** 1893 **Profile** A national organisation that provides support systems for Irish language schools, Irish language classes and other activities to further the use of Irish. It organises the Irish language festival, *An tOireachtas* (dating from 1897), which includes literary, cultural, artistic and stage presentations and competitions.

DEPARTMENT OF IRISH FOLKLORE *University College Dublin, Belfield, Dublin.* **email** hennigan@macollamh.ucd.ie **Tel** 01-706-8216 **Established** 1971 **Profile** The dept took over the work of the Irish Folklore Commission (1935–1971) which collected a vast amount of folklore and ethnological data from around Ireland. The dept studies and collates this data and is in continual co-operation with folklorists around the world. It holds two manuscript series: the Main Manuscripts comprising 2,238 bound volumes, and the Schools' Collection, which runs to 1,128 bound volumes and 1,124 boxes of unbound material. There are also collections of sound recordings, about 40,000 photographs, films and videos and other pictorial representations. The dept also has a library of some 38,000 printed books, pamphlets and periodicals on folklore and related fields. Around 75% of its manuscripts and recordings are in Irish, and most remaining items are in English. The collections have items in Scots Gaelic and in Manx and Breton.

EUROPEAN BUREAU FOR LESSER USED LANGUAGES *10 Lower Hatch Street, Dublin 2.* eblul@indigo.ie **Tel:** *01-661 2205* **Established** 1982 **Profile** the aim of the bureau is to promote the lesser used languages of Europe. It issues publications with research on the lesser used languages, helps language bodies to apply for EU funding, and defines legal structures for official EU bodies to adhere by. The prime piece of legislation it contributed towards was *The European Charter for Regional and Minority Languages.* It also holds a council for delegates from minority languages, which meets around twice a year. The bureau acts on a consultancy basis for the Council of Europe and UNESCO.

GAEL-LINN *26 Merrion Square, Dublin 2.* **email** gaellinn@tinet.ie **Tel** 01-676 7283. **Established** 1953. **Profile** A non-political, non-governmental agency working to promote and gain recognition for the Irish language and culture throughout Ireland. Its work covers four areas of activity: education, youthwork, the arts and its own traditional music label. It also organises the National Youth Arts and Music Festival, *Slógadh.*

THE IRISH WORLD MUSIC CENTRE *Foundation Building, University of Limerick, Limerick.* **email** Ellen.Byrne@ul.ie **Tel** 061-202 575 / 202590 **Established** 1994 **Profile** set up by Mícheál Ó Súilleabháin when he became the Chair of Music at the University of Limerick, the centre has engaged in significant research in Irish and Irish-related music and dance as well as developing a number of taught post-graduate programmes over a five-year period, coming to completion this year. Research and taught programmes are available at masters and doctoral level. The centre hosts a number of concerts and seminars featuring music, dancers and scholars from both Irish traditional and contemporary fields of music and dance.

THE MUSIC NETWORK *Coach House, Dublin Castle, Dublin 2* **email** info@musicnetwork.ie **Tel** 01-676 1930 **Established** 1986 **Profile** The network is the national music development organisation which aids in the promotion of classical, jazz and traditional music in Ireland. It is grant-aided by the Arts Council and sponsored by the ESB. It also provides information and educational services and issues the Irish Music Handbook and a Directory of Musicians in Ireland. Among its many activities is the organisation of the Crann tour - a 12-venue tour of musicians around the country.

OIDEAS GAEL *Glenn Cholm Cille, Co. Donegal.* **email** oidsgael@iol.ie **Tel** (073) 30248 **Profile** It organises Irish language courses together with cultural activities.

NA PÍOBAIRÍ UILLEANN (the society of uilleann pipers) *15 Henrietta Street, Dublin 1.* **email** npupipes@iol.ie **Tel** 01-873 0093. **Profile** the aim of the society is to promote uilleann piping and holds classes and public performances.

RAIDIÓ NA GAELTACHTA *see Media chapter.*

RAIDIÓ NA LIFE *see Media chapter.*

RAIDIÓ TEILIFÍS ÉIREANN *see Media chapter.*

TAISCE CHEOL DÚCHAIS ÉIREANN (The Irish Traditional Music Archive) *63 Merrion Square, Dublin 2.* **web** www.itma.ie **Tel** 01-661 9699 **Established** 1987. **Profile** It acts as a resource centre for research and information on Irish traditional music. It now holds the largest collection of books, sound recordings, videos, photographs and manuscripts on Irish traditional music, covering Ireland and areas of Irish settlement abroad. A representative collection of the traditional music of other countries is also being made.

TG4 (formerly Teilifís na Gaelige) *see Media chapter.*

ÚDARÁS NA GAELTACHTA *Na Forbacha, Galway.* **email** eolas@udaras.ie **web** www.udaras.ie **Tel** 091-503 100 **Established** 1980 **Profile** formerly Gaeltarra Éireann (1957–1979), Udaras is a regional development agency responsible for the economic, social and cultural development of Gaeltacht regions and for ensuring the continuation of Irish as the spoken language of the Gaeltacht areas. Through its economic development activities, it has facilitated the creation of 7,880 full-time jobs. Its language and culture dept is responsible for all aspects of language and culture promotion and development throughout the Gaeltacht.

THE ULSTER FOLK AND TRANSPORT MUSEUM *Cultra, Holywood, Co Down, BT18 0EU.* **Tel** 01232-428 428. Holds recordings and archives, along with some instruments. Also holds performances.

ENTERTAINMENT

Music

Irish No. 1 Single Charts (October 1998-October 1999)

Week ending	Album Title	Artist(s)	Weeks at No. 1	Record Label	Previous Highest Position	Country of Origin
19.09.98	Millennium	Robbie Williams	2	Chrysalis	1	England
08.10.98	I Don't Want To Miss A Thing	Aerosmith	2	Sony	3	USA
22.10.98	Sweetest Thing	U2	2	Island	*	Ireland
05.11.98	Irreplaceable	Kerri Ann	1	Polygram	2	Ireland
12.11.98	Believe	Cher	6	Warner	3	USA
24.12.98	Goodbye	Spice Girls	1	Virgin	2	England
31.12.98	Chocolate Salty Balls	Chef	4	Sony	2	USA
28.01.99	Pretty Fly (For A White Guy)	Offspring	3	Sony	5	USA
18.02.99	Baby One More Time	Britney Spears	6	Zamba	*	USA
01.04.99	Swear It Again	Westlife	5	BMG	*	Ireland
06.05.99	No Scrubs	TLC	2	BMG	2	USA
20.05.99	Candle For Kosovo	Various	2	Ritz	*	Ireland
03.06.99	Everybody's Free (To Wear Sunscreen)	Baz Luhrmann	2	EMI	*	USA
17.06.99	That Don't Impress Me Much	Shania Twain	1	Universal	2	USA
24.06.99	9pm (Till I Come)	ATB	3	Interactive	9	USA
22.07.99	Livin' La Vida Loca	Ricky Martin	1	Columbia	3	Puerto Rico
29.07.99	When You Say Nothing At All	Ronan Keating	2	Polydor	*	Ireland
12.09.99	If I Let You Go	Westlife	2	RCA	*	Ireland
26.08.99	Mamba No. 5	Lou Bega	3	RCA	2	Germany
16.09.99 -						
30.09.99	Blue (Da Ba Dee)	Eiffel 65	3	Eternal	15	Germany

Irish No. 1 Album Charts (October 1998-October 1999)

Week ending	Album Title	Artist(s)	Weeks at No. 1	Record Label	Previous Highest Position	Country of Origin
17.09.98 ·						
08.10.98	This Is My Truth Tell Me Yours	Manic Street Preachers	4	Sony	*	Wales
15.10.98	Hits	Phil Collins	2	Virgin	14	England
29.10.98	I've Been Expecting You	Robbie Williams	1	EMI	*	England
05.11.98 -						
17.12.98	The Best of 1989-1990, B Sides	U2	7	Island	*	Ireland
24.12.98 -						
07.01.99	Ladies & Gentlemen, The Best of	George Michael	3	Sony	2	England
14.01.99 -						
25.02.99	You've Come A Long Way Baby	Fatboy Slim	7	Sony	9	England
04.03.99	Tears of Stone	Chieftains/Various	1	BMG	3	Ireland
11.03.99	The Miseducation of Lauryn Hill	Lauryn Hill	1	Sony	2	England
18.03.99	13	Blur	1	EMI	*	England
25.03.99	Tears of Stone	Chieftains/Various	1	BMG	1	Ireland
01.04.99 -						
29.04.99	Now That's What I Call Music! 42	Various	5	Various[1]	*	Various
06.05.99 -						
27.05.99	Gold - Greatest Hits	Abba	4	Universal	2	Sweden
03.06.99 -						
17.06.99	By Request - The Best of Boyzone	Boyzone	3	Universal	*	Ireland
24.06.99 -						
08.07.99	Dawson's Creek	Original Soundtrack	3	Sony	1	USA
22.07.99	Now That's What I Call Music! 42	Various	4	Various	*	Various

Continued from previous page

Week ending	Album Title	Artist(s)	Weeks at No. 1	Record Label	Previous Highest Position	Country of Origin
26.08.99	Big Hits 99	Various	5	Various	*	Various
30.09.99	Traveller	Christy Moore	1	Columbia	*	Ireland

* Indicates single/album entered Charts at Number 1. **1** EMI, Virgin, Polygram
Compiled by ChartTrack on behalf of IRMA ©

Irish Artists in British Top 40 Single Charts

● (October 3, 1998 - October 2, 1999)

Date of Entry Day / mth	Single Title	Artist(s)	No. entered at	Highest position	Weeks at No 1	Weeks spent in Top 40
03.10.98	Rollercoaster	B*Witched	*	1	2	9
03.10.98[1]	No Matter What	Boyzone	*	1	3	15
03.10.98	Jesus Says	Ash	15	15	-	2
03.10.98[2]	What Can I Do (Remix)	The Corrs	3	3	-	?
17.10.98	The Magic is There	Daniel O'Donnell	16	16	-	2
31.10.98	Sweetest Thing	U2	3	3	-	6
07.11.98	Tell Me Ma	Sham Rock	13	13	-	5
28.11.98	So Young	The Corrs	6	6	-	8
05.12.98	I Love the Way You Love Me	Boyzone	2	2	-	10
05.12.98	Wild Surf	Ash	31	31	-	1
19.12.98	To You I Belong	B*Witched	*	1	1	7
06.02.99	National Express	The Divine Comedy	8	8	-	5
27.02.99	Runaway (Remix)	The Corrs	2	2	-	9
27.02.99	To You I Belong	B*Witched	37	37	-	1
06.03.99	Precious Times	Van Morrison	36	36	-	1
13.03.99	When the Going Gets Tough	Boyzone	*	1	2	9
13.03.99	Party All Night	Mytown	22	22	-	1
20.03.99	The Way Dreams Are	Daniel O'Donnell	18	18	-	2
27.03.99	Blame it on the Weatherman	B*Witched	*	1	1	6
17.04.99	Promises	The Cranberries	13	13	-	3
01.05.99	Swear It Again	Westlife	*	1	2	8
22.05.99	You Needed Me	Boyzone	*	1	1	7
05.06.99	Saltwater	Chicane feat. Maire Brennan	6	6	-	6
12.06.99	I Know My Love	The Chieftains feat. The Corrs	37	37	-	1
24.07.99	Uno Mas	Daniel O'Donnell	25	25	-	1
07.08.99	When You Say Nothing At All	Ronan Keating	*	1	3	9
21.08.99	If I Let You Go	Westlife	*	1	1	7
21.08.99	The Pop Singer's Fear of the Pollen Count	The Divine Comedy	17	17	-	2

1 The **Boyzone** single No Matter What had already been in the Single charts for 7 weeks prior to 03.10.98
2 The **Corrs** single What Can I Do (Remix) had already been in the Single charts for 5 weeks prior to 03.10.98

Compiled by **CIN** (Chart Information Network) ©

Irish Artists in British Top 40 Album Charts

● (October 3, 1998 - October 2, 1999)

Date of Entry Day / mth	Album Title	Artist(s)	No. entered at	Highest position	Weeks at No 1	Weeks spent in Top 40
03.10.98	Talk On Corners[1]	The Corrs	-	1	4	96
03.10.98	Where We Belong[2]	Boyzone	1	1	3	53
03.10.98[3]	Fin De Siecle[3]	The Divine Comedy	9	9	-	4
17.10.98	Nu-clear Sounds	Ash	7	7	-	3

Continued from previous page

● (October 1998 - October 1999) Date of Entry Day / mth	Album Title	Artist(s)	No. entered at	Highest position	Weeks at No 1	Weeks spent in Top 40
24.10.98	B*Witched	B*Witched	3	3	-	30
24.10.98	Songs From Sun Street	The Saw Doctors	24	24	-	1
24.10.98	Forgiven, Not Forgotten⁴	The Corrs	40	40	-	1
31.10.98	Love Songs	Daniel O'Donnell	9	9	-	3
14.11.98	The Best Of, 1980-1990 & B Sides	U2	*	1	-	8
21.11.98	The Best Of, 1980-1990	U2	8	4	-	19
16.01.99	Forgiven, Not Forgotten	The Corrs	22	2	-	28
13.02.99	Fin De Siecle	The Divine Comedy	36	26	-	4
06.03.99	Tears Of Stone	The Chieftains	36	36	-	2
20.03.99	Back On Top	Van Morrison	11	11	-	12
17.04.99	The Best of 1980-1990	U2	36	36	-	2
01.05.99	Bury The Hatchet	The Cranberries	7	7	-	4
12.06.99	By Request⁶	Boyzone	*	1	8	17
11.09.99	A Secret History	The Divine Comedy	3	3	-	4
02.10.99	Greatest Hits	Daniel O'Donnell	10	10	-	1
02.10.99	Quiet Revolution	Chris De Burgh	23	23	-	1

1 **The Corrs** album Talk On Corners *had already been in the Album charts for 43 weeks prior to 03.10.98. It reached Number 1 on 27.02.99 after 64 weeks in the Top 75, staying there for 3 weeks. On 10.04.99 the album again reached Number 1 for a further week and* Forgiven, Not Forgotten *climbed to Number 2 giving the Dundalk band a unique double.*

2 **Boyzone** *had already spent 17 weeks in the Album Charts with* Where We Belong *prior to 03.10.98*

3 **The Divine Comedy** *had already spent 3 weeks in the Album Charts with* Fin De Siecle *prior to 03.10.98*

4 **The Corrs** *had already spent 36 weeks in the Top 75 Album Charts with* Forgiven, Not Forgotten *prior to 24.10.98*

5 **Boyzone's** By Request *entered the Charts at Number 1 on 12.06.99, staying there for 2 weeks. On 10.07.99 the album again reached Number 1, staying there for 6 weeks.*

Compiled by **CIN** (Chart Information Network) ©

B*witched

Westlife

Neil Hannon
- The Divine Comedy

U2

The Chieftains

Irish Eurovision Song Contest Entries

Year	Venue	Song Title (Ireland)	Irish Performer(s) & Placing	Winning Country
1965	Naples	I'm Walking the Streets in the Rain	Butch Moore (6th)	Luxembourg
1966	Luxembourg	Come Back to Stay	Dickie Rock (=4th)	Austria
1967	Vienna	If I Could Choose	Sean Dunphy (2nd)	United Kingdom
1968	London	Chance of a Lifetime	Pat McGeegan (4th)	Spain

Continued from previous page

Year	Venue	Song Title (Ireland)	Irish Performer(s) & Placing	Winning Country
1969	Madrid	*The Wages of Love*	Muriel Day & The Lindsays *(=7th)*	*
1970	**Amsterdam**	***All Kinds of Everything***	**Dana *(1st)***	Ireland
1971	Dublin	*One Day Love*	Angela Farrell *(11th)*	Monaco
1972	Edinburgh	*Ceol an Ghrá*	Sandie Jones *(15th)*	Luxembourg
1973	Luxembourg	*Do I Dream?*	Maxi *(=10th)*	Luxembourg
1974	Brighton	*Cross your Heart*	Tina *(=7th)*	Sweden
1975	Stockholm	*That's What Friends Are For*	Jimmy & Tommy Swarbrigg *(9th)*	Netherlands
1976	The Hague	*When*	Red Hurley *(10th)*	United Kingdom
1977	London	*It's Nice to be in Love Again*	The Swarbriggs Plus Two *(3rd)*	France
1978	Paris	*Born to Sing*	Colm C.T. Wilkinson *(5th)*	Israel
1979	Jerusalem	*Happy Man*	Cathal Dunne *(5th)*	Israel
1980	**The Hague**	***What's Another Year?***	**Johnny Logan *(1st)***	Ireland
1981	Dublin	*Horoscopes*	Sheeba *(5th)*	United Kingdom
1982	Harrogate	*Here Today, Gone Tomorrow*	The Duskey's *(11th)*	Germany
1983	Munich		No Entry	Luxembourg
1984	Luxembourg	*Terminal 3*	Linda Martin (2nd)	Sweden
1985	Gothenburg	*Wait Until the Weekend Comes*	Maria Christian *(6th)*	Norway
1986	Bergen	*You Can Count on Me*	Luv Bug *(4th)*	Belgium
1987	**Brussels**	***Hold me Now***	**Johnny Logan *(1st)***	Ireland
1988	Dublin	*Take Him Home*	Jump The Gun *(8th)*	Switzerland
1989	Lausanne	& *The Real Me*	Klev Connolly & The Missing Passengers *(18th)*	Yugoslavia
1990	Zagreb	*Somewhere in Europe*	Liam Reilly *(=2nd)*	Italy
1991	Rome	*Could it Be That I'm in Love*	Kim Jackson *(=10th)*	Sweden
1992	**Malmö**	***Why Me?***	**Linda Martin *(1st)***	Ireland
1993	**Cork**	***In your Eyes***	**Niamh Kavanagh *(1st)***	Ireland
1994	**Dublin**	***Rock 'n' Roll Kids***	**Paul Harrington & Charlie McGettigan *(1st)***	Ireland
1995	Dublin	*Dreamin'*	Eddie Friel *(14th)*	Norway
1996	**Oslo**	***The Voice***	**Eimear Ouinn *(1st)***	Ireland
1997	Dublin	*Mysterious Woman*	Marc Roberts (2nd)	United Kingdom
1998	Birmingham	*Is Always Over Now*	Dawn Martin *(9th)*	Israel
1999	Jerusalem	*When You Need Me*	Bronagh and Karen Mullan *(17th)*	Sweden

* *Spain, UK, Netherlands, France*

Cinema

	1995	1996	1997
Cinema Admissions	9.8 million	11.5 million	11.5 million
Cinema Attendances Revenues	IR£27.6m	IR£40.25m	IR£40.25m
Cinema Screens	197	215	261

Lottery

An Post National Lottery

● **FACTFILE**

Established	1987
Chairman	John Hynes
National Lottery Director	Ray Bates
Total surplus (1987-1998)	IR£900 million

● **1998 MAJOR STATISTICS**

Total sales	IR£336.8m
Sales increase 1997-1998	3.8%
Total prizes	IR£173.6m
Gross Surplus	IR£163.2m

Agents' Commission and Bonuses	IR£20.9m
Printing, Marketing, Distribution costs	IR£9.2m
On-Line Facilities, Services Costs	IR£13.3m
Administrative Costs	£IR£8.3m
Total Operating expenses	IR£51.9m
Beneficiary projects surplus	IR£111.3m
Lotto Sales	IR£219.3m
Lotto Prizes	IR£109.6m
Instant Game Sales	IR£108.6m
Instant Game Prizes	IR£59m
Lotto 5-4-3-2-1 Sales	IR£8.9m
Lotto 5-4-3-2-1 Prizes	IR£4.9m
Largest individual jackpot	IR£2.96m
Number of Staff	77

● **LOTTO JACKPOT STATISTICS**

IR£2m+ and up to and including IR£3m 3
IR£1m+ and up to and including IR£2m 24
IR£750,000+ and up to and including IR£1m 11
IR£500,000+ and up to and including IR£750,000 ...15
IR£250,000+ and up to and including IR£500,000 15
IR£100,000+ and up to and including IR£250,000 10
Total...78

● **BENEFICIARY FUNDING 1998**

Youth, Sport, Recreation, Amenities ...£43.507m *(36%)*
Health and Welfare...........................£41.713m *(34%)*
Arts, Culture, National Heritage ....£27.408m *(23%)*
Irish Language.....................................£8.230m *(7%)*
Total..£120.858m

● **TOTAL BENEFICIARY FUNDING 1987-98**

Youth, Sport, Recreation, Amenities £305.923m
Health and Welfare £318.074m
Arts, Culture, National Heritage £223.187m
Irish Language £67.252m
Total...£914.436m

Lottery Grants by Government Department

Department	1987	1988	1989	1990	1991	1992
Finance			28,946	107,538	71,202	336,000
OPW		1,736,913	1,497,000	2,441,000	1,366,000	1,296,000
Environment	350,000	6,122,795	5,335,678	4,948,123	6,536,151	5,964,969
Education	3,588,794	21,637,746	22,231,485	28,051,151	28,993,454	28,640,305
Defence			620,000	670,000	704,000	1,026,000
Foreign Affairs		319,186	529,883	438,096	422,521	212,864
Int. Co-operation		800,000			690,000	0
Social Welfare		850,000	900,000	750,000	2,360,000	3,485,000
Health	3,357,500	6,412,634	7,120,741	8,671,950	28,135,000	41,292,000
Arts/Cult./Gael.					0	
Heritage Co.		109,093	273,236	596,514	1,020,753	1,435,504
National Gallery				99,216	36,794	231,373
Arts Council	1,800,000	1,880,000	2,948,000	4,948,000	4,988,000	4,988,000
Trans/Ener/Comm					0	2,965,000
Taoiseach	1,347,852	2,711,987	2,035,020	3,328,404	4,346,036	4,268,913
Tourism & Trans				558,000	442,000	0
Communications				500,000	999,391	0
Gaeltacht		836,937	3,370,563	4,111,650	3,912,449	4,358,026
Agriculture					940,581	0
TOTAL:	**10,444,146**	**43,417,291**	**46,890,552**	**60,219,642**	**85,964,332**	**100,499,954**

Department	1993	1994	1995	1996	1997	Total
Finance	100,000	98,000	358,943	94,077	4,663,000	5,887,706
OPW	80,000	753,000	1,150,000	378,755	0	10,698,668
Environment	4,784,968	3,540,000	6,290,000	6,600,000	6,719,704[1]	57,192,388
Education	30,406,537	36,969,383	33,008,475	36,027,295	28,519,073[2]	298,073,698
Defence	1,078,000	1,050,000	1,194,000	1,328,000	1,348,000	9,018,000
Foreign Affairs	212,468	250,000	219,991	179,959	225,054	3,010,022
Int. Co-operation	0	0	0	1,000,000		2,490,000
Social Welfare	4,729,000	4,728,000	4,430,000	4,460,084	5,600,000[3]	32,292,084
Health	29,436,000	30,012,000	22,181,000	22,144,000	24,020,000[4]	222,782,825
Arts/Cult./Gael.	8,907,736	7,496,419	8,520,927	10,312,895	11,429,611[5]	46,667,588
Heritage Co.	1,265,722	1,544,372	1,560,820	1,796,150	2,787,448	12,389,612
Nat Gallery	83,275	201,305	227,855	191,897	257,000	1,328,715
Arts Council	4,988,000	4,988,000	3,707,000	3,970,000	4,400,000	43,605,000
Trans/Ener/Comm	729,000	0	0	0	0	3,694,000
Taoiseach	0	0	0	0	0	18,038,212
Tourism & Trans	0	0	0	0	0	1,000,000
Communications	0	0	0	0	0	1,499,391
Gaeltacht	0	0	0	0	0	16,589,625
Agriculture	0	0	0	0	0	940,581
Tourism, Sport, Recreation	0	0	0	0	6,564,428	6,564,428
TOTAL:	**86,800,706**	**91,630,479**	**82,849,011**	**88,483,112**	**96,533,318**	**793,762,543**

1 = Environment is now Environment and Local Government. *2* = Education is now Education and Science.
3 = Social Welfare is now Social, Community and Family Affairs. *4* = Health is now Health and Children.
5 = Arts, Culture and Gaeltacht is now Arts, Heritage, Gaeltacht and Islands.

TOURISM

Tourism: Ireland's new billion-pound Industry

By **Dr James McDaid TD,**
Minister for Tourism, Sport & Recreation

ON the cusp of the Millennium, the outlook for Irish tourism is better than ever, In terms of our recent performance, Ireland is at the top of the league. In the last ten years, visitor numbers have doubled, foreign-exchange revenue has almost trebled to £2.3 billion in 1998, and tourism looks set to emerge as Ireland's single, largest industry. It is no wonder that we are the envy of many of our larger European neighbours.

It is unlikely that visitors to Ireland ever stop to consider what a vital role they are playing in our economy. Nevertheless, the once-Cinderella industry is now sustaining an estimated 127,000 full-time jobs, many of them in areas substantially lacking in other types of economic development. That is important to us as a nation, not only in terms of economics, but also in terms of our psyche. The Irish are, after all, a people who have, for generations, known the scourge of emigration, often the result of sustained economic deprivation. It is a historic irony that many of the visitors who come to Ireland nowadays, do so in search of their roots, their ancestors having left for Botany Bay, Van Diemens Land or Ellis Island, sometimes a century or two ago.

One of the clear successes of Irish tourism is the prosperity and economic activity it has brought to the traditionally less developed areas of the country. Many communities scattered along the remote western sea-board, in particular, owe their livelihood to the relatively new tourism phenomenon. The people of those rural communities have a central role to play in the future of Irish tourism, whether they are involved in the B&B sector, the broader hospitality area of pubs, hotels and restaurants or in the myriad arts and crafts enterprises that have taken hold of the imaginations of visitors from Milan to Melbourne, from Boston to Brisbane.

Today, Ireland's accommodation 'product' is of the first order. We cater for every budget, from family-run guesthouses and B&Bs to self catering cottages, and from small country-house hotels, to those in the international four and five-star category. Moreover, getting to Ireland has never been easier. Government and industry are working closely with the air and sea carriers to facilitate optimum tourism access, and to judge by the figures, we must be succeeding. Our own domestic market too continues to be important to us and our high quality tourism product has become very attractive to the Irish consumer.

All of us involved in Irish tourism are acutely aware of the huge responsibility that comes with our success. Sustainability and conservation are central to tourism planning, to guaranteeing a future for the industry and for ensuring the integrity and uniqueness of the Ireland offering. When emigration reached crisis proportions in the 1950s, the cry was, "you can't eat the scenery". Neither, today, can we afford to ravage it. Our success must be well managed.

We must not destroy those special things that draw visitors to Ireland in the first instance. Attractions such as the Cliffs of Moher, the Aran Islands and the celebrated Ring of Kerry find themselves under pressure at peak times of the year. Congestion here must be tackled well and quickly. Clearly sustainability is crucial, so right now we're spending £2.3 million on our new Tourism and the Environment Initiative which involves 20 pilot environmental management projects, chosen from more than 120 applications. This Initiative should facilitate the development of appropriate strategies to meet the challenges of growth and expansion within the industry.

There are, of course, issues other than sustainability. All of us in the industry are working hard to extend the traditional summer season into the shoulder and off-peak periods and we have made good progress in this regard over the past five years. Special interest and activity holidays, whether in the arts, sports or other leisure pursuits all have excellent potential to boost the shoulder and off-peak seasons. Golf, fishing, painting, gourmet events, and opera and theatre festivals are not confined to summer, and Ireland is now set to offer a vast range of events and activities that will cater for practically every taste on a year-round basis.

One of my major policy priorities is to ensure that everything possible is done to see that tourism revenue is spread across all seasons and across all regions. Traditionally popular areas such as the South-East, South-West and West of Ireland continue to do well in the tourism stakes, but the move must now be to extend the reach of tourism more strongly into the midlands and the North-West. Our finely honed heritage and culture projects are doing much to correct the regional imbalance. So too are the myriad festivals and events that tourism bodies, communities and businesses working together are creating all over the country. Vintage weeks, international jazz weekends, comedy festivals and choral festivals are all attracting visitors to their enterprising regions.

The tourism industry is not unaffected by the recruitment difficulties currently facing many sectors. Over the next five years the industry here in Ireland will need an additional 105,000 personnel, with 40,000 of them filling newly-created posts. Staff turnover in tourism is high, but the industry is focusing on ensuring that it emerges as a credible, serious choice for school and college leavers, those seeking to come back into the workforce and for those considering a new career choice. It is reassuring to see that our national tourism and catering training body, CERT, is in co-operation with the industry, making a determined drive in this area. The future looks good.

It is difficult for the written word to capture the essence of Ireland and its people Nevertheless, it is our people who are our greatest tourism asset. Visitor attitudes surveys confirm that their warmth and friendliness are unparalleled elsewhere in the world. It's not for nothing that we are known as the land of the *Céad Mile Fáilte* - the hundred thousand welcomes.

Dr James McDaid TD
October 1999

Dr James McDaid is Minister for the Department of Tourism, Sports and Recreation and is a TD for the Donegal North-East constituency. He qualified and worked as a medical doctor (GP) and has been a member of the Dáil since 1989.

Republic of Ireland

- **MAIN FIGURES "AT A GLANCE"**
Visitors to (000s) ....6,064[1]
Visitor Revenue (Ir£m) ....2,281.00[1]
Persons employed in tourism.....................126,700[2]
Total bednights (Ir£m) 44.6
Most popular attraction....................Rock of Cashel[2]
Most popular destination....................Dublin Region

1 does not include domestic trips
2 approximately
2 Dúchas attractions

Northern Ireland

- **MAIN FIGURES "AT A GLANCE"**
Visitors to (000s) ....1,477[1]
Visitor Revenue (Stg£m)................................217.00[1]
Persons employed in tourism.......................15,000[2]
Total bednights (million)..7.8
Most popular attraction.................Botanic Gardens
Most popular destination.............Down and Belfast

1 does not include domestic trips
2 approximately
2 Dúchas attractions

Visitors and Expenditure

Visitors to RoI and Revenue by Country of Origin

Country of Origin	1996		1997		1998	
	Visitors 000s	Revenue IR£m	Visitors 000s	Revenue IR£m	Visitors 000s	Revenue IR£m
Britain	2,590	574.0	2,850	683.0	3,199	749.6
Mainland Europe:						
Germany	339	148.9	303	121.8	310	123.4
France	262	88.1	250	89.1	270	89.8
Italy	119	53.5	111	50.9	141	57.7
Netherlands	109	35.4	131	44.0	134	43.1
Belgium/Luxembourg	60	-	73	-	71	-
Spain	66	-	71	-	82	-
Denmark	23	-	28	-	30	-
Norway/Sweden	55	-	60	-	67	-
Switzerland	62	-	58	-	54	-
Other	83	140.7	85	151.9	97	153.2
Total: Europe	1,178	466.6	1,170	457.7	1,256	467.2
North America:						
USA	660	-	718	-	789	-
Canada	69	-	60	-	69	-
Total: North America	729	316.6	778	348.2	858	384.4
Rest of World:						
Australia/N. Zealand	88	-	107	-	124	-
Japan	33	-	36	-	26	-
Other	65	-	71	-	71	-
Total: Rest of World	186	93.8	214	99.7	221	103.0
TOTAL:	**4,683**	**1,451.0**	**5,012**	**1,588.6**	**5,534**	**1,704.2**
Northern Ireland	607	85.0	580	101.9	530	97.1
TOTAL (incl. N.I.)	**5,290**	**1,536.0**	**5,592**	**1,690.5**	**6,064**	**1,801.3**
Excursionist Revenue	-	8.0	-	14.5	-	18.7
Carrier Receipts	-	345.0	-	400.0	-	461.0
Total:	-	1,889.0	-	2,105.0	-	2,281.0
Domestic Trips	6,170	578.8	6,850	670.8	6,934	751.0
Total Revenue:	-	2,467.8	-	2,775.8	-	3032.0

Visitors to NI and Revenue by Country of Origin

Country of Origin	1996		1997		1998	
	Visitors 000s	Revenue £m	Visitors 000s	Revenue £m	Visitors 000s	Revenue £m
Britain:						
England	588	82.4	571	85.1	578	88.5
Scotland	221	25.5	214	26.0	243	29.0
Wales	16	2.1	14	1.9	17	2.5

Continued from previous page

Country of Origin	1996 Visitors 000s	1996 Revenue £m	1997 Visitors 000s	1997 Revenue £m	1998 Visitors 000s	1998 Revenue £m
Total: Britain	825	110.0	799	113.0	838	120.0
Europe	97	22.0	105	21.0	108	25.0
North America	100	29.0	109	31.0	115	30.0
Republic of Ireland	370	30.0	345	27.0	360	28.0
Other	44	15.0	57	16.0	56	14.0
TOTAL:	1,436	206.0	1,415	208.0	1,477	217.0
Domestic Trips	607	60.0	570	60.0	543	63.0
Total Revenue:	-	266.0	-	268.0	-	280.0

RoI & NI: Tourists Classified by Accommodation

Accommodation 1998	Republic of Ireland (million nights)	(%)
Hotels	6.2	14
Guesthouses / B&Bs	7.6	17
Rented	7.6	17
Caravan & Camping	1.3	3
Hostels	1.8	4
Friends / Relatives	14.7	33
Other	5.4	12
Total:	44.6	100

Accommodation 1998	Northern Ireland (million nights)	(%)
Hotels	0.9	12
Guesthouses / B&Bs	0.6	8
Rented	0.6	7
Caravan & Camping	0.1	1
Hostels	-	-
Friends / Relatives	4.9	63
Other (incl. hostels)	0.7	9
Total:	7.8	100

RoI: Destination & Revenue by Region, 1998

Region	Total Visitors 000s	Total IR£m	Overseas Visitors 000	Overseas IR£m	Home Visitors 000s	Home IR£m	Northern Ireland Visitors 000s	Northern Ireland IR£m
Dublin	4,095	627.8	2,933	525.2	1,039	76.1	123	26.5
Midlands / East	1,693	275.0	869	194.2	787	74.7	37	6.1
North-West	1,397	200.6	602	113.2	548	60.3	247	27.1
Shannon	1,988	266.9	1,066	167.0	892	93.8	30	6.1
South-East	2,030	267.0	917	131.9	1,090	130.0	23	5.1
South-West	2,790	508.3	1,455	336.1	1,308	159.8	27	12.4
West	2,467	406.7	1,071	236.6	1,323	156.3	73	13.8
TOTAL:	16,460	2,552.3	8,913	1,704.2	6,987	751.0	560	97.1

RoI: Visitors by Reason for Journey

Reason	1993	1994	1995	1996	1997	1998[1]
Business	497,000	547,000	597,000	757,000	785,000	661,000
Holiday	1,622,000	1,807,000	2,314,000	2,466,000	2,768,000	2,568,000
Visiting	980,000	1,031,000	1,014,000	1,139,000	1,231,000	963,000
Other	233,000	297,000	332,000	376,000	380,000	362,000
TOTAL:	3,332,000	3,682,000	4,257,000	4,738,000	5,164,000	4,554,000

1 *January to September only*

RoI: Visitors by Country of Origin

Country	1993	1994	1995	1996	1997	1998
Britain	1,887,000	2,087,000	2,365,000	2,698,000	3,025,000	3,383,000
Europe	924,000	970,000	1,085,000	1,164,000	1,175,000	1,262,000
USA and Canada	406,000	474,000	617,000	703,000	764,000	855,000
Other	116,000	150,000	190,000	174,000	201,000	216,000
TOTAL:	3,333,000	3,681,000	4,257,000	4,739,000	5,165,000	5,716,000

NI: Visitors by Reason for Journey & Country of Origin, 1998

Country	Business	Holiday	Visiting	Other	Total
Britain:					
England	225,420	40,460	294,780	17,340	578,000
Scotland	68,040	36,450	126,360	12,150	243,000
Wales	5,610	3,400	6,630	1,360	17,000
Total: Britain	299,070	80,310	427,770	30,850	838,000
Europe	34,560	34,560	31,320	7,560	108,000
North America	10,350	49,450	41,400	13,800	115,000
Other	7,280	22,400	22,400	3,920	56,000
Republic of Ireland	79,200	90,000	97,200	93,600	360,000
TOTAL:	430,460	276,720	620,090	149,730	1,477,000

Visits Abroad and Expenditure by RoI Residents

Category	1996		1997		1998	
	Visits 000s	Expenditure £m	Visits 000s	Expenditure £m	Visits 000s	Expenditure £m
Route of Travel:						
Air	1,398	725	1,570	793	1,641	-
Sea	458	133	491	145	490	-
Continental	725	501	830	567	1,022	-
Transatlantic	153	163	161	178	178	-
Total: Route of Travel	2,734	1,522	3,052	1,683	3,331	-
Cross Border Visits	431	85	432	82	-	-
Total: Expenditure	-	1,607	-	1,765	-	-
Payments*	-	235	-	298	-	-
Total	-	1,372	-	1,467	-	1,353[1]
Reason for Journey:						
Business	551	393	530	357	444	-
Holiday	1,182	680	1,299	752	1,219	-
Visiting	721	286	864	358	677	-
Other	278	162	360	216	266	-
Total: Reason for Journey	2,732	1,521	3,053	1,683	2,606	-

* Passenger fares by Irish visitors abroad to Irish carriers   **1** *January - September 1998 (provisional)*

Visits at Home and Abroad and Expenditure by NI Residents

Description	1996		1997		1998	
	000s	£m	000s	£m	000s	£m
All Holidays:						
Short Holidays	808	94.0	845	87.0	791	89.0
Long Holidays	1,093	507.0	1,105	521.0	1,065	520.0
Total: All Holidays	1,901	601.0	1,950	608.0	1,856	609.0
Domestic Holidays:						
Short Holidays	410	26.0	350	20.0	340	20.0
Long Holidays	197	34.0	220	40.0	203	43.0
Total: Domestic Holidays	607	60.00	570	60.0	543	63.0

Visitor Attractions

RoI & NI: Most Popular Visitor Attractions, 1998

Republic of Ireland*		Republic of Ireland*	
Attraction (County)	No. of Visitors	Attraction (County)	No. of Visitors
Rock of Cashel (Tipperary)	229,012	**Brú na Bóinne** (Meath)	221,492

Continued from previous page

Republic of Ireland* Attraction (County)	No. of Visitors
Muckross House (Kerry)	220,195
Kilkenny Castle (Kilkenny)	168,335
Clonmacnoise (Offaly)	140,604
Glendalough Visitor Centre (Wicklow)	113,207
Kilmainham Gaol (Dublin)	108,055
Illnacullin - Garinish Island (Cork)	78,042
Connemara National Park (Galway)	77,882
Glenveagh Castle & National Park (Donegal)	75,218
Cahir Castle (Tipperary)	68,065
John F. Kennedy Park (Wexford)	50,186
Ionad an Bhlascaoid Mhoir (Kerry)	40,178
Céide Fields (Mayo)	40,104
Charles Fort (Cork)	37,319
Jerpoint Abbey (Kilkenny)	34,443
Donegal Castle (Donegal)	32,868
Dunmore Cave (Kilkenny)	31,852
Ross Castle (Kerry)	28,885
Carrowmore (Sligo)	27,965

* Dúchas Heritage Sites only

Northern Ireland Attraction (County)	No. of Visitors
Botanic Gardens (Belfast)	650,000
Giant's Causeway Visitor Centre (Antrim)	407,806
Belvoir Forest Park (Belfast)	380,000
Cave Hill Country Park (Belfast)	380,000
Pickie Family Fun Park (Down)	300,000
Carnfunnock Country Park (Antrim)	256,080
Sir Thomas & Lady Dixon Park (Belfast)	250,000
Ulster Museum (Belfast)	235,694
Scrabo Country Park (Down)	200,000
Tollymore Forest Park (Down)	192,000
Belfast Zoo (Belfast)	183,273
Belleek Pottery (Fermanagh)	171,757
Ulster Folk & Transport Museum (Down)	168,623
Oxford Island Nature Reserve (Armagh)	158,000
Murlough National Nature Reserve (Down)	129,000
Castlewellan Forest Park (Down)	127,000
Exploris (Down)	127,000
Ulster American Folk Park (Tyrone)	111,250
Delamont Country Park (Down)	107,600
Fantasy Island (Antrim)	103,000

Awards

RoI & NI: Blue Flag Beaches (1999)

In 1999, 83 beaches (ROI - 77, NI - 5) and 5 marinas (ROI - 4, NI - 1) were awarded the Blue Flag status from the EU.

County	Marinas	Beaches
Antrim	0	2
Clare	2	8
Cork	1	9
Derry	0	1
Donegal	0	12
Down	1	2
Dublin	0	2
Galway	0	5
Kerry	0	13
Mayo	0	13
Sligo	0	3
Waterford	0	3
Westmeath	0	2
Wexford	1	4
Wicklow	0	3
Total:	5	83

Beaches are listed below unless otherwise stated

● **ANTRIM**
Ballycastle, Portrush West Strand.

● **CLARE**
Ballycuggeran Beach, Cappa Pier, Fanore, Kilkee, Lehinch, Mountshannon Beach, White Strand Doonbeg, White Strand Miltown Malbay. *Marinas - Kilrush Creek Marina, Mountshannon Marina.*

● **CORK**
Barleycove, Garrylucas, Garryvoe, Inchydoney, Ownahincha, The Warren, Tragumna, Youghal Claycastle, Youghal Front Strand. *Marinas - Kinsale Yacht Club.*

● **DERRY**
Benone.

● **DONEGAL**
Bundoran, Carrickfinn, Culdaff, Downings, Fintra, Killahoey, Lisfannon, Marble Hill, Murvagh, Portnoo (Narin), Portsalon, Rossnowlagh.

● **DOWN**
Millisle Lagoon, Tyrella. *Marinas - Bangor Marina.*

● **DUBLIN**
Killiney, Seapoint.

● **GALWAY**
Kilmurvey, Loughrea, Tra an Doilin, Tra na mBan, Traught.

● **KERRY**
Ballinskelligs, Ballybunion North, Ballybunion South, Ballyheigue, Banna, Derrynane, Fenit, Inch, Kells, Maherbeg, Rossbeigh, Ventry, White Strand Caherciveen.

● **MAYO**
Bertra, Carrowmore, Clare Island, Dooega, Dugort, Elly Bay, Golden Strand, Keel, Keem, Maullaghroe, Mulranny, Old Head, Ross.

● **SLIGO**
Enniscrone, Mullaghmore, Rosses Point.

● **WATERFORD**
Bonmahon, Clonea Strand, Counsellor's Strand.

● **WESTMEATH**

Lilliput Lough Ennell, The Cut Lough Lene.

● **WEXFORD**

Courtown, Curracloe, Duncannon, Rosslare. *Marinas -*

Kilmore Quay.

● **WICKLOW**

Brittas Bay North, Brittas Bay South, Greystones South.

RoI & NI: Best Kept Towns Competition (1999)

The Best Kept Towns Competition is organised by the Department of the Environment in the Republic of Ireland, the Northern Ireland Amenity Council and is sponsored by the Super Valu Supermarket Chain. Winners were announced in Dublin Castle in June 1999.

Title	Winner
Ireland's Best Kept Town	Ardagh (*Co. Longford*)
Ireland's Best Kept Village	Ardagh (*Co. Longford*)
Best Kept Small Town	Waringstown (*Co. Down*)
Best Kept Large Town	Kilkenny City

RoI: Tidy Town Awards (1999)

The Tidy Town Awards were announced by the Minister for the Environment, Mr. Noel Dempsey, at Dublin Castle in September 1999.

Title	Winner
National Award Winner	Clonakilty (*Co. Cork*)
Ireland's Tidiest Village	Rathbarry (*Co. Cork*)
Ireland's Tidiest Small Town	Clonakilty (*Co. Cork*)
Ireland's Tidiest Large Town	Carrickmacross (*Co. Monaghan*)

RoI: Tidy Town / Village Awards by County (1999)

County	Winner (Runners-up)	County	Winner (Runners-up)
Carlow	Rathvilly (*Leighlinbridge, Ardattin*)	Louth	Tallanstown (*Knockbridge, Greenore*)
Cavan	Loch Gowna (*Butlersbridge, Cootehill, Cavan*)	Mayo	Westport (*Belcarra, Aughagower*)
Clare	Ennis / Mountshannon (*Kilkee, Quin*)	Meath	Moynalty (*Slane, Carlanstown*)
Cork	Clonakilty (*Rathbarry, Kinsale, Eyeries*)	Monaghan	Carrickmacross (*Glaslough, Milltown*)
Donegal	Malin (*Dunfanaghy, Glenties, Letterkenny*)	Offaly	Clonbullogue (*Geashill, Tullamore, Banagher*)
Dublin	Skerries (*Malahide, Dalkey Town*)	Roscommon	Keadue (*Cloontuskert, Ballintubber*)
Galway	Milltown (*Mountbellew, Portumna*)	Sligo	Coolaney (*Riverstown, Easkey*)
Kerry	Kenmare (*Sneem, Killarney*)	Tipperary NR	Terryglass (*Garrykennedy, Silvermines*)
Kildare	Kill (*Johnstown, Rathangan*)	Tipperary SR	Emly (*Rossadrehid, Kilsheelan*)
Kilkenny	Kilkenny (*Inistioge, Bennetsbridge*)	Waterford	Lismore (*Ardmore, Passage East*)
Laois	Castletown (*Ballacolla, Errill*)	Westmeath	Tyrrellspass (*Finea, Glasson Village, Ballinahown Village*)
Leitrim	Dromod (*Carrick-on-Shannon, Dromahair*)	Wexford	Ballymun (*Blackwater, Enniscorthy, The Harrow*)
Limerick	Adare (*Galbally, Ardpatrick, Athea Village*)	Wicklow	Aughrim (*Enniskerry, Stratford-on-Slaney*)
Longford	Ardagh (*Newtowncashel, Abbeyshrule*)		

SPORT

The Championship:
New century, new format.

By Damian Dowds

THE GAA Championship as we have known it for most of the twentieth century will emerge in the twenty first century in a radically new format. Since 1889 the Championship has been played on a knock-out basis within each province (in 1887 the Championship was played as an open draw and in 1888 it was not completed). The first dilution of the knock-out nature of the Championship came in 1997 when the so-called 'back door' was introduced in hurling where the runners-up in Leinster and Munster were readmitted to the All-Ireland quarter-finals. Now, change in both the hurling and football championships in all provinces seems inevitable. More games for county players has become the catch cry of the late 1990s. It seems that county players will indeed get more Championship games but at what cost to the humble club player and other competitions?

For several years now the Championship has become increasingly well marketed and packaged. Live television, major sponsorship, page upon page of newsprint and improved facilities at GAA grounds have all contributed to the increased popularity of the country's premier sports competition. The hype starts building early each New Year when thoughts turn to summer days, the dry sod and the fervour of the Championship. There have been casualties of this hype. The National League seems to be dying a Railway Cup-like death. It has become a phoney war which precedes the intensity of summer battle. Managers treat it with contempt and with 23,000 people attending this year's finals, it appears the public are are seeing it for what it is – a warm up. People are only interested in the main event and are starting to vote with their feet. The various provincial cup competitions such as the Dr McKenna Cup and the O'Byrne Cup have gone the same way. They are now slotted into unfashionable Saturday dates and played in front of paltry crowds. Players, managers and spectators take these competitions even less seriously than the League.

Despite assertions to the contrary, there has never been a shortage of matches for intercounty players, but with the focus now entirely on the Championship the significance of other competitions has diminished. Winning a League title is no longer considered a success if your team does not perform well in the Championship, as a recent Limerick hurling manager would testify.

The Championship leaves no room for error and it draws its appeal from its 'win at all costs' mentality. With the exception of the Leinster and Munster hurling finals if a team is beaten it is eliminated. It is as simple and straightforward as that. The Championship is the real article, there is no shadow boxing , or fielding second string players to give them experience; the stakes are too high. We do not witness any 'dead' games in the Championship, no team has already qualified for anything and each game must be played as though it is the last of the season. The introduction of any system which causes the diminution of the 'win at all costs' nature of the Championship will destroy the very fabric of the competition. The advancement of the argument that because the Leinster and Munster hurling finals have remained competitive since the introduction of the back door, early rounds of the new Championship will remain competitive, is unsustainable. The Leinster and Munster finals are competitive because the provincial titles are there to be won. It is conceivable that in the future a team may choose to lose an earlier round and take the loser's route to avoid a particularly difficult clash. This must be avoided at all costs to maintain the integrity of the competition.

The great Kerry team of the 1970s and 1980s has a lot to answer for! It was that team, and to a lesser extent Dublin, which introduced high levels of fitness into Gaelic games. That they did it with no little amount of skill is not in doubt, but with all teams now aspiring to ever higher levels of fitness the cost to the intercounty player is great. Training commences in many cases in October and the number of sessions is normally well into three figures by the time the Championship comes eight or nine months later. It calls for an enormous collective effort which often proves expensive in financial, personal and professional terms. It is completely understandable that a feeling of minimal return for maximum effort follows a first round Championship exit and colours the opinions of those involved. Dublin hurling manager Michael O'Grady grabbed headlines this year after his side were narrowly defeated by Wexford in May when he said that his players would not play competitive hurling until spring 2000. That was not strictly true; his players went on to play with their clubs in the Dublin hurling championship and league. This perfectly illustrates the position the Championship has come to occupy in the GAA mindset; it is the only competition which counts and club games are a poor substitute.

If the Championship is changed and counties get more games the club versus county conflict, which has thus far not emerged on a large scale, will become one of the biggest problems facing the GAA in the early part of the new century. It is without question that county players put a tremendous effort into training but the fact that many club players also put in a similarly large effort often goes without notice. Most senior and intermediate clubs commence training in January or February and the focus of their season is the county championship which commences in the summer. County players are central to the fortunes of the clubs they belong to, without them many clubs would struggle. It is both unreasonable and unrealistic to expect clubs to play important games without their star players as some commentators have suggested.

Furthermore, a good run in the Championship interrupts club competitions in counties as it is. Club players generally do not grumble about this as it is not an annual occurrence, but can they be expected to train hard while their competitions are interrupted each year by the county team having four or more games in the Championship. A lack of matches and interruption to competition is certain to turn club players away from the GAA, and without a vibrant club scene county football will stagnate because the pool from which it draws its players becomes more shallow. Take the example of Armagh this year. The club championship was interrupted and did not reach even the semi-final stage until October because of the county team's involvement in the All-Ireland series. In Down competitions were disrupted because of the involvement of the county *minor* team in the All-Ireland final.

The moves to reformat the Championship so that it has more games is assuming an air of inevitably. The guiding principle of this must be the protection of the integrity of club competitions. A new system which is biased towards the intercounty player must attempt to be fair to club players. If the new format means club players are to go weeks without games it will mark the beginning of a two-tier GAA where competition formats are biased towards the perceived needs of an elite group of players. With 33 teams in the football Championship and 17 in hurling the number of players to benefit from the new structures will be approximately 1,500 (allowing 30 players per panel). Should the most important competition in Gaelic Games be changed for such a small number of players and to the detriment of the tens of thousands of players who play each week for the honour of their parish? The GAA will have to think carefully about the path it chooses to tread.

Gaelic Games

Cumann Lúthchleas Gael

Páirc an Chrócaigh, Baile Átha Cliath 3.
Tel. (01) 8363222.
Website: www.gaa.ie
email: info@gaa.ie

Founded	1884
President	Joe McDonagh
President elect	Sean McCague
Director General	Liam Mulvhill
Number of Provincial Councils	4
Number of Clubs	2,664
Number of Members	750,000
Number of Teams	20,000
Number of Coaches	2,000
Biggest Attendance	
Football	90,556 (1961 Down v Offaly)
Hurling	84,856 (1954 Cork v Wexford)
Main Stadium	Croke Park (Capacity: 63,000)

● 1999 HURLING CHAMPIONS

All-Ireland	Cork
Connacht	Galway
Leinster	Kilkenny
Munster	Cork
Ulster	Antrim
National League	Tipperary
Interprovincial (1998 Champions)	Leinster
All-Ireland Minor	Galway
All-Ireland U21	Kilkenny
All-Ireland Club	St Joseph's/Doora-Barefield (Clare)

● 1999 FOOTBALL CHAMPIONS

All-Ireland	Meath
Connacht	Mayo
Leinster	Meath
Munster	Cork
Ulster	Armagh
National League	Cork
Interprovincial	Munster
All-Ireland Minor	Down
All-Ireland U21	Westmeath
All-Ireland Club	Crossmaglen Rangers (Armagh)

TOP SCORERS 1999 SENIOR CHAMPIONSHIP

Hurling	Joe Deane (Cork)	1-24
	Henry Shefflin (Kilkenny)	1-24
Football	Oisín McConville (Armagh)	3-18

Championship Results

1999 SENIOR HURLING CHAMPIONSHIP
● Connacht

10.07.99 Final	Galway...4-26	Roscommon ...2-8

● Leinster

30.05.99 1st rnd....Wexford...1-13	Dublin 1-12
20.06.99 s/f..........Kilkenny...6-21	Laois..............1-14
20.06.99 s/f..............Offaly...3-17	Wexford 0-15
11.07.99 Final......Kilkenny...5-14	Offaly 1-16

● Munster

22.05.99 1st rnd..Tipperary...4-29	Kerry..............2-6
30.05.99 1st rnd .Waterford...1-16	Limerick 1-14
06.06.99 s/f..............Clare...2-12	Tipperary 0-18
12.06.99 s/f (R).........Clare...1-21	Tipperary......1-11
13.06.99 s/f..............Cork...0-24	Waterford......1-15
04.07.99 Final............Cork...1-15	Clare.............0-14

● Ulster

19.06.99 s/f..............Derry...4-16	Down 4-8
19.06.99 s/f..............Antrim...3-23	London 1-6
10.07.99 Final.........Antrim...2-19	Down 1-9

● All-Ireland Series

25.07.99 q/f............Offaly...4-22	Antrim 0-12
25.07.99 q/f............Clare...3-15	Galway 2-18
02.08.99 q/f (R) ....Clare...3-18	Galway 2-14
08.08.99 s/f..............Cork...0-19	Offaly 0-16
15.08.99 s/f.........Kilkenny...2-14	Clare.............1-13
12.09.99 Final............Cork...0-13	Kilkenny 0-12

1999 SENIOR FOOTBALL CHAMPIONSHIP
● Connacht

29.05.99 1st rnd ....Mayo...3-13	New York 0-10
30.05.99 1st rnd ......Leitrim...1-7	Roscommon .0-14
06.06.99 1st rnd ....London...1-8	Galway 1-18
13.06.99 s/f..............Mayo...0-21	Roscommon .0-10
27.06.99 s/f ....Galway...1-13	Sligo 3-7
04.07.99 s/f (R) ......Galway...1-17	Sligo 0-7
18.07.99 Final...........Mayo...1-14	Galway 1-10

● Leinster

09.05.99 P ....Wexford...0-16	Longford 1-13
09.05.99 P...........Carlow.....1-8	Westmeath ...2-10
16.05.99 P (R) ....Longford...2-15	Wexford 0-11
30.05.99 P........Westmeath...3-17	Longford 2-9
06.06.99 1st rnd ......Dublin...2-15	Louth 0-14
06.06.99 1st rnd ....Meath...2-20	Wicklow 0-6
13.06.99 1st rnd ......Laois...1-16	Westmeath 1-8
13.06.99 1st rnd.......Offaly...0-11	Kildare 0-7
27.06.99 s/f ....Dublin...1-11	Laois.............0-14
04.07.99 s/f ....Meath...1-13	Offaly 0-9
18.07.99 s/f (R) ....Dublin...0-16	Laois 1-11
01.08.99 Final ....Meath...1-14	Dublin 0-12

● Munster

23.05.99 1st rnd ....Kerry...1-11	Tipperary 0-8
23.05.99 1st rnd .Waterford...0-4	Cork..............3-23
19.06.99 s/f..............Cork...4-13	Limerick 1-6
20.06.99 s/f..............Kerry...3-17	Clare.............0-12
18.07.99 Final..........Cork...2-10	Kerry 2-4

● Ulster

30.05.99 P........Monaghan...1-10	Fermanagh ...2-12
06.06.99 1st rnd....Donegal.....2-9	Armagh.........1-12
13.06.99 1st rnd ......Derry...2-8	Cavan 2-15
13.06.99 1st rnd (R)Armagh..2-11	Donegal 0-12
20.06.99 1st rnd......Down...1-15	Antrim 0-14
20.06.99 1st rnd (R).Cavan.....0-5	Derry.............2-14
27.06.99 1st rnd......Tyrone...0-18	Fermanagh 0-8
04.07.99 s/f............Armagh...1-10	Derry.............0-12

11.07.99 s/f ....Down...2-14   Tyrone 0-15
01.08.99 Final........Armagh...3-12   Down 0-10
● **All-Ireland Series**
22.08.99 s/f................Cork...2-12   Mayo............0-12
29.08.99 s/f ....Meath...0-15   Armagh..........2-5
26.09.99 Final ....Meath...1-11   Cork...............1-8

1999 MINOR HURLING CHAMPIONSHIP
● **Leinster**
11.07.99 Final ......Wexford...0-13   Kilkenny........0-13
16.07.99 Final (R).Kilkenny...2-13   Wexford 1-11
● **Munster**
04.07.99 Final .....Tipperary...1-13   Clare..............0-7
● **Ulster**
10.07.99 Final ....Antrim...2-13   Down 0-3
● **All-Ireland Series**
24.07.99 q/f ....Wexford...2-17   Antrim 1-9
25.07.99 q/f ....Galway...5-11   Clare............1-10
08.08.99 s/f ....Tipperary...3-13   Wexford 1-8
15.08.99 s/f ....Galway...1-18   Kilkenny..........3-9
12.09.99 Final ......Galway...0-13   Tipperary 0-10

1999 MINOR FOOTBALL CHAMPIONSHIP
● **Connacht**
18.07.99 Final...........Mayo.....3-3   Galway 1-10
● **Leinster**
01.08.99 Final ....Dublin...1-13   Wexford 2-10
08.08.99 Final (R) ....Dublin...2-13   Wexford 1-12
● **Munster**
18.07.99 Final.............Cork...2-16   Kerry..............1-8
● **Ulster**
01.08.99 Final ....Down...0-10   Donegal 0-10
08.08.99 Final (R) .....Down.....2-7   Donegal 0-9

● **All-Ireland Series**
22.08.99 s/f................Mayo...1-19   Cork...............2-9
29.08.99 s/f ....Down...0-13   Dublin 1-10
03.09.99 s/f (R) ....Down...2-14   Dublin 1-9
26.09.99 Final ....Down...1-14   Mayo............0-14

1999 U21 HURLING CHAMPIONSHIP
● **Leinster**
17.07.99 Final.......Kilkenny...1-17   Offaly 1-6
● **Munster**
31.08.99 Final .....Tipperary...1-18   Clare............1-15
● **Ulster**
18.07.99 Final ....Antrim...2-14   Derry............0-12
● **All-Ireland Series**
29.08.99 s/f ....Kilkenny...6-27   Antrim 0-10
04.09.99 s/f ....Galway...3-12   Tipperary 1-16
19.09.99 final ....Kilkenny...1-13   Galway 0-14

1999 U21 FOOTBALL CHAMPIONSHIP
● **Connacht**
17.04.99 Final Roscommon...1-12   Sligo 0-9
● **Leinster**
11.04.99 Final ..Westmeath.....1-9   Laois............0-10
● **Munster**
14.04.99 Final...........Kerry...1-10   Cork...............0-7
● **Ulster**
19.04.99 Final ...Monaghan...0-12   Donegal 1-8
● **All-Ireland Series**
01.05.99 s/f................Kerry...3-15   Roscommon ...1-8
02.05.99 s/f ......Westmeath...2-10   Monaghan 0-8
15.05.99 Final ..Westmeath...0-12   Kerry 0-9

1999 All-Ireland Football Final Statistics

Croke Park, September 26. Attendance: 63,276 **Meath 1-11, Cork 1-8.**

Meath, Team and Scorers: Cormac Sullivan; Mark O'Reilly, Darren Fay, Cormac Murphy; Paddy Reynolds, Enda McManus, Hank Traynor; Nigel Crawford, John McDermott; Evan Kelly (0-3), Trevor Giles (0-4), Nigel Nestor; Ollie Murphy (1-0), Graham Geraghty (0-3), Donal Curtis (0-1). **Subs:** Richie Kealy for Nestor (56 mins), Barry Callaghan for Traynor (62 mins), Tommy Dowd for Kelly (70 mins). **Manager:** Sean Boylan.

Cork, Team and Scorers: Kevin O'Dwyer; Ronan McCarthy, Seán Óg Ó hAilpín, Anthony Lynch; Ciaran O'Sullivan, Owen Sexton, Martin Cronin; Nicholas Murphy, Micheál O'Sullivan; Micheál Cronin, Joe Kavanagh (1-1), Padraig O'Mahony (0-1); Philip Clifford (Captain 0-5), Don Davis, Mark O'Sullivan (0-1). **Subs:** Fionan Murray for Mark O'Sullivan (43 mins), Fachtna Collins for Micheál Cronin (49 mins), Michael O'Donovan for O'Mahony (62 mins). **Manager:** Larry Tompkins.

Half-time score: Meath 1-5, Cork 0-5. **Top Scorer:** Philip Clifford (Cork 0-5, 3 frees). **Man-of-the-Match:** Mark O'Reilly (Meath). **Referee:** Mick Curley (Gaway). **Booked:** Hank Traynor, John McDermott (both Meath). **Sent off:** None.

1999 All-Ireland Hurling Final Statistics

Croke Park, September 12. Attendance: 62,989. **Cork 0-13, Kilkenny 0-12.**

Cork, Team and Scorers: Donal Óg Cusack; Fergal Ryan, Diarmuid O'Sullivan, John Browne; Wayne Sherlock, Brian Corcoran, Seán Óg Ó hAilpín; Mark Landers (Captain 0-1), Mickey O'Connell; Timmy McCarthy (0-3), Fergal McCormack, Neil Ronan; Seanie McGrath (0-3), Joe Deane (0-3), Ben O'Connor (0-1). **Subs:** Alan Browne (0-1) for N. Ronan (half-time), Kevin Murray (0-1) for M. Landers (51 mins). **Manager:** Jimmy Barry–Murphy.

Kilkenny, Team and Scorers: James McGarry; Philly Larkin, Canice Brennan, Willie O'Connor; Michael Kavanagh, Pat O'Neill, Peter Barry; Andy Comerford (0-2), Denis Byrne (0-1); DJ Carey, John Power (0-1), Brian McEvoy (0-1); Ken O'Shea, Henry Shefflin (0-5), Charlie Carter (0-2). **Subs:** PJ Delaney for J. Power (64 mins), Niall Moloney for C. Carter (64 mins). **Manager:** Brian Cody.

Half time score: Cork 0-4, Kilkenny 0-5. **Top Scorer:** Henry Shefflin (Kilkenny 0-5, 4 frees). **Man-of-the-Match:** Brian Corcoran. **Referee:** Pat O'Connor (Limerick). **Booked:** None. **Sent off:** None.

The National Leagues

● HURLING

02.05.99 s/f ....Galway...2-15   Kilkenny 1-15
02.05.99 s/f ....Tipperary...0-19   Clare 1-15
16.05.99 Final ....Tipperary...1-14   Galway 1-10

Division 1A	P	W	D	L	Pts
Galway	6	6	0	0	12
Clare	6	4	1	1	9
Offaly	6	3	0	3	6
Antrim	6	3	0	3	6
Dublin	6	2	1	3	5
Limerick	6	2	0	4	4
Kerry	6	0	0	6	0

Division 1B	P	W	D	L	Pts
Tipperary	6	5	0	1	10
Kilkenny	6	5	0	1	10
Cork	6	4	0	2	8
Laois	6	3	0	3	6
Waterford	6	2	0	4	4
Wexford	6	2	0	4	4
Down	6	0	0	6	0

Division 1 relegation playoff
16.05.99 ....Kerry...2-13   Down 0-12

Division 2	P	W	D	L	Pts
Wicklow	9	8	0	1	16
Derry	9	8	0	1	16
Roscommon	9	6	1	2	13
Kildare	9	5	0	4	10
Carlow	9	4	1	4	9
Westmeath	9	4	0	5	8
Meath	9	3	1	5	7
London	9	3	1	5	7
Tyrone	9	2	0	7	4
Monaghan	9	0	0	9	0

Division 2 Final
30.05.99 ....Derry...1-14   Wicklow 0-13

Division 3	P	W	D	L	Pts
Mayo	8	7	0	1	14
Armagh	8	6	1	1	13
Louth	8	6	0	2	12
Sligo	8	6	0	2	12
Fermanagh	8	4	0	4	8
Leitrim	8	2	0	6	4
Longford	8	2	0	6	4
Cavan	8	1	1	6	3

Donegal ....8 ....0 ....0 ....8 0
Division 3 Final:10.10.99 Armagh...0-13   Mayo 1-6

● FOOTBALL

11.04.99 q/f ....Armagh.....0-6   Sligo 0-6
11.04.99 q/f ....Meath...0-14   Kerry 0-10
11.04.99 q/f ....Cork...3-14   Derry 1-6
11.04.99 q/f ....Dublin...1-17   Kildare 2-8
25.04.99 s/f ....Cork...0-6   Meath 0-3
25.04.99 s/f ....Dublin...0-11   Armagh 0-11
02.05.99 s/f. (r) ....Dublin...1-14   Armagh.......0-12
09.05.99 Final............Cork...0-12   Dublin 1-7

Division 1A	P	W	D	L	Pts
Armagh	7	5	1	1	11
Cork	7	4	1	2	9
Dublin	7	3	2	2	8
Tyrone	7	3	2	2	8
Galway	7	3	1	3	7
Donegal	7	3	0	4	7
Offaly	7	2	2	3	6
Leitrim	7	0	1	6	1

Division 1B	P	W	D	L	Pts
Meath	7	4	1	2	9
Kildare	7	4	1	2	9
Derry	7	3	2	2	8
Mayo	7	3	2	2	8
Clare	7	3	1	3	7
Down	7	3	1	3	7
Monaghan	7	3	1	3	7
Laois	7	0	1	6	1

Division 2A	P	W	D	L	Pts
Kerry	8	7	0	1	14
Roscommon	8	7	0	1	14
Westmeath	8	6	0	2	12
Wicklow	8	6	0	2	12
Louth	8	4	0	4	8
Antrim	8	2	0	6	4
Limerick	8	2	0	6	4
London	8	2	0	6	4
Kilkenny	8	0	0	8	0

Division 2B	P	W	D	L	Pts
Sligo	7	5	1	1	11
Fermanagh	7	4	2	1	10
Carlow	7	5	0	2	10
Wexford	7	4	0	3	8
Cavan	7	4	0	3	8
Longford	7	3	0	4	6
Tipperary	7	1	1	5	3
Waterford	7	0	0	7	0

1998 All-Stars

HURLING: Stephen Byrne Offaly; **Willie O'Connor** Kilkenny, **Kevin Kinahan** Offaly, **Martin Hanamy** Offaly; **Anthony Daly** Clare, **Sean McMahon** Clare, **Kevin Martin** Offaly; **Tony Browne** Waterford, **Ollie Baker** Clare; **James O'Connor** Clare, **Martin Storey** Wexford, **Michael Duignan** Offaly; **Joe Dooley** Offaly, **Brian Whelahan** Offaly, **Charlie Carter** Kilkenny. **Player of the Year:** Tony Browne (Waterford).
FOOTBALL: Martin McNamara Galway; **Brian Lacey** Kildare, **Sean Martin Lockhart** Derry, **Tomás Mannion** Galway; **John Finn** Kildare, **Glen Ryan** Kildare, **Seán Óg de Paor** Galway; **Kevin Walsh** Galway, **John McDermott** Meath; **Michael Donnellan** Galway, **Jarlath Fallon** Galway, **Dermot Earley** Kildare; **Karl O'Dwyer** Kildare; **Padraig Joyce** Galway, **Declan Browne** Tipperary. **Player of the Year:** Jarlath Fallon (Galway).

Roll of Honour

● **ALL-IRELAND SENIOR FOOTBALL**
31 Kerry 1903, 1904, 1909, 1913, 1914, 1924, 1926, 1929, 1930, 1931, 1932, 1937, 1939, 1940, 1941, 1946, 1953, 1955, 1959, 1962, 1969, 1970, 1975, 1978, 1979, 1980, 1981, 1984, 1985, 1986, 1997.
22 Dublin 1891, 1892, 1894, 1897, 1898, 1899, 1901, 1902, 1906, 1907, 1908, 1921, 1922, 1923, 1942, 1958, 1963, 1974, 1976, 1977, 1983, 1995.
8 Galway 1925, 1934, 1938, 1956, 1964, 1965, 1966, 1998.
7 Meath 1949, 1954, 1967, 1987, 1988, 1996, 1999.
6 Cork 1890, 1911, 1945, 1973, 1989, 1990.
5 Cavan 1933, 1935, 1947, 1948, 1952. **Down** 1960, 1961, 1968, 1991, 1994. **Wexford** 1893, 1915, 1916, 1917, 1918.
4 Kildare 1905, 1919, 1927, 1928. **Tipperary** 1889, 1895, 1900, 1920.
3 Louth 1910, 1912, 1957. **Mayo** 1936, 1950, 1951. **Offaly** 1971, 1972, 1982.
2 Limerick 1887, 1896. **Roscommon** 1943, 1944.
1 Donegal 1992. **Derry** 1993.

● **ALL-IRELAND SENIOR HURLING**
28 Cork 1890, 1892, 1893, 1894, 1902, 1903, 1919, 1926, 1928, 1929, 1931, 1941, 1942, 1943, 1944, 1946, 1952, 1953, 1954, 1966, 1970, 1976, 1977, 1978, 1984, 1986, 1990, 1999.
25 Kilkenny 1904, 1905, 1907, 1909, 1911, 1912, 1913, 1922, 1932, 1933, 1935, 1939, 1947, 1957, 1963, 1967, 1969, 1972, 1974, 1975, 1979, 1982, 1983, 1992, 1993.
24 Tipperary 1887, 1895, 1896, 1898, 1899, 1900, 1906, 1908, 1916, 1925, 1930, 1937, 1945, 1949, 1950, 1951, 1958, 1961, 1962, 1964, 1965, 1971, 1989, 1991.
7 Limerick 1897, 1918, 1921, 1934, 1936, 1940, 1973.
6 Dublin 1889, 1917, 1920, 1924, 1927, 1938. **Wexford** 1910, 1955, 1956, 1960, 1968, 1996.
4 Galway 1923, 1980, 1987, 1988. **Offaly** 1981, 1985, 1994, 1998.
3 Clare 1914, 1995, 1997.
2 Waterford 1948, 1959.
1 Kerry 1891. **Laois** 1915. **London** 1901.

● **NATIONAL FOOTBALL LEAGUE**
16 Kerry 1928, 1929, 1931, 1932, 1959, 1961, 1963, 1969, 1971, 1972, 1973, 1974, 1977, 1982, 1984, 1997.
10 Mayo 1934, 1935, 1936, 1937, 1938, 1939, 1941, 1949, 1954, 1970.
8 Dublin 1953, 1955, 1958, 1976, 1978, 1987, 1991, 1993.
7 Meath 1933, 1946, 1951, 1975, 1988, 1990, 1994.
5 Cork 1952, 1956, 1980, 1989, 1999.
4 Derry 1947, 1992, 1995, 1996. **Down** 1960, 1962, 1968, 1983. **Galway** 1940, 1957, 1965, 1981.
3 New York 1950, 1964, 1967.
2 Laois 1927, 1986.
1 Cavan 1948. **Longford** 1966. **Monaghan** 1985. **Offaly** 1998. **Roscommon** 1979.
● **NATIONAL HURLING LEAGUE**
17 Tipperary 1928, 1949, 1950, 1952, 1954, 1955, 1957, 1959, 1960, 1961, 1964, 1965, 1968, 1979, 1988, 1994, 1999.
14 Cork 1926, 1930, 1940, 1941, 1948, 1953, 1969, 1970, 1972, 1974, 1980, 1981, 1993, 1998.
11 Limerick 1934, 1935, 1936, 1937, 1938, 1947, 1971, 1984, 1985, 1992, 1997.
9 Kilkenny 1933, 1962, 1966, 1976, 1982, 1983, 1986, 1990, 1995.
6 Galway 1932, 1951, 1975, 1987, 1989, 1996.
4 Wexford 1956, 1958, 1967, 1973.
3 Clare 1946, 1977, 1978.
2 Dublin 1929, 1939.
1 Offaly 1991. **Waterford** 1963.

● **ALL-IRELAND MINOR (UNDER 18) FOOTBALL**
11 Kerry 1931, 1932, 1933, 1946, 1950, 1962, 1963, 1975, 1980, 1988, 1994.
10 Dublin 1930, 1945, 1954, 1955, 1956, 1958, 1959, 1979, 1982, 1984.
9 Cork 1961, 1967, 1968, 1969, 1972, 1974, 1981, 1991, 1993.
6 Mayo 1935, 1953, 1966, 1971, 1978, 1985.
5 Galway 1952, 1960, 1970, 1976, 1986.
4 Tyrone 1947, 1948, 1973, 1998.
3 Derry 1965, 1983, 1989. **Down** 1977, 1987, 1999. **Meath** 1957, 1990, 1992. **Roscommon** 1939, 1941, 1951.
2 Cavan 1937, 1938. **Laois** 1996, 1997. **Louth** 1936, 1940.
1 Armagh 1949. **Clare** 1929. **Offaly** 1964. **Tipperary** 1934. **Westmeath** 1995.

● **ALL-IRELAND MINOR (UNDER 18) HURLING**
17 Cork 1928, 1937, 1938, 1939, 1941, 1951, 1964, 1967, 1969, 1970, 1971, 1974, 1978, 1979, 1985, 1995, 1998.
16 Kilkenny 1931, 1935, 1936, 1950, 1960, 1961, 1962, 1972, 1973, 1975, 1977, 1981, 1988, 1990, 1991, 1993. **Tipperary** 1930, 1932, 1933, 1934, 1947, 1949, 1952, 1953, 1955, 1956, 1957, 1959, 1976, 1980, 1982, 1996.
4 Galway 1983, 1992, 1994, 1999. **Dublin** 1945, 1946, 1954, 1965.
3 Limerick 1940, 1958, 1984. **Offaly** 1986, 1987, 1989. **Wexford** 1963, 1966, 1968.
2 Waterford 1929, 1948.
1 Clare 1997.

● **ALL-IRELAND UNDER 21 HURLING**
11 Cork 1966, 1968, 1969, 1970, 1971, 1973, 1976, 1982, 1988, 1997, 1998.
8 Tipperary 1964, 1967, 1979, 1980, 1981, 1985, 1989, 1995.
7 Galway 1972, 1978, 1983, 1986, 1991, 1993, 1996. **Kilkenny** 1974, 1975, 1977, 1984, 1990, 1994, 1999.
1 Limerick 1987. **Waterford** 1992. **Wexford** 1965.

● **ALL-IRELAND UNDER 21 FOOTBALL**
9 Cork 1970, 1971, 1980, 1981, 1984, 1985, 1986, 1989, 1994. **Kerry** 1964, 1973, 1975, 1976, 1977, 1990, 1995, 1996, 1998.
3 Mayo 1967, 1974, 1983.
2 Donegal 1982, 1987. **Derry** 1968, 1997. **Roscommon** 1966, 1978. **Tyrone** 1991, 1992.
1 Antrim 1969. **Down** 1979. **Galway** 1972. **Kildare** 1965. **Meath** 1993. **Offaly** 1988. **Westmeath** 1999.

Camogie

Cumann Camógaíochta na nGael
Páirc an Chrócaigh, Áth Cliath 3. Tel. (01) 8554257.

Founded...1904
President.....................................Fileas Ní Bhreasláin
Secretary.....................................Síle De Bhailís
Number of Affiliated Clubs 498
Number of Members.....................................78,000
● 1999 CHAMPIONS
All-Ireland Senior...Tipperary
All-Ireland Intermediate ....Clare
All-Ireland Junior...Cork

All-Ireland Minor...Cork
National League Senior ....Cork
National League Junior ....Derry

● 1999 SENIOR CHAMPIONSHIP RESULTS

03.07.99 preliminary ...Cork...7-24	Wexford 0-2
10.07.99 q/f.............Down...3-14	Dublin 3-9
17.07.99 q/f.......Tipperary...1-18	Clare............1-6
18.07.99 q/f.............Cork...5-18	Limerick 0-2
18.07.99 q/f.........Kilkenny.....2-8	Galway 1-8
07.08.99 s/f.........Kilkenny...2-12	Cork.............1-13
07.08.99 s/f ....Tipperary...6-22	Down 1-3
05.09.99 Final .....Tipperary...0-12	Kilkenny.........1-8

1999 All-Ireland Camogie Final Statistics

Croke Park, September 5. Attendance: 15,084. **Tipperary 0-12, Kilkenny 1-8.**
Tipperary Team and Scorers: J. Delaney; S. Kelly, U. O'Dwyer, C. Madden; M. Stokes Captain, C. Gaynor, S. Nealon; E. Hayden, A. McDermott; N. Kennedy (0-6), T. Brophy, H. Kiely; E. McDonnell (0-1), D. Hughes (0-3), N. Harkin. **Subs:** P. Fogarty for Kiely; C. Hennessy (0-2) for Harkin.
Kilkenny Team and Scorers: M. Holland; T. Millea, M. Hickey, U. Murphy; S. Costelloe, J. Maher, M. Costelloe; K. Long, S. Millea (0-7); S. Gleeson, B. Mullaly, M. Downey; M. Comerford, M. Maher (0-1), L. Lyng (1-0). **Subs:** A Downey for M. Downey.
Referee: A. Derham (Dublin).

Roll of Honour

● **ALL-IRELAND SENIOR**
26 Dublin 1932, 1933, 1937, 1938, 1942, 1943, 1944, 1948, 1949, 1950, 1951, 1952, 1953, 1954, 1955, 1957, 1958, 1959, 1960, 1961, 1962, 1963, 1964, 1965, 1966, 1984.
19 Cork 1934, 1935, 1936, 1939, 1940, 1941, 1970, 1971, 1972, 1973, 1978, 1980, 1982, 1983, 1992, 1993, 1995, 1997, 1998.
12 Kilkenny 1974, 1976, 1977, 1981, 1985, 1986, 1987, 1988, 1989, 1990, 1991, 1994.
6 Antrim 1945, 1946, 1947, 1956, 1967, 1979.
3 Wexford 1968, 1969, 1975.
1 Galway 1996. **Tipperary** 1999.

● **ALL-IRELAND INTERMEDIATE**
2 Clare 1993, 1995.
1 Dublin 1992. **Armagh** 1994. **Limerick** 1996.

Tipperary 1997. **Down** 1998.

● **ALL-IRELAND JUNIOR**
6 Cork 1973, 1980, 1983, 1984, 1996, 1999. **Galway** 1972, 1979, 1985, 1988, 1994, 1998.
3 Clare 1974, 1981, 1986. **Down** 1968, 1976, 1991. **Dublin** 1970, 1971, 1975. **Kildare** 1987, 1989, 1990.
2 Derry 1969, 1978. **Limerick** 1977, 1995.
1 Antrim 1997. **Armagh** 1993. **Louth** 1982. **Tipperary** 1992.

● **ALL-IRELAND MINOR**
9 Cork 1975, 1976, 1978, 1979, 1980, 1983, 1984, 1985, 1998.
7 Galway 1977, 1981, 1986, 1987, 1994, 1996, 1997.
3 Kilkenny 1988, 1989, 1991. **Tipperary** 1990, 1992, 1993.
1 Down 1974. **Dublin** 1982. **Wexford** 1995.

Women's Gaelic Football

Cumann Peíl Gael na mBan
House of Sport, Long Mile Road, Dublin 12. Tel. (01) 4569113. website: www.ladiesgaelic.ie.
email: info@ladiesgaelic.ie.
Founded...1974
President.............................Noel Murray (Waterford)
President Elect.................Walter Thompson (Dublin)
Secretary ....Helen O'Rourke (Dublin)
Number of Affiliated Clubs 600

Number of Members.....................................70,000
● 1999 CHAMPIONS
All-Ireland Senior ....Mayo
All-Ireland Intermediate ....Louth
All-Ireland Junior ....Tyrone
All-Ireland Minor ....Monaghan
National League Division 1 ....Monaghan
National League Division 2 ....Tyrone
National League Division 3 ....Cork

1999 SENIOR CHAMPIONSHIP RESULTS

● **Leinster**

04.07.99 q/f	.....Westmeath.....0-9	Meath	1-11
04.07.99 q/f	........Longford...3-11	Louth	1-8
04.07.99 q/f	.............Dublin...2-11	Wexford	2-6
11.07.99 s/f	...............Laois...1-10	Dublin	0-9
11.07.99 s/f	...............Meath...0-14	Longford	1-10
25.07.99 Final	.........Meath...1-12	Laois	1-7

● **Munster**

19.07.99 s/f........Waterford....w/o Clare ....

19.07.99 s/f..............Kerry.....1-7 Cork 0-11
15.08.99..............Waterford...6-12 Cork................2-8

● **All-Ireland Series**

04.09.99 s/f	.......Waterford...1-15	Monaghan	1-9
04.09.99 s/f	..............Mayo...3-13	Meath	2-7
03.10.99 Final	..........Mayo...0-12	Waterford	0-8

1999 All-Ireland Final Statistics

Croke Park, October 3. Attendance: 15,159 **Mayo 0-12, Waterford 0-8.**
Mayo, Team and Scorers: D. Horan; N. Ó Shé, H. Lohan, I. Mullarkey (0-1); M. Heffernan, Y. Byrne, N. Lally; C. Egan, C. Heffernan (0-4); M. Staunton, C. Staunton, S. Costello (0-1); D. O'Hora (0-5), S. Bailey (0-1), M. O'Malley. **Subs:** O. Casby for C. Staunton (1 min); S. Gibbons for M. O'Malley (54 mins).
Waterford, Team and Scorers: S. Hickey; T. Whyte, A. Crotty, N. Walsh; M. Troy, S. O'Ryan, J. Torpey (0-1); M. O'Ryan, O. Condon; F. Crotty, M. O'Donnell, N. Barry (0-2); A. Wall, C. Ryan (0-2), G. Ryan (0-3). **Subs:** B. Nagle for F. Crotty (39 mins); P. Walsh for M. O'Ryan (53 mins).
Referee: Finbarr O'Driscoll (Dublin).

Roll of Honour

● **ALL-IRELAND SENIOR**
11 Kerry 1976, 1982, 1983, 1984, 1985, 1986, 1987, 1988, 1989, 1990, 1993
5 Waterford 1991, 1992, 1994, 1995, 1998
3 Tipperary 1974, 1975, 1980
2 Monaghan 1996, 1997
2 Offaly 1979, 1981
1 Cavan 1977
1 Roscommon 1978
1 Mayo 1999.

● **ALL-IRELAND JUNIOR**
2 Clare 1991, 1996
1 Cork 1995
1 Dublin 1989

1 Leitrim 1988
1 London 1993
1 Longford 1997
1 Louth 1998
1 Mayo 1987
1 Meath 1994
1 Monaghan 1992
1 Waterford 1986
1 Wicklow 1990
1 Tyrone 1999.

● **NATIONAL LEAGUE**
11 Kerry 1980, 1981, 1982, 1983, 1984, 1985, 1987, 1988, 1989, 1990, 1991
3 Monaghan 1994, 1996, 1997
3 Waterford 1992, 1995, 1998
1 Laois 1993
1 Tipperary 1979
1 Wexford 1986

Handball

Comhairle Liathróid Láimhe na hÉireann

Páric an Chrócaigh, Baile Átha Cliath 3. Tel. (01) 8741360. email: ihc@tinet.ie

Founded	1924
President	..................................Peter Carter
Secretary	....Lorcán Ó Ruairc
Number of Affilliated Clubs	180
Number of Members	7,365

● **1999 Senior All-Ireland Champions**
Softball Singles.....................Michael Walsh - Kilkenny
Softball DoublesWalter O'Connor, Tom Sheridan - Meath
40x20 Singles ....Tony Healy - Cork
40x20 Doubles............Tony Healy, John Herlihy - Cork

● **1999 Intermediate All-Ireland Champions**
Softball Singles.........................Eoin Kennedy - Dublin
Softball Doubles.........David King, John Ryan - Carlow
40x20 Singles.................................Paul Brady - Cavan
40x20 Doubles..Dominic Lynch, Anthony Lynch - Kerry

● **1999 Junior All-Ireland Champions**
Softball Singles ....Eamon O'Neill - Limerick
Softball DoublesEamon O'Neill, Martin Kiely - Limerick
Hardball Singles...................Eamon O'Neill - Limerick
Hardball DoublesEamon Law, Eddie Bourke - Kilkenny
40x20 Singles ....Jimmy King - Carlow
40x20 Doubles ....Pat Madden, Pat Coughlab - Clare

Roll of Honour

● **SENIOR SOFTBALL DOUBLES**
10 M. Walsh & E. Downey Kilkenny 1985, 1987, 1988, 1989, 1990, 1991, 1993, 1995, 1996, 1997.
7 P. Downey & J. O'Brien Kerry 1955, 1956, 1960, 1961, 1962, 1963, 1964.
5 J. Hassett & E. Hassett Tipperary 1934, 1935, 1936, 1937, 1938.
3 J.J. Gilmartin & J. Dunne Kilkenny 1939, 1940, 1941. **T. Quish & J. Quish** Limerick 1983, 1984, 1986. **R. Lyng & S. Buggy** Wexford 1970, 1977, 1979.
2 L. Rowe & G. Rowe Dublin 1946, 1948. **J. Hassett & J. O'Brien** 1951, 1952. **T. McEllistrim & M. McEllistrim** all Kerry 1968, 1971. **T. McGarry & M. Mullins** Limerick 1958, 1959. **T. Sheridan & J. McGovern** 1992, 1994. **T. Sheridan & W. O'Connor** all Meath 1997, 1998. **P. Perry & A. Mullaney** Roscommon 1932, 1933. **J. Bergin & J. Sweeney** Tipperary 1949, 1950. **P. Murphy & J. Quigley** Wexford 1972, 1974. **M. O'Neill & L. Sherry** Wicklow 1930, 1931.
1 J. Kirby & D. Kirby Clare 1978. **M. Griffin & M. Walsh** Cork 1953. **M. Joyce & C. Ryan** Dublin 1927. **J. Whyte & C. Barrett** Galway 1926. **M. McEllistrim & N. Kerins** Kerry 1973. **A. Greene & P. Hughes** 1981. **C. Delaney & J. Dunne** 1954. **D. Brennan & J. Lucas** 1929. **J. Delaney & T. Ryan** 1965. **O. Harold & P. Reilly** 1980. **T. Behan & J. Norton** all Kilkenny 1925. **P. McGarry & M. Hogan** Limerick 1976. **M. Walsh & P. McGee** Mayo 1966. **L. Molloy & D. McGovern** Meath 1967. **J. Bergin & J. O'Rourke** Sligo 1947. **J. Collins & C. Collins** Tipperary 1942. **J. Flavin & M. Battersberry** Waterford 1928. **J. Ryan & J. Doyle** 1957. **P. Murphy & R. Lyng** 1975. **R. Lyng & J. Goggins** all Wexford 1982. **P. Lee & J. Cleary** Wicklow 1969.

● **SENIOR SOFTBALL SINGLES**
14 M. Walsh Kilkenny 1985, 1986, 1987, 1988, 1989, 1990, 1991, 1992, 1993, 1994, 1995, 1996, 1997, 1999.
8 P. Perry Roscommon 1930, 1931, 1932, 1933, 1934, 1935, 1936, 1937.
6 J. Maher Louth 1963, 1964, 1968, 1969, 1970, 1973.
5 J. Ryan Wexford 1952, 1954, 1955, 1956, 1957.
4 P. Kirby Clare 1974, 1975, 1976, 1977.
3 L. Rowe Dublin 1947, 1949, 1951. **J.J. Gilmartin** Kilkenny 1938, 1939, 1946. **R. Lyng** Wexford 1965, 1971, 1978.
2 P. Downey Kerry 1958, 1961. **T. O'Rourke** Kildare 1979, 1984. **F. Confrey** Louth 1959, 1960. **S. McCabe** Monaghan 1966, 1967. **J. Bergin** Tipperary 1948, 1950.
1 M. Griffin Cork 1953. **M. Joyce** 1925. **P. Ryan** 1980. **W. McGuire** all Dublin 1927. **M. Walsh** Galway 1940. **D. Brennan** 1929. **J. Delaney** 1962. **J. Dunne** 1941. **O. Harold** 1982. **P. Reilly** 1981. **T. Behan** all Kilkenny 1926. **J. McNally** Mayo 1928. **W. O'Connor** Meath 1988. **A. Ryan** Tipperary 1983. **P. Murphy** Wexford

1972.

● **SENIOR HARDBALL DOUBLES**
6 J. Ryan & J. Doyle Wexford 1952, 1954, 1955, 1956, 1957, 1956.
4 J.J. Gilmartin & P. Dalton Kilkenny 1940, 1945, 1946, 1947. **T. Quish & J. Quish** Limerick 1984, 1985, 1986, 1987.
3 P. Downey & J. O'Brien Kerry 1959, 1960, 1963. **P. McGarry & J. Bennis** Limerick 1978, 1979, 1980. **P. McGee & P. Bolingbrook** Mayo 1965, 1966, 1967. **P. Bell & J. Doyle** Meath 1932, 1933, 1935. **W. O'Connor & T. Sheridan** Meath 1992, 1993, 1998.
2 W. Walsh & D. Keogh Cork 1943, 1944. **T. Soye & T. O'Reilly** Dublin 1927, 1928. **P. Winders & C. Winders** Kildare 1982, 1983. **W. O'Connor & D. Gough** Meath 1994, 1996. **P. Hickey & C. Cleere** Tipperary 1968, 1972. **P. Ormonde & C. Maloney** Tipperary 1929, 1931.
1 W. Walsh & T. Morrissey Cork 1948. **A. Clarke & G. Moran** 1950. **A. Clarke & J. Clarke** 1942. **M. Sullivan & J. Doyle** 1971. **T. Soye & G. Brown** all Dublin 1930. **J. Hassett & J. O'Brien** 1951. **J. Hassett & P. Downey** all Kerry 1953. **C. Winders & G. Lawlor** 1977. **P. Winders & M. Purcell** 1981. **R. Grattan & J. Bolger** 1949. **T. O'Rourke & M. Dowling** 1990. **T. O'Rourke & P. McCormack** 1998. **W. Doran & G. Lawlor** all Kildare 1969. **B. Bourke & W. Pratt** 1991. **J. Delaney & C. Delaney** 1961. **J. Lucas & T. Cherry** 1934. **J.J. Gilmartin & A. Cullen** 1937. **J.J. Gilmartin & J. Dunne** 1941. **J.J. Gilmartin & T. Cherry** 1938. **J.J. Gilmartin & T. Jordan** all Kilkenny 1939. **J.J. Bowles & S. Gleeson** Limerick 1926. **J. Maher & P. Reilly** Louth 1964. **P. McGee & B. Colleran** 1974. **P. McGee & P. McCormack** all Mayo 1976. **S. McCabe & L. Gilmore** Monaghan 1970. **P. Perry & P. Reid** Roscommon 1939. **E. Corbett & N. Ryan** 1995. **J. Ryan & M. Shanahan** 1962. **P. Hickey & J. Cleere** 1975. **W. McCarthy & N. Ryan** all Tipperary 1989. **A. Byrne & W. Mullins** Westmeath 1973.

● **SENIOR HARDBALL SINGLES**
10 J.J. Gilmartin Kilkenny 1936, 1937, 1938, 1939, 1940, 1941, 1942, 1945, 1946, 1947. **P. McGee** Mayo 1965, 1967, 1972, 1973, 1974, 1975, 1976, 1977, 1982, 1983.
6 A. Clarke 1944, 1948, 1949, 1951, 1954, 1955. **T. Soye** both Dublin 1926, 1927, 1928, 1929, 1930, 1931. **J. Maher** 1961, 1963, 1964, 1968, 1969, 1970. **P. McAuley** both Louth 1991, 1993, 1994, 1995, 1996, 1997.
4 P. Downey Kerry 1958, 1959, 1960, 1962. **T. O'Rourke** Kildare 1985, 1988, 1989, 1990. **J. Ryan** Wexford 1952, 1953, 1956, 1957.
2 P. Winders Kildare 1981, 1984. **B. Bourke** Kilkenny 1986, 1992. **P. McGarry** Limerick 1979, 1980. **P. Hickey** Tipperary 1966, 1971.
1 P. Reid Carlow 1934. **C. Winders** 1978. **M. Dowling** 1943. **R. Grattan** 1950. **W. Aldridge** all Kildare 1925. **J. Lucas** Kilkenny 1932. **P. Bell** 1933. **S. Tormey** 1935. **W. O'Connor** all Meath 1998. **M. Walsh** Roscommon 1987.

SOCCER

Republic of Ireland

THE FOOTBALL ASSOCIATION OF IRELAND
80 Merrion Square, Dublin 2.
Tel. (01) 6766864
website: www.fai.ie
email: info@fai.ie

Founded..1921
President.....................................Pat Quigley
Chief Executive ....Bernard J. O'Byrne
Number of Affiliated Clubs 4,139
Number of Coaches ....4,000 (at various levels)

1998/99 Champions
Premier Division...........................St Patrick's Athletic
First Division..................................Drogheda United
Harp Lager F.A.I. Cup ....Bray Wanderers
FAI League Cup...Cork City
Top Scorers 1998/99
Premier Division..T. Molloy (14) St Patrick's Athletic
First Division ....Tony Izzi (17) Cobh Ramblers
National League Player of the Year.....Colin Hawkins
Main Stadium ....Dalymount Park, capacity 18,000

International
National Manager...............................Mick McCarthy
Biggest Recorded Attendance 47,000
World Ranking –as of September 1999...............34th
Most Capped Player ....Tony Cascarino (86)
Most Caps won as Captain ....Andy Townsend (40)
Most International Goals ....Frank Stapleton (20)
1998 Senior Player of the Year ...Kenny Cunningham
1998 Young Player of the Year.............Robbie Keane
1998 Youths Player of the Year ....Barry Quinn
1998 Ladies Player of the Year ....Yvonne Lyons
Record International Victory ....8-0 (v Malta 1983)
Record International Defeat ....0-7 (v Brazil 1982)
Best World Cup Result ....Quarter-finalists 1990

International Results

European Championship Qualifiers,Senior
● Lansdowne Road 5 September 1998. **Republic of Ireland 2** (Irwin pen 4, Roy Keane 15), **Croatia 0.** *Republic of Ireland:* Given; Irwin, Cunningham, Babb, Staunton; McAteer, Roy Keane, Kinsella, Duff (Kenna 46); Robbie Keane (Carsley 61), O'Neill (Cascarino 8). *Referee:* V. Pereira (Portugal).
● Lansdowne Road, 14 October 1998. **Republic of Ireland 5** (Robbie Keane 16, 18, Roy Keane 54, Quinn 63, Breen 82), **Malta 0.** *Republic of Ireland:* Given; Kenna, Staunton, Breen, Cunningham; Roy Keane, McAteer (Carsley 84), Kinsella, Duff; Quinn (Cascarino 74), Robbie Keane (Kennedy 83). *Referee:* R. Olsen (Norway).
● Belgrade, 18 November 1998. **Yugoslavia 1** (Mijatovic), **Republic of Ireland 0.** *Republic of Ireland:*

Given; Irwin, Cunningham, Breen, Staunton; McAteer (O'Neill 82), Roy Keane, Kinsella, McLoughlin (Connolly 73); Duff, Quinn (Cascarino 73). *Referee:* K.E. Nilson (Sweden).
● Lansdowne Road, 9 June 1999. **Republic of Ireland 1** (Quinn 66), **FYR Macedonia 0.** *Republic of Ireland:* A. Kelly, Carr, Cunningham, Breen, Irwin; Carsley, Kennedy, Kinsella, Duff (Kilbane 63); Quinn (Connolly 82), Keane (Cascarino 69). *Referee:* U. Meier (Switzerland).
● Lansdowne Road, 1 September 1999. **Republic of Ireland 2** (Robbie Keane 53, Kennedy 68), **Yugoslavia 0.** *Republic of Ireland:* A. Kelly; Irwin (Carr 66), Breen, Cunningham, Staunton; Kennedy, Kinsella, Roy Keane (Carsley 68), Kilbane; Quinn (Cascarino 79), Robbie Keane. *Referee:* P. Collina (Italy).
● Zagreb, 4 September 1999. **Croatia 1, Republic of Ireland 0.** *Republic of Ireland:* A. Kelly; Carr, Cunningham, Breen, Staunton; Carsley, McLoughlin, Kinsella, G. Kelly (Harte 72), Duff (Kilbane 56); Cascarino (Quinn 82). *Referee:* M. Diaz-Vega (Spain).
● Valetta, 8 September 1999. **Malta 2, Republic of Ireland 3** (Robbie Keane 13, Breen 21, Staunton 74). *Republic of Ireland:* A. Kelly; Carr, Breen (Harte 73), Cunningham, Staunton; Kennedy (McLoughlin 55), Carsley, Kinsella, Kilbane (Duff 65), Robbie Keane, Quinn. *Referee:* S. Capodban (Romania).
● Skopje, 9 October 1999. **Macedonia 1, Republic of Ireland 1** (Quinn 17). *Republic of Ireland:* A. Kelly; Irwin, Breen, Cunningham, Stauntonl G. Kelly, Kinsella, McLoughlin, Kennedy (Holland 85); Robbie Keane (O'Neill 65), Quinn (Cascarino 78). *Referee:* Fernandez Marin (Spain).

GROUP 8 FINAL STANDINGS

	P	W	D	L	F	A	Pts
Yugoslavia	8	5	2	1	18	8	17
Republic of Ireland	8	5	1	2	14	6	16
Croatia	8	4	3	1	13	9	15
FYR Macedonia	8	2	2	4	13	14	8
Malta	8	0	0	8	6	27	0

Friendlies, Senior
● Lansdowne Road, 10 February 1999. **Republic of Ireland 2** (Irwin 37pen, Connolly 74), **Paraguay 0.** *Republic of Ireland:* Given (A. Kelly 68); Irwin, Cunningham, Breen, Harte (Babb 73); McAteer (McLoughlin 83), Roy Keane, Kinsella (Carsley 68), Duff; Quinn (Cascarino 70) Robbie Keane (Connolly 68). *Referee:* Gyfli Thor Orrason (Iceland).
● Lansdowne Road, 28 April 1999. **Republic of Ireland 2** (Kavanagh 75, Kennedy 77), **Sweden 0.** *Republic of Ireland:* Given; Carr, Cunningham, Breen (Babb 46); Staunton; McLoughlin, McAteer (Kilbane 46), Kinsella (Kavanagh 46), Kennedy (Duff 79); Quinn (Robbie Keane 79), Connolly (Cascarino 71).
● Lansdowne Road, May 29 1999. **Republic of Ireland 0, Northern Ireland 1** (Griffin 85). *Republic of Ireland:* Given; Carr, Cunningham, Babb, Maybury; Kennedy, Carsley (McLoughlin 45), Kinsella (Kavanagh

82), Duff (O'Neill 56); Quinn (Cascarino 72), Robbie Keane (Connolly 56). *Referee:* K Richards (Wales).

U21
EUROPEAN QUALIFIERS
● Kilkenny, 4 September 1998. **Republic of Ireland 2** (Conlon, S. Baker), **Croatia 2.**
● Arklow, 13 October 1998. **Republic of Ireland 2** (McClare 30, Worrell 90) **Malta 1.**
● Smederevo, Yugoslavia, 18 November 1998. **Yugoslavia 1, Republic of Ireland 1** (Kilbane 90 pen).
● Galway, 8 June 1999. **Republic of Ireland 0, Macedonia 0.**
● Tolka Park, 31 August 1999. **Republic of Ireland 0, Yugoslavia 2.**
● Zagreb, 3 September 1999. **Croatia 5, Ireland 1** (Hawkins).
● Valetta, 7 September 1999. **Malta 1, Republic of Ireland 3** (Malta og, Mahon, Fenn).
● Ohrid, 8 October 1999. **Macedonia 0, Republic of Ireland 1** (Rowlands).

U20
WORLD CUP in Nigeria
● Ibadan, 4 April 1999. **Republic of Ireland 0, Mexico 1.**
● Ibadan, 7 April 1999. **Republic of Ireland 2** (McPhail 42, Duff 64), **Saudi Arabia 0.**
● Ibadan, 10 April 1999. **Republic of Ireland 4** (Sadlier 20, Duff 73, Healy 74, Crossley 90), **Australia 0.**
● Kano, 14 April 1999. **Republic of Ireland 1** (Sadlier 35), **Nigeria 1.** Republic of Ireland lost 5-3 on penalties.

U18
EUROPEAN YOUTH CHAMPIONSHIPS
Qualifying Playoff
● The Oval, 9 March 1999. **Northern Ireland 1, Republic of Ireland 2** (Fitzpatrick 17, Doherty 73).
● Tolka Park, 11 May 1999. **Republic of Ireland 2** (Crossley 26, Doherty 67), **Northern Ireland 1.**
● Republic of Ireland win 4-2 on aggregate to qualify for European Championships in Sweden.
European Youth Championship Finals, Sweden
● Atvidaberg, 19 July 1999. **Republic of Ireland 1** (Crossley 60 pen), **Spain 0.**
● Finspang, 21 July 1999. **Republic of Ireland 3** (Barrett 4, Fitzpatrick 70, Doherty 87), **Georgia 3.**
● Norrköping, 23 July 1999. **Republic of Ireland 0, Italy 2.**
● Linköping, 25 July 1999. **Republic of Ireland 1** (C. Delaney 47), **Greece 0.**
Republic of Ireland finish third overall.

Domestic Results

FAI CUP
2nd rnd	Bohemians........0	Shelbourne 1	
2nd rnd	St Pats Athletic........1	UCD..................0	
2nd rnd	St Marys Cork........0	Kilkenny City......3	
2nd rnd	Galway United........1	H. FarmEverton .0	

2nd rnd	Bray Wanderers........3	Cherry Orchard..0	
2nd rnd	Sligo Rovers........2	Cobh Ramblers..1	
2nd rnd	Derry City........2	Dundalk 0	
2nd rnd	Cork City........0	Finn Harps........0	
2nd rnd (r)	Finn Harps........1	Cork City............0	
05.03.99 q/f	Galway Utd........1	St Pats Athletic ..0	
06.03.99 q/f	Kilkenny City........2	Finn Harps........2	
06.03.99 q/f	Sligo Rovers........1	Bray Wanderers.1	
07.03.99 q/f	Derry City........0	Shelbourne 2	
09.03.99 q/f (r)	Finn Harps ...w.o.	Kilkenny City........	
10.03.99 q/f (r)	Bray W........0	Sligo Rovers 0	
16.03.99 q/f (r2)	Bray W........1	Sligo Rovers 0	
02.04.99 s/f	Shelbourne........1	Bray Wanderers.2	
04.04.99 s/f	Galway Utd........1	Finn Harps........2	
09.05.99 Final	Bray W........0	Finn Harps 0	
15.05.99 Final (r)	Bray W........2	Finn Harps........2	
20.05.99 Final (r2)	Bray W........2	Finn Harps........1	

FINAL. Tolka Park 20 May 1999. Attendance: 4,350.
Bray Wanderers 2, Finn Harps 1.
Bray Wanderers: Walsh; Kenny, Doohan, Lynch, Farrell (Smyth 87); O'Connor, Tresson, Fox, Keogh; Byrne, O'Brien. Goals: Byrne 37 mins, 72 mins.
Finn Harps: McKenna; Scanlon (R. Boyle 63), Dykes, D. Boyle, Minnock; Mohan (S. Bradley 83), O'Brien, Harkin, McGrenaghan (Sheridan 76); Mulligan, Speak. Goal: Speak 11 mins.
Referee: J. McDermott (Dublin).

PREMIER DIVISION FINAL LEAGUE TABLE 1998/99
	P	W	D	L	F	A	Pts
St Patrick's Athletic	33	22	7	4	58	21	73
Cork City	33	21	7	5	62	25	70
Shelbourne	33	13	8	12	37	35	47
Finn Harps	33	12	10	11	39	40	46
Derry City	33	12	9	12	34	32	45
U.C.D.	33	10	12	11	31	32	42
Waterford United	33	11	9	13	21	37	42
Shamrock Rovers	33	9	13	11	34	40	40
Sligo Rovers	33	9	11	13	37	50	38
Bohemians	33	10	7	16	28	37	37
Bray Wanderers	33	8	8	17	30	45	32
Dundalk	33	6	9	18	23	40	27

Champions: **St Patrick's Athletic** *Relegated:* **Bray Wanderers** *and* **Dundalk.**

FIRST DIVISION FINAL LEAGUE TABLE 1998/99
	P	W	D	L	F	A	Pts
Drogheda United	36	17	13	6	57	32	64
Galway United	36	16	16	4	53	34	64
Cobh Ramblers	36	17	7	12	55	43	58
Longford Town	36	15	9	12	41	33	54
Kilkenny City	36	14	11	11	49	46	53
Limerick	36	13	13	10	39	35	52
Monaghan United	36	10	14	12	44	44	44
Athlone Town	36	10	10	16	45	61	40
Home Farm Everton	36	11	5	20	42	54	38
St Francis	36	2	12	22	25	68	18

Champions: **Drogheda United** *Promoted:* **Galway United.** Cobh Ramblers lost 7-0 on aggregate to Bohemians in the two leg Promotion/Relegation playoff.

1998/99 FAI Premier Division Results

	1	2	3	4	5	6	7	8	9	10	11	12
1. Bohemians	--	1-2	0-2	0-1	1-0	2-3	1-1	1-1	2-0	0-1	3-0	0-1
	--	0-0	0-2		2-1	0-1						0-1
2. Bray Wanderers	0-1	--	0-1	0-1	0-0	0-0	1-4	3-4	1-0	1-1	0-0	6-0
		--	1-3		1-0				0-1	1-2		0-1
3. Cork City	0-0	3-0	--	2-1	4-1	2-0	1-2	3-1	2-1	1-0	1-2	5-0
			--	0-1	2-0	2-1		3-0	2-1			0-0
4. Derry City	0-2	5-1	1-1	--	0-1	2-1	0-1	1-1	0-1	2-0	2-0	1-0
	0-1	1-1		--		1-0	0-0		1-0			
5. Dundalk	0-1	0-1	1-1	2-2	--	0-0	2-0	1-1	1-2	0-2	2-0	2-0
				0-1	--			1-1	1-2	3-2	0-2	
6. Finn Harps	1-0	6-2	1-1	2-2	0-0	--	2-1	2-1	3-2	1-1	0-0	1-2
		0-3			1-0	--	0-3	4-1			1-0	2-0
7. St Patrick's Athletic	3-0	3-0	2-0	1-0	3-1	2-2	--	3-0	2-1	4-1	1-0	2-0
	1-3	1-0	1-0		1-0		--			4-0	0-0	
8. Shamrock Rovers	3-0	0-1	0-3	0-0	1-1	2-0	2-1	--	2-1	1-1	2-0	0-0
	1-1	0-0		1-0			0-1	--			0-0	
9. Shelbourne	2-1	1-0	3-3	2-0	1-2	0-0	0-1	2-2	--	1-1	1-1	1-0
	1-2					2-0	1-1	1-0	--	1-0		0-2
10. Sligo Rovers	2-2	0-0	0-2	3-3	2-0	1-1	1-4	2-3	1-3	--	0-1	1-1
	2-1		2-5	2-0		2-0		1-0		--		2-1
11. UCD	2-0	3-1	0-1	2-2	0-0	3-0	2-2	0-2	1-1	2-0	--	1-1
	2-0	1-3	2-2	2-1					0-1	0-0	--	
12. Waterford	0-0	1-0	0-2	1-2	1-0	0-3	0-2	1-1	0-0	1-1	1-0	--
				1-0	2-0		0-0	1-0			1-2	--

1998/99 FAI 1ST DIVISION RESULTS

	1	2	3	4	5	6	7	8	9	10
1. Athlone Town	--	1-0	1-2	2-2	3-1	2-2	0-2	3-1	3-0	2-0
	--	2-3	0-1	1-1	1-1	2-0	1-1	1-1	4-1	1-1
2. Cobh Ramblers	4-0	--	2-0	3-0	2-1	3-1	1-0	0-2	3-0	4-1
	2-2	--	1-2	0-3	2-2	4-0	1-1	2-0	1-1	1-1
3. Drogheda Utd	4-0	1-1	--	1-1	1-0	0-1	1-0	1-2	2-0	1-1
	1-1	4-1	--	0-2	3-2	1-0	1-1	1-0	1-1	2-2
4. Galway Utd	2-0	0-2	2-2	--	2-1	1-0	0-0	0-0	1-1	1-1
	4-0	2-0	2-1	--	2-1	0-0	2-1	0-0	3-0	2-0
5. Home Farm Everton	3-0	2-3	1-5	0-2	--	2-1	3-1	2-0	2-1	3-2
	2-1	0-1	0-2	2-3	--	1-2	1-2	1-3	1-1	2-0
6. Kilkenny City	1-2	0-2	2-2	4-2	1-0	--	1-1	3-1	3-3	2-2
	4-1	3-1	1-1	1-1	1-0	--	2-1	2-2	0-2	1-0
7. Limerick	3-2	3-0	0-3	0-1	1-0	0-2	--	2-0	1-0	3-0
	3-1	1-1	1-0	1-1	0-1	1-1	--	0-0	1-1	2-1
8. Longford Town	1-0	2-0	1-2	1-1	2-0	3-1	3-0	--	2-0	2-3
	0-1	0-1	1-1	1-1	1-0	1-0	0-1	--	2-1	2-0
9. Monaghan United	5-1	1-0	0-0	3-3	1-1	0-1	1-1	0-1	--	3-1
	1-0	2-0	1-1	2-0	0-0	1-1	0-1	2-1	--	4-0
10. St Francis	1-1	1-0	0-3	2-2	1-2	0-3	2-2	0-2	0-3	--
	0-2	2-2	0-3	0-1	0-1	0-1	0-0	0-0	1-1	--

International Squad 1998-99

Name	Club	d.o.b.	Born	Pos	Debut	Caps	Goals
BABB, Phil	Liverpool	30.11.70	Lambeth	D	23.03.94	29	0
BREEN, Gary	Coventry City	12.12.73	London	D	29.05.96	24	4
CARR, Stephen	Tottenham Hotspur	29.08.76	Dublin	D	28.04.98	6	0
CARSLEY, Lee	Blackburn Rovers	28.02.74	Birmingham	M	11.10.97	14	0
CASCARINO, Tony	A.S. Nancy	01.09.62	Kent	S	11.09.85	86	19
CONNOLLY, David	Feyenoord	06.06.77	Willesden	S	29.05.96	18	7
CUNNINGHAM, Kenny	Wimbledon	28.06.71	Dublin	D	24.04.96	27	0
DUFF, Damian	Blackburn Rovers	02.03.79	Dublin	S	25.03.98	11	0
GIVEN, Shay	Newcastle United	20.04.76	Lifford	GK	29.03.96	23	0

Continued from previous page

Name	Club	d.o.b.	Born	Pos	Debut	Caps	Goals
HARTE, Ian	Leeds United	31.08.77	Drogheda	D	02.06.96	21	2
HOLLAND, Matt	Ipswich Town	11.04.74	Bury	M	09.10.99	1	0
IRWIN, Denis	Manchester United	31.10.65	Cork	D	12.09.90	54	4
KAVANAGH, Graham	Stoke City	02.12.73	Dublin	M	25.03.98	3	1
KEANE, Robbie	Coventry City	08.09.80	Dublin	S	25.03.98	12	4
KEANE, Roy	Manchester United	10.08.71	Cork	M	22.05.91	43	5
KELLY, Alan	Blackburn Rovers	11.08.68	Preston	GK	17.02.93	25	0
KELLY, Gary	Leeds United	09.07.74	Louth	M	23.03.94	30	1
KENNA, Jeff	Blackburn Rovers	27.08.70	Dublin	D	26.04.95	26	0
KENNEDY, Mark	Manchester City	15.05.76	Dublin	M	06.09.95	25	3
KILBANE, Kevin	West Bromwich Albion	01.02.77	Preston	S	06.09.98	8	0
KINSELLA, Mark	Charlton Athletic	12.08.72	Dublin	M	25.03.98	13	0
MAYBURY, Alan	Leeds United	08.08.78	Dublin	D	25.03.98	2	0
McATEER, Jason	Blackburn Rovers	18.06.71	Liverpool	M	23.03.94	30	1
McLOUGHLIN, Alan	Portsmouth	20.04.67	Manchester	M	03.06.90	41	2
O'NEILL, Keith	Middlesbrough	16.02.76	Dublin	S	29.05.96	13	4
QUINN, Niall	Sunderland	06.10.66	Dublin	S	25.05.86	73	19
STAUNTON, Steve	Liverpool	19.01.69	Drogheda	D	19.10.88	82	7

Information correct as of October 9 1999.

D.o.b.= Date of birth; Pos = Position; D=Defender; M=Midfielder; S=Striker.

Records

● CHAMPIONSHIP WINNERS

15 Shamrock Rovers 1922-23, 1924-25, 1926-27, 1931-32, 1937-38, 1938-39, 1953-54, 1956-57, 1958-59, 1963-64, 1983-84, 1984-85, 1985-86, 1986-87, 1993-94.

9 Dundalk 1932-33, 1962-63, 1966-67, 1975-76, 1978-79, 1981-82, 1987-88, 1990-91, 1994-95.

8 Shelbourne 1926-26, 1928-29, 1930-31, 1943-44, 1946-47, 1952-53, 1961-62, 1991-92.

7 Bohemians 1923-24, 1927-28, 1929-30, 1933-34, 1935-36, 1974-75, 1977-78. **St Patrick's Athletic** 1951-52, 1954-55, 1955-56, 1989-90, 1995-96, 1997-98, 1998-99.

6 Waterford United 1965-66, 1967-68, 1968-69, 1969-70, 1971-72, 1972-73.

5 Cork United 1940-41, 1941-42, 1942-43, 1944-45, 1945-46. **Drumcondra** 1947-48, 1948-49, 1957-58, 1960-61, 1964-65.

2 Athlone Town 1980-81, 1982-83. **Cork Athletic** 1949-50, 1950-51. **Derry City** 1988-89, 1996-97. **Limerick** 1959-60, 1979-80. **St James' Gate** 1921-22, 1939-40.

1 Cork Celtic 1973-74. **Cork Hibernians** 1970-71. **Dolphin** 1934-35.

Since the 1985-86 season the National League has had a Premier Division and a First Division.
First Division winners
3 Drogheda United 1988-89, 1990-91, 1998-99.
2 Bray Wanderers 1985-86, 1995-96. **Waterford United** 1989-90, 1997-98.
1 Athlone Town 1987-88. **Derry City** 1986-87. **Galway United** 1992-93. **Kilkenny City** 1996-97. **Limerick City** 1991-92. **Sligo Rovers** 1993-94. **U.C.D.** 1994-95

● FAI CUP WINNERS

24 Shamrock Rovers 1925, 1929, 1930, 1931, 1932, 1933, 1936, 1940, 1944, 1945, 1948, 1955, 1956, 1962, 1964, 1965, 1966, 1967, 1968, 1969, 1978, 1985, 1986, 1987.

8 Dundalk 1942, 1949, 1952, 1958, 1977, 1979, 1981, 1988.

6 Shelbourne 1939, 1960, 1963, 1993, 1996, 1997.

5 Bohemians 1928, 1935, 1970, 1976, 1992. **Drumcondra** 1927, 1943, 1946, 1954, 1957.

2 Bray Wanderers 1990, 1999. **Cork Athletic** 1951, 1953. **Cork United** 1941, 1947. **Derry City** 1989, 1995. **Limerick** 1971, 1982. **St James' Gate** 1922, 1938. **St Patrick's Athletic** 1959, 1961. **Sligo Rovers** 1983, 1994. **Waterford United** 1937, 1980.

1 Alton United 1923. **Athlone Town** 1924. **Cork** 1934. **Cork City** 1998. **Finn Harps** 1974. **Fordsons** 1926. **Galway United** 1991. **Home Farm** 1975. **Transport** 1950. **U.C.D.** 1984.

Most International Goals

Player	No. of Goals
1. Frank Stapleton	20
2. Tony Cascarino	19
3. John Aldridge	19
4. Don Givens	19
5. Niall Quinn	19
6. Noel Cantwell	14
7. Gerry Daly	13
8. Jimmy Dunne	12
9. Liam Brady	9
10. Kevin Sheedy	9

Northern Ireland

Irish Football Association

20 Windsor Avenue, Belfast BT9 6EG.
Tel. (01232) 669458

Founded..1880
President..Jim Boyce
Main Stadium..........Windsor Park (Capacity: 28,500)

INTERNATIONAL
Northern Ireland Manager............Lawrie McMenemy
FIFA World Ranking –as of September 1999......71st
Most International Goals.................Colin Clarke (13)
Most Capped Player.....................Pat Jennings (119)
Best World Cup Result ....Quarter finalists 1958

International Results

SENIOR
European Championship Qualifiers
● Istanbul, 05.09.98 **Turkey 3, Northern Ireland 0.**
Northern Ireland: Fettis, Horlock, Hill, Morrow, A.
Hughes, Rowland (Quinn 45), Lennon, Mulryne,
Gillespie (Whitley 73), M. Hughes, Dowie. Subs Not
Used: Taylor, Kennedy, McCarthy, O'Boyle. Booked:
Lennon. *Referee:* R. Wojcik (Poland).
● Windsor Park, 10.10.98 **Northern Ireland 1**
(Rowland), **Finland 0.** *Northern Ireland:* Fettis; A.
Hughes, Morrow, Patterson, Horlock; Gillespie
(McCarthy 74 mins), Mulryne, Lennon, Rowland (Quinn
87 mins); M. Hughes, Dowie (O'Boyle 80 mins).
Referee: Z. Arsic (Yugoslavia).
● Windsor Park, 18.11.98 **Northern Ireland 2** (Dowie,
Lennon), **Moldova 2.** *Northern Ireland:* Fettis; Griffin,
Patterson, Morrow, Kennedy; Gillespie (McCarthy 87
mins), Lomas, Lennon, Rowland (Gray 78 mins);
Dowie, M. Hughes. *Referee:* V. Hrinak (Slovakia).
● Windsor Park, 27.03.99 **Northern Ireland 0,**
Germany 3. *Northern Ireland:* Taylor; Patterson,
Williams, Morrow, Horlock; Gillespie (McCarthy 83
mins), Lomas, Lennon (Sonner 68 mins), Rowland
(Kennedy 68 mins); Dowie, M. Hughes. *Referee:* G.
Cesari (Italy).
● Chisinau, 31.03.99 **Moldova 0, Northern Ireland 0.**
Northern Ireland: Taylor; Patterson (A. Hughes 63
mins), Horlock, Lomas, Williams, Morrow, Gillespie,
Lennon, Robinson; Dowie, M. Hughes. *Referee:* E.
Trivcovic (Croatia).
● Windsor Park, 04.09.99 **Northern Ireland 0, Turkey**
3. *Northern Ireland:* Taylor; Horlock, Williams, Hunter,
A. Hughes, Kennedy; Lennon, Lomas, McCarthy
(Gillespie 63), M. Hughes; Dowie (Quinn 77). *Referee:*
A. Sars (France).
● Dortmund, 08.09.99 **Germany 4, Northern Ireland**
0. *Northrern Ireland:* Taylor; Horlock, Williams, Morrow,
Nolan, Kennedy; Lennon (Gillespie 46), Lomas,
McCarthy, M. Hughes; Dowie (Quinn 46). *Referee:* G.
Bikas (Greece).
● Helsinki, 09.10.99. **Finland 4, Northern Ireland 1**
(Whitley 59). *Northern Ireland:* Taylor; Jenkins (Jim

Whitley 79), Williams, Morrow, Nolan; McCarthy, Jeff
Whitley, Lennon, Kennedy, Hughes (Johnson 74),
Quinn (Coote 68). *Referee:* A. Ancion (Belgium)

GROUP 3 FINAL STANDINGS
	P	W	D	L	F	A	Pts
Germany	8	6	1	1	20	4	19
Turkey	8	5	2	1	15	6	17
Finland	8	3	1	4	13	13	10
Northern Ireland	8	1	2	5	4	19	5
Moldova	8	0	4	4	7	17	4

Friendlies
● Windsor Park, 27.04.99 **Northern Ireland 1** (Parker
og), **Canada 1.** *Northern Ireland:* Taylor (Wright 46),
Hughes, Horlock, Lomas, Williams, Hunter, McCarthy
(Hamill 59), Mulryne (Sonner 82), Dowie (McVeigh 74),
Coote (Ferguson 74), Rowland. *Referee:* M. McCurry
(Scotland).
● Lansdowne Road, 29.05.99 **Republic of Ireland 0,**
Northern Ireland 1 (Griffin). *Northern Ireland:* M Taylor
(Carroll 45 mins); Patterson; Williams; Hunter; Hughes;
McCarthy, Robinson, Lennon (Griffin 78 mins);
Rowland (Johnson 74 mins); Quinn, Dowie (Coote 45
mins). *Referee:* K. Richards (Wales).
● Windsor Park, 18.08.99 **Northern Ireland 0, France**
1. *Northern Ireland:* Taylor (Wright 46 mins); A Hughes,
Williams, Hunter, Horlock; McCarthy, Lennon, Lomas,
Kennedy (Gillespie 73 mins); Dowie (Quinn 55 mins); M
Hughes. *Referee:* W. Young (Scotland).

UNDER 21
European U21 Championship Qualifiers
Cocaeli, 04.09.98 **Turkey 2 Northern Ireland 0.**
Ballymena, 09.10.98 **Northern Ireland 1** (Coote),
Finland 1.
Coleraine, 17.11.98 **Northern Ireland 1** (Healy),
Moldova 1.
The Oval, 26.03.99 **Northern Ireland 1** (Hertzsch og),
Germany 0.
Chisinau, 30.03.99 **Moldova 0, Northern Ireland 0.**
Mourneview Park, 03.09.99 **Northern Ireland 1**
(Griffin), **Turkey 2.**
Ludenscheid, 07.09.99 **Germany 1, Northern Ireland 0.**
Valkeakoski, 08.10.99 **Finland 2, N. Ireland 1** (Feeney).

UNDER 18
European U18 Championship Qualifiers
Connah's Bay, 22.08.98 **Azerbaijan 0, Northern**
Ireland 3 (Hawe 2, G.McCann).
Bangor, 24.08.98 **Wales 1, Northern Ireland 2**
(Hamilton, McAreavey).
Bangor, 26.08.98 **Moldova 0, Northern Ireland 2**
(Hamilton, McAreavey)
European U18 Championship play offs
The Oval, 08.03.99 **Northern Ireland 1** (Hamilton),
Republic of Ireland 2.
Tolka Park, 11.05.99 **Republic of Ireland 2, Northern**
Ireland 1 (Hamilton).
Friendlies
Coleraine, 22.09.98 **Northern Ireland 1** (Convery),
Germany 2.
Ballymena, 24.09.98 **Northern Ireland 0, Germany 0.**

Domestic Results

Premier Division Final League Table 1998/99

	P	W	D	L	F	A	Pts
Glentoran	36	24	6	6	74	35	78
Linfield	36	20	10	6	68	39	70
Crusaders	36	18	8	10	48	39	62
Newry Town	36	17	9	10	52	46	60
Glenavon	36	13	12	11	49	35	51
Ballymena United	36	11	8	17	40	42	41
Coleraine	36	10	9	17	34	53	39
Portadown	36	9	10	17	41	47	37
Cliftonville	36	7	14	15	31	47	35
Omagh Town	36	5	6	25	25	79	21

Champions: Glentoran Relegated: Omagh Town.

First Division Final League Table 1998/999

	P	W	D	L	F	A	Pts
Distillery	28	17	4	7	44	30	55
Ards	28	16	1	11	47	34	49
Bangor	28	15	3	10	37	35	48
Ballyclare Comrades	28	11	5	12	55	44	38
Dungannon Swifts	28	11	5	12	36	46	38
Carrick Rangers	28	10	4	14	41	41	34
Larne	28	9	5	14	28	32	32
Limavady Utd	28	6	7	15	37	63	25

Promoted: Distillery.
Promotion relegation playoff: Ards 0, Cliftonville 1. Cliftonville 4 Ards 2. Cliftonville win 5-2 on aggregate.

Premier Division Results

	1	2	3	4	5	6	7	8	9	10
1. Ballymena United	--	1-2	1-0	2-0	1-0	1-1	1-0	1-1	0-0	1-0
	--	2-2	0-1	1-2	0-1	3-6	4-2	0-0	1-2	2-2
2. Cliftonville	0-1	--	1-1	2-3	2-2	2-4	1-1	1-4	2-1	0-2
	1-0	--	0-0	1-1	0-0	0-0	0-1	0-2	2-1	0-0
3. Coleraine	2-1	1-1	--	0-2	1-3	1-3	0-0	2-2	2-1	1-0
	0-1	3-1	--	0-2	0-0	0-1	2-1	3-0	1-0	0-2
4. Crusaders	2-0	2-1	0-1	--	1-0	0-0	1-4	2-0	5-0	1-1
	1-0	1-0	2-0	--	1-1	0-3	3-2	3-2	2-0	0-0
5. Glenavon	0-0	0-1	3-1	3-0	--	0-1	1-1	1-2	2-0	1-0
	1-0	0-0	3-1	2-0	--	0-1	2-2	1-1	6-1	2-2
6. Glentoran	2-1	0-1	5-4	1-4	5-2	--	0-1	1-3	2-0	1-0
	1-0	1-1	5-0	2-1	1-0	--	1-2	5-1	2-0	3-1
7. Linfield	1-0	1-0	2-1	2-1	2-0	1-1	--	2-2	2-0	2-2
	4-1	2-1	1-1	4-2	3-1	1-1	--	2-1	3-0	3-1
8. Newry Town	0-0	2-1	1-1	0-0	1-0	1-2	2-1	--	0-2	3-2
	1-0	1-0	1-0	3-0	0-2	1-0	2-1	--	1-1	1-2
9. Omagh Town	1-4	2-2	2-0	0-0	0-3	0-2	1-3	1-3	--	1-0
	0-5	1-1	1-1	1-2	0-3	1-4	1-5	2-3	--	1-0
10. Portadown	1-3	0-1	3-0	0-1	1-1	0-3	0-2	2-3	2-0	--
	2-1	3-0	1-2	0-0	2-2	1-3	1-1	2-1	3-0	--

First Division Results

	1	2	3	4	5	6	7	8
1. Ards	--	2-1	2-0	1-0	2-0	2-1	1-0	3-0
	--	0-2	1-2	2-4	0-2	1-0	5-1	1-2
2. Ballyclare Comrades	2-5	--	3-0	2-1	0-1	1-2	2-0	5-1
	2-0	--	0-1	1-1	3-1	6-0	0-1	4-4
3. Bangor	1-0	3-2	--	0-1	2-0	2-1	0-1	0-0
	0-0	1-4	--	2-2	1-0	3-1	1-0	3-4
4. Carrick Rangers	4-1	3-2	1-2	--	0-1	3-2	1-0	2-3
	1-0	0-2	0-1	--	2-3	0-1	1-1	4-0
5. Distillery	0-2	3-3	0-3	0-0	--	1-1	1-0	3-1
	4-3	1-0	2-0	3-2	--	3-1	0-0	1-0
6. Dungannon Swifts	2-1	1-0	3-2	2-1	1-5	--	1-1	2-0
	1-2	1-1	1-3	2-0	2-1	--	1-0	1-2
7. Larne	0-2	4-1	0-1	1-0	0-1	1-0	--	4-0
	0-2	5-3	2-0	3-2	0-1	0-1	--	0-0
8. Limavady United	2-3	0-1	3-0	1-2	1-5	1-1	3-3	--
	0-3	2-2	1-3	2-3	0-1	3-3	1-0	--

IRISH CUP FINAL
Portadown were awarded the Irish Cup when the IFA established that finalists Cliftonville had fielded an ineligible player in the semi-final replay with Linfield and disqualified them from the competition.

NATIONWIDE GOLD CUP FINAL
Windsor Park, 15.12.98 **Glentoran 3** (Hamill 11, Kirk 64, Devine 88), **Portadown 1** (Arkins 90).

COCA-COLA LEAGUE CUP FINAL
Windsor Park, 04.05.99 **Linfield 2** (Ferguson 94, 112), **Glentoran 1** (Young 97) aet.

CALOR COUNTY ANTRIM SHIELD FINAL
Windsor Park, 02.02.99 **Glentoran 2** (Kirk 40, Elliott 45), **Cliftonville 0.**

IRISH NEWS CUP FINAL
Ballybofey, 29.04.99 **Finn Harps 2** (McGrenaghan 41, Harkin 55), **Ballymena United 0.**

MID-ULSTER CUP FINAL
Mourneview Park, 13.04.99 **Glenavon 3** (McMenemy 27, Grant 61, Ginty 79), **Ards 1** (Arthur 73 pen)

International Squad 1998-99

Name:	Club	Dob	Born	Pos	Debut	Caps	Goals
CARROLL, Roy	Wigan Athletic	30.09.77	Enniskillen	GK	21.05.97	2	0
COOTE, Adrian	Norwich City	03.08.78	Gt Yarmouth	S	27.04.99	3	0
FERGUSON, Glenn	Linfield	10.07.69	Belfast	S	27.04.99	1	0
DOWIE, Iain	QPR	09.01.65	Hatfield	S	27.03.90	59	12
FETTIS, Alan	Blackburn Rovers	01.02.71	Belfast	GK	13.11.91	25	0
GILLESPIE, Keith	Blackburn Rovers	18.02.75	Larne	M	07.09.74	29	1
GRIFFIN, Danny	St. Johnstone	10.08.77	Belfast	D	29.05.96	9	1
HAMILL, Rory	Glentoran	04.05.76	Coleraine	S	27.04.99	1	0
HORLOCK, Kevin	Manchester City	01.11.72	Erith	M	26.04.95	20	0
HUGHES, Aaron	Newcastle United	08.11.79	Magherafelt	D	25.03.98	10	0
HUGHES, Michael	Wimbledon	02.08.71	Larne	M	13.11.91	51	3
HUNTER, Barry	Reading	18.11.68	Coleraine	D	26.04.95	15	1
JENKINS, Iain	Dundee United	24.12.72	Whiston	D	30.04.97	6	0
JOHNSON, Damien	Blackburn Rovers	18.11.78	Lisburn	M	29.05.99	2	0
KENNEDY, Peter	Watford	10.09.73	Lisburn	D	18.11.98	6	0
LENNON, Neil	Leicester City	25.06.71	Lurgan	M	11.06.94	31	2
LOMAS, Steve	West Ham	18.01.74	Hanover	M	23.03.94	33	2
MAGILTON, Jim	Ipswich Town	06.05.69	Belfast	M	05.02.91	39	5
McCARTHY, Jon	Birmingham City	18.08.70	Middlesbrough	M	24.04.96	16	0
McVEIGH, Paul	Tottenham	06.12.77	Belfast	S	27.04.99	1	0
MORROW, Steve	QPR	02.07.70	Bangor	D	18.05.90	39	1
MULRYNE, Philip	Norwich C	01.01.78	Belfast	M	11.02.97	8	1
NOLAN, Ian	Sheffield Wed	09.07.70	Liverpool	D	05.10.96	10	1
O'BOYLE, George	St.Johnstone	14.12.67	Belfast	S	03.06.94	13	1
PATTERSON, Darren	Dundee United	15.10.69	Belfast	D	03.06.94	17	1
QUINN, James	WBA	15.12.74	Coventry	S	24.04.96	19	1
ROBINSON, Stephen	Bournemouth	10.12.74	Crumlin	S	21.05.97	3	0
ROWLAND, Keith	QPR	01.09.71	Portadown	D	08.09.93	19	1
SONNER, Danny	Sheffield Wed	09.01.72	Wigan	M	10.09.97	3	0
TAGGART, Gerry	Leicester City	18.10.70	Belfast	D	27.03.90	45	7
TAYLOR, Maik	Fulham	04.09.71	Germany	GK	27.03.99	8	0
WHITLEY, Jim	Manchester City	14.04.75	Zambia	M	03.06.98	3	0
WHITLEY, Jeff	Manchester City	28.01.79	Zambia	D	11.02.97	4	1
WILLIAMS, Mark	Watford	28.09.70	Stalybridge	D	27.03.99	8	0
WRIGHT, Tommy	Manchester City	29.08.63	Belfast	GK	26.04.89	31	0

Caps Correct as of 9th October 1999.
Dob=Date of birth; Pos = Position; D=Defender; M=Midfielder; S=Striker; GK=Goalkeeper

Records

● **IRISH CUP CHAMPIONS**

35 Linfield 1891, 1892, 1893, 1895, 1898, 1899, 1902, 1904, 1912, 1913, 1915, 1916, 1919, 1922, 1923, 1930, 1932, 1934, 1936, 1939, 1942, 1945, 1946, 1948, 1950, 1953, 1960, 1962, 1963, 1970, 1978, 1980, 1982, 1994, 1995.

17 Glentoran 1914, 1917, 1921, 1932, 1933, 1935, 1951, 1966, 1973, 1983, 1985, 1986, 1987, 1988, 1990, 1996, 1998.

12 Distillery 1884, 1885, 1886, 1889, 1894, 1896, 1903, 1905, 1910, 1925, 1956, 1971.

8 Belfast Celtic 1918, 1926, 1937, 1938, 1941, 1943, 1944, 1947.

Cliftonville 1883, 1888, 1897, 1900, 1901, 1907, 1909, 1979.

6 Ballymena 1929, 1940, 1958, 1981, 1984, 1989.

5 Glenavon 1957, 1959, 1961, 1992, 1997.

4 Ards 1927, 1952, 1969, 1974.

Coleraine 1965, 1972, 1975, 1977.

3 Derry City 1949, 1954, 1964.

Shelbourne 1906, 1911, 1920.

Portadown 1991, 1999.

2 Crusaders 1967, 1968.

Queen's Island 1882, 1924.

1 Bangor 1993.

Bohemians 1908.

Carrick Rangers 1976.

Dundela 1955.

Gordon Highlanders 1890.

Moyola Park 1881.

Ulster 1887.

Willowfield 1928.

● **IRISH LEAGUE CHAMPIONS**
42 Linfield 1890-91, 1891-92, 1892-93, 1894-95, 1897-98, 1901-02, 1903-04, 1906-07, 1907-08, 1908-09, 1910-11, 1913-14, 1921-22, 1922-23, 1929-30, 1931-32, 1933-34, 1934-35, 1948-49, 1949-50, 1953-54, 1954-55, 1955-56, 1958-59, 1960-61, 1961-62, 1965-66, 1968-69, 1970-71, 1974-75, 1977-78, 1978-79, 1979-80, 1981-82, 1982-83, 1983-84, 1984-85, 1985-86, 1986-87, 1988-89, 1992-93, 1993-94.
20 Glentoran 1893-94, 1896-97, 1904-05, 1911-12, 1912-13, 1920-21, 1924-25, 1930-31, 1950-51, 1952-53, 1963-64, 1966-67, 1967-68, 1969-70, 1971-72, 1976-77, 1980-81, 1987-88, 1991-92, 1998-99.
14 Belfast Celtic 1899-1900, 1914-15, 1919-20, 1925-26, 1926-27, 1927-28, 1928-29, 1932-33, 1935-36, 1936-37, 1937-38, 1938-39, 1939-40, 1947-48.
6 Distillery 1895-96, 1898-99, 1900-01, 1902-03, 1905-06, 1962-63.
4 Crusaders 1972-73, 1975-76, 1994-95, 1996-97.
3 Cliftonville 1905-06, 1909-10, 1997-98.
Portadown 1989-90, 1990-91, 1995-96.
1 Ards 1957-58.
Coleraine 1973-74.
Derry City 1964-65.
Queen's Island 1923-24.
Since the 1995-96 season the Irish League has been split into a Premier Division and First Division.
First Division Winners
1 Ballymena 1996-97.
Coleraine 1995-96.
Newry Town 1997-98.
Distillery 1998-99.

● **TOP INTERNATIONAL GOALSCORERS**

Player	No. of Goals
Colin Clarke	13
Gerry Armstrong	12
Joe Bambrick	12
Willie Gillespie	12
Jimmy Quinn	12
Iain Dowie	12
Olphie Stanfield	11
Billy Bingham	10
Johnny Crossan	10
Jimmy McIlroy	10
Peter McParland	10

● **PAST PRESIDENTS**
Lord Moyola, Captain Sir James Wilson, Austin Donnelly, Fred Cochrane, Joe McBride, Harry Cavan, Sammy Walker, Jimmy Boyce.

Rugby

Irish Rugby Football Union
62 Lansdowne Road, Ballsbridge, Dublin 4.
Tel. (01) 6684601
website: www.irfu.ie
email: office.webmaster@irfu.ie

Founded 1874
Number of Provincial Unions 4
Number of Clubs...250
Number of Members (men) 60,000
Number of Members (women) 500
President...Bill Lavery
Secretary and Treasurer..........................P.R. Browne
Biggest Attendance..............55,000 (Lansdowne Rd)
Main Stadium.......Lansdowne Road (capacity 49,638)
Oldest Club ....Dublin University (founded 1854)
1998/99 Interpovinal Champions.................Munster

1998/99 All Ireland League
Division One Champions ....Cork Constitution
Division Two Champions.........................Dungannon
Division Three Champions................................UCD
Division Four Champions...........................Midleton

INTERNATIONAL
National Manager..............................Donal Lenihan
National Coach ....Warren Gatland
Most Capped International .........C.M.H. Gibson (69)
Most International Points .............M.J. Kiernan (308)
Most International Tries ....................B.J. Mullin (17)

First International Game ....versus England, 1875
Best World Cup Performance Quarter-finalists (1987, 1991 and 1995)
Grand Slams 1 (1948)
Triple Crowns........6 (1894, 1899, 1948, '49, '82, '85)
International Championships ....18 (10 outright wins)

International Results

WORLD CUP QUALIFIERS
● 14 November 1998, Lansdowne Road. **Ireland 70 (10T, 10C) Georgia 0. IRELAND:** C. O'Shea; J. Bishop, P. Duignan, J. Bell, K. Maggs, E. Elwood, C. McGuinness (C.Scally 54 mins); P. Clohessy (J. Fitzpatrick 63 mins), R. Nesdale (A. Clarke 29 mins), P. Wallace, P. Johns Captain, M. O'Kelly (J. Davidson 60 mins), E. Miller, V. Costello (D. O Cuinneagain 60 mins), A. Ward. **Scorers:** *Tries:* Dempsey (2), Bell, Costello, Duignan, Johns, Maggs, O'Shea, Scally, Wallace; *Conversions:* Elwood (10). **Referee:** Robert Davies (Wales).
● 21 November 1998, Lansdowne Road. **Ireland 53 (7T, 6C, 2PG) Romania 35 (5T, 2C, 2PG). IRELAND:** C. O'Shea; J. Bishop, J. Bell, P. Duignan (K. Maggs half-time), D. O'Mahony, E. Elwood (D. Humphreys 55 mins), C. Scally (C. McGuinness 59 mins); P. Clohessy, A. Clarke (K. Wood half-time), P. Wallace (J. Fitzpatrick 49 mins), P. Johns Captain (J. Davidson half-time), M. O'Kelly, E. Miller (half-time), V. Costello, A. Ward. **Scorers:** *Tries:* Bell (2), O'Shea, Scally, Ward, Penalty tries (2); *Conversions:* Elwood (3), Humphreys (3);

Penalty Goals Elwood (2). **Referee:** P. Honiss (New Zealand).

FIVE NATIONS

● **7 February 1999, Lansdowne Road. Ireland 9 (3PG) France 10 (1T, 1PG, 1C).** IRELAND: C. O'Shea; J. Bishop, K. Maggs, J. Bell (R. Henderson 15 mins), G. Dempsey; D. Humphreys, C. McGuinness; P. Clohessy (J. Fitzpatrick 62 mins), K. Wood, P. Wallace (J. Fitzpatrick temporary), P. Johns Captain, J. Davidson, E. Miller, D. O Cuinneagain, V. Costello (T. Brennan 51 mins). **Scorers:** *Penalties:* Humphreys (3). **Referee:** P. Marshall (Australia).

● **20 February 1999, Wembley. Wales 23 (2 T, 3 PG, 2C) Ireland 29 (2T, 3PG, 2DG, 2C).** IRELAND: C. O'Shea; J. Bishop, K. Maggs, J. Bell, N. Woods; D. Humphreys, C. McGuinness; P. Clohessy (J. Fitzpatrick 66 mins), K. Wood, P. Wallace, P. Johns Captain (M. Galwey 80 mins), J. Davidson, D. O Cuinneagain, A. Ward, E. Miller (V. Costello 66 mins). **Scorers:** *Tries:* Maggs, Wood; *Penalty Goals:* Humphreys (3); *Drop Goals:* Humpheys (2); *Conversions:* Humphreys (2). **Referee:** S. Young (Australia).

● **6 March 1999, Lansdowne Road. Ireland 15 (5P) England 27 (4P, 2T, 1C, 1DG).** IRELAND: C. O'Shea; J. Bishop, K. Maggs, R. Henderson, G. Dempsey; D. Humphreys, C. McGuinness; P. Clohessy (J. Fitzpatrick 66 mins), K. Wood, P. Wallace, P. Johns, J. Davidson, D. O Cuinneagain, V. Costello (E. Miller 65 mins), A Ward. **Scorers:** *Penalty Goals:* Humphreys (5). **Referee:** P O'Brien (New Zealand).

● **20 March 1999, Murrayfield. Scotland 30 (4T, 2C, 2PG) Ireland 13 (1T, 1C, 2PG).** IRELAND: C. O'Shea; J. Bishop, K. Maggs, J. Bell (R. Henderson 64 mins), G. Dempsey, D. Humphreys, C. McGuinness (C. Scally 76 mins); P. Clohessy, K. Wood, P. Wallace, P. Johns Captain, J. Davidson, D. O Cuinneagain, E. Miller (V. Costello 17 mins), A. Ward (T. Brennan 65 mins). **Scorers:** *Tries:* Humphreys; *Conversions:* Humphreys; *Penalty Goals:* Humphreys. **Referee:** D. Bevan (Wales).

FRIENDLIES

● **28 November 1998, Lansdowne Road. Ireland 13 (1T, 1C, 2PG) South Africa 27 (3T, 3C, 2PG).** IRELAND: C. O'Shea; J. Bishop, J. Bell, K. Maggs, G. Dempsey, E. Elwood, C. McGuinness; J. Fitzpatrick (R. Corrigan 55 mins), K. Wood (R. Nesdale 81 mins), P. Clohessy, P. Johns Captain, M. O'Kelly (J. Davidson 55 mins), D. O Cuinneagain, A. Ward, V. Costello. **Scorers:** *Tries:* Wood; *Conversions:* Elwood; *Penalty Goals:* Elwood (2). **Referee:** C. Thomas (Wales).

● **10 April 1999, Lansdowne Road. Ireland 39 (5T, 4PG, 1C) Italy 30 (3T, 2DG, 1PG, 3C).** IRELAND: C. O'Shea; J. Bishop, K. Maggs, R. Henderson (J. Bell 38 mins), G. Dempsey, E. Elwood, C. Scally; J. Fitzpatrick (P. Wallace 55 mins), R. Nesdale (K. Wood 55 mins), P. Clohessy, P. Johns Captain, J. Davidson, T. Brennan, D. O Cuinneagain, V. Costello (A. Ward half time). **Scorers:** *Tries:* C. O'Shea (2), J. Bishop, G. Dempsey,

P. Johns; *Conversions:* Elwood; *Penalty Goals:* Elwood; *Penalty Goals:* Elwood (4). **Referee:** F. Gillet (France).

● **12 June 1999, Brisbane. Australia 46 (6T, 2PG, 5C), Ireland 10 (1T, 1PG, 1C).** IRELAND: C. O'Shea; J. Bishop, B. O'Driscoll, K. Maggs, M. Mostyn, D. Humphreys, T. Tierney; P. Clohessy (R. Corrigan 53 mins), K. Wood, P. Wallace, P. Johns (M. O'Kelly 53 mins), J. Davidson, D. O Cuinneagain Captain, V. Costello (D. Corkery 62 mins), A. Ward. **Scorers:** *Tries:* K. Maggs; *Conversions:* Humphreys; *Penalty Goals:* Humphreys. **Referee:** A. Watson (South Africa).

● **19 June 1999, Perth. Australia 32 (2T, 6PG, 2C), Ireland 26 (3T, 3PG, 1C).** IRELAND: G. Dempsey; J. Bishop, B. O'Driscoll, K. Maggs, J. Bell, D. Humphreys, T. Tierney; P. Clohessy (R. Corrigan 71 mins), K. Wood (R. Nesdale 56 mins), P. Wallace, P. Johns (J. Davidson 67 mins), M. O'Kelly, T. Brennan (D. Corkery 76 mins), D. O Cuinneagain Captain, A. Ward. **Scorers:** *Tries:* Clohessy, Bishop, Maggs; *Conversions:* Humphreys; *Penalty Goals:* Humphreys (3). **Referee:** A. Watson (South Africa).

● **28 August 1999, Lansdowne Road. Ireland 32 (4T, 4PG), Argentina 24 (3T, 1PG, 3C).** IRELAND: C. O'Shea; J. Bishop, B. O'Driscoll, K. Maggs (M. Mullins 54 mins), M. Moyston, D. Humphreys (E. Elwood 71 mins), T. Tierney; P. Clohessy, K. Wood, P. Wallace (J. Fitzpatrick 36 mins), P. Johns (M. O'Kelly 65 mins), J. Davidson, T. Brennan (E. Miller 59 mins), A. Ward, D. O Cuinneagain Captain. **Scorers:** *Tries:* Moyston (3), Woods; *Penalty Goals:* Humphreys (4). **Referee:** Derek Bevan (Wales).

Interprovincial Results

EUROPEAN CUP
Pool A

09.10.98 ....Leinster........9	Begles/Bordeaux.3	
31.10.98..Begles/Bordeaux......31	Leinster 10	
06.11.98................Leinster......27	Llanelli...............34	

Pool B

10.10.98............Perpignan......41	Munster 24
31.10.98................Munster......13	Perpignan............5
08.11.98................Padova......21	Munster 35

Pool C

10.10.98 ....Ebbw Vale......28	Ulster................61
16.10.98................Ulster......29	Toulouse...........24
30.10.98................Ulster......43	Ebbw Vale 18
08.11.98Edinburgh Reivers......21	Ulster................23

EUROPEAN SHIELD

07.10.98.............Connacht......29	Perigeux...........28
31.10.98 ....Caerphilly......39	Connacht............8
11.10.98................Rovigo......20	Connacht...........21
07.11.98.............Connacht......14	Racing Club 19

European Cup Quarter Finals

11.12.98................Ulster......15	Toulouse...........13
13.12.98.............Colomiers......23	Munster 9

European Cup Semi-Final

09.01.99.................Ulster......33	Stade Francais..27

European Cup Final

30.01.99.................Ulster......21	Colomiers 6

EUROPEAN CUP FINAL TABLES

Pool A	P	W	D	L	F	A	Pts
Stade Francais	6	5	0	1	.216	.117	.10
Llanelli	6	3	0	3	.113	.180	.6
Begles-Bordeaux	6	2	0	4	.141	.124	.4
Leinster	6	2	0	4	.127	.176	.4

Pool B	P	W	D	L	F	A	Pts
Perpignan	6	5	0	1	.238	.108	.10
Munster	6	4	1	1	.144	.108	.9
Neath	6	1	1	4	.118	.194	.3
Padova	6	1	0	5	.79	.169	.2

Pool C	P	W	D	L	F	A	Pts
Ulster	6	4	1	1	.97	.168	.9
Toulouse	6	4	0	2	.154	.110	.8
Edinburgh Reivers	6	2	1	3	.179	.156	.5
Ebbw Vale	6	1	0	5	.114	.307	.2

EUROPEAN SHIELD

	P	W	D	L	F	A	Pts
Narbonne	6	6	0	0	.228	.98	.12
Caerphilly	6	4	0	2	.167	.154	.8
Perigueux	6	3	0	3	.168	.119	.6
Connacht	6	3	0	3	.129	.159	.6
Racing Club	6	3	0	3	.127	.184	.6
Rovigo	6	1	0	5	.108	.156	.2
Newport	6	1	0	5	.123	.183	.2

INTERPROVINCIAL CHAMPIONSHIP 1998
Results

14.08.98	Donnybrook	Leinster ...14	..Ulster	34
15.08.98	Sportsgrounds	..Connacht 13	..Munster	18
21.08.98	Dooradoyle	Munster...18	..Leinster	24
22.08.98	Sportsgrounds	..Connacht.21	..Ulster	18
28.08.98	Donnybrook	Leinster ...29	..Connacht	..24
04.09.98	Ravenhill	Ulster	29 ..Munster	..12
11.09.98	Ravenhill	Ulster	11 ..Leinster	35
12.09.98	Dooradoyle	Munster...21	..Connacht	...7
03.10.98	Sportsgrounds	..Connacht.24	..Leinster	23
03.10.98	Musgrave Park	.Munster...31	..Ulster	9
23.10.98	Donnybrook	Leinster ...10	..Munster	25
23.10.98	Ravenhill	Ulster	36 ..Connacht	6

Final Table

	P	W	D	L	F	A	B	Pts
Munster	6	4	0	2	.125	...92	...2	...18
Ulster	6	4	0	2	.137	..119	...3	...15
Leinster	6	3	0	3	.135	..136	...2	...14
Connacht	6	2	0	4	...95	..145	...3	...11

Club Tables

ALL IRELAND LEAGUE 1998-99 FINAL TABLES

DIVISION ONE	P	W	D	L	F	A	Pts
Garryowen	11	8	0	3	.237	.140	.16
Cork Constitution	11	8	0	3	.265	.170	.16
Buccaneers	11	8	0	3	.196	.202	.16
St. Mary's	11	7	0	4	.215	.177	.14
Lansdowne	11	7	0	4	.189	.184	.14
Shannon	11	6	0	5	.224	.164	.12
Young Munster	11	4	1	6	.134	.135	...9
Terenure College	11	4	1	6	.175	.182	...9
Ballymena	11	4	0	7	.190	.224	...8
Clontarf	11	4	0	7	.198	.246	...8
Blackrock	11	4	0	7	.180	.232	...8
Galwegians	11	1	0	10	.117	.264	...2

DIVISION TWO	P	W	D	L	F	A	Pts
Dungannon	15	13	2	0	.479	.259	.26
De La Salle Palmerston	15	10	3	2	.284	.211	.22
Wanderers	15	10	5	0	.342	.293	.20
Old Belvedere	15	9	5	1	.276	.212	.19
Malone	15	9	5	1	.233	.206	.19
Bective Rangers	15	8	5	2	.240	.269	.18
Portadown	15	8	6	1	.250	.268	.17
Greystones	15	8	7	0	.334	.313	.16
Old Crescent	15	7	7	1	.305	.236	.15
Sunday's Well	15	7	8	0	.270	.246	.14
City of Derry	15	7	8	0	.284	.293	.14
University College Cork	15	5	6	4	.248	.303	.14
Dolphin	15	5	9	1	.218	.256	.11
Skerries	15	3	11	1	.199	.262	...7
Old Wesley	15	2	11	2	.181	.315	...6
Ballynahinch	15	1	14	0	.171	.372	...2

DIVISION THREE

Section A	P	W	D	L	F	A	Pts
UCD	13	10	0	3	.362	.176	.20
NIFC	13	9	0	4	.246	.186	.18
Monkstown	13	8	0	5	.209	.238	.16
Instonians	13	7	1	5	.277	.178	.15
Bohemians	13	6	0	7	.179	.225	.12

Section B	P	W	D	L	F	A	Pts
Richmond	13	7	0	6	.156	.208	.14
Carlow	13	6	0	7	.212	.208	.12
Corinthians	13	5	1	7	.256	.223	.11
Dublin University	13	4	0	9	.193	.253	...8
Highfield	13	2	0	11	.130	.325	...4

DIVISION FOUR	P	W	D	L	F	A	Pts
Midleton	10	7	1	2	.194	83	.15
Ballina	10	7	1	2	.167	...96	.15
Banbridge	10	7	0	3	.161	.129	.14
Waterpark	10	5	0	5	.155	.121	.10
Omagh	10	5	0	5	.142	.123	.10
Suttonians	10	5	0	5	.161	.146	.10
Queen's	10	5	0	5	.152	.226	.10
Bangor	10	4	1	5	.113	.153	...9
Ards	10	4	0	6	.134	.153	...8
Collegians	10	3	1	6	.150	.159	...7
CIYMS	10	1	0	9	55	.195	...2

Thomond and Barnhall promoted to Division Four.

AIL Division One semi-final and final results

24.04.99	s/f	.Garryowen	19	..St Marys College	.17
25.04.99	s/f	.Cork Con.	32	..Buccaneers	20
01.05.99	final	...Cork Con	14	..Garryowen	11

International Squad Factfile

Name	Club	Position	D.O.B.	Caps	Points	Debut
BELL, Johnathon	Dungannon	Centre	07.02.74	30	6T	1994
BISHOP, Justin	London Irish	Wing	08.11.74	13	3T	1998
BRENNAN, Trevor	St Mary's College	Lock	22.09.73	7	–	1998
CASEY, Bob	Blackrock College	Lock	18.07.78	0	–	–
CLOHESSY, Peter	Young Munster	Prop	22.03.66	31	2T	1993
CORKERY, David	Cork Constitution	Flanker	06.11.72	27	3T	1994
CORRIGAN, Reggie	Greystones	Prop	10.11.70	9	–	1997
COSTELLO, Victor	St Mary's College	No. 8	23.10.70	22	3T	1996
D'ARCY, Gordon	Lansdowne	Full Back/Winger	10.02.80	–	–	–
DAVIDSON, Jeremy	Castres	Lock	28.04.74	23	–	1995
DAWSON, Kieron	London Irish	Flanker	29.01.75	3	–	1997
DEMPSEY, Girvan	Terenure College	Wing	02.10.75	6	3T	1999
DUIGNAN, Pat	Galwegians	Centre	01.05.72	2	1T	1998
ELWOOD, Eric	Galwegians	Out-half	26.02.69	32	.66PG, 2DG, 36C	1993
FITZPATRICK, Justin	Dungannon	Prop	21.11.73	10	–	1998
FULCHER, Gabriel	Lansdowne	Lock	27.11.69	21	1T	1994
GALWEY, Mick	Shannon	Lock	08.10.66	24	1T	1991
HENDERSON, Rob	Wasps	Centre	27.10.72	11	–	1996
HUMPHREYS, David	Dungannon	Out-half	10.09.71	18	28PG,4DG, 11C, 1T	1996
JOHNS, Paddy	Dungannon	Lock	19.02.68	54	4T	1990
MAGGS, Kevin	Bath	Centre	03.06.74	20	5T	1997
McGUINNESS, Conor	St Mary's College	Scrum-half	29.03.75	14	1T	1997
McKEEN, Angus	Lansdowne	Prop	13.02.69	0	–	–
MILLER, Eric	Terenure College	No. 8	23.09.75	15	1T	1997
MOYSTON, Matt	Galwegians	Wing	18.08.72	2	3T	1999
MULLINS, Mike	Young Munster	Centre	29.10.70	1	–	1999
NESDALE, Ross	Newcastle	Hooker	30.07.69	11	–	1997
O CUINNEAGAIN, Dion	Ballymena	Flanker/No. 8	24.05.72	12	–	1998
O'DRISCOLL, Brian	Blackrock College	Centre		3	–	1999
O'KELLY, Malcolm	St Mary's College	Lock	19.07.74	15	–	1997
O'MEARA, Brian	Cork Constitution	Scrum-half	05.04.76	4	–	1997
O'SHEA, Conor	London Irish	Full Back	21.10.70	30	4T, 3PG, 1DG, 1C	1993
SCALLY, Ciaran	Blackrock	Scrum-half	15.10.78	4	2T	1998
TIERNEY, Tom	Garryowen	Scrum-half	01.09.76	3	–	1999
TOPPING, James	Ballymena	Wing	18.12.74	5	–	1996
WALLACE, Paul	Saracens	Prop	30.12.71	30	3T	1995
WARD, Andy	Ballynahinch	Flanker	08.09.70	15	2T	1998
WOOD, Keith	Garryowen	Hooker	27.01.72	27	5T	1994
WOODS, Niall	London Irish	Wing	21.06.71	8	–	1994

Caps correct as of September 30th 1999.
D.O.B. = Date of Birth

Athletics

Bord Lúthchleas na hÉireann

11 Prospect Road, Glasnevin, Dublin 9. Tel. (01) 8309901. website: www.ble.ie. email: admin@ble.ie

Founded..1967
President ....Nick Davis
Honorary Secretary ....Dermot Nagle

Number of Senior Clubs 144
Number of Junior Clubs......................................135
Total Membership 18,129
Principal Venue........Morton Stadium, Dublin (10,000)
Biggest Crowd
..................30,000 1979. World C.C. C'ships, Limerick

Domestic Results

TRACK & FIELD, NATIONAL CHAMPIONS 1999

Event	Men's Champion	Performance	Women's Champion	Performance
100m	Gary Ryan	10.45*	Emily Maher	11.75

Continued from previous page

Event	Men's Champion	Performance	Women's Champion	Performance
200m	Gary Ryan	21.21	Ciara Sheehy	24.40
400m	Paul McBurney	47.09	Karen Shinkins	53.40
800m	Gareth Turnbull	1.48.57	Maura Prendiville	2.05.69
1,500m	Mark Carroll	3.46.20	Elaine Fitzgerald	4.16.99
5,000m	Mark Carroll	14.07.90	Una English	16.00.65
10,000m	Noel Berkeley	29.16.66	-	-
3,000m steeplechase	Cormac Smith	8.50.35	-	-
110m Hurdles	Peter Coghlan	13.51	-	-
100m Hurdles	-	-	Susan Smith-Walsh	13.49*
400m Hurdles	Brian Liddy	51.19	Susan Smith-Walsh	55.54
4x100m Relay	Dublin City Harriers	41.89	Leevale AC	48.72
10,000m Walk	Pierce O'Callaghan	41.47.50	-	-
5,000m Walk	-	-	Olive Loughnane	22.58.27
High Jump	Brendan Reilly	2.28m*	Brigid Corrigan	1.76m
Long Jump	Ciaran McDonagh	8.04m	Jacqui Stokes	6.06m
Triple Jump	Michael McDonald	14.94m	Siobhan Hoey	12.28m
Javelin	Terry McHugh	74.24m	Alison Moffitt	43.51m
Hammer	Patrick McGrath	72.01m	Nicola Coffey	55.79m
Shot Putt	John Dermody	18.61m	Emma Gavin	13.45m
Discus	Nicky Sweeney	59.56m	Ailish O'Brien	48.14m
Pole Vault	John Hallissey	4.50m	Bridget Pearson	3.20m*
56lbs Distance	Nicky Sweeney	8.95m*	-	-

*National Record

International Results

WORLD CROSS COUNTRY CHAMPIONSHIPS
Belfast 27/28 March 1999

● MEN'S LONG RACE INDIVIDUAL

Name	Country	Time
1. Paul Tergat	Kenya	38:28
2. Patrick Ivuti	Kenya	38:32
3. Paulo Guerra	Portugal	38:46
45. John Ferrin	Ireland	42:12
57. Dermot Donnelly	Ireland	42:38
77. Martin McCarthy	Ireland	43:14
78. David Burke	Ireland	43:15
96. Pauric McKinney	Ireland	44:06
100. Noel Cullen	Ireland	44:10

● MEN'S LONG RACE TEAM EVENT

Country	Points
1. Kenya	12
2. Ethiopia	57
3. Portugal	76
10. Ireland	253

● MEN'S SHORT RACE INDIVIDUAL

Name	Country	Time
1. Benjamin Limo	Kenya	12:28
2. Paul Kosegi	Kenya	12:31
3. Hailu Mekonnen	Ethiopia	12:35
21. Mark Carroll	Ireland	13:07
41. Paolo Daglio	Ireland	13:22
67. Cormac Finnerty	Ireland	13:41
69. Cormac Smith	Ireland	13:41
74. Brian Treacy	Ireland	13:43
85. Cian McLoughlin	Ireland	13:52

● MEN'S SHORT RACE TEAM EVENT

Country	Points
1. Kenya	14
2. Morocco	46
3. Ethiopia	55
11. Ireland	198

● WOMEN'S LONG RACE

Name	Country	Time
1. Gete Wami	Ethiopia	28:00
2. MerimaDenboba	Ethiopia	28:12
3. Paula Radcliffe	Britain	28:12
38. Rosemary Ryan	Ireland	29:58
72. Teresa Duffy	Ireland	31:07
77. Marie McMahon	Ireland	31:34
83. Maureen Harrington	Ireland	32:13
87. Louise Cavanagh	Ireland	32:37
97. Helena Crossan	Ireland	34:05

● WOMEN'S LONG RACE TEAM EVENT

Country	Points
1. Ethiopia	18
2. Kenya	27
3. Portugal	94
13. Ireland	270

● WOMEN'S SHORT RACE INDIVIDUAL

Name	Country	Time
1. Jackline Maranga	Kenya	15:09
2. Yamna Oubouhou-Belkacem	France	15:16
3. Annemari Sandell	Finland	15:17
22. Anne Keenan-Buckley	Ireland	16:02
28. Brid Dennehy	Ireland	16:09

Name	Country	Time
54. Una English	Ireland	16:44
55. Niamh Beirne	Ireland	16:45
66. Elaine Fitzgerald	Ireland	17:04
76. Mairead Murphy	Ireland	17:24

● WOMEN'S SHORT RACE TEAM EVENT

Country	Points
1. France	40
2. Ethiopia	48
3. Morocco	69
7. Ireland	159

WORLD ATHLETICS CHAMPIONSHIPS
Seville, 20-29 August 1999

MEN

Date	Event	Round	Winner	Perf	Irish Competitior	Perf	Status
21.08.99	Hammer	Pool B	I. Astapkovich (BLR)	77.75m	34. Patrick McGrath	68.96m	DNQ
21.08.99	HighJump	Pool B	M. Boswell (CAN)	2.29m	12. Brendan Reilly	2.26m	Qual. for final
22.08.99	Discus	Pool B	J. Schult (GER)	65.65m	25. Nick Sweeney	58.62m	DNQ
22.08.99	400m	1st rnd	A. Cardenas (MEX)	45.34	8. Paul McBurney	46.87	DNQ
23.08.99	110m Hurdles	1st rnd	M. Crear (USA)	13.30	4. Peter Coghlan	13.64	Qual. for q/f
23.08.99	110m Hurdles	Q/F	R. Duane (USA)	13.13	4. Peter Coghlan	13.37	Qual. for s/f
23.08.99	High Jump	Final	V. Vyacheslav (RUS)	2.37m	8. Brendan Reilly	2.29m*	8th overall
24.08.99	200m	1st rnd	K. Konstantinos (GRE)	20.68	4. Paul Brizzell	21.02	DNQ
24.08.99	200m	1st rnd	O. Thompson (BAR)	20.70	5. Gary Ryan	20.86	DNQ
24.08.99	110m Hurdles	S/F	R. Duane (UGA)	13.14	5. Peter Coghlan	13.35	DNQ
25.08.99	50km Walk	Final	G. Skurygin (RUS)	3:44:23	29. Jeff Cassin	4:20:43	29th overall
25.08.99	5,000m	S/F	M. Mourhit (BEL)	13:28.96	9. Mark Carroll	13:34.98	Qual. for final
26.08.99	Long Jump	Pool A	G. Cankar (SLO)	8.23m	5. Ciaran McDonagh	8.00m*	Qual. for final
26.08.99	800m	1st rnd	A. Longo (ITA)	1:45.01	4. James Nolan	1:46.38	Qual. for s/f
26.08.99	800m	1st rnd	W. Kirwa (FIN)	1:46.20	6. David Matthews	1:49.52	DNQ
27.08.99	800m	S/F	H. Sepeng (RSA)	1:45.20	7. James Nolan	1:47.07	DNQ
27.08.99	Javelin	Pool A	J. Zelezny (CZE)	84.31m	10. Terry McHugh	77.23m	DNQ
28.09.99	Long Jump	Final	I. Pedroso (CUB)	8.56m	10. Ciaran McDonagh	7.90m	10th overall
28.08.99	5,000m	Final	S. Hissou (MAR)	12:58.13	14. Mark Carroll	13:52.23	14th overall
28.08.99	4x400m Relay	1st rnd	USA	3:00.79	5. Ireland	3:05.81	DNQ

Irish 4x400m relay team: Gary Ryan, Paul McBurney, Tomas Coman, Paul McKee

WOMEN

Date	Event	Round	Winner	Perf	Irish Competitior	Perf	Status
22.08.99	400m Hurdles	1st rnd	D. Hemmings (JAM)	54.27	4. Susan Smith-Walsh	55.06	Qual. for s/f
22.08.99	400m	1st rnd	O. Falilat (NGR)	45.34	4. Karen Shinkins	52.12	Qual. for q/f
23.08.99	400m Hurdles	S/F	N. Bidouane (MOR)	53.95	6. Susan Smith-Walsh	55.20	DNQ
23.08.99	400m Hurdles	Q/F	A. Rücker (GER)	50.62	7. Karen Shinkins	52.08	DNQ
24.08.99	200m	1st rnd	D. Ferguson (BAH)	22.68	5. Ciara Sheehy	23.54	DNQ
27.08.99	20km Walk	Final	H. Liu (CHN)	1:30:50	32. Gillian O'Sullivan	1:40:51	32nd overall
27.08.99	1,500m	1st rnd	R. Jacobs (USA)	4:04.75	12. Elaine Fitzgerald	4:12.77	DNQ

* National Record

Perf = Performance. Performance is expressed in time unless otherwise stated;
DNQ = Did not qualify for next round;
Qual. = Qualified

Records

MEN

Event	Irish Record Holder	Perf	Date	World Record Holder	Perf	Date
100m	Neil Ryan	10.46	30.06.97	Maurice Greene (USA)	9.79	16.06.99
200m	Gary Ryan	20.67	26.08.97	Michael Johnson (USA)	19.32	01.08.96
400m	Derek O'Connor	45.73	05.06.86	Michael Johnson (USA)	43.18	26.08.99
800m	David Matthews	1:44.82	05.09.95	Wilson Kipjeter (DEN)	1:41.11	24.08.97
1,500m	Ray Flynn	3:33.5	07.07.82	Hicham El Guerrouj (MAR)	3:26.00	14.07.98
1 Mile	Ray Flynn	3:49.77	07.07.82	Hicham El Guerrouj (MAR)	3:43.13	07.07.99
3,000m	Mark Carroll	7:30.36	28.07.99	Daniel Komen (KEN)	7:20.67	01.09.96
5,000m	Mark Carroll	13:03.93	01.09.98	Haile Gebrselassie (ETH)	12:39.36	13.06.98
10,000m	John Treacy	27:48.7	22.08.80	Haile Gebrselassie (ETH)	26:22.75	01.06.98
Steeplechase	Brendan Quinn	8:24.09	30.08.85	Bernard Barmasai (KEN)	7:55.72	24.08.97
110m Hurdles	Peter Coghlan	13.30	07.08.99	Colin Jackson (GBR)	12.91	20.08.93
400m Hurdles	Tom McGuirk	49.73	01.06.96	Kevin Young (USA)	46.78	06.08.92
High Jump	Brendan Reilly	2.28m	23.08.99	Javier Sotomayor (CUB)	2.45m	27.07.93

Continued from previous page

Event	Irish Record Holder	Perf	Date	World Record Holder	Perf	Date
Pole Vault	Alan Bourke	5.00m	13.08.89	Sergey Bubka (UKR)	6.14m	31.07.94
Long Jump	Ciaran McDonagh	8.00m	26.08.99	Mike Powell (USA)	8.95m	30.08.91
Triple Jump	Colm Cronin	15.89m	26.06.77	Jonathon Edwards (GBR)	18.29m	07.08.95
Shot Putt	Paul Quirke	20.04m	07.07.92	Randy Barnes (USA)	23.12m	20.05.90
Discus	Nicky Sweeney	67.59m	04.09.98	Jürgen Schult (GDR)	74.08m	06.06.86
Hammer	Declan Hegarty	77.80m	28.04.85	Yuriy Sedykh (USSR)	86.74m	30.08.86
Javelin	Terry McHugh	82.14m	07.08.94	Jan Zelezny (CZE)	98.48m	25.05.96
4x100m Relay	National Team	39.46	09.08.97	United States of America	37.40	21.08.93
4x100m Relay	National Team	3:05.45	06.06.99	United States of America	2:54.20	22.07.98

WOMEN						
Event	Irish Record Holder	Perf	Date	World Record Holder	Perf	Date
100m	Michele Carroll	11.43	17.06.78	Florence Griffith-Joyner (USA)	10.49	16.07.88
200m	Ciara Sheehy	23.49	08.08.99	Florence Griffith-Joyner (USA)	21.34	29.09.88
400m	Karen Shinkins	51.07	12.07.99	Marita Koch (GDR)	47.60	06.10.85
800m	Sonia O'Sullivan	2:00.69	15.07.94	Jarmila Kratochílová (TCH)	1:53.28	26.07.83
1,500m	Sonia O'Sullivan	3:58.85	25.07.95	Yunxia Qu (CHN)	3:50.46	11.09.93
1 Mile	Sonia O'Sullivan	4:17.26	23.07.94	Svetlana Masterkova (RUS)	4:12.56	14.08.96
2,000m	Sonia O'Sullivan	5:25.36	08.07.94	Sonia O'Sullivan (IRL)	5:25.36	08.07.94
3,000m	Sonia O'Sullivan	8:21.65	15.07.94	Junxia Wang (CHN)	8:06.11	13.09.93
5,000m	Sonia O'Sullivan	14:41.40	01.09.95	Bo Jiang (CHN)	14:28.09	23.10.97
10,000m	Catherina McKiernan	31:08.41	17.06.95	Junxia Wang (CHN)	29:31.78	08.09.93
100m Hurdles	Susan Smith	13.12	09.08.98	Yordanka Donkova (BUL)	12.21	20.08.88
400m Hurdles	Susan Smith	54.31	12.08.98	Kim Batten (USA)	52.61	11.08.95
High Jump	Laura Sharpe	1.89m	03.07.94	Stefka Kostadinova (BUL)	2.09m	30.08.87
Long Jump	Terrie Horgan	6.48m	14.06.92	Galina Chistyakova (RUS)	7.52m	11.06.88
Triple Jump	Siobhan Hoey	12.38m	19.06.98	Inessa Kravets (UKR)	15.50m	10.08.95
Shot Putt	Marita Walton	16.99m	02.04.83	Natalya Lisovskaya (USSR)	22.63m	07.06.87
Discus	Patricia Walsh	57.60m	07.07.84	Gabriele Reinsch (GDR)	76.80m	09.07.88
Hammer	Olivia Kelleher	57.53m	24.04.99	Mihaela Melinte (ROM)	76.07m	29.08.99
Javelin	Mary T. Real	50.42m	20.06.92	Trine Sollberg-Hattertad (NOR)	68.19m	28.07.99
4x100m Relay	National Team	45.60	11.06.92	German Democratic Republic	41.37	06.10.85
4x400m Relay	National Team	3:32.56	05.09.87	Soviet Union	3:15.17	01.10.88

Irish and World records are correct as of 28 September 1999.

Boxing

Irish Amateur Boxing Association

National Boxing Stadium, South Circular Road, Dublin 8. Tel. (01) 4533371. email: info@tinet.ie
website:www.local.ie/sports_and_leisure/combat_sports

Honorary Secretary ....Seán Crowley
Number of County Boards 26
Number of Clubs 330
Principal Venue
....................National Boxing Stadium (capacity 2,000)

Founded 1911
President ....Breandán Ó Conaire

● IRISH AMATEUR BOXING SENIOR CHAMPIONS 1999

Weight	Winner	Club
48kg Light Flyweight	Jim Rooney	Star, Belfast
51kg Flyweight	Liam Cunningham	Saints, Belfast
54kg Bantamweight	Damien McKenna	Holy Family, Drogheda
57kg Featherweight	Bernard Dunne	CIE, Dublin
60kg Lightweight	Aodh Carlyle	Sacred Heart, Dublin
63.5kg Light Welterweight	Sean Barret	Rylane, Cork
67kg Welterweight	Neil Gough	St Paul's, Waterford
71kg Light Middleweight	Michael Roche	Sunnyside, Cork
75kg Middleweight	Conal Carmichael	Holy Trinity, Belfast
81kg Light Heavyweight	Alan Reynolds	St Jospehs Sligo
91kg Heavyweight	Stephen Reynolds	St Josephs, Sligo
91+kg Super Heavyweight	John Kinsella	Crumlin, Dublin

● IRISH AMATEUR BOXING INTERMEDIATE CHAMPIONS 1998

Weight	Winner	Club
48kg Light Flyweight	John Owens	St Colmans, Sligo
51kg Flyweight	Harry Cunningham	Saints, Belfast
54kg Bantamweight	William Waite	Holy Trinity, G/G, Belfast
57kg Featherweight	Edward Hyland	Golden Cobra, Dublin
60kg Lightweight	Karl Crawley	Glasnevin, Dublin
63.5kg Light Welterweight	Joe Harkin	Dunfanaghy, Donegal
67kg Welterweight	Kevin Cumiskey	Tralee, Kerry
71kg Light Middleweight	Terence McDermott	Bishop Kelly
75kg Middleweight	Conal Carmichael	Holy Trinity, Belfast
81kg Light Heavyweight	Alan Reynolds	St Jospehs, Sligo
91kg Heavyweight	John McDonagh	St Annes, Westport
91+kg Super Heavyweight	Colin Kenna	Mount Tallant

● IRISH AMATEUR BOXING JUNIOR CHAMPIONS 1999

Weight	Winner	Club
48kg Light Flyweight	J.P. Kinsella	Ballybrack ABC, Dublin
51kg Flyweight	Kevin Butler	St Colmans, Cork
54kg Bantamweight	Jamie Dowling	Paulstown, Kilkenny
57kg Featherweight	Francis Maughan	Drimnagh, Dublin
60kg Lightweight	Fergus Turner	St Ibars, Wexford
63.5kg Light Welterweight	Ciaran Smithers	Bunclody, Wexford
67kg Welterweight	Ger McAuley	Star, Belfast
71kg Light Middleweight	Michael Mullaney	Claremorris BC, Mayo
75kg Middleweight	Shane Dalton	Ennis, Clare
81kg Light Heavyweight	Coleman Barret	Olympic, Galway
91kg Heavyweight	Daniel Finn	Loughglynn, Roscommon
91+kg Super Heavyweight	Paul O'Rourke	Ballybrack, Dublin

Swimming

Swim Ireland

House of Sport, Long Mile Road, Dublin 12. Tel. (01) 4501739. email: swimirl@gofree.indigo.ie

Founded............1999
Number of Clubs............149
Number of Members............6,500
Number of Swimming Pools nationwide............219

President............Alice McKibben
Honorary Secretary............Mrs. Pat Donovan
Number of Coaches............50
Number of Teachers............1,500
Biggest Attendance 2,000 Leisureland, Galway 1997

1999 Irish National Swimming Champions

Event	Women's Champion	Club	Time	Men's Champion	Club	Time
50m Freestyle	J. Douglas	Alliance	0:26.35	W. Carey	Limerick	0:23.77
100m Freestyle	J. Douglas	Alliance	0:58.06	J.P. Williamson	Waterford	0:52.05
200m Freestyle	C. Gibney	Trojan	2:02.32	J.P. Williamson	Waterford	1:52.05
400m Freestyle	F. Kinsella	Trojan	4:23.93	N. Cameron	Leander	3:58.61
800m Freestyle	J. Doyle	Terenure	9.19.03	-	-	-
1500m Freestyle	-	-	-	B. Hoey	Templeogue	15:41.76
50m Backstroke	C. Hogan	St Pauls	0:30.86	H. O'Connor	New Ross	0:26.16
100m Backstroke	S. McNally	Longford	1:05.04	J. Thiele	Hamburg	0:56.86
200m Backstroke	S. McNally	Longford	2:18.86	H. O'Connor	New Ross	2:00.13
50m Breaststroke	E. Robinson	Bangor	0:32.94	G. Beegan	Cormorant	0:30.09
100m Breaststroke	L. Robinson	Bangor	1:11.06	M. Williamson	Lisburn	1:04.89
200m Breaststroke	K. Marshall	Ards	2:38.62	A. Bree	Ards	2:17.17
50m Butterfly	L. Kelleher	Sundays Well	0:29.28	A. Reid	Larne Junior	0:24.75
100m Butterfly	L. Kelleher	Sundays Well	1:03.55	A. Reid	Larne Junior	0:55.11
200m Butterfly	L. Kelleher	Sundays Well	2:18.49	G. Beegan	Cormorant	2:06.74
100m Individual Medley	C. Hogan	St Pauls	1:06.04	J. Thiele	Hamburg	0:58.71
200m Individual Medley	L. Kelleher	Sundays Well	2:21.23	G. Beegan	Cormorant	2:05.55
400m Individual Medley	N. Pepper	Cormorant	4:59.54	G. Beegan	Cormorant	4:28.36

➤ *Continued from previous page*

Event	Women's Champion	Time	Men's Champion	Time
Team Relays				
4x100m Freestlye Relay	..Bangor	4:02.02	Terenure	3:31.83
4x200m Freestyle Relay	..Templeogue	9:09.82	Terenure	7:48.28
4x100m Medley Relay	.....Bangor	4:26.41	New Ross	3:51.57

The 1999 Irish Open Swimming Championships were held at the Grove Pool in Belfast between July 21st and 24th.

Records

SHORT COURSE

WOMEN

Event	Irish Record Holder	Time	World Record Holder	Time
50m Freestyle	Michelle Smith	0:25.85	Jingyi Le (CHN)	0:24.23
100m Freestyle	Michelle Smith	0:54.87	Jingyi Le (CHN)	0:53.01
200m Freestyle	Michelle Smith	1:59.69	Claudia Poll (CRC)	1:54.17
400m Freestyle	Michelle Smith	4:14.02	Claudia Poll (CRC)	4:00.03
800m Freestyle	Michelle Smith	8:44.06	World Standard	8:15.34
1,500m Freestyle	Michelle Smith	16:46.75	World Standard	15:43.31
50m Backstroke	Niamh O'Connor	0:29.44	Sandra Voelker (GER)	0:27.27
100m Backstroke	Michelle Smith	1:02.36	Angel Martino (USA)	0:58.50
200m Backstroke	Michelle Smith	2:10.76	Cihong He (CHN)	2:06.09
50m Breaststroke	Gina Galligan	0:32.47	Xue Han (CHN)	0:30.77
100m Breaststroke	Siobhan Doyle	1:10.71	Samantha Riley (AUS)	1:05.70
200m Breaststroke	Sharlene Brown	2:32.26	Masami Tanaka (JPN)	2:20.22
50m Butterfly	Michelle Smith	0:28.15	Jennifer Thompson (USA)	0:26.05
100m Butterfly	Michelle Smith	0:59.99	Jennifer Thompson (USA)	0:56.90
200m Butterfly	Michelle Smith	2:07.04	Susan O'Neill (AUS)	2:05.37
100m Individual Medley	Michelle Smith	1:02.70	Jennifer Thompson (USA)	0:59.30
200m Individual Medley	Michelle Smith	2:13.46	Allison Wagner (USA)	2:07.79
400m Individual Medley	Michelle Smith	4:36.84	Guohong Dai (CHN)	4:29.00
4x100 Freestyle Relay	National Team	3:54.72	China	3:34.55
4x200 Freestyle Relay	National Team	8:25.94	Sweden	7:51.70
4x100 Medley Relay	National Team	4:15.90	Japan	3:57.62

MEN

Event	Irish Record Holder	Time	World Record Holder	Time
50m Freestyle	Nick O'Hare	0:22.76	Mark Foster (GBR)	0:21.31
100m Freestyle	Nick O'Hare	0:50.02	Alexandr Popov (RUS)	0:46.74
200m Freestyle	Ken Turner	1:49.38	Ian Thorpe (AUS)	1:43.28
400m Freestyle	Ken Turner	3:53.82	Grant Hackett (AUS)	3:35.01
800m Freestyle	Ken Turner	8:02.88	Kieren Perkins (AUS)	7:34.90
1,500m Freestyle	Ken Turner	15:33.57	Grant Hackett (AUS)	14:19.55
50m Backstroke	Adrian O'Connor	0:25.76	Thomas Rupprath (GER)	0:24.13
100m Backstroke	Adrian O'Connor	0:55.23	Jeff Rouse (USA)	0:51.43
200m Backstroke	Hugh O'Connor	1:59.33	M. Lopez-Zubero (ESP)	1:52.51
50m Breaststroke	Gary O'Toole	0:28.59	Mark Warnecke (GER)	0:26.70
100m Breaststroke	Gary O'Toole	1:01.87	F. Deburghgraeve (BEL)	0:58.79
200m Breaststroke	Gary O'Toole	2:11.35	Andrei Korneev (RUS)	2:07.79
50m Butterfly	Andrew Reid	0:24.67	Milos Milosevic (CRO)	0:23.30
100m Butterfly	Declan Byrne	0:55.41	James Hickman (GBR)	0:51.02
200m Butterfly	Colin Lowth	2:00.65	James Hickman (GBR)	1:51.76
100m Individual Medley	Standard	0:57.39	Jani Sievinen (FIN)	0:53.10
200m Individual Medley	Gary O'Toole	2:02.23	Jani Sievinen (FIN)	1:54.65
400m Individual Medley	Gary O'Toole	4:22.97	Matthew Dunn (AUS)	4:04.24
4x100m Freestyle Relay	National Team	3:24.66	Brazil	3:10.45
4x200m Freestyle Relay	National Team	7:27.78	Australia	7:02.74
4x100m Medley Relay	National Team	3:45.66	Australia	3:29.88

Irish records correct as of April 25, 1998. Swim Ireland have not updated the records at time of going to print. World records correct as of April 13, 1999.

Horse Racing

Irish Horseracing Authority

Leopardstown Racecourse, Foxrock, Dublin 18. Tel. (01) 2892888. website: www.iha.ie. email: info@iha.ie

Founded	1994
Chairman	Denis Brosnan
Chief Financial Officer	Martin J. Moore
Secretary	Paddy Walsh
Number of Meetings	258
Number of Races	1,819
Total Betting	£636,934,000
On-course	£115,934,000
Off-course	£521,000,000
Total Prizemoney	£16,576,000
Total Attendances	1,218,953
Main tracks	The Curragh, Leopardstown, Fairyhouse, Punchestown and Ballybrit

National Hunt 1997/98

Number of Races	1,116
Total Prizemoney	£8,121,000
Champion Trainer	Aidan O'Brien (94 winners)
Champion Jockey	Charlie Swan (90 winners)
Champion Apprentice	Ruby Walsh (40 winners)

Leading Trainers (97/98)	Runs	Wins	Prizemoney
Aidan O'Brien	795	94	£733,289
Noel Meade	367	70	£414,875
Michael Hourigan	405	49	£385,452
W.P. Mullins	319	41	£275,509
P. Mullins	241	39	£236,578

Leading Jockeys (97/98)	Rides	Wins	Prizemoney
Charlie Swan	521	90	£643,022
Conor O'Dwyer	479	64	£471,381
T.P. Treacy	439	58	£408,816
Richard Dunwoody	199	49	£466,016
Ruby Walsh	221	40	£222,199

Flat 1998

Number of Races	703
Total Prizemoney	£8,455,000
Champion Trainer	Dermot Weld (83 winners)
Champion Jockey	John Murtagh (87 winners)
Champion Apprentice	Shane Kelly (36 winners)

Leading Trainers	Runs	Wins	Prizemoney
Dermot Weld	541	83	£921,123
John Oxx	372	68	£832,563
Aidan O'Brien	427	65	£979,155
Jim Bolger	436	50	£435,490
Kevin Prendergast	303	29	£334,223

Leading Jockeys	Rides	Wins	Prizemoney
Johnny Murtagh	396	87	£1,028,623
Mick Kinane	299	63	£724,088
Kevin Manning	373	53	£521,645
Shane Kelly	352	36	£316,855
Patrick Smullen	365	35	£393,021

1999 Winners

NATIONAL HUNT

Race	Winner	Jockey	Trainer	SP	Prize
Ladbroke Handicap Hurdle	Archive Footage (GB)	D. Evans	D.K. Weld	25/1	£48,975
AIG European Champion Hurdle	Istabraq	C.F. Swan	A.P. O'Brien	8/15	£37,250
Jameson Irish Grand National	Glebe Lad	T.P. Rudd	M.J.P. O'Brien	8/1	£78,350
Power Gold Cup	Rince Rí	R. Walsh	T. Walsh	9/2	£32,850
Compaq Galway Plate	Moscow Express	R. Walsh	F.M. Crowley	4/1	£40,162
Kerry National Chase	Lanturn	P. A. Carberry	P. Hughes	7/1	£43,400

FLAT

Race	Winner	Jockey	Trainer	SP	Prize
Airlie Coolmore 2,000 Guineas	Saffron Walden (Fr)	O. Peslier	A.P. O'Brien	12/1	£112,700
Hibernia Foods 1,000 Guineas	Hula Angel (USA)	M. Hills	B.W. Hills	16/1	£112,750
Budweiser Irish Derby	Montjeu	C. Asmussen	J.E. Hammond	13/8	£440,555
Kildangan Stud Irish Oaks	Ramruma (USA)	K. Fallon	H.R.A. Cecil	4/9	£118,700
Heinz 57 Phoenix Stakes	Fasliyev (USA)	M.J. Kinane	A.P. O'Brien	2/7	£65,350
ESAT Digifone Champion Stakes	Daylami	L. Dettori	S.B. Surroor	6/4	£42,400
Jefferson Smurfit Memorial St Leger	Kayf Tara	L. Dettori	S.B. Surroor	1/2	£108,800
Aga Khan Studs National Stakes	Sinndar	J.P. Murtagh	John Oxx	7/1	£26,000

Golf

Amateur

Golfing Union of Ireland

Glencar House, 81 Eglinton Road, Donnybrook, Dublin 4. Tel. (01) 269 4111. website: www.gui.ie. email:

Founded	1891
Number of Affiliated Clubs	384
President	Tom Grealy, Roscommon
President Elect	Paddy Murphy, Newlands
Honorary Secretary	J. Gerard O'Brien, Clontarf
Number of Coaches	5
Number of Club Members	200,000
Oldest Club	Royal Belfast (1881)

Results

● IRISH AMATEUR CLOSE CHAMPIONSHIP

Killarney Golf Club, June 12-16

Quarter-finals

M. Sinclair	bt	G. McGimpsey	4/3
S. Browne	bt	E. Power	2/1
C. McMonagle	bt	P. Gribben	19th
B. Smyth	bt	G. McNeill	5/4

Semi-finals

M. Sinclair	bt	S. Browne	7/5
C. McMonagle	bt	B. Smyth	2/1

Final

C. McMonagle	bt	M. Sinclair	2/1

● IRISH AMATEUR OPEN CHAMPIONSHIP

Royal Dublin Golf Club May 14-16

282	G. Cullen	72...71...72...67
283	J. Fanagan	67...71...71...74
284	G. McGimpsey	69...73...67...75
284	A. McCormick	69...72...71...72
288	N. Fox	68...75...73...72
289	J. Foster	69...71...73...76
290	D. Dunne	77...71...71...71
290	C. McMonagle	70...73...72...75
291	C. Moriarty	73...70...77...71
292	P. Cowley	71...74...71...76
292	A. Pierse	69...74...76...73

● WEST OF IRELAND CHAMPIONSHIP

Enniscrone Golf Club, May 1-5

Quarter-Finals

R. Leonard	bt	M. Sinclair	5/3
G. Cullen	bt	M. Strandvik	5/3
H. Salonen	bt	S. D. Moloney	1 Hole
M. Ilonen	bt	J. Fanagan	2/1

Semi-Finals

R. Leonard	bt	G. Cullen	2/1
M. Ilonen	bt	H. Salonen	3/2

Final

M. Ilonen	bt	R. Leonard	4/2

● NORTH OF IRELAND CHAMPIONSHIP

Royal Portrush, July 5-9

Quarter finals

P. Gribben	bt	D. Coyle	1 hole
G. McGimpsey	bt	A. Morris	4/3
R. Elliott	bt	B. Omelia	6/5
D. Gibson	bt	L. Dalton	4/3

Semi-finals

P. Gribben	bt	G. McGimpsey	5/4
D. Gibson	bt	R. Elliott	2/1

Final

P. Gribben	bt	D. Gibson	2/1

● SOUTH OF IRELAND CHAMPIONSHIP

Lahinch, July 24-28

Quarter-finals

A. Morrow	bt	A. McCormick	2 holes
M. Campbell	bt	S. Browne	1 hole
C. Wisler	bt	J. Semelsberger	3/2
P. Martin	bt	R. Leonard	1 hole

Semi-finals

M. Campbell	bt	A. Morrow	1 hole
P. Martin	bt	C. Wisler	4/3

Final:

M. Campbell	bt	P. Martin	21st

● EAST OF IRELAND CHAMPIONSHIP

Co. Louth Golf Club, 5-7 June

277	K. Kearney	69...66...67...75
283	C. Williams	71...72...69...71
286	O. David	73...70...68...75
287	C. McMonagle	70...74...73...70
289	J. Olver	74...72...71...72
289	M. Sinclair	70...73...71...75
291	E. Power	71...77...71...71
291	J. Kehoe	69...75...73...74
292	G. McGimpsey	73...78...71...70
292	S. Branger	72...72...73...73

Ladies

Irish Ladies Golf Union

1 Clonskeagh Square, Clonskeagh Road, Dublin 14. Tel. (01) 2696244. email: ilgu@tinet.ie

Founded	1893
President	Teddy Mayne
Secretary	Terese Thompson
Number of Affiliated Clubs	358
Number of Club Members	46,500

● 1999 CHAMPIONSHIPS / WINNERS

Irish Close	Claire Coughlan (Cork)
Irish Open	Hazel Kavanagh (Grange)
Connacht	Deirdre Smith (Co. Louth)
Leinster	Jennifer Gannon (Co. Louth)
Midland	Rebecca Caokley (Australia)
Munster	Valerie Hassett (Ennis)
Ulster	Alison Coffey (Warrenpoint)

Results

● IRISH LADIES CLOSE CHAMPIONSHIP
Carlow G.C. 18-22 May 1999
Quarter finals
Lillian Behan.............bt........Yvonne Cassidy........2/1
Eileen Rose Power....bt.........Emma Dickson.......20th
Claire Coghlan..........bt......Miriam Abernethy....1 hole
Bronagh Lunney.......bt...........Sinead Keane........2/1
Semi Finals
Eileen Rose Power....bt.............Lillian Behan.......21st
Claire Coghlan..........bt.......Bronagh Lunney.........2/1
Final
Claire Coghlan..........bt....Eileen Rose Power........4/3

● IRISH LADIES OPEN CHAMPIONSHIP
Waterford Castle

1.	Hazel Kavanagh	73	69	75	217
2.	Elaine Dowdall	71	75	73	219
3.	Claire Hargan	72	76	73	221
4.	Sinead Keane	73	76	73	222
=5.	Deirdre Walsh	77	70	78	225
=5.	Bronagh Lunney	76	76	73	225
=5.	Mary McKenna	69	75	81	225
8.	Sheena Wood	70	84	73	227
9.	Suzanne Van Wezel	72	80	76	228
10.	Evelyn Hearn	76	75	78	229

Professional

● IRISH OPEN (Druid's Glen 1-4 July)
Final Leaderboard (Top 16)

268 (-16) €233,320
1........Sergio Garcia (Spa)..................69...68...67...64
271 (-13) €155,540
2........Angel Cabrera (Arg) ....70...66...66...69
273 (-11) €87,640
3........Jarrod Moseley (Aus) ....66...69...69...69
276 (-8) €59,453
=4......Eamonn Darcy (Ire)....................68...67...71...70
=4......Miguel Angel Martin (Spa) ....71...71...72...62
=4......Thomas Björn (Den) ....70...66...71...69
277 (-7) €34,055
=7......Malcolm Mackenzie (Eng) ....72...70...67...68
=7......Sven Strüver (Ger) ....69...70...70...68
=7......Colin Montgomerie (Sco)..........68...67...71...71
=7......Lee Westwood (Eng) ....70...68...71...68
278 (-6) €24,890
=11....Phil Price (Wal) ....67...65...75...71
=11....Gary Orr (Sco) ....68...71...72...67
279 (-5) €21,970
=13....Craig Hainline (USA) ....65...72...72...70
=13....Emanuele Canonica (Ita)..........68...72...72...67
280 (-4) €18,573
=15....David Howell (Eng)....................69...73...67...71
=15....Stephen Leaney (Aus) ....70...71...67...72
=15....Russell Claydon (Eng) ....69...69...71...71
=15....Alex Cejka (Ger) ....67...68...72...73
=15....Ricardo Gonzalez (Arg) ....71...69...68...72
=15....John Mellor (Eng) ....68...71...73...68

Other Irish finishers
282 (-2) €14,070
=25....Des Smyth (Ire) ....73...69...67...73
297 (+13) €2,094
68......Richard Coughlan (Ire) ....71...71...76...79

● EUROPEAN OPEN (The K Club 30 July-2August)
Final Leaderboard (Top 16)

271 (-17) €316,660
1........Lee Westwood (Eng) ....69...67...70...65
274 (-14) €165,020
=2......Darren Clarke (N. Ire) ....73...60...66...75
=2......Peter O'Malley (Aus) ....68...69...68...69
277 (-11) €87,760
=4......Constantino Rocca (Ita) ....69...73...70...65
=4......Robert Karlsson (Swe) ....70...72...69...66
278 (-10) €53,350
=6......John Senden (Aus) ....67...73...69...69
=6......Gary Emerson (Eng) ....70...69...70...69
=6......José Coceres (Arg)....................67...70...70...71
=6......Angel Cabrera (Arg) ....69...69...70...70
279 (-9) €33,044
=10....Richard Green (Aus)..................71...69...69...70
=10....Per-Ulrik Johansson (Swe) ....73...66...72...68
=10....Russell Claydon (Eng) ....72...69...68...70
=10....Peter Lonard (Aus) ....72...67...72...68
=10....Andrew Coltart (Sco) ....71...67...71...70
280 (-8) €26,776
=15....Katsuyoshi Tomori (Jpn) ....66...69...73...72
=15....Colin Montgomerie (Sco)..........67...71...69...73
=15....Paul Lawrie (Sco) ....67...71...72...70

Other Irish finishers
281 (-7) €22,641
=18....Padraig Harrington (Ire) ....69...73...71...68
285 (-3) €10,450
=45....Des Smyth (Ire) ....72...70...72...71
287 (-1) €6,127
=55....Damien McGrane (Ire)...............72...70...72...73
297 (+9) €2,832
72......Philip Walton (Ire) ....72...71...76...78

● WEST OF IRELAND GOLF CLASSIC
(Galway Bay 12-15 August)
Final Leaderboard (Top 16)

276 (-12) €58,330
1........Constantino Rocca (Ita) ....70...68...68...70
278 (-10) €38,380
2........Padraig Harrington (Ire)............69...69...68...72
279 (-9) €18,080
=3......Des Smyth (Ire) ....71...68...69...71
=3......Paul Broadhurst (Eng) ....73...66...72...68
=3......Gary Evans (Eng) ....70...66...71...72
280 (-8) €10,500
=6......Anders Hansen (Den) ....67...74...71...68
=6......Michael Long (NZ) ....69...72...73...66
=6......Paul McGinley (Ire) ....68...69...74...69
281 (-7) €7,410
=9......Eric Carlberg (Swe) ....68...67...74...72
=9......Mats Hallberg (Swe) ....70...71...71...69
282 (-6) €6,440

11......Gary Emerson (Eng)................68...71...72...71
          283 (-5) €5,666
=12....Elliot Boult (NZ) ....66...75...71...71
=12....Knud Storegaard (Den) ....68...71...74...70
=12....Soren Hansen (Den)................67...72...72...72
          284 (-4) €4,931
=15....Maarten Lafeber (Hol) ....71...68...73...72
=15....Andrew Raitt (Eng) ....68...75...66...75
=15....Benoit Teilleria (Fra).................70...72...72...70

Other Irish finishers
          285 (-3) €4,287
=18....Peter Lawrie (Ire) ....70...76...72...67
          288 (Par) €2,520
=35....Gary Murphy (Ire) ....72...72...73...71
          290 (+2) €1,505
=50....Eamon Darcy (Ire) ....71...75...72...72
          292 (+4) €1,015
=59....Philip Walton (Ire) ....75...70...75...72
          298 (+10) €528
=76....Damien Mooney (NI) ....73...71...77...77

● **DONEGAL IRISH OPEN**
2-5 September 1999, Letterkenny Golf Club
          286
1. S. Mendiburu (Fra).......................71...72...71...72
=2. L. Davies (Gbr) ....77...70...70...69

=2. R. Carriedo (Spa) ....76...72...71...67
=2. E. Esterl (Ger)...............................75...68...71...72
Mendiburu won at second hole of sudden-death play-off
          287
5. A. Nicholas (Gbr) ....72...70...73...72
          288
=6. T. Johnson (Gbr)...........................75...75...69...69
=6. M. Hedblom (Swe) ....72...72...74...70
=6. N. Karlsson (Swe).........................76...66...72...74
=6. D. Reid (Gbr) ....74...71...68...75
          289
=10. J. Morley (Gbr)............................77...72...71...69
=10. W. Dicks (Gbr) ....70...72...71...76
          290
=12. L. Kreutz (Fra) ....73...76...70...70
=12. R. Hakkarainen (Fin) ....75...67...77...71
=12. K. Taylor.......................................71...73...73...73
          291
=15. E. Steen (Swe) ....75...71...76...69
=15. A. Munt (Aus) ....77...74...70...70
=15. J. Mills (Aus) ....76...70...72...73
=15. N. Fink (Aus)................................71...75...72...73
=15. M. Hageman (Ned) ....71...74...70...76

Angling

Sea Angling

Irish Federation of Sea Anglers
27 Seafield Avenue, Dollymount, Dublin 3.
Tel. (01) 8336218

Founded..1953
President ....Capt. Christy O'Toole
Secretary.......................................Hugh O'Rorke
Number of Affiliated Councils .4 (Connacht, Leinster,
Munster and Ulster)
Number of Affiliated Clubs 182
Connacht 16
Leinster 64
Munster 43
Ulster..59

Coarse Fishing

National Coarse Fishing Federation of Ireland
"Blaithin", Dublin Road, Cavan, Co. Cavan.
Tel. (049) 32367.

President ....Ned O'Farrell
Secretary ....Brendan Coulter
Number of Clubs..50-60
Number of Councils ...4 (Connacht, Leinster, Munster
and Ulster)

Badminton

Badminton Union of Ireland
Baldoyle Badminton Centre, Baldoyle Industrial Estate,
Grange Road, Baldoyle, Dublin 13. Tel. (01) 8393028.

Founded..1899
President.......................................Audrey E. Kinkead
General Secretary ....John Feeney
Number of Clubs...600
Number of Branches ....4: Connacht,

...................................Leinster, Munster and Ulster
Number of Teams..2,500
Number of Members..Men (20,500); Women (21,000)

● **1999 Irish Senior Champions**
Ladies Singles ....Sonya McGinn
Men's Singles ....Michael Watt
Ladies Doubles ....Sonya McGinn & Keelin Fox
Men's Doubles ....Donie O'Halloran & Mark Peard

Mixed Doubles ....Bruce Topping & Jayne Plunkett	Men's Singles ....Ciaran Darcy
	Ladies Doubles......Teresa Donohue & Fiona Glennon
● 1999 Irish Under 19 Champions	Men's Doubles ....Ciaran Darcy & Neil Lynch
Ladies Singles.....................................Sarah Ross	Mixed Doubles ....Neil Lynch & Fiona Glennon

Basketball

Irish Basketball Association

National Basketball Arena, Tymon Park, Dublin 24.
Tel. (01) 4590211. website: www.indigio.ie/iba.
email: info@iba.ie

Founded..1945
Number of Clubs Affiliated to I.B.A. 300
Number of Local Area Boards...............................15
Number of Clubs Affiliated to Local Boards....1,200
Number of Registered Players (Men)................5,341
Number of Registered Players (Women).........5,896
Number of Registered Players (Schools)......80,000
President...Finn Ahern
Chief Executive Officer.....................Scott McCarthy
General Secretary ....Sheila Gillick
Number of Coaches..1,100
Main VenueNational Basketball Arena (capacity 2,500)

● 1998/99 NATIONAL MEN'S CHAMPIONS
Superleague ....Star of the Sea
Cup ....Denny Notre Dame
National Championship ....Marathon St Vincents
Division One.................................Team West Ballina
Junior Cup...Killester
Junior Cup Southern Region ....Kilkenny
Junior Cup North-Eastern Region ....Ballina Colts
Junior Cup North-Western Region.............Portlaoise

● 1998/99 NATIONAL WOMEN'S CHAMPIONS
Superleague ....Avonmore Snowcream Wildcats
Cup ....Tolka Rovers
National C'ship.........Avonmore Snowcream Wildcats
Regional League ....Crusaders
Junior Cup.............Avonmore Snowcream Wildcats
Junior Cup Southern Region ....Glanmire
Junior Cup North-Eastern Region.............Crusaders
Junior Cup North-Western Region..............Kilkenny

League Tables 1998/99

● MEN'S SUPERLEAGUE

	P	W	L	Pts
Star of the Sea 26		21	5	68
Waterford Crystal................26		19	7	64
Killester..............................26		17	9	60
Esat Telecom Demons.........26		17	9	60
Marathon St. Vincents 26		17	9	60
Denny Notre Dame...............26		16	10	58
Burger King Limerick 26		12	14	50
Neptune...............................26		12	14	50
UCD Marian 26		12	14	50
Kerry Spring Killarney.........26		11	15	48

Team Sligo Dairies.................26	10	16	46
Dungannon..........................26	8	18	42
Dublin Bay Vikings 26	8	18	42
Tolka Rovers........................26	2	24	30

● MEN'S FIRST DIVISION

Northern Conference	P	W	L	Pts
Team West Ballina 9		9	0	27
Moycullen 9		5	4	19
Queens................................9		4	5	17
Belfast Rockets 9		0	9*	8

Southern Conference	P	W	L	Pts
Tralee Tigers........................15		13	2	41
Clare Jets............................15		11	4*	36
Neptune...............................15		9	6	33
St Mary's Castleisland..........15		7	8	28
Esat Telecom Demons..........15		5	10*	24
Marathon Limerick 15		0	15*	14

*Forfeit = no points

● WOMEN'S SUPERLEAGUE

	P	W	L	Pts
Snowcream Wildcats............16		14	2	44
Tolka Rovers........................16		9	7	34
Meteors...............................16		9	7	34
Killester..............................16		6	10	28
Supermacs Limerick.............16		2	14	20

● WOMEN'S REGIONAL LEAGUE

North-East Region	P	W	L	Pts
Crusaders 8		7	1	22
Firhouse..............................8		4	4	16
Drimnagh 8		4	4	16
Tridents 8		4	4	16
New Ross Bullets..................8		1	7	10

North-Western Region	P	W	L	Pts
Team Sligo Dairies 6		4	2	14
Castlebar Rockets 6		4	2	14
Sporting Belfast...................6		3	3	12
Longford Falcons 6		1	5	8

South Region	P	W	L	Pts
Waterford Wildcats 8		7	1	22
Blarney...............................8		6	2	20
St Mary's 8		5	3	18
Glanmire 8		2	6	12
Waterford Glass 8		0	8	8

Bowling

Bowling League of Ireland

c/o 32 Iona Villas, Glasnevin, Dublin 9.
Tel: (01) 830 5548
Founded..1927
President...W.J.Morrissey
Secretary...B.J.Heade
Number of Clubs...22
Number of Coaches...12
Number of Members...1,950
● 1999 Senior Champions
Singles ....John J. Murphy (Crumlin)
Pairs..........Derek McCarthy, Frank McCarthy (C.Y.M.)
Triples..................................Bray (Skip: Blair Somers)
Fours.......................C. Y. M. (Skip: Bernard Vaughan)
Under 25 Singles........................Blair Somers (Bray)
● 1999 Junior Champions
Singles.................Richard Leonard (St. James Gate)
Pairs ....Chris Cushen, Pat O'Looney (Westmanstown)
Triples................Westmanstown (Skip: Tony Hegarty)
Fours...Ierne (Skip: Joe Tyrell)

Ladies' Bowling League of Ireland

17 Kimmage Road West, Dublin 12. Tel. (01) 4555302
President..Marie Barber
Honorary Secretary...............................June Fincher
Number of Clubs...18
Number of Senior Coaches 5
Number of Club Coaches.....................................16
Number of Umpires 12
● 1999 Senior Champions
Singles ....Phillis Nolan (Blackrock)
Pairs ....H.Cahill, C.O'Gorman (Blackrock)
Triples............M. Tormey, P.McCann, P.Day (Leinster)

Fours...I.Culligan, M.Elliott, D.McCulloch, M.Hoey CYM
● 1999 Junior Champions
Singles ....Jean Kane (IGB)
Pairs......................C.Morrissey, T. Tate (Greystones)
Triples.........C.Morrissey, L. de Buitlear, Margt. Smyth
(Greystones)
Fours.....D. Neilan, H.Buggy, L.Lyons, V.Doddy (R.U.)

Irish Indoor Bowling Association

c/o 204 Kings Road, Knock, Belfast BT5 7HX.
Founded..1962
President...R. McDermott
Secretary ....D. Hunter
Number of Clubs..1,084
Number of Members...................................30,000+

Irish Bowling Association

2 Ashdene Road, Moneyreagh, Co. Down, BT23 6DD.
Tel. (01232) 448348
Founded..1904
President.......................................Hugh Montgomery
Secretary ....J. North McQuay
Number of Clubs...130
Number of Coaches..41
Number of Members...6,700
● 1999 Champions
Singles ....John J. Murphy (Crumlin)
Pairs ....Ron Hastings, Gary Scott, (Bangor)
Triples.................Ballymoney (Skip: Ronney Milliken)
Fours.......................C. Y. M. (Skip: Bernard Vaughan)
Under 25 Singles........................Blair Somers (Bray)

Canoeing

Irish Canoe Union

House of Sport, Long Mile Road, Dublin 12. Tel. (01)
450 9838.
website: www.irishcanoeunion.ie
email: office@irishcanoeunion.ie

Founded..1960
President...John Carolan
Secretary ....John Keogh
Number of Associate Members.......................4,500
Number of Intructors...450
Number of Clubs...105

1999 DOMESTIC RESULTS
Liffey Descent 4 September 1999
Men
Senior K2 ....Gary Mawer, John Mawer IRL
Junior K2 ....Dan Sillito, Jim Mumford ENG
Senior K1 ....Malcolm Banks IRL
Junior K1 ....David O'Connor IRL
Senior Wild Water ....Michael O'Meara IRL

Junior Wild Water..........................Shaun Smith ENG
Senior Open Singles ....Patrick Kelly IRL
Junior Open Singles ....Dean Dalton IRL

Women
Senior K1 ....Michelle Barry IRL
Senior Wild Water ....Anne Mynes IRL
Senior Open Singles...................Heather Clarke IRL
Junior Open singles ....Ruth O'Connor IRL

Veterans
Veterans K1 ....Nick Daniels ENG
Veterans Wild Water ....Robert Sherburn IRL
Veterans Open Singles ....Derek Hall ENG

Men's K1 Irish Freestyle Champion ....Ali Donald
Women's K1 Irish Freestyle Champion
....Eodaoin Ní Challaráin

Cricket

Irish Cricket Union

45 Foxrock Park, Foxrock, Dublin 18. Tel. (01) 2893943
website: www.ulsterweb.com/cricket/icu/home.shtml
Founded..1923
President...Dermott Monteith
Honorary Secretary ....John Wright
Number of Clubs Affiliated to I.C.U.................170
Number of Teams...400
Number of Registered Players 9,000
Number of Coaches..70
Largest Attendance.....4,0001993, Ireland v. Australia
Highest Score...198 I.J. Anderson v. Canada XI, 1973
Number of Provincial Unions 4
National Coach......Mike Hendrick (until Dec 31 1999)
Most Capped Player .D.A. Lewis 121 caps 1984-1997
Most Runs...................4,275 (S.J.S. Warke, 1981-96)
Most Centuries.................7 (I.J. Anderson, 1966-85)
Most Wickets..................326 (J.D. Monteith, 1965-84)
Best Bowling Analyses9-26 (F. Fee v. Scotland 1957)
Most Catches...............................57 (A.J. O'Riordan)
Quickest Century
....51 minutes, 51 balls J.A. Prior v. Warwickshire 1982

● **1999 Champions**
Royal Liver Irish Senior Cup ....Brigade
Northern Cricket Union League ....North Down
Northern Cricket Union Cup ........................N.I.C.C.
North-West Cricket Union League ....Limavady
North-West Cricket Union Cip...................Limavady
Munster Cricket Union League..............Cork County
Munster Cricket Union Cup ....Cork County
Leinster Leagues
    W.M.&K Senior League (Section A)........Clontarf
    W.M.&K Senior League (Section B) ....Merrion
    Lewis Traub League...............................Merrion
Leinster Cricket Union Cup ....Pembroke
Senior Interprovincials ....Leinster
World Ranking of the Irish Team 13th

● **1999 IRISH SENIOR CUP RESULTS**
1st Round
Limavady ....bt...................CYM ..162 runs
NICC ....bt.....Railway Union ....32 runs
2nd Round
Merrion..........................bt........Balymena ....36 runs
Brigade ....bt........Muckamore ....70 runs
Cliftonville ....bt ....Rush .....9 wkts
Bready ....bt........Cork County .....6 wkts

Donemana ....bt ....Lisburn ......3 wkts
Downpatrick ....bt ....Clontarf ......7 wkts
North County ....bt..............Eglinton ..164 runs
Fox Lodge....................bt ....Malahide ......5 wkts
Instonians ....bt ....YMCA ....74 runs
Limavady ....bt ....Phoenix ......5 wkts
Lurgan...........................bt ....Leinster ...42 runs
Strabane ....bt........North Down ....36 runs
Old Belvedere ....bt ....Ardmore ....10 runs
Pembroke ....bt ....NICC ....12 runs
The Hills.......................bt ....Sion Mills ....97 runs
Glendermott ....bt...........Woodvale ......9 wkts
3rd Round
Limavady ....bt ....Bready ......5 wkts
Strabane ....bt...............Lurgan ....27 runs
Brigade ....bt.......Downpatrick ....13 runs
Fox Lodge.....................bt ....Instonians ....4 wkts
Merrion..........................bt ....North County ......5 wkts
Cliftonville...................bt....Old Belvedere ....w.o.
Glendermott ....bt ....Pembroke ....19 runs
Donemana ....bt ....The Hills ....79 runs
4th Round
Limavady ....bt ....Cliftonville ....1 wkt
Fox Lodge....................bt ....Strabane ....21 runs
Merrion...........................bt ....Glendermott ......6 wkts
Brigade ....bt ....Donemana...112 runs
Semi-finals
Limavady ....bt...........Fox Lodge ..144 runs
Brigade ....bt............Merrion ..105 runs
Final
Brigade ....bt ....Limavady ......4 wkts

IRISH WOMEN'S CRICKET UNION

50 St.Alban's Park, Sandymount, Dublin 4.
Founded..1982
President..Hilary O'Reilly
Honorary Secretary................................Ursula Lewis
Number of Provincial Unions
................3 (South Leinster, North Leinster and Ulster)
Number of Clubs...17
Number of Registered Players 1,500
Number of Coaches..1
Most Capped Player ....Mary Pat Moore (46)
Most Runs.................................956 (Mary Pat Moore)
Most Centuries .... 1 (Mary Pat Moore)
Most Wickets.................................40 (Susan Bray)
Best Bowling Analyses.................5-27 (Susan Bray)
Biggest Attendance...300 (1995, European Cup final)

Croquet

Croquet Association of Ireland

Carrickmines Croquet & Lawn Tennis Club, Glenamuck
Road, Carrickmines, Co. Dublin. Tel. 01 2955744

Founded..1900
President...Niall McInerney
Secretary ....Jane Shorten

Number of Affiliated Clubs 6
Number of Associate Members 144

Cycling

Irish Cycling Federation

Kelly Roche House, 619 North Circular Road, Dublin 1.
Tel. (01) 855 1522. **website:** www.fic.ie

Founded...1988
President...Pat McQuaid
Honorary Secretary................................Jack Watson
Number of Clubs...................................127
Number of Regions.4 (Connacht, Leinster, Munster & Ulster)
Total Membership (1999)....................................2,520

● **INTERNATIONAL RESULTS 1998-99**
World Championships, Valkenberg, Holland.
07.10.98 Men's Junior Time trial (23kms).

Name & Position	Country	Time
1.....Fabian Cancellara	SUI	29:39.15
2.....Torsten Hiekmann	GER	29:41.61
3.....Filippo Pozzato	ITA	29:46.41
22...Mark Scanlon	IRL	31:42.54
37...Dermot Nally	IRL	32:29.06

10.10.98 Men's Junior Road Race (120 kms)

Name & Position	Country	Time
1.....Mark Scanlon	IRL	2:54:36
2.....Filippo Pozzato	ITA	2:54:36
3.....Eduard Kivichev	RUS	2:54:36
35...Dermot Nally	IRL	2:54:58
47...Stephen Gallagher	IRL	2:55:17
82...Shane Prendergast	IRL	3:07:29
84...David Kenneally	IRL	3:08:45

● **DOMESTIC RESULTS 1999**

Race	Winner
FBD Milk Rás	Philip Cassidy (Ireland)
Junior Tour of Ireland	Brian Ahern (Ireland)
Senior Road Race	Tommy Evans (Clarke Nissan)
Junior Road Race	Michael Dennehy (Kanturk)
Veterans Road Race	Sean McIlroy (Carrick Wheelers)
Ladies Road Race	Geraldine Gill(Velo Lannion France)
Senior 40k TT	Andrew Roche (Emmyvale)
Senior 16k TT	Philip Cassidy (Navan)
Junior 16k TT	Brendan O'Brien (Clarke Contracts)
Ladies 16k TT	Marie Reilly (Bohermeen)
Senior 80k TT	Patrick Moriarty (Les Jeunes/Dublin)
1998 Senior Cyclo Cross	Robin Seymour (Giant)
U23 Men's Championships	David McQuaid (UCD)

Darts

Irish National Darts Organisation

Raheen, Ballyneety, Co. Limerick. Tel. (061) 351018.
Founded..1979
President...Marian McDermott
Chairman ....Liam Kerins
Secretary ....John Keane
Treasurer ....Patrick Murphy
Number of Clubs...1,500
Number of Teams...2,120
Main Venue.............Limerick Inn Hotel (Capacity: 700)
Biggest Attendance....900 (1989 at Lucan Spa Hotel)
National Senior Coach....................John Joe O'Shea

National Managers.....................................John Keane
................Patrick Murphy, Gerry O'Dowd, Liam Kerins
Most Caps ....John Joe O'Shea and Jack McKenna

● **1999 National Champions**
National Singles, Men.............Sean McGowan, Sligo
National Singles, Women........Olive McIntyre, Leitrim
Mens Intercounty, Team ....Galway
Ladies Intercounty, Team................................Carlow
National Youth Singles..........Kevin Keegan, Wexford
Youths Intercounty, Team ....Wexford

Greyhound Racing

Bord na gCon

104 Henry Street, Limerick. Tel. (061) 316788
Founded..1958
Chairman..Paschal Taggert
Chief Executive..................................Michael J. Field
Number of Meetings (1998)................................1,818
Number of Races (1998)..................................16,536
Attendance (1998)..............................754,000
Total Prizemoney (1998)....................£2,578,853
Betting (Tote & Bookmaker 1998) £32,156,846
Main Venue ....Shelbourne Park

● **1999 Winners**
Irish Derby Winner....................................Springtime
Irish Oaks ....Born A Survivor
Breeders Cup Stakes (Sprint) ....Quarter-to-five
Breeders Cup Stakes 525 yards........Quare Princess
Breeders Cup Stakes 750 yards ....Get Connected
Irish St Leger (1998) ....Deer Field Sunset
National Breeders Produce Stakes...Born A Survivor
Irish Laurels.....Tiger's Eye/Lumber Boss (Dead heat)
Champion Stakes....................................Mister Bozz

Equestrian Sport

Equestrian Federation of Ireland

Ashton House, Castleknock, Dublin 15. Tel. (01) 8387611
Founded..1931
Number of Organisations...14
Total Number of Members................................9,000
    Men 6,000
    Women 3,000
President..Lewis Lowry

Secretary General ....Col. E. V. Campion
Number of Coaches...400
Biggest Attendance 150,000
..........Punchestown 1991 European Three Day Event
Principal Venues..........................R.D.S. 7,000 seats;
................Millstreet 5,000 seats; Punchestown 21,000
● **1999 Champions**
Dressage........................Katy Bradley riding Cabalo
Eventing............Jane O'Flynn riding Kilnadeema Star

Hockey

Irish Hockey Union

6A Woodbine Park, Blackrock, Co. Dublin. Tel. (01) 2600028
Founded..1893
President ....J. Smyth
Honorary Secretary ....J. Andrew Kershaw
Number of Clubs...76
Number of Provincial Unions..3 (Ulster, Munster and Leinster)
Main Stadium................UCD, Belfield. Capacity 1,500

1999 Champions	Winners
Irish Senior Cup	Cork Church of Ireland
Irish League	Instonians
Irish Junior Cup	Harlequins
Irish Schools Cup	Ashton
Leinster Senior Cup	Pembroke Wanderers
Ulster Senior Cup (Kirk)	Lisnagarvey
Ulster Senior Cup (Anderson)	Lisnagarvey
Munster Senior Cup	Cork Church of Ireland

INTERNATIONAL

Irish Senior Coach...John Clarke
Number of Senior Coaches 19
Most Capped Player..............Marty Sloan (149 caps)
Top Scorer..Jimmy Kirkwood
Biggest Attendance ...5,000 (1995, European Nations Cup finals)

● **1999 IRISH SENIOR CUP RESULTS**
Fifth Round

Cork Col	11	Aer Lingus	0
Avoca	2	Banbridge	1
Cliftonville	2	Instonians	3
Annadale	3	Monkstown	2
Mossley	1	Three Rock Rovers	6
YMCA	3	Glenanne	5
Harlequins	0	Pembroke Wanderers	1
Raphoe	1	Lisnagarvey	5

Quarter-finals

Cork Col	2	Avoca	1
Instonians	4	Annadale	5 aet
Glenanne	1	Three Rock Rovers	3
Pemborke Wanderers	1	Lisnagarvey	2

Semi-finals

Cork Col	3	Annadale	2
Three Rock Rovers	2	Lisnagarvey	1

Final

Cork Col	4	Three Rock Rovers	3

Irish Ladies Hockey Union

95 Sandymount Road, Dublin 4. Tel. (01) 6606780
Founded..1894
President....................................Catriona O'Brien
Honorary Secretary................................Joan McCloy
Number of Clubs...126
Number of Provincial Unions ....5 (Ulster, Munster, Leinster, Connacht and South-East)
Number of Members.30,000 (of which 20,364 are registered as players)
Main Stadium ....University College Dublin, Belfield. Capacity 1,500

1999 Champions	Winners
Irish Senior Cup	Hermes
Irish League	Pegasus
Irish Junior Cup	Our Lady's Terenure
Irish Junior League	Pegasus II
Irish Schools Cup	Mount Saville
Senior Interprovincial	Ulster
Leinster Senior Cup	Old Alexandria
Ulster Senior Cup	Pegasus
Munster Senior Cup	Harlequins
Connacht Senior Cup	Yeats County
Inter varsity	Trinity College, Dublin

INTERNATIONAL

Irish Senior Ladies Coach ....Riet Kuper
Number of Coaches...8
Most Capped Player......................Mary Logue (135)
Top Scorer ....Sarah Kelleher
International Ranking 14th
Biggest Attendance....6,000 (August 1994, Women's Hockey World Cup final)
Biggest Recorded Victory
..........................11-0 (v Wales 1907 & v. Poland 1997)

● **1999 IRISH SENIOR CUP RESULTS**
1st Round

North Down	1	Muckross	5
Pegasus	4	Pembroke Wanderers	0
NUIG	0	Harlequins	8

Yeats County 0	Randalstown................4	Harlequins 1	Belvedere 0
Glenanne......................1	Railway Union 1	Pegasus ....w.o.	Bandon ....
Glenanne won replay		**Quarter finals**	
Galway 2	Col Cork 4	Randalstown................1	Coleraine 2
Portadown 1	UCC...............................0	Pegasus 3	Harlequins 0
Old Alexandra..............3	Loreto 1	Muckross 5	Col Cork 0
2nd Round		Old Alexandra..............0	Hermes.........................3
Old Alexandra..............3	Portadown 2	**Semi-finals**	
Muckross 4	Victorians.....................0	Pegaus 3	Muckross 0
Col Cork 2	Trinity............................1	Coleraine 0	Hermes.........................7
Collegians....................0	Randalstown................1	**Final**	
Ards 0	Hermes.........................5	Hermes.........................3	Pegasus........................2
Coleraine 4	Glenanne......................1		

Motorsports

Motor Cycling

Motor Cycle Union of Ireland
35 Lambay Road, Glasnevin, Dublin 9.
Tel. (01) 8378090. website: www.mcui.ie
email: mcuireland@yahoo.com
Founded..1902
Number of Centres....................2: Southern (Leinster, Connacht & Munster) and Ulster
Number of Clubs...66
Number of Members..............................1,700
President...Sam McClelland
Secretary...Andrew Campbell
Number of Coaches...2
Biggest Attendance...100,000 (North-West 200 Road Races, Portrush Co. Antrim)
Main Venue (Short Circuit)
..........Mondello Park, Naas; Nutts Corner, Co. Antrim.
Main Venues (Road Racing)
.............Cookstown, Tandragee, Portstewart, Skerries.

⬤ IRISH CHAMPIONS 1999
Road Racing
125 cc ....Simon Byrne
Supersport 600...............................Barry Gill
Senior Class ....John Cahill
400 c.c. Support Class ....Martin Finnegan
401-750 c.c. Support Class ....Alan Egan

Short Circuit
125 cc ....Simon Byrne
400 cc...Matt Niland
600 cc.......................................Enda Corrigan
Senior Class...............................Derek Wilson
Sidecar Driver............................Terry O'Reilly
Sidecar Passenger..........................Arron Galligan

Motor Rallying

Motorsport Ireland
34 Dawson Street, Dublin 2. Tel. (01) 6775628
website: www.motorsportireland.com
email: asinclair@motorsportireland.com
Founded..1901
Number of Clubs...35
Total Membership 3,600
Chairman...Cecil Sparks
Secretary..Alex Sinclair
Biggest Attendance 100,000
Phoenix Park, 1929 Irish Grand Prix
Main Venue ....Mondello Park, Naas, Co. Kildare
Irish Land Speed Record, flying km 179.31mph
1994 Brendan O'Mahony, Porsche 962

⬤ IRISH RALLY CHAMPIONS 1999
Donegal International Rally ....James Cullen
Galway International Rally ......Bertie Fisher (Subaru)
Killarney International Rally ....Ian Greer

⬤ IRISH CHAMPIONS 1999
Sexton Trophy (1998)....................Neil Shanahan RIP
Hillclimb ....Donal Griffin
Touring Car/RT 2000 ....Jonathon Fildes
National Rally Navigation ......Michael O'Connor/Paul Phelan
Hewison ....Eamon Byrne
Vard Rally ....Niall Maguire
Forestry Rally ....Dermot Kelly
Rallycross ....Laurence Gibson

Formula 1

JORDAN RECORD 1991-98

Year	Starts	Points	Poles	Wins	Final Position	Drivers	Engine
1991	31	13	0	0	5th	A. deCesaris, B. Cachot	Ford

Continued from previous page

Year	Starts	Points	Poles	Wins	Final Position	Drivers	Engine
1992	28	1	0	0	13th	S. modena, M. Gugelmin	Yamaha
1993	31	3	0	0	11th	R. Barrichello, T. Boutsen	Hart
1994	31	28	1	0	5th	R. Barrichello, E. Irvine	Peugeot
1995	34	21	0	0	6th	R. Barrichello, E. Irvine	Peugeot
1996	32	22	0	0	5th	R. Barrichello, M. Brundle	Peugeot
1997	34	33	0	0	5th	R. Schumacher, G. Fisichella	Peugeot
1998	32	34	0	1	4th	R. Schumacher, D. Hill	Honda
Total	**253**	**155**	**1**	**1**			

JORDAN'S 1999 RECORD (up to and including September 26th)
Number of Races: 14; Number of Pole Positions: 1; Number of Podium Finishes: 6 (First: 2; Second: 1;Third: 3).
Number of Points: 57, Number of Retirements: 11.

1999 WORLD DRIVERS' CHAMPIONSHIP (up to and including September 26th)

	1st	2nd	3rd	4th	5th	6th	Other	Retired	Points
Eddie Irvine (Ferrari)	3	2	2	2	1	2	1	1	60
H-H Frentzen (Jordan)	2	1	3	4	0	0	0	4	50
Damon Hill (Jordan)	0	0	0	1	1	2	3	7	7

Netball

NI Netball Association
Netball Office, House of Sport, Upper Malone Road, Belfast BT9 5LA. Tel. (01232) 383806

Founded 1949
President ....Maureen Drennan
Secretary ....Claire Curran
Number of Clubs 35
Number of Teams 54

Number of Members 1,000
Number of Coaches 40
Internationa Coach (senior) ....Marion Lofthouse
Most Capped Player ....Elizabeth Rodgers
Top Scorer (international) ....Helen McCambridge
Biggest Attendance ....1,100. N.I. v Jamaica 1996

Orienteering

Irish Orienteering Association
c/o AFAS, House of Sport, Longmile Road, Walkinstown, Dublin 12. Tel. (01) 4509845.
website: http://homepage.tinet.ie/~ioa/
email: irishoa@tinet.ie
Founded 1970
Chairman ....Brendan Creedon
Honorary Secretary ....Ken Griffin
Number of Regions..3, Connacht, Leinster & Munster
Number of Clubs 25
National Coaching Officer ....Frank Ryan
Most Caps ....Eileen Loughman (1976-97)

● **1999 Shamrock O-Ringen Winners**
Elite Men ....Colm O'Halloran (Cork)
Mens Long ....Stefan Schlatter (Switzerland)
Mens Short ....Graham turner (Australia)
Mens 18 ....Ewan McCarthy (Britain)
Mens 20 ....Robert Palmer (Wales)
Mens 35 ....Charles Bromley Gardner (Britain)
Mens 40 ....Juha Liukkonen (Finland)
Mens 45 ....Steven Templeton (England)
Mens 50 ....Peter Gorvett (England)
Mens 55 ....Brian Shaw (England)

Mens 60 ....Jim Heardman (Scotland)
Elite Women ....Toni O'Donovan (Cork)
Womens Long ....Natasha Davison (England)
Womens Short ....Julia Simpson (England)
Womens 18 ....Caroline Dennehy (Cork)
Womens 20 ....fionne Austin (Cork)
Womens 35 ....Dorothy Pelly (England)
Womens 40 ....Lotti Spalinger (Switzerland)
Womens 45 ....MMalfa Peter (Switzerland)
Womens 50 ....Monica Nowlan (Dublin)
Womens 55 ....Ann Hughes (England)
Womens 60 ....Rita Jacobsen (Denmark)

The Shamrock O-Ringen is held annually in Kerry and west Cork. It is a World Ranking event and incorporates the Irish individual championships.

Pitch and Putt

The Pitch and Putt Union of Ireland

House of Sport, Long Mile Road, Walkinstown, Dublin 12. Tel. (01) 4509299. email: ppui@iol.ie
website: www.iol.ie/ppui

Founded	1961
Number of Clubs	148
Number of Provincial Councils	2
Total Number of Members	12,000
Number of Coaches	215

Honorary Secretary ....Peg Smith

● **1999 Champions**
Gents Matchplay ....Sean Harkin (St Bridgets)
Gents Strokeplay ....Niall Cuffe (Kilbeggan)
Ladies Matchplay......Bernadette Coffey (St Bridgets)
Ladies Strokeplay ....Marian Byrne (St Bridgets)

Racquetball

Racquetball Association of Ireland

c/o John Comerford, 5 Edenvale Close, Kilkenny.
Founded 1979
President ....Philip Duignan
General Secretary................................John Comerford
Number of Clubs ....40 (approx)

● **1998 Irish Open Champions**
Men's Open Singles ....Noel O'Callaghan
Ladies Singles (Olympic) ....Elma Gibney

Men's Open Doubles ....Stephen O'Loan
....Martin McConnon
Ladies Open Doubles ....Karen Grumbridge
A. Marie Grumbridge

● **1998 Irish Open Champions**
Boys U18 Singles ....Michael Keane
Girls U18 Singles ....Elma Gibney
Boys U16 Singles ....Pa Boyce
Girls U16 Singles................................Sonya Donnelly

Rowing

Irish Amateur Rowing Union

House of Sport, Long Mile Road, Walkinstown, Dublin 12. Tel. (01) 4509831. email: info@iaru.ie

Founded	1899
Number of Clubs	70
Number of Members	8,290
President	Thomas Fennessy
Honorary Secretary	James Bermingham
Administrator	Peadar Casey
International Team Manager	Dermot Henihan

● **1999 DOMESTIC RESULTS**
National Championships
Iniscarra, Co. Cork 16-18 July 1999.
Men's Champions
Senior Eights ....Neptune
Senior Coxed Fours ....Neptune
Senior Coxless Fours ....Neptune
Senior Coxless Pairs ....Neptune
Senior Quadruple Sculls ....Neptune
Senior Double Sculls ....Fermoy/St Michaels

Senior Single Scull.......................................Neptune
Lightweight Single Scull..........................Lee Valley
Intermediate Eights............University College Cork
Intermediate Coxed Fours.....University College Cork
Intermediate Coxless Pairs................Trinity College
Intermediate Single Sculls ....Neptune
Novice Eights ....Commercial
Novice Coxed Fours..............................NUI Galway
Novice Single Scull ....Muckross

Women's Champions
Senior Eights ....Commercial
Senior Coxless Fours............................Commercial
Senior Coxless Pairs.............................Commerical
Senior Double Sculls ....Commercial
Senior Single Scull ....Commerical
Intermediate Eights ....Neptune
Intermediate Coxed Fours ....Neptune
Intermediate Single Sculls ....Killorglin
Novice Eights ....Carlow
Novice Coxed Fours......................................Carlow
Novice Single Scull ....Killorglin

● **1999 INTERNATIONAL RESULTS**
World Rowing Championships 22-29 August 1999, St Catharines, Canada.
Men
27.08.99 ....Single Scull ....D Final....1. Slovenia ....7:20.83....2. Russia ....7:22.14....5. Ireland ....7:31.67 A. Maher
28.08.99 ....LW Double Scull .B Final....1. Japan ....6:18.43....2. Netherlands6:20.84 ...6. Ireland ....6:25.48 Niall O'Toole and Derek Holland

Continued from previous page

28.08.99 ....LW Single Scull...A Final....1. Denmark ....6:47.97....2. Czech Rep 6:51.14....4. Ireland 6:55.05
Sam Lynch
29.08.99 ....LW Quad. Scull...A Final....1. Italy ....6:27.71....2. Germany....6:32.41....3. Ireland 6:32.81
Neal Byrne, Gearoid Towey, James Lindsay-Fynn and Noel Monahan
29.08.99 ....LW Pair ....A Final....1. Italy ....7:28.35....2. Chile ....7:29.05....3. Ireland 7:29.18
Neville Maxwell and Tony O'Connor.

Women
27.08.99 ....Double Scull ......C Final....1. South Africa ...7:44.45....2. Ireland 7:54.54
Ireland: M. Hussey and D. Stack.
LW = Lightweight

Sailing

Irish Sailing Association

3 Park Road, Dun Laoghaire, Co. Dublin. Tel. (01) 2800239. website: www.sailing.ie ; email: isa@iol.ie

Founded	1946
Number of Branches	4 (North, South, East and West)
Number of Category One Clubs	43
Number of Members (Category One)	16,000
President	Paddy Maguire
General Secretary	Paddy Boyd
1998 Senior Helmsmen	Tom Fitzpatrick & David McHugh
1999 Junior Helmsman	Nicholas O'Leary
1998 Junior Helmsman	Gerbil Owens
Principle Venues	Dublin Bay, Howth, Cork, Kinsale

Royal Yachting Association

Northern Ireland Council, House of Sport, Upper Malone Road, Belfast BT9 5LA. Tel. (01232) 381222

Founded	1875
Number of Clubs	35
Chairman	Patrick Knatchbull
Honorary Secretary	Harold Boyle
Number of Coaches	250 (approx.)
Principal Venues	Belfast Lough, Strangford Lough, Lough Neagh and Lough Erne

Snooker

Republic of Ireland Billiards & Snooker Association

House of Sport, Longmile Road, Dublin 12. Tel. (01) 450 9850

Founded	1959
President	Tommy Martin
Secretary	Eamon Kearns
Number of Clubs	82
Number of Coaches	6

● **1999 Champions**

Irish Senior Open	Joe Canny (Celbridge)
Leinster Open	Robert Murphy (Monkstown, Dublin)
Munster Open	Tom Gleeson (New Institute)

Ladies Open	Ann McMahon
Billiards Championship	Phil Martin

● **1999 IRISH SNOOKER CHAMPIONSHIP**
Quarter finals (best of 9 frames)

Jason Watson	bt	Mick Farrell	5-1
Joe Canny	bt	Carl Murphy	5-3
Stanley Murphy	bt	Robert Redmond	5-2
Tom Gleeson	bt	Rodney Goggins	5-3

Semi-finals (best of 11 frames)

Joe Canny	bt	Jason Watson	6-4
Stanley Murphy	bt	Tom Gleeson	6-4

Final (best of 15 frames)

Joe Canny	bt	Stanley Murphy	8-3

Special Sports

Special Olympics Ireland

Ormond House, Upper Ormond Quay, Dublin 7.   Tel. (01) 8720300. **email:** specialo@iol.ie

Founded	1978
Chairman	Cyril Freaney
Secretary	Myra O'Leary

Sports	Athletics, Basketball, Tenpin Bowling, Swimming, Table Tennis, Gymnastics, Soccer, Equestrian, Golf, PolyHockey and Alpine Skiing.
Number of Clubs (*approx.*)	100
Number of Members (*approx.*)	12,000

Irish BlindSports

c/o 25 Turvey Close, Donabate, Co. Dublin. Tel. (01) 8436501

Founded	1989
President	Liam Nolan
Secretary	Catherine Walsh
Sports	athletics, judo, water-skiing, tenpin bowling, adventure weekends
Number of Members	300

Northern Ireland Blind Sports

12 Sandford Avenue, Belfast, BT5 5NW. Tel. (01232) 657156

Founded	1989
Secretary	Lisa Royal
Number of Members	600
Sports	football, bowls, tandem cycling, golf, sailing, angling, water-skiing, athletics, ten pin bowling

Squash

Irish Squash

House of Sport, Long Mile Road, Dublin 12. Tel. (01) 4501564
website: www.ucc.ie/ucc/socs/squash/irish_squash.html
email: irishsquash@clubi.ie

Founded	1993
Number of Clubs	111
Total Number of Members	250
President	Patrick Madigan
Secretary	to be elected
Number of Provincial Associations	4
National Senior Mens Coach	Eoin Ryan
National Senior Ladies Coach	Elvy D'Costa
Ireland's European Ranking (women)	13th
Ireland's European Ranking (men)	13th
1998 Irish Women's Champion	Madeline Perry
1998 Irish Men's Men Champion	Derek Ryan

Most Capped Competitor	Derek Ryan
Top Ranked Irish Player (women)	Aisling McArdle

Ulster Squash

House of Sport, 2a Upper Malone Road, Belfast, BT9 5LA. Tel. (01232) 381222

Founded	1995
Number of Clubs	49
Total Number of Teams	119
Total Number of Members	967
President	David Irvine
Biggest Attendance	300
	Maysfield Leisure Centre 1992
Principal Centre	
	Centre of Excellence for Squash, Newtownards

Surfing

Irish Surfing Association

Easkey Surf and Information Centre, Easkey, Co. Sligo. Tel. (096) 49020. email: isasurf@iol.ie
www.iol.ie/~isasurf/

Founded	1967
Number of Clubs	12
Total Number of Members (approx.) Men	1,150
Total Number of Members (approx.) Women	350
President	Brian Britton
Administrator	Zoë Lally

Number of Coaches	75
1998 National Champion (Men)	Colin O'Hare
1998 National Champion (Women)	Zoë Lally
1999 Intercounty Champions	Waterford
European Ranking (Senior)	6th
European Ranking (Junior)	4th
World Ranking	18th
Principal Venues	Portrush, Rossnowlagh, Bundoran, Strandhill, Lahinch, Ballybunion and Tramore

Tennis

Tennis Ireland

Argyle Square, Morehampton Road, Donnybrook, Dublin 4. Tel. (01) 6681841.
websitewww.tennisireland.ie. email: tennis@iol.ie

Founded	1908
Number of Clubs	220
Total Number of Members	92,500
Men	25,500
Women	21,000
U18s	46,000
President	Walter Hall
Honorary Secretary	Ciaran O'Donovan
Top Irish Player (men)	John Doran

Top Irish Player (women)	Kelly Liggan
Number of Coaches	191
Principal Venue	Riverview, Donnybrook

● 1999 Singles Champions

	Men	Women
Irish Open	T. Spinks	Lucie Ahl
Irish Indoor	Scott Baron	Yvonne Doyle

● 1999 Junior Singles Champions

	Men	Women
Irish Open	C. Niland	E. Ó Riain

Taekwondo

Taekwondo Association of NI
20 Lester Avenue, Lisburn, Co. Antrim BT28 3QD.
Tel. (01846) 604293

Founded...1978
Chairman ....Glen Culbert
Honorary Secretary ....Bertie Nicholson
Number of Clubs...16

Number of Teams..2
Number of Members (Northern Ireland) 600
Number of Coaches..15
Biggest Recorded Attendanc 650
National Senior Coach (international)......Paul Gibson
Most Capped Competitor (international) ....Jason
Creighton

Tug of War

Irish Tug of War Association
c/o Longhouse, Ballymore-Eustace, Co. Kildare.
Tel. (045) 864222.
Founded 1967
President ....Eddie Hubbard
Secretary ....Martha Buckley
Branches ..4 (Connacht, Leinster, Munster and Ulster)
Number of Clubs 41
Number of Members ....1,400 (approx)

Number of Coaches ....2 per club
Best International Result.Youth Team, Silver at 1997
European Championships (Jersey)
Most Capped Competitor Martin Keogh, won 13 gold
medals in European and World Championships
World Rankings ....Top 6

Volleyball

Volleyball Association of Ireland
Unit C1, Crosbie Business Centre, Ossory Road, East
Wall, Dublin 3. Tel. (01) 8552993. website: www.
clubi/volleyball.ie; email: volleyball@clubi.ie

Founded..Feb: 1968
President ....Susan O'Donnell
Secretary..Wouther Lewis
Treasurer ....Fergal Collins
Number of Clubs...23
Number of Schools..81

● 1998/99 Mens Champions
Division 1 ....Portmarnock
Division 2 ....Naas
Senior Championship ....Dublin City University
Intermediate Championship ....Naas
1998/99 Womens Champions
Division 1 ....Santry
Division 2 ....Naas
Senior Championship ....Dublin City University

Intermediate Championship ....Santry
Junior Championship ....Naas
Premier 32, All-Ireland Men ....Belfast City
Premier 32, All-Ireland Women...East Coast Cruisers

NI Volleyball Association
House of Sport, Upper Malone Road, Belfast.
Tel. (01232) 381222.

Founded..1970
President ....Patrick Murphy
Secretary ....Simon Hunter
Number of Clubs...30
Number of Coaches..26

● 1997/98 Champions
Men's Senior League.........................Larne Old Boys
Women's Senior League ....Belfast City
Men's Cup.....................................Portadown Aztecs
Women's Cup..Belfast City

Wrestling

Irish Amateur Wrestling Association
c/o 54 Elm Mount Drive, Beaumont, Dublin 9.
Tel. (01) 8315522

Founded..1947
President..Michael Whelan
Honorary Secretary ....Michael McAuley

Number of Coaches..............................20 (freestyle)
Most Capped Competitor ....Joe Feeney
won British welterweight title, 1957-64
● Best International Results
Team ....1994 Small Nations Champions
Individual ....R. Dunleavy (1st)
1994 Small Nations Championships

Olympics

Medalists Representing Ireland since 1924

Games	Name	Event	Medal
Amsterdam, 1928	Dr. Pat O'Callaghan	Hammer	Gold
Los Angeles, 1932	Dr. Pat O'Callaghan	Hammer	Gold
	Bob Tisdall	400m Hurdles	Gold
Helsinki, 1952	John McNally	Boxing (bantam weight)	Silver
Melbourne, 1956	Ronnie Delaney	1,500m	Gold
	Fred Tiedt	Boxing (welter weight)	Silver
	Freddie Gilroy	Boxing (bantam weight)	Bronze
	John Caldwell	Boxing (fly weight)	Bronze
	Tony Byrne	Boxing (light weight)	Bronze
Tokyo, 1964	Jim McCourt	Boxing (light weight)	Bronze
Moscow, 1980	David Wilkins & Jamie Wilkinson	Yachting (Flying Dutchman)	Silver
	Hugh Russell	Boxing (fly weight)	Bronze
Los Angeles, 1984	John Treacy	Marathon	Silver
Barcelona, 1992	Michael Carruth	Boxing (welter weight)	Gold
	Wayne McCullough	Boxing (bantan weight)	Silver
Atlanta, 1996	Michelle Smith	Swimming (400m Individual Medley)	Gold
	Michelle Smith	Swimming (400m Freestyle)	Gold
	Michelle Smith	Swimming (200m Individual Medley)	Gold
	Michelle Smith	Swimming (200m Butterfly)	Bronze

TOTAL: Gold 8, **Silver** 5, **Bronze** 6.

Irish born* Medallists representing countries other than Ireland

Games	Name	Country Represented	Event	Medal
Athens (1896)	John Pius Boland	Ireland	Tennis (singles)	Gold
Athens (1896)	John Pius Boland	Ireland	Tennis (doubles)	Gold
Paris (1900)	John Flanagan	USA	Athletics (Hammer)	Gold
Paris (1900)	Denis St. George Daly	Britain	Polo†	Gold
Paris (1900)	Pat Leahy	Ireland	Athletics (High Jump)	Silver
Paris (1900)	Harold Mahony	Britain	Tennis (singles)	Silver
Paris (1900)	Harold Mahony	Britain	Tennis (mixed doubles)	Silver
Paris (1900)	John Cregan	USA	Athletics (800m)	Silver
Paris (1900)	Pat Leahy	Britain	Athletics (Long Jump)	Bronze
Paris (1900)	Harold Mahony	Britain	Tennis (mens doubles)	Bronze
St. Louis (1904)	John Flanagan	USA	Athletics (Hammer)	Gold
St. Louis (1904)	Tom Kiely	Ireland	Athletics (Decathlon)	Gold
St. Louis (1904)	Martin Sheridan	USA	Athletics (Discus)	Gold
St. Louis (1904)	Pat Flanagan	USA	Tug-of-War	Gold
St. Louis (1904)	James Mitchell	USA	Athletics (56lb Weight Throw)	Silver
St. Louis (1904)	John J. Daly	Ireland	Athletics (Steeplechase)	Silver
St. Louis (1904)	Albert Newton	USA	Athletics (Marathon)	Bronze
St. Louis (1904)	Albert Newton	USA	Athletics (Steeplechase)	Bronze
St. Louis (1904)	Martin Sheridan	USA	Athletics (Long Jump)	Bronze
Athens (1906)§	Peter O'Connor	Ireland	Athletics (Triple Jump)	Gold
Athens (1906)§	Con Leahy	Britain	Athletics (High Jump)	Gold
Athens (1906)§	Martin Sheridan	USA	Athletics (Discus)	Gold
Athens (1906)§	Martin Sheridan	USA	Athletics (Shot Putt)	Gold
Athens (1906)§	Martin Sheridan	USA	Athletics (Stone Thrower)	Silver
Athens (1906)§	Martin Sheridan	USA	Athletics (Long Jump)	Silver
Athens (1906)§	Peter O'Connor	Ireland	Athletics (Long Jump)	Silver
Athens (1906)§	Con Leahy	Britain	Athletics (Triple Jump)	Silver
Athens (1906)§	John McGough	Britain	Athletics (1,500m)	Silver
London (1908)	John Flanagan	USA	Athletics (Hammer)	Gold
London (1908)	Martin Sheridan	USA	Athletics (Discus-Freestyle)	Gold
London (1908)	Martin Sheridan	USA	Athletics (Discus-Greek Style)	Gold
London (1908)	Robert Kerr	Canada	Athletics (200m)	Gold
London (1908)	Joe Deakin	Britain	Athletics (3 mile)†	Gold

Continued from previous page

Games	Name	Country Represented	Event	Medal
London (1908)	Johnny Hayes	USA	Athletics (Marathon)	Gold
London (1908)	Tim Aherne	Britain	Athletics (Triple Jump)	Gold
London (1908)	Con O'Kelly	Britain	Wrestling	Gold
London (1908)	Edward Barrett	Britain	Tug-of-War	Gold
London (1908)	Matt McGrath	USA	Athletics (Hammer)	Silver
London (1908)	Con Leahy	Ireland	Athletics (High Jump)	Silver
London (1908)	Denis Horgan	Britain	Athletics (Shot Putt)	Silver
London (1908)	James Clark	Britain	Tug-of-War	Silver
London (1908)	James Cecil Parke	Britain	Tennis (mens doubles)	Silver
London (1908)	-	Ireland	Mens Hockey†	Silver
	Eric Allman-Smith	Ireland	Mens Hockey	Silver
	Henry Brown	Ireland	Mens Hockey	Silver
	Walter Campbell	Ireland	Mens Hockey	Silver
	Walter Peterson	Ireland	Mens Hockey	Silver
	C. F. Power	Ireland	Mens Hockey	Silver
	G. S. Gregg	Ireland	Mens Hockey	Silver
	E. P. C. Holmes	Ireland	Mens Hockey	Silver
	Robert Kennedy	Ireland	Mens Hockey	Silver
	Henry Murphy	Ireland	Mens Hockey	Silver
	W. G. McCormack	Ireland	Mens Hockey	Silver
	Frank Robinson	Ireland	Mens Hockey	Silver
London (1908)	Martin Sheridan	USA	Athletics (Long Jump)	Bronze
London (1908)	Robert Kerr	Canada	Athletics (100m)	Bronze
London (1908)	Edward Barrett	Britain	Wrestling	Bronze
London (1908)	Con Walsh	Canada	Athletics (Hammer)	Bronze
London (1908)†	-	Ireland	Polo†	Bronze
London (1908)	John McCann		Polo	Bronze
Stockholm (1912)	Kennedy McArthur	South Africa	Athletics (Marathon)	Gold
Stockholm (1912)	Pat McDonald	USA	Athletics (Shot Putt)	Gold
Stockholm (1912)	Matt McGrath	USA	Athletics (Hammer)	Gold
Stockholm (1912)	Matt Hynes	Britain	Tug-of-War	Silver
Antwerp (1920)	Pat McDonald	USA	Athletics (56lb Weight Throw)	Gold
Antwerp (1920)	Paddy Ryan	USA	Athletics (Hammer)	Gold
Antwerp (1920)	Noel Mary Purcell	Britain	Water Polo	Gold
Antwerp (1920)	Capt. Frederick Barrett	Britain	Polo†	Gold
Antwerp (1920)	Percy O'Reilly	Britain	Polo†	Gold
Antwerp (1920)	Frank Heggarty	Britain	Athletics (8,000m)†	Silver
Paris (1920)	Terence Saunders	UK	Rowing (Coxless Fours)	Gold
Paris (1924)	Matt McGrath	USA	Athletics (Hammer)	Silver
Paris (1924)	Capt. Frederick Barrett	Britain	Polo†	Bronze
Los Angeles (1932)	Sam Ferris	Britain	Athletics (Marathon)	Silver
Berlin (1936)	B. J. Fowler	Britain	Polo	Silver

* 32 counties; § Unofficial Olympic Games; † team events. Total Gold: 29; Total Silver: 21; Total Bronze: 11.

NI medalists, representing Britain

Games	Name	Event	Result	Medal
Los Angeles (1932)	Sam Ferris (b. Co. Down)	Marathon	2:31.18	Silver
Melbourne (1956)	Thelma Hopkins (b. England*)	High Jump	1.67m	Silver
Innsbruck (1964)†	Robin Dixon, Lord Glentoran (b. Co. Antrim)	Two-man bobsleigh	4:21.90	Gold
Munich (1972)	Mary Peters (b. England)	Pentathlon	4801 points	Gold
Los Angeles (1984)	Billy McConnell (b. Co. Down)	Hockey	-	Bronze
Los Angeles (1984)	Stephen Martin (b. Co. Down)	Hockey	-	Bronze
Seoul (1988)	Stephen Martin (b. Co. Down)	Hockey	-	Gold
Seoul (1988)	Jimmy Kirkwood (b. Co. Antrim)	Hockey	-	Gold
Barcelona (1992)	Jackie Burns-McWilliams (b. Co. Antrim)	Hockey	-	Bronze

* worked / lived in Northern Ireland; † Winter Olympic Games Total Gold: 3; Total Silver: 2; Total Bronze: 2.

Irish Summer Olympians, 1924-96

1924 PARIS *(Athletics):* John Kelly, W. J. Lowe, Sean Lavan, Norman McEachern, J. O'Connor, John O'Grady, Larry Stanley, J. J. Ryan. *(Boxing):* M. Doyle, Sgt. P. Dwyer, Pte. J. Flaherty, R. M. Hilliard, Pte. J. Kelleher, Pte. J. Kidley, Pte. M. McDonagh, W. J. Murphy. *(Lawn Tennis):* W. G. Ireland, E. D. McCrea, H. Wallis, P. Blair-White. *(Water Polo):* S. Barrett, J. Beckett, J. S. Brady, P. Convery, C. Fagan, M. A. O'Connor, N. M. Purcell.

1928 AMSTERDAM *(Athletics):* Pat Anglim, Alister F. Clarke, G. N. Coughlan, L. D. E. Cullen, Denis Cussen, Sean Lavan, Norman McEachern, Dr. Pat O'Callaghan, Con O'Callaghan, Theo Phelan. *(Cycling):* Bertie Donnelly, J. B. Woodcock. *(Boxing):* Garda J. Chase, Gda. Matt Flanagan, G. Kelly, P. J. Lenihan, Cpl. M. McDonagh, Gda. W. J. Murphy, Pte. W. O'Shea, Edward Traynor. *(Swimming):* J. S. Brady, W. D. Broderick, M. Dockrell, T. H. Dockrell, H. B. Ellerker, C. Fagan, N. Judd, T. McClure, J. A. O'Connor, M. A. O'Connor.

1932 LOS ANGELES *(Athletics):* Eamonn Fitzgerald, M. J. Murphy, Bob Tisdall, Dr. Pat O'Callaghan. *(Boxing):* John Flood, Patrick Hughes, James Murphy, Ernest Smith.

1936 BERLIN No Irish team travelled.

1948 LONDON *(Athletics):* J. J. Barry, Cummin Clancy, Dan Coyle, Charles Denroche, Paul Dolan, Pat Fahy, Dave Guiney, Jimmy Reardon, Frank Mulvihill, Reggie Myles. *(Basketball):* H. Boland, Lt. P. Crehan, Lt. J. Flynn, Sgt. W. Jackson, Pte. T. Keenan, G. McLaughlin, Cadet J. R. McGee, Cpl. T. Malone, Cdt. F. B. O'Connor, Lt. D. O'Donovan, Sgt. D. Reddin, Pte. D. Sheriff, Pte. P. Sheriff, Sgt. C. Walsh. *(Boxing):* William E. Barnes, Peter Foran, Willie Lenihan, Maxie McCullagh, Mick McKeon, Kevin Martin, Gearoid O'Colmain, Hugh O'Hagan. *(Equestrian):* Cmdt. Fred Ahern, Cmdt. Dan J. Corry, Lt. Col. John J. Lewis. *(Fencing):* Dorothy Dermody, Patrick Duffy, T. Smith, Nick Thuillier, Owen Tuohy. *(Football):* W. Barry, W. Brennan, J. Cleary, F. Glennon, P Kavanagh, P. Lawlor, P. McDonald, Lt. P. McGonagle, E. McLoughlin, W. O'Grady, B. O'Kelly, W. Richardson, R. Smith. *(Rowing):* H. R. Chantler, P.G. Dooley, T. G. Dowdall, S. Hanley, P. D. Harrold, D. Lambert-Sugrue, B. McDonnell, E. M. A. McElligott, J. Nolan, W. J Stevens, R. W. R. Tamplin, D. B. C. Taylor. *(Yachting):* R.H. Allen, A.J. Mooney.

1952 HELSINKI *(Athletics):* Paul Dolan, Joe West. *(Boxing):* Peter Crotty, William Duggan, John Lyttle, John McNally, Kevin Martin, Terry Milligan, Andrew Reddy, Thomas Reddy. *(Equestrian):* Capt. Mark Darley, Harry Freeman-Jackson, Ian Hume-Dudgeon. *(Fencing):* George Carpenter, Paddy Duffy, Harry Thuillier, Tom Rafter. *(Wrestling):* Jack Vard. *(Yachting):* Dr. Alf Delaney.

1956 MELBOURNE *(Athletics):* Ronnie Delany, Eamonn Kinsella, Maeve Kyle. *(Boxing):* Anthony Byrne, John Caldwell, Freddie Gilroy, Harry Perry, Patrick Sharkey, Martin Smyth, Fred Tiedt. *(Equestrian):* Capt. Kevin Barry, Harry Freeman-Jackson, Ian Hume-Dudgeon, Lt. Patrick Kiernan, William Mullin, Lt. William Ringrose. *(Wrestling):*

Gerald Martina. *(Yachting):* John Somers-Payne.

1960 ROME *(Athletics):* Ronnie Delany, Willie Dunne, Michael Hoey, Maeve Kyle, John Lawlor, Patrick Lowry, Gerald McIntyre, Bertie Messitt, Frank O'Reilly. *(Boxing):* Joseph Casey, Patrick Kenny, Adam McClean, Colm McCoy, Eamonn McKeon, Bernard Meli, Danny O'Brien, Harry Perry, Ando Reddy, Michael Reid. *(Cycling):* Peter Crinion, Anthony Cullen, Seamus Herron, Michael Horgan, Martin McKay. *(Equestrian):* Lt. John Daly, Lt. Edward O'Donohoe, Capt. William Ringrose. *(Eventing):* Anthony Cameron, Ian Hume Dudgeon, Harry Freeman-Jackson, Edward Harty. *(Fencing):* Shirley Armstrong, Chris Bland, George Carpenter, Brian Hamilton, Tom Kearney, Harry Thuillier. *(Weightlifting):* Sammy Dalzell, Tommy Hayden. *(Wrestling):* Dermot Dunne, Joseph Feeney, Gerry Martina, Sean O'Connor. *(Yachting):* Dr R. G. Benson, Charles Gray, Jimmy Hooper, Dr A. J. Mooney, Dr D. A. Ryder, John Somers-Payne.

1964 TOKYO *(Athletics):* Noel Carroll, Basil Clifford, Jim Hogan, Maeve Kyle, John Lawlor, Derek McCleane, Tom O'Riordan. *(Boxing):* Brian Anderson, Paddy Fitzsimons, Sean McCafferty, Jim McCourt, Chris Rafter. *(Fencing):* John Bouchier-Hayes, Michael Ryan. *(Judo):* John Ryan. *(Wrestling):* Joseph Feeney, Sean O'Connor. *(Yachting):* Robin D'Alton, Johnny Hooper, Eddie Kelliher, Harry Maguire. *(Equestrian):* Tommy Brennan, Tony Cameron, John Harty, Harry Freeman-Jackson.

1968 MEXICO *(Athletics):* Noel Carroll, John Kelly, Pat McMahon, Mick Molloy, Frank Murphy. *(Boxing):* Mick Dowling, Brendan McCarthy, Jim McCourt, Eamonn McCusker, Martin Quinn, Eddie Tracey. *(Cycling):* Peter Doyle, Morrison Foster, Liam Horner. *(Fencing):* John Bouchier-Hayes, Finbarr Farrell, Colm O'Brien, Michael Ryan. *(Shooting):* Dr. Gerry Brady, Dermot Kelly, Arthur McMahon. *(Swimming):* Liam Ball, Anne O'Connor, Donnacha O'Dea, Vivienne Smith. *(Equestrian):* Tommy Brennan, Capt. Ned Campion, Diana Conolly-Carew, Juliet Jobling-Purser, Ada Matheson, Penny Moreton, Diana Wilson.

1972 MUNICH *(Athletics):* Phil Conway, Neil Cusack, John Hartnett, Mike Keogh, Eddie Leddy, Danny McDaid, Dessie McGann, Fanahan McSweeney, Frank Murphy, Margaret Murphy, Mary Tracey, Claire Walsh, Donie Walsh. *(Boxing):* Mick Dowling, Christy Elliott, Neil McLaughlin, James Montague, Charlie Nash, John Rodgers. *(Canoeing):* Gerry Collins, Ann McQuaid, Brendan O'Connell, Howard Watkins. *(Cycling):* Peter Doyle, Liam Horner, Kieran McQuaid, Noel Taggart. *(Equestrian):* Bill Butler, Patrick Conolly-Carew, Juliet Jobling-Purser, Bill McLernon, Ronnie McMahon. *(Fencing):* John Bouchier-Hayes. *(Judo):* Anto Clarke, Liam Carroll, Matthew Folan, Patrick Murphy, Terry Watt. *(Rowing):* Sean Drea. *(Clay Pigeon Shooting):* Dr. Gerry Brady, William Campbell, Arthur McMahon, Dermot Kelly. *(Swimming):* Liam Ball, Brian Clifford, Christine Fulcher, Andrew Hunter, Brenda McGrory, Ann O'Connor, Aisling O'Leary. *(Weighlifting):* Frank

Rothwell. *(Yachting):* Harry Byrne, Harold Cudmore, Owen Delaney, Robert Hennessy, Kevin McLaverty, Richard O'Shea, David Wilkins, Sean Whittaker.
1976 MONTREAL *(Archery):* Jim Conroy. *(Athletics):* Eamonn Coghlan, Neil Cusack, Eddie Leddy, Danny McDaid, Jim McNamara, Niall O'Shaughnessy, Mary Purcell. (Boxing): Brian Byrne, Brendan Dunne, Gerry Hammill, Dave Larmour, Christy McLaughlin. *(Canoeing):* Declan Burns, Ian Pringle, Brendan O'Connell, Howard Watkins. *(Cycling):* Alan McCormack, Oliver McQuaid. *(Equestrian):* Eric Horgan, Ronnie McMahon, Gerry Sinnott, Norman Van der Vater. *(Rowing):* Sean Drea, Martin Feeley, Ian Kennedy, Andrew McDonough, James Muldoon, Christopher O'Brien, Liam Redmond, James Renehan, Michael Ryan, William Ryan. *(Clay Pigeon Shooting):* Richard Flynn. *(Swimming):* Miriam Hopkins, Robert Howard, Deirdre Sheehan, Kevin Williamson. *(Yachting):* Robert Dix, Peter Dix, Derek Jago, Barry O'Neill, James Wilkinson, David Wilkins.
1980 MOSCOW *(Archery):* Jim Conroy, Hazel Greene, Willie Swords. *(Athletics):* Eamonn Coghlan, Sean Egan, Ray Flynn, Pat Hooper, Dick Hooper, Mick O'Shea, John Treacy. *(Boxing):* Martin Brerton, P. J. Davitt, Sean Doylelt, Gerry Hawkins, Barry McGuigan, Hugh Russell, Phil Sutcliffe. *(Canoeing):* Declan Burns, Ian Pringle. *(Clay Pigeon Shooting):* Nicholas Cooney, Thomas Hewitt, Albert Thompson. *(Rifle & Pistol Shooting):* Ken Stanford. *(Cycling):* Billy Kerr, Tony Lally, Stephen Roche. *(Judo):* Alonzo Henderson, Dave McManus. *(Modern Pentathlon):* Mark Hartigan, Jerome Hartigan, Sackville Curry. *(Rowing):* Christy O'Brien, Frances Cryan, Noel Graham, Pat Gannon, David Gray, Iain Kennedy, Ted McDonagh, Willie Ryan, Ted Ryan, Denis Rice, Liam Williams. *(Swimming):* David Cummins, Catherine Bohan, Kevin Williamson. *(Yachting):* David Wilkins, James Wilkinson.
1984 LOS ANGELES *(Archery):* Hazel Greene, Mary Vaughan. *(Athletics):* Ray Flynn, Declan Hegarty, Dick Hooper, Monica Joyce, Regina Joyce, Jerry Kiernan, Conor McCullough, Carey May, Caroline O'Shea, Marcus O'Sullivan, Frank O'Mara, Paul Donovan, Liam O'Brien, Mary Parr, Roisin Smith, John Treacy, Patricia Walsh. *(Boxing):* Tommy Corr, Paul Fitzgerald, Gerry Hawkins, Kieran Joyce, Sam Storey, Phil Sutcliffe. *(Canoeing):* Ian Pringle. *(Cycling):* Philip Cassidy, Seamus Downey, Martin Earley, Paul Kimmage, Gary Thompson. *(Equestrian):* Capt. David Foster, Sarah Gordon, Margaret Tolerton, Fiona Wentges, Capt. Gerry Mullins. *(Judo):* Kieran Foley. *(Clay Pigeon Shooting):* Roy Magowen, Albert Thompson. *(Swimming):* Carol-Anne Heavey, Julie Parkes. *(Yachting):* Bill O'Hara.
1988 SEOUL *(Archery):* Noel Lynch, Joe Malone, Hazel Greene-Pereira. *(Athletics):* Marcus O'Sullivan, Gerry O'Reilly, Ann Keenan-Buckley, Brendan Quinn, Eamonn Coghlan, Frank O'Mara, John Doherty, John Treacy, John Woods, Dick Hooper, Marie Murphy-Rollins, Ailish Smyth, Conor McCullough, Terry McHugh, Carlos O'Connell, Jimmy McDonald, T. J. Kearns, Barbara Johnson. *(Boxing):* Wayne McCullough, Joe Lawlor, Paul Fitzgerald, John

Lowey, Michael Carruth, Billy Walsh, Kieran Joyce. *(Canoeing):* Alan Carey, Pat Holmes, Pete Connor, Declan Bums. *(Cycling):* Phil Cassidy, Cormac McCann, Paul McCormack, John McQuaid, Stephen Spratt. *(Equestrian):* Cmdt. Gerry Mullins, Capt John Ledingham, Paul Darragh, Jack Doyle, Capt. David Foster, John Watson, Shea Walsh. *(Judo):* Eugene McManus. *(Rowing):* Frank Moore, Pat McDonagh, Liam Williams. *(Swimming):* Michelle Smith, Stephen Cullen, Aileen Convery, Richard Gheel, Gary O'Toole. *(Tennis):* Owen Casey, Eoin Collins. *(Wrestling):* David Harmon. *(Yachting):* Bill O'Hara, David Wilkins, Peter Kennedy, Cathy McAleavy, Aisling Byrne.
1992 BARCELONA *(Archery):* Noel Lynch. *(Athletics):* Sonia O'Sullivan, Catherina McKiernan, Marcus O'Sullivan, Paul Donovan, John Doherty, Frank O'Mara, Noel Berkeley, Sean Dollman, John Treacy, Andy Ronan, Tommy Hughes, Victor Costello, Paul Quirke, Terry McHugh, Nicky Sweeney, Perri Williams, Bobby O'Leary, Jimmy McDonald, T. J. Kearns. *(Boxing):* Paul Buttimer, Wayne McCullough, Paul Griffin, Michael Carruth, Paul Douglas, Kevin McBride. *(Canoeing):* Ian Wiley, Mike Corcoran, Pat Holmes, Conor Holmes, Alan Carey. *(Cycling):* Paul Slane, Mark Kane, Kevin Kimmage, Robert Power, Conor Henry. *(Equestrian):* Mairead Curran, Melanie Duff, Olivia Holohan, Eric Smiley, Anna Merveldt, Peter Charles, Francis Connors, Paul Darragh, James Kernan, Eddie Macken. *(Fencing):* Michael O'Brien. *(Judo):* Keith Gough, Ciaran Ward. *(Rowing):* Niall O'Toole. *(Swimming):* Gary O'Toole, Michelle Smith. *(Tennis):* Owen Casey, Eoin Collins. *(Yachting):* David Wilkins, Peter Kennedy, Mark Mansfield, Tom McWilliams, Denise Lyttle.
1996 ATLANTA *(Athletics):* Neil Ryan, Gary Ryan, Eugene Farrell, David Matthews, Niall Bruton, Shane Healy, Marcus O'Sullivan, Cormac Finnerty, Sean Dollman, T.J. Kearns, Sean Cahill, Tom McGuirk, Jimmy McDonald, Mark Mandy, Nicky Sweeney,Terry McHugh, Roman Linscheid, Sinead Delahunty, Sonia O'Sullivan, Kathy McCandless, Marie McMahon, Catherina McKiernan, Susan Smlth, Deirdre Gallagher. *(Boxing):* Damaen Kelly, Brian Magee, Francis Barrett, Cathal O'Grady. *(Canoeing):* Ian Wiley, Michael Corcoran, Andrew Boland, Stephen O'Flaherty, Conor Moloney, Gary Mawer. *(Clay Pigeon Shoot):* Thomas Allen. *(Cycling):* Declan Lonergan, Philip Collins, Martin Earley, Alister Martin, David McCann. *(Equestrian):* Jessica Chesney, Capt John Ledingham, Eddie Macken, Peter Charles. *(Three Day Event):* Mick Barry, Alfie Buller, David Foster, Virginia McGrath, Eric Smiley. *(Dressage):* Heike Holstein. *(Gymnastics):* Barry McDonald. *(Rowing):* Brendan Dolan, Niall O'Toole, John Holland, Neville Maxwell, Tony O'Connor, Sam Lynch, Derek Holland. *(Yachting):* Mark Lyttle, Mark Mansfield, David Burrows, Marshall King, Dan O'Grady, Garrett Connolly, Denise Lyttle, Louise Cole, Aisling Bowman, John Driscoll. *(Judo):* Kieran Ward. *(Swimming):* Marion Madine, Michelle Smith, Earl McCarthy, Adrian O'Connor, Nick O'Hare. *(Shooting):* Gary Duff, Ronagh Barry. *(Tennis):* Eoin Casey, Scott Barron.

Sports Directory

The Irish Sports Council 21 Fitzwilliam Square, Dublin 2. Tel. (01) 6763847.

House of Sport Long Mile Road, Walkinstown, Dublin 12. Tel. (01) 4501633.

Sports Council of NI House of Sport, Upper Malone Road, Belfast BT89 5LA. Tel. (01232) 381222.

Olympic Council of Ireland 27 Mespil Road, Dublin 4. Tel. (01) 6680444.

Badminton Union of Ireland Baldoyle Industrial Estate, Grange Road, Baldoyle, Dublin 13. Tel. (01) 8393028.

Ból Chumann na hÉireann (Bowling) *Mr. Pat O'Sullivan*, Lower Froe, Rosscarbery, Co. Cork. Tel. (023) 48128.

Bord Lúthchleas na hÉireann (Athletics), 11 Prospect Road, Glasnevin, Dublin 9. Tel. (01) 8309901.

Bord na gCon (Irish Greyhound Board), 104 Henry Street, Limerick. Tel. (061) 316788.

Bowling League of Ireland (*J. B. Duff*), c/o 7 Glendoher Close, Dublin 16.

Canoe Association of Northern Ireland (*Mr. M. Murray*), 143 Oakhurst Avenue, Belfast BT10 0PD.

Cerebral Palsy Sport Ireland (*Ms. Brenda Green*), Sandymount Avenue, Dublin 4. Tel. (01) 2695355

Comhairle Liathróid Láimhe na hÉireann (Handball) Páirc an Chrócaigh, Baile Átha Cliath 3. Tel. (01) 8741360.

Community Games National Community Games, 5 Lower Abbey Street, Dublin 1. Tel. (01) 8788095.

Croquet Association of Ireland c/o

Carrickmines Croquet & Lawn Tennis Club, Glenamuck Road, Carrickmines, Co. Dublin.

Cumann Camógaíochta na nGael Páirc an Chrócaigh, Baile Átha Cliath 3. Tel. (01) 8554257.

Cumann Lúthchleas Gael (GAA) Páirc an Chrócaigh, Baile Átha Cliath 3. Tel. (01) 8363222.

Equestrian Federation of Ireland Ashton House, Castleknock, Dublin 15. Tel. (01) 8387611.

Irish Cycling Federation Kelly Roche House, 619 North Circular Road, Dublin 1. Tel. (01) 8551522.

Football Association of Ireland, The 80 Merrion Square, Dublin 2. Tel. (01) 6766864.

Golfing Union of Ireland Glencar House, 81 Eglinton Road, Donnybrook, Dublin 4. Tel. (01) 2694111.

Irish Amateur Archery Association 61 Ashwood Road, Clondalkin, Dublin 22. Tel.(01) 4573186.

Irish Amateur Boxing Association National Boxing Stadium, South Circular Road, Dublin 8. Tel. (01) 4533371.

Irish Amateur Fencing Association Branksome Dene, Frankfort Park, Dundrum, Dublin 14. Tel. (01) 6793888.

Irish Amateur Gymnastics Association House of Sport, Long Mile Road, Walkinstown, Dublin 12. Tel. (01) 4501805.

Irish Amateur Rowing Union House of Sport, Long Mile Road, Walkinstown, Dublin 12. Tel. (01) 4509831.

Swim Ireland House of Sport, Long Mile Road, Walkinstown, Dublin 12. Tel. (01) 4501739.

Irish Amateur Weightlifting Association 27 O'Connell

Gardens, Bath Avenue, Dublin 4. Tel. (01) 6601390.

Irish Amateur Wrestling Association c/o 54 Elm Mount Drive, Beaumont, Dublin 9. Tel. (01) 8315522.

Irish Aviation Council c/o 38 Pembroke Road, Dublin 4. Tel. (01) 2874474.

Irish Baseball & Softball Association 14 Innishmaan Road, Whitehall, Dublin 9. Tel. (01) 8378118.

Irish Basketball Association National Basketball Arena, Tymon Park, Dublin 24. Tel. (01) 4590211.

Irish BlindSports c/o 25 Turvey Close, Donabate, Co. Dublin. Tel. (01) 8436501.

Irish Bowling Association (*Mr. J. N. McQuay*), 2 Ashdene Road, Moneyreagh, Co. Down BT23 6DD. Tel. (01232) 448348.

Irish Canoe Union House of Sport, Long Mile Road, Walkinstown, Dublin 12. Tel. (01) 4509838.

Irish Cricket Union 45 Foxrock Park, Foxrock, Dublin 18. Tel. (01) 2893943.

Irish Deaf Sports Association (*Mr. Dermot Saunders*), 8 Dun Emer Drive, Dundrum, Dublin 16. Tel. (01) 2956030.

Irish Federation of Sea Anglers 67 Windsor Drive, Monkstown, Co. Dublin. Tel. (01) 2806873.

Irish Football Association 20 Windsor Avenue, Belfast BT9 6EG. Tel. (01232) 669458.

Irish Hang Gliding Association House of Sport, Long Mile Road, Walkinstown, Dublin 12. Tel. (01) 4509845.

Irish Hockey Union 6A Woodbine Park, Blackrock, Co. Dublin. Tel. (01) 2600087.

Irish Horseracing Authority Leopardstown Racecourse, Foxrock, Dublin 18. Tel. (01) 2892888.

Irish Indoor Bowling Association (Mr. D. Hunter), c/o 204 Kings Road, Knock, Belfast BT5 7HX.

Irish Judo Association 79 Upper Dorset Street, Dublin 1. Tel. (01) 8308233.

Irish Ladies Golf Union 1 Clonskeagh Square, Clonskeagh Road, Dublin 14. Tel. (01) 2696244.

Irish Ladies Hockey Union 95 Sandymount Road, Dublin 4. Tel. (01) 6606780.

Irish Olympic Handball Association Tymon Bawn Community Centre, Firhouse Road West, Old Bawn, Tallaght, Dublin 24. Tel. (01) 4599142.

Irish Orienteering Association c/o AFAS, House of Sport, Long Mile Road, Walkinstown, Dublin 12. Tel. (01) 4501633.

Irish Rugby Football Union 62 Lansdowne Road, Ballsbridge, Dublin 4. Tel. (01) 6684601.

Irish Sailing Association 3 Park Road, Dun Laoghaire, Co. Dublin. Tel. (01) 2800239.

Irish Squash House of Sport, Long Mile Road, Walkinstown, Dublin 12. Tel. (01) 4501564.

Irish Surfing Association Easkey House, Easkey, Co. Sligo. Tel. (096) 49020.

Irish Table-Tennis Association 46 Lorcan Villas, Santry, Dublin 9. Tel. (01) 8421679.

Irish Ten Pin Bowling Association (Ms. Ros O'Reilly), 40 Cabinteely Green, Dublin 18. Tel. (01) 2857529.

Irish Triathlon Association 202 St. Donagh's Road, Donaghmede, Dublin 13. Tel. (01) 8470818.

Irish Trout Fly Fishing Association (Mr. James McNally), Cullies, Co. Cavan. Tel. (049) 31501.

Irish Tug of War Association (Mrs. Nuala Hubbard), c/o Longhouse, Ballymore Eustace, Co. Kildare. Tel. (045) 864222.

Irish Water-Polo Association 3 Strand Mews, Lea Road, Sandymount, Dublin 4. Tel. (01) 2693918.

Irish Waterski Federation 91 South Mall, Cork. Tel. (021) 334605.

Irish Windsurfing Association (Mr. Chris Sparron), Boherboy, Dunlavin, Co. Wicklow.

Irish Women's Bowling Association (Mrs. V. Canning), 1 Beach Road, Whitehead, Co. Antrim BT38 9QS. Tel. (01960) 378563.

Irish Women's Cricket Union "Woodcroft", 50 St. Alban's Park, Sandymount, Dublin 4.

Irish Women's Indoor Bowling Association (Mrs. D. Miskelly), 101 Skyline Drive, Lambeg, Lisburn, Co. Antrim BT27 4HW. Tel. (01846) 663516.

Ladies Football Association of Ireland 80 Merrion Square, Dublin 2. Tel. (01) 6766864.

Ladies Gaelic Football Association, The House of Sport, Long Mile Road, Walkinstown, Dublin 12. Tel. (01) 4569113.

Ladies' Bowling League of Ireland (Mrs. June Fincher), c/o Kimmage Road West, Dublin 12. Tel. (01) 4555302.

Motor Cycling Union of Ireland 35 Lambay Road, Glasnevin, Dublin 9. Tel. (01) 8378090.

Mountaineering Council of Ireland c/o AFAS, House of Sport, Long Mile Road, Walkinstown, Dublin 12. Tel. (01) 4509845.

National Chinese and Associated Martial Arts (Mr. C. Walsh), 72 Ramoan Gardens, Belfast BT11 8LN.

National Coarse Fishing Federation of Ireland (Mr. Brendan Coulter), "Blaithin", Dublin Road, Cavan, Co. Cavan. Tel. (049) 32367.

Northern Ireland Amateur Fencing Association (Miss. K. Lowry), 40 Groomsport Road, Bangor, Co. Down BT20 5LR. Tel. (01247) 454000.

Northern Ireland Amateur Gymnastics Association (Miss. D. Orme), 31 Palmerstown Road, Belfast BT4 1QB. Tel. (01232) 381414.

Northern Ireland Amateur Weightlifters Association (Mr. J. Sheppard), 71 Beechgrove Avenue, Belfast BT6 0ND. Tel. (01232) 798464.

Northern Ireland Archery Association (Mr. Wellesley McGown), 17 Bridge Road, Kilmore, Lurgan, Co. Armagh, BT67 9LA. Tel. (01762) 326987.

Northern Ireland Billiards & Snooker Control (Mr. A. Rainey), 52 Jonesboro Park, Belfast BT5 5FY.

Northern Ireland Blind Sports (Ms. L. Royal), 12 Sandford Avenue, Belfast BT5 5NW. Tel. (01232) 657156.

Northern Ireland Ice Hockey (Mr. Jim Graves), c/o 88 Coronation Park, Dundonald, Belfast BT16 0HF. Tel. (01232) 483859.

Northern Ireland Jiu Jitsu Association (Mr. J. Canning), 279 Coalisland Road, Dungannon, Co. Tyrone BT71 6ET. Tel. (018687) 40467.

Northern Ireland Judo Federation House of Sport, Upper Malone Road, Belfast BT9 5LA. Tel. (01232) 383814.

Northern Ireland Karate Board (Mr. M. Leydon), 33 Corrina Park, Upper Dunmurry Lane, Belfast BT17 0HA. Tel. (01232) 240558.

Northern Ireland Netball Association House of Sport, Upper Malone Road, Belfast BT9

5LA. Tel. (01232) 383806.

Northern Ireland Orienteering Association (*Ms. K. Millinson*), 311 Ballynahinch Road, Hillsborough, Co. Down. Tel. (01846) 638185.

Northern Ireland Sports Association for People with Learning Disabilities (*Ms. A. Shane*), 11b Belsize Road, Lisburn, Co. Antrim BT27 4AL. Tel. (01820) 662357.

Northern Ireland Surfing Association (*Mr. R. Allen*), 'Shague', Tempo Road, Enniskillen, Co. Fermanagh BT74 6HR. Tel. (01365) 322591.

Northern Ireland Tug of War Association (*Mr. P. Doherty*), 56 Belrangh Road, Garvagh, Co. Derry. Tel. (01265) 868697.

Northern Ireland Volleyball Association House of Sport, Upper Malone Road, Belfast. Tel. (01232) 381222/

Parachute Association of Ireland c/o AFAS, House of Sport, Long Mile Road, Walkinstown, Dublin 12. Tel. (01) 4509845.

Pitch and Putt Union of Ireland, The House of Sport, Long Mile Road, Walkinstown, Dublin 12. Tel. (01) 4509299.

Racquetball Association of Ireland (*Mr. John Comerford*), 5 Edenvale Close, Kilkenny.

Republic of Ireland Billiards & Snooker Association House of Sport, Longmile Road, Walkinstown, Dublin 12. Tel. (01) 4509850.

Republic of Ireland Netball Association 10 Barry Avenue, Finglas, Dublin 11. Tel. (01) 8347634.

Royal Irish Automobile Club RIAC, 34 Dawson Street, Dublin 2. Tel. (01) 6775628.

Royal Yachting Association House of Sport, Upper Malone Road, Belfast BT9 5LA. Tel. (01232) 381222.

Ski Club of Ireland, The Kilternan Hotel, Kilternan, Co. Dublin. Tel. (01) 2955658.

Special Olympics Ireland Ormond House, Upper Ormond Quay,

Dublin 7. Tel. (01) 8720300.

Speleological Union of Ireland c/o AFAS, House of Sport, Long Mile Road, Walkinstown, Dublin 12. Tel. (01) 4509845.

Taekwondo Association of Northern Ireland (*Mr. B. Nicholson*), 20 Lester Avenue, Lisburn, Co. Antrim BT28 3QD. Tel. (01846) 604293.

Tennis Ireland Argyle Square, Morehampton Road, Donnybrook, Dublin 4. Tel. (01) 6681841.

Ulster Deaf Sports Council (*Mr. E. McCaffrey*), 3 Richmond Grove, Glengormley, Co. Antrim.

Ulster Squash House of Sport, 2a Upper Malone Road, Belfast BT9 5LA. Tel. (01232) 381222.

Volleyball Association of Ireland Unit C1, Crosbie Business Centre, Ossory Road, East Wall, Dublin 3. Tel. (01) 8552993.

Lottery Sports Funding

Elite Athlete Grants

Sport	No. of Recipients	£
Archery	1	5,000
Athletics	48	278,000
Badminton	3	14,000
Blindsports	7	22,200
Boxing	25	82,600
Canoeing	14	78,400
Cerebral Palsy	8	31,500
Clay Pigeon	2	14,000
Equestrian	4	28,000
Cycling	10	32,400
Fencing	1	7,000
Handball	4	4,200
Judo	1	7,000
Motor Sports	2	4,200
Orienteering	5	8,500
Rowing	28	177,400
Sailing	9	72,400
Snooker	2	6,600
Squash	5	30,400
Surfing	2	4,000
Table Tennis	5	6,000
Tennis	3	7,800
Triathlon	1	1,000
Weightlifting	2	14,000
Wheelchair Sports	15	72,400
TOTAL	**207**	**1,009,000**

Local Community Projects

County	No. of Projects	£
Carlow	5	95,000
Cavan	8	163,000
Clare	9	155,000
Cork	44	2,409,000
Donegal	34	1,671,000
Dublin	51	3,693,000
Galway	26	1,437,000
Kerry	20	510,000
Kildare	31	1,781,000
Kilkenny	9	167,000
Laois	8	190,000
Leitrim	4	60,000
Limerick	13	628,000
Longford	6	87,000
Louth	13	217,000
Mayo	9	296,000
Meath	11	220,000
Monaghan	7	196,000
Offaly	15	316,000
Roscommon	9	130,000
Sligo	5	167,000
Tipperary	19	390,000
Waterford	10	236,000
Westmeath	16	677,000
Wexford	13	388,000
Wicklow	9	211,000
TOTAL	**404**	**16,490,000**

WHO WAS WHO

Art

ANTRIM, Lady (1911-1974) b. Yorkshire, sculptor and cartoonist. Former Governor of the Ulster College of Art. Commissions include bronze sculptor and stained glass, Moyle Hospital, Larne; stone sculptors for St. Joseph's Church, Ballygally; the parliament buildings, Newfoundland.

ARMSTRONG, Arthur (1921-1996) b. Carrickfergus, self-taught landscape painter. Featured in collections worldwide. Former member of the RHA. Exhibited widely in Ireland, Europe and US.

BACON, Francis (1909-92) b. Dublin, one of the most important artists of the 20th century. His father forced him to leave home at an early age. Moved to London and worked as an interior designer and started painting with no formal training. Initially inspired by Surrealism but borrowed imagery from the old masters. Made a major impact with the painting *Three figures at the Base of a Crucifixion*. Best known for his disjointed, violent figures.

BARRY, James (1741-1806) b. Cork, historical painter. A protégé of EDMUND BURKE, he was appointed professor of painting at the Royal Academy. His most celebrated paintings are *Adam & Eve* (1771) and *Venus Rising from the Waves* (1772). Many of his works are on display in Cork's Crawford Gallery.

BEATTY, Sir Chester (1875-1968) b. New York, philanthropist and art collector. Amassed the greatest collection of oriental manuscripts ever held by a private collector. Left this collection to the Irish nation. Was made an honorary citizen of Ireland - the first to be given this honour.

BEIT, Sir Alfred (1903-94) philanthropist and art collector. Restored Russborough House, Co. Wicklow, using the family wealth (made from gold and diamond trading in South Africa). His art collection was at one time the most valuable private collection in the world. A governor of the National Gallery, established a trust for the house and the lands. Donated 17 Old Masters to the National Gallery but they were stolen (by the infamous Martin Cahill) before they were transferred - all but three were recovered. Made an honorary citizen of Ireland with his wife in 1993.

BIGGS, Michael (1928-1993) sculptor. Primarily known for stone carving and letter cutting. Created many public and private inscriptions in stone, wood and bronze between 1950-1992.

BINDON, Francis (d. 1765) b. Clare, portrait painter and architect. Many contemporaries, including JOHNATHAN SWIFT, sat for him. Worked with acclaimed architect Richard Cassels in designing the Palladian style Russborough House in Co. Wicklow.

BRANDT, Muriel (1909-1981) b. Belfast, painter and portrait artist. Commissions include a series of decorative murals in the Franciscan Church of Adam and Eve, Dublin. Member of RHA. Mother of artist RUTH BRANDT.

BRANDT, Ruth (1936-1989) b. Dublin, artist and lecturer at NCAD (1976-1988). Participated in the *Irish Exhibition of Living Art*. Commissions include the Glasnevin Met Office and stained-glass windows at Artane Oratory, Dublin. Solo exhibits throughout Ireland.

BROWN, Fr. Francis (1923-1989) b. Cork, photographer and Jesuit priest. His photographs of the Titanic (as it departed on its maiden voyage) were sent around the world after the ship sunk. More than 42,000 of his negatives were found in 1985, chronicling his travels in Australia, Ireland and Britain.

BYRNE, Michael (1923-1989) painter. Worked for the Arts Council and NCAD. Founder member of the Independent Artists. Committee member of the Project Arts Centre, Dublin.

CAMPBELL, George (1917-79) b. Co. Wicklow, artist. Founding member of the Living Art Exhibition (after WWII), won many awards, his finest works are considered his paintings of Spain.

CASTLE, Richard (c.1695-1751) architect, collaborated with Edward Lovett Pearce in the design of Parliament House and designed Leinster House. He also designed Westport house in Mayo, Powerscourt House in Wicklow and Carton House in Kildare.

CLARKE, Harry (1889-1931) b. Dublin, illustrator and stained-glass artist. Possibly the country's best-known stained glass artist. His style evidences influences from the Art Noveau work of Aubrey Beardsley as well as Celtic dawn influences, which had come into vogue at the beginning of the century. Works represented in the Honan College Chapel, Cork; St. Patrick's Basilica, Lough Derg; the Catholic parish churches of Ballinrobe and Carrickmacross.

COLLINS, Patrick (1910-1994) b. Co. Sligo, painter. Featured in numerous public and private collections worldwide. Elected tSaoi in 1987.

CONNOR, Jerome (1876-1943) b. Kerry, sculptor. Commissions included the Walt Whitman Memorial and Robert Emmet statue for the Smithsonian Institution, Washington.

CONOR, William (1884-1968) b. Belfast, painter. First exhibited as war artist followed by portraits of city scenes and shipyard workers. Member of RHA. His works are on permanent exhibition in the Ulster Folk Museum. Awarded an OBE in 1952.

DANBY, Francis (1793-1861) b. Co. Wexford, landscape artist. Was a regular exhibitor at the Royal Academy in England but was never made a full member. Patented a new type of ship's anchor in 1861.

DEANE, Sir Thomas Newenhan (1828-99) b. Co. Cork, architect. Some of his best known works include The National Library and National Museum in Kildare Street, Dublin.

DILLON, Gerard (1916-1971) b. Belfast, artist. Worked with oils, tapestry and murals. Set designer for Abbey Theatre. Best known for Connemara landscapes. Represented Ireland at the *Guggenheim International*

Exhibition.

DOYLE, John (1797-1868) b. Dublin, political cartoonist. Espoused CATHOLIC EMANCIPATION. His caricatures revolutionised the art of the cartoon, moving them way from the grotesque to the likeness of subjects. Created the persona of 'John Bull' to embody public opinion. His sons were also artists, and his grandson was Arthur Conan Doyle, creator of Sherlock Holmes.

DUNLOP, Ronald Ossary (1894-1973) b. Dublin, painter. A member of the London group, he is best remembered for his palette-knife paintings with their rich colours. Works on view in the Tate Gallery, London, in addition to many other public galleries. His writings on art include *Landscape Painting* (1954) and *Struggling with Paint* (1956).

FOLEY, John Henry (1818-74) b. Dublin, sculptor. Produced statues of public figures, including one of Prince Albert for the Albert Memorial. Other commissions include EDMUND BURKE and GOLDSMITH at Trinity College and HENRY GRATTAN on College Green, Dublin.

FOWKE, Captain Francis (1823-65) b. Belfast, appointed architect and engineer to the British department of science and art, he designed many of the major museums in Britain, including the Albert Hall in London, the Victoria & Albert Museum in London (later completed by Sir Aston Webb) and the National Gallery of Ireland in Dublin.

FURNISS, Harry (1854-1925) b. Wexford, caricaturist. Emigrated to London and worked as a caricaturist on the *Illustrated London News* (1876-84) and *Punch* (1884-94). Illustrated Lewis Carroll's *Sylvie and Bruno* and editions of Dickens and Thackeray. Embarked on a career in film with Thomas Edison, pioneering animated cartoons (1914).

GANDON, James (1743-1823) b. London, architect who designed some of the finest buildings in 19th-century Dublin, including the Custom House, the Four Courts and King's Inns.

GIBBINGS, Robert John (1889-1958) b. Cork, illustrator and writer. Revived the art of wood engraving and was the first artist to use diving equipment and make underwater drawings. Famous works include the river books - *Sweet Thames Run Softly* (1940), *Lovely is the Lee* (1945), *Sweet Cork of Thee* (1951).

HARRISON, Celia (1863-1941) b. Co. Down, painter and advocate for women's rights.

HEALY, Michael (1873-1941) b. Dublin, illustrator and stained-glass artist. Commissions included illustrations for the Dominican's journal *Irish Rosary* and windows for Loughrea Cathedral, Galway, among many other church buildings throughout Ireland.

HENRY, Paul (1877-1958) b. Belfast, oil painter. Best remembered for his evocative and bold west of Ireland landscapes, with their strong blocks of colour and defined shapes. Member of RHA. (1929). Received poster commissions for the Irish Tourist Board and the London & Scottish Railway.

HERON, Hilary (1923-1977) b. Dublin, artist. Awarded the first MAINIE JELLETT memorial travelling scholarships (1947) for work in carved wood, limestone and marble. Exhibited at the *Irish Exhibition of Living Art.* Represented Ireland with LOUIS LE BROCQUY at the *Venice Biennale* (1956).

HOBART, Henry (1858-1938) b. Co. Down, noted Ulster architect.

HOBSON, Florence (1881) b. Kildare, Ireland's first female architect (qualified 1893).

HONE, Evie (1894-1955) b. Dublin, painter and stained-glass artist. Overcame polio and joined her friend MAINIE JELLETT to study in Paris. Become one of the foremost Irish stained glass artists of the 20th century. Produced many stained glass windows, including *My Four Green Fields* and a number of oils and watercolours.

HONE, Nathaniel (1831-1917) b. Dublin, landscape artist. Studied in Paris and moved to Barbizon and worked closely with Millet, painting landscapes. Returned to Dublin (1875) and was elected to RHA (1880). Held an exhibition with JACK BUTLER YEATS. Some 500 oil paintings and 900 watercolours were bequeathed to the National Gallery by his widow.

JELLETT, Mainie (1897-1944) b. Dublin, abstract artist. One of Ireland's leading modern artists, studied in Paris with EVIE HONE, joined the cubist integral movement. Moved back to Ireland (1930) and was a founder member of the Irish Exhibition of Living Art (1943).

JERVAS, Charles (c.1675-1739) b. Offaly, a member of the Courts of George I and II of England, was an official portrait artist.

JOHNSTON, Francis (1760-1829) architect who designed the General Post Office in Dublin. Founding member of the Royal Hibernian Academy and President of that body from 1824 until 1829.

KEATING, Sean (1889-1977) b. Limerick, artist. Studied Dublin, Aran Islands and London. Elected to RHA (1923) and its president (1949-62), was a professor of painting and made many visits to US. Completed many government commissions, including one for the World's Fair, New York (1939) and a mural for International Labour Office, Geneva.

KING, Cecil (1921-1986) b. Dublin, self-taught artist and sculptor. Featured in many public and private collections. Co-founded the Contemporary Irish Art Society. Commissions include the brilliant yellow structure outside the UCG science block.

LAMB, Charles (1893-1964) b. Armagh, landscape painter and member of RHA.

LANE, Sir Hugh Percy (1875-1915) b. Cork, art critic and collector. Amid great controversy, founded a gallery of modern art in Dublin at the beginning of the 20th century and championed contemporary Irish artists of the time, including JACK B YEATS and WILLIAM ORPEN. Was director of the National Gallery of Ireland in 1914 but drowned on the Lusitania when it was torpedoed in 1915.

LAVERY, Sir John (1856-1941) b. Belfast, painter. After studying in Glasgow, London and Paris, became a portrait painter and enjoyed great success with his paintings of women. Famous works include a portrait of his wife, Hazel (used on Irish banknotes for half a century and still used as the watermark on Irish currency notes) and MICHAEL COLLINS lying in state. Knighted in 1918. Wrote an autobiography (1940).

LEECH, William (1881-1968) b. Dublin, impressionist artist. Studied in Dublin under WALTER OSBORNE and in Paris. Moved to France but exhibited in Dublin and was elected to the RHA (1910) and was associated with the group that included AE and COUNTESS MARKIEVICZ, moved to England (1916) but was still a regular contributor to Irish exhibitions.

LOVER, Samuel (1797-1868) b. Dublin; artist, writer and songwriter. Established himself in Dublin as a marine painter and miniaturist. Assisted Dickens in founding Bentley's Miscellany.

McCORMICK, Liam (1916-96) b. Derry, influential church architect, his most famous work is the circular Church of St Aengus at Burt in Co. Donegal.

McGUIRE, Edward (1932-1986) b. Dublin, painter. Participated in many prominent group exhibitions. Received numerous awards for his work. Works displayed at Ulster Museum, Belfast, National Gallery of Ireland, Hugh Lane Gallery, Dublin and Dublin City University.

MacLISE, Daniel (1806-70) b. Cork, painter. After studying at the Royal Academy in London, painted the Royal Gallery frescoes in the House of Lords. Most famous works are *The Meeting of Wellington and Blücher* (1861) and *The Death of Nelson* (1864). Also illustrated books for Tennyson and Dickens.

McWILLIAM, F.E. (1902-92) b. Banbridge, Co. Down; sculptor. Studied in London and Paris - a fine example of his work - 'Legs Static' (1978) - is on public display in Banbridge Civic Building grounds.

ORPEN, Sir William (1878-1931) b. Dublin, artist. Studied at the Slade, London, received many commissions, elected as an associate of the Royal Academy and as a member of the RHA (1908). Taught in Ireland and in London with Augustus John. An official war artist (1917-19), his paintings from this time hang in the Imperial War Museum in London. After the war he became a much sought after portrait artist.

OSBORNE, Walter (1859-1903) b. Dublin, impressionist artist. Studied in Ireland at RHA and in Antwerp under a scholarship, mastering both oils and watercolours. Painted English and Irish landscapes, elected to the RHA and taught there. Many of his paintings can be seen at the National Gallery. His works have become increasing popular at auction. Acclaimed works include *Beneath St Jacques, Antwerp*.

PEARCE, Edward Lovett (c. 1699-1733) b. England, Palladian architect. Collaborated in the design of Castletown House in Kildare but is most famous for designing the building at College Green in Dublin which housed the Irish Parliament from 1730 to 1800.

POWERS, Mary Farl (1948-92) b. Minnesota, artist. Known for printmaking and working with paper. Former director of the Graphic Studio, Dublin.

PURSER, Sarah (1848-1943) b. Dun Laoghaire, artist. Studied in Dublin and in Paris. In London, received many portrait commissions from the aristocracy. Became a wealthy woman from investing her earnings and helped purchase the building that is now the Hugh Lane Gallery. Her best-known paintings are those of her famous Irish contemporaries such as MAUD GONNE MACBRIDE.

REID, Nano (1905-81) b. Louth, noted landscape artist.

VANSTON, Dáirine (1903-88) painter who exhibited widely in Ireland and abroad. Work featured in *Horizon* magazine. Details of her work and career given to the Archives of Modern European Art, Venice.

WEJCHERT, Alexandra (1920-95) b. Poland, architect. Moved to Ireland (1965). Worked here until her death.

YEATS, Jack Butler (1871- 1957) b. London, artist and writer. Brother of W.B. YEATS. Regarded as one the most influential and talented artists in Ireland. Illustrated many pen-and-ink drawings for journals and books - known as W. *Bird* for cartoon work in *Punch* magazine (1910-48). Famous works include *At the Galway Races, On Drumcliffe Strand* and *Memory Harbour*. Retrospectives of work mounted in London (1942, 1948), Dublin (1945) and the US (1951-52). Literary works include *Sailing, Sailing Swiftly* (1933) and *Ah Well* (1942).

Business

ANDERSON, John (c.1760-1820) b. Scotland, established first Irish mail coach service at Cork in 1789. Based in Fermoy he rebuilt much of the town and opened the Fermoy Bank in 1800.

ANDREWS, Christopher Stephen 'Todd' (1901-85) b. Dublin, leader in the semi-state sector. Placed in charge of turf development in 1932, set up a structured commercial enterprise, Bord na Móna, which thrived under his stewardship. Also headed CIE and RTÉ.

BEDDY, James (1900-76) b. Cobh, public servant. Managing director of the Industrial Credit Company (1952). Was the first chairman of both the IDA and An Foras Tionscal and made a valuable contribution to the financing and development of industry in Ireland.

BEERE, Thekla (1902-91) b. Kells, public servant. An expert on shipping, rail transport and labour relations, appointed Secretary of the Department of Transport and Power in 1959 she was the first woman to be appointed head of a government department.

BYRNE, Edward influential member of the CATHOLIC COMMITTEE in the 1790s he was a very successful merchant and distiller.

CANTILLON, Richard (1680-1735) b. Kerry, enjoyed successful banking career in France. Published *General Essay on Commerce* in 1755 on understanding economic processes.

CLARK, Sir George Smith (1861-1935) founded the Workman-Clark ship building firm in Belfast in 1880. Unionist MP for Belfast 1907-1910.

CROMMELLIN, Samuel Louis (1652-1727) a key figure in establishing the linen industry in Ulster.

DOYLE, Vincent (1923-88) b. Donegal, hotelier. Recognising an emerging affluent middle class he built a number of luxury hotels including the Montrose and the Burlington, he also bought hotels in the US and Britain. Appointed chairman of Bord Fáilte (1973) and was retained in the post for several terms.

EASON, John (1880-1976) b. Dublin, businessman. Managing director of the family firm of Eason and Son – wholesale newsagents and book distributors (1926-

50), played a prominent role in getting the business community to become reconciled with the nascent Irish State.

GALLAGHER, Pat 'the Cope' (1873-1964) b. Donegal, set up an extremely successful co-operative society in Dungloe, senior figure in the IRISH AGRICULTURAL ORGANISATION SOCIETY.

HARLAND, Edward (1831-1895) b. Yorkshire, established Harland and Wolff shipyard in Belfast in 1862. Mayor of Belfast in 1885 and 1886 he was a Unionist MP (1889-95).

PIRRIE, William James (1847-1924) worked his way up from apprentice to chairman at Harland & Wolff he oversaw the building of the Titanic. Lord Mayor of Belfast in 1896 and 1897 he served as a Unionist Party senator at Stormont.

WOLFF, Gustav (1834-1913) b. Germany, founded Harland & Wolff ship building firm in Belfast in 1861, Unionist MP for Belfast 1892-1910.

History

ALEXANDER, Harold R. (1891-1969) b. Tyrone, British army officer in both World Wars, made Field Marshal in 1944, played vital role in expelling Axis forces from North Africa in WWII. Governor-General of Canada (1946-52); elevated to the peerage 1959.

ANDREWS, John Miller (1871-1956) b. Co. Down, Prime Minister of Northern Ireland (1940-43), NI MP (1921-53) he was Minister for Labour (1921-37) and Minister for Finance (1937-40). Grand Master of ORANGE ORDER in Ireland (1948-54) he was Grand Master of the Imperial Grand Council of the World (1949-54).

ANNESLEY, James (1715-60) b. Co. Wexford. Claimant to the earldom of Anglesea and inspiration for Robert Louis Stevenson's *Kidnapped.*

ASHE, Thomas (1885-1917) b. Kerry, veteran of 1916 Rising; force fed, he died on hunger strike protesting his right to be treated as a prisoner of war.

AUCHINLECK, Claude (1884-1981) b. Tyrone, served as a British army officer in World War I. A general during World War II; promoted to field-marshal in 1946.

BALLANCE, John (1839-93) b. Antrim, Prime Minister of New Zealand (1891-93).

BARNARDO, Thomas (1845-1905) b. Dublin, set up Dr. Barnardo's homes for homeless children (1867).

BARRINGTON, Sir Jonah (1760-1834) b. Co. Laois, Protestant judge and memorialist who was found to be pilfering court funds. Settled in France, where he wrote the racy *The Rise and Fall of the Irish Nation* (1833).

BARRY, John (1745-1803) b. Wexford, known as the 'Father of the American Navy'. Active during the War of Independence, he presided over the US navy from 1782 until his death.

BARRY, Kevin (1902-20) b. Dublin, medical student and member of the IRA, captured and hanged. His extreme youth at his death aroused widespread condemnation and led to many students joining the IRA.

BARRY, Tom (1897-1980) b. Cork, IRA 'flying column' leader during War of Independence.

BARTON, Robert (1881-1975) b. Wicklow, signatory of the ANGLO-IRISH TREATY.

BERGIN, Osborn (1873-1950) b. Cork, gaelic scholar and professor of Early and Medieval Irish at UCD.

BIANCONI, Charles (1786-1875) b. Italy and arrived in Ireland (1786), set up the road-car service. Became a naturalised Irish citizen.

BING, Geoffrey (1909-77) b. Down, lawyer and politician, opposed the Stormont administration and raised many questions about civil liberties in Northern Ireland. His pamphlet *John Bull's Other Ireland* (1950) on these issues was a best-seller.

BLACKBURN, Helen (1842-1903) b. Knightstown, Co. Kerry. Secretary of the National Society for Women's Suffrage in England (1874-95), she published many books on women's suffrage.

BLANEY, Neil T. (1922-95) b. Donegal, a TD (1948-95) and MEP (1979-84 & 1989-94), held various ministries in FIANNA FÁIL. Charged with gunrunning in 1970 but had charges dismissed.

BLYTHE, Ernest (1889-1975) b. Antrim, MP and TD (1918-33); held various ministries in CUMANN NA NGAEDHEAL governments; supporter of the restoration of the Irish language.

BLOOD, Thomas *'Captain Blood'* (c. 1618-1680) adventurer who plotted to seize Dublin Castle but was found out. In 1671, he stole the crown and orb from the Tower of London, was captured but pardoned.

BÓRÚ, Brian (*c.* 926-1014) high king of Ireland (1002-14). His forces were victorious in the decisive defeat of the Vikings in Ireland at the Battle of Clontarf, but he himself was killed.

BOYCOTT, Captain Charles Cunningham (1832-97) gave the word 'boycott' to the English Language. The tenants of the Mayo estate where he was a land agent protested at his refusal to reduce rents by not working the land.

BRENNAN, Robert (1881-1964) b. Wexford, leader of 1916 Rising in Wexford. Irish Ambassador to the US during WWII.

BROOKE, Alan Francis *1st Viscount Alanbrooke* (1883-1963) b. Fermanagh, British field marshal. Chief of Imperial General Staff in 1941, regarded as Churchill's most trusted military adviser, accompanied him to the Allied Forces conferences in 1943.

BROOKE, Sir Basil (1888-1973) b. Fermanagh, Prime Minister of Northern Ireland (1943-63), NI MP (1929-67) he was Minister for Agriculture (1933-41) and Minister for Commerce and Production (1941-45). A veteran of World War One his government introduced the far reaching Education Act in 1947 and ruthlessly suppressed the IRA's border campaign (1956-62). Created Viscount Brookeborough 1952.

BROWN, William (1777-1857) b. Mayo, founder of the Argentine navy (1813) and veteran of the Royal Navy.

BROWNE, Noël (1915-1997) b. Waterford, TD (1948-82). Minister at the centre of controversial 'mother and child scheme' in 1951. Implemented a radical plan to eliminate TB (prepared by Dr. James Deeny) which greatly reduced the occurrence of the disease.

BROWNING, Miciaih (d. 1689) b. Derry, his vessel ended the Siege of Derry (1689) by breaking the boom across the Foyle.

BROY, Eamonn (1887-1972) b. Kildare, Garda

Commissioner (1932-38). Enlisted former IRA members (the BROY HARRIERS) to counter the Blueshirts.

BRUGHA, Cathal (1874-1922) b. Dublin, veteran of 1916 Rising. TD (1918-22), Minister for Defence (1919-22); fought with anti-treaty forces during the civil war and was killed.

BURKE, Edmund (1729-97) b. Dublin, MP (1765-97); author of *Reflections on the Revolution in France* (1790) which condemned the revolution; advocated reform of the penal laws and Irish self-government.

BURKE, Robert O'Hara (1820-61) b. Galway, one of the first white men to cross Australia but died of starvation on his return journey.

BURKE, William (1792-1829) with his partner William Hare (1790-1860) he committed a series of murders in Edinburgh to supply dissection cadavers to Dr Robert Knox, the anatomist. Was hanged.

BUTT, Isaac (1813-79) b. Co. Donegal, politician and advocate for HOME RULE. Called to he Irish bar in 1838, he soon became active in politics. Led the IRISH PARLIAMENTARY PARTY in the House of Commons (1871-79), espousing Home Rule in the House of Commons with little success.

CADE, Jack (d. 1450) leader of the 1450 insurrection. Worked in Kent as a physician. Marched on London and defeated the king's forces. Lost control over his men and was killed in Sussex.

CARSON, Sir Edward (1854-1935) b. Dublin, a barrister, leader of Irish Unionists at Westminster (1910-21). Supported the formation of the ULSTER VOLUNTEER FORCE, led 218,000 Ulster unionists in the signing of the SOLEMN LEAGUE AND COVENANT in 1913. Prosecuted the homosexual writer OSCAR WILDE. Elevated to the peerage in 1921 as Lord Carson of Duncairn.

CASEMENT, Roger (1864-1916) b. Dublin, knighted in 1911 for his work with the British colonial service. A member of the IRISH VOLUNTEERS, he secured some German weapons for the 1916 Rising but was captured at Banna Strand, Co. Kerry, tried for treason and hanged. His remains were re-interred in Dublin in 1965.

CEANNT, Eamonn (1881-1916) b. Galway, veteran of 1916 Rising and signatory of the Proclamation of the Republic. Executed by firing squad.

CHILDERS, Erskine (1905-74) b. London, fourth President of Ireland (1973-74). FIANNA FÁIL TD (1938-73) he was Minister for Posts and Telegraphs (1951-54 and 1966-69), Minister for Lands (1957-59), Minister for Transport and Power (1959-69) and Tánaiste (1969-73). He is the only President to have died while in office.

CHILDERS, Robert Erskine (1870-1922) b. London, veteran of Boer War, wrote the successful spy novel *The Riddle of the Sands* (1903), involved in Howth gun-running in 1914. Served in the British navy during WWI, secretary to the Irish delegation at ANGLO-IRISH TREATY negotiations, executed by Free State authorities during the Civil War.

CHURCH, Sir Richard (1785-1873) b. Cork, led the revolution in Greece. Took part in the Greek War of Independence (1821-32), appointed generalissimo of the Greek insurgent forces, earning the title 'Liberator of Greece' and becoming a Greek citizen.

CLARKE, Thomas James (1858-1916) b. Isle of Wight, revolutionary. Credited with a huge influence on the Easter Rising in 1916, after which he was court-martialled and shot.

CLUSKEY, Frank (1930-98) b. Dublin, LABOUR PARTY Politician. In government from 1973, introduced wide-ranging social welfare reforms. Resigned his ministerial post over the controversial supply of natural gas from Kinsale.

COLLEY, George (1925-83) b. Dublin, politician. Elected a TD (1961) and held various ministerial posts, was an unsuccessful candidate for the leadership of FIANNA FÁIL.

COLLINS, Michael (1890-1922) b. Cork, veteran of the 1916 Rising. Leader of the IRISH REPUBLICAN BROTHERHOOD during War of Independence. Elected to the first Dáil, Minister of Finance in the Republican government, signatory of the ANGLO-IRISH TREATY 1921. Chairman of the Provisional government (January-August 1922), Commander-in-Chief of the Free State army during the civil war. Killed in an ambush.

CONNOLLY, James (1868-1916) b. Edinburgh of Irish parents, revolutionary. Founded Independent Labour Party of Ireland in 1912, founded CITIZEN'S ARMY in 1913 to protect workers from police attacks during the Dublin Lockout, joined IRISH REPUBLICAN BROTHERHOOD 1915. A signatory of the Proclamation of the Republic, he served as commanding officer in the General Post Office during the 1916 Rising. Executed while in a chair (tied to it because of his wounds).

COSGRAVE, William Thomas (1880-1965) b. Dublin, President of Executive Council (1922-32), Chairman of Provisional Government (August-December 1922), Minister for Finance (1922-23), Minister for Defence (1924) and Minister for Justice (1927). TD (1919-44), MP (1917-1919), Leader CUMANN NA GAEDHEAL (1922-33) and FINE GAEL (1935-44). A veteran of the 1916 Rising his government dealt ruthlessly with the republican side during the Civil War. While in office he led the Irish Free State into the League of Nations, initiated the Shannon hydro-electric scheme and used the Imperial Conferences to lay the foundations for independence.

COSTELLO, John A. (1891-1976) b. Dublin, Taoiseach (1948-51 and 1954-57), Minister for Health (1951), FINE GAEL TD (1933-69), Attorney General (1926-32). Although never leader of Fine Gael he was Taoiseach of Inter-party governments which he formed from disparate groups. His government passed the REPUBLIC OF IRELAND ACT in 1948 taking Ireland out of the British Commonwealth and it successfully negotiated admittance to the United Nations in 1955.

COUSINS, Margaret (1878-1954) b. Roscommon, major figure in Irish suffragette movement. Emigrated to India 1915 where she became that country's first female magistrate.

CRAIG, Sir James (1871-1940) b. Belfast, Prime Minister of Northern Ireland (1921-40), NI MP (1921-40). An ardent opponent of HOME RULE he was Quarter Master General of the ULSTER VOLUNTEER FORCE 1914-16. His government implemented a draconian SPECIAL POWERS ACT in 1922 (giving the authorities virtually unlimited powers of arrest and detention) and abolished proportional representation for local government in 1922 and for Stormont elections in 1929. Knighted in 1918 and created Viscount Craigavon in 1927.

CROKER, Thomas Wilson (1780-1857) b. Galway; politician and essayist. In 1802, he was called to the Irish bar and his two essays produced around this time were brilliant successes as was his pamphlet advocating CATHOLIC EMANCIPATION.

CROKER, Richard 'Boss' (1841- 1922) b. Cork; US politician infamous for his control of the Tammany Hall political machine. He entered New York City politics in 1862. As 'Boss Croker' he controlled Democratic party politics for the next 16 years. After political reforms in 1901, he left the US and lived out his life in Ireland.

CROZIER, Captain Francis (1796-1848) b. Banbridge, Co. Down, naval explorer. Died in an ill-fated polar expedition searching for the North-West Passage.

DARCY, Patrick (1598-1668) b. Galway, constitutional nationalist, who argued before the Commons that no law of the English parliament can have any force in Ireland unless enacted by the Irish Parliament.

DAVIES, Christian 'Mother Ross' (1667-1739) b. Dublin, woman soldier who served for many years in the army as a man, fighting in the battle of Blenheim and other battles.

DAVIS, Thomas (1814-45) b. Cork, YOUNG IRELANDER and founding member of its newspaper The Nation. A noted poet, he wrote A Nation Once Again and The West's Awake.

DAVITT, Michael (1846-1906) b. Mayo, founder of the Irish NATIONAL LAND LEAGUE in 1879. Imprisoned in England as a FENIAN in 1870, released in 1877.

de VALERA, Éamon (1882-1975) b. New York, President of the Dáil (1919-22), President of the Executive Council (1932-37), Taoiseach (1937-48, 1951-54 and 1954-59), the third President of Ireland (1959-73). A Commandant in the 1916 Rising he escaped execution because of his American birth. A member of Dáil Éireann from 1919 he withdrew from it in protest at its ratification of the ANGLO-IRISH TREATY. TD (1919-59), MP (1917-1919), leader of FIANNA FÁIL (1926-59) he was Minister for External Affairs (1932-48), Minister for Education (1939-40) and Local Government (1941). Active in world politics he was President of the Council of the League of Nations (September-October 1932) and President of the Assembly of the League of Nations (1938). As President of the Executive Council he abolished the Oath of Allegiance for members of the Oireachtas in 1933, removed all reference to the king from the constitution during the abdication crisis of 1936 and was the key figure in drafting the 1937 Constitution. Pursued a prolonged and damaging 'Economic War' with Britain in the 1930s he secured the 'Treaty Ports' on the eve of World War Two enabling him to steer Ireland, in the teeth of severe international criticism, on a neutral course during the conflict. Elected President in 1959 he is the only person to have held the offices of President and Taoiseach.

DEVLIN, Anne (c. 1778-1851) devoted servant of Robert Emmet who carried messages between him and his friends after the failure of the rising in 1803. Arrested and tortured, she refused to reveal any information.

DEVLIN, Joe (1871) b. Belfast, MP (1902-34) at Westminster and Stormont. Member of IRISH PARLIAMENTARY PARTY, president of ANCIENT ORDER OF HIBERNIANS (1905-34). Died 1934.

DEVOY, John (1842-1928) b. Kill, Co. Kildare, journalist and nationalist. A member of the IRB, later an influential figure in CLAN NA GAEL, he raised finance for republican groups in Ireland. Wrote the Recollections of an Irish Rebel (1928).

DILL, Sir John (1881-1944) b. Armagh, Boer War and World War I veteran. Field Marshal and Chief of Staff of the British army 1940.

DILLON, John (1851-1927) b. Dublin, MP (1885-1918). Exponent of HOME RULE and leading figure in IRISH PARLIAMENTARY PARTY.

DONNELLY, Charles (1910-37) b. Tyrone, poet who fought and died with the 15th International Brigade in the Spanish Civil War.

DUFFY, Charles Gavan (1816-1903) b. Monaghan, member of YOUNG IRELAND movement. Co-founded The Nation in 1842, Prime Minister of Victoria, Australia (1871-72); knighted 1873.

DUGGAN, Eamonn (1874-1936) b. Meath, TD (1918-33). Signatory of ANGLO-IRISH TREATY.

DUNLAP, John (1747-1812) b. Tyrone, founded the first daily newspaper in North America, the Pennsylvania Packet; was first to print the US Declaration of Independence.

EMMET, Robert (1778-1803) b. Dublin, leader of an abortive rebellion in Dublin in 1803. Remembered for his speech from the dock he was hanged and beheaded.

EDGEWORTH (de Firmont), Henry Essex (1745-1807) b. Edgeworthstown, Co. Longford, known as the 'Abbé Edgeworth'. Son of a Protestant rector, ordained a Jesuit priest and became confessor to both Louis XVI and his sister. Narrowly escaped death during the Revolution.

FAIR, James G. (1831-1894) b. Tyrone, gold prospector in California. Founded Bank of Nevada, American Senator (1881-87).

FAULKNER, Brian (1921-77) b. Co. Down, Prime Minister of Northern Ireland (1971-72), NI MP (1949-72), he was Minister for Home Affairs (1959-63), Minister for Commerce (1963-69) and Minister of Development (1969-71). The last Prime Minister of Northern Ireland his government introduced internment without trial in 1971 and was in charge of the army when thirteen civilians were killed on a civil rights march in Derry. These events precipitated the British government's decision to impose Direct Rule from Westminster. Chief Minister of the short-lived 'Power Sharing Executive (January-May 1974) he was elevated to the peerage as Baron Faulkner of Downpatrick in 1977.

FITZGERALD, Lord Edward (1763-98) b. Kildare, veteran of the American War of Independence. Leading member of the UNITED IRISHMEN, captured May 1798, he died from his wounds before he could be tried.

FITZGERALD, Thomas Lord Offaly Silken Thomas

(1513-37) b. Kildare, appointed Lord Deputy in 1534. Instigated a rebellion almost immediately; surrendered in 1535, assured of a pardon but was hanged, drawn and quartered.

FITZMAURICE, James C. (1898-1965) b. Dublin, veteran of WWI. Subsequently officer in the Irish Air Corps, accompanied by two Germans he completed the first east-west crossing of the Atlantic by air in 1928.

FLOOD, Henry (1723-91) b. Kilkenny, MP in Irish House of Commons, leader of Patriot Party which agitated for legislative independence. Appointed vice-treasurer of Ireland in 1775 but removed in 1781 for being strongly nationalist.

GLENDY, John (1778-1832) b. Derry, Presbyterian minister and member of UNITED IRISHMEN, emigrated to the US and became a Commodore in the US navy.

GOUGH, Sir Hubert de la Poer (1870-1963) b. Waterford, veteran of the Boer war, served as Lieutenant-General during World War I.

GRATTAN, Henry (1746-1820) b. Dublin; statesman. Became an active supporter of HENRY FLOOD, who led the Irish independence movement, and left law in 1775 to enter into the Irish parliament. Secured the abolition of all claims by the British parliament to legislate for Ireland in 1782 but could not prevent the ACT OF UNION (1800) and sat in the parliament at Westminster until his death.

GRAVES, Thomas (1747-1814) b. Derry, Admiral in the British navy (1812-14).

GRIFFITH, Arthur (1871-1922) b. Dublin, founded SINN FÉIN 1905, proposed Irish abstentionism from Westminster and establishment of indigenous assembly; MP (1917-22). Served as Minister for Justice and Minister for Foreign Affairs, signatory of 1921 ANGLO-IRISH TREATY, President of Dáil Éireann (January-August 1922).

GUINNESS, Arthur (1725-1803) b. Kildare, founded Guinness brewery at St James' Gate in 1759. Under his grandson's stewardship (Sir Benjamin Lee Guinness), the brewery's stout became famous and the business grew into the largest of its kind in the world.

HAMILTON, Gustavus (1639-1723) b. Fermanagh, founded the 'Enniskilleners'- a Williamite regiment; fought at the Battle of the Boyne.

HEALY, Cahir (1877-1970) b. Donegal, nationalist representative at Stormont from 1925-65 for Fermanagh South and MP for Fermanagh and South Tyrone 1950-55 at Westminster.

HEALY, Timothy (1855-1931) b. Cork, MP (1880-1918). Governor-General of Irish Free State (1922-28).

HENNESSY, Richard (1720-1800) b. Cork, fought with Irish regiments on continental Europe. Founded the Hennessy Brandy distillery in 1763.

HILL, Wills (1718-93) b. Co. Down, minister in various British governments. Became Marquis of Downshire in 1789, rebuilt Hillsborough castle.

HINCKS, Francis (1807-85) b. Belfast, Prime Minister of Canada (1851-54). Subsequently Governor of Barbados.

HOBSON, Bulmer (1883-1969) b. Co. Down, founding member of Fianna Éireann (1909), member of the IRB but opposed the 1916 Rising.

HUGHES, Desmond (1919-1992) b. Belfast, fighter pilot and veteran of WWII. Deputy commander of British forces in Cyprus (1972-74).

HUSSEY, Thomas (1741-1803) b. Meath, noted for his diplomatic skills in the service of George III in continental Europe. First president of Maynooth College and later Bishop of Waterford and Lismore.

HYDE, Douglas (1860-1949) b. Castlerea, Co. Roscommon, the first President of Ireland (1938-45). To the forefront of the cultural revival at the end of the nineteenth century he was co-founder of CONRADH NA GAEILGE (The Gaelic League) in 1893 and its President until 1915. Professor of Modern Irish at UCD (1909-32) he wrote *Casadh an tSúgáin* (the first Irish language play to be staged professionally). Member of Free State Senate.

KANE, Richard (1666-1736) b. Antrim, Governor of Gibraltar and Minorca (1720-25).

KEARNEY, Peadar (1883-1942) b. Dublin, wrote the words to the Irish national anthem, *Amhrán na bhFiann*. Veteran of 1916 Rising.

KENNEDY, Arthur (1810-1883) b. Co. Down, Governor of Hong Kong (1872-77) and Queensland (1877-83).

KING, John (1838-72) b. Tyrone, explorer. Was the first white man to travel across Australia, accompanying the Burke and Wills expedition (1860), and survive. The other members of the expedition died on the return journey, but King was rescued by the Aborigines and survived.

KITCHENER, Horatio Herbert (1850-1916) b. Ballylongford, Co. Kerry. General in WWI and statesman. Appointed secretary for war in 1914, raised a huge army before he went down with the HMS Hampshire off Orkney in 1916.

LACY, Count Peter (1678-1751) b. Limerick, field marshal in Russia. In 1691, served in the Irish Brigade and joined the army of Peter the Great in 1698, fought in the Swedish war and was wounded. Appointed governor of Latvia (1728) and promoted to field marshal (1736).

LARKIN, Jim (1876-1947) b. Liverpool, founding member of IRISH TRANSPORT AND GENERAL WORKERS UNION (1908). Charismatic workers' leader during the Dublin Lock-out (1913-14), founded Workers' Union of Ireland (1924), TD (1928-32, 1937-38 & 1943-44).

LEMASS, Seán (1899-1971) b. Dublin, Taoiseach (1959-66), TD (1924-69), Minister for Industry and Commerce (1932-39, 1941-48, 1951-54 and 1957-59), Minister for Supplies (1939-45) and Tánaiste (1945-48, 1951-54 and 1957-59). A veteran of the 1916 Rising he was a founding member of FIANNA FÁIL in 1926 and party leader (1959-66). As Minister for Industry and Commerce he established Aer Lingus (1936), Irish Shipping (1941) and Bórd Fáilte (1952). His period as Taoiseach marked the end of the policy of economic protectionism which had stifled Irish industry and the beginning of Ireland's open economy era. He also held groundbreaking talks with TERENCE O'NEILL, the Prime Minister of Northern Ireland in 1965.

Le MESURIER McCLURE, Robert John (1807-73) b. Wexford, discovered the North-west Passage - the link between the Pacific and Atlantic via the Arctic

Ocean.

LENIHAN, Brian (1930-95) b. Louth, TD (1961-73 & 1977-95), MEP (1973-79); held various ministries including Tánaiste in FIANNA FÁIL governments. Defeated candidate in 1990 Presidential election.

LESTER, Seán (1888-1959) b. Antrim, Irish Free State representative to League of Nations, appointed Acting Secretary General of the League in 1940.

LOGAN, James (1674-1751) b. Armagh, appointed Governor of Pennsylvania 1736.

LOWE, Sir Hudson (1769-1844) b. Galway, soldier and diplomat. Fought with the British army during the Napoleonic wars and was made governor of Santa Maura, Ithaca and Cephalonia. Afterwards, was attached to the Prussian army of Blücher, and in 1816, was made governor of St Helena were he kept guard over Napoleon.

LUNDY, Robert Governor of Derry when King James and his army lay siege to the city in 1689. Removed from office by the citizens of Derry when suggested surrendering. Escaped but was later imprisoned in the Tower of London. His effigy is burned annually.

MacBRIDE, John (1865-1916) b. Mayo, fought in the Boer War against the British. Fought in the 1916 Rising and was executed. Married Maude Gone.

MacBRIDE, Maude Gonne (1865-1953) Irish nationalist and muse for the poet W.B. YEATS. Espoused the cause of Irish independence and edited a nationalist newspaper, *L'Irlande libre*, in Paris. Married MAJOR JOHN MACBRIDE. After his death she became an active Sinn Féiner in Ireland. A celebrated beauty, Yeats pursued her for many years. Her son SEAN MACBRIDE founded Amnesty International.

MacBRIDE, Seán (1904-88). b. Dublin, fought with republicans during the civil war. Chief-of-staff of the IRA (1936-37), founder and leader of the republican party CLANN NA POBLACHTA (1946-65), TD (1947-1957), Minister for Foreign Affairs (1948-51), UN commissioner for Namibia (1973-75), chairman of Amnesty International 1973-76. Awarded Nobel Prize for Peace (1974) and Lenin Peace Prize (1978).

McCLURE, Sir Robert John le Mesurier (1807-73) b. Wexford; Arctic explorer. He participated in two Arctic expeditions in 1836 and 1848. As commander of a ship in the Franklin expedition (1850-54), he penetrated eastwards and was officially accredited with the discovery of the North-west Passage (subsequently attributed to Sir John Franklin) for which he won a parliamentary award.

McCRACKEN, Henry Joy (1767-98) b. Belfast, Presbyterian and founding member of the UNITED IRISHMEN. Led the United Irishmen rebellion in Antrim in 1798 and was captured and hanged.

MacDIARMADA, Seán (1884-1916) b. Leitrim, revolutionary. Joined the IRISH REPUBLICAN BROTHERHOOD and was responsible for organising its infiltration of other organisations. Crippled after contracting polio (1912). Signatory of the PROCLAMATION OF THE IRISH REPUBLIC he was executed for his role in the 1916 Rising.

McDONAGH, Thomas (1878-1916) b. Tipperary, poet and revolutionary. Published much highly acclaimed poetry and translations from Irish. Was active in the IRISH VOLUNTEERS and belatedly joined the prepara-

tions for the 1916 Rising, taking command of Jacob's Factory during the fighting for which he was executed.

MacEOIN, Seán (1893-1973) b. Longford, the most successful guerrilla leader in the War of Independence. Supported the ANGLO-IRISH TREATY and became Chief-of-Staff of the Free State army. FINE GAEL TD (1929-65) he served as Minister in two Coalition Governments.

MacMURCHADA, Diarmait (1110-71) b. Wicklow, king of Leinster. Banished by high king RUAIDRÍ UA CONCHOBAIR in 1166, solicited help from Henry II of England, succeeded in attracting Richard de Clare (STRONGBOW) to Ireland by offering him his daughter in marriage and succession to the kingship of Leinster.

MacNEILL, Eoin (1867-1945) b. Antrim, co-founder of the GAELIC LEAGUE (1893) and IRISH VOLUNTEERS (1913). TD (1918-27), Minister for Education (1922-25). Irish representative to the Boundary Commission (1924-25) but resigned. Noted Gaelic scholar.

MacNEILL, James (1869-1938) b. Antrim, Governor-General of Irish Free State (1928-32).

MacSWINEY, Terence (1879-1920) b. Cork, prominent member of the IRISH VOLUNTEERS. Elected Lord Mayor of Cork in 1920. Imprisoned in August 1920, commenced a hunger strike and died after 74 days.

MARKIEWICZ, Constance Georgine *née Gore-Booth* (1868-1927) b. London, reared in Sligo, nationalist. While studying art at the Slade School in London, met and married Count Casimir Markiewicz. The couple settled in Dublin. Became involved in SINN FEIN and met MAUD GONNE MCBRIDE. She and her husband parted in 1913. Fought in the 1916 Rising and was sentenced to death but sentence reprieved. The first woman MP elected (1918) to the English parliament, but never took her seat. Elected to Dail Éireann (1919) and assigned the labour portfolio, but was arrested twice. After the Civil War, was a member of the Dail from 1923.

MARTIN, Richard (1754-1834) b. Dublin, lawyer and humanitarian. As MP for Galway (1801-26), pushed a bill to proscribe the cruel treatment of cattle. Through his work the Royal Society for the Prevention of Cruelty to Animals (RSPCA) was founded.

MEAGHER, Thomas Francis (1823-1867) b. Waterford, deported to Van Diemen's land for his part in the abortive Rising of 1848. Escaped and went to the US. Became a general in the Union Army in the American Civil War and later Governor of Montana.

MITCHEL, John (1815-75) b. Co. Derry; patriot. Founded the UNITED IRISHMAN (1848) and was arrested and tried for treason-felony. Transported to Van Diemen's Land, escaped to the US, published his famous *Jail Journal* (1854). Returned to Ireland and elected as MP for Tipperary, but was not allowed to take his seat and died the same month.

MULCAHY, Richard (1886-1971) b. Waterford, veteran of 1916 Rising. Fought with the Free State forces during the civil war becoming Commander-in-Chief following the death of Michael Collins. TD (1918-37, 1938-43 & 1944-61), member of CUMANN NA NGAEDHEAL and FINE GAEL, served in various government ministries.

MURPHY, Fr. John (1753-98) b. Wexford, Leader of Rising of 1798 in Wexford taking the towns of

Enniscorthy, Wexford and Ferns. Captured following defeats at Arklow and Vinegar Hill he was executed by hanging.

Ó BUACHALLA, Domhnall (1866-1963) b. Kildare, 1916 veteran, Governor-General of the Irish Free State (1932-37).

Ó CEALLAIGH, Seán T. (1882-1966) b. Dublin, second President of Ireland (1945-59). A founding member of SINN FÉIN (1907) and FIANNA FÁIL (1926) he was a veteran of the 1916 Rising. TD (1918-45) he was Minister for Local Government and Public Health (1932-39), Minister for Finance (1939-45), Vice-President of the Executive Council (1932-37) and Tánaiste (1937-45).

O'CONNELL, Daniel *'The Liberator'* (1775-1847) b. Kerry, founded CATHOLIC ASSOCIATION in 1823 to lobby for Catholic Emancipation which was achieved in 1829. In 1828, became first Roman Catholic elected to the House of Commons. Lobbied for the repeal of the Act of Union but was unsuccessful.

Ó DALAIGH, Cearbhall (1911-78) b. Wicklow, fifth President of Ireland (1974-76). Attorney General (1946-48 and 1951-53), a Supreme Court judge from 1953 he was Chief Justice from 1961-73, and President of the First Chamber of the Court of Justice of the European Communities from 1974. He resigned as President to protect the dignity of the office after a government Minister branded him a 'thundering disgrace' when he sent a Criminal Justice Bill to the Supreme Court to attest its constitutionality.

O'DONNELL, Red Hugh (c. 1571-1602) b. Donegal, inaugurated Chief of O'Donnell Clan in 1592. Allied with HUGH O'NEILL, he engaged in the 'Nine Years' War'. Left Ireland after the Battle of Kinsale in 1602 to obtain further Spanish aid, but was poisoned at the Spanish court.

O'DOHERTY, Cahir (1587-1608) b. Donegal, the last Irish Chieftain. Was killed after attacking Derry and Strabane.

O'DUFFY, Eoin (1892-1944) b. Monaghan, Garda Commissioner (1922-33). Previously Chief-of-Staff of the Free State Army. Founded the ARMY COMRADES ASSOCIATION (Blueshirts) in 1932; founding member and first leader of FINE GAEL (1933-34). Leader of an Irish Brigade (1936-38) which fought in the Spanish civil war on the side of General Franco's fascists.

O'HIGGINS, Kevin (1892-1927) b. Laois, CUMANN NA NGAEDHEAL TD (1918-27) Supported *Anglo-Irish Treaty*. Minister for Justice in first Free State government, 77 anti-treaty IRA members were executed in reprisals by this government during the civil war. Influential in establishing the Garda Síochana. He was assassinated and his killers were never caught.

O'LEARY, John (1830-1907) b. Tipperary, FENIAN. Studied law and medicine but never qualified. Became strongly associated with the Fenian movement. Edited the *Irish People*, a newspaper voicing Fenian views, but was betrayed and arrested in 1865, sentenced to 20 years but released after nine and banished from the country, returning in 1885. A strong influence on the poet W.B YEATS.

O'MALLEY, Donogh (1921-1968) b. Limerick, FIANNA FÁIL TD (1954-68), as minister for education he introduced free post primary education in 1966.

O'MALLEY, Grace *Gráinne Ní Mháille* (c. 1530-1603) b. Mayo, legendary pirate queen along the Mayo coast. Allegedly visited Queen Elizabeth in London, speaking to her as one queen to another. Married twice, was seized after the death of her second husband. Managed to escape to Ulster and stayed with The O'Neill, was subsequently pardoned by Queen Elizabeth.

O'NEILL, Hugh (1550-1616) b. Tyrone, Earl of Tyrone and chief of the O'Neill Clan from 1583; his forces and the forces of RED HUGH O'DONNELL engaged the English in the Nine Years War, culminating in his surrender and the Treaty of Mellifont in 1603. Unable to adapt to the new circumstances, fled Ireland with other Gaelic chieftains in the 'Flight of Earls' in 1607.

O'NEILL, Owen Roe (c. 1590-1649) b. Tyrone, nephew of Hugh. Served with distinction in Spanish army, arrived in Ulster in 1642 and became military leader of the rebellion. Was victorious over Monro at Battle of Benburb.

O'NEILL, Phelim (1604-1653) leader of the 1641 Rising, he was executed for that role.

O'NEILL, Terence (1914-90) b. London, Prime Minister of Northern Ireland (1963-69), NI MP (1946-70) he was Minister of Finance (1956-63). A veteran of World War Two he was elevated to the peerage as Lord O'Neill of the Maine in 1970. While Prime Minister he held two ground breaking meetings with Taoiseach SEÁN LEMASS and attempted to introduce limited civil rights for Catholics. The Unionist party effectively split over the issue in 1969 and he resigned as leader.

O'SHEA, Katherine (1845-1921) CHARLES STEWART PARNELL'S mistress, she married him after he was ousted from the leadership of the IRISH PARLIAMENTARY PARTY.

PARKER, Debra (1882-1963) b. Derry, NI MP (1921-29 & 1933-60); Minister of Health (1949-57), the only woman to serve as Minister in any Northern Ireland government.

PARNELL, Anna (1852-91) b. Wicklow, sister of CHARLES STEWART PARNELL, established LADIES LAND LEAGUE in Ireland, January 1881. First radical female agitator in Irish history. The league's activities were suppressed by her brother.

PARNELL, Charles Stewart *'the uncrowned king of Ireland'* (1846-91) b. Wicklow, leader of Home Rule Movement from 1877 and leader of IRISH PARLIAMENTARY PARTY (1880-90). Lobbied the House of Commons successfully for land reform and manoeuvred Irish public opinion in favour of HOME RULE. Ousted from leadership of the IPP in 1890 when cited as co-respondent in a divorce petition. Married divorcee KATHERINE O'SHEA in 1891.

PEARSE, Pádraig (1879-1916) b. Dublin, poet and veteran of 1916 Rising. Founded the all-Irish Scoil Éanna (1908), founding member of Irish Volunteers (1913) member of the IRISH REPUBLICAN BROTHERHOOD. Commander-in-Chief of the Volunteers during the Rising, President of the Provisional Government and signatory of the PROCLAMATION OF THE IRISH REPUBLIC, executed for his role in the Rising.

PLUNKETT, Joseph Mary (1887-1916) b. Dublin, poet and veteran of 1916 Rising. Member of IRISH REPUBLICAN BROTHERHOOD and the IRISH VOLUNTEERS.

Chief military strategist for the Volunteers during the Rising, signatory of PROCLAMATION OF THE IRISH REPUBLIC, executed for his role in the Rising.

REDMOND, John (1856-1918) b. Wexford, MP (1881-1918), leader of IRISH PARLIAMENTARY PARTY (1900-18). A major figure in the passage of the 1912 HOME RULE BILL (1914), called on the IRISH VOLUNTEERS to join British Army – almost 200,000 did.

RYAN, Frank (1902-44) b. Limerick, fought with anti-treaty IRA during civil war. Founded Saor Éire, led 200 Irish volunteers to fight with the socialists in the Spanish civil war (1936-37).

SANDS, Bobby (1954-81) born Belfast, member of the PROVISIONAL IRA he was imprisoned in 1977, commenced hunger strike (March 1, 1981) to regain political status for prisoners. Elected MP for Fermanagh & South Tyrone he died on the 66th day of his protest.

SARSFIELD, Patrick (d. 1693) born Dublin, Brigadier General in army of James II. Signed the TREATY OF LIMERICK which allowed him and his men safe passage to join James in France. Killed at Battle of Landen.

STRONGBOW - Richard Fitz Gilbert de Clare (d. 1176) b. Wales; Norman adventurer who arrived in 1170 at the request of DIARMAIT MACMURCHADA. MacMurchada promised him his daughter in marriage and succession to the kingship of Leinster; king of Leinster from 1171.

TANDY, James Napper (1740-1803) b. Dublin, founding member of UNITED IRISHMEN, leader of French expeditionary force in 1798 which landed in Donegal but retreated. Captured and sentenced to death, Napoleon demanded and obtained his extradition in 1802.

TAYLOR, George (b. 1716) member of American Continental Congress, he was a signatory of the American Declaration of Independence.

WOLFE TONE, Theobald (1763-98) b. Dublin, founding member of the SOCIETY OF UNITED IRISHMEN in 1791. Solicited French aid for the 1798 rebellion. Captured at Buncrana, he was found guilty of treason and sentenced to be hanged. Committed suicide while awaiting execution.

Literature

ALLINGHAM, William (1824-1889) b. Ballyshannon, poet. Became involved with the pre-Raphaelites - his poetry collection *Day and Night Songs* was illustrated by Rossetti and Millais - best remembered for poem *The Fairies* which opens with 'Up the airy mountains, down the rushy glen...'

BALL, Francis Elrington (1863-1928) b. Dublin, historian. The son of a Lord Chancellor, educated privately because of poor health. His treatise *The Judges in Ireland 1221-1921* is now an important source as much of the information in it was based on documents in the Irish Record Office which was destroyed in 1922.

BANIM, John (1798-1842) b. Kilkenny, novelist and playwright who collaborated with his brother Michael

(1796-1874) on the *Tales of the O'Hara Family* (1826) portraying humble Irish folk.

BECKETT, Samuel (1906-1989) b. Dublin - writer, poet, playwright and translator. Educated in Enniskillen and TCD. Taught in Paris and becoming friendly with JAMES JOYCE. Involved with the French Resistance during the Second World War he was awarded the Croix de Guerre. Usually wrote in French and made the translation in English. Works include *Dream of Fair to Middling Women* (1932), *More Pricks than Kicks* (1934), *Murphy* (1938), the trilogy *Molloy, Malone Dies* and *The Unnamable* (1950), *Waiting for Godot* (1952), *Endgame* (1957), *Krapp's Last Tape* (1958), *Happy Days* (1961) and *Collected Poems* (1984). Awarded Nobel Prize for Literature in 1969.

BEHAN, Brendan (1923-1964) b. Dublin; celebrated wit, dramatist, author and poet. His family was steeped in Irish literature and song, joined the IRA and was arrested and sent to a Borstal for possession of explosives in Liverpool. Returned to Dublin and again arrested for shooting at policeman. Learned Irish from native speakers in the Curragh prison and began to write. Worked with Joan Littlewood to produce plays, the most famous of which include *The Quare Fellow* (1954) and *An Giall/The Hostage* (1958), and the autobiographical *The Borstal Boy* (1958). His drinking was legendary and eventually led to his death.

BEHAN, Dominic (1928-89) b. Dublin, writer and folklorist. A brother of BRENDAN BEHAN, emigrated and wrote scripts for the BBC. His songs include *The Patriot Game* and *Liverpool Lou*. His works include *Posterity Be Damned, My Brother Brendan* (1965), *the Folk Singer* (1972), *Teems of Times* (1979) and the novel *The Public Life of Parable Jones*.

BICKERSTAFFE, Isaac (c. 1735-1812) b. Dublin, playwright. An officer in the marines, he was dismissed and had to flee the country in 1772. The best known of his plays is *The Maid of the Mill*.

BOUCICAULT, Dion Lardner (c.1820-90) b. Dublin, dramatist. He is credited with writing around 150 plays (including translations and adaptations), the most notable of these being the *Colleen Bawn* (based on Griffin's *The Collegians*).

BOWEN, Elizabeth (1899-1973) b. Dublin, novelist in Anglo-Irish literary genre. Works include *The Last September* (1929), *The Death of the Heart* (1938), *A World of Love* (1955).

BRODERICK, John (1927-89) b. Athlone, novelist. Travelled extensively and met Ernest Hemmingway and Gore Vidal. His first novel, *The Pilgrimage* (1961), was banned in Ireland. Other works include *An Apology for Roses* (1973), *Oh, What a Beautiful City* (1974), *The Irish Magdalene* (1991).

BROOKE, Henry (1703-83) b. Co. Cavan, dramatist and novelist. Was friendly with the poet Alexander Pope and married his ward. His novel *The Fool of Quality* (1766) is the sole survivor of his reputedly numerous works.

BROWN, Christy (1932-1981) b. Dublin, writer. Despite suffering from cerebral palsy, completed his autobiography *My Left Foot* (1964) – made into an Oscar-winning film – and *Down all the Days* (1970).

Poetry includes *Come Softly to My Wake* (1971).

CARBERY, Ethna (1866-1911) b. Co. Antrim, writer. Her contributions to nationalist papers did much to contribute to SINN FÉIN's cause.

CARLETON, William (1794-1869) b. Co. Tyrone; novelist. Most famous for *Traits and Stories of the Irish Peasantry* (1830), a portrait of nineteenth century rural Irish life.

CENTLIVRE, Susanna (1667-1722) b. Co. Tyrone, dramatist. Wrote many successful comedies, including *The Wonder! A Woman Keeps a Secret* (1714) which gave the actor Garrick one of his best roles.

CLARKE, Austin (1896-1974) b. Dublin, poet and dramatist. Worked in England as a literary critic and journalist before returning to Dublin in 1937. The first of his 18 books, *The Vengeance of Fion*, was published in 1917. Famous poems include *The Planters Daughter* and *Lost Heifer*. Works include *Flight to Africa* (1963), *A Penny in the Clouds* (1968), *Collected Poems* (1974).

COBBE, Frances Power (1822-1904) b. Newbridge, a supporter of women's rights and prominent anti-vivisectionist. Travelled in Italy and the East and wrote *Cities of the Past* (1864) and *Italics* (1864).

COFFEY, Brian (1905-1995) b. Dublin; poet, translator and editor. Works include *Third Person* (1938), *The Big Laugh* (1976), *Death of Hektor* (1984), *Advent* (1986).

COLUM, Patrick (1881-1972) b. Longford; primarily a poet, wrote the famous haunting song *She Moved Through the Fair*. Works include the biography of ARTHUR GRIFFITH - *Ourselves Alone* (1959) and a collection of anecdotes about JAMES JOYCE – *Our Friend James Joyce* (1958).

CONGREVE, William (1670-1729) dramatist and poet who was educated at Kilkenny School and Trinity where he was a fellow student of JOHNATHAN SWIFT. His masterpiece *Love for Love* was first produced in 1695. Died after a coach accident and is buried Westminster Abbey.

CORKERY, Daniel (1878-1964) b. Cork, writer and cultural leader. His book, *The Hidden Ireland* (1925), criticised the literary historians who saw Ireland in terms of the 18th-century ascendancy. Had a profound influence on writers such as SEAN O'FAOLAIN and FRANK O'CONNOR. Member of Seanad Eireann (1951-54).

DAY-LEWIS, Cecil (1904-72) b. Co. Mayo; poet and writer. Educated at Oxford, published his first book of poetry in 1925. Became associated with the poetry movement of the 1930s with Auden and Spender and espoused left-wing causes, becoming a member of the Communist party (which he later renounced). After WWII, was a professor of poetry at Oxford (1951-56) and Harvard (1964-65) and was made Poet Laureate in 1968. Also wrote literary criticism, translations and detective novels (under the pseudonym Nicholas Blake). Father of film star Daniel Day-Lewis.

DENHAM, Sir John (1615-69) b. Dublin, poet. Published *Cooper's Hill* (1642), a topographical poem which Pope imitated in *Windsor Forest*. Buried in Poets' Corner in Westminster Abbey.

De VERE WHITE, Terence (1912-1994) writer and literary editor for *The Irish Times* (1961-77). Works include *Kevin O'Higgins* (1948), *A Fretful Midge*

(1957), *Lucifer Falling* (1965), *The Parents of Oscar Wilde* (1967), *The Anglo-Irish* (1972), *Chimes at Midnight* (1977) and *Chat Show* (1987).

DILLON, Eilís (1920-1994) b. Galway, novelist and playwright. Works include *The Island of Horses* (1956), *A Page of History* (1966), *Across the Bitter Sea* (1973), *Blood Relations* (1977), *The Cats' Opera* (1981), *Wild Geese* (1981), *Down in the World* (1983), *Children of Bach* (1993).

DUNSANY, Edward John 18th Baron (1878-1957) b. London, poet and playwright. Fought in the Boer War and afterwards, settled in Dunsany Castle, Meath. At W.B. YEATS's request, he wrote many plays for the ABBEY THEATRE, including *The Glittering Gate* (1909) and *The Laughter of the Gods* (1919). His poetry includes *Fifty Poems* (1930) and *Mirage Water* (1939).

EDGEWORTH, Maria (1767-1849) b. Oxfordshire, novelist. After an education in England, returned to Longford to help her father raise his many children. Published her first novel *Castle Rackrent* (1800) to immediate acclaim and went on to publish a series of social novels on Irish life.

ERVINE, St. John Greer (1883-1971) b. Belfast, playwright and novelist. Drama critic for the *Observer* until 1939. Works include *Boyd's Shop* (1936) and *Friend and Relations* (1941), as well as biographies of *Charles Stewart Parnell* (1925), *Sir James Craig* (1949) and *George Bernard Shaw* (1956).

FARQUHAR, George (c. 1677-1707) b. Derry, playwright. Educated at Trinity and an actor in Dublin, the accidental wounding of another actor shocked him into leaving. Wrote his first work, *Love and a Bottle* in 1698. His most famous plays, *The Beaux' Strategem* and *The Recruiting Officer*, were written during his final illness. He died in poverty.

GÉBLER, Ernest (1915-1998) b. Dublin, novelist. The son of an Austro-Hungarian itinerant musician, his novel *The Voyage Of The Mayflower* (1950) was a hugely successful blockbuster, selling 4 million copies in the US. Married to writer EDNA O'BRIEN, he separated from her in 1961, soon after her book *The Country Girls* was published. Screenplays include *Call Me Daddy, The Lonely Girl (Girl with Green Eyes), Women can be Monsters, Why Aren't You Famous?* and *A Little Milk of Human Kindness*.

GOGARTY, Oliver St. John (1878-1957) b. Dublin, poet and surgeon. Works include *An Offering of Swans* (1923) and *Elbow Room* (1939).

GOLDSMITH, Oliver (1728-1774) b. Longford, poet and author. Became known in literary spheres and associated with Samuel Johnson. Works include *The Citizen of the World* (1762), the acclaimed *The Vicar of Wakefield* (1766), his most famous verse being *The Deserted Village* (1770). Plays include *The Good-Natur'd Man* (1768) and the still successful *She Stoops to Conquer* (1773).

GRAVES, Alfred (1846-1931) b. Dublin; writer and educationalist. An inspector of schools in England, he was a leader of the Celtic Revival, writing a good deal of Irish folk verse and songs. He also wrote an autobiography *To Return to All That* (1930).

GREGORY, Lady Isabella Augusta (1852-1932) playwright and founder of the Irish Theatre movement.

After her marriage to Sir William Gregory, governor of Ceylon, met and became friendly with WB YEATS, founding the ABBEY THEATRE and the Irish Players. Wrote many short plays including *Spreading the News* (1904) and *The Rising of the Moon* (1907). Also transcribed Irish legends and translated Molière.

GRIFFIN, Gerald (1803-40) b. Limerick, novelist. Travelled to London and published short stories of Irish life. His book, *The Collegians* (1829), was used as the basis of Boucicault's *Colleen Bawn*. In 1838 he destroyed his manuscripts and entered a monastery.

HANLEY, Gerard (1916-1992) b. England, writer. Works include *The Consul at Sunset* (1951), *The Year of the Lion, Gilligan's Last Elephant, See You in Yasukuni* and the screenplay *The Blue Max*. (1966).

JAMESON, Anna Brownell (1794-1860) b. Dublin, critic and author. Her writings include *Diary of an Ennuyée* (1826), *Characteristics of Shakespeare's Women* (1832), *Beauties of the Court of Charles II* (1833) and works on art.

JOHNSTON, Denis (1901-84) b. Dublin, playwright. Educated in Dublin, Edinburgh, Cambridge and Harvard. Joined the English and Northern Ireland bars. His works include *The Old Lady Says 'No'* (1929) and *The Moon on the Yellow River* (1931). Autobiographical works include *Nine Rivers from Jordan* (1953), which tells of his years as a war correspondent. His daughter Jennifer Johnston is also a novelist.

JOYCE, James Augustine Aloysius (1882-1941) b. Dublin, writer. Educated at Clongowes, Belvedere and University College, Dublin. A linguist and a prolific reader, he corresponded with Ibsen. The Catholic Church's hold on Ireland compelled him to move to Paris. Returned briefly after his mother's death and returned to exile from Ireland with Nora Barnacle who was to be his partner for the rest of his life. Had written two books by the end of WWI, *Chamber Music* (1907) and *Dubliners* (1914), a collection of short stories. Ezra Pound became his champion and the auto-biographical *A Portrait of the Artist as a Young Man* appeared in instalments in *The Egoist* (1914-15). Pound and W.B. YEATS petitioned on Joyce's behalf and he obtained a grant from the Royal Literary Fund in 1915. However, his eyesight was failing. Was also deeply disturbed by his daughter's schizophrenia. Published his most famous work, *Ulysses* (1922), in Paris to much criticism. Now regarded as a watershed in literature, it narrates a day in the life of Leopold Bloom as he wanders through Dublin (Bloomsday is now celebrated every year in Dublin). His subsequent work, *Finnegan's Wake*, was published in 1939.

KAVANAGH, Patrick (1905-67) b. Monaghan, poet and novelist. Left Monaghan for Dublin (1939) to pursue a literary career. Arguably his best work is *The Great Hunger* (1942), a poem which exposes the harsh reality of farming. In 1948, wrote the autobiographical *Tarry Flynn*. His antisocial, unorthodox lifestyle was anonymously written about in the press and led to a libel action, from which he never recovered. Works include *Collected Poems* (1964).

KEANE, Molly (1904-1996) b. Kildare, novelist. Used her Anglo-Irish ascendancy background as the basis for her books. Adopted the pen-name MJ Farrell and wrote her first book, *The Knight of Cheerful Countenance*. Wrote ten books between 1928 and 1952, stopping when her husband died. However, resumed writing and her book, *Good Behaviour* (1981), was shortlisted for the Booker Prize.

KEATING, Geoffrey also known as Seathrún Céitinn (c. 1570-1645) b. Tipperary; historian. His chief work, *Foras Feasa ar Éirinn* (History of Ireland) was allegedly written in a cave. Supposedly killed in a church by Cromwellian soldiers.

KICKHAM, Charles (1828-82) b. Tipperary, FENIAN, journalist and novelist. Editor of Fenian newspaper, *The Irish People*. Best known for novels *Sally Kavanagh* and *Knocknagow* (1879) and poem *Rory of the Hill*.

LAVIN, Mary (1912-96) b. Massachusetts (came to Ireland as a child), best-known as a short story writer. Her first short story *Miss Holland* was published in the *Dublin Magazine*. Other works include *Tales from Bective Bridge* (1942), *Mary O'Grady* (1950), *A Memory and other Stories* (1972),*The Shrine and Other Stories* (1977) and *A Family Likeness* (1985). Was awarded the Katherine Mansfield prize and the Gregory Medal.

LECKY, William Edward Hartpole (1838-1903) b. Dublin, philosopher and historian. Educated at TCD, his works include *History of Rationalism* (1865), *History of England in the 18th Century* (1878), *Democracy and Liberty* (1896) and *The Map of Life* (1899), a Unionist MP (1895-1902).

Le FANU, Joseph Sheridan (1814-73) b. Dublin, gothic horror novelist and journalist. Left law to take up journalism and went on to become owner and editor of the *Dublin University Magazine* as well as three other Dublin newspapers. His novels are marked by their preoccupation with the supernatural. His 14 works include The *House by the Churchyard* (1863), *Uncle Silas* (1864) and *In a Glass Darkly* (1872).

LESLIE, Sir Shane (1885-1971) b. Co. Cavan, writer. Born into the Protestant ascendancy, converted to Roman Catholicism and espoused nationalism. Wrote *The End of a Chapter*, an analysis of the pre-WWI generation, and followed it with *The Celt and the World, Doomsland, The Oppidan* and *The Cantab*.

LEWIS, C.S. (1898-1963) b. Belfast, writer, academic and Christian apologist. Professor of medieval and Renaissance English at Cambridge from 1954. His first book *Dymer* (1926) is a narrative poem that is both satirical and idealistic – a quality that suffuses most of his work. Other works include *Allegory of Love* (1936), *The Screwtape Letters* (1942), *The Problem of Pain* (1940), *Beyond Personality* (1944) and *Mere Christianity* (1952). Also wrote science fiction and children's books, the most famous of which are *The Chronicles of Narnia*.

LYNCH, Liam (1937-96) b. Dublin, writer and playwright. Works include *Do Thrushes Sing in Birmingham?* (1962), *Soldier* (1969), *Strange Dreams Unending* (1974), *Krieg* (1982), *Voids* (1982), *Shell Sea Shell* (1983).

LYNCH, Patricia (1900-72) b. Cork, popular children's author. Published more than 50 children's books including *The Turf Cutter's Donkey* (1934), *The Grey Goose of Kilnevan* (1941) and *Story Teller's Holiday*

(1947).

LYONS, Francis Stewart (1923-83) b. Derry; historian and biographer. Professor of history at the University of Kent from 1964 he was Provost of Trinity College Dublin 1974-81. His works include The *Fall of Parnell* (1960), *John Dillon* (1968), *Ireland Since the Famine* (1971), *Charles Stewart Parnell* (1977) and *Culture and Anarchy in Ireland 1890-1939* (1978).

McDONAGH, Donagh (1912-68) b. Dublin, playwright. Son of the revolutionary THOMAS McDONAGH, edited The *Oxford Book of Irish Verse* with Lennox Robinson. Plays include *Happy as Larry* (1946), *God's Gentry* (1951) and *Step-in-the-Hollow (1957)*.

McGEE, Thomas D'Arcy (1825-68) b. Co. Louth, writer and politician. Emigrated to Canada in 1842 and espoused numerous nationalist causes. Published Romantic poetry, as well as *A History of the Irish settlers in North America* (1851), *A Popular History of Ireland* (1862-69) and *Poems* (1869). Elected an MP, was assassinated in Ottawa for opposing a proposed Fenian invasion of Canada.

McMAHON, Brian (1909-1998) b. Listowel, writer and playwright. Works include The *Bugle in the Blood, The Song of the Anvil, The Honey Spike, The Death of Biddy Early, The Lion Tamer, Children of the Rainbow, Red Petticoat, The Sound of Hooves* (1985), *The Master* (autobiography 1992), *The Tallystick* (1994).

MacGILL, Patrick (1890-1963) b. Donegal, poet and novelist. Worked in Scotland as a farm-labourer and navvy. Works include *Children of the Dead End* (1914) and *The Rat-Pit* (1914), among many other books. Emigrated to the US (1930) and died there in poverty.

MacNEICE, Louis (1907-63) b. Belfast, poet. A lecturer in the classics, became aligned with left-wing British poets of the 1930s, particularly Auden. Works include *Blind Fireworks* (1929), *Collected Poems* (1949), *Autumn Sequel* (1954), *Eighty-Five Poems* (1961) and *Solstices* (1961). Also renowned for his radio plays and his literary criticism.

MACKEN, Walter (1915-67) b. Galway; novelist, actor and playwright. Remembered for historical trilogy *Seek the Fair Land* (1959), *The Silent People* (1962) *The Scorching Wind* (1964) and *Brown Lord of the Mountain.*

MALONE, Edmund (1741-1812) b. Dublin, editor of Shakespeare. Called to the Irish bar but worked in the London literary sphere. Wrote an eleven-volume edition of Shakespeare (1790) and was one of the first people to discredit Chatterton's Rowley poems and denounced William Henry Ireland's Shakespeare forgeries. The Malone Society was formed in 1907 in his honour.

MANGAN, James Clarence (1803-49) b. Dublin, poet. His life was marked by failed love, poverty and alcoholism. Published translations of Irish poetry in The *Poets and Poetry of Munster* (1849), which includes *My Dark Rosaleen, The Nameless One* and *The Woman of Three Cows.* Also published translated German poetry - *Anthologia Germanica* (1845).

MERRIMAN, Brian (1747-1805) b. Ennistymon, Co. Clare, Gaelic poet. His poem *Cúirt an Mheáin Oidhche* (The Midnight Court) is the most translated

poem in the Irish language. A bawdy epic, it mocks sexual morals, celibacy, the clergy and male chauvinism. The poem had the notable distinction of being banned in English but allowed in its original Irish.

MOORE, Thomas (1779-1852) b. Dublin, poet and socialite, most notably in Regency London. Published many works, including his *Irish Melodies* (1807-1834) with accompanying music, some of which he composed himself. Also wrote satires and prose. A close friend of Lord Byron he was noted for his wit, charm, liberalism and singing voice. Other works include *Lalla Rookh* (1817) and *Life of Byron* (1830). Melodies include *Believe Me If All those Endearing Young Charms, The Harp that Once through Tara's Halls* and *The Time I've Lost in Wooing.*

O'BRIEN, Flann/Myles na gCopaleen Brian O'Nolan (1911-66) b. Co. Tyrone, playwright and novelist. Wrote a satirical column *An Cruiskeen Lawn* in The *Irish Times* for two decades. Works include *At Swim-two birds* (1939), *The Third Policeman* (1940/67), *An Béal Bocht* (1941), *The Hard Life* (1961), *Faustus Kelly* (1943), *The Dalky Archive* (1964).

O'CADHAIN, Máirtín (1906-70) b. Galway, noted Irish language writer. Most famous for novel *Cré na Cille* (1949), translated into several European languages. First Irish-writer elected to the Irish Academy of Letters.

O'CASEY, Seán (1880-64) b. Dublin, dramatist. Best remembered for the trilogy of plays dealing with struggle for Irish Independence: *The Shadow of a Gunman* (1923), *Juno and the Paycock* (1924) and *The Plough and the Stars* (1926), which remain among the most popular of productions on the Irish theatre circuit. *The Silver Tassie,* his next play, was rejected by the ABBEY THEATRE and O'Casey moved to London, wrote more plays and a six-volume autobiography.

Ó CLÉIRIGH, Mícheál (1575-1643) b. Donegal, Compiled the *Annals of the Four Masters* in Irish, assisted by Cuigcoigriche Ó'Duigeanáin, Fearfeasa Ó'Maolconaire, and Cuigcoigriche Ó'Cléirigh.

Ó CONAIRE, Pádraic (1883-1928) b. Galway, Irish language novelist and short story writer. Best known for *M'Asal Beag Dubh* and *Fearfasa MacFeasa* (1930).

O'CONNOR, Frank (1903-66) b. Cork, novelist, short story writer and translator. Best known for short stories, collected in volumes such as *Guests of the Nation* (1931) and *Crab Apple Jelly* (1944). Works include *Bones of Contention* (1936), *The Saint and Mary Kate* (1932), *Dutch Interior* (1940), *An Only Child* (1961), *My Father's Sons* (1968), *The Backward Look* (1967).

Ó CRIOMHTHAIN, Tomás (1856-1937) b. Great Blasket Island, Kerry. Best known for the diary, *Allagar na h-Inise* (1928) and the autobiography *An t-Oileánach* (1929).

Ó DOIRNÍN, Peadar (1682-1769) b. Louth, poet. Best known for works as political and humorous verse writer.

O'DONNELL, Peadar (1893-1986) b. Donegal, novelist and playwright. Works include *Storm* (1925), *Islands* (1928), *The Knife* (1930), *The Gates Flew Open* (1932), *On the Edge of the Stream* (1934), *Salud: An Irishman in Spain* (1937), *The Big Windows* (1955), *There Will Be Another Day* (1963), *Proud Island*

(1975).

O'FAOLÁIN, Seán (1900-91) b. Cork, novelist and biographer. Works include *Midsummer Night Madness* (1932), *King of the Beggars;* (1938), *De Valera* (1939), *Come Back to Erin* (1940), *The Great O'Neill* (1942), *Constance Markievicz* (1943), *Vive Moi!* (1964), *Foreign Affairs* (1976), *Collected Stories* (1980-82).

O'FLAHERTY, Liam (1896-1984) b. Inishmór, novelist. Works include *The Black Soul* (1924),*The Assassin* (1928), *Skerrett* (1932), *Famine* (1937), *The Short Stories of Liam O'Flaherty* (1937), *Duil* (1953), *The Pedlar's Revenge and Other Stories* (1976).

O'GRADY, Standish (1846-1928) b. Cork, a writer of historical novels. Works include *The Heroic Period* (1878) and *Red Hugh's Captivity* (1889).

Ó GRIANNA, Séamus (1891-1969) b. Donegal, novelist and short story writer, known by pen-name *Máire*. Best known for *Cith is Dealain* (1926) and *Caislean Óir* (1924).

Ó RATHAILLE, Aodhagán (1670-1726) b. Kerry, Irish language poet.

Ó SÚILLEABHÁIN, Eoghan Rua (1748-84) b. Kerry, poet. Wrote in Irish about experiences as a school teacher, seaman and wandering labourer.

Ó SÚILLEABHÁIN, Muiris (1904-50) b. Great Blasket Island, Kerry; Irish-language writer. Best known for autobiography *Fiche Blian ag Fás* - Twenty Years a-Growing (1933).

Ó TUAIRISC, Eoghan (1919-82) b. Ballinasloe; poet, writer, playwright and translator. Works include *L'Attaque, Dé Luain, An Lomnochtán, Rogha na Fhile, Dialann sa Diseart, Na Mairnéalaigh, La Fhéile Mhichíl, An Hairyfella in Ifreann, Fornocht do Chonac.*

Ó hUIGINN, Tadhg Dall (1550-91) b. Sligo, bardic poet who dedicated his poems to the Gaelic lords in his surrounding area.

PARKER, Stewart (1941-88) b. Belfast, playwright. Works include *The Casualty Meditation* (1966), *Spokesong* (1975), *Catchpenny Twist* (1977), *Nightshade* (1985), *Northern Star* (1985).

REID, Forrest (1875-1947) b. Belfast, novelist and literary critic. Works include *The Kingdom of Twilight* (1904), *Following Darkness* (1912), *At the Door of the Gate* (1915), *Uncle Stephen* (1931), *The Retreat* (1936), *Young Man, or Very Mixed Company* (1944).

RUSSELL, George 'AE' (1867-1935) b. Co. Armagh, artist and poet. Went to art school in Dublin where he met and became a lifelong friend of YEATS. Broadened his interests and became involved in theosophy. Wrote on a wide variety of subjects including the agricultural co-operative movement. Hosted meetings for those interested in the arts and economic future of Ireland. Published *Collected Poems* (1913) and was editor of the *Irish Homestead* and the *Irish Statesman*.

SAYERS, Peig (1873-1958) b. Kerry, skilled storywriter gifted with a wealth of folklore on the Great Blasket Island. Recordings of her folktales and stories were made by Irish Folklore Commission and later published as her autobiography *Peig* (1936).

SHERIDAN, Richard Brinsley (1715-1816) b. Dublin, playwright and politician. As a young man, eloped with a society beauty and married her. To support their lavish lifestyle, turned to writing for the stage. Bought a share in the Drury Lane Theatre from the actor Garrick. Found success in comic writing. Was elected to Parliament (1780-1812). A strong opponent of the Union and an advocate for free speech, noted as a brilliant orator. The theatre burnt down and Sheridan's extravagance led him into penury, in which he died. Works include *The Rivals* (1775), his most famous and popular play *The School for Scandal* (1777), *The Critic* (1779)

STEPHENS, James (1880-1950) b. Dublin, writer. Best known works include *The Charwoman's Daughter* and *Crock of Gold,* which dealt with Irish folklore and fantasy, and *The Insurrection in Dublin* (1916) about the Easter Rising.

STOKER, Bram (1847-1912.) b. Dublin, best remembered for *Dracula* (1897), which took six years to create and inspired dozens of other works. Published a total of 18 books on mostly gothic themes. Manager of the Lyceum Theatre, London, for 27 years working with the actor Henry Irving. Final work was *Personal Reminiscences of Henry Irving* (1906).

SHAW, George Bernard (1856-1950) b. Dublin, playwright, essayist and music critic. Awarded Nobel Prize for Literature (1925). Heavily involved in the Fabian society he was a ardent socialist. Initially successful in America, his works were recognised by English theatrical producer and writer, Granville-Barker, as masterpieces. Fell out of favour for his pacifist stance during WWI and for advocating the cause of his native country after the 1916 Rising. For many years refused to allow film versions of his work but was reconciled to the idea by Gabrial Pascal. Works include *Arms and the Man, Mrs Warren's Profession, Pygmalion, Major Barbara, Caesar & Cleopatra, Androcles and the Lion, Saint Joan, The Doctor's Dilemma, Heartbreak House, The Millionairess.*

SWIFT, Jonathan (1667-1745) b. Dublin, writer and dean of St Patrick's Cathedral. Took holy orders (1694) and was appointed to a Co. Antrim parish, returned to Surrey to act as a tutor to Hester Johnson 'Stella'. Given a vicarage near Trim, travelled between Ireland and London, and was noted as a wit and conversationalist. Was sought out and acted as an advocate of the Tories, attacking the Whigs. Given the deanery of St Patrick's and was followed by Esther Vanhomrigh – 'Vanessa' (controversy surrounds the roles played by Stella and Vanessa in his life). Works include *A Tale of a Tub, The Battle of the Books* (1704), *Drapier's Letters* (1724), and the satirical *Gulliver's Travels* (1726).

SYNGE, John Millington (1871-1909) b. Co. Dublin, dramatist. Settled in Paris but returned to visit the Aran Islands. Met W.B. YEATS, who advised him to return to the islands. Did so (1899-1902) and started *The Aran Islands* (published 1907). Became involved with the Irish National Theatre and wrote the plays *The Shadow of the Glen* (1903), *Riders to the Sea* (1907) and *The Playboy of the Western World* (1907, causing a riot when first staged in the Abbey), *The Tinker's Wedding* (1908) and the unfinished *Deirdre of the Sorrows.*

WADDELL, Helen (1889-1965) renowned medieval Latin scholar with strong ties to Banbridge, Co. Down, where she is buried.

WALSH, Maurice (1879-1964) b. Kerry, novelist. Best known for *Blackrock's Feather* (1932) and *The Quiet Man*, a short story from his collection *Green Rushes* (1935), which was made into *The Quiet Man*, one of Ireland's most famous films with John Wayne and Maureen O'Hara (1952).

WILDE, Oscar Fingal O'Flahertie Wills (1854-1900) b. Dublin, noted wit and playwright. Educated at TCD and Oxford, won Newdigate Prize for poetry and graduated with double first. Founded aesthetic cult 'art for art's sake', first published *Poems* (1898), *The Happy Prince and Other Tales* (1891),*The Picture of Dorian Gray* (1891), *A House of Pomegranates* (1891), the plays *Vera* (1883), *The Duchess of Padua* (1891) and *Salome* (1891, written in French and banned in England). Achieved overnight success with first comedy, *Lady Windermere's Fan* (1892) and continued with three more comedies *A Woman of No Importance* (1893 - 1st production), *An Ideal Husband* and The *Importance of Being Earnest* (both produced in 1895). Downfall came through his liaison with Lord Alfred Douglas, whose father, the Marquis of Queensberry, called Wilde a homosexual. Wilde sued and lost the libel action and was subsequently arrested and found guilty on charges of homosexuality, prosecuted by EDWARD CARSON. Served two years in Reading Jail, and afterwards went into exile in France. Wrote the moving *The Ballad of Reading Gaol* (1898) and had *De Profundis* published posthumously in 1905. Died in 1900 and is buried in Paris.

YEATS, William Butler (1865-1939) b. Dublin, playwright and one of Ireland's most celebrated poets. Family moved to London but spent childhood in Sligo with grandparents. Attended art school, became friendly with GEORGE RUSSELL and other mystics. Began writing and was influenced by JOHN O'LEARY and others to include Irish themes in his work. Involved in Madame Blavatsky's Theosophism, helped found NATIONAL LITERARY SOCIETY to publicise the literature of Ireland. Published *The Wanderings of Oisin* (1889), *The Countess Cathleen* (1892) *The Celtic Twilight* (1893), and prose books the *Secret Rose*, *The Tables of Law* and *The Adoration of the Magi* (1897). Began his infatuation with MAUD GONNE MACBRIDE (1889) and met LADY AUGUSTA GREGORY with whom he founded the Irish Literary Theatre (1889). Wrote the play *On Baile's Strand* and *Cathleen Ni Houlihan* (1902) and founded ABBEY THEATRE (1904). Also met Ezra Pound who influenced his plays, married George Hyde-Lees (1917). Other plays include *Four Plays for Dancers - At the Hawk's Well, The only Jealousy of Emer, The Dreaming of the Bones* and *Calvary*. Published poetry books *The Green Helmet and Other Poems* (1910), *Responsibilities* (1914). *The Wild Swans at Coole* (1919), *Michael Robartes and the Dancer* (1921) *The Tower* (1928) and *The Winding Stair* (1933). Member of Free State Senate he was awarded the Nobel Prize for Literature in 1923. Most famous poems are *Lake Isle of Innisfree, September 1913, Easter 1916* and *The Circus Animal's Desertion*. Died in France in 1939 and was re-interred in Sligo in 1948.

Music

BALFE, Michael William (1808-70) b. Dublin, opera composer and violinist. Debuted as a violinist, aged 9 years. In 1823, went to London, then to Italy to study under Rossini. Returned to England in 1833 and wrote many operas for Drury Lane. The most enduring of his compositions is *The Bohemian Girl* (1843) and the music to La Scala's ballet, *La Pérouse*.

BAX, Sir Arnold (1883-1953) b. London, composer. Was inspired by YEATS's *The Wanderings of Oisín*. Wrote poetry commemorating the Easter Rising and included among his friends PEARSE and other 1916 revolutionaries. His works include 7 symphonies, concertos and chamber music.

BECKETT, Walter (1914-96) musician and composer. Educated at Portora Royal School, Enniskillen and TCD. Lectured in TCD, was music critic for the *Irish Times* During the 1950s, wrote arrangements and original compositions for RTÉ. Professor of Harmony and composition at, and was elected as fellow of, the RIAM.

BOWLES, Michael (1909-98) composer.

BRACKEN, Thomas Irish born poet who wrote the National Anthem of New Zealand - *God Save New Zealand*.

CLANCY, Willie (1918-75) b. Clare, instrumental musician. Noted as a master of several traditional instruments, but acclaimed as a piper. Now commemorated by international summer school Scoil Samhraidh Willie Clancy.

DOWLAND, John (1562-1626) b. Dublin, composer to Royal Courts at Copenhagen and London. Wrote three volumes of *'Books of Songs or Ayres'*.

FIELD, John (1782-1837) b. Dublin, pianist, composer and pioneer of the nocturne. An infant prodigy, he studied under Clementi, who used him to show the capabilities of his pianos. In 1802, accompanied Clementi to Paris, Vienna and St Petersburg and stayed and worked as a music teacher. His 19 Nocturnes and other musical works were said to have influenced Chopin. Spent most of his life in Russia where he died.

FLEISCHMANN, Aloys (1910-92) b. Munich, composer. Made professor of music at UCC and stayed there until he retired (1934-1980). Regarded as one of the most influential figures in musical life in Ireland, founding the Cork Symphony Orchestra (1939) and the Cork International Choral and Folk Dance Festival (1954), as well as being an active member of numerous organisations - was a member of the RIAM and Aosdána. Compositions include 6 works for orchestra, 3 works for chamber orchestra and 15 works for vocal and choral performance.

FRENCH, Percy (1854-1920) b. Roscommon, singer/songwriter and artist. His most famous compositions are *The Mountains of Mourne* and *Are Ye Right There Michael*.

GALLAGHER, Rory (1948-1995) b. Donegal. Internationally renowned rock/blues guitarist. Voted World's Top Guitarist. Formed Taste (1966) - Albums: *Taste* (1969); *On The Boards* (UK No 18 - 1970).

Went solo (1971) - Albums (1971-90): *Rory Gallagher; Deuce; Blueprint; Tattoo; Against The Grain; Calling Card; Photo Finish; Top Priority; Jinx; Defender; Fresh Evidence.* Live albums: *Live! In Europe* (1972); *Irish Tour 1974* (1974); *Stage Struck.* Compilations include: *Rory Gallagher Boxed* (1992).

GILMORE, Patrick Sarsfield (1829-92) b. Dublin, bandmaster. Emigrated to the US, formed a band and toured the country, served during the US Civil War. Composed military band pieces, dances and songs, including *'When Johnny Comes Marching Home'.*

GROOCOCK, Joseph (1913-97) composer.

HARTY, Sir Hamilton (1880-1941) b. Hillsborough, Co. Down, composer and arranger. Conducted the Hallé Orchestra. Compositions include *An Irish Symphony* and many songs. Also made well-known arrangements of Handel's *Fireworks* and *Watermusic* suites.

HERBERT, Victor (1859-1924) b. Dublin, composer. A cellist, played in the orchestras of Johann Strauss and at the Stuttgart court. Moved to New York and became the leading cellist in the Metropolitan Opera Company's orchestra. Composed a popular comic opera - *Prince Ananias* - and serious operas *Natoma* (1911) and *Madeleine* (1914).

KELLY, Luke singer with the THE DUBLINERS, formed Dublin (1962), with himself, Ronnie Drew, Barney McKenna, Kieron Bourke and later John Sheehan. Toured extensively and enjoyed much success all over Europe.

KENNEDY, Frankie (d. 1994) member of ALTAN, one of Ireland's top traditional music groups. Married to Band member Mairéad Ní Mhaonaigh.

KENNEDY, Jimmy (1902-84) b. Tyrone, wrote songs *'The Hokey Cokey', 'Red Sails in the Sunset', 'South of the Border, Down Mexico Way'* and *'The Teddy Bears Picnic'.*

McCORMACK, Count John Francis (1884-1945) b. Athlone, tenor singer. After studying in Milan, was taken on by the Covent Garden Opera for the 1905-6 season. Due to his nationalist beliefs, did not appear in England during WWI and took US citizenship in 1919. For the rest of his career, sang popular sentimental songs, films include *Song O' My Heart* (1930) and *Wings of the Morning* (1937). Made a papal count in 1945.

NELSON, Havelock (1917-96) composer.

LYNOTT, Phil (1951-1986) formed THIN LIZZY in Dublin in 1969 after short spell with Brian Downey, Eric Bell, Eric Wrixon. Disbanded 1983. Lynott released two solo albums: *Solo in Soho* ('80); *The Phil Lynott Album* ('82). His heroin addiction ultimately led to his death

O'RIADA, Seán (1931-71) b. Cork, composer and musician who made a huge contribution to Irish musical culture. Studied music extensively in Ireland, Italy and France. Musical director to the ABBEY THEATRE, composed the score for *Mise Éire* (1959). Formed Ceoltóirí Cualann, a traditional ensemble much celebrated via a radio series. It included Paddy Maloney, Martin Fay and Sean Keane. Composed score to the film *The Playboy of the Western World* ('62).

POTTER, A.J. (1918-80) b. Belfast, composer, broadcaster and teacher. Studied composition under Vaughan Williams. Moved to Dublin and was Professor of Composition at the RIAM (1955-73). A prolific composer, his music incorporated a wide variety of techniques and his orchestration is recognised as being outstanding. Notable works include his *Missa Brevis* (1936 rev. 1940) which won the 1951 Festival of Britain Prize, *Overture to a Kitchen Comedy* (1950) and *Sinfonia de Profundis* (1969).

VICTORY, Gerard (1921-95) b. Dublin, composer and member of Aosdána. Director of Music at RTÉ (1967-82) and president of UNESCO's International Rostrum of Composers (1981-83). During a career as a composer spanning over 40 years, wrote around 200 works, including four symphonies, eight operas, a large-scale cantata, two piano concertos and scores for films, plays and celebratory events. The most notable of these being *Chatterton, An Evening for Three, The Rendezvous* and *Ultima Rerum.*

Printing, Publishing & Broadcasting

ANDREWS, Eamon (1922-87) b. Dublin, broadcaster; newspaper columnist, amateur champion boxer, best-known for presenting *This is Your Life.* An astute analyser of the television business, set up his own production company and was served on the board that saw the launch of RTÉ.

BLOW, James (d. 1759) a printer and bookseller who specialised in religious literature in eighteenth century Belfast.

BRACKEN, Brendan 1st Viscount (1901-58) b. Kilmallock, journalist and Conservative politician. Managing director of *The Economist* (1928-45).

BURKE, Sir John Bernard (1787-1848) b. Tipperary, genealogist and compiler of "Burke's Peerage" which he published annually from 1847 (the first directory of British peers).

CAMPBELL, Patrick (1913-80) b. Dublin, broadcaster and author. Wrote for the *Irish Times* and the *Sunday Times* and devised scripts for the BBC, taking up broadcasting for them. Most famous for the TV programme *Call My Bluff.*

COLLIER, Peter (1846-1909) b. Co. Carlow, pioneered the field of subscription publishing. Emigrated to the US and started printing books from a basement, which were then sold on an instalment plan. Established the national weekly *Collier's* (1895) which grew to have a subscription of over 3 million.

COYNE, Richard (d. 1856) a printer, publisher and bookseller who specialised in Catholic literature in nineteenth century Dublin.

CRAWFORD, Emily (*c.* 1840-1915) b. Co. Longford, foreign correspondent. Lived in Paris and wrote articles on Paris's social and political life for English publications. Reported on the Franco-Prussian war, at considerable risk to herself, and became Paris correspondent of the *Daily News* and the *New York Tribune.*

DANIEL, William (d. 1628) Anglican Archbishop of Tuam from 1609, translated the *New Testament* and *The Book of Common Prayer* into Irish and had them published.

DUFFY, James (1809-71) publisher who produced work for the Young Irelanders.

FAULKNER, George (1703-1775) a printer and bookseller. Proprietor of the *Dublin Journal* he also published the works of JOHNATHAN SWIFT.

GILL, Michael (1794-1879) b. Dublin, acknowledged as the father of printing in Dublin. Established a publishing house in Dublin (1856) M.H. Gill and Son which was later associated with Macmillan of London, becoming Gill and Macmillan (1968).

HARMSWORTH, Alfred Charles William *1st Viscount Northcliffe* (1865-1922) b. Dublin, journalist and newspaper magnate. Revolutionised Fleet Street with his *Daily Mail*, which had an American-style layout and news presentation. Launched a number of papers and bought many provincial papers with his brother Harold. Also launched the first newspaper for women, the *Daily Mirror*, and founded the Amalgamated Press for educational journals. In 1908, took over *The Times* and boosted its circulation.

HARRIS, Frank (1856-1931) b. Galway; journalist and writer. His autobiography (1923-7) was banned for pornography. Was the editor of the *Fortnightly Review, Saturday Review, Vanity Fair* and the *Evening News*, the latter being a pioneer in sensationalist journalism.

JOY, Francis (c.1697-1790) established the Belfast Newsletter in 1737 which is the oldest daily newspaper in Ireland.

MORAN, D.P. (1871-1936) b. Waterford, founder and editor of the *Leader* renowned for its fierce nationalist tone.

MURPHY, William Martin (1844-1919) b. Cork, MP (1885-92); founder of the *Irish Independent* (1905), led the employers' federation during the 1913 Dublin Lock-out.

NEWMAN, Alec (1905-72) b. Waterford, editor of The *Irish Times* (1954-61).

O'HEHIR, Micheál (1920-1996) b. Dublin, legendary RTÉ commentator on Gaelic games and horse-racing, commented on 99 All-Ireland finals between 1939 and 1984.

POWELL, Humphrey The first printer in Ireland he printed *The Book of Common Prayer* in 1551.

SWINEY, Eugene (d. 1781) printer and bookseller in eighteenth century Cork who specialised in Catholic literature.

Religion

AIKENHEAD, Mary (1787-1858) b. Cork, founded the Irish Sisters of Charity. Born a Protestant, converted to Catholicism after the death of her father, founded ten houses and St. Vincent's Hospital – the first in Ireland administered by nuns.

ALEXANDER, Cecil Frances (1818-95) b. Dublin, hymn composer; most famous hymns are *All Things Bright and Beautiful* and *Once in Royal David's City.*

BEDELL, William (1571-1642) b. Essex, bishop and provost at Trinity College. Opposed the oppression of

Catholics and ensured that students of divinity studied Irish. Had the Old Testament translated into Irish, later translated and printed as Bedell's Bible.

BERESFORD, John G. (1773-1862) b. Dublin, Church of Ireland Archbishop of Armagh and Primate of All Ireland (1822-62).

BERKELEY, George (1685-1753) b. Kilkenny, Church of Ireland Bishop of Cloyne (1734-52) and philosopher. His most important treatises were *Essay towards a New Theory of Vision* (1709), *A Treatise concerning the Principles of Human Knowledge* (1710) and *Three Dialogues between Hylas & Philonous* (1713), in which he developed the concept 'to be is to be perceived' - the contents of the material world are ideas that only exist when they are perceived by a mind. Obsessed with founding a college in America to propagate Christianity among the 'American savages' but was never to see this college founded in his lifetime.

BERNARD, John Henry (1860-1927) b. Wicklow, Church of Ireland Archbishop of Dublin (1915-27) and Provost of Trinity College (1919-27).

BRONTË, Patrick (1777-1861) b. Co. Down, his daughters were the famous writers Charlotte, Emily and Anne.

CONWAY, William (1913-1977) b. Belfast, Roman Catholic Archbishop of Armagh and Primate of All Ireland from 1963, created Cardinal 1965.

COOKE, Henry (1788-1868) b. Derry, moderator of Presbyterian General Assembly (1841 & 1862). Vociferous opponent of Repeal of the Union and the Disestablishment of the Church of Ireland.

CROKE, Thomas W. (1824-1902) b. Cork, Roman Catholic Archbishop of Cashel from 1875 and Patron of the GAELIC ATHLETIC ASSOCIATION who named their headquarters after him.

CULLEN, Paul (1803-78) b. Kildare, Ireland's first Cardinal. Archbishop of Armagh (1850-52), Archbishop of Dublin from 1852. Founded Catholic University (1854) and Clonliffe College (1859). Primate of All Ireland from June 1866 until his death.

CUSACK, Margaret Anna *'the Nun of Kenmare'* (1829-1899) b. Dublin; social thinker and writer. An Anglican, converted to Catholicism (1858) and founded a convent in Kenmare. After coming into conflict with the church hierarchy, went to England and founded the Sisters of St Joseph of Peace. Honoured for setting up the Famine Relief Fund in 1879, but later fell out of favour for her work for women's suffrage - the Vatican ordered her name be removed as founder of her order. Returned to her Anglican beliefs and spent her final years lecturing and writing. Published 100 books of biography, history, poetry, music and social reform.

D'ALTON, John (1883-1963) b. Mayo, Roman Catholic Archbishop of Armagh and Primate of All Ireland from 1946, created Cardinal 1953.

D'ARCY, Charles F. (1859-1938) born Dublin, Church of Ireland Archbishop of Armagh and Primate of All Ireland (1920-38).

DUNS SCOTTUS, Johannes (c. 1260-1308) medieval scholar. Held the Oxford chair of divinity. In the 16th century his teachings were ridiculed by humanists and others, and a derivation of his name –dunce–

referring to his adherents came to mean slow-witted. **ERIGENA, John Scotus** (c. 810-c. 877) philosopher and theologian. A unique figure outside the mainstream of medieval thought, taught at the court of Charles I in France. Gave his support to the predestination controversy which was condemned as *sultes Scotorum* (Irishman's porridge) by the Council of Valence. His major work attempted to amalgamate Christianity and neo-Platonism but was condemned. According to legend, he was stabbed to death by his scholars with their pens 'for trying to make them think'.

FARLEY, John (1842-1918) b. Armagh, Archbishop of New York (1902-18), created Cardinal 1911.

HORAN, James (1912-86) b. Mayo, parish priest at Knock, Co. Mayo (1967-86). Built a new 10,000-capacity basilica, hosted Pope John Paul II on his trip to Ireland in 1979, driving force behind the building of Knock airport (completed 1986).

HUGHES, John (1797-1864) b. Tyrone, first Roman Catholic Archbishop of New York (1850-64).

KERNOHAN, Joseph (1869-1923) b. Derry, founded Presbyterian Historical Society (1906).

KILLEN, William (1806-1902) b. Antrim, President of the Presbyterian College Belfast in 1870s.

KING, William (1650-1729) b. Antrim, Church of Ireland Archbishop of Derry (1690-1703), Archbishop of Dublin (1703-1729).

LOGUE, Michael (1840-1924) b. Donegal, Archbishop of Armagh (1887-1924), created Cardinal 1893.

McAULEY, Catherine (1778-1841) b. Dublin, founded the Sisters of Mercy (1831). The Mercy order has been responsible for educating hundreds of thousands of Irish students (although controversy has grown around the treatment of orphans in their care). Her portrait is on the current Irish five-pound note.

McQUAID, John Charles (1895-1973) b. Cavan, archbishop, who had a strong influence on Irish social and political life. Ordained a priest in the Holy Ghost Fathers (1924), became the dean of studies and then president (1931) at Blackrock College, Dublin. Greatly influenced Éamon de Valera and was made archbishop of Dublin (1940) by Pius XII. Led opposition to Dr. Nöel Browne's Mother and Child scheme, a secular national health scheme (which ultimately led to the fall of the then government in 1951) and, being opposed to multi-denominational education, banned Catholics from attending Trinity College. Retired in 1972.

MacHALE, John (1791-1881) b. Mayo, Archbishop of Tuam (1834-1881). An outspoken nationalist, he backed CATHOLIC EMANCIPATION, Repeal of the Union and Land Reform.

McKENZIE, John (1648-96) b. Tyrone, Presbyterian minister who survived the Siege of Derry and published his account of it in 1690, *'Narrative of the Siege of Londonderry'.*

McNAMARA, Kevin (1926-1987) b. Clare, Roman Catholic Archbishop of Dublin (1985-87).

MacRORY, Joseph (1861-1945) b. Tyrone, Roman Catholic Archbishop of Armagh and Primate of All Ireland (1928-45), created Cardinal 1929.

MATTHEW, Fr Theobald (1790-1856) b. Tipperary, formed a temperance society in 1838, a forerunner of the current Pioneer Total Abstinence Association.

Ó FIAICH, Tomás (1923-90) b. Armagh, President of Maynooth College (1974-77). Roman Catholic Archbishop of Armagh and Primate of All Ireland (1977-90), created Cardinal 1979. Widely learned and popular, welcomed Pope John Paul II to Ireland during his visit (1979). Held strong nationalist views, but advocated a united Ireland through peaceful means. Was also active in promoting the ecumenical movement.

O'GROWNEY, Fr Eugene (1863-1899) b. Meath, a key figure in the revival of the Irish language in the last century, he was vice-president of the Gaelic League from 1893 and Professor of Irish at Maynooth College (1891-96).

RICE, Edmund (1762-1844) b. Kilkenny, founded his first school in 1803 in what was to be the beginning of the Christian Brothers. Pope Pius VII recognised the Brothers in 1820 and Brother Ignatius as he was then known became Superior-General. Beatified 1996.

SCRIVEN, Joseph (1819-86) b. Banbridge, Co. Down, wrote the hymn – 'What a Friend We have in Jesus' – which has been sung throughout the world and translated into many languages.

SHANAHAN, Joseph (1871-1943) b. Tipperary, Roman Catholic missionary priest to Nigeria from 1902, bishop in Nigeria (1920-31).

ST. BRENDAN (c.484-578) b. Kerry, 'Brendan the Navigator'. Believed to have discovered America between 535 and 553.

ST. BRIGID (d. 525) b. Louth, patron saint. Founded religious house in Kildare. Her miracles are said to have derived from legends about a Celtic goddess. Her feast day is February 1st, marked throughout Ireland by the construction of crosses made from rushes.

ST. COLUMN CILLE (521-97) b. Donegal, patron saint. Founded monastic settlements at Derry and Kells, and the monastery at Iona in 563 from which missionaries brought Christianity to Scotland and northern England.

ST. PATRICK (d. 460) b. Wales, foremost of Ireland's three patron saints. A missionary bishop, he arrived in 432 bringing Christianity to Ireland. Established See at Armagh. His life was said to have been a confabulation to get the Primacy of the Irish church established at Armagh.

PLUNKETT, Saint Oliver (1625-81) b. Meath, Archbishop of Armagh from 1669. Hanged, drawn and quartered following spurious charges of involvement in a 'Popish Plot'. Canonised 1975.

TALBOT, Matthew (1856-1925) born Dublin, took a pledge of total abstinence in 1884 following an early life of heavy drinking. Devoted himself to religion and good deeds. Conferred with the title Venerable by the Catholic Church 1976.

WALKER, Rev George (1618) b. Tyrone, Protestant minister who was joint governor of Derry during the siege (1689). Appointed bishop of Derry following the siege, he was killed in battle in 1690.

Science & Medicine

ADAMS, Robert (1791-1875) b. Dublin, surgeon. Noted in his field in Ireland, he wrote *Treatise on Rheumatic Gout* (1857), which was a seminal work on the subject.

ALLMAN, George James (1812-98) b. Cork, noted pioneer in marine zoology. Best known for his work on hydroids.

ANDREWS, Thomas (1813-85) b. Belfast. Although a physician, most noted for his work as a physical chemist. Discovered the composition of ozone and the critical temperature of gases, above which they cannot be liquified, however great the pressure applied.

BALL, John (1818-89) b. Dublin; botanist, alpinist and author of the *Alpine Guide*. Wrote on the botany of Morocco and South America.

BARCROFT, Sir Joseph (1872-1947) b. Newry, Co. Down, physiologist who invented device for blood-gas analysis. Also studied the oxygen-carrying function of haemoglobin and led an expedition to the Andes to study acclimatisation.

BATES *née O'Dwyer*, **Daisy May** (1863-1951) b. Tipperary, anthropologist. Emigrated to Australia in 1884. Renowned for investigating the condition of aborigines, became known as Kabbarli (grandmother) as she worked for aboriginal welfare and set up camps for the aged.

BEAUFORT, Francis (1774-1857) b. Meath, hydrographer. Served in the British navy as a hydrographer (1829-55). Devised the *Beaufort Scale* of wind measurement which is still in use today, it defines 12 wind conditions from dead calm to hurricane force.

BENNETT, Edward Hallaran (1837-1907) b. Cork, surgeon and authority on bone fractures. A professor of surgery, specialised in and made a collection of fractures and dislocations for the University of Dublin. Best known for his description of a fracture of the thumb now known as 'Bennett's fracture'.

BERNAL, John Desmond (1901-71) b. Nenagh, Co. Tipperary, regarded as the father of modern crystallography, founder of molecular biology and a pioneer worker on the structure of water. An ardent communist, actively supported international efforts for peace during the Cold War. Included among his major theses is *The Origin of Life* (1967) as well as the work *The Social Function of Science* (1939).

BLACK, Joseph (1728-99) b. Bordeaux of Belfast parents, established many of the basic principles of modern chemistry.

BOURKE, Austin (1913-95) b. Waterford, meteorologist. Appointed director of Ireland's Meteorological Service in 1964, developed an interest in agricultural meteorology and devised a technique for predicting the occurrence of potato blight, still in use today.

BOYLE, Robert (1627-91) b. Waterford, pioneer of modern chemistry. Son of the great earl of Cork, studied Galileo's works in Florence, took up residence in London and played a leading role in the college of contemporary philosophers, later the Royal Society. Performed experiments on the properties of air which led to his proposition that the volume of gas is inversely proportional to its pressure at a constant temperature (Boyle's Law). Investigated many other subjects in science - electricity, chemistry, specific gravity, refraction and crystallography.

BRENNAN, Louis (1852-1932) b. Castlebar, inventor. Emigrated to Australia, invented dirigible torpedo, gyrostat monorail and worked on the development of the helicopter.

BROUNCKER, William *2nd Viscount* (1620-84) mathematician, who was the first to express π as a continuous fraction and found expressions for the logarithm as an infinite series.

BULL, Lucien (1876-1972) b. Dublin, invented electrocardiograph (1908) and pioneer in the development of rapid cinematography.

BURKITT, Denis (1911-93) b. Fermanagh, medical scientist. Served in Africa, diagnosed a form of cancer, now known as Burkitt's lymphoma, also was one of the first people to establish the link between fibre deficiency in the diet and many diseases of developed world.

CALLAN, Fr. Nicholas (1799-1864) b. Louth, inventor of the induction coil (fore-runner of modern transformer) and pioneer in the field of electrical science.

COLLES, Abraham (1750-98) b. Kilkenny, surgeon. Professor of anatomy and surgery in the College of Surgeons, was the first to precisely diagnose 'Colles' fracture,' a fracture just above the wrist.

COOPER, Edward (1798-63) b. Dublin, astronomer. Built an observatory at Markree Castle, Co. Sligo. Systematically recorded stars and the minor planets and kept meteorological records (1833-63). His catalogue of stars contained the approximate location of 60,066 (of which only over 8,000 were already known).

DEASE, William (1750-98) b. Cavan, founded Royal College of Surgeons in Dublin 1784.

DUNLOP, John (1840-1921) b. Scotland, moved to Belfast in 1860s, produced the first pneumatic tyre.

EDGEWORTH, Richard Lovell (1744-1817) b. Bath, educationalist and inventor, father of Maria Edgeworth. After time spent in England and France, returned to the family estate in Co. Longford. He came in contact with Erasmus Darwin and the Lichfield circle. He fathered 22 children and practised many of his educational theories on them. He also advocated parliamentary reform and CATHOLIC EMANCIPATION.

FERGUSON, Harry George (1884-1960) b. Hillsborough, Co. Down, inventor and engineer. Built his own aeroplane, the first to fly from Irish soil in December 1909. Over many years he developed the renowned Ferguson farm tractor with a hydraulic linkage which controlled the depth of ploughing. These tractors went on to play a large role in the mechanisation of agriculture during and after WWII.

FITZGERALD, George Francis (1851-1901) a professor of natural philosophy, made important discoveries in the fields of electrolysis and electromagnetic radiation. His name is linked with that of Hendrik Antoon Lorentz for the Fitzgerald-Lorentz contraction in the phenomenon of change in moving bodies as observed in the Michelson-Morley experiment.

GRAVES, Robert James (1796-1853) b. Dublin, physician. Studied medicine and after spending time on the continent, returned to Dublin and appointed to the Meath Hospital. Organized medical teaching there along the lines of the French system - with emphasis placed on note taking, physical examination, and autopsies. Noted for his diagnosis of Graves' Disease, a form of hyperthyroidism.

GREATRAKES, Valentine (1629-83) b. Waterford, physician known as the touch doctor. He became famous for curing all types of illnesses by touching or stroking. Failed to demonstrate his powers before the king but his cures were attested by ROBERT BOYLE and others. His *Brief Account* (1666) was published as a rebuttal to his sceptics.

GREGG, John Robert (1867-1948) b. Monaghan, inventor of shorthand system and publisher. Working in Liverpool, he devised a new shorthand system and in 1888, published his system in the *Gregg Shorthand Manual*. Emigrated to the US in 1893 and set up a publishing company.

GRIFFITH, Sir Richard (1784-1878) b. Dublin, geologist and engineer. Surveyed Leinster and examined Irish bogs for a government commission. After the Irish Valuation Act, 1827, devised 'Griffith's Valuations' for country rate assessments and published his *Geological Map of Ireland* (1855). Consulted on all major building projects in Ireland, including the National Gallery and the Museum of Natural History.

HALPIN, Captain Robert Charles (1836-1894) b. Wicklow, laid first transatlantic cable (completed 1866) from Valentia to Newfoundland.

HAMILTON, Sir William Rowan (1805-65) b. Dublin, mathematician, inventor of quaternions. A child prodigy, knew 13 languages and at 15 had begun his own mathematical investigations, inspired by Newton's *Principia*. Appointed professor of astronomy at Trinity College while an undergraduate and developed a new approach to dynamics which had a major bearing on the 20th-century development of quantum mechanics. Introduced quaternions as a new algebraic approach to three-dimensional geometry, since proved to be the foundation of much modern algebra.

HARVEY, William Henry (1811-66) b. Limerick, botanist. Colonial treasurer at Cape Town, created a large herbarium collection of South African plants. Published *Genera of South African Plants* (1838) and *Manual of British Algae* (1840). Appointed Keeper of the Herbarium at TCD (1840) and travelled extensively to collect seaweeds.

JOLY, John (1857-1933) inventor and physicist, developed first practical colour photography system and radioactivity treatment for cancer.

KELVIN, William Thomson *1st Baron* (1824-1907) b. Belfast, physicist and mathematician. At 22, became professor of mathematics and natural philosophy. Proposed the absolute, or Kelvin, temperature scale in 1848 and, simultaneously with Rudolf Clausius, devised the second law of thermodynamics. His investigations covered geomagnetism and hydrodynamics, particularly wave and vortex motion. Oversaw the laying of the first Atlantic submarine cable and grew wealthy by patenting a mirror galvanometer for accelerating telegraphic transmission. Created 1st Baron Kelvin of Largs (1892) and is buried in Westminster Abbey beside Isaac Newton.

KENNELLY, Arthur Edwin (1861-1939) engineer. Emigrated to the US (1887) and assisted Edison, becoming a professor at Harvard (1902-1930). Proposed, simultaneously with Heaviside, the existence of an ionized layer in the atmosphere, termed the Kennelly-Heaviside layer.

KIRWAN, Richard (1733-1812) b. Galway, chemist. Published the first systematic English thesis on mineralogy (1784) and was one of the main proponents of the phlogiston theory - whereby a substance, supposed to exist in all combustible bodies, is released in combustion.

KYAN, John Howard (1774-1850) b. Dublin, inventor. Through his work in a brewery in England, he discovered a method of preserving wood –kyanizing– which he subsequently patented in 1832.

LARDNER, Dionysius (1793-1859) b. Dublin, scientific writer. His works on algebraic geometry (1823) and calculus (1825) attracted much attention. Was made professor of natural philosophy and astronomy at London University. Remembered as creator and editor of *Lardner's Cabinet Cyclopaedia* (1829-49).

LONSDALE *née Yardley*, **Dame Kathleen** (1903-71) b. Newbridge, Co. KIldare, eminent crystallographer. After studying physics at Bedford College, London, she joined William Bragg's research team. Using Bragg's X-ray diffraction method, she obtained the molecular structure of hexamethylbenzene (1929) and hexachlorobenzene (1931), using the Fourier analysis for the first time, a method which was later adopted as a common technique. Professor of chemistry at University College, London, and the first female fellow of the Royal Society (1945).

MALLET, Robert (1810-81) b. Dublin, pioneer of seismology (the study and measurement of earthquakes).

PARSONS, Charles (1854-1931) b. Offaly, invented turbine for use in ships and founded his own firm for its manufacture. Also produced optical glass and many noted astronomical instruments.

PARSONS, Lawrence (d. 1908) brother of Charles, determined the temperature of moon's surface.

PARSONS, William *Third Earl of Rosse* (1800-67) b. York, lived in Offaly, astronomer. Constructed the largest telescope of its time (mid-19th century), workmen from his Offaly estate helped to make its mirrors. This telescope was subsequently used by many prominent astronomers of the time who made important discoveries about star clusters. The earl himself discovered the spiral shape of galaxies.

STONEY, George Johnstone (d. 1911) first to propose existence of electrons.

WALTON, Ernest T.S. (1903-95) b. Waterford, awarded the Nobel Prize for Physics in 1951 with John Cockcroft for their work splitting the atom. Invented the Cockcroft-Walton accelerator used in this procedure.

Sport

AHEARNE, Tim (1885-1968) b. Co. Limerick, athlete. Representing Britain in the triple jump at the 1908 games in London Ahearne won the gold medal. His jump of 14.91m was a world record. His brother Dan set a new world record two years later.

BLANCHFLOWER, Jackie (1933-98) international soccer player. Capped 12 times by Northern Ireland. A Manchester United player he survived the Munich air crash in 1958 but the injuries he sustained ended his career prematurely.

BRADSHAW, Harry (1913-90) born Wicklow, golfer. Winner of the Irish Professional ten times he also won the Irish Open twice (1947 and 1949) and the Dunlop Masters twice (1953 and 1955). A member of three Ryder Cup teams (1953, 1955 and 1957). He and Christy O'Connor Senior won the Canada Cup (now the World Cup) in 1958.

CARROLL, Noel (1941-1998) b. Louth, athlete. Won a scholarship to Villanova University in the US. A member of the All-American Athletics teams of 1963 and 1965. He and his Villanova team mates set a world record for the 4x880 yards relay. He competed in the Olympics in 1964 and 1968. Won a total of 14 Irish titles, at 440 and 880 yards, three British AAA titles, three European Indoor titles and held for a time the European 880 yards record.

CUSACK, Michael (1847-1906) b. Clare, founding member of the GAELIC ATHLETIC ASSOCIATION in 1884. A stand is named after him in Croke Park.

DALY, Fred (1911-1990) b. Antrim, professional golfer. The only Irish golfer to have won a Major (the British Open in 1947), he won several professional titles including the 1946 Irish Open. Played in the Ryder Cup on three occasions (1947, 1949 and 1953).

DEMPSEY, Jack (1862-1895) b. *John Kelly* Kildare, boxer. Held the World Middleweight title for seven years from 1884. Fighting in America, he defended his title successfully on five occasions.

ELLIOTT, Shay (1934-1971) b. Dublin, professional cyclist. He was the first Irishman to wear the yellow jersey in the Tour de France. Winner of the Roubaix stage in the Tour in 1963, he completed three Tours with his best finish (47th place) coming in 1961. Silver medallist in the 1962 World Road Championship.

GALLAGHER, Charlie (d. 1989) Gaelic footballer, an outstanding forward he won three Ulster SFC with Cavan (1964, 1967 and 1969).

GALLAGHER, Patsy (1894-1954) b. Donegal, international soccer player. Scorer of 184 goals in his 436-game, 15-year career with Celtic where he won four Scottish Cups and six League Championships. Capped eleven times by Northern Ireland between 1920 and 1927, he won one international cap with the Free State.

FLANAGAN, John J. (1873-1938) b. Limerick, athlete. After emigrating to the US Flanagan became a three time gold medal winner in the hammer event at three different Olympics: Paris 1900, St. Louis 1904, and London 1908. Won an Olympic silver medal in 1904 for throwing the 56lb weight.

FLANAGAN, Seán (1922-1993) Gaelic footballer, captain of the Mayo All-Ireland winning teams of 1950 and 1951, also won two National Football League medals (1949 and 1954) and five Connacht football medals (1948-51 and 1955). FIANNA FÁIL TD 1951-77, Minister for Health (1966-69) and Minister for Lands (1969-73), MEP 1979-84.

HAMLET, George T. (1881-1959) rugby international, won 30 caps between 1902 and 1911, a member of the team which shared the International Championship with Wales in 1906. IRFU President 1926-27.

HERRON, Tommy (1950-1980) b. Down, motorcyclist. Regarded as one of the top motorcycle riders in the world in the 1970s. Won three Isle of Man TTs.

KEANE, John (1916-75), hurler, winner of an All-Ireland SHC with Waterford in 1948 and two Munster SHC (1938 and 1948).

MACKEY, Mick (1912-1982) b. Limerick, hurler. Won three All-Ireland Hurling medals with Limerick (1934, 1936 and 1940) captaining the team twice. Won eight Railway Cup medals between 1934 and 1945 and five National Hurling League medals (1934-38). Managed the Limerick hurling team in the 1950s.

MAGEE, Louis (1874-1945) rugby international, won 27 caps (1895-1904), member of Championship winning side in 1896 and captain of the Triple Crown winning side 1899.

MAGUIRE, Sam (1879-1927) b. Cork, Gaelic footballer who played championship football for London in the early 1900s. Maguire had the distinction of swearing Michael Collins into the IRB, and the cup which All-Ireland Football winning captains now receive bears his name.

MEAGHER, Lory (1899-1973), hurler, winner of three All-Ireland SHC with Kilkenny (1932, 1933 and 1935) captaining the team in 1935, one National Hurling League (1933) and seven Leinster SHC (1926, 1931-33 and 1935-37).

MURPHY, Tommy (1921-85) Gaelic footballer, midfielder who won three Leinster SFC with Laois (1937, 1938 and 1946).

MONAGHAN, Rinty (1920-1984) b. Belfast, boxer. Became undisputed flyweight champion of the world in March 1948 when he defeated Scotland's Jackie Patterson in the King's Hall, Belfast. In a great career, Monaghan won Irish, British and European titles. Because of various medical ailments, he was forced to retire in early 1950, ending his career on a high as undefeated World title holder.

McCARTHY, Liam (1853-1928) b. London of Irish parents, McCarthy was the first treasurer of the London GAA County Board. The cup which All-Ireland Hurling winning captains now receive bears his name. The cup was first presented in 1923 and a new Liam McCarthy cup was presented for the first time in 1992.

McTIGUE, Mike (1892-1966) b. Clare, boxer. On St. Patrick's Day 1923 in the La Scala Opera House in Dublin McTigue won the World Light-heavyweight title beating Battling Siki, of Senagal, on points in a 20 round contest. It proved to be the last world title fight at any weight to go more than 15 rounds. He held the title for two years.

O'CALLAGHAN, Dr. Pat (1905-1991) b. Cork, athlete.

Double Olympic Gold Medallist for the Irish Free State, winning the hammer in Amsterdam (1928) and Los Angeles (1932). In addition to numerous national titles and a European Record of 56.95m (1933) he recorded an unofficial World Record of 59.56m (1937).

O'DONNELL, Nick (1925-88) hurler, the winner of an All-Ireland SHC medal as a sub with Kilkenny in 1947 he won a further three medals with Wexford 1955, 1956 and 1960 (as captain in 1955 and 1960). Winner of two National Hurling League Medals (1956 and 1958) and six Leinster SHC medals (1951, 1954-56, 1960 and 1962. Texaco Hurler of the Year 1960.

O'REILLY, Joe (1932-39) international soccer player. Capped 20 times by the Irish Free State between 1932 and 1939 the Second World War ended his international career. Captain of St James' Gate when the won the FAI Cup (1938) and the League of Ireland (1939/40).

O'REILLY, John Joe (d. 1952) Gaelic footballer, captain of the Cavan teams which won the All-Ireland in 1947 (at the Polo Grounds in New York) and 1948, won a National Football League Medal in 1948 and 11 Ulster SFC (1937, 1939-45 and 1947-49).

RING, Christy (1920-1979) b. Cork, hurler. Winner of eight All-Ireland Hurling medals 1941-44, 1946, 1952-54 including three as captain, 18 Railway Cup medals between 1942 and 1963, and four National Hurling League medals, 1940, 1941, 1948, 1953. Ring played with Cork from 1939 until 1962.

SCOTT, Elisha 'Lee' (1894-1959) b. Belfast, soccer player and manager. Played 429 games in a 22-year career with Liverpool winning two League Championships. Hugely successful manager with Belfast Celtic (1936-49), he led them to six League titles and six Irish Cups. Capped 31 times for Northern Ireland (1920-36).

SHERIDAN, Marty (1881-1918) b. Mayo, athlete. Set 16 world records in his career and regarded as the finest athlete in the world at his peak. In 1902 he became the first man to throw the discus over 40 metres, holding the world record for ten years, breaking it eight times himself until he reached his all-time best of 43.69 metres. Representing the US, he won a total of nine Olympic medals including five gold, three silver and two bronze. His gold medals came in the discus (St. Louis 1904, Athens 1906 and London 1908), the Shot Putt (Athens 1906) and the Discus Greek Style (London 1908).

STEPHENSON, George (1901-1970) rugby international, won 42 caps between 1920 and 1930 scoring 14 tries. Member of the side which shared the International Championship in 1926 and 1927.

WHELAN, Liam (1935-1958) b. Dublin, international soccer player. Winner of two League Championships with Manchester United in 1955/56 and 1956/57, he was capped four times by the Republic of Ireland before he tragically lost his life in February 1958 in the Munich plane crash which killed eight Manchester United players.

Theatre, Television & Film

ALLGOOD, Molly *Máire O'Neill* (1887-1952) b. Dublin, actress, sister of SARA ALLGOOD. Played Pegeen Mike in the controversial 1907 production of Synge's *The Playboy of the Western World*. Engaged to Synge she acted in his *Deirdre of the Sorrows* (1909). Films include *Juno and the Paycock* (1930),*Someone at the Door* (1950) and *Treasure Hunt* (1952).

ALLGOOD, Sara (1883-1950) b. Dublin, actress. Film debut in *Riders to the Sea* (1904), repeated her greatest stage success in Hitchcock's *Juno and the Paycock* (1930). Emigrated to Hollywood (1940) and played motherly roles. Films include *How Green was My Valley* (1941), *Jane Eyre* (1944), *Challenge to Lassie* (1949).

BARRY, Spranger (1719-1777) b. Dublin, actor. Played Othello and was highly acclaimed. An intense rivalry grew between himself and Garrick. Opened theatres in Dublin and Cork, but his extravagant lifestyle forced him to return to the stage in London.

BYRNE, Eddie (1911-81) character actor in many films which include *The Gentle Gunman* (1946), *The Mummy* (1959), *Mutiny on the Bounty* (1962) and *Star Wars* (1977).

CAREY, Patrick (1916-94) born London, documentary film-maker. Founded Aengus Films (1962). Films include *Journey into Spring* (1956), *Waves*, *Wild Wings*, *Yeats Country*, *Oisín* (1962-74), *Flamingo - Variations on a theme*, *The Algonquin Trilogy* (1975-83). Worked on *A Man for All Seasons*, *Ryan's Daughter* and *Barry Lyndon*.

CUSACK, Cyril (1910-93) b. South Africa, actor and star of over 57 films (1917-1990). Performed with Abbey, Gate and Old Vic theatres and the Royal Shakespeare Company. Film debut in *Knocknagow* (1917). Major success with Carol Reed's *Odd Man Out* (1947). Acclaimed Broadway performance in Eugene O'Neill's *A Moon for the Misbegotten* (1957) opposite Wendy Hiller. Films include *The Spy Who Came in from the Cold* (1965), *Fahrenheit 451* (1967), *Little Dorrit* (1988), *Far and Away* (1992) and *As You Like it* (1992). Father of actresses Sinéad, Niamh and Sorcha Cusack with whom he co-starred in the Gate Theatre production of Chekhov's *Three Sisters*. (1990).

DEVLIN, J.G. (1907-91) b. Belfast, actor in theatre, TV and in films such *The Rising of the Moon* (1957), *Darby O'Gill and the Little People* (1959) and *The Raggedy Rawney* (1988).

DONLEVY, Brian (1899-1972) b. Portadown, actor, starred in 65 films over 40 years. Male model for shirts, made acting debut (1924), with a walk-on in a Broadway play and cameo role in a film. Played tough villain roles. Most notable in *Beau Geste* (1939), earning an Oscar nomination for Best Supporting Actor. Films include *Jesse James* (1939), *Billy the Kid* (1941), *The Curse of the Fly* (1969), *Pit Stop* (1969).

EDWARDS, Hilton (1903-82) b. London, actor and producer. Founded a new theatre company with MICHEÁL MACLIAMMÓIR at the Peacock (1928), subsequently moved to the Gate (1930). Directed over 400 productions and introduced new systems of theatre production. The company made successful tours abroad and introduced European classics, such as *Peer Gynt*, and new Irish works to Irish audiences. Directed a short film *Road to Glenascaul* (1951) nominated for an Academy Award. Also head of drama for RTÉ.

FITZGERALD, Barry *William Shields* (1888-1961) b. Dublin, actor. Film debut in *Land of Her Fathers* (1924) and Hitchcock's *Juno and the Paycock* (1930). Lured to Hollywood by John Ford, reprising his stage role in O'Casey's The *Plough and the Stars* (1937). Won an Oscar for Best Supporting Actor in *Going My Way (1944)*. Films include *Bringing up Baby* (1938), *How Green Was My Valley* (1941), *The Quiet Man* (1952) and *Broth of a Boy* (1959).

GIBBONS, Cedric (1893-1960) b. Dublin, art director for over 76 films. MGM's Art Department Head, he designed the Oscar statuette, which he won 11 times for design and once for 'consistent excellence' (1950). Married actress Dolores del Rio (1930-1941). He worked on *Ben-Hur* (1926), *Tarzan and his Mate* (1934), *Treasure Island* (1934), *The Wizard of Oz* (1939), *Madame Curie* (1943), *National Velvet* (1944), *The Postman Always Rings Twice* (1946), *The Yearling* (1946), *Little Women* (1949), *Annie Get Your Gun* (1950), *An American in Paris* (1951) and *Forbidden Planet* (1956).

HICKEY, Kieran (1936-93) b. Dublin, film director. One of the first film-makers to develop the Irish film industry. Produced films on JONATHAN SWIFT and JAMES JOYCE in 1960s. Film/documentaries include *Stage Irishman* (1968), *Faithful Departed* (1969), *A Child's Voice* (1977), *Criminal Conversation* (1980), *Attracta* (1983), *Short Story - Irish Movies 1945-1958* (1986) and *The Rockingham Shoot* (1987).

HUSTON, John Marcellus (1906-87) b. Missouri, film director. Started off as an actor and contributed to a number of screenplays, before making his directorial debut with *The Maltese Falcon* (1941). Proved to be adept in the action and film noir genres as displayed in *Key Largo* (1948), *The African Queen* (1951), *The Misfits* (1960), *The Man Who Would be King* (1975), but also made a haunting adaptation of James Joyce's *The Dead*, his last film. He became an Irish citizen in 1964 and lived periodically in Connemara. His daughter, Angelica, is the star of the film *The Mammy*, made in Ireland in 1998.

INGRAM, Rex (1893-1950) b. Dublin, film director, directed over 27 films. Emigrated to US and worked for Edison, Vitagraph, Fox (1913), Universal (1916) and Metro Film Studios (1920). Directed Rudolph Valentino in *The Four Horsemen of the Apocalypse* (1921) and *The Conquering Power* (1921). Set up film studio Victorine with aid of MGM after a row over direction of *Ben-Hur* but the advent of sound affected his future films. Made only one talking picture *Baroud* (1933). Worked as a sculptor, painter and novelist.

JORDAN, Dorothy (1761-1816) b. Waterford, a popular actress in Dublin, moved to London where she had great success at Drury Lane. Began a liaison with the Duke of Clarence (later William IV) in 1790, which lasted until 1811, bearing him ten children, the eldest of whom was made Earl of Munster by the king.

KERRIGAN, J.M. (1887-1964) b. Dublin, actor. Joined Abbey Players (1907), emigrated to US (1917) and played Irish characters on Broadway and in Hollywood. Films include *O'Neill of the Glen* (1916), *Song O' My Heart* (1930), *Werewolf of London* (1935), *The Plough and the Stars* (1936), *20,000 Leagues under the Sea* (1954), *The Fastest Gun Alive* (1956).

KNOWLES, James Sheridan (1784-1862) b. Cork, dramatist. Son of a schoolmaster and cousin to Richard Brinsley Sheridan, studied medicine but opted for a career on the stage. Did not succeed and opened a school in Belfast. His most famous works were *Love, The Hunchback* (1832), *The Wife* (1833), and *The Love Chase* (1837). He acted with much success in his own plays but changed career again becoming a Baptist preacher and drawing large crowds.

McANALLY, Ray (1925-89) b. Buncrana, versatile and prolific character actor on film, stage and TV. Screen debut (1930s). Best known for *The Mission* (1986) and *My Left Foot* (1989). Other films include *Shake Hands with the Devil* (1959), *Billy Budd* (1962), *Angel* (1984), *Cal* (1984), *The Fourth Protocol* (1987), *The Sicilian* (1987), *White Mischief* (1988) and *We're No Angels* (1989).

McCORMACK, F.J. *Peter Judge* (1891-1947) Irish character actor with ABBEY THEATRE. Films include *Odd Man Out* (1946), *The Plough and the Stars* (1937) and *Hungry Hill* (1946).

McGINNIS, Niall (1913) film debut with *Turn of the Tide* (1935). Films include *Henry V* (1944), *The Nun's Story* (1958), *Becket* (1964), *Sinful Davy* (1969) and *The Mackintosh Man* (1973).

MacGOWRAN, Jack (1916-73) character actor. Films include The *Quiet Man* (1952), *The Gentle Gunman* (1952), *The Rising of the Moon* (1957), *Darby O'Gill & the Little People* (1959), *Doctor Zhivago* (1965) and *The Exorcist* (1973).

McKENNA, Siobhán (1923-1986) b. Belfast, actress. Starred in both Irish and English language theatre/film. Films include *Daughter of Darkness* (1948), *The Playboy of the Western World* (1962), *The Lost People* (1949), *King of Kings* (1961), *Of Human Bondage* (1964) and *Doctor Zhivago* (1965). Her last performance as Mommo in the Druid Theatre production of Tom Murphy's *Bailegangaire* (1985) was highly acclaimed.

MacLIAMMÓIR, Mícheál (1899-1978) b. Cork, actor, writer, painter and theatre impressario. A child actor, became into a renowned painter and designer. Founded the Gate Theatre in Dublin with his lifelong partner HILTON EDWARDS. The theatre company capitalised on new Irish writing, drawing inspiration from and staging European drama, as well as the classics. Played Iago in Orson Welles' film of *Othello* (1949) and was the narrator in the film *Tom Jones* (1963). Also published fiction, plays and memoirs in both English and Irish. His one-man shows during the 1960s drew critical acclaim in Ireland and internationally. Works include *The Importance of Being Oscar* (1960), *I Must Be Talking to My Friends* (1963) and *Mostly About Yeats* (1970).

MACKLIN, Charles (c.1697-1797) b. Donegal, writer and actor. Acted in Drury Lane, but killed a fellow actor in an argument over a wig and was tried for murder. Wrote a tragedy and many farces and comedies, including *Love á la Mode* (1759) and *The Man of the World* (1781).

MOORE, Owen (1886-1939) b. Meath, actor. Star of US silents and early talkies. Film debut in *Biograph* (1908) and appeared in many of D.W. Griffith's early productions, Mary Pickford's regular leading man in early stages of her career, married her secretly (1910) but they were later divorced (1920). Films include *The Honour of Thieves* (1909), *Women Love Diamonds* (1927), *Husbands for Rent* (1928), *She Done Him Wrong* (1933) and *A Star is Born* (1937).

O'CONNOR, Una *Agnes Teresa McGlade* (1880-1959) actress born Belfast, portrayed maid, spinster and gossip characters. Her ear-piercing shriek was used to great effect in horror films. Films include *The Invisible Man* (1933), *The Bride of Frankenstein* (1935), *The Adventures of Robin Hood* (1938), *The Adventures of Don Juan* (1948) and *Witness for the Prosecution* (1957).

O'DEA, Denis (1905-1978) actor. Films include *The Informer* (1935), *The Plough and the Stars* (1947), *Treasure Island* (1950) and *The Rising of the Moon* (1957).

O'DEA, Jimmy (1899-1965) b. Dublin, comedian and actor. Well-known on the variety circuit in Dublin theatre, formed a successful comedy partnership with Maureen Potter in the early fifties, which lasted until his death. Starred in the film *Darby O'Gill and the Little People* (1959). Other films include *Casey's Millions* (1922), *Jimmy Boy* (1935), *Blarney* (1938), *The Rising of the Moon* (1957), *Johnny Nobody* (1960).

O'LEARY, Liam (1910-92) b. Cork, actor, director and archivist. Co-founded Irish Film Society (1936). Former Abbey Theatre Director. Made one of Ireland's most rousing propaganda films *Our Country* (1948). Starred in *Stranger at My Door/At a Dublin Inn* (1950). Published works include *Silent Cinema* (1965), *Invitation to the Film* (1945) and the first *Rex Ingram Biography* (1980).

O'NEILL, Eugene (1888-1953) Irish-American playwright with screen-play adaptations. Films include *Anna Christie* with Blanche Sweet (1923), and Greta Garbo (1930), *Strange Interlude* (1932), *The Emperor Jones* (1933), *The Long Voyage Home* (1940), *Summer Holiday* (1947), *Long Day's Journey into Night* (1960) and *The Iceman Cometh* (1973).

O'SULLIVAN, Maureen (1911-98) b. Roscommon, actress. Discovered at Dublin's International Horse Show (1930) by American Frank Borzage. Best remembered as Jane in the *Tarzan* jungle adventures. Married writer John Farrow and retired to raise their seven children, including actress Mia Farrow. Later hosted a syndicated TV series. Films include *Song O' My Heart* (1930), *David Copperfield* (1935), *Pride and Prejudice* (1940), *All I Desire* (1953), *Never too Late* (1965).

PURCELL, Noel (1900-85) actor and comedian. Films include *Captain Boycott* (1947), *Moby Dick* (1956), *Mutiny on the Bounty* (1962), *Lord Jim* (1965), *McKenzie Break* (1969), *Flight of the Doves* (1971),*The Mackintosh Man* (1973).

RYAN, Kathleen (1922-1985) actress. Films include *Odd Man Out* (1947), *Captain Boycott* (1947), *Esther Waters* (1948), *The Yellow Balloon* (1952), *Captain Lightfoot* (1953), *Jacqueline* (1956) and *Sail into Danger* (1958).

SHIELDS, Arthur (d. 1970) born Dublin, actor. Brother of actor Barry Fitzgerald, player with Dublin's ABBEY THEATRE, emigrated to US. Played priests, missionaries and fanatics. Films include *The Plough and the Stars* (1936), *How Green was My Valley* (1941), *National Velvet* (1944), *She Wore a Yellow Ribbon* (1949), *The Quiet Man* (1952) and *The Pigeon that Took Rome* (1962).

TAYLOR, William Desmond *William Tanner* (1877-1922) actor and director. Director of 39 films he rose to fame as director of Mary Pickford films. Former president of the Screen Directors Guild. Films include *The Beggar Child* (1914), *Anne of Green Gables* (1919), *Huckleberry Finn* (1920), *The Green Temptation* (1922) and *The Top of New York* (1922). Shot under suspicious circumstances in Hollywood.

Acknowledgements

The Editorial Staff and DnD Research Ltd would like to thank the following people and organisations for their much valued assistance in compiling information for this publication. Without their time and expertise, this book would not have been possible.

John McAteer, Tom O'Brien, Marie Duffy - Department of the Marine and Natural Resources; Edward Crean, Morgan McDonagh - Department of Enterprise, Trade & Employment; Carmel Whitemore - Department of the Environment and Local Government; Tom Duffy - Department of Social, Community and Family Affairs; Ann Bredin - Department of Public Enterprise; Elizabeth Cameron, Irene McAllister - Department of Economic Development; Ivor Graham, David O'Neill - Fisheries Division Northern Ireland; Mark R. Wilson - Forest Service Northern Ireland; Department of Agriculture for Northern Ireland; Department of Finance; Department of Agriculture & Food; Yvonne O'Hara - Office of the Revenue Commissioners; Margaret O'Reilly; Mary Murphy, Bernie O'Keeffe, Norma O'Connell - Central Statistics Office, Cork and the Central Statistics Office Library, Rathmines, Dublin; Noreen Gibney - Irish Organic Farmers & Growers Association; Cherie Kennedy - Livestock & Meat Commission for Northern Ireland; Irish Dairy Board; Teagasc - Agriculture and Food Development Authority; Paula McGrath - Irish Congress of Trade Unions; Katherine - Industrial Development Board for Northern Ireland; Bord Iascaigh Mhara; An Bord Glas; Coillte; Ian Hyland - Business & Finance magazine; Angie Haslett - Ulster Business magazine.

Ledu; Forfás; Enterprise Ireland; Electricity Supply Board; Viridian; Bord Gais Éireann; IDA Ireland; National Lottery; An Post; CFM Capital; National Treasury Management Agency; The Central Bank of Ireland; Deloitte & Touche; Dúchas; Bord Fáilte Éireann; Northern Ireland Tourist Board; Ernst & Young; Dublin Airport; Cork Airport; Shannon Airport; Brendán Ó Baoill - Aerphort Dún na nGall; Siobhán Collins - Kerry Airport; Michael McGrath - Knock International Airport; Judith Steele - Belfast International Airport; Chris Lundy - Belfast City Airport; Galway Airport; Joe Corcoran - Sligo Airport; Damien Tierney - City of Derry Airport; Peter Tawse - Waterford Regional Airport; Aer Lingus; Shay Warren - Ryanair; Margaret Stevens - Ulster Bus; Bus Éireann; Translink; Grace Fitzgerald - Irish Rail; Norman Maynes - Northern Ireland Railways; David Glynn - Ports and Shipping; Joe Kavanagh - Department of Environment & Local Government; Claire Alexander, Chris Crawford - Department of Environment Northern Ireland; Society of Irish Motor Industry (SIMI); Harry Walker - NI Automobile Association.

Alison Weir, Martin McDermott - Press Office, Dept. of Health & Social Services; Hugh McGee, Clare Grant, Aidan Mulligan - Information Management Unit, Dept. of Health & Children; Eastern Health Board, Midland Health Board, Mid-Western Health Board, North-Eastern Health Board, North-Western Health Board, South-Eastern Health Board, Southern Health Board, Western Health Board; Al-Anon Family Groups Information Centre, Dublin; the Arthritis Foundation of Ireland; Avril Gillatt - Irish Caner Society; Cystic Fibrosis Association of Ireland; Susanne Kennedy - National Association for Deaf People; Down's Syndrome Association of Ireland; AWARE; Diabetes Foundation of Ireland; BODYWHYS; Marian Wilkinson - the Irish Epilepsy Association; Kathleen Kirwan - The Irish Heart Foundation; the Irish Haemophilia Society; Headway Ireland the National Head Injuries Association.

Denise Staunton - Roscommon County Library; Paddy Behan - Naas Local History Group; Northern Ireland Tourist Board; Deirdre - Carlow County Library; I Millan - North Down Council Development Services, Bangor; Kathy Murphy - Dundalk County Library; Michelle Murray - Longford County Library; Geraldine McHugh - Donegal County Library; Cathy Bennett - Meath County Library; Portlaoise County Library; Omagh District Council Tourist Information; Dublin Tourism Centre; Padraig McLaughlin - North West Tourism; Craigavon Borough Council; Carrick-on-Shannon County Library; Jarlath Glynn - Wexford County Library; Athlone Library; Eileen - Bray Tourist Information Office; Clonmel Library.

Liz Powell - The Arts Council; The Arts Council of Northern Ireland; Audiovisual Federation - IBEC; Caroline Maloney - Eason & Sons Ltd; Clé - The Irish Book Publishers' Association; Dónoil ó Maolfabhail - Bord na Gaeilge; An Coimisiún le Rincí Gaelacha; Comhaltas Ceoltóirí Éireann; Comhdháil Náisiúnta na Gaeilge; Yann Rivallain - the European Bureau for Lesser Used Languages; Music Network; The Irish World Music Centre, University of Limerick; Contemporary Music Centre; all of the local regional arts officers; Principle Management; Polygram Records; BMG Records; Virgin Records; Atlantic Records; Setanta Records; Sony Records; RCA Records; Clive Lacey - IRMA; Chart Information Network; Majella O'Doherty, Alacoque Kealy, Paul Mulligan - RTÉ; David Moore - TG4; TV3; Caroline - BBC NI; Barbara Clarke - UTV; Sinéad Owens - Independent Radio and Television Commission; Ann-Marie Lenihan - National Newspapers of Ireland; Katriona Burke - Regional Newspapers Advertising Network; Caroline Maloney - Eason & Son Ltd; Monica O'Connor - Department of Foreign Affairs; All Editors of Local and National newspapers listed *(see Media chapter)*; All Editors of Magazines, Journals and Periodicals listed *(see Media chapter)*; Jane O'Keefe - Today FM; Paula Carey - ICTU.

Caoimhe Hudson, Jan Cromie, Bill Stewart - Statistics and Research Branch, Dept. of Education Northern Ireland; Nicola Brien, Statistics Section, Dept. of Education and Science; Brian Dennehy, Higher Education Authority; Educate Together Schools; Gaelscoileanna.

The Catholic Press Office; Elaine Whitehouse - Church of Ireland; Stephen Lynas - The Presbyterian Church in Ireland; Rev Edmund Mawhinney - Methodist Church; Pastor Noel McCormick - Brethren Church; Teresa Ward - Council for Research & Development; The Seventh-Day Adventist Church in Ireland; Arif Fitzsimon - Islamic Cultural Centre of of Ireland; The National Spiritual Assembly of the Baháís of the Republic of Ireland; Pauline Maguire - Dublin Meditation Centre; Baptist Union of Ireland; Gerard Ryan - Church of Scientology; Rachel M. Bewley-Bateman - Religious Society of Friends; Lutheran Church in Ireland; Ewen G. Watt - Watch Tower Bible and Tract Society of Ireland; The Irish District of Moravian Church; The Church of Jesus Christ of Latter-Day Saints; Fr Ireneu Craciun - The Greek Orthodox Church in Ireland; Rev John Nelson - Non-Subscribing Presbyterian Church; Rev Bill Darlinson - Unitarian Church; Free Presbyterian Church; Fr Kevin O'Doherty - Newtowncunningham.

Eanna Hickey - Office of the Chief Justice; Marianne Nolan - Department of Finance Public Services Section; Susan Boardman, Corina McGrath - General Council of County Councils; Air Corps - Press Office; Max Hanlon - Army Press Office, Lisburn; Sergeant Chris Smith - Defence Forces Press Office Dublin; Seamus - Press Office Department of Justice, Equality and Law Reform; Maureen Erne - Press Office, Northern Ireland Prisons Service; Dr Richard Erskine, Gillian Hunter - RUC Central Statistics Unit; An Garda Síochána Press Office; Linda Telford - Communications Office, Northern Ireland Court Service.

Catherine Hughes - Department of Education for Northern Ireland; Dominic Whelan - Information Division, Department of Foreign Affairs; Siobhan Lacey - Department of Enterprise, Trade and Employment; Jackie Coogan - Department of the Taoiseach; Department of the Environment; Seamus Hempenstall - Press and Information Office, Department of Justice, Equality and Law Reform; Tom McGrath - Department of Public Enterprise; Siobhan Tweedie - Department for the Environment for Northern Ireland; Margaret - Northern Ireland Office; Nigel Crosbie - Department of Finance and Personnel for Northern Ireland; Dearbhla Doyle - Department of Foreign Affairs.

Marie Scully - Irish Basketball Association; Marshall Gillespie, author, Northern Ireland Soccer Yearbook; Brian Morton - Irish Bowling Association; Gerard N. Byrne - Irish Cricket Union; June Fincher - Ladies Bowling League of Ireland; Naomi Magee, Press Officer, Northern Ireland Unionist Party; Finbar O'Driscoll - Ladies Gaelic Football Association; Catherine Meaney - Turf Club; Veronica Byrne - Swim Ireland; Zoë Lally - Irish Surfing Association; Paula Jordan - Republic of Ireland Billiards and Snooker Association; Slattery PR; Eamon - Pitch and Putt Union of Ireland; Janice O'Hara - Motorsport Ireland; Irene Johnston - Irish Ladies Hockey Union; Joan Morgan - Irish Hockey Union; Teresa Thompson - Irish Ladies Golf Union; Lorcan Ó Ruairc - Comhairle Liathróid Láimhe na hÉire-ann; Equestrian Federation of Ireland; John Keane - Irish National Darts Organisation; Tony Allen - Irish Cycling Federation; Jon Hynes - Irish Canoe Union; Síle De Bhailis - Cumann Camógaíochta na nGael; Dermot Nagle - Bord Lúthchleas na hÉireann; Badminton Union of Ireland; Irish Amateur Boxing Association; Irish Horse Racing Authority; Bord na gCon; Motor Cycle Union of Ireland; Irish Amateur Rowing Association; Irish Sailing Association; Press Office - Department of Tourism and Sport and Recreation.

D. Waddell - Antrim Borough Council; Ards Borough Council; Wendy Geary - Armagh City and District Council; Ballymena Borough Council; Ballymoney Borough Council; Andrea Little - Banbridge District Council; Wilma Stewart - Belfast City Council; Anne Beacom - Carrickfergus Borough Council; Mandy Eakins - Castlereagh Borough Council; Coleraine Borough Council; Adrian McCreesh - Cookstown District Council; G. Bartley - Craigavon Borough Council; Derry City Council; Down District Council; Alison Hudson - Dungannon District Council; Eliz Connor - Fermanagh District Council; Liz Wilkin - Larne Borough Council; Elizabeth Beattie - Limavady Borough Council; Lisburn Borough Council; Melissa - Magherafelt District Council; Richard Lewis - Moyle District Council; Bernie - Newry and Mourne District Council; Mary Claire Deane and Gillian - Newtownabbey Borough Council; North Down Borough Council; Omagh District Council; Strabane District Council.

Kristina Fallenius - Nobel Foundation, Sweden; Sheila Clifford - the Minister's Office, Dept of Arts, Heritage, Gaeltacht and the Islands; Peter Scally - Jesuit Communications Centre; Gerry Malone - Bord Fáilte, Baggot St; Jennifer Lynch - NALA; David Nowlan - The Irish Times; Dave Spratt, Dept of Tourism, Sport and Recreation; David McCormack - Pacemaker; Kathy O'Neill - Buncrana; Colm McKenna - Muff, Co Donegal; Philip and Eugenie O'Dwyer; Tommy Walsh, Mayo; Donal Mulligan and Glen; Stuart Brennan; Feargal MacGiolla; Denise McLaughlin; Cormac, Jack and Rosaleen Campbell.

Gerry McGovern, Micheal Kelliher, Ronan Flood, Margaret Sheane, Emmet Kelly, Stephen Faloon, Robert Downes, Charlotte Breen, Andrew Eager, Olwyn Leo, Kevin Sweeney, Eoin Mac Giolla Rí, Patrick Coffey, Keith O'Suillivan, John Kelly, Neil Hegarty and all the other staff @ Local Ireland. Seán Egan and all at Techman.

INDEX

a local heart with a global beat

35% off the 2001 Local Ireland Almanac if you complete and return the following questionnaire.

First Name: _____ Surname: _____

Address1: _____

Address 2: _____

City:_____ State:_____ Country:_____ Postcode:_____

Gender: Male ☐ Female ☐ Nationality

Age: ☐☐ Homeowner: yes/no Marital status: single / married

Occupation:

☐ Executive/Managerial
☐ Professional (Doctor, Lawyer, etc.)
☐ Academic/Educator
☐ Computer Technical/Engineering
☐ Service/Customer support
☐ Clerical/Administrative
☐ Sales/Marketing/Media
☐ Other (please specify)

☐ Tradesperson/Craftsperson
☐ College/University/Graduate student
☐ Student
☐ Homemaker
☐ Self-employed/Own company
☐ Retired

Interests:
This will help us choose the kind of content to improve future editions.

☐ Arts & Culture
☐ Sports & Outdoors
☐ Current Affairs/Politics
☐ Entertainment
☐ Music
☐ Travel
☐ Other (please specify)

☐ Computers & Technology
☐ Health & Fitness
☐ Economics
☐ Shopping
☐ Environment
☐ Home & Family

We will contact you next September to order your copy of the 2001 Local Ireland Almanac at a 35% discount on the recommended retail price. Postage and carriage will be charged at cost.

All information supplied will be kept confidential and not disclosed to any other organisation for commercial interest.

Free post is available to customers in the Republic of Ireland only.

By completing this questionnaire you are under no obligation to purchase the 2001 Local Ireland Almanac.

www.local.ie

Local Ireland Almanac
Merrion House
Merrion Road
FREE POST
Dublin 4